THE STONE-CAMPBELL MOVEMENT

THE STONE-CAMPBELL MOVEMENT

A GLOBAL HISTORY

D. NEWELL WILLIAMS
DOUGLAS A. FOSTER
PAUL M. BLOWERS
GENERAL EDITORS

SCOTT D. SEAY, MANAGING EDITOR

CONTRIBUTORS

CARMELO ÁLVAREZ   LAWRENCE A. Q. BURNLEY
STANLEY GRANBERG   JOHN MARK HICKS
LORETTA LONG HUNNICUTT   TIMOTHY LEE
EDWARD J. ROBINSON   DAVID THOMPSON
MARK TOULOUSE   GLENN ZUBER

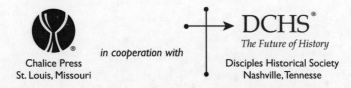

Chalice Press
St. Louis, Missouri

in cooperation with

DCHS®
The Future of History
Disciples Historical Society
Nashville, Tennesse

Visit www.chalicepress.com

Print: 9780827235274   EPUB: 9780827235281   EPDF: 9780827235298

Library of Congress Cataloging-in-Publication Data

The Stone-Campbell movement : a global history / edited by D. Newell Williams, Douglas A. Foster, Paul M. Blowers.
p. cm.
ISBN 978-0-8272-3527-4 (pbk.)
1. Restoration movement (Christianity)—History. I. Williams, D. Newell. II. Foster, Douglas A. (Douglas Allen), 1952- III. Blowers, Paul M., 1955-

BX7315.S77 2012
286.609--dc23   2012030350

Printed in the United States of America

Contents

We would like to express our enduring gratitude to the following major donors. It is because of their generosity that this book went from project to publication.

Bethany Christian Church (Disciples of Christ)
Fort Washington, Maryland

Ms. MaryAnn Brown

Rev. and Mrs. David Caldwell

Mr. John David McAllister Caldwell

Dr. and Mrs. Glenn Thomas Carson

Disciples of Christ Historical Society

First Christian Church (Disciples of Christ)
Duncan, Oklahoma

Dr. Cynthia L. Hale

Mr. and Mrs. Oscar Haynes

The Estate of Jayne Hopson

The Estate of Lester McAllister

Otter Creek (Church of Christ)
Brentwood, Tennessee

Ray of Hope Christian Church (Disciples of Christ)
Decatur, Georgia

The James and Dudley Seale Publications Fund

Dr. and Mrs. Douglas Smith

Vine Street Christian Church (Disciples of Christ)
Nashville, Tennessee

Woodmont Christian Church (Disciples of Christ)
Nashville, Tennessee

Preface

In January 2003, Paul M. Blowers, of Christian Churches/Churches of Christ, Douglas A. Foster, of Churches of Christ, and D. Newell Williams, of the Christian Church (Disciples of Christ) wrote the final paragraphs of the introduction to *The Encyclopedia of the Stone-Campbell Movement:*

> A comprehensive history of the Movement written jointly by scholars from each of the three major streams may be on the horizon. Points of consensus regarding the telling of the common story are emerging. Moreover, the historians involved in this effort have come to recognize each other as persons of faith, commitment, and insight.

Having labored for many years on *The Encyclopedia,* each confessed relief that as exciting as such a project would be, it would surely be the task of a future generation of historians. *The Encyclopedia* was published in 2004 and within a year Cyrus White, publisher of Chalice Press, and Glenn Carson, president of the Disciples of Christ Historical Society, approached Williams with a proposal that he write a comprehensive history of the Stone-Campbell Movement. Williams replied that such a history would have to explore not only the Movement's North American streams, but its significant global development, and therefore would require a diverse team of historians working over a period of several years.

In response, White and Carson asked Williams to draw up a proposal. Williams called a meeting with Blowers and Foster at the Annual Meeting of the AAR and SBL in Philadelphia in November 2005, at which the three developed a plan for producing a global history that would involve Stone-Campbell scholars from all parts of the world. Blowers, Foster, and Williams would serve not only as researchers and writers, but as general editors of the project. The plan also called for the appointment of a managing editor who, in addition to being one of the writers, would handle details of arranging writers' conferences, communicate with the writing team, and correspond with outside reviewers. In total, the project would employ fourteen historians as researchers and writers, and they would meet face-to-face in three intensive writers' conferences over a period of three years.

In the eighteen months following submission of "final" drafts, the three general editors and the managing editor would, in correspondence with the full team, edit the manuscript for submission to Chalice Press.

Chalice Press and the Disciples of Christ Historical Society accepted the proposal in substance, and during the spring and summer of 2006 refined the details of the covenant by which the DCHS would raise funds for the project and Chalice would publish the work. The general editors asked Scott Seay, assistant professor of Church History at Christian Theological Seminary (CTS), to serve as managing editor. In support of the project, CTS agreed to provide meeting rooms and overnight accommodations for the three writers' conferences.

During the summer of 2006 the general editors and managing editor recruited ten other historians from a pool of over three hundred potential contributors to join them in writing what they were soon calling "A World History of the Stone-Campbell Movement." The group gathered for the first time at CTS on January 7-10, 2007. This first writers' conference began with worship in the Seminary's Sweeney Chapel and included a litany of commissioning led by Glenn Carson and Cyrus White in which all of the writers participated. Several members of the writing team met each other for the first time in this opening worship in which participants prayed for each other. Each day of the conference began with corporate spiritual exercises, and the conference concluded with a closing act of worship. The group followed a similar pattern of worship and spiritual practices in each of the following conferences. Through a process of small group and plenary sessions, the writers constructed an initial outline and assigned research and writing tasks. Each of the writers made a commitment to highlight in the central narrative the contributions of groups that had received less attention in previous histories, including women, African Americans, Hispanic Americans, Asian Americans, and the Stone-Campbell Movement outside North America.

First drafts from all fourteen writers were due to the managing editor by December 1, 2007. On January 6-9, 2008, the writers met at CTS for their second conference. Having reviewed each other's work, the writers identified gaps in the previous outline which led to a significant revision of the book's structure and a new set of assignments. The goal was to submit individual contributions for a second draft of the manuscript to the managing editor by August 31, 2008. In addition, the writing team affirmed at the second conference that since the early years of the Stone-Campbell Movement in North America had already been told in multiple publications, they would give greater attention to the more recent story of its worldwide expansion, partnerships, and twenty-first century challenges.

The writers gathered at CTS for their third and final conference on November 14-16, 2008. After reviewing the second draft, the group further revised and refined the outline and identified additional tasks for each of the writers, including in some cases consultations with persons from outside the writing team. The writers also determined that since no chapter would emerge as the work of any one member of the team, and since the overall outline, revised at every conference, was a product of their corporate discernment, chapters would not be identified in the final text as having been written by particular members of the team. The new history was a genuinely multi-authored work.

Third drafts were due to the managing editor by December 1, 2009, but as could be expected, not all of the writers were able to submit their contributions on schedule. Nevertheless, by summer 2010, Williams and Foster, who had received research leaves from their respective academic institutions, Brite Divinity School and Abilene Christian University, and assumed primary responsibilities as general editors, were able to begin preparing a fourth draft that ultimately would be sent to outside reviewers. In the process, it became clear that there were still a number of topics and issues missing from the manuscript that needed to be added to fulfill the goals of the project. The general editors, managing editor, and several members of the larger team took on new research and writing assignments, and other writers provided essential resources for editing existing sections of the manuscript.

The writers and outside reviewers received the fourth draft in two installments, the first in December 2010 and the second in March 2011. Appreciation is expressed to outside readers James O. Duke, Everett Ferguson, Sheila Gillams, Robert F. Rae, Laurie Maffly-Kipp, Thomas H. Olbricht, and Randi Walker, who offered helpful comments on the manuscript. Carefully considering responses from both members of the writing team and the outside reviewers, Foster and Williams undertook

significant further editing of the manuscript from May 2011 through February 2012, while managing editor Scott Seay edited footnotes and tracked down missing sources. Special thanks are due to Sheila Gillams who, at the request of the editors, provided information on developments since the 1960s in the Church of Christ, Disciples of Christ, a predominantly African American stream of the Movement.

Though Williams, Foster, and Blowers had not expected to be involved in writing the history they saw on the horizon in 2003, they are grateful to have shared in this project. They are also grateful to have partnered with the eleven colleagues with whom they have co-authored this first attempt at a world history of the Stone-Campbell Movement. In addition, they are grateful to the academic institutions that granted members of the writing team leave time to devote to this project, especially Abilene Christian University, Brite Divinity School, and Christian Theological Seminary. Finally, they are grateful for the bold vision of Chalice Press and the Disciples of Christ Historical Society in inviting such a proposal and for the commitment and energy of the Disciples of Christ Historical Society in funding it.

D. Newell Williams, Brite Divinity School

Douglas A. Foster, Abilene Christian University

Paul M. Blowers, Emmanuel Christian Seminary

Contributors

Carmelo Álvarez (Ph.D., Free University of Amsterdam) is an ordained minister in the Christian Church (Disciples of Christ). He serves as a missionary-consultant for the Global Ministries (Christian Church and United Church of Christ) in Latin America and the Caribbean. Álvarez teaches in several theological schools and seminaries in Latin America and the Caribbean. Always committed to ecumenism, he has served a term as General Secretary of the Ecumenical Association of Third World Theologians (EATWOT) and Regional Secretary in the Caribbean for the Latin American Council of Churches.

Paul Blowers (Ph.D., University of Notre Dame) has taught on the faculty of Emmanuel Christian Seminary since 1989. Although he is a recognized scholar of early Christianity, he also is widely published in the history of the Stone-Campbell Movement. His work aims at improving the self-understanding of the Movement across its various expressions. He is a member of the Christian Churches/Churches of Christ.

Lawrence A. Q. Burnley (Ph.D., University of Pennsylvania) is an ordained minister in the Christian Church (Disciples of Christ) and currently serves as assistant vice president for diversity and intercultural relations, and assistant professor of history at Whitworth University. For many years he served as an executive for Global Ministries of the Christian Church (Disciples of Christ), travelling abroad and conducting seminars and workshops to improve race relations in the churches.

Douglas A. Foster (Ph.D., Vanderbilt University) is Professor of Church History in the Graduate School of Theology of Abilene Christian University and Director of the Center for Restoration Studies. The author and editor of many articles and books, his work concentrates on the place of the Stone-Campbell Movement in American Christianity and the nature of Christian unity.

Stanley Granberg (Ph.D., Open University, Oxford Centre for Mission Studies) served for ten years as a missionary in Kenya. He has taught Bible, missiology, evangelism and at several theological schools associated with the Stone-Campbell Movement. Currently, he is director of Kairos Church Planting Support, an organization that helps recruit, equip, and support church planters in the Churches of Christ and Christian Churches/Churches of Christ.

John Mark Hicks (Ph.D., Westminster Theological Seminary) teaches theology and church history at Lipscomb University where he has served since 2000. Ordained in the Churches of Christ, he has held a number of positions in educational ministries in churches and authored ten books for both scholarly and popular audiences.

Loretta Long Hunnicutt (Ph.D., Georgetown University) has taught church history at Pepperdine University since 2002. Her teaching and research focuses mainly on colonial and early national American history, especially the history of women during these periods. A member of the Churches of Christ, she is the author of a biography of Selina Campbell.

Timothy Lee (Ph.D., University of Chicago) joined the faculty of Brite Divinity School in 2002. His current research focuses on the history of Christianity in Korea and among Asian Americans, a topic about which he has written a number of works. He co-chaired the Korean Religions Group of the American Academy of Religion, 2007-2013. An ordained minister of the Christian Church (Disciples of Christ) he also served as moderator of North American Pacific Asian Disciples (NAPAD).

Edward J. Robinson (Ph. D. Mississippi State University), after serving at Abilene Christian University for six years, joined the faculty at Southwestern Christian College in Terrell, Texas, in 2010. The author of five books, his work focuses on pioneer leaders in African American Churches of Christ.

Scott Seay (Ph.D., Vanderbilt University) joined the faculty of Christian Theological Seminary in 2005. A specialist in colonial and early national New England religion and culture, he also has published in the history of the Stone-Campbell Movement. Raised in the Christian Churches/Churches of Christ, he now is an ordained minister in the Christian Church (Disciples of Christ) and has served a number of churches as an educator, consultant, and interim minister.

David Thompson (Ph.D., B.D., University of Cambridge) is Emeritus Professor of Modern Church History in the University of Cambridge. He has published on English nonconformity (including Churches of Christ), baptism, ecumenism, and church, state and society in Europe. A former President of the Annual Conference of Churches of Christ in Great Britain and of the World Convention, he is an ordained minister of the United Reformed Church.

Mark Toulouse (Ph.D., University of Chicago) currently serves as principal and professor of the history of Christianity at Emmanuel College and in the Department for the Study of Religion at the University of Toronto. An ordained minister of the Christian Church (Disciples of Christ), he taught for twenty-five years at Disciples-related schools before assuming his current position in 2009. His research specializes in North American Christianity and culture, and in topics connecting both religion and public life.

D. Newell Williams (Ph.D., Vanderbilt University) has been president and professor of modern and American church history of Brite Divinity School since 2003. His numerous articles and five books have focused on the history of the Stone-Campbell Movement. He has served the Christian Church (Disciples of Christ) in many ways, recently finishing a term as moderator. An ordained Disciples minister, he regularly preaches and teaches in congregations and other church venues.

Glenn Zuber (Ph.D., Indiana University) is an ordained minister in the Christian Churches/Churches of Christ. He has taught in American studies, history, and theology at several schools, where his work focuses on twentieth-century American history, race relations, and revivalism. His interests in the Stone-Campbell Movement focus primarily on the questions of women's leadership and the church growth movement.

Introduction

A New History of the Stone-Campbell Movement

"History is providence illustrated."[1] So begins William Thomas Moore's *A Comprehensive History of the Disciples of Christ*, published in 1909 to celebrate the Centennial of Thomas Campbell's *Declaration and Address*. Moore's volume reflected the view of history that had reigned supreme in American Protestant thought in the nineteenth century. Far from a series of random events, history was the theater of God's action. For Moore, the Stone-Campbell Movement was the climax of the forward march of New Testament Christianity.

The Stone-Campbell Movement was born of the union in the 1830s of two frontier American reform efforts— the "Christians" led by Barton W. Stone, and the "Reformers" or "disciples of Christ" led by Alexander Campbell. Unable to decide on one name, members of the Stone-Campbell Movement were known variously as Christians and Disciples of Christ, and their churches were identified as Christian Churches or Churches of Christ. By the end of the nineteenth century they had divided in North America into two streams, one taking the name Churches of Christ, the other taking the names Christian Churches and Disciples of Christ. A division in the Christian Churches/Disciples of Christ stream was under way by the 1920s and eventually gave rise to groups known as the Christian Church (Disciples of Christ), often referred to as the Disciples, and Christian Churches/Churches of Christ, sometimes referred to as the independent Christian Churches. Churches in Britain, Australia, and New Zealand were known as Churches of Christ.

For leaders of the generation of Stone and the Campbells, and for many in Moore's own time, the idea of the "fall of the church" developed by early Protestants had an undeniable logic. The story had three stages beginning with the apostolic age that was Christianity's creative and normative era. This was followed by a long period of decline during the patristic and medieval periods, finally yielding to an age of recovery or restoration begun by the Protestant Reformation. The Stone-Campbell Movement, then, could be understood as the completion of that long yet incomplete reformation. Identifying the goal of his efforts as the *restoration* of apostolic Christianity, rather than a mere reform of existing Christianity, Alexander Campbell's 1825 words still resounded loudly in 1909: "Celebrated as the era of reformation is, we doubt not but that the era of restoration will transcend it in importance and fame, through the long and blissful Millennium."[2]

Moore expanded this providential perspective with the idea of a law of development that was part of "the very fabric of the world." It unfolded in three phases: creation, chaos, and reconstruction. The opening of Genesis already previewed these phases: the completed and perfected creation (Gen. 1:1); the chaos that threatened to overthrow its order (1:2); and the reconstruction of the world in the progressive development of created things culminating with humankind (1:3-27).[3] All great movements in salvation history went through the same stages, including the Stone-Campbell Movement.

For Moore, the creative age of the Movement had begun with Thomas Campbell's appeal for Christian unity in the *Declaration and Address* (1809). "In the beginning," wrote Moore, "God created the movement, and simply used Thomas Campbell to put its great principles into a language that might be read by the people of the ages to come."[4] Soon, however, the Movement found itself caught in the chaos of denominational rivalry, drifting from its true vocation. Then, in the early 1830s, particularly with the start of Alexander Campbell's monthly journal the *Millennial Harbinger*, the Movement regained its compass, reconstructing its true mission to overcome Christian division once and for all and to spread New Testament Christianity to the far corners of the earth.

Early histories of the Stone-Campbell Movement largely shared Moore's providential outlook. They usually assumed the Movement to be at the vanguard of the final phase of Christian history.[5] Writings like Robert Richardson's *Memoirs of Alexander Campbell* (1868-69) and John Rogers' *Biography of Elder Barton Warren Stone* (1847), praised the heroes of the Movement as champions against the sectarianism of their time. The

1

most triumphalistic version, a study by John Rowe, made them into larger-than-life figures who transcended the faults of ordinary humans. First published in 1884 and in subsequent editions to 1913, Rowe's history contrasted the restoration of primitive Christianity with the apostasies that had littered church history for centuries.

> Where, among all the existing sects, do you find such sentiments uttered as were uttered by Thomas Campbell? Is there one prominent man among any of the denominations, at this time, who proposes such measures of reform as were instituted by Thomas Campbell? Do you hear any of our Protestant divines talk as he talked, and do you see any of them labor as he labored, to crush out sectarianism and to purify the Church of all tradition? Do you find one Protestant minister among ten thousand ministers making the least plea for Christian union upon the basis of the Bible? Not one. Intellectually and morally, in comparison with Thomas Campbell, they were all pigmies.[6]

Regardless of the hyperbole, Rowe's logic rang true for many members of the Stone-Campbell Movement at the close of the nineteenth century: the Stone-Campbell Movement was the culmination of previous Protestant reforms. Another option was to argue that it was the heir to a line of persecuted, often invisible New Testament Christians who had resisted apostate Roman Catholicism. Alexander Campbell, who often referred to the Movement as "the current Reformation," could also use the second approach as he did in his 1829 debate with Bishop John Purcell.[7] This argument paralleled Baptist Landmarkism and provided a ready-made historical pedigree and legitimization of the Movement. It would be used in the twentieth century by the conservative Disciple James DeForest Murch in a history of the Movement widely circulated among Christian Churches/ Churches of Christ.[8]

Moore's portrait was more modest by comparison, but hardly less romantic and apologetic. The Disciples of Christ, he wrote, "have been called by Divine Providence to meet this emergency [of restoring apostolic Christianity] in the onward course of Christianity around the world."[9] Moore's contemporary James H. Garrison, who produced another history of the Movement the same year, *The Story of a Century*, hoped that as members faced a new century with new challenges they would exercise constructive self-criticism so the Movement might remain true to its calling. It was not enough to rest on the laurels of the past. The Disciples of Christ,

Garrison argued, had to adapt to changing times, to be open to new truth while faithful to their own principles.[10] If they could do this they had every hope of leading the way toward Christian unity in the dawning ecumenical age, the "Period of Reunion" as Garrison dubbed it.[11]

David Lipscomb, an early twentieth century leader in the North American Churches of Christ, also held hope for the future of the Stone-Campbell Movement in the changing landscape of Protestant Christianity, but on very different terms. Unlike Garrison, who saw the Movement working in "federation" (cooperative union) with other denominations on the way to unity,[12] Lipscomb declared that only by reducing Christianity to its divine simplicity and purity through a thoroughgoing restoration of precise doctrines and practices could the Movement fulfill its mission. As reliable as the voice of the Campbells and Stone had been, they were still only human voices. God would have to fight the ultimate battle for unity through his unfailing Word.[13] The Stone-Campbell Movement was only as good as its testimony to that Word.

The voices of Garrison and Lipscomb, added to those of Moore, Rowe, and other writers, show the diverse ethos of Stone-Campbell historiography at the one-hundredth anniversary of Thomas Campbell's *Declaration and Address*. An unmistakable triumphalism resounded in all these writers, though in far more somber tones in Lipscomb. For them, the Stone-Campbell Movement was well on its way to fulfilling its mission to serve the unity of the church and the evangelization of the world. The future held uncertainties, to be sure, but there was profound confidence in the rightness of the Movement's dedication to the Lordship of Christ, the banishment of creeds as tests of fellowship, the honoring of liberty of theological opinion, and the reign of Scripture in matters of faith and practice in the church.

The Critical Turn in Stone-Campbell Historiography

The centennial histories of Thomas Campbell's *Declaration and Address* appeared just as critical historicism was emerging in the academic centers of Europe, Great Britain, and North America. This new approach viewed history as the result of patterns of cause and effect in social, cultural, and economic forces. Moore mirrored, to some degree, the influence of historicism with his notion of a "law of development" in church history. Nineteenth-century history writing, influenced by Idealism, Romanticism, and the newly expanding social sciences, had focused on macro-histories, "totalizing" narratives that took in whole sweeps in the advance of human culture.[14] By the early twentieth century, however, Ernst Troeltsch and others were pointing out that historiography had come to a new crisis with the exclusion of the divine dimension of history and the recognition of the absolute relativity of all cultural values.[15]

Moore and his generation of Stone-Campbell historians were far too committed to the supernatural factor in Christian history, and to the transcendent integrity of biblical revelation, to heed the more radical, secularist forms of historical interpretation. However, in the early twentieth century a new generation of Stone-Campbell historians began to reflect parts of the newer critical methods. Far less openly apologetic, these writers attempted to achieve some critical distance from the Movement while still remaining faithful to it. One early example was the admission that the Movement had never been uniform, but had included differing, even conflicting ideas and views from its very beginning. As early as 1905 Errett Gates observed in his history *The Disciples of Christ* what would later become common, that the core principles of Christian unity and the restoration of apostolic Christianity were not as compatible as the Campbells and others had supposed. The potential for division was present early, capable of undermining the Movement's mission.

By 1961 Winfred Garrison was saying this more candidly. Liberals and conservatives were both present in the founding generation, he argued, and there were liberal and conservative elements even in the thinking of individual figures. The early leaders, Garrison wrote, "did not all hold the same views and transmit the same heritage of ideas."[16] Such insights into the complexity of the Stone-Campbell Movement would in time be crucial for historians trying to understand the divisions that took shape in the twentieth century.[17]

Another signal of this critical turn in Stone-Campbell historiography was an acknowledgment of the early Movement's American character. The early twentieth century was an important transitional period in the writing of American history. The so-called New or Progressive History attempted to move beyond the "mythic" constructions of American identity in an earlier era. As Ernst Breisach notes of this school of thought, "abstractions like providence, nation, and democracy had evoked a false sense of continuity between past, present, and future and had helped to preserve injustice." Progressive historians instead proposed to describe history on the ground, free from old ideological perspectives, and

to reveal hidden factors moving America toward a just society—though they often overlooked major problems like racism in favor of socio-economic theories of conflict and social progress.[18]

A transitional figure in the emergence of the New History was Frederick Jackson Turner. Though Turner upheld the old ideal of American "exceptionalism,"—its unique role in the history of nations—he believed that historians must look at social, economic, demographic, and geographic factors to tell how this nation of immigrants became an authentic democracy.[19] Turner's organizing principle was his famous "frontier thesis." The westward expansion of America across the frontier was the key to its self-realization as a nation and ultimate independence from Europe.

> The peculiarity of American institutions is, the fact that they have been compelled to adapt themselves to the changes of an expanding people—to the changes involved in crossing a continent, in winning a wilderness, and in developing…out of the primitive economic and political conditions of the frontier…the complexity of city life.[20]

Given the importance of the western frontier in the history of the Stone-Campbell Movement, it is little surprise that some of the Movement's own historians were drawn to Turner's thesis. Winfred E. Garrison, in particular, appropriated this frontier model in his *Religion Follows the Frontier: A History of the Disciples of Christ* (1931). Garrison identified three stages in the expansion of the American frontier: the colonial, the revolutionary, and the western pioneer phases. The third phase, including the Second Great Awakening and the development of a distinct culture in the trans-Appalachian frontier, was the birthplace of the Stone-Campbell Movement. Like Turner, Garrison focused heavily on a profile of the western pioneer as sturdy, enterprising, independently-minded, and self-reliant. These were the movers and shakers of the Stone-Campbell reformation. They were "prophets among the pioneers." But after the Civil War, with the vanishing of the old frontier, the Movement's advocates faced the new frontier of urbanization:

> The Disciples never quite kept pace with their rivals in the cities. They lacked both the financial and the cultural resources which others drew from their constituencies in the East. Born on the frontier, they had only frontier materials out of which to develop the instruments of advancement, and this they did with laudable energy and notable

success, but subject to the limitations imposed by their origin. But if they fell behind in the cities, they were at home in the county-seat towns throughout the Mississippi Valley and, for the most part, kept abreast with their economic and cultural development as well as their growth in population.[21]

Garrison's emphasis on the uniquely American and frontier character of the Stone-Campbell Movement was the first of many such studies. It became typical of histories of the Movement to include a preliminary chapter on its American background.[22] Some of these studies would be written by outsiders looking in. For example, the so-called "Chicago School" historians, including Jerald Brauer and Martin Marty, emphasized the irony of a Movement dedicated to the destruction of denominationalism in an American context which encouraged denominationalism, itself becoming a denomination—indeed not one but three.[23] As recently as 1989, historian of American Evangelicalism Nathan Hatch profiled the Movement as a quintessential example of the process of "democratization" in the Second Great Awakening, again accentuating the uniquely American shape of Disciples and Christians.[24]

Garrison further influenced the historiography of the Movement by his reconsideration of its beginnings. Early histories, including Garrison's own *Religion Follows the Frontier* (1931), followed Robert Richardson's two-volume *Memoirs of Alexander Campbell* that regarded Stone's movement as a tributary that flowed into the Campbell reform rather late in the story. Moore published *A Comprehensive History* in 1909 because it was the centennial year of Thomas Campbell's *Declaration and Address*, then widely viewed as the beginning of the Movement. In contrast, Garrison's *An American Religious Movement* (1945) begins with the statement that the Movement "began early in the nineteenth century with the union of two separate movements." The assumption of a Campbellite mainstream with a less-important Stoneite tributary had been abandoned.

This shift in understanding of Stone's role in the Movement had been anticipated in B. B. Tyler's *A History of the Disciples of Christ*, published in 1894 as part of the "American Church History" series. The change in Garrison's thinking between the publication of *Religion Follows the Frontier* and *An American Religious Movement* appears to have been a result, however, not of Tyler's work, but the publication of two books highlighting the ministry of Stone and the Christians: A. W. Fortune's *The*

Disciples in Kentucky and Charles Crossfield Ware's *Barton Warren Stone: Pathfinder of Christian Union*. Both books were published in 1932 to commemorate the union of the followers of Stone and Campbell and reflected not only regional pride (Stone lived in Kentucky), but also the authors' desires to celebrate a founder of the Movement whose influence they believed was less susceptible than that of Alexander Campbell to legalism and exclusivism. Reflecting this shift in perception of Stone's role in the formation of the Movement, Leroy Garrett titled his 1981 history *The Stone-Campbell Movement*. The authors of this history have also chosen that designation as the Movement's most appropriate name.

Perhaps the most dramatic critical turn in Stone-Campbell historiography was the adoption of social-scientific models of interpretation by insider historians. David Edwin Harrell, Jr., a scholar from Churches of Christ, published the most extensive early treatment. Harrell's *A Social History of the Disciples of Christ* appeared in two volumes: *Quest for a Christian America: The Disciples of Christ and American Society to 1866* (1966) and *The Social Sources of Division in the Disciples of Christ, 1865-1900* (1973). These studies broke new ground in exploring how millennialism, nationalism ("Manifest Destiny"), and the desire for religious and social reform interacted and shaped the Stone-Campbell Movement's early reformers.

Most influential, perhaps, was Harrell's argument that ideological differences over slavery, and eventually the Civil War itself, had created a *de facto* sectional alienation that underlay other sources of division between Disciples groups north and south of the Mason-Dixon Line. A number of historians agreed with Harrell's thesis and came to see sectionalism as a major factor in the eventual breach between Disciples and Churches of Christ.

One of the virtues of Harrell's work was his attention to minorities in the Stone-Campbell Movement. His was one of the first histories to give concentrated attention to the plight of African Americans in the Movement and their role in shaping it despite the often-discriminatory record of white churches. Although Garrison and DeGroot's chapter "Negro Work" in *The Disciples of Christ: A History* (1948) discusses the work of African Americans, Harrell called attention to the reality of racism in the Movement, even after most members had discarded biblically argued theories of racial inferiority.

Such socio-historical studies of the Movement had great influence in helping its streams develop a healthy self-criticism about their internal life and their relations to the broader religious culture. In recent decades such studies have been on the increase, and, together with more traditional approaches that focus on the Movement's intellectual history, have cumulatively created what Douglas Foster and Michael Casey have called a "new historiography" in the Stone-Campbell tradition.[25]

Globalization, Postmodernity, and the Rewriting of Stone-Campbell History

In his *Comprehensive History of the Disciples of Christ*, W. T. Moore argued that in Christian history there is a "law of progress, which is always practically Westward." Christianity's eastward advance was rare, he asserted, and its "zig-zagging" northward and southward had been modest from the time it began in ancient Palestine. Moore generalized that if one examined all the facts, this law of Westward progress would be seen as universally true throughout history. He concluded that Christianity had always followed and contributed to this law of progress, and that its future success would continue to be Westward.[26] Writing before the World Wars doused confidence in the unrelenting progress of Western Protestant civilization, Moore believed that the Stone-Campbell Movement was a microcosm of this law of Christianity's westward progress and mirrored the ideal of American manifest destiny.

A century later, this vision seems overconfident, narrow, and unsustainable, though some may still find sympathy with it. For one thing, it hardly does justice to the fact that Christianity has always been moving in many directions. Examples include the early southward expansion into Africa, the important eastward missions of Nestorian Christians to India and China as early as the seventh century, and the northward track of Byzantine Christianity into Slavic lands in the ninth and tenth centuries.

Even in the modern missionary age, amid the "discovery" of the Americas, Christianity's penetration of the Far East and of the southern hemisphere, notably Latin America and sub-Saharan Africa, are a major part of its story. In fact, as missiologists now can demonstrate, the center of world Christianity has moved from the West (Europe, Britain, and America) to the global South including Africa, Latin America, and parts of Asia. Already these regions are sending missionaries to re-evangelize the West.

But neither does Moore's vision of a constant westward progress do justice to the Stone-Campbell Movement itself. Early in its history the Stone-Campbell Movement in the United State moved eastward to interact with its British roots—influencing and being influenced by restorationist groups there. The Movement in Canada intersected with and was shaped by its southern neighbors as well as British immigrants. Stone-Campbell Christians from the northern hemisphere soon carried their faith to the southern, and churches formed in New Zealand and Australia. The first international missionaries from North America went to the Middle East, to Turkish-occupied Palestine, south to Jamaica in the Caribbean, and to Africa. In the twentieth century Stone-Campbell missions proliferated all over the world, and numerous indigenous traditions took a life of their own far beyond the English-speaking world. Any history of the Stone-Campbell Movement written today requires telling the story of this global reality.

Globalization has already dramatically reshaped historiography. In the study of American history alone, significant changes in the reconstruction of the American past call into question older limited analyses. Thomas Bender, for example, speaks of the campaign to "deprovincialize the narrative of American history" and "to integrate the stories of American history with other, larger stories from which, with a kind of continental self-sufficiency, the United States has isolated itself."[27] America is not a self-enclosed identity but a complex construction of the multiple historical trajectories of its constituent peoples and nationalities; not a melting pot, if that means a single coherent narrative of national identity, but a kaleidoscope of multiple identities. These new global approaches aspire to dethrone the "nation" as the key historiographic category. Whether or not they can produce coherent and compelling understandings rather than simply being reactionary to older versions of American history and identity, the critics will judge.

Another watershed in historical studies is the acknowledgment of the shift from modernity to post-modernity. In Moore's time, historiography was geared to macro-history and totalizing narratives, especially those focused on "progress" or "modernization." A shift away from macro-history began in the 1970s, especially rejecting history written from the standpoint of dominant institutions or socio-political elites. Instead, the focus was on "micro-histories" and the stories of outsiders and marginalized groups, especially immigrants, racial minorities, and women.[28] The question of how—or whether—these stories should be included in a larger narrative has generated considerable debate. Are they merely detached stories and perspectives, or can they be made integral parts of an overarching story?

Furthermore, how do historians construct or "impose" such a larger story?

The impact of globalization and postmodernism on the historical field in general also poses important challenges for church historians, including historians of the Stone-Campbell Movement. For many years scholars have produced histories of the Stone-Campbell Movement in specific geographical contexts. While indispensable for the information they provide, these studies tend to fit the specific story into a macro-narrative of the Movement that emphases its American origins and development.

In 1958, for example, Robert G. Nelson, former Disciples missionary to Jamaica, produced a centennial history, *Disciples of Christ in Jamaica, 1858-1958*. The book is largely a chronicle of the institutional dimensions of the Disciples mission in Jamaica, but also an apology for the ecumenical mission principles of the Disciples of Christ in the United States.[29] While Nelson briefly refers to the challenges of native Jamaican leaders to take over the work, the missing element is the story of how indigenous Jamaicans embraced and shaped the Stone-Campbell Movement.

In contrast, Daisy L. Machado's 2003 study *Of Borders and Margins: Hispanic Disciples in Texas, 1888-1945*, is "history from a 'margins' perspective." Machado speaks in a postmodern and "postcolonial" manner about Anglo Disciples' experience of the "other" in the Hispanics of the borderlands whom they encountered and eventually evangelized beginning in the late nineteenth century. For Machado, this was not a mere abstraction or set of historical data—it was reality "shaped by a past that lives on in the present and continues to affect Hispanic Disciples living in the United States."[30]

Machado parallels the telling of national history "by those who had the power to impose themselves… [and] to name themselves and to exclude others from that self-definition" with the recounting of the clash of identities between largely Anglo-American Disciples and Texas Hispanics who had deep roots in a Latino Catholic culture.[31] In this context, Machado argues, the American ideal of conquering the western frontier, which found expression in Stone-Campbell Movement missions, had important and often disturbing implications, including the missionaries' sense of cultural and racial superiority. The Movement succeeded, in her view, only to the extent that it was able to raise up Mexican-Texan church leaders who endured the prejudices and fostered the Movement's virtues on their own terms.

Machado's work shows the need for histories of the indigenization of the Stone-Campbell Movement, even if they disrupt consensus interpretations of the Movement's expansion. Another such history is that of the General Assembly of the Church of Christ, Disciples of Christ, International, sometimes referred to as the Assembly Churches. The African American body has remained largely independent of the predominantly white North American streams of the Movement.

Narrating the stories of women in the Stone-Campbell Movement has also been an important dimension of the postmodern reframing. Numerous studies have appeared in recent years, some of a more biographical or anecdotal character, including Debra Hull's *Christian Church Women* and Loretta Long's *The Life of Selina Campbell*.[32] Others openly engaged the concerns of feminist historians and theologians, including Mary Ellen Lantzer Pereira's *Women Preaching in the Christian Church*.[33]

Because ideas (theological, ecclesiological, missiological, etc.) and identities have no reality apart from their embodiment in human lives, seeking to recapture the unique experiences of individual leaders has been crucial. An excellent example is Edward Robinson's work on the ministry and legacy of Samuel Robert Cassius (1853-1931). Cassius was born in Virginia as an enslaved African, but became an effective evangelist and organizer among African American Churches of Christ. He also worked against American racism, writing a powerful attack on discrimination in 1920 titled *Third Birth of a Nation*, a response to the D. W. Griffith movie *Birth of a Nation*.[34] The likes of Cassius raise questions about who were the true "progressives" in an era when liberal Protestantism was laying sole claim to the "social gospel." D. Duane Cummins's biographies of A. Dale Fiers and Kenneth L. Teegarden highlighted their leadership in regard to controversial social issues.[35]

The new historiography of the Stone-Campbell Movement has also provided different self-definitions of the Movement's streams. For example, recent studies of Churches of Christ show how factors besides legalism or exclusivism, such as counter-cultural millennialism, shaped the consciousness of churches alienated from "mainline" Disciples of Christ.[36] Another area of fruitful study has been the debate among scholars from Christian Churches/Churches of Christ and Churches of Christ over whether their streams legitimately qualify as "Evangelicals" in the American Protestant context,[37] even amid the larger dispute over the usefulness of the term.[38]

The Challenge of a New History of the Stone-Campbell Movement

Clearly among the foremost challenges of writing a new history of the Stone-Campbell Movement is telling the story in a way that includes its multiple dimensions, but also explains the ways in which those streams continue to intersect and interact. When *The Encyclopedia of the Stone-Campbell Movement* was published in 2004, it opened up new opportunities for the Movement's constituencies to explore the history that has both held them together and broken them apart. This study is in part a follow-up to that project. Its contributors serve as guides to the "movements within the Movement." Major attention is given to dimensions of those movements that have received little notice in earlier histories or which deserve to be revisited and reassessed.

An especially great burden of the present study is to expand the understanding of the international scope of the Stone-Campbell Movement. The World Convention of Churches of Christ has reported from research conducted by Clinton Holloway that the Stone-Campbell Movement has manifestations in at least 180 nations.[39] Though many are the outgrowth of missionary work and remain relatively small, the missiological and ecclesiological dynamics of these communities and their unique developments of Stone-Campbell identity constitute a whole new field of exploration.

This study follows a generally chronological order beginning with the emergence of the Movement in the United States. Chapter one recounts the story of the Stone and Campbell movements and their union in the 1830s. Chapters two through five continue the story in the United States up to the first decade of the twentieth century. The influences of sectionalism, war, race and gender receive special attention. Separate chapters are devoted to the emergence of African American institutions and women's organizations, topics that have not received extensive examination in general Stone-Campbell histories. In chapter five, both social and theological factors receive attention in the description of the division in North America into Churches of Christ and Disciples of Christ at the end of the nineteenth century. The chapter also identifies important differences within these two streams.

Chapter six examines the origins of the Movement in the United Kingdom and the British Empire and the development of British, Canadian, Australian, and New Zealand streams of the Stone-Campbell Movement. While the churches in the UK and British Empire were similar to those in the United States, these are nevertheless unique stories shaped by distinct origins and cultural contexts. One significant difference was the absence of influences from Barton Stone in the development of these streams.

Chapter seven traces the remarkable global expansion of the Stone-Campbell Movement undertaken by the churches in Britain, New Zealand, Australia, and North America from the 1870s to the 1920s. This is a first attempt to write this wide-ranging and diverse story. The chapter relates this missionary effort with an eye both to chronology and geography, from beginnings in Scandinavia, France, and Turkey, to Asia, the South Pacific, Africa, Latin America, and the Caribbean. The chapter also gives attention to the development of differing theologies and strategies of mission, noting the significant influence of the 1910 Edinburgh World Missionary Conference.

The next six chapters continue the story of developments in North America, the UK, and the British Commonwealth. Chapter eight describes the consolidation and complexity of North American Churches of Christ. The focus of chapter nine is the growing cooperation yet ultimate division within North American Disciples of Christ. The 1971 *Yearbook of American and Canadian Churches* recorded that division with separate listings for the Christian Church (Disciples of Christ) and the Christian Churches/Churches of Christ. The following chapter expands the story of the emergence and development of Christian Churches/Churches of Christ. The next two chapters describe responses of the North American streams to social changes that began in the 1960s, and distinctive theological and institutional developments in those streams. Chapter thirteen discusses developments in the UK and British Commonwealth, including division, growing cooperative efforts, and unions with other churches. It also gives attention to the churches' response to issues of war, gender, sexuality, and race.

Chapters fourteen through seventeen pick up the story of the spread and development of the Stone-Campbell Movement internationally, in Asia, Latin America and the Caribbean, Africa, and Europe. Though indigenization is a major theme in these accounts, reflecting the current state of historical research and writing on the Stone-Campbell Movement the authors of this text relied largely on sources written by missionaries. The writers hope that this first attempt at a global history will stimulate the writing of additional indigenous histories.

Chapter eighteen focuses on the theme that birthed the Stone-Campbell Movement and that became the greatest irony of its existence—Christian unity. Though established by advocates of the unity of Christ's church, the movement itself has divided more than once. Yet at the same time, the quest for unity has continued at the heart of this global movement.

An important new horizon of Stone-Campbell history, embodied in the present work and reflected by initiatives such as the World Convention of Churches of Christ, the Stone-Campbell Dialogue, and *The Encyclopedia of the Stone-Campbell Movement*, is expression of a common identity among the Movement's faithful—an identity transcending those things that have divided us, whether doctrine, practice, race, ethnicity, gender, or local heritage. Claiming that common ground will be a crucial gauge of whether the Stone-Campbell Movement will continue to move, witnessing faithfully to the gospel of reconciliation and the reign of Jesus Christ in and for the world.

1

Emergence of the Stone-Campbell Movement

The Stone-Campbell Movement began with the union in the 1830s of two North American groups: the Christians led by Barton W. Stone, and the Reformers led by Thomas and Alexander Campbell. Influenced by a host of people, ideas, and events, both groups affirmed that Christian unity was critical to the evangelization of the world and the in-breaking of Christ's earthly reign of peace and justice. The founders of both groups were identified with Presbyterian denominations—Stone in the United States, and the Campbells in Northern Ireland. Also, each group attracted significant numbers of Baptists. Yet despite these similarities, there were significant differences between the two groups.

Christians

The Christians emerged from the Presbyterian Church in the United States of America, a body profoundly shaped by colonial revivalism. The revivals that appeared among New Jersey Presbyterians in the 1720s proved controversial. The central issue was the revivalists' insistence that religion was a "sensible thing," an *experience* of the work of the Holy Spirit, and not merely a matter of believing the right doctrines and living

The Old Northwest

a moral life. Matters came to a head in 1741 when the anti-revival Old Light party expelled the pro-revival New Light party from the Synod of Philadelphia. Following the division, the New Lights constituted themselves as the Synod of New York and continued to grow, while the Old Lights declined. In 1758, the two parties reunited largely on New Light terms.[1] The Presbyterian Church from which the Christians emerged in the early nineteenth century was the church formed by the reunion of 1758.

Barton Warren Stone (1772-1844) joined this church while studying at the classical academy of Presbyterian minister David Caldwell in Guilford County, North Carolina. When he entered the academy in January 1790, a neighboring Presbyterian pastor, James McGready, was leading a revival among the fifty or so students of the academy. McGready stood squarely in the tradition of the colonial awakening, preaching that human beings were created to know and enjoy God. Having lost this capacity because of the first sin, however, they sought happiness through the satisfaction of their "animal nature," the possession of "riches" and "honors," and a "religion of external duties" which they thought appeased God who remained unknown and unloved. Yet none of these substitutes could satisfy their longings for happiness. At death they would be separated from God eternally and suffer torments beyond human comprehension.[2]

McGready urged that salvation delivered God's elect from future punishment and enabled them to experience in this life the happiness for which they were created—the happiness of knowing and enjoying God. Heaven was a continuation of this happiness. Salvation through faith in Jesus Christ caused the sinner to fall in love with God and come to Christ, both for pardon from the penalty of sin and release from its power. Though this faith was a gift from God, only sinners who *applied to Christ*—who sought faith—could have assurance of receiving it. One applied to Christ by using the "means of grace," which included withdrawing from distracting activities such as dancing and playing cards, asking God to change one's heart, and meditating on the horrors of sin and the full and free salvation in Jesus Christ.

Stone had entered Caldwell's academy with the intention of pursuing a career in law, a career he believed would enable him to attain the wealth, status, and pleasures that, according to the popular literature of his day, would bring him happiness. Born December 24, 1772, near Port Tobacco, Maryland, he had grown up in an Anglican family long accustomed to wealth and social standing. His father, John Stone, whose holdings in land and sixteen enslaved Africans identified the family as upper middle class, had died when Barton was three. Four years later, in the midst of the American Revolution, his mother Mary had moved the family to Pittsylvania County, Virginia, where they had continued to identify with the Church of England.

Though Stone tried to ignore the revival, he could not deny that the converts seemed to enjoy a happiness he did not know. Hearing McGready preach, he resolved to seek the gift of faith. In keeping with Presbyterian teaching of the time, his period of seeking faith lasted a full year. At one point he despaired of ever receiving it. He reported that he received the faith he sought through a sermon delivered by McGready's colleague, William Hodge.

> With much animation, and with many tears, he spoke of the love of God to sinners, and of what that love had done for sinners. My heart warmed with love for that lovely character described... My mind was absorbed in the doctrine—to me it appeared new.

According to revivalist Presbyterians, to find one's heart "warmed" with love to God and to find something "new" in the preaching of what God had done for sinners through Jesus Christ were signs of faith. Stone reported that the truth of God's love triumphed, and that he fell at the feet of Christ, "a willing subject."[3]

Following his conversion, Stone felt a call to preach the gospel. Completing his studies at Caldwell's academy, he became a candidate for the ministry in the Orange Presbytery of North Carolina in spring 1793. This was the beginning of a struggle, which, though it would not prevent him from being ordained as a Presbyterian minister, would ultimately lead him to separate from the Presbyterian Church—a struggle between Presbyterian doctrine and Enlightenment reason.

The Presbytery directed Stone and former classmate Samuel Holmes to prepare for an examination on the doctrine of the Trinity by reading a work by the seventeenth century Dutch Reformed theologian, Herman Witsius.[4] Stone remembered that

> Witsius would first prove that there was but one God, and then that there were three persons in this one God, the Father, Son and Holy Ghost—that the Father was unbegotten—the Son eternally begotten, and the Holy Ghost eternally proceeding from the Father and the Son—that it was idolatry to worship more Gods than one, and yet equal worship must be given to the Father, the Son, and Holy Ghost.

Engraving of Barton W. Stone from a portrait by Alexander Bradford who lived in Georgetown, Kentucky, in the 1820s. It appeared in the *Biography of Elder Barton Warren Stone Written by Himself, With Additions and Reflections by Elder John Rogers*, published in 1847.

Previously Stone had prayed to the Son without fear of idolatry or concern for equal worship to the members of the Trinity. The result of his effort to follow Witsius' Trinitarian teaching was that he no longer knew how to pray, which greatly diminished the enjoyment of God he had known since his conversion. "Till now," he wrote, "secret prayer and meditation had been my delightful employ. It was a heaven on earth to approach my God, and Saviour; but now this heavenly exercise was checked, and gloominess and fear filled my troubled mind." When he and Holmes discovered that each was having the same problem, they stopped studying Witsius, convinced that his text obscured rather than enlightened the truth and had disrupted their spiritual development.[5]

Like other Americans of the Revolutionary generation, Stone had been influenced by the Enlightenment dictum of John Locke that propositions inconsistent with clear and distinct ideas were "contrary to reason." To Stone, the idea that there was more than one God, which he found implied in Witsius' teaching that equal worship must be given to the Father, Son, and Holy Ghost, was inconsistent with the clear and distinct idea that there is one God. Not considering the possibility of holding in tension seemingly contradictory propositions, Stone concluded that Witsius' treatment was unintelligible.[6]

Witsius' work, however, was not the only treatment of the doctrine of the Trinity. Henry Patillo (1726-1801), a respected member of the Orange Presbytery, championed the views of Isaac Watts (1674-1748) who had been influenced by the Enlightenment. Watts argued that the scriptural doctrine of the Trinity was not contrary to reason. To be sure, the idea that "three Gods are one God, or three persons are one person" was contrary to reason. The Scriptures, according to Watts, taught that "the same true Godhead belongs to the Father, Son and Spirit, and… that the Father, Son and Spirit, are three distinct agents or principles of action, as may reasonably be called persons." Thus, to say "the Father is God, the Son is God, and the Spirit is God" was not contrary to the proposition that there is one God.[7]

As to the proper worship owed to the members of the Trinity, Watts asserted that the Scriptures revealed all that was necessary. One could be sure that it was proper to worship Father, Son, and Spirit because Scripture clearly reveals that they share in the divine nature or godhead, implying that we should worship the members of the Trinity with an eye to the specific place, work, and character Scripture attributes to each.[8]

Stone and Holmes obtained Watts' "treatise" and accepted his views.[9] Stone's struggles with Presbyterian doctrine and Enlightenment reason, however, did not end with his discovery of Watts' treatise. By spring 1794, he had decided to pursue some other calling. "My mind," he wrote, "was embarrassed with many abstruse doctrines, which I admitted as true; yet could not satisfactorily reconcile with others which were plainly taught in the Bible." As before, when Stone had struggled with the doctrine of the Trinity, his intellectual difficulties affected his devotion: "Having been so long engaged and confined to the study of systematic divinity from the Calvinistic mould, my zeal, comfort, and spiritual life became considerably abated."[10]

Yet he could not shake his call to ministry. After teaching for a time in Georgia, he returned to North Carolina in spring 1796, successfully completed his theological examinations, and received a license from the Orange Presbytery to preach the gospel as a probationer. He had not, however, overcome his earlier difficulties with Calvinist theology. He admitted that during his first years of ministry, he accepted the Calvinist doctrine of predestination as true but beyond human understanding. As a result, he avoided it in preaching.[11] David Caldwell had advised just such a course of action to another of his students, Samuel McAdow, who later became a leader of the Cumberland Presbyterians.[12]

In late 1797, the Presbyterian congregations at Cane Ridge and Concord in central Kentucky invited Stone to serve as a probationer. The following spring, he received a call through the Transylvania Presbytery to become pastor of the two congregations. October 4, 1798, was set for his ordination.[13] Knowing that he would be required to "sincerely receive and adopt" the Westminster Confession of Faith as "containing the system of doctrine taught in the Holy Scriptures," he undertook a careful re-examination of the document. This resulted in an even greater crisis than before. He could not believe the doctrine of the Trinity as expressed in the Confession. Furthermore, he had great doubts about the Confession's teaching on predestination. Convinced that God *gives* faith, he struggled to understand how a God who loves sinners could give faith to some by a special work of the Spirit and condemn others for not believing.[14] In Lockean terms, the clear and distinct idea was that God loves sinners and desires that they come to faith.

As the day of his ordination at the Cane Ridge meeting house arrived, Stone informed James Blythe (1765-1842) and Robert Marshall (1760-1833), two leaders of the Presbytery, of his difficulties with the Confession's teaching on the Trinity. He did not, however, share his doubts regarding the doctrine of predestination. The Adopting Act of 1729 had allowed Presbyterian ordination of ministerial candidates who would only partially subscribe to the Confession of Faith if, in the view of the presbytery, the candidate's objections to the Confession concerned "non-essentials." Though later repealed by the Old Light Synod of Philadelphia, the Adopting Act's ideas continued to guide many Presbyterians.

Failing to relieve Stone of his difficulties with the Confession, Blythe and Marshall asked him how far he would be willing to adopt it. Stone answered that he would be willing to do so as far as he saw it consistent with the Word of God. Blythe and Marshall indicated that Stone's partial subscription was sufficient, and the ordination proceeded.[15]

Meanwhile, a revival had begun in Logan County, Kentucky, forty miles north of Nashville, Tennessee, that would help Stone resolve his difficulties with the question of how a God who loved sinners could give faith to some and condemn others for not having it. James McGready, whose preaching had fueled the revival at Caldwell's Academy, had become pastor in 1796 of three congregations named after Logan County rivers—Red, Muddy, and Gasper. By spring 1797, a brief awakening had occurred at the Gasper River church. During summer and fall 1798, awakenings had begun at the Gasper, Muddy, and Red River congregations.

These revivals grew out of sacramental meetings—a Scottish tradition widely adopted by eighteenth-century American Presbyterians. On Friday, Saturday, and Sunday, ministers from several congregations preached on themes related to conversion and the Christian life. On Sunday they observed the Lord's Supper, with a thanksgiving service often following on Monday. The pattern begun in 1798 of heightened religious interest and conversions associated with sacramental meetings was repeated the next summer. The hallmarks of what became known as the Great Revival in the West (1797-1805)—large crowds, camping on the grounds, and the phenomenon of "falling"—first appeared during the summer of 1800.[16]

Stone, who attended one of McGready's Logan County camp meetings in early spring 1801, described the falling. "Many, very many fell down, as men slain in battle, and continued for hours together in an apparently breathless and motionless state—sometimes for a few moments reviving, and exhibiting symptoms of life by a deep groan, or piercing shriek, or by a prayer for mercy most fervently uttered." Gradually the "gloomy cloud, which had covered their faces" gave way to smiles of hope and joy; then they rose "shouting deliverance" and addressing the surrounding crowd "in language truly eloquent and impressive."[17]

Even more amazing than the falling was that sinners appeared to obtain faith within a matter of hours. In the late eighteenth century, Presbyterians, along with Baptists and Methodists, assumed that the sinner's application to Christ, or seeking of faith, would last from several weeks to a year, as it had for Stone. McGready taught that it was only when sinners had been thoroughly convinced of their helplessness to save themselves that they would perceive the excellence and glory of what God had done for sinners in Jesus Christ. Presbyterians understood this process of "conviction" to be a work of the Spirit that prepared the sinner to believe.[18]

Before attending McGready's sacramental meeting in Logan County Stone had developed the view that God gives faith through the hearing of the gospel without a special work of the Spirit to prepare one to believe. Yet difficulties with the idea had prevented him from declaring it publicly. Stone reported in 1805 that his difficulties were removed by what he believed was the work of God in the revival. "Many old and young, even little children, professed religion, and all declared the same simple gospel of Jesus. I knew the voice and felt the power."[19]

Stone believed this voice was the voice of God speaking through the gospel. The power he felt was the power of the gospel to make sinners fall in love with God and desire both forgiveness of sin and release from its power. Stone reported, "I saw that faith was the sovereign gift of God to all sinners, not the act of faith, but the object or foundation of faith, which is the testimony of Jesus, or the gospel; that sinners had power to believe this gospel, and then come to God and obtain grace and salvation."[20]

Convinced that God gives faith through hearing the gospel without a previous work of the Spirit, Stone returned to central Kentucky and urged sinners to "believe now, and be saved." Soon reports of falling at meetings spread throughout the region. In June, Stone conducted a sacramental meeting at his Concord church in which Baptists and Methodists, as well as Presbyterians, participated. The outdoor meeting continued for five days and nights. Colonel Robert Patterson, longtime member of the Lexington Presbyterian Church, attended and began a chronicle of the rising tide of revival in central Kentucky. Patterson estimated the attendance at Concord as 4,000 and the number who fell as 150. Presbyterian communion services marked by falling and the participation of Baptists and Methodists continued in the region through July.[21]

Stone's sacramental meeting at Cane Ridge, later known as the Cane Ridge Revival, began Friday, August 6, 1801, and continued through Thursday. Observers estimated the number of wagons on the grounds on Saturday and Sunday at between 125 and 148, covering the equivalent of four city blocks. Estimates of the number of people on Saturday and Sunday ranged from 10,000 to 20,000. One participant counted seven ministers preaching at the same time in different parts of the camp, some using stumps and wagons as platforms. Eighteen Presbyterian and four Methodist ministers participated. Between eight and eleven hundred took the Lord's Supper, administered Scottish Presbyterian style to successive groups of communicants seated at tables in the meeting house. Estimates of the number who fell ranged from three hundred to three thousand.[22]

An unidentified black preacher who addressed a circle of African Americans was likely a Baptist.[23] There is no evidence, however, of widespread mingling of blacks and whites at the Cane Ridge meeting. Blacks were members of Presbyterian churches, but worship services were segregated. Black members at Cane Ridge sat in a loft that they entered by a ladder from outside the building.[24]

Stone's Presbyterian colleagues Richard McNemar, Robert Marshall, John Thompson, and John Dunlavy accepted his "new light" concerning faith. However, not all Presbyterians were pleased. Stone recounted that the strict orthodox Presbyterian clergy "writhed" under the doctrines, but did not publicly oppose them at first because of the phenomenal success they seemed to have among the people.

By fall 1802 the situation had changed. Suffering membership losses to the Baptists and Methodists, some Presbyterians began aggressively preaching the doctrines of the Westminster Confession of Faith. In response, the Methodist and Baptist preachers focused on their distinctive doctrines. Desiring to maintain the unity that had characterized the Revival, Stone, McNemar, Marshall, Thompson, and Dunlavy refused to preach the distinctive doctrines of the Presbyterians, continuing, instead, to call simply for sinners to believe the gospel and be saved.[25]

By summer 1803, differences arose over order in the services, especially "mingled exercises"—the simultaneous offering aloud of individual prayers and exhortations. This practice, which had been a feature of the revival in Logan County, appeared in central Kentucky in fall 1801, following the Cane Ridge meeting.

As the revival continued, physical manifestations such as jerking and laughing increasingly accompanied the mingled exercises.[26]

Ironically, Stone and the other ministers who believed that faith came by hearing the gospel without a special work of the Spirit supported mingled exercises, which would seem to have made it difficult to hear the gospel. Furthermore, they did little to discourage the growing catalog of physical manifestations, including dancing and singing. Some of the ministers who opposed Stone's view of faith approved of at least some of the disputed practices. Generally, however, Presbyterians who opposed the new doctrine tended to view mingled exercises as unauthorized.[27]

Matters came to a head at the Synod of Kentucky that opened in Lexington September 6, 1803. Stone and his colleagues could see that the majority of the Synod was determined to suspend them from the ministry over their doctrinal stance. On September 10, the ministers presented a protest declaring their withdrawal from the Synod's jurisdiction rather than be "prosecuted before a Judge (Confession of Faith), whose authority to decide, we cannot in Conscience acknowledge."[28]

The Synod's efforts to heal the breach were unsuccessful, and the five formally united as the "Springfield Presbytery." They chose that name because of the support they had received at the Washington Presbytery meeting at Springfield, Ohio in 1803, and the "evident displays of divine power" during the sacrament held at that meeting. In January 1804, the Springfield Presbytery published a one-hundred-page pamphlet titled *An Apology for Renouncing the Jurisdiction of the Synod of Kentucky.* This document stated their position on faith and called for the renunciation of creeds as a means of maintaining the unity of the church. The Revival, they insisted, had demonstrated that unity was a gift of the Spirit and that the Bible was a sufficient rule of faith and practice. They also were clear that they continued to regard the members of the Synod "as brethren in the Lord," and that they did not desire to separate from their communion, or to exclude them from theirs.[29]

Stone reported that the *Apology* alleviated much of the prejudice against them that resulted from the Synod's opposition to their doctrine and convinced many of the truth of their teachings. He noted that positions expressed in the pamphlet resulted in positive relations with the Methodists, who apparently assumed there would be a quick union with the Springfield Presbytery. The very popularity of the Presbytery, however, made it hard not to think of themselves as a distinct party, undermining their intention to maintain the unity witnessed in the Revival.[30]

At the June 1804 meeting of the Presbytery at Cane Ridge, Richard McNemar offered a solution. He proposed adoption of a document he had drafted titled *Last Will and Testament of Springfield Presbytery*. It declared: "We *will*, that this body die, be dissolved, and sink into union with the Body of Christ at large." On June 28, 1804, the members of the Presbytery signed their names as witnesses to the document. Appended to the *Last Will and Testament* was "The Witnesses' Address," in which the subscribers declared that it was "from a principle of love to Christians of every name, the precious cause of Jesus, and dying sinners who are kept from the Lord by the existence of sects and parties in the church" that they had consented "to die the death."[31]

The witnesses did not, however, give up their prerogatives as Presbyterian ministers. Like all Presbyterians, they rejected legislating for the church on their own authority rather than the authority of Scripture. They renounced licensing and ordaining ministers on the basis of the candidate's adherence to a creed or confession of faith. Yet, they did not give up their responsibility as ordained ministers to examine, license, and ordain qualified candidates recommended by congregations.[32]

At the June 1804 meeting the witnesses also determined to be known exclusively as Christians. Rice Haggard (1769-1819) had recommended this in a sermon at Bethel Church two months earlier, arguing that Acts 11:26 should be interpreted as meaning that God had given the disciples the name Christian. A decade earlier Haggard had convinced Virginia and North Carolina Methodists led by James O'Kelly (1735-1826) who rejected Bishop Francis Asbury's appointment system to adopt the name Christian.[33]

Marshall and Thompson noted that the Presbytery's belief that the millennium was near was a major influence in their adoption of the *Last Will and Testament*.[34] As early as the sixteenth century English Puritans had associated the thousand-year rule of Christ that many saw prophesied in Revelation 20:1-6 with a sudden growth of Christianity. David Rice (1733-1816), the father of Presbyterianism in Kentucky, had identified overcoming division among Christians and renunciation of slaveholding as other marks of the millennium's approach.

The witnesses believed the Revival had overcome division among Christians. Stone also believed slavery was ending—a belief supported by the public record. Emancipations in Stone's county increased during the course of the revival, largely as a result of deeds

of manumission filed by members of the Cane Ridge congregation.[35] Reared in a slaveholding family, Stone had become an opponent of slavery in 1797. In a letter to neighboring Presbyterian pastor Samuel Rennels he had argued against the biblical defense of slavery. "Slavery," he declared, "dissolves the ties of God and man; ties the most strong and indissoluble of all others. One of these ties is conjugal affection. The loving husband is torn from the weeping distracted embraces of the most affectionate wife[,] carried far off & sold like a beast…how must the happiness of this loving pair be forever destroyed!…can this be right? Can it be agreeable to a good God?"

Stone argued that Scripture interprets Scripture and that no interpretation could be authoritative if it stood in conflict with the biblical revelation of God's love for all.[36] In 1800 he had presented a resolution from the Cane Ridge and Concord churches to the West Lexington Presbytery declaring that slavery was "a moral evil, very heinous, and consequently sufficient to exclude such as will continue in the practice of it from the privileges of the church." A year later, he had filed a deed of manumission for two enslaved Africans, Ned and Lucy, whom he had received as a bequest from his mother the year before.[37]

The signers of the *Last Will and Testament of Springfield Presbytery* thought they were promoting the unity of the church and thus hastening the coming of the millennium. However, the seven years following the publication of the document were marked by both external and internal controversy. During 1804, they were "sorely pressed" by the Synod's charge that their preaching that Jesus died for all and not merely for an elect implied universal salvation. Key to the Synod's charge was the doctrine of substitutionary atonement by which Jesus' death purchased salvation for all for whom he died. They replied that Christ died to restore sinners to union with God by a radical display of grace and not as a substitute for sinners. Stone developed the new doctrine in a thirty-six-page pamphlet titled *Atonement: The Substance of Two Letters Written to a Friend*, published in spring 1805. This publication sparked a written controversy with members of the Synod that expanded to Stone's doctrine of the Trinity.[38]

In the midst of this controversy, Shaker missionaries from New York visited the Christians in 1805 proclaiming that Christ had returned to earth in the person of Ann Lee (1736-1784) and promising perfect holiness to all who accepted celibacy and communal ownership of property. Two of Stone's closest colleagues, Richard McNemar and John Dunlavy, became Shakers, along with members of their congregations. Stone attributed the success of the Shaker mission among the Christians to the desire of some in his movement for perfect holiness and what he called the "wild, enthusiastic speculations" of his fellow preachers, including the claim that the Millennium had begun.[39] Stone, who had married Elizabeth Campbell just prior to the Cane Ridge Meeting, could not believe he would be a more perfect Christian without her and strongly opposed the Shakers wherever they went.[40]

The major issue at an October 1808 ministers meeting was slavery. Some ministers from Ohio proposed that the churches withdraw Christian fellowship from slaveholders. Stone and David Purviance, another Kentucky preacher who opposed slavery, argued against making it a matter of fellowship. Stone reportedly said that the conduct and character of every slaveholder in their churches was exemplary in every other way. Furthermore, many of them had "suffered great persecutions for the Christian cause and name, and that to declare them out of fellowship would be ungenerous and cruel in the extreme."[41] This was quite a change for Stone, who eight years earlier had proposed to the West Lexington Presbytery the exclusion of slaveholders, and may reflect his fear of losing members after suffering significant losses to the Shakers. Stone may also have come to believe that the best way to influence erring Christians was not to expel them, but to remain in fellowship.

The Christians also struggled with the issue of doctrinal uniformity that emerged over differences regarding baptism. At an 1807 conference held to discuss the subject the group decided

> …that every brother and sister should act freely, and according to their conviction of right—and that we should cultivate the long-neglected grace of forbearance towards each other—they who should be immersed, should not despise those who were not, and *vice versa*.

Several Christian preachers, including Stone, adopted believers' immersion and were immersed.[42]

Stone reported that despite the 1807 decision allowing wide leeway on believers' immersion, some ministers were unhappy that members of their congregations were submitting to it. Among those ministers were Marshall and Thompson who began to recommend that the Christians should have a formal statement of belief, a "*formulary*…by which uniformity might be promoted and preserved." Stone and others opposed the idea, insisting that the arguments for a "formulary" were the same used for the creation of every divisive human creed ever written.[43]

At a general conference at Bethel, Kentucky, in August 1810, the ministers decided that the Christians would establish a formal union and publish a statement of their current views, but not adopt a formulary. The formal union amounted to nothing more than the participants subscribing to a resolution to "unite themselves together *formally*, taking the word of God as their only rule and standard for doctrine, discipline and government, and promising subjection to each other in the Lord." The group appointed ministers Marshall, Thompson, Stone, Purviance, and Hugh Andrews to write a document expressing the Christians' current beliefs concerning doctrine and church government. They hoped such a statement would eliminate prejudice by individuals who believed they denied the divinity and atonement of Christ and rejected church order, and would open a door for cordial relations with other denominations.[44]

Seven months later, at a general conference at Mount Tabor, Kentucky, the committeee reported that they could not come to a consensus on their current views. Marshall, Thompson, and Andrews insisted on orthodox statements on the Trinity and atonement, which Stone and Purviance opposed. After discussion, the conference declared that a consensus statement was not necessary. They asserted that they could simply continue in love and unity, bearing with one another despite differences in doctrine.[45] The conference also took back the formal union that had been approved at the Bethel conference. Deeply disappointed at their failure to bring doctrinal uniformity to the Christians, Marshall and Thompson returned to the Presbyterians.[46]

Though internal controversy subsided after the Mt. Tabor conference, external controversy continued unabated. In 1811, Marshall and Thompson published a pamphlet criticizing the Christians for their false doctrine and "their disorganized state."[47] David Purviance responded to Marshall and Thompson with *Observations. Constitution, Unity, and Discipline of the Church of Christ, addressed to the brethren of the Christian Church*. Three years later, Stone published a statement of the Christians' doctrines based on a draft he had prepared for the committee charged with preparing a statement of beliefs for the 1811 Mount Tabor conference. Titled *An Address to the Christian Churches in Kentucky, Tennessee and Ohio. On Several Important Doctrines of Religion*, his purpose, as when a member of the failed drafting committee, was to open a door to fellowship with believers who viewed them as heretics.[48]

Stone's delay in publishing *An Address* was likely due to changes in his personal circumstances, beginning in May 1810 with the death of his wife Elizabeth. In October 1811, a thirty-nine-year-old widower with four daughters, he married Elizabeth's nineteen-year-old cousin, Celia Wilson Bowen, and moved to middle Tennessee.[49]

As with his earlier publication on *Atonement*, this new treatise did not satisfy critics. In 1815 Presbyterian minister Thomas Cleland of Mercer County, Kentucky, published a response titled *The Socini-Arian Detected*, attacking Stone's views of the atonement and Christology. Stone would not publish again for seven years, again likely due to a series of changes in personal circumstances including a move to Lexington, Kentucky, then to a farm near Georgetown, Kentucky, and the births of two daughters and a son. During this interval he revised his Christology in light of Cleland's criticism, but his revised edition of *An Address* published in 1821 still did not satisfy his Presbyterian critics, nor did his rejoinders answer their objections.[50]

In 1826, Stone began publication of the monthly *Christian Messenger*. In addition to calling for Christian unity on the Bible alone, the journal supported the American Colonization Society, founded in 1816. The society's founders believed slaveholders would manumit enslaved Africans if assured of their removal from white society, reflecting the racism of both supporters and opponents of slavery. In 1821, the Society purchased land in West Africa and established the colony of Liberia to demonstrate to the federal and state governments the feasibility of colonizing free blacks in Africa. Stone continued to support the Colonization Society through the 1830s.[51]

Within two decades of the return of Marshall and Thompson to the Presbyterians in 1811, the Christian Church in the West numbered more than sixteen thousand members in Kentucky, Tennessee, Alabama, Ohio and Indiana. Many had joined through profession of faith and baptism. Others had come from the Christian Church movement in Virginia and North Carolina associated with former Methodist James O'Kelly. A sizable number of Baptists—not only individuals and congregations, but whole Baptist associations—had united with the Christians in response to their call for Christian union on the Bible alone.[52] The lineage of most of these associations was Separate Baptist, a movement that had emerged from the Great Awakening in New England. By 1827, a sixth of Kentucky Baptist churches of Separate lineage had become Christian Churches.[53]

In the fourth issue of *The Christian Messenger*, Stone began a nine-part "History of the Christian Church in the West." The words "in the West" recognized that there were Christian Churches in Virginia and North Carolina and also in New England. The Christians in New England had emerged from the Baptists in the early years of the nineteenth century and were led by Abner Jones (1772-1841) and Elias Smith (1769-1846). In 1808 Smith founded the *Herald of Gospel Liberty*, reprinting in the first issue the *Last Will and Testament of Springfield Presbytery*. Smith opposed state-supported churches and their clergy, infant baptism, and the doctrines of the Trinity and predestination.[54]

Stone began his account of the Christian Church in the West with a report of prayers for revival at the beginning of the century which, he declared, God had answered by pouring out his spirit "in a way almost miraculous" in Tennessee and Kentucky. The final event in his *History* was the return of Marshall and Thompson to the Presbyterians in 1811. For Stone, the response of the Christians to Marshall and Thompson's proposal of a creed had established their identity as a Christian unity movement. Acknowledging continued opposition to the Christians he declared, "We trust in the living God, and labor to be accepted of him not doubting but that on the ground we now occupy, the whole church of God on earth will ultimately settle."[55] Meanwhile, Stone had observed the emergence of a movement among Baptists in Virginia, Pennsylvania, the Western Reserve (Ohio) and Kentucky known as "Reformers" or "New Testament Baptists," which, in his view, had much in common with the Christians.

Reformers

Two Scots Irish Presbyterians—Thomas (1763-1854) and Alexander Campbell (1788-1866), father and son—were leaders of this other group. Alexander Campbell claimed that his family had descended from the clan Campbell of Argyll, Scotland, headed by the first Duke of Argyll, Sir Archibald Campbell, a leader in the Glorious Revolution of 1688. Sources give contradictory testimony, however, concerning whether Archibald's father, Thomas, immigrated to Ireland from western Scotland in 1710 or was born in Ireland.[56]

Alexander recorded that his grandfather, also named Archibald, had converted from Catholicism to Anglicanism (the Church of Ireland) after serving in the British military in Canada during the Seven Years War.[57] While Catholicism was the majority faith of the

Irish, it was certainly not typical of Scottish emigrants to Ulster, who were almost universally Presbyterian. Archibald's conversion to Anglicanism would have given him privileges unavailable to either Irish Catholics or Presbyterians. Anglicans were "the ascendancy," the ruling class of Ireland, though vastly outnumbered by both Catholics and Presbyterian "dissenters." In counties of Northern Ireland where Presbyterians were in the majority, identification with Presbyterianism could also provide social and economic opportunities. All four of Archibald's sons became members of the Antiburgher Seceder Presbyterian Church, one of many factions among the fiercely independent Scottish Presbyterians in Ireland.[58]

In the early 1700s Scottish "Seceders" had come to Northern Ireland proselytizing. These zealous "dissenting dissenters" had rejected the reintroduction of patronage into the (Presbyterian) Church of Scotland in 1712. Patronage was the right of the hereditary owner of church property to select and install the minister in the parish church. The Scottish General Assembly had abandoned the practice in 1690 after William and Mary officially reestablished Presbyterianism in the Church of Scotland.

The British Parliament, however, brought it back as an incentive to Scottish landowners to support Queen Anne instead of the Catholic Stuarts who had been ousted in the 1688 Glorious Revolution. Those who continued to support the Stuarts were called Jacobites from the Latin for James—*Jacobus*—the deposed Stuart King. While the General Assembly of the Church of Scotland opposed patronage, they accepted it with the understanding that local presbyteries had the right to overrule any appointment. The Seceders, however, refused to allow patronage at all and withdrew to form their own Associate Synod opposed to the General Synod of the Church of Scotland in 1733.

Later, the Seceders themselves divided between Burghers and Antiburghers. This was a dispute over the "Burgess Oath" imposed on city officials in Glasgow, Edinburgh, and Perth to keep Catholics out of public office after the 1745 Jacobite Rebellion.[59] The officials were required to swear that they would abide in and defend "the true religion presently professed within this realm, and authorized by the laws thereof…renouncing the Roman Religion called Papistry."[60] The clash was over whether or not the term "true religion" could be interpreted as referring to the Seceders. The Burghers believed it could, and therefore supported the oath; the

Antiburghers believed it could not, so opposed it.

The Seceders also suffered an Old Light-New Light division over subscription to the Westminster Confession of Faith. The New Lights opposed subscription because of the clause concerning upholding "the true religion" which implied, they believed, the established church from which they had seceded—the church that had accommodated lay patronage. Between 1799 and 1806 both the Burghers and Antiburghers divided into Old Lights and New Lights. New Lights tended to ease strict adherence to Calvinist doctrine. The Old Lights, on the other hand, sought to maintain rigorous loyalty to orthodox doctrine.[61]

Religion in Northern Ireland had been shaped by constant conflict. Much of it reflected the divisions inherited from Scotland just described. But there were additional sources of conflict as well. Unlike in Scotland, where the state church was Presbyterian, in Ireland Presbyterians were dissenters, their political loyalty always under question by English officials. Ulster Presbyterianism, therefore, was formed largely by its experience of restrictions imposed by the (Anglican) Church of Ireland.

Conflict in Northern Ireland also reflected tensions between the majority Catholic population and Protestant communities consisting of the politically dominant Church of Ireland and Presbyterian dissenters who exercised considerable control in certain northern counties. The Peep O'Day Boys formed as a violent organization to protect and advance the economic well being of lower-class Protestants against Catholics and their "Protestant co-conspirators." In response, the Defenders, formerly a body dedicated to land reform for all, transformed itself into a Catholic defense organization.[62]

In the midst of the struggles, however, some Non-Seceder Presbyterians in eastern Ulster exhibited remarkable levels of religious tolerance. In Belfast, New Light leaders who opposed required subscription to any confession of faith other than the Bible raised most of the funds for the construction of St. Mary's Catholic Chapel and attended its dedication ceremony in 1784. They also helped form the Society of United Irishmen in 1791 that called for full political rights for Catholics, uniting Catholics and Protestants in a campaign for Irish independence from Britain. In 1793, their General Synod of Ulster went on record as favoring reform in the Irish Parliament and emancipation of Catholics, praying "that the time may never more return when religious distinctions shall be used as a pretext for disturbing society or arming man against his neighbour."[63] Jane Corneigle, wife of Thomas Campbell and mother of Alexander Campbell, grew up in County Antrim, a center of New Light strength.

Though Thomas Campbell's affiliation was with the strict Antiburgher Seceders, his personal sentiments tended toward the liberal and tolerant. Before his Anglican father consented for him to begin training for the Antiburgher ministry, Thomas had established a school for the poor in heavily Catholic Connaught.[64] He refused to be involved with any of the religio-political intrigues of the day, publicly opposing the secret societies that pitted Catholic against Protestant and Irish against British.[65]

In the last quarter of the eighteenth century, missionary societies that emerged from the English Evangelical Revival began a campaign to evangelize "heathen" around the world. Evangelicalism, largely in the form of Methodism, began to take shape in Northern Ireland before the Campbells departed for America. Methodists, particularly those supported by the Countess of Huntingdon, were leaders in forming the General Evangelical Society in Dublin in 1787 to furnish "a succession of zealous and popular ministers of every denomination who shall be employed to preach… wherever an opportunity shall offer."[66]

Eleven years later, in the aftermath of the failure of the United Irishmen to throw off the yoke of Britain in the Rebellion of 1798, Thomas Campbell was a founder and the only Antiburgher member of the Evangelical Society of Ulster (ESU).[67] Like the Dublin Society, the ESU proposed to send preachers, regardless of denomination, to preach the gospel to the lost. Over the next year the ESU gained support and members.

In July 1799, however, Thomas Campbell's Antiburgher Synod posed the question, "Is the Evangelical Society of Ulster constituted on principles consistent with the Secession Testimony?" After considerable discussion the Synod voted that it was not, and after a conference with three elders, Thomas Campbell submitted to the verdict by promising to "try to see eye to eye" with the Synod and to withdraw from any leadership role in the ESU.[68] By 1803 the Synod had forbidden any connection with the organization.

Campbell was also frustrated in his efforts to bring about union among the Seceders in Ireland. The Burgher and Antiburgher division had to do with political matters unique to Scotland. The burgess oaths had never been required in Ireland, yet the two parties remained

separated there just as in Scotland. In 1790 Ulster had twenty-five Antiburgher congregations and forty-two Burgher.[69] Though Thomas Campbell and other leaders felt there was no reason for them to be separated, the churches remained under the jurisdiction of the Scottish Synods that saw the distinctions as essential.

In October 1804 Campbell participated in a consultation at Richhill that drew up a formal proposal for the union of the Burghers and Antiburghers in Ireland. The Synod meeting in Belfast later that year received the proposal favorably. However, when the General Associate Synod—the Scottish body over all the Antiburgher churches—heard of the proposed reunion, it squelched any formal proposal being brought to its assembly. Nevertheless, in 1806 the Associate Synod of Ulster sent Thomas Campbell to the General Synod meeting in Glasgow, with a formal application to allow the Irish churches to make their own decision about this matter. The Synod allowed him to argue his case, but refused to allow the proposition to come to a vote.[70]

Deep disappointment with this failure, coupled with the burdens of operating a school, pastoring a congregation in Ahorey, and continuing political and religious unrest resulted in serious illness. Campbell's physician advised him that he would only get worse if he did not remove himself from the cause of his stress. In 1807 Campbell decided to do what tens of thousands of people from Ulster had already done—sail to America.[71]

By 1790, Irish immigrants and their descendants made up a fourth of the white population of Pennsylvania.[72] Networks of family members already in America, along with recruiters and merchants, fueled Irish emigration, capitalizing on their desire for a better life—economically and, in the case of Thomas Campbell, religiously.[73] The merchant networks that developed were shaped by region, religion, kinship, political allegiances, and economic priorities, and rarely overlapped.[74] Campbell could be assured that ships sailing from Londonderry would link him immediately with his kind of Irish Presbyterians who had already settled in the United States. Arriving in Londonderry April 1, 1807, he contracted passage with the captain of an American ship, the *Brutus*, sailing for Philadelphia on April 8.

Campbell landed in Philadelphia after a thirty-five day voyage and discovered that the Associate Synod of North America, which combined the Burgher and Antiburgher Seceders in the United States, was meeting in the city. Presenting himself and his letters from the Presbytery of Market Hill and the church at Ahorey, he was welcomed and assigned to the Chartiers Presbytery in western Pennsylvania. His base of operations was near the town of Washington, an area where many people he knew were already living.

He did not, however, achieve the goal of removing himself from the stresses he had experienced among the Seceder Presbyterians in Northern Ireland. His commitment to Christian unity and cooperation surfaced quickly in the American context. His actions in late August 1807, on a preaching trip to a small Presbyterian group at Cannamaugh, a community on the Allegheny River above Pittsburgh, began a series of events that would sever his formal ties with the Associate Synod. Traveling with a fellow minister, William Wilson, Campbell felt compelled to invite Presbyterians not part of his Associate Synod to share in the Lord's Supper.

As Wilson and Campbell traveled together to and from Cannamaugh (today Conemaugh), the younger and more doctrinally strict Wilson must have been distressed to hear some of Campbell's ideas. In a sermon before serving the Lord's Supper, Campbell expressed his belief that it is through faith that one receives Christ, and that there was no divine authority for requiring confessions of faith, covenants, or fasting before administering the Lord's Supper. These were matters over which the Seceders had been wrestling for some time as they revised their confession of faith titled *Narrative and Testimony*.[75]

Wilson evidently expressed his displeasure with Campbell's views to several other ministers of the Chartiers Presbytery. One of those ministers, John Anderson (1748-1830), had been appointed to accompany Campbell to a sacramental service at Buffaloe, but refused to go because of his belief that Campbell was teaching doctrines "inconsistent with some articles of our testimony." Campbell's troubles began when at the October meeting of the Presbytery someone raised a question as to why Anderson had neglected to fill his assignment at Buffaloe. Anderson stated his reason, and after considerable discussion the Presbytery voted that he was justified.[76]

The next day Thomas Campbell moved that Anderson's excuse be reconsidered. Though he had some support, the majority ruled against him, and Campbell angrily left the meeting. The Presbytery appointed a committee of five to look into his supposed heresy and ruled he was to receive no more preaching appointments because he had left the meeting the previous day. The committee included his antagonist John Anderson and three of Anderson's former pupils.

At the January 5, 1808, meeting, Anderson and the committee presented a list of seven formal charges.

In addition to heresies concerning the Lord's Supper, confessions of faith, and two other doctrinal matters, they accused Campbell of advocating that lay ruling elders had the responsibility of preaching in congregations without a minister, and that it was acceptable to hear ministers not part of the Secession church. Furthermore, they charged him with preaching in a church with a settled minister without being assigned to do so by the Presbytery.[77]

Engraving of a portrait of Thomas Campbell by Thomas Sully, prominent Philadelphia portrait painter, that appears in Alexander Campbell's *Memoirs of Elder Thomas Campbell*, published in 1861.

The Presbytery delayed a full discussion of the charges until February, allowing Campbell to prepare written responses to the accusations. The Presbytery judged his answers on two of the doctrinal matters to be satisfactory, but on the rest they judged Campbell's answers to be either evasive or actually admitting the charge. The Presbytery then voted to censure Campbell and suspend his ministerial standing.

In May Campbell appealed his case to the Associate Synod of North America meeting in Philadelphia. While the Synod reprimanded the Presbytery for allowing Anderson to refuse to fill his appointment and removed the suspension of Campbell's ministerial standing, it voted to censure Campbell with a rebuke and admonition. Though disappointed and angry, Campbell submitted to the rebuke of the Synod and spent the next two months ministering in Philadelphia at the direction of that body. When he returned home in August he discovered that the Chartiers Presbytery had given him no preaching assignments.

At the September 14, 1808, meeting of the Presbytery, Campbell presented a paper renouncing its jurisdiction and that of the Associate Synod. Following up on this action, he submitted another paper to the May 1809 meeting of the Synod titled "Declaration and Address to the Associate Synod" in which he removed himself from the authority of the Presbytery and Synod.[78]

With no ministerial appointment and no immediate means of support, a few supporters stepped forward to help. He continued to preach in the vicinity of Washington, Pennsylvania, to people who sympathized with his ideas. By early summer, however, many felt they needed a more organized way of proceeding. Abraham Altars, in whose home Campbell was living, hosted a meeting to discuss possibilities. Campbell laid out his ideas concerning the unity of the church based on the simple teachings of Scripture, which were, he insisted, the foundation for evangelizing the world. However, when he proposed that the group's operating principle be "where the Scriptures speak, we speak; and where the Scriptures are silent, we are silent," some objected, thinking it cast doubt on infant baptism. Infant baptism had already been controversial in the group, though Campbell did not believe that rejection of infant baptism was an inevitable conclusion from Scripture.

At the next meeting of the group in August, Campbell proposed the formation of an evangelical society for the spread of the gospel—to be called the Christian Association of Washington. A committee commissioned Campbell to write an organizational document and apology. By September he had completed a "Declaration and Address"—the second he had written that year. This time, however, it was not a document of separation, but a call for Christians of all denominations to come together to "promote simple evangelical Christianity." Reflecting many of the sentiments of the Evangelical Society of Ulster Campbell had helped form eleven years earlier, the *Declaration and Address* described the work of the Association as supporting ministers who would preach only those things that conformed to the "original standard"—Scripture—and who actually practiced simple New Testament Christianity.[79]

To accomplish this, Campbell insisted, cooperation across denominational lines would be necessary. Campbell attacked divisions among Christians and urged all to come together in one fold under the one Shepherd. Reflecting millennial hopes of the day, he asked why any Christian would think it incredible that the church's original unity, peace, and purity should resume "in this highly favored country"? By reading Scripture rightly, all would agree on the great central truths—in fact, they already did. Inferences and opinions divided Christians. He admitted that he had prejudices like all other humans, but stated his willingness to surrender anything not explicitly taught in Scripture if it meant returning "to the original constitutional unity of the Christian Church; and, in this happy unity, [to] enjoy full communion with all our brethren, in peace and charity."[80]

Thomas Campbell had sent word for his family to join him in America in a letter written January 1, 1808. Because of an outbreak of smallpox, the family was unable to make arrangements until late August when Alexander traveled to Londonderry to find a ship. He contracted passage with the captain of the *Hibernia*, and the family set sail on Saturday, October 1, 1808. The group consisted of Jane Campbell and six children, who ranged from twenty-one year old Alexander to Alicia who was two. The ship was caught in a storm off the coast of Scotland the following Wednesday and the Captain anchored in Loch Indaal near the Isle of Islay, for three days. On Friday evening, October 7, strong winds caused the ship to drag its anchor and strike a rock that pierced the hull. The wreck forced the Campbells to delay their journey to the United States by ten months.

Yet the delay proved to be an important time for Alexander Campbell's intellectual and spiritual formation. The family decided to stay in Glasgow until sailing weather was better. Two things shaped Alexander during the next nine months—his studies at the University of Glasgow, and his association with religious leaders seeking to reform the Church of Scotland.

At the University Campbell learned the Scottish common sense philosophy of Thomas Reid (1710-1796) from George Jardine (1742-1827), who had studied under Reid and who became one of Campbell's favorite professors. This philosophy affirmed that the data of the human senses, when confirmed by the testimony of others, was a reliable source of knowledge. The other major influence was his friendship with Greville Ewing (1767-1841), formerly a minister in the Church of Scotland, but then a leader in the religious reform led by James (1768-1851) and Robert (1764-1842) Haldane. When the Church of Scotland opposed the Haldanes' formation of the Society for the Propagation of the Gospel at Home in 1798, they began to form independent Congregational churches.

Portrait of Alexander Campbell from the late 1820s or mid-1830s by Washington Bogart Cooper, prominent Nashville painter.

In Ewing's home Campbell heard discussions on topics ranging from weekly Lord's Supper to church structure and baptism. The legitimacy of infant baptism, which Ewing strongly supported, had divided the independents, especially after the Haldane brothers received immersion—though they had never made it a term of communion. This would become a major issue in the Christian Association and the reform that Alexander and his father would launch in America.

When the University school term ended in May, the Campbell family began preparation to travel, though it took three months to secure passage. In the meantime, the semiannual "communion season" observed by the Seceder Church arrived. Though the Westminster Confession of Faith had recommended "frequent communion," the Church of Scotland had retained the medieval custom of taking it twice a year. The Confession directed that when communion was infrequent, congregational elders should examine the spiritual state of each member in preparation for the sacrament. For anyone the elders already knew, this might mean simply showing up to receive the metal token necessary for entrance to the communion service. Since Alexander did not have a letter from the Irish Synod certifying his good standing, the elders asked him to appear before them for an oral examination. Apparently they had no problem with his answers, and he received the token.

Campbell had changed during the previous six months, however. His actions on the day of the communion service have come to symbolize Alexander Campbell's growing anti-sectarianism and passion for religious reform. The method of serving the sacrament was the Scottish tradition of seating people in shifts at large tables to partake of the elements. He presented his token and was admitted, but waited until the last table of communicants was seated. When the bread and wine came around, he passed them on without taking them. This was not unheard of—Reformed literature spoke of the dangers of taking the Lord's Supper "in an unworthy manner." Apparently Campbell's refusal caused no stir. But this act, though largely private, marked for Campbell a rejection of what he now saw as sectarianism and a turn in his journey toward reform.

Finally, the family set sail from Greenock, Scotland, on August 3, 1809, on the ship *Latonia*. After an almost two-month voyage they arrived in New York on September 29, and set off immediately for Philadelphia. There Alexander contracted for transportation across the mountains to Washington, Pennsylvania, a distance of three hundred fifty miles.

In early October Thomas received word that his family had arrived in New York, so he and a friend, John McElroy, left immediately, encountering them on October 19. Over the next days they filled one another in on the details of the past two years—Thomas's formation of the Christian Association, the family's shipwreck and stay in Glasgow, Alexander's refusal to take communion at the sacramental service in Glasgow. Alexander examined his father's *Declaration and Address* and embraced the ideals it expressed.

Thomas Campbell recommended that Alexander spend six months studying Scripture, which he did, reading widely in theology and church history as well. On July 15, 1810, Alexander preached his first official sermon, eliciting strong approval from his audience. Within a few weeks he was receiving frequent calls to preach. That Thomas encouraged his son to accept these invitations despite Alexander's lack of ordination, however, proved to be a major obstacle to Thomas's petition for ministerial affiliation with the Synod of Pittsburgh of the Presbyterian Church in the United States of America (PCUSA). The Synod rejected Campbell's petition in October 1810.[81]

Though Thomas Campbell had made it clear in the *Declaration and Address* that the Christian Association was not a church, it had begun to look increasingly like one. Both Campbells preached on Sundays for members. When Thomas's efforts to affiliate with the PCUSA failed, it appeared inevitable that the group would organize itself into a church. They did so on May 4, 1811, calling it the "First Church of the Christian Association, meeting at Crossroads and Brush Run."[82] On New Year's Day the following year, Thomas Campbell formally ordained Alexander to Christian ministry.

Thomas Campbell felt uneasy about creating one more church in the dizzying array already present on the American scene. His vision for unity expressed in the *Declaration and Address* simply had not materialized. Events of 1812, however, would result in affiliation with another body calling for a return to New Testament Christianity.

Alexander Campbell had met Margaret Brown (1791-1827) in late 1810, and they were married on March 11 the following year. By summer 1811 they were expecting their first child. The Browns were Presbyterians and joyfully anticipated the baptism of their grandchild. Alexander Campbell had been thinking about infant baptism since hearing the arguments and witnessing the sharp controversy among the independents in Scotland. Now, however, the issue was personal. After studying the matter for several months, he concluded there was no scriptural warrant for infant baptism and refused the rite for his daughter Jane, who was born March 13, 1812.

Alexander's rejection of infant baptism had obvious implications. If he took his position seriously, his own infant baptism was now in question. The Haldanes had not made immersion a term of communion, and he himself had preached that it was unscriptural to do so. Yet he now felt compelled, contrary to his earlier views, to submit to immersion.[83]

The previous year Thomas Campbell had immersed three members of the Christian Association. Though he opposed immersing persons who had been baptized as infants, Joseph Bryant, Margaret Fullerton, and Abraham Altars, had never been baptized in any form. Because Bryant insisted that immersion was the only true baptism, Thomas Campbell immersed the three on July 4, 1811.[84]

Alexander assumed his father would refuse to administer immersion to him and others who had received infant baptism. The Baptists were the only ones who consistently practiced believer's immersion, yet Campbell had strong prejudices against them as ignorant and uneducated.[85] Finally he approached a Baptist minister named Matthias Luce (1764-1841) who he felt would be open to immersing him. In their initial conversation, Luce was more than happy to immerse Campbell and any others who desired it according to normal Calvinist Baptist practice, which included relating a conversion experience. When Campbell explained that he wanted the act performed on the basis of a simple confession of faith in Jesus as Son of God, Luce balked. Campbell had been studying the issue intensely for some time by then, and he was thoroughly prepared to argue his position. Campbell's persuasive abilities prevailed, and Luce, despite possible censure by his Baptist Association, agreed to perform the baptisms as Campbell stipulated.

Wednesday, June 12, 1812, was the day appointed. Thomas Campbell had been convinced by his son's arguments, and prior to the immersions stated in a lengthy address that it was his duty to submit to this important divine institution. Alexander also spoke on the importance of immersion. Luce then immersed Alexander and Margaret Campbell, Thomas and Jane Campbell, Alexander's sister Dorothea, along with James and Sarah Hanen in Buffalo Creek. Within a short time, almost all the members of the former Christian Association, now called the Brush Run Church, had either submitted to immersion or left.[86]

With the acceptance of believer's immersion, it seemed natural to many that the Brush Run Church would affiliate with the Baptist denomination. Alexander Campbell, however, still viewed Baptist preachers as "narrow, contracted, illiberal and uneducated." Furthermore, he opposed subscription to the Baptists' Philadelphia Confession of Faith as a term of fellowship.

Yet Campbell's experience with the Baptist people generally was much more positive, seeing them as committed to Scripture and true conversion.[87] Over the next year Baptist churches in the area issued Campbell multiple invitations to preach and urged the Brush Run congregation to join the local Redstone Baptist Association. Both Alexander and his father believed they should pursue their reforms with other Christians. So after consultation, Brush Run agreed to become part of the Redstone Association on the condition that they would be allowed to preach and teach whatever they learned from the Holy Scriptures regardless of any creed or confession. A majority of the association agreed to the condition, and from 1815 until the 1830s the Campbells advocated their reforms as Baptists.

Meanwhile, Alexander Campbell became a master at spreading his ideas through the popular media of his day, especially public debates and journalism. Though at first he had agreed with his father that debates were contrary to the Christian spirit, he eventually came to view "a week's debating [as] worth a year's preaching."[88] In 1820 he published his first debate, conducted with Presbyterian John Walker on baptism. The book became something of a sensation, leading Campbell to reissue it in an expanded edition in 1822.

The popularity of the published Walker debate led Campbell to open his own printing shop in 1823 in Bethany, (West) Virginia, on land deeded to him by his father-in-law. For the next seven years he published a monthly journal, the *Christian Baptist*. In 1826 he published the first edition of a version of the New Testament he edited titled *The Living Oracles*. Two years later he issued the first of many hymnals.[89]

Through the *Christian Baptist*, Campbell called for a "restoration of the ancient order of things," including weekly observance of the Lord's Supper and weekly contributions for the poor. He also attacked confessions of faith, "modern missionary schemes," and the clergy.[90] Campbell argued that the ancient faith was not the metaphysical dogmas of the creeds, but the gospel or good news of what God had done through Jesus Christ, as testified by the apostles. To be a Christian was to believe that Jesus was the Messiah upon the testimony of the apostles, and to be baptized in accord with apostolic practice into the name of the Father, Son, and Holy Spirit.[91]

Moreover, he declared that the confession that Jesus is the Christ, followed by baptism, was the only basis necessary for the union of Christians. Human beings would never unite on a human creed, since creeds were composed of inferences made from the revelation of what God had done in Jesus Christ and were subject to all the defects of human reasoning. Attempts to establish unity on a human creed were contrary to "the prayer and plan of the Lord Messiah," that is, Jesus' prayer in John 17:20-21: "I do not pray for these only (for the unity and success of the apostles) but for those also who shall believe on me through, or by means of *their word*—that they all may be one—that the world may believe that Thou hast sent me."[92]

For Campbell, the testimony of the apostles, the unity of the disciples, and the world's belief that Jesus is the Christ were bound together. Only when the church was united through faith in the apostles' testimony would the world believe that Jesus was the Christ. Missionary "schemes" prior to the restoration of the unity of the church would be futile.[93]

Campbell also attacked the "clergy system" and the two props he said supported it. The first was the "alleged special call of God" to ministry, which clergy used to enhance their authority. The second was the supposed necessity of an association of the called ones for the better administration of the church. The real purpose of such associations was to protect the authority and stipends of the clergy. The clergy system resulted in people not hearing and reading the Bible, since when congregations could not afford the services of the clergy, they did not meet.[94]

Campbell's opposition to the clergy, however, did not extend to what he identified as the church's rightly authorized ministry. The first issue of the *Christian Baptist* carried the following caution in bold type: "In our remarks upon the 'Christian clergy,' we never include the elders or deacons of a Christian assembly, or those in the New Testament called the overseers and servants of the Christian Church."[95] In the *Christian Baptist* and later publications, Campbell outlined what he understood to be the qualifications and duties of the divinely instituted ministry.

The ministry of the Christian community consisted of bishops, deacons, and evangelists. Bishops, meaning overseers, also identified as elders or pastors, were to teach, preside at meetings of the church, shepherd the members of the congregation, and rule in matters of discipline.[96] Campbell did not include the word "preach" in his description of the bishop's distinctive duties since he saw preaching as simply sharing the Christian gospel, which was the duty of all Christians. Campbell understood the bishop's duty to teach as explaining a passage of Scripture or interpreting the Christian faith.[97] Administration of the Lord's Supper was included in "presiding" at meetings of the congregation.[98]

Campbell believed that elders or bishops should give full time to the office and should be remunerated for their service.[99] Bishops differed from clergy in that they were elected to pastoral office from the congregation of which they were a member and were officers only of that congregation. Campbell argued that the qualifications necessary to fulfill the duties of an elder were not likely to be found in a younger person or in a new convert of any age. By 1826 he was convinced that there should be a plurality of elders, which he also called a "presbytery," in every congregation.[100]

Deacons were servants of the church. Campbell noted with approval that it was a custom of the ancient church to "commit to the deacons care of the Lord's table, the bishop's table, and the table of the poor." Since the duties of a deacon were often "too oppressive for a single individual" and included keeping the treasury of the church, Campbell believed it advisable to establish a plurality of deacons in every congregation.[101]

In contrast to bishops and deacons who were officers of the congregation, evangelists were sent out by the congregation or a group of congregations to preach the gospel, baptize converts, organize congregations, administer discipline, and teach the assembled Christians until they were able to elect elders. Evangelists were to receive both compensation and supervision from the church or churches that sent them. Presumably because he read 1 Timothy 4 ("Let no one despise your youth") as instructions to an evangelist, and because the evangelist was not set over the church but worked under its supervision, Campbell believed that an evangelist could be a young person.[102]

In 1830 Campbell replaced the *Christian Baptist* with the *Millennial Harbinger*, though he published both through July. In the prospectus Campbell stated, "This work shall be devoted to the destruction of Sectarianism, Infidelity, and Antichristian doctrine and practice." The journal's object was to develop and introduce the millennium, which he defined as the achievement of the ultimate perfection of society described in the Bible.[103]

Campbell used the *Millennial Harbinger*, as he had the *Christian Baptist*, to oppose slavery. Having made Virginia his home, he was familiar with the institution of slavery and personally acquainted with Africans. As early as 1820, Africans had been included on the rolls of the Brush Run Church.[104] In the inaugural issue of the *Christian Baptist*, he had criticized American Christians who praised the civil and religious freedom of the United States, yet maintained at the same time "a system of the most cruel oppression, separating the wife from the embraces of her husband, and the mother from her tender offspring…because might gives right and… skin is a shade darker than the standard color of the times."[105] He again acknowledged the evil of slavery in the first issue the *Millennial Harbinger*, alluding to it as an injustice that would be righted under any government embodying Christian principles. He also promised to publish articles that would pave the way for the elevation and emancipation of enslaved Africans.[106]

In 1829, Campbell served as representative from Brooke County to the Virginia State Constitutional Convention, intending to introduce gradual emancipation of enslaved Africans into the document. His failure led him to conclude that he would focus his efforts on eradicating the evil through religious and not political action. Like Stone, however, Campbell later became a supporter of the objectives of the Colonization Society, even proposing in 1832 that the federal government allocate ten million dollars a year to fund the work of the Society, including the purchase of enslaved females from slaveholders who would not emancipate them so as to reduce the potential number of persons born into slavery.[107]

Despite his professed opposition to slavery, Campbell purchased two brothers, James and Charley Pool from a Methodist preacher during the months between the death of his first wife, Margaret, late in 1827, and his marriage to Selina Huntington Bakewell in July 1828. In keeping with his advice to others, he freed them when they reached the age of twenty-eight. He also owned at least two other enslaved Africans, all of whom were freed after a period of service.[108]

Campbell engaged in five public debates, and several others in print. Three public debates were with Presbyterian ministers—John Walker in 1820, William Maccalla in 1823, and N. L. Rice in 1843. All focused on baptism, though the Rice debate included discussions of the role of the Holy Spirit and the authority of creeds. In 1829 he met the skeptic Robert Owen (1771-1858), and in 1837 Catholic Bishop John Baptist Purcell (1800-1883) of Cincinnati. These last two contests propelled him into the national spotlight as one of the chief defenders of Protestant Christianity.[109]

One of the most distinctive doctrinal developments in the Campbell reform was its understanding of the purpose of baptism. Campbell first fully developed the position that baptism is for assurance of the remission of sins and admission to the Kingdom of Christ in his debate with Maccalla. This view contrasted sharply with the Baptist position that the church should administer baptism only to candidates who had already received inward assurance of the remission of their sins. Campbell's view of the purpose of baptism along with his sharp distinction between the Old and New Covenants, which eliminated the role of the law in bringing persons to faith, disturbed many Baptists and led to increasing tensions between Campbell and other Baptist leaders.[110]

The person often credited with the numerical growth of the Reformers was Walter Scott (1796-1861). Scott was born in Moffat, Scotland, in 1796 and raised in the Church of Scotland. While his parents had hoped he would become a Presbyterian minister, after study at the University of Edinburgh he immigrated to Long Island, New York, at age 22 to teach school at the invitation of his uncle, George Innes. The following year he moved to Pittsburgh, Pennsylvania. There Haldane minister George Forrester invited Scott to teach in a school Forrester operated. Under Forrester's tutelage, Scott accepted his reform ideas and was immersed.

Portrait of Walter Scott painted between 1832 and 1844 while serving as pastor of the Christian Church at Carthage, Ohio. The artist is unknown.

Acceptance of believers' immersion led Scott to re-examine all his religious views. When Forrester drowned in 1820, Scott assumed leadership of the school and church, and spent much time reading in his former mentor's library. The next year he traveled to New York in search of the author of a pamphlet that argued convincingly that baptism was for the remission of sins. His disappointment at the legalism of the Scotch Baptist congregation where the tract's author, Henry Errett (d. 1825), was a member, led the melancholy Scott on a months-long journey through New Jersey, Maryland, and Washington, D.C., in search of authentic Christianity. He finally returned to Pittsburgh at the invitation of Robert Richardson, father of one of his former pupils, to tutor fifteen students.

Scott met Alexander Campbell when Campbell visited Pittsburgh during the winter of 1821-22. Though temperamentally very different, they forged a relationship that would lead to forty years of collaboration in religious reform. Within five years Scott had married, moved to Ohio, and become active in the Mahoning Baptist Association of which Campbell was then a part.

Campbell endorsed Scott as one who understood the ancient order of things like few others. At the 1827 meeting of the Mahoning Association, Scott accepted the invitation to serve as the group's evangelist to "proclaim the word to those without, and to teach those within to walk in the Lord."[111] This opportunity, and Scott's development of the evangelistic method known as the "five-finger exercise," made him the foremost evangelist among the Campbell Reformers. Pointing one by one to the fingers of a hand, Scott proclaimed that *faith* in the gospel of Jesus Christ leads to *repentance*, which leads to *baptism*, which is followed by God's *forgiveness of sins* and the *gift of the Holy Spirit*. Scott said that if he had a sixth finger, it would be "eternal life."

To many who assumed a Calvinist model in which sinners could only pray for the Holy Spirit to give them faith, this message was a marvelous word of hope. Scott—like Stone—was preaching that anyone could hear and accept the gospel without waiting for a special work of the Spirit. God had already acted, and they had only to accept the good news to begin the inward process that would lead to eternal life. According to contemporary accounts, Scott baptized an average of 1,000 persons annually for the next three years.[112]

As Reformed Baptist churches spread through Pennsylvania, Virginia, the Western Reserve of Ohio, and Kentucky, antagonism also grew between the Reformers and those who rejected Campbell's beliefs. In 1829 the Beaver Baptist Association in Pennsylvania issued an "anathema" condemning the Campbell reformers, a move that spread to other associations and led to the expulsion of members and churches that sympathized with the reform. By the end of the decade a clear break existed between the groups. In Kentucky up to one third of Baptists, numbering as many as ten thousand, sided with Campbell.[113]

Union of Christians and Reformers

Barton Stone and Alexander Campbell met in fall 1824, while Campbell was conducting a two-month preaching tour of Kentucky. At Stone's invitation, Campbell spoke at the Christian Church in Georgetown and stayed in Stone's home. In 1827, they engaged in a brief published exchange regarding the doctrine of the Trinity and the confession required for Christian fellowship.[114] In the September 1829 *Christian Messenger* Stone reported that a Baptist brother had recently asked him why the Christians and the "New Testament Baptists" did not become one people. Stone responded that if there was any difference between the two groups, he did not know it. "We have nothing in us to prevent a union," he declared, "and if they have nothing in them in opposition to it, we are in spirit one."[115]

Despite Stone's professed ignorance, significant differences did exist between the two groups. Like other Baptists, Campbell believed that only congregations had the right to ordain ministers. Stone, maintaining his Presbyterian heritage, held that ministers could be ordained only with the approval of both a congregation and a conference of ordained ministers. He also held that ministers charged with teaching false doctrine were to be tried by a conference of ministers rather than a congregation. Like other Baptists, Campbell made believer's immersion a qualification for participation in the Lord's Supper. Though the Christians had generally adopted believer's immersion, they refused to make it a qualification for membership or receiving the Lord's Supper.[116]

Campbell feared that union with the Christians, known for their non-traditional views of the Son of God and atonement, would hinder his influence with more orthodox Christians. Rather than responding directly to Stone's statement that they were already one in spirit, Campbell published the views of correspondents who believed there would be negative consequences in associating too closely with the Christians. A letter from an Irish writer identified Stone as an Arian and chided Campbell for calling Stone "brother" in their exchange on the doctrine of the Trinity.[117]

Another correspondent, referring to the New England Christians associated with former Baptists Abner Jones and Elias Smith, reported hearing of a Christian church that was Unitarian, ignorant, and enthusiastic. The writer observed that he would certainly use the name Christian exclusively if such disreputable groups had not already appropriated it, but that as things were, he thought he would keep the name Baptist.[118] Stone responded that based on this reasoning, one would have to reject Christianity itself because of abuses. And, certainly, Stone ventured, this correspondent would have to reject the Reformed Baptists, for in the West their enemies would assert that "they were Unitarian in their sentiments, and enthusiastic too, and that many of them were ignorant as well."[119]

Campbell claimed he had always favored the name Christian. However, if Christian had come to imply Unitarian or Trinitarian in a technical theological sense, he would choose the ancient name disciple over Christian and recommend "disciples of Christ" as the best designation.[120]

Despite Campbell's negative responses, Stone raised the issue of union again in the August 1830 *Christian Messenger.* He asserted that both groups were working "to unite all christians in the spirit and truth of the New Testament," a cause he had advanced for almost thirty years. Furthermore, some among the Christians had long advocated immersion for the forgiveness of sins and the gift of the Holy Spirit. He warned, however, that if the Reformers were to make their view of baptism a requirement for fellowship, they would become sectarians with a one-article unwritten creed that excluded more followers of Christ than any written one.

Responding in the *Millennial Harbinger,* Campbell expressed hope that his "Extra" on "Remission of Sins" would convince Stone that the immersion commanded by Christ was for the remission of sins. If obedience to the commands of Christ was sectarianism, Campbell declared, it would be impossible to refute the charge. "No opinion, creed, or dogma of human invention shall be with us a term of communion; but *obedience* to the commands of Jesus will always be, unless we should unhappily renounce the Lord Jesus as our Lord, King, and Lawgiver."[121]

In February Campbell continued to develop the distinction between opinions and obedience in response to an article by Stone the previous month. Stone had stated that it was his opinion that immersion was true baptism. If, however, he were to make this opinion a term of fellowship, where would such action stop? Campbell responded that opinions were always speculative, doubtful matters. However, the word could not be applied to "matters of testimony, to laws, institutions, or religious worship," otherwise the church would have no way of determining its faith and practice.[122]

In the September 1830 *Christian Messenger* Stone endorsed weekly observance of the Lord's Supper.[123] However, Stone rejected Campbell's view that churches should make believer's immersion a qualification for participation in the Lord's Supper. "What authority have we for inviting or debarring any pious, holy believer from the Lord's table? The King's will is, that his friends do this in remembrance of him—and all that his law [1 Corinthians 11:28] expressed on the subject is, 'Let a man examine himself and so let him eat and drink.'" Stone declared that Christ never instituted barriers to keep unimmersed persons from worshipping him. As for names, he had no objection to the biblical "disciple." He could not, however, give up the name Christian, since according to his reading of Acts 11:26, God had given it to the church and it was a means of uniting followers of Christ.[124]

Stone raised the issue of a union of the Christians and Reformers a third time in the August 1831 *Christian Messenger*. "The question is going the round of society, and is often proposed to us, Why are not you and the Reformed Baptists, one people? or, Why are you not united?" Stone again responded that he believed the two groups were united in spirit, and that there was no barrier on the Christians' side to their union in form.[125]

Campbell's reply in the *Millennial Harbinger* challenged Stone to define what he meant by "union in form." If he meant creating a formal confederation of all the "christians" and "disciples," what would be the "articles of confederation," and how would they be adopted? Should there be a convention of messengers from the churches, or a general assembly of all the members? He noted that Stone had made no proposal for a formal union, nor had he heard of any general meeting among the Christians to discuss terms for such a union. Did Stone think, he asked, that one or two people had the power to "propose and effect a formal union among the hundreds of congregations scattered over this continent, called christians or disciples, without calling upon the different congregations to express an opinion or a wish upon the subject?[126]

Campbell also questioned Stone's claim that the Reformers had adopted positions taught by the Christians many years before. Identification of his reformation with earlier anti-creedal movements was precisely what he wanted to prevent.

> Many persons, both in Europe and America, have inveighed against sects, creeds, confessions, councils, and human dogmas, during the last two centuries, and some even before Luther's time; but what have these to do with the present proposed reformation? This is only the work of a pioneer: it is clearing the forests, girdling the trees, and burning the brush.

It was not the anti-creedal, anti-council, and anti-sectarian impulse that was central to his reformation,

Campbell claimed. Rather, the quest for the ancient gospel and ancient order of things distinguished it "from every other cause plead on this continent or in Europe since the great apostasy."[127]

Campbell's critiques could not stop Stone's efforts to bring Christians and Reformers into union. Early in 1831, Stone had established a cordial relationship with Reformer John T. Johnson. Johnson, a lawyer and former member of Congress, had been a member of the Baptist church at Great Crossings, Kentucky, just west of Georgetown. When the Great Crossings Baptist Church refused to become part of Campbell's reformation, Johnson and two others had formed a new congregation in February 1831. In October the new church began worshipping with a group of Christians in the vicinity.[128]

As part of a strategy for uniting Christians and Reformers, Stone invited Johnson to join him as co-editor of the *Christian Messenger* to begin in 1832. At a meeting at Georgetown in late November 1831, Reformer John Smith and Christian John Rogers expressed their willingness to travel together throughout Kentucky to unite congregations of the two groups. Those present also agreed that before sending Smith and Rogers, they would conduct a four-day meeting at Georgetown over Christmas day and a similar meeting at Lexington over New Year's Day to which they would invite Christians and Reformers from across the state.[129]

According to John Smith's biographer, John Augustus Williams, the four-day Christmas and New Year's meetings were well attended by both Christians and Reformers who "worshipped and counseled together with one spirit and one accord." Though no official records exist of either meeting, Williams provided an account of the Lexington gathering. Smith, speaking on behalf of the Reformers, stated that the union God commands was founded on the Bible alone as the rule of faith and practice. He admitted that the two groups differed on some speculative teachings such as "the mode of divine existence" and Christ's atoning work, matters that had been controversial among Christians for centuries. He claimed that for several years, he had attempted to use only the language of the Bible when speaking about such things since no one could be offended by using the very words of the Lord himself.

Distinguishing between opinion and faith, he asserted that followers of Christ could never be united in opinions, but that they must be one in faith. He concluded, "Let us, then, my brethren, be no longer Campbellites or Stoneites, New Lights or Old Lights, or any other kind of *lights*, but let us all come to the Bible and to the Bible alone, as the only book in the world that can give us all the Light we need."[130]

Stone responded, agreeing that they could never unite on speculations regarding the subjects Smith had mentioned. While philosophical discussions of these topics might be interesting, they could never build up the church. He confessed that after the Christians had given up creeds for the Bible alone, he had delivered some speculative discourses on such subjects, though they never feasted his heart. He agreed with Smith that such speculations should never be preached, and that if speaking of these issues at all, only the words of Scripture should be used. He concluded, "I have not one objection to the ground laid down by him as the true scriptural basis of union among the people of God; and I am willing to give him, now and here, my hand."[131]

Williams reported that Stone turned and offered Smith his hand symbolizing the pledge of fellowship. Someone then proposed that all who were willing to unite on these principles follow Stone's example, and leaders from both groups moved forward to clasp one another's hands and ratify their union. The next day, Sunday, January 1, 1832, the Christians and Disciples present met together to share the Lord's Supper, symbolizing their unity.[132]

The *Christian Messenger* for January 1832 announced the Lexington union. It also announced that John Smith from the Reformers and John Rogers from the Christians, supported equally by contributions from both groups, had been set apart to visit the churches to encourage similar unions. When asked if the Christians and Reformers in other places would now unite, Stone and Johnson answered: "If they are sincere in their profession, and destitute of a party spirit, they will undoubtedly unite." The two editors rejoiced to report unions in Rush County, Indiana, and Maury County, Tennessee, noting that the union had been manifested already in three states. They encouraged members everywhere to send news of the progress of the cause in their regions, describing such news as "worth more than volumes of dull theology, and vain speculations."[133]

Despite Campbell's reservations, two individuals, Smith and Stone, had proposed and initiated a union of the two communions. There had been no general meeting of messengers from all the congregations of Christians and Disciples to deliberate on terms and conditions. Though the meetings in Georgetown and Lexington had consisted of members and preachers from

several churches, neither meeting could be described as a general assembly of both bodies. Both were simply regional gatherings with immediate results limited to the union of the local congregations in their respective towns. Every congregation was free to decide how to proceed.

The union of Christians and Reformers begun at Lexington would grow only if embraced by individual congregations and leaders, and there were members of both groups who were not happy with the prospect. In an early effort to head-off objections to the union, Stone and Johnson published a joint editorial in April 1832 insisting that neither side had "joined" the other. They noted that "One will say, the Christians have given up all their former opinions of many doctrines, and have received ours—another will say, the Reformers have relinquished their views on many points, and embraced ours." Such statements, they observed, were harming the union effort by provoking jealousy between the groups. Furthermore, they declared, such statements were not true. Neither group had dropped any beliefs or practices

John T. Johnson joined Stone as co-editor of the *Christian Messenger* in 1832. From a prominent Kentucky family, Johnson had served two terms in the U.S. Congress before becoming a minister. His brother Robert M. Johnson was vice-president under Martin Van Buren.

held before the union; that had not been a condition for bringing it about. All had pledged, they insisted, simply to follow Christ as he directed in Scripture.[134]

Union, of course, did lead to changes for both sides. Campbell's view of the authority of the local congregation to ordain ministers prevailed over Stone's belief that a body of ordained ministers also had a role.[135] Stone's insistence on open communion prevailed over Campbell's exclusion of the unimmersed, reflected in Stone's widely adopted admonition that the table is the Lord's and that Christians do not have authority to invite or debar.

At the same time, Campbell's practice of limiting church membership to the immersed became the norm. This was a departure from the Christians' open membership practice, which allowed individuals to decide whether they had fulfilled the command to be baptized. Reflecting, perhaps, a move toward Campbell's understanding of immersion as an institution commanded by Christ, and not a matter of opinion, Stone defended this change by observing that the Christian Church was founded on the New Testament and that in the New Testament baptism was not sprinkling or pouring, but immersion.[136] The matter of the name remained unresolved, with individual congregations being known as Church of Christ or Christian Church while the united movement was often identified as Disciples of Christ.

That many of the Christians had adopted Campbell's understanding of the purpose of baptism made the union easier, as it had a direct influence on Christian assemblies. Well into the 1820s, the Christians' assemblies had resembled gatherings of the Great Revival. Describing the preaching of the Christians prior to their adoption of baptism for remission of sins, preacher B.F. Hall wrote, "We would clap and rub our hands, stamp with our feet, slam down and tear up the Bible, speak as loud as possible and scream at the top of our voice, to get up an excitement." Though the falling, jerking, and laughing had disappeared, emotional outbursts and simultaneous prayers had continued to mark the worship of the Christians, especially when praying for "mourners" to receive an assurance of the remission of sins from the Holy Spirit.[137] Campbell's teaching of the purpose of baptism changed the congregations' expectations regarding how the Spirit would be received, and correspondingly, their behavior in seeking the Spirit.[138]

Christians who had not accepted Campbell's views of immersion had the greatest difficulty with the union. This included leaders of the Elias Smith-Abner Jones movement in New England and the James O'Kelly movement in Virginia and North Carolina.[139] It also included leaders of Stone's Christians in the West, such as David Purviance who, like other opponents of Campbell's views, argued that identifying immersion with assurance of the remission of sins crowded out inward evidences of the remission of sins, substituting cold legalism for a lively spiritual faith.[140]

Stone called on Christians to unite with the Reformers despite differences on the purpose of baptism. All of the disputants, he noted, believed immersion was baptism. With this fundamental agreement why should they fight and divide because they didn't agree on every aspect of the design of baptism? Reminding the Christians of their historic refusal to impose opinions as tests of fellowship, he admonished: "Let the unity of christians be our polar star. To this let our eyes be continually turned, and to this let our united efforts be directed—that the world may believe, and be saved."[141]

Stone insisted that he could see the presence of Christ in Campbell's movement—the chief test of fellowship for both groups. Christians who opposed Campbell's views replied, however, that the Campbell churches made their position on the purpose of baptism and other doctrines tests of fellowship, thereby excluding the Christians from fellowship.[142] Despite Stone's efforts, many churches of his movement in Ohio and some in Indiana refused to unite with the Reformers. Instead, they remained in communion with the Smith-Jones and O'Kelly Christians in what became known as the Christian Connection. In 1931 the Christian Connection, by then known as the Christian Church, merged with the Congregational Churches to form the Congregational Christian Churches. In 1957 congregations of the Congregational Christian Churches (each deciding for itself) merged with the Evangelical and Reformed Church to become the United Church of Christ.

Stone grieved that not all the Christians united with the Reformers. Nevertheless, the union brought together roughly ten thousand Christians and perhaps twelve thousand Reformers to form a new movement of over twenty thousand. Over the next three decades the Stone-Campbell Movement would become one of the ten largest denominational bodies in the United States, with an estimated membership of two hundred thousand.[143]

2

Developments in the United States to 1866

The new movement, despite its growth, faced many challenges. Alexander Campbell's teaching on the purpose of immersion remained controversial. New initiatives included the establishment of schools and extra-congregational organizations for mission. In addition, the churches' view of their role in bringing in the millennium made it impossible to avoid the pressing social issues of slavery and race, the treatment of Native Americans, and war. As they struggled to respond, they found their commitment to Christian unity challenged by the sometimes radically different positions held by Stone-Campbell Christians.

Immersion

The distinctiveness of Alexander Campbell's teaching of immersion for remission of sins insured that it would continue to be an issue. In the minds of many, Campbell's stance implied that immersion of believers was essential to being a Christian. Yet when challenged by a correspondent from Lunenburg, Virginia, about a statement referring to Christians in the Protestant sects, Campbell exclaimed in the September 1837 *Millennial Harbinger* that he could not

> make any one duty the standard of Christian state or character, not even immersion into the name of the Father, of the Son, and of the Holy Spirit, and in my heart regard all that have been sprinkled in infancy without their own knowledge and consent, as aliens from Christ and the well-grounded hope of heaven.[1]

However, he ended this statement with the caveat that anyone who willfully neglected or was willfully ignorant of any ordinance of Christ, or who refused to obey because it was possible for someone to be saved without it, could not be counted as a Christian.

Campbell soon discovered that his position concerning "Christians in the sects" was not universally held among members of the Movement. In response to his critics, he provided ample evidence from previous writings that he had always held the position expressed in the disputed article. He could not consider as enemies of Christ those who, though having received only infant baptism, showed their absolute loyalty to Christ through their active love for others and constant love and devotion to God. It was an error, he declared, to deny that such people were Christians. Such denial was even more repugnant when it came from those who, though they happened to hold what he considered a scriptural view of baptism, lacked the very evidences of Christ in their lives seen in those they condemned.[2]

While Campbell continued to insist that New Testament baptism was believers' immersion, he rejected the idea that one's submission to immersion was the evidence of Christian identity.

> It is the image of Christ the Christian looks for and loves; and this does not consist in being exact in a few items, but in general devotion to the truth as far as known.[3]
>
> …the term *Christian* was given first to immersed believers and to none else; but we do not think that it was given to them because they were immersed, but because they had put on Christ;…Can a person who simply, not perversely, *mistakes* the outward baptism, have the inward? I answer that, in my opinion, *it is possible*.

For Campbell, as for Stone, it was the image of Christ in one's life that confirmed Christian identity. He never wavered from urging "faith, repentance and baptism… as essential to their constitutional citizenship in the Messiah's Kingdom, and to their sanctification and comfort as Christians."[4] Yet he consistently taught that the person who lived a life shaped like Christ is the true Christian.

Campbell's theology of baptism, however, did influence his understanding of the church. He continued to insist that immersion was a requirement for formal entry into the church. He was equally firm in his assertion that his stance on baptism did not deny the Christian identity of the unimmersed, in whom one could see the face of Christ. This tension in Campbell's ecclesiology would contribute to a later reemergence of the issue of open membership.

Education and Organization for Mission

A key element in the growth and stability of the Stone-Campbell Movement was the establishment of schools. Barton Stone taught in schools located in Lexington and Georgetown, Kentucky, and Thomas and Alexander Campbell taught in and operated schools in both Ireland and the United States. The Movement's earliest institution of higher education was Bacon College, established in Georgetown, Kentucky, in 1836, and named after the empiricist philosopher Francis Bacon. Other early schools included Alexander Campbell's Bethany College in Virginia, now West Virginia, begun in 1840, and Tolbert Fanning's Franklin College started in 1845 near Nashville, Tennessee.

These schools did not see themselves as denominational institutions serving only members of the Stone-Campbell Movement. Each was privately chartered and governed, followed a liberal arts curriculum, and solicited students regardless of religious background. They did, however, require Bible instruction for all students. Furthermore, though their founders and leaders resisted the idea of being theological seminaries for the training of ministers, the colleges definitely served that function. Many nineteenth-century leaders of the Movement were products of the colleges.[5] Given the pervasive racism of American society, these schools were accessible, however, only to whites.

Both Stone and the Campbells opposed church structures that were obstacles to Christian union and reform. Though Stone believed conferences of ordained ministers exercised legitimate authority in ordination and trying ministers for false doctrine, his experience with the Synod of Kentucky had fueled his resistance toward the efforts of Marshall and Thompson to impose uniformity on the Christians. The Irish Antiburgher Synod's censure of Thomas Campbell in 1797 for his

work with the Evangelical Society of Ulster, his expulsion in 1809 from the Associate Synod of North America, and the rejection of his petition to become a minister of the Presbyterian Church in the United States of America provided ample evidence to Thomas and Alexander Campbell of the repressive and divisive potential of such structures. Yet both Stone and the Campbells valued extra-congregational structures and believed that they could serve the church's mission.

The Campbells' adoption of believer's immersion led to their connection with Baptist associations. These associations, consisting of local congregations in specified regions, served as cooperative structures for mutual edification, pooling of resources for evangelism, and helping resolve church disputes. Though they had no formal jurisdiction over the churches, they did function as centers of accountability.[6] In 1830, the Mahoning Baptist Association, of which Alexander Campbell was then a member, met in Austintown, Ohio. Despite the success of the Association's evangelistic efforts through its support of Walter Scott, many supporters of Campbell's reform feared the associations were becoming coercive structures. Attempts by some associations to expel the Campbell reformers, such as the 1829 Beaver Association's "Anathema," had confirmed their fear.

As the 1830 Association meeting began, Walter Scott moved that the Mahoning Association be dissolved as "an advisory council" or "an ecclesiastical tribunal." Before Alexander Campbell could argue against the motion, Scott called for a vote, and the motion carried. Somewhat irritated, Campbell responded that despite this action, the group would still have to continue to meet and work together in some way. Campbell's biographer, Robert Richardson, put a positive spin on the move, describing it as the Association having "resolved itself into a simple annual meeting." Campbell himself gave a positive account of the meeting in the *Millennial Harbinger*, noting that the group planned to have a voluntary meeting for reporting on evangelistic and reform efforts the following year at New Lisbon, Ohio.[7]

The next year Campbell began a series of articles in the *Millennial Harbinger* on "The Co-Operation of Churches," a series that would continue in various forms during the next two decades. In the first article he argued that just as a church can do more than an individual, a district of churches can do more than a single congregation. He argued from Scripture that churches in the New Testament were organized into districts and cooperated in both benevolence—aiding the suffering churches in Judea—and other religious work, including evangelism, citing the example of 2 Cor. 8:19 where the churches had appointed an evangelist to travel with Paul.[8]

In his October 1831 report of the New Lisbon annual meeting—successor of the Mahoning Association— Campbell stated that the gathering's most significant action was to propose a plan of cooperation in evangelism by the churches. The proposal suggested annual meetings of the churches in four counties of the former Association, as well as continuing an annual meeting of all the churches for worship, hearing reports, and discussing how to organize and fund cooperative evangelism. According to Campbell, everyone present accepted the proposal.[9] Though they had rejected the name, in reality the functions of the old Association had been continued in the new annual meeting.

Nevertheless, opposition even to this minimal form of extra-congregational organization arose. In the May 1832 *Millennial Harbinger*, A. B. G. warned that he saw in the recent discussions an "association in embryo." It was from such small beginnings, he asserted, that the many-headed monster would grow. He insisted that there had never been nor could there ever be any legitimate reason to create any such combination of churches to advance the Kingdom.[10]

Despite criticism, the annual meeting of the former Mahoning Association churches continued, and other groups followed the same pattern, with regional and state meetings for worship, preaching, and cooperation in evangelism becoming the norm by the 1840s.[11] Yet Campbell had come to believe that something more was needed. In conjunction with a notice warning readers of a dishonest minister named James McVay, Campbell asserted in November 1841 that as long as the churches had only the uncoordinated efforts then in place, people like McVay would continue to plague the churches. What was needed, he believed, was a general cooperation, a national organization. Campbell then proposed to demonstrate from Scripture that a Christian community existed beyond the local congregation, and that it was authorized to select and appoint public leaders.[12]

In a brief article in 1842, Campbell listed the areas in which he believed the churches needed to cooperate, including missions, Bible publication, benevolence, and the ordering of the ministry. He further stated that the churches could not have adequate cooperation without a more extensive organization.[13] This began an extended discussion of the topic in the *Millennial Harbinger*. Between 1842 and 1848 Campbell published no fewer than twenty-nine articles on church organization and church

cooperation—the majority in the first part of the decade. In January 1849 he promised readers another series on the topic, informing them that he intended to appoint a committee to determine whether there was a scriptural model or divine precedent for a specific form of church organization. In April he reported that the committee had only been able to meet once and had not yet come to a conclusion. In an article examining the word *ekklesia*, he concluded that each congregation is responsible to Christ for its own actions, and that nowhere in Scripture is there any authorization for a national or regional church. Yet he also stated his belief that the independent character of the churches did not prohibit cooperation of congregations— even at the national level—to advance the Kingdom.[14]

Campbell continued developing his ideas of how the church functioned at both local and universal levels. Not only were there officers or servants in each local congregation, he insisted that Scripture clearly showed that certain officers also functioned for the universal church—in the first age they were Apostles, Prophets, Evangelists, and public messengers; and in the current day, missionaries and messengers of the churches. Furthermore, no divine statutes regulated the church in its organization and pooling of resources for evangelizing the world. As long as a plan preserved the independence of the individual congregations and provided for cooperation through covenant relationships, it was within the bounds of apostolic authority. That is why, he concluded, the Baptist association had always been for him the most acceptable form of cooperation in Christendom.[15] As for a general organization for the churches of his reform, Campbell must have had in mind the model of the Triennial Convention created in 1814 by Baptists in the United States for cooperation in foreign missions.

Campbell asked for responses to the idea of calling a general meeting of the churches for Cincinnati, Lexington, Louisville, or Pittsburgh. In July he reprinted a proposal from Walter Scott's *Christian Age & Unionist* calling for the meeting to be in Cincinnati in October. Campbell was convinced, however, that because of a recent cholera outbreak in the city, people would not attend in October. He suggested the following May would be best. Furthermore, he insisted that it be a meeting of "messengers of churches, selected and constituted such by the churches—one from each church, if possible, or if impossible, one from a district, or some definite number of churches." It was not to be a meeting of self-appointed messengers, or of representatives of only a few districts, but a true general convention.[16]

Despite his suggestion to wait until May, organizers moved ahead with a meeting that convened on October 23-27, 1849, in the Christian Church at the corner of Fourth and Walnut Streets in Cincinnati. Campbell himself did not attend, explaining later that he had been suffering from "an unusually severe indisposition." However, he published a glowing report of the convention written by W. K. Pendleton that included the constitution of the American Christian Missionary Society, created at the convention and modeled after the mission agency of the Congregational Churches.

Pendleton reported that one hundred fifty messengers from almost as many congregations had attended. While he made this number out to be remarkable, it was certainly only a fraction of what Campbell had hoped for. Nevertheless, following Pendleton's report Campbell exclaimed that his expectations for the convention had been more than realized, and he saw its accomplishments as "a very happy pledge of good things to come."[17]

Campbell's evaluation was overly optimistic. Opposition reflecting earlier fears of such organizations immediately arose. The Church of Christ at Connelsville, Pennsylvania, composed a list of resolutions opposing the missionary society created by the Cincinnati convention. Not only was a missionary society not authorized by Scripture, they insisted, but the method of membership was based on annual dues that would exclude many Christians—even the apostles themselves who had no silver or gold. They cited the cooperative method used for evangelization in Tennessee as their preferred model.[18]

The so-called Tennessee plan, though not confined to that state, seemed to reflect Alexander Campbell's own understanding of scriptural cooperation. A system of collaborative efforts between local congregations was begun in Middle Tennessee in the early 1840s first in certain counties, then later in "districts" of two or more counties, and finally in a state cooperation in 1847. These gatherings were voluntary and strictly confined to consultation and cooperation in raising funds for the work of evangelists in areas targeted by local church leaders attending the meetings. These cooperations did not preclude evangelism done independently by churches or individuals, nor did they have power to interfere with any congregation. Representatives of the congregations themselves, not a separate board of directors, selected evangelists, determined support, and targeted areas for work.[19]

After the Civil War when the scriptural legitimacy of extra-congregational structures became particularly divisive, some insisted that Campbell had opposed them

early in his reform efforts, but had reversed his view either because of senility or vanity. Campbell served as President of the American Christian Missionary Society from its beginning in 1849 until his death in 1866. Yet, in the 1823 *Christian Baptist* he had seemed to oppose such organizations, exclaiming, for example, that no Christian should dare to "transfer to a missionary society, or Bible society, or education society, a cent or a prayer, lest in doing so they should rob the church of its glory, and exalt the inventions of men above the wisdom of God."[20] Campbell himself explained, however, that his objections were never against Christians cooperating for a good and scriptural end. It was the abuse of such structures he had opposed, not the structures themselves.[21]

Despite Campbell's support, the American Christian Missionary Society (ACMS) experienced only limited success between its establishment in 1849 and Campbell's death in 1866. Its first missionaries were Dr. James T. (1807-1874) and Julia (1813-1908) Barclay of Virginia. Antislavery leaders in the Movement criticized the ACMS because the Barclays were holders of several enslaved Africans. Though they divested themselves of all such persons when they received their missionary appointment, they were never acceptable to some members of the Movement.[22]

The Society chose Jerusalem for its initial effort based on millennial expectations about the conversion of the Jews that would precede Christ's second coming. After three years, the ACMS's lack of funding forced the Barclays to return to the United States in 1854.[23] Barclay was disappointed with the results of the Jerusalem Mission. The nearly six thousand Jewish inhabitants of the city suffered under an oppressive Muslim regime and resented the presence of all other religious traditions. Roman Catholic and Orthodox groups also resisted his evangelistic work.

Though frustrated in his attempts to evangelize Jews, Barclay, a medical doctor, treated more than 2,000 cases of malaria during an epidemic that broke out during his first year in Jerusalem. In addition, he pursued his avocation of archaeology, and even assisted Edward Robinson—often known as the father of biblical archaeology—in his excavations around Jerusalem. Barclay published the results of this work in 1858 as *The City of the Great King*, which expressed his millennial beliefs and remains an important resource for the topography of nineteenth-century Jerusalem.[24]

The Barclays returned to Jerusalem in the summer of 1858. During this second mission, the doctor's millennial expectations grew even stronger. In articles published in the *Millennial Harbinger* in 1860-1861, Barclay claimed that God had sworn to the Jewish people through their prophets that they would one day be restored to their homeland. Included in that restoration was their return to "spiritual favor" with God by their conversion to apostolic Christianity. He called on the churches of the United States and Great Britain to support the repatriation of the world's Jews to Palestine so that their conversion might be accomplished more easily and quickly. The end of time was near, he believed, and the conversion of the Jews would usher in the Second Coming of Christ.[25] However, Barclay's disappointment only increased. His fervent millennialism became an embarrassment to leaders who had previously supported him, and as support from the ACMS diminished due to the Civil War, the Barclays abandoned the mission in 1862 and returned home permanently the next year.[26]

Perhaps in response to criticism lodged by antislavery members of the Movement, the ACMS's second missionary was Alexander Cross, a black man who went to Monrovia, Liberia, in 1854. The idea of sending a missionary to Liberia had been circulating among Stone-Campbell leaders since the late 1840s. In his address to the national convention in 1853, Alexander Campbell announced what already had been done to begin the work. Ephraim Smith had visited Liberia at his own expense and recommended that the ACMS establish a mission there. The churches of Kentucky had identified "a colored brother, a gifted preacher of the gospel" who was willing to go. This was the model already established by other Protestant denominations: to commission a formerly enslaved person to immigrate to Liberia to preach among "his own people."[27]

The "colored brother" of whom Campbell spoke was Alexander Cross (1811-1854). He was an enslaved man and a member of Ninth Street Christian Church in Hopkinsville, Kentucky. D. S. Burnet, Vice-President of the ACMS, visited the church in 1852 and heard Cross deliver an address on temperance which convinced him that this "pious and orderly man" was the ideal candidate for the Liberian Mission. Burnet appealed to the members of the congregation, who purchased Cross's freedom and provided him with the necessary education so that "by the time he was ready to depart he had been well qualified for his duties and responsibilities." Other churches throughout Kentucky contributed to Cross's support, and by late 1853, enough money had been collected to fund his work for the first year. Cross and his family landed in Monrovia, Liberia, as the first Stone-Campbell missionaries to Africa in early January 1854.

Two months after arriving, he contracted malaria and died, ending the effort.[28]

The Society's third missionary was Julius Oliver Beardslee (1814-1879). Shortly after his graduation from Oberlin College in 1838, Beardslee had begun mission work in Jamaica as a Congregationalist. An ardent abolitionist, he had gone to the island to organize churches among formerly enslaved persons in St. Andrews Parish on the southeastern part of the island. He continued this work for sixteen years, but in 1855, concern for his health forced him to return to the United States.[29]

Even before returning to the United States Beardslee had questioned the practice of infant baptism. While serving Congregationalist churches in northeast Ohio he came in contact with Stone-Campbell leaders and became convinced that immersion of believers was scriptural baptism.[30] After his immersion, Alexander Campbell and William K. Pendleton strongly supported the idea of sending Beardslee back to Jamaica, this time as an agent of the ACMS. The board of the ACMS unanimously approved his appointment in 1857, and for several months he traveled among the churches raising funds for the Jamaica Mission.[31]

Beardslee and his wife Eliza returned to Jamaica in January 1858, and within a few months had organized Christian Chapel in Kingston—now Duke Street Christian Church—as a base for their mission work. Although membership remained small, the church offered morning and evening services on Sunday, a Sunday school for children and a Bible study for adults, a lecture on Wednesday evening, and occasional prayer and praise meetings. By 1860, the mission reported that because of the efforts of Jamaican leaders, four additional churches had been planted within a short distance from Kingston.[32]

Undoubtedly, the Beardslees' prior connections in Jamaica helped them begin this new mission. Some of the founders of Christian Chapel had been part of the Congregationalist Freeman's Chapel before the missionaries' departure. Moreover, John Crole, "a young preacher…in [the Beardslees'] former ecclesiastical connection," became the preacher for one of the four new churches in 1860. Beardslee boasted that he had "converted" a leading Methodist missionary, and claimed that leaders of that denomination had been trying for some time to prevent their people from affiliating with the new mission, "but with poor success."[33] Nevertheless, by 1864, funds to support the Jamaica Mission had dried up and the Beardslees again returned to the United States.

Slavery and Race

For several years Stone and Campbell supported the American Colonization Society. In late fall 1834, Stone moved from Georgetown, Kentucky, to Jacksonville, Illinois, to remove his family from slavery. This move coincided with his endorsement of William Lloyd Garrison's call for immediate abolition without the removal of Africans from the United States.

In the April 1835 issue of the *Christian Messenger*, Stone wrote that while he had planned to write several articles for his readers on the subject of slavery, he had decided instead to reprint a tract sent him by a friend. The tract, titled "Address to the People of the United States on Slavery," was originally published by the New England Anti-Slavery Society, organized by Garrison in 1832. The "Address" noted that many believed the enslaved Africans were not prepared for liberty. The tract countered that if Americans would acknowledge them as humans and confess the wrong done to them, rejecting the evil notion that people can be property, this would be the first step toward "civilizing and Christianizing the negro."[34]

Stone stopped printing the "Address" after three installments. In its place, he published in the July 1835 issue of the *Christian Messenger* two articles defending immediate abolition. The first was a letter to the editor of the *Vermont Chronicle* by a resident of Barbados, testifying that the 1834 abolition of slavery in the British colonies had proven not only safe, but beneficial. Eighty thousand formerly enslaved Africans had been freed, and blacks outnumbered whites ten to one. There was such order and industry among the population that those who had formerly opposed emancipation had reversed their opinion. In Barbados, he exclaimed, "I would as soon sleep with open doors, as I would in any town on the banks of the Connecticut River."[35]

The second article was a report of hopeful prospects of emancipation in the French colonies based on a speech by the Duc de Broglie of the French Chamber of Peers on February 23, 1835. The Duc de Broglie argued that the successful abolition of slavery in the British colonies proved that apprehensions regarding the consequences of abolition were exaggerated. Such a transition was thus shown possible without breakdown of order or threat to property holders. The example of successful abolition of slavery in the British colonies had eliminated the last justification for its continued existence.[36]

In November Stone explained why he had discontinued reprinting the "Address." Not long after he had begun publishing it, he had heard of riots and acts of violence in the North *against* abolitionists and growing resistance to all efforts to abolish slavery. Some of his readers in the East and South had cancelled their subscriptions to the *Christian Messenger* because of the articles. He lamented that though he had opposed slavery for nearly forty years, he was at a loss as to how to end the evil.[37] However, Stone did not retract his endorsement of immediate abolition. Rather, in 1842, like many radical abolitionists, he called on Christians to prepare for Christ's coming to establish a millennium of justice and peace by withdrawing from participation in civil governments and by living instead by the laws of Christ.[38]

The connection between Stone's call for Christian withdrawal from participation in civil government and his support for the immediate abolition of slavery was evident in "An Interview Between an Old and Young Preacher," published in December 1844, a month after Stone's death. The Young Preacher raised objections to the Old Preacher's call for Christians to withdraw from participation in civil government based on a reading of the King James Version of Romans 13:1, which counsels Christians to "be subject to the higher powers." In response, the Old Preacher observed that "[i]f it be the duty of Christians under one worldly government to uphold and support that government, then it is the duty of Christians living in every worldly government to uphold and support that government; those living in N[orth] America must uphold and support the democracy of *all* the U[nited] States ..." Stone's placement of the word *all* before the United States clearly pointed to federal and state laws supporting slavery. Stone pointed out that the Apostles in Acts 4 had chosen to obey God rather than human laws.[39]

Despite Stone's endorsement of immediate abolition without colonization, Stone-Campbell Christians continued to support colonization. Georgia philanthropist Emily Tubman (1794-1885) provides a striking example. In 1843, sixty-nine enslaved persons accepted her offer of freedom and assistance to immigrate to Liberia. She worked through the Maryland Colonization Society to charter a ship at great personal expense and to accompany them on their journey. Tubman's example is certainly exceptional, and it is impossible to determine with certainty how many members of Stone-Campbell churches freed enslaved persons and assisted in their emigration to Liberia. Still, colonization continued to find support among members of the churches.[40]

Meanwhile, Alexander Campbell's alarm over the increasing divisiveness of the issue of slavery was leading him to examine his position. In May 1844, just six months before Barton Stone's death, the General Conference of the Methodist Episcopal Church had clashed over whether a bishop could hold enslaved Africans, resulting the next year in the separation of the southern conferences to form the Methodist Episcopal Church, South. Baptist churches in the South pulled out of the Triennial Convention that same year after both Home and Foreign Mission Societies refused to appoint missionaries who held enslaved Africans, forming the Southern Baptist Convention in Louisville, Kentucky.

Emily Tubman's efforts to free and "colonize" enslaved Africans were aided by Kentucky Senator Henry Clay, who had been her legal guardian after her father's death and who became President of the American Colonization Society in 1836.

These events deeply affected Campbell's hopes and fears for the destiny of his own movement. In his millennial optimism, Campbell had come to believe that in America religious freedom would lead to the restoration of the ancient gospel and order of things, which would in turn lead to the unity of all Christians. This unity would result in the conversion of the world, which would usher in the millennium, in which slavery would be abolished.[41] If, instead, the very nation prepared by God for this wonderful scenario destroyed itself over the issue of slavery, all would be lost.

In the January 1845 *Millennial Harbinger* Campbell printed a letter written four years earlier by his father to Cyrus McNealy that revealed his position regarding slavery in light of its divisive potential. McNealy had taken a strong antislavery position, asserting that slavery was sinful, the result of violence, and unauthorized by Scripture. Thomas Campbell began by quoting every Scripture he could find that mentioned slavery. Using a literalistic interpretation of each passage, he attempted to refute McNealy's assertions. God had allowed Abraham to have slaves in the Old Testament, and Paul and Peter told slaves to be obedient to their masters in Titus and 1 Peter, therefore slavery could not be inherently sinful. Yet Thomas Campbell closed his letter by stating that Americans, as citizens and Christians, should do all they could for the ultimate abolition of slavery, because of the tendency for abuse inherent in the American system.[42]

In the next issue, Alexander Campbell began a series of eight articles detailing his view of the Christian position regarding American slavery. In the final article, Campbell summarized his position in three propositions: the simple relation of master and slave is nowhere condemned by Scripture; slavery is inexpedient because it is not in harmony with the spirit of the age; but no Christian community claiming to follow the Bible can make the simple relation of master and slave a term of fellowship or a subject of discipline.[43] Campbell's so-called moderate views were founded on a literalistic interpretation of Scripture, his deep fear that this issue had the potential of destroying his life's work of reform, and deeply embedded racist assumptions that blinded him to the perspective of enslaved Africans. In the series he had stated, "Much as I may sympathize with a black man, I love a white man more.[44]

The slavery controversy took an unexpected turn for Campbell during an 1847 trip to visit churches and raise funds for Bethany College in Great Britain and Ireland. After arriving in Liverpool on May 29, he began a rigorous schedule of travel and speaking throughout England and Scotland. When he reached Edinburgh on August 5, 1847, Campbell found himself challenged by members of the Scottish Anti-Slavery Society. American slavery had become an enflamed issue in Scotland during the previous two years, sparked by the visit of formerly enslaved African and anti-slavery advocate Frederick Douglass. During his tour Douglass had spoken widely against Britain's complicity with American slavery. Joined by William Lloyd Garrison, the two had especially stirred passions in the fledgling Free Church of Scotland by calling on the body to refuse support from American Presbyterians who supported slavery.[45]

The Anti-Slavery Society posted placards in Edinburgh labeling Campbell a slaveholder and "defender of manstealers," terms used by Douglass and Garrison in their recent campaign. The charges disrupted Campbell's speaking engagements in Edinburgh. The Society's secretary, Rev. James Robertson, challenged Campbell to a debate, and placards with this challenge followed him to every city in which he was to speak.

In late August Campbell finally accepted the challenge through a letter published in the *Edinburgh Journal*. Campbell's supporters, however, began an attack on the integrity of Robertson. They posted notices questioning Robertson's status as a "reverend" and asking if he were the James Robertson who had been put out of the Baptist Church in Dundee for abusing his mother. Robertson and his supporters immediately filed libel charges against Campbell with a warrant forbidding him to leave Scotland until the case had been decided. The warrant was judged legal in a series of appeals, and the trial was set for ten days later.

Campbell, apparently seeing an opportunity for bringing attention to his cause, refused to allow his friends to post bail and went to jail. When the judge, Lord Murray, finally heard the case, he declared the warrant illegal and ordered Campbell's release.[46] Campbell denied ever supporting American slavery or defending "manstealers." Yet his insistence that slavery was not inherently evil, his opposition to immediate emancipation, and his racist attitudes made him suspect to abolitionists.

Ultimately, Campbell's attempt to avoid division by promoting a "moderate" position on slavery proved futile. The Fugitive Slave Law of 1850 required all citizens to cooperate in the return of runaways or suffer severe penalties. Campbell's denunciation of those who advocated civil disobedience to the Law was a lightening rod. John Kirk of Ohio labeled Campbell a heretic for advocating that it was right to hold humans forcibly as property and that a Christian minister could be a slaveholder. He challenged Campbell's support of the Fugitive Slave Law as in direct conflict with the teachings of Scripture. "I have come to the conclusion that I will neither patronize priest nor paper that is not strictly anti-slavery." Campbell replied that Kirk himself needed emancipation from his extreme "opinionism," calling

him "a very good miniature Pope." Such exchanges contributed to rising tensions in the Stone-Campbell Movement and led Campbell to complain that whatever position he took he was condemned.[47]

In 1856 several students at Campbell's Bethany College defied a de facto gag order on the subject of slavery. The school expelled five students for disruptive conduct, and several others left. Some were accepted immediately at North-Western Christian University in Indianapolis (now Butler University), which had been established to provide a "free state" anti-slavery option to members of the Stone-Campbell Movement.[48]

A clear voice for the anti-slavery position was Indiana preacher Pardee Butler (1816-1888), who took his campaign to Kansas in 1855. Lacking feathers, pro-slavery activists tarred and "cottoned" him, threatening to hang him if he persisted in his work. Not deterred, in 1858 Butler requested financial support for his work in Kansas from the ACMS. Isaac Errett (1820-1888), ACMS Corresponding Secretary, responded: "It must… be distinctly understood that if we embark in a missionary enterprise in Kansas, this question of slavery and anti-slavery must be ignored." Interpreting Errett's stipulation as a gag order, Butler replied:

> For myself, I will be no party, now or hereafter, to such an arrangement as that contemplated in your letter now before me. I would not make this 'Reformation of the nineteenth century' a withered and blasted trunk, scattered by the lightnings of heaven, because it took part with the rich and powerful against the poor and oppressed, and because we have been recreant to those maxims of free discussion which we have ostentatiously heralded to the world as our cherished principles.[49]

In protest to the ACMS position, founder of North-Western Christian University Ovid Butler (1801-1881, no relation to Pardee), Cincinnati preacher John Boggs (1810-1897), and several others organized in 1858 an anti-slavery convention in Cleveland, Ohio, and founded the Christian Missionary Society as a rival to the ACMS the following year. This society provided modest funding of Pardee Butler's work in Kansas.[50]

Stone-Campbell Christians also produced two important anti-slavery publications. One was an abolitionist paper begun in 1854 by John Boggs, first titled the *North-Western Christian Magazine* then changed to the *Christian Luminary* in 1858. The other was an anti-slavery manual published in 1848 by John Fee, founder of an interracial school in Berea, Kentucky. Fee supported immediate emancipation and attacked the position that the Bible sanctioned slavery.[51]

In his book *The Philosophy of Slavery*, educator and minister James Shannon asserted a philosophical and theological defense of hereditary bondage as embodied in American slavery.

Outspoken advocates of immediate abolition could be found even in Campbell's family. His sister, Jane Campbell McKeever, principal of the Pleasant Hill Female Seminary, and her husband Matthew operated a station on the Underground Railroad in West Middletown, Pennsylvania—within ten miles of Alexander Campbell's Bethany, (West) Virginia home. In 1854 she clearly intended to take her brother to task in a letter addressed to John Boggs and published in Boggs' *North-Western Christian Magazine* (italics and capital letters are hers).

> I truly rejoice to find that ONE of *our brotherhood* has had the fortitude, and [independence] of mind, to rise superior to the reproach and opposition of so many of his *professed Christian brethren*, in behalf of the poor, oppressed and degraded slaves…I trust that you will be encouraged to persevere, believing

that God, who in all generations has been the God of the oppressed…will strengthen you, and bless your efforts in the good cause for which you plead.[52]

Campbell's sister Dorothea and her husband, Joseph Bryant, were also participants in the Underground Railroad. In the early 1840s, the Bryants recruited their son, Bethany College student Thomas Campbell Bryant, to conduct escaped slaves from Wheeling (West) Virginia through Bethany to the McKeever home in West Middletown. Campbell's sister Alicia was married to Matthew Clapp, yet another supporter of the Underground Railroad, who, like Jane McKeever, publicly castigated Campbell for his position on slavery.[53]

At the same time, the Stone-Campbell Movement also included pro-slavery activists. James Shannon (1799-1859) was a prominent scholar who served as president of the University of Missouri, Bacon College, and Christian University (now Culver-Stockton College). His 1855 address to a pro-slavery convention reflects attitudes characteristic of advocates in both the North and South:

> …if, as we have seen, right of property in slaves is sanctioned by the light of Nature, the Constitution of the United States, and the clear teaching of the Bible, a deliberate and persistent violation of that right, even by government, is villainous as highway robbery; and when peaceable modes of redress are exhausted, is a just cause of war between separate states, and of revolution in the same state.[54]

Such sharp polarization thwarted Alexander Campbell's attempts to prevent fissures in the Stone-Campbell Movement over the issue of slavery. Furthermore, his opposition to slavery on practical grounds had no more impact on the number of slaveholders and enslaved Africans in the Movement than calls for immediate abolition on moral grounds by Barton Stone and others. Statistics from the American and Foreign Anti-Slavery Society of 1851 showed that members of the Stone-Campbell Movement owned 101,000 slaves, making them, per capita, the largest slave-owning religious body in the nation.[55]

Evidence of racism in Stone-Campbell churches could be found in remarks like the 1851 appeal for financial assistance to a northern church from an evangelist in Mississippi. He urged support because the whites he was evangelizing were "of the same superior race as yourselves."[56] A letter to Alexander Campbell in 1861 by white evangelist Edward E. Gacey detailed his violent treatment at the hands of church leaders in Virginia upon discovering he was married to a "mulatto" woman who was able to pass as white.[57] Having reviewed much of the early literature of the Movement, historian David Edwin Harrell, Jr., concluded that white superiority always lurked just below the surface in the thought of white members of the Stone-Campbell Movement.[58]

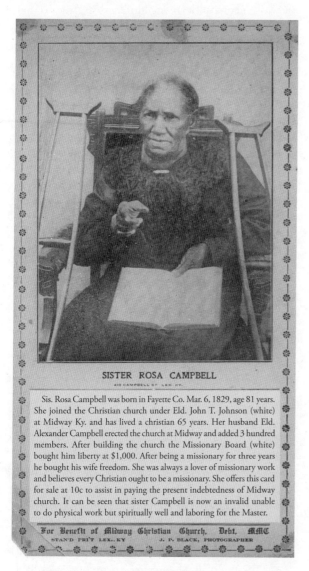

SISTER ROSA CAMPBELL
410 CAMPBELL ST. LEX. KY.

Sis. Rosa Campbell was born in Fayette Co. Mar. 6, 1829, age 81 years. She joined the Christian church under Eld. John T. Johnson (white) at Midway Ky. and has lived a christian 65 years. Her husband Eld. Alexander Campbell erected the church at Midway and added 3 hundred members. After building the church the Missionary Board (white) bought him liberty at $1,000. After being a missionary for three years he bought his wife freedom. She was always a lover of missionary work and believes every Christian ought to be a missionary. She offers this card for sale at 10c to assist in paying the present indebtedness of Midway church. It can be seen that sister Campbell is now an invalid unable to do physical work but spiritually well and laboring for the Master.

For Benefit of Midway Christian Church, Debt, MMC
STAND PRI'T LEX. KY   J. P. BLACK, PHOTOGRAPHER

Despite the pervasive racism, blacks continued to be part of the Movement. As was the case with Protestant churches throughout the South, black membership most often resulted from association with a "Christian" owner or overseer. For some, exposure to the preached word came as a result of driving whites to church. Sometimes plantation owners allowed slaves to attend their services, though in segregated seating. Despite being relegated to back seats and balconies, many blacks heard the gospel, believed it, confessed their acceptance of Christ, and received baptism.[59]

Black participation in white-controlled churches, however, was limited. Sometimes blacks served as custodians. Occasionally they filled the office of deacon, although ministering only to black members. There is no record of black elders.[60]

Though written records are lacking, oral tradition holds that an African American congregation, possibly the first in the Movement, was established at Midway, Kentucky, in the mid-1830s, with a black minister named Alexander Campbell serving as pastor. Records definitely show the church to be in existence by 1852. The Kentucky Christian Missionary Society eventually purchased Campbell for $1,000.00 to allow him to devote his time to preaching. Kentucky law would have required that he leave the state if they had given him his freedom. It is also possible that the first school for black pupils in the area, which likely met on Sunday, was started in this church.[61]

Other black congregations had been established in Kentucky, Ohio, North Carolina, Georgia, and Tennessee by 1863. At least one of them, begun in Pickerelltown, Logan County, Ohio, in 1838, also functioned as an Underground Railroad station. Peter Lowery, a black businessman and church leader, became pastor of the Grapevine Christian Church, begun near Nashville, Tennessee, in 1859. According to the best available figures, black membership in the Stone-Campbell Movement totaled seven thousand in 1862.[62]

Treatment of Native Americans

Few in Native American communities became members of Stone-Campbell churches. This may have reflected the attitudes of Alexander Campbell whose growing accommodation to slavery was mirrored in his response to Native Americans. In January 1830 Campbell expressed outrage at the treatment of Cherokee Indians by the state of Georgia. Between 1827 and 1831 the Georgia legislature, prompted by demand for arable land for cotton and the discovery of gold on Cherokee property, passed legislation abolishing Cherokee laws and government and set in motion a process to seize their land, divide it into parcels, and offer the parcels in a lottery to white Georgians.

Campbell argued that if any property owner could be deprived of land "because he is red, or yellow, or some other unfashionable color," then the "rights of man" were only what anyone in power said they were. He also contended that the United States government must honor its treaties, including those with the Cherokee; otherwise it was "the right of the strong always to plunder the property and insult the person of the weak." Finally, he agreed with William Lloyd Garrison's argument that the Cherokee were not under the jurisdiction of the state of Georgia, or any other state.[63]

Following this January 1830 editorial, however, Campbell was silent on the plight of Native Americans. Readers of his *Millennial Harbinger* would scarcely have known that there were Native Americans within the borders of the United States. Given Campbell's expression of complete sympathy for the Cherokee cause in 1830, one might have expected him to protest in 1838 when the U.S. Army entered the Cherokee Nation, rounded up as many Cherokee as they could into temporary stockades and subsequently marched the captives to what the government named Indian Territory, now the State of Oklahoma. Four to five thousand Cherokee died along what became known as the "Trail of Tears."

The most prominent advocate for evangelism among Native Americans in the Stone-Campbell churches was James Jenkins Trott of Tennessee. Trott had joined the Methodist Episcopal Church in 1821 and was working as a missionary among the Cherokee in Georgia by 1826. The state of Georgia imprisoned him and several other missionaries in 1831 when they refused to take an oath of loyalty to the state. While in prison, Trott read some writings of Alexander Campbell, and when he was released, he became a convert to "the primitive gospel." The Methodists eventually cut ties with him after he preached doctrines about baptism that contradicted accepted Methodist teaching. In 1831 he wrote to Campbell about his experiences stating, "My heart's desire and prayer to God is that the primitive gospel may be introduced, prevail and triumph among this oppressed people."[64]

Over the next two decades Trott worked as an evangelist among native Americans in Tennessee, Georgia, and other parts of the South. His home was near Franklin College, and he worked with Tolbert Fanning to organize cooperative mission efforts throughout Tennessee.[65] By 1856, he grew frustrated with the lack of support for missions to Native Americans among the Stone-Campbell churches. He particularly criticized the thousands of dollars raised for colleges compared to the hundreds given to help convert the Cherokee.[66]

After campaigning for several months, he secured financial support from the Franklin congregation for his return to work among the Cherokee in Indian Territory. He also wrote an eloquent plea for missions among the Cherokee to Alexander Campbell in 1860, which Campbell published in the *Millennial Harbinger*.[67] The American Civil War and Trott's own poor health undermined his work and led to his death in 1868. Nonetheless, Trott's contribution to the advancement of the Movement's work among the Cherokee was without parallel.

War

Members of the Stone-Campbell Movement were greatly mixed in their attitudes toward war. Many leaders, however, came to embrace pacifism. In July 1835, Barton Stone showed his support of the peace movement by publishing parts of a letter written by Stephen Thurston refusing a commission from the governor of Maine to be chaplain of a militia regiment. Thurston stated that he opposed war and therefore could not participate in support of military training. If he served as a chaplain and war did break out, he would be required to pray for the success of the United States. Would that not, he asserted, be the same as "praying that God would… enable us to shoot, cut, stab, and destroy our fellow men with great skill, and rapidity; and lay them at our feet, weltering in their gore?" Would such a prayer be consistent with the conduct expected of a Christian minister, he asked. "Can…prayer for victory over our enemies, when that victory is to be gained by butchery and blood, be justified in the sight of that God who requires us to love our enemies, and pray for them?"[68]

In the same issue of the *Christian Messenger,* Stone published extracts from a recently published pamphlet by William Ladd calling for the formation of a Congress of Nations to interpret international law and a Court of Nations to apply it. Ladd had led in the formation of the American Peace Society in 1828. Although Stone would eventually advocate an antigovernment stance, having lost faith in the power of human governments to achieve justice, he was still calling for a Congress of Nations as late as June 1841.[69]

Most members of the peace movement did not oppose the use of force in defense against unprovoked aggression. However, in 1838, "ultraists" within the movement, led by Henry Clarke Wright and William Lloyd Garrison, formed a Non-Resistance Society to oppose the use of force even in self-defense. Wright and Garrison argued that the practice of non-resistance would usher in Christ's reign on earth. Stone was open, as late as 1827, to arguments in support of Christians defending themselves against aggression. In response to the question, "Is war right or wrong in the Kingdom of Christ?" he answered that although the gospel "aims a death blow at the very root and principle of war," yet "if an assassin were to enter our houses to kill us, our wives or children, should we not act right in endeavoring to defend ourselves and families?" Assuming the answer to this question to be "yes," he argued by analogy that a nation would be justified in repelling aggressors by force.[70]

William Lloyd Garrison (1805-1879), quoted by Alexander Campbell in his opposition to government treatment of the Cherokee, significantly shaped Stone's later views on slavery and war. (National Portrait Gallery)

In 1842, Stone addressed the question of whether Christians should go to war in the form of a dialogue between two "Christian brethren." The brother representing Stone's views noted that when Peter cut off the ear of the High Priest's servant in defense of Jesus, the Lord had rebuked him, telling him to put his sword away, for those who took up the sword would die by it. Nothing was as repugnant to Christ's Kingdom as war, he asserted, regardless of whether it was Christians against Christians, or Christians who were supposedly fighting "against the wicked, and hurrying them unprepared into eternal punishment." He stopped short, however, of condemning war in every situation, stating instead that as the gospel had its effect on human hearts, war would recede. Therefore, in the millennial age "nations shall learn war no more." He concluded, "Lord! hasten the happy day!"[71]

By July 1844, Stone had ceased to justify war in any case. In a lecture on Jesus' Sermon on the Mount he noted that non-resistance toward an aggressor was the meaning of Jesus' teaching in Matthew 5:39: "But I say unto you, that ye resist not evil; but whosoever shall smite thee on thy right cheek, turn to him the other also." Stone advised that by observing this teaching Christians might overcome aggressors and impress upon them the truth of the gospel. If genuine Christianity were to spread throughout the earth, wars would cease and the world would be bound together. "A nation professing christianity, yet teaching, learning and practicing the arts of war," he warned, "cannot be the Kingdom of Christ, nor do they live in obedience to the laws of Christ." Such a government, he declared, was "anti-christian, and must reap the fruits of their infidelity at some future day."[72] In Stone's view, the government of the United States stood under the judgment of God.

Stone's call for non-resistance appeared in one of four articles calling for Christians to withdraw from participation in civil government, all published between 1842 and 1844. Stone advanced two arguments for why Christians should not seek or hold office in government. The first was that participation in politics had a negative impact on Christian spirituality. In the dialogue between two Christian brethren, the brother representing Stone's view asserted, "It is a stubborn fact, that whenever a Christian seeks for, or holds a civil or military office in the governments of this world, he loses the savor of religion, his zeal, and ardent desire to promote the interest of Zion."[73] The negative impact of politics on spirituality extended to all Christians who participated in politics, as it diverted their attention from Christ and his Kingdom of peace.[74]

Stone's second argument against Christians participating in civil government was that the government and laws of Jesus were sufficient to rule the world. Human laws, like their makers, were always changing. The result was "continual jars, collision, strife and war. Even our best of human governments, for this very reason, is now tottering and unstable, and must ultimately submit to the divine government, and unchanging laws of our king, before it becomes right."[75] He asserted that if all were to submit to Jesus' government, "peace, love and harmony would unite, and keep united the now jarring, wretched world." In any event, the lawful king, Christ Jesus, would soon put down all other powers and reign with the Saints on earth for a thousand years without rival. Then peace would be restored and all human laws and governments annihilated.[76]

Stone contrasted the effect of human laws and the "law of God"—or the gospel—on human behavior.

The purpose of human laws and government was for human happiness, but the facts showed that under human laws the world had been "a slaughter-pen of human victims—hatred, strife, war, contention, division and every evil work have followed." Furthermore, crime actually increased with the proliferation of human laws. The root of the problem was that human laws were incapable of ruling the evil world because the worldly mind was subject neither to human laws nor the law of God. The gospel, however, would provide divine power, the Spirit of God, that would allow humans to overcome the carnal mind and become new creatures in Christ Jesus. As new creatures in Christ, he argued, "God's law is written on our hearts, and becomes the principle of action, we delight in it, and it is our pleasure to walk in it continually."[77]

What, then, was the Christian's duty to civil government? Stone stated that the Christian was to pray for human governments and to be subject to their ordinances, as long as they did not oppose the ordinances of Christ. He further admonished Christians to so live under Christ's government, "as to show its superiority over all human governments and by this means engage others to receive it and be saved."[78]

Stone knew that there would be opposition in the church to his view that Christians should not participate in civil government. In the 1842 dialogue, the character representing Stone's view indicated that he hesitated to speak, knowing that his views would be classified as "fanaticism or ultraism." As Stone saw it, however, his views on participation in civil government were only an extension of the Christians' long held views on church government. "Our brethren have not seen the legitimate issue of what they have been doing, in arguing against human creeds and laws for the government of the church. In doing this they were clearing away the rubbish from the foundation of God's government of the world."[79] In other words, the law of Christ was to govern the world just as it was to govern the church.

Alexander Campbell also embraced pacifism. As early as the first issue of the *Christian Baptist* he attacked the glaring inconsistency of Christian generals and Christian chaplains praying for God to give their soldiers success in "making as many widows and orphans" as possible.[80] He believed that God's triumph in the millennium would include a complete eradication of war. Following the end of the Mexican War in 1848, Campbell delivered a widely publicized *Address on War* to the Wheeling, (West) Virginia, Lyceum. He declared that "War is not now, nor was it ever, a process of justice. It

never was a test of truth - a criterion of right. It is either a mere game of chance or a violent outrage of the strong upon the weak."[81]

As Campbell speculated on ways to end conflicts between nations, he proposed, as had Stone in 1835—affirming the agenda of the American Peace Society—that a world court be established that would be empowered to serve as an umpire to stop the outbreak of war. "Why not, as often proposed, and as eloquently, ably, and humanely argued, by the advocates of peace, have a congress of nations and a high court of nations for adjudicating and terminating all international misunderstandings and complaints, redressing and remedying all wrongs and grievances?"[82]

He insisted that even worse than the lives and property destroyed by wars was their devastating moral influence, creating and perpetuating fear, hatred, and national jealousy. He urged his hearers to do everything in their power to foster a peaceful spirit, pointing out objections to war at every opportunity.[83] He ended his *Address* with this admission:

> I must confess that I both wonder at myself and am ashamed to think that I have never before spoken out my views, nor even written an essay on this subject. True, I had, indeed, no apprehension of ever again seeing or even hearing of a war in the United States. It came upon me so suddenly, and it so soon became a party question, that, preserving, as I do, a strict neutrality between party politics…I could not for a time decide whether to speak out or be silent. I finally determined not to touch the subject till the war was over…I am sorry to think—very sorry indeed…that probably even this much published by me some three years or even two years ago, might have saved some lives…[84]

Campbell's pacifist sentiments, coupled with his belief that the institution of slavery was not condemned in Scripture, contributed to his opposition to civil disobedience in the case of the Fugitive Slave law of 1850.[85] Yet, believing that the Scriptures unequivocally condemned Christian participation in warfare, he advocated resistance to government conscription to military service, especially after the outbreak of the Civil War. No Christian, he insisted, "who fears God and desires to be loyal to the Messiah, the Prince of Peace" would join the ranks of that unholy warfare.[86]

Determined not to repeat the mistake he had made during the Mexican War, Campbell included the 1848 "Address on War" in his *Popular Lectures and Addresses* prepared for publication on the brink of the Civil War. Campbell was devastated by news of the attack on Fort Sumter by Southern forces in April 1861. In June, the *Millennial Harbinger* published his anguished cry:

> Civilized America! Civilized UNITED STATES! Boasting of a humane and Christian paternity and fraternity, unsheathing your swords, discharging your cannon, boasting of your heathen brutality, gluttonously satiating your furious appetites for fraternal blood, caps the climax of all human inconsistencies inscribed on the blurred and moth-eaten pages of time in all its records.[87]

Among the leaders of the Movement, a significant minority maintained neutrality throughout the war.[88] In addition to Campbell, Jacob Creath, Jr. (1799-1886), Benjamin Franklin (1812-1878), John W. McGarvey (1829-1911), and Tolbert Fanning (1810-1874) stood firmly on neutral ground. Challenged in Paris, Missouri, for not praying for the President of the United States, Creath replied that he did not intend to introduce politics into the pulpit. Benjamin Franklin, editor of the *American Christian Review*, declared that he would not take up arms to kill persons he had labored for twenty years to bring into the Kingdom of God. McGarvey was one of fourteen Stone-Campbell ministers to sign a "Circular from Preachers in Missouri" urging all members of the churches to join them in refusing to do military service. Echoing views published by Stone in the 1840s, Middle Tennesseans led by Tolbert Fanning advised Jefferson Davis, president of the Confederate States of America, that the Bible was for them a higher authority than the laws of any human government and asked to be relieved of "requirements repulsive to their religious faith."[89]

Despite this opposition to war by prominent leaders of the Stone-Campbell Movement, most members and many leaders of the churches supported the military and political goals of their respective section. In the North, Elijah Goodwin (1807-1879), editor of the Indianapolis based *Christian Record*, championed the Union cause and criticized the neutral position of Franklin's *American Christian Review*. W. T. Moore preached a pro-Union sermon in Frankfort, Kentucky, on the "Duty of Christians in the Present Crisis" the Sunday before the state legislature declared its loyalty to the Union—a message he believed had helped determine the outcome of the vote. James A. Garfield (1831-1881) resigned as principal of the Western Reserve Eclectic Institute (now Hiram College) to join the Union army. He commanded the Forty-second Ohio Regiment and rose in rank to

major general. James H. Garrison (1842-1931), later editor of *The Christian-Evangelist*, enlisted in Company F of the Twenty-fourth Missouri Infantry. Dr. Lewis L. Pinkerton (1812-1875) served as both surgeon and chaplain of the Eleventh Kentucky Cavalry.

Stone-Campbell leaders in the South supported the military efforts of the Confederacy. Dr. Winthrop H. Hopson (1823-1889) gave up his pastorate in Lexington, Kentucky, to serve as a chaplain under General John H. Morgan. Thomas W. Caskey (1816-1896) served as chaplain of the Eighteenth Mississippi Regiment of Volunteers. As was the case with many Civil War chaplains, he participated in battle, claiming that he had not sought to break arms or to kill enemy soldiers, but to break their legs, since it took two soldiers to remove from the field a soldier with a broken leg. On the other hand, Benjamin Franklin Hall (1803-1873), who also served as a chaplain, was reported to have demanded "that when there was any chance of killing Yankees he must be allowed the privilege of bagging as many as possible." Despite the pacifism of their fathers, Alexander Campbell, Jr., and Barton W. Stone, Jr., both served in the Confederate army, the latter rising to the rank of Colonel.[90]

Prior to the War, the ACMS had, as in the case of anti-slavery advocate Pardee Butler's request for support, avoided taking a stand on sectional issues. When the war began, however, the Cincinnati-based body was pressured to declare its support of the Union. At the Missionary Society's 1861 meeting in Cincinnati at which no Southern leaders were present, Dr. J. P. Robison proposed a resolution urging members of the churches "to do all in their power to sustain the proper and constitutional authorities of the Union." Isaac Errett who was presiding over the meeting ruled it out of order for consideration by the ACMS. He then called a ten-minute recess, however, and David S. Burnet called an ad hoc meeting that proceeded to pass the resolution with only one dissenting vote.

Two years later, meeting again in Cincinnati without any Southern members present, a substantial majority of the ACMS officially passed a resolution that unequivocally aligned the society with the Union:

> *Resolved*, That we unqualifiedly declare our allegiance to said government [the United States], and repudiate as false and slanderous any statements to the contrary.
>
> *Resolved*, That we tender our sympathies to our brave soldiers in the fields, who are defending us

from the attempts of armed traitors to overthrow our Government, and also to those bereaved and rendered desolate by the ravages of war.

Resolved, That we earnestly and constantly pray to God to give our legislators and rulers wisdom to enact and power to execute such laws as will speedily bring to us the enjoyment of a peace that God will deign to bless.

Sectionalism and Division

The sectional tensions that led to the American Civil War divided virtually every Protestant denomination in the country. The Stone-Campbell Movement could not escape the social and political pressures saturating American society in the era. Yet the body's fierce congregationalism made impossible the kind of structural division experienced by the Baptists and Methodists in the 1840s. Still, it appeared that the churches of the Movement had, in some sense, divided along the sectional lines seen in other denominational groups.

In April 1866, Moses E. Lard (1818-1880), Kentucky church leader and editor of *Lard's Quarterly*, published an article titled "Can We Divide?" Lard began by detailing his view of the church's unity. Issues over which Christians differed had arisen throughout the church's history, he wrote. However, matters like missionary societies and Christian participation in war could never be the cause of division because they were not explicitly discussed in Scripture. If anyone made their opinions of such issues tests of fellowship, they must be regarded as factionalists and repudiated. If, however, individuals or churches added things clearly condemned in Scripture— which in his view included creeds, instrumental music, and dancing—that was a different matter. The church must renounce and exclude such heretics. That was not a division in the church, however, but a departure from it. The church was still united.[91] Ironically, Lard's definition of unity that denied the very possibility of division, while identifying the use of instrumental music as appropriate grounds for exclusion, would itself contribute to division in the Movement.

Lard then moved to a discussion of sectional issues. The issue of slavery had been a topic of discussion from the beginning, he stated. The churches in both North and South had felt the growing mistrust of one another that characterized the nation. When war broke out, the ordeal, in Lard's words, had "cooled many an ardent feeling, and caused old friends to regard one another

a little shyly." Still, he insisted, the war had caused no division in the churches. He then boldly exclaimed, "We can never divide."[92]

Though Lard's definition of unity had ruled out the possibility of division, in reality the war had contributed to the creation of deep cracks among the churches of the Stone-Campbell Movement. Events of the war years helped transform several issues previously regarded as opinions into matters of fellowship. One was the American Christian Missionary Society—an issue on

In 1863, pacifist Moses E. Lard moved to Canada rather than take the oath of loyalty to the Union required of ministers by the Missouri legislature. He later moved to Georgetown and then Lexington, Kentucky where he edited *Lard's Quarterly* and later *Apostolic Times*.

which Lard said the church could not divide!

Tolbert Fanning of Tennessee had begun the *Gospel Advocate* in Nashville in 1855, in part to examine the question of the legitimacy of missionary societies.[93] Though by the late 1850s Fanning apparently had serious misgivings about structures like the ACMS, he had been an active participant in the State Cooperation of Tennessee and apparently had endorsed Campbell's call for a national cooperation in 1849—though unable to attend the Cincinnati Convention that formed the ACMS.[94]

In 1859, on the eve of the Civil War, Fanning traveled to Cincinnati to attend the annual convention. When asked to give a report on the work in Tennessee, he contrasted the way Tennessee congregations cooperated in evangelism with "institutions not recognized by the Scriptures" that did the work of the churches for them like the ACMS. Yet at the end of his presentation, published in the December 1859 *Gospel Advocate*, he exclaimed, "I am happy to say, that from what I have heard on the floor, we are one people."[95]

Within two years, however, Fanning had condemned the society and all extra-congregational organizations and denounced those who supported them. His declaration of non-fellowship with those who supported the ACMS was not based on further study of Scripture or new theological insights. Rather, it was in response to the anti-South resolutions passed by the Society in 1861 and 1863.

Fanning, a pacifist, accused the ACMS of calling for the murder of fellow Christians. He declared he could never have fellowship with the society unless it repented of this sin. David Lipscomb would write in 1866 that the "Society committed a great wrong against the church and cause of God."[96] Fanning and Lipscomb's shift to non-fellowship with those who supported the

Society did not happen until the body's actions during the Civil War. While issues of theology and polity were involved, the socio-political events associated with the war turned support of the Missionary Society into an issue of fellowship.

In a similar way, the socio-economic disparities between North and South following the war helped make the issue of instrumental music a matter of fellowship. The South suffered massive social and economic disruption during and after the war, including the freeing of enslaved persons who had formerly composed much of the wealth of white southerners. Because of significant population loss due to the war and migration during Reconstruction, many Southern churches were destitute and scores simply disappeared. In the North the end of the war brought prosperity, evidenced partly by the construction of new church buildings. Many of the new structures included musical instruments as a reflection of "more sophisticated" tastes of members now enjoying the economic boom. The use of instrumental music in worship had been discussed in the journals as early as 1851, yet like the missionary society, the issue did not become divisive until after the American Civil War.

Missionary societies, instrumental music, and other issues did eventually contribute to division in the late nineteenth and early twentieth centuries. Contributing to the complexity of this division would be massive changes in the status of formerly enslaved Africans and shifts in the role of women in society and church.

3

Growth of African American Institutions to 1920

No group was more deeply affected by the Civil War and its outcome than formerly enslaved African Americans. For these people, the end of the war meant freedom to develop and exercise leadership in ways never afforded under slavery. In the church it provided the prospect of organizing congregations free of white oversight, starting extra-congregational organizations of their own, and establishing schools. Yet racism challenged these efforts at every point. Whites often tried to control the destiny of blacks, disregarding their desires and newly gained rights. Landmark Supreme Court decisions and the extension of Jim Crow legislation heightened challenges to black Americans beginning in the 1890s.

Two African American Leaders

One of the best-known black leaders in the Stone-Campbell Movement was Preston Taylor (1849-1931). Much of Taylor's early life is unknown. He was born to enslaved Africans in Shreveport, Louisiana, on November 7, 1849. Sometime before the Civil War he moved with his parents to Kentucky, then served as a drummer in Company G of the 116th United States Colored Infantry. After emancipation Taylor secured a contract to build several sections of the Big Sandy Railway between Mt. Sterling, Kentucky, and Richmond, Virginia, garnering a reputation as a hard worker and efficient leader.[1]

After Taylor joined the Stone-Campbell Movement in the 1870s, he preached for a large African American Christian Church in Mt. Sterling, Kentucky. In 1879 he began editing the column, "Our Colored Brethren," in the *Christian Standard*. This column, the first in a Stone-Campbell paper to highlight the activities of African Americans, gave him considerable visibility as a leader. Taylor also served as national evangelist for the General Christian Missionary Convention (the name adopted by the American Christian Missionary Society from 1869-1895) from 1883 to 1886, spearheading the establishment in New Castle, Kentucky, of a ministerial training school funded by African Americans.

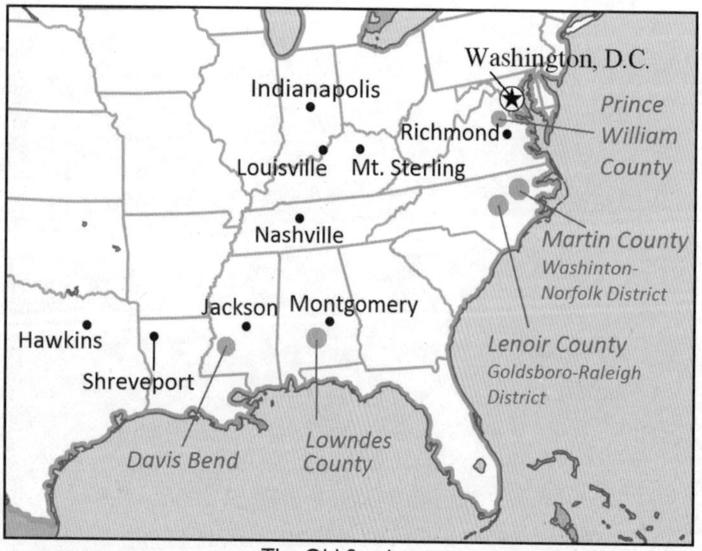

In 1886 Taylor moved to Nashville, Tennessee, where he became minister of the Gay Street Christian Church. Two years later allegations of sexual misconduct, though shown to be unsubstantiated, forced him from that position. Taylor founded the Lea Avenue Christian Church in 1891.[2]

While already known as a religious leader in Nashville's black community, Taylor soon emerged as an influential business leader as well. Taylor learned the funeral trade from M. S. Combs, a white minister and undertaker, and opened his own funeral home in 1888. He promoted black commerce through Nashville's Negro Business League.[3] Taylor also helped

The Old Southwest

46

form the Tennessee Agricultural and Industrial State Normal School for Negroes that opened in 1912, known since 1968 as Tennessee State University. He interacted freely with religious leaders from other denominations, such as Baptist publisher R. H. Boyd. Taylor continued his work as entrepreneur, pastor, evangelist, and civic leader until his death in 1931.

Because he suffered constant racism from leaders in the Disciples missionary organizations, Samuel R. Cassius eventually rejected such organizations and became an early leader in black Churches of Christ.

A lesser-known contemporary of Taylor was Samuel Robert Cassius (1853-1931). Cassius was born in Prince William County, Virginia, May 8, 1853, the son of an enslaved African named Jane and her master James Macrae. Following the Emancipation Proclamation in 1863, Jane and Samuel joined thousands of refugees who flocked to Washington, D.C., to seek a new life of freedom. While there, a white schoolteacher, likely Frances W. Perkins of the New England Freedman's Aid Society, made a deep impression on him. She taught Cassius not only secular subjects, but also the New Testament. He would later say that her instruction was central in steering him toward spiritual pursuits.[4]

It was not until after he moved to Indiana in the early 1880s and found a job as a mineworker, however, that Cassius first heard a preacher from the Stone-Campbell Movement. The minister preached on faith, and though Cassius was the only black person in the audience, he was so convinced by the message that he immediately responded to the invitation. He and a white man were baptized that evening. Soon, with the encouragement of two white preachers from Illinois, Hiram Woods and W. R. Jewell, Cassius quit his job in the mines and began a life of ministry.[5]

First taught to read by his mother, Cassius came to love both secular literature and the publications of the Stone-Campbell Movement. He read carefully the Campbell-Purcell and Campbell-Rice debates and wrote extensively for the *Christian Leader* and other papers. Though he was convinced of the truth of Stone-Campbell doctrinal positions, including the view of baptism, he strongly opposed the pervasive racial discrimination he experienced in the churches. He began his ministry in Iowa, but moved to Oklahoma Territory in 1891, believing blacks could be free of racial prejudice there. He also preached in California, Texas, and Colorado, yet struggled constantly to raise support for his ministry. He complained that he had to deal with prejudice both against his race and against the Stone-Campbell Movement.[6] Nevertheless, Cassius continued his work as an evangelist until his death in 1931.

Taylor and Cassius were representative of countless other African Americans who dedicated their lives to the Stone-Campbell Movement. Their dedication, often in the face of discrimination and meager resources, led to the establishment of congregations, schools, and missionary institutions. In subtle and sometimes not so subtle ways, they challenged the racial inequalities permeating American society as contrary to the gospel.

African American Congregations

At the end of the Civil War the largest numbers of African Americans in the Stone-Campbell churches were in the former slave states of Kentucky, Tennessee, Georgia, Virginia, and North Carolina. Most had been members of predominantly white congregations, but, like blacks in other Christian bodies where there were sufficient numbers, African American members after the war usually chose to form their own congregations, often assisted financially by white members.

In the decades following the Civil War the number of African Americans in Stone-Campbell churches grew dramatically—from around seven thousand in 1862, to twenty thousand in 1876, to an estimated fifty-six thousand three hundred by the end of the century. This growth was due almost exclusively to the work of black evangelists who traveled regionally baptizing converts and starting churches, many with little or no support. Some received support from white regional conventions or from individuals such as the philanthropist Emily H. Tubman of Georgia. In North Carolina, significant funding came from black Christians who had been free before the war.[7]

One of the best known of these evangelists was Levin Woods of Mississippi who received support from the General Christian Missionary Convention (GCMC). The remarkable success of Woods's ministry may have been related to the distinctive background of the persons among whom he ministered. Early reports to the GCMC described Woods as pastor of five congregations with eight hundred members on the "former plantations" of Joseph Davis and his brother, former Confederate President Jefferson Davis. These five congregations may have been attracted to the Stone-Campbell Movement because of Woods's commitment to continue the self-organized worship and ministry they had experienced in the Davis Bend plantation churches before the War.[8]

Joseph Davis had implemented the educational and social ideals of utopian Robert Owen among the enslaved Africans on the Davis family plantations. Owen believed that the role of teachers was to guide students in observing objects in the natural world. Students were encouraged to learn cause and effect through experimental trials. Despite legal prohibitions, Davis ensured that the enslaved Africans on Davis Bend learned to read, write, and perform basic mathematical calculations, as well as develop trades and practice self-expression. Benjamin Montgomery gained proficiency as a civil engineer, learned several foreign languages, and operated the general store at Davis Bend. Following emancipation, Montgomery was elected to the board of an educational institution for blacks sponsored by the GCMS, and his oldest daughter graduated from Oberlin College in Ohio.

Based on the idea developed in Owens's 1813 *A New View of Society* that the less people are governed the more submissive they will be, Davis encouraged enslaved Africans to form families and permitted females to purchase time out of the fields to care for children. He created a system of black sheriffs, courts, and an appellate structure with himself as the judge of final appeal. He also appears to have permitted enslaved Africans on the Davis plantations to organize their own worship services.[9]

Levin Woods, likely a formerly enslaved African on one of the Davis plantations, had served as an evangelist for the black Baptist Missionary Convention (later known as the General Baptist Missionary Convention of Mississippi) since its beginning in 1869. He met officials of the Stone-Campbell GCMC while on a fund raising trip to the North on behalf of the Baptist group, and in 1872 the GCMC sent him a large number of Bibles and hymnals to aid his work. By the end of that year he had become an employee of the GCMC, though still affiliated with the Baptist Convention.

Woods may have felt a tension between the Baptist Convention's requirement that ministers teach according to its Articles of Faith, and the encouragement of Stone-Campbell leaders to read and interpret the Bible for himself. The Stone-Campbell leaders emphasized that the "simple gospel" they saw in Scripture mattered more than official denominational teachings. These principles, in contrast to what could be seen as an imposed creed, may have appealed to many who had been formed in the non-authoritarian environment of Davis Bend.[10]

William T. Withers reported having learned of Woods at the Mississippi Annual State Meeting at Jackson in November 1872. George Owen of Jacksonville, Illinois, described Woods as having independently come to the conclusion "that it was his duty to receive members into the church upon confession of their faith in Jesus Christ as the Son of God, and immersion, without requiring any such experience as the Baptists usually do." Woods was "disposed to take his stand on the Bible, and the Bible alone, to the exclusion of all human creeds." At Withers's instigation, Woods united with the Christian Church in Jackson the last Sunday in May 1873 and received from the church a letter endorsing him as an evangelist. Five of Woods's churches had already adopted "the Bible alone" as their rule of faith and practice, and soon adopted the name Christian.[11]

The president of the Baptist agency retaliated by claiming the churches had followed Woods because they were "babes in the doctrine."[12] The Baptist Missionary Convention expelled Woods in July 1873 for preaching contrary to the Baptist faith and for leading congregations to call themselves Christian rather than Missionary Baptist. Earlier that summer he had conducted a series of evangelistic meetings that resulted in the founding of ten additional congregations totaling 1,261 members. In 1874 Woods reported adding 3,500 members with a total membership of 4,300 in twenty-five churches. He also reported ten Sunday schools and twenty-four meetinghouses.[13]

Though the Davis Bend plantations provided a unique context, Levin Woods's ministry mirrored the activities of other black evangelists and church planters of the era. Moreover, the distinctive background of the persons among whom Woods ministered, in particular their experience of making decisions as individuals, may help to explain why some individuals and communities found the distinctive message of Stone-Campbell evangelists especially appealing.

African American Regional Conventions

Soon after Emancipation, African Americans in all Christian bodies began forming state organizations. In Kentucky, black Stone-Campbell Christians organized their first regional convention in 1873—the State Missionary Convention of the Colored Christian Church. Other black statewide conventions followed in Alabama and Tennessee in 1880, Texas in 1881, Mississippi in 1887, and Georgia in 1891.

Kentucky provides a case study of the development of these organizations. At its first meeting in 1873 the convention elected as its president H. Malcolm Ayers of Lexington, minister of one of the earliest black congregations in the state. Over the years, the missionary convention went by different names, including State Missionary Society of Christian Churches in Kentucky, Kentucky Christian Churches (Colored), and Kentucky Christian Missionary Convention. Regardless of the name, the churches made it clear that the Convention's rulings were strictly advisory. All resolutions required congregational approval to go into effect—no convention could tell a congregation what to do.[14]

A primary goal of the Kentucky Missionary Convention was to support an evangelist. The first was William P. Richards, who served from 1885 to 1889 while also serving as minister of the Hancock Street Church in Louisville. In November 1887, he reported holding twenty-five meetings, performing eight baptisms, and receiving another five persons into membership. By 1888, the Missionary Convention reported 4,064 members in forty-one churches, with another thirteen congregations not submitting membership statistics. In 1893 the Convention meeting at Winchester adopted a constitution that set membership dues at one dollar per year, with life memberships for twelve dollars—which could be paid in installments of three dollars a year over four years. The Convention appointed an Executive Board of nine to guide the organization between conventions.[15]

The Convention also sought to advance the evangelization of Kentucky by recommending specific actions to the churches and promoting a regional journal. In 1900 the Convention, in an effort to strengthen the churches'

Christian education programs, called for congregations to work with other denominations to reach every family in their neighborhoods, enrolling as many as possible in Sunday schools. Eleven years later the Convention tried to save a struggling magazine, the *Christian Soldier*, by naming it the primary organ of communication for the churches. Leaders intended to publish the journal monthly, fully funded by subscriptions at no cost to the Convention. Though the plan was not successful, the paper appeared occasionally for several years.[16]

African American women also created organizations. The founding of the Christian Woman's Board of Missions (CWBM) in 1874 by white members led to the formation of CWBM chapters in black churches and black regional conventions. Black women began the Kentucky Christian Woman's Board of Missions Convention in 1880 that focused on both domestic and foreign missions.[17]

African Americans in Kentucky also organized a Sunday School Convention in 1880, adding a third element to their emerging regional program. In contrast to gender divisions in the leadership of the State Missionary Convention and the Christian Woman's Board of Missions, both women and men (mostly non-ordained) led the Sunday School Convention. At one point Maggie L. Freeman served as president of both the CWBM and the Sunday School Convention. Lexington business leader D. I. Reid served several terms as President of the Missionary Convention and was also active in the Sunday School Convention. The Sunday School Convention sought to improve and increase the number of Sunday schools by holding teacher training events and, on occasion, sending an evangelist to organize Sunday schools and demonstrate how they could be used as a method of evangelism.[18]

Eventually the three conventions developed a pattern of meeting consecutively in the same location, for a total of five days, with the last day reserved for the women's meeting. Other than occasional greetings by delegates of the CWBM, the black conventions and their white counterparts in Kentucky had little connection. Contacts between the Kentucky Christian Bible School Association (white) and the Sunday School Convention (black) were also rare. Black members of the Movement in Kentucky had more contact with the national CWBM and the General Christian Missionary Convention than with the white conventions in Kentucky.[19]

While black conventions in Kentucky and other states chose to work with the national CWBM and the GCMC, Samuel Robert Cassius reflected a deep ambivalence toward the national bodies. He consistently attacked society leaders who

> preach about the goodness of God, and pray about loving one another, and being one in Christ, but… scorn me on account of my race and color, and tell me that their people will not tolerate me as an equal, I am compelled to say to all such, "Thou hypocrite!" Do you believe the Bible when it says that God is no respecter of persons, or that God made of one blood all men?[20]

Cassius openly expressed his disdain of the paternalism evident in the white dominated organizations. After attending the GCMC meeting in Louisville in 1889 he wrote a scathing letter to the *Christian-Evangelist* protesting the appointment of a white, J. W. Jenkins, as superintendent of colored missions. The report of the meeting, Cassius complained, implied that blacks were so inferior intellectually and spiritually that it was impossible to find a black man "with enough common sense to do evangelistic work among his own people." He insisted that there were black preachers who were every bit as fit to do the work the Convention had commissioned Jenkins to do.[21]

In 1893 C. C. Smith, corresponding secretary of the GCMC's Board of Negro Education and Evangelization, published an article in the *Christian-Evangelist* labeling American blacks "ignorant, inexperienced, improvident, and childish," asserting that it was the responsibility of whites to educate and make them fit for society as skilled laborers. Smith's assertions enraged Cassius and were a factor in his formation in 1909 of a black society free from white control—the Missionary Executive Board of the Colored Disciples of Oklahoma, which he served as president for two years. Eventually, however, Cassius came to oppose all regional and general organizations—not because they were inherently "unscriptural," but because the whites who controlled them refused to place black evangelists in leadership roles or to support separate black societies. The blatant racism of the white leadership turned him against the organizations.[22]

The Assembly Churches

African Americans in eastern North Carolina developed organizational structures that were significantly different from those of other regions. After the American Civil War, white Stone-Campbell preachers John Philips and John J. Harper preached among formerly enslaved Africans in Lenoir County. As a result, Alfred Lovick, Demas Hargett, and Allen Chestnut received ordination by white preachers. These black leaders also received financial assistance and administrative advice from white leaders regarding incorporation of churches, documentation of meetings, and literature of the Movement.[23]

Beginning in 1872, churches in Lenoir County met in annual conferences composed of elders, ministers, and delegates. Elders were men licensed and ordained to serve as pastors, while ministers were licentiates who had not yet passed their ordination examination. Delegates were the members of churches in attendance at the conference, all of whom had equal voting privileges. The conference elected one elder as moderator who presided over the three- to four-day session and appointed members to serve on committees. Committees included Preaching (appointing preachers for the conference), Lord's Day Schools, Finance, and Ministerial Affairs. Elders and ministers of the conference evangelized in Lenoir, Wake, Johnston, Sampson, and Wayne counties west of the Tar River.[24]

In 1854 a group of free blacks, Native Americans, and whites had formed the Free Union Disciple Church in Martin County east of the Tar River. This congregation, with its history of independence and the financial resources of free blacks, became a training ground and strategic base for post-emancipation ministers including Robert Esom Green, Alfred "Offie" Pettiford, William A. James, and Joseph F. Whitley to establish new African American churches in the region. Though the exact date is unknown, at some point sixteen African American churches in that part of the state had formed the Martin County Convention, which included Martin, Manteo, Beaufort, Hyde, Washington, Dare, Currituck, and Craven counties east of the Tar River.[25]

In 1886 Robert Esom Green made the fifty-mile journey from his home in Hyde County, east of the Tar River, to Lenoir County, west of the Tar River, to participate in the Fifteenth Annual Conference of Disciples held at Vine Swamp, October 21-24. Six churches of the Lenoir County Conference attended. Green represented the Martin County Convention and proposed a union of the two organizations. On a motion by Alfred Lovick the convention accepted the proposal on October 23, 1886.[26]

The union of African Americans from both sides of the Tar River created the General Assembly of Disciples of Christ, later known as the Church of Christ, Disciples of Christ. By 1897, these congregations, sometimes referred to as the Assembly Churches, reported a membership of 2,910.[27]

The General Assembly's major responsibilities included overseeing the ministry, advancing the establishment of new churches, and strengthening existing congregations. Resolutions approved by the Assembly were compiled into a book of discipline. Among requirements were that ministers have a "normal" education (the equivalent of twelve grades of schooling), be tested on their understanding of faith and doctrine by the Committee on Examination and Ordination, and receive a minister's license from the General Assembly. Unions comprised of ministers already serving congregations directed training for new ministers, and the Committee on Ministerial Character conducted an annual review of each one's behavior.[28]

The Assembly advanced the planting and strengthening of congregations through the work of evangelists appointed by the elder elected to serve as moderator. Evangelists were responsible for building up the churches through regular preaching, though some also had administrative duties. In 1897 the General Assembly appointed two finance evangelists, two Sunday school evangelists, and thirteen general evangelists. Finance evangelists collected dues from churches to support the General Assembly. Sunday school evangelists organized new Sunday schools and assisted local Sunday school superintendents in securing literature. The Council of Seven, also appointed by the moderator of the Assembly, carried out administrative decisions and served as a board of appeals between meetings of the Assembly. In 1899, the General Assembly passed resolutions forbidding elders to start a church within one-half mile of an existing church if in a town, or five miles if in the country.[29]

In the 1890s, leaders of the General Assembly made a conscious commitment to use biblical models and language in their corporate life. The 1891 minutes reflect this commitment in the use of "propose" and "agree" instead of "motion" and "second," "chief elder" instead of "president" or "moderator," "scribe" instead of "secretary," "proceedings" for "minutes," and "assembly" instead of "convention." White Stone-Campbell leaders in North Carolina criticized the body for insisting on biblical language for their contemporary affairs, but the General Assembly remained firm in this commitment. This development set the Assembly churches apart doctrinally as well as organizationally from the white North Carolina Convention. Like other North American Stone-Campbell churches that eventually were known exclusively as Churches of Christ, the Assembly churches increasingly sought to ground all aspects of their practice in what they saw as New Testament commands and precedents.[30]

The white North Carolina State Convention made its last financial contribution to the General Assembly in 1891. After that date, the relationship between the white convention and the Assembly Churches became increasingly distant. One exception were ties created by John J. Harper in the development of the Lenoir Conference, which facilitated occasional cooperation in educational projects between black and white members.[31]

A controversy in 1910 over the location of a school led the General Assembly, which in 1906 reported over six thousand members, to divide into two districts with the Tar River as the dividing line. Churches west of the river were called the Goldsboro-Raleigh District, and those east of the river the Washington-Norfolk District, each with its own assembly. The action also established a Council of Seven for each district and a quadrennial General Assembly of representatives from both.[32]

One of the distinctive worship practices of the Assembly Churches was feet-washing. Participants separated into pairs, and with a white cotton towel girded about the waist, washed each other's feet following Jesus' example in John 13:1-17. The churches practiced this act following communion, observed quarterly (later monthly) rather than weekly.[33] With their hierarchical structure and such worship practices, the Assembly Churches formed a distinctive tradition within the Stone-Campbell Movement.

African American Schools

After the church itself, nothing received greater attention among black Stone-Campbell Christians following emancipation than education. This, they believed, was key to their economic, intellectual, and spiritual advancement. African Americans looked to white members to partner with them in achieving their educational objectives. However, white commitment to education for blacks, though real, never matched the aspirations of black leaders. Moreover, racism limited the types of educational initiatives whites were willing to support.

John Shackelford and Lewis Pinkerton of Kentucky were among the few white members of the Movement who strongly supported literacy and schooling for blacks. Shackelford, ACMS Secretary in 1866, made what may have been the most radical proposal of his time concerning black education—that blacks be admitted to the Stone-Campbell Movement's colleges. Even Northern members who had been outspoken opponents of slavery passionately rejected Shackelford's proposal. Burke Hinsdale, president of Hiram College in Ohio, argued that practical difficulties of educating blacks and whites in the same institution made the proposal unacceptable. When Pinkerton called members of the churches in Kentucky to establish schools for blacks, the responses confirmed his 1866 appraisal of the attitude of former slaveholders in Kentucky.[34] "There are a majority of the late slave-holders of Kentucky, well pleased to hear of the failures that over take the negro."[35]

In 1867 Charles Loos, Robert Milligan, and Isaac Errett lectured at Hiram College on the adverse impact on the United States if blacks were granted suffrage without education. Taking the message to heart, a small group of students formed the Freedmen's Missionary Society to provide the needed instruction. In November two students, Orrin Gates and Mary Atwater, traveled to Lowndes County, Alabama, as missionaries of the Society, joined by Laura Brown in 1869. Intense opposition from the Stone-Campbell churches there as well as white hostility in general thwarted their efforts. The Society was unable to raise adequate funding and finally disbanded in 1870.[36]

Though not all Southern whites opposed schooling for blacks, nearly all were deeply concerned about who would control it. Most felt strongly that meddling Northerners should return home and mind their own business. Nashville editor David Lipscomb reflected the general attitude of Southern whites when he advised the Hiram students of the Freedmen's Missionary Society to take care of the dissolute Dutch in Cleveland and let the Southern people do the work God had given them to "improve, convert and save the negro."[37]

However, blacks did not wait for whites to provide their education. Many took the initiative, often beginning with establishing Sunday schools that provided both religious and literacy education. Some Sunday schools, such as the one at Second Christian Church in Indianapolis, Indiana, eventually developed into full-fledged public schools.[38] In 1874, the Mississippi General Convention listed ten black Sunday schools and twenty-five churches as part of Levin Woods's ministry. In 1893, Alabama churches reported thirty-eight black congregations with 2,485 members and fifteen Sunday schools with six hundred fifty members.[39] These Sunday schools were often under the leadership of women.

Peter Lowery of Nashville, Tennessee, founded the Movement's first African American educational institution outside of the Sunday schools. Lowery, pastor of the Grapevine Christian Church, had purchased his freedom and that of his mother, three brothers, and two sisters in the 1830s. A respected business and religious leader, he secured a charter to establish the Tennessee Manual Labor University (TMLU) in December 1867. The charter stated that the school was "for the elevation of the Freedmen...[for the promotion of] Education, Industry, and Pure Christianity."[40] After purchasing three-hundred acres of farm land at Ebenezer, Tennessee, near Murfreesboro, TMLU opened in 1868.

TMLU had the support of white leaders of the Movement, including *Millennial Harbinger* editor W. K. Pendleton, *Christian Standard* editor Isaac Errett, and *Gospel Advocate* editor David Lipscomb. Lipscomb published an endorsement of the school by sixty Nashville business leaders. White support collapsed, however, when a financial scandal broke involving not Lowery, but agents—including Lowery's son—appointed to raise funds for the school. After an article in the October 1870 *Christian Standard* charging that the project was a fraud, the school's end was inevitable. Despite having one hundred eighty students enrolled, the school closed after little more than two years of operation.[41]

The short life of TMLU did not, however, end interest in the development of educational institutions for blacks. In 1872, the GCMC established the Committee on the Education of a Colored Ministry at its meeting in Louisville, Kentucky. Thomas Munnell, Secretary of the GCMC, reported that correspondence with Southern church members showed they were in favor of the effort.[42] The Convention appointed an agent to raise funds, and the Louisville Bible School (LBS) opened its doors in 1873.

The school's primary purpose was to train black ministers for evangelism and leadership in local congregations. The curriculum included geography, grammar, arithmetic, and study of the Old and New Testaments. White Louisville physician Winthrop H. Hopson, along with black members in the area, provided key leadership in the founding of LBS. The Convention appointed an all white board to oversee the school, which in turn appointed a white principal, Pitt H. Holmes. Economic depression in the 1870s coupled with funding shortages already experienced by the GCMC forced the closing of LBS in June 1877.[43]

Despite the closings of Tennessee Manual Labor University and Louisville Bible School, interest in black education continued. At the General Convention of 1877, W. A. Belding, in his report on the work of the Committee on the Evangelization of the Freedmen, concluded, "It is impossible to Christianize them [blacks] without educating them." He submitted a resolution that the Convention make a concerted effort to establish a school in Mississippi for the education of black ministers that was already being contemplated.[44] This school would become Southern Christian Institute (SCI) in Edwards, Mississippi.

Faculty of Southern Christian Institute. Joel Lehman, appointed SCI president in 1891 by the CWBM, is pictured on the front row, third from right.

The founding of SCI was the fruit of a collaborative effort between Northern and Southern whites. With the encouragement of James A. Garfield, William T. Withers offered to donate 160 acres of farmland near Edwards, in the part of Mississippi where Levin Woods had evangelized. Ovid Butler of Indianapolis drew up the charter for SCI as a capital stock company organized to raise money for a black junior college with an emphasis on teacher preparation. Mississippi's Republican-dominated Reconstruction legislature approved the charter on April 8, 1875, urged on by the black Secretary of State James Hill. The stock company's Board of Commissioners included eight Northerners and eight Southerners, among them African American Benjamin Montgomery, who had operated the general store on the Davis plantations, and GCMC evangelist Levin Woods. Two years later Montgomery died.[45] In December 1877 the company elected a second board, this time composed of six white men—five from Mississippi and one from Indiana—but only one black, Levin Woods.

Stipulations as to improvements that had to be completed by a stated time led the board to reject Withers's offer of land for the school. However, the Board found and purchased an eight-hundred-acre plantation in the same vicinity and the school opened its doors in October 1882.[46] Before SCI formally began, two schools had been launched under its charter. William Irelan (white) had opened the first in 1881 at Hemmingway, Mississippi, with the help of Thomas Munnell, though

white pressure soon forced Irelan to close the school and leave Hemmingway. Later the same year a black man named A. I. Williams tried again, this time near Jackson and under the supervision of Randal and Letitia Faurot (white). Faurot, a Northerner, had started teaching blacks while serving as a medical assistant in a Union military camp in Tennessee before the war's end.[47]

Though thirty students enrolled the first year, no member of the Stone-Campbell Movement entered until five years later in 1887. In 1883, the Board elected Jephthan Hobbs (white) as president of SCI, who directed the institution until 1891.[48] In 1889 the GCMC had secured control of the school by purchasing a majority of its stock. The following year the GCMC transferred ownership to the Christian Woman's Board of Missions. The CWBM appointed Joel B. Lehman (white) as Hobbs's successor. SCI offered academic courses in Bible, teacher training, music, and vocational instruction in farming, carpentry, and home economics. The school also offered general education at the elementary and high school levels.[49]

The demise of Louisville Bible School in 1877 left an educational void in that region of the country. In 1883, Preston Taylor, then serving as national black evangelist for the GCMC, launched an effort in Mt. Sterling, Kentucky, to establish a ministerial training school. After raising $1,000, Taylor joined black leaders H. Malcolm Ayers and T. Augustus Reid in securing the endorsement of the State Missionary Convention of the Colored Christian Church in Kentucky. Black churches contributed most of the $2,500 needed to purchase buildings belonging to the defunct Brinker College in New Castle, with Taylor raising the balance. Five black and six white leaders constituted a Board to govern the school's operations. The Christian Bible College (CBC) opened its doors in September 1886.[50] The *Gospel Advocate* described CBC's principal T. Augustus Reid as scholarly and highly regarded as an educator among blacks, informing readers that he had left a well-paying public school position to serve CBC.[51]

Financial problems led the school's board to cease operations during the 1887-1888 academic year and to turn to the GCMC for assistance. The body agreed to help—but only if the Board would place the property under the General Convention's control. In 1889, John Jenkins, GCMC Superintendent of Missions and Schools Among the Colored People, did an assessment of the school and discovered it was operating as a co-educational institution. In his report to the Convention, he declared that the "negro race has not yet reached the plane of civilization that will admit of co-education when the college is in [the] charge of one of their own color."[52] The GCMC closed the school in 1892, using the proceeds to reopen Louisville Bible School as the Louisville Christian Bible School. LCBS provided ministerial training for African Americans for twenty-two years before closing in 1914.[53]

Principal James H. Thomas and family with faculty of the Piedmont School of Industry. Thomas opened the school with seven students, a blackboard, a box of chalk, and two erasers.

African Americans in Lowndes County, Alabama, saw a serious need for education at the primary and high school levels. The Lum Graded School opened on October 15, 1894, under the direction of H. Jackson Brayboy and Robert Brooks, both graduates of Southern Christian Institute. Brooks, a native of Lowndes County, had taken the Alabama teacher's examination after returning from SCI and secured the highest certification available. The school's first board consisted of members of the black churches of Lowndes County, with the board's first president a minister who had graduated from Louisville Christian Bible School. A local white landowner initially donated five acres, and the GCMC's Board of Negro Education and Evangelism (BNEE) later purchased and donated another sixty.[54] By 1899, the school had an enrollment of 128 pupils. A decade later, C. C. Smith, then Field Secretary of the CWBM which had assumed responsibility for the BNEE, reported that black leaders had done all of the work at Lum with minimal guidance from him.[55]

Financial challenges, made worse by an October 1907 storm that kept many students from enrolling for the fall term, forced school leaders to appeal to the CWBM for financial support. The CWBM leaders agreed to provide $1,000 in return for the privilege of naming the school, which officially became the Alabama Christian Institute (ACI) in October 1914. The CWBM closed the school in 1923, explaining that it believed the Alabama public school system was then able to supply all the education blacks needed.[56]

African Americans in the Piedmont sections of Virginia and North Carolina worked to provide a distinctively Christian education for their youth. The Piedmont School of Industry (PSI) opened in the one-room building of the Fayette Street Christian Church of Martinsville, Virginia, on October 8, 1900. Black leaders formed a corporation—the Piedmont Disciples of Christ—to operate the school. In 1901 the corporation purchased land and buildings with two hundred dollars donated by local African American members and a six hundred dollar advance from the CWBM. Within a year, school officials had repaid the advance along with the cost of repairs to the facilities.[57]

James H. Thomas served as PSI's only principal from its opening in 1900 until its closing in 1932. In a 1901 article Thomas described the school's purpose, denying that its only aim was to train pupils in industrial skills and thrift. No one, he insisted, regardless of how thrifty and industrious they may be, can be a credit to God without also being moral and intelligent; "while we are training our pupils in industry and thrift, we shall lay equally as much stress upon Bible and moral and intellectual training, and shall endeavor to give them a practical training for citizenship." This approach, he believed, would come nearest to preparing his students for the demands of the twentieth century.[58]

Purposes similar to those of the founders of PSI seem to have motivated black Christians in East Tennessee to purchase facilities previously used by a school in Jonesboro for $1,500. Local black leadership raised four hundred dollars, with the balance secured through a loan from CWBM. On October 26, 1908, Principal James E. Baker and two teachers began operating Tennessee Christian Institute (TCI). The school operated for six years before closing in 1914.[59]

As early as 1880, black churches in Texas had begun serious discussions concerning establishing a school for the education of ministers. In 1893 leaders proposed such a school for Waco. A committee selected H. S. Howell to head a fundraising effort to establish the National Colored Christian College. Howell traveled extensively to rally support for the Texas school and reportedly secured donations of land and eight hundred dollars in cash. Promoters of the project eagerly began construction of a building. All efforts halted, however, when Howell absconded with the money.[60]

African American leader Mary Alphin, wife of preacher William Alphin, led a second attempt to establish a school for blacks in Texas in the 1910s. Potential black donors initially resisted Alphin's efforts, reminding her of H. S. Howell's fraud over a decade earlier when raising funds for such a project.[61] The CWBM was willing to help, but their offer presented its own challenges. As Texas CWBM organizer Bertha Mason Fuller observed, "The CWBM promised financial help and supervision, but in turn required all funds and property to pass through their hands for accounting.… To this, the Negroes demurred. They had been deceived by one of their leaders. They did not know the white folk too intimately and they stiffly withheld their approval of assets and funds being sent to Indianapolis."[62]

Mary Alphin, elected President of the Texas Women's Missionary Society in 1908, had been a school teacher in Topeka, Kansas, for fifteen years before moving to Texas. *(From Jarvis Christian College website)*

Not willing to see the effort fail, Fuller invited Sarah Lue Bostick (1868-1948), National President of the Negro CWBM, to come to Texas and reconcile the two parties. Bostick accepted the invitation. She worked effectively among black congregations in Texas, organizing missionary societies for women and promoting Mary Alphin's dream of a school for black young people in Texas.[63] Alphin expressed her vision for the school in the report of a two-week fundraising trip in 1910.

> How much our work suffers among our people for lack of leaders…We are trying to impress on people to give in a way so they show that they want a school in Texas…We tried to impress the splendid

opportunity CWBM was offering the young people by preparing them for their life work by training the head, hand, and heart.[64]

Alphin's use of "head, hand, and heart" was a coded reference to her desire for the Texas school to include higher education and not simply vocational training.

Alphin's dream began to be realized when on January 15, 1913, Jarvis Christian Institute (later renamed Jarvis Christian College) opened its doors in Hawkins, Texas. African American educator J. N. Ervin served as president from its founding until 1938. Jarvis achieved high school status in 1914 and received accreditation as a junior college in 1928.[65]

Samuel Robert Cassius had moved to Oklahoma Territory in 1891 to be part of what many blacks viewed as an opportunity for advancement in their own communities free from white domination. By 1895 Cassius had begun expressing his dream of a school to train black youth in industrial trades and religion. Two years later he began publishing a paper, the *Industrial Christian*, to promote the school and raise funds. The response was meager, however, so the following year he published a booklet soliciting donations for what he called the "Tohee Industrial School." He explained that his own lack of early opportunities for education and learning a trade had motivated him to make this effort. Cassius also informed readers that the school would be a tool to evangelize blacks, whose religion, he asserted, was not what the Bible taught. He intended to combine the industrial school model of Booker T. Washington with strong religious instruction.[66]

By 1899 Cassius had received enough money to construct a building, though he still needed books, charts, black boards, and other teaching supplies. The school finally opened in July, but much to Cassius's distress, he was forced to close after only four months of operation because of lack of funds. Though friends tried to revive it in 1902, the school never reopened. Cassius's appeal for funding had been almost exclusively aimed at members of the Stone-Campbell Movement and sometimes took a sectarian tone. He had strong competition from nearby state-supported Colored Agricultural and Normal University, now Langston University, begun in 1897. This, along with the fact that he refused to take a deferential approach to potential white donors, narrowed his base of support and ensured he would never receive sufficient funding for the school or his evangelistic efforts.[67]

A younger contemporary of Cassius, George Phillip Bowser, had served as an itinerant preacher in Tennessee and had begun a paper for African Americans titled the *Christian Echo* in 1902. On October 8, 1907, Bowser opened a school in Nashville, Tennessee, with Samuel W. Womack as superintendent and Beulah Christopher as assistant and instructor. Bowser's curriculum balanced learning with manual labor, though he stated his intention to operate the school under the standards set for state "normal" institutions for training teachers, with the addition of classes in Bible. Beginning with seventeen students, the school operated out of the Jackson Street Church of Christ.[68]

In 1914, after securing property in Putnam County, Tennessee, Bowser moved the school from Nashville to Silver Point. Bowser was encouraged by an increase in enrollment to fifty-seven students and the school's eight-acre campus with a two-story frame building free of debt.[69] Bowser rejected extra-congregational organizations such as the General Christian Missionary Convention and the Christian Woman's Board of Missions as "unscriptural," so he did not have that source of financial assistance. He aimed his appeals for support at individual Christians both black and white.

Following a visit to the school in 1916, A. M. Burton, a white leader in Middle Tennessee and founder of the Life and Casualty Insurance Company wrote, "The devotion of these ex-slaves impressed me more clearly than anything else that it is our Christian duty to help put the school on a self-sustaining basis. They have certainly been trying to teach the word of God under many disadvantages and among more trials and tribulations than anything I have ever witnessed."[70] Burton's appeal resulted in $550.41 in donations, of which David Lipscomb and his wife contributed one hundred dollars, and their nephew, David Lipscomb, Jr., a horse.[71]

A number of whites became interested in Bowser's Silver Point Christian Institute because of the advocacy of African American Annie C. Tuggle who served as teacher and fund-raiser.[72] Bowser continued to operate the Silver Point school until it closed in 1920. He later operated schools in Fort Smith, Arkansas; Detroit, Michigan; and Fort Worth, Texas.[73]

Early home of the Goldsboro Christian Institute, established by the Goldsboro-Raleigh District of the General Assembly of the Disciples of Christ in Eastern North Carolina.

In 1910 the Goldsboro-Raleigh District of the General Assembly of Disciples of Christ in Eastern North Carolina purchased a sixteen-acre tract to establish a school for church leaders. Under the direction of Elder Edgar S. L. Whitfield, Assembly Churches built a seventeen-room two-story building to house the Goldsboro Christian Institute (GCI). They did not appeal to the CWBM or ACMS for funds. They did, however, solicit support from both blacks and whites with some success. GCI operated into the 1920s as an accredited high school.[74]

National Conventions

African Americans moved to establish a national organization as soon as they had the opportunity. Under the leadership of Rufus Conrad, a group of

G. P. and Francis Bowser pose in front of a chart outlining three dispensations of God's communication to humanity.

black ministers in Nashville, Tennessee, organized the American Christian Evangelizing and Education Association (ACEEA) in May 1867. The ACEEA's efforts resulted in the establishment of several congregations in east Tennessee. Though the ACEEA appealed to the ACMS for support, it received little help from any source, and the effort collapsed by the early 1870s.[75]

In 1873, Preston Taylor, then pastor of the Colored Christian Church of Mt. Sterling, Kentucky, and H. Malcolm Ayers of Lexington, Kentucky, organized the National Convention of the Churches of Christ (NCCC). The NCCC pressed for a role in organized mission work among blacks, forming an advisory committee to work with the GCMC on black-related issues. In 1879, Taylor appealed to the GCMC to share leadership with the NCCC on matters related to black evangelism and education. The GCMC did meet with the committee at least once, but after it formed its own Board of Negro Evangelism and Education (BNEE) in 1890, the GCMC appears to have ignored the NCCC and its advisory committee.[76]

The membership of the BNEE reflected the General Convention's view that control of the education of blacks should be in the hands of white Southerners. M. F. Robinson, pastor of Hancock Christian Church in Louisville, was the only black member of the board, and his appointment came only after a white nominee declined. Recognizing the need for a greater effort in black education, the 1891 Convention authorized the selection of a full-time Field Secretary to coordinate educational work among black people. The Board determined that the Secretary should be white, claiming, "negro religious hucksters had caused Blacks not to trust their own."[77]

In January 1892, the GCMC appointed C. C. Smith to serve as Corresponding Secretary of the BNEE. By all accounts, Smith, whose 1893 racist comments angered Samuel Robert Cassius and contributed to his ultimate opposition to missionary organizations, brought administrative ability, energy, and dedication to his work. Financial support of the GCMC's African American work improved steadily under his leadership, though not as much as Smith believed was needed. Faced with ongoing financial challenges, Smith appealed to the CWBM in 1900 to take responsibility for all work in African American education and evangelization, which they did.

In 1912 the CWBM appointed Joel B. Lehman, previously president of Southern Christian Institute, as national Superintendent of Negro Work. Lehman was committed to industrial education as the primary, if not only, form of education for blacks. In statements published while president of SCI, Lehman clearly revealed his belief that industrial education for blacks was important primarily for the well being of Southern whites. He attributed the success of SCI to the policy of doing "no injustice to the Christian white people," and making sure that the students were "humble and deferential," seeing the world's problems from the viewpoint of whites as well as their own. Unless blacks were properly educated, he explained, their degeneration would undermine white society.[78] Lehman's privileging the concerns of Southern whites reflected white racist attitudes that had shaped the Stone-Campbell Movement and North American Christianity in general since before emancipation. The apparent disregard of the NCCC by the General Convention reflects that body's discomfort with allowing blacks to influence their own educational agenda.

Preston Taylor, the primary spokesperson for the NCCC, had challenged the GCMC to support higher education for African Americans, in addition to industrial education. In 1917 Taylor led in establishing the National

Successful Nashville entrepreneur and African American community advocate, Preston Taylor, pictured with his wife Ida, was both a leader and benefactor of black Disciples organizations.

Christian Missionary Convention (NCMC) as successor to the NCCC. One of the issues leading to its formation was black dissatisfaction with the educational policies of CWBM Superintendent of Negro Education Joel Lehman. In particular, leaders wanted at least one school that offered African Americans a "standard college curriculum where our leaders, especially those entering the ministry, may be adequately equipped for their work."[79]

In his inaugural address as president of the new Convention, Taylor charged the white church establishment with failing to help develop black leaders because of simple lack of commitment.[80] Mincing no words to an audience that included Lehman as well as the presidents of the CWBM and the ACMS, Taylor declared, "The attitude of our white brotherhood on the race question accounts largely for our smallness."[81] Taylor and other black leaders believed the new organization could help initiate a more effective partnership between black and white Disciples. Taylor urged his hearers to consider the theological and spiritual importance of maintaining one church.

> The Disciples of Christ, strange as it may seem, need the colored people, if for no other reason, as the acid test of Christian orthodoxy and willingness to follow the Christ all the way in his program of human redemption. For if the white brother can include in his religious theory and practice the colored people as real brothers, he will have avoided the heresy of all heresies.[82]

The assembly of forty-one leaders who gathered in Nashville, Tennessee, for the organization of the Convention included Sarah Lue Bostick of the CWBM.[83] It did not include representatives of the Assembly Churches, though in the next decade Taylor would seek unsuccessfully to unite the General Assembly and the NCMC. Neither did it include Samuel Robert Cassius who had given up on extra-congregational organizations, or George Phillip Bowser who believed they were unscriptural.

Heightened Challenges to Black Americans

While white racism had never ceased to be an obstacle to the advancement of African Americans, the virulent racism between 1890 and 1920 made this era one of the most challenging in the history of black Americans.[84] The inauguration of the so-called Mississippi Plan in 1890 deprived black Southerners of

their voting and other civil rights through the imposition of poll taxes and literacy tests administered by white registrars. Mississippi's disfranchisement program quickly spread to other southern states depriving black citizens of their rights under the Fourteenth and Fifteenth Amendments.[85] The 1896 U.S. Supreme Court decision *Plessy v. Ferguson* legalized segregation in the entire nation and effectively reduced people of color to second-class citizenship. Three years later in *Cummings v. the Board of Education*, the Court ruled, "The education of people in schools maintained by state taxation is a matter belonging to the respective states."[86] This allowed states legally to deny adequate state funding for black public education. Segregation became universally entrenched in the South and in much of the North—including elevators and waiting rooms in hospitals, water fountains, Bibles used for swearing in in courtrooms, theaters, hotels, swimming pools, libraries, churches, schools, and cemeteries.[87]

A proliferation of racist literature enflamed black-white relations across America, uniformly branding black men as lustful, immoral, and vicious. Works such as Thomas Dixon's 1905 *The Clansman*, inspiration for the 1915 movie *Birth of a Nation*, were widely endorsed by white educators and politicians, stimulating a revival of the Ku Klux Klan and spurring an increase of lynching of blacks in both the North and South.[88] White apologists portrayed lynching as white society's desperate response to black men raping white women, even though the record did not sustain this perception.[89]

In this repressive setting, African Americans launched their own reform efforts. Booker T. Washington formed the Negro Business League in 1901 to encourage blacks to enter business. Four years later, W. E. B. Du Bois gathered black and white leaders in Niagara Falls, Canada, to organize the Niagara Movement that called for immediate civil rights for African Americans. In 1906 black students at New York's Cornell University founded the first black fraternity—Alpha Phi Alpha, and two years later black students at Howard University in Washington, D.C., established the first black sorority—Alpha Kappa Alpha. In 1909 African Americans, prompted by a violent race riot in Springfield, Illinois, organized the NAACP (National Association for the Advancement of Colored People) to abolish forced segregation and to agitate for equal rights. Two years later African Americans established the National Urban League to assist black migrants relocating from rural to urban centers.[90]

The responses of white leaders of the Stone-Campbell Movement to the circumstances of African

Americans were similar to those of other white Americans. Predictably, Southern white leaders opposed black voting rights; yet Northern leaders also regarded black suffrage with mixed feelings. One leading editor confided that he had always believed the Federal government had acted unwisely in bestowing suffrage upon the former slaves. During the late 1880s and 1890s when the Southern states were systematically disfranchising black voters, Northern editors often supported the actions, not with overt defenses of racial discrimination in voting, but by repeated characterizations of blacks as irresponsible voters, thereby creating the need for educational qualifications.[91]

In response to the virulently racist movie *Birth of a Nation* based on the book *The Clansman*, Samuel R. Cassius published in 1920 his own book *Third Birth of a Nation* in which he advocated equal opportunity for blacks, but strict prohibition of racial intermarriage.

In accord with the Stone-Campbell Movement's history of accommodation to Southern white attitudes, an 1899 *Christian-Evangelist* editorial virtually endorsed the practice of lynching. The editor suggested that Northerners could scarcely understand the conditions in the South that led Southerners to such extreme measures. "The sudden emancipation of the negro race, together with their enfranchisement, has precipitated a condition of things in many parts of the South which is responsible for these appalling crimes," he explained. Southern women had suffered "brutal abuse by the negroes" and Southerners were doing what they had to do to preserve the social order.[92]

The most popular national black leader in the United States was Booker T. Washington.[93] Having assumed leadership in 1881 of the Tuskegee Institute, a newly established Alabama teachers college for African Americans, Washington had become famous for his advocacy of industrial training aimed at making African Americans competitive in the work force. Responding to the needs of black people and the desires of white segregationists, Washington, in his famous Atlanta address of September, 1895, stated, "In all things that are purely social we can be as separate as the fingers, yet one as the hand in all things essential to mutual progress."[94]

Two years later, Washington was invited to deliver a keynote address to the meeting of the American Christian Missionary Society at Indianapolis. A *Christian-Evangelist* editorial expressed the opinion of Washington held by many in the churches:

> His address on the subject of the negro problem in the South was one of the most remarkable speeches, in its point, power and pathos, to which we have ever listened....Mr. Washington seems to be a philosopher, an orator, a teacher, a prophet, and a practical philanthropist, all in one. He has remarkable powers of oratory, and a clear grasp of the situation and its needs. He understands the possibilities and the weaknesses of his race, and is doing a work among them which no one else is doing, or perhaps could do.[95]

Black leaders in Stone-Campbell churches typically took an accommodationist political stance. Edgar S. L. Whitfield's *A Message to Negro Disciples,* a 1906 tract aimed at blacks both inside and outside of the General Assembly of the Disciples of Christ of Eastern North Carolina, advised making peace with white people, because they were the majority property and business owners of America. "Teach your children to make friends with the white man, and despise him not because of slavery."[96] Commenting in 1915 on a eulogy of Booker T. Washington written by Samuel Robert Cassius, Annie Tuggle, ardent supporter of G. P. Bowser's Silver Point School, argued that "will power" had enabled Washington "to accomplish such a great work." Tuggle urged members of the churches to emulate Washington's persistence and courage by supporting the Silver Point School's mission of educating the heads, hands, and hearts of African Americans.[97]

Few members—black or white—openly opposed the separation and subordination of blacks institutionalized by the so-called Jim Crow laws. W.E.B. Du Bois's 1905 call for immediate civil rights for African Americans received little support. One notable exception was Preston Taylor, who was not only a minister, but a successful entrepreneur and leader of Nashville's Negro Business League. His efforts with other prominent Nashville blacks to stage a boycott protesting the passage of segregation laws were not typical of Stone-Campbell Christians of the era.[98] Most did not openly challenge racial segregation or the systematic denial of the civil rights of black Americans. More common among Stone-Campbell Christians was Annie Tuggle who addressed only the spiritual plight of her oppressed brothers and sisters, not their bodies or social condition.[99]

Yet blacks in the Stone-Campbell Movement did resist the virulent racial discrimination of their era, signaling in restrained and sometimes more overt ways their refusal to allow others to determine their destiny. Despite obstacles placed before them they acted on their own understandings of the church's mission, continuing to plant and maintain congregations and to design and support regional and national conventions and assemblies as different as the General Assembly of Disciples of Christ of Eastern North Carolina and the National Christian Missionary Convention. They also established educational institutions. While white leaders such as Joel B. Lehman insisted on the industrial education model, black leaders including James Thomas, George Phillip Bowser, Preston Taylor, Mary Alphin, and James Ervin were determined to provide more than a trade school education for African Americans. Armed with bravery and persistence, blacks would play an increasingly important role in the Stone-Campbell Movement.

4

The Expanding Role of Women in the United States, 1874-1920

Blacks were not the only Americans to exercise increased leadership in the church following the Civil War. The war claimed the lives of nearly 650,000 men, leading some women, both black and white, to assume roles previously held by men. Industrialization accelerated this development, especially in the North.[1]

A critical factor in the growth of woman's leadership among Stone-Campbell Christians, as in other Protestant traditions, was the development of national women's societies. These societies gave women something the churches of America had not: public roles, widespread networks, and a new self-concept as important agents in furthering God's Kingdom on earth. Yet even women who were not members of national women's societies assumed new roles in the churches.

National Women's Societies

A new chapter in the role of women in the Stone-Campbell Movement began in 1874 with the founding of two national societies: the interdenominational Woman's Christian Temperance Union (WCTU) and the Stone-Campbell Movement's Christian Woman's Board of Missions (CWBM). Another significant event took place in 1886 when women in St. Louis organized the National Benevolent Association (NBA) to care for widows and orphans.[2]

A grassroots movement of women who organized against saloons and alcohol during the winter of 1873-1874 sparked this new wave of organizing. Inspired by the temperance movement that emerged in the U.S. during the early decades of the nineteenth century, women in villages and small towns throughout Ohio marched into saloons, fell on their knees, and implored saloonkeepers and patrons to give up drinking. Many did, at least temporarily. The press in Cincinnati,

Chicago, and New York spread the news of the "Women's Crusade," with one writer reporting that the effort had wiped out the saloons and doubled church attendance in over 250 towns and villages in Ohio.[3] Never before had women joined in public action with such success. At the 1874 Chautauqua summer resort in western New York, a group of women met to discuss the implications of the crusade. These women planned a national convention that met in November in Cleveland, Ohio, and organized the Woman's Christian Temperance Union (WCTU).[4]

In October of the same year, women in the Stone-Campbell Movement organized what many would come to consider the most successful of the Movement's mission societies—the Christian Woman's Board of Missions (CWBM). Between 1869 and 1874 women in the Baptist, Congregational, Episcopal, Methodist, and Presbyterian Churches had all formed missionary agencies. Unlike the other women's societies, however, the CWBM was not a women's auxiliary to an established missionary organization. Rather, it was an independent agency run entirely by women, not subject to oversight by any denominational official or agency.

The organization of the WCTU and CWBM represented a significant shift in conventional wisdom regarding women's roles. What historians label "the cult of true womanhood" or the "cult of domesticity" had dominated upper and middle class American thought since the 1820s, especially in the more industrialized North. This idea assumed that only men were suited by nature for the harsh public world of business and politics. Women—seen as humble, pious, submissive, and meek—were the natural protectors of the home, nurturers of children, and pillars of the church, all essential but non-public functions.[5]

The scriptural basis for prohibiting women from public roles in church came from passages like 1 Timothy 2:8-12, "Let the woman learn in silence with all subjection...I suffer not a woman to teach, nor to usurp authority over the man." Many Christians interpreted these injunctions as prohibiting any public speech by women in the church. Alexander Campbell had articulated such views in a series of articles in the *Millennial Harbinger* in the 1850s, asserting that a woman's most important role was head of the "school of the home." His widow, Selina Huntington Bakewell Campbell (1802-1897), continued to espouse this position in letters and articles after Campbell's death.[6]

Other leaders, however, began calling for a larger role for women in the church. The editor of the *Christian Standard*, Isaac Errett, though he embraced a restrictive understanding of Paul's injunction for women to submit to male authority, supported women speaking at prayer meetings. He criticized the "unrighteous embargo" that prevented women from organizing and addressing their own meetings or even praying publicly at the bedside of a dying person. Such restrictions were unnecessary and a hindrance to women communicating the gospel to their women neighbors. "We have known instances in which the dying have called on their sisters to pray with them, and there was a blushing refusal and acknowledged incompetency—not because those who refused lacked faith or piety, but simply because the customs of society had never allowed them to pray in the presence of others." Errett insisted that women should be able to form organizations to minister to orphans, the unemployed, the poor, and sick.[7]

Editor Elijah Goodwin of the *Christian* went even further by claiming that under certain conditions women could preach. He, like Errett, believed that Scripture prohibited women from exercising authority over men, but he did not believe that all preaching was necessarily done from a position of authority. Goodwin wrote in 1875 that women could speak for "the edification and comfort of saints, and for the conversion of sinners" as long as they did not speak "in a manner, or under circumstances that would indicate a desire to rule over the man, or a want of regard for their husband's authority."[8] Though their endorsements usually included such limitations, these and other male leaders increasingly encouraged women to use their gifts for the cause of Christ, and many did.

The catalyst for the Christian Woman's Board of Missions was Caroline Neville Pearre, wife of the minister of the Christian Church in Iowa City, Iowa.

Pearre had become frustrated with the General Christian Missionary Convention's ineffectiveness in raising money and sending missionaries. According to her own account, after her morning devotion on April 10, 1874, Pearre became powerfully convinced that she was to lead a new women's mission effort. She immediately organized a local women's missionary group and began a letter-writing campaign that garnered the support of editors Isaac Errett and James H. Garrison for a national effort. At the General Convention in October, she led a group of seventy-five women in drafting a constitution for the CWBM. The document specified that the body would engage in both home and foreign missions and would be under the complete control of women. The General Christian Missionary Convention unanimously approved and recognized the new body.[9]

Most supporters of the CWBM saw it as an institution that would operate quietly behind the scenes. Isaac Errett, in his 1874 *Christian Standard* editorial titled "Help These Women" in which he endorsed a woman's society, commented that the church had wrongfully confined women's work to the Sunday school, and that the women's missionary societies would allow them another acceptable avenue of service.[10] Errett envisioned the national CWBM, like its local predecessor at Iowa City, as meeting once a month for prayer and discussion and enlisting women to contribute regularly to foreign missions. The society was a way women could participate in mission work without violating presumed scriptural prohibitions. Errett apparently believed that, by advocating no public role for women, the CWBM could earn the approval of all the churches.

The CWBM's official statement of goals in 1874 reflected the same assumptions—their activities would not be public. The organization was to cultivate a missionary spirit among church members, particularly women. Members of local auxiliaries were to invite non-Christian friends to meetings and encourage children to consider missionary careers. Furthermore, the groups were to disseminate news about mission work—what they labeled "missionary intelligence." Finally, auxiliaries were to train their members to give to local and national CWBM causes. Every woman would thus be involved through prayer, education, and regular contributions.

Errett's hope that all Stone-Campbell churches would support the CWBM proved unrealistic. Some critics argued, as they had with the ACMS and GCMC, that the Bible did not authorize conventions and missionary societies at all and therefore they were contrary to God's will. The very possibility of creating public leadership roles for women stirred controversy with some, as did the development of separate men's and women's conventions. *Gospel Advocate* editor David Lipscomb, who opposed the societies as unscriptural, added this objection when he wrote, "They know the Bible plainly: 'There is neither male or female, but ye are all one in Christ;' yet you divide the Christians into male and female societies."[11]

Caroline Neville Pearre, organizer of the CWBM, had a successful teaching career at Christian Female College in Columbia, Missouri, before marrying Sterling Elwood Pearre in 1869.

Lipscomb was among those who opposed any public role for women in church or society. To him, even the 1897 Congress of Mothers which led to the formation of the National Parent-Teacher Association was a danger. Instead of encouraging women to become better mothers, such meetings enticed women away from the joy of raising children and tending the home. "The child of a mother that does not love home, the home life and home duties will suffer in its most vital interests," Lipscomb insisted.[12] Other *Gospel Advocate* writers were even more explicit. J. W. Sewell believed it impossible that a woman could be a good mother and a committed member of a women's group: "...the mothers of...[rebellious] boys are the women most often found in the front rank of the

W.C.T.U., the C.W.B.M., and like organizations, there praying the loudest and longest, and talking the most and fastest."[13]

According to anti-society leaders, women who attended conventions, and especially those who spoke publicly, acted in a masculine manner that violated scriptural limits. These critics based their opposition on a key component of the cult of true womanhood—that women should not draw attention to themselves. A woman could teach the gospel to her children or a husband more ignorant than herself, but in the church she could only act in a "modest way, neither taking the lead, assuming authority or attracting public attention to herself."[14] Lipscomb claimed that even when women gathered in their own conventions they were assuming male roles. It was inconsistent for women to claim moral superiority because of their uniquely feminine characteristics—another major component of the cult of true womanhood—when they acted like men by attending conventions and "assuming the rights of the strong."[15]

Such attitudes were not confined to men. After hearing reports of women preaching in 1880, Selina Campbell pled with her sisters "to abandon the practice, and consider it as rebellion against God's will. And let man, whom God has appointed, take the oversight of the church."[16] Annie Tuggle, who later raised funds for G. P. Bowser's Silver Point Christian Institute, immediately began evangelizing among her family and friends after her baptism in 1908 at the age of seventeen. Two of her sisters, her mother, and a cousin were baptized because of Tuggle's efforts. Yet when her cousin, Ellen Reed, asked Annie to baptize her, she refused because she believed it was not scriptural for a woman to baptize. Though she often led the worship service in the all-woman congregation near her home, her autobiography makes it clear that she did so only because in that context she would not be exercising authority over men.[17]

CWBM leaders tried to find a middle position between secular "women's rights" advocates and traditional members of Stone-Campbell churches who insisted women remain silent. Missionary Candace Lhamon Smith's address at the 1896 CWBM National Convention illustrated this middle position:

I am not an advocate of "Woman's Rights," popularly so called. I only plead for her the freedom in Christ Jesus to use the rights she has ...Let us forget the things that are behind, including the sphere prescribed by us in the days of our ignorance. Let us press forward to the things that are before, making for ourselves a sphere that shall be bounded but by the limits of humanity's need, and the love of humanity's Redeemer.[18]

CWBM leaders found that changing women's concept of their proper role was among their most difficult challenges. Articles and speeches designed to rouse women from their apathy and become active in the society's work abound in the Board's early years. Domestic duties were not an excuse to refuse to be active in the CWBM. Emma Campbell, in a delicate balance of advocating both increased women's action and the cult of true womanhood, asserted that while nowhere was the work of godly women needed more than in the home, it was also true that Jesus commended Mary for sitting at the feet of Christ, labeling her choice "the better part." Women would be better and accomplish more, she suggested, if they occasionally set aside "all thought of the wearisome round of domestic duties," to do something directly related to their spiritual development.[19]

CWBM leaders bristled at the notion that to be "proper," a woman must embrace a life exclusively devoted to her home and family. They responded that a proper woman was one who spread the gospel in public ways, and certainly not a woman who selfishly devoted all her time to herself. CWBM leader Marcia M. B. Goodwin sharply attacked traditional views of women's work in an 1881 article in the *Christian Standard*.

A woman may live an idle, useless life, or devote her days to fashion and folly, and she will be applauded for having kept her 'proper sphere;' but let her take the Bible and publicly proclaim its truth—let her, in God's house, raise her voice in defense of virtue and in warning against error—and sneers and calumny are her portion. And this is consistency! This is Christianity! This is brotherly love that "thinketh no evil."[20]

CWBM convention speakers tried to convince women that the missionary cause took priority over the care of their homes. With so much still to be accomplished on the mission field, it was deplorable that churchwomen paid so much attention to their personal adornment and the cleanliness of their house and so little to missions. "While the home must not be neglected, if it is made an excuse for not obeying and serving the Lord, if it fills the first place in our hearts, which only Christ should occupy, the blessing is turned to a curse, and we

are its poor slaves."[21] Louise Kelly in 1896 pointed to the new meaning life had taken on for many CWBM women now that the home was not their only concern. "Christian Women! When God has called us to a mission above that entrusted to angels, let us not thwart His divine purpose by refusing to see this heavenly vision, and sink back into the valley of sordid selfishness from which we have been rescued."[22]

The dedication of the CWBM's College of Missions in Indianapolis in 1910.

The CWBM soon left behind its modest beginnings as a small network of women's fellowship groups for discussion, prayer, and fundraising. The founders had always seen its primary function as recruiting women to advance the missionary cause, not providing an opportunity to socialize. By the 1890s, the organization had fully developed its own independent structure, including traveling speakers, tens of thousands of contributing and praying members, its own publications, and a full calendar of conventions and public meetings. By 1910 the organization had even established its own educational institution, the College of Missions in Indianapolis.

The CWBM justified its ever-expanding agenda with a new twist on the Movement's plea for the restoration of the ancient order. Women had experienced a perfect freedom in the time of Christ, they asserted, but male church leaders during the "Dark Ages" had taken away that freedom. By appealing to the model of the primitive church, they were making the case to powerful men that women had the freedom in Christ to proclaim the gospel in any way possible. They used the same argument male leaders had used against denominational structures to challenge efforts to stop women's organizing and speaking. M.M.B. Goodwin declared that those who would prevent women from teaching "the Living Oracles" followed in the footsteps of medieval clerics, not the apostles.[23] Even the founding women directors of the National Benevolent Association saw their purpose as organizing women to restore something that had been lost since the days of the apostles: "The purpose of the organization was to restore to the church that brotherly love and benevolence taught by Christ and practiced by the disciples in the early days of the church."[24]

The Role of Organizers

To address the twin problems of apathy and opposition, the CWBM and WCTU developed systems for inspiring, recruiting, training, and deploying women into church and society as advocates of mission, not unlike methods used by labor and political organizers. CWBM organizers were the female counterparts of male state missionary society evangelists as they inspired and organized women in the small, sometimes scattered, churches of their region.

An effective organizer was first of all an effective lecturer whose words could change lives. Lecturers gave addresses designed to attract large audiences and create enthusiasm for the organized temperance and missionary causes. One woman stated the purpose of an organizer as not simply conveying information, but as giving "instruction that awakens, arouses and sets on fire the many indifferent women of our land, consumes them even—consumes self, indifference, lethargy—and then recreates them—makes them new women in Christ." In the words of another author, an organizer had to "inspire the women with an inspiration for heroic sacrifice and service for the Master."[25] One organizer insisted that her responsibility was not to raise money, "but to act as a missionary to the needy places—to sow the seed." The organizer's most long-lasting work was, like that of evangelists, not the kind that would necessarily make "the largest showing."[26]

While the primary job of CWBM organizers was to form auxiliaries, women often started auxiliaries in their churches without the leadership of an official organizer. Sometimes women from an auxiliary in one church visited a nearby congregation and helped organize a new one. CWBM leaders at the county and district levels often designated persons to speak at churches in their area and to organize any women they could gather.

Starting in 1909, the CWBM used the titles of Organizer, State Field Missionary, Field Missionary, and State Missionary interchangeably for its women lecturers. The WCTU called its lecturers Evangelists, as did the Sunday school societies. Woman lecturers could invite members of their audience to come forward to join a chapter of the organization they represented. Although not calling hearers to convert to Christianity per se, the practice mirrored the conversion process for unbelievers at revival services.

Challenges facing organizers included difficult travel conditions and opposition to women speakers and missionary societies. They had to be prepared for every contingency. Through the pages of *Missionary Tidings* and convention speeches, women shared advice on how to overcome the problems they faced. One needed to be as "wise as a serpent, but harmless as a dove" when dealing with opposition to women in public leadership. When such resistance arose, the organizer should only hold an afternoon meeting with the church's women.[27] Other women spoke of how to address opposition to missionary societies. One lecturer suggested that an organizer must make sure her points "apply to that particular place so forcibly they will strike home." She must, however, be kind and avoid launching a personal attack on the individual raising the objection.[28]

CWBM leaders identified skills that organizers would have to develop to win over indifferent or skeptical audiences. For example, the organizer had to have a strong, clear voice, overcoming any soft-spokeness and self-consciousness. Organizer Mary Lyons recommended, "A woman who expects to stand before the public should have a voice that can be heard by the entire audience. If, by nature, she has not a strong, clear voice, then by careful training [she must] obtain it."[29]

Serving as organizers forced numerous women in the Movement to assume a more public presence, a difficult transition for women not accustomed to public speaking. South Dakota State Organizer Millie Vercoe confessed to *Missionary Tidings* readers in 1902: "The terrible feeling of shyness was hard to fight against. I am learning how to do what others have learned in the past—how to speak in public. These difficulties have been, and are to be overcome."[30]

The establishment of an active, growing auxiliary required more than an effective speech, however. The organizer had to recruit and train volunteers in a very short time, usually one to three days. This included talking to women who had expressed interest and discerning local financial, leadership, and spiritual resources. She had to recognize those with leadership abilities and cultivate others. Susie Sublette of Kentucky described the usual pattern to *Missionary Tidings* readers—a hasty organization of an auxiliary, appointing a few committees, and setting a date for the first meeting before traveling to the next church.[31]

Organizer Clara Hazelrigg, wife of W. A. Hazelrigg, was a school teacher and a superintendent of Butler County, Indiana, schools. In 1895 she wrote *A New History of Kansas Designed Expressly for Use in the Public Schools*. She served as minister of the West Side Christian Church in Topeka, Kansas, from 1914-1931.

In training women in local congregations to run auxiliaries, organizers impressed on them the importance of their work. These women "should be leaders, women who have a large view of Christ and a large view of woman's work in the world."[32] Only leaders with such a vision would be able to enlarge the local church's view of the world. Organizers lamented, however, the scarcity of women willing to assume leadership positions. Anna M. Hale reported that "[t]he greatest need in so many places is women who are willing to fill the places of officers and head the Auxiliary in its great work of enlarging the horizon of the home congregation."[33] When no such women surfaced, the work suffered. South Carolinian Cora Brunson listed women's indifference and lack of self-confidence to serve as leaders as the two prime hindrances to the missionary cause.[34]

CWBM speakers also inspired women to see their auxiliary as one of the most important groups in their local church and in the Stone-Campbell Movement as a whole. The local auxiliary, said one national leader, "remains today the strongest spiritual factor in many of our congregations."[35] Many came to believe that much of a church's spiritual power depended on the local CWBM auxiliary. "It is the guardian of our most sacred interests of the church and the home, for it represents the mother-heart of the church. No one in all the world but a mother knows how to love next to God."[36]

Organizers traveled constantly, speaking before state, Sunday school, and Christian Endeavor conventions. Clara Hazelrigg (1859-1937) reported in 1897 that she had traveled 9,000 miles as Organizer for the Kansas CWBM.[37] Over ten months in 1904 Texas State CWBM Secretary Bertha Mason, who later played a role in founding Jarvis Christian College, reported organizing auxiliaries, speaking at twelve district, four county, and two state conventions, as well as the black state convention. In addition, she spoke daily for six weeks in three camp meetings.[38]

Lura V. Thompson traveled extensively through six states and territories in late 1901 and most of 1902, visiting eighty-eight churches and establishing ten new auxiliaries. Local women organized another nine after her departure. She calculated that she had traveled 221 days, given 114 public addresses, delivered 62 afternoon talks, and spoken to 35 children's groups under less than ideal travel conditions:

> To reach some of the churches required miles of travel across country in conveyances varying all the way from the running gears of a wagon to the latest improved rubber-tired carriage, and in all conditions of weather. But these rides are counted among the delights of the year's work. In some parts of the country a sixty-mile drive between eight o'clock in the morning and six in the evening, and an address at eight o'clock the same evening, is counted a light day's work.[39]

In search of recruits, CWBM leaders eventually began speaking from pulpits, further blurring the already loose distinctions between preaching and missionary speaking. While most church members did not see filling the pulpit for the CWBM as the same as preaching, it was a significant step in that direction. CWBM Corresponding Secretary Marion E. Harlan reported speaking at three church services in a two-day stop in Denver in 1912 as she returned from a western speaking tour.[40] In a description in *Missionary Tidings* of her work as an organizer, Mary A. Lyons shared her recruiting methods with readers. While she began by canvassing the district and visiting interested women, she reported "fill[ing] the pulpit on Sunday in most instances," and holding women's meetings in the afternoons. According to Rachel Crouch, the usual pattern became to hold a children's meeting in the morning, a women's meeting in the afternoon, and a public meeting at night for the whole church.[41]

By the 1890s such public meetings held by local auxiliaries were part of a national CWBM effort to advertise and gain support for the missionary cause. Though not all auxiliaries were equally active or public, CWBM leaders believed that public meetings in the church added members to local groups and enlarged their base of supporters. Sunday afternoon or night services usually included hymns, addresses, and poems by several women. Local chapters also held such services on the annual CWBM day during which organizers asked churches to take a special offering for their mission efforts. Some state organizations, like the Montana CWBM, asked their auxiliaries to hold such public meetings quarterly.

An 1892 issue of *Missionary Tidings* featured an example of such a CWBM service. The Ladies' Missionary Auxiliary of Missoula, Montana, sent an invitation to church members advertising a 7:30 p.m. Sunday service. There was a Scripture lesson, prayers, addresses, hymns, duets, and a collection. Two days later the *Morning Missoulian* reported that the evening was entertaining and instructive, and furthermore was "witnessed by the largest number of people which has ever gathered within the doors."[42] Rather than women speaking in public causing damaging controversy, local CWBM auxiliaries often found that the experience generated positive publicity and drew curious onlookers.

Men in the CWBM

The CWBM also recruited men because of the society's unique program of missionary education. The fact that men joined the CWBM underscores the fact that the organization was not viewed as a women's fellowship group. It was, rather, a missionary society run by women leaders consisting of pastors, laymen, laywomen, and children. In no other area of church life would it have been accepted for women to lead and instruct men. Such authority was not available to women in regular church services or local church government. But since women were the "experts" in missionary education and organizing, men who were interested in the missionary cause often had to learn from the local CWBM auxiliary. Many women asked CWBM leaders if interested men

could join their chapters. While some questioned allowing men to become members, Organizer Rachel Crouch explained in a 1903 *Missionary Tidings* article that their constitution was clear on this question: "Any person may become a member."[43]

Since the CWBM did not report membership figures by gender, the exact number of men in local auxiliaries is unknown. In some places, however, men composed up to one third of the membership and were among its most avid supporters. The Effington, South Dakota, auxiliary, organized on September 21, 1902, began with seven men and fifteen women. Millie Vercoe commented that in South Dakota, "The interest in the brethren wherever our work is presented has been great…many [men] are reading the TIDINGS more faithfully than the sisters."[44] At the church in Kelso, Washington, fifteen women and five men organized a chapter in 1899. A Texas organizer reported in 1897 that several pastors belonged to the auxiliary and attended every meeting.[45] CWBM leaders especially encouraged the interest of pastors because of their access to pulpits where they could preach on missions and deepen their congregation's commitment to the cause.

Children's Societies

Another indication that the CWBM was not merely a women's fellowship group was its development of a children's program. CWBM leaders argued that if they were not diligent, children would grow up without an interest in the success of missions. Mrs. T. I. Stockman argued, "The children are the future church; to neglect them is to reproduce an anti-missionary element, which has cost so much labor and loss of time in the past."[46] The CWBM's children's program was intended to train, not just inform. It taught children about missionaries' lives and countries of operation, the importance of prayer, the necessity to give money for the missionary cause, and the need for more missionaries—both men and women. Cordie B. Knowles noted, "If we simply teach a child, he may forget; but train him in right principles, fix them in his heart and conscience, not simply by his hearing them but by his putting them into daily and hourly practice, and they will become so truly a part of the warp and woof of his life that when he is old he *can not* depart from them."[47]

The CWBM children's work was unique. While Sunday schools usually had women teachers, senior leadership was all male. The same was true of Christian Endeavor, a popular interdenominational youth program begun in 1888. Women composed the entire leadership in the CWBM's Young People's Societies, usually referred to as children's bands. In contrast to the other programs, the children's work allowed women not only to teach children, but to lead and develop the organizations that taught them.

The missionary education of children and youth in these organizations reached a high level of success by the mid-1880s. In 1888 the CWBM began a children's monthly titled *Little Builders at Work*. By 1893 eight states had CWBM Young People's Departments with Superintendents, and the number doubled to sixteen the next year. Later the CWBM organized societies specifically for young women and girls. By 1914, the Southern California-Arizona CWBM reported that they had a plan for a CWBM "trinity" in each church—"women, girls and children all linked together in missionary work in the name of Jesus Christ."[48]

In 1893, Stockman recommended that the CWBM organize Junior Christian Endeavor societies to present the CWBM missionary cause.[49] Though Christian Endeavor (CE) was not part of the CWBM, Stockman and others sought to bring CE state organizations and local chapters into its orbit. For CWBM leaders, all organizations of the churches should actively participate in the missionary cause—anything less was a scandal. In many states CWBM organizers controlled the Stone-Campbell churches' CE chapters. Just prior to the 1894 CWBM convention, Cordie B. Knowles urged local chapters to reach out to Christian Endeavor. "[A]s we can have no *legal* hold upon them as an organization, see to it, pastors and sisters of our Auxiliaries, that in the very start your Juniors are made to feel the *responsibility* of our missionary work."[50]

The CWBM frequently found CE leaders to be willing partners. In fact, the same women who organized CWBM auxiliaries and Mission Bands were often the ones who had started the Christian Endeavor societies in their congregations. In 1889, California State Organizer, Mrs. I. A. Conklin, reported in *Missionary Tidings* that she had organized thirty-four auxiliaries, with four hundred forty members; six Young People's (CE) Societies, with one hundred nine members; and thirty-four Mission Bands, with nine hundred forty-eight members.[51] At other times, CWBM leaders recruited CE leaders to join their auxiliaries, ensuring that more CE children would receive missionary training and that the CWBM would increase its audience.

In organizing CE chapters among Texas churches, Olivia Baldwin found that most were not contributing to the CWBM. She found no trouble interesting the children in the CWBM's work and quickly secured promises from CE leaders that they would present CWBM materials. Some CE Superintendents also joined the cause.[52] In Iowa, for example, one woman served as head of the CWBM Young People's Department and Superintendent of the Junior CE.[53]

Members of CWBM auxiliaries and children's organizations, often the mothers of the children, identified and equipped countless future missionaries and missions supporters. Many CWBM leaders regarded this as the body's most important accomplishment. The Southern California-Arizona State CWBM secretary, Mrs. G.M. Anderson, reported with pride in 1916, "A number of Triangle Mission Clubs and Circles [for young children] have been organized and several young people have volunteered and will prepare themselves for missionary work."[54] A correspondent from North Carolina reported that among the CWBM's greatest accomplishments for 1913 was that "some of our young people are seriously considering a missionary life."[55]

The story of the women of the Farrar family of Richmond, Virginia, underscores the influence of the CWBM on mothers and their daughters long after the CWBM ceased to exist as an independent organization in 1920. Bessie (1872-1947) and Francis "Birdie" (1874-1970) Farrar had been inspired to serve in the CWBM in the 1880s under the influence of their mother, a leader in the local auxiliary. Both girls grew up to become CWBM organizers for Virginia in the 1890s and then CWBM missionaries. Bessie served in India, while Francis served in Mexico. Francis, who would later marry Moses Louis Omer, became one of the first women preachers among Stone-Campbell churches.

The CWBM and Race

The CWBM was a predominantly white organization. Black women, however, were welcome to organize their own auxiliaries and did so. In 1880 black women began the Kentucky Christian Woman's Board of Missions Convention—just six years after the founding of the national organization. In 1896, black women formed the Mississippi Women's Missionary Society.[56] These organizations cooperated with the national CWBM, but operated separately from the white regional organizations.

In 1896, Sarah Lue Bostick organized the first black auxiliary to the CWBM in Arkansas. In 1899 she organized two more, and the next year, another three.

In 1901 Bostick brought these six auxiliaries together to form the black Arkansas Christian Woman's Board of Missions. In the report of its first meeting, almost ninety percent of a total offering of $43.00 had been sent to the national body with only $5.00 kept for local projects.[57] The following year the white Arkansas Christian Woman's Board of Missions appointed Bostick Organizer of black auxiliaries.

The women of the black Arkansas Christian Woman's Board of Missions elected Bostick president of the Negro CWBM in 1907. In this role, she traveled extensively, giving leadership to black auxiliaries and advocating the cause of missions in black congregations. An avid reader, she became known for her impressive ability to employ from memory a wide range of materials in her missionary addresses and other presentations.[58]

By 1912, dues and offerings of the black Kentucky Christian Woman's Board of Missions were sufficient to allow the employment of a second organizer to travel among the churches establishing and advising local auxiliaries. The Board divided the state into two districts and appointed an Organizer for each—Susie Brown in the Eastern district, Susie King in the Western. Their assignment included ensuring that all auxiliaries became affiliated with the national CWBM.[59]

In the early twentieth century, shifts occurred in the relationship between the white societies and work among African Americans. At the request of C. C. Smith, Corresponding Secretary of the American Christian Missionary Society's Board of Negro Education and Evangelism, the national CWBM assumed responsibility in 1900 for all work in African American education and evangelism. Smith continued to serve as executive until 1912, when the CWBM appointed Joel B. Lehman, president of Southern Christian Institute, as national Superintendent of Negro Work.

Despite the commitment of black women to co-operation with the national CWBM, blacks expressed growing dislike of oversight by a predominantly white organization, especially after the appointment of Lehman as Superintendent. Though highly respected by the white leadership of the CWBM, Lehman was widely viewed by black leaders as authoritarian, patronizing, and unresponsive. In response to complaints of black leaders, the CWBM appointed two African Americans to work with black churches in 1917. P. H. Moss was selected as the national church school and young people's worker. Rosa Brown Bracy became the national women's worker. Continuing black dissatisfaction with

Lehman's leadership, especially his limited view of black education, contributed to the formation in 1917 of the African American-led National Christian Missionary Convention.[60]

Rosa Brown Bracy (1896-1960) grew up in Port Gibson, Mississippi, the daughter of a pastor. A graduate of Southern Christian Institute, she taught school before being named the first Field Secretary for Negro Work of the CWBM.

Women Organizers Become Women Preachers

After decades of organizing, CWBM leaders began to conclude that they had reached the limit of their ability to grow their membership within established churches. In 1906, Laura Gerould Craig reported that since there were more auxiliaries and Young Women's Circles than churches in New York, "evidently our organizing work is restricted."[61] Organizers found themselves spending time and effort maintaining the health of scattered auxiliaries in small, pastorless churches. In 1915, two North Carolina CWBM officials commented that since there was already an auxiliary in practically every town and city with a church, they would have to target rural churches for members if they were to continue to grow.[62] But many of these churches had no minister to pull together a church program of any kind. Small rural churches, which in some states made up a majority of Stone-Campbell congregations, had their own challenges. The Ohio organizer reported in 1913 that only about a third of the almost six hundred churches had regular preaching, while in North Carolina in 1915, only sixteen churches out of one hundred fifty had it.[63] Members often could not see the point in sponsoring a CWBM auxiliary.

It became clear to many CWBM leaders that only by addressing the pressing problems of the numerous struggling congregations could they secure more members for the organization and convince women to invest in foreign missions. The next stage in the growth of the CWBM would come from infusing new life into these struggling churches. As Laura Gerould Craig commented, "The Organizer must give attention to the difficult problems of the Church as well as the Auxiliaries."[64] The question of how to help the struggling churches became one of the chief motivations for women organizers to begin preaching.

Louise Kelly, a CWBM district organizer in Kansas who eventually became a national organizer, frequently addressed entire congregations. In 1902 and 1903, she reported spending "much time…in seeking to infuse new life and hope in discouraged churches and sowing the seed in virgin soil." During this time she visited thirty-two churches and delivered thirty-six public addresses, but visited only sixteen auxiliaries. Kelly reported that during her month-long visit to Wisconsin, for example, she had taught widely among the churches, but had not organized new auxiliaries because of the weakness of the congregations.[65]

As talented women speakers gave their CWBM lectures in struggling churches, they found that people often responded as if they were sermons. Clearly, some believed that CWBM organizers were preaching, not just "lecturing," despite their lack of ordination, institutional authority, and official title. Frances "Birdie" Farrar was twenty-two years old and single when she became an organizer for the Virginia CWBM in 1896. At one place on her speaking tour that year, Farrar noted, "Many, I knew had come from curiosity to hear what a woman had to say, for, in some parts of Virginia, the people think it very strange to hear a woman speak in public." Often in the mountain churches, she reported, people in the audience asked the people sitting around them, "Do she preach? Do she take a text?" The mountaineers wondered whether Farrar was preaching from a biblical text or merely exhorting the faithful.[66]

Farrar's experiences show that women organizers gave many listeners the impression they were actually preaching. Farrar complied with the unspoken rules that allowed her to "lecture" but not "preach"—she did not call herself an evangelist or invite the unconverted forward to profess Jesus Christ as Lord and Savior. Yet her audience still wondered if she was preaching. Furthermore, she herself believed her CWBM speaking was, in some ways, a form of preaching. To the common question asked by mountaineers, she answered that "Yes, she did take a text."[67]

Farrar did what hundreds of other organizers did—preach specifically to the women in the room. "It was a woman," she told her audiences, "who first carried tidings of the Risen Lord, and ever since Mary Magdalene gave that first joyous message…women would continue to tell the old story until every knee should bow and every tongue confess Jesus as Lord to the glory of God the Father."[68] As long as she did not ask her hearers to accept Jesus or plan to stay long, an organizer could preach the gospel.

While Farrar did not assume the role of evangelist in 1896, other CWBM organizers did. Some not only informed audiences of the missionary cause but performed missionary work themselves. In 1897 Clara Hazelrigg asked her Kansas audiences to come forward and confess their faith. Of Hazelrigg's one hundred twenty-five addresses that year, a contemporary noted that she "frequently had confessions at the close of her addresses." In fact, Hazelrigg was ordained the same year she was organizing for the CWBM and began holding revivals as an evangelist.[69] Wisconsin CWBM Organizer Isabelle Goodacre recalled later in life that "I was a state organizer [for the CWBM in the mid-1890s]… and preached or spoke in all our Churches."[70] In the 1910s, Daisy Schultz served as regional superintendent for the CWBM's Young People's Department in the Inland Empire (North Idaho and East Washington) while performing pulpit supply as an ordained preacher.[71]

Being perceived as a preacher while promoting the women's missionary cause was an important step toward preparing CWBM organizers to fill that role. Other early women preachers first received authority to preach from the positive reactions of audiences to their temperance lectures. Clara Babcock (1850-1925), Whiteside County, Illinois, WCTU President and perhaps the first woman to be ordained in the Stone-Campbell Movement, became a preacher in an Erie, Illinois, church because of a chance speaking engagement in 1888. The only record of Babcock's reasons for being in Erie that day in 1888 is found in the 1915 *History of the Disciples in Illinois.* The author explained that after Babcock left the Methodists and became part of the Stone-Campbell Movement, she went out into the service of the W.C.T.U. in Illinois. Being in Erie on a Sunday, she was induced to speak to the Christian congregation in the forenoon. The presence and approval of God were so manifest that she was led to continue in the service of that congregation. Later, after wise counsel and mature deliberation, she was ordained to the Christian ministry in 1888.[72]

Ordained at the Erie, Illinois, Christian Church August 2, 1889, Clara Hale Babcock was a popular evangelist and temperance speaker. She held pastorates in Illinois, Iowa, North Dakota, and Ontario, Canada.

Although the specific reasons that "induced" Babcock to speak to the Erie, Ilinois, Christian Church are vague, one can presume that Babcock was there to speak for the WCTU. Whether Babcock preached or gave a WCTU lecture, the church would not likely have asked her to speak had she not been president of the Whiteside County WCTU. As a WCTU leader and speaker, her responsibilities would have honed her speaking abilities and earned her the respect of temperance supporters, including many Stone-Campbell Christians.

Another former temperance lecturer, Sadie McCoy (1863-1948), became a minister after discovering her preaching talents through her work in organizing Sunday

schools. An unplanned revival followed one child's desire to become a Christian after a Sunday school organizing address. McCoy often told of how "she was led from a school teacher to a temperance lecturer and Sunday school worker, never dreaming that she would become a 'Preacher of the Gospel.'" In fact, over the next fifty years she became one of the most successful evangelists and pastors in the Stone-Campbell Movement. Even while she preached the gospel, she never completely left her roots in temperance lecturing. She was equally comfortable holding revivals and temperance rallies, both of which her many hearers appreciated.[73]

Some women were ordained before assuming regional or national leadership of the CWBM, but became known as preachers through their CWBM leadership. This was the case with Bertha Mason (1876-1959), daughter of Texas pastor J. C. Mason (1845-1934). Bertha Mason graduated from Add-Ran College in Thorp Spring and was ordained by her father's Houston congregation in 1896.[74] Having previously worked under her father's direction in organizing a Spanish Sunday school in Houston with another young person from the congregation, Samuel Guy Inman, her first

After serving as a CWBM organizer in Texas and a missionary in Mexico, Bertha Mason Fuller was secretary of the Arkansas Christian Women's Missionary Board from 1922 to 1942. After retiring, she wrote biographies of her father, Rev. J. C. Mason, and CWBM colleague Sarah Lue Bostick.

assignment as an ordained minister was to teach for a year in a missionary school at Juarez, Mexico (1896-97). In 1897 she became Corresponding Secretary of the Texas CWBM. From 1900-1903 she served a three-year missionary assignment in Monterrey, Mexico, before returning to serve an additional five-year term as Corresponding Secretary of the Texas CWBM. It was through her service as head of the Texas CWBM that Mason, who married J. H. Fuller in 1907, became known as a preacher.[75]

A native of Kentucky, Sarah Lue Bostick's lineage was Native American, black, and French. Widowed at an early age, she married Arkansas preacher Mancil Mathis Bostick.

A similar progression of circumstances may have propelled Sarah Lue Bostick into the role of the first known African American woman preacher in the Stone-Campbell Movement. According to one tradition, Sarah Lue Young married Mancil Mathis Bostick, a cotton farmer and deacon of the Pea Ridge Christian Church in Arkansas, on April 24, 1892, and both were ordained to the ministry the same day.[76] According to another tradition, the date of Bostick's ordination is unknown, though she apparently assisted her husband on evangelistic missions from the beginning of their marriage.[77] In any case, it was through her service to the CWBM that she became widely known as a preacher.

The rise of women preachers is, perhaps, the most dramatic example of the influence of the national women's societies on Stone-Campbell churches. Francis Farrar Omer, Bertha Mason Fuller, and Sarah Lue Bostick were like many other women whose service as preachers was directly connected to the CWBM. Clara Babcock demonstrated the transformative power of the WCTU on women to become leaders and speakers. In addition to those who became preachers, the CWBM and WCTU transformed the self-understanding of countless other women, giving them confidence that they could serve Christ beyond the roles previously assigned to them. They expanded the meaning of the Stone-Campbell call for restoration, imploring male leaders to return to them the freedom women had to serve Christ in the primitive church.

Other Organizations

Women associated with the CWBM and the WCTU, however, were not the only Stone-Campbell women to assume new roles in the churches. The four decades following the Civil War was a period of significant growth for the Sunday school in American Protestantism. By 1872, when the Interdenominational Sunday School Convention approved its uniform lesson plan as a strategy for Bible study throughout U.S. Protestantism, the Stone-Campbell Movement ranked fifth in size of Sunday school participation.[78] Though senior leadership was reserved for males, women assumed primary roles in the establishment and growth of Sunday schools. Among African Americans, these schools often provided both religious and literacy education and, in some cases, developed into public schools. Women were also organizers of Christian Endeavor societies in their congregations, though senior leadership of this interdenominational youth program, as with the Sunday schools, was reserved for males.

Annie C. Tuggle did not believe that organizations such as the CWBM were scriptural. Neither did she believe that a woman should speak in church gatherings that included both men and women.[79] Nevertheless, in 1914, when travel was difficult for any African American, and even more so for a female African American, she accepted the role of fundraiser for G. P. Bowser's Silver Point Christian Institute, a task that required her to traverse the southern states in pursuit of donors.

In the Assembly Churches, the 1910 division of the General Assembly into the Goldsboro-Raleigh and Washington-Norfolk districts led to women assuming new responsibilities. Although the moderator (chief elder) of the General Assembly in 1892 had established a "Sisters Union" to solicit aid and send funds to the General Assembly, pastors had not encouraged the work and little was done. With each district now responsible for a full range of committees—on new churches, discipline, statistics, and finance—the work could no longer be confined to ministers. Lay people had to assume many of the mandated responsibilities, and that opened the door for women to become active in the business of the church.[80]

In 1917, the women of the Goldsboro-Raleigh District reinstated the Woman's Home Mission Convention (WHMC), dormant since its establishment as a Sisters Union in 1892. By 1923, the WHMC had its own annual sessions, usually scheduled one week prior to the district assembly. The WHMC also served as a model for the women of the Washington-Norfolk District who, in 1925, petitioned their annual assembly to begin a missionary auxiliary called the Woman's Missionary Society.[81]

Continuing Debate on Woman's Role in Church and Society

By the beginning of the twentieth century, churches of the Stone-Campbell Movement reflected a wide range of positions on women's roles. Churches that rejected the legitimacy of extra-congregational organizations generally excluded women from leadership in both church and society.[82] In these churches in Tennessee and Texas, women could not serve as evangelists and preachers and were forbidden to speak in public worship except in singing hymns and confessing their faith in baptism.[83] In Indiana, however, Daniel Sommer held that though women were not to serve as evangelists and preachers, it was their privilege to pray, read Scripture, and exhort believers audibly in the public assembly.[84]

Restrictive views, however, did not go unchallenged, even in churches that rejected the societies. One of the most prominent women associated with those churches was Silena Moore Holman (1850-1915). Wife of an elder in the Washington Street Church of Christ in Fayetteville, Tennessee, she was an effective leader of the Tennessee WCTU. Holman combined her work as a temperance advocate with powerful appeals for a wider role for women in the churches. As early as 1880 she contributed articles to the *Gospel Advocate* advocating increased educational opportunities for women. As was the case with many CWBM leaders, Holman argued her points from within the assumptions of the "cult of true womanhood." In the case of women's education, for example, she insisted that to be good mothers, women

must be educated.[85]

In 1888, the same year that Clara Babcock became a pastor in Illinois, Holman began a series of articles in the *Gospel Advocate* sharply challenging traditional assumptions about women's roles. The articles were prompted by a response from *Advocate* editor David Lipscomb to a question from a church leader in Missouri about women Sunday school teachers. Lipscomb asserted that Scripture clearly condemned women's public teaching in formal gatherings of the church. While Lipscomb admitted that it was difficult to know exactly where to draw the line, he believed that the only proper role for women was to "engage in those acts of service in the church assembly that she can do in a modest way, neither taking the lead, assuming authority or attracting public attention to herself." He concluded that teaching children in Sunday school was permissible.[86]

Within a few weeks Holman had composed a rejoinder to Lipscomb's assertions. She agreed that the passages used to restrict women's public roles in the church (especially 1 Cor. 14:34-35; 1 Tim. 2:11-15) were difficult to harmonize with other Scriptures that clearly indicated women had such roles (for example, 1 Cor. 11:5; Acts 21:9). She appealed to the long-established hermeneutical principle that every Scripture must be interpreted in light of every other passage, and not in isolation. If the words "let your women keep silence in the churches" were to be taken literally and in isolation from other Scriptures, women could not sing, pray, teach Sunday school, or ask questions. In fact, they could not go to church at all, because they were instructed to learn at home from their husbands.[87]

She went on to cite numerous instances of prominent roles women played in the early church, including the women who followed and supported Jesus and Paul, those present at the crucifixion, those charged with proclaiming the good news of Jesus' resurrection, and those who were part of the company on Pentecost who received the Holy Spirit. She ended with a rebuke of the attitudes of the church of her day.

In those days Philip's daughters prophesied in the presence of Luke and of Paul. But the modern woman is deemed unworthy to read or even to ask questions about the Bible in the presence of a nineteenth century man. Priscilla was wise enough, and in no wise considered unworthy to instruct Apollos, one of the most learned and eloquent of the early teachers in the doctrine of the new religion. But the modern woman must not venture to express an opinion on any religious subject in the presence of the vast amount of dignity and learning and wisdom and goodness embodied in the presence of some of our brethren of the present day.[88]

In the June 20 issue, Lipscomb printed a challenge to Holman's article written by A. A. Bunner, who would become one of her sparring partners on the issue of women's roles. In a somewhat flippant tone, Bunner said that since Holman had spoken from a woman's standpoint, he would now treat the question from a scriptural one. He charged that none of Holman's examples invalidated Paul's clear and unassailable command for women to keep silent in the church. Whatever those other passages meant, they could not negate that injunction. None of those passages, therefore, should be understood as women teaching in a formal public assembly.[89]

Holman's response, published in the August 1 issue, did not concede any of her earlier points. She continued to insist that one must harmonize Scriptures with one another and not choose which ones will take precedence, which her detractors clearly did with the restrictive passages. She barraged Bunner with dozens of questions, trying to force him to admit that the matter was not as clear as he asserted. Are women who have the talent to speak publicly sinning against God when they teach the gospel to the unsaved? How can women sing in church and obey the command to keep silence? Since many of the hymns sung in church were written by women, is it a violation of God's will for women and men to sing them together, since they are women's words? Does a woman have to cover her head when she prays in her own home at night? Was it a meaningless accident that Christ appeared first to a woman after his resurrection and charged her with telling the good news to others?

This was only the beginning. Holman would continue writing extensively on the subject over the next months and years. David Lipscomb did not censor Holman's articles. Rather, he published them and responded, repeating the restrictive theological positions concerning woman's nature and role and warning that any change to that position would result in disaster for both church and society. The fact that Holman could not understand the plain teaching of Paul to keep silence was itself an indication, Lipscomb said, of the inherent unfitness of women for public leadership.

Her unfitness to lead and teach arises from her strong emotional nature causing her to be easily deceived and to be ready to run after anything or body that might strike her fancy against reason and facts. This is still strongly woman's characteristic, as the article of our sister plainly shows. Paul says, notwithstanding this characteristic that unfits woman for a leader and teacher of assemblies, if she will devote herself to bearing children, in faith and charity and holiness, as her true work, she shall be saved.[90]

Lipscomb dismissed Holman's arguments by saying that her logic was typical of women—she wanted her points to be true, so they were true, regardless of any evidence to the contrary. She might have made the same argument about Lipscomb's position, but did not.

Holman went on to become prominent in the WCTU, which wielded considerable political power in Tennessee. In 1899 she became president of the state organization, serving in that role until 1914. Under Holman's leadership, the organization increased its membership from two hundred to four thousand, and she led a successful campaign for prohibition enacted by the Tennessee legislature in 1909.

In September 1915 Holman underwent an emergency appendectomy and died several days later from complications. Her last article in the *Gospel Advocate* had been published in 1913. She never relented in her position that women could exercise their gifts in a public way to serve the church without "usurping authority" over men.[91] At Holman's request, evangelist T. B. Larimore conducted her funeral, attended by over two thousand people. He had refused to take sides on the issues of extra-congregational organizations and women's roles, and Holman knew he would not "apologize for her work."[92]

The debate over women's roles also continued in churches that accepted extra-congregational organizations. In 1892, T. W. Caskey challenged J. B. Briney to debate the following proposition on the pages of the *Christian Evangelist*: "According to New Testament teaching, a woman may be an evangelist or pastor of a church and do any work in the ministry or fill any office in the church, that a man may do or fill." Taking the affirmative, Caskey argued that women and men are equal in creation and redemption and that in the New Testament women preached the gospel. The admonition for women to keep silent was a local custom not binding on the whole church.[93] Briney answered that the Lord had forbidden women to preach in public assemblies and therefore to send or call a woman to that work was "open rebellion to the King."[94] Earlier the same year, Clara

Babcock had defended women preachers in the *Christian Standard* on much the same grounds as Caskey: men and women were created equal; though woman lost her high estate in the fall, the gospel had restored the equality of men and women. The Scriptures must harmonize; women did teach and were commended for doing so by Paul, the admonition to keep silent notwithstanding.[95]

The following year Morgan Hayden took up Briney's position on the pages of the *Christian Standard*.[96] Among several respondents to Hayden was a former state evangelist from Illinois, N. S. Haynes. Haynes asserted that women have all of the abilities necessary to preach the gospel, adding: "If other evidence of woman's equal business abilities be needed, it may be found in our Christian Woman's Board of Missions."[97]

Despite Haynes's reference to women having the abilities necessary to preach the gospel, both the Caskey-Briney and Hayden debates on women's preaching focused on the interpretation of Scripture. Was the admonition for women to keep silent the law of Christ or merely the "custom" of a particular church? As one correspondent stated in a letter to the *Christian Standard*, "I believe with all my heart in the inspiration of Paul the apostle but do not regard Bro. Hayden as an infallible translator of Paul."[98]

The earliest editions of the annual yearbook published by the American Christian Missionary Society included a small list of women described as "pastoral helpers." Beginning in 1906, however, the yearbook included a "List of Women Preachers," including as many as seventy-five names.[99] By 1913 there was no longer a separate list for women; those names were simply included in a combined list of preachers. This seems to represent a slowly developing recognition of the legitimacy of women's preaching. Moreover, the CWBM continued to grow in numbers into the second decade of the twentieth century. Yet, the rising number of women preachers and the astounding growth of the CWBM can easily mask the continuing tensions over the role of women leaders in churches that accepted the extra-congregational organizations.

By 1920, women, whose voices had been largely marginalized prior to the Civil War, had emerged as leaders in their own right across the Stone-Campbell Movement. Women were teachers and administrators of the Sunday school movement. With the formation of the CWBM in 1874, women created the most effective general organization to emerge in the Stone-Campbell Movement and ventured into forms of service including ordained ministry that would have been unimaginable to the Movement's leaders a generation before. Though tensions over the role of women continued, even in those parts of the movement least open to women's leadership the female voice had been heard.

Prominent Tennessee WCTU leader Silena Moore Holman (seated at left) and her husband Dr. Thomas Pinkney Holman, with family. *(From TheRestorationMovement.com website)*

5

Divisions in North America

The Emergence of Churches of Christ and Disciples of Christ

When Alexander Campbell died March 4, 1866, he left a movement too diverse for any single person to lead. That year the *Gospel Advocate* in Nashville, Tennessee, begun in 1855 but discontinued during the American Civil War (1861-1865), resumed publication under the editorship of David Lipscomb (1831-1917), and the *Christian Standard* of Cincinnati, Ohio, began publication under the editorship of Isaac Errett (1820-1888). The combination of these events on the heels of the War foreshadowed the future of the Stone-Campbell Movement in North America. By the late 1880s, the *Gospel Advocate* and the *Christian Standard* would symbolize a division into two distinct and increasingly distant church bodies, Churches of Christ and Disciples of Christ—a division documented by the 1906 U.S. Census of Religious Bodies.

When Campbell died, the Movement's leading paper with 8,500 subscribers was the *American Christian Review*, published in Cincinnati and edited by Benjamin Franklin (1812-1878). Stone-Campbell Christians who resented the *Review*'s lukewarm support of the American Christian Missionary Society and its wartime neutrality began the *Christian Standard* as an alternative.[1] The *Gospel Advocate*, while sympathetic to the *Review*'s theological positions, was reborn out of the perceived need for a paper that reflected Southern sentiments. Franklin would soon become a minority voice in the North, and though his ideas continued to resonate with many Southern readers, sectional attitudes limited his influence there. The *Gospel Advocate* would become the primary source for shaping the attitudes and doctrinal positions of many Southern Stone-Campbell congregations well into the twentieth century.

David Lipscomb and Southern Churches

David Lipscomb emerged as the most prominent leader of the Stone-Campbell Movement in the former Confederate states. His mentor, Middle Tennessee educator and editor Tolbert Fanning (1810-1874), had founded the *Christian Review* in 1844, Franklin College near Nashville in 1845, and the *Gospel Advocate* in 1855. Fanning's early religious formation had come from preachers in the Stone movement, including B. F. Hall (1803-1873), Ephraim D. Moore (1784-1859), and James E. Matthews (1799-1867) in northeast Alabama. After arriving in Tennessee in 1831 to attend the University of Nashville, Fanning came under the influence of Alexander Campbell, who was closely associated with the congregation there. He accompanied Campbell on extended preaching tours in 1835 and 1836.[2]

Theologically, then, both Stone and Campbell shaped Fanning. From the Barton Stone of the 1840s, whose growing frustration with the failure of state and federal governments to abolish slavery led him to reject participation in civil government, Fanning received a strong sense of what Richard Hughes has called the "apocalyptic worldview."[3] He was apolitical (he did not vote after 1845), a pacifist (long before the American Civil War), Kingdom-oriented (the Kingdom of God will triumph over all earthly powers), and counter-cultural (a Southerner who opposed slavery). At the same time, Campbell's commitment to the primitive church elaborated in his *Christian Baptist* series "A Restoration of the Ancient Order of Things" deeply influenced Fanning's thinking. In turn, Fanning's ideas influenced Lipscomb. When Fanning and Lipscomb revived the *Gospel Advocate* in 1866 they were a united front—a theological fusion of late Stoneite apocalypticism and Campbellite primitivism with a strong sectional bias.

Thus, three thought streams shaped Stone-Campbell churches in Middle Tennessee after the Civil War: an "apocalyptic" stream originating with Barton W. Stone, a socio-sectional stream shaped by the experience of the Upper South, and a legalistic stream of biblical interpretation rooted in Campbell's primitivism. All three merged in Tolbert Fanning and were also present in David Lipscomb as editor of the *Gospel Advocate* from 1866 until his death in 1917.

An advocate of American democracy before the American Civil War, David Lipscomb was profoundly changed by the conflict, becoming a pacifist and rejecting the Christian's participation in civil government.

Of the three thought streams, the apocalyptic was the most distinctive. It was a counter-cultural stance holding that the coming of God's Kingdom would annihilate all human authority. In a treatise on the Christian's relation to civil government, Lipscomb wrote that the work of the Kingdom of God was to destroy every human kingdom.[4] Similarly, James A. Harding (1848-1922)—co-founder with Lipscomb of the Nashville

Bible School in 1891—taught that the Kingdom Christ established was opposed to all human and governmental authority and had as its purpose the destruction of all such earthly powers.[5]

Lipscomb and Harding did not define the Kingdom of God in institutional terms. They certainly believed that the church was part of Christ's Kingdom, but the Kingdom embraced much more. It included everything and everyone who had submitted to God as sovereign.[6] God's mission was to introduce the Kingdom into a fallen world, a mission that would continue until the Kingdom reached everlasting perfection.[7] The kingdoms of the fallen world were Satanic; therefore God's followers should reject allegiance to anything in the world. Lipscomb's vision was thoroughly God-centered and mission-oriented, and included opposition to nationalism and war, and the pursuit of a counter-cultural lifestyle with the Sermon on the Mount as the model.[8]

One cannot understand the *Gospel Advocate*'s rejection of missionary societies without recognizing this counter-cultural vision. Lipscomb viewed such organizations as institutional machinery with political ends that served the interests of the kingdom of this world rather than the Kingdom of God. Fanning wrote in 1866 that he and Lipscomb were absolutely convinced that "the adoption or substitution of any expedient, society or plan for Christian work besides the 'Kingdom not of this world' is an insult to God, and a disgrace to the Christian profession."[9] As Richard Hughes points out, the rejection of human innovations (whether missionary societies or instrumental music) and the refusal to vote were "two sides of the same apocalyptic coin" in the eyes of Fanning, Lipscomb, and Harding.[10]

The socio-sectional stream gave a geographical character to Churches of Christ. While sectional and sociological differences existed prior to the Civil War, they rose to prominence in the postwar period. Resolutions in support of the Union passed in 1861 and 1863 by the American Christian Missionary Society had become the flashpoint of the sectional difference. After learning of the first resolution, Tolbert Fanning exclaimed, "Should we ever meet them in the flesh, can we fraternize with them as brethren? How can the servants of the Lord of this section ever strike hands with the men who now seek their life's blood?"[11]

After 1866 the *Gospel Advocate* clearly reflected a Southern bias. Lipscomb tried to tone down sectional tensions by enlisting Kentucky Christians in the venture, even asking J. W. McGarvey (1829-1911) to edit the journal. Most members of Stone-Campbell churches in Kentucky, however, including many writers for Franklin's *American Christian Review*, regarded the new *Gospel Advocate* as a sectional paper intent on opposing missionary societies. Lipscomb admitted, "The fact that we had not a single paper known to us that Southern people could read without having their feelings wounded by political insinuations and slurs, had more to do with calling the Advocate into existence than all other circumstances combined."[12]

A signal event in 1866 reflecting the sectional formation of Churches of Christ was a consultation meeting of church leaders from Alabama, Georgia, Tennessee, Kentucky (Louisville and Bowling Green, but not Lexington), and Virginia in Murfreesboro, Tennessee, from June 9-16. Those present discussed the poverty-stricken condition of many Southern Christians, congregational cooperation, the "true bond of Christian union," the relationship between State and Church, and how to equip members in local congregations.[13] In many ways, according to Robert Hooper, this meeting set the *Advocate*'s agenda for the last decades of the nineteenth century.[14] Many Southern congregations ultimately formed an identity shaped by the *Advocate* as their major organ of fellowship and teaching.[15]

An example of the complex mixture of sociological and sectional tensions at work can be seen in the 1872 controversy over the new building for the Central Christian Church in Cincinnati. The congregation spent $140,000 on the building and $8,000 on an organ. Benjamin Franklin led an assault against such extravagant spending as evidence of worldly pride. It stood in contrast with the $100,000 that the *Advocate* had raised mostly from the former Confederate and border states for destitute Southerners in 1866-1868.[16] The fact that a Northern congregation could spend $140,000 on a single building but only $100,000 could be raised to help the poor in the South accentuated, especially in the minds of *Advocate* readers, the contrast between the values of Christians in the wealthy North and the impoverished South.

Another example of the complex mix of tensions at work was Lipscomb's treatment of the *Christian Hymn Book*, long used by Stone-Campbell churches throughout the nation. When the American Christian Missionary Society received the rights to publish the hymnal and began to promote a revised edition in Southern churches after the war, Lipscomb was outraged. He confessed that his opposition to the hymnal was largely because of the "blood stains, that to our mind it acquired in passing

through the bloody-hearted *Christian Missionary Society*."[17] He also attacked it for its elitist literary style and its substitution of unfamiliar hymns for older ones. Most Southern Christians, he asserted, were poor laboring-class people whose religious language was the simple words of Scripture. Furthermore, he asserted that the poverty-stricken South lacked the resources to purchase and use such an elitist hymnal. Lipscomb promoted a Canadian hymnbook published by James Beatty of Toronto rather than contribute to the coffers of the bloodstained missionary society.[18]

The legalistic stream transcended sectional differences and is best understood in light of the question of instrumental music in worship. Why did this issue so radically divide churches? Simply put, for many the instrument defiled the assembly. This understanding was based on a Puritan principle inherited through the Stone-Campbell Movement's Reformed roots. It assumed that God's positive law, which includes ceremonial matters as distinguished from morality, governs the worship assembly, and that obedience to positive law is a test of loyalty. The Reformed tradition had long debated what acts constituted necessary elements of worship— which ones were commanded by God and which were merely acceptable ways of fulfilling those commands. The Movement's controversies in the 1860s and 1870s solidified a particular understanding of this regulative principle among the developing Churches of Christ.[19]

Perhaps a correspondent named Turner posed the classic statement of the issue in 1870 when he asked, "Does the New Testament determine the elements of the public worship?" As far as he knew, Turner continued, the churches were agreed on what a sinner should do to be saved, but not on the elements of public worship. Turner asserted that every legitimate act of worship must have a specific command from God and that there are five such acts in the New Testament—teaching, singing, praying, contributing, and communing at the table.[20] Only these five acts should be practiced in worship assemblies, and all of these acts should be present in the assembly every first day of the week.

Benjamin Franklin, perhaps more than any other writer of the era, stressed the nature of the assembly as obedience to positive law. He explained the difference between it and moral law in his sermon "Divine Positive Law." Obedience to positive law, he insisted, was the ultimate evidence of reverence for divine authority because it revealed the true condition of the heart at the deepest levels. Obedience to positive law reflected pure faith and therefore was higher than obedience to moral law, which generally reflected simple good judgment and included incentives and rewards. Examples of positive law in Scripture included placing blood on the door-posts (Exodus 12:1-13), Abraham's sacrifice of Isaac (Genesis 22), Naaman's immersing himself in the Jordan (2 Kings 5), marching around the walls of Jericho (Joshua 2), and immersion in water for the remission of sins (Mark 16:16). Obedience to positive command, unencumbered by the crutches of moral law, truly showed a person's loyalty. Defiance of positive law revealed a "spirit of disobedience" that would lead to damnation. Regarding immersion, Franklin explained:

> Baptism is the test of [the sinner's] belief in Christ—the trial of his loyalty to the King. There, at the entrance of the Kingdom, the question comes before the sinner of *obedience* in a matter of the most trying nature—obedience to a commandment, where the sinner can see no reason for *obedience* only that the King requires it. If the sinner stops at this first formal act required, and refuses to *obey*, what may we expect of him at any subsequent time?"[21]

The instrumental music controversy was largely irrelevant to Southern churches in the decades immediately after the Civil War. Most simply could not afford instruments even if they had wanted them. Lipscomb himself did not discuss the question until 1873 when he agreed with Franklin that anything not specifically ordained by God in the New Testament was without divine authority.[22] However, this issue would become for many the most hotly debated and long-lasting source of antagonism between Churches of Christ and Disciples. For members of Churches of Christ it became a visible symbol of whether one was loyal or rebellious toward God. There was a positive command to sing, but there was no such command that authorized playing musical instruments. To add them, therefore, was disobedience.

Yet another issue that divided Churches of Christ and Disciples was the question of calling a resident preacher from outside the congregation. Alexander Campbell's vision of a full-time ministry elected from, ordained, and compensated by each congregation was rarely achieved. In many congregations no single person, let alone a plurality of persons, seemed qualified to fill the duties of Campbell's office of elder. Elders were elected and ordained, but did not serve full time, often did little teaching and were not compensated. Desiring a teaching ministry, some churches, especially in the North, began to hire evangelists to stay with them and devote full time

to their congregation.[23]

Tolbert Fanning believed that this development would rob the evangelist's office of persons needed for the important work of preaching, baptizing, and planting congregations. It would also hinder the development of talent within congregations, since the hired pastor would have a tendency to perform all of the activities that the members themselves should do.[24] Lipscomb made it clear that while he opposed calling pastors from outside the congregation, he did not oppose paying them. "The eldership," he wrote, "has not been honored, respected, and supported as it should have been, but this evil will never be remedied by supplanting the elders with peripatetic pastors."[25]

Growth of Innovations in the North

In the missionary society, instrumental music, and resident preacher controversies, those who would become known as Disciples of Christ, the majority of whom were in the North, could not fathom the reasoning behind the growing militant opposition to these practices. Shaped by their experience of post-Civil War prosperity and renewed enthusiasm for the role of the United States in the advance of God's Kingdom, the majority of Disciples

Christian Standard editor Isaac Errett defended hiring a resident preacher from outside the congregation as a temporary measure toward achieving Campbell's ideal of a plurality of full-time compensated elders who would share in leading the local church.

either rejected or misunderstood the commitment to positive law of those who viewed the innovations as open rebellion against God. To Disciples, such accusations seemed irrational and mean spirited. This stream was drawing from other historical Stone-Campbell commitments as its foundation.

Since its beginning, the Stone-Campbell Movement had regarded avoidance of doctrinal tests of fellowship as a core value. Both the *Last Will and Testament* and the *Declaration and Address* identified compulsory confessions of faith as a source of religious tyranny and division. In a five-part series on the nature of Christian doctrine published in the *Millennial Harbinger* in 1856, Robert Richardson detailed what he saw as central to the Movement's identity. He began by insisting that Christian doctrine must be distinguished from the Christian gospel. Protestants had tended to teach doctrine, where Christ and the apostles preached the gospel. Conversion, Richardson lamented, had become for many "the adoption of a religious theory, rather than of a religious life." Christ was a person, not a doctrine. Trust in Christ, not commitment to doctrine, was the key to a proper understanding of Christianity.[26] For Disciples this position was summed up in the slogan "No creed but Christ, no book but the Bible, no law but love."[27]

For Richardson and many others in the North, commitment to Christ meant willingness to embrace new ways of advancing Christ's Kingdom. In the post-Civil War era, Stone-Campbell Christians in the North established five national societies in addition to the American Christian Missionary Society that had been organized in 1849. The Christian Woman's Board of Missions was founded in 1874. Following a meeting of men called by W. T. Moore during the 1874 General Christian Missionary Convention (GCMC), the Foreign Christian Missionary Society was formed in 1875. In 1887 women in St. Louis, led by Matilda Hart Younkin (1843-1899), chartered the National Benevolent Association to care for the sick and homeless. The following year, as other Protestant bodies were establishing church extension funds to assist congregations with facilities, the GCMC organized the Board of Church Extension. In 1895, the GCMC voted to organize a Board of Ministerial Relief to raise funds to aid destitute ministers and their families.[28]

Socio-economic and sectional factors played a powerful role in determining the paths Stone-Campbell Christians would take. Many in the defeated and impoverished South were increasingly inclined to reject the kingdoms of this world and seek the certainty of having fulfilled all that God required. In contrast, the booming economy of the victorious North encouraged enthusiasm for what many in the North perceived as improved methods of advancing God's mission—a mission they increasingly identified with the mission of the United States to extend democracy and freedom throughout the world.[29]

After moving to St. Louis with her family in 1875, Matilda Hart Younkin became increasingly disturbed by the failure of the church to address the needs of the urban homeless. In 1886 she gathered six women in a basement room of the First Christian Church in St. Louis to pray, leading a year later to the establishment of the National Benevolent Association.

No one exemplified the latter attitude more than James H. Garrison (1842-1931), editor of the St. Louis based *Christian-Evangelist*. Though he first viewed missionary societies as simply one expedient method to take the gospel to the world, he eventually came to see them as essential to the Movement's maturity. If we are to become adults and not children, he exclaimed, we must have organizations to do our work "in an orderly and systematic way."[30] This view of organizational development would eventually lead him to advocate Alexander Campbell's vision of a representative convention that would speak and act for the whole Movement, though without legislative power.[31]

Growing Divergence

Two events symbolized the growing divergence of outlook in the Movement. The first took place on August 17, 1889, near the Sand Creek Church in rural Shelby County, Illinois. Nearly six thousand people had gathered for an annual fellowship meeting begun in 1873. The 1889 meeting provided a stage for church leaders from several Illinois congregations to declare non-fellowship with those who had introduced "innovations."

In a document that came to be known as the Sand Creek "Address and Declaration"—a play on Thomas Campbell's call for unity in the "Declaration and Address"—writers warned churches that they could no longer tolerate the unauthorized practices. The list included instrumental music and choirs in worship, missionary societies, hiring of preacher-pastors, raising money outside the Sunday contribution, and other unnamed offenses.[32] After a lengthy admonition asserting that those who practiced such things were not as informed in the Scriptures as those who rejected them, the document concluded,

> And now, in closing up this address and declaration, we state that we are impelled from a sense of duty to say, that all such as are guilty of teaching, or allowing and practicing the many innovations to which we have referred, that after being admonished and having had sufficient time for reflection, if they do not turn away from such abominations, that we can not and will not regard them as brethren.[33]

Significantly, both David Lipscomb and James H. Garrison condemned the "Address and Declaration." Garrison ridiculed the seceders and their leader, preacher-editor Daniel Sommer, as a handful of factionists who posed no real threat to the Movement.[34] Lipscomb, while in sympathy with the theological positions taken at Sand Creek, believed the meeting and the resulting document to be just as unscriptural as the missionary societies they denounced.[35] Nevertheless, the Sand Creek event and its aftermath provided a visible marker of how far the division had already developed.

Another marker event in the widening division took place in late October 1892, when the General Christian Missionary Convention met in Nashville, Tennessee. Those who supported missionary societies had organized the Tennessee Christian Missionary Society just two years earlier, but under the influence of David Lipscomb and the *Gospel Advocate* the vast majority of churches in the state did not support it. Lipscomb and others who had participated in pre-Civil War cooperative efforts saw the new state society—as well as the national bodies—as usurping the churches' responsibility for evangelization. The GCMC's choice of Nashville for its meeting was apparently an effort to create a more favorable attitude toward the societies in Tennessee.

Lipscomb and others who opposed extra-congregational structures attended the meetings. Later Lipscomb would write that he believed the convention had actually strengthened the cause of those who opposed the societies. He was not surprised at the attitudes he witnessed that, in his view, disregarded the clear teachings of the Bible. The one thing that seemed to anger him most, however, was the appearance on the program of women speakers from the Christian Woman's Board of Missions.

In an article describing his experiences at the Convention, he described hearing a young woman make a "rambling talk" on missions that "lowered the standard of womanly modesty" and was an embarrassment to all present. If the clear teachings of Scripture on the nature and role of women could be set aside as flagrantly as this, he exclaimed, then we can substitute sprinkling for baptism or eliminate it entirely, reject Christ's divinity, and toss out the Bible completely for a creed that says whatever we want to hear. The Convention, he concluded, was "an open, defiant rejection of God and his holy word."[36] After this event, Lipscomb seemed resigned to the reality of division.

The 1906 Census

The first division of the North American Stone-Campbell Movement received formal recognition in the 1906 Census of Religious Bodies. As early as 1850, Congress had instructed census takers to gather certain "social statistics," including religious data like number of churches, membership, and value of church property for all American religious bodies.[37] The churches of the Stone-Campbell Movement had been identified in the published data under the heading Disciples of Christ.

When the Census Bureau became a permanent agency in 1902, specialized surveys distinct from the ten-year population count became possible. The first of five stand-alone religious censuses conducted by the Bureau was begun in 1906, led by Census Director S. N. D. North. As census officials geared up for data collection, they noticed in their monitoring of journals that the *Gospel Advocate*, which in previous data was part of Disciples of Christ, seemed at times to distance itself from that body. In addition, North had received a letter from William J. Campbell of Marshalltown, Iowa, informing him that three thousand "churches of Christ" formerly connected with Disciples of Christ no longer were. Campbell included a list of preachers for this body published by McQuiddy Publishing Company (publisher of the *Gospel Advocate*). The list included David Lipscomb, E. A. Elam, and other editors of the magazine. Hoping this would solve the problem, North double-checked the directory of preachers from the Disciples yearbook and found that Lipscomb and Elam were listed there too![38]

In a letter to David Lipscomb dated June 17, 1907, published in the July 18, 1907, *Gospel Advocate*, North described his confusion and asked,

> 1. Whether there is a religious body called "Church of Christ," not identified with the Disciples of Christ, or any other Baptist body? 2. If there is such a body, has it any general organization, with headquarters, officers, district or general conventions, associations or conferences? 3. How did it originate, and what are its distinctive principles? 4. How best can there be secured a complete list of the churches?

Lipscomb's reply explained in detail why he believed there was now such a body separate from the Disciples. He gave a history lesson on the origins of the Stone-Campbell Movement, as much for the readers of the *Advocate* as for North. He explained that some in the Movement had come to advocate the very things it had opposed since the beginning—the organization of the churches into a missionary society and use of instrumental music in worship. Their motivation was a desire for popularity fueled by increased numbers and wealth that subverted the very principles on which they were founded. He concluded with the declaration, "There is a distinct people taking the word of God as their only and sufficient rule of faith, calling their churches 'churches of Christ' or 'churches of God,' distinct and separate in name, work, and rule of faith from all other bodies of people."[39]

James H. Garrison reacted with disbelief to Lipscomb's reply to North. This showed, Garrison exclaimed, that sectarianism and a desire for a following at the expense of Christian unity was alive and well.[40] Lipscomb responded that he had not initiated the inquiry concerning a separate body. Census officials had seen the difference, asked, and Lipscomb gave them the facts. He had done nothing but "try to be true to God and his word."[41]

These salvos led to a yearlong barrage of accusations and counter-accusations between Garrison and Lipscomb in their respective papers. Each was fully convinced of the obvious rightness of his position and unable to understand the other's reasoning. Frustration and personal attacks mounted. Garrison accused Lipscomb of attempting to promote a formal division.[42] Lipscomb insisted he had done nothing to cause the division; he had merely answered truthfully when Census Director North had asked him a direct question.[43]

Before Lipscomb's correspondence with Director North, Census officials had authorized G. A. Hoffmann, editor of the Disciples yearbook, to gather data for the Stone-Campbell churches.[44] After receiving Lipscomb's letter, North visited the Nashville editor in late 1907 to ask him to choose an agent to gather statistics for "churches of Christ." Lipscomb asked *Gospel Advocate* office manager J. W. Shepherd to gather the data and issued a strong appeal to the churches to return the census forms Shepherd would be sending: "When the government requests such things at our hands, we think they ought to be furnished. Not to do this is to violate the obligation God has placed us under to the government."[45]

Hoffmann, however, had already begun sending forms to the same churches. Some had supplied the requested information to him before receiving Shepherd's material. Others had discarded Hoffmann's request, regarding him as a "digressive." When these churches received Shepherd's forms, many assumed it was another mailing from Hoffmann and failed to respond. In repeated pleas, Hoffmann in the *Christian Standard* and *Christian-Evangelist*, and Shepherd in the *Gospel Advocate*, urged churches to send in their statistics.[46] Information received from congregations wishing to be distinguished from Disciples was uneven at best.

When the census data was published, first in a bulletin in 1909, then in two oversized volumes in 1910, Churches of Christ appeared second in a chart listing seventeen "New Denominations and Denominational Families," noted as formerly included with Disciples of Christ. The number of congregations listed for Churches of Christ was 2,642 with 159,123 members. Disciples of Christ reported 7,799 congregations with 923,698 members.[47] Though the figures were far from perfect, they reflected the separation that had been under way for several decades.

African American Churches of Christ

The division reflected in the census data cut across racial lines. Published figures listed 9,705 black Disciples in one hundred twenty-nine congregations, while black

Churches of Christ numbered 1,528 members in forty-one churches.[48] Apparently the Assembly Churches were numbered among black Disciples of Christ since no separate listing appears in the data.

The separation between what would become black Disciples and black Churches of Christ had become evident in the late 1890s in Nashville, Tennessee, where Preston Taylor served as preacher, first for the Gay Street Christian Church and later the Lea Avenue congregation. Taylor had long-supported cooperative efforts, leading in the formation of the National Convention of Churches of Christ in 1878 and serving as an evangelist for the General Christian Missionary Convention beginning in 1884. Both of Taylor's congregations had active auxiliaries of the Christian Woman's Board of Missions

Early meeting place of the Jackson Street Church of Christ in Nashville, Tennessee, the "Mother Church" of Black Churches of Christ. *(From website of the Jackson Street Church of Christ, http://www.jacksonst.org/)*

(CWBM) and used instrumental music in worship.

Some of his parishioners, however, especially two preachers named Alexander Campbell (1862-1930) and Samuel W. Womack (1851-1920), came to oppose missionary societies and instrumental music in worship. Around 1900 Campbell left Lea Avenue and began meeting with others in his home for, in his words, "the pure worship." A few months later, S. W. Womack left the Gay Street church to join Campbell. From this beginning Campbell and Womack formed the Jackson Street Church of Christ in Nashville, Tennessee, the "mother church" of African American Churches of Christ.[49]

Though Campbell's life prior to his separation from the Disciples is largely unknown, he quickly became an energetic leader of African American Churches of Christ in Middle Tennessee. In addition to planting churches across the state, he was a fierce debater. In 1920 he debated J. B. Booth, presiding Elder of the African Methodist Episcopal Church in Marshall County,

Tennessee. Campbell affirmed, "The church of Christ, with which I stand identified, is apostolic in origin, doctrine, and practice." Booth denied the proposition. According to a white Church of Christ observer, when the debate ended, Campbell challenged Booth to a public discussion of water baptism, but Booth refused, "saying he never expected to debate again."[50]

Womack, Campbell's senior by more than a decade, had been a leader in Stone-Campbell churches in Tennessee for more than twenty years before joining Campbell in the formation of the Jackson Street Church. Baptized in Lynchburg, Tennessee, in 1866 by a white preacher, T. J. Shaw, Womack became a regular contributor to the *Christian Standard* in the 1870s. In the 1880s he was active in preaching across the state and in organizing the black Tennessee state meeting.[51] However, by the early years of the twentieth century Womack had rejected such organizations and was declaring his determination to adhere strictly to what he perceived to be scriptural teachings, asserting, "I know of no way taught in the Book to succeed in the work, but to work, talk, and trust God by doing what he says, just as he says it."[52]

Womack and Campbell both published often in the *Gospel Advocate*, using reports of their evangelistic endeavors to solicit support for their efforts to plant and nurture congregations across the region. Womack was influenced by the views of editor David Lipscomb and frequently sought his counsel. When Lipscomb died in 1917, Womack eulogized him in an article published in the *Advocate*, noting: "So many times I have met him at the office, and any part of the Book that I did not understand, he was ready to help me out on it."[53]

Among the first persons that Campbell and Womack drew to the Jackson Street Church was George Philip Bowser (1874-1950). Bowser, who had been licensed to preach in the African Methodist Episcopal Church, left Methodism in 1897 under the teaching of an elderly preacher named Sam Davis and united with the Gay Street Christian Church. Later explaining his move to the Jackson Street Church of Christ, Bowser recounted that he had "determined to follow Christ according to the plan laid down by the apostles in the book of God, and to follow nothing else."[54]

In February 1902, black preachers in Churches of Christ announced plans to publish a paper for "the teaching of pure New Testament Christianity in the interest of the church of Christ in the United States." Organizers intended the paper to appear first as a monthly, expanding later into a weekly. The paper, to be called the *Minister's Bulletin*, evidently never materialized.[55] In the aftermath of that failed project, however, Bowser began publication of the *Christian Echo*, a journal for and by African Americans in Churches of Christ that would become one of the longest-lived journals in the history of the Stone-Campbell Movement. Under Bowser's leadership, the Jackson Street Church helped birth the Silver Point Christian Institute in Silver Point, Tennessee, in 1907. From the Jackson Street congregation also would come one of the most effective black preachers in the history of Churches of Christ, Womack's son-in-law, Marshall Keeble (1878-1968).[56]

The stories of Campbell, Womack, Bowser, and Keeble suggest that in the challenging social and economic circumstances of the post-Civil War American South, a spirituality that rejected the kingdoms of this world and offered assurance of having fulfilled all God required proved attractive to many blacks.

Division Accomplished

The 1906 Census of Religious Bodies pushed congregations to decide with which group they would identify—a choice not available in the same way before. By requiring a decision the census exacerbated the antagonism between those already taking sides in the conflict, leading each to blame the other for division and unfaithfulness to God. The Census became the symbol of a process of separation that was nearing completion.[57]

The division's roots, however, were firmly planted in socio-economic and sectional factors related to the American Civil War. In the impoverished and defeated South, most members of the Stone-Campbell Movement identified faithfulness to Christ as obedience to the positive commands of the New Testament. In the prosperous and victorious North, most Stone-Campbell Christians defined faithfulness as trust in the person of Christ. Both commitments had been present in the Movement since the beginning. Socio-economic and sectional factors had disposed members of the Movement to emphasize one over the other, resulting in division. Though sharing a common heritage, Churches of Christ and Disciples of Christ would now continue as separate streams of the Stone-Campbell Movement.

Neither stream, however, was homogeneous. Each came into existence with significant internal differences that would lead to further realignments. These differences were already evident by the 1909 publication of the 1906 Census of Religious Bodies. Like the division between the streams, these differences within the streams were related to socio-economic and sectional factors.

Disciples of Christ

Social and intellectual influences that were most prominent in the Northern United States greatly influenced the emerging Disciples of Christ. Industrial growth, massive immigration, and economic strength created vibrant cities and a growing gap between the urban rich and poor that highlighted the inability of a divided church to address urban needs. Meanwhile, new intellectual currents challenged Christianity on several fronts. Scientific advances including Darwin's theory of evolution threatened the traditional Christian creation story. New comparative studies of religion claimed that Christian theology had always reflected both its cultural surroundings and non-Christian religious expressions. The new disciplines of sociology and psychology raised questions about the origins of religious ideas. In addition, a new method from Germany for studying the Bible, known as higher criticism, began to affect views of Scripture and its interpretation in the United States. Historical critics asked questions about the text's social background, date, authorship, literary characteristics, and sources, challenging traditional interpretations like Moses's authorship of the Pentateuch and the apostolic authorship and historical reliability of the gospels. Controversies raised by these developments led to sharp differences among Disciples.

Higher Criticism

Disciples began debating the merits of higher criticism of the Bible in the 1880s. John W. McGarvey was the best-known opponent of biblical higher criticism among Disciples. McGarvey, who had joined the faculty of Kentucky University's College of the Bible in 1865 and served as president beginning in 1895, authored a weekly column in the *Christian Standard* titled "Biblical Criticism" from 1893 to 1904. In these articles he opposed higher criticism as an attack on the Bible's inspiration and credibility.[58] Henry E. Webb describes McGarvey's essays as written "on a popular level and spiced with humor, sarcasm, and ridicule."[59]

Alexander Campbell had identified Peter's confession that Jesus is the Christ, the Son of the living God (Matthew 16:16) as the only confession required for baptism. McGarvey declared his position on the qualifications for baptism in response to the hypothetical case of a man who would request to be baptized upon his confession of faith in Christ, but claim not to believe "those old stories in Genesis, nor such tales as that about Jonah."

I would say to him, "My friend, your faith in Christ is not sufficient to justify baptizing you into his name. If you really believe in him, you can not refuse to believe anything that he believed, and you can not deny any fact which he declared real. He has declared true the very stories in Genesis which you say you do not believe, and he has endorsed as a reality the story of Jonah. You must learn the way of the Lord more perfectly before I can baptize you."[60]

Learning that E. B. Cake, minister of the Maysville, Kentucky, Christian Church and a recent graduate of the College of the Bible had referred to allegories and legends in Genesis in a series of "Half Hour Talks," McGarvey declared that Cake "has deserted and repudiated the religious body with which the Maysville church has been indentified hitherto, and he has neither the moral nor the civil right to occupy that pulpit another Lord's day."[61] James B. North observes that McGarvey's harsh denunciation of higher critics often alienated even people who accepted his views.[62]

Alexander Procter (1825-1900) represented the more liberal response to the new intellectual currents. Procter was one of four well-known Missouri pastors (including Thomas P. Haley, Allen B. Jones, and George Longan) who embraced openness to the new theological trends among Disciples. Procter and McGarvey overlapped as students at Bethany College, and Procter had ordained McGarvey to the ministry and officiated at his wedding, but their careers took considerably different turns.

Though Procter published little, his views were well known to Disciples leaders. Like Congregationalists Horace Bushnell and Henry Ward Beecher, Procter promoted a spirit of inquiry, critical methods of Bible study, the centrality of love to Christian theology, the evolutionary nature of God's creative action, and a fascination with science of all kinds. Procter believed that science revealed many errors in the Bible, and he was willing even to debate the veracity of the virgin birth. Yet, he was certain that "Christ was the central truth of the universe." For this reason, he remained solidly within Disciples life in spite of some of his theologically liberal positions.[63]

The paradigm represented by Procter gained some support among Disciples. Yet a third, more moderate position seen in leaders like James H. Garrison also gained influence. Garrison sought to maintain what he saw as the essentials of historic Christian faith while linking it to the best science had to offer. Chief among these essentials was the Christian affirmation of God's love. Though Garrison did not endorse truly liberal theological initiatives very often, he reported on them and was quite open to new ideas.

In contrast to McGarvey, who emphasized literal belief of the Bible, Garrison expressed a commitment to the person and example of Jesus. Here he stood in the tradition of Robert Richardson and Alexander Campbell in their distinction between belief in doctrines and belief in Jesus Christ. Garrison added, in response to leaders like McGarvey, that the Christian's belief was ultimately in Christ, not in the Bible. His belief in the evolutionary emergence of truth led him to identify Christ's concerns with the best of his own culture, linking Christianity and North American democracy.

Garrison's moderate stance is evident in his response to an event that occurred in 1889. On December 8, Robert C. Cave, Garrison's minister at the Central Church in St. Louis, preached a sermon that was reprinted in the *St. Louis Republic* under the title "Clerical Sensation." In the sermon Cave introduced several ideas based on higher critical studies of Scripture, including that the Bible was not the inerrant word of God but a record of humanity's gradual and fallible discernment of the nature of God. He also denied the virgin birth, the bodily resurrection of Christ, and the existence of divinely mandated conditions of salvation.[64]

Garrison at first counseled forbearance. When Cave preached that it made no difference whether one believed Christ to be a historical or fictitious figure, however, Garrison launched a campaign against Cave's ideas. This view of Christ, Garrison believed, hit at the very heart of Stone-Campbell commitments. He personally attacked Cave as having surrendered New Testament teachings vital to Christianity and the church.[65] Though Cave had much support in the congregation, by the end of the year he had resigned as minister under the pressure of Garrison's attacks and widespread opposition.

In an effort to counter Cave's teachings, Garrison solicited articles for the *Christian-Evangelist* from prominent preachers reaffirming basic Stone-Campbell beliefs. He edited and reprinted the articles in 1891 in a volume titled *The Old Faith Restated*. The list of writers reflected the broad divergence already present in Disciples. J.W. McGarvey asserted that the Bible was "the only rule of faith and practice" and that critics who questioned the truth contained in the Bible were both unintelligent and lacking in moral judgment.[66] Missouri pastor George W.

Longan wrote an essay on Jesus in which he insisted that knowledge of Jesus had not been substantially altered as a result of critical scholarly work, though the gospels may have been shown to contain mistakes.[67] Other subjects treated included sin, revelation, justification, repentance, baptism, the Lord's Supper, the Holy Spirit, the Church, evangelism, and mission.

In his concluding essay, Garrison defined what he believed had to be continued from the Movement's past. He warned against the narrow, sectarian spirit that equated its own interests with the Kingdom of God or closed itself to new understandings. He defended the Christian liberty to believe things differently from others when the Bible did not contain a definitive word. He condemned doctrinal extremes that reduced all mystery to rational explanation and put conclusions about the proper order of faith, repentance, confession, baptism, pardon, and church membership above heart-felt experience of Christ. These tendencies, when accompanied by "extreme church independency," a "controversial spirit," and "pugilistic preaching," Garrison warned readers, jeopardized the Movement's future.

Instead, the Movement needed to stand for the "vital principles" of its past:

> …the unity of God's people, the supreme authority and sufficiency of the Scriptures, the Christo-centric view of Christianity,…a return to the simple, traditional method of New Testament evangelization,…an intelligent treatment of the Biblical literature, the assertion of the common priesthood of believers and the necessity for a practical, beneficent faith which applies the gospel to all our human ills.[68]

Isaac Errett, twenty years Garrison's senior, was another moderate leader. In 1873 he had published *Our Position*, in which he identified what he saw as agreements and differences between the Stone-Campbell Movement and other Protestant Christians. Number one on his list of agreements was the Divine inspiration of the Bible.[69] Nevertheless, in a famous encounter with McGarvey at the Missouri Christian Lectures at Independence, Missouri, in 1883, he refused to affirm that the Scriptures were free from error or to apply the word "infallible" to the Bible. Though he did not use higher critical methods, Errett acknowledged the limitations of human language. He had no interest in defending any theory of inspiration or infallibility; rather he understood Christ as the foundation of faith and trusted the Bible as a reliable guide.[70]

Christian Unity

New approaches to Christian unity also divided Disciples. By the turn of the century, many Disciples worked cooperatively with Methodists, Presbyterians, Baptists, and others. These Disciples took for granted the Christian status of these bodies and worked alongside them rather than trying to convert their members to the Disciples of Christ.

Soon, biblical critical methods combined with these ecumenical practices to create a new understanding of Christian unity, especially for urban Disciples. One example is B. B. Tyler, pastor of the Church of Christ on West 56th Street in New York City from 1883-1896. During those years, he served often as President of the Chautauqua Union, as President of the Christian Endeavor Union in New York and surrounding areas, on the Board of Managers of the American Bible Society, and as an officer of the ministerial arm of the People's Municipal League, which required him to be in regular contact with Protestant, Catholic, and Jewish religious leaders. These experiences broadened Tyler's understanding of Christian unity.

In 1893, Tyler delivered the closing address for the Disciples congress at the Chicago World's Fair. He argued that signs of union could be seen everywhere—not just in religion, but in all areas of life. This meant, he believed, that "theological dogmas are being relegated to the background" and the "personal Christ is made prominent as never before." He spoke of the growing maturity of Disciples. "There has been no talk," he told the audience, "about the Bible being the creed of the church." Instead, Disciples and other Christians were recognizing that the "creed that needs no revision is this: Jesus of Nazareth is the Christ, the Son of the living God."[71]

W. T. Moore, who spoke earlier at the congress, made much the same point. Among such Disciples, unity had moved away from text-based agreements about the nature of the apostolic church and toward practical efforts to find ways to work with all Christians to accomplish such goals as world evangelization and social change. Disciples, Moore said in 1893, "are beginning to seek for practical channels through which to display our energies, instead of in theological hair-splitting, which serves only to confuse thought rather than clarify it, to hinder Christian unity rather than foster it." This approach gave Moore and other liberal Disciples great confidence that the future would be better than the past: "The age to come will be especially distinguished for its great victories in all the departments of human progress. It will be strongly marked by the spirit of unity which will prevail everywhere."[72]

Yet even as some Disciples leaders became excited by prospects of greater unity, others became more vocal about restoring primitive Christianity. In 1902, Errett Gates noted what he saw as a resurgence of the struggle between primitivism and unity, attributing it to the new Christian union efforts among the churches.[73] The liberals' emphasis on unity in service was reflected in a *Christian-Evangelist* editorial that railed against the divided church's waste of time and resources in bolstering efforts that contributed little to human well being. Meanwhile the truly vital causes of world evangelism, suppressing the liquor traffic, solving labor problems, and reforming politics languished. A new rationale for union among liberal Disciples became the "overthrow of these works of the devil."[74] As conservatives rightly pointed out, this call for cooperation for the sake of social service was not the same as Thomas Campbell's call for unity through the restoration of New Testament Christianity.

By the 1909 Centennial Convention celebrating Thomas Campbell's *Declaration and Address,* nearly all the liberal leaders among Disciples echoed the rejection of a restoration of primitive Christianity seen in Tyler's 1893 speech. In addresses to the Convention, I. M. Spencer and J. M. Philputt insisted that unity depended on a personal Christ, not on agreement about the Bible. To make the Bible the basis of unity meant that Disciples were no different from all other Christians who understood unity as coming together on their understandings of Scripture.[75]

What did it mean, however, to say that unity depended upon a personal Christ? Liberal Disciples had fashioned rather vague notions of Christ that portrayed him as primarily interested in advancing civilization.[76] Christ's goal was to effect political and social reforms that would establish God's righteousness as the foundation of human society and national governments.[77] Jesus became all things to all good-hearted people who believed they could see what was good for everyone else in the world.

Samuel H. Church, the grandson of Walter Scott, a businessman and lay Disciples leader, delivered by far the most controversial address at the Centennial Convention. Reflecting the far left wing emerging among Disciples, Church called for an abandonment of immersion as a requirement for membership and urged unity not only with other Protestants, but with Catholics and Jews as well. He reminded listeners that Jesus had done all his earthly work without the help of a New Testament and asserted that the only difference Jesus would see between a Jew, an Episcopalian, a Catholic, and a Unitarian would

be in how righteous they were and how much they loved. Reflecting the racist assumptions of many progressives, Church argued that America was "the melting pot in which all the white races must be amalgamated and all their religions blended."[78] He did not mention how other races of Christians would be included or how they were to contribute to civilization.

After Church's address, the majority present passed a resolution disavowing it. However, Charles Clayton Morrison (1874-1966), who had purchased the *Christian Century* in 1908, published it with notes of both critique and appreciation. The journal's next issue contained a letter from Addison Clark, a founder of Texas Christian University, who concluded, "With all its faults, Mr. Church's address is one of the greatest addresses of the Convention."[79]

Peter Ainslie's presidential address one year later, though challenging traditional boundaries, persuaded the majority present at the 1910 Convention to establish the Council on Christian Union.[80] Presenting what he asserted was the view from "God's balcony," Ainslie declared:

> What a host of saints! Some were called "Naza-renes," others "Christians," still others "Roman Catholics,"…but, whatever be their names, all these are our brethren…What a host of saints! They are called "Presbyterians," "Baptists," "Episcopalians," "Congregationalists," "Lutherans," "Methodists" and "Disciples," but, whatever be their names, all these likewise are our brethren… Some may doubt this fellowship, but I will not.

Ainslie told the assembly that what was needed was not so much that the Disciples change their attitude, but that *some* Disciples change their attitude.[81]

These sentiments were reinforced by a letter written by W. T. Moore on his seventy-ninth birthday encouraging the Convention to send letters to other denominations calling for mutual study of Christian unity. Commenting approvingly, a *Christian Century* editorial lamented that "the long line of overtures on unity issued by the Disciples of Christ to their Christian brethren have been vitiated by the sectarian insistence upon something that has been called 'our position.'" The writer asserted that such overtures were nothing more than the invitation of a sect for all others to join it. Moore's letter urged Disciples to join the entire Christian world in studying together the matter of union.[82]

Not everyone was pleased, however, with Moore's letter or Ainslie's address. Ainslie endorsed the "federation" movement that had created the Federal Council of the

Churches of Christ in America in 1908, predecessor to the National Council of Churches. Disciples had participated in the Council's founding and were present through most of the serious discussions leading up to its creation, beginning around 1900. Conservative Disciples had opposed the federation movement, which emphasized unity based on service. At the 1902 Convention in Omaha, Elias B. Sanford, a Congregational pastor, had been invited to present the plan of federation to the assembly. J.A. Lord, editor of the *Christian Standard*, had immediately objected, stating that any such action would "recognize the denominations."[83] Nevertheless, after considerable debate the Convention adopted the resolution for federation.

Within weeks, the *Christian Standard* had announced that "*Christian union is not our plea* ... the *right* basis of union, and not union itself, is the thing that distinguishes us." That right basis was Scripture, understood in a traditional pre-critical and literal sense. The article linked federation with other unacceptable ideas, railing against higher criticism and evolution as forms of "secular thought which would create the universe without God and build the church without Christ."[84] For conservative Disciples, support of federation was disloyal to the historic plea of the Disciples of Christ.

Closely related to federation was open membership—an issue that had nearly prevented the union of Stone and Campbell forces in the 1830s. In 1878, the Foreign Christian Missionary Society (FCMS) sent W.T. Moore to London to begin his fifteen-year ministry at the West End Tabernacle. The congregation included both immersed and unimmersed members. Though Moore had accepted the congregation's call on the basis that the church would practice only immersion, the congregation, with his blessing, continued to accept all forms of baptism. Isaac Errett defended Moore's position against critics like H. G. Allen, editor of the *Old Path Guide*, who wrote a scathing editorial in 1885 about the practice that came to be known as the "London Plan."

The issue of open membership became increasingly controversial when a handful of high-profile North American congregations adopted the practice, beginning in 1885 with the Cedar Avenue Church of Cleveland, Ohio. The *Christian Standard*, which took a decidedly conservative turn following the death of Isaac Errett in 1888, argued that missionary gifts from this congregation should not be accepted by the FCMS. James H. Garrison's *Christian-Evangelist*, following in Errett's irenic tradition, took the opposite position, but without condoning the practice of open membership. In 1903 Edward Scribner

Ames brought the practice to the Hyde Park Church of Christ in Chicago, and thee years later C. C. Morrison adopted the London Plan for the Monroe Street Church in Chicago. When two years later Morrison assumed ownership of the *Christian Century*, he used the journal to advocate the practice, along with federation and other ecumenical ventures.[85]

Conservatives, Liberals, and Moderates

A battle between liberal and conservative Disciples was clearly evident by 1909. The new understandings of Christian unity aggravated the tensions begun in the late nineteenth century with the advent of biblical criticism. The pages of the *Christian Standard* were filled with relentless condemnation of the developing liberalism of the universities and compromising approaches to unity. On the other hand, the *Christian Century* worked to rally liberal forces.[86] Each group's course seemed set in stone.

James H. Garrison, editor of the *Christian-Evangelist*, assumed leadership of moderate Disciples of Christ following the death of Isaac Errett.

There were, however, not two, but at least three distinct groups among Disciples. Strict restorationists, many of whom followed the *Christian Standard*, read the Bible with literal eyes, believing the perfect church to be modeled after forms they deduced from the New Testament. The Assembly Churches, though not involved in the battle between the *Christian Standard* and the *Christian Century*, were in this group, having increasingly identified their practices with New Testament models beginning in the 1890s. On the other end of the spectrum were those who relied upon Christ's example and human experience as authorities for Christian faith. These liberals argued that the goal of all Christianity was to make human life more successful. Christians should not fear the conclusions of science, but embrace them.

Most Disciples leaders stood between these views, representing a moderate form of restorationism. Like James H. Garrison, they were not legalistic in their reading of the Bible. They emphasized Christ, rather than a text, as the guiding spirit of the Stone-Campbell Movement and avoided "tests of fellowship." Yet they also stressed Disciples distinctives associated with a restored church and called all other Christians to recognize the wisdom of their approach. They believed in the value of science and reason, but also affirmed the need for the church to look to the Bible for patterns to guide its life and expression. These leaders sought to draw liberals and conservatives toward the center to avoid further division. Their efforts, though noteworthy, were not successful. In 1971 conservatives identified as Christian Churches/Churches of Christ asked to be listed in the *Yearbook of American and Canadian Churches* as a body separate from the Disciples of Christ.

Churches of Christ: Three Traditions

Disciples viewed Churches of Christ as uniformly conservative. In reality, at least three major traditions existed in this stream of the Movement: (1) the Tennessee Tradition, led by David Lipscomb and James A. Harding; (2) the Indiana Tradition, led by Daniel Sommer (1859-1940); and (3) the Texas Tradition, led by Austin McGary (1846-1928). These three struggled for dominance as Churches of Christ tried to define the boundaries of their distinct identity in the post-Civil War era. The labels do not mean that the traditions were restricted to their respective geographical regions or that everyone in those regions agreed with the dominant tradition in that area. Rather, they identify theological orientations that reflect the primary geographical origin of each.

The Tennessee Tradition. In 1891 David Lipscomb and James A. Harding co-founded the Nashville Bible School in Nashville, Tennessee. The founders had multiple reasons to begin the new school. It would serve as a local effort for the poor in contrast to the wealth of Vanderbilt

University; it would compete with a Baptist school begun in the city; and it would provide an alternative to existing Stone-Campbell institutions that had adopted the innovations.[87] Embodying the educational ideals of Alexander Campbell, Lipscomb and Harding saw Nashville Bible School equipping men and women for living in the Kingdom of God in whatever careers they chose. Thirty-two students from Kentucky, Tennessee, Alabama, Arkansas, Texas, and California enrolled the first year.

James A. Harding, after graduating from Bethany College in 1869, had become a full-time itinerant evangelist in the mid-1870s. He conducted over three hundred evangelistic meetings from Canada to Florida and from New York to New Mexico, as well as fifty debates.[88] In 1891 he moved to Nashville at Lipscomb's invitation to serve as superintendent of the Nashville Bible School. Harding also edited *The Way* (1899-1903) and co-edited *The Christian Leader & the Way* (1903-1912). Harding moved to Bowling Green, Kentucky, in 1901 to become founding President of Potter Bible College.

Lipscomb and Harding were the most significant Stone-Campbell editors and educators east of the Mississippi and south of the Ohio in the early twentieth century. Many regard Lipscomb as the "father" of Southern Churches of Christ and Harding as the "father" of twentieth century Bible schools (colleges) among the group. Their students would go on to found schools in Meaford, Ontario; Nova Scotia; Armenia (Persia); Valdosta, Georgia; Denton, Gunter, and Abilene, Texas; Bridgeport, Alabama; Odessa, Missouri; Tokyo, Japan; Cordell, Oklahoma; and Harper, Kansas. Their efforts created a high regard for education in Churches of Christ despite the doubts of some concerning the propriety of church-related schools.

Theologically, Lipscomb and Harding represented a fusion of the apocalyptic and positive law traditions of the Stone-Campbell Movement.[89] While Nashville Bible School embraced the positive law tradition, it was framed by an apocalyptic vision of the dynamic in-breaking of the reign of God. God acted to carry out the divine will rather than remaining passive in some deistic or semi-deistic fashion. God empowered holy living by the indwelling of the Spirit (Harding was much more emphatic on this than Lipscomb). They opposed all political involvement as compromise with the world, yet insisted that the church's mission was much broader than evangelism. The church—as the presence of Jesus in the world—preferred the poor and shared its wealth with the disadvantaged. The inspiration for discipleship was not law, but the reign of God in the person of Jesus as taught in the Sermon on the Mount. This apocalyptic orientation prevented their positive law emphases from degenerating into mere legalism.

The Indiana Tradition. The thought of Benjamin Franklin, founder and editor of the *American Christian Review* from 1856 until his death in 1878, provided the roots of the conservative stream north of the Ohio. Franklin moved his base of operations to Anderson, Indiana, from Cincinnati in 1864. Though northern and southern conservatives often cross-fertilized each other's thought, they operated not only in different geographical and cultural settings, but also with different theological orientations. While Lipscomb's focus was a strong counter-cultural view of the Kingdom and Christian life, Benjamin Franklin and other northern conservatives accentuated the positive law tradition. Without an apocalyptic orientation, such a focus often reduced divine grace and presence to law and obedience.

Daniel Sommer, a protégé of Franklin's, would become one of the prime examples of the Indiana Tradition. Sommer, who wrote for Franklin's *American Christian Review* in the 1870s, had become disenchanted with the direction of the churches and what he saw as the insidious effects of colleges after attending Bethany College from 1869-1872. Though John F. Rowe (1827-1897) became editor of the *American Christian Review* when Franklin died in 1878, Sommer purchased the paper in 1886 and merged it with his own *Octograph* to form the *Octographic Review* (renamed *Apostolic Review* in 1913). Sommer's paper, edited from Indianapolis, Indiana, had between seven and ten thousand subscribers during the years of his greatest influence.

Sommer shared the Tennessee Tradition's antipathy toward sophistication, worldliness, and the power of the industrialists. Both Lipscomb and Sommer railed against proud, wealthy members of urban churches who manifested a worldly spirit and desire for popularity. They shared disdain for hired pastors, choirs and musical instruments in worship, missionary societies, and expensive church buildings.[90]

Sommer's influence, however, was mainly north of the Ohio River, stretching through the Midwestern states. He claimed that his opposition to the church-related schools saved Churches of Christ in that region from the "college craze" common in the South.[91] Members of Churches of Christ did not establish colleges in Ohio, Indiana, and Illinois—the area of his greatest influence. The Colleges, he believed, centralized power, promoted elitism, and impoverished the church by constructing brick and mortar buildings rather than disciples.[92] Yet his chief opposition was the positive law rationale that they were unauthorized by Scripture.

The Texas Tradition. Despite the relatively close relationship between Texas conservatives and the *Gospel Advocate* in the 1850s-1870s, Texans did not receive the apocalyptic message well. Unlike Middle Tennessee, many Stone-Campbell leaders in Texas had fought in the Civil War. The other two ideological streams that shaped Churches of Christ—the positive law and socio-sectional—dominated Texas Churches of Christ. Austin McGary, founding editor of the *Firm Foundation* in 1884, epitomized the origin of the Texas tradition.

McGary, a Confederate veteran and twice sheriff of Madison County, Texas, had become part of Churches of Christ in 1881 at age thirty-five. When he attended the 1884 Texas State Meeting at Bryan he became disturbed that "the majority of brethren were drifting away from the ancient landmarks."[93] McGary, however, was not only concerned about the digressives in Texas; he also feared what he viewed as the more liberal influence of the *Gospel Advocate*. In particular, he opposed Lipscomb's position that the simple desire to obey God was a sufficient motive for baptism, even when candidates did not know that baptism was for the remission of sins.

McGary began publishing the *Firm Foundation* in September 1884 to oppose both the liberalism of the *Gospel Advocate* and the digression in Texas churches. At the time the *Advocate* had over seven thousand subscribers, many of them in Texas. McGary considered it a subversive influence. The *Firm Foundation* embraced the view that only those immersed with the specific understanding that baptism was for the remission of sins and necessary for salvation are genuinely baptized, taught that the Holy Spirit only dwelled representatively in the believer through the word of God, embraced a deistic understanding of providence, and fully identified the church with the Kingdom.

At the beginning of the twentieth century the Tennessee and Texas theological traditions dominated Southern Churches of Christ while Sommer's influence held sway over much of the Midwest. These streams overlapped in many ways, but they were often at odds. They held many beliefs and practices in common—weekly Lord's Supper, immersion of believers for the remission of sins, a biblical pattern for the church expressed by positive law, plurality of elders, and a cappella music in worship. In form they appeared as one. The logic behind their theological perspectives, however, was quite different.

Differences among Churches of Christ showed up in practical polity issues like selection and authority of elders as well as in theological understandings such as the nature of the human soul and its fate after death. The churches debated proper uses of the Sunday contribution, the relation of the Kingdom to the church, and involvement in social movements. Several key questions, however, were particularly significant as they reflected the theological orientation of the three traditions.

Rebaptism and Sectarianism

Both Lipscomb (Tennessee) and Sommer (Indiana) believed the Texas practice of requiring re-immersion of persons who had been immersed without understanding that baptism was for remission of sins was pure sectarianism. Sommer condemned the "rebaptists" as judges of people's fitness for baptism.[94] As early as 1891 he published a tract defending the proposition: "Single immersion performed in the name of the Godhead even by a sectarian and even in connection with certain sectarian errors is valid baptism when rendered for the purpose of obeying Christ." He published it because he believed the *Firm Foundation* was intent on causing a division on the issue and he refused to allow any discussion of the question in the *Octographic Review*.[95]

For the Texas Tradition, whether Baptists who seek to unite with a Church of Christ should be re-immersed was a "gospel" issue.[96] McGary, for example, suggested that the *Advocate* was imitating the digressive innovators by teaching that sinners could be saved and enter the Kingdom in ways not taught in Scripture.[97] This was the same spirit that presumed to force the societies and instruments on the church.[98] Members of the Texas Tradition saw the Tennessee practice of "giving the right hand of fellowship" to Baptists, accepting them as members of their churches—labeled "shaking in the Baptists"—as embracing a broad unscriptural vision of the Kingdom.[99]

Lipscomb believed that anyone who elevated re-mission of sin above all the other scriptural teachings about baptism was a sectarian and thereby responsible for creating a sinful faction.[100] The insistence that people immersed upon their faith in Jesus should be re-immersed because they did not understand it was for the remission of sins was, according to Harding, pure sectarian extremism that added to Christ's commands and resulted in division.[101]

The Texas charge that the practice of "shaking in the Baptists" acknowledged there are Christians outside of Churches of Christ was true. Harding was clear that

people in all Christian denominations "who have believed in Christ with their whole hearts, who in deep penitence of soul have confessed his holy name, who have been buried in baptism and raised to walk in newness of life, who are diligently studying his holy law and who are daily striving to do his will….we may expect to be saved." Harding's understanding of baptismal and sanctifying grace included the conviction that God is gracious with people's failings if not rooted in a rebellious spirit.[102] The editors of the *Firm Foundation* feared this attitude because it enlarged the Kingdom beyond the borders of their vision of the "Church of Christ."

There were frequent debates on this subject from 1884 into the 1910s. One of the last published debates on the topic was between Texan John W. Durst and Tennessean J. C. McQuiddy in 1914—simultaneously published by the Firm Foundation and Gospel Advocate publishing houses.[103] Some suggest that this debate marked a turning point in the discussion since afterward the Texas position began to gain ground.

Spirituality and the Holy Spirit

Other than rebaptism, Churches of Christ contested no topic more hotly than the nature and function of the Holy Spirit. Though this debate raged primarily between the Texas and Tennessee Traditions, Indiana had no patience with the Texas position.[104] The Texas Tradition rejected as sectarian and unscriptural any understanding of the indwelling of the Spirit other than through the word, by faith.[105] Those who advocated a personal enabling indwelling were "in the fog of sectarian mysticism."[106] The words of Scripture, they insisted, are sufficient to lead and guide us in every way, therefore God's Spirit does not need to be personally present to do so. Furthermore, the idea of a personal enabling indwelling of the Spirit would imply that the Spirit still works miracles, but the time of miracles ended with the apostles.[107]

At the root of this perspective was not only a kind of semi-Deism which rejected the idea of God's personal involvement in the world, but an understanding of knowledge that assumed human beings can be influenced only by words or ideas. The Spirit does not act on the heart because this would be metaphysical coercion rather than intelligent moral persuasion. If the Holy Spirit used means other than the revealed will of God in Scripture to persuade people, it would mean that the Bible was insufficient. Therefore, God does not act on the human heart "separate or apart from the word."[108]

Many in the Tennessee Tradition were horrified

by this kind of language, including James A. Harding, T. R. Burnett, and C. E. W. Dorris. Burnett called it the "word alone doctrine," where people mistakenly understood the Holy Spirit to be an idea or thought in the Bible.[109] Harding believed a denial of the indwelling, enabling, and transforming Spirit was tantamount to "semi-infidel[ity]," a "withering, deadly curse to those that believe it."[110] On the contrary, Bible study was not the only way one received help from God. Harding and others influenced by the Nashville Bible School believed that the personal presence of the Spirit in the Christian provided necessary supernatural power for living a holy life.[111]

A graduate of Bethany College in 1869, James A. Harding became a major evangelist and debater in Churches of Christ. He began a journal, *The Way*, in 1899, which reflected his view of the indwelling of the Holy Spirit in the life of the Christian.

Nevertheless, those in the Texas Tradition continued to distance themselves from these ideas. L. C. Chisholm spoke for many when he linked the baptism and Holy Spirit controversies. It was no wonder, he declared, that those who were asking questions about the influence of the Holy Spirit were the same ones who "have said that men need not know just when God forgives their sins."[112] To Chisholm, both originated from denominational

theology and demonstrated the impurity of the Tennessee Tradition.

Institutionalized Power

Daniel Sommer labeled the Texas Tradition's handling of rebaptism and the Holy Spirit, as well as the Tennessee Tradition's apocalypticism, as "hobbyism." But it was Tennessee's seemingly incessant promotion of the institutional innovations of the Sunday school, Sunday school literature, and colleges that especially alarmed him.[113] Because of what he believed to be agitation by Southern churches, Sommer began a campaign against both colleges and Sunday schools at the beginning of the twentieth century.[114]

Sommer objected to colleges at several levels. Recalling Alexander Campbell's founding of Bethany College in 1840, Sommer noted that Campbell "erred in connecting the church with the world in both *fact* and *form* when he established Bethany College as a religio-secular institution with the Lord's money." Campbell's action had implied that the church was not enough to defend and promote the truth, but that an institution was needed to fill in gaps such as the training of preachers.[115] The college was, in effect, just like the missionary societies.[116] Moreover, such worldly organizations tempted Christians "to make a show of greatness" and thereby manifest a "lack of gospel humility." Colleges like Bethany were human institutions designed to usurp the work of the church, squander the Lord's money, and promote worldly values.[117]

Many in the *Firm Foundation* orbit shared Sommer's misgivings about Tennessee "institutionism." J. D. Tant (1861-1941), for example, feared that "many good brethren in Texas are going Bible College crazy" and that "the work of the church to teach the Bible and make gospel preachers is fast being turned over to the Bible colleges, and the church is losing its identity along the line."[118]

The Female Voice: Privileged or Forbidden?

The "cult of true womanhood" deeply shaped the Tennessee Tradition.[119] This movement made domesticity and submissiveness the true marks of femininity while restricting the reins of public leadership and power to masculine hands. The editors of the Tennessee Tradition at the turn of the twentieth century consistently excluded women from any public role—including speaking and leadership in both society and church.[120] When some congregations permitted women to lead prayers or preach, James A. Harding contended they were flagrantly violating God's law of male leadership.[121] Yet even in Tennessee, voices like that of Selina Holman challenged this position.

The Indiana Tradition shared an understanding similar to Holman's in terms of church gatherings. Daniel Sommer regarded the position of his Southern brothers as extreme and believed that his own position was a kind of *via media* between the Tennessee Tradition and the Disciples. While rejecting female elders and evangelists, Sommer argued that it was a woman's privilege to pray audibly, read Scripture, and exhort believers gathered in the public assembly.[122] Indeed, in the Indiana Tradition the phrase "rights, privileges, and duties" was almost a mantra that sought to uphold the sanctity of the female voice in the assembly.[123]

Dominance of the Tennessee Tradition

In the first decade of the twentieth century, the Tennessee Tradition, through the *Gospel Advocate*, *Christian Leader & the Way*, and the growing number of colleges, was the most dominant influence among Churches of Christ. The Texas Tradition, however, was fast gaining traction. The Indiana Tradition, a minority Midwestern voice in the Stone-Campbell Movement (there were ten thousand members of Churches of Christ in Indiana in 1906, the largest number in any state north of the Ohio), had little influence on Southern churches in Texas and Tennessee. The sheer numbers and influence of Southern Churches of Christ ultimately overwhelmed the distinctiveness of the Indiana Tradition. At the same time, however, some in the South shared the non-institutional emphases of the Indiana Tradition, and this cleavage would reveal itself in the separation of the non-institutional Churches of Christ in the mid-twentieth century.

Seeking Unity within the Movement

By the first decade of the twentieth century North American followers of Stone and the Campbells were traveling on remarkably diverse paths. The differences were so great that one might ask if it is appropriate to speak any longer of a single Stone-Campbell Movement. Despite the differences, however, some North American leaders continued to call members of the Stone-Campbell churches to recognize their unity in Jesus Christ.

Among these figures was evangelist and educator T. B. Larimore (1843-1929). Though he came to be most closely associated with Churches of Christ, Larimore refused to line up with one side against another in the rancorous fights. In 1897 a former student challenged Larimore through the pages of the *Christian Standard*

to declare his positions on the divisive issues. Larimore pointed out in his response that the fact that no one knew his positions, despite the fact that he had preached constantly all over the country, was proof that he had simply left the issues alone. Larimore regarded them as matters over which sisters and brothers could disagree and still maintain fellowship. In a striking passage he exclaimed:

> When Brother [Enos] Campbell took my confession, on my twenty-first birthday, he questioned me relative to none of these "matters now retarding the progress of the cause of Christ." While thousands have stood before me, hand in mine, and made "the good confession," I have never questioned one of them about these "matters." Shall I now renounce and disfellowship all of these who do not understand these things exactly as I understand them? They may refuse to recognize or fellowship or affiliate with ME; but I will NEVER refuse to recognize or fellowship or affiliate with them—NEVER.[124]

Educator Frederick D. Kershner (1875-1953), thirty-two years Larimore's junior, also refused to disfellowship those who took positions different from his own. Within Disciples of Christ, Kershner maintained relationships with conservatives, liberals, and moderates alike. He published in both the *Christian Standard*, which after the death of Isaac Errett in 1888 was the voice of conservative Disciples, and the moderate *Christian-Evangelist*. Open to the possibilities of Disciples participation in the ecumenical movement, he served on the Council on Christian Union spearheaded by Peter Ainslie. He also developed a personal friendship with Indiana Church of Christ leader Daniel Sommer.[125]

The differences between and within Churches of Christ and Disciples of Christ would lead members of the Stone-Campbell Movement in North America in diverse directions. Yet the deep commitment to unity seen in figures like Larimore and Kershner would always be present.

6

Origins and Developments in the United Kingdom and British Dominions to the 1920s

Often understood as uniquely American, the Stone-Campbell Movement also had beginnings in Britain in the first half of the nineteenth century. The first church associated with the Movement in the U.K. was formed in December 1836, and British emigrants soon established congregations in Canada, New Zealand, and Australia. Though in the United States Barton Stone contributed significantly to the Movement's thought, leaders in the United Kingdom were influenced primarily by the writings of Alexander Campbell. This, along with other differences in origin and context, contributed to distinctive developments in the U.K. and British Empire.

The United Kingdom

The fact that North America became the most popular destination for British emigrants in the nineteenth century has tended to make trans-Atlantic influences seem natural. In fact, there was nothing natural or inevitable about the influence of Alexander Campbell's writings in the British Isles. At the beginning of the 1830s memories of the War of Independence and the War of 1812 were still fresh, and Britain viewed the United States with mixed feelings. Relations between the Church of England and the Episcopal Church were cool, and American Methodism by its adoption of episcopacy had moved decisively away from British Methodism. Camp meeting revivalism alarmed British church officials, prompting the newly formed Congregational and Baptist Unions to send delegations to the U.S. in the early 1830s partly to discover if disturbing reports about American religion had been exaggerated.[1] Still, from the start of his *Christian Baptist* in 1823, and especially with the publication of the Campbell-Maccalla debate on baptism in 1824, Campbell's publications found their way across the Atlantic, usually mailed by emigrants to relatives back home.[2]

After the restoration of episcopacy and the Book of Common Prayer to the Church of England in 1662, dissenters—Protestants who disagreed with the Anglican Church—usually organized independent Baptist, Congregationalist, or Presbyterian congregations. Striving to live out the principle that "the Bible, and the Bible only, is the religion of Protestants,"[3] some tried to model church life on a literal adherence to what they saw as the teachings of the New Testament. Some of these congregations eventually identified with the Stone-Campbell Movement after coming in contact with either Campbell's writings or James Wallis's *Christian Messenger and Reformer* after 1837.[4] In other cases, members of Churches of Christ[5] convinced Methodist lay preachers of their doctrine of immersion. The first British groups attracted to Campbell's ideas, however, were Baptist.

Some of these churches surfaced in response to a circular letter dated March 1818, titled "The Church professing obedience to the faith of Jesus Christ, assembling together in New York; to the Churches of Christ scattered over the earth." Reprinted in the November 1827 *Christian Baptist*, the letter described the congregation's public worship and discipline and invited other churches conformed "to the simplicity of the apostolic faith and practice" to correspond with them. In the same issue, Alexander Campbell began publishing responses to the invitation from churches in the United Kingdom.[6] All shared a similar pattern of Sunday worship, and several seem to have been related to the movement known as Scotch Baptists.[7] Campbell's writings appealed to these groups because of his emphasis on "a restoration of the ancient order of things."

William Jones, minister of a Scotch Baptist church in Windmill Street, London, referred to this correspondence in the first issue of his *Millennial Harbinger and Voluntary Church Advocate* in March 1835.[8] Jones eventually published many of Campbell's *Christian Baptist* articles in his *Millennial Harbinger*, which circulated mostly among Scotch Baptists. Jones soon realized, however, that several of Campbell's teachings conflicted with his own. Jones labeled Campbell's teaching of baptism for the remission of sins "baptismal regeneration" and warned his readers against it. The question of creeds was also sensitive for Jones. He seems to have deliberately omitted the fourth article in Campbell's "Restoration of the Ancient Order of Things" series, which insisted, "the word of the apostles shall be the only creed, formula, and directory of faith, worship, and Christian practice."[9] In the fifth of his "Letters to England," Campbell alluded to Jones's accusation that he had departed from the faith in denying total depravity and the necessity of special divine action in conversion, as well as his teaching of baptismal regeneration.[10] Nevertheless, many Scotch Baptists found Campbell's arguments persuasive. One was James Wallis, who became the most significant leader of British Churches of Christ in their first thirty years.

First Generation Leadership

Baptized in 1812 as a member of Andrew Fuller's Particular Baptist congregation in Kettering, James Wallis moved in 1814 to Leicester, then to Nottingham in 1816.[11] He became part of the Scotch Baptists in 1834, and it was among them that he encountered Jones's *Millennial Harbinger*. His exposure to Campbell's ideas also developed through correspondence with Joseph Harpham, a friend who had emigrated from Nottingham to Philadelphia around 1822 and discovered Campbell's writings four years later. Harpham, "tired of their system of worship and their confession of faith," had left the Particular Baptists and become part of a Campbell Reformer congregation in 1831.[12]

Campbell's articles along with his 1835 *Christianity Restored* (later titled *The Christian System*) convinced Wallis. At odds now with Scotch Baptist baptismal teachings, he and others led a series of secessions from Scotch Baptist churches to create the first Churches of Christ. No Scotch Baptist congregation, except much later Rose Street, in Kirkcaldy, Scotland, became a Church of Christ. Rather, individuals from various Baptist and other groups, including a number of Methodists, formed these first churches.

Jones ceased publication of his magazine after June 1836, and Wallis published the first issue of his *Christian Messenger and Reformer* in March 1837.[13] Between those two dates controversy had broken out in the Scotch Baptist church in Park Street, Nottingham, over whether baptism was for the remission of sins. Wallis and his friends took Campbell's position in affirming that it was, while the others stood with Jones in denying it. Wallis's group met separately to break bread on December 25, 1836, in an upper room of Jonathan Hine's warehouse in Mount Street, Nottingham, forming the first Church of Christ in Great Britain associated with the Stone-Campbell Movement.[14]

In 1840-41 G. C. Reid, who had been pastor of an independent evangelical congregation in Dundee, Scotland, toured Scotland, England, and Wales visiting most, if not all, of the Churches of Christ. He warned them against what he saw as Scotch Baptist reluctance to engage in evangelism and urged the formation of "a co-operative plan" to support evangelists.[15] Wallis picked up this idea in the *Christian Messenger* and helped organize the first "Co-operation Meeting" for August 18-22, 1842, in Edinburgh. The presence of former Methodists in British Churches of Christ may have predisposed the body to favor this development.

Fourteen churches were represented, with letters from eleven others. The meeting received statistics from forty-three churches with a total membership of 1,233 in England, Scotland, and Wales.[16] The meeting unanimously passed as its first resolution "that this meeting deem it binding upon them, as disciples of Jesus Christ, to cooperate for the maintenance of evangelists to proclaim the gospel" and appointed a committee of four to gather contributions.[17] Though an economic depression in the early 1840s contributed to the Co-operation's slow start, internal controversy also took a toll. Wallis noted as early as 1843 that some churches refused to give anything for evangelists for fear of "a hireling priesthood," while others felt that the evangelists already working among the churches did not stay long enough in one place.

In addition, some in British Churches of Christ had become wary of Campbell's influence. They were suspicious of his founding of Bethany College, despite his assurances that it was not established to train "clergy." In 1844-45, British churches discussed Campbell's debate with Presbyterian minister, N.L. Rice, which some feared implied an endorsement of open communion. Though Campbell had generally opposed the practice, Stone's view that Christians neither invite nor debar because Jesus is host at the table had prevailed in the American Churches. Campbell's response to the letter from a woman in Lunenburg County, Virginia, published in the September 1837 *Millennial Harbinger* as "Any Christians among Protestant Parties," had earlier raised some of the same issues.

Another area of controversy in the churches surrounded premillennial expectations for the second coming of Christ. The depression heightened the desire for deliverance from threatening economic circumstances, drawing many to teachings like those of American Baptist preacher William Miller (1782-1849), who calculated dates for the Second Coming in 1843-44. Even more influential among Churches of Christ were the premillennial arguments of British physician John Thomas (1805-1871), editor of the *Apostolic Advocate* and later founder of the Christadelphians.

A draper by profession, James Wallis's travels to his suppliers enabled him to spread Campbell's ideas in the cloth-making areas of Lancashire and Yorkshire.

A division in the Edinburgh church in 1844, probably over millennial issues, led many in Scotland to press for another Co-operation Meeting as a means of avoiding further division. Campbell's presence as chair of that second Co-operation Meeting in 1847 served to reconcile him to the British leadership. His address, which focused on the importance of evangelism rather than matters of discipline and fellowship, led to renewed

efforts to support evangelists. By this time there were eighty churches with a membership of 2,300.

By 1854 the controversies had subsided, the economy was beginning to improve, and new leaders appeared— J.B. Rotherham in Wales, David King in the southern counties of England, and T.H. Milner in Scotland. Rotherham was originally a Methodist who became a Baptist minister in 1853, then converted to Churches of Christ a year later. King, born in London, had also been a Methodist but was baptized in the Church of Christ at Camden Town in 1842. Milner was originally a Haldane Baptist in Edinburgh who became part of Churches of Christ in 1857. Both King and Milner founded journals—King the *Bible Advocate* in 1847 and Milner the *Christian Advocate* in 1857.

The Co-operation's Evangelist Committee targeted major cities, establishing new churches in Manchester in 1855 and Birmingham in 1858. At the Annual Meeting in Leicester in 1861, Timothy Coop of Wigan, originally a Methodist, assumed principal leadership of the organization. The Meeting also passed three resolutions, which in effect became the constitution of the Co-operation for the rest of its life. The first stated in part:

That this Coöperation shall embrace such of the churches contending for the primitive faith and order, as shall willingly be placed upon the list of churches printed in its Annual Report. That the churches thus coöperating disavow any intention or desire to recognize themselves as a denomination, or to limit their fellowship to the churches thus co-operating; but on the contrary they avow it both a duty and a pleasure to visit, receive, and co-operate with Christian churches, without reference to their taking part in the meetings and efforts of this Co-operation. Also that this Co-operation has for its object evangelization only, and disclaims all power to settle matters of discipline, or differences between brethren or churches.[18]

At the end of 1861, Wallis handed over the editorship of the *British Millennial Harbinger* to King, who had assisted him for some time. King wrote in the preface to his first volume that the *Harbinger* "no longer exists mainly for the purpose of reproducing the thoughts of brethren who labour in distant lands." Whether he was referring to Campbell or not, he reduced both the number of articles reprinted from U.S. journals and coverage of events in the U.S. except as they related to emigrants from Britain.

Second Generation Leadership

By the mid-1860s the first generation of leaders was dying. When T.H. Milner died in 1866 at the age of forty-one, King was left with no rival as leading editor in the British churches.[19] He retained that position until 1879 when G. Y. Tickle became editor of *The Christian Advocate*. When James Wallis died in 1867 at the age of 73, King wrote that Wallis had "to a larger extent than any other, living or dead…in this country…pleaded a return in all things to the good laws and right statutes of the Apostolic Church." He noted that while Wallis never doubted the presence of Christians in the sects, he rejected the rationale that the existence of Christians in the sects could make the sects Christian, insisting that a true church of Christ was more than merely "a company of Christians."[20] King's statement reflected a hardening of attitudes toward other Christians that came to characterize the movement for the next forty years.

While an increasing number of American churches were employing college-trained evangelists as resident pastors, British Churches of Christ continued to rely on a model of mutual edification. Some British members, however, began to argue that their churches could benefit from resident evangelists. This issue became linked to the earlier issue of open communion in the person of Henry Samuel Earl (1831-1919), a British citizen whose family had immigrated to America where he studied at Bethany College under Alexander Campbell. At a worship service at Camden Town with his unimmersed mother after returning to England in 1861, he became offended when she was not given communion. That incident and his connection with the American churches led the Annual Meeting that year to question him about his position on communion when he offered his services as an evangelist. Though he replied that he was not willing to exclude anyone, he convinced the Meeting that he favored closed communion and received support for nearly three years. During this period he reported three hundred thirty-one conversions before moving to Australia in May 1864.[21]

In 1865, the Annual Meeting asked David King to explore the possibility of securing assistance from the U.S. after Benjamin Franklin recommended "two reliable evangelists" to work in Britain.[22] The following year, however, when the chair raised the question of evangelistic help from America, the response reflected British suspicion of American doctrinal positions. The consensus was that they would repudiate any evangelist, American or English, who advocated "communing at the table of the Lord with unbaptized persons." The resolution expressed regret that some American evangelists communed with "unbaptized persons, who without formal invitation, and as it is alleged, on their own responsibility partake."[23] Timothy Coop, treasurer of the Evangelist Committee, and several other members, however, dissented against the statement.[24]

The 1872 Annual Meeting at Leicester declined another offer of an evangelist to be secured by Franklin and John F. Rowe. The controversy intensified in 1875 when Henry Earl asked the U. S. Stone-Campbell Movement's Foreign Christian Missionary Society (FCMS) to support him as a missionary to England. After unsuccessfully trying to persuade him to go instead to a "non-Christian land," the FCMS finally agreed. Arriving in Southampton, Earl rented the Philharmonic Hall and was soon preaching to audiences of between one and two thousand. By September 1876 he had formed a church of thirty-three members, thirty of whom he had baptized.[25] The membership of the Southampton church passed one hundred in 1877, and Earl wrote to America that a great harvest could be reaped in England.

United Kingdom

The Annual Meeting responded by appointing William Linn, G.Y. Tickle, and David King "affectionately to expostulate" with the Americans about their deviations from apostolic practice. This included communion with the unimmersed, paid evangelists serving as resident pastors, colleges intended to supply such evangelists, and organizations independent of the churches that employed and supported such evangelists.[26]

Despite the Annual Meeting's action, the FCMS sent Marion D. Todd to Chester in January 1878. The church in Chester had dwindled in size and lacked leadership when Todd arrived and began an evangelistic campaign.[27] Meanwhile, Timothy Coop, probably the wealthiest member of the British Churches of Christ, had become disillusioned with the General Evangelist Committee. In spring 1878 he visited FCMS headquarters in Cincinnati and offered to give £1,000 for every £2,000 it would contribute towards supporting American evangelists in England. The FCMS Board agreed to send three evangelists, and W.T. Moore, pastor of Central Christian Church in Cincinnati, who was present, immediately volunteered.[28]

Coop invited Moore to preach in Southport, where Coop had settled in 1863. When the Southport church later divided, Moore began a congregation in Liverpool. In July 1881, James H. Garrison replaced Moore in Liverpool when he moved to the West London Tabernacle, an independent evangelical mission previously led by the evangelist Henry Varley.[29] On August 1, members of the churches at Chester, Liverpool, and Southport, whose ministers were supported by the FCMS, held a meeting at Helsby in Cheshire, and after an address by Henry Varley, agreed to form the Christian Association.[30] Over the next thirty-five years membership in the Association reached a maximum of seventeen churches with about half in Lancashire and Cheshire, three in Liverpool, and one in Birkenhead. The Association had as many as three churches in London, as well as congregations in Gloucester, Cheltenham, Southampton, and Woolston.

In 1894 the Christian Association set up an Evangelist Committee to which the FCMS made an annual grant rather than paying missionaries directly. In 1917 virtually all the Association churches had ministers, while the two hundred churches of the Co-operation had only fifteen resident evangelists. The majority of Christian Association ministers were from the U.S. and only stayed a few years. Among those with longer ministries were W.T. Moore, Henry Earl, and Leslie W. Morgan—the latter also editing the *Christian Monthly* and

serving as General Secretary of the Association.[31] Some of the English ministers served a single congregation for decades, a situation completely unknown in the older Churches of Christ.

Although the total number of congregations in the Christian Association was small, their location was strategic. FCMS missionaries traveling to fields in Africa, India, and China almost always visited the FCMS churches in England en route. As a result, the Association churches always had a high awareness of overseas missions. Nearly every church had a chapter of the Christian Woman's Board of Missions, and support for CWBM efforts continued in those congregations even

David King, prominent editor in British Churches of Christ in the late 1800s, was appointed by the General Evangelist Committee in 1855 to plant a church in Manchester and in 1858 in Birmingham.

after the Christian Association ceased to exist.[32]

Association churches published a number of journals during their history. W.T. Moore established *The Evangelist* soon after arriving in England. In 1881 Moore and Henry Varley founded the *Christian Commonwealth* as a general journal rather than exclusively for Churches of Christ.[33] *The Disciple* and *The Missionary Gleaner* both had a strong focus on missionary fundraising. With the motto "That They May All Be One," *The Christian Quarterly and Missionary Gleaner* appeared in 1903, but four years later became the *Christian Monthly*, which continued until

March 1921.

American evangelists who spent time in Christian Association churches in England included some of the most distinguished of their day, including Moore and Garrison. The English evangelists, though less well known, were also significant. T.S. Buckingham served for many years as pastor of the Southampton church and was responsible for beginning the work at Woolston. Originally a preacher for the Co-operation Churches at Mollington and Cam-yr-Alyn, in 1878 he became pastor of the church in Chester that would later join the Christian Association.[34] William Durban (1841-1912), for many years editor of the *Christian Monthly*, conducted Garfield Bible College—a correspondence school similar to one operated by Lancelot Oliver for the Co-operation. He also served as editor with W. T. Moore of the *Christian Commonwealth* for more than twenty years.[35] While working as a missionary to Berhampore, India, for the General Baptist Missionary Society, Eli Brearley had met M.D. Adams of the FCMS mission at Bilaspur and was attracted to Stone-Campbell principles. On Brearley's return to England, W. T. Moore influenced him to become part of the Christian Association where he served two churches for a total of twenty-three years.[36]

One of the main differences between the churches of the Christian Association and those of the Co-operation was the greater emphasis the Association placed on evangelism and evangelistic campaigns. These efforts focused on winning non-Christians rather than convincing other Christians of right church order. One striking example of this difference was that not all Christian Association churches had communion on Sunday mornings.[37] Morning services were often seen as evangelistic, so the Lord's Supper was reserved for Sunday evening. With their emphasis on evangelism, the Christian Association churches had much in common with the wider evangelical world. They found it more natural to work with other denominations than did the older Churches of Christ.

By the first decade of the twentieth century, growth of the Christian Association had slowed in comparison with the Co-operation churches. One reason was a steady drain of potential leaders to the United States as young men who went there to train often never returned. Establishing a college in Britain became a significant part of union discussions with the Co-operation in 1917.[38]

The formation of the Christian Association separately from the churches of the Co-operation in 1881 did not end the controversy over evangelists. Though the Annual Meeting of 1890 agreed almost unanimously to appeal to the churches to raise the yearly income of the Evangelist Committee by £5,000, many in the older churches opposed the evangelists' innovative methods. These included instrumental music in worship, receiving offerings from non-members, and inclusion of non-members in the choir. The result was a sequence of Conference Papers at the Annual Meeting critical of such practices. David King wrote several of these papers, exclaiming in his 1892 Jubilee Conference paper that "to *Hold the Fort* is a first essential; preserving, intact, every element of the Faith and Worship of the Church of Christ."[39] King's views did not go unchallenged, however, even in the churches of the Co-operation. A younger, more progressive generation, epitomized by Halstaff Coles and Sydney Black, pressed for a "Forward Movement." Coles insisted, "Caution has its dangers as well as enterprise and courage."[40]

The 1890 Annual Meeting of the Co-operation established an official journal to replace both King's *Ecclesiastical Observer* and the Scottish *Christian Advocate*. Called the *Bible Advocate*, the body appointed King editor-in-chief and put Coles in charge of the Sunday School Notes. Tensions soon escalated between the two. In October King criticized a pamphlet in which Coles had suggested that the churches were spending too much time on proselytizing and not enough on conversion. Coles responded with a letter to the editor lamenting King's "spiritual insularity." By December Coles was no longer associated with the *Bible Advocate*, and the next month he began as editor of a new journal, *The Young Christian*, published by John Crockatt.[41]

King's death in 1894 was as much the end of an era as that of James Wallis a generation earlier. Although those closest to King, especially those he trained, recalled "his patience, thoughtful kindness, and encouragement," those who only knew him by his writings saw a different person—lucid, logical, but focusing more on the errors of others than their virtues.[42] The future now lay with the Forward Movement under the leadership of evangelists like Sydney Black (1860-1903).

The Forward Movement

Women from Co-operation churches held their first "Sisters' Conference" during the 1880 Annual Meeting at Huddersfield. Under the leadership of Louise King, Mary Tickle, and Sarah Black (James Wallis's daughter), these meetings provided an opportunity for women to report on the work they were doing in their congregations. In 1881, Louise King noted the increased numbers of women in occupations previously denied them and asked whether women should not be equally active in the church, listing examples of such work from several congregations.[43] In his 1889 Conference Paper on "The Position and Work of Sisters in Evangelization," Sydney Black insisted that Christian women not be confined to traditional roles, dismissing restrictive interpretations of texts about women being in subjection and keeping silent. Black declared that the Churches were "losing incalculable blessing and power by keeping our beloved sisters in such an unscriptural and senseless position." When the paper appeared in the *Year Book*, a footnote explained that Black's views did not represent the thought of the churches as a whole.[44] The continued resistance to the expansion of women's work in the British Churches of Christ is reflected in the fact that the Sisters' Committee did not achieve equal status with other committees until 1937.

Several British Churches had contributed to the support of Dr. James Turner Barclay, the American Christian Missionary Society's first missionary, sent to Jerusalem in 1851. In the 1860s David King collected money to support the ACMS mission in Jamaica. However, the father of overseas missions in the British Churches of Christ was John Crook. Crook's parents had been Baptists, his father a minister. But after her husband's death, Crook's mother had become a member of the Rodney Street Church of Christ in Wigan. When Crook returned to Britain from a trip to America, he also joined the congregation. He became a member of the General Evangelist Committee in 1872, and served as its secretary from 1873 to 1900.

In 1886, though Crook had published four articles in the *Christian Advocate* on the importance of foreign missions, the Annual Meeting rejected beginning any work for lack of funds. Though the 1887 Conference paper by Bartley Ellis on "Aggressive Christianity" raised the issue again, not until Crook's Conference Paper on foreign missions at the 1891 Annual Meeting in Wigan did things begin to change. In that presentation he strongly affirmed that it was time for the churches to participate in the evangelization of the world. Milner Black, a brother of Sydney Black, was present as a delegate from Churches of Christ in Victoria, Australia, and urged British support for a new work in India. Subsequent discussion led to a resolution that the Conference begin foreign mission work despite David King's opposition. George Collin, in a move to delay action, proposed forming a committee to investigate the subject.

When the committee reported on their investigations to the Annual Meeting in 1892, they proposed that the churches begin work in Central India or Burma. Ninety-three of the one hundred ten churches approved, and the Conference appointed a Foreign Missionary Committee made up of a representative cross-section of the churches, including George Collin, David King, and John Crook, to decide on the location. At its meeting on October 12, 1892, the Committee decided to begin work in Burma, and on October 31 Crook and the first three missionaries sailed from Liverpool to Rangoon.[45]

Among the consequences of the Forward Movement was a greater willingness by members of British Churches of Christ to engage in politics. In the early twentieth century some began to discuss the relation of the Churches to socialism.[46] Perhaps the most divisive political issue, however, was the question of pacifism and conscientious objection to conscription during the World War I. The question of pacifism first surfaced during the South African War of 1899-1902. In an 1899 "News and Views" column in the *Bible Advocate*, Henry Tickle criticized government policy in the Transvaal in southern Africa as preparing for war rather than pursuing diplomacy. Protests from readers and editor Lancelot Oliver's desire to avoid conflict led Tickle to resign from the paper in January 1900. That development, however, prompted several letters supporting Tickle's views.

The 1900 Annual Meeting passed a resolution condemning the military spirit "now so prevalent in British society generally," including "many sections of the churches." They invited Tickle to prepare a Conference Paper for 1901 on "the attitude of the Churches of Christ toward service in the Army or Navy, compulsory or voluntary."[47] Tickle's paper reviewed biblical evidence and views of members of the movement from Alexander Campbell onwards, concluding that Christianity did not sanction war in general, and that its whole genius was antagonistic to the spirit of war. Though he conceded that under certain circumstances war became "a dread inevitability," it was still "the privilege and duty of the individual to decline all such [military] service, whether voluntary or compulsory, even if such a course should involve penalties in person and property."[48]

Another political question arose with the passage of the Education Act of 1902, which provided support for Anglican and Catholic schools out of local education taxes. Many non-Anglicans refused to pay the "sectarian" part of the tax. Backed by Annual Meeting resolutions in 1903-5, many members of British Churches of Christ became "passive resisters," refusing to pay the tax as late as 1914. Although the issue did not divide Churches of Christ, the resistance set a precedent that pacifists would soon employ.

The British declaration of war in 1914 took the British public by surprise. The *Bible Advocate* of August 7 did not mention it, apparently because it had gone to press before it happened. The next week Lancelot Oliver's front page editorial focused on the war, ending with the hope that the coming catastrophe would "convince us of the delusion that peace is preserved by being prepared for war, and a more rational and Christian arrangement be introduced."[49] On September 4, Bartley Ellis and John M'Cartney argued that the Christian profession was inconsistent with taking up arms; and the following week Oliver, though personally convinced that no one should take part in war, pleaded for mutual respect between those who enlisted and those who refused. He urged readers to contribute to the Prince of Wales' National Relief Fund to help all affected by the war.[50]

In October 1914 William Mottershaw wrote a letter asking for a list of the names of volunteers so they could connect with one another in the camps. J.G. Rotherham sent the names of eight young enlistees from a church in London, but T.E. Entwistle quickly responded that the names should not be published for fear of appearing to sanction militarism. He suggested the names be sent to one individual who would be responsible for keeping them in touch with one another.[51]

Differences over the issue of Christians in military service became sharper in 1915. Articles in the *Bible Advocate* expressing views for and against continued, with even more explosive statements appearing in the Letters to the Editor. In April William Robinson reported his experience of entering a church in uniform: "One of the more prominent members came to me and said, 'I am sorry to see you. You are a traitor to the Prince of Peace.'"

With rising casualties and a decline in recruits, the government launched a final effort at voluntary recruitment in October, setting up local tribunals to assist. When conscription began in 1916, these tribunals became the bodies that heard the appeals of conscientious objectors—a task for which they had not been prepared.[52] Mounting military losses in 1916 and 1917 made the public increasingly unwilling to tolerate conscientious objectors. "Absolutists," who refused even noncombatant work to assist the war effort, received no sympathy.

At first, some who opposed military service hoped that government provisions for exemption might work. However, a report of decisions by eleven tribunals published by Robert Price in January 1916 revealed that no one had been granted exemption, and only seven had

been given conditional exemption (all miners). Some had accepted non-combatant service, but the majority had rejected it and appealed. A week later, after many of the appeals had been rejected, Price warned that those who regarded non-combatant service as aiding and abetting a crime and refused it were liable to be rounded up as deserters.[53]

On April 22 representatives from Wigan, Ashton-under-Lyne, Blackburn, Manchester, and Swindon held a conference at Platt Bridge church, Wigan. The group formed a Central Working Committee to support those who might be arrested for refusing to serve and urged members in other areas to form similar committees. They also organized a national conference in Wigan that agreed to establish a relief fund for conscientious objectors.[54]

The 1916 Annual Meeting tried very hard to respect the range of views in the churches. Julian Elwes, who was in charge of communicating with members serving in the armed forces, organized a service for those suffering because of the war on the Monday night before the Meeting.[55] H. E. Tickle spoke and noted that, while the service was primarily to remember those who had died and to show sympathy to their families, they remembered all who were suffering, including those in prison for conscience's sake.[56] The Annual Meeting passed a resolution of sympathy with those who faced death in battle, the wounded and prisoners of war, and all who had lost loved ones. It also remembered those who were suffering for conscience's sake, and called on the government "to release them for work of national importance not under the control of the military authorities." An anti-war amendment failed to gain support.[57]

Another issue raised by the controversy over the war was the question of who could claim to speak for Churches of Christ. Determined pacifists did not want to be regarded merely as individuals with a conscience but as people maintaining loyalty to the principles of their tradition. Success before a tribunal depended on being able to demonstrate that pacifism was a principle of the religious body to which they belonged. Churches of Christ, however, had no such "official position" to which pacifists could appeal.

Moving stories of individuals on both sides began to appear. In June Robert Price described the treatment of conscientious objector Arthur Travis at Richmond Castle, who prison authorities severely abused and placed in detention for fourteen days. In September, Price reported on Clifford Cartwright, also at Richmond

Castle, who was shipped off to France, court-martialed, and sentenced to death, though the death sentence was later commuted to ten years of penal servitude.[58] The number of combat deaths reported by the churches rose almost every week. In November William Robinson wrote a tribute to his friend William Wilson, a well-known preacher killed in action at age 25, in which he quoted John Oxenham as saying that "the noblest death a man may die" was "fighting for God and Right and Liberty." In protest, T. E. Entwistle the next week labeled Robinson's description a "false sentiment," which in turn elicited letters of protest.[59]

Controversy continued through 1917 and 1918. Lancelot Oliver's health failed and he resigned as editor of the *Bible Advocate* at the Annual Meeting in 1917, succeeded by R.K. Francis. Though concern about the treatment of conscientious objectors increased, anxiety about the deteriorating military situation heightened tensions. Entwistle appealed to members to write the Government protesting its breaking of promises to respect conscientious objectors, particularly those who refused alternative service.[60] One example was Arthur Wilson, a member of the church at Hamilton Street, Blackburn, and his three brothers. Both the military representative and the chair of his hearing acknowledged Arthur's convictions, but the Central Tribunal refused his appeal. After four courts martial, Wilson was forced to do hard labor for over two years in various prisons until his health broke. He died of influenza in Strangeways prison in December 1918.[61]

Some have suggested that pacifism was a cause for the later division among the British churches, a symbol of developing separation between working-class sectarians and a more educated middle class.[62] Conscientious objection, however, was not a function of working class social status. Ultimately the divisions were theological, involving different understandings of the movement's purpose, which ranged from strict adherence to a perceived apostolic pattern to a broad recognition of the unity of Christians. Though pacifism may have been a presenting issue, the reason for the division was related to understandings of Scripture.

Paralleling changes in the Stone-Campbell Movement in the United States, the range of understandings of Scripture had broadened in British Churches of Christ beginning in the 1890s. From the beginning, the *Young Christian* favored a historical-critical approach to interpreting Scripture. In its fourth issue an editorial noted that many Methodist, Anglican, and Free Church authors no longer held the theory of verbal inspiration

and asserted that the Bible itself was "the greatest foe to this theory." Two months later Bartley Ellis responded, "I cannot conceive how we can hold the Scriptures to be inspired, and yet reject verbal inspiration." He asserted it was impossible to hold book inspiration without verbal inspiration and that the next step would be to deny divine revelation altogether. Ellis also used the anti-intellectual argument that a certain class of "*learned men*" had harmed the cause of Christ, claiming such learning led to the "yoke of the apostasy," i.e., Roman Catholicism. In July the *Young Christian* countered that the abandonment of the doctrine of verbal inspiration actually increased appreciation of the Bible.[63]

In May 1892 the magazine began a series of seven articles written by Joseph Smith titled "The Higher Criticism." His sources included critical works like S.R. Driver's *Introduction to the Literature of the Old Testament*, Robertson Smith's *The Old Testament in the Jewish Church*, and Herbert Ryle's *History of the Old Testament Canon*. He concluded that the New Testament lent no support to the traditional theory that Moses wrote the Pentateuch or was responsible for its present form. "Loyalty to our Lord does not bind us to an untenable theory which gives an inadequate explanation of the facts, and which grew out of the teaching of post-reformation dogmatic theologians." Christ's use of the Old Testament simply reflected its use in that era and required no theory about the limitation of Christ's knowledge.[64]

By comparison, Lancelot Oliver's address on "Biblical Criticism" at the Wednesday evening meeting of the 1892 Annual Conference in Edinburgh and published in David King's journal *The Old Paths* seems tame. Oliver demonstrated familiarity with the principal books on the subject, but suggested that it was too early to assume everything the critics said was right.[65] The *Young Christian* labeled Oliver's paper "a very cautious performance," criticizing what it judged to be his readiness to accept the results of criticism only when they confirmed traditional views. It also lamented the Annual Meeting's refusal to commission a Conference Paper on the subject.[66]

Nevertheless, in 1893, the *Young Christian* published a series of articles by R.P. Anderson titled "The Other Side," intended as a response to Joseph Smith's articles the year before. Anderson offered a traditional interpretation of historical critical findings, including a sophisticated defense of Mosaic authorship of the Pentateuch. According to Anderson, who had spent several years in Russia, before he left Britain it had been easy to convince people that Churches of Christ had the New Testament order because they accepted the

Scriptures as binding. After his return, however, most people no longer regarded them as such, implying this was due to the influence of higher critical ideas.[67]

Though the controversy had died down after 1894, Joseph Smith again raised the question in his 1910 Conference Paper on how to stop the "Alienation of the Masses from the Church." He acknowledged changing understandings of inspiration, even among ordinary people, and asserted that the old approach would convince no one. He was convinced, however, that the gospel, if "proclaimed with religious fervour, intellectual grasp and honesty, moral power and spiritual insight,…disassociated from primeval views of the cosmos, patriarchal ideas of the construction of society, and unproved dogmatic conceptions of the record of Revelation, will still find its way to the heart of man."[68]

Next year the Meeting finally agreed to commission a paper on the subject, asking Charles Greig to speak on "A Review of the Work of the Higher Criticism and Its Bearing on New Testament Christianity." Greig was a well-respected member of the Sunday School and Publishing Committees who had taught himself New Testament Greek. His paper was a judicious assessment of the current state of the field. Greig concentrated on critics whose theological orthodoxy was indisputable. He showed an easy familiarity with the latest discoveries in biblical archaeology and their implications for understanding the biblical text. He expressed joy that biblical criticism left intact the traditional plea of Churches of Christ for New Testament Christianity.[69] Despite Greig's positive evaluation, T.E. Entwistle reported that the discussion of the paper revealed "little disposition to accept the leading of the higher critics."[70] Articles and letters to the editor for and against biblical criticism continued in the *Bible Advocate* and other papers through the rest of the year.[71]

Reunion

The growing acceptance of higher criticism among leaders of the Co-operation, limited as it was, may have helped open the door for a renewed relationship with the Christian Association. Though the two organizations had existed separately since 1881, they had continued to view each other as members of the same movement. In 1901 the Annual Conference of the Christian Association meeting in London passed a resolution urging consideration of "ways and means to produce a closer co-operation among those in this country pleading for a restoration of New Testament Christianity."[72] In response, the General Evangelist Committee of the

Co-operation appointed seven people to confer with representatives of the Christian Association to see what was possible "without compromise of N.T. truth."[73] The two groups met at Southport on March 16-17, 1902, to discuss open communion. Though the representatives engaged in extensive correspondence over the next three years, the conversation ended by mutual consent without an agreement.[74] The Co-operation's 1910 Annual Meeting appointed another seven leaders to renew talks with the Christian Association, but they were unable to make any progress.[75]

Six years later, after the two groups had been in separate conversations concerning a proposed World Conference on Faith and Order, George W. Buckner, President of the Christian Association Conference at Chester, made a strong appeal for closer fellowship with the Co-operation Churches.[76] This time the response was notably different. The two groups organized a meeting in Leicester for March 2, 1917. The May 4 *Bible Advocate* reported that for the first time they had proposed a complete union. Representatives drafted six principles as a basis for the union, the first four based on agreements made in 1902. These included a confession of "the Christhood and Divinity of Jesus" as the basis of human relationship to God; the "great commission" of the risen Christ as the basis for human pardon and relationship to the Church; entry to the Church "by faith in Christ, repentance from sin, and, upon confession of faith, immersion in water, in the name of the Lord Jesus Christ"; and the Lord's Supper as "an ordinance inside the Church" with "Scriptural qualification to participate" by compliance with the conditions of entry to the Church.

Two additional principles, written by Christian Association representatives, were designed to eliminate differences in practice regarding communion and affirm respect for mutual ministry. It was their duty, they said, "to induce any unimmersed believers who present themselves at the Lord's Table to obey Christ in believer's immersion" as soon as possible; and that it was also their duty to "develop the abilities of all the members of the Church capable of taking part in the Lord's work, and to afford them suitable opportunities."[77] The Christian Association representatives assured their Conference that the principles were not to be regarded as a creedal standard or general statement of Christian truth, but as a way of resolving differences. Other details concerned provisions for handling legacies to the Christian Association, the merging of the two Chapel Building Funds, and the addition of three members to represent the Christian Association on the General

Evangelist Committee for six years, during which time the FCMS guaranteed to continue support for the salaries of Association preachers.

A Special Conference of the Christian Association at Cheltenham July 16-17, 1917, accepted the report unanimously. On August 7, the Annual Meeting of the Co-operation Churches also adopted it by a vote of 115 to 12. After the resolution to unite passed, the Meeting summoned the Christian Association representatives from their hotel, and they addressed the assembly in a scene the *Bible Advocate* described as historic.[78] All but one (Southampton) of the fifteen churches then in the Christian Association joined the united body.

The union succeeded in 1917 after two earlier failed attempts because of the death of some opponents in the Co-operation, and the willingness of Christian Association representatives to commit to persuading the unimmersed who took communion to be immersed. Many leaders on both sides were committed to participation in larger ecumenical efforts, and felt that such efforts had to begin within Churches of Christ.[79]

Emigration

In contrast to the United States, where the Stone-Campbell Movement advanced with the settlement of an agricultural frontier, British Churches of Christ were located almost exclusively in urban or industrial areas. Typically members of the Churches were not farmers, but shopkeepers, craftspeople, or trades people. Churches established in the major towns of the Midlands, the North of England, and Scotland by the 1860s would form the heart of the Movement in Britain for the next century.[80]

Britain, however, was a very different country than it had been when the first Church of Christ was begun there thirty years earlier. The political system had become more representative, the economy had grown significantly, and population had continued to grow rapidly, particularly in the north. By 1851 half the population was under the age of twenty, and unemployment had risen to new highs. Emigration was one solution to the lack of work, and various plans for sponsored emigration to North America, Australia, and New Zealand were developed in this period. A significant number of emigrants were from Nonconformist (non-Anglican) traditions. Most from England and Wales were Baptists, Independents, and Quakers, with a growing number of Methodists. Most from Scotland were Seceder Presbyterians, but some were Scotch Baptists.

The 1849 *British Millennial Harbinger* published three articles from a correspondent identified as D.L. who suggested that Churches of Christ form an emigration company. The Potters' Emigration Society which proposed making attractively priced farmland available in Wisconsin served as his model. Such a program, he believed, would aid the poor—the majority of church members—and extend the reach of the churches.[81] Citing the success of the Free Church of Scotland's effort in Otago, New Zealand, in support of his idea, he suggested Upper Canada and the Western U.S. as possible destinations. After publishing D.L.'s third article and a letter supporting the project, Wallis wrote that he believed the proposal was unworkable. Nevertheless, he agreed that since the effort would help the poor, he would assist D.L. by forwarding names and contributions from supporters.[82]

Though D.L.'s plan for a Churches of Christ emigration company never materialized, many members did immigrate to the United States, strengthening the Stone-Campbell Movement there. British emigrants also started churches in New Zealand and Australia, and helped sustain growth in Canada. The *British Millennial Harbinger* first published statistics of churches in the colonies in 1865, listing eight in South Australia, two in New South Wales, three in New Zealand, and one in Jamaica.[83] Though the list was by no means complete, it reflected the role emigration was already beginning to play in the expansion of the British Movement.

Assisted emigration plans always presumed that the emigrant would be involved in agriculture. When members of Churches of Christ emigrated, most of whom were shopkeepers, craftspeople, or tradespeople, they immediately found themselves in a world in which their skills and experience could help them do very well economically. In contrast to Churches of Christ in Britain, many emigrants became important figures in colonial politics, which had an impact on the development of the Movement in the colonies.

Many of the same issues that concerned the British Churches of Christ in the decades between the 1830s and 1920s affected the development of the churches planted by British immigrants to the colonies of Canada, Australia, and New Zealand. These matters included the raising of funds for and training of evangelists; employing resident evangelists or relying on mutual edification; open communion; women's leadership; and higher criticism. Yet different contexts and influences produced distinctive communities in each place.

Canada

Canadian immigration was complex and included

Canada

significant numbers of Scottish followers of James and Robert Haldane, as well as a smaller number of Scotch Baptists.[84] Stone-Campbell Christians in Canada often came from such churches, with, in some cases, whole Canadian congregations switching allegiance to the Stone-Campbell Movement. The churches in some early settlements initially had no clear denominational affiliation, making the precise dating of such changes difficult. The identity of these churches is further complicated by the fact that in the past some Canadian scholars equated "Scotch Baptists" with Haldanes. Joseph Ash, a pioneer in Canadian Stone-Campbell churches, did this in his *Reminiscences*, which became a standard source for later historians.[85] Reuben Butchart also made this mistake in his 1949 study *The Disciples of Christ in Canada Since 1830*. Though Butchart had an encyclopedic knowledge of people and congregations, he failed to distinguish Scotch Baptists from both Haldanes and "English" Baptists from Scotland.

Each group brought distinctive beliefs and practices to the Canadian context. Scotch Baptists required a plurality of elders in each church rather than a single pastor. Sunday worship featured "mutual edification" rather than a sermon delivered by a single elder or pastor. They strongly affirmed predestination and rational faith, and opposed revivalism. "English" Baptists generally expected a single pastor for each church, were more moderate in affirming predestination, and did not always believe that baptism was necessary for church membership. The Haldanes were strongly committed to revivalism and, though some of their churches had single pastors, generally believed in mutual edification in Sunday worship. They also practiced weekly celebration of the Lord's Supper with an ordained minister presiding.[86] Each of these traditions had a role in the shaping of the Stone-Campbell Movement in Canada.

The earliest Churches of Christ in Canada emerged in the Maritime Provinces of Prince Edward Island, Nova Scotia, and New Brunswick, influenced by Hadanes, Scotch Baptists, Regular Baptists, and evangelists from the American Christian Missionary Society.[87] The first congregation was organized in

1810 by Scottish immigrant John R. Stewart at Cross Roads, Prince Edward Island. Though without clear denominational affiliation, the congregation celebrated weekly communion apparently from its beginning. The next year evangelist Alexander Crawford, who had been baptized by the Haldanes and had immigrated to Yarmouth, Nova Scotia, in 1809, visited Prince Edward Island and immersed several people, including Stewart. For the next few years, Stewart founded churches associated with Regular Baptists,[88] many of which joined the Nova Scotia Baptist Association after his death in 1828. Cross Roads was the exception, and began using the name "Disciples of Christ" in 1830.[89]

The New Glasgow church on the north coast of Prince Edward Island had Scotch Baptist origins. Led by John Stevenson, a deacon in the Paisley Scotch Baptist Church, a group of young Scottish emigrants formed the congregation in 1820. When a committee asked Stevenson to receive ordination from the Regular Baptists, he declined, apparently because he wanted to be free from ecclesiastical control. The New Glasgow church moved toward a Stone-Campbell position on baptism for the remission of sins in 1855 with the arrival of Donald Crawford, an evangelist funded by the American Christian Missionary Society who made the island his base of evangelistic activity for forty years.[90]

Like the Cross Roads congregation, the Stone-Campbell church in Halifax, Nova Scotia, had Regular Baptist origins. Richard Creed, an immigrant from England in 1820, became a preacher among Halifax Baptists but disagreed with the majority view in his advocacy of weekly communion. Lewis Johnston, an ex-Anglican medical doctor who had become a deacon in the Granville Street Baptist Church in Halifax, also became interested in Stone-Campbell teaching. In 1833 he began editing *The Christian Gleaner*, which reprinted articles from Campbell's *Millennial Harbinger* and circulated among Baptists until 1838.[91]

In 1830, Johnston, Granville Street's minister Henry Green, and over half the congregation were expelled because of sympathy with Stone-Campbell positions.[92] The expelled group organized as Second Baptist Church and gradually moved towards a Stone-Campbell identity under the influence of Creed and Johnston. In 1836, the church withdrew from the Regular Baptist Association, received evangelists from the U.S. the next year, and by 1841 was known simply as the Church of Christ in Halifax.[93]

In New Brunswick the movement reflects a pattern of direct contact with Stone-Campbell churches in the U.S. The first congregation, Duke Street, St John, began as early as 1835 and received partial financial support from a Church of Christ in Eastport, Maine.[94] A Baptist congregation at L'Etete begun in 1835 invited George Garraty, supported by the American Christian Missionary Society, to preach for them in 1856. As a result, the congregation became a Christian Church, organizing formally in March 1863. Garraty also worked with two other congregations that affiliated with the Stone-Campbell Movement.[95]

In Ontario influences came from Haldanes, Regular Baptists, Free Will Baptists, Baptists from Scotland, and the Christian Connection. Free Will Baptists were distinguished from Regular Baptists by their rejection of the doctrine of predestination. James Black, a key figure in the early Ontario churches, had been baptized at Lochawe, Argyll, Scotland in 1817, by Baptist missionary Dugald Sinclair.[96] When Black immigrated to Canada in 1820, he settled in Aldborough Township in southern Ontario and joined a Scottish Baptist church. Over the next decade most of the members of Dugald Sinclair's congregation immigrated to the same area, and Sinclair himself followed in 1831.[97] Members from Aldborough moved to Mosa in 1826 and to Howard Township in 1829, and established new churches.[98] These, along with the Lobo church west of London, Ontario, adopted the name "Disciples" in 1855 after a visit from Alexander Campbell.[99]

Haldanes John Menzies and Alexander Stewart began a congregation in Esquesing in 1820, which by 1828 had adopted Campbell's view of baptism for remission of sins.[100] In 1826, Stewart established a church at York (Toronto) that became the source of several other Stone-Campbell congregations. When James Beaty, James Lesslie, and other members separated from Stewart's church in 1834, apparently over personality clashes, they formed what would become the Shuter Street Church of Christ. In 1842, Thomas Scott joined Shuter Street and with Beaty planted churches in Pickering Township in 1843 and Cooksville in 1845.[101]

Another important leader of Ontario churches was former Presbyterian Daniel Wiers. Immersed in the Baptist church at Beamsville in 1827, the congregation quickly invited him to become their part time minister. Doubts about the validity of creeds and predestination, despite a year's study at the Baptist Seminary at Hamilton, New York, led him to the writings of Alexander Campbell. As a result, the congregation excluded Wiers in February 1830. Befriended by Freewill Baptist preachers David Marks and Freeborn W. Straight, Wiers was ordained into that church and began a congregation at Clinton township. In late 1831 or early 1832 Wiers and Straight purchased and read a bound set of Alexander Campbell's *Christian Baptist*, and by August 1832, Wiers was preaching baptism for the remission of sins.[102]

Joseph Ash of the Christian Connection in Canada provided yet another tributary into the Stone-Campbell Movement. At first Ash hoped that Christian Connection churches would unite with the Campbell movement like the union then taking place between many Stone and Campbell congregations in the United States. While some from Christian Connection churches in Canada did so, most resisted. In the 1830s, Ash and his friend John Ford, a former Irish Baptist, organized Stone-Campbell churches in Cobourg, Oshawa (Whitby), Bowmanville, and Port Hope.[103]

The Canadian churches held their first Cooperation meeting in June 1843 at Norval, Ontario, attended by sixteen congregations.[104] Unlike the British Co-operation which met a year earlier, the Canadian meeting took no steps to support evangelism. Instead, groups of local churches assumed responsibility for evangelistic efforts. Provincial cooperations which collected and disbursed funds for the support of evangelists began in the Maritimes in 1840 and in Ontario in 1845 and 1846. Though meetings were at first occasional rather than annual, eventually the churches formed annual associations, beginning in Prince Edward Island in the early 1850s, with the Maritimes following in 1855.[105]

The most important development for the Canadian Churches in the last decades of the nineteenth century was the opening of the Western Provinces of Manitoba, Saskatchewan, Alberta, and British Columbia. As new farmland became available in the 1890s, significant migration from Ontario and the Maritimes, as well as from Britain and the U.S., attracted Stone-Campbell Christians who established congregations throughout western Canada. Churches in Ontario supported these efforts, as did the ACMS, the Board of Church Extension, and new regional Canadian missionary societies.[106]

Ontario had become the heartland of Canadian Churches of Christ, aided in the 1870s by American evangelists from as far south as Texas. By 1881, 16,000 out of 20,000 members were in Ontario, though numbers declined sharply as a result of westward migration and rural-urban population shifts.[107] Though an earlier organization had ceased because of financial difficulties, delegates from thirty-two churches formed the Co-operation of Disciples of Christ in Ontario at a convention in Everton in June 1886. Eight churches pledged $330 for the work.

The Ontario Co-operation held its first "June meeting," as the annual conventions became known, in Guelph in June 1887. It quickly formed an Ontario chapter of the CWBM, which inspired the formation of other chapters in the Western Provinces. The financial report revealed that the body had received $1,953 and spent $1,484. The Co-operation's chief activities were employing a provincial evangelist, providing financial aid to new or mission churches, and raising funds for evangelization, including occasional long-term support for a resident evangelist in a specific location. The body later revised its initial constitution of 1889 to include support for overseas missions and the education of ministers.[108]

Though ministerial education in Canadian churches began when Donald Crawford tutored students in his home in Prince Edward Island, like the U.K., Canada suffered the loss of potential ministers to the United States. Many Canadians graduating from Toronto University in the 1890s went to schools in the United States and never returned. The first attempt to stop this pattern was to establish lectureships in Toronto that would serve both students and the general membership, but this proved unsuccessful. In 1895, leaders established a college that met in the church at St Thomas, Ontario. Under the presidency of John Campbell, supporters had constructed a brick building, hired faculty, and enrolled forty-one students by February 1897. However, during the administration of W. C. MacDougall (1903-1906), the school lost significant support when the Cincinnati-based *Christian Standard* attacked MacDougal's endorsement of higher criticism.[109] By 1910 the school had closed, and the churches made no further efforts until after World War I.[110]

Despite small numbers, Stone-Campbell churches in Canada produced a plethora of journals, partly because of the size of the country and their relatively localized circulation. Unlike Britain, where there were never more than two major periodicals, Canada had at least nine between 1860 and 1917 serving a membership only twice the size. Not surprisingly, many failed for lack of subscriptions. Those that survived were subsidized either by their editors or by the co-operations.

David Oliphant, Jr. (1821-1885), who had studied under Alexander Campbell at Bethany, was significant both as an evangelist and editor. His monthly magazines went through five names between 1845 and 1865, beginning with the *Witness of Truth* (1845-1850) and ending with the *Message of Goodwill to All Men* (1864-1865). More controversial was the *Bible Index* (1872-1892), originally begun by John Trout and James Beaty, Jr. The paper advocated mutual ministry and engaged in a debate with the *Christian Standard* over the legitimacy of paying evangelists or elders. It rejected instruments and choirs in worship, though the extent to which these were actually employed in Canada at this time is unclear. The *Bible Index* also strongly criticized the proposal for an Ontario Co-operation in 1882-83.[111]

The Christian Worker (1881-1886), initially a magazine of the Georgian Bay Co-operation that later moved to Meaford, urged support for both the FCMS and the CWBM. So did *The Christian*, which began as the magazine of the Maritimes Home Mission Board in 1883, was later renamed *The Christian Messenger*, and was the main journal for eastern Canada beginning in 1897. Still another paper, the *Gospel Messenger* (1894-1896), shared the concerns, though not the tone, of the *Bible Index*, and reached a stable circulation under a new title after World War I.[112]

A clear contrast existed between two types of periodicals. The first, like the *Bible Index*, was mainly concerned with articles on the interpretation of Scripture and what the writers perceived as apostolic practices, with church news less important. The second, like the *Christian Worker* or the *Christian*, was primarily concerned with reporting the work of evangelists and supporting the various Co-operations. Historian E. C. Perry concluded that the papers were not responsible for creating divisions, but "served groups who were already distinct from each other."[113]

In any case, by the late 1800s a growing division in the Canadian churches was evident. The Beamsville Church, originally a strong supporter of cooperative activity, in the 1890s employed preachers who opposed the co-operations, especially H.M. Evans, founder of the *Gospel Messenger*. Evans also had ties to the church at Meaford, which was strongly influenced in the early 1890s by James A. Harding, co-founder with David Lipscomb of the Nashville Bible School. Through Harding's influence, a number of preachers from Nashville came to Canada to preach, and twenty-three Canadians attended Nashville Bible School between 1895 and 1917. In 1900, Tennessean S.M. Jones moved to Beamsville from Nashville and founded Beamsville Bible School. In 1910 Jones was at the center of a controversy over instrumental music that split the Beamsville church.[114]

Meaford also provided the springboard for a similar movement in Manitoba when several of its members founded the church at Carman in 1890-91, and Abraham Foster from Nashville founded the Carman

Bible School in 1897.[115] With few formal ties binding local congregations, determining when divisions became final is difficult. The Canadian Census of 1901 listed sixty-seven churches with 4,711 members as "Disciples" and eleven churches with 750 members as "Churches of Christ," numbers that reflected proportions similar to those in the 1906 U.S. Census of Religious Bodies.[116]

New Zealand

The founders of the Stone-Campbell Movement in New Zealand were all from British Churches of Christ.[117] Four years after the Treaty of Waitangi in 1840 established New Zealand as a Crown Colony, Thomas Jackson and his family left Scotland for New Zealand. They established a church of five members in Nelson on the north end of the South Island on March 2, 1844, and immediately requested that James Wallis send hymnbooks and copies of Campbell's New Testament and *Christianity Restored*. Though Wallis remarked that Jackson had not been "regularly called, ordained and sent forth by his brethren," he sent the requested books.[118]

In 1846 Thomas Jackson and his wife left for Auckland on the North Island where they established another Church of Christ. The small group that stayed at Nelson continued to meet but did not grow, mirroring the town's lack of development until the discovery of gold on the northwest coast of the South Island in 1860.[119] Though the Auckland church grew slowly at first, it experienced two periods of rapid growth, first in 1852 with the arrival of a Captain Rattray and his family from Scotland, and in 1864 when a group from London migrated to the city. In 1862, a group from the Manchester, England, Church of Christ had arrived that included Matthew Green, who became one of the leading evangelists in Australasia.[120]

In Dunedin on the South Island, twenty-five members of the Church of Christ in Cupar, Fife, Scotland had arrived in 1858 and organized a church. By 1862, they had constructed a building and started a Sunday school— the first Church of Christ in New Zealand to do either. Still, they grew only slowly until they invited Bethany-educated Englishman Henry S. Earl to serve as their evangelist in 1867. Two of the Cupar members moved to Invercargill, south of Dunedin, where, with arrivals from the churches in Birmingham and Manchester, they started another congregation in 1859.[121] By 1903, A.B. Maston's *Jubilee Pictorial History* of Churches of Christ in Australasia reported forty Churches of Christ in New Zealand, seven of which had more than one hundred members.

In the late nineteenth century the churches in New Zealand developed conferences to employ evangelists along the same lines as the British churches. The Northern Conference, formed in Auckland in 1883, supported Henry Exley to found churches in the Auckland suburbs and the surrounding country. The Southern Conference followed in 1884, made up of the churches of Westland, Canterbury, Otago, and Southland. The Nelson District on the South Island founded five new churches in the 1890s. The Wellington District on the North Island, across Cook Strait from Nelson, started new churches in Wellington's suburbs. In 1906 Nelson and Wellington combined in a Middle District Conference and increased support for evangelists, though they remained the smallest

New Zealand

of the three Conferences.

The New Zealand churches held their first Dominion Conference in Wellington on January 1, 1901. Although decision-making authority still lay in the area conferences, the Dominion Conference discussed a number of matters of interest to all the churches, including foreign missions, a Bible college and a national magazine. Dominion Conferences were held in 1904, 1909, and 1912, but

did not became annual until after World War I. By 1905 there were fifty churches with a membership of more than 2,400.[122]

The churches also initiated new efforts in women's work and foreign missions. In 1908 L.F. Stephens and his wife formed a chapter of the Christian Woman's Board of Missions in Wanganui, on the North Island. Supporters soon formed other chapters, which eventually supported two Home Mission preachers. Representatives from local Sisters' Guilds that were affiliated with the Auckland and Middle District Conferences held national Sisters' Conferences and undertook a variety of work in local churches including sewing circles, Dorcas societies, and hospital and home visitation. The second Dominion Conference in Dunedin in 1904 assumed responsibility for the Churches of Christ mission in Bulawayo, Southern Rhodesia.[123]

Immediately before World War I, the number of new churches being established in New Zealand dropped, barely exceeding the number that closed.[124] Unlike in Canada where Churches of Christ experienced most of their growth in urban areas, the population of New Zealand was more evenly distributed between town and country. The many rural churches tended to be small and difficult to sustain. Though the New Zealand population was growing more rapidly than that of any European country, the rate of growth of Churches of Christ was slowing.[125]

After the war, the churches' stalled growth along with a worldwide economic slowdown prevented the New Zealand Conferences from raising sufficient funds for evangelism and church construction. The Presidents of the three Conferences proposed a merger into a single Dominion Conference. On April 6, 1920, the New Zealand churches held their first Annual Dominion Conference in its new unified form in Wellington. One of the new Conference's first acts was to replace the magazines of the old Northern and Southern Conferences with *The New Zealand Christian*, appointing Ira Paternoster as editor.[126] The New Zealand Churches of Christ had moved from scattered beginnings to a national identity in less than eighty years.

Australia

The background of the Stone-Campbell Movement in Australia included Scotch Baptists, Wesleyan Methodists, as well as members of New Zealand and British Churches of Christ.[127] In 1845 Thomas Magarey, a leader of the Church of Christ in Nelson, New Zealand, moved to Adelaide, Australia. Uniting with a

Scotch Baptist church, he introduced the members to the writings of Alexander Campbell and circulated copies of the *British Millennial Harbinger*. In 1847, Thomas Jackson from New Zealand visited and lectured on baptism for the remission of sins. The result was a split, the Scotch Baptists departing in July 1848, leaving those who agreed with Campbell's position in possession of the congregation's Franklin Street building.[128] About the same time, a group who had emigrated from the New Mills Church of Christ in Ayrshire, Scotland, established a Church of Christ at Willunga, south of Adelaide. Philip Santo, a member of the Franklin Street church, formed other congregations at Burra Burra north of Adelaide in 1850, and Hindmarsh in 1854.[129]

Though the discovery of gold in Victoria in the early 1850s lured many to leave Adelaide, within less than a year the gold fever faded, and many began trickling back. By June 1853, Magarey was distributing forty copies of Wallis's *British Millennial Harbinger* each month to Christians in and around Adelaide.[130] In 1855, several who had been part of the 1848 split returned, further strengthening the Franklin Street congregation.[131]

In New South Wales, Churches of Christ had a Wesleyan Methodist background. The first congregation was established most likely in Western Sydney around 1851, led by William Stimson and John Hodges, both Wesleyan immigrants from England.[132] Another English Wesleyan immigrant, Albert Griffin, formed a second church in Sydney in 1852. When he had become disturbed at what he perceived as the lack of a sign of the Holy Spirit in his life, he was helped by reading copies of the *British Millennial Harbinger* sent by his brother, Eleazer, a member of the Church of Christ in London. Griffin soon met Henry Mitchell, formerly a member of a Church of Christ in New Zealand, and in 1852 they began to meet to take the Lord's Supper. They also began to preach in the open air in nearby Hyde Park.

When local Wesleyans sent one of their newly arrived preachers, Joseph Kingsbury, to talk to Griffin, Griffin succeeded in converting him to the Stone-Campbell position and immersed him in September 1853. Griffin and Mitchell established a congregation at Hyde Park, most of which later moved to the Sydney suburb of Enmore.[133] Those who remained formed a third Sydney congregation, constructing a building which opened in 1869 on Elizabeth Street. In 1864 the Enmore church

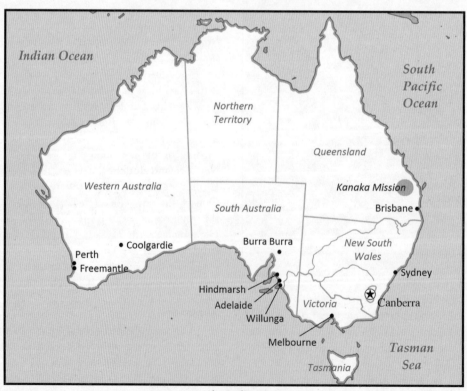

Australia

set apart Edward Lewis as an evangelist, and in 1866 the three churches formed an Evangelist Committee, which employed Matthew Green the following year.[134]

In Victoria members of British Churches of Christ attracted to Australia by the gold rush in the 1850s founded churches in and around Melbourne. The first church gathered in the home of John Ingram, but in January 1853 became part of a congregation meeting in the home of H. G. Picton in the suburb of Prahran.[135] In May 1854, members from Prahran founded a second church in Melbourne, and four years later another group from Prahran began to meet in Brighton. The first Church of Christ in western Victoria was established at Ballerat in 1859.[136]

The churches in Victoria grew more rapidly than those in both New South Wales and South Australia, partly because of the use of evangelistic campaigns. T. H. Milner, who arrived in Australia from Edinburgh in 1862, encouraged the Australian churches to ask for assistance from both British and American churches, but neither was then in a position to help. When the Victoria Evangelist Committee, formed in 1863, appealed to British evangelist Henry S. Earl, he agreed to come, arriving in 1864. Earl and Milner conducted evangelistic meetings over the next two years on a scale larger than anything experienced by the Australian Churches of Christ.

By the mid-1860s, Victoria had twelve churches with a total of two hundred thirty members. South Australia and New South Wales each had three churches, with total memberships of eighty-four and just over a hundred respectively. The growth of Australian Churches of Christ over the next fifty years mirrored general population growth. By the beginning of the twentieth century, half of Australia's population lived in the six largest cities, and between 1901 and 1911, urban population increased by fifty percent. The 1911 Commonwealth Census listed the number of adherents in Churches of Christ as 38,748.[137]

Much of that increase could be attributed to the work of evangelists like Milner and Earl. Earl's work in Adelaide in 1865, for example, added over three hundred members to the congregation. Marrying a daughter of Australian church leader Thomas Magarey, Earl remained in South Australia for the next seven years building up the church at Hindmarsh and establishing new churches in several country towns.[138] In 1867, U.S. evangelists G.L. Surber and T.J. Gore arrived, Surber serving the Lygon Street church in Melbourne for five

years, and Gore in Adelaide for over fifty. Matthew Wood Green moved to Sydney from Auckland in 1867, working with the church there until 1870 and later serving in

Born in Ireland, Thomas Magarey (1825-1902) immigrated with his family to New Zealand in 1841 where he was converted by members of the Stone-Campbell Movement.

Melbourne and Adelaide.[139]

In addition, beginning in the 1870s an increasing number of young Australians traveled to the College of the Bible in Lexington, Kentucky, to prepare to become evangelists. Though not all returned, many did, and contributed to the growth of the churches. T.H. Bates from Melbourne, for example, was one of the first Australians to go to the U.S. in 1868. He returned in 1873 and began a ministry in Adelaide and Western Australia.[140]

The Australian churches also revived efforts at evangelistic cooperation. Churches in both Victoria and New South Wales had formed Evangelist Committees in the 1860s, but the Victoria committee and annual meeting had disbanded in 1868 over a disagreement concerning whether its decisions were binding on the churches.[141] In 1873, Victoria church leaders met at Prahran to consider reestablishing an Annual Meeting, and convened the first gathering of this second series on April 14.[142]

The South Australian churches organized in 1875 when the Hindmarsh congregation initiated a Preliminary Co-operation Meeting on March 29 with twelve churches represented. Though the issue of open communion threatened the effort, the meeting appointed Philip Santo as chair and created an Evangelist Committee to raise funds to support evangelists for country churches.[143] Representatives of seven churches with the support of four others met in Adelaide in 1883 to form a second Evangelistic Union in South Australia. Reflecting the earlier tensions over open communion, two of the nineteen articles of its constitution condemned churches and evangelists that "knowingly" had fellowship with the unimmersed at the Lord's Table. Churches supporting the earlier Evangelist Committee (sometimes called the "liberal" churches) wanted these clauses removed. The two groups, consisting of twenty-five churches, reached an agreement in 1885, with all promising to reject open communion but to avoid inflammatory statements like

Henry S. Earl, pictured here in an Australian church, was an effective evangelist in England, Australia, and New Zealand.

those in the 1883 Constitution.[144]

The pattern of organization was consistent throughout Australia. Congregations in New South Wales formed a Co-operation in 1885. In 1898 the churches at Perth, Fremantle, and Coolgardie in Western Australia formed a conference and within a year had established six new churches. Tasmanian churches began a Conference in 1894, though progress was slow with only twelve churches founded by 1901.[145] Also, by 1901, the twenty-three churches in Queensland had also created an Annual Conference. In 1889 and 1891, the Australian churches held Inter-colonial Conferences, and following the creation of the Commonwealth of Australia in 1901, held their first Federal Conference in 1906. Domestic mission work followed the British pattern, with a Committee responsible to a representative conference instead of the Missionary Society pattern common in America.

Along with the need for full-time evangelists, the Australian churches quickly recognized the need for a college. In a December 1870 article, T.H. Bates, then studying at the College of the Bible in Lexington, Kentucky, urged Australian Christians to follow through on their desire to establish a Bible college. That year Henry Earl raised $5,000 for a school, and two years later G. L. Surber promised to raise additional funds in the United States.[146] Securing adequate support for such a school proved difficult. Churches in South Australia finally executed a trust deed for a college to be located in Adelaide in 1881, but six years later Matthew Wood Green was still trying to raise more money on a trip to the United States and Great Britain. He brought back $3,700 and £93, together with a promise from the FCMS to pay $700 annually for five years once the college opened.

Despite the desire for a national school, the first efforts were small and regional. T.J. Gore, J.K. Henshelwood, W.C. Morro, and James Johnson began short-lived efforts between 1888 and 1903, two of them in Melbourne. Finally, the Federal Conference took action. Hiring the highly respected evangelist H.G. Howard as professor, classes began in February 1907 in Melbourne. The Conference appointed Howard principal in the middle of the year, and in 1909 purchased property in the Melbourne suburb of Glen Iris. The college began classes on the new campus in 1910 with A.R. Main as principal.[147]

Separate women's work began in Victoria, with prayer meetings organized in the mid-1860s. A Sisters' Conference first met in 1886 with Mrs. C.L. Thurgood, wife of an American evangelist, chosen the first President. The monthly officers meeting quickly began considering the role of women in overseas missions. Christian women in New South Wales began a Sisters' Conference in 1894 with Mrs. W.T. Clapham as the first President. Despite a strong plea in favor of women's rights by Matthew Wood

Green at the 1893 Conference, women in South Australia were not given a place on the Conference program to present reports of their Dorcas Societies until 1904. [148]

Though many women had opposed establishing a Sisters' Auxiliary to the General Conference when first proposed, by 1905 attitudes had reversed. After reports by Mrs. E.W. Pittman and Mrs. D.A. Ewers about the home and foreign mission work by women in Victoria and Western Australia, a majority agreed to organize a Sisters' Auxiliary Conference in conjunction with the General Conference in September 1906. This body raised significant sums of money for a wide range of work. [149] Though the Sisters' Conferences were like those in the U.K., their dedication to raising funds for overseas missions, to which there was no parallel in the British Sisters' Conference, reflects the influence of the Christian Woman's Board of Missions.

Much of the Australian enthusiasm for overseas missions at the end of the 1880s came from women. When FCMS missionaries to India Emma and Greene L. Wharton visited Australia in 1889, Emma Wharton spoke at the Victoria Sisters' Conference. The following year Greene L. Wharton addressed the first Inter-Colonial Conference, which expressed its "full sympathy with foreign missions." The Australian churches formed their first Foreign Missions Committee in Victoria, with others organized in South Australia in 1891 and in New South Wales in 1892. Together the three constituted the General Foreign Missions Committee, based in Melbourne. [150]

In addition to a growing commitment to overseas missions, the Australian churches increased the scope of their work to include minority populations at home. In 1892 the South Australian churches began to support the "Kanaka" mission. Kanakas were South Sea islanders used as indentured labor on the Queensland sugar plantations until 1907, when an intensification of the "White Australia" policy forced their repatriation. The churches sent John Thompson, who had worked with the Kanakas in Queensland, to the New Hebrides (now Vanuatu) in 1903. [151] In 1893 Australian churches began work among Chinese immigrants in Melbourne, and later in Sydney in 1899 and in Adelaide in 1900. [152]

Another significant development was the consolidation of Australian periodicals. Until 1868 Churches of Christ had no Australian paper, and the *British Millennial Harbinger* was still the main source of news. T.J. Gore founded the *Australian Christian Pioneer* in 1868, and over the next thirty years a variety of papers in different colonies came and went. A.B. Maston, an American evangelist who arrived in Australia via New Zealand in

the 1880s, was the leading figure in bringing the journals together. In 1891 he formed the Austral Printing and Publishing Company in Melbourne, and in 1898 founded the *Australian Christian*. This paper became a nationwide periodical, drawing on the expertise of F.G. Dunn (editor of the Victoria *Australian Christian Standard*) and D.A. Ewers (editor of the South Australian *Christian Pioneer*).

By the outbreak of World War I many of the issues that had once been controversial no longer troubled most in Australian Churches of Christ. With the increased number of candidates, more congregations could call a full-time evangelist, leading to the virtual disappearance of mutual ministry by 1900. The churches had discussed the use of instruments in worship in the 1880s, but this no longer seemed a crucial issue. With the establishment of the College of the Bible at Glen Iris, the churches increasingly recognized that evangelists needed training that extended beyond Bible knowledge to engage theology, history, and other church traditions. [153] Though the Australian Conferences passed resolutions of loyalty to King and Empire in 1915 and 1916, Australia's rejection of conscription by popular referendum removed military service as a potentially divisive issue from the Australian Churches.

Ministry and Evangelism in the U.K. and British Dominions

The development of the Stone-Campbell tradition in the three British dominions reflects the influence of different American and British traditions regarding ministry and evangelism. In the past scholars presented the issue as a question of whether or not ministers or evangelists (the term used in Britain to describe full-time preachers until 1947) were paid, as became the norm in the United States, or unpaid, as was more often the case in Britain. Previous studies of Canada and Australia show that growth was more rapid wherever there was a paid ministry, suggesting an explanation for the more dramatic growth of the Movement in the U.S. than in the U.K. and British dominions. These earlier studies suggest that the Scotch Baptist practice of "mutual ministry" was the source of the British tradition of an unpaid ministry. [154]

The British movement's origins, however, were only partly from the Scotch Baptists. Early British Churches of Christ persuaded some Scotch Baptists to join them, but in fact they seem to have recruited more Methodists. This is not surprising in view of their rejection of Calvinist theology, which still prevailed among Baptists and Congregationalists. Furthermore, though the British churches valued mutual ministry, the very purpose of the

Co-operation was to raise money to support evangelists. Though never as successful as they had hoped, British Churches of Christ were paying evangelists through the General Evangelist Committee as early as the 1840s. However, following a Methodist pattern of traveling preachers, they expected evangelists to stay with one church for only a few months, rather than several years.

In the same way, Scotch Baptist origins of the churches in the British colonies were less than previous studies suggested. In Canada, where there was significant Scottish influence, Stone-Campbell churches drew mostly from Haldane sources. In New Zealand, the Scotch Baptist influence was almost non-existent. In Australia there was some, but it was confined to South Australia. The earlier estimate of the influence of the Scotch Baptists may have come from the fact that the Haldanes also believed in mutual edification. Still, they had less hesitation about paid evangelists—in fact, they pioneered their use in Scotland. Clearly, mutual edification and paid evangelists were not mutually exclusive.

Why then did Churches of Christ in the U.K. and British dominions tend to rely on unpaid elders rather than paid evangelists? One reason is simply the lack of money. The British experience shows that raising the funds necessary to pay a preacher was very difficult before the 1870s. Another explanation is the lack of opportunities for training. Unlike in the U.S. where Stone-Campbell leaders began colleges very early, in the U.K. and British dominions the churches did not establish colleges until the twentieth century. David King did begin an informal training system in the late 1860s, and the Annual Meeting appointed a Training Committee to carry on that work beginning in 1876 with some success, but a uniform program of ministerial education did not exist.[155] In the earliest period, several who became leaders in British Churches of Christ had already received theological training in another denomination. Another factor was that several of the denominations from which the Stone-Campbell Movement drew had a tradition of lay preaching. This was certainly true of the Methodists, but Baptists and Congregationalists had also developed such patterns in the early nineteenth century.[156]

It cannot be denied, however, that the British churches also had a decidedly anti-clerical strain. T.H. Milner, for example, was ardently anti-clerical. Before he joined Churches of Christ, Milner had been a Baptist in Scotland and edited the group's magazine, *The Evangelist*. He came to reject Calvinism and adopted the view that the Holy Spirit worked only through the words of Scripture. Eventually he also began to question the Baptist understanding of the authority of pastors and elders and in 1852 formed a new church that withdrew from the Baptist Union and joined Churches of Christ in 1855.[157] David King also strongly opposed the creation of a professional clergy, an attitude probably rooted in his Wesleyan formation during the 1840s when British Methodism had tried to extend the control of traveling preachers over the churches. This anti-clericalism, together with a lack of funding and educational institutions, and strong precedents for lay preaching, helped establish mutual edification as the dominant pattern of ministry in Churches of Christ in the United Kingdom and British dominions for more than 60 years.

Global Influence of the Churches of the U.K. and British Dominions

The combined numerical strength of the Churches in the United Kingdom, Canada, New Zealand, and Australia was never as great as in the United States. However, the significance of these churches far exceeded their numbers in the worldwide spread of the Stone-Campbell Movement. Each supplied key leaders who, along with U.S. missionaries, took both the gospel and their distinctive expressions of the Stone-Campbell Movement to the continents of Africa and Asia.

7

The Expansion of World Missions, 1874-1929

Stone-Campbell world missions began in 1849 with the formation of the American Christian Missionary Society (ACMS). Though results of the Society's efforts in Jerusalem, Jamaica, and Liberia were mixed, they reflected a growing commitment to world missions. New efforts began in the late nineteenth century with the establishment of other societies. In the United States leaders organized the Christian Woman's Board of Missions (CWBM) in 1874 and the Foreign Christian Missionary Society (FCMS) in 1875. By the 1890s, these organizations were partnering with the Scottish Conference of the British Churches of Christ and the newly formed Foreign Missionary Committees of the Australian and British Churches of Christ. In addition, direct support missions from the United States began in the 1890s with Wilson Kendrick Azbill (1848-1929) and John Moody McCaleb (1862-1953). These leaders pioneered world missions for the emerging Churches of Christ and Christian Churches/Churches of Christ.

A major development in Christian missions in the late nineteenth and early twentieth centuries was a move toward cooperation among denominations. Stone-Campbell missions had often focused on "converting" Christians of other bodies through an appeal to restore the New Testament church. A shift toward converting non-Christians to Christian faith began in the 1880s. The Edinburgh World Missionary Conference of 1910, often identified as the beginning of modern ecumenism, was attended by leaders of Protestant mission agencies from Britain, Europe, and the United States, including representatives of U.S. and British churches of the Stone-Campbell Movement. It called denominational bodies to avoid duplication of efforts and unite in evangelizing the non-Christian world. Many associated with Stone-Campbell mission organizations embraced this ecumenical vision, but others did not, producing new missions "independent" of the missionary societies and separate from missions of U.S. Churches of Christ.

These new missions, most often designated "direct support missions" in Stone-Campbell history, opposed comity agreements with other denominations and the alleged practice of open membership by the missionary societies, and were a key marker of the emergence of Christian Churches/Churches of Christ.[1] This book also uses "direct support" at times to identify mission work conducted by North American Churches of Christ, which opposed missionary societies as inherently unscriptural. In both cases, missionaries solicited support from individuals and congregations that sent funds directly to the missionary rather than to the ACMS, the CWBM, the FCMS, or their successor, the United Christian Missionary Society (UCMS).

This arrangement posed numerous problems, however, including how to raise and collect funds, transfer money, and maintain accountability for both supporters and missionaries. Among the emerging Christian Churches/Churches of Christ, two agencies—the Christian Restoration Association and the *Christian Standard*—offered to serve as clearinghouses for mission contributions, receiving and dispersing funds to missionaries. Often, however, missionaries created their own parachurch agencies, usually with boards in the United States, to receive and distribute funds and maintain financial records. Another method, though not confined to direct support missions, was the "living link" church in which a local congregation essentially adopted a missionary, supplying full or partial support and ongoing personal contact.

Still another approach used by those who opposed the societies was the forwarding agent. In this case, a volunteer collected funds and sent them to the missionary, serving as a liaison between supporters and the worker in the field. One prominent example was Don Carlos Janes (1877-1944). Janes began serving as forwarding agent for several missionaries from U.S. Churches of Christ as early as 1911 after the elders of the Highland Church of Christ in Louisville, Kentucky, appointed him treasurer of the church's "missionary office." Janes went on to become the most important forwarding agent and promoter of international missions among U.S. Churches of Christ before World War II.[2]

The 1910 Edinburgh Conference had called for indigenization of missions, beginning with the education of local leaders with the eventual transfer of responsibility for the churches and mission institutions to them. Though Stone-Campbell missions had barely begun this process, developing nationalisms and the economic collapse of the Great Depression heightened a sense of urgency for the missions to become indigenous churches. Edinburgh also recommended better education of missionaries, and in response the CWBM established the College of Missions in Indianapolis in September 1910. Before it merged with the Kennedy School of Missions in Hartford, Connecticut, in 1928, more than three hundred fifty missionaries had graduated from the school, most of whom were employed by one of the Stone-Campbell missionary societies.[3]

Between 1911 and 1928, students at the College of Missions in Indianapolis studied a wide range of subjects—including languages—often taught by indigenous leaders from Stone-Campbell mission fields. (Charles Paul, *The Call of China*, 1919)

Scandinavia

Following the European revolutions of 1848, religious toleration spread to the Scandinavian countries, beginning with Denmark. Dr. A. O. Holck (1844-1907), a native of Denmark and member of Central Christian Church in Cincinnati, believed that this development

presented an opportunity for the Stone-Campbell Movement.[4] In November 1876, Holck and his wife, Elizabeth, began work in Copenhagen as missionaries of the FCMS. Though opposition by the state church was stronger than expected, by 1880 they had established a congregation, begun publishing a monthly newspaper called *The Old Paths*, and ministered in the nearby village of Lyngby. By the beginning of the twentieth century, the Danish Mission claimed two well-established churches, and the monthly paper had a circulation of nearly 6,000. Much to Holck's disappointment, however, the combined membership of the two congregations never grew much larger than two hundred.[5]

Even before the Holcks's arrival, the Scottish Conference of the British Churches of Christ supported several small free churches in and around Fredrikshald, Norway. In the early 1880s, a Norwegian sailor carried copies of *The Old Paths* to these congregations, and Holck eventually began working with them as well. To support the expanding work, now known as the Scandinavian Mission, the Scottish Conference and FCMS sent three additional missionaries in the early 1880s: Julius Cramer, O. C. Mikkelsen, and R. P. Anderson. While Mikkelsen and Cramer served mainly in Copenhagen, Holck and Anderson worked to stabilize and expand the work in Norway.[6]

By the late 1880s, the mission claimed at least a dozen small congregations in Norway. When Anderson and his wife returned to Scotland in 1904, and the Scottish Conference ended support of the Scandinavian Mission, the FCMS dispatched Yale-educated E. W. Pease and his wife, who served until 1908. Two Swedish congregations at Melano-Limhamn (1897) and Helsingborg-Ramlosa (1899) were also part of the Scandinavian Mission. Sustaining the work in Sweden without the regular presence of missionaries, however, was a struggle.[7]

Pentecostalism made significant progress in churches throughout Norway between 1905 and 1910, including the Stone-Campbell congregations. Initially Anderson and Pease welcomed what they saw as a "religious awakening." Later, however, Pentecostal doctrines and practices caused conflict, leading the missionaries to lament the influence of "tongue-speakers" and "prophesiers." The annual report for 1909 complained that Pentecostals "have affected our work in every place…so that it is difficult to tell how many members are actually with the Church of Christ."[8] Likely more than half of the 1,000 Norwegian members had affiliated with Pentecostalism by the 1920s.

Influenced by growing ecumenical contacts even before the 1910 Edinburgh Conference, the FCMS had begun to shift its priorities toward "non-Christian" populations. Partly due to this shift, it moved to close the Scandinavian Mission after Dr. Holck's death in 1907, ending all support by 1910. However, small contributions from U. S. individuals and churches apparently continued for some time. By 1948, the two Copenhagen churches had merged, first with one another, and then with the Baptists, the strongest dissenter denomination in Denmark at the time.[9] What became of the churches in Norway and Sweden is not known.

France

Before 1920, the Stone-Campbell Movement made two attempts to establish a mission in France. Jules and Annie DeLaunay, both former Roman Catholics who had joined Central Christian Church in Cincinnati, arrived in Paris in November 1877, supported by the FCMS. They eventually settled in Vaugirard, one of the city's most disreputable suburbs.[10] Through the late 1870s and early 1880s, the DeLaunays held evangelistic meetings three nights a week. They wrote and distributed tracts, published a hymnal, and began a small school to train evangelists for the mission. Eventually they established a small church, a Sunday school, and several auxiliary organizations. Despite these initial successes, the FCMS voted to close the mission in 1886, claiming the Delaunays were unable to manage the mission's finances and operations effectively. Delauany, however, asserted that the real issue was FCMS opposition to his support of the British practice of closed communion.[11]

The Movement's second attempt to establish a permanent presence in France came after the French government enacted the 1905 Law on the Separation of the Churches and the State. A priest who left the Catholic Church after its disestablishment, Victor Hautefeuille, began l'Œuvre des Anciens Pretres Catholique (The Work of Former Catholic Priests) to assist his colleagues in finding employment. He envisioned the creation of a new, ecumenical French national church based on the "restoration of primitive Christianity in doctrine, ordinances, and fruit." Former priests with strong evangelical Protestant commitments, he believed, could serve as the most effective evangelists both in France and abroad.[12]

Hautefeuille's movement caught the attention of Alfred E. Seddon (1846-1939), a London-born journalist, minister, missionary, and social reformer affiliated with the Stone-Campbell Movement. He corresponded with

Hautefeuille in 1908-1909 and tried to raise support for a renewed mission in France. Though the FCMS, reflecting emerging ecumenical mission priorities, refused to support Seddon, in 1909 the *Christian Standard* appointed him its European correspondent. With direct financial support of *Standard* readers, he began the "hors-de-Rome" (out of Rome) movement with Hautefeuille. The two published the monthly *Le Messager Chretién (The Christian Messenger)* advocating the restoration of New Testament Christianity and organized several small churches in Paris and the surrounding area.

Controversy over funding plagued the work, some suspecting Seddon of misappropriation of money, though it was never proved. Seddon's failing health, controversies in the congregations, mounting secularism in French society, and World War I disrupted the hors-de-Rome movement and scattered its congregations. The Stone-Campbell Movement would establish no lasting presence in France until after World War II.

Turkey

In 1879 the FCMS appointed G. N. Shishmanian as a missionary to Constantinople. Born in Turkey, Shishmanian was a Christian before immigrating to the United States, where he came in contact with the Stone-Campbell Movement and was immersed in Dallas, Texas. He later studied under J. W. McGarvey at the College of the Bible for two years. Through McGarvey's influence, Shishmanian received assistance from churches in Kentucky and surrounding states in addition to support from the FCMS.[13] All Stone-Campbell mission work in Turkey was done among Armenian and Orthodox Christian groups since the government made proselytizing Muslims virtually impossible. Shishmanian preached and distributed tracts in and around Constantinople and helped establish house churches in more than a dozen cities, though none became self-supporting.

In 1884, the FCMS added medical doctor Garabed Kevorkian to the Turkish mission to supervise five outstations, and in 1886, Hohanes Karagiozian began work in Cilicia and two places in Russia.[14] Two years later, Andrew (1869-1937) and Mae Chapman arrived to work with Shishmanian in Constantinople, and Mihran Baghdasarian went to Aroomia, then to Salmas, in neighboring Iran, to work among the Armenian population. All were supported by the FCMS. Though Baghdasarian began the Persian Mission with high hopes, by September 1899 he left because of persecution and difficult living conditions. The Chapmans returned to the United States in 1901 for the same reasons.[15]

In 1887 C. L. Loos reported in the *Christian Standard* that Congregationalist missionaries in Turkey supported by the American Board of Commissioners for Foreign Missions had strongly criticized their Stone-Campbell counterparts for encroaching on their territory and converts. Stone-Campbell missionaries and Armenian members of their churches were aggressively teaching their baptismal beliefs and immersing Armenian Congregationalists. In response to the charges, Loos accused the Congregationalists of showing the same intolerance as Catholics, denying others the right to teach their religious beliefs and make converts. Loos asserted that this was not a matter on which they could yield. "We will never cease…to teach with earnestness and insistence all whom we can approach, believers and unbelievers, what the law of God teaches in this regard."[16]

Stone-Campbell missionaries also experienced Muslim hostility, which increased as the Ottoman Empire disintegrated amid rising nationalism. Turkish Muslims who converted to Christianity were forced into military service, often never to return. All new churches, schools, and publications had to receive the approval of Sultan Abdul-Hamid, and permission was almost never granted. The diversity of language, ethnicity, and traditional religion made evangelism even more difficult. Shishmanian and Kevorkian, despite their U.S. citizenship, often experienced harassment and imprisonment. In 1905, after twenty-six years of support, the FCMS ended its work in Turkey, citing a lack of results. Reflecting its increasing ecumenical commitments and in stark contrast to Loos's 1887 response to Congregationalist criticisms, the FCMS also cited the mission's overlap with the work of the American Board of Commissioners for Foreign Missions.[17]

Though no Stone-Campbell mission existed in Turkey after 1905, the systematic extermination of Armenians by the Turkish Ottoman government during World War I prompted many Stone-Campbell Christians to action. L. B. Phillian, an Armenian who was a member of a Christian Church in Pennsylvania and a friend of *Christian Standard* editor S. S. Lappin, pled with the churches to aid Armenian Christians during the genocide of 1915-1919. In January 1916, the paper ran a large ad titled "Help Armenian Refugees," urging readers to raise money to bring a group of 4,200 to the United States.[18]

The American Committee for Armenian and Syrian Relief, formed in 1915 with the leadership of U.S. ambassador to the Ottoman Empire, Henry Morgenthau, Sr., served as a clearinghouse for all contributions. The *Christian Standard* began collecting funds for Armenia in summer 1916, quickly raising almost $1,500. The journal published photos of refugees and continued appeals for relief money over the next several years. By 1920 it had sent over $39,000 to the American Committee, mostly from small individual contributions.[19] This was the last known Stone-Campbell effort of the period in this part of the world.

India

At the 1881 Annual Convention, church leaders intent on focusing mission efforts on converting non-Christians urged the FCMS and CWBM to cooperate in establishing a mission in Japan, India, or China. In October the two boards chose India, and in September 1882, eight missionaries left the United States for Bombay (today Mumbai). The FCMS supported Greene L. (1846-1906) and Emma (d. 1922) Wharton, and Albert (1847-1922) and Mary Kelly Norton. The CWBM supported four single women: Ada Boyd (d. 1915), Laura Kinsey (d. 1926), Mary Graybiel (1846-1935), and Mary Kingsbury (1857-1926). The FCMS missionaries were to establish churches and train Indian leaders, while the CWBM missionaries were responsible for working with Indian women, educating children, and providing medical services.[20]

Eventually the missionaries settled in Harda, Central Provinces, a railway town four hundred miles northeast of Bombay. They began learning Hindi, preaching in village streets and bazaars, organizing children's Sunday schools, and operating a bookstore. English-speaking Methodists eventually gave the Mission their building. As other workers arrived, the mission expanded its work along the Great Indian Peninsular Railway. Bilaspur, in Madhyar Pradesh state, established in 1885, quickly became the largest station of the Disciples India Mission and became known for providing education for girls. Mungeli, established in 1886, became known for its evangelistic work among the Satnamis, a branch of the leather workers' caste. By 1889, the mission had its first medical personnel—Dr. C. S. Durand at Harda, and Drs. Olivia Baldwin (1858-1931) and Arabella Merrill at Bilaspur.[21]

Abdul Khadir (1863-1888), a twenty-two-year-old Muslim railway conductor in Harda, was the Mission's first convert and illustrates the difficulties such people faced. After reading a tract explaining the "Scripture plan of salvation" and contacting its author, G. L. Wharton, he was baptized in January 1885. As a result, his wife returned to her father's house with his two children, and friends tried to force him to renounce his faith. At times he sought protection in the mission. Because of Khadir's preaching in the bazaars around Harda, the railway transferred him to Pune, which was infamous for its monsoons, and less than three years after his conversion he died of cholera.[22]

A key to missionary success for all denominations was the recruitment of indigenous helpers. Mary Graybiel wrote in 1887, "Do all that we foreigners may, we shall never convert the people of this country to Christ. The most we can hope to do is to influence the few through whom the many are to be reached."[23] Two indigenous men, Jagganath and Nathoolal, and their wives came to the Mission from the Presbyterians at Rajputna, and proved to be effective evangelists. Of major significance were Bible women, converts who traveled with female missionaries to help introduce Christianity to other Indian women. In 1892 the missionaries briefly employed Joseph Jaahaw as a preacher and his wife Agnes Bai as a Bible woman to teach persons who came to the dispensaries and assist in the schools. Another Bible

woman, Susan Bai, also helped in the dispensary and Sunday schools.[24]

Like other missions in India with women missionaries, Disciples developed "zenana work." The zenana was the enclosure in a house to which male visitors were never admitted, where the women lived and spent most of their day. Women missionaries were able to visit zenanas where they taught the Bible and other subjects, and provided medical care. By 1893 Ada Boyd had twenty-four houses on her visiting list. The zenana work was particularly attractive to women missionary physicians. Of the eighteen doctors who served in India for the FCMS and CWBM before 1920, thirteen were women.[25]

The Mission's first orphanage began when two very poor parents brought their sixteen-month-old boy, Siriwan, to Ada Boyd on New Year's Day 1884. Two years later Boyd brought Benji, aged three, back from Lucknow, where his mother had died in a Home for Homeless Women. By March 1890 there were fifteen children at Bilaspur. Several of the children were

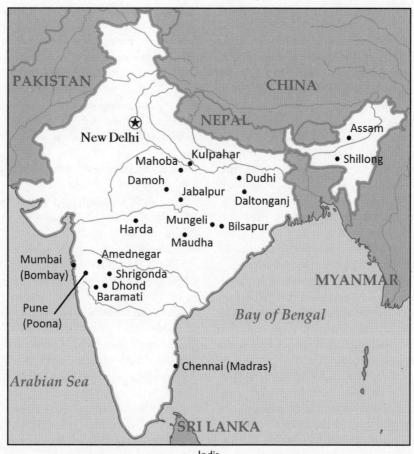

India

eventually baptized, Siriwan and Benji being the first on May 21, 1893. By 1894 two of the girls, Phulmani and Patia, were assisting in the schools. In May 1895, Mary Kingsbury reported that eleven girls from the orphanage had been baptized.[26]

Until parents became suspicious of a missionary takeover, Laura Kinsey and Mary Kingsbury were allowed to teach in the government school at Harda. When that ended, Kinsey established a mission school for boys in February 1885 and later that year added a school for girls. She and G. L. Wharton also started a Sunday school for boys of middle and higher castes. In Bilaspur, Mary Kingsbury opened the Chata girls' school in August 1887, with the assistance of the daughter of a Bible woman who worked with Mary Graybiel. The Mission began other schools for boys, girls, and women at Gol Bazaar and Chata over the next few years.[27]

Between 1893 and 1907, the FCMS and CWBM opened eleven new stations in the United and Central Provinces, sending an additional fifty-nine missionaries, thirty-six of whom remained in India for twenty years or more.[28] In the midst of this expansion, a severe famine killed an estimated three million people in the Central and United Provinces between 1896 and 1901. Unable to meet the massive need for care of orphans, the Disciples Mission was forced to send children from its orphanages at Bilaspur, Mahoba, Deoghar, and Damoh to other Christian missions. This experience created a positive attitude toward ecumenical cooperation among the missionaries, expressed in an 1889 *Christian Standard* article by William Forrest, though insisting that the missionaries remained committed to the distinctive beliefs and practices of the Stone-Campbell Movement.[29] Publicity given to the famine resulted in increased financial support for the mission, with the *Christian Herald,* the *Christian Standard,* and the *Bible Advocate* helping raise funds. The mission's famine relief work also greatly improved its relationship with the Indian people. W. E. Rambo (1861-1932), who established the boys' orphanage at Damoh in 1895, recalled that "when we moved in the people hooted us in the street and tried to keep us out. After the famine, they knew us in the remotest villages and welcomed us as friends who saved life when there was none to deliver."[30]

The tragedy of the famine clearly strengthened the mission and ensured its survival. Yet, in the view of some, it proved to be an ambiguous legacy. The orphanages and schools became the main work of the Mission, resulting in the institutionalization of mission stations. Former Disciples missionary to India, Donald McGavran, would later criticize this development, arguing that concentration on relief work by Christian missions generally came at the expense of preaching the gospel.[31]

The work of George (1870-1932) and Virginia (1865-1954) Brown illustrates the effectiveness of many of the missionaries. In 1903, George began pressing the need for a school to train indigenous helpers. In less than two years Stone-Campbell churches raised over $25,000 to purchase land and open Jabalpur Bible College. Brown established the mission's first printing press in Jabalpur in 1904 and began publishing the Hindi-English *Sahayak Patrika* (*The Christian Helper*). The press also served the printing needs of several other Protestant missions in the city, with all profits supporting the Mission's work. The Browns administered the Bible College and ran the mission press until their retirement in 1917.[32] By 1907 the mission included twelve churches with a combined membership of nearly 1,400. Sunday schools and day schools provided instruction to over 6,000 students, and orphanages cared for nearly 650 children.

The growth of the India Mission prompted leaders to begin moving more decisively toward indigenization. In 1909 they organized the Indian Christian Missionary Society, a "home missions" board composed of both missionaries and Indian Christians supported entirely by the Indian churches. The society opened work in Kotah north of Bilaspur and in several other villages, caring for orphans, supporting new Christians disowned by their families and castes, and teaching agricultural and industrial skills.[33] Further moves toward indigenization occurred in 1912 when the FCMS and CWBM consolidated their work and property in India, creating a joint advisory committee to administer the mission. In 1915, the India Disciples Church Council, composed of equal numbers of missionaries and Indian leaders, assumed leadership of the mission.

Two of the most visible Indian leaders were Hira Lal (1875-1955) and his wife Sunarin Bai (d. 1952). A product of the mission school at Mungeli, Hira Lal was baptized in 1891, and Sunarin shortly afterward. For many years, he served as senior assistant in the hospital in Mungeli, and during the absence of missionary physicians administered it himself. He was also an effective village evangelist, largely because he ignored caste distinctions. The mission ordained him in 1917, and Sunarin Bai worked with the Bible women in Mungeli.[34]

The Conference of the Australian Churches of Christ began expressing interest in foreign missions in response to an 1890 visit from G. L. Wharton. Support, however, came almost entirely from individuals and congregations rather than the Conference. The first missionary from Australia was Mary Thompson, who left for India in 1891. South Australian women's groups supported the training of Yakub Masih and Nathoo Lal as evangelists. Henry H. Strutton and his wife arrived in 1895 to work with the Poona and Indian Village Mission (PIVM), with several other long-term missionaries from Australia joining them before 1920: Florence Cameron, Roy and Ethel Coventry, Elsie Caldicott, Vera Blake, and Tom and Flora Escott. Each served in India for more than twenty-five years.[35]

The Foreign Missionary Committee (FMC) of the British Churches of Christ began work in India in 1909, when they acquired a mission in Daltonganj, Palamau, begun by Paul Singh, an Indian pastor in the Methodist Episcopal Church. Singh had been converted to Churches of Christ by R. H. Parker, a medical missionary in the Central Provinces. The Daltonganj mission recognized the need to provide industrial training and work for converts from the higher castes since they often lost their employment and social support.

Parker later traveled to Melbourne, Australia, where he persuaded G. P. Pittman and his wife to go as missionaries to India. By 1911, several Australian churches were supporting the FMC mission in Daltonganj, contributing primarily to the support of indigenous evangelists.[36] By late 1912, the FMC had opened a second station at Garhwa, twenty miles from Daltonganj, directed by Paul Singh and his wife. A third followed at Latehar for work among the aboriginal Oraous.[37]

Most Stone-Campbell women missionaries in India relied on Bible women to help with a variety of tasks, especially the zenana work. Missionary Bessie Madsen is pictured here with Bible women in 1921.

In 1914 the London Missionary Society (LMS) offered the FMC a mission station at Dudhi, which the Pittmans moved to oversee. The FMC sent A.C. Watters and his wife, who had been training to go to Africa, to assume leadership of the Daltonganj Mission. The LMS had worked in Dudhi more than fifty years, and the Christians there were reluctant to accept the "new" teachings of the British Churches of Christ regarding baptism and the Lord's Supper. Though the LMS missionaries helped smooth the transition, pastor Jhunga Babu left the Dudhi Mission, apparently in protest over the new teachings.[38]

Direct support missionaries who worked apart from the missionary agencies were also in India before 1920. Edward S. Jelley (1878-1962), who had served as a Holiness missionary in India in the late 1890s, became part of Churches of Christ in Vancouver, British Columbia, sometime before 1911. Early that year he responded to a call for missionaries in the *Gospel Advocate* and received a hearty endorsement from editor J. C. McQuiddy (1858-1924). As a result, a number of congregations in California, Texas, and Vancouver pledged their support to Jelley, his wife Theodora, and their children. They arrived in Bombay in August 1911.[39]

Jelley preached and established churches along with several Indian evangelists, especially Marawat Rao and R. K. Pardhe, primarily in Ahmednagar in the Bombay Presidency. By early 1913, the mission reported twelve churches and more than 1,200 baptisms. Because the Jelleys believed that "the establishment of a school is equivalent to the establishment of a church," they began an education mission in Bombay and a number of surrounding villages. The Mangs—a lower caste with little access to education—responded eagerly to this offer of Western education. Jelley made it clear that conversion to Christianity was not a prerequisite to receiving an education from the mission.[40]

Three additional couples joined the Jelleys in the early years of their work. Dr. Salini Armstrong-Hopkins and her husband George (1855-1918) had been pioneer Methodist missionaries in India for twenty-five years. They joined the Jelleys in 1912, but were never able to raise adequate financial support from Stone-Campbell churches. By 1916 they began accepting support from other denominations. George Armstrong-Hopkins died in 1918, and his wife retired shortly afterward. W. Hume (b. 1890) and Nora McHenry joined the Jelleys in 1914, and S. O. and Alice Martin in 1916. The three couples continued to build the mission, establishing a printing press and doing evangelistic work among Indian soldiers in the British army during World War I.[41]

In 1916, a doctrinal conflict broke out between Jelley and the other missionaries that reflected a growing premillennial controversy among U.S. Churches of Christ. The McHenrys and Martins held premillennial views of the second coming of Christ, a view Jelley strongly opposed. The McHenrys and Martins accused Jelley of treating them in ways that showed he was morally unfit for the mission field. Though the editors of the *Gospel Advocate* investigated the accusations and exonerated Jelley in 1918, editorial endorsements and reports of his work virtually disappeared from the periodicals. By 1919, the McHenrys and the Martins had joined the Seventh Day Adventist Church and begun working in its Bombay mission.[42] Financial support for the Jelleys dried up. Exhausted and embittered, the Jelleys had to pay their own way to return to the United States for a furlough in 1923.[43] Jelley appealed to readers of the *Christian Standard* and received enough support to continue working in India until 1933.[44]

When they converted to Christianity in 1891, Hira Lal and Sunarin Bai experienced great opposition from their higher caste Hindu families. Thirty years later the majority of members in the mission's church at Mungeli were their relatives.

When George Desha and his wife arrived in India in 1925 as new missionaries from U.S. Churches of Christ, they expected to find three thousand members in at least a dozen churches and several schools in and around Bombay. They discovered, however, that two Indian evangelists who supposedly had been sustaining the Jelleys' mission apparently were defrauding the supporting congregations. The Deshas moved across the subcontinent to Darjeeling in hopes of establishing "an entirely new field not afflicted with certain disadvantages inherited from the past." Before they could begin a lasting

work, however, poor health forced them to return to the United States in 1927. North American Churches of Christ would send no other missionaries to India until after World War II.[45]

Japan

In 1873, the reform-minded Meiji government rescinded a 250-year-old edict outlawing Christianity in Japan. Though Protestant missionaries had entered Okinawa as early as 1846 and the mainland in 1859, this opening of Japan to outside contact led British and North American mission agencies to send significant numbers of missionaries beginning in the 1880s. The FCMS sent George T. (1843-1920) and Josephine (1850-1885) Smith, and Charles E. (1853-1898) and Laura (1861-1925) Garst to Yokohama in October, 1883. After their arrival, the Smiths and Garsts spent several months collaborating with other missionaries and learning Japanese, then settled in Akita, a city of 40,000 on the northwestern coast of Honshu, Japan's main island.

Baptist missionary Thomas Pratt Poate and his Japanese associate Kudo San "smoothed the path for them many times and assisted them in their preaching and teaching." Since they and Poate were the only Protestant workers in the area, they struck an informal comity agreement for evangelizing the northern region of Honshu: the Baptists would focus on the east, the Disciples on the west.[46] The missionaries perceived the people as largely indifferent to their message. Still, they baptized their first converts in 1884—Matsumura San and Ino Funasaka—and by 1889, had organized a church in Akita. George Smith, Charles Garst, and Kudo San itinerated throughout northern Honshu, preaching and distributing tracts. In 1888, they opened outstations in Tsuruoka, ninety miles south of Akita, and at Innai, where a group of converts who were miners met daily to read and discuss the Scriptures. Eventually the mission had over a dozen outstations. Six additional missionaries arrived before 1890, establishing seven small churches and opening a school for training Japanese evangelists in Akita.[47]

By the late 1880s, however, opposition to the Churches of Christ Mission in Japan (CCJM) began to develop. The Meiji government's efforts to reshape the empire's political and economic life to resemble that of Western powers provoked resistance by many Japanese, especially in rural areas. A nationalist movement arose to foster Japanese unity and patriotism and to resist Western colonialism, including Christianity. FCMS president Archibald McLean explained that the Japanese viewed

Christianity as "a foreign religion," making it appear "unpatriotic for them to forsake the faith of their fathers and to become Christians."[48] CCJM and other Christian missions became targets of vandalism, slander in the press (including the appellation "Jesus dogs"), and persecution of converts.[49]

In 1890, the CCJM relocated from Akita to Tokyo, partly because of the opposition. Leaders believed they would be more successful among students in the capital as the imperial university system developed. The work in Akita continued under Japanese leadership until Sherman (1861-1921) and Dr. Nina Asbury Stevens (1866-1951) Wells resumed leadership of the work in 1895. The mission also opened centers in Honshu in the Fukushima district between Akita and Tokyo and in Osaka in the southwest. By 1899 the mission reported a membership of six hundred eleven with seven preachers and three Bible women.[50]

The second Stone-Campbell mission effort in Japan began in 1892 when W. K. Azbill assembled a group to work in Tokyo. Though Azbill did not oppose missionary societies, to gain support from congregations

that did oppose them he raised funds from churches and individuals that went directly to the missionaries. A Japanese Christian who had studied in the United States, Kakujiro Ishikawa, was part of the group and served as translator and occasional preacher. While Abzill was occupied with raising funds, three single women—Lucia Scott, Carme Hostetter, and Alice Miller—laid the foundation of what would become the Yotsuya Mission, the first lasting direct-support mission of the Stone-Campbell Movement.[51]

Among this group of missionaries was John Moody McCaleb (1861-1953). Soon after arriving in Tokyo McCaleb, who unlike Azbill did have strong objections to missionary societies, parted ways with the rest of the group because Azbill had accepted money from an Ohio church that also supported the FCMS. To this violation of conscience was added McCaleb's unhappiness with Azbill's constant appeals for money to churches in Britain and the United States. McCaleb believed missionaries should be satisfied with whatever churches and individuals contributed, and he supplemented his funds by teaching English and operating a farm.

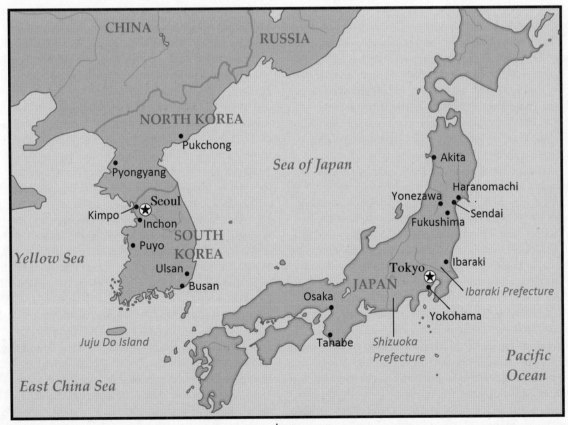

Japan

This, he believed, was the model of missionary work described in the New Testament, though eventually he accepted regular support from Churches of Christ in Kentucky and Tennessee.[52] McCaleb was one of the first international missionaries who identified with North American Churches of Christ.

Once the CCJM relocated to Tokyo, it developed a strong education ministry, led for almost twenty years by experienced teachers Lavenia Oldham (1862-1927) and Mary Rioch (d. 1957). The two operated "charity schools" in the slums of Tokyo for poor and orphaned children who could not afford to attend government schools. They also taught English and Bible classes for male students at nearby Tokyo Senmon Gakko (now Waseda University), introducing many future Japanese leaders to the CCJM.[53]

Between 1900 and 1909, the FCMS sent at least twenty-four additional missionaries to Japan, mostly to expand the educational work. With a generous bequest from Francis Morton Drake (1830-1903), the mission opened Seigakuin Shingakko, later known as Seigakuin Seminary, in Takinogawa, a suburb of Tokyo, in 1903. Known in English as Drake Bible College, the school offered a four-year course to educate church leaders like its namesake in Des Moines, Iowa. Rollin McCoy (1878-1959) served as dean and professor between 1907 and 1923, when the college merged with the Methodist Aoyama Gakuin Seminary. After World War II, this school merged with several others to become Tokyo Union Theological Seminary. The Japanese members of the Drake faculty included Kakujiro Ishikawa and Frank Naotaro Otsuka, the latter with degrees from Bethany College, Yale, and the University of Chicago.[54]

Perhaps the most influential general educational institution of the CCJM was the Joshi Sei Gakuin, called in English the Margaret K. Long Girls' School, begun in 1905. By 1920, the school was considered one of the best in Japan.[55] The mission had also established a successful Boys' School in 1906.[56] Missionaries established other schools in Fukushima and Osaka, as well as the Asakusa (East Tokyo) Institute which also provided social and religious services in a depressed part of the city.[57]

In 1906, the CCJM began publishing the monthly *Japan Harbinger*. Printed in English with occasional material in Japanese, the paper reported the mission's work to potential supporters in the United States and Canada. Each issue contained missionary reports by both FCMS-supported and direct support missionaries, articles by Japanese leaders, and news from congregations and mission stations. The paper also championed union

efforts being discussed among Protestant missions in Japan. Rose Theresa Armbruster (1875-1950), long-time editor of the paper, wrote in 1906, "We are hoping and praying that thru the Holy Spirit's guidance such a union work may be established in Japan and all the separate elements be welded into the 'Church of Christ in Japan.'"[58]

Also in 1906, the McCaleb mission began the Zoshigaya Gakuin, a boarding school in central Tokyo that taught English and Christianity to nearly two hundred students. At least fourteen Japanese workers assisted the missionaries. In addition, McCaleb, C. G. Vincent and Yunosuke Hiratsuka edited an English language periodical titled *Missionary Messenger* from July 1913 to May/June 1923.[59] McCaleb and his colleagues had established twenty-one small house churches throughout Tokyo by 1920, in cooperation with at least two dozen missionaries from Churches of Christ in the U. S., Canada, and Australia.[60]

One characteristic of McCaleb's work was a reluctance to permit Japanese leaders to assume significant responsibilities. McCaleb and his colleagues suspected that many in Protestant missions had "converted" to benefit from educational opportunities provided at the mission schools. The fact that many converts seemed to have no strong theological convictions and evangelists often left their work for better-paying government jobs seemed to corroborate their suspicions.[61] One Japanese Christian who did rise to leadership was Yunosuke Hiratsuka (1873-1953). Hiratsuka had studied English under McCaleb in Tokyo and was baptized by him in 1895. After working briefly with Presbyterian Churches in San Francisco and Salinas, California, as well as a Japanese YMCA in San Francisco, Hiratsuka returned to Japan in 1903. McCaleb's associate William J. Bishop (1872-1913), who seemed more open to encouraging Japanese leadership than McCaleb, quickly invited Hiratsuka to preach for the Kamitonizaka Church of Christ, where he served for more than forty years. Hiratsuka became one of the most influential leaders in Japanese Churches of Christ before World War II.[62]

William D. (1864-1936) and Emily (1873-1953) Cunningham eventually assumed leadership of the Yotsuya Mission begun by Azbill volunteers Lucia Scott, Carme Hostetter, and Alice Miller, developing it into one of the most successful direct-support missions in the history of the Stone-Campbell Movement. In 1899, shortly before they were to go to Japan as FCMS missionaries, William was diagnosed with polio. As a result, the Society deemed him unfit for foreign service.

The CWBM also refused to sponsor the Cunninghams, citing lack of resources. Nevertheless, they arrived in Tokyo in October 1901, supported by a number of churches and individuals. Within a month, they began publishing the monthly *Tokyo Christian*, organizing churches, conducting schools, and developing service organizations. [63]

Despite their earlier difficulties with the missionary societies, the Cunninghams maintained a positive working relationship with the FCMS missionaries. "We have entertained none but the kindliest feelings for all the members of the Board and desire that our friends should do the same."[64] They also developed a positive working relationship with those working with McCaleb. The Cunninghams were impatient with anyone who provoked conflict between "organized" and direct support work. "Yes, I believe in organized work," he wrote, "not because it is organized, but because it is work…It's the Lord's work that claims my first attention and I have no time to waste in quarrelling over the method of doing it."[65]

Yunosuke Hiratsuka (left), minister for Kamitomizaka Church of Christ in Tokyo, with I. Kamikura and T. Yokoo, who served with him as elders of the congregation. J. M. McCaleb left funds with Hiratsuka to care for Churches of Christ missionaries Lillie Cypert and Sarah Andrews and Disciples missionary Grace Farnham, three who remained in Japan during World War II. (Don Carlos Janes, *Our World Tour*, 1924)

By 1920 the Stone-Campbell Movement sustained three substantial mission efforts in Japan: the CCJM supported by the FCMS, the direct support Yotsuya Mission begun by W. K. Azbill, and the work of J. M. McCaleb and others from Churches of Christ in the United States, Canada, and Australia. Each had dozens of missionaries who preached, began churches, and established schools and other ministries. And while each maintained its own work, the missions operated in relative harmony.

China

In 1886, the Foreign Christian Missionary Society sent Canadian physician William Macklin (1860-1947) to establish the China Mission—the third of the non-Christian nations targeted in 1881. After settling in Nanjing, Macklin immediately called for additional workers. Edwin P. Hearnden (d. 1896) and Albert F. H. Saw (1865-1898) of the Christian Association in Britain, also supported by the FCMS, joined him that same year. Two additional couples from the United States—Frank Eugene (1851-1915) and Martha Redford (1865-1935) Meigs, and Edward Thomas (1854-1944) and Carrie Loos (1856-1892) Williams—arrived in early 1887. For their first two years the seven missionaries studied the languages and customs of the people while living in an abandoned Buddhist temple they renamed Thistle Abbey.[66]

By 1888, the China Mission had implemented a division of labor. Macklin provided medical care, becoming particularly well known for his success in treating opium addiction. Because of their mastery of Chinese languages, the Williamses took primary responsibility for evangelistic work, preaching regularly in Drum Tower, South Gate, and Hsiakwan.[67] Hearnden and Saw opened a second station in Chuchow, forty miles northwest of Nanjing. The Meigs began a boarding school for boys that by 1891 developed into the Jidu Shuyuan, or "Christian College." When Charles and Lily Molland arrived in 1889, they opened a third station at Wuhu, sixty miles southwest of Nanjing. A year later James Ware opened a fourth station at Shanghai. Rosa Tonkin, former Secretary of the South Australian Overseas Missions Committee and supported by the Australian Churches of Christ, joined him in 1901. Tonkin worked until 1920 with factory workers in Shanghai, particularly women and children.[68]

Sentiment against foreigners had been growing in China since the middle of the nineteenth century. A series of treaties with Western powers had forced China to allow Christian missionary activity, legalize the opium trade, and grant political and economic control of key port cities to European colonizers. To many

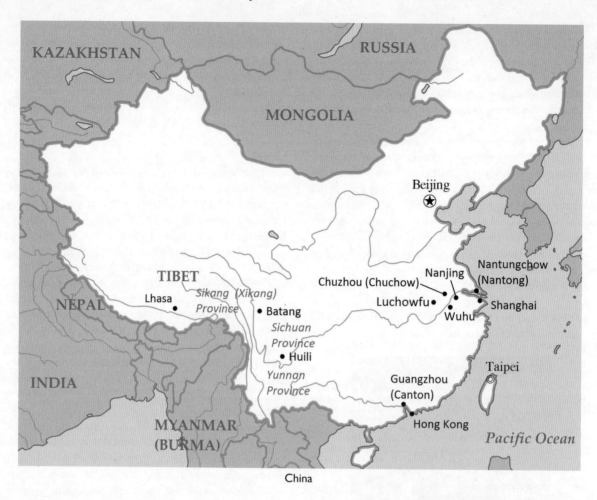

China

Chinese, missionaries were an example of unwanted foreign intrusion.[69] In 1890, the China Mission planned a dedication for the new medical clinic and chapel in Drum Tower at Nanjing. A large mob gathered outside the chapel and before Chinese soldiers could disperse the crowd, rioters had torn down the doors and pelted the missionaries with stones. Later that day, another mob gathered outside the clinic, but soldiers arrived before violence broke out. Opposition was strongest in Chuchow, where locals posted signs threatening those who sent their children to the mission's day schools, attempted to burn down mission property, and assaulted the missionaries when they appeared in public.[70]

Despite the opposition, the China Mission baptized its first convert in 1888. Shi Kwei-biao was a travelling story-teller and actor who lived in a small village outside of Chuchow. He had heard the gospel years earlier, but an opium addiction had kept him from deciding to become a Christian. After trying seven times, Shi finally

completed Macklin's addiction treatment program and soon began to serve the China Mission as one of its most effective evangelists. FCMS executive Archibald McLean wrote of Shi in 1919, "When he began his ministry, the people who knew his career before his conversion spat on his clothes and in his face; now, when it is known that he is to preach in the same places, it is necessary to have a succession of services to accommodate the crowds who wish to hear him."[71] Shi worked in the Mission until his death in 1925.

The extensive medical outreach of the China Mission significantly lessened prejudice against the missionaries. In addition to Macklin, twelve other medical missionaries served in China before 1920, some for more than twenty-five years.[72] Still, opposition to Christianity remained. The Boxer Uprising of 1898-1901 was an attempt by Chinese nationalists to drive Western people and culture from China. Fomented by Empress Dowager Cixi, fighters who believed themselves impervious to bullets led the rebellion. Christians bore the brunt of the Boxers' attack: almost two thousand Protestant and thirty thousand Catholic Chinese were killed during the uprising, in addition to at least one hundred eighty-eight Protestant missionaries and family members, and almost fifty Catholic bishops, priests, and sisters.[73] Though the Uprising did not take place in areas of Disciples work, missionaries in the lower Yangtze Valley evacuated to Shanghai until the Uprising was over, leaving local officials to protect the stations.[74]

Shi Kwei-biao (right) became one of the most effective evangelists of the China Mission. His wife, Shi Kwei-plao (left), was known as the "Dorcas" of her village because of her skill in making and selling clothes to support the work of the churches around Chuchow. (Elliot Osgood, *Breaking Down Chinese Walls,* 1908)

Sun Yat-sen's republican revolution of 1911-1912, brought fighting to the entire country, including Nanjing. Revolutionary forces attacked the city, which was defended by six thousand Imperial troops. When the Imperial leader sent two hundred of his wounded to Macklin's hospital, the doctor urged him to evacuate and retreat northward to stop further destruction of the city and loss of innocent lives. Macklin, along with FCMS missionary Frank Garrett and a companion, slipped through the lines and obtained the promise from the invading forces that they would protect the city from looting if the Imperial commander withdrew. When the commander and his troops fled northward on December 1, 1911, the task of surrendering the city fell to Macklin

and his fellow missionaries. When the retreating Imperial army arrived in Chuchow, another FCMS missionary, Dr. E. I. Osgood, was instrumental in negotiating peace and convincing the forces not to enter the city.[75]

By the 1920s the Stone-Campbell Movement could claim several significant achievements in China. In Nanjing the mission had established three churches and three stations. It also operated six primary and secondary schools and two major health care facilities. In addition, missionaries helped form four major educational institutions through ecumenical work with other denominations, including the University of Nanjing, Nanjing Theological Seminary, the Bible Teachers' Training School for Women, and Ginling College for Women.[76] Missionaries also established churches, schools, and hospitals in Chuchow, Wuhu, and Nantong.[77]

From the beginning, Chinese converts worked closely with the missionaries. In addition to Shi Kwei-biao was Peng Yang-Hwa, who had converted at age sixty-one and spent the next twenty-five years evangelizing. Chen His-ren, one of the first two graduates of the Nanjing Christian Girls' School in June 1905, taught at the school for almost thirty years, influencing two thousand girls for Christian leadership. Chang Li-Seng, a pastor trained at the Bible Institute in Nanjing, was instrumental in leading a revival in Chuchow in 1908.[78]

Nevertheless, until 1921 authority was vested almost entirely in the missionaries. Organized in station groups, an annual convention established in 1889, and a seven-member Advisory Committee that functioned between convention meetings, the missionaries made all decisions about the mission's work under the authority of the FCMS. Though the missionaries helped form a convention for Chinese Disciples, the two had little interaction. In 1912 the missionaries began sharing their convention minutes with the Chinese convention, and the following year, Chinese leader Li Hou-fu began meeting with the Advisory Committee. In 1919 missionaries reconfigured the Advisory Committee to include three Chinese elected by the Chinese convention. Still, the missionaries remained in control.[79]

From 1921 to 1924 the missionaries began to implement a more equitable arrangement, abolishing the two separate conventions and establishing a new convention and administrative committee of which both Chinese and missionaries were members. Any member of a Stone-Campbell congregation in China would be eligible for a position in the new structure. The churches selected the administrative committee, composed of equal numbers of Chinese and missionaries. Beginning in 1925, missionary Edwin Marx and the first Chinese secretary of the mission, Li Hou-fu, shared administrative responsibility.[80]

Evangelist Koh Luen-pu assisted Chang Li-Seng in leading the 1908 revival in Chuchow. Pictured here with his wife "Esther" and one of their children. (Elliot Osgood, *Breaking Down Chinese Walls*, 1908)

Tibet

Canadian physician Susie Rijnhart (1868-1908) and her husband Petrus reached Tibet in 1894 as direct support missionaries sponsored by the newly formed Cecil Street Church of Christ in Toronto. For three years they provided medical care to the people in Lanzhou, and learned the languages and customs of the peoples of the Qinghai Province. In 1898 they began an ill-fated journey to the Tibetan capital, Lhasa, during which their ten-month-old child died, robbers attacked their caravan, and their Sherpa guides abandoned them. Shortly afterward, Petrus mysteriously disappeared while looking for help. With assistance from the interdenominational China Inland Mission, Dr. Rijnhart returned to Canada in 1901, where she published an account of her ordeal and lectured to raise support for a renewed Tibetan mission.[81]

In 1903, the FCMS began support of Dr. Rijnhart, along with Dr. Albert (1875-1922) and Flora Shelton. Initially, they established a station at Tachienlu, in the Sichuan Province, not far from the China Inland Mission. Dr. Rijnhart soon resigned because of poor health, but the Sheltons continued for three more years, learning

languages and providing medical care. In 1906, James and Minnie Ogden joined the mission, and two years later they all relocated further inland to the town of Batang where they were joined by Harold and Josephine Baker. Though the local lamas—politically powerful Buddhist monks—resented this foreign intrusion, Chinese occupation of the province three years earlier made FCMS entry into Tibet possible.[82]

Shelton immediately established a hospital, which was for many Tibetans the only medical facility with a formally trained physician within a month's journey. The mission also opened a day school and an orphanage. The Tibetan Christian Mission operated in Batang until 1911 when severe fighting between Tibetan and Chinese forces compelled the missionaries to abandon the mission temporarily. The fall of China's Qing Dynasty inspired Tibetan guerillas to fight even more fiercely to drive out Chinese occupying forces.

Dr. Albert Shelton developed close relationships with Tibetan Buddhist leaders who eventually supported his medical work in Batang. Here Shelton meets with the local lama about 1920. (Flora Shelton, *Shelton of Tibet*, 1923)

When the missionaries returned to Batang in 1914, they found their facilities in ruins, requiring them to spend the next few years reestablishing the mission.[83] By 1920, the hospital, Christian day school, and orphanage had resumed full operation under the direction of five missionary couples, and a church of twenty-five members worshipped each Sunday. Government travel restrictions on the missionaries gradually eased, and they began making long journeys into the villages surrounding Batang.[84]

In 1918 the Dalai Lama surprisingly granted permission to the Tibetan Christian Mission to open a second station at Chamdo, halfway between Batang and Lhasa. For more than six months, at the request of a Tibetan army general, Shelton had been making occasional trips to Chamdo to provide medical services to injured Tibetans and Chinese. In addition he taught basic medical skills, preached, and distributed tracts.[85] The Dalai Lama even appeared open to Shelton's doing medical work in the capital. He wrote to supporters in 1919, "Our prospects were never so bright as they are today."[86]

Burma and Thailand

Following the Third Anglo-Burmese War in 1885, all of Burma came under British colonial rule as a province of British India. Though European influence—especially British—was strong in neighboring Thailand, it was not under direct colonial rule. Protestant missionaries had worked in Southeast Asia since the early nineteenth century, but the expansion of British colonialism increased missionary activity. The Stone-Campbell Movement arrived in Burma and Thailand as a direct consequence of these developments.[87]

In 1892, the Foreign Missionary Committee of the British Churches of Christ began work in Burma. Robert (1864-1933) and Agnes (d. 1894) Halliday, and A. E. Hudson established a mission at Ye, a seaport and major train terminal in Tenasserim province. They began an English school and offered basic medical care, and Robert Halliday became an expert in the Mon language of the local Talaing people. The missionaries of the FMC

Burma, Thailand, and Singapore

received help from the long-established American Baptist Mission, which was at the time no longer working at Ye.

Hudson baptized the mission's first convert in February 1895. In June he wrote, "These natives will not be won by harshly crying down Buddhism, or the religion of their ancestors…There is no weapon that touches the heart and conscience as the story of redemption through the blood of [Christ's] cross."[88] In 1896 Halliday began translating the Bible into the Mon language, completing the Psalms in 1905. Mon Christians assisted with language study, translation, and evangelism, but even after ten years of labor, the Burma Mission remained small.[89]

Between 1900 and 1905, additional missionaries arrived at Ye, and the Committee reorganized the work into three areas. Halliday directed evangelism with the assistance of Mon preachers Ko Win, Saya Kori (also associated with the American Baptist Mission), and Le He. G. F. Munro directed general education efforts, establishing a boarding school with sixty students and four Mon teachers. Finally, John Wood led a program to teach the Mon people improved agricultural skills.[90]

Though growing in staff and service, the Burma mission at Ye suffered from several problems. Opposition from phongyi—politically powerful Buddhist monks—made local people reluctant to associate with the mission. Some in the British churches began questioning whether the mission's results were worth the high cost. In response Halliday accused the FMC of failing to trust the missionaries to organize the work. In addition, the American Baptist mission had begun to expand work in the area, restricting the British Mission's expansion. Finally, in 1907, the British colonial government raised educational standards so that the mission schools were not able to gain government approval.[91]

Between 1908 and 1910, the FMC considered opening a new work among the Talaing people nearer Moulmein to the North of Ye. After a report from Halliday, who had spent several months in Siam (Thailand) on his return from furlough in 1910, the FMC decided to suspend their work in Ye. Though Ko Win, the "old and respected pastor of the church," assumed leadership, he died a year later. In 1912 the American Baptists agreed to take responsibility for the mission at Ye, and within three years, the FMC deeded them the mission property.[92]

As early as 1903 the FMC had begun work across the border in Phrapatom (now known as Nakhon Pathom), situated in northwest Siam, where the Talaing people also lived. Alfred Hudson and Percy Clark (1879-1957) used a motor boat, the *Dayspring*, to reach villages, a method they had used in Burma.[93] For almost fifty years, Clark and his wife Mary provided medical care, taught school, evangelized, and organized churches among the ethnically mixed Mon, Thai, and Chinese people. Percy also served for many years as president of the National Christian Council of Churches in Thailand. Interned in prisoner of war camps during World War II, the Clarks earned the esteem of Thai officials, with Percy eventually holding important government positions.[94]

By 1910, the mission had organized congregations and schools in the provincial cities of Nakon Choom and Phra Pathom. Native evangelists Chun Kwang and Ki Hong assisted Percy Clark in leading the churches, while Mary Clark and two native teachers—Boon Nak and Me Woo—taught in boarding schools in each station. Medical work also became an important part of the mission, with Clark administering over one thousand treatments annually by 1910, especially during outbreaks of cholera, yellow fever, and bubonic plague.[95]

In 1913, just before the FMC transferred the Burma mission at Ye to the American Baptists, the Hallidays joined the Clarks, in Thailand. The Clarks led the work among the Thai and Chinese, continuing their holistic approach of evangelistic and pastoral work, education, and medical services. By contrast, the Hallidays led the work among the Mons, focusing exclusively on evangelism. Two Mon evangelists at Ye—Mg Phe and Mg Shwe Diak—followed the Hallidays to Thailand and with the Clarks developed a lasting mission among the people of central Thailand.[96]

At the outbreak of World War I, Siamese King Vajiravudh (1881-1925) aligned his kingdom with the Allied Powers partly because of foreign pressure. He removed German and Austrian officials from leadership positions in industry, education, and finance, and instituted a draft to build a Thai unit to serve in Europe. These unpopular decisions fueled anti-European nationalism that impacted all aspects of Thai life, including Protestant missions. Church membership in the mission fluctuated, financial support diminished, and Thai Christians sometimes regarded missionary personnel with suspicion.[97]

Nevertheless, the Thailand mission continued to grow slowly. Before 1920, the congregation at Nakon Choom divided into two churches, one Siamese and the other Chinese, each with its own native pastor. Although they conducted separate Bible studies, they worshipped together as one church in both Mandarin Chinese and Thai. Two new congregations developed out of "prayer rooms" established in Tah Moang and

Tah Rua, villages near Nakon Choom. Though these congregations remained small, they were important witnesses to the work of the Clarks and the mission's Thai evangelists. Medical treatments provided at the Nakon Choom dispensary grew dramatically because of Clark's growing reputation and the worldwide influenza pandemic of 1918-1919.[98] Evangelism among the Mon people continued, and in the 1910s the Hallidays and their indigenous co-workers published a Mon translation of the Old Testament—a major contribution to the publication in 1928 of the Mon Bible.[99]

Philippines

The Philippine Revolution against Spanish colonialism begun in 1896 had lasted almost two years when the United States, already moving toward war with Spain in the Caribbean, aligned itself with the revolutionaries. When the Spanish-American War ended in 1898, however, the coalition broke down and the Philippine-American War raged for three more years. Finally, after a brutal campaign, most Filipino revolutionaries surrendered in 1901 and swore allegiance to the United States. The new U.S.-dominated government quickly abolished slavery and ended Catholicism as the state religion[100]

The opening of the Philippines to Protestant missions prompted Herman Williams (1872-1958), a chaplain during the Philippine-American War, to convince the FCMS to send him and his wife back to the islands as missionaries. The FCMS also sent W. H. (1872-1948) and Elinor (1876-1947) Hanna. Arriving in 1901, the couples settled first in Manila and for two years worked primarily among United States servicemen and English-speaking Filipinos.[101]

Before the FCMS missionaries arrived, however, three Protestant missionary societies had formed the Evangelical Union of the Philippines and partitioned the islands into comity areas. Manila already had stations supported by Episcopal, Presbyterian, and United Brethren societies. Because of this, in 1903 the Williamses and Hannas moved to Laoag in the north of the island of Luzon and began learning the Ilocano language.[102]

Other FCMS supported missionaries quickly followed, and by 1910 they had established four Filipino mission stations. Drs. Cyrus (1869-1956) and Leta (1874-1928) Pickett took over the Laoag work in 1904, establishing a medical mission that became the Sally Read Memorial Hospital in 1913. The Williamses relocated to Vigan, fifty miles to the south, establishing a mission press in 1906 to print periodicals, tracts, educational materials,

and Ilocano Bibles. Bruce (1871-1949) and Ethel (1874-1967) Kershner arrived in 1905 to reestablish the station in Manila, serving both United States servicemen and teaching in a Bible training school that, in 1916, became the Albert Allen Memorial Bible College. Leslie (1876-1945) and Carrie (1882-1966) Wolfe joined the Kershners in Manila in 1907. The missionaries established a fourth station in Aparri in 1906, where Filipino workers were in charge from the beginning.

Because the islands were not involved in World War I, the Philippine Mission continued to grow during the 1910s. Medical work expanded in 1911-1912, when Drs. W. N. Lemmon (1872-1944) and L. Bruce Kline opened clinics at the Manila and Vigan stations that began nurses' training programs for Filipino women under the direction of Daisy Lemmon and Florence Kline. Eventually these clinics developed into the Mary Chiles Hospital (1914) in Manila and the Frank Dunn Memorial Hospital (1916) in Vigan. Two Filipino doctors—Dr. Isadore Santos of Manila and Dr. Domingo Samonte of Vigan—helped establish and administer these hospitals with the missionaries. Continuing their medical work in Laoag, the Picketts developed a successful treatment for

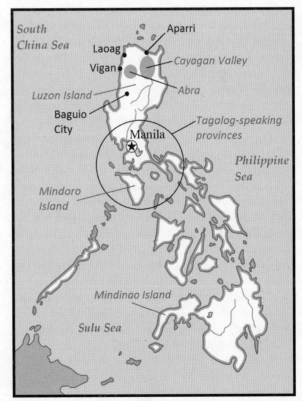

Philippines

"oriental yaws," a bacterial infection that causes painful lesions on the skin.[103]

In its 1910 report to the FCMS, Philippine Mission leaders listed forty-seven churches under the leadership of fourteen missionaries and more than eighty Filipino workers, with a total membership of 4,783.[104] The 1918 annual report listed eighty-three churches led by twenty-two missionaries and sixty-two Filipino workers, with a combined membership of 6,975, making the Philippine Mission one of the largest of the Stone-Campbell Movement.[105]

As the mission grew, Filipino Christians pushed for a greater role in leadership. When Stephen Corey (1873-1962), secretary of the FCMS, visited in 1914, Filipino leaders stressed their desire for "liberty, both in church and in matters of national government."[106] Beginning in 1916, missionaries expected Filipino evangelists to receive two years of study at Union Theological Seminary in Manila in addition to their Albert Allen Bible College training. In 1923, the Disciples missionaries closed the Bible College to merge its work completely with the Union Seminary, a cooperative effort of the Presbyterian, Methodist, and United Brethren missions.[107]

The 1920s was a golden era for the Disciples Philippine mission. Hospitals, men's and women's training institutes, and nursing schools were thriving. In 1922, twenty-five missionaries served the Islands, the largest number in the mission's history, and by 1924 the number of Filipino Disciples had reached 9,289. In keeping with the mission's stated goal of establishing indigenous churches, much of the teaching and evangelism was being done by Filipino Christians.[108]

Yet in the same decade the mission experienced two crises that would affect its development and that of the Disciples of Christ significantly. Both the FCMS and the CWBM had been part of comity agreements in their expanding international work, a policy continued by the United Christian Missionary Society, which in 1920 united the FCMS, the CWBM, and four other Disciples mission organizations. Though the Philippine Evangelical Union's comity arrangement had been finalized before Disciples arrived, they worked in harmony with the other mission churches. In 1923 through a formal agreement with the Methodist mission, Disciples received several churches in the Abra region and ceded Disciples churches in the Cagayan Valley to the Methodists.[109]

Leslie and Carrie Wolfe strongly opposed comity agreements that made any area off limits to Disciples missionaries. They also actively resisted the practice of

open membership, which they believed missionary E. K. Higdon (1887-1961) was practicing in the Taft Avenue Church in Manila and which they feared was implied in the comity agreement with the Methodist Church. In April 1925, nine Disciples missionaries wrote a formal petition to the UCMS for the recall of the Wolfes. The petition cited incompatibility, accused the couple of obstructing the plans of the majority of missionaries and of waging a campaign to turn the Filipino Christians

The indigenization of the Philippine Mission accelerated partly because well-educated Filipinos emerged as leaders. Emiliano Quigano, pictured here with his wife and daughters, held a responsible position in the colonial government and also served as pastor of a church in Manila. (*Missionary Intelligencer*, April 1915)

against them.[110]

Leslie Wolfe made an aggressive response, accusing the other missionaries of being sympathetic to open membership and attacking the decision to close the Albert Allen Bible College and collaborate with the Union Theological Seminary. The conflict escalated over the next year and became a cause célèbre in the United States, with the *Christian Standard* and a new publication titled *Touchstone* championing the cause of the Wolfes. In February 1926 the UCMS sent a "Commission to the Orient" to, among other things, investigate the controversy in the Philippines. Upon the recommendation of the Commission and approval by the 1926 General Convention at Memphis, the UCMS terminated the Wolfes' support.[111]

Conservative Disciples in the United States rallied to their support. The *Christian Standard* appealed for funds and the Christian Restoration Association, which coordinated missions conducted independently of the UCMS, served as the clearinghouse for donations. By the end of 1926 the Wolfes had secured sufficient funding to resume work in the Philippines, continuing until after World War II.[112] Many of the churches influenced by Wolfe in the Manila area identified with the new independent movement, marking a major rift in the Disciples mission.

The second crisis for the Disciples mission came in the form of the worldwide financial collapse in the late 1920s. The crash of the U.S. stock markets in October 1929 and the accompanying economic downturn led to a massive reduction in mission funding by all American mission agencies, including the UCMS. Ironically, the great success of the Disciples Philippine mission led the UCMS to assume that the churches there could continue without the level of support previously provided. By the early 1930s, no UCMS missionary was left, and mission properties had been either turned over to the local congregations or sold.[113]

New Hebrides

In the late nineteenth century Australian landowners brought thousands of Pacific Islanders to work on cotton and sugar plantations under conditions often no better than slavery. As early as the 1880s, John Thompson (1859-1945) began evangelistic work among the Kanaka—a somewhat pejorative term for Pacific Islanders—and in 1891 the Queensland Conference of the Australian Churches of Christ began supporting him. Soon he had established congregations in Doolbi, Cordalbor, and Childers, small towns in southeastern Queensland, and before the turn of the century, the Kanaka Mission claimed around two hundred members.[114]

In 1901, a series of laws forced the repatriation of most Pacific Islanders then living in Australia. Willie Tabimancon, one of John Thompson's earliest converts, returned home to Pentecost Island in the New Hebrides and established a mission in Ranwadi, conducting Bible classes every day and three times on Sunday. When Thompson arrived in 1903 in response to Tabimancon's appeals to the Queensland churches, he found fifty converts ready for baptism. Though Thompson contracted malaria and returned to Australia, he maintained contact with Tabimancon.[115]

Meanwhile, the Stone-Campbell Movement was developing on two other islands of the New Hebrides. As early as 1880, a former plantation worker named Manasseh and his son were conducting evangelistic work among the people of Aoba Island. Peter Pentecost, one of Tabimancon's early converts, joined them and by 1902 or 1903 they had established a small church in Amata.[116] With financial support from individuals, F. J. Purdy of the Australian Churches of Christ came to Aoba Island in 1906 to assist these indigenous leaders. Within five years, he reported that the island had fifty-three teachers working in the villages among a Christian community numbering at least four hundred members.[117] On Maewo Island, the beginnings of the Movement are less clear, but by 1900 there were as many as 2,000 members of Stone-Campbell churches there. In each case, Thompson, Purdy, and indigenous leaders cooperated with existing Protestant missions on the islands—especially those of the Presbyterian Church and the Plymouth Brethren—all of whom regarded one another as fellow evangelicals.[118] The Overseas Mission Board of the Australian Churches of Christ sent several missionaries to the New Hebrides before World War I.[119] With the death of Willie Tabimancon in 1918, the growth of the Stone-Campbell Movement on the New Hebrides (now Vanuatu) slowed until after World War II.

Liberia

Partly inspired by the story of Alexander Cross's mission to Liberia in 1854, a young African American named Jacob Kenoly (1876-1911) took up the work, first independently and then with the support of the CWBM. The oldest of thirteen children born to formerly enslaved parents, Kenoly was working as a porter in an Atlanta hotel when he met D. A. Brindle, a Georgia evangelist. With Brindle's encouragement, Kenoly began attending Southern Christian Institute and committed himself to go to Africa as a missionary. After his graduation in 1902, he preached in Georgia, Missouri, Oklahoma, and Arkansas, saving 20 percent of his income to finance his work in Africa. With no support other than what he had saved and raised, Kenoly landed in Monrovia in July 1905. Initially he worked as a cook and a carpenter, but eventually moved sixty miles outside of the capital to immerse himself in the culture and language of the indigenous Liberians. For more than a year he preached and conducted a village school for boys.[120]

Kenoly relocated to the coastal town of Schieffelin in 1906 after receiving two hundred acres of land from the government and some modest financial support from former teachers at Southern Christian Institute. Over the next five years he built a school eventually named the Liberian Christian Institute, organized a church and a temperance society, and preached among descendants of formerly enslaved persons from the United States and the indigenous people of Liberia. Impressed with his initiative and his accomplishments, the CWBM began supporting his work in 1908. Kenoly spent almost all of his annual salary of $300, however, to support the school and its students.[121]

Kenoly's school served as the heart of the Liberian Mission. He reported that most of the thirty to fifty students were indigenous Liberians whose parents brought them to his school because of his reputation for teaching them "civilized ways." In a typical day Kenoly taught primary classes in the morning, secondary classes in the afternoon, and then returned each evening for singing class and Bible study. In addition to teaching, Jacob and Ruth Kenoly fed, clothed, and provided medical care for all the students.[122]

Kenoly dreamed of sending students to further their education in the United States, especially at his alma mater, Southern Christian Institute. With the support of the CWBM and congregations familiar with Kenoly's work, at least three of his students graduated from SCI and returned to Liberia as missionaries.[123] One of these students, Jerome Freeman, returned in 1930 to establish the Jacob Kenoly Memorial Institute, a school similar to the one Kenoly himself had begun. Freeman continued to lead the Institute until it closed in the 1950s.[124]

In early 1911, Dr. Royal (1874-1966) and Eva Nichols (1877-1951) Dye, CWBM missionaries in the Belgian Congo, visited the mission in Schieffelin on their way back to the United States. They reported to Kenoly that the CWBM would increase its support of the Liberian Mission by doubling his salary and sending an assistant teacher as soon as the society could raise funds to do so.[125] Before the CWBM could fulfill these commitments, however, Kenoly drowned while fishing to provide food for his students in June 1911.

The CWBM's commitment to the Liberian Mission only strengthened as a result of Kenoly's death. His wife, Ruth, led the work for almost two years, maintaining the grounds, teaching in the school, and holding prayer meetings in the church. The CWBM paid her the same salary that her husband had received, sent shipments of supplies, and promised to send experienced missionaries to aid the work. Meanwhile, C. C. Smith (1845-1919), a long-time supporter of SCI, raised more than $3,000 as

a "Jacob Kenoly Memorial Fund" in order to support the Liberian Mission.[126]

Harry (1892-1967) and Lula (d. 1966) Smith, both SCI graduates, joined the Liberian Mission shortly after Kenoly's death. From 1912-1914, a team of four missionaries led by Emory Ross (1887-1973) sought to expand the Mission's educational and medical work. In spite of increased finances and personnel, by 1916 the missionaries concluded that "the life and means expended would bring smaller returns there than in other fields," and recommended that the CWBM close the Liberian Mission. CWBM leaders agreed, judging that "the results in Liberia have never been encouraging." By 1917 the Board had turned over its property in Scheiffelin to the Liberian government.[127] Despite accusations of abandonment by Ruth Kenoly and demands from the *Christian Standard* that the CWBM provide a full explanation for closing the mission, by 1920 there was no continuing presence of the Stone-Campbell Movement in Liberia.[128]

South Africa

The British had gained control of the Cape Colony from the Dutch in 1814, though most early British settlers confined themselves to Cape Town on the southern coast. To the north and east was the Zulu kingdom and the descendants of Dutch settlers, known as Boers, both of whom resisted British attempts to expand control throughout southern Africa. By 1879 the Zulu kingdom had fallen and its province of Natal came under British control. To preserve their independence, the Boers organized republics, notably the Orange Free State and the Transvaal.[129]

After the discovery of diamonds in the Orange Free State in 1870, the British moved to annex the territories, leading to the First Boer War (1880-1881). Though the war ended with a devastating loss for the British and the continued independence of the Boer republics, colonists from Britain, Australia, and New Zealand poured into the region during the 1880s and 1890s. When gold was discovered in the Transvaal in 1886, the British again tried to annex the territory, resulting in the Second Boer War (1899-1902). This time the British won, and immigration accelerated even further. By 1910, the British had consolidated the Orange Free State, Transvaal, Natal, and the Cape Colony into the Union of South Africa.[130]

Henry Elliott Tickle, one of the original members of the Foreign Missionary Committee of the British Churches of Christ, played a critical role in the early

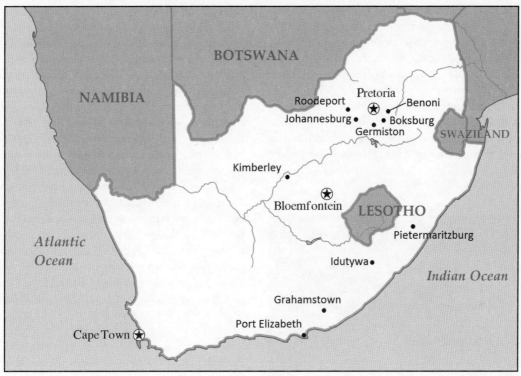

South Africa

formation of the Stone-Campbell Movement in South Africa.[131] He had come to the colony in 1892 for health reasons, and began contacting other members of Churches of Christ who had immigrated. By linking scattered Christians and encouraging them to meet to take the Lord's Supper, Tickle fostered the formation of several congregations.

The Second Boer War forced the disbanding of these early congregations.[132]After the war, however, the FMC appealed for an evangelist for South Africa, and in 1902 sent R. K. Francis. Within two years Francis had reestablished the congregations in Johannesburg and Pretoria.[133] In 1903 the FMC also employed Scottish evangelist Fred Cowin who revived the church at Cape Town. In 1905 these South African churches held their first annual conference in Johannesburg.[134]

All the churches thus far were white. That would change in 1906 when a new church at Roodeport began "work among the natives" with the support of the South African Conference. The Roodeport church employed Agrippa Mzozoiyana and later George Khosa—both associated with the mission in Bulawayo, Southern Rhodesia—for the work. Despite opposition from its white neighbors, the Roodeport church moved ahead,

especially motivated by the exploitation of black mine workers. By early 1909 the mission claimed almost a hundred black converts.[135]

By the early 1920s, the Pretoria congregation had closed, and the combined membership of the Johannesburg and Capetown congregations was less than fifty. The growth at Roodeport, however, continued, with the number of black and colored members growing to at least 3,500 under Khosa's leadership.[136]

About the time Khosa began his work in Roodeport, another black South African named Thomas Kalane (d. 1924) was studying at Wilberforce University in Ohio. Under the influence of W. H. Book (1863-1946), Kalane was baptized and pledged to return to his homeland as a missionary. Though the FCMS declined to support Kalane, Book's Tabernacle Christian Church in Columbus, Indiana, established the East Africa Missionary Society to oversee his work and serve as trustee of any property acquired. In 1921, Kalane began his work in Kimberley, the most important diamond-mining center in the colony. He established a church and began evangelistic work in several stations. One report credits 3,000 conversions to his efforts.[137]

Controversy soon erupted, however, when Kalane

was accused of living with a woman to whom he was not married. She charged him with abuse, and Kalane served six months in prison. White missionaries from the United States, including O. E. Payne, were dispatched to Kimberley to assume leadership of the mission, but Kalane's problems were only beginning. Missionaries from another denomination accused him of fomenting opposition to the colonial government in South Africa. Convicted of sedition, Kalane was deported to his homeland, Portuguese East Africa (Mozambique) where he died in 1924 from complications from an injury received in prison.[138]

The success of Thomas Kalane's evangelistic work in the mining towns around Kimberley alarmed colonial authorities who feared large gatherings of black South Africans as potentially violent. (*Christian Standard*, October 11, 1913)

Missionary Charles Buttz Titus (1863-1953) assumed leadership of the Kimberley mission in 1925, serving as pastor and organizing a Bible training institute. A former FCMS worker in China, Titus had become a supporter of direct-support missionary work as early as 1911. In 1927, Carl and Clara Lewis joined Titus and helped him organize the African Christian Missionary Society "to plant and develop, after the New Testament pattern, churches of Christ in South Africa." The Christian Restoration Association quickly endorsed the new agency. By the end of the 1920s, the mission reported twenty stations and 63 outstations among the mining towns of north central South Africa, with at least two dozen indigenous evangelists assisting the white missionaries.[139] In 1925, a $20,000 gift from Dallas businessman M. H. Thomas sent Jesse Kellems (1892-1980) and Charles Richards on a three-year evangelistic campaign through South Africa. Known as the Thomas Evangelistic Mission, this initiative eventually gained support from the Federal Conference of Churches of Christ in Australia, the annual Conference of the Churches of Christ in Great Britain, the Convention of Churches of Christ in South Africa, and proponents of direct support missions in the United States. The *Christian Standard* and the mission's periodical, the *South African Christian,* carried regular reports. The Thomas Mission baptized thousands from all South African racial groups, and helped revitalize the older congregations at Cape Town and Johannesburg. Some hoped that the Stone-Campbell Movement's message of Christian unity might help overcome the racial divisions then hardening in the colony.[140]

However, financial support for the Thomas Mission dwindled because of the Great Depression and controversy over open membership allegedly promoted by the missionary societies. Kellems repeatedly emphasized the independence of the Thomas Mission from the missionary societies and highlighted its commitment to believer's baptism. He even published his debates on baptism with members of the Dutch Reformed Church to prove his fidelity to the historic Stone-Campbell teaching, but to no avail. By 1930 the Thomas Mission had closed.

Northern and Southern Rhodesia

Armed with a charter from Queen Victoria and ambiguous treaties with local tribal leaders, the British South Africa Company arrived in 1889 to establish a colony north of the Transvaal. After two wars with the indigenous people, they officially established Southern Rhodesia in 1897. Immigrants from Britain, Australia, and New Zealand poured into the new colony and developed large plantations of cotton, tobacco, and coffee. After the turn of the century as white immigrants gained control of more land, the colonial government forced the indigenous people onto reservations. By 1911, the British South Africa Company pushed further north and organized a second colony, Northern Rhodesia. Though the British government granted Southern Rhodesia the right to self-rule as an imperial colony in 1923, Northern Rhodesia remained a British protectorate until the early 1950s.[141]

The Stone-Campbell Movement made significant progress in these colonies, largely due to the efforts of John Sherriff (1864-1935). A native of New Zealand, Sherriff arrived in South Africa in 1896 and began evangelistic work, first in Cape Town, and later in Kimberley, Johannesburg, and Pretoria. By 1897, he had settled in Bulawayo, an important industrial and commercial center of Southern Rhodesia. There he opened a night school for black and colored mine workers, and by 1903 had baptized three of his students—George McKenna, Agrippa Mzozoiyana, and Charles Kakha. Another of Sherriff's early converts was George Khosa, evangelist at Roodeport. Sherriff supported himself and the Bulawayo mission through his trade of stonemasonry.[142]

While in New Zealand during the Second Boer War, Sherriff recruited additional missionaries who returned with him in 1906, including New Zealander F. L. Hadfield (d. 1966) and Australian Emma Dobson (1875-1960), whom Sherriff later married. The Foreign Mission Council of the New Zealand Churches of Christ assumed responsibility for the mission, supporting Agrippa Mzozoiyana and later Daniel Shandhavu as evangelists and translators.[143] The British Churches of Christ also supported the mission in Bulawayo as a part of their work in South Africa.[144]

Once Hadfield was in place, Sherriff bought a 412-acre farm at Forrest Vale outside Bulawayo to use as a practical training institution in association with, but not part of, the Mission, to be supported by independent contributions. Meanwhile, several Churches of Christ in Texas began contributing to a "South African Fund," and by 1907 were providing a monthly sum to support the work of Sherriff and his colleagues.[145] By the time the other missionaries arrived, membership in the church had grown to one hundred nineteen.

Though the work in Bulawayo continued, in 1913 the missionaries relocated the mission's headquarters to Intini, forty miles southeast. This provided a strategic location for the mission to expand throughout the populous Belingwe Reserve, using indigenous evangelists trained at a school the missionaries had established. However, by 1918, accusations of immorality directed at some of the evangelists prompted colonial authorities to demand tighter missionary control. Partly because of this controversy, missionaries again relocated the headquarters and training school to Dadaya. From this new location, the missionaries and a growing number of indigenous workers established congregations and schools at Dadaya, Fishu, Ignome, and Shabani by the mid-1920s.[146]

In 1920 the Bulawayo congregation moved from its initial location in a white residential area to a new site provided by the Government in an indigenous area.[147] Though the schools at Bulawayo were integrated, Hadfield had previously held separate worship services for white, colored, and black church members. At the new location, missionaries and local Christians began sharing oversight of the work through a central committee. The mission began a monthly periodical, *Foreign Mission News*, to publicize the work at Bulawayo and raise funds for its support. The monthly paper included articles by and news about both missionaries and indigenous Christian leaders. The mission at Bulawayo increasingly reflected Sherriff's conviction that no racial barriers should be allowed in the churches.[148]

John Sherriff (center) with staff and students at the Church of Christ Mission School, Bulawayo, Southern Rhodesia. His wife, Emma, is seated in front of him, and missionary F. L. Hadfield stands behind him. In 1904, the school had 32 students. (*Bible Advocate*, January 15, 1904)

In 1920-1921, the Sherriffs made a fundraising and missionary recruiting trip to churches in Canada, the United States, Australia, and New Zealand. As a result, several from U. S. Churches of Christ moved to Southern Rhodesia to serve as missionaries. Among them were

W. N. and A'Delia Short in 1923; Ray and Zelma Lawyer in 1924; Dow Merritt and his family in 1926; and George M. Scott and his family in 1927.[149] Most served a brief time in Southern Rhodesia, then became pioneers of Stone-Campbell missions in Northern Rhodesia—especially at Sinde and Kalomo—in the 1930s and 1940s.

On the eve of the Great Depression, the mission in Southern Rhodesia consisted of twenty-two churches in Bulawayo and the Belingwe Reserve, fifteen schools scattered throughout the Reserve, and a Central Day School and Boarding School at Dadaya with an enrollment of nearly 1,500. The Native Evangelist and Teacher Training College, also at Dadaya, enrolled twenty-three African students preparing for leadership in the mission.[150] The Bulawayo congregation was fully self-supporting and employed an indigenous preacher.

Nyasaland

Though the Portuguese had controlled the narrow strip of land along the eastern shoreline of Lake Nyasa since the sixteenth century, in the late 1880s the British targeted it as key to their building a transcontinental railway from Cairo to Cape Town. Based on the presence of Scottish and English missionaries who had been working in the area since the 1870s, the British set up a colonial administration and forced the Portuguese to withdraw in 1890. As in Southern Rhodesia, large numbers of settlers from Britain, Australia, and New Zealand immigrated to the new colony, known initially as the British Central Africa Protectorate. In 1907, the protectorate was renamed Nyasaland, a name it carried until becoming independent Malawi in 1964.[151]

In 1906, John Sherriff had converted Ellerton Kundago, a mine worker living near Bulawayo. Returning to his home in the Zomba province of Nyasaland the next year, Kundago met three African leaders of the Church of Scotland mission and convinced them to be immersed—George Masangano, Ronald Kaunda, and Frederick Nkhonde. By late 1907, the four had established the first Church of Christ in Nyasaland. Because of this early connection, many early converts came from the Church of Scotland. This created tension between the groups, especially since some apparently had been under discipline by the Church of Scotland, and others had come because Churches of Christ would baptize them simply on a confession of faith rather than after years of study.[152]

An English missionary named Joseph Booth (1851-1932) with ties to the Seventh Day Baptists, the Seventh-Day Adventists, and the Watch Tower Movement had been working in the region since the early 1890s. He had established several missions with schools that taught industrial skills, basic literacy, and Christian faith.[153] When Booth lost his support from the Adventist General Conference in Birmingham, England, in August 1905, he joined one of the Birmingham Churches of Christ and asked the FMC for support to educate Africans in Britain. When the FMC rejected his request ostensibly for lack of funds, he sent letters asking for support from Churches of Christ in Great Britain, Canada, Australasia, and the United States. Lancelot Oliver repudiated Booth in the *Bible Advocate*, explaining that Booth's plan involved "matters of grave political implications," apparently a reference to his proposal to restore Nyasaland to its African inhabitants within twenty-one years.[154]

Continuing his fundraising efforts in the Cape Town Church of Christ, Booth persuaded George Hubert Hollis and George Hills to join him in missionary work in Nyasaland. The three missionaries sent a letter in July 1907 to churches in South Africa and Great Britain, appealing for funds for the "Church of Christ Central African Mission." The letter implied that the mission already existed and that the Cape Town church supported it. The Cape Town church, however, openly repudiated the appeal, recommending support for the churches at Roodeport and Bulawayo instead.[155]

After Hollis and Hills cut their ties with Booth, they secured recognition from the Conference of Churches in South Africa. In June 1908, a letter in the *Bible Advocate* endorsed their work, and the Annual Meeting that year authorized the FMC to raise support.[156] Later that year Sherriff asked Hollis and Hills to travel from Cape Town to Nyasaland to direct the work being done by the African evangelists. Upon their arrival they found Kundago leading a church of twenty-six members.[157] The FMC began support of the mission in 1909, with the first British missionaries, Mary Bannister and Henry and Etta Philpott, arriving in 1912 and 1913 respectively. With Namiwawa serving as the mission headquarters, it grew quickly to include four stations and numerous outstations in the Zomba and Blantyre districts.[158]

The missionaries and indigenous leaders cooperated in aggressive evangelism, building churches, establishing day schools, and providing free medical care. Hollis wrote in 1910 that he was persuaded "if Africa is to be won for Christ the work will be chiefly done by the native."[159] In 1911, indigenous evangelists began making extended journeys to areas where no missions existed. On one such trip that year, Masangano and Kaunda discovered several thousand Christians in Bandawe, to the north in the Nkhata Bay district. These Christians had "formed themselves into churches more or less resembling those of primitive times," and reportedly were eager to have the help of the mission. Occasionally, these preaching tours included Portuguese East Africa (Mozambique), where the Catholic Church was dominant.[160]

In early 1915, John Chilembwe (1871-1915), a former associate of Joseph Booth, led an uprising against the British in Nyasaland. Chilembwe had accompanied Booth to the United States in 1897, where he studied for two years at Virginia Theological Seminary in Lynchburg and was exposed to the developing black nationalism of African American leaders such as W. E. B. DuBois. Chilembwe returned to Nyasaland in 1900 as a Baptist missionary, establishing schools and churches, and gaining a reputation as an inspiring preacher. By 1914, Chilembwe was speaking out against British colonialism, especially the harsh treatment of refugees from Mozambique and the conscription of Africans to fight in the British army in German East Africa during World War I. Eventually, he led two hundred followers in an uprising against white plantation owners in January 1915, killing at least three. Chilembwe then fled to Mozambique where he was killed by border police.[161]

Although instrumental in founding the first Church of Christ in Nyasaland in 1907, Ellerton Kundago eventually broke with the Stone-Campbell Movement and began a new church characterized by more aggressive African nationalism. (*Bible Advocate*, October 1, 1909)

During the uprising and for some weeks afterwards the government moved the missionaries and white settlers to the military camp at Zomba for their protection. When the settlers were allowed to return to their homes, however, authorities detained the five missionaries without explanation for seven weeks. Finally, colonial authorities expelled Hollis and prohibited the others from teaching or holding meetings. They also destroyed the church and school building at Mlanje. Attempts by the FMC to gain an explanation from the Colonial Office failed.

The colonial government had connected Churches of Christ with the Chilembwe uprising based on allegations that leaders of the Nyasaland mission had known about it beforehand. Apparently Frederick Nkhonde had informed Hollis of Chilembwe's plans, but Hollis had dismissed the reports as rumor. The mission's African leaders testified that they had tried to persuade Chilembwe to abandon his plans. The government sentenced Nkhonde, Masangano, and Kaunda to seven years in prison, but would have executed them if it had possessed evidence of their participation. Two former leaders of the mission, Barton Makwangwala and Simon Kadewere, were put to death for their part in the uprising. The colonial government bought the mission property for a nominal sum in 1917, and local leaders took charge of the four churches and eight schools that were left.[162] The FMC transferred the Philpotts to the Indian Mission, and Mary Bannister, after spending time in Bulawayo, returned to Britain. The colonial government refused to allow FMC missionaries to return to Nyasaland until 1927.[163]

Belgian Congo

The FCMS first proposed work in the Congo in 1884 before the region became a Belgian colony. The Society abandoned its plans, however, after explorer Henry Morton Stanley estimated a beginning cost of $25,000. The Society's second attempt began in 1895 with the commissioning of Ellsworth E. Faris (1874-1953) to work in the Congo Free State, then privately controlled by King Leopold II of Belgium. A physician, Dr. Harry Biddle (1872-1898), agreed to accompany Faris, and the two departed in March 1897. After consulting experienced missionaries and buying supplies in London, they arrived in the Congo near the end of May. For more than a year the two searched for a suitable location, finding opposition at nearly every turn. Belgian colonial authorities, angry at criticism about human rights violations from Protestant missionaries, were reluctant to permit new ones to operate in the colony. Biddle became seriously ill and died on his way back to the United States, but Faris remained to negotiate the purchase of an existing mission station at Bolenge.[164]

Situated seven hundred miles from the mouth of the Congo River, Bolenge had been established by the Livingstone Inland Mission in 1883, and later supported by the American Baptist Missionary Union (ABMU). By the time Faris arrived in 1899, however, the ABMU had chosen to concentrate its efforts in the Lower Congo. The ABMU offered the Bolenge station to the FCMS for $2,500, roughly half of what they had invested in it, and helped Faris get settled.[165]

After the purchase, Dr. Royal and Eva Dye joined the Disciples of Christ Congo Mission. Dr. Dye immediately opened a clinic while his wife opened a school for girls. Three Congolese Christians, presumably converts of the American Baptist mission, provided assistance: Ikoko, a carpenter; his wife Bokama; and Josefa, a crippled fisherman. Josefa became an effective evangelist and was largely responsible for the mission's first baptisms in 1902.[166]

From the beginning, the Disciples of Christ Congo Mission (DCCM) intended to develop an indigenous church that would "transform the whole Congo social order through the vital application of the principles and life of Jesus." The two goals—indigenous church and social change—sometimes proved to be in tension. In March, 1903, the DCCM organized its first congregation with twenty-four members in which missionaries and Congolese Christians shared leadership. Polygamy, however, quickly became a central issue. The missionaries could not see this strongly embedded indigenous practice as part of a Christian social order. Eventually native leaders agreed with the missionaries that converts should abandon the practice as a requirement for church membership.[167]

The missionaries emphasized stewardship, hoping the congregation would quickly become self-supporting. The church responded by making tithing a minimum standard of membership. The churches of the DCCM also developed a tradition of "thank-offerings" at both Christmas and Easter, expecting members to give sacrificially beyond their tithe.[168]

One of the most significant early leaders of the DCCM was Mark Njoji. Njoji's father belonged to the chiefly aristocracy of Central Africa, and his brother was a celebrated *sangoma* (shaman-healer) in the Congo River basin. Njoji began attending the mission school in Bolenge around 1900 and soon showed promise as a leader. He was among the first converts baptized in 1902 and a charter member of the church in Bolenge the following year. For several years, he served as an evangelist in the villages around Bolenge and helped establish additional mission stations.

In 1907-1909 Njoji accompanied the Dyes on a trip to the United States. While there he studied at Eureka College and at a sanitarium in Battle Creek, Michigan. In 1914, DCCM leaders chose him to be the mission's first indigenous pastor, serving the church in Bolenge for many years. A large crowd gathered at the church on July 4, 1920 to witness his ordination. Beyond Bolenge, he served the wider community of Congolese Disciples as its primary spokesperson until poor health forced his retirement in the late 1950s.[169]

One of the most pressing challenges in the DCCM's early years was the blatant human rights violations committed by the Belgian colonial government. Between 1885 and 1908, King Leopold II controlled the territory of the upper Congo River basin through the International African Association. The agency claimed to provide humanitarian assistance to the people of central Africa, but in reality it gave Leopold sole access to colonize the territory and plunder its natural resources. The Congo Free State's economy relied on forced labor by Congolese, who harvested rubber, mined copper, and collected ivory under conditions no better than chattel slavery. By 1908, between 5 and 10 million Congolese had perished from starvation or disease, and the hands of countless others were cut off as punishment for failing to meet quotas.[170]

Beginning in 1902, a coalition of politicians, literary figures, journalists, and church leaders both in the United States and Great Britain began to call worldwide attention to these human rights violations. Their efforts forced the Belgian Parliament in 1908 to wrest control of the colony from their king and to institute immediate reforms. The territory remained a Belgian colony, but its administration was subject to international scrutiny.[171] Though the DCCM missionaries knew about the human rights violations from the beginning, they had confined their criticisms to diaries, private correspondence, and reports to the FCMS because the mission's existence required a measure of cooperation with the Belgian government. Between 1904 and 1908, however, DCCM missionaries became more vocal. They published scathing critiques of the colonial system in Stone-Campbell journals. Most significantly, in 1904 a small group of Protestant leaders—including FCMS president Archibald McLean, and DCCM missionaries Dr. Edward A. Layton and Robert Ray Eldred—unsuccessfully lobbied the U.S. government to intervene. After the removal of Leopold in 1908, DCCM personnel—like all Protestant missionaries—rarely involved themselves in the affairs of the colonial government.[172]

Within five years of their arrival in 1899, DCCM missionaries believed they had mastered the Lonkundo language enough to begin developing a written version and publishing material to support their work. For years, Eva Nichols Dye had relied heavily on "word hunters," young people from her school who consulted tribal leaders and helped her learn the vocabulary and structure of Lonkundo. Using the English alphabet, she developed a written version of the language between 1905 and 1907. Though years later Dye reflected on just how inadequate their understanding of the language had been, the foot-powered mission press began churning out hymnbooks, educational materials, and tracts. In 1917, DCCM missionaries began collaborating with colleagues at the interdenominational Congo-Balolo Mission and with leading Congolese Christians to produce the first Lomongo-Lonkundo translation of the Bible. In 1921, after more than four years' work, they published the *Bonkanda wa Nzakomba*—the "Book of God"—making the Bible available to an estimated one million Lomongo-Lonkundo-speaking people in central Africa.[173]

The central role of the Congo River as a transportation route led Stone-Campbell churches in the Pacific Northwest to raise more than $15,000 to purchase a steamship for the DCCM. The Pittsburgh Centennial Convention of 1909 dedicated the *S. S. Oregon* which made its first trip up the Congo River a year later. For the next forty years, the *S. S. Oregon* served the mission, for most of that time captained by Congolese Christian John Inkema. Following his lead, Congolese Christians and missionaries alike referred to the vessel as *Nsango Ea Ndoce*, in Lonkundo, "Good News." "She is a Gospel boat," Inkema preached from one of its decks in 1938, "so that our people may know the God of love, our heavenly Father, that they may be released from the dreadful fear of the spirits, the strong bonds of ignorance, of superstition, of sin"[174]

Partly because of the *Oregon*, by the 1920s, DCCM had expanded up the Congo River's tributaries into six additional stations: Longa (1908), Lotumbe (1910), Moneika (1912), Mondombe (1920), Wema (1925), and Coquilhatville (1925). The basic pattern begun at Bolenge was duplicated in these stations. Missionaries organized churches and boarding schools for boys and girls, and large numbers of indigenous evangelists itinerated throughout surrounding villages. Each mission station was responsible for a territory approximately 10,000 miles square with an estimated population of 100,000. The central station was a training center, mainly for evangelists, who traveled for months at a time in the surrounding villages. They regularly returned to the mission station for an *ekitelo*, an ingathering of all evangelists from the back country to worship and baptize converts. As often as possible, the missionaries themselves also itinerated in the villages to provide counsel and support to the developing Christian communities.[175]

As the DCCM expanded, so did its missionary staff, with a total of eighty-four serving before 1929. The work of two couples stands out. A linguist, Andrew F. Hensey (1880-1951) arrived in 1905 and began helping Eva Nichols Dye design a written version of Lonkundo. Though not a printer by trade, he spent almost twenty-five years running the mission press at Bolenge.[176] One of the publications was *Ekim'ea Nsango* (*News Messenger*), a quarterly Lonkundo-language journal begun in 1913. Because of his skill as a diplomat and his knowledge of the Congolese people, he served on the Belgian government's Royal Commission for Protection of Natives. Arriving in Congo in 1907, Hensey's wife Alice (1885-1950) was a musician and poet, and was responsible for translating hymns and teaching them to Congolese Christians. Known as the "official hostess of Bolenge," she entertained government officials, denominational executives, and representatives from other Protestant missions in their home.[177]

Herbert (1880-1954) and Mary Hopkins (1881-1952) Smith arrived in 1909, and served at DCCM for the next thirty-seven years. They were primarily responsible for opening the station at Lotumbe in 1910, and served as the station's only missionaries for a number of years. In 1928, they led the way in establishing a central training school for indigenous evangelists at Bolenge—later known as the Congo Christian Institute—and taught there until 1946 when they both retired. In celebration of the Golden Jubilee of the mission, they wrote *Fifty Years in Congo: Disciples of Christ at the Equator*.[178]

In addition to the Henseys and Smiths, by the 1920s at least six missionary physicians led the expanding medical work of DCCM. Dr. Louis Jaggard (1877-1951) arrived in 1908 and served for the next thirty-six years. Initially Bolenge, Lotumbe, and Moneika were the centers of medical work, but the missionary physicians itinerated at the other stations and surrounding villages. Particularly significant was their success using the new antibiotic Salvarsan to treat children suffering from the chronic bacterial skin infection called "yaws."[179]

A spirit of ecumenism characterized the work of the mission from the beginning. DCCM personnel participated in the General Conference of Protestant Missionaries, a gathering held roughly every five years that brought together missionaries from all denominations serving in the Congo for fellowship, worship, and addressing common challenges. In 1911, DCCM hosted the conference at the Bolenge station. Out of this meeting came two significant developments. First, the DCCM press began publishing the quarterly *Congo Mission News*, an interdenominational journal for Protestant missionaries; and second, the group formed the Congo Continuation Committee according to the model suggested by the 1910 World Missionary Conference in Edinburgh. This ecumenical committee served in an advisory capacity to all of the Protestant missions in the Congo, often representing those missions to the Belgian colonial government. Moreover, DCCM was one of six Protestant missions that cooperated in opening the Union Mission House in Kinshasa in 1922. This house served for many years as a center of training and collaboration for Protestant missionaries serving in the Congo.[180]

Mark Njoji (left) served as pastor of the church in Bolenge with assistant pastor Paul Lofembe, superintendent of the Bolenge printing office. Lofembe eventually became an evangelist for DCCM in Leopoldville.

By the 1910s, education was widely regarded as the most important work of the DCCM. When FCMS

Secretary Stephen J. Corey (1873-1962) visited in 1912 to assess the mission's progress and help plan its future, he became convinced that education was a prerequisite for establishing strong churches and developing indigenous leaders for both church and society. Reflecting the racist assumptions of most white Westerners, the curriculum of the mission schools focused on industrial education and "character formation" as defined by the missionaries. In 1921, representatives of the Phelps-Stokes Commission, begun in 1911 to promote the educational models used in the United States for African Americans, visited the DCCM schools and found them to be models of the kind of education they judged best.[181]

In 1923 DCCM had six fully functioning mission stations employing 689 Congolese workers who evangelized and taught in almost 350 outstations. There were 549 churches and regular places of worship, and 275 schools serving 4,414 students. Perhaps most impressive of all, church membership in 1923 was 8,679. In just over twenty-five years, DCCM had grown to be the largest and most successful of all the Stone-Campbell Movement's foreign missions.[182]

Jamaica

The results of the early Jamaica Mission had been impressive. By 1861 there were nine churches with a combined membership of 470, six preachers, regular Sunday schools and Bible classes at most of the churches, and three fully operative day schools with three others just beginning. Over the next three years the number of members grew to a high of 821, and the British churches had begun sending some support to the mission. Two years later there were fifteen stations still with a membership of 821. By the time J. O. Beardslee ended his work with the ACMS and returned to the United States in 1864, there were eighteen stations with 721 members.

When Beardslee attempted to resume work in Jamaica in 1866, he discovered that the mission's growth had slowed significantly. This was partly due to unsettled conditions resulting from the rebellion against British rule led by Baptist deacon Paul Bogle the year before. Though Beardslee appealed to the ACMS to resume his support, the agency was unable to raise the funds.[183]

In 1876, the Christian Woman's Board of Missions voted unanimously to assume responsibility for the Jamaica Mission. It had declined to only five small churches under the leadership of two Jamaican evangelists. CWBM leaders discovered that the Mission suffered from serious problems. First, it had gained a

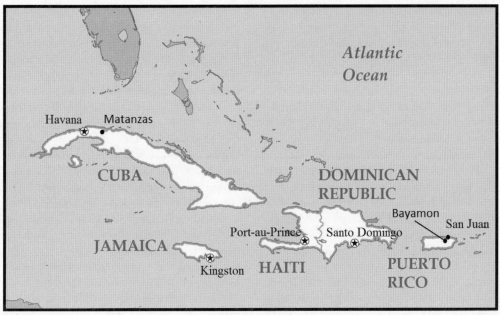

Greater Antilles

bad reputation because of Beardslee's earlier strategy of bringing whole congregations from other denominations into the mission. Secondly, the ACMS had naively assumed that the Jamaica Mission would be self-sufficient in a few years. Beardslee had rarely emphasized stewardship education, however, and he and the early missionaries had confined their work primarily to the poor.[184]

In January 1876, the CWBM appointed William H. (1842-1928) and Martha Jane Williams to lead the Jamaica Mission. Though the Williams family left in March 1879 because of ill-health, and most workers stayed no longer than three years, the CWBM supplied missionaries for the Jamaica Mission for the next four decades, with assistance from the British Christian Association and the Jamaican Mission itself.[185]

The work of W. K. and Anne Azbill from 1882 to 1886 marked an attempt to shift the Jamaican work in two significant ways. First, unlike previous missionaries who had stayed for short periods and had not become integrated into Jamaican life, the Azbills lived in a "good house" in Kingston and made a conscious effort to become part of the life of the island. Second, Azbill revived the Jamaica Christian Missionary Association, formed in 1865 to employ Jamaican workers.[186] John Thompson, originally an English Baptist missionary, joined the Mission with his church in 1882 and served

until his retirement in 1891. Another English Baptist, Caleb Randall, became a Disciples missionary in 1885 and later chair of the Mission. Randall enlisted the help of W.T. Moore of the West London Tabernacle to send recruits beginning in the late 1880s. The number of Jamaican pastors increased as well, one of the earliest being Louis S. Thomas, who began studies at Southern Christian Institute in Edwards, Mississippi, in 1896.[187]

In 1907 a disastrous earthquake hit the eastern part of Jamaica where the Disciples work was located. Fourteen churches and mission homes were wrecked, but the quick action of Jamaican Christians to rebuild reflected the mission's growing strength. Immediately afterward a revival added 1,500 people to the churches.[188] By 1918 the Jamaica Mission reported 2,685 members, with 15,000 adherents in at least thirty-six churches. Four missionaries, seven ministers, and seven teachers were at work, along with ten women's missionary auxiliaries with 364 members and seven schools with 671 students.[189]

In 1926, the Jamaica Mission celebrated the Golden Jubilee of the work of the Christian Woman's Board of Missions (CWBM) on the island. The mission had twenty-five churches—located mainly in the St. Andrew and St. Catherine Parishes—with a combined membership of 3,606. It also administered nine elementary schools, subsidized by the UCMS and government funding, with a total enrollment of 880. Eight UCMS missionaries and twenty-three Jamaican pastors and teachers led the work of the mission.[190] Still, the most pressing issue was the need for the churches to become financially self-sufficient and autonomous.[191]

Mexico

In summer 1895, Merritt L. Hoblit (b. 1866) urged the Texas Christian Convention in Gainesville to begin a Mexican mission. After providing a brief review of the nation's history since independence in 1822, he exclaimed, "The Mexican drinks from the same fountain of liberty that has been opened to us." Other Protestant denominations had been in Mexico for more than twenty years with great success, he continued. "Is it not an opportune time for *us* to enter this field?" Later that fall, the CWBM appointed Hoblit its first missionary to Mexico.[192]

In November 1895, Hoblit crossed the Rio Grande near El Paso, and with $200 support began work in Ciudad Juarez. Two months later he wrote the CWBM, "We have a mission chapel and a schoolroom, well-furnished with benches, blackboard, book case, tables, chairs, lamps, and organ." Soon others joined him, including his mother, a missionary couple from England, and Bertha Mason from Texas. They began a school for children, organized a congregation, published a Spanish-language newspaper titled *El Evangelista*, and visited prisoners in local jails. Despite these efforts, after a year and a half they still had no converts.[193]

By early 1897, discouragement and the growing threat of yellow fever in Ciudad Juarez led the CWBM to relocate the mission to Monterrey, seven hundred miles to the southeast. The CWBM chose this site partly because the city was rapidly industrializing and was a center of railway traffic in northern Mexico. La Puerta Abierta (the Open Door)—Hoblit's name for the relocated mission—opened in the fall with Hoblit as the only missionary. The large mission house contained a classroom, several reading rooms, a director's office, and a printing room. The mission was located on one of the city's busiest streets and attracted constant visitors, especially students from the nearby Colegio Civil, who used the reading rooms and took night classes.[194]

Hoblit's work in Monterrey was hampered, however, by lack of personnel, outbreaks of yellow fever and smallpox, and personal discouragement at the lack of response. His regular reports to the CWBM grew increasingly frustrated, and by August 1899 he had resigned. The CWBM, however, did not abandon the Mexican mission. Between 1900 and 1905, a dozen

missionaries came to Monterrey to continue the work, including Bertha Mason, who had been a member of the Juarez mission. The new workers rejuvenated the mission, organizing a congregation, reviving the school, beginning house-to-house evangelism, and printing material in both Spanish and English, most notably a weekly bi-lingual newsletter titled *La Via de Paz* (*The Way of Peace*), with a circulation of nearly thirty thousand at its height.[195]

The mission witnessed its first Mexican converts in summer 1900—Concha, a young student in Mason's day school, and the girl's employer, Natalia Flores. As numbers increased, the missionaries quickly put Mexican Christians into leadership roles. Francisco Puebla served as an evangelist, and Cleto Flores, a respected Mexican businessman, served as one of the first deacons in the Monterrey congregation.[196]

Among the most influential early leaders of the Mexican mission were Thomas Westrup (1837-1909), his Mexican-born wife Francesca Barocio (1853-1910), and three of their children. Veteran Baptist missionaries, the Westrups were ministering in a small church in Monterrey when they began work with the CWBM in 1902. Thomas translated literature into Spanish, published the mission's weekly newsletter, and preached regularly. Because of his work in translating hymns, he became known—both inside and outside of the Stone-Campbell Movement—as the "father of Mexican hymnody." Francesca cared for dozens of children enrolled at the school and taught kindergarten until her death. Together they served as the primary leaders of the Monterrey mission for almost a decade.[197]

The mission's school, the Instituto Cristiano, experienced explosive growth in the early twentieth century. In 1900, enrollment was only 35, but three years later the school had more than 400 pupils taking classes in both Spanish and English.[198] The mission built a new school building in 1905 at the cost of $10,000. In addition to missionary teachers, the Instituto Cristiano employed several Mexican teachers, including Manuel Lozano, Elisa Rocha, and Francisco Flores.[199]

Although the center of the Mexican mission remained at Monterrey, the work expanded northward into the states of Nuevo León and Coahuila, and later across the Rio Grande into south Texas. Between 1905 and 1908, Samuel Guy Inman (1877-1965), Enrique Westrup (1880-1967), and Felipe Jimenez taught in the small mining and ranching communities of Coahuila with the support of the CWBM. They established congregations and schools, and mentored Mexican Christians to serve as leaders. Though the CWBM reassigned Inman in 1915, and Jimenez died a year later, the Movement's mission in northeast Mexico and south Texas flourished and expanded into six additional communities, including Piedras Negras and Sabinas where missionaries established schools with enrollments of nearly two hundred students.[200]

In 1908, the Monterrey congregation sent Manuel Lozano as a missionary to Mexican Americans in San Antonio, Texas. As early as 1899, Mexican Americans there had organized a Spanish-speaking congregation with Mexican-born pastor Ignacio Quintero. According to a 1928 account, though this church had made some headway against "superstition [and] sectarianism"— the Protestant view of Catholicism—and the "sin in a populous and wicked part of the city," by 1906 it had disbanded. Upon his arrival Lozano reorganized the congregation, and with the help of his sister-in-law, Crispina Ramirez, ran a day school for boys and girls. By 1916, they had established seven Mexican American congregations in and around San Antonio. These churches were fragile, however, because they were considered an extension of the Mexican mission rather than an indigenous U.S. ministry and depended on poorly financed missionary leadership from Mexico.[201]

The Mexican Revolution (1910-1917) significantly disrupted the mission's work. In Piedras Negras, revolutionary factions often held control of the town, occupying the mission's buildings and using its supplies. The missionaries and many Mexican civilians fled to Eagle Pass, Texas, to escape the turmoil. In Monterrey, classes at the Instituto Cristiano were suspended for long periods because students were afraid to attend; the church and school buildings were pock-marked with bullet holes; and at least one person associated with the mission was beaten for trying to prevent revolutionaries from occupying the school building. Furthermore, increased military intervention by the United States after 1914 sparked strong anti-American sentiment. In their published reports, the missionaries frequently advised United States leaders to stay out of the conflict so that Mexican democracy could develop without foreign intrusion.[202]

In 1914 all Protestant missionaries left Mexico due to the violence of the revolution. The mission survived the revolution primarily because of Mexican leaders, especially Felipe Jimenez, who had worked with Inman and Enrique Westrup in Coahuila. Immersed at the age of nineteen by a Baptist missionary, his parents had disowned him for becoming a Protestant. For many years he served as pastor of the Baptist church in Saltillo, but

in 1903 led his congregation to unite with the Stone-Campbell Movement because of developing friendships with the missionaries in Monterrey. In 1907, he led one of the most significant revivals to that date which resulted in more than a hundred additions in Monterrey. In 1912, he became the first Mexican-born pastor of the mission's original church in Monterrey.[203]

Jimenez died in 1916 amid the turmoil of the revolution and a brief illness. In his obituary, Inman observed that "countless hundreds owe their knowledge of Christ and their power for efficient service to this great soul."[204] Other Mexican leaders included Isaac Uranga (San Luisito), Manuel Beltrán (Sabinas), and Juan Flores (Piedras Negras) who maintained the churches and schools and ministered to refugees from the revolution.[205]

Latin America had not been included on the agenda of the 1910 Edinburgh World Missionary Conference because it was considered part of Christendom and, therefore, not a mission field. Nevertheless, Stone-Campbell leaders in the United States and Canada shared the North American Protestant perspective that Catholicism had failed the people of Latin America and that Protestant missions were needed to bring these nations to Christ. In 1916, Protestant mission boards convened the "Latin American Congress on Christian Work" in Panama. The group elected Inman executive secretary of a newly formed Committee on Cooperation in Latin America. At a meeting convened by Inman's committee in Mexico City in early 1919, the boards approved a plan to increase cooperation in the evangelization of Mexico that included dividing the country into comity areas assigned to specific boards.[206]

The CWBM agreed to relocate its mission work to central Mexico, asserting that the congregations they had established no longer needed their assistance. Though the Board sold the Monterrey school building to the Methodists, the congregations were to retain their church buildings.[207]

Enrique Westrup, who had ended his work with the mission in 1912, opposed the decision, stating that the congregations were not capable of self-support. He argued that the comity agreements might have served some purpose if introduced at the beginning, but now there were Baptists, Presbyterians and Methodists in central Mexico as well as in the region of Monterrey, and the Baptist boards had refused to participate in the plan. He did not consider the other bodies as rivals, he said. He had been cooperating with the Presbyterians, though without compromising distinctive Disciples teachings. He insisted, however, that support for "the great message our people have for the rest of the Christian world" should continue. Westrup organized the Mexican Society for Christian Missions, and with funds received from churches and individuals in North America opened a school and supported evangelists to serve the churches in the Monterrey area.[208]

Meanwhile, with the proceeds from the sale of their property in Monterrey, the CWBM purchased land in central Mexico and began work on December 1, 1919. Within less than a decade, the mission reported churches at San Luis Potosí, Charcas, and Aguascalientes, as well as four schools. The mission also reported cooperating with Northern and Southern Methodists, Northern and Southern Presbyterians, Congregationalists, and the International YMCA in a Union Press and in the Union Theological Seminary at Mexico City.[209]

The presence of North American Churches of Christ in Mexico before 1920 came in the form of attempts to establish "Christian colonies." After a survey trip in 1897, C. M. Wilmeth persuaded a group of Texas Christians to move to a site near Tampico early the following year. However, after Wilmeth's death in October, probably from malaria, the effort collapsed. Austin McGary attempted a second colony in 1899 by advertising inexpensive land in the northern state of Coahuila through the *Firm Foundation* and a new paper titled *The Mexico Pioneer*, but failed to attract sufficient interest. The final colonization effort launched by W. A. Schultz in 1911 saw fifteen families move to Xicatinte, Tamaulipas, the following year. Schultz and others preached to both American settlers and Mexicans with some success, but the Mexican Revolution effectively ended the endeavor. Though a few small congregations continued, primarily among settlers from the United States, no significant work by Churches of Christ in Mexico remained.[210]

By the 1920s, two missions represented the Stone-Campbell Movement in Mexico: one in Monterrey that received funds from churches and individuals independently from the Disciples mission boards, the other in central Mexico under the direction of the CWBM that worked in collaboration with several North American mission boards.

Cuba

Following the Spanish-American War (1898), the United States governed Cuba until 1902 while a civilian government was being created. Seizing this opportunity, in 1899 the FCMS sent two couples—both graduates of Eureka College—to begin a Mission in Havana: Lowell (1861-1949) and Clara (1869-1929) McPherson; and Melvin (1868-1929) and Sue Menges. The couples began their work among U. S. servicemen and other English speakers, but by 1902 the Mengeses were fluent enough to begin Spanish-language work in Matanzas, fifty miles to the east.[211]

The work in Havana was exceptionally difficult. Catholic leaders strongly opposed the mission, and it experienced considerable competition from Presbyterian, Episcopalian, and American Baptist missions. In addition, the population of Havana, with significant numbers of U. S. military personnel and civilians, was highly transient. "Half the audience of one Sunday service would be in America before the next Sunday," FCMS president Archibald McLean complained. The war itself had demoralized, impoverished, and embittered the Cuban people who came to view the United States as a colonial occupier.[212]

Still, the Cuban mission experienced modest success. Angel Godinez, a Cuban evangelist, preached in four or five locations throughout Havana, while the McPhersons focused their attention on the English-speaking population. In 1904-05, FCMS missionaries Willamina Meldrum and Mark Peckham opened a school for training Cuban evangelists. The McPhersons returned to the United States in 1907, and the FCMS decided to close the Havana work for lack of suitable replacements. The Presbyterian mission assumed leadership of the school in 1908 after the FCMS reassigned Meldrum and Peckham to Matanzas.

The work in Matanzas lasted longer. In addition to the Mengeses, the mission employed two Cuban evangelists, Jacobo Gonzalez and Julio Fuentes, after the turn of the century. Between 1906 and 1915, they opened outstations in five towns, each of which included a small house church. Together, membership in the churches in Matanzas and the surrounding area was about 250 at its height. In 1905, the Cuban Mission opened a school for training evangelists similar to the one in Havana, though rapid turnover of missionary personnel hampered the school's effectiveness.[213]

In September 1917, on the advice of the missionaries, the FCMS closed the Cuban mission. By March 1918 the Presbyterian Church in the United States of America had purchased the mission's property for $18,000.00. The congregation at Matanzas, under the leadership of Cuban evangelists, unanimously voted to unite with the Presbyterians, despite differences of doctrine and practice. The last annual report of the Cuban Mission to the FCMS reported "The members are very grateful to the Foreign Christian Missionary Society for all it has been to them and reluctantly sever this closer union, but they welcome this larger union with others whose ideals and desires are so similar."[214]

Puerto Rico

In August 1898, at the beginning of the Spanish American War, U.S. military forces occupied the Spanish colony of Puerto Rico. By October the island had become a possession of the United States, a fact confirmed by the Treaty of Paris in December. For the first time in its history, the island was open to Protestant missionaries.

At the Disciples annual convention in Chattanooga, Tennessee, in October, J. A. Erwin asserted that "the Lord sent the armies of America down there to open up a door for the ambassadors of the Prince of Peace, hitherto closed against them." Reflecting the jingoism of the era, Erwin insisted that just as Disciples had supported U.S. efforts to bring liberty to the people of Cuba and Puerto Rico, they must now do everything necessary to bring them the Kingdom of Christ. The alternatives were to let them "remain in the possession of Rome, drift away from God into infidelity, or be given to sectarianism."[215] The ACMS immediately sent Erwin to Puerto Rico to survey possibilities for a mission, and in January 1899 appointed him and his wife missionaries. They arrived in Ponce in April and moved at once to San Juan where they began studying Spanish and conducting English

language services for U.S. soldiers. They soon opened a day school for children and began teaching Bible classes and distributing tracts.[216]

Despite Erwin's fear of the island being "given to sectarianism"—that is, to denominations other than the Disciples—Disciples were original participants in a comity agreement reached in 1899 with the major Protestant denominations in Puerto Rico. Disciples were assigned the district of Bayamon and the surrounding rural areas in the mid-North section of the island.[217] Though some tension existed over strict adherence to the agreement, it proved to be an important foundation for interdenominational cooperation in the twentieth century.[218]

As the Erwins learned Spanish and expanded their preaching and Bible teaching, they had their first responses, baptizing five Puerto Ricans on June 10, 1900. Erwin, however, who had been a lawyer before coming to Puerto Rico, unexpectedly resigned his position as missionary in 1901 to become district judge in Mayaguez. Mr. and Mrs. William M. Taylor of Tennessee followed the Erwins and organized the first Puerto Rican congregation, the Central Church in Bayamon. Taylor was a tireless evangelist who baptized 137 people in his first year of work, but stayed only two years.[219]

The most significant Disciples work in the early period resulted from the devastating effects of the San Ciriaco hurricane, which struck the island on August 8 and 9, 1899. The storm destroyed buildings and most of the agriculture of the island, killing almost 3,500 people. The hurricane also orphaned hundreds of children who

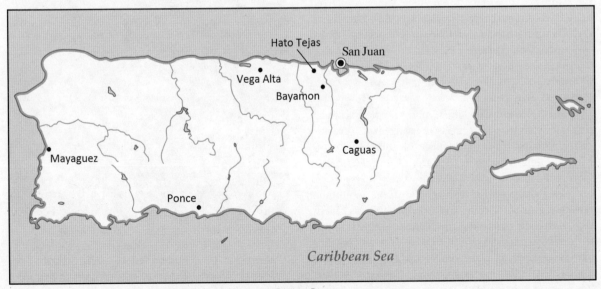

Puerto Rico

were forced to live in the open without homes or secure sources of food or clothing.[220]

In light of this critical need, the town of Bayamon offered an old municipal building to the Disciples if they would repair it and organize an orphanage for girls. When the Erwins urged the CWBM to take on this task, the agency quickly raised $800 to repair the building and secured the services of J. A. Erwin's sister, Mrs. A. M. Fullen, as superintendent. On August 1, 1900, Disciples opened the first Protestant orphanage in Puerto Rico, giving Disciples a good name in the community and diminishing suspicion of "los Protestantes."[221]

Based on the success of the girls orphanage, in June 1902 the missionaries began exploring the possibility of opening a second orphanage for boys. With the support of the CWBM, the mission purchased a 114-acre farm outside of Bayamon in a community named Hato Tejas. The CWBM contracted H. G. and Rose Wilkinson in 1903 to organize a farm and construct a building on the property, then to open and direct the orphanage. After Wilkinson contracted a tropical disease that forced him to return to the United States in 1905, the CWBM asked Dr. William A. and Edna Alton who were conducting a medical mission in Mayaguez to take charge of the project. Under the direction of the Altons, the orphanage finally opened in December 1906. The following year, the girls orphanage was moved from downtown Bayamon to across the street from the boys orphanage.[222]

The schools associated with the orphanages quickly gained a reputation for excellent teaching. The boys orphanage also became a source of recruitment for the ministry. After Merritt and Alice Vanneter arrived in 1910 to direct the boys orphanage, they established the "Training School for Christian Workers." From this school would emerge some of the most important leaders in the Puerto Rican churches, including the first ministers to receive Disciples ordination, Augusto Cotto Reyes and Juan Ortiz.[223]

The 1906 arrival of Vere C. and Mayme Carpenter marked a shift to more aggressive evangelism. Vere had just graduated from the College of the Bible, while Mayme had graduated in 1901 from Central Christian College. Rural people themselves, the Carpenters focused on taking the gospel to the people of the mountains outside the island's cities and towns. Vere was chiefly responsible for overseeing the building projects of the early mission, including the first Disciples church building in the community of Dajaos in 1910. Mayme taught Bible schools, led music services, and taught classes for women. They spent thirty-eight years preaching, establishing

churches, and nurturing Christians in Puerto Rico.[224]

By 1914, it was clear that funding was inadequate to operate the orphanages and schools and to continue extensive evangelism. The CWBM decided to close the orphanages in June 1915. The children had already begun attending nearby public schools during the final year of operation. Merritt B. Wood, who had arrived in 1909 to be minister of the Central Church in Bayamon, continued to operate the Training School at Hato Tejas until 1919. During their existence, the orphanages cared for and educated over three hundred children, many of whom became leaders in the Puerto Rican churches.[225]

Three significant events took place between 1919 and 1922 in the life of Puerto Rican Disciples that marked new levels of ecumenism and a move toward indigenization. The first was the formation of a cooperative educational institution for the training of ministers. Like the Disciples, other denominations had begun small schools in their respective areas of the island. Discussions between mission leaders led to a proposal for the merging of these schools into a strong seminary that would serve all the Protestant groups. Though the newly formed United Christian Missionary Society had at first decided against Disciples participation in the seminary, missionary Vere Carpenter made such a strong appeal for cooperation that the board reversed its stance and Disciples became founding members of the Seminario Evangélico de Puerto Rico in 1919. This school would

As in the United States, Stone-Campbell women in Puerto Rico organized local chapters of the Christian Woman's Board of Mission. The women of Central Christian Church in Bayamon organized this chapter in 1924. (*World Call*, January 1924)

become the chief training center for Protestant ministers in Puerto Rico and other Latin American countries.[226]

A second event took place in 1921-1922 when, in keeping with the comity agreement, the Presbyterian Church in the USA ceded three congregations to the Disciples. These churches were adjacent to the Disciples mission lead by Vere Carpenter in Dajaos. The CWBM paid the Presbyterian Board of Home Missions $6,000 for the properties. The correspondence between W. R. Patterson, treasurer for the Presbyterian Board, and Anna Atwater of the CWBM reflected a clear sense of cooperation in mission.[227]

The final event was the admission in July 1922 of Augusto Cotto Reyes and Juan B. Ortiz, the only ordained national ministers, to the monthly meetings of the Mission, a gathering previously open only to the missionaries. Though without voting privileges, they could express their views fully concerning the administration of the mission.[228] In 1930 full control of the mission's work would be turned over to a committee of eleven elected by the annual convention of the Puerto Rican churches.[229]

During its first two decades the Puerto Rican mission had struggled with frequent turnover of missionaries, the high cost of operating the orphanages, and the small number of members relative to other Protestant groups. In 1919 Disciples had only 687 members, roughly a fourth of the numbers of both Methodists and Baptists. As the third decade began, however, Puerto Rican leaders, many of whom had studied in the Training School for Christian Workers, began to take on increased responsibility for preaching, teaching and directing the work. By 1922, membership had risen to 847, and within the next decade had more than doubled.[230] A remarkable but sometimes uneasy partnership was developing between UCMS missionaries and Puerto Rican leaders that would lead to a truly indigenous Disciples church in Puerto Rico.

Argentina

The Stone-Campbell Movement arrived in Argentina in 1906, when CWBM missionaries Willis (1870-1957) and Lulu (d. 1927) Burner settled in Belgrano, a neighborhood of Buenos Aires. Using part of their home as a chapel, they began worship services that attracted both European immigrants and Argentine citizens. Four additional missionaries soon arrived: Maria Reynolds Ford (1873-1964) and Zona Smith (1874-1952) in 1909; and Tolbert (1877-1959) and Mabel (1883-1935) Reavis in 1912. They established a second church at Colegiales,

another Buenos Aires neighborhood, and began a monthly paper, *La Luz y la Verdad* (*The Light and the Truth*).[231]

After the 1916 Panama Conference, the Argentine Mission began cooperating with other Protestant groups in a number of ecumenical projects. The first was a union seminary established originally in Uruguay in 1884 by the Methodist Episcopal Church and the Waldensians. The school moved to Buenos Aires in 1889, and when Manuel Blanco, an early convert of the Argentine Mission, began his studies there in 1916, the CWBM began supporting it. After the school added CWBM missionary Tolbert Reavis to its faculty, several of the Mission's young men began preparing for ministry there.[232] In 1916, the CWBM Argentine Mission joined efforts with Methodists in their secondary school Colegio Americano, renamed Colegio Ward in 1928, and in 1926 helped found a union bookstore called *La Aurora* (the Dawn).[233]

Though at first barred from becoming ministers, women exercised leadership through several organizations. Zona Smith and several Methodist women founded the Liga Nacional de Mujeres Evangélicas (National League of Evangelical Women) in 1916. Through the League, women from eight denominational missions cooperated in educational and benevolence ministries. By 1922, they had established the Instituto Modelo de Obreras Christianas (Women's Training School) to prepare young women for service in Christian education.[234] After twenty years of separate operation, the Instituto merged with Union Theological Seminary in Buenos Aires in 1942 to provide comprehensive, interdenominational programs of theological education for both women and men.

In the 1920s missionaries began seriously to consider the indigenization of the mission. They opened three additional stations in Buenos Aires led by Argentine leaders Emilia Echauriz, Antonio De Césare, and José Urso.[235] Rafael Galizia became the first Argentine pastor, appointed to serve the Belgrano Christian Church in 1925 when missionaries Tolbert and Mabel Reavis resigned. Galizia served only one year, however, when differences with other leaders of the mission—possibly concerning open membership—led him to accept the pastorate of a Baptist church in Corientes.[236]

Paraguay

At the 1916 Panama Conference, the CWBM accepted responsibility for Paraguay as part of its South American comity area. Protestant presence in the nation had been limited to small communities of immigrants from Europe and the United States who showed little interest in mission work. The revolution of 1904 began a long period of almost feudal control of the nation by various political factions, especially in rural areas. Having seen the chaos first-hand, CWBM missionary Samuel Guy Inman spoke at the 1917 International Convention in Kansas City on "The Pain of Paraguay," highlighting the suffering of the Paraguayan people and the seeming indifference of the church, both Catholic and Protestant.[237] The next year, C. Manly (1884-1976) and Selah (1886-1970) Morton arrived in Asunción as CWBM missionaries to resume educational and evangelistic work formerly conducted by the Methodist Episcopal Church.[238]

In 1919, the CWBM purchased property in Asunción from a local aristocratic family, where the Mortons established Colegio Internacional, a co-educational boarding school that attracted children of well-to-do families.[239] Dr. Arthur Elliott (b. 1891) became the first permanent director of the school in 1920, and served until 1937. His wife Ivy (1895-1973), and another missionary couple, Robert (1891-1985) and Mary (1890-1951) Lemmon, were long-time teachers at the school.[240] The work of the mission was almost entirely focused on the school, and by 1928 enrollment had grown to more than two hundred.[241]

Conclusion

By the 1920s, Stone-Campbell Christians were engaged in missions around the world. While the focus of the missionary organizations had shifted toward areas of the world without historic Christian communities, work had expanded into Latin America and the Caribbean. The Great Depression of the 1920s and 1930s would have a massive negative impact on financial support of missions, but would also hasten the process of indigenization in many places.

Some Stone-Campbell leaders had accepted the call of the 1910 Edinburgh World Missionary Conference for cooperation among mission boards, entering comity agreements and participating in union educational and publishing enterprises. Others held firmly to the view that the Stone-Campbell Movement's distinctive call to the restoration of New Testament practices would be compromised by such arrangements. This disagreement was a major factor in the division between what would become the Christian Church (Disciples of Christ) and Christian Churches/Churches of Christ.

In time, the ecumenical commitments of the Christian Church (Disciples of Christ) would lead them to partner with existing churches rather than establish new churches where Christian communities already existed. Meanwhile, the experience of World War II would raise the global consciousness of Churches of Christ as never before, inspiring members who had served in the U.S. military around the world to return to plant new churches. These new Churches of Christ, along with mission efforts of the emerging North American Christian Churches/Churches of Christ and Disciples ecumenical partnerships, would transform the Stone-Campbell Movement into a truly global phenomenon by the beginning of the twenty-first century.

8

Churches of Christ

Consolidation and Complexity

In 1916, the majority of U.S. Churches of Christ were located in the Upper South within 100 miles of a geographical band between Nashville, Tennessee, and Abilene, Texas. Two-thirds of the membership lived in Texas, Tennessee, Arkansas, Kentucky, and Oklahoma; and when northern Alabama and northern Mississippi were added, the percentage rose to more than 70 percent. Not surprisingly, as a result of their division with Disciples of Christ, Churches of Christ were a mostly Southern, largely agrarian, community. In 1916 only about 10 percent of members lived north of the Ohio River, with less than 20 percent in states west of Texas, north of Oklahoma, and in the deep South states of Georgia, Louisiana, and South Carolina.[1]

Between 1906 and 1916, census figures indicate that Churches of Christ doubled in membership to 317,937, then grew 25 percent more from 1916 to 1926 to a total of 433,174. Such a phenomenal increase reflects several things: churches choosing to align with Churches of Christ instead of Disciples, new congregations formed out of church splits, and evangelization of regions where Churches of Christ were relatively unknown.[2]

In 1916 Churches of Christ were strongest in middle Tennessee and central Texas, though each region represented a different and competing theological tradition. Not everyone in the geographical boundaries of Texas or Tennessee was committed to their regional tradition, nor were the traditions monolithic. Some, like G. C. Brewer (1884-1956), were transitional figures—his theology of grace was clearly Tennessean, but his politics were Texan. Nevertheless, the traditions were real and embodied strongly held convictions. In the early decades of the twentieth century, the Texas Tradition thrived

in the world influenced by the *Firm Foundation*, with the Tennessee Tradition equally powerful in the world influenced by the *Gospel Advocate*. The institutional and numerical strength of the Tennessee and Texas Traditions eventually marginalized the Indiana Tradition, though it remained significant in the early twentieth century.

The Tennessee Tradition as a theological consensus, however, came increasingly under attack by leaders of the other two over its positions on special providence, rebaptism, miracles, millennialism, the Holy Spirit, and the role of civil government. By mid-century the tradition had largely collapsed as an identifiable trajectory, and a subtle deism emerged. Pacifism almost disappeared. Rebaptism became the majority position, even in Tennessee. Millennialism was driven out. The personal indwelling of the Spirit became the minority view. Many came to ridicule special providence.

The breakdown of the Tennessee Tradition was a slow process, but by the late 1930s it was almost complete. The majority of members of Churches of Christ became nationalistic patriots during World War II. With few exceptions they embraced segregation as a cultural identity. As a whole, the body benefited from post-World War II prosperity and gained cultural respectability in the 1940s-50s. The Texas Tradition became the new consensus in Churches of Christ and dominated the body until new paradigms arose in the 1960s.

The Texas Tradition Reigns

Though the Tennessee and Texas Traditions had always clashed on many points, their adherents had often maintained strong personal relationships and made repeated attempts to display unity. For example, in 1895 Jefferson Davis Tant (1861-1941) became the Texas field editor for the *Gospel Advocate* despite the fact that he shared the theological perspectives of the *Firm Foundation*. He hoped his "association with the *Advocate* family might have a tendency to bring about a better state of feelings between some of the readers of the two papers."[3] When Tant came to Nashville in 1899, he stayed seven weeks, taught at the Nashville Bible School, held meetings in churches, and shared a genuine camaraderie with Lipscomb and Harding. But he also noted that he had been served opposition to rebaptism "for breakfast, dinner and supper."[4]

The rivalry between Texas and Tennessee continued strong throughout the first decades of the twentieth century. T. B. Larimore who hailed from middle Tennessee and northern Alabama often traveled to Texas for evangelistic meetings. He noted that when Texas Christians subscribed to the *Firm Foundation* their intent was not so much to subscribe to a Christian paper but to a Texas paper.[5] Apparently, many Texans resented the presence of Tennessee preachers who arrived in Texas as if "the salvation of Texas depended upon" them, though, as Foy E. Wallace, Sr. (1871-1949), cautioned, every gospel preacher who comes to reap the harvest should be welcomed.[6] Nevertheless, there was a strong feeling that Tennessee preachers, and the *Advocate* in particular, had been "ruling the church of Christ with a high hand," according to William T. Owen of Alhambra, California. Breaking this "ecclesiastical body within the church," Owen asserted, would be one of his generation's greatest accomplishments.[7]

Theologically, the Tennessee stream regarded the church as a manifestation of the Kingdom, but not identical with it as the Texas tradition insisted. Tennessee's eschatology yearned for a renewed earth whereas Texas expected the annihilation of the earth along with a platonic spiritual existence in heaven. Tennessee taught the presence of the Holy Spirit in Christians as a dynamic, personal presence that enables holy living, while Texas limited the work of the Spirit to the written word. Tennessee's preaching was Christocentric, focusing on the good news of God's redemption through Jesus; Texas saw the task of preaching as making plain God's requirements in the plan of salvation. Tennessee rooted discipleship in the ministry of Jesus and therefore had a much larger view of the social dimensions of the church's mission; Texas focused on the marks of the true church found in Acts and the Epistles, such as its name, terms of admission, and organization. Tennessee's understanding of baptism was theocentric, seeing it as obedience that

trusted in God's saving work; Texas was anthropocentric, understanding baptism as the final step of human obedience necessary to obtain salvation. Tennessee affirmed an exclusive allegiance to the Kingdom of God, while Texas affirmed a dual—though tiered—allegiance to the church and nation. These two traditions agreed on the forms the church should take, but their basic theological and spiritual orientations were quite different.

Though the Texas Tradition emerged in full view with the beginning of the *Firm Foundation* in 1884, twentieth-century leaders like J. D. Tant and Robertson L. Whiteside (1869-1951) developed and promoted it. Originally a Methodist preacher, Tant became part of the Stone-Campbell Movement in 1881 without rebaptism since he had been immersed as a believer among the Methodists. However, in 1886 he was reimmersed by J. S. Durst and became, along with Durst and Austin McGary, one of the major proponents of rebaptism in Churches of Christ. Tant was a controversial but effective popularizer of the Texas Tradition, writing for both the *Firm Foundation* and the *Gospel Advocate*. He held over 200 debates and probably baptized more people than any other evangelist among Churches of Christ in the early twentieth century.

If Tant was the popularizer of the Texas Tradition, Whiteside was the systematizer, sometimes even called the "David Lipscomb of Texas."[8] Though a graduate of the Nashville Bible School (1898), he rejected its counter-cultural apocalyptic vision. In 1925, he and C. R. Nichol (1876-1961) wrote the first major work opposing Robert H. Boll's (1875-1956) premillennial views.[9] Noting Boll's pessimistic view of human nature, Whiteside sensed that the deeper issue with Boll was a competing understanding of Christianity. While Whiteside focused on the human mechanics of restoring the church, Boll stressed the Kingdom's breaking into the world through God's action.

Whiteside epitomized the Texas Tradition and is perhaps most responsible for the development of a consensus theology among Churches of Christ in the 1930s-1950s. He led the fight against the Nashville Bible School's apocalyptic orientation, including its pacifism, focus on grace, and reliance on the personal indwelling of the Spirit. His theology saturated Churches of Christ through his commentary on Romans, his five-volume *Sound Doctrine* co-authored with C. R. Nichol, and his Sunday school literature for both the Firm Foundation (1928-1930) and Gospel Advocate publishing houses (1937-1944).[10] *Sound Doctrine*, studied in congregations nationwide, had a profound impact on people in the pews as Whiteside provided a compelling alternative to the Tennessee Tradition. Foy E. Wallace, Jr. (1896-1979), who would champion the Texas Tradition past mid-century, affirmed that no other teacher had been more of a "mentor and model" to him than Whiteside.[11]

In 1930, as subscribers to the *Gospel Advocate* decreased in Texas, the publisher invited Texan Foy E. Wallace, Jr., to the editor's chair. Wallace in turn appointed Whiteside to the *Advocate*'s editorial staff. Initially Wallace enjoyed success and popularity, but he soon filled the paper with contentious advocacy. Wallace resigned in 1934 due to personal financial problems, but his replacement, John T. Hinds (1866-1938), was another Texan. Wallace and Hinds had both written for the *Firm Foundation* in the 1920s with Hinds the front-page editor of the Texas paper.

As a result, Wallace and Hinds brought Texas attitudes and convictions to the Tennessee paper. Many Texans were afraid that Wallace had gone soft when he went to the *Advocate*. Tant, for example, confessed that he "feared when [Wallace] went to Nashville that he was wandering from his earlier training," but his fears were alleviated when Wallace added Nichol and Whiteside to the staff. He felt assured that they would bring the *Advocate* around to biblical truth on all issues.[12] In effect, the Texans moved into Tennessee and aligned the *Advocate* with the Texas tradition during the 1930s. This shift significantly curtailed the influence of the Nashville Bible School, especially its apocalyptic vision.

The Eclipse of the Apocalyptic Worldview

By 1945 Churches of Christ had effectively removed the apocalyptic worldview from the mainstream of the movement, a shift symbolized by the resignation of E. H. Ijams (1886-1982) from the presidency of David Lipscomb College (formerly the Nashville Bible School) and the publication of Foy E. Wallace, Jr.'s anti-premillennial treatise *God's Prophetic Word*.[13] Though some have tended to equate the Tennessee orientation with premillennialism, it is much broader than any specific millennial view. Richard Hughes defines apocalyptic as living "as if the final rule of the kingdom of God were present in the here and now."[14] As the Tennessee Tradition lived out this vision in the 1880s-1920s, it assumed the ongoing action of God in creation. This counter-cultural spirituality embraced, among other things, the enabling power of the indwelling Spirit, pacifism accompanied by rejection of nationalism and patriotism, a vibrant understanding of grace as both the ground and power of the Christian life, and a belief in God's ultimate triumph over Satan and creation of a new earth on which to reign. Each of these came under assault from the anthropocentric "positive law" emphases of the Texas Tradition.

Presence of the Holy Spirit. The sanctifying indwelling presence of the Holy Spirit became a point of contention in the 1900s-1920s. James A. Harding, in contrast to the Texas Tradition, pressed the absolute necessity of this divine presence for holy living. Harding became so identified with this perspective that some came to believe that his students and the Bible Schools they founded were theological innovators.[15]

Harding's pessimistic view of human nature meant that it was primarily God's action that transforms humans into the image of Christ. Reflecting Paul's cry in Romans 7, Harding exclaimed, "I would do right, that is I desire, to do the very thing that Jesus would do were he in my place, and to do it just as he would do it. Alas! How wretchedly I fail in doing the thing I would."[16] Believers must have the help of the Spirit to overcome their fallen nature. Everyone knows at the deepest levels, Harding asserted, that we are utterly incapable of caring for, guiding, or strengthening ourselves.[17]

Writers for the *Christian Leader & The Way* debated different views of the work of the Holy Spirit thoroughly in the first decade of the twentieth century. That contest ended with an apparent tie, but when the debate reemerged in the late 1920s in the *Firm Foundation*, the Texas position was clearly dominant. A key player in the debate, Kenny Carl Moser (1893-1976), had questioned the anti-indwelling orthodoxy of 1920s Texas. Moser had attended Thorp Spring Christian College from 1915 to 1919, where he heard Texas orthodoxy from C. R. Nichol and the Tennessee perspective from R. C. Bell (1877-1964). In 1930 Moser confessed that he had at first denied the indwelling of the Spirit simply because his teachers had taught him to deny it. Later, however, he had come to believe that the doctrine was plainly taught in Scripture.[18] Those who would deny that God's Spirit dwells in the Christian, he asserted, had left grace for law and replaced the security Christ gives for the miserable condition Paul describes in Romans. "Legalism is the father of the denial of the personal indwelling of the Spirit," he exclaimed.[19]

Firm Foundation editor G. H. P. Showalter (1870-1954) immediately banned Moser from the pages of the *Firm Foundation*, and by September 1933 Foy Wallace had dismissed him as a contributing editor of the *Gospel Advocate*. By the 1930s, denial of the Spirit's personal indwelling was a fairly settled position in Churches of Christ. After Harding's departure from the Nashville

Bible School (NBS) in 1901, many of his former students moved toward the Texas Tradition on this point. H. Leo Boles (1874-1946), a 1906 NBS graduate and President of the school from 1913-1920 and 1923-1932, is one example.[20] Most came to agree with the Texas position that to admit the Spirit works outside the written word undermines the sufficiency of Scripture.

Millennialism. Many in the Tennessee Tradition, including James A. Harding and J. N. Armstrong, held premillennial beliefs (e.g., that Jesus would destroy his enemies and reign a thousand years on the earth prior to the new heaven and new earth). Lipscomb himself was non-committal concerning a specific view of premillennialism. The real heart of apocalyptic eschatology was the imminent return of Christ, the necessity of divine action in the world, and renewed earth eschatology. The foundational principle of the Tennessee Tradition was that God was working to bring the universe fully under divine rule—to usher in completely the Kingdom of God.

Premillennial eschatology itself, however, took center stage in the late 1910s, especially through the work of R. H. Boll. A German immigrant, Boll had been baptized in a Church of Christ in Tennessee in 1895 and graduated from the Nashville Bible School in 1900. A popular writer, by 1909 he had become front-page editor of the *Gospel Advocate*. Opposition to his essays on unfulfilled prophecy, millennialism, and the book of Revelation, however, resulted in his resignation in 1915. The next year he became editor of the New Orleans-based premillennial *Word and Work* and moved it to Louisville, Kentucky, where he lived.

In 1924 Boll published *The Kingdom of God: A Survey-Study of the Bible's Principal Themes* in which he explored his premillennial understandings in the context of the relationship of the church and Kingdom.[21] Nichol and Whiteside responded with a book condemning Boll and his position.[22] A series of debates followed, intended to clarify the issue yet maintain a modicum of fellowship between the two groups. The most significant were a written discussion between Boll and H. Leo Boles in 1927 and two oral debates in 1933 between Charles M. Neal and Foy E. Wallace, Jr., then editor of the *Gospel Advocate*, in Winchester, Kentucky, and Chattanooga, Tennessee. The written discussion was congenial, but the oral debates were bitter and ultimately divisive.

Statements made by Boles, then President of David Lipscomb College, illustrate a crucial shift in attitude between 1925 and 1935. At the end of the 1927 debate, Boles wrote that he regarded Boll as a pious

Christian whom he esteemed "very highly as a brother in Jesus Christ."[23] By 1935, however, he had reversed his judgment. While he had not previously regarded the premillennial question as a fellowship issue, he explained, the question had become so divisive, he could no longer consider himself in fellowship with Boll.[24]

Robert Henry Boll, a major leader in Churches of Christ in the early twentieth century, was increasingly ostracized for his promotion of premillennial views of the relationship of the church to the Kingdom of God. *(Courtesy Center for Restoration Studies, Abilene Christian University)*

Despite G. C. Brewer's plea for forbearance and his warning against Pharisaic partyism at the 1934 Abilene Lectures, Churches of Christ generally followed the lead of Foy E. Wallace, Jr. Wallace insisted that premillennialism's claim that the Kingdom had not yet fully come was a menace to Churches of Christ, making the church a mere accident.[25] In 1935 W. W. Otey (1867-1961) summoned the church to "mark" and "turn away" from all premillennialists and those who would not oppose them.[26]

As indicated by Otey's censure, "Bollism" described not only those who taught premillennialism, but also those who sympathized with and refused to disfellowship them. L. L. Brigance (1879-1950), a Bible teacher at

Freed-Hardeman College, played on the cultural fears of the day, urging every college president and preacher to publicly denounce "Bollshevism" and oppose the "Boll Evil."[27] In effect, the major papers and colleges with the exception of Harding College President J. N. Armstrong—son-in-law of James A. Harding—gave in to the pressure to exclude premillennialists as writers, speakers, and teachers in their papers, schools, and churches.

The exclusion of premillennialists from Churches of Christ resulted in the loss of eschatology as a fundamental impulse of faith and practice. Amillennialism became the groups's view, along with rejection of the idea that God would create a new earth and a loss of urgency about the second coming of Christ. At the root of the exclusion of the premillennialists was the accusation that their understanding of the Kingdom undermined the importance of the church. Their removal from the mainstream signaled the triumph of a theological position that equated the church and the Kingdom. The Texas theological agenda focused more on human action to restore the true church rather than on God's work, and its spirituality focused more on human achievement than the work of the Spirit and God's bringing in the Kingdom.

Pacifism. The Tennessee Tradition's pacifism rose out of a sense of alienation from the fallen world and went hand-in-hand with hostility toward the agendas of civil governments. In this view, the spirit of this age was completely incompatible with God's Kingdom. The spirit of civil government was "force, violence and destruction of life," in contrast to the righteousness, peace, and life of the Kingdom of God.[28]

The death of pacifism among Churches of Christ is the tale of the two world wars. In late 1917, opposition from the local council of defense forced Cordell Christian College in Oklahoma to close its doors. President J. N. Armstrong had counseled male students to serve as noncombatants; but when faculty member S. A. Bell denounced all military service by Christians in an article in Armstrong's *Gospel Herald*, the council demanded the school's closure. World War I also silenced the pacifist witness of the *Gospel Advocate*. Publisher J. C. McQuiddy closed the journal to anti-war writing after Federal agents threatened him with arrest for publishing seditious articles.[29]

In contrast, G. H. P. Showalter (1870-1954), editor of the *Firm Foundation*, embraced militarism from the start. Conscientious objectors, according to Showalter, were German agents seeking to undermine the war effort.

He advocated that the church support the government rather than such imposters.[30]

Despite a resurgence of pacifism in some parts of Churches of Christ in the 1920s and 1930s, World War II marked the death of pacifism in the mainstream with R. L. Whiteside and Foy E. Wallace, Jr., leading the charge. Through the pages of his *Bible Banner*, Wallace attacked everyone who lacked the patriotism to defend the United States. Whiteside called the Nashville Bible School heritage on war and civil government a "nondescript religio-politico cult" which was "unethical and unbiblical and in all respects untrue."[31] The shift from allegiance to the Kingdom of God, peace, and opposition to participation in civil government, to patriotism, nationalism, and support of war moved Churches of Christ from cultural isolation to cultural respectability in the American nation.

A "middle" position, however, developed among some who rejected "pacifism" as a modernist secular philosophy, yet still insisted that Christians could not be involved with killing for their country. Among them was premillennial leader R. H. Boll who was clear that he regarded pacifists during World War I as political agitators who had no right "to interfere with the Civil Government in its purposes, policies, or rights." Though Christians were not to kill, governments had the God-given responsibility to bear the sword.[32]

G.C. Brewer expressed the same attitude in the buildup to World War II. While Christians could not kill, those who went to prison for refusing to support their country were aiding the enemy. He advised Christians to enlist quickly, advise officials of their conscientious objection to killing, and insist on a non-combatant assignment. He urged them to express their opposition as strictly personal and not that of the church to which they belonged because many in Churches of Christ did not share these convictions.[33]

Grace. In 1932 the Gospel Advocate Publishing Company printed K. C. Moser's *The Way of Salvation*. It was a frontal assault on the Texas Tradition's understanding of grace, faith, and works. There was no doubt in Moser's mind that by a "subtle but steady polemic: somebody was misconstruing the saving work of Christ and seriously compromising the gospel."[34] The fundamental misunderstanding, according to Moser, was the substitution of human righteousness for divine righteousness. Moser understood that the concept of righteousness as completely independent of human effort was difficult to grasp for many of his contemporaries. A righteousness not tied to good deeds seemed impossible.

Nevertheless, he contended that righteousness is a gift from God through faith in Christ's work rather than something resulting from acts of obedience.[35]

The reaction to Moser was immediate and hostile. Whiteside sarcastically commented that Moser's words sounded like something a Universalist or ultra-Calvinist would write. "Not only am I not able to grasp the idea of a righteousness that does not depend on human effort," he wrote, "but I do not believe there is such righteousness in any human being."[36] Whiteside's commentary on Romans, first appearing as a series in the *Gospel Advocate*, was a sustained reply to Moser's book.[37] Wallace, then editor of the paper, responded that Moser's emphasis was certainly not "more effective than the plain Bible preaching of faith, repentance, confession, and baptism" that faithful preachers had always proclaimed.[38] Though Wallace had just appointed Moser to the *Gospel Advocate* staff on January 1, 1933, most likely due to the influence of G. C. Brewer, by September Wallace had dropped him, explaining that the other staff (including Boles, Nichol, and Whiteside) objected to Moser's "peculiar ideas" as "contrary to the gospel."[39]

Nevertheless, G. C. Brewer (1884-1956), a 1911 graduate of the Nashville Bible School, supported his friend. *The Way of Salvation* was one of the "best little books that came from any press in 1932," he wrote. "I commend it heartily. If there is a conclusion in it with which I differ, I do not now recall it."[40] In 1952 when the controversy over grace and faith arose again after the publication of Moser's pamphlet *Christ Versus a Plan*, Brewer reminded his Abilene Lectureship audience that Lipscomb and Harding had known these truths and taught them faithfully.[41] If, in fact, our actions—our obedience to commandments or observance of laws—made us righteous, Moser insisted, we would make the death of Christ unnecessary.[42]

From the 1930s through the 1950s, Moser and Brewer were minority voices in Churches of Christ. When a young preacher named Roy Key wrote an article on the "righteousness of God" for the 1945 *Gospel Advocate* in which he rehearsed some of the same ideas, the reaction was strongly negative. His article promoted ideas, one reader said, "that I have not been accustomed to hearing."[43] A Texas understanding of the righteousness of God had so saturated the minds of *Gospel Advocate* readers by 1945 that the Tennessee Tradition's own theology of grace sounded strange, innovative, and unsound.

R. C. Bell was a staunch advocate of the Tennessee Tradition and one of the strongest supporters of higher education among Churches of Christ in the first half of the twentieth century. Bell had graduated from the Nashville Bible School, taught at Potter Bible College, Western Bible and Literary College, and Cordell Christian College. Later he served as President of Thorp Spring Christian College, Dean of Harding College, and a faculty member of Abilene Christian College.

Bell sensed a change among Churches of Christ in the mid-twentieth century. The church was "booming," with hundreds of new church buildings and a new post-World War II mission emphasis. These things were reflections of the real shift, Bell believed—that the body no longer embraced its alien status. During World War II patriotism and nationalism had swamped the church and it became socially comfortable, at peace with American culture. Theologically the church denied the enabling personal presence of the indwelling Spirit. In their five-step "plan of salvation" (hear, believe, repent, confess, and be baptized), Churches of Christ focused on human action rather than on God's. Church growth seemed a matter of executing the "plan" and building buildings. In a 1951 autobiographical article, Bell expressed his view that the church needed revival by an infusion of Harding's apocalyptic theology in order "to save [it] from changing divine dynamics to human mechanics."[44]

The Rise of Schools in Churches of Christ

When Lipscomb and Harding founded the Nashville Bible School in 1891, there had been some objecting voices from the North. J. W. McGarvey of the College of the Bible in Lexington, Kentucky, for example, questioned the wisdom of establishing another school when, in his view, a sufficient number already existed in the region. In the first decade of the twentieth century Daniel Sommer of the Indiana Tradition began to question the very existence of the schools.

Sommer had blamed the "modern school men" in 1889 for the division between Churches of Christ and the Disciples of Christ.[45] The increasing number of schools among Churches of Christ in the early twentieth century revived his fears. In 1936 Foy E. Wallace, Jr., similarly complained that the colleges encouraged professionalism among preachers.[46] Some feared the schools would come to control the churches through these professional pastors.

Yet both the Tennessee and Texas Traditions were active in defending the rightness and establishing of institutions of higher education. Nashville Bible School leaders were clear that they never intended it to be a professional school for preachers but a liberal arts institution where Bible study was part of the required curriculum for all pupils. From the beginning, the school educated men and women to be wise and useful Christians, equipped to choose their profession upon graduation. Lipscomb and Harding believed the church needed more schools rather than fewer. By 1904, Nashville Bible School graduates had established four other institutions in the United States (Gunter Bible College in Gunter, Texas; Potter Bible College in Bowling Green, Kentucky; Southwestern Christian College in Denton, Texas; and Valdosta Bible School in Georgia), one in Persia, one in Canada, and one in Japan.[47]

J. N. Armstrong, son-in-law of James A. Harding, was another enthusiastic promoter of schools. After graduating from and teaching at Nashville Bible School, he followed Harding to Potter Bible College in Bowling Green, Kentucky, in 1901. In 1905 he began the Western Bible and Literary College in Odessa, Missouri, along with R. C. Bell.[48] In 1908 Armstrong became president of Cordell Christian College in Oklahoma, which had been established the previous year. After the forced closure of Cordell in 1918, Armstrong became President of Harper College in Kansas in 1919. In 1924 Harper College merged with Arkansas Christian College in Morrilton, Arkansas, and was renamed Harding College. The school moved to Searcy, Arkansas, in 1934 where Armstrong served as President until 1936.

Another fervent advocate of the schools was pioneer educator Jesse P. Sewell (1876-1969). An 1898 graduate of Nashville Bible School, he served on the editorial staff of the *Gospel Advocate* and wrote frequently for the *Christian Leader & the Way*. He encouraged the founding of Southwestern Christian College in Denton, Texas, in 1904. He also persuaded A. B. Barret, a native of Tennessee and graduate of Nashville Bible School, to leave Southwestern to establish what is now Abilene Christian University in 1906.[49] In addition, he played a significant role in the purchase of the Thorp Spring property for the beginning of Thorp Spring Christian College in 1910. He served as Abilene's president from 1912 to 1924 and spent his twilight years teaching Bible at Harding College (1950-1957).

Education in Texas, however, predated Nashville Bible School in the series of schools located at Thorp Spring. Starting with Add Ran College in 1873 (which would later move and become Texas Christian University), schools continued in various forms at Thorp Spring until a board comprised exclusively of members of Churches of Christ purchased the property in 1910 and called it Thorp Spring Christian College. The

school operated until 1928. In 1894, members of Texas Churches of Christ had founded a school at Lockney between Lubbock and Amarillo, which operated until 1918.

Foy E. Wallace, Jr., son of a Texas preacher, was appointed editor of the *Gospel Advocate* in 1930 as a result of his highly successful evangelism. An effective debater, he addressed such issues as premillennialism, the Christian's responsibility to civil government, and church support of colleges. *(Courtesy Center for Restoration Studies, Abilene Christian University)*

The series of schools that created Freed-Hardeman College in Henderson, Tennessee, falls outside the influence of the Nashville Bible School. In 1885 members of the Stone-Campbell Movement purchased the property of the Henderson Masonic Male and Female Institute and organized a board that renamed the school West Tennessee Christian College.[50] In 1895 the school united with A. G. Freed's (1863-1931) Southern Tennessee Normal College and in 1897 was renamed Georgie Robertson Christian College, after the daughter of a major donor and Board member. Uncomfortable with the growing influence of the Christian Church in Henderson, Freed moved in 1905 to become President of Southwestern Christian College in Denton, Texas, at the end of his ten-year commitment. Georgie Robertson Christian College folded in 1907 and trustees sold the property to the city of Henderson. However, in 1908 Freed returned with former student N. B. Hardeman (1874-1965) to establish a new school—National Teachers' Normal and Business College. The Board renamed the school Freed-Hardeman College in 1919.

Reflecting the growing strength of Churches of Christ in southern California, George Pepperdine (1886-1962), founder of Western Auto, funded the establishment of Pepperdine College in Los Angeles in 1937 under the presidency of Batsell Baxter (1886-1956). Pepperdine College established the first permanent graduate theological school among Churches of Christ in 1944 under W. B. West, Jr. (1907-1994). Pepperdine was also the first school in Churches of Christ to admit students of all races.

Churches of Christ in North America experienced an educational boom in the first decades of the twentieth century, at the very time they were taking shape as an identifiable stream of the Stone-Campbell Movement. The colleges established then served as powerful centers of influence on the body's thought and development throughout the century.

The Theological Identity of Churches of Christ

Churches of Christ stabilized their theological identity in the first half of the twentieth century by three methods: large urban revivals, institutional lectureships, and "brotherhood" literature. Large urban revival meetings attracted thousands to hear well-known preachers. The most famous of these was the Hardeman Tabernacle Meetings in Nashville, Tennessee. The most successful of the institutional lectureships was the annual Abilene Christian College Lectures, drawing thousands from around the country. Practically every preacher in Churches of Christ read a handful of significant books that also found their way into church libraries and the homes of many members. These books, studied at home and church, solidified the distinct theological perspectives of members of Churches of Christ. Each factor contributed to the creation of a powerful theological consensus that allowed little divergence.

By 1920, Nashville, Tennessee, had the largest contingent of members of Churches of Christ of any city in the United States. Consequently, it became a leader in significant ways, especially east of the Mississippi. In 1921 Nashville churches agreed to cooperate in a three-week evangelistic meeting in March-April 1922. They selected N. B. Hardeman to conduct the meeting,

which drew as many as 8,000 for some services.[51] Local newspapers published the sermons immediately after they were presented, and the Gospel Advocate Company published the series in book form. Hardeman returned in 1923, 1928, 1938, and 1942 for a total of one hundred and twenty-five sermons.[52]

Hardeman's topics covered a range of issues, but three themes dominated: the church, the Bible, and conversion. From the marks of the church to the authority of the Bible to the five steps of salvation, Hardeman covered the ground that would identify Churches of Christ. William Woodson has suggested that these sermons provided members of Churches of Christ with a clear sense of their identity as Hardeman systematized and put in plain words their main teachings.[53] Hardeman himself commented that these meetings gave the larger Nashville community a sense of who Churches of Christ were like nothing else could have.[54] The Hardeman Tabernacle sermons continued to influence Churches of Christ through dissemination and imitation through the rest of the century.

These meetings, along with his 1923 Nashville debate with Ira Boswell on instrumental music,[55] confirmed Hardeman's reputation as a defender of the faith who could be trusted with training preachers at Freed-Hardeman College. The college, with Hardeman as President, produced hundreds of preachers who served Churches of Christ during the middle of the twentieth century, especially after World War II when the G.I. Bill enabled many rural students to attend college.

College Lectureships also became powerful sources of identity, becoming places to discuss issues, solidify perspectives, and exchange practical ideas. In essence, they became a mode of communal discernment for Churches of Christ. The Abilene Christian College Lectures, begun in February 1918, became an annual gathering that attracted preachers and members from every part of the United States and the world. In a 1965 study of forty-six years of the Lectures, William Banowsky offered a window into how members discussed, discerned, and decided issues, creating a widespread consensus.[56] Annual lectureships began at Freed-Hardeman in 1935 and at Pepperdine in 1942. At the beginning of the twenty-first century, the Abilene, Pepperdine, and Freed-Hardeman lectureships were still among the largest gatherings of members of Churches of Christ.

The Freed-Hardeman lectureship was particularly important for advancing and solidifying the Texas Tradition in Tennessee. Guy N. Woods (1908-1993), a skilled debater and controversialist, typified the theology of the Texas stream. He shaped generations through his writing, especially as a staff writer and later editor of the *Gospel Advocate* from 1943 till his death. He was probably most well known in Freed-Hardeman circles, however, for conducting the annual lectureship's "Open Forum" for thirty years. Continuing the legacy of N. B. Hardeman, Woods extended his mentor's theology with definitive answers to all questions raised.[57]

Nicholas Brody Hardeman became the model preacher for a generation of leaders in Churches of Christ. His widely disseminated Tabernacle Sermons set a doctrinal standard for the body. (*Courtesy Center for Restoration Studies, Abilene Christian University*)

In some ways the lectureships served the same purpose as denominational conventions. At the very least, they contributed to the stabilization of the identity of Churches of Christ by providing fellowship and a forum for discussion that fostered the formation of a consensus theology.

In addition to revivals and lectureships, certain widely used publications helped make the Texas Tradition dominant in Churches of Christ. Texas-oriented authors R. L. Whiteside and Guy N. Woods shaped the churches' perspectives through the Gospel Advocate Company's adult Sunday school literature. Whiteside authored the *Gospel Advocate Adult Quarterly* (1932-1936) and the *Adult Lesson Commentary* (1937-1944), and Woods followed as the author of the *Adult Gospel Quarterly* from 1948 to 1978. The Firm Foundation Publishing House also published Sunday school literature for all ages throughout the twentieth century, catechizing congregations in the Texas Tradition.

Whiteside and Nichol's five-volume series *Sound Doctrine*, popular for its pocket size and simple writing style, became one of the most effective pieces of literature in the history of Churches of Christ. Another influential book of the mid-twentieth century was Leroy Brownlow's *Why I am a Member of the Church of Christ*.[58] With over one million copies in print, it is probably the single highest selling book written for Churches of Christ. First printed in 1945, and read by most members of Churches of Christ from 1945-1965, it was still used in some congregations as a basic catechism at the beginning of the twenty-first century. Brownlow explained that he was a member of the Church of Christ because it had the scriptural founder, foundation, name, organization, and creed. It rightly interpreted Scripture, was undenominational, conducted mission work scripturally, equated the church and Kingdom, taught the five steps of salvation, and practiced the five authorized acts of worship in the Sunday assembly (praying, singing, reading Scripture, taking the Lord's Supper, and giving). Ecclesiology—the doctrine of the church—was the focus of the theology of mid-twentieth-century Churches of Christ and became the body's theological identity.

The Positive Law Tradition in Conflict

By the early twentieth century Churches of Christ had adopted a three-fold hermeneutic asserting that the parts of Scripture binding on Christians today were the explicit commands, apostolic examples, and necessary inferences of the New Testament. As early as 1883 James A. Harding argued that whatever "is not taught therein by precept, or by approved example, or by a *necessary* inference is not taught by the Heavenly Father at all."[59] In 1901 Harding could say: "I have been taught all my life that the Scriptures teach 'by precept by approved apostolic example and by necessary inference,' and it is certain that this is correct."[60] With this way of understanding Scripture the Christian could discern the details of biblical positive law and thus implement correct church forms and practices.

Leaders originally applied this hermeneutic to matters like congregational music and missionary societies, but eventually they applied it to other practices including ordaining elders with the laying on of hands and extending the right hand of fellowship as a formal worship practice. The issues that proved most divisive in the early twentieth century were the use of Sunday schools, located or resident evangelists, and multiple cups in communion. Shaped by the positive law mindset and hermeneutic, some in Churches of Christ viewed these as vital matters. The controversies reflected a struggle between institutionalized forms and "modern methods," though always couched in terms of faithfulness to Scripture.

Sunday Schools. The use of literature other than the Bible, the division of the Sunday assembly into classes, and the role of female teachers became prominent issues among Churches of Christ in the first decades of the twentieth century. These questions became particularly volatile in Texas. Lee P. Mansfield noted in 1916 that twenty years earlier there had been only a few congregations with Sunday schools, but in his day every church had one.[61] By 1926, Churches of Christ were conducting 4,403 Sunday schools with 274,571 students.[62]

While Daniel Sommer opposed the Sunday school as an institution that subverted parental obligations and became an appendage to the church,[63] some in the Texas Tradition opposed it on positive law grounds, focusing on the unauthorized division of the church into classes and the use of women as teachers. N. L. Clark led the fight when he declared in a January 1907 *Firm Foundation* editorial that he could not view the Sunday school as anything but an unauthorized innovation.[64] He opposed the Sunday school, he insisted, "because it is not in the Book."[65] Clearly it was scriptural for the church to meet and, under the direction of the elders, to worship and be taught. It was equally scriptural for churches to send evangelists to preach the gospel, and for parents to instruct their children at home. Why, then, divide the church by introducing a Sunday school about which Scripture is silent?

R. L. Whiteside immediately began a lengthy discussion opposing Clark in the *Firm Foundation*, and Clark resigned as editor two years later. A tract war and series of debates ensued including the Clark-Young debate in Fort Worth, Texas, in June 1911. J. D. Tant, along with Whiteside, led in the promotion of Sunday schools and attacks on those who opposed them.

Though Clark himself believed the issue was not significant enough to break fellowship, he could not stem the tide.[66] The *Apostolic Way*, a paper established

in 1913 that came to champion the non-Bible class stance, published a list of faithful churches in 1925. In 1936 Gene Shelburne began publishing *Gospel Tidings* as a voice for the non-class congregations and in 1946 founded what became the South Houston Bible Institute. As the churches condemned and excluded one another over the issue, the non-class churches formed themselves into a cohesive group through their meetings, papers, and school. The group totaled 18,779 members in 458 churches in 2009.[67]

Located or Resident Preachers. At the beginning of the twentieth century the general practice among U.S. Churches of Christ, as in Britain, was for several men to instruct the church each Sunday, often called mutual edification. Most churches opposed an educated professional class of preachers. Evangelists were itinerants who conducted revival meetings, baptized new converts, and planted churches. However, this was already changing in some places by the late nineteenth century. Instead of employing evangelists to plant churches in unevangelized areas, Churches of Christ began employing evangelists to preach weekly, a practice that had emerged earlier in the Disciples stream of the U.S. Stone-Campbell Movement. Lipscomb, among others, continued to oppose this move.[68]

However, M. C. Kurfees in Louisville, Kentucky, W. L. Logan in Murfreeesboro, Tennessee, and L. S. White in Gallatin, Tennessee, were functioning as located preachers by 1900. Kurfees and others persuaded most *Gospel Advocate* readers that there was a difference between the "modern pastor system" where one person rules the church, and a preacher who served one local congregation for a period of time.[69] By mid-century an educated ministry serving particular congregations had become the dominant model.

Daniel Sommer, nevertheless, continued to insist that mutual edification was the only biblical model, and many in the Indiana Tradition would continue Sommer's opposition. Carl Ketcherside—champion of the Indiana Tradition in the mid-twentieth century—debated the question with G. K. Wallace in 1952 at Paragould, Arkansas, and in 1953 at St. Louis, Missouri.[70] The resulting division produced a small group of Mutual Edification congregations that in 2009 counted 4,800 members in 115 churches.[71]

One Cup. Churches of Christ, like all other churches, had always used a single cup in the Lord's Supper, though large congregations sometimes used one cup for each side of the building. Following the lead of congregations from several denominations that began using individual cups to prevent the spread of disease in the 1890s, C. E. Holt of Florence, Alabama, suggested the use of individual cups in a 1911 *Gospel Advocate* article. David Lipscomb responded that one must maintain the "divine appointments" as they were given.[72]

The reaction from writers such as H. C. Harper in the *Firm Foundation* was much stronger.[73] Harper was also an editor of the *Apostolic Way*, and many in the non-class churches came to regard multiple cups as an innovation that subverted the apostolic pattern. When Harper and Clark debated the question in the *Apostolic Way*, the tension became so great that Harper and G. A. Trott resigned from the paper and began a new one titled *The Truth*. The paper continued as *The Old Paths Advocate* after a 1932 name change under the editorship of Homer L. King.

Lipscomb, though having always opposed individual cups, in 1915 wrote one of his last articles suggesting there might be freedom in this matter.[74] G. C. Brewer, who had urged Lipscomb to write the article, had been a leader in introducing individual communion cups—first at the Central Church of Christ in Chattanooga, Tennessee, then in Columbia, Tennessee, in 1915. At the same time, G. Dallas Smith (1870-1920) introduced individual cups into the Fayetteville and Murfreesboro, Tennessee, churches, and the tide quickly turned in both Tennessee and Texas. After Lipscomb's article permitting individual cups, Brewer reported that most Churches of Christ began using them, though the churches in Nashville took much longer to adopt the practice. One Cup churches numbered 551 congregations with 17,313 members in 2009.[75]

The Institutional Controversy

By the end of World War II, mainstream Churches of Christ were an identifiable group with shared beliefs and practices (plurality of elders and deacons, five steps of salvation, five acts of worship), institutions (David Lipscomb College, Abilene Christian College, Freed-Hardeman College, Pepperdine College, Harding College), papers (*Gospel Advocate, Firm Foundation*), and events (Abilene Christian College Lectureship, Freed-Hardeman Lectureship, Pepperdine Lectureship). Other aspects of their identity had been clear by the late nineteenth century—*a cappella* music, autonomy of local congregations, and exclusion of women from the pulpit, in addition to more widely held Stone-Campbell stances on believers' immersion for the remission of sins

and weekly communion. As the Texas and Tennessee Traditions had battled for prominence, with the marginalized Indiana Tradition steadily losing ground, mainstream Churches of Christ had slowly reached a consensus on theological issues that had previously divided them. By the early 1930s, the Texas Tradition had the upper hand in shaping that consensus, and by 1945 it had won the day.

Churches of Christ had also continued to grow. Though the government never funded publication of the U. S. religious census of 1946, M. Norvel Young collected data that indicated Churches of Christ had increased by 1946 to over 680,000 members in more than 10,000 congregations in the United States.[76] Though the figure is likely inflated since it represented a 50 percent increase over the 1936 census, it reflects a group rooted in Southern culture spreading by migration across the whole nation, particularly the West Coast. In 1957 Young reported to the *Britannica Yearbook* that Churches of Christ numbered over 1,600,000 with more than 15,500 congregations;[77] and some suggested—with caution—2,000,000 members in 1959.[78] These numbers were surely overstated since total United States membership in 1980 was only 1,200,000, and data from 2006 showed roughly 1,260,000 members.[79] A better estimate for membership in the United States in 1960 is somewhere in the range of 900,000-1,000,000.

Nevertheless, the numbers indicated substantial growth. With this growth came a sociological shift toward affluence and cultural respectability. This sociological shift was nowhere more evident than in the growth and academic standing of schools related to Churches of Christ. While George Pepperdine College was the only accredited educational institution among Churches of Christ in 1950, during that decade Abilene (1951), Harding (1953), Lipscomb (1954), and Freed-Hardeman (1956) achieved accreditation. In addition, eight other colleges began operation during the 1940s and 1950s: Montgomery Bible School (1942; now Faulkner University) in Montgomery, Alabama; Florida Christian College (1946; now Florida College) in Temple Terrace; Central Christian College (1950; now Oklahoma Christian University) in Bartlesville and later Oklahoma City; York College (1956) in York, Nebraska; Ohio Valley College (1958) in Parkersburg, West Virginia; Lubbock Christian College (1957) in Texas; Columbia Christian College (1956; later Cascade College, closed in 2009) in Portland, Oregon; Michigan Christian College (1959; now Rochester College) in Rochester, Michigan; and

Northeastern Christian College (1959; merged with Ohio Valley in 1993) in Villanova, Pennsylvania.

At the same time, mainstream Churches of Christ reflected a complex variety of attitudes toward the relation of the church to its surrounding culture: some embraced it, others isolated themselves from it, while still others were aggressively hostile to it. The "institutional" controversy that surfaced in the 1940s and 1950s was rooted in these differing attitudes. Those more accepting of culture created extra-congregational institutions for evangelism and social services. Isolationists tried desperately to stop what they saw as the rising tide of institutionalism and cultural accommodation.

Nevertheless, Churches of Christ remained largely united hermeneutically. That the restoration of the primitive church of the New Testament was achieved by obeying positive law was a shared assumption. Embedded in that understanding was the three-fold biblical hermeneutic: explicit command, binding example, and necessary inference was what mattered. This approach to Scripture, they agreed, would provide Christians with legal authority for all true ecclesial practices. Therefore, when questions surfaced regarding accommodation to their affluent and upwardly mobile American culture and the legitimacy of creating institutions for evangelism and benevolence, the discussion focused on legal authority for particular actions. May a congregation support an organization such as an orphan's home or a Christian college? Both sides used the same positive law hermeneutic to support their positions.

Their failure to resolve these issues points to the role of social change in fueling the institutional controversy. In the post-World War II era, Churches of Christ were emerging as a cultural force. They were no longer marginalized, poor, and insignificant. Some who viewed culture positively as providing opportunities for service sought to engage that culture through enlarging the institutional base of Churches of Christ through children's homes, retirement homes, organized missions, and colleges. Congregational treasuries, they believed, should support these ventures. Isolationists, referred to by David Edwin Harrell, Jr., as "cultural separationists," saw these "worldly affairs" as having nothing to do with their Christian lives. Their concern was "saving souls, restoring the church, and escaping the corruption of the world."[80] In some sense this was the concern of both sides as both limited the mission of the church to what they deemed spiritual concerns and excluded any social agenda. Yet these separatists held a deep fear that the rise of church-supported institutions would destroy the spiritual identity of the church.[81]

Beginnings of the Controversy

As early as the 1930s the development of institutions raised questions. The 1936 religious census reported seven colleges, seven orphanages, and two homes for the aged. Foy E. Wallace, Jr., with some disgust, recognized that "we are institutional already."[82] This development, however, had gone largely unnoticed because of the body's preoccupation with the premillennial controversy and the older Sommerite opposition to colleges. Generally, churches had not supported colleges out of their treasuries.[83] When F. B. Srygley and Daniel Sommer met in Nashville in 1933, they agreed that colleges had a right to exist, but congregational treasuries should not support them.[84]

Not everyone agreed, however. At the 1931 Abilene Christian College Lectures G. C. Brewer encouraged churches to support the school. As a result the *Gospel Advocate* printed a series of articles on both sides of the issue. Texans such as Foy E. Wallace, Jr., John T. Hinds (*Gospel Advocate* editor from 1934-1938), and C. R. Nichol opposed Brewer.[85] Some Tennesseans, like C. E. W. Dorris, who were influenced by David Lipscomb's own version of non-institutionalism, also opposed Brewer. World War II again distracted Churches of Christ from the issue, but as the postwar college boom materialized, it resurfaced. By then, however, cultural attitudes had shifted in many congregations.

The postwar years saw the rise of organized missions, a significant increase in the number of children's homes from seven to forty, and the dramatic growth of colleges. Missions became an institutional issue when some larger congregations began to serve as "sponsoring churches" to whom other congregations or individuals could send contributions for missionaries in targeted fields. In 1943 G. C. Brewer announced the intention of the Broadway Church of Christ in Lubbock, Texas, to "sponsor" missionary activities in Europe after the war.[86] Otis Gatewood (1911-1999) led the effort to evangelize Germany under the oversight of the Broadway elders. Other congregations assumed coordination and sponsorship of work in Japan and Italy. This centralization of mission funding was disconcerting to some, but many congregations across the country adopted the method.

In 1947 N. B. Hardeman in the *Gospel Advocate* encouraged churches to support the colleges financially.

Robert L. Whiteside along with brothers Cled and Foy E. Wallace, Jr., opposed him in the *Bible Banner*.[87] Hardeman paralleled the work of a children's home with the work of a college. If a congregation could contribute to a children's home as part of its benevolence budget, then it could contribute to a college as part of its edification work. Furthermore, he contended, a school was an extension of the home, not the church.

As had Daniel Sommer earlier, Foy Wallace and others saw the potential danger in a college wielding power over churches. J. D. Tant asserted that the battle was already lost, charging the colleges with gaining control of the churches early in the twentieth century and producing "preachers to entertain the sects." Those preachers were now in the pulpits of churches pushing the support of colleges, orphans' homes, and sponsoring churches.[88] Throughout the late 1940s and early 1950s articles for and against saturated the papers among Churches of Christ.

The Division

In 1949, just as Foy E. Wallace, Jr., ceased publication of the *Bible Banner*, Roy Cogdill (1907-1985) and Fanning Yater Tant (1908-1997) began the *Gospel Guardian*, the paper that would serve as the chief voice of the non-institutional churches. Institutional programs proliferated even as the discussion continued. The nationally broadcast Herald of Truth radio program, begun in 1952 under the sponsorship of the Fifth and Highland Church of Christ in Abilene, Texas, became hotly contested and a major focus of attention since churches from across the country supported the program. Wallace himself receded into the background as he lost the confidence of non-institutional leaders like Cogdill and Tant and continued to be distrusted by old adversaries. Wallace would not re-emerge as a significant player in the mainstream of Churches of Christ until the late 1960s, and then with a new issue—the "liberalization" of the church through new Bible translations.[89]

Those who opposed the institutions compared them to the missionary society. Though the institutions themselves were not evil, they argued, when they become linked with the church they become centers of power and control over congregations. Consequently, opponents invoked what they regarded as the New Testament legal pattern as divine protection for congregations from such control. Since there is no New Testament authority for sponsoring churches or churches contributing to human institutions in the New Testament, churches must maintain their autonomy by refusing to support such organizations. Individuals could support them if they so desired.

The controversy, as Harrell notes, "quickly reached an impasse because of the unusually bitter personal direction that it took."[90] Brewer, for example, regarded the "antis" (a derisive term for those opposed to institutionalism) as Foy E. Wallace, Jr.'s "cantankerous" supporters.[91] The right wing of the Texas Tradition formed the base of the non-institutional movement, though there were significant influences in the minority Tennessee Tradition as well. The personal feelings that emerged during the controversy were rooted in earlier battles between the Tennessee, Texas, and Indiana streams in the 1910s-1930s. Though Texas won the day in the 1930s, the postwar tide moved most members into a more accommodative stance that rejected the cultural separatism that had dominated Churches of Christ in the early twentieth century in all three Traditions.

In the 1950s the *Gospel Guardian* and Florida Christian College (renamed Florida College in 1963) became the rallying centers for the non-institutional movement. Leaders began other papers to support the *Guardian*, including the *Preceptor* (1951), *Truth Magazine* (1956), and *Searching the Scriptures* (1960). On the other hand, the *Gospel Advocate* and *Firm Foundation* supported the institutional moves, though the latter did so slowly. B. C. Goodpasture (1895-1977), editor of the *Gospel Advocate* from 1939 until his death, turned the tide in many ways.[92] Goodpasture's ability to gauge the issues of the day was unparalleled and he wielded tremendous influence among the churches. Ultimately, he banned non-institutionalists from writing in the *Advocate* and called for a quarantine of all such preachers by the churches. As preachers shifted sides in the 1950s, Goodpasture eagerly printed their "conversions." Non-institutional preachers resented what they regarded as his exercise of political power.[93]

As the papers battled, churches split. One of the most heated divisions took place in 1951 in Lufkin, Texas. Led by Cled Wallace, the Lufkin church excommunicated Roy E. Cogdill, publisher of the *Gospel Guardian*. A wildfire of congregational divisions followed for the next fifteen years. The high water mark of the polemical exchange was the debate between Guy N. Woods and Cogdill in Birmingham, Alabama, in November, 1957.[94] The last major attempt to reconcile the two groups in the early years of the division was at the so-called Arlington Meeting in Arlington, Texas, in 1968.[95] While participants thoroughly debated the hermeneutical issues, the two sides had already become settled in their convictions.

By 1960 the division was set. Batsell Barrett Baxter's 1959 directory of ministers, compiled from information submitted by ministers themselves, included very few non-institutional preachers. Harrell estimated that just over 10 percent of the total membership aligned themselves with non-institutional churches, roughly equivalent to the ratio of the 1906 division between Churches of Christ and Disciples.[96] In 2009 the non-institutional group had 113,656 members in 1,898 congregations, with the largest percentage in Texas.[97]

Dissonant Voices

As Churches of Christ grew in the 1940s and 1950s, then divided in the 1950s and 1960s, dissenting voices grew tired of the infighting and prepared the way for a different path in the late 1960s and beyond. One of these voices was W. Carl Ketcherside (1908-1989). Ketcherside had been nurtured in the Indiana Tradition, the recipient of Daniel Sommer's mantle. He took the lead in opposing colleges and located preachers, continuing the Sommerite vision through his *Mission Messenger* begun in 1940. By 1957, however, Ketcherside had undergone a transformation. While he had not changed his understanding of the issues, he turned his periodical toward the goal of unity much as Sommer himself had done in the 1930s and 1940s. He rejected the exclusivist sectarian part of his heritage and promoted unity meetings among the streams of the Stone-Campbell Movement in North America. Christians cannot experience unity through conformity, he insisted, but only through Christ in the midst of diversity.[98]

Another such voice was Leroy Garrett (b. 1918). After attending Freed-Hardeman and Abilene Christian Colleges, he pursued graduate degrees at Southern Methodist University (M.A., 1943), Princeton Theological Seminary (B.D., 1948), and Harvard University (Ph.D., 1957). Rooted theologically in the Texas Tradition, his years of experience and education moved him toward a more ecumenical position. Through his journals *Bible Talk* begun in 1952 and *Restoration Review* begun in 1959, Garrett exposed sectarian exclusivity in Churches of Christ and called for the recognition of unity among all followers of Christ.[99]

Ketcherside and Garrett represented an alternative vision of the Stone-Campbell Movement not often found among Churches of Christ at the time. Indeed, it stood in stark contrast with the church's debating, disfellowshipping, and hard-fighting style in the institu-

tional controversy. Because their message was at first too radical for most in Churches of Christ, it did not have significant impact until other shifts took place. While their anti-sectarianism exploded on the national scene with the 1966 book *Voices of Concern* edited by Robert Meyers, it was only in the 1980s that many in Churches of Christ began to accept the call to unity of Ketcherside and Garrett.[100]

However, other voices emerged in the 1950s that also provided an alternative to the infighting. One of those voices was K. C. Moser. In 1952 Harding College published his *Christ Versus a "Plan*," a scathing rebuttal of the widespread "plan-of-salvation" mentality."[101] Rather than thinking about steps to salvation, Moser argued, faith and trust in Jesus as savior is the means of salvation, and baptism is the embodiment of faith. Moser had been the focus of the "grace" debates of the early 1930s and his work now renewed that discussion.

In 1957 Moser privately published *The Gist of Romans*, which the Gospel Light Publishing Company in Delight, Arkansas, reissued the next year.[102] For many young ministers, this survey of Romans was a surprising revelation of grace in the midst of fights over ecclesiological perfectionism. Within a few years several college professors, including Jimmy Allen at Harding, began using *The Gist of Romans* in classes. It was in this atmosphere that F. W. Mattox (1909-2001), who had known Moser in Oklahoma City and studied at the feet of J. N. Armstrong at Harding College, invited Moser to teach at Lubbock Christian College in 1964. Moser spent his last years teaching the doctrine of grace to eager students.

Another dissident voice in mainstream Churches of Christ was Andy T. Richie, Jr., at Harding College, who was a quiet embodiment of the Tennessee Tradition. As the turbulent 1960s began, Ketcherside, Garrett, Moser, Richie, and others would have increasing influence in eroding the positive law hermeneutic and exclusivist view of the church characteristic of the Texas Tradition that had dominated Churches of Christ since the 1940s.

African American Church Growth

The development of black Churches of Christ into a vibrant American religious force was one of the most significant developments in the body in the first half of the twentieth century. Much of this story is tied to two figures—George Phillip (G. P.) Bowser and Marshall Keeble. Both Bowser and Keeble shared the positive law hermeneutic dominant among white Churches of Christ, which they identified as the means of turning

African Americans "from darkness to light, from human institutions to the church of our Lord."[103] Yet they differed from each other in several important respects.

Bowser was an educated Methodist preacher in Nashville, Tennessee, before uniting with the Stone-Campbell Movement. Keeble, a former Baptist with a seventh-grade education, received baptism at the hands of Preston Taylor and spiritual guidance at the feet of his father-in-law, S. W. Womack of the Jackson Street Church of Christ in Nashville.[104] In addition to their differences in background and education, Bowser and Keeble had different preaching styles. Bowser filled his sermons with Scripture citations, while Keeble filled his with homespun parables and personal stories.[105]

More significantly, Bowser and Keeble took different stances on the issue of racial segregation. Bowser vigorously opposed white racism in American churches and society. In 1920, C. E. W. Dorris, white superintendent of the all-black Southern Practical Institute (SPI) in Nashville, Tennessee, required students to enter the school building through the back door. Bowser, who had recently closed his school at Silver Point and accepted a position as principal of SPI, vehemently denounced the practice and resigned as principal, forcing the school's abrupt closing.[106] While Bowser protested, "I can't treat my boys and girls like that," Keeble pled with Bowser: "Let us come in the back. All you want is to give a Christian education."[107] For Bowser, black dignity was more important than gaining educational opportunities under the auspices of white racists. For Keeble, educational opportunities for black youth were essential even if it meant accommodation to a racist society.

Bowser's opposition to white racism cost him dearly. A decade later a white minister from Texas saw Bowser and noted that he "had barely enough clothes to cover him, and they were decidedly threadbare."[108] Because of his firm stance against racial discrimination, Bowser never garnered the financial support from white Christians that Keeble did. Keeble, aided by white philanthropists in Churches of Christ, always dressed nicely, often dined sumptuously, and eventually traveled globally. While preaching in Pecos, Texas, for example, Keeble reported, "The white brethren gave all of the boys [students from the Nashville Christian Institute] new suits and they fixed me up nicely."[109]

Two factors made Bowser and Keeble effective in the growth of black Churches of Christ despite their significant differences. First, both benefited from the support of white believers.[110] Though Bowser's resistance to racism meant that he would receive relatively little white support, he still acknowledged that he had received help from white sponsors. Keeble had the substantial and enduring assistance of A. M. Burton, a wealthy Christian businessman from Nashville, Tennessee. Burton, who had briefly supported Bowser's school at Silver Point, became a major benefactor for Keeble. In 1925, Keeble acknowledged Burton as the "greatest missionary in the church today."[111] After tallying more than one thousand baptisms in 1932, Keeble was quick to proclaim openly that white congregations had sponsored all of his work.[112]

Marshall Keeble became president of Nashville Christian Institute in 1942, two years after its founding. Pictured here with his chief benefactor, insurance executive A. M. Burton, who became chair of the Board in 1943. *(Courtesy Center for Restoration Studies, Abilene Christian University)*

Second, both Bowser and Keeble were educators. Bowser taught and mentored a host of young aspiring preachers, including R. N. Hogan (1902-1997). After Bowser's death in 1950, Hogan assumed oversight of the *Christian Echo* and clearly emerged as one of the most powerful preachers in African American Churches of Christ. Driven by a passion to bring lost souls to God and stamp out racial discrimination in Churches of Christ, Hogan advanced a gospel that attacked both what he believed to be religious error in the churches and white racism in the body's colleges.

After establishing congregations in Texas and Oklahoma, Hogan relocated to California in 1937 and established the Figueroa Church of Christ. From his post in southern California, Hogan answered evangelistic calls from across the country, cast his support behind Bowser's newly-established Southwestern Christian College in Terrell, Texas, and through the pages of the *Christian Echo* assailed white school administrators who barred African Americans from their campuses. Hogan charged that the fear of black men having sex with white women was at the heart of white racism in the nation and in Churches of Christ. Black men in Churches of Christ, he drolly asserted, "just want to be the white man's brother and *not* his brother-in-law."[113]

R. N. Hogan (left) and J. S. Winston in a 1939 Gospel Meeting in the Lower Rio Grande Valley in Texas. Both were mentored by G. P. Bowser and shared his fierce opposition to segregation and racial discrimination. *(From therestorationmovement.com website)*

J. S. Winston (1906-2001) was another protégé of G. P. Bowser. In the early 1930s, Marshall Keeble and white minister T. W. Brents had encouraged Winston to preach. Winston soon helped Hogan establish a congregation in Sherman, Texas, before working with African American Churches of Christ in Fort Worth, Marlin, Sweeny, and Van Alstyne, Texas. Winston's greatest legacy, however, was unquestionably his push for trained leaders in black Churches of Christ. He worked tirelessly and closely with G. P. Bowser to launch Southwestern Christian College in Terrell, Texas, the only accredited college controlled by African Americans in Churches of Christ. In 1948, Winston served as president of the Southern Bible Institute in Fort Worth, the precursor of Southwestern Christian College, which relocated to Terrell the following year. According to historian Edward Robinson, "Bowser dreamed the dream, but his protégés, R. N. Hogan, Levi Kennedy, and J. S. Winston, executed his dream."[114]

Bowser's protégés, who he referred to as sons, worked primarily outside of the South. R. N. Hogan preached for more than five decades in southern California. J. S. Winston ministered many years in the state of Ohio. Levi Kennedy labored to build the Sheldon Heights Church of Christ in Chicago, Illinois. These men, for the most part, were willing to work independently of white support. Furthermore, they unabashedly condemned racial discrimination practiced by whites in Churches of Christ.[115]

Like Bowser, Keeble mentored and trained black men who themselves entered the ministry, planted churches, and shepherded congregations. Luke Miller was one of the most influential. Born and reared in Alabama, Miller received baptism from his spiritual father and soon became a song-leader and preacher in Churches of Christ. Miller accomplished his greatest work in East Texas where he established several congregations.[116] John R. Vaughner, another Keeble protégé, left an enduring mark on African American Churches of Christ in 1947, when he immersed a Baptist minister, Wilton H. Cook, and his entire congregation in Hopewell, Virginia. Cook shortly thereafter enrolled at Keeble's Nashville Christian Institute and preached in African American Churches of Christ in Florida and Texas.[117] Like their spiritual father, many of those who Keeble mentored assumed a non-threatening posture on racism and relied heavily on white Christians for support. However, some of the young men shaped by Keeble at the Nashville Christian Institute, especially in his later years, became leaders in the Civil Rights Movement.

Because of the selfless work of black evangelists, African American Churches of Christ grew at a phenomenal rate in the twentieth century. In 2009 predominantly black congregations numbered 1,191 with a combined membership of 216,082.[118]

Conclusion

Churches of Christ in the first half of the twentieth century—both black and white—reflected the tumultuous social and cultural changes that surrounded them, sometimes accommodating to those changes, sometimes resisting them. A positive law approach profoundly shaped their commitments to both Scripture and the centrality of the church. Though suffering several small schisms in this period, by mid-century they had emerged from the earlier division from the Disciples with an optimism and self-confidence characteristic of post-World War II America. Churches of Christ also mirrored the segregated American society. Yet the dedicated work of black evangelists led to a proliferation of black congregations in the United States.

As Churches of Christ moved toward the new millennium, the turmoil of the mid-twentieth century continued to affect them, causing many to question and reject the consensus that had given the mainstream its identity. This identity crisis developed among many congregations and individual members and posed a major challenge to the mainstream's sectarian self-assurance.

9

Disciples of Christ

Cooperation and Division

The Pittsburgh Centennial Convention in 1909 had witnessed a growing divergence over new approaches to the Bible and Christian unity. It also marked an increasing commitment to cooperation among Disciples. By 1909 many leaders had come to believe that the loose congregational polity of the nineteenth century had enabled an unhealthy spirit of competition. Any individual with an entrepreneurial bent could start a new organization and promote it as important to Disciples life. James H. Garrison described the growth of Disciples institutions in his 1909 *The Story of a Century*. The body had nearly 12,000 congregations, twenty-seven educational institutions, three missionary societies as well as other service organizations, and interdenominational Bible school work through Christian Endeavor, all conducting remarkable ministries.[1] Though Garrison saw this growth as evidence of progress, competition for support between agencies prompted many Disciples to call for a centralization of ministries. After 1909, Disciples began to create a more extensive cooperative structure, one that would have significant implications for African Americans and women, and also for Disciples social action, ecumenism, education, and mission.

The battle between liberals and conservatives evident in 1909 heightened as advocates of the higher criticism of the Bible and ecumenism assumed leadership in the developing cooperative structure. This conflict was most evident in relation to education and mission. In 1934 the Convention authorized a Commission on Restudy of the Disciples of Christ to address differences among Disciples. Though the Commission met regularly for fourteen years and produced a number of insightful reports, it was unable to reverse the growing divergence among Disciples.

Continuing commitment to cooperation and a Disciples theological renaissance in the 1950s stimulated reflection on the nature and purpose of the church. This reflection contributed to the adoption of "The Strategy of World Mission" in 1959 and "A Provisional Design for the Christian Church (Disciples of Christ)" in 1968. Following the adoption of the "Provisional Design," more than 2,300 congregations requested removal from the *Year Book of the Disciples of Christ*, leaving 4,046 participating Disciples congregations by 1970.

Disciples membership, however, had declined even before the adoption of the "Provisional Design." Paralleling the twentieth-century growth patterns of several other U.S. Protestant denominations, Disciples experienced numerical growth during the first half of the century followed by a steep decline that began in the 1960s.

The listing of Christian Churches/Churches of Christ in the 1971 *Yearbook of American and Canadian Churches* as a body separate from both the Christian Church (Disciples of Christ) and Churches of Christ formally marked the second major division of the North American Movement. At the same time, some organizations such as the World Convention of Churches of Christ and the Disciples of Christ Historical Society maintained paths of fellowship between all three of the major North American streams.

Forming a Cooperative Structure

W. T. Moore noted in his 1909 history of the Movement that a slight tendency toward centralization had begun with the establishment of the American Christian Missionary Society (ACMS) in 1849. By the early twentieth century, however, all aspects of American life were "characterized by bigness" and consolidation as great department stores replaced small neighborhood shops and large corporations subsumed small companies. Disciples, he asserted, "have reached an era where such centralization is absolutely necessary in order that they may achieve the triumphs that are awaiting them in the near future."[2]

At the 1906 Convention at Buffalo, New York, a committee appointed to consider further centralization had recommended creating a delegate convention representing all congregations, an idea first advanced by Alexander Campbell in the 1840s. This convention would decide on behalf of the congregations what societies, colleges, publishing houses, and social benevolence organizations Disciples in North America would recognize. Conflicting appeals to congregations could then be controlled and restricted.

After Pittsburgh in 1909, conventions included "general" sessions to consider matters affecting all Disciples congregations. The 1912 Louisville Convention even adopted a constitution for "The General Convention of Churches of Christ." However, the 1906 committee's proposal to create a representative delegate convention proved controversial. Congregations and individuals who feared too much authority becoming vested in a convention to the detriment of their long-established autonomy refused to implement the proposal. Though the constitution called for delegate votes, in practice every person in attendance continued to vote on every item before the convention.

In 1917, the Kansas City Convention adopted a revised constitution that created the International Convention of the Disciples of Christ; international because it included members of congregations from both the United States and Canada. The document solidified the power of the mass meeting, with the exception that close voice votes would be decided by ballot with each congregation present having one vote. More significantly, the new constitution created a Committee on Recommendations composed of representative delegates who would screen all items brought before the assembly.

The 1906 Buffalo committee's report also had recommended unifying home and foreign missionary work. Both the Foreign Christian Missionary Society (FCMS) and the Christian Woman's Board of Missions (CWBM) had work in India, Africa, and China, and the ACMS and CWBM had missions in the United States and its territories, as well as efforts in Canada. Each

society had its own magazine, its own congregational advocates, and its own leadership, duplicating and, in the eyes of many, wasting both effort and resources.

In 1913, the societies created the Men and Millions Movement, which ultimately raised over $6 million for Disciples agencies and encouraged young people to consider missionary or church service. This campaign demonstrated the Disciples' ability to cooperate at every level of church life. After the 1917 Kansas City Convention, a committee composed of members of several Disciples boards and societies recommended forming a united organization with equal governance by men and women.

Two years later in Cincinnati, the committee recommended creating the United Christian Missionary Society (UCMS). This new agency would combine the American Christian Missionary Society, the Christian Woman's Board of Missions, the Foreign Christian Missionary Society, the Board of Church Extension, the National Benevolent Association, and the Board of Ministerial Relief. A few months earlier the journals of five of the organizations had merged to form *World Call*, and many felt the result was a better accounting of mission than any of the societies could have managed alone. A unification of the boards themselves possessed a compelling logic, so compelling that conservatives voted for the unification despite misgivings that a more consolidated organization would increase the influence of liberals.[3] Legal incorporation of the UCMS took place on June 22, 1920, with Frederick Burnham, formerly president of the American Christian Missionary Society, serving as president, and Archibald McLean of the Foreign Christian Missionary Society, and Anna Atwater of the Christian Woman's Board of Missions, as its first vice-presidents. Headquarters were in St. Louis from 1920-1928, moving to the former CWBM College of Missions building in Indianapolis in 1928.

In 1907 Disciples had formed a committee to suggest solutions to the problem of privately owned publishing houses competing for support from congregations. By the end of 1909, lumber tycoon R. A. Long had bought out James H. Garrison's interest in the Christian Publishing Company, including *The Christian-Evangelist*, and established a board of trustees to run the company in the interest of all Disciples. The board reinvested profits as needed to strengthen the company, but otherwise redistributed funds to support other Disciples groups. Disciples now had a recognized publishing company in direct competition with private publishers such as the

Standard Publishing Company, publisher of the *Christian Standard*.

Continuing concern over multiple financial appeals to congregations prompted in 1935 the formation of Unified Promotion, a cooperative fundraising and distribution agency. The UCMS along with six other general boards, twenty-three state missionary societies, and five educational institutions were founding members. Though not all cooperative agencies that reported to the International Convention joined, Unified Promotion became an effective means by which most general and state boards, societies, and many of the colleges cooperated in their appeals to the churches.[4]

Meanwhile, questions concerning ordination of ministers arose. Disciples increasingly realized that their congregational ministers were functioning as neither the congregational elder nor traveling evangelist as Alexander Campbell had described. Many concluded that since ministers served several congregations over time, ordination should not be the responsibility of individual congregations operating independently. At the very least, there needed to be mutually accepted standards that would be applied by all the churches.

In 1935 the International Convention appointed a Commission on Ordination to study the issue. The Commission's report, approved by the 1939 Convention, recommended three standards:

1. Good moral character and personal fitness for ministry.
2. A full college course, and, if possible, graduate training in religion.
3. Experience in Christian work that shows real leadership, vision, pastoral qualities, and preaching ability.[5]

The report also recommended that ordination be authorized by an ordination council assembled by a congregation and recognized by the regional committee on ordination if such a committee existed. The council was to consist of the minister and one or more elders from each of three or more congregations. Upon the vote of this council and the signing of the ordination certificate by three ministers, the council was to arrange a service of ordination in the candidate's local church, the regional convention, or the candidate's college or seminary.[6]

The implementation of the ordination council approach was uneven. Some congregations continued to ordain persons to ministry without consulting anyone else. The direction of Disciples thinking reflected in the Commission's report, however, was clearly toward shifting responsibility for ordination to a body representative of the larger church. In 1964 the International Convention stated that ordination is a "rite, or ceremony, of the whole Church, local and ecumenical, current and eternal" and is to be performed "under the guidance of the state or area Committee or Commission on the Ministry."[7]

The effectiveness of this cooperative approach to ordination, when coupled with the Disciples continuing commitment to freedom, was tested in the case of James Warren ("Jim") Jones (1931-1978). In 1954, Jones established an independent Pentecostal church in Indianapolis eventually called the People's Temple Full Gospel Church. The racially integrated congregation developed into a model of social gospel ministry, and Jones became a popular, though controversial, civic leader. In 1960, the People's Temple was granted standing in the Indiana Christian Churches (Disciples of Christ), and in 1964 Jones was ordained as a Disciples minister.[8]

In 1965, Jones and over a hundred followers relocated to Redwood Valley, California, partly in response to his vision of a nuclear holocaust destroying the Midwest. Granted standing by the Northern California-Nevada Disciples churches, the People's Temple grew to more than three thousand members in the 1970s. Jones became active in California politics, and the church administered a variety of social service ministries.[9]

By the early 1970s Jones derided traditional Christianity as a "fly away religion" and claimed power to raise the dead. He became exploitive and abusive, demanding absolute loyalty from People's Temple members and misappropriating church funds.[10] Disciples leaders refused to intervene, however, citing the denomination's "longstanding tradition of freedom of the pulpit and the rights of congregations to determine their internal affairs."[11]

After negative press reports triggered federal and state investigations, Jones and nearly a thousand followers migrated to Jonestown, Guyana, in summer 1977. When a delegation sent by the U.S. government in 1978 to investigate reports of abuse prepared to depart Jonestown, People's Temple guards opened fire, killing Congressman Leo Ryan and several others. Jones and nine hundred fourteen of his followers then committed "revolutionary suicide" by drinking Flavor-Aid laced with poison.[12]

Just prior to the People's Temple move to Guyana, the Northern California-Nevada Region had established a special committee to review Jones's standing as a Disciples minister and to distance themselves from him and the People's Temple. Because Jones never returned to the United States, the review was never completed.[13]

Following the tragedy, Disciples leaders acknowledged deep anguish but consistently cited the denomination's commitment to congregational freedom as the reason for their reluctance to intervene.[14] In 1979, Disciples leaders chose not to develop denominational procedures for such cases, but to encourage each region to develop annual review processes to help "shepherd" its ministers and congregations.[15]

Commitments to both cooperation and freedom, evident in the development of Disciples policies and criteria for ordering ministry, were also reflected in the development of the National Christian Missionary Convention.

The National Christian Missionary Convention

Preston Taylor and other black leaders had begun the National Christian Missionary Convention (NCMC) one month prior to the formation of the International Convention in 1917. Though black Disciples refused to give up their newly formed organization to become part of the International Convention, they voted to make the NCMC an auxiliary.[16] Moreover, the NCMC did not duplicate services that could be secured through existing agencies like the CWBM. In 1917 the CWBM had employed African Americans Rosa Brown Bracy (1895-1960) as Women's Worker and Patrick Henry Moss (1875-1935) as Church School and Young People's Worker to provide services to African American churches. Bracy and Moss continued to provide services to African American churches following the organization of the NCMC, first as employees of the CWBM and later as employees of the UCMS.

With the formation of the UCMS, a Joint Executive Committee with an equal number of members from the NCMC and the UCMS oversaw services to predominantly African American congregations. In turn, the NCMC was asked to cover half the cost of UCMS services to black churches. Under these arrangements, Robert Hayes Peoples (1903-1983) became the first African American national secretary of Negro evangelism and religious education in 1935 and served until 1944. Carnella Jamison (1911-1997) succeeded Bracy as Women's Worker in 1938. In 1942 the UCMS replaced the Joint Executive Committee with the Inter-Agency Council, which encouraged general, state, and area staff to provide services to African American churches and related organizations.[17]

The year after Peoples's resignation in 1944, a long-range planning committee of the NCMC, in consultation with UCMS leadership, proposed restructuring the way services were being provided to black Disciples churches. The Committee explained that while they wanted to preserve the NCMC's relationship with the UCMS, they felt it was important to give the NCMC a larger part in determining policies and directing work among African Americans. The proposal called for the NCMC's National Board to assume functions of the African American work previously administered by the UCMS and other agencies.

The NCMC Board was to establish its own headquarters in Indianapolis and employ its own staff, which would direct programs of Evangelism, Religious Education, Church Development, Pensions, Benevolence, Scholarships, Church Extension, Higher Education, Financial Resources, Enlistment of full-time workers, and an African American Disciples paper—*The Christian Plea.* In turn, the NCMC would amend its constitution to allow representatives from the UCMS and other Disciples agencies on its National Board, with each agency providing financial support to the Convention.[18]

W. H. Taylor, NCMC president for 1944, opposed the proposal as giving too much authority to white-run agencies, which he charged favored open membership. Despite Taylor's opposition, the NCMC approved the proposal. Under this new structure, Emmett J. Dickson (1909-1995), former Jarvis College faculty member, became Executive Secretary of the NCMC in 1945. Dickson's staff included Carnella Jamison Barnes (who married Anderson B. Barnes in 1945) in women's work, and C. L. Parks in ministerial institutes and evangelism, both of whom had been employees of the UCMS. In 1946 Dickson added Lorenzo Evans as director of Christian education, and in 1949 Charles H. Webb as director of church development and evangelism.[19]

In addition to sharing support staff for conventions and other gatherings, the cooperating agencies continued to share African American program costs. The 1944 restructuring, however, made increased giving by congregations to the NCMC necessary to cover costs of expanded program services. In 1956, the organization received a total of $20,350 from the UCMS and other agencies, $15,137 from churches related to the NCMC, and $4,000 from the Preston Taylor Estate. Eighty of the five hundred sixty-six African American congregations gave consistently, with thirty-eight contributing 95 percent of the money from black churches.[20]

Robert Hays Peoples had become pastor of Second Christian Church in Indianapolis after resigning his national staff position in 1944. As president of the National Convention in 1955, Peoples proposed a merger of NCMC services with those of the International Convention and the UCMS. The NCMC was to remain a "fellowship-assembly" for inspiration and education, and a legal corporation that could hold property. Its executive secretary would be employed by the International Convention with the status of associate executive secretary.[21]

Peoples' proposal reflected the fact that during the 1950s NCMC personnel had increasingly worked with staff from the UCMS and other agencies in annual NCMC sessions, worker's conferences, schools of mission, and work with children and youth. The 1953 International Convention in Portland, Oregon, had adopted a resolution that committed the body to a policy of non-segregation in all convention sessions, its constituent agencies, and in hotel and meal facilities. The Convention had formally approved this policy the following year in Miami, Florida. A Social Action Commission formed by the NCMC in 1952 monitored this commitment, working closely with Louis Deer, director of the UCMS Department of Social Welfare.

A graduate of the University of Chicago, William K. Fox, served as Administrative Secretary of the National Convocation and assistant to the General Minister and President from 1972-1982, and co-authored *Journey Toward Wholeness*, a history of African American Disciples of Christ.

The Social Action Commission also encouraged NCMC members to become full participants in the life and work of the International Convention.[22]

In 1959, an NCMC Commission on Merger of Program and Services approved Peoples' plan in principle. It identified the first step as transfer of program staff from NCMC supervision to UCMS staff positions with the same professional status as other staff performing similar jobs. The Commission also called for the UCMS to maintain a minimum of four African American executive staff, to appoint African Americans to the policy-making boards of all agencies, to make African Americans visible in the public life of the church, and to form an Interracial Commission to promote employment of African Americans at all levels. Funding for the administrative secretary of the Interracial Commission was to come from the NCMC and the cooperating agencies. The Commission anticipated that most of the support for the annual NCMC assembly would come from registrations. They also called for increased support of the UCMS by NCMC congregations through Unified Promotion. [23]

The 44th annual session of the NCMC in Columbus, Ohio, August 22, 1960, approved the Commission's report. By 1961, Willard Wickizer, UCMS executive secretary of the Division of Church Life and Work, reported that the merger of program and services at the general level was underway. In addition, black and white state conventions had merged in both Kansas and Ohio.[24]

The agencies formed a Joint Committee on Merger and New Brotherhood Relations in January 1966 with five members each from the NCMC, the UCMS, and the International Convention. They proposed that all business procedures of the NCMC move to the International Convention by 1968 and that other functions of the NCMC continue under a new name. The new organization would meet biennially opposite from the biennial meetings of the International Convention or its successor. The NCMC approved "A proposed Recommendation on Principles for the Merger of the National Christian Missionary Convention and the International Convention of the Christian Churches (Disciples of Christ)" at its August 1968 meeting at Jarvis Christian College. The International Convention took the same action at Kansas City the following month.[25]

A task force developed the next steps, which the NCMC approved at its final meeting in Lexington, Kentucky, August 5-10, 1969. The new organization would be named the National Convocation of the Christian Church (Disciples of Christ). The Administrative Secretary of the Convocation was to be selected by the

General Office (formerly the office of Executive Secretary of the International Convention) in consultation with the Convocation's own executive committee and UCMS administration. John R. Compton (1926-2003) became the Convocation's first administrative secretary.[26]

The preamble to the proposal approved in 1959 by the NCMC Commission on Merger of Program and Services stated the merger's theological basis:

> Christian Churches (Disciples of Christ) have always held the firm conviction that the church is one as Christ prayed, "That they all may be one." While this has been commonly applied to denominational divisions, our basic philosophy also affirms that there can be no wholeness if any segment is excluded because of culture, race, or national origin. The church is the creation of our Lord and Savior, Jesus Christ, composed of all those who profess His name…[27]

These theological principles were not new. They had undergirded the two previous structures for relating African American Disciples to the denomination's cooperative life. In each case, African American Disciples developed a structure to manifest Christian unity while strengthening the African American witness in a racist movement and society. In 2011 the National Convocation embraced nearly five hundred congregations with over 68,000 members.

Renewed Associations with the Church of Christ, Disciples of Christ

Disciples associated with the emerging cooperative structure also sought to strengthen relations with the Church of Christ, Disciples of Christ of eastern North Carolina and Virginia. Beginning in 1910, the American Christian Missionary Society's monthly publication included a listing of General Assembly ministers.[28] In 1913, Joel Baer Lehman, the CWBM's newly appointed national Superintendent of Negro Work, attended the annual assembly of the Washington-Norfolk District.[29]

An important connection between Disciples associated with the cooperative structure and the General Assembly was the Rev. George Calvin Campbell (1872-1949), president of Goldsboro Christian Institute from 1922-1926. Campbell, born in Pinetown, North Carolina, began his ministry in the Church of Christ, Disciples of Christ. His education, however, took him first to Disciples-related Hiram College in Ohio where he received ordination, then to Wilberforce and Fisk Universities, and later to Lane Theological Seminary

in Cincinnati. From 1898-1912, he served Disciples congregations in Lockland, Ohio; Carlisle and Lexington, Kentucky; and Nashville, Tennessee. From 1912-1921, while earning a Bachelor of Philosophy, a Master of Arts, and a Bachelor of Divinity from the University of Chicago, he was pastor of the Amour Avenue Christian Church in Chicago. In 1918 he became a member of the National Christian Missionary Convention.[30]

From Campbell's perspective, there was no reason why the Church of Christ, Disciples of Christ could not work with other Disciples. Campbell did not hesitate to use the white Disciples' newspaper, the *North Carolina Christian*, to appeal for funds to support the Goldsboro Institute. He also sought to establish connections between the NCMC and the General Assembly districts. At the 1923 Goldsboro-Raleigh District Assembly, he announced that the NCMC had pledged two hundred dollars to the Institute. Though the funds never arrived, probably because of financial challenges worsened by the Depression, the following year Campbell lobbied unsuccessfully for Goldsboro-Raleigh to send a contribution to the NCMC as a sign of good faith.

In 1926 Patrick Henry Moss became the first African American UCMS executive to attend the Quadrennial General Assembly. Moss conducted a seminar for ministers, establishing a precedent for relations between the General Assembly and Disciples affiliated with the International Convention. Executives of the NCMC and UCMS conducted classes for General Assembly leaders in finance, ministry, and education. In turn, the NCMC continued to encourage the Church of Christ, Disciples of Christ to become part of it.

Elder John F. Whitfield also sought to unite the two groups. From 1918-1926 Whitfield served General Assembly congregations throughout eastern North Carolina. In 1926 he moved to Roanoke, Virginia, and became a member of the National Christian Missionary Convention. Through his efforts, the NCMC approved a resolution in 1927 to extend a formal invitation to the Church of Christ, Disciples of Christ to cooperate with it.

> Whereas, the Disciples of Christ of Eastern North Carolina and Eastern Virginia are desirous of co-operating with the larger work of the brotherhood and thereby having fellowship in all the work of the brotherhood; be it Resolved, That a commission of seven be appointed by the President of the National Convention to meet a similar commission of seven appointed by the brethren of that district to consult, suggest and recommend ways and means by which

they (the brethren of Eastern North Carolina and Virginia) may cooperate with the larger work.[31]

NCMC president Preston Taylor led a delegation of black and white Disciples leaders to the October 1927 Goldsboro-Raleigh District Assembly. Whitfield, who continued to serve as the district's scribe, wrote that the delegation was well received, adding that Assembly leaders were especially impressed by Preston Taylor.

Elder Taylor brought a wonderful message on "Brotherhood and Fellowship Cooperation." He explained the object and aim of the National Convention and its various standing committees or boards that work with the United Christian Missionary Society. He also offered to explain any question as far as possible that any one might ask relative to the general work. He made a profound impression upon all who heard him because of the plain and Christian-like way he made his plea.[32]

The leadership of the Goldsboro-Raleigh Assembly called a special session for January 10, 1928, at Greenville, North Carolina, to gather the leadership of the two assemblies. Taylor and others from the NCMC attended, and in an address titled "Gather Up the Fragments," he again invited the Church of Christ, Disciples of Christ to affiliate with the NCMC. In response, the General Assembly leaders appointed Chief Elders W. A. Fordham (Goldsboro-Raleigh) and W. R. Steeley (Washington-Norfolk) to serve as delegates to the August 1928 NCMC meeting in Chicago.[33]

Although authorized to make decisions regarding their affiliation with the NCMC, Fordham and Steeley deferred to a consensus of the churches that was reached outside of a regular business meeting. Though no official records exist, it is clear the churches decided against affiliation, most likely because there had been little previous interaction between congregations and people of the two groups. Though leaders of the NCMC had attended assemblies, widespread fellowship between the two groups had never developed.[34]

Neither of the chief elders appeared at the meeting in Chicago, thus setting a boundary between themselves and the NCMC. Nevertheless, Moss returned to offer seminars at Goldsboro-Raleigh in 1928 and 1929. The relationship between the two organizations had by no means been severed.[35]

At the invitation of Goldsboro-Raleigh Chief Elder Hardy D. Davis, a staunch advocate of affiliation with the NCMC, officials from the North Carolina Christian

Missionary Convention and executives of the NCMC resumed regular visits to Goldsboro-Raleigh in 1940. The visitation team typically included a representative of the NCMC, a minister from the Disciples' Piedmont District, and a staff member from the North Carolina regional office or the general office in Indianapolis. NCMC and UCMS leaders, including Robert Hays Peoples, John F. Whitfield, Emmet J. Dickson, and C.L. Parks, offered seminars, later extending their offerings to the Washington-Norfolk District.[36] In 1948, the Goldsboro-Raleigh District began a partnership with the UCMS to restore the Goldsboro Christian Institute that had closed in 1926. C.L. Parks, of the NCMC national staff, became the Institute's director of instruction.[37]

Bishop W. D. Keyes of the Church of Christ, Disciples of Christ visits the offices of the Christian Church (Disciples of Christ) in 1974.

The NCMC and the UCMS and their successor organizations continued to provide services to the Church of Christ, Disciples of Christ through the 1970s. "Reconciliation," a Disciples program in response to the 1960s urban crisis, funded a project operated by the Washington and Norfolk District Assembly. In August 1972 the National Convocation held its second Biennial Session at Atlantic Christian (now Barton) College in Wilson, North Carolina, to encourage attendance of members of the Church of Christ, Disciples of Christ. Later in the decade, the Division of Homeland Ministries, a successor to the UCMS, supported a continuing education program designed primarily for Church of Christ, Disciples of Christ ministers at Atlantic Christian College.[38]

At the same time, some in the Church of Christ, Disciples of Christ worked against fellowship with other Disciples. In 1950, Oscar S. Lucas published an influential book titled *The Disciple's Voice,* which presented the doctrines of the Church of Christ, Disciples of Christ as the only means of personal salvation. Lucas pointed to the church's practice of feet-washing and the title "disciple" for followers of Christ as proofs of its superior witness. In his judgment, all other churches, including Disciples related to the International Convention, were lost.[39]

The long association between the Christian Church (Disciples of Christ) and the Church of Christ, Disciples of Christ, including listing of General Assembly churches in the Disciples *Year Book,* led to confusion regarding their relationship. In 1954 the Disciples Assemblies resolved to use Church of Christ, Disciples of Christ as their official name. By that time, they had expanded beyond their Eastern North Carolina base to the northeastern United States, following the Northern migration of members. By 2011 the Church of Christ, Disciples of Christ had seven district assemblies, with congregations in North and South Carolina, Virginia, New York, New Jersey, Connecticut, Washington D.C., Maryland, Pennsylvania, Georgia, Florida, Tennessee, and Texas; as well as Liberia, Ghana, and Togo, West Africa; with missions in Panama, Central America, and Guyana, South America.[40] Despite the efforts of the NCMC and its successors to relate the Church of Christ, Disciples of Christ to the Christian Church (Disciples of Christ), no formal relationship existed. Historian of the Church of Christ, Disciples of Christ Sheila H. Gillams describes the group as a "fourth branch of American restorationism" alongside the Christian Church (Disciples of Christ), Churches of Christ, and Christian Churches/Churches of Christ.[41]

Internally, the 1980s and 1990s proved transformational for the General Assembly. General Bishop MacDonald Moses had developed a global vision for the Church of Christ, Disciples of Christ because of contact with indigenous evangelists from Liberia and Guyana who sought affiliation with the body. He found himself faced with the challenge of bringing the Church of Christ, Disciples of Christ out of its localized kinship network of the southern and northeastern districts to create an international church. After being re-elected to the general bishopric in 1993, Moses resolved to reorganize the General Assembly with a departmentalized corporate order to centralize the work of evangelism, education, missions, ushering, music, nursing, and special events. Because of increased presence outside of the United States, the body incorporated under the name General Assembly Church of Christ, Disciples of Christ, International.[42]

Women

Though leadership roles for women continued to emerge as the cooperative structure developed, women leaders became increasingly skeptical of their position in the new UCMS. Despite promises to distribute leadership positions equally between women and men, it never happened. Furthermore, women employees of the UCMS quickly discovered that they suffered from an unfair salary structure.

Hazel A. Lewis (1886-1978) and Cynthia Pearl Maus (1880-1970) provided strong leadership in children's and youth work for the UCMS, including the development of a highly successful camp and conference program. Both accepted their positions under protest because they were not paid the same as men who held equivalent positions. A January 1927 letter noted that the men in the Religious Education Department had received increases between $300 and $600 each over the previous six years, while the women, making $2,500 per year, had received no increases, even though they had started at $500 less per year than the men. This was true, the letter continued, even though both Lewis and Maus had seniority over all the men in the department except for its executive, Robert M. Hopkins.[43]

In the early 1930s, the women of the UCMS issued a statement that concluded, "After twelve years of experience we are convinced that neither the present setup of our work nor the place accorded the women has met the needs of womanhood for its largest development, its best service, and its greatest contribution to the work."[44] The original UCMS officers in 1920 included sixteen men and nine women. In 1933, the women noted that the disparity, instead of being equalized as pledged in 1920, had actually grown to seventeen men and four women.[45] Effie Cunningham expressed her feelings in a 1931 letter to UCMS colleague Lela Taylor:

…we who helped prepare for our United Society thought we had safeguarded the work and workers from this very thing. Our women were free in Christ,…There was no other place in the whole world where this could have developed as it did in our brotherhood. Christian freedom for our women in leadership service has constantly decreased since the United Society was organized, in spite of its fair and good promises for rightness along these lines. The disappointment in this failure hurts almost as much as the thing itself, only the thing itself is so dangerous.[46]

After decades of UCMS women seeking equal pay for equal work, the board finally adopted "one schedule for men and women" in 1956. Still, it took over five years before women's compensation caught up with men's, especially in pension payments.

A 1953 study of women's status among Disciples of Christ noted that in the two hundred seventy-seven congregations reporting, only five women in three churches served as elders. The study found that of the twenty Disciples national policy-making boards, seven had no women members, three had one woman, two had two women, and the rest (except the UCMS, which then had equal numbers) possessed a clear majority of men. The International Conventions from 1940 to 1952 had invited only seven women to give major addresses out of the more than one hundred speakers. The report concluded that "full opportunity for ministerial service for women has not yet come into being even among the Disciples."[47]

In 1956, a study of women serving in the UCMS revealed that women were outnumbered as executive secretaries (11-3), assistant and associate secretaries (4-1), and national directors (22-15).[48] The same year Professor Edward D. Hamner of Phillips University conducted a survey titled "Women in the Ministry of the Disciples of Christ." Of the fifty-four who responded, sixteen served as pastors (thirteen ordained, two licensed, and one laywoman), and another twenty-one reported having served as pastors in the past. Of the sixteen pastors, only two had served for ten years or more. Hamner's study showed that the husbands of most women ministers also served in ministry, and the most common reason given for entering ministry was their experiences helping husbands. Other reasons included the need of churches, a sense of call, and continuing a ministry after a husband's illness or death. Their salaries were very small, often barely covering expenses.

Women struggled against all odds in the pastorate and even lost ground during the 1960s. As late as 1973, the Disciples yearbook reported only eight women among the 2,651 Disciples pastors. Over the next three decades, this figure would climb to 27.8 percent of all 2,469 pastors of recognized congregations.[49] During most of the twentieth century, however, women's ministry was largely limited to the mission field. Writing in 1953,

Pioneer leader in youth work, Cynthia Pearl Maus also authored numerous volumes on religion and the fine arts.

Mossie Allman Wyker, an ordained Disciples woman, lamented that though women had become educators, lawyers, doctors, government officials, and successful businesspeople, they remained second-class members of the church.[50]

Nevertheless, women made significant contributions to the Disciples witness throughout the twentieth century. Anna Atwater, first woman vice-president of the UCMS (1920-1925), significantly shaped Disciples missionary activities during these years. In 1949, under the leadership of Jessie M. Trout, UCMS vice-president from 1950-1961, Disciples women formed the Christian Women's Fellowship (CWF), uniting missionary societies and women's guilds into one organization. CWF included a major focus on missionary education and support. Four years later women formed the International Christian Women's Fellowship (ICWF) to unite congregational groups in the United States and Canada. Beginning in

1957, the ICWF conducted quadrennial assemblies where thousands of women from the United States, Canada, and around the globe gathered for fellowship and leadership development. In 1955, over 1,500 CWF members organized the World Christian Women's Fellowship.[51]

Rosa Page Welch also significantly influenced the Disciples' witness. An African American civil rights activist, classically trained mezzo-soprano, and educator, Welch played a key role in the racial integration of Disciples' organizations in the mid-twentieth century. While attending Southern Christian Institute she had discovered a love for music, and after graduation began leading singing at evangelistic meetings. White Disciples soon began asking her to lead singing and perform at youth conferences and other church meetings. Often the only person of color present, her efforts helped erode racial barriers. In 1952 she traveled and sang throughout Africa, Asia, Europe, and South America, becoming known among Disciples as the "Ambassador of Good Will." After serving as a missionary to Nigeria for the Church of the Brethren in the early 1960s, she supported the Disciples cooperative program as an employee of Unified Promotion.[52]

Social Action

As Disciples were developing their cooperative church structure, they encountered significant changes in American life. As modern industry expanded in urban areas, so did poverty, leading to social unrest and conflict between labor and management. In response, the social gospel movement combined evangelical piety with a call for social transformation that challenged Christians to focus on social reform.

Disciples had embraced some social-gospel trends earlier in their history. An "institutional church" movement had emerged among many American denominations in the late nineteenth century with congregations building gymnasiums, libraries, schools, and food kitchens to serve their neighborhoods. Central Christian Church in Des Moines, Iowa, was one example. Disciples also contributed to settlement houses—an effort in which middle-class "social workers" lived with the poor to help alleviate ignorance and poverty. In 1896, George Albert Bellamy (1879-1960) organized Hiram House in Cleveland, Ohio, which he led for fifty years. This growing embrace of social transformation as Christian ministry was also reflected in the number of Disciples applying for missionary service who articulated objectives such as "social justice and world order" in their applications for service.[53]

Walter Rauschenbusch, a Baptist minister teaching church history at Rochester Theological Seminary, had provided early leadership for the social gospel movement. His *Christianity and the Social Crisis*, published in 1907, helped raise the consciousness of many in the churches. By 1908, the efforts of Rauschenbusch and others to rally American denominations to Christianize society had paid high dividends when Protestants organized the Federal Council of the Churches of Christ (FCC). Uniting the efforts of thirty-three denominations representing eighteen million church members, the FCC immediately created a Commission on Church and Social Service.

Though some Disciples participated in the social gospel movement through their association with the FCC, most preachers continued to insist that the only way to transform society was to transform individuals by bringing them to Christ. Among the few exceptions was Alva Taylor (1871-1957), who chaired the International Convention's Commission on Social Service and the Rural Church from its formation in 1911 until 1928. James Crain (1886-1971), Taylor's successor, also worked to educate Disciples about the gospel's relationship to social issues.[54]

With the outbreak of World War I, Peter Ainslie and Frederick D. Kershner expressed historic Stone-Campbell pacifist convictions, though few Disciples agreed with them. Disillusionment following the war among many Americans, including Disciples, led to the formation in 1935 of the Disciples Peace Fellowship (DPF). Kirby Page (1890-1957), who published *War: Its Causes, Consequences, and Cure* in 1923, became one of the best-known Disciples pacifists. Both the Department of Social Welfare, the successor to Alva Taylor's original commission, and the DPF supported international peace movements and Disciples conscientious objectors during World War II, though neither was totally pacifist. Disciples also joined other Protestants to aid war refugees and orphans, creating the Week of Compassion in February 1944.

Disciples remained notoriously slow, however, to respond to most social issues. Even though Crain successfully elected a black member to his board in 1933, Disciples as a whole did little to counter racial segregation in the nation. Disciples seminaries began to integrate in the early 1950s, though most Disciples colleges waited until the mid-to-late 1960s to integrate their student bodies and were even slower in integrating their faculties.

Ecumenism

The Council on Christian Union, established through the leadership of Peter Ainslie in 1910, was the major vehicle of Disciples participation in the ecumenical movement. Though theological moderates such as Frederick D. Kershner supported the Council, most Disciples involved in the emerging ecumenical movement advocated the new approaches to the Bible and Christian unity. These leaders, however, kept at least one traditional Stone-Campbell understanding of Christian unity: that it was based on the individual's relationship to Christ. As a result, Disciples continued to see unity as a gift of God, an essential attribute of the body of Christ and not something human beings create.

They also continued to view denominationalism as a "sin." Yet some leaders began to admit that Disciples themselves participated in this "sin." They asserted that, no matter how much they might want to deny it, Disciples of Christ were a denomination and had never been free of the influences of historical and cultural development. This recognition led to the more important admission that Disciples fell under the same judgment as all other denominations and that every denomination "including the Disciples of Christ, was a partial and relative expression of a faith which would be fully known only in unity."[55] In coming to terms with their identity as a denomination, some Disciples had discovered yet another justification for seeking the unity of the church.

These Disciples, however, departed from earlier understandings of Christian unity in an important way. Alexander Campbell, Barton Stone, and other early leaders had viewed unity as something the church had to "restore." They claimed that the early church had been united but that this unity was lost due to divisive human opinions. The key to restoring that unity involved a return to the simple gospel, stripped of human opinion. Disciples who were influenced by the higher criticism and ecumenism abandoned this view of restoration for an understanding that no human community could avoid being shaped by historical factors.

With a new understanding and appreciation of the inevitable diversity of the church in different times and circumstances, these Disciples expressed a more positive appraisal of other denominations. Their increasing awareness of the inability of any group of humans to capture the divine message in its entirety led them to recognize that Disciples of Christ had much in common with other Protestant denominations struggling to find the most appropriate forms of Christian expression and witness. Many became more humble about their understandings and more tolerant of the expressions of others. This insight enabled later Disciples to work

for unity with other denominations in the ecumenical movement.

Education

Stone-Campbell enthusiasm for education in the nineteenth century had led to founding more colleges than the Movement would adequately support. Though most schools struggled financially and eventually collapsed, some survived and became influential educational institutions. In 1910, E. V. Zollars organized an "educational congress" to discuss problems facing Disciples colleges. This led to the establishment of the Association of Colleges of the Disciples of Christ, with President R. H. Crossfield of Transylvania University as its first president. R. A. Long pledged to give one million dollars if Disciples would give an additional five million for benevolence, education, and mission, three and a half million of which would go to the colleges.

In 1914, Disciples created a permanent Board of Education to develop this campaign, at first composed of the presidents of the twenty-six Disciples-affiliated institutions of higher education. The Board affiliated with the International Convention after its creation in 1917, and in 1922 added other church leaders as members in equal numbers to the college presidents. Through these efforts, Disciples colleges in the twentieth century gained a level of financial security. Because each school maintained its own self-perpetuating board of trustees, colleges were able to adjust their programs to the academic demands of modern higher education without denominational interference. Furthermore, as accrediting agencies developed, Disciples schools rapidly sought certification, continuing to fine-tune academic programs according to accepted educational standards.

By 1910, most ministerial training schools in North America, including Disciples schools, had become graduate institutions offering bachelor of divinity degrees. The College of the Bible in Lexington, founded as the ministerial training department of Kentucky (now Transylvania) University in 1865, and the College of the Bible at Texas Christian University, founded as the Bible department of Add Ran College in 1873, began emphasizing professional and graduate programs, eventually becoming Lexington Theological Seminary and Brite Divinity School. The College of the Bible at Phillips University founded in 1907, now Phillips Theological Seminary, and the College of Religion at Butler University founded in 1925, now Christian Theological Seminary, also began professional and graduate programs. When the Association of Theological Schools (ATS) in the United States and Canada developed in 1936 with criteria for evaluating theological institutions, Disciples seminaries quickly sought affiliation. Many Disciples ministerial students also studied at Yale and the University of Chicago. At Chicago, Disciples chartered a Disciples Divinity House in 1894 to cultivate Disciples identity and provide financial assistance to Disciples enrolled in the Divinity School.

Ministers graduating from these institutions acquired new perspectives, ultimately fueling the conflicts over the Bible and approaches to Christian unity that had emerged by the beginning of the twentieth century. The most public battle occurred in 1917 at the College of the Bible in Lexington. Ben Battenfield, a student who worked closely with the *Christian Standard*, used the magazine to urge the school's trustees to investigate charges of liberal teaching. When the majority of faculty members stated clearly they would be no party to such proceedings, the trustees backed away from a formal inquiry, citing the incompatibility of heresy trials with Disciples commitments.

Informally, however, the trustees looked into the matter and concluded that the faculty had done nothing that deserved disciplinary action. The dean of the faculty, Hall L. Calhoun (1863-1935), had sympathies similar to Battenfield's. He had worked closely with J.W. McGarvey and believed Disciples educational institutions were becoming too accepting of modern critical methods of biblical interpretation. Calhoun left the College of the Bible to teach in the more conservative environment of Bethany College.[56] After this, most Bible appointments in older Disciples schools went to faculty educated in doctoral programs in such places as Yale Divinity School and the University of Chicago.

By 1946, twenty-seven institutions of higher education were affiliated with the Board of Higher Education of the Disciples. They represented more than thirty-seven million dollars in assets in thirteen colleges or universities, seven seminaries, two junior colleges focusing on women's education, and five Bible chairs located at state universities. Over one thousand students were preparing for Christian ministry, including at least four hundred enrolled at the graduate level.[57]

Higher education opportunities for blacks in America had increased significantly. However, education for blacks at Disciples-related institutions other than Jarvis and Southern Christian Institute remained elusive.

When Emmett J. Dickson and Robert Hays Peoples applied to the Disciples Divinity House at the University of Chicago for fellowships, both were turned down. After widespread coverage of the event in the NCMC's journal, *The Christian Plea*, Edward Scribner Ames, Dean of the Disciples House, promised that any person who met both the University's and the House's criteria would receive a fellowship. Despite Ames's promise, when the Divinity School at Chicago accepted and granted a scholarship to William K. Fox, a graduate of Tennessee State College, the Disciples House did not grant him a fellowship providing housing and a stipend. Again, *The Christian Plea* kept the matter in the news. Finally, near the end of his first year in April 1941, Fox received a personal call from Ames informing him that the Disciples House would provide a fellowship for his studies.

In 1949, Charles Berry, Jr., and Earl W. Rand conducted a study titled "Negro Education in the Disciple Brotherhood," which asked, "To what extent does the Disciple Brotherhood perpetuate the ideals of freedom, justice and dignity of the individual by offering to its Negro youth an educational program comparable to that of its white youth?" Recognizing the central role of education in achieving equity, Berry and Rand contended that the colleges, especially church-related schools, were responsible for taking the lead in resolving racial conflict. They urged quick action to achieve "peace, goodwill and fraternity" and avoid racial strife.[58]

Mission

Differences among Disciples over new approaches to the Bible and Christian unity were most prominent in regard to mission. The primary issue was open membership. In 1919, Frank Garrett, secretary of the Central China Mission, asked the UCMS to be part of a united church that would integrate Presbyterian, Congregational, and London Missions congregations in China. Participation would necessarily include accepting into church membership those sprinkled as infants.

The conservative response was swift. Robert E. Elmore (1878-1968), who had served as recording secretary of the Foreign Christian Missionary Society, vehemently protested the proposal, resigning his FCMS position to aid the *Christian Standard* in its opposition to the society and its policies. Others withheld congregational contributions and rallied behind a series of resolutions at International Conventions calling for the UCMS to recall missionaries practicing open membership. Immediately before the 1919 International Convention, conservatives held a "Restoration Congress" to rally against what they saw as destructive liberalism in the incipient UCMS, with regional congresses continuing for years.[59] In reaction to the resolutions and public outcry, the society promised to recall missionaries who publicly supported open membership. However, under the influence of UCMS Vice-President Stephen J. Corey (1873-1962), the organization refused to infringe on private opinion or liberty of individual conscience.

In 1925, the International Convention passed a "Peace Resolution" explicitly declaring that the UCMS must sever ties with any missionary who "committed him or herself to the belief in or practice of the reception of unimmersed persons into the membership." The UCMS Board of Managers refused to enforce the Resolution, standing by the Stone-Campbell Movement's commitment against creedalism and heretic hunting. They stated that the phrase "committed...to belief in" never referred to someone's private opinion about open membership, but only to agitation about it that could lead to division. Conservatives cried foul. More studies and debates followed, but after the 1926 Memphis International Convention conservatives began exploring ways to organize outside the International Convention and work around the UCMS.

In 1927 conservatives created the North American Christian Convention (NACC), not overtly as a rival to the International Convention, but as an occasional meeting for fellowship. Some proponents, including Frederick D. Kershner, insisted that it was not schismatic.[60] However, many NACC organizers were deeply disillusioned by the perceived obstinacy of the UCMS bureaucracy and the institutional focus of the International Convention. They wanted a convention that would focus on doctrinal matters rather than social issues, and that would highlight inspiring preaching rather than institutional reports. By 1950 when NACC directors voted to hold the convention annually, it had grown into a gathering focused on preaching, holding up world evangelism and ministries independent of the cooperative agencies of the Disciples of Christ.

As conservatives had correctly perceived, the 1926 Memphis Convention had marked a public acknowledgment of the mission approach the UCMS would increasingly embrace. In response to the report of a special commission sent by the UCMS to investigate charges of open membership in its China mission, Convention president A.D. Harman argued that the UCMS could not simply develop a policy for bringing

Christ to the world as if everyone were the same. Disciples could not, he insisted, act as if their missionary policy "were an inanimate something, detached from life, built in Memphis, boxed and ready to be shipped to the world." Instead, he argued, the UCMS must become aware of the ways God's Spirit was illuminating the lives of those they sought to evangelize apart from the missionaries' understandings of the gospel.[61]

Stephen J. Corey, who became president of the UCMS in 1930, recorded in his diary how the 1928 meeting of the International Missionary Council shaped his developing approach to mission: "Indigenous, self-governing, self-operating, self-supportive, the burning topic at Jerusalem. Shift from paternalism to partnership."[62] These were principles that would guide the UCMS in following decades.

Despite these growing commitments, an often unconscious assumption of white North Americans that American civilization was destined to encompass the globe hindered their efforts, even at home. In the mid-1950s, Disciples had only ten U.S. Hispanic congregations with 636 members with an additional 754 Hispanic members of predominantly white congregations. This number reflected Disciples' inability to understand needs outside the boundaries of "their racially comfortable congregations." Daisy Machado shows that though some Disciples had become aware by 1900 of the need to minister to Hispanics in Texas, the body provided little support to produce materials or aid ministers working to develop congregations. Believing that persons living in the U. S. should speak English, Disciples established no work to educate Spanish-speaking ministers in Texas. Instead, such ministers usually had graduated from Disciples missionary schools in Mexico.[63]

Puerto Rican Disciples migrating to New York established their own congregations, finding little support among existing Disciples churches. Ministers for these bodies usually came from Puerto Rico and were often graduates of the Seminario Evangélico de Puerto Rico. Puerto Ricans started the first of these congregations, La Hermosa Christian Church in New York City, in 1939. At first, the congregation had no official relationship to North American Disciples. When the congregation hired Puerto Rican Disciples minister Pablo Cotto in 1943, however, he moved to associate it with Disciples in the U.S. and Canada. La Hermosa became the "mother church" for most Hispanic Disciples in the northeast United States, helping establish other Hispanic congregations in New York and assisting non-affiliated congregations as they chose to join Disciples life. Many leaders among Hispanic Disciples in the United States came from Puerto Rico.[64]

Domingo Rodriguez, who served La Hermosa Christian Church from 1953 to 1955, would become Director of Hispanic and Bilingual Congregations for Homeland Ministries in 1969.

Disciples also had difficulty supporting work among Asian Americans. In 1891, First Christian Church of Portland, Oregon, collaborated with the CWBM and Chinese residents of the area to found Portland Chinese Christian Mission. This was the first Asian Disciples community in America, led for a time by Drake-trained Chinese pastors Jeu Hawk and Louie Hugh, before they returned to China. In 1907, the CWBM helped found the Chinese Christian Mission in San Francisco.[65]

In 1908 similar work with Japanese immigrants in Los Angeles led to the founding of Japanese Christian Church, the precursor of All Peoples Church (later Center) and West Adams Christian Church. Japanese Disciples formed three other communities in California—in San Bernardino, Imperial Valley, and Berkeley—and one more in Rocky Ford, Colorado.[66] In 1933, collaboration between whites and Filipinos led to

the founding of the first Filipino Disciples congregation, also in Los Angeles.[67]

Despite missionary concern that led to the founding of these churches, Asian American Disciples found themselves marginalized, dependent on the dominant white church. The flow of power was clear—well-meaning white Disciples did missionary work for Asians and made all decisions for them. When society marginalized them or the white church experienced financial distress, Asian Disciples had little recourse. Not surprisingly, seven of the eight Asian Disciples churches closed before 1965, though one managed to reconstitute itself.[68]

The closure of Portland Chinese Mission was announced in the February 1924 issue of *World Call*. The local advisory board entrusted with supervising the Chinese mission explained:

On account of…peculiar conditions among the Chinese, such as the decreasing Chinese population, the inability to secure trained native leadership… and the consequent small attendance at religious services we do not feel it wise to spend so much missionary money for the results obtained. …we recommend to the home department of the United Christian Missionary Society…that the Chinese Mission at Portland, Oregon, be discontinued, effective February 1, 1924.

A UCMS pamphlet frankly stated the most important of the "peculiar conditions:" "Chinese exclusion laws and bitter race prejudice caused the depletion of the Chinese community. Therefore, in 1923, it seemed best to close the mission."[69]

Eventually, San Francisco's Chinese Institute also closed, and when President Franklin D. Roosevelt issued Executive Order 9066 authorizing the internment of 120,000 Japanese immigrants and their children, the five Japanese Disciples communities, too, suffered closure.[70] Maureen Osuga, a U.S.-born Disciple who suffered internment with her family at Heart Mountain, Wyoming, recalled, "When World War II broke out, our family was allowed to take only what we could carry to the concentration camp. Vultures swooped down on my father's two drug stores, jewelry store and five and ten cent store, swindling him out of his life's work."[71] Disciples leadership offered no protest. Of the early Asian-American church starts, only the Filipino church escaped closure and continued to thrive.

Some Asian American Disciples were members of predominantly white Disciples congregations, though they often felt less than fully welcome. Describing her experience in such congregations, Osuga wrote: "None of the churches in my life included me in any overt, positive way. Hence I was included on their terms, and my 'Japaneseness' was nonessential and invisible."[72] White Disciples, confident of the superiority of American civilization, had little interest in the distinctive identity and experiences of other nationalities.

In 1900, when Jeu Hawk returned to China, co-worker Louie Hugh, pictured with his wife Grace and their first child, was placed in charge of the Portland Chinese Mission, where he served until his return to China in 1909.

The open membership controversy and the development of independent missions reduced UCMS funding, losses made worse by the Great Depression. Congregations suffered and some, unable to pay their mortgages, went into foreclosure. Ministers were forced to work at reduced wages, some losing their jobs. Giving for the work of the general church dried up, and enthusiasm for cooperative work waned. The UCMS had faced financial shortfalls even before the depression, and deficits climbed to over $700,000 by 1930 and well over a million by December 1932. The UCMS cut jobs and salaries as it worked to maintain its financial footing. This strategy enabled the UCMS to keep its deficit in check, but the society would not show a gain in income until 1936.

In 1928, responding to legal requirements, Disciples were forced to separate pension funds from all other church finances. When the Pension Fund split from the UCMS, two other boards asked the International Convention to allow them to work independently as well. In 1933, the National Benevolent Association separated and sought funding directly from Disciples in the regions of the country where it did most of its work. The next year, the Board of Church Extension also began operating separately from the UCMS.

Theological Liberalism

The new approaches to the Bible and Christian unity that divided Disciples were identified with liberal Protestant theology, which at the beginning of the twentieth century was of two types. Many Disciples leaders represented the version known as "Evangelical" or "Christocentric" liberalism, which held to traditional doctrine and practice except where "modern circumstances required adjustment or change." Evangelical liberals called for a focus on the life and teachings of Jesus, which appealed to many Disciples. A much smaller number of Disciples accepted the form of Protestant liberalism known as "modernistic liberalism," or "scientific modernism." These Protestants began with the "scientific method, scholarly discipline, empirical fact, and prevailing forms of contemporary philosophy," approaching religion "as a human phenomenon" and "the Bible as one great religious document among others." Scientific modernism especially flourished at the University of Chicago.[73]

Among Disciples, scientific modernism's most influential voice was Edward Scribner Ames (1870-1958). Ames taught philosophy at the University of Chicago beginning in 1895, the year he earned the first Ph.D. offered by the school's philosophy department. In addition, Ames served as pastor of the Hyde Park Church (later known as the University Church) for forty years. As early as 1918, Ames explained the meaning of scientific modernism for Disciples in *The New Orthodoxy*, drawing his theology from natural and social sciences rather than biblical sources.

Human experience was the only authority for religion, Ames asserted. Human beings are completely autonomous, "perfectly free souls, unawed by any authority over us or by any superstition within us, yet reverent toward the things which experience has taught us and eagerly in quest of clear perceptions of the ideal possibilities of life." Faith for Ames sprang from the fact that the "world has immense possibilities" that "may be realized through the industry, intelligence, and good-will of men working in harmony with the highest knowledge and deepest convictions they possess." God is not distant; rather humans find God in their life with others—especially when it is hopeful and constructive. God is in "the moral values and the spiritual realities of life."[74] Christ was a moral example—he taught Christians how to live.[75] Ames believed theology, traditionally conceived, was limiting and shortsighted. His autobiography, *Beyond Theology*, reveals how strongly he felt the church needed to overcome such limitations.[76]

Yet, most Disciples at the University of Chicago were not scientific modernists. Herbert L. Willett (1864-1944) was an evangelical liberal. After college at Bethany and four years as a pastor in Ohio, Willett attended Yale, then became the first Disciple to earn a Ph.D. in Bible from the University of Chicago in 1896. He accepted a faculty appointment but continued to serve as pastor for churches in Chicago throughout his career. Though not a radical biblical critic, Willett became controversial because he accepted moderate conclusions of higher criticism.[77]

In 1903, Willett published *Basic Truths of the Christian Faith*, aimed at a popular audience and reflecting several liberal shifts in Disciples theology. He replaced a focus on restoration of the early church and an emphasis on the epistles and Acts with a serious engagement with the gospels. "It must be remembered," Willett told his readers, "that the Gospels, containing as they do the teachings of our Lord, are the greatest of all documents for Christian culture."[78] For Willett, Christ's teachings were far more important than any ecclesiastical declaration of Christ's divinity.

Inspiration for Willett was not in the words of the Bible, but in the actual historical events of Israel and the early Christians. As he put it in 1917, "The Bible as a result of these critical studies is not less divine but more human. It is seen to be less a supernaturally perfect record of history and science than a faithful and inspiring account of the most impressive movement of the divine activity in the world."[79] For Willett, the Bible's authority was found more in what it enabled people to do than in what it was.[80]

Willett's *Basic Truths* emphasized human initiative and participation in the Kingdom of God. Baptism became "the public ceremony of allegiance by which the Christian knight takes upon himself the service of his Lord." Where Campbell had seen the church as a harbinger of God's Kingdom, Willett argued that God "has no other way of getting the Kingdom organized in

the world than by the ministries of his people." Instead of a literal second coming of Christ, Willett described a second coming that was "continuous and spiritual," found not in a literal millennium, but in the advance of God's love among human beings.[81] These themes heightened awareness of social problems and fostered a renewed commitment to church unity. Yet they also led to an uncritical vision of history as progress, and to an overconfidence in human ability to accomplish great things in the name of God.

Herbert Lockwood Willett was a popularizer of biblical higher criticism who wrote for the *Christian-Evangelist* and the *Christian Century*.

For over four decades, another Chicagoan, Charles Clayton Morrison (1874-1966), editor of the *Christian Century*, also advanced evangelical liberalism and the social gospel among Disciples. In his book *What Is Christianity?* Morrison defined the Christian community as "the revelation of God in history." For Morrison, revelation was God's activity seen in historical events through "a historical community whose corporate life is oriented toward him."[82] Though Morrison's insistence that Christians take seriously both history and God's involvement in it was a part of Stone-Campbell theological tradition, he had no interest in restoring an ancient church. His vision was completely oriented toward growth and progress.

Morrison's theology departed significantly from traditional Stone-Campbell understandings, emphasizing human experience in Christ and social transformation over fidelity to biblical authority and the necessity of individual conversion. He did, however, continue the anti-Jewish and anti-Catholic characteristics of traditional Protestant theology. Seeing the Christian community as the unique revelation of God, Morrison's theology included clear anti-Jewish tones. Furthermore, Morrison's commitment to church unity was largely limited to Protestant unity, viewing Catholicism as something authentic Christianity had to overcome.[83]

Ames and Willett were founding members of the Campbell Institute, with Morrison joining a few years later. Begun in 1896, the Institute's purpose was "to encourage and keep alive a scholarly spirit and to enable its members to help each other to a riper scholarship by the free discussion of vital problems." For the most part, the Institute represented values associated with liberalism and university-educated Disciples. It served to bolster the morale of liberal-leaning Disciples who hoped to change the conservative culture they felt characterized most of Disciples life.[84] With the exception of Albertina Forrest, the Institute admitted only male members in its early years.[85]

The Institute's liberalism weathered the growing strength of neo-orthodoxy in North American Protestantism during the 1930s largely unscathed. This theological movement emerged to challenge liberalism's naïve optimism about human nature and God after the horrors of World War I. Ames described the work of Karl Barth and Reinhold Niebuhr as a "reversion…to the general attitude and doctrinal position of the old systems of speculative theology."[86] A few Disciples, like Harold Lunger in 1935, later professor at Brite Divinity School from1956 to1977, spoke positively about neo-orthodoxy in the pages of *The Scroll*, the Institute's journal. Charles Clayton Morrison also strongly supported the expression of neo-orthodoxy in the pages of *The Christian Century*. For the most part, however, Disciples associated with the Institute remained thoroughgoing liberals.

Commission on Restudy of the Disciples of Christ

In response to the growing divergence of Disciples over the Bible and Christian unity, the International Convention established a commission in 1934 to "restudy the origin, history, slogans, methods, successes and failures of the…Disciples …with the purpose of a more effective and a more united program." Convention president, William F. Rothenburger, pastor of the 2,300-member Third Christian Church of Indianapolis, specified that the commission be composed of persons "proportionately representing the varied phases and schools of thought and the institutional life among us."[87]

Drake University president, D. W. Morehouse, president of the 1935 International Convention, appointed nineteen prominent pastors, educators, editors, and mission executives to the commission. Over the next dozen years, the Convention elected additional commissioners nominated by the Commission. Morehouse designated Frederick D. Kershner, Dean of the College of Religion at Butler University, as chair and Rothenburger as secretary.

The Commission initially met twice a year, alternating between Indianapolis and Chicago. At most meetings commissioners presented and discussed two or more papers. Topics included Stone-Campbell origins, sources of schism, possibilities for union with other Christians, and Disciples polity. Every meeting also included worship. In addition, the Commission held business sessions, usually over lunch, during meetings of the International Convention.

Though attendance at Commission meetings was irregular, Kershner and Rothenburger, along with eleven other men (no women served) provided continuity and direction to the Commission's work. On the back of his copy of the Minutes of the July 13-14, 1939, meeting, Kershner plotted the members along a left to right continuum. Kershner placed six on the left, including Edward Scribner Ames and Charles Clayton Morrison, Rothenburger and one other in the middle but leaning left, himself in the middle leaning right, and three on the right.[88]

The Commission submitted a report to the 1946 Columbus International Convention that was a compilation of papers on "Causes of Unrest and Dissension Among the Disciples of Christ." Morrison and Dean E. Walker, Professor of Church History at Butler, identified by Kershner as on the right, presented the report. First on a list of "causes of tension among us" was the practice of admitting unimmersed Christians to membership in Disciples congregations.

> Some hold that, under the authority of Christ we have no right to receive any who have not been scripturally baptized, and that we are bound to apply this principle to the penitent believer and the unimmersed Christian without discrimination. It is maintained that any such discrimination is a surrender of the witness which we have been called to bear with respect to the scriptural action of baptism.
>
> Others hold that in making the distinction

between a penitent believer and one who brings credentials from a sister church of Christ, they are acting under the authority of the Christ. They believe that inasmuch as Christ has received such a person into the membership of his church, they would be disloyal to Christ in not recognizing the full status of such a person as a Christian, a member of the Church of Christ, and receiving him as such without re-baptism, unless he desire to be re-baptized.[89]

Two other causes of tension were the development of the North American Christian Convention as an expression of dissatisfaction with the International Convention, and "challenges" from both the left and the right to the "simple, scriptural and truly catholic creed, namely faith in Jesus Christ as the Son of God and man's Savior."[90]

The report also identified differences regarding four other issues: whether Disciples should deny denominational status or accept it while testifying against denominationalism and seeking common ground with all Christians; whether agencies and conventions threaten local church autonomy, or provide leadership the churches want and voluntarily accept; whether the New Testament provides a divine authoritative pattern for the form and organization of the local church, or principles to guide the form and organization of the local church; and whether the absence of any clear evidence of organizations beyond the local church in the New Testament prohibits such organizations, or leaves the churches free to create agencies as needed to relate to each other and fulfill their mission in the most adequate and responsible manner.

The commissioners asserted that a major cause of the conflicts among Disciples was that for many the principles of restoration and unity had come to be understood as contradictory. They pointed out that some affirm "that Christian unity is possible only on the basis of the restoration of the primitive church," while others "are content to abandon the concept of the restoration of the primitive church and center our emphasis upon union." Still others, they observed, "believe that a new synthesis of these two concepts of unity and restoration is possible."[91]

The report recommended that all segments of the Disciples press, as well as their conventions and boards, conduct a wide-ranging and open discussion of the questions the Commission had identified and any others pertinent to Disciples unity. The commissioners also related how they had grown to respect and trust each other across the theological spectrum, describing their relationship as "an exceedingly precious fellowship." They declared that it was their highest desire and prayer that the same spirit would spread through "the brotherhood" as it pursued the discussion of issues outlined in the report.[92]

Far from encouraging discussion of the issues, the *Christian Standard* refused to publish the Commission's report. Editor Burris Butler (1909-1982) drafted a response blasting the Commission's efforts as assuming the Disciples "brotherhood" wanted to remain united regardless of differences. He charged that the Commission's listing of open membership as a "cause of tension" among Disciples "acknowledges that it occupies a legitimate place *'within the brotherhood.'*" According to Butler, the Commission had confused the New Testament bond of fellowship that requires obedience to Christ with an artificial or denominational unity, placing "matters of faith in the category of opinion."

Butler was especially sorry to see the names of opponents of open membership associated with the report. Referring to those members of the Commission, Butler asked, "In their 'exceedingly precious fellowship' with men of *every shade of unbelief* have these men, hitherto concerned about New Testament teaching, come to place human friendships and social amenities above loyalty to the direct commands of Christ?" What the Commission had failed to realize, he asserted, was that the differences were not causes of tension, but "irreconcilable principles that no amount of restudy can harmonize."[93]

The Commission's report to the 1947 Buffalo Convention was largely the work of Walker and George W. Buckner identified by Kershner as on the left. Buckner was head of the Association for the Promotion of Christian Unity, the name adopted by the Council on Christian Union in 1916. The report began by declaring the Commission's belief that "unity does not demand uniformity in all things." It then listed items the Commission declared all Disciples held, beginning with "The acknowledgment of Jesus Christ as Lord and Savior is the sole affirmation of faith necessary to the fellowship of Christians," followed by, "The New Testament is the primary source of our knowledge concerning the will of God and the revelation of God in Christ." In response to Butler's charge that the Commission was trying to maintain the unity of a denomination rather than the church, the Commissioners stated that their efforts were not simply for their immediate fellowship, but for the whole church. Finding solutions to these problems, they insisted, could lead to overcoming the evils of division.[94]

The Commission's 1948 report was largely the work of Walker. It urged Disciples not to think of themselves as a sect, but as a manifestation of the unity Christ wants for the entire church. The plea for unity on the simple confession of Christ was not merely for unity's sake or to abolish human creeds, but so that the world could see Christ, believe in him, and be saved.[95]

The Commission held its final meeting in Indianapolis, July 5-6, 1949. The group revised and approved a preface and conclusion to the 1946, 1947, and 1948 reports prepared by Walker, O. L. Shelton (1895-1959), and Winfred E. Garrison (1874-1969). Shelton, formerly pastor of Independence Boulevard Christian Church in Kansas City, Missouri, had been elected both to the Commission and to succeed Kershner as dean of the Butler School (formerly known as College) of Religion in 1944. Using Kershner's continuum, Shelton appears to have been in the middle leaning left. Garrison, literary editor of the *Christian Century*, Disciples historian, and retired professor of church history from the University of Chicago, was clearly on the left.[96]

Answering Butler's charge that personal fellowship had blinded members who opposed open membership, the Commissioners observed that their close association had not blunted, but sharpened their convictions, their understanding of each other, and the problems facing Disciples. They encouraged all Disciples to engage in similar studies, meeting in small groups for serious discussion that would require careful preparation by the participants. Declaring that they agreed on much more than they disagreed on, Commissioners admonished Disciples to find truth, not by expressing their ideas to people with whom they already agreed, but by being willing to submit to mutual criticism.[97] The Commission took its final action at its October 26, 1949, luncheon meeting in Cincinnati. It voted not to dissolve, but to become "an invisible fellowship of prayer."[98]

Theological Reflection and Emerging Notions of Mission and Church

While few Disciples had been at the forefront of theological inquiry during the emergence of neo-orthodoxy in the 1930s, by the mid-1950s many Disciples leaders were ready to engage in serious theological reflection. W. Barnett Blakemore, Jr. (1912-1975), Dean of the Disciples Divinity House at the University of Chicago, asserted in 1955 that Disciples were a "non-theological people" who found themselves in the midst of an "intellectual crisis." He argued that "the times have

shifted from a philosophical search to justify our faith, to a theological search to justify our philosophizing."[99] The Campbell Institute's journal, *The Scroll*, published essays on theological method, the relationship between theology and worship, theological foundations for church unity, recovery of biblical theology, and Christology.[100]

The concern for theological reflection showed up most notably, however, in the work of the Panel of Scholars (1957-1961), a Commission sponsored by the UCMS and the Board of Higher Education to examine Disciples doctrine in light of contemporary scholarship. The panel met for four years and, reflecting its white male composition, presented papers on nearly every conceivable aspect of Disciples life except gender and race. In 1963, Blakemore served as general editor for the publication of these papers in a three-volume series titled *The Renewal of the Church*. In a 1991 analysis of the Panel's work, James O. Duke and Joseph D. Driskill identify three major areas of focus: "The task and place of theology in the church, past and present; Christology or christocentrism …; and issues in ecclesiology."

Though Duke and Driskill conclude that the reports contain hardly any proposals and therefore little that is truly original, they maintain that the Panel of Scholars made two significant theological advances. The first was the realization that Disciples did have a theological tradition—Jesus Christ. The nineteenth-century Disciples slogan "No creed but Christ" was not anti-theological but was itself a theological assertion. This made it possible for Disciples theologians to (re) connect the Disciples heritage to apostolic preaching of Jesus Christ, to Protestant theology, and above all to contemporary Christian thought. The second advance was the recognition that their theological tradition gave them freedom to disavow certain traditional formulations and develop new expressions in keeping with their present understandings of God's self-disclosure in Jesus Christ. These moves made the historic Disciples questioning of tradition appropriate to contemporary theological dialogue.[101]

Both of these advances were clearly evident in Ronald E. Osborn's "One Holy Catholic and Apostolic Church"—the concluding essay of volume I of the Panel's report. Osborn asserted that "Apostolicity was an explicit ideal of Disciples from the outset," but that Thomas Campbell had taken a fatal turn when he defined it as restoration of a New Testament constitution for the worship, discipline, and government of the church. While Campbell's intentions were catholic, seeking to serve unity and freedom, his ideology proved to be sectarian because it was founded on a series of false assumptions that he shared with others of his era.[102]

First among these false assumptions was that the New Testament is a constitution for the church. A comparison of any book in the New Testament with Leviticus would quickly reveal that the New Testament is not a constitution, nor does it contain one, in the sense of specific prescriptions for the order, worship, faith, and life of the church. Another false assumption was that the New Testament gave shape to the church. Rather, the church was formed by the gospel as proclaimed by the apostles. The New Testament contained samples of their preaching and directives to the churches, but "fidelity to the gospel rather than to deductions about ancient church organization should give shape to the church." Finally, it was a false assumption that once the books of the New Testament had been completed, the Holy Spirit ceased to guide the church except by these writings. If true, the church could no longer follow the first-century practice of facing a problem prayerfully and taking counsel in the light of its best understanding of the gospel, as was the case in the decision to admit Gentiles to the church. Osborn concluded, "The subsequent divisions within the movement are due not so much to the bad spirit of a people whose professions of unity must be regarded as hypocritical as they are to the ambiguity, confusion, and contradiction arising from the ill-starred attempt to make a constitution out of the New Testament."[103]

If restoration was no longer justifiable as an interpretation of apostolicity, was there a defensible interpretation of the concept? Osborn answered that there was, and that Thomas Campbell had pointed toward that interpretation when he wrote that "nothing ought to be inculcated upon Christians as articles of faith; nor required of them as terms of communion; but what is expressly taught and enjoined upon them, in the word of God." Apostolic faith and order viewed in this light, Osborn argued, points to what is essential to the life of the church over against that which is peripheral or transitory.[104]

Osborn defined apostolic faith as "utter trust in God resulting from the understanding of his saving deeds wrought through Jesus of Nazareth, whom the apostles gladly confessed as Son of God, Savior, and Lord." Such faith was primarily a matter of relationship, but it was a "special type of relationship with a unique Reality—namely the God and Father of our Lord Jesus Christ." At their best, Disciples had contended for apostolic faith in this sense, over against "the highly intellectualized dogmatic formulations which under the influence of Greek philosophy and of eighteenth-century rationalism the church had come to regard as the sole authentic expressions of the faith."[105]

Osborn argued that the order of the church established by the end of the apostolic period must have contained all that was essential to its life. The contemporary church was therefore under obligation to bring a sympathetic and intelligent understanding to the forms of the apostolic church in order to distinguish what was historically conditioned and therefore transitory from what bore witness to the gospel. Disciples must be careful neither to insist on elements that the apostolic church did not require nor to overlook concerns to which it gave attention through its developing patterns of order.[106]

Osborn commented on four elements of what he identified as the original order of the apostolic church: ministry, baptism, communion, and confession. The ministry of reconciliation in the apostolic age belonged to the whole people of God, but also to a specialized ministry recognized by the church and set apart for service. Baptism in the New Testament was a means of grace; an appropriate attitude toward baptism was gratitude, not legalism concerning the manner of its administration. Communion in the New Testament bore witness to and mediated the gospel of divine grace. Confessions of faith in the apostolic church were "joyful outpourings of whole-souled devotion to Jesus Christ as the Revealer of God, not hair-splitting definitions of dogma."[107]

The Disciples theological renaissance of the 1950s represented by Osborn and others made possible a reconsideration of both mission and polity. Having often neglected the theological implications of their missionary endeavors, Disciples began to give theological attention to their emerging understanding of world mission. The practical impetus for this reflection came from the 1952 World Meeting of the International Missionary Council at Willengen, Germany. There, younger churches in countries struggling against Western colonialism asked missionary organizations to end their paternalism and embrace a new spirit of partnership. Representatives from those parts of the world identified mission work as an example of colonial power, a realization that was leading their churches to seek greater freedom from the missionary organizations.

In response, Virgil Sly guided the foreign division of the UCMS to reconsider and restate its theology of missions. Study papers prepared by a Commission on the Theology of Mission (1958-1962), cosponsored by the UCMS and the Council on Christian Unity (the name adopted by the Association for the Promotion of Christian Unity in 1954), aided this work. In 1956, Sly changed the name of the Division of Foreign Missions to the Division of World Mission. By 1959, he had also changed the title of "The Strategy for World Missions," a document first developed in 1955, to "The Strategy for World Mission." These changes, in Sly's words, resulted from the recognition that "the mission…is God's mission." With this shift, the UCMS affirmed the move from exporting "missions" to foreign locations to seeking to serve as participants in God's mission, which began long before any Christians arrived.[108]

The theological renaissance also encouraged Disciples to reconsider their cooperative church structure. As the Panel of Scholars finished its work, Disciples established a Commission on Brotherhood Restructure. The continuing competition and overlap of Disciples organizational life, with its multiple national agencies and state societies, contributed significantly to the desire for a more effective church structure. Restructure would attempt to address these concerns with a representative convention (the General Assembly) and an understanding of local, regional, and general "manifestations" of the church, each with its appropriate rights and responsibilities.

The rationale for such a distinctive structure, neither hierarchical nor radically congregational, had been developed by W. Barnett Blakemore in his Panel of Scholars chapter "The Issue of Polity for Disciples Today." Blakemore had argued that the association of Christians, at any level, for the promotion of the church's mission creates new power and new ability, new responsibility and therefore new authority. This power and authority, however, was not hierarchical.

> …these rights and powers originate with the association [and] have not derived from some other specific association, either more local or wider, higher or lower. Each level of association is to be understood as the highest authority with respect to the churchly functions which it is peculiarly able to carry out. With respect to churchly functions which it cannot fulfill, it must place itself at the service of those associations which can fulfill those functions, though never at the expense of destroying its ability to fulfill its own appropriate functions…there are areas in which a local congregation is "autonomous," and other areas where it is not. That same

[is true]…of a state convention, or a benevolent association, or any other association established to carry out a function that belongs to the church.[109]

Blakemore was describing the cooperative structure that had developed among Disciples. Though agencies recognized by the International Convention, such as the UCMS and the Board of Church Extension, reported to the International Convention, they were accountable to their separate boards for the fulfillment of their specific ministries. Responsible to Jesus Christ as the ultimate authority of the church, and not to some other organization, these boards cooperated with other ministries to serve God's mission.

The Commission began by examining biblical metaphors for the church that focus on the church's dependence on Christ, God's initiative in creating and sustaining the church, and the church's responsibility as witness to God's redeeming work. This exercise reminded commissioners that the covenant of God's love seen in Jesus Christ is the source of the church. This covenant, Ronald Osborn argued, was intensely personal but never merely individual. To be in covenant with God was to be in covenant with God's people. Christians did not make this covenant. Rather, they declared or acknowledged God's covenant and its consequences. Because of God's covenant, all Christians were responsible to one another and to God's mission of reconciliation.

Osborn also offered three theses to help the Commission understand the place of theology in matters of church structure: (1) no doctrine of the church could dictate the complete details of any church structure— theology had its limits; (2) every doctrine of the church contained implications for church structure and every church structure contained theological implications; and (3) because theology had limits, "common sense and practical experience" should take over when theology had reached its end. The question of the number of regions, for example, might be decided on pragmatic grounds alone, but the question of whether regional representatives should include women and men, ministers and non-ordained laity, and persons of various racial and ethnic groups should be decided on theological grounds.[110]

The Commission presented "A Provisional Design for the Christian Church (Disciples of Christ)" to the 1966 Dallas International Convention. Following extensive discussion, the Convention voted by more than two-thirds to receive the document and transmit it to congregations, agencies, regions, and institutions for study and response. Among the responders was an anonymous Committee for the Preservation of the Brotherhood that distributed two anonymous pamphlets, *Freedom or Restructure?* and *The Truth About Restructure*. Both were authored by James DeForest Murch and emphasized perceived threats to the freedom of congregations and their property rights. Most members of the Committee had not supported the Disciples cooperative agencies since the 1920s. Opposition to the Provisional Design also came from Robert Burns (1904-1991), a member of the Commission on Brotherhood Restructure and pastor of the Peachtree Christian Church of Atlanta, Georgia. Burns, secretary of a committee that circulated the "Atlanta Declaration of Convictions and Concerns," charged that the proposed design would endanger congregational liberty, especially in regard to a possible union with other denominations.

In August 1967, members of the Atlanta group met with members of the Commission. The commissioners refused to comply with the group's demand that the word "autonomy" be added to the Provisional Design, arguing that although congregations are free, no part of the body of Christ can be autonomous. However, in response to their concern, a statement defining congregational rights was included in the final draft of the Provisional Design.

The work of the Commission on Restructure concluded on September 26, 1968, when Disciples voted in Kansas City to accept the Provisional Design. Though received by the Assembly's singing of the doxology, this action changed Disciples structure very little. Essentially, the cooperative structure that had been developing since the first decade of the twentieth century was reaffirmed with minor refinements meant to increase the efficiency of Disciples in their mission of witness and service. The number and structure of agencies (referred to in 1968 as general units and later as general ministries), state societies (referred to as regions), the International Convention (now a representative General Assembly rather than a mass meeting), remained visibly the same, each with separate governing boards. Only the UCMS was notably transformed, being divided into separately governed divisions of homeland and overseas ministries, so there would no longer be one general ministry that was so much larger than the others. The structure and freedom of congregations remained unchanged.

The major change of restructure was the formal definition of church. With restructure, Disciples shifted from using "church" as referring only to congregations, to an understanding of church as composed of congregations, regions, and general ministries joined together by God's covenant of love which binds Christians to God and to one another. This definition, informed by New Testament images of church, reflected the actual experience of Disciples for more than half a century. The group's formal name shifted from Christian Churches (Disciples of Christ) to the Christian Church (Disciples of Christ). The singular "Christian Church" acknowledged that they were bound together into one body rather than simply a grouping of separate congregations. The parenthetical "Disciples of Christ" recognized that Disciples did not constitute the whole church, but only one partial and fragmentary expression of Christ's body.[111]

Numerical Growth and Decline

From 1890 to 1906 the Stone-Campbell Movement had been the fastest growing of the large Protestant bodies, increasing at a rate nearly twice that of all Protestants combined and over twice that of the total population. At the start of the twentieth century, Disciples claimed a membership exceeding 1,100,000 members. The 1906 Census of Religious Bodies recorded the Movement's first formal split, listing a separate body of Churches of Christ with about 160,000 members. Churches of Christ outnumbered Disciples in Tennessee, Arkansas, and Alabama and had almost as many members as the Disciples in Texas. Outside of the South, however, the division had little effect on Disciples membership.[112]

Mirroring developments in other North American Protestant denominations, a small group of professional evangelists had emerged among Disciples at the turn of the century, creating the National Evangelistic Association in 1904. Leaders included Charles Reign Scoville (1869-1937), Charles R. L. Vawter (1879-1935), and Jesse M. Bader (1886-1963). Bader served in 1920 as the first superintendent of evangelism for the UCMS. In 1932 he left the UCMS to lead the Department of Evangelism of the Federal Council of the Churches of Christ in America.

Through the efforts of such professional evangelists and others, Disciples grew by more than eighty percent between 1906 and 1952, reaching a total of 1.8 million members in 1952. This reflected a rate of growth that was roughly equal to that of the U.S. population, though somewhat lower than that of other large Protestant groups, including Baptists, Lutherans, and Methodists. Nevertheless, Disciples membership increased in all but the five New England states and North Dakota. Growth was most notable in high population growth states of the South and West to which Disciples migrated.

Disciples also increased with the growth of population in cities where they already had significant numbers and infrastructure in place. Membership grew by 40,000 in Los Angeles, 25,000 in Dallas and Fort Worth, and 21,000 in Indianapolis. Kansas City, Oklahoma City, Tulsa, and Wichita each added over 10,000 Disciples.[113]

In 1968, after Disciples approved the Provisional Design, more than a third of the congregations listed in the Disciples' *Year Book* formally withdrew from the Christian Church (Disciples of Christ). Many of these congregations had not supported the cooperative program of the Disciples for many years. Over the next few years, other congregations that had earlier stopped support for the Disciples' cooperative program also withdrew. But, even before the removal of those churches from the *Year Book*, Disciples numbers had begun to decline. In 1971 the Christian Church (Disciples of Christ) and Christian Churches/Churches of Christ combined claimed 70,000 fewer members than the Disciples had reported in 1952, a decline of nearly 4 percent during a period when the U.S. population had increased by 35 percent.[114] After the separation of Christian Churches/Churches of Christ, the number of Disciples in 1971 was 950,000—a decrease of nearly 50 percent from the number reported in 1952.[115]

Paths of Fellowship

Even as Christian Churches/Churches of Christ formally withdrew from the Christian Church (Disciples of Christ), the World Convention of Churches of Christ and the Disciples of Christ Historical Society maintained paths of fellowship for members of these two North American streams of the Movement. These two organizations also opened doors for fellowship with members of North American Churches of Christ.

The World Convention of Churches of Christ had begun in 1930 as a means of international fellowship and cooperation among the churches of the Stone-Campbell Movement. Six other Christian World Communions had established international forums, and the founder of World Convention, Jesse M. Bader, believed it was time for the Stone-Campbell Movement to do the same. The first convention had been in Washington, D.C., immediately following the 1930 Washington, D.C., Disciples International Convention. Though North American Churches of Christ were not involved in the founding of the World Convention, members were always welcome, and some became involved. With the formal separation of the Christian Church (Disciples of Christ) and Christian Churches/Churches of Christ, the World Convention rejected the temptation to identify with one of the two bodies, making a commitment to serve the whole of the Stone-Campbell Movement.[116] The global gatherings held by World Convention continued to include persons from across the streams of the North American Movement and from around the globe.

The Disciples of Christ Historical Society also included persons from across the streams of the Stone-Campbell Movement. The Society had been created by action of the International Convention in 1941. Initially located at Culver-Stockton College, where librarian Claude Spencer had begun a collection nearly

Australian Delegation to the World Convention in 1930

Thomas W. Phillips Memorial building in Nashville, Tennessee, home of the Disciples of Christ Historical Society since 1958. The massive library and archives serves all streams of the Stone-Campbell Movement.

a decade before, the Society had soon needed larger quarters to house its growing collection. A location near Vanderbilt University in Nashville, Tennessee, had been chosen because of Vanderbilt's offer of free space for five years, the work of community and church leaders to raise the funds to move the collection there, and the fact that Vanderbilt was a neutral location not identified with any one of the streams of the Movement. In 1958 the Society moved into the Thomas W. Phillips Memorial building, a gift from the family of Mr. Phillips, a millionaire oilman and well-known lay leader of the Movement. Basic funding for the Society came from the cooperative fund-raising program of the Disciples of Christ, but the Society's membership, board, authors, and speakers were always drawn from across the streams of the Movement.[117] These efforts and those of other organizations promoted connections and mutual understanding among members of the divided North American Stone-Campbell Movement.

10

The Emergence of Christian Churches/ Churches of Christ

The second major division of the North American Stone-Campbell Movement followed the pattern of denominational schisms seen in the American Fundamentalist-Modernist controversy. Sociologists of religion Sutton and Chaves identified "a new nonlocal organization" that "successfully mobilizes the loyalty and the resources of a subset of existing congregations" as a necessary development for such a division.[1] Beginning in the 1920s, that nonlocal organization for conservative Disciples was the North American Christian Convention, accompanied by mission efforts and new Bible colleges, providing a system that functioned independently from the Disciples International Convention.

Conflict between conservative and liberal Disciples, however, continued well beyond the American Fundamentalists' rejection of theological liberalism in the 1920s and 1930s, extending over three generations and resulting in a heavier cost than for most other Protestant denominations. More than 40 percent of Disciples would eventually break ranks with the body's mainline institutions. Clearly the Disciples schism reflected issues seen in the larger Fundamentalist-Modernist controversy—liberal theology, critical approaches to Scripture, and the nature of biblical authority.[2] Yet the strife also involved debates rooted in nineteenth-century Stone-Campbell issues, such as the policies, structure, and leadership of missionary societies. At a deeper level, it was a battle over whether the nineteenth-century Stone-Campbell plea for Christian unity and a restoration of the ancient order was to be reinvented for a new era or preserved as a bulwark against modernist assaults.

The central role of the United Christian Missionary Society in the controversy suggests that it was broader than merely a clash over theological liberalism. Labels most often used by the competing factions, for example, are not "conservative" and "liberal," or even "fundamentalist" and "modernist," but rather "cooperative" and "independent," terms indicating support or rejection of the UCMS and other agencies. Yet, as with the first division, there was no clean break between the groups. The process through which preachers, laypersons, and churches identified with either "cooperative" or "independent" Disciples was long and complicated and left deep scars between and within each group. Eventually the "independent" Christian Churches/Churches of Christ would emerge as a separate stream of the North American Stone-Campbell Movement.

Toward a Second Division in the North American Movement

At the heart of the division were differences over interpretation and application of the Stone-Campbell principles of restoration and unity. Yet differences over church organization, evangelism, and social reform existed as well. In the late nineteenth century, Disciples supported new missionary societies and evangelistic outreach, and promoted social reform movements such as temperance. By the 1920s, Disciples "cooperatives" increasingly defined themselves by loyalty to a network of church agencies interconnected through the International Convention whose leaders were often disposed toward liberal theology and ecumenism. Some of these leaders rejected restoration altogether in favor of a progressive agenda. "Independents" increasingly defined themselves in reaction to the cooperatives, rejecting what they saw as powerful and unresponsive mission organizations and developing their own direct-support missions. While defending a version of restoration, they articulated Christian unity in increasingly narrow terms, especially as they saw their progressive rivals cultivating relationships with the emerging ecumenical movement. Once Prohibition became law in 1919 with passage of the 18th amendment to the United States Constitution, independents no longer actively pursued social reform, instead focusing almost entirely on evangelism.

For the conservatives or independents, the United Christian Missionary Society became the symbol of the disastrous direction of cooperative Disciples. The UCMS mirrored a pattern of consolidation seen in other denominations. In the early twentieth century, unified denominational boards and structures appeared to be the wave of the future, bringing a businesslike efficiency to the work of the churches.[3] While most conservatives came to view such consolidation itself as bad, more importantly they believed that the UCMS was challenging biblical authority and the pattern of the New Testament church. A perceived wave of "progressive" movements infiltrating all Protestant churches further alarmed conservative Disciples. This alarm was exacerbated by the climate of fear created by the United States' mobilization in World War I and the Red Scare following the Bolshevik Revolution of 1917, which led to new levels of opposition to liberalism. Conservative Protestants connected rumors of foreign invasion, Communist subversion, and growing Catholic immigration with the advance of theological liberalism.[4] Such fears, shared by conservative Midwestern Disciples, helped to fuel the 1920s rebirth of the Ku Klux Klan with its Anti-Catholic focus.[5]

Though the controversy at the College of the Bible in 1917 involved a flagship Disciples institution, it did not become the catalyst for a national rupture. In fact, the loose affiliation of Disciples schools, agencies, societies, and conventions made such a rupture almost impossible. This all changed, however, with the creation of the UCMS. Now conservatives had a clear target at which to aim their attacks, one that concentrated all the perceived dangers in one place.

Mission efforts independent of the UCMS rallied conservative Disciples against the agency and provided alternative, less bureaucratic structures. In the early years, the Christian Restoration Association (CRA) established in 1925 provided a clearinghouse for many conservative missionaries, and the *Christian Standard* gave extensive coverage and editorial encouragement to them. In many respects, the Disciples "independent missions movement" paralleled the "faith missions" emerging

among American Fundamentalists. They too resisted mainline denominational agencies by creating alternate organizations to propagate what they saw as the "faith once delivered."[6]

Distinctive Stone-Campbell traditions, however, played a significant role in the alternative mission structures developed by conservative Disciples. They largely agreed with Churches of Christ that local congregations, working together according to New Testament examples, held the key to Christian unity and world evangelization. Only congregations, then, could guarantee that the missionaries they supported would proclaim the true plan of salvation and establish the "New Testament church" abroad.

The need for greater cooperation, however, especially acknowledged by missionaries on the field, led to the establishment of multiple targeted missionary agencies with minimal bureaucracy that still claimed to uphold "independent" principles. In 1944 the Africa Christian Mission opened with a U.S. based board of trustees, and five years later the South Africa Church of Christ mission, pioneered by Max Ward Randall (1917-2000), also incorporated and formed a board. Other more general agencies included Missions Services, Inc., established in 1945 to publish information on direct-support missions and provide purchasing services for missionaries on the field, and the National Missionary Convention, begun in 1948 to promote increased world evangelism.

The mission agencies quickly drew criticism from advocates of a strict direct-support model. Randall reported that one supporting congregation on the West Coast began insisting that the South Africa Mission was unscriptural and that the organization's work "must be handed over to the eldership of that particular church who could do the job more efficiently." While Randall believed that a modest form of centralization and accountability was inevitable, he continued to contrast the "independent" model with the "organized method" of the UCMS with its compromising ecumenical commitments and liberal outlook.[7] Clearly, however, the South Africa Church of Christ Mission went beyond a purely congregational-based direct-support model, thereby moving outside of what many conservatives considered the New Testament norm.

Meanwhile, missionaries anxiously looked for consistent, reliable means for raising funds and encouraging congregational support. One was the "living link" method in which one congregation committed to finance an individual missionary on the field—a method the FCMS had used in the early twentieth century. Some direct-support missionaries developed multiple living link congregations, though extreme conservatives viewed this as a violation of what they saw as the normative relation between a single congregation and a missionary. Another innovation was the "forwarding agent," an individual who collected funds from churches and conveyed them to missionaries on the field. Conservatives justified this as a non-bureaucratic and more personal way of dealing with administrative necessities.[8]

Independents continued to create missionary organizations with boards and financial networking in the 1950s and 60s. Most controversial, however, was the Christian Missionary Fellowship (CMF), founded in 1949 under the leadership of O. D. Johnson, a former direct-support missionary in Kulpahar, India. For staunch independents, it was bad enough that CMF, like the Brazil Christian Mission and the European Evangelistic Society, had a board of trustees and continued to have its officers and missionaries listed in the Disciples Yearbook. But in its articles of incorporation, CMF embraced the specific identity of a missionary "society" in all its aims.[9] In light of their experience with the UCMS, "society" was an explosive word for hard-line conservatives. *Christian Standard* editor Burris Butler reflected the opposition in a 1951 editorial.

> The Christian Missionary Fellowship is organized as a missionary society. That any group of brethren has a right to organize such a society is a principle for which the *Standard* has always contended. That it is wise or expedient for such a society to be organized at this juncture we deny. In view of the successful growth of independent missions during the past twenty years, the formation of such an organization is entirely unnecessary.[10]

With the battle now joined against a "missionary society" among Christian Churches/Churches of Christ, O.D. Johnson immediately went on the defensive. Johnson asserted that many of the boards of existing direct-support mission agencies would likely not hold up under legal scrutiny. Furthermore, in administrative functions many of the denominational societies had frankly been more efficient.[11] Modest centralization in matters of funding, accountability, recruitment, networking of supporting congregations, and the like would maximize effectiveness. Johnson and other CMF apologists insisted that the new society would not compete with independent missionaries but aid them.

At a deeper level, however, hermeneutical and ecclesiological differences were at play. Strong conservatives in Christian Churches/Churches of Christ, like their counterparts in Churches of Christ, clung to a nineteenth-century positive law approach to the Bible, confident in a New Testament pattern for all crucial matters of faith and practice. Johnson was no liberal, but he and the supporters of CMF were adamant on the principles of expediency and organizational freedom where there was no clear scriptural precedent. They claimed these principles were rooted in the Stone-Campbell heritage itself.[12] Not impressed by Johnson's reasoning, Mark Maxey, independent missionary in Japan, retorted, "the use of the 'expediency' argument as a reason for the existence of an organization to do the work of the church is in itself a dangerous expedient. It has often proved to be the nose of the camel under the tent."[13]

Leaders of the Christian Missionary Fellowship met at the Disciples of Christ Historical Society in 1966. Pictured (left to right) are Howard Hauser, Russell Blowers, Dean E. Walker, Jess Johnson, Richard Owen, and Harry Baird.

Early leaders and supporters of CMF also conveyed a relatively more ecumenical spirit that further aggravated critics. Many of these leaders were graduates of Butler University School of Religion and had been influenced by the "free church catholic" idealism of Frederick D. Kershner, Dean E. Walker, and William Robinson, the British theologian who taught for a time at the School of Religion. O. D. Johnson envisioned a middle way between overly accommodating ecumenism on one extreme, and restorationist sectarianism on the other. He cautioned against slamming the door on other denominational groups on the mission field, against "sheep stealing" from denominational missions, against pressing haphazardly into areas assigned to other denominations by ecumenical agreements, and against planting "New Testament churches" that would become little indigenous "denominations" of their own.[14]

In the same vein, Johnson encouraged acceptance of all Stone-Campbell missions, including those of the UCMS in places like India that were "sufficiently committed to faith in Christ as Lord and Deity, immersion of penitent believers for the remission of sins, wearing the name Christian, and weekly observance of the Lord's Supper." He urged missionaries to encourage indigenous churches to cultivate the principles of New Testament Christianity in their own contexts, embodying the restoration ideal in ways that would draw indigenous people into its embrace.[15]

Another significant development that gave identity to conservative Disciples was the Bible college movement. Though Johnson Bible College (now Johnson University) was founded in 1893, the most active period of establishment of new Bible colleges began in the 1920s. These schools were havens for conservative biblical instruction, protected from the influences of biblical higher criticism and other modernist cultural trends.[16]

Cincinnati Bible Seminary (now Cincinnati Christian University), a merger of McGarvey Bible College (Louisville) and Cincinnati Bible Institute, was an example of conservative Disciples Bible colleges. Cincinnati Bible Institute was supported by the Clarke Fund, originally begun by James DeForest Murch (1892-1973) to support evangelists starting new churches. The Institute was closely aligned with the *Christian Standard*, whose editorial board members served as faculty. The new Cincinnati Bible Seminary, founded in 1924, declared it would fight "infidelity" and train leaders who would nurture the restoration agenda in local churches.[17]

Conservatives established several other Bible colleges from the 1920s through the 1950s. Many benefited from Christian Service Camps, established to encourage young people toward ministerial vocations. Judge T. O. Hathcock founded the first Camp in Georgia in 1924. A year later Hathcock and his wife donated land for the founding of Atlanta Christian College, now Point University. James DeForest Murch also helped found service camps nationwide.[18]

Two of the most distinctive Bible colleges were the College of the Scriptures in Louisville, Kentucky, and the Christian Institute, later named Winston-Salem Bible College, in North Carolina, both established in 1945. Each college had a racially integrated staff, board, and student body, though organized primarily to educate African American ministers. The College of the Scriptures was under the leadership of President

Tibbs Maxey (1910-2002) and Dean George Calvin Campbell who had led the Goldsboro Christian Institute in the 1920s. Maxey used his influence as a white male to bridge the gap between the races in both church and society. Robert Lee Peters (1867-1951), a successful black church planter in North Carolina and Virginia, organized the Winston-Salem school, though it was forced to close briefly in 1949 because of lack of funds. However, two white ministers, Aubrey Payne (1907-1999) and Leland Tyrrell (1912-1985), helped reorganize the school in 1950 with Payne serving as president and Peters as dean.

Though similar in many ways, the two schools differed in their attitude toward Disciples institutions. The College of the Scriptures reflected the same antagonism seen in schools like Cincinnati, while Winston-Salem retained more positive relations with cooperative Disciples. This difference continued throughout the century and was evident in the attitudes of each institution's alumni.[19]

Conservatives sometimes located new Bible colleges close to Disciples liberal arts schools they believed were disloyal to the restoration cause. Some schools came to see themselves as bases of regional evangelism, training preachers to uphold restorationist understandings of the gospel and plant new churches.[20] In later decades, however, many Bible colleges increased course offerings in the liberal arts and sciences and added non-ministerial degree programs.[21]

A Separate Fellowship of Christian Churches/ Churches of Christ

Historians of the Stone-Campbell Movement disagree on precisely when the second North American division reached the point of no return. Some contend that the division was already in place by the end of the 1920s in light of the UCMS open membership controversy, the creation of Bible colleges, the establishment of the North American Christian Convention, and the proliferation of independent missions. In addition, journalistic strife mounted as the Cincinnati-based *Christian Standard* increasingly represented conservative causes in opposition to the *Christian-Evangelist* and other Disciples periodicals.

Other historians, however, place the division of "cooperative" and "independent" Disciples in the 1940s and 1950s, seen especially in the failure of the Commission on Restudy of the Disciples of Christ (1934-1949) to unify conservatives and liberals and to strengthen the position of those in the middle.[22] Furthermore, in 1947, *Christian Standard* editor Burris Butler began publishing the "Honor Roll of the Faithful," a list of local congregations willing to separate themselves from the UCMS and other perceived institutional and doctrinal aberrations of the Disciples of Christ. The Honor Roll provided an initial rallying point for conservative churches, but also anticipated the publication in 1955 of an ongoing "Directory of the Ministry," marking an even stronger collective identity of "loyal" churches, ministers, and missions.[23]

At the end of the 1950s, a group of leaders from both independent and cooperative groups initiated a series of Consultations on Internal Unity, presenting essays on unity, ecclesiology, and doctrine to try to stop further division. The seventh and last consultation met at Phillips University in Oklahoma in 1966. While cultivating positive relations among participants, many of whom remained friends well after the meetings, the Consultations did little to heal the alienation between Disciples and Christian Churches/Churches of Christ.[24]

During the 1950s, the International Convention increasingly reflected its alignment with the cooperatives as opposed to the independents. A pamphlet authorized in the mid-1960s by the Commission on Cooperative Policy and Practice, titled "What Brotherhood Cooperation Means," claimed that

> "Independents" have for all intents and purposes formed the equivalent of another denomination. They have their own separate North American Christian Convention, their separate direct and not-so-direct missionary work, their separate churches, their separate colleges, their separate publishing house and journal, their separate ministerial associations, separate evangelizing societies, separate benevolent homes, and similar agencies, all of which serve the Independent brethren... It is not their independence so much as their separateness that sets Independents apart from the Brotherhood and from the ecumenical world.[25]

The pamphlet chided independents for spreading the "idle tale" that the UCMS sought to dictate to ministers and missionaries and to violate individual conscience. It further charged that independents tended toward legalism and theological rigidity, noting that some insisted on creedal statements far more extensive than the simple confession that Jesus is the Christ. The writer observed that independents who rejected Disciples churches or organizations that maintained fellowship with those that practiced open membership—even if they did not practice it themselves—violated the independents' own principle of congregational autonomy.[26] Cooperative missionary work, the tract declared, was more responsible and efficient than that done by independents.[27] If independents were to claim the status of a persecuted minority, they needed to remember: "The right of minority groups to protest carries with it certain obligations to cooperate."[28]

The differences over how to date the cooperative-independent division reflect the fact that it was a lengthy process not definable by any single development. Simply put, like the Stone-Campbell Movement's first North American division, it was not a clean break. Scholars do agree, however, that the implementation of the restructure of the Christian Church (Disciples of Christ) in the late 1960s and early 1970s was the final, formal confirmation that two bodies now existed.[29]

In the planning stages before restructure, conservatives had expressed deep concerns that the adoption of a more denominational structure was at best premature and at worst unbiblical. The Panel of Scholars Reports that they saw as challenging much of the Movement's traditional theology and polity had already disturbed them. With restructure on the horizon, some conservatives accused the Panel not only of ignoring Scripture and abandoning the restoration principle, but of redefining authority, taking liberties with the principle of expedience,[30] and driving a wedge between the authority of Christ and the authority of the New Testament.[31] Dean Walker, formerly of the Butler School of Religion and one-time President of both Milligan College and Emmanuel School of Religion, wrote:

> Christ of course is the only ultimate authority for Christians. It is just for this reason and at this point that the liberal devotion to what they call a democratic process of creating the Church's structure is shown to be completely void of understanding of the nature of God's Revelation in Christ. While these liberals accuse Campbell of obsession with the idea of a written constitution, yet these same liberals would adopt, as revelation by the Spirit, the conflicts and compromises in the political arena out of which issues the democratic constitution in forms and concepts of life. They would make the Church essentially a political institution to take its place in the pressure politics of the modern democratic state...[32]

Walker suggested that the architects of restructure were shaping a church polity on the model of the "Federal Republic" rather than the "Christocracy," or monarchy of Christ, envisioned by the Campbells.[33] As the momentum toward restructure intensified, so did the grievances of its critics. James DeForest Murch criticized the restructure notions of covenant, freedom, and congregational, regional, and general manifestations of the church.[34] The new model appeared to be ecclesiastical engineering orchestrated by a select few allegedly acting on behalf of all local churches and individual Disciples. It was bound to lead to vertical hierarchy or authoritarianism. Local church autonomy would be sacrificed in the name of covenantal loyalty to the denomination; any freedom left would be relative.

Most conservatives saw the situation as a clear-cut choice between a cooperative ecclesiology based on loyalty to a centralized denominational structure, and a free church ecclesiology based on the voluntary association of congregations in shared efforts. They pointed to the statement by Disciples historian W Winfred E. Garrison calling restructure a "fork in the road," and probably the wrong fork as far as models of association in the Stone-Campbell tradition.[35] Moderate independents Dean Walker and Robert Fife argued that church order was less a matter of structure than of the fellowship of persons—a family relationship centered in the worshipping congregation and the local community of disciples committed to ongoing study of, and adherence to, the New Testament model of communion.[36]

By the time Disciples leaders formally implemented restructure, many "independent" churches had already decided not to participate, though a small minority held out hope for reconciliation and allowed their names to remain in the Disciples *Year Book*. As Henry Webb noted, though restructure dramatically thinned Disciples numbers, it did not itself cause a split. Independent churches had long been associating with one another, and remained free to associate with one another in whatever ways they desired.[37] By 1968, many had so few ties to Disciples agencies, that they gave little attention to and felt no threat from the restructure process.

The *Christian Standard* and its editor Edwin Hayden unapologetically repudiated the Provisional Design as it began to take effect in 1968 and advised churches on how to withdraw from the Disciples *Year Book*.[38] Hayden published the withdrawal resolution of First Christian Church, Carrollton, Georgia, as a model of how to protect legal ownership of congregational property.[39] Eventually over 3,000 congregations with a total membership of over 800,000 withdrew from the *Disciples Year Book*.[40]

In contrast to Churches of Christ, which in 1906 were largely southern and outnumbered Disciples of Christ only in Tennessee, Alabama, and Arkansas, the Christian Churches/Churches of Christ had a nationwide distribution that outnumbered the Christian Church (Disciples of Christ) in half of the continental states. Christian Churches/Churches of Christ were most successful in parts of the Midwest, much of the West, a few northeastern states, and the southeastern states of Georgia and Florida. In Ohio, Indiana, and Illinois sixty percent of the membership previously reported in the Disciples *Year Book* identified with Christian Churches/Churches of Christ.

Disciples maintained a majority in Texas, Oklahoma, Kansas, Missouri, Iowa, Kentucky, California, many eastern states, and scattered states across the South and West. Disciples also consistently outnumbered Christian Churches/Churches of Christ in urban counties. This seems to confirm David Edwin Harrell's suggestion of sociological aspects of the division, with the more liberal Disciples having an advantage in urban settings and the more conservative Christian Churches/Churches of Christ in rural areas.[41]

The location of Churches of Christ also appears to have been a factor in the division between Disciples and Christian Churches/Churches of Christ. Conservative Disciples were least likely to identify with the independents in areas where Churches of Christ were most numerous. By offering a strong restorationist alternative, Churches of Christ may have attracted conservative members dissatisfied with progressive trends among Disciples, making it unnecessary for them to form new congregations.[42]

The separation between Disciples and Christian Churches/Churches of Christ raised a host of questions about continuing connections. Would the Pension Fund or the Disciples of Christ Historical Society still serve independent ministers and churches? B. D. Phillips, whose family wealth had helped construct the Historical Society's building in Nashville, issued a strong protest to its trustees concerning the Provisional Design's mandate that general agencies of the Disciples conform their constitutions and bylaws to the Design.[43] One Illinois Disciples leader warned that in withdrawing from the restructured denomination, ministers would risk losing tax-exempt status and eligibility for the Pension Fund and the services of other Disciples agencies. Edwin Hayden fired back that ministers' tax-exempt status did not depend on any *Year Book* listing but on affiliation with a local church.[44]

In the end, the services of the Pension Fund as well as most other Disciples agencies remained open to all persons in the Stone-Campbell Movement, including Churches of Christ. Only a small minority of independent ministers and professors continued to participate in the Pension Fund, however. As credentialing questions arose, Christian Churches/Churches of Christ eventually developed their own institutions, including a Chaplaincy Endorsement Commission.[45]

Diversification in the Christian Churches/ Churches of Christ

In 1962, Charles Gresham (1928-2002) spoke confidently of the "unity of the independent movement" based on shared opposition to restructure, the perceived power of cooperative institutions, and support for the rights of local congregations.[46] The independent churches also demonstrated solidarity in their zeal for global missions and evangelism. Yet conservative leaders differed, sometimes strongly, on theological, ecclesiological, missiological, and even hermeneutical matters, including their perspectives on the past and future of the Stone-Campbell Movement.

Christian Churches/Churches of Christ have often been caricatured as ideologically and sociologically homogenous, the embodiment of a Fundamentalist revolt among Disciples of Christ. In reality, independents developed three significantly different schools of thought that endured and in some cases deepened after the division. While the danger of imposing or oversimplifying categories is real, it is hard to deny that this diversification continued to shape the identity of Christian Churches/ Churches of Christ in relation both to other Stone-Campbell streams and to the larger church well into the twenty-first century.[47] The growth of Christian Churches/Churches of Christ in non-Western contexts increased their diversity all the more.

Identifying marks of the three groups include convictions about restoration of apostolic Christianity and Christian unity; views on biblical authority; commitments concerning church organization, education, and mission; and loyalty to the Stone-Campbell heritage, including attitudes toward other streams of the tradition and ecumenical Christianity.

I. *Foundationalist Restorationists.*[48] The first group had its roots in the most hard line opposition to perceived Disciples liberalism and "ecclesiasticism"—a term used to refer to hierarchical and authoritarian rule. It began as a large and vocal group, but in the late twentieth century diminished considerably and by the beginning of the twenty-first was a small minority. The group drew its inspiration from a group of leaders, many from the Bible

college movement, who viewed Disciples in the 1920s as standing at a fork in the road. The two options were rigorous adherence to what they saw as the restoration program (the "old paths"), or accommodation to Protestant liberalism, which they believed would lead to the rapid annihilation of the Stone-Campbell Movement. In this respect these staunch restorationists look like classic Fundamentalists who saw the church embroiled in an all-out war with modernism. Nevertheless, significant theological differences with American Fundamentalists such as use of confessions of faith and the dominance of Calvinism made the label confusing and inaccurate.[49]

An early representative of this group was Rupert C. Foster (1888-1970) of Cincinnati Bible Seminary, a veritable prophet of the Bible college movement whose own education at Harvard Divinity School and Yale University gave him credibility to attack liberal Protestantism among Disciples.[50] Foster had no use for what he saw as Reformed creedal Fundamentalism and distanced himself from many of its doctrinal positions, such as its view of baptism. Nevertheless, he shared its ongoing commitment to the nineteenth-century positive law hermeneutic with its understanding of the Bible as a revealed system of facts, propositions, and precepts. Foster likewise shared the Fundamentalists' abhorrence of biblical higher criticism, their devotion to the *King James Version* and their repudiation of the *Revised Standard Version*.[51] Foster deemed the RSV "a massive piece of radical [modernist] propaganda," exemplified, among other things, in the translators' blatant attempt to undermine the divine dignity of Christ by changing "Thee" (KJV) to "you" (RSV).[52]

Foster rejected the idea that controversy was detrimental to the wellbeing of the church. Finding inspiration in Alexander Campbell's public debates, he identified issues worth fighting for as "the ever recurring compromises of Christianity with heathen philosophies and systems of religion or rationalistic theories of science."[53] For Foster, the Bible college would provide a safe haven for teaching sound biblical doctrine. Yet, he also challenged the churches to work aggressively to Christianize the curricula, faculties, and campus life of private and state universities lest atheists and rationalists overrun them.[54] Even Disciples liberal arts colleges were targets for such transformation, since in Foster's view they were already infested with modernists.[55]

Foster was by no means alone in his crusade. His fighting style manifested itself in a "Restoration Congress" in Louisville in 1921, which threw down the gauntlet against Disciples progressives and the

UCMS, and demonstrated the conservatives' ability to organize serious opposition. The Christian Restoration Association conducted a similar campaign, with nine regional rallies, intending among other things "to challenge the brotherhood to choose between modernism and the old paths…between the 'Bible plan' and 'open membership'…between loyalty and diplomacy…between friendly cooperation and dictatorial consolidation."[56]

Secretary of the Executive Committee of the FCMS in 1920, Robert E. Elmore vehemently opposed the proposal of China missionaries to enter a union with Presbyterians and Congregationalists that would have required accepting non-immersed persons as members. As editor of *The Touchstone* from 1925-1927, and later the *Restoration Herald* from 1938 to 1960, he sought to hold Disciples to a strict restoration standard of unity, ecclesiology, and mission.

Robert Elmore was, along with James DeForest Murch, a leading standard-bearer of the Christian Restoration Association. In the Protestant culture war of the time, he matched Rupert Foster's combativeness with his own attack on rationalism, understood as any form of enthroning human reason over the rule of revelation.[57] Biblical criticism, liberal theology, and "low" Christology were all part of Enlightenment rationalism now infiltrating liberal Protestantism, he asserted. Elmore

even attacked Francis Bacon, long esteemed as a hero in the Movement for liberating reason from the shackles of theological opinion, as an instigator of this deviation from true Christianity.[58] The ecumenism Elmore detected in the UCMS became another major target as he led the charge against open membership as a blatant departure from New Testament teaching on baptism.

Not surprisingly, foundationalist restorationists were among the strongest advocates for minimal church bureaucracy and independent (direct support) missions.[59] Their lasting legacy, however, was their insistence that Christian unity and world evangelism could be achieved only by a strict return to New Testament Christianity, which included their conception of the biblical plan of salvation, believers' immersion, weekly observance of the Lord's Supper, and congregational autonomy. Restoration—not ecumenical compromise or "secular" agendas like "Social Christianity"—was the true vocation of the Stone-Campbell Movement.[60]

Tensions within this group developed as early as the 1920s when R.C. Foster complained that some hard-line preachers were undermining the restoration cause by embracing controversy for its own sake.[61] By the 1940s, the conservative restorationist consensus was teetering, especially because of the work of James DeForest Murch. Despite his strong support of the restoration agenda, Murch feared that restorationism could fall into sheer parochialism. By the 1960s this "old paths" group was increasingly regionalized and marginalized, especially as Bible colleges adapted to new educational trends, some older independent missions faltered while new missionary organizations proliferated, and later, as a younger generation of church leaders grew weary of a biblicism that thrived on controversy.

The regionalizing of the "old paths" group is evident in the Kiamichi Mission in rural Oklahoma, founded in 1940 by A. B. McReynolds (1897-1980). The ministry focused on church planting, missions to Native Americans, and encouraging Bible-college-trained preachers. But it also organized camps and preaching "clinics" to support conservative political activism, especially anti-communism, gun rights, and the reintroduction of conservative Christian influences in public schools.[62] Also, certain Bible colleges like Florida Christian College in Kissimmee developed close-knit regional support networks for conservative restorationism. School leaders clearly stated a restoration agenda in their "philosophy of education," which included a commitment to the Fundamentalist tenet of the inerrancy of Scripture. Its "position statement" embraced other beliefs shared with Fundamentalism, including the virgin birth of Christ and the divine nature of the church. The statement continued, however, with a list of truths not shared with Fundamentalists, which must also be restored, including immersion for remission of sins and the gift of the Holy Spirit, and faithfulness to the ancient order in such matters as congregational polity and weekly observance of the Lord's Supper.[63]

Such detail stood in contrast to other regional Bible colleges that minimized their doctrinal statements in public documents. Cincinnati Christian University (originally Cincinnati Bible Seminary) in the early twenty-first century continued to require faculty, administration, and trustees to subscribe to a doctrinal statement that included an affirmation of biblical inerrancy and the New Testament "plan of salvation."[64] In documents portraying itself to the public, however, the once bastion of restorationist conservatism published only a very general mission statement: "To teach men and women to live by biblical principles and to equip and empower them with character, skills, insight, and vision to lead the church and impact society for Christ."[65] Such generality could hardly have satisfied R. C. Foster and other conservatives of an earlier era. Meanwhile, Cincinnati Christian University made significant changes in its vision and curriculum to engage its urban location and recruit students from non-Stone-Campbell churches. Other Bible colleges with roots in strict restorationism followed similar patterns of adjustment.

While some foundationalist restorationists adapted and softened their rhetoric, others endured and accepted inevitable marginalization. The so-called "Ottumwa Brethren," launched principally from Portland, Oregon, and Ottumwa, Iowa, in the 1940s, resembled a "holiness movement," adding to the restoration agenda bans on drinking, smoking, dancing, and opulent dress, along with strong advocacy of the subjection of women to men.[66] An early Brethren champion, Archie Word (1901-1988), was a revivalist and evangelist from Oregon whose fighting style and exclusivism far exceeded even that of Foster and Elmore.

Convinced that even the Bible colleges were failing to advance restoration and defend the truth, the Ottumwa Brethren founded Midwestern School of Evangelism in Ottumwa, Iowa, in 1947, and the Churches of Christ School of Evangelists, now Northwest College of the Bible, in Portland, Oregon, in 1952. Through effective networking they also began Bible training schools in local churches and a broad program of camps, church growth clinics, and other missions. For the Ottumwa Brethren, "evangelism" remained virtually a byword for spreading their view of the restoration gospel. Yet their uncompromising spirit brought criticism even from other conservative restorationists in Christian Churches/Churches of Christ, and led to almost total marginalization.[67]

II. *Neo-Restorationists and Neo-Evangelicals.* A second identifiable group included two dynamically related subsets: "neo-restorationists" and "neo-evangelicals."[68] Representing a majority of Christian Churches/Churches of Christ in North America at the beginning of the twenty-first century, this group ran the gamut from desire to recover a restoration agenda, to a willingness to downplay the restoration ideal to find common cause with mainstream Evangelicalism. What gave them a common identity was their rejection of what they saw as a declining mainline Protestantism that had lost its doctrinal grounding and zeal for evangelism and missions. All would agree that restoration must be cast as an inviting appeal reflecting current cultural realities rather than a stark appeal to scriptural conformity.

Without question, one major visionary of this group was James DeForest Murch, whose own thinking on the nature of restoration evolved over his long career. In his early editorial work for Standard Publishing and his leadership in the Christian Restoration Association, Murch helped rally conservative Disciples against the full array of liberal sins. A staunch critic of the UCMS, he also vigorously supported independent missions and the Associated Free Agencies, an affiliate of the Christian Restoration Association that served as a coalition of independent evangelistic enterprises.[69]

Though some historians have classified Murch, at least in this early stage, as a Fundamentalist, he resisted the label.[70] What Murch offered conservatives was more than merely another voice of opposition to Disciples progressives. In his writings he framed the Stone-Campbell restoration agenda as part of the centuries-long crusade of "free churches" against ecclesiastical tyranny. Faithful restorationists were part of an anti-tradition tradition, a lineage of New Testament Christians that had endured persecution from established churches since the second century. They were champions in the larger "Protestant Revolt" and historic players in the embodiment of a free church ecclesiology.[71]

In the Stone-Campbell Movement itself, Murch identified Christian Churches/Churches of Christ as "Centrists," poised between extremist Churches of

Christ on the right and liberal Disciples on the left.[72] Murch used the label as a way to shore up solidarity among "independents," knowing full well that different perspectives existed among them.

Indeed, Murch experienced his own conflicts with foundationalist restorationists, who criticized his willingness to maintain lines of communication with the left as well as the right. In 1938, for example, he proposed holding unity meetings that would include "progressives" as well as conservatives.[73] In 1945, Standard Publishing, having assumed an avowedly more rigorous position against Disciples agencies, fired Murch from his editorial position, accusing him of being a compromiser.[74]

James DeForest Murch, editor of the National Association of Evangelicals *United Evangelical Action*, offered conservative Disciples an alternative to foundationalist restorationism.

The censure came just before the National Association of Evangelicals (est. 1942) invited Murch to edit its magazine, *United Evangelical Action*. Murch's presence in this national conservative coalition provided a powerful example for later leaders who began to forge new alliances and cultivate new resources that would have been unacceptable to an earlier generation of restorationists reluctant to associate with Calvinists and Pentecostals.[75] Along with this was Murch's critical assessment of the

liberal ecumenism of the World Council of Churches: "if there is to be effective, practical, visible, organic unity such as distinguished the New Testament Church there is little evidence of commitment to the essential elements in this *mélange*."[76]

The Protestant Neo-Evangelicalism that developed in American Christianity in the mid-twentieth century was a fragile coalition from the beginning because of its internal diversity (the prefix "neo" was dropped in the 1960s). Historian D. G. Hart has argued that "Evangelicalism" has become so vague that it is useless as a label,[77] while others insist that though Evangelicalism reflects a kaleidoscopic diversity, it still possesses a coherent core.[78] Whatever the case, the American Evangelicalism of the 1950s provided Disciples neo-restorationists a fresh context to voice their platform of biblical truth. This was true despite the differences that surfaced and the fact that Evangelicals did not have conservative Disciples on their theological radar screen.[79] Just as some earlier Disciples progressives had seen the Stone-Campbell unity plea as a leavening force for the ecumenical movement, Murch envisioned the restoration plea as a catalyst to galvanize Evangelical Protestants.[80]

In the 1950s and 1960s, some Christian Churches/Churches of Christ, following Murch's example, began to support the Billy Graham Crusades, to use Christian education resources from Evangelical publishing houses, and later to interact with Evangelical church growth and mission organizations and find their place in campaigns against abortion and other social causes important to Evangelicals. Eventually non-Stone-Campbell creationists and premillennialists appeared on the program of the North American Christian Convention. Bible college professors took graduate degrees from Evangelical seminaries and joined Evangelical scholarly societies. Some like Jack Cottrell fought long and hard to convince Christian Churches/Churches of Christ to embrace biblical inerrancy (as distinct from "infallibility") as a *restoration* principle.[81]

III. *"Free Church Catholics."* The third group in Christian Churches/Churches of Christ was probably the smallest at the beginning of the twenty-first century, and reflected the legacy of certain influential individuals who struggled to find a middle way during the alienation of conservative and progressive Disciples before and after restructure. This group has variously been called "Old Conservative Disciples"[82] and "high church sacramentalists."[83] Many in their ranks, however, called themselves "free church catholics," a name coined by Disciples historian and theologian Alfred T. DeGroot (1903-1992). The group's identity was centered in academic institutions like Milligan College and Emmanuel School of Religion (now Emmanuel Christian Seminary), schools more open to higher-critical biblical scholarship.

Milligan, in contrast to the Bible colleges founded in the twentieth century, had its origins in the nineteenth century and was for many years the only liberal arts college associated with Christian Churches/Churches of Christ. Emmanuel School of Religion (renamed Emmanuel Christian Seminary in 2011), chartered in 1961 under the leadership of Dean E. Walker, then president of Milligan, was located across the street from the Milligan campus. The faculties of other schools such as Hope International University, Northwest Christian University, Crossroads College, Manhattan Christian College, Johnson Bible College (now Johnson University), and Atlanta Christian College (now Point University) also reflected a level of sympathy with this group. At the beginning of the twenty-first century, however, only a tiny fraction of local congregations retained any significant identification with this "free church catholic" ethos.

Most of this group's heroic figures were voices of moderation among mid-twentieth century Disciples. Frederick D. Kershner, Dean and Professor of Christian Doctrine at the Butler University School of Religion, now Christian Theological Seminary, from 1924 to 1944, was especially revered. Kershner consciously put himself into the very heart of the debates of the 1920s and beyond. Ecumenical in spirit and friendly to early Disciples involvement in the ecumenical movement, he nonetheless opposed the practice of open membership and insisted that restoration would hold its own in the new ecumenical atmosphere of the twentieth century.[84]

Another important figure was British Disciple William Robinson (1888-1963). Robinson was one of the most prominent representatives of the free churches in the emerging Faith and Order movement before coming to teach from 1951-1956 at Butler School of Religion. Robinson, like Kershner, sought to press conservative Disciples beyond legalistic restorationism to embrace the historic Christian *consensus fidelium*—what the faithful have believed through the centuries—along with careful study of the New Testament. Both Kershner and Robinson, in their reading of the Stone-Campbell plea, maintained a "high" congregational ecclesiology, the view that the local congregation is an expression of the whole church in its fullness; that the unity and "sacramentality" of the Church universal is grounded in the congregation—the local gathering of the faithful. They were committed to

restoring the "one holy, catholic, and apostolic Church" and the sacramental character of the ordinances of baptism and the Lord's Supper.[85]

An irenic voice in conservative Disciples who cautioned against rigid patternism, Robert Fife defined Christian unity as both gift and imperative that required ongoing reformation.

A number of younger figures guaranteed a place for the legacy of free church catholicism, among them Dean E. Walker (1899-1988), James Van Buren (1914-1997) of Manhattan Christian College, and Robert Fife (1918-2003) of Milligan College. Walker called for refocusing the restoration ideal on the person of Jesus Christ rather than an "ancient order" of apostolic Christianity—though he too opposed open membership, hierarchical and authoritarian church structures, and other perceived deviations from the New Testament.[86]

Van Buren, a former student of Kershner, opposed both foundationalist restorationsts and Murch's Evangelicalism as viable options for the Christian Churches/Churches of Christ, the one breeding legalism and the other courting denominationalism.[87] He particularly targeted the National Association of Evangelicals' original statement of faith, which endorsed the view that the whole Bible is the Word of God. Instead he advised churches to hold true to Alexander Campbell's affirmation that the Bible contains the Word of God but is not *in toto* the Word of God.[88] Other free church catholics also criticized the doctrines of inerrancy and plenary verbal inspiration as misrepresenting the nature of biblical authority and as having no precedent in the Stone-Campbell tradition.[89]

Robert Fife, like Van Buren and Walker, insisted that the true goal of "restoration" was to recover the virtues and the ideals of the New Testament rather than some static pattern of faith and practice. Restoration was a matter of grace, not law.[90] Fearful that "closed membership" would undermine the ecumenical credibility of conservative Disciples, Fife argued that church membership was itself a dynamic principle in the New Testament, and that the practice of "open communion" among Christian Churches/Churches of Christ recognized the gift of membership sacramentally extended to all the faithful by Christ through the Eucharist.[91]

For free church catholics, the consensus-building work of the Commission on Restudy of the Disciples of Christ (1934-1949) was the last best hope for reconciling conservatives, moderates, and progressives. Frederick D. Kershner, who chaired the Commission for much of its life, attempted to build consensus across the board. The Commission's failure to convince alienated Disciples to stay together created an identity crisis for moderate conservatives. It was free church catholics who, between 1959 and 1966, organized the Consultations on Internal Unity to study points of consensus they hoped could counteract division. James DeForest Murch and other neo-evangelicals contributed, as did cooperative Disciples Ronald E. Osborn (1917-1998), A. T. DeGroot (1903-1992), and Stephen J. England (1895-1987).

At the beginning of the twenty-first century, considerable fluidity still remained among the three discernable groups in Christian Churches/Churches of Christ. Each segment shared a concern to present the restoration project to a postmodern world that is quite different from the world of the early Stone-Campbell Movement. Each group had adapted to the polarizing and pluralistic culture of North America. Furthermore, colleges, seminaries, missionary organizations, and congregations had become more complex and not always easily labeled. Individual leaders often crossed between these groups and resisted alignment with any single one. The *Christian Standard*, principal journalistic voice of Christian Churches/Churches of Christ, had ranged editorially across all three groups: free church catholics having a voice in Edwin Errett (editor, 1929-44), foundationalist restorationists in Burris Butler (editor, 1944-57), and neo-restorationists and evangelicals in Sam Stone (editor, 1978-2003) and Mark Taylor (editor since 2003). Similarly, the North American Christian Convention had seen representation from all three groups, though gradually the preeminent voice in its planning and programming had been that of Neo-Restorationists/Neo-Evangelicals.

Christian Churches/Churches of Christ in North America at the beginning of the twenty-first century found themselves in a crisis of identity, challenged to find their true center.[92] They also faced the challenge of mediating between their historic Stone-Campbell identity and their relation to the wider Christian world. In this challenge, however, they did not differ from Churches of Christ and the Christian Church (Disciples of Christ). Each of these streams struggled with its identity in the midst of the pluralism, polarization, and massive shifts in United States culture from the 1960s through the first decades of the twenty-first century.

11

Responses to United States Social Change, 1960s–2011

The pluralism and polarization of United States culture from the 1960s through the first decades of the twenty-first century resulted from several factors. The wider occupational opportunities afforded to blacks and women during World War II fueled both the Civil Rights and Women's movements. Inspired by these movements, gay, lesbian, bisexual, and transgender persons also sought rights that had been denied them. In addition, many returning U.S. service personnel, having witnessed the results of Nazi bigotry in the Holocaust, vowed to overcome such evils in the United States. Emerging from World War II as the dominant world powers, the U.S. and the Soviet Union engaged in a Cold War that became a protracted hot war in Southeast Asia, further dividing the American public. With the fall of the Soviet Union in 1991, the United States was the only superpower and became a target of radical Islamist terrorism, responding with prolonged military actions in Afghanistan and Iraq, again raising the issue of war. Meanwhile, the 1965 Immigration and Naturalization Act had eliminated quotas, furthering a process that made the United States the most ethnically and religiously diverse country in the world.[1] In response to the increasing social, ethnic, and religious pluralism since the 1960s, U.S. culture entered a period of sharp polarization characterized by conflicting views of the nation's ideal future. In this context, Stone-Campbell Christians addressed issues of race, war, ethnic diversity, gender equality, sexuality, and religious pluralism.

Race

African Americans in the 1960s continued to face systemic racism in every aspect of American life. Most U.S. churches, however, were slow to respond to racism, and many actively resisted change. In 1963, the National Council of Churches (NCC), responding to the black-led Civil Rights Movement that employed nonviolent direct action, appealed to Christian bodies in the U.S. to confess their sin of failing to affirm that every person is a child of God and to mobilize resources for securing civil rights for all Americans. NCC president and Disciples lay leader J. Irwin Miller stated the Council's position: "racial discrimination violates Christian love and is man's denial of God's rule."[2]

Gaines M. Cook, Executive Secretary of the Disciples International Convention, expressed full support for the NCC's appeal. With authorization from the Convention's Administrative Committee, Cook recommended that all Disciples agencies, boards, and institutions take immediate action. To facilitate Disciples efforts, the Convention established the Coordinating Committee for Moral and Civil Rights.[3]

The United Christian Missionary Society (UCMS) responded to the NCC's appeal by authorizing an emergency $50,000 loan from fixed reserves to cover immediate program costs approved by the Coordinating Committee. The UCMS also developed principles for staff involvement in civil rights demonstrations and direct action. Individuals could decide for themselves whether or not to participate, and nonviolent direct action was to be used only after negotiations proved unsuccessful. In local situations leaders were to work for racial equality in partnership with both black and white congregations. UCMS president A. Dale Fiers (1906-2003) modeled these principles by participating in civil rights marches in a number of southern cities. In addition, five hundred and sixty-one Disciples ministers pledged to work for passage of the 1964 Civil Rights Act, and ten served as NCC observers during a voter registration drive in Canton, Mississippi.[4]

Some Disciples-related schools also participated in the Civil Rights Movement. In 1954, the Disciples' historically black Southern Christian Institute had merged with Tougaloo College in Jackson, Mississippi. In the early 1960s, Tougaloo students, with the support of President Adam Beittel, protested racial discrimination in Jackson, leading a boycott of restaurants that refused to serve blacks. Many were arrested for trying to attend segregated white churches and concerts. Tougaloo also hosted voter registration and nonviolence workshops led by Student Nonviolent Coordinating Committee members Bob Moses and James Lawson.[5] In addition, Christian Theological Seminary (CTS) in Indianapolis supported the Civil Rights Movement by sending eight students to Washington, D.C., in 1964 to participate in the Theological Students' Vigil, and CTS Dean Ronald E. Osborn participated in Indianapolis civil rights initiatives and the 1965 Selma-to-Montgomery voting rights marches.[6]

Leaders in Disciples regional organizations also joined the civil rights struggle through regional assembly resolutions. The 1963 Kentucky regional assembly approved a resolution commending the state Commission on Human Rights for promoting "equal service in places of public accommodations" regardless of race. A year later, the assembly urged state and federal lawmakers to open public accommodations to all people. After Congress passed the Civil Rights Act of 1964, Kentucky Disciples adopted a resolution expressing appreciation to Kentucky members of the House and Senate for supporting the legislation.[7]

Not all Disciples, however, supported such efforts. In 1963, the International Convention proposed that congregations take up a special contribution for civil rights initiatives. By October 31, only 10 percent of congregations listed in the *Year Book* had ordered promotional materials, and by the end of the campaign, churches had contributed only slightly over a third of the goal of $300,000. Most regions had virtually no civil rights programs in place. With the exception of the seminaries, which admitted blacks in the 1950s, segregated Disciples-related schools did not change their admissions policies until required to do so by the Civil Rights Act of 1964. Furthermore, some members of the Disciples Coordinating Committee for Moral and Civil Rights were critical of its actions, leading several regions and congregations to withhold funds from Unified Promotion. When asked to endorse Martin Luther King, Jr.'s 1963 March on Washington for Jobs and Freedom, the majority of the members of the Committee

responded that the march was not within the committee's "stated area of concern."[8]

In 1966, Disciples leaders in Dallas, Texas, tried to prevent King from speaking at the International Convention, which was to be held in their city. Dale Fiers, then the Convention's executive secretary, told the local arrangements committee that if King was not coming to Dallas, neither was the International Convention. Ultimately leaders reached a compromise that allowed King to serve as one of four members of a panel.[9]

Dale Fiers, Judge Robert G. Storey of Dallas, and Roman Catholic Bishop John Wright of Pittsburgh with Martin Luther King, Jr. Storey and Wright participated on a panel with King moderated by J. Irwin Miller (not pictured) at the 1966 International Convention. Storey, who had served as a judge at the Nuremburg Trials after World War II, opposed King's advocacy of civil disobedience.

African American Disciples expressed distress at what they perceived to be a lack of support for racial justice among Disciples at the August 23-28, 1966, meeting of the National Christian Missionary Convention at Park Manor Christian Church in Chicago. The Convention passed two resolutions dealing with civil rights. The first, titled "Support for Chicago Housing Protests," endorsed action then underway in the Chicago area against "un-American housing practices" led by Dr. Martin Luther King, Jr. The other, titled "Racially Discriminatory Employment of Ministers," condemned racial discrimination in ministerial call and field placement of seminarians by local Disciples churches, seminaries, and state and national manifestations of the church.[10]

In response to the concerns of black Disciples, and motivated by the 1965 Watts riots, the St. Louis Assembly in October 1967 urged congregations and church agencies to make urban needs a priority, and in March 1968 the Council of Agencies issued "A Call for the Response of the Christian Churches." Martin Luther King, Jr.'s assassination a month later and the urban rioting that followed added even more urgency to their call. As a result, the UCMS created the Urban Emergency Action Committee, which developed the "Reconciliation" program. With an initial two-year funding goal of two million dollars above regular budgets, Reconciliation supported programs and projects designed to help people help themselves in areas of employment, economic opportunity, housing, and educational programs.[11]

In the following decades, appointments to Disciples general and regional structures reflected an intentional dismantling of historic racial barriers to leadership. John R. Compton served as the first director of the Reconciliation program from 1968-1970, and in 1977 became the first African American Regional Minister (Indiana). Other African Americans later served as Regional Ministers, including Lonnie Oates (Northeastern), William Morrison (Florida), Jack Sullivan (Northwest), and Sotello Long (South Carolina). In 1971 Walter Bingham became the first African American elected as Moderator of the General Assembly, followed by K. David Cole in 1989, Alvin Jackson in 2001, Charisse Gillett in 2003, William Lee in 2005, and Regina Morton in 2011.

The 1982 General Assembly adopted extensive guidelines for the implementation of Affirmative Action in church agencies. The next year, Compton was elected President of the Division of Homeland Ministries, becoming the first African American to serve as president of a general unit. Other milestones included the appointment in 1987 of Raymond E. Brown, as Senior Vice President of Church Extension. Janice M. Newborn began her tenure as Director of Program Implementation for the Department of Church Women in 1986. The twenty-first century saw the trend continue with Lois Artis elected President of the Church Finance Council in 2000, William Edwards appointed Associate General Minister and President in 2002, and Marilyn Fiddmont Vice President of the Southwest Zone of the Christian Church Foundation in 2010.

In 1989 the Assembly reaffirmed the Disciples commitment to Affirmative Action and Civil Rights and instructed the General Minister and President to communicate to the U.S. President and Congressional leaders the Assembly's concern about apparent reversals in these areas. The body directed the General Minister

and President to hold consultations across the U.S. to inform the church of recent Supreme Court decisions eroding civil rights and to develop strategies of justice to change these reversals legislatively. A decade later, the General Board adopted "becoming an anti-racist/pro-reconciling church" as one of the major priorities of its 2020 Vision—a "whole church initiative" for the years 2000-2020.

Many in Churches of Christ took the position that engagement with "social issues" was outside the church's focus.[12] A classic statement of this position appeared at the height of the Civil Rights Movement in the March 31, 1964, issue of *Firm Foundation*. James Fowler asserted that Christians before the U.S. Civil War "did not turn from their primary purpose of preaching Christ to become involved in revolutionary demands and social reforms." In the early church, he asserted, the apostles never tried to disrupt "the legal, social system that prevailed, and they did not make the church party to political movements and pressure groups." Fowler charged Christians who became preoccupied with social efforts like the Civil Rights Movement of acting contrary to the spirit of Christianity, embracing values that were actually contrary to the cause of justice.[13]

However, leaders in African American Churches of Christ took strong exception to such views. R. N. Hogan, editor of the *Christian Echo*, unflinchingly exposed the racism of schools affiliated with Churches of Christ in his paper. With the exception of Pepperdine College, which admitted African Americans from its opening in 1937 (though denying them on-campus housing), all the schools excluded blacks. Hogan rebuked white administrators who consistently denied American blacks admission into their colleges, yet admitted students of color from other nations. Such raw discrimination, Hogan charged, was "proof that God is not there; for where God is, no man is barred because of the color of his skin."[14]

Although Marshall Keeble in his public statements was an accommodationist to white racism, several of the students he mentored at the Nashville Christian Institute (NCI) became civil rights leaders. Alabamian Fred D. Gray vowed at an early age to destroy "everything segregated I could find."[15] At age twelve, he enrolled in NCI and accompanied Keeble on some of his preaching tours. After graduation Gray completed an undergraduate degree at Alabama State College in Montgomery and earned a law degree at Case Western Reserve University in Cleveland, Ohio. In the 1950s Gray represented E. D. Nixon, Rosa Parks, and Martin Luther

King, Jr., attacking segregation in Alabama and beyond. When NCI closed in 1967, Gray argued for the plaintiffs who sued Marshall Keeble and the largely white board to prevent them from transferring $500,000 in assets to David Lipscomb College, which had historically refused to admit black students.[16]

Fred D. Gray, attorney for Rosa Parks, Martin Luther King, Jr., and E. D. Nixon, was minister of the Tuskegee (Alabama) Institute Church of Christ when it merged with the predominately white East End Church of Christ in 1974. Here he receives a Distinguished Service Award from Pepperdine University. *(Courtesy Center for Restoration Studies, Abilene Christian University)*

Another Keeble student who became a Civil Rights leader was Arthur Smith, Jr., who while a doctoral student at the University of California at Los Angeles immersed himself in the Civil Rights and Black Power movements and changed his name to Molefi Kete Asante. Asante, considered by many the father of Afrocentrism, became one of the most prolific authors and scholars on African and African American history and racism in the United States.[17]

Jack Evans, longtime President of Southwestern Christian College in Terrell, Texas, and another Keeble student, was unyielding in his stance against racial discrimination. In 1974 he debated white Missionary

Baptist pastor Vernon L. Barr in Dallas, Texas, denouncing Barr for his racism. Floyd Rose, also a product of NCI, championed the cause of racial justice and social equality, becoming a leader in civil rights and community development in Detroit. Similarly, Franklin Florence, Sr., still another graduate of NCI, while preaching in New York worked closely with Malcolm X to stamp out racial disparity in employment.[18]

Prompted by growing tensions and the failure of Churches of Christ generally to confront racial issues, minister David Jones and members of the African American Schrader Lane Church of Christ in Nashville, Tennessee, hosted a Race Relations Workshop, March 4–8, 1968. Jones pointedly asked white members if recent growth in Churches of Christ was the result of welcoming racists into their congregations without demanding repentance.[19] Lawrence L. (Bud) Stumbaugh, white Nashville entrepreneur and member of the Madison Church of Christ, delivered a blistering speech decrying "the past, present, and persistent failure of the church to be what it ought to be." In words reminiscent of Martin Luther King, Jr., Stumbaugh declared that "one does not have to be grossly wicked to be immoral—just spineless."[20]

The Schrader Lane Race Workshop was the first major effort in Churches of Christ to address civil rights issues. A special supplement to the *Christian Chronicle* published shortly after the meeting included many of the speeches and stirred considerable debate. A second Race Conference took place on June 25–26, 1968, two months after the assassination of Martin Luther King, Jr., and the death of Marshall Keeble. The conference included thirty-seven white and black preachers, businessmen, and college administrators who met in Atlanta, Georgia. Several participants urged that preachers speak out against racial injustice from the pulpit, that the "Herald of Truth" television program address issues of race, that Lectureship directors invite black preachers to speak, and that colleges hire "qualified" blacks to teach. However, at the end of the conference, several white leaders refused to sign or endorse a statement that included these and other recommendations, heightening black frustration and alienation.

Southwestern Christian College President Jack Evans expressed the feelings of many in a *Christian Chronicle* editorial later that year when he declared that black Churches of Christ were "ready to exchange servility and dependence for independence and, if need be, estrangement." During the Civil Rights era, black Churches of Christ, already segregated and patronized by whites, developed into a completely separate and independent body, identified by their own institutions: the *Christian Echo*, Southwestern Christian College, the National Lectureship and the Annual National Youth Conference.[21] What one commentator described as "an angry peace" prevailed.[22] Though the schools affiliated with Churches of Christ were racially integrated by the early 1970s, relatively few students of color entered, and the churches remained almost entirely segregated. The only publication in Churches of Christ other than the African American *Christian Echo* that consistently condemned segregation and white supremacy was *Mission Journal*. Begun in 1968 as a voice for progressives, *Mission* addressed the churches' complicity in racism by charging elders, ministers, and editors of other journals of refusing to deal with the issue.[23] Not until the 1990s did school administrators make public acknowledgment of their institutions' sin of racism. In 1999, for example, Abilene Christian University President Royce Money publicly confessed ACU's sin of racial discrimination to the Southwestern Christian College annual Lectureship.[24] Like most other Christian bodies in America, however, Churches of Christ continued to be largely segregated.

Christian Churches/Churches of Christ gave virtually no support to the Civil Rights Movement. Since most congregations were predominantly white and either rural or suburban, they were often insulated from racial minorities.[25] Like Churches of Christ, they had no formal institutions to rally action for social justice. Furthermore, their bitter separation from the more socially active Disciples disposed them to view social justice as part of the liberal agenda they so much abhorred.

The ideological justification for the lack of action on civil rights by the Christian Churches/Churches of Christ was largely constructed by James DeForest Murch. In the late 1960s, Murch and *Christian Standard* editor Edwin Hayden (1904-1995) regularly attacked what they labeled moral socialism, a secular agenda for achieving racial equality through political posturing and social engineering. Murch warned against mainline Protestant support of the social gospel that he believed mirrored this secular agenda:

> Psychologists, psychiatrists, social activists, and liberal educators are not going to make a better world without making better men with spiritual motivations, disciplines, and resources that are distinctly and Biblically Christian. To talk of building a better world without changing the people in it is sheer lunacy, and people are beginning to find that out.[26]

Hayden condemned as "racism in reverse" the plan of the Consultation on Church Union (COCU), of which Disciples were part, to appoint a black as the first presiding bishop of the proposed "Church of Christ Uniting." He viewed it as evidence of mainline subservience to "engineered"—and therefore superficial—racial reform.[27] He also criticized the National Black Economic Development Conference in Detroit for its inflammatory demands for $500 million in reparations from white churches and Jewish synagogues.[28] Similarly Hayden denounced Coretta Scott King's innuendo that all whites were implicated in the murder of Dr. Martin Luther King, Jr. He asserted that the "distraught widow" was "echoing the ultimate illogic of the social gospel, thrusting aside individual responsibility, judgment, and salvation in favor of dealing with 'the system.'"[29] The message, then, was simple: by making devout disciples of Jesus Christ, racial reconciliation would happen on its own in the context of individual relationships and accountability. Racism was not the problem but a symptom of the deeper problem of human sinfulness.

Not all leaders in Christian Churches/Churches of Christ, however, agreed with Murch's and Hayden's assessments. Some remained deeply concerned that congregations were ignoring systemic racism and using opposition to social activism in liberal churches (especially the Disciples) to excuse themselves of responsibility for working toward racial justice. In the late 1960s, W. Graham Barnes, who had studied Stone-Campbell race relations and helped organize a Fellowship of Concerned Individuals (FOCI), led a Call to Action for ministers and congregations of the Christian Churches/Churches of Christ to address the racial crisis. Forty-four ministers, scholars, and other professionals, white and African American, signed its petition and committed to combat racism and discrimination and to break down racial barriers.[30]

One of the most vocal in that group was Robert O. Fife, professor of history at Milligan College, who insisted that addressing issues of social justice and racial reconciliation was a "restoration" principle. Fife had been a chaplain in World War II and was with the allied troops that liberated the Nazi death camp at Dachau, Germany—an experience that inspired a lifelong commitment to racial and ethnic reconciliation as central to the Christian gospel. Fife later published his Indiana University Ph.D. dissertation under the title *Teeth on Edge*, a study of the slavery controversy in the early Stone-Campbell Movement, to which he appended an appeal to the churches to break through "the chumminess of likeminded people" and work to reflect "the diversity of the world brought to the feet of Jesus."[31]

Fife was not alone. James Van Buren, a popular writer and professor at Manhattan Christian College, urged suburban Christian Churches/Churches of Christ to overcome their insularity and begin turning toward ministry in the racially and ethnically diverse inner city.[32] Though affirming Van Buren's call, Christian Churches/ Churches of Christ largely framed racial reconciliation in terms of evangelism and missions rather than social transformation. Leland Tyrrell and W. Ray Kelley, both presidents of the African American Winston-Salem Bible College, now Carolina Christian College, insisted that a key to overcoming the sin of racism and achieving racial equality in America was a partnership between black and white preachers to evangelize the black community. This, they asserted, was what was needed to demonstrate the commitment of predominantly white churches to the challenges facing African Americans.[33]

In the 1980s and 1990s, Christian Churches/ Churches of Christ, like many American Evangelicals, "rediscovered" aspects of the social gospel and came to view concerns for urban ministry and racial reconciliation as part of evangelism. Many congregations became self-conscious of their social homogeneity, prompting calls to embrace the needs of the inner city and mushrooming ethnic populations.[34] Prophetic voices from within African American Christian Churches/Churches of Christ, such as Denzil Holness of Central Christian Church in Atlanta, also began to clamor for reappraisal of the racial imbalances and alienation still existing in many congregations.[35] Experiments in "intentional" integration began in churches like Westlane Christian Church, Community Christian Church, Englewood Christian Church, and New Paradigm Christian Church, all in Indianapolis.[36] This trend paralleled an accelerating pattern of white congregations "hosting" Korean or Hispanic churches by sharing buildings, resources, and worship.

Nevertheless, coming to grips with persistent subtle bigotry remained a struggle.[37] In October 2010, the *Christian Standard* devoted an entire issue to the troubling record of Christian Churches/Churches of Christ in cultivating racially integrated congregations and addressing the complex problems of racism. African American minister Byron Davis commented that developing multicultural and multi-ethnic church staffs would become increasingly important as whites become a minority in many parts of the United States.[38]

One avenue Christian Churches/Churches of Christ took in the early twenty-first century as a result of renewed concern for racial reconciliation was increased attention to urban poverty. Ozark Christian College Professor Mark Moore observed in 2009 that the churches historically neglected social justice because they associated it with the secular and political left.[39] Strong commitment of resources and personnel to urban ministry overseas by the Christian Missionary Fellowship and other organizations had raised consciousness of the need to respond to poverty at home as well.[40] The *Christian Standard* increasingly profiled churches involved in urban ministry and instructed congregations how to use resources to serve the poor and cultivate a moral conscience concerning the needs of inner-city populations.[41] Among the group's schools, Cincinnati Christian University created an undergraduate degree in Urban and Intercultural Ministries and an Urban Scholars program to provide scholarships for students from urban environments.[42]

War

At the time of their emergence as a separate body, many in Churches of Christ embraced the legacy of pacifism begun by Stone and Campbell and later reinforced by David Lipscomb. However, the First and Second World Wars had taken a toll on that legacy. During the Vietnam War (1959-1975), journals in Churches of Christ rarely mentioned the conflict except to condemn anti-war protesters as part of a Communist conspiracy to overthrow the United States government.[43] Soon after U.S. military advisors arrived to aid the French in Vietnam in 1950, a group of five influential leaders in Churches of Christ, including G. C. Brewer, B. C. Goodpasture, and Batsell Barrett Baxter, began the journal *Voice of Freedom*. The paper implicitly supported the war, mirroring conservative Protestant fears of Catholicism and Communism to promote American nationalism as a key religious commitment.[44]

The pacifist vision among Churches of Christ never completely vanished, however. Among the one-cup fellowship, pacifism remained a core principle.[45] Even among mainstream Churches of Christ small pockets of support for pacifism and conscientious objection to military service remained, especially in North Alabama and Middle Tennessee. While few openly challenged the mainstream position, materials like Alexander Campbell's "Address on War" and Bennie Lee Fudge's 1943 tract "Can a Christian Kill for His Government?" continued to be reprinted and circulated.[46]

One of the most respected leaders in Churches of Christ in the mid-twentieth century was Batsell Barrett Baxter (1916-1982), chair of the Bible Department at Lipscomb University and speaker for the "Herald of Truth" radio and television programs. Baxter, through one of the founders of *Voice of Freedom*, had taken a conscientious objector position during World War II and continued to oppose Christians killing in warfare.[47] On March 8, 1968, as the Vietnam War intensified, Baxter delivered a chapel message to the Lipscomb student body titled "The Christian and Warfare."

Baxter began with the assertion that "warfare is inconsistent with the basic message and spirit of Christianity." After citing an array of Scriptures from the Sermon on the Mount to Jesus' rebuke of Peter for using his sword against an enemy, Baxter affirmed, "Christians are to be obedient to government in all matters, with one exception—when government's requirements conflict with God's teachings, they must obey God." He then quoted from early church and Stone-Campbell leaders who took this position and answered potential objections to his position, closing with a restatement of his conviction that no scriptural case could be made for Christian participation in warfare.

Nevertheless, reflecting his pro-American sentiments he added that the United States was "the finest government in the world." Christians should be grateful for being able to live in this nation, he said, especially since the government allowed those who conscientiously objected to participation in war to perform alternative service. He then recommended that young men from Churches of Christ offer to serve in the Medical Corps to save and preserve life rather than take it.[48] Baxter's "limited conscientious objector" position, however, displeased both those who believed Christians should fight for their country and those who took an absolute pacifist position.

Three years later, at the height of the Vietnam War, Leabert (Lee) M. Rogers, then living in northwest Alabama, published a book titled *God and Government* in which he advocated absolute pacifism and total separation of the Christian from civil government. Starting with the familiar positive law approach, Rogers insisted that the only scripturally authorized relations between Christians and government were paying taxes, obeying laws not in conflict with God's law, and praying for rulers.[49] To go beyond those actions would be to go beyond God's instructions.

Yet Rogers did not confine his argument to a simplistic positive law approach. In ten detailed chapters reminiscent of David Lipscomb's *Civil Government*, he examined the history, nature, and purpose of human governments, contrasting them with the Kingdom of God. Warfare, he asserted, has a standard of values inherently in conflict with Christian standards. The Christian must view every casualty of war as "a *man made in the image of God*, [a] precious soul for whom Christ died." Since the mission of God's church is to save the lost, it is in absolute opposition to the mission of war.[50]

Pacifism would continue as a minority position in Churches of Christ in the late twentieth and early twenty-first centuries.[51] Yet the overt display of American nationalism as a key religious commitment by many in that stream seemed to be reflected by an increase in the display of the American flag in church buildings. While U.S. and Christian flags had long been a fixture in many mainline (including Disciples) and Evangelical church sanctuaries, Churches of Christ had maintained a strong tradition of separation of church and state in this matter, even when most members supported Christian participation in the military.[52] After the terrorist attacks of September 11, 2001, some congregations and schools began to display the U.S. flag in and around their buildings.[53] For example, the Brentwood Hills Church of Christ in Nashville, Tennessee, hung a huge American flag on the side of its building for a time, and Lipscomb University, namesake of David Lipscomb, hung a large flag above the entrance to the auditorium used for daily chapel.[54]

An informal survey of a small number of Churches of Christ taken in November 2010 revealed that twenty congregations in eleven states had U.S. flags in their worship space. A few also had Christian flags. Some leaders and members resisted what they saw as an illegitimate display of nationalism that conflicted with the Christian's allegiance to the Kingdom of God. In the same survey fifteen widely informed national leaders across the United States expressed surprise that any Church of Christ would display a flag in its sanctuary.[55] In the early twenty-first century, members of Churches of Christ reflected a variety of positions regarding the Christian and warfare and the related issue of American nationalism. Overall, however, the vast majority had little problem endorsing participation in the military and in government at all levels.

Christian Churches/Churches of Christ distinguished themselves from Churches of Christ and Disciples by the virtual non-existence of pacifist sentiment. A two-part article in the 1982 *Christian Standard* written by Jack Cottrell, Professor of Theology at Cincinnati

Bible College, reflected the majority view. Cottrell identified what he saw as four errors of pacifists, including misunderstandings of God's nature, the purpose of government, the sanctity of life, and the life and teachings of Jesus. Cottrell asserted that one could not imitate Jesus on matters of government and war because "what Jesus taught and modeled was not intended to be a complete ethical system." Everything God created government to do, including waging war, Cottrell insisted, "was no less good and moral and righteous than what He has ordained for individuals and the church to do within their own spheres of activity."[56]

A 1984 survey of ministers and elders in Stone-Campbell churches on the Pacific slope conducted by sociologist Laurence Keene revealed that 60 percent of leaders of Christian Churches/Churches of Christ agreed with the statement, "Christians should accept, as part of their responsibility as citizens, the 'call to bear arms' in the event our country goes to war," with only 7 percent strongly disagreeing.[57] A 1990 textbook widely used in schools affiliated with Christian Churches/Churches of Christ articulated again the majority view. Titled *What the Bible Says About Civil Government*, author Paul Butler asserted that every Christian man must serve in the military except for missionaries and ministers "actively preaching the gospel." He went on to add, however, that even missionaries and ministers might need to serve in the military if required to "hasten the overthrow of evil aggressive forces in the world."[58]

Disciples continued to recognize the pacifist tradition. Opponents of the Vietnam War included both pacifists and others who perceived a widening gap between American values and the actions of the United States government in the conflict. Americans valued democracy and the right of people everywhere to determine their own destiny. Yet in Vietnam, the United States seemed to many to be involved in a war that denied these values. To a growing number of Americans, including Disciples, the South Vietnamese people did not appear to want the destiny the United States was trying to give them.[59]

Students and faculty on several Disciples campuses organized peace marches, demonstrations, and moratoria to protest the War. Often school administrators sanctioned such actions, as was the case in the October 1968 peace march at Drury College.[60] On October 15, 1969, peace advocates staged a national Vietnam War Moratorium after President Nixon's "Vietnamization" policy failed to end the conflict. Brite Divinity School dismissed classes to allow faculty and students to participate. The school held

prayer services in Texas Christian University's Robert Carr Chapel, and students met to discuss theological understandings of war.[61]

Widely respected preacher and educator Batsell Barrett Baxter advocated the position in 1968 that Christians could not participate in military combat, but should instead serve in the medical corps. *(Courtesy Center for Restoration Studies, Abilene Christian University)*

Three years earlier, in 1966, the Disciples' International Convention had approved a series of resolutions supporting the legal protection of pacifists as well as those who, while not opposed to all war, conscientiously objected to a specific war like the one in Vietnam. A year later, after military chaplain E. Tipton Carroll, Jr., argued on the floor of the Convention that such a position undermined young men who were defending their country, the body reversed the previous Convention's decision in a standing vote with no count required. In 1968, the first General Assembly of the Christian Church (Disciples of Christ) reversed the 1967 Convention's decision, this time with a vote of 1,725 in favor of selective conscientious objection and 845 against.[62] At the same time, delegates affirmed their support of men and women serving in the armed forces and pledged to continue to support them regardless of the political climate at home and the military policies of the U.S. government. Though Disciples never issued an official statement opposing the War in Vietnam, the 1976 Assembly adopted a resolution expressing relief at the end of the Indochina War and urging the U.S. government to establish relations with the new communist governments of Vietnam, Laos, and Cambodia.

The right to oppose a particular war emerged again among Disciples in response to the War in Iraq. Resolution 0728 submitted by the Disciples Peace Fellowship called the 2007 Assembly to affirm the right to oppose a particular war by those who had volunteered for military service but who, on the grounds of Christian conviction, refused deployment to Iraq. This resolution also asked the assembly to go on record as conscientiously opposing the war in Iraq as inconsistent with the teachings of Jesus and as violating the traditional standards of just war. In keeping with the concern for U.S. military personnel reflected in the Vietnam era actions, this resolution asked Disciples to commend the men and women of the armed forces stationed in Iraq for their courage and sacrifice and to hold them and their families in prayer. Following a lively and impassioned debate, the Assembly adopted the resolution, though the vote was far from unanimous.[63]

Ethnic Diversity

The Immigration Act of 1965 initiated a new wave of migration to the United States. Seeking to learn from past failures, Disciples reached out to these new immigrants through their newly formed Division of Homeland Ministries, created during restructure from the UCMS. Church Extension also played a major role through its training program for new church planters.

In 1969, Domingo Rodriguez (1918-2006) became the first Hispanic to serve as director of the Homeland Ministries Office of Programs and Services for Hispanic and Bilingual Congregations. Born, raised, and educated in Puerto Rico, he had served as pastor of La Hermosa Christian Church in New York City from 1953-1955 and was the first executive secretary of the Christian Church (Disciples of Christ) in Puerto Rico from 1958-1962. Rodriguez initiated an aggressive program of church planting and revitalization. He also called a conference of Hispanic ministers that created a Committee on Guidelines for Strategy and Action. The Committee morphed into a board, then a conference, then another committee, and finally the Hispanic Caucus, which, in 1980, developed the National Hispanic and Bilingual

Fellowship of the Christian Church (Disciples of Christ). The Hispanic and Bilingual Fellowship held its first Assembly in 1981.

Rodriguez's successor, Lucas Torres (1933-2008), had served congregations in the Bronx, New York, and rural Puerto Rico before assuming the position of Director in 1973. His service included educational initiatives like the 1975 Christian Men's Fellowship/Christian Women's Fellowship study *Dignidad: Hispanic Americans and Their Struggle for Dignity.* Torres examined the diverse Hispanic heritage of the U.S. that included Puerto Ricans, Mexicans, Mexican-Americans, Cubans, Dominicans, and Central Americans, each challenged by cultural assimilation and racial prejudice. He stressed the need for self-determination, political and economic development, and education and leadership in both church and society. He challenged Disciples to recognize Hispanic members as an integral part of the church and to affirm the cultural diversity shared in genuine Christian community.

Torres's message, however, did not reach all Disciples. Daisy L. Machado, who ministered with Hispanic congregations in New York City and Houston, Texas, described challenges she encountered while organizing churches among Hispanic immigrants in the 1980s and 1990s. When attempting to partner with existing congregations, Machado discovered churches that "didn't want any more 'Mexicans' in their building," including white mothers who believed all Mexican children carried lice. Machado noted that many Disciples continued to expect Hispanic immigrants to move into white churches and assimilate as English-speaking Americans, a far cry from Torres's call to cultural diversity.[64]

Tensions between emerging Hispanic leaders and Homeland Ministries led to the establishment of the Central Pastoral Office for Hispanic Ministries in 1991. This new general ministry was to provide programs and pastoral care to Hispanic ministers and congregations, advise regional and general ministries on Hispanic ministry, and serve as an advocate for Hispanic Disciples. By 2011, the National Pastor for Hispanic Ministries had oversight of 182 congregations with a membership of over 9,800.[65]

Asians were also part of the new wave of immigration. In 1976 Wilshire Korean Christian Church became the first Korean Disciples congregation. Evangelism executive Harold Johnson of Homeland Ministries collaborated with Asian Disciples including David Kagiwada(1929-1985), Soongook Choi (1933-2002) and Itoko Maeda (1918-2008) to organize a consultation on Asian ministries in Indianapolis in 1978 to affirm the unique identity of Asian American Disciples, raise Disciples consciousness about the Asian presence, and help Disciples attend to the needs of the growing Asian American population. Participants organized the Fellowship of Asian American Disciples (FAAD), renamed American-Asian Disciples (AAD) a year later, which the 1979 St. Louis General Assembly formally acknowledged as a constituency. The group held its first convocation in October 1980 in Indianapolis, with sixteen Asian Disciples and three General staff. The group decided to hold convocations biannually alternating with the General Assembly.

Nine years later there were eight Asian American congregations. An October 1989 Homeland Ministries consultation called for developing Asian ministerial leadership, establishing congregations, fostering Asian representation on boards of the church, and appointing an Asian staff person in Homeland Ministries for American Asian ministries. Koreans were to be the initial target because of the rapid growth of the Korean immigrant population and the growth of Korean Christianity. The 1991 Tulsa General Assembly approved this initiative, and in 1992 Geunhee Yu was called to the new position. Yu, a Ph.D. in pastoral care and counseling from Vanderbilt University, was also a graduate of Seoul Christian University, affiliated with Christian Churches/ Churches of Christ. In 1996, the group changed its name to the North American Pacific/Asian Disciples (NAPAD) to be more inclusive. By 2011, there were sixty-five NAPAD churches, totaling more than 3,300 Disciples. Approximately 75 percent of the congregations were Korean, with the rest Chinese, Japanese, Filipino, Vietnamese, Indonesian, and Samoan.[66]

In April 2009 the General Board adopted a proposal to confer general ministry status to the Office of the Executive Pastor of NAPAD. This action gave responsibility and accountability for programming to the NAPAD Convocation. In January 2010 NAPAD began to function much like the Central Pastoral Office for Hispanic Ministries as a general ministry administratively separate from Home Missions (the name adopted by Homeland Ministries in 2004).

While Disciples were seeking to strengthen their witness among Hispanic and Asian Americans, Haitians were discovering the Disciples of Christ. In 1973, Haitian immigrant Philius Nicolas, an ordained minister in the Church of God in Christ, organized a Church of God among Haitian immigrants in the Flatbush section of Brooklyn, New York. While taking courses at Union

Theological Seminary, he learned of the Disciples from Winthrop Hudson's *Religion in America*. In an interview in 1988, Nicolas remarked that he had been looking for a "larger and more catholic group with which to affiliate" and was immediately attracted by Hudson's description of the Stone-Campbell Movement. His investigations led him to Puerto Rican Disciples in New York City, whose worship services appealed to him and to his French-speaking, Pentecostal congregation. In 1976 Nicolas's Evangelical Crusade officially affiliated with the Disciples of Christ.[67]

By 1986 Evangelical Crusade reported an active membership of 1,225 and could point to a network of Haitian Disciples congregations. Two years later, Charles Lamb, regional minister of the Northeastern Region, estimated that one-fourth of all active Disciples in New York were Haitians.[68] Haitian congregations also developed in twelve other states, the District of Columbia, and Quebec. Haitian Disciples held their first general church meeting July 14-15, 2010, in Indianapolis.[69] The group discussed ways to help Haitian Disciples better connect to Disciples structures and understand Disciples beliefs and practices. It also highlighted the wider church's need to become better acquainted with the Haitian church and culture.[70] By 2011, the number of congregations had reached forty-three with a membership of 2,332.[71]

Christian Churches/Churches of Christ demonstrated institutional commitment to Hispanic and other ethnic church plants through parachurch organizations and voluntary congregational activism. Established in 1964, Spanish-American Evangelistic Ministries (SAEM) focused primarily on starting churches in Mexico, but it eventually broadened its work to the U.S. and published the *Spanish Directory of the Ministry* for all known work among Spanish-speaking communities by Christian Churches/Churches of Christ. Starting in 1998, the Christian Missionary Fellowship (CMF) began "inter-cultural ministries" to Hispanics in Los Angeles and Indianapolis. Team Expansion, a Louisville-based organization, started Spanish-speaking churches in Miami and the Pacific Northwest. In addition, the Hisportic Christian Mission, established in 1984, started seventeen Portuguese-speaking churches from Rhode Island to New Jersey. Other congregations hosted Spanish-speaking churches or started Spanish language services.[72]

In the first decade of the twenty-first century some Christian Churches/Churches of Christ sought to be more intentional about creating greater ethnic and cultural diversity. The group's substantial track record in international missions raised consciousness in many U.S. congregations of the need to reflect the global face of Christianity.[73] Stadia New Church Strategies, one of the leading church-planting organizations in Christian Churches/Churches of Christ, began working more

Evangelical Crusade of Fishers of Men, meeting in 1977 on Rogers Street in Brooklyn, had affiliated with Disciples of Christ the previous year, becoming the "mother church" of Haitian Disciples.

actively to start and underwrite new churches in ethnic minority communities—especially Spanish-speaking. Stadia also brought attention to the challenges of breaking down barriers between white congregations and their ethnic neighbors. Some megachurches began a critical assessment of their sociological homogeneity and organized initiatives for change. One example was the "Dream of Destiny" campaign of Shepherd of the Hills Christian Church near Los Angeles, California, which sought to encourage churches to work proactively and evangelistically toward greater racial and ethnic diversity. Shepherd of the Hills saw a significant change in its own ethnic make-up to approximately 55 percent ethnic minorities and 45 percent Caucasian.[74]

Among Churches of Christ, Iglesias de Cristo (Hispanic Churches of Christ) had existed in Texas as early as the 1910s and had spread to locations with significant Hispanic populations like California and Puerto Rico. Like black Churches of Christ, these congregations had often lived in the racist shadow of the white establishment. The Civil Rights Movement and increased immigration forced Churches of Christ to confront the white majority's accommodation to racism and complacency toward minority populations. Prompted by former missionaries, a number of leaders and congregations began looking for ways to serve the growing body of new Americans.

One prominent outreach of Churches of Christ was FriendSpeak, a program adapted for the United States from an international program in which participants taught conversational English using a simple translation of Luke. FriendSpeak encouraged instructors to cultivate friendships with the new arrivals rather than teach traditional evangelistic lessons. As conversations arose in the course of reading Luke, teachers had opportunity to share their faith.[75] This, along with more traditional efforts, led to the formation of dozens of ethnic Churches of Christ and an even larger number ministries to immigrants in the late twentieth and early twenty-first centuries.[76]

Yet Churches of Christ also reflected the conflicts in American society over how to respond to increased immigration. Fears of the erosion of traditional American values due to the changing population were evident in events at the Farmer's Branch, Texas, Church of Christ in 2006. The city of Farmer's Branch made headlines that year when its municipal council passed ordinances fining landlords for renting to illegal immigrants and making English the city's official language. Though a federal judge ruled the ordinances unconstitutional, the city appealed the ruling. Three members of the city council that passed the ordinance were members of the Farmers Branch Church of Christ, including the lawyer who made the initial proposal. Soon after the passage of the ordinances, however, the congregation began bilingual services in English and Spanish.[77] The church's desire to serve their changing community clashed with a fear of rapid change. Ironically, the separate bilingual services lasted only a short time because Hispanic members and attendees felt they were being excluded from the main service.[78]

Despite such tensions, by the beginning of the twenty-first century, Churches of Christ in the United States had established congregations and ministries involving at least ten ethnic groups. Among these were twelve Korean and twelve Native American congregations, eight Chinese, four each of Haitians and Filipinos, two each of Cambodians, Portuguese, and Liberians, and one Laotian/Thai church. In addition, as with the other North American streams, scores of predominately white churches conducted services and ministries in all of these languages as well as Spanish, Russian, and Mienh.[79] Based on reports in the *Christian Chronicle*, steady increases in services conducted in languages other than English occurred in the late twentieth and early twenty-first centuries.[80]

Gender Equality

Disciples women provided significant support for the emerging women's movement of the 1970s. The 1974 centennial of the CWBM's founding became an occasion to promote the movement through General Assembly resolutions, including urging congregational, regional, and general ministries to give full consideration to women in hiring and to provide equal pay for equal work. Another resolution called on churches to establish a single diaconate with both men and women, and urged regional organizations and educational institutions to give preference to women when candidates of equal qualifications were available. The Assembly also endorsed the Equal Rights Amendment (ERA) and advised churches to work for its ratification.

Some Disciples, though, rejected the Assembly's resolutions, including Philius Nicolas's newly affiliated Haitian congregation that firmly opposed the Equal Rights Amendment.[81] Acceptance of women's leadership in congregations, though more common among middle-class whites, continued to be uneven, with some congregations admitting women as deacons and elders, and others refusing to do so. By the end of the twentieth century, however, a majority of congregations had women deacons and elders, and almost all had discussed the issue.[82]

The number of women clergy among Disciples of Christ also continued to grow in the late twentieth century. In 1984, 4.2 percent of Disciples senior ministers and 32.8 percent of associate ministers were women. While the number of women associate ministers had mushroomed since the early 1970s, the number of lead ministers had increased only 4 percent since 1972. Though more than half of all students in Master of Divinity programs at Disciples schools were women by the end of the twentieth century, many seeking ordination, women still made up only 20 percent of Disciples clergy.

Most Disciples women ministers were white, though some Disciples women of color gained prominence both in Disciples circles and beyond. Cynthia Hale, Robin Hedgeman, Delores Carpenter, and Deborah Thompson were among the first African American women pastors. In addition to serving congregations, Thompson would become Director of New Congregation Development, and Hedgeman Associate Regional Minister of Ohio. In 1997 *Ebony* magazine named Carpenter, pastor of the Michigan Park Christian Church of Washington, D.C., one of fifteen great black women preachers based on a poll of black leaders. The magazine also added Hale, founder of Ray of Hope Christian Church of Atlanta, Georgia, to its Honor Roll of Great Preachers.[83]

In 1988 a group of black clergy urged the National Convocation to integrate women clergy more fully into the life of the church by calling more black women to local congregations, addressing "deep-rooted theological issues concerning women in ministry," and sensitizing clergy as well as regional and area ministers to the issue.[84] By the end of the twentieth century, the number of black women serving as pastors had increased significantly, indicated by the seventy women who attended the African American Clergy Women's Retreat in March 2000.

Though not institutionally part of the Christian Church (Disciples of Christ), the Church of Christ, Disciples of Christ also reflected growing recognition of women's leadership among African Americans of the Stone-Campbell tradition. The 1972 General Assembly affirmed ordination of women.[85] One of the group's women leaders was Sheila H. Gillams, who served as General Evangelist of the Church of Christ, Disciples of Christ International from 1991-2005, directing the evangelism and education departments that supported church planting in West Africa, Guyana, Jamaica, and the United States.

Asian American women also had increasing prominence among Disciples. Itoka Maeda helped organize the first Asian American Disciples gathering in 1978, urging the group to include both North and South American Asians in its scope. April Lewton served as NAPAD moderator, and others such as Binh Hunt of Richmond, Virginia, served as church planters. In 2004, Sandyha Jha, pastor of First Christian Church of Oakland, California, and Minister of Transformation for the Christian Church of Northern California-Nevada, became co-Moderator of the Disciples of Christ anti-racism commission.[86]

Among Hispanic women, Miriam Cruz served as assistant to Chicago mayor Richard Daley to establish programs for Hispanics, and later worked for the Jimmy Carter administration. In Puerto Rican churches in New York City, women assisted in ministry and evangelization from the beginning. By the 1960s, several Puerto Rican women had received ordination, mostly as assistant pastors, though Juana Santana served as preaching minister of the Bridgeport, Connecticut, church. By the 1980s Hispanic women were enrolling in seminaries and serving on national boards. Cuban American Daisy L. Machado joined the Brite Divinity School faculty in 1992. In 1996, the *Confraternidad Nacional de Mujeres Hispanas y Bilingües* (National Fellowship of Hispanic and Bilingual Women) was organized to support Disciples women's ministry in Hispanic congregations and provide opportunities for fellowship among Hispanic women.[87]

Several Disciples women made contributions in theological scholarship, including Delores H. Carpenter who served as Professor of Religious Education at Howard University Divinity School and edited the *African American Heritage Hymnal* published in 2001. Serene Jones taught theology at Yale for seventeen years, publishing *Feminist Theory and Christian Theology* in 2000 and becoming president of Union Theological Seminary in New York in 2008. Kristine Culp, Dean of the Disciples Divinity House at the University of Chicago, published *Vulnerability and Glory: A Theological Account* in 2010. In addition to teaching at Brite Divinity School, Daisy Machado served as Director of the Hispanic Theological Initiative at Emory University from 1996-99. In 2005 she became dean of Lexington Theological Seminary, and later joined the faculty of Union Theological Seminary in New York where she became Dean of Academic Affairs in 2010.

Rita Nakashima Brock published *Journeys by Heart: A Christology of Erotic Power*, which won the Crossroads/Continuum Publishing Company award for the most outstanding manuscript in women's studies in 1988. She also co-authored two widely discussed volumes: *Casting Stones: Prostitution and Liberation in Asia and the United States*, which won the Catholic Press Award in Gender Studies in 1996, and *Saving Paradise: How Christianity Traded Love of the World for Crucifixion and Empire* (2008). In 1995 Brock and Jones joined Texas Christian University Hebrew Bible scholar Claudia Camp as editors of *Setting the Table: Women in Theological Conversation*. The fourteen authors acknowledged their shared Disciples identity.

> We have been particularly struck by how much we share based on our common grounding in the Disciples tradition and in Disciples communities…

> We reflected often on our common experience of being shaped by a tradition that is low church in its polity and yet highly liturgical with regard to its weekly practice of communion, and we slowly discovered together that as Disciples, we stand uniquely positioned to speak theologically to traditions ranging from Baptist to Episcopal and Roman Catholic.[88]

Identified by Stephen V. Sprinkle as a one-volume Panel of Scholars report, this collection of essays was a feminist project offered for the benefit of the whole church.[89]

In 2005, the General Assembly in Portland, Oregon, elected Sharon E. Watkins General Minister and President of the Christian Church (Disciples of Christ), the first woman to serve as head of a major American denomination. Watkins had served Disciples Overseas Ministries for two years in Kinshasa, Zaire, and later worked for Phillips University. She was the pastor of churches in Indiana and Oklahoma before being chosen General Minister. Watkins's leadership did much to raise the profile of women across the Christian Church (Disciples of Christ). In January 2009, at the request of President Barack Obama, Dr. Watkins became the first woman to preach at an inaugural prayer service. In 2011 she was included in the online Huffington Post's list of Ten Inspiring Religious Leaders.[90]

Sharon Watkins is installed as General Minister and President of the Christian Church (Disciples of Christ) at the 2005 General Assembly at Portland, Oregon.

In Churches of Christ, traditional views of women's roles remained dominant, though significant changes had begun by the late twentieth century. The group's public response to the Equal Rights Amendment was almost universal opposition. Writers condemned the Amendment and warned of dire consequences on church life and, most importantly, the family.[91] Some women in Churches of Christ argued that women with careers outside the home had effectively abandoned their home and family, and that the separate income created barriers in marriage. Career women, therefore, were responsible for the growing divorce rate and the resulting destruction of the family.[92] Others warned of the impact on the family if mothers were drafted to fight in a war.[93] Several hundred women from both Churches of Christ and Christian Churches/Churches of Christ participated in anti-ERA activities in connection with the International Woman's Year Conference in Houston, Texas in November 1977.[94]

Even after the furor over the Equal Rights Amendment died down, women's issues remained volatile. For example, a 1992 *Firm Foundation* article by Irene Taylor insisted the ERA had been a cover for a radical agenda to legalize homosexuality. She asserted that many well-meaning Christian women had supported ratification of the Amendment thinking that it would improve their condition, unaware of the Amendment's real intent. Conservatives like Taylor feared that legal moves for gender equality would lead to the destruction of American society.[95]

Nevertheless, many in Churches of Christ celebrated the prospect of a new society characterized by gender equality and reevaluated their position on women's leadership in the church. Some congregations opened roles once reserved solely for men to all Christians, including leading public prayers and presiding at the Lord's Supper.[96] Conferences on the role of women reinforced this trend. In 1998, the Center for Christian Education, a preacher training school in Irving, Texas, convened a forum on "The Role of Women" that drew four hundred participants from across the country.[97] Speakers included professors from church-affiliated schools and prominent preachers who addressed scriptural injunctions on female behavior and the traditional role of women in Churches of Christ. Most concluded that interpretations of Scripture that excluded women from public leadership in church were unnecessarily strict. This conference and others like it supported the movement of women into new positions of leadership already happening in some Churches of Christ.

Advocates for expanded women's ministry created a "Gender Justice and Churches of Christ" website that offered a forum for discussion and provided materials for

churches and individuals considering this topic. Many church members welcomed the changes in women's roles as an enlargement of the churches' resources for reaching more people. In addition, the growing number of women serving in ministry positions prompted the formation of the Women in Ministry Network. The Network sponsored national and regional gatherings annually and posted articles, sermons, and other materials written by women ministers.[98]

Some in Canadian Churches of Christ suggested that one reason for their declining numbers, particularly in Ontario, was restrictions on women's role. Several Canadian women shared their reasons for leaving Churches of Christ in a 2005 volume edited by Warren Lewis and Hans Rollmann titled *Restoring the First-Century Church in the Twenty-First Century*. A lack of leadership opportunities and the pressure to remain silent in the worship life of the church were at the top of the list.[99]

In 1994, Dr. Jeanene Reese began the Center for Women in Christian Service at Abilene Christian University and directed an annual Equipping Women for Ministry Workshop at the school. In an interview in 2001, Reese listed the most common paid ministries filled by women in Churches of Christ as children's, youth, and adult education ministers; after-school and childcare administrators; counseling staff; pastoral and elder care providers; and chaplains and church administrative staff. Women also served in outreach, benevolence, and inner-city programs; worship and theater ministries; and in parachurch groups.[100] Conspicuously absent were pulpit minister and elder, two roles that even more inclusive churches generally reserved for men.

The experience of Katie Hays while serving as a preaching minister in Churches of Christ illustrated the difficulties of such service in this stream of the Stone-Campbell Movement. Some in her Birmingham, Alabama, congregation welcomed her to leadership, but women often were among her fiercest critics. Hays suggested that the opposition might have reflected a fear by those women that her public leadership undercut their lifelong commitment to traditional women's ministries.[101] Other women who served as ministers among Churches of Christ in the late twentieth and early twenty-first centuries included D'Esta Love who was chaplain for Pepperdine University, Charme Robarts who served Skillman Church of Christ in Dallas as Involvement Minister, and Sara Barton who was Campus Minister for Rochester College in Rochester Hills, Michigan.

Black Churches of Christ were generally less open to women's leadership than white churches. While journals serving a mostly white audience debated the role of women in church leadership, the *Christian Echo*, the most widely read publication among black Churches of Christ, reminded women that

> in the church there are some things we as ladies must be cautious about. We must always recognize that God has an order of headship when it comes to church. I Corinthians 11:3. According to this Scripture, man has someone over Him: Christ, Christ has someone over Him: God, and woman has someone over Her: Man.[102]

Yet, even among black Churches of Christ some women were able to assume leadership roles within certain boundaries. Ruby Holland, for example, organized the Ladies Auxiliary for Christian Education, which provided significant funding for Southwestern Christian College. Holland also participated in the creation of the Black and White Group of Los Angeles, later called the Multi-Ethnic Group, with the goal of bridging racial boundaries among women in Churches of Christ.

Hispanic women in Churches of Christ initially had little opportunity for public leadership. By the beginning of the twenty-first century, however, Latinas shared in some of the changes taking place among Anglo women. Josephine Decierdo-Mock, daughter of a Filipino father and a Mexican mother, earned teaching credentials from Pepperdine University, then served churches with her husband Steve in ten European countries as well as the Philippines, Ecuador, Peru, Chile, and Mexico, in addition to years of service among Latinos/as in southern California. She described her ministry largely in terms of working among women in jails, migrant camps, and churches and urged Christians to avoid placing church traditions over servanthood in reaching the lost. Encouraging church members in Mexico and the Philippines not to feel constrained by American methods of worship, Decierdo-Mock reflected the growing cultural diversity of Churches of Christ and the challenges that diversity posed to traditional white practices.[103]

While the number of women majoring in Bible or religion in fourteen colleges and universities affiliated with Churches of Christ increased in some cases in the late twentieth and early twenty-first centuries, trends were mixed. A Fall 2010 survey of enrollments indicated relatively small numbers of such women overall, and among schools providing longitudinal data, seven showed a decline after 2007. Decreases in the number of all Bible majors kept the relative percentages of males and females stable in most cases, yet none of the schools,

which included both undergraduate and seminary level programs, showed a pattern of increasing numbers of female students after 2007. The proportion of female students from Churches of Christ enrolled in Bible degree programs in these schools ranged between 3 and 25 percent, the highest being in undergraduate programs, though actual numbers were often very small. Women generally made up between 10 and 20 percent of seminary programs, though one had none, and two others had only one or two.[104]

The small numbers and apparent decrease of women from Churches of Christ in theological or ministerial education in the stream's schools is difficult to assess. Not all women who were members of Churches of Christ attended schools affiliated with the group. Resistance to the idea of "women ministers" in some of the schools likely played a role. An increasing level of frustration among some women about possibilities for exercising their gifts of ministry in Churches of Christ may also have been a factor.

While extremely few women served as preaching ministers in Churches of Christ, a number of congregations began to open up other worship leadership roles.[105] A research project conducted by Abilene Christian University professors Stephen Johnson and Lynette Sharp Penya in 2010 identified a sample of sixty-six Churches of Christ that considered themselves to be gender inclusive. Most of the responding congregations reported that women led in worship by reading Scripture, praying, leading singing, presenting devotional or communion thoughts, and waiting on the Lord's Table. Only 20 percent, however, reported having women preach on Wednesday nights or Sunday mornings.[106]

Though concrete data is difficult to obtain, the number of women in Churches of Christ engaged in professional ministry did seem to be increasing at the beginning of the twenty-first century. Long-time ministry leader in Churches of Christ D'Esta Love expressed her view in a 2010 memorandum: "…it is fair to say that we are a growing number and that women in Churches of Christ who are trained in ministry are finding their way into positions of ministry as they wait for our churches to receive their gifts and open more opportunities."[107]

Christian Churches/Churches of Christ generally took an equally firm stand in favor of traditional roles for women. An article in the *Christian Standard* in 1975 warned that the humanistic desire to obliterate distinctions between male and female had invaded even the church, a matter that for some in this stream became even more important than "Biblical restoration."[108] The controversy surrounding the Equal Rights Amendment in the 1970s only hardened attitudes concerning women's leadership. In a 2007 *Christian Standard* interview, Christian educator Eleanor Daniel argued that the controversy over the ERA made it more difficult for women to become ordained ministers because many churches, in reaction to the cultural conflicts of the 1970s, began to refuse to endorse anything that seemed sympathetic to what they saw as radical views. "The ERA, for people who were committed to Scripture and wanted to retain values that were important to them, seemed like another challenge to everything they had held dear for a long time."[109]

The two sides of the debate over women's leadership were summarized by Brant Lee Doty's report on a 1988 Open Forum panel. "[Tom] Thurman and [Ronald] Fisher affirmed a divine order in creation which establishes the relative functions and works of men and women; [Joe] Webb and [David] Root contended that the New Testament reflects a cultural first-century order which is not relevant to the present scene." As was true with other discussions on women's roles, those involved in the discussion (mostly men) focused on how to interpret and apply Paul's views on women found in Galatians 3:28; 1 Timothy 2:8-15; 1 Corinthians 11: 2-16; and 1 Corinthians 14: 34-36.[110]

Many in Christian Churches/Churches of Christ believed the debates over women's roles were related to the issue of biblical inerrancy. Those who held a hard line in support of inerrancy usually rejected women's leadership and tended to identify with a particular stream of traditional Fundamentalism. On the other hand, those who rejected Fundamentalist understandings of inerrancy for a more Evangelical view often supported women's leadership, which brought them closer theologically to groups like the Church of God (Anderson, Indiana).

Leaders in Christian Churches/Churches of Christ began dialogues with Church of God leaders in the 1980s and discovered a group that was both conservative in theology and supportive of women's ordination. This was a new possibility for many in the Christian Churches/Churches of Christ. In his report on the 1990 dialogue, James B. North mentioned the Church of God's acceptance of women preachers first on his list of significant differences between the two groups.[111] Often forgotten was the fact that a number of women had served Christian Churches/Churches of Christ with distinction between 1910 and 1940 as revivalists, missionary leaders, singing evangelists, and other kinds of ordained ministers.[112]

Despite persistent opposition to female preachers and elders, women continued to move into leadership positions in Christian Churches/Churches of Christ. While only one or two served as preachers, churches ordained and hired an increasing number of women as associate ministers. A study by Eleanor A. Daniel found that the number of women listed in the *Directory of the Ministry* between 1997 and 2001 more than doubled from four hundred to over eight hundred in the categories of Associate Minister, Youth Minister, Children's Minister, and Music Minister.[113] Women also taught ministry courses in colleges and seminaries affiliated with Christian Churches/Churches of Christ after 1970. These included Daniel herself who taught Christian education at Cincinnati Bible College, now Cincinnati Christian University; Mary Ellen Lantzer Pereira who taught biblical studies at Northwest Christian College, now Northwest Christian University; and Nealy Brown who taught counseling at Lincoln Christian University.

The most visible indication of the renewed respect of women as leaders came with the selection of Marsha Relyea Miles as President of the 2007 National Missionary Convention. In an interview after her selection, Miles admitted that serving "was an idea I had to pray about and talk about with my husband and my home church elders." Though she consulted with her husband and elders about the propriety of taking such a role, she was aware that Isabelle Dittemore had served as President of the Convention in 1951, a reminder of the significant ministry roles filled by women in Christian Churches and Disciples of of Christ since the 1920s.[114]

Leadership among African American women in Christian Churches/Churches of Christ could be seen in the Annual Christian Women's Retreat. Organized in 1980 by female alumni of the College of the Scriptures, the retreat gathered African American women to focus on social, spiritual, emotional, and physical issues related to their experience. Among the retreat's original organizers was Magnolia Clark who, after working with emotionally disturbed children for a number of years, returned to the College of the Scriptures to serve as its first dean of women. Later she also served as the school's Academic Dean and Registrar.[115]

Sexuality

By the 1970s, issues of gender for many Americans included abortion and homosexuality. In the case of abortion, advocates of choice argued that women had a fundamental right to choose whether and when to have children. Though birth control was the best option, abortion must be available for women to exercise that basic right of choice, since birth control methods were not always effective.[116] Advocates of gay and lesbian rights called for an extension of civil rights to all Americans.

Though no Disciples General Assembly advocated abortion, assemblies consistently supported the right of women to choose an abortion, even while acknowledging the complexity of the issue and a variety of stances among Disciples. At the 1974 and 1976 meetings Disciples asserted that decisions about abortion should lie with the woman and not with the government while strongly encouraging congregations to study the issue and provide support to those who must decide. Affirming the right of women to choose an abortion, the 1984 Assembly asserted that abortion was not the best method of birth control and encouraged greater efforts on the part of society and the churches to educate young people on avoiding unwanted pregnancies. The Assembly also stated that the optimal place of sexual activity was in the context of marriage. Affirming its earlier actions, the 1989 Assembly passed a resolution opposing laws restricting women's access to abortions.

More controversial for Disciples was the role of gays and lesbians in the church. Sharp disagreement over this issue erupted at the 1977 Kansas City Assembly, which considered four resolutions on the issue.[117] One asked the assembly to oppose homosexuality as a lifestyle for Christians and was rejected by a vote of 2,304 to 1,538. Another urged the passage of legislation to end the denial of civil rights because of sexual orientation, which the assembly adopted by a vote of 2,541 to 1,312. The third was an eleven-page study document from the Task Force on Family Life and Human Sexuality prepared under the auspices of Homeland Ministries. The document did not endorse homosexuality, though some delegates accused it of being an apologetic for a homosexual lifestyle. After an emotional debate and threats to withdraw from the denomination if the document were accepted, the Assembly approved it for research and reflection by the churches.

The fourth resolution asked the Assembly to deny ordination to "any candidate who declares he or she practices or prefers homosexuality as a lifestyle." The denomination was to offer counseling to such candidates, and the church was to remain open to the possibility of their changing. Exhausted by the debate over the three previous resolutions, the Assembly referred this one to the Task Force on Ministry for further investigation, with a report to be presented to the 1979 gathering in St. Louis.

After the Assembly, General Minister and President Kenneth L. Teagarden surveyed the chairs of all regional commissions on ministry. The results indicated that none had knowingly ordained a candidate who claimed to be homosexual, but neither had they asked about lifestyle or sexual orientation. The chairs had no intention of ordaining a homosexual person, yet they did not want the General Assembly establishing detailed definitions of emotional stability or standards of morality that would be difficult to follow. None of the regions had studied the issue of homosexuality, and few had any process in place for counseling and guidance.

During 1978, several regions considered resolutions prohibiting the ordination of homosexual candidates. That summer a civil court judge ruled in a suit against Lexington Theological Seminary that it must award a degree to a homosexual candidate who had completed all academic requirements since the seminary's statement of requirements did not support its refusal. In that environment of heightened tension, Disciples opened their 1979 General Assembly.

The report of the Task Force on Ministry noted that some Disciples now affirmed that homosexual practice could be an appropriate way of life for consenting adult Christians. It also noted that while the 1971 *Policies and Criteria for the Order of the Ministry* had established qualifications for ministry, interpreting and implementing them was the responsibility of regions in collaboration with their congregations.

In light of these findings, the Task Force reached a twofold conclusion: "(a) Recent studies have not convinced us nor the Church at large that ordaining persons who engage in homosexual practices is in accord with God's will for the Church, and (b) The Christian Church (Disciples of Christ) intends to continue its current pattern of assigning responsibility to the regions with respect to the nurture, certification and ordination of ministers." By affirming established procedures for examining candidates for ministry at the regional level, the Task Force, while not supporting the ordination of homosexuals, left open the door for regions to choose to ordain gay and lesbian candidates. The 1979 Assembly approved the Task Force's report.

The issue of homosexuality and ordination re-emerged at the 1991 Tulsa Assembly in the nomination of Michael Kinnamon for General Minister and President. Kinnamon, the author of numerous books and articles on ecumenism, had been dean and professor of theology and ecumenical studies at Lexington Theological Seminary since 1988. Earlier he had taught on the faculty of Christian Theological Seminary (1983-1988) and served as executive secretary of the World Council of Churches Commission on Faith and Order (1980-83). For many Disciples his nomination was exhilarating, but for others his inclusive stand on the ordination of gays and lesbians was unacceptable.[118] Kinnamon failed to achieve the two-thirds majority approval required for election by sixty-five votes—less than two-thirds of one percent.

The discussion before the vote, however, had elicited statements so hurtful to many delegates and Assembly participants that the Assembly passed a resolution calling the church to a season of prayer for healing and guidance. It asked Disciples to engage in reflection and education regarding issues such as biblical interpretation and the church's response to homosexual persons and those who affirm them, and to commit to work together toward a clear vision of the inclusivity of Christ's church.

By the first decade of the twenty-first century, two regions were known to openly ordain gay and lesbian candidates, while others refused to ordain such candidates. Still others operated with a "Don't Ask/Don't Tell" policy. Many Disciples expressed support for gay, lesbian, bisexual, and transgender persons. The Disciples *Year Book* listed the Gay, Lesbian and Affirming Disciples Alliance (GLAD), formed in 1979, under "Other Organizations" sponsored by the Office of the General Minister and President. Nevertheless, only a few Disciples congregations had called an openly gay or lesbian person as their minister.

Among Churches of Christ relatively little was published that overtly engaged the issues of abortion or homosexuality. In a 1996 *Restoration Quarterly* article, Craig Churchill of Abilene Christian University asserted that the group's response to the 1973 *Roe v. Wade* Supreme Court decision had been woefully inadequate. While *Integrity* and *Mission* journals had printed a few articles examining both sides of the issue, most writers in Churches of Christ strongly rejected abortion as evil but without providing an adequate theological basis or recognizing its complexities. Among possible reasons for the lack of adequate discussion of abortion in Churches of Christ, Churchill proposed, was the view held by many that it was a social or political issue rather than a theological one, coupled with conservative aversion toward talking openly about any matter of sexuality.[119]

As in the case of abortion, Churches of Christ almost universally regarded homosexuality as contrary to God's will. While most writers agreed that all humans deserved to be treated with dignity and guaranteed equal treatment under law, they saw homosexual practice as a sinful lifestyle choice. An unofficial "Church of Christ Internet Ministries" website answered the question "Is Homosexuality acceptable within the church of Christ?" by quoting biblical passages in Genesis, Leviticus, Romans, and 1 Corinthians, insisting that a homosexual lifestyle was unacceptable to God and the church. Homosexuals could, the author stated, repent and be forgiven of the sin, but homosexual practice was unjustifiable under any circumstances.[120]

As in every religious body, however, closeted gay and lesbian persons had always been members of Churches of Christ. In 1979, a group of homosexual members in Houston, Texas, began an organization named "A Cappella Chorus" to provide support and fellowship for one another. Soon chapters formed in Los Angeles, Nashville, Seattle, Tampa, and other urban areas, and the group began publication of a newsletter titled *Holy Kiss* that by the late 1980s was distributed to gay members of Churches of Christ in twenty-seven states, South Africa, and Micronesia. In a tract published in the mid-1980s, the group pled for acceptance in Churches of Christ.

> How disappointing it is, when we are rejected not only by the world, but also by the Church that has taught and nurtured us. It is difficult, if not impossible, to fully celebrate Christ in our lives, let alone encourage others to know the selfless love of Jesus, in a church that rejects, or at best ignores, Christians because of the norms of general society.[121]

In a 1979 interview by Lynn Mitchell with leaders of the A Cappella Chorus, a spokesperson explained that one of the group's goals was to reclaim for the church those who had "dropped out" because of their sexual orientation. They also sought to foster discussion in Churches of Christ about what Scripture actually said about homosexuality. Another leader confessed that the attitude he had experienced in Churches of Christ had alienated him from the fellowship. Still another described the pain of being publicly disfellowshipped by a Houston congregation. Mitchell's report concluded with one member's hope that A Cappella Chorus could provide "the fellowship and love that the redemptive community of the church should be providing."[122]

In the mid-1980s Leroy Garrett provided brief notices of A Cappella Chorus and its publication *Holy Kiss* in the section of his *Restoration Review* titled "Our Changing

World."[123] After that, however, the group seemed to disappear. Possibly reflecting the general erosion of denominational loyalty in American Christianity, many who had been active in A Cappella Chorus may have left Churches of Christ for groups such as the Universal Fellowship of Metropolitan Community Churches begun in 1968, or open and affirming congregations of mainstream denominations.

In the early twenty-first century, the Lesbian-Gay-Bisexual-Transgender (LGBT) activist group Soulforce conducted Equality Rides by visiting schools in the United States with anti-homosexual policies. The group visited several universities affiliated with Churches of Christ, including Abilene Christian University in 2006 and 2010, Pepperdine University in 2007, and Heritage Christian University in Florence, Alabama, in 2008.[124] While ACU and Pepperdine engaged Equality Ride participants in university-organized dialogue, Heritage Christian formally refused to meet with the group and ordered three of the riders arrested for trespassing.[125] While Soulforce expressed gratitude to ACU "for the dialogue we have had here with students, faculty and administration," the group still labeled the campus unsafe for LGBT students because of its continuing anti-gay policies.[126]

In the 1990s Sally Gary, then professor of Communication at Abilene Christian University, began CenterPeace, an organization that invited "all men and women who experience same-sex attraction to the table, wherever we may be in our thinking on this issue." Though regarding homosexuality as a type of human brokenness, CenterPeace explicitly rejected "condemnation of God's children who experience same-sex attraction" and welcomed all who acknowledged Christ to "grace-filled dialogue and respectful disagreement." CenterPeace sponsored national conferences and retreats for Christians with same-sex attraction, as well as their ministers and parents.[127]

Among Christian Churches/Churches of Christ, growing fear that abortion and homosexuality threatened the moral foundations of the nation and its families led many leaders and members into political organizing. When Operation Rescue moved its "Summer of Mercy" anti-abortion protests to Wichita, Kansas, in 1991, two large Christian Churches lent their aid to the effort. Pastors Gene Carlson of the 7,000-member Westlink Christian Church and Joe Wright of the equally large Central Christian Church helped organize sit-ins at a local abortion clinic. Carlson was arrested as leader of a group composed of forty ministers and hundreds of

parishioners that blocked access to the clinic.[128] Lincoln Christian University's Imago Dei student organization participated annually in the March for Life from 1989-2008, with University President Charles McNeely and Professor Robert Rea leading the event's opening prayer in different years. Imago Dei also hosted national anti-abortion speakers and spearheaded meetings for Illinois marchers with members of Congress.[129]

Flyer advertising gatherings for homosexual members of Churches of Christ at the Montrose Church of Christ in Houston, Texas, around 1979. The congregation also published the globally circulated paper, *Holy Kiss.* (*Courtesy Center for Restoration Studies, Abilene Christian University*)

Writers in Christian Churches/Churches of Christ sought to keep abortion visible as a major moral issue confronting American society in the late twentieth century. The *Christian Standard* published scores of articles that studied the issue from both moral and biblical standpoints and rallied churches to oppose abortion rights. Some writers urged churches not to label women who had undergone abortions as "murderers," but to acknowledge the anguish of especially poor and minority women who had experienced the pain of an unwanted pregnancy. They also insisted that churches should support ministries that aided single mothers who had chosen to have their babies rather than to abort them.[130]

Others, however, focused on what they regarded as the self-evident immorality of abortion, defending the full humanity of unborn infants created in the image of God.[131] Some denounced what they viewed as the pro-choice lobby's co-opting of the term "choice," insisting that biblically virtuous free "choice" is one thing and the humanistic invention of "reproductive rights" quite another.[132] On the whole, views on abortion in Christian Churches/Churches of Christ reflected those of American Evangelical groups, upholding the "sanctity of life" and dismissing the civil rights of pregnant women as a legitimate issue.

The matter of gay and lesbian rights also prompted some leaders in Christian Church/Churches of Christ to enter politics. After the Massachusetts Supreme Court ruled in favor of same-sex marriage in 2004, religious right groups sponsored a series of successful referenda to ban the practice in their states. Russell Johnson of Fairfield Christian Church near Columbus, Ohio, organized the Ohio Restoration Project, an initiative to enlist 1,000 "patriot pastors" who would oppose same-sex marriage and gay and lesbian rights. The effort enlisted nine hundred supporters within ten weeks, inspiring similar networks in Texas and Pennsylvania.[133] During the 2004 election, Southeast Christian Church in Louisville promoted a similar movement in Kentucky, running ads and articles in the church's 40,000-circulation paper, the *Southeast Outlook*, asking residents to vote for a "Marriage Protection Amendment" to ban same-sex marriages.[134]

At the beginning of the twenty-first century most members of Christian Churches/Churches of Christ reflected conservative Evangelical positions on sexuality. The same was true of Churches of Christ, though they had been less involved in political efforts opposing abortion and same-sex marriages than Christian Churches/Churches of Christ. While Disciples were much more diverse in their stances on these issues, all three streams manifested an increasing sense of the need to consider how best to respond to the brokenness and complexity of the world in faithfulness to the gospel of Jesus Christ.

Religious Pluralism

Though religious pluralism had long been a feature of life in the United States, Americans became increasingly aware of religious diversity following World War II.

Disciples leadership responded by seeking to strengthen interfaith relationships and foster understanding of other religious traditions. Judaism received particular attention in response to the role of Christianity in the Holocaust. The 1978 General Assembly affirmed the kinship of Christian and Jewish faith, applauded courses in Jewish Studies at Disciples schools, and resolved to promote greater dialogue between Christians and Jews to prevent the reoccurrence of events such as the Holocaust.

Such an open stance toward other religions, however, raised fears in some Disciples of compromise of Christian faith. In 1987 a group called Disciple Renewal submitted resolution 8728 to the General Assembly declaring Jesus Christ as the only path to salvation. Believing the resolution's drafters designed it to challenge efforts at interfaith dialogue and provoke divisive debate, Assembly leaders referred the resolution to the Commission on Theology of the Council on Christian Unity to prepare a report for the next Assembly.[135] The Commission's 1989 report, though affirming salvation through Christ, also stated that "eligibility for salvation is God's decision... human judgment cannot place parameters on the grace of God." The Assembly adopted the report with the provision that it did not speak for everyone in the church.

The 1989 Assembly also passed a resolution encouraging interfaith dialogue between Christians and Jews and requesting the Commission on Theology to prepare a report on Jewish-Christian relations for the 1991 General Assembly. That report called for further prayer, study, and conversations by Disciples with their Jewish neighbors at the local, regional, and national levels. In 1993 the Assembly accepted a report from the Commission on Theology that encouraged congregational involvement in restudying the church's relation to Jews on biblical, historical, and theological grounds, but stopped short of condemning the evangelization of Jews.

Clark M. Williamson, Professor of Theology at Christian Theological Seminary, was a major influence on Disciples attitudes toward Jewish-Christian relations. His 1982 book, *Has God Rejected His People?* focused on Christian anti-Jewish ideology, offering practical and theological proposals for overcoming it. In 1993 Williamson argued in *A Guest in the House of Israel* that "the mission of the church is one that it shares *with* the people Israel."[136] As a member of the Christian Scholars Group on Christian-Jewish Relations, Williamson helped draft the 2002 statement "A Sacred Obligation: Rethinking Christian Faith in Relation to Judaism and the Jewish

People" that affirmed Jews were still in a saving covenant with God and rejected Christian missions to convert Jews.[137]

Prompted partly by the September 11, 2001, terrorist attacks, the Disciples Council on Christian Unity and the Council for Ecumenism of the United Church of Christ convened a Consultation on Interreligious Dialogue and Relations in October 2002. The gathering focused on two questions: "Why engage in interfaith dialogue?" and "What are the special gifts we can bring to such work?" Subsequent meetings produced "Disciples of Christ and Interreligious Engagement," commended for teaching and study by the 2005 General Assembly.[138] The report declared that though sent into the world to testify to the love of God through Christ, Disciples had "not always embodied this love in our relationships with people of other religious traditions." It expressed the call "to develop mutual respect, and to discover areas of commonality" with people of other faiths, and to balance evangelism with receptivity to the witnessing of others for the sake of truth. For most Disciples at the beginning of the twenty-first century, neither Jews nor Muslims were targets of evangelization.

The response of members of Churches of Christ to the increase of non-Christian religions, particularly Islam, often reflected the concerns growing from the events of September 11, 2001. Some writers expressed deep fear that Islam's growth was a major threat both to the United States and to Christianity. One congregation's website supplied links to anti-Islamic articles, including one that began with the warning "The events of September 11, 2001 were not unique from an Islamic perspective. Islam has been an aggressive violent religion from the very beginning. Islam was born in bloodshed, nurtured in violence, and matured in conquest. Why should anyone think it has changed?"[139]

Others, while viewing Muslims as objects of evangelism, refused to fall into fearful condemnatory judgments. Two professors, both with extensive mission experience and personal interaction with Islam, published books dealing with Christianity and Islam at the beginning of the twenty-first century. Evertt L. Huffard taught at Harding and Freed Hardeman Universities after ministering for thirteen years in Jordan, Israel, and Lebanon. In February 2001, seven months before the 9-11 attacks, Huffard published *Christ or the Qur'an?*, a primer for members of Churches of Christ on basic Islam. He related his experience of Muslim hospitality and honesty and explained why tensions existed between Islam and Christianity. He compared Muslim and Western worldviews, showing noble commitments and a deep attitude of respect for others in Islam in contrast to Western secularism and individualism.[140]

In 2002, in direct response to the September 11 attacks, Glover Shipp, longtime missionary in Brazil, managing editor of the *Christian Chronicle* and professor at Oklahoma Christian University, published *Christianity and Islam: Bridging Two Worlds*. While admitting his own imperfect understanding of the Muslim mindset, Shipp drew on decades of research and teaching on world religions to give an overview similar to the one published the year before by Huffard. Shipp explained Islamic beliefs in a straightforward and often positive way, focusing on strategies for winning Muslims to Christ. He closed with the hope that the book would help Christians prepare "for a truly *spiritual* holy war for the souls of [Islam's] 1.2 billion disciples worldwide."[141]

In 2011, Lee Camp of Lipscomb University published a penetrating study titled *Who Is My Enemy? Questions American Christians Must Face About Islam—and Themselves*. He contended that just as Christians have acted in violent ways without making Christianity and all Christians violent and bloodthirsty, the same is true of Islam. Camp called for a reexamination of the teachings of both Christianity and Islam regarding war and peacemaking.[142]

Another approach was seen in the work of Lynn Mitchell, long-time minister and elder in Churches of Christ, who served as Resident Scholar in Religion at the University of Houston beginning in 1985. Mitchell served on the Houston Committee for Muslim-Christian Dialogue and was a founding board member of the Institute for Interfaith Dialog. The institute's roots were in a moderate Muslim movement founded by Turkish leader Fethullah Gülen to promote understanding and peaceful relations between Americans and Islamic peoples worldwide. Mitchell also helped organize the Gülen Institute on the Campus of the University of Houston to promote research into the Muslim leader's religious and philosophical principles.[143]

Some universities associated with Churches of Christ also began limited attempts at interfaith dialogue in the early twenty-first century. The 2010 annual "Summit" at Abilene Christian University offered sessions featuring interaction between a Muslim scholar and a Christian faculty member. Publicity urged the importance of "honest but respectful conversation between people of different religions" to promote mutual understanding in a polarized world. Classes focused on questions Christians have for Muslims and how Christians and Muslims view Muhammad.[144] In addition, faculty and administrators at Lubbock (Texas) Christian University formed positive relations with the Gülen Institute for Interfaith Dialog, participating in conferences and travel programs designed to introduce students and others to that form of moderate Islam.[145]

Among responses of Christian Churches/Churches of Christ to the growth of non-Christian religions in North America was the 1994 hiring of Robert C. Douglas as Professor of Intercultural Studies at Lincoln Christian College (now University). Douglas had previously served for eight years as Executive Director of the Zwemer Institute of Muslim Studies in Pasadena, California. In the wake of the events of September 11, 2001, many congregations invited Douglas to speak on Islam. His approach was to teach the basic principles of Islam, to point out that many Muslims reject radical jihad, to challenge Christians to understand Islam before reacting to it, and to remind them that their interactions with Muslims should witness to the grace of God in Jesus Christ.[146]

Conclusion

The diversity of responses among Stone-Campbell Christians since the 1960s to issues of race, war, ethnic diversity, gender equality, sexuality, and religious pluralism is a case study in the pluralism and polarization of United States culture. Stone-Campbell Christians were united on none of these matters. Differences could be seen in widely varying attitudes toward social action, the roles of women and men and related issues of sexuality, and American nationalism, both within and among the North American streams. Often members came to see themselves as having more in common with people in other parts of the culture (i.e., American Evangelicals or mainline churches) than with other Stone-Campbell Christians. At the same time, certain aspects of their common heritage were evident in a continuing witness to peace, and the understanding that the Christian's call in interfaith dialogue is to witness to God's love revealed in Jesus Christ. In the midst of great social and cultural upheaval, important theological and institutional shifts also were occurring in each of the North American streams of the Stone-Campbell Movement.

12

Significant Theological & Institutional Shifts in the United States

The massive social changes that began in the 1960s combined with the distinctive histories of each of the major U. S. streams of the Stone-Campbell Movement to produce identity-shaping shifts. A growing number of leaders in Churches of Christ challenged the dominant positive law approach to Scripture and Christianity, calling members to reclaim a focus on God's work and grace rather than human attainment of precise doctrines and practices. Other leaders in Churches of Christ rejected this call, raising the possibility of yet another division. Many in Christian Churches/Churches of Christ redirected their energies away from defending what they viewed as the restored church to a passion for evangelism and church growth. This passion produced a phenomenal number of mega-churches—congregations with a sustained weekly attendance of 2000 or more. The Christian Church (Disciples of Christ) established priorities in 2001 that combined becoming an anti-racist/pro-reconciling church with the establishment of 1,000 new congregations and the revitalization of 1,000 existing ones by the year 2020. These shifts perhaps more than anything else defined these streams at the beginning of the twenty-first century.

A Rediscovery of Grace in Churches of Christ

Major shifts in Churches of Christ in the late twentieth century were rooted in the body's development of new perspectives on Scripture. At least two factors shaped this change: revulsion by many toward the legalistic haggling of previous years, and a heightened concern to address racial justice, poverty, and war. Many leaders rejected the body's past resistance to engage social issues, looked at the Bible through lenses other than those of the positive law hermeneutic, and reexamined their

history in ways that challenged traditional views and re-appropriated forgotten commitments.

A key factor that sparked this serious reevaluation of traditional positions was increased access to graduate theological education for members of Churches of Christ. Permanent graduate theological programs in schools affiliated with Churches of Christ began under the direction of W. B. West, Jr. (1907-1994), first at Pepperdine in 1944 and then at Harding in 1952. West received a Th.D. from the University of Southern California in 1943, the first person from Churches of Christ to receive a doctorate in theological studies. Two brothers, LeMoine G. Lewis (1916-1987) and Jack P. Lewis, were also major figures in the rise of graduate theological education among Churches of Christ, LeMoine at Abilene Christian University and Jack at Harding. Both received doctorates from Harvard University in the 1940s, in Church History and New Testament respectively, and Jack also received a doctorate in Old Testament from Hebrew Union College. These pioneers encouraged others to pursue doctoral work, and during the 1950s and 1960s a growing number of graduate-trained scholars returned to teach at schools affiliated with Churches of Christ.

In 1958, Abraham Malherbe and Pat Harrell founded *Restoration Quarterly* (*RQ*) as a place for dialogue among this growing community of scholars. *RQ* published several articles that anticipated a hermeneutical shift in Churches of Christ, one of the most significant being Roy Bowen Ward's "'The Restoration Principle': A Critical Analysis." Reflecting some of the same impulses seen in the Disciples Panel of Scholars *Reformation of Tradition* volume published two years earlier, Ward discussed the development of the canon and the nature of the New

Testament documents, suggesting a move away from the positive law hermeneutic. "The Restoration Principle," he wrote, "is meaningless unless the hermeneutical problem is carefully considered." Ward redefined restoration as understanding the theology of the New Testament and reapplying it to new contexts, not duplication of New Testament forms.[1]

Meanwhile, the rapid growth of Churches of Christ in the 1940s and 1950s had produced a need for more ministers. By the 1960s a significant shortage developed, with the colleges unable keep up with demand. To relieve the pressure, leaders in several cities began "schools of preaching." Though their original purpose was to fill pulpits, those who distrusted the colleges also saw the new schools as "safe" places to train preachers. The first was Sunset School of Preaching in Lubbock, Texas, in 1963, followed quickly by others in Tennessee, Colorado, Texas, and Louisiana. These schools taught only Bible, focused on training evangelistic pulpit ministers, and did not offer accredited degrees. Most students studied for two years and then entered the ministry. In the 1970s 25 percent of preachers among Churches of Christ were educated at these schools.[2]

The difference in ministerial training between the schools of preaching and the colleges significantly affected the discussions regarding biblical interpretation. Schools of preaching generally continued a positive law reading of the Bible that was antagonistic toward higher criticism of the Bible. Most of the colleges, on the other hand, exposed students increasingly to biblical higher criticism. As a result, two hermeneutical groups developed in the 1970s-1980s, each gravitating toward a preferred set of commentaries. More traditional ministers tended to use the *Gospel Advocate Commentary*; more progressive ministers the *Living Word Commentary* published by Sweet Publishing Company.

By the mid-1980s the serious nature of this hermeneutical divide was apparent. In 1986 Rubel Shelly and Monroe Hawley conducted an exchange with William Woodson and Alan E. Highers at Freed-Hardeman University in which Shelly stated that the critical "task of this generation is the serious topic of hermeneutics."[3] Unless the hermeneutical orientation shifts, Shelley contended, Churches of Christ were bound to repeat their divisive history as new issues arose. The traditional hermeneutic of command, example, and inference was, he argued, ill-suited both to the nature of Scripture and the mission of the church.

The battle of the late 1980s and early 1990s was

between the "old" and "new" hermeneutics. Conservatives, defending the positive law reading of the New Testament, decried the arrogance of the scholars who called for a hermeneutical adjustment. Abilene Christian University Bible professor J. D. Thomas (1910-2004) attempted to mediate between the sides while defending the old hermeneutic.[4] In his 1958 study *We Be Brethren*, Thomas had anticipated challenges raised in the 1960s and 1970s against the traditional approach.[5] F. LaGard Smith also entered the fray with a new twist on the old hermeneutic that still retained the positive law orientation.[6]

From 1987 to 1993, hermeneutics became a major topic of discussion at the annual Christian Scholar's Conferences hosted by various universities affiliated with Churches of Christ. The 1989 and 1990 conferences at Pepperdine University and Abilene Christian University were largely dedicated to the topic.[7] Presenters increasingly asserted that the hermeneutical task was a theological one. The shift was not merely one of exegetical method, but of understanding the core gospel and its theological meaning.

One leader in this shift was Thomas H. Olbricht who taught biblical theology at Abilene Christian University (1967-1986) and Pepperdine University (1986-1996). Olbricht sought to reorient the hermeneutical focus of the church away from "command, example, and inference" to "God, Christ, and the Holy Spirit." According to Olbricht, the church needed to recover the central theological message of Scripture in light of the mighty acts of God. Theology was rehearsing those mighty acts rather than dissecting the text through the lens of a positive law hermeneutic. Olbricht's 1996 book *Hearing God's Voice* described his journey to this position through the hermeneutical landscape of post-World War II Churches of Christ.[8]

The hermeneutical discussion did not stay at the academic level, however. It was at the heart of conflicts ranging from "worship wars" to the church's very mission. Debates over worship practices ranging from handclapping to drama in the assembly reflected growing differences in biblical interpretation in local congregations. The shift also renewed discussion about instrumental music in worship as some congregations added instrumental services in the early twenty-first century.[9]

While conservatives feared that any move away from the traditional stance would result in the loss of beliefs and practices essential for remaining true to

Scripture, progressives believed a hermeneutical change was essential for the group's survival. Tim Woodruff, for example, suggested that function is more important than form. "Has our obsession with New Testament patterns and duly authorized forms," he asked, "resulted in a more loving and united community?" He answered that it had not and counseled that "drastic surgery" was needed or the patient would die.[10]

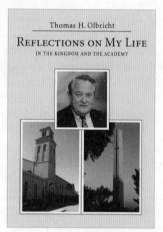

Thomas H. Olbricht helped reshape the understandings of Scripture and the nature of God in mainstream Churches of Christ over a sixty-year career of teaching and ministry. In 2012, Olbricht published an autobiography chronicling his theological journey. *(From Wipf and Stock Publishers)*

Rather than reproducing patterns found in the New Testament through the positive law approach, progressives looked for the theological roots that should shape Christian life. Several books pursued this theological agenda using terms like the "core gospel" and the "crux of the matter."[11] From the 1990s into the twenty-first century, many in Churches of Christ reoriented their theology and ecclesiology away from patterns of positive law to a reclamation of Christ as the center of God's message. This shift involved focusing on the gospel rather than patterns of church as the key element of Christianity.

This move was in some ways a renewal of the grace-oriented perspectives of Lipscomb and Harding and a reformulation of themes K. C. Moser pressed in the 1930s-1960s. These educational and hermeneutical shifts created a new openness to the message of grace that had always been present to some degree in the teaching of leaders like G. C. Brewer, R. C. Bell, Jesse P. Sewell,

R. H. Boll, F. W. Mattox, and Andy T. Richie, Jr., but had not been affirmed publicly by the majority of leaders in twentieth-century Churches of Christ.

The renewal of a grace-oriented theology was symbolized by the personal journey of Rubel Shelly (b. 1945). Trained at Freed-Hardeman College, he absorbed the Texas Tradition from his mentors, including debater and theologian Thomas B. Warren (1920-2000). In the late 1960s and 1970s, Shelley became a major standard bearer for conservative positive law positions. Later describing those early years as graceless sectarianism, his theology began to change in the early 1980s when he encountered the ideas of some of the founding leaders of Churches of Christ, particularly those in the Nashville Bible School (Tennessee) tradition. In March 1983, Shelley made a speech at a Preacher's Forum in Centerville, Tennessee, in which he publicly repudiated his past sectarianism. The following year he published *I Just Want to Be a Christian*, a book that began a storm of controversy between conservatives and progressives.[12] The book's appendix reprinted essays from writers friendly with the Tennessee Tradition's focus on grace and non-sectarianism, such as David Lipscomb, F. D. Srygley, M. C. Kurfees, and G. C. Brewer. Shelley's embrace of these ideas brought them to the attention of a host of ministers and academics in Churches of Christ and provided a welcome relief for many, opening doors for renewed discussion of grace and an expanded view of unity.

An indication of the new openness was a volume edited in 2001 by Lynn Anderson and Leonard Allen titled *The Transforming of a Tradition: Churches of Christ in the New Millennium.*[13] The authors—who included women as well as men—painted a picture of the group's future that included renewal in areas of worship, relationships, mission, and dreams for the entire Stone-Campbell heritage. Rather than attempting to reproduce a static set of New Testament practices, they sought to renew Churches of Christ using the resources of historic Christian spiritual practices as well as "forgotten" voices from within the Stone-Campbell tradition itself.

This renewal was supported by a series of books called "The Heart of the Restoration" published by Abilene Christian University Press and written by ACU theological faculty. The first, *The Crux of the Matter: Crisis, Tradition and the Future of Churches of Christ*, identified central issues for Churches of Christ in the twenty-first century, including the group's sectarian self-concept and shifts in assumptions about the nature and function of Scripture. Other volumes focused on hermeneutics, the Christological foundations of the faith, and what it means to live as the church in the twenty-first century.[14] Another example of the shift was a series of books by theologian John Mark Hicks. Instead of viewing the Lord's Supper, the Sunday assembly, and baptism as legal ordinances regulated by "positive law," he portrayed them as moments of divine encounter and genuine means of grace.[15]

Conservatives, alarmed at these changes, did not remain passive. As early as 1973 preachers and elders in Memphis, Tennessee, called a meeting with representatives of the Highland Church of Christ of Abilene, Texas, who then sponsored the nationally broadcast "Herald of Truth" radio and television program. When the broadcasts had begun in 1952, they had focused on traditional stances in Churches of Christ. Over time, the content of the broadcast had shifted to the felt needs of its audience and how the gospel could address those needs. Widely respected minister and educator Batsell Barrett Baxter (1916-1982), the main speaker for the program during the shift, had roots in the Tennessee Tradition. Though conservatives demanded that the program return to its original message, the Highland representatives refused.[16]

Another indication of growing polarization was the founding of two new journals. As *Firm Foundation* editor Reuel Lemons began to move into the more progressive camp in the early 1970s, rejecting the authority of inference and example, conservatives H. A. (Buster) Dobbs and Bill Cline purchased the paper in 1983.[17] Progressives responded by establishing *Image* in 1985, where Lemmons continued his editorial work. In 1992, Rubel Shelly, Philip Morrison, and Mike Cope launched another journal titled *Wineskins* that reflected the hermeneutical, evangelical, and emerging ecumenical shift within Churches of Christ. Writers addressed issues such as social justice, women's leadership, and ecumenical concerns in new ways.[18]

Two other influential leaders who challenged the exclusivism of Churches of Christ in the late twentieth century were Max Lucado and Rick Atchley. Lucado, a graduate of Abilene Christian University and missionary to Rio de Janeiro, Brazil, for five years, joined the ministry staff of the Oak Hills Church of Christ in San Antonio in 1988. His writing skill soon made him a best-selling author in the Evangelical Christian market. His public association with Christians from other bodies led some in Churches of Christ to question his faithfulness,

while others saw it as a welcome move away from the sectarianism of their past.

In a much-publicized 1996 speech to a Promise Keepers Clergy Conference in Atlanta, Georgia, Lucado urged the 40,000 attendees to embrace a version of a slogan widely used in the nineteenth-century Stone-Campbell Movement—"In essentials unity, in non-essentials liberty, and in all things charity." He called on those present to repent to those around them if they had ever spoken against their denomination. This call, along with similar ones in other Promise Keeper rallies and national forums, led some in Churches of Christ to denounce Lucado and others like Lynn Anderson who openly associated with Christians from other bodies. Lucado increasingly called for a focus on the things that united Christians rather than on the differences.[19]

Rick Atchley was minister of the Richland Hills (later simply "The Hills") Church of Christ near Fort Worth, Texas, the largest congregation in that stream of the Movement, with 6,400 members at the beginning of the twenty-first century. In 2006 Atchley co-authored *Together Again* with Bob Russell, then minister of the largest congregation of the Christian Churches/Churches of Christ in the United States—Southeast in Louisville. The authors consciously published the book to coincide with the centennial of the 1906 U.S. Census of Religious Bodies which listed Churches of Christ and Disciples separately for the first time and issued a strong call for a new recognition of the unity God has created in Christ's church.[20]

Three other distinct but interrelated developments reflected the growing theological tensions over the positive law tradition in Churches of Christ: a brief but sharp controversy over views of the Holy Spirit, shifts in the focus of campus ministry, and the rise of the International Churches of Christ (ICOC). At the 1966 Abilene Christian College Lectureship, four speakers advocated the literal, personal indwelling of the Holy Spirit in the Christian, a direct challenge to the Texas Tradition's teaching that the Spirit worked only through the written word.[21] A flood of articles appeared in the *Firm Foundation* over the next couple of years both opposing and supporting the view.[22] Though the vast majority of members of Churches of Christ who challenged the word-only view did not believe in speaking in tongues or miraculous healing, the Charismatic conversions of several prominent leaders and members, including entertainer Pat Boone, made conservatives even more fearful of abandoning the "word-only" stance.[23]

To many, anyone who believed in an active role of the Spirit apart from Scripture became suspect.

At the same time as the Holy Spirit controversy, a shift in the nature of campus ministry in Churches of Christ made them a target of that suspicion. The dominant model in the group was the Bible Chair, usually sponsored by one or more congregations and offering Bible and religion courses to Christian students in state universities.[24] In contrast, in the 1960s Evangelical groups such as InterVarsity Fellowship and Campus Crusade for Christ focused on training Christian college students to be effective evangelists. In 1967, Jim Bevis and Rex Vermillion of the Broadway Church of Christ in Lubbock, Texas, began a national effort they labeled "Campus Evangelism" with the goal of making "the present college works on state campuses more evangelistic." Drawing from training received from Campus Crusade, they designed an approach that began with persuading students to receive training in personal evangelism, then having them begin aggressive evangelism on their campuses using dorm Bible studies or "Christian bull sessions," and personal testimonies.[25]

Many in Churches of Christ applauded the new emphasis on evangelism. Yet to some, Campus Evangelism with its openness to Evangelical Christians and criticism of traditional practices seemed a threat. Critics also feared that Campus Evangelism was being influenced by charismatic ideas that emphasized religious experience at the expense of doctrinal faithfulness. Growing uneasiness about Campus Evangelism led the Broadway Church to end its support in 1969. Though sponsored for a few more months by the Burke Road Church in Houston, Campus Evangelism as a national organization ended in spring 1970.[26]

Just as Campus Evangelism came into being in 1967, Chuck Lucas began what would become one of the most highly successful of the new campus ministries at the Crossroads Church of Christ in Gainesville, Florida. In the 1970s, Lucas adopted an aggressive discipling approach, borrowed in part from the charismatic movement, which pressured students to spend large amounts of time weekly in personal evangelism and assigned each convert a "discipler" to whom they answered for every aspect of their lives.[27] Lucas's dramatic success in making converts made him a sought-after speaker at campus ministry events, and Crossroads became a model for many, though it drew increasing criticism for manipulative practices.

In 1979, one of Lucas's converts, Kip McKean, became minister of a dying congregation in Lexington,

Massachusetts. Shortly after arriving, he restructured the congregation using the aggressive evangelism and discipling techniques he had learned at Crossroads. Experiencing rapid growth, the Lexington church eventually moved its services to the Boston Gardens and renamed itself the Boston Church of Christ. McKean's vision for evangelism, discipleship, and church growth drew many to the Boston model, and church leaders began training eager evangelists to take their discipleship methods to other places.[28]

At first, the Boston Movement continued to focus much of its effort on college and university students; but when a growing number of people around the country accused it of being a cult, many campuses banned the group.[29] Experiencing only limited success in restructuring existing congregations, the Boston Church of Christ switched its strategy to sending church planters into cities across the United States and the world to establish "faithful" churches. In some ways the group came to reflect an extreme version of the positive law tradition in Churches of Christ in its unrelenting evangelism and condemnation of all other Christian bodies. By the mid-1980s, the group had broken with mainstream Churches of Christ, a schism formally marked by the 1993 incorporation as the International Churches of Christ with headquarters in Los Angeles, California.[30]

While a broad middle remained in the 1990s, twenty-first-century Churches of Christ reflected a clear bifurcation between conservatives and progressives. The Freed-Hardeman Lectureship and smaller regional lectureships, along with publications like *Spiritual Sword*, *Firm Foundation*, and *Gospel Advocate* represented the former, though not themselves identical on every issue. Publishing houses such as ACU Press and Leafwood publishers represented the latter, along with the Pepperdine and Abilene Christian University Lectureships, *New Wineskins* and *Leaven* journals, as well as the theological faculties of several universities and leaders of many large urban and suburban congregations.

Progressives increasingly focused on aspects of the Christian faith that had often been neglected or opposed in Churches of Christ. Urban ministries gave significant attention to social justice and attacked institutionalized racism. Women exercised increasing leadership in the public assemblies, and a growing liturgical freedom allowed new ways to worship and proclaim the gospel. Many became aware of the rich insights of the twenty centuries of Christian history, including the traditions of Christian spiritual formation as churches sought to deepen their relationship with God. Progressives claimed these moves were rooted in both Scripture and the Stone-Campbell heritage of freedom and unity.

Conservatives were active in evangelizing their neighbors, and were heavily involved in global missions. They continued to promote the values of the Texas Tradition through lectureships, periodicals, electronic media, and gospel meetings. They generally opposed church involvement in social justice, rejected a larger role for women in the public assembly, were suspicious of the disciplines of spiritual formation rooted in Christian history, and opposed changes in worship style.

The relative strength of each of these positions was difficult to measure. Each had its own schools, papers, and spokespersons; and each had its own ministries and world mission work. A survey of ministers in Churches of Christ taken in 2000 indicated that those who identified themselves as theologically "moderate" served congregations that together made up slightly more than 40 percent of members of the group. Just over 50 percent of the total membership was in congregations whose ministers labeled themselves as "conservative." The study also showed that over half of congregations with "conservative" ministers had experienced decline during the years immediately before the survey, as compared to 40 percent of churches with "moderate" ministers. Thirty-seven percent of the churches with "moderate" ministers had grown in size as compared to slightly over 30 percent of those with "conservative" preachers.[31]

Despite what appeared to be increasing polarization, at the beginning of the twenty-first century support for relief agencies such as Global Samaritan of Abilene, Texas, and Churches of Christ Disaster Relief in Nashville, Tennessee, revealed a significant degree of ongoing cooperation between conservatives and progressives and a strong sense of Christian responsibility to serve the hurting of the world. A number of leaders still held hope for a "broad middle" that would find unity "rooted in the person and work of Christ."[32]

The Growth of Mega-Churches in the Christian Churches/Churches of Christ

While congregations in Christian Churches/Churches of Christ had largely been defined by the pursuit of separatism and theological purity from the 1920s-1960s, new evangelistic movements transformed these churches after 1971. Five events paved the way for the ascendency of the Neo-Restorationist/Neo-Evangelical group in this stream. Perhaps the most significant was the listing of Christian Churches/Churches of Christ as separate

from the Christian Church (Disciples of Christ) in the *Yearbook of American and Canadian Churches* in 1971. For many, this represented the last step in the long process of division.[33] Without Disciples institutions against which to define themselves, Christian Churches/Churches of Christ looked for a new, more positive rationale for their existence.

Four additional events proved critical in the reshaping of Christian Churches/Churches of Christ. First, in 1969, a group of church planters meeting at Great Lakes Bible College in Lansing, Michigan, organized what would become the National New Church Conference.[34] The next year, former Disciples missionary Donald A. McGavran (1897-1990) popularized his scholarly insights on church growth in a seminal work, *Understanding Church Growth.*[35] Then in 1973, the Supreme Court legalized abortion in its *Roe v. Wade* decision, helping ignite the Religious Right in American politics and pulling some leaders in Christian Churches/Churches of Christ into new political alliances with other conservative Christians. Finally, in 1976, Bob Russell's Southeast Christian Church passed 1,000 in attendance as the congregation pioneered the mega-church style of evangelism among Christian Churches/Churches of Christ.[36]

A major source of strategy and inspiration for the new church growth initiative in Christian Churches/Churches of Christ came from the theories of Donald McGavran. His ideas had emerged from dissatisfaction with the meager results of Disciples' missionary efforts in India, where both his parents and grandparents had served. Mainline missions, including Disciples, proclaimed the gospel primarily through education, preaching, and medical care, justifying their small results by maintaining that their job was to "sow the seed" and wait for God to produce the fruit. McGavran disagreed and argued that missionaries should pare down their social ministries and focus on native-led evangelism among specific tribes and ethnic communities, which he called "people groups."[37]

First publishing his ideas in *Bridges to God* (1955), McGavran founded the Institute of Church Growth in 1961 at Northwest Christian College, now Northwest Christian University, in Eugene, Oregon. In 1965, he accepted Fuller Theological Seminary's invitation to become the founding dean of the School of World Mission and moved his Institute to Pasadena, California. Initially influencing mostly missionaries, McGavran's ideas appealed to U. S. church leaders after the 1970 release of *Understanding Church Growth.* McGavran presented his ideas to pastors at the first annual Church

Growth Colloquium sponsored by Emmanuel School of Religion, now Emmanuel Christian Seminary, and Milligan College in June 1969. The four-day conference addressed topics such as "The Scientifically Measurable Factors of Church Growth," "Why Churches Stop Growing," and "How to Activate Churches."[38]

McGavran's ideas found a receptive audience among churches and pastors interested in a new approach to reaching their communities with the gospel. Church growth theory encouraged evangelism that focused on reaching one homogenous segment of a community—a "people group." Those who adopted this idea self-consciously sought to present the gospel in culturally relevant and nuanced ways that led to concrete results. Whereas an older generation of ministers in Christian Churches/Churches of Christ had grown up focused on doctrinal purity, the church growth generation focused on practical results—the number of converts.[39]

Church planting networks assumed an increasingly important role in Christian Churches/Churches of Christ after the first National Colloquy on New Church Evangelism in May 1969. In many ways this meeting of thirty-eight ministers at Great Lakes Bible College marked a new chapter in the group's history. The question posed to those in attendance was "How Can the Church of Christ Keep Up With a Growing Population that Will Double in the Next 30 Years?" The ministers concluded that the Christian Churches/Churches of Christ needed a "crash program" in how to plant new churches. The group began holding annual conferences they would eventually name the National New Church Conference (NNCC).[40]

Two other institutions provided important models that strengthened this church-planting movement. On the East Coast, Orchard Group brought together experienced church planters Tom Jones and Paul Williams in 1992 to launch the Princeton Community Church. Inspired by what they had learned from a Rick Warren/Saddleback conference, the sponsors of the Princeton launch team experimented with new methods such as seeking contributions from several church plant agencies and local churches, using a large team of four families, and launching a professional marketing campaign. The opening service of the Princeton church attracted 400 people, an unheard of number in 1992. In the process of launching the Princeton Church, the participating groups created a new model for church planting that emphasized the importance of cooperation and teamwork. On the West Coast, the Northern California Evangelistic

Association began using a similar approach, and by the late 1990s was averaging one new church every month. In 2003, the Northern California Evangelistic Association merged with the Church Development Fund to create Stadia: New Church Strategies. With this move, the regional body became a national church-planting agency.

In 2005, planners for the NNCC, later renamed the Exponential Conference, began to invite leaders from other Evangelical denominations, and the next year nine hundred people attended. Numbers continued to surge, with three thousand from thirty-five different groups and denominations attending in 2008. Conference director Brent Foulke explained how the Exponential Conference fulfilled Restoration ideals: "Church planters share a hunger to introduce people to Christ, and that common mission unites us. The conference really is a safe place to share ideas without denominational drums being beaten. Our autonomy ideally positions us as a conduit to bring this event, and that kind of collaboration is what our movement is all about."[41] This attitude, which made Christ and a shared evangelistic mission central rather than a restored church, marked a major change of self-concept in this part of Christian Churches/Churches of Christ.[42]

Though connected in important ways to the church growth movement, the development of mega-churches in American Christianity took on a character of its own. Bob Russell's ministry at Southeast Christian Church in Louisville, Kentucky, illustrates the way mega-churches began reshaping Christian Churches/Churches of Christ in the 1970s and 1980s. Russell led Southeast from a weekly attendance of around a hundred with one minister in 1966, to 18,000 in attendance and a staff of four hundred in 2006 at his retirement. That year, Southeast was listed as the largest church in Kentucky and the sixth largest in the United States. Over the years, Russell developed a board of elders that included businessmen and successful executives from companies like Procter & Gamble and UPS. In 1998 the church moved into a one hundred-acre building complex located at the intersection of two major highways.[43]

Soon after weekly attendance reached 1,000 in 1976, Russell began hosting other large church pastors in the Christian Churches/Churches of Christ for a yearly three-day conference, providing a new model of ministry to aspiring ministers.[44] By the early twenty-first century, 4 percent of all mega-churches were affiliated with Christian Churches/Churches of Christ—more than any other denomination in the United States.[45]

Mega-churches among Christian Churches/Churches of Christ engaged their culture primarily in two ways. First, some mega-church pastors became heavily involved in political action, especially when they perceived a need to defend what they viewed as the Christian moral foundations of America on issues involving sexuality. Though press coverage often made it seem that all mega-churches were involved in conservative politics, in fact, many avoided political statements completely. Second, many mega-church pastors used social surveys and demographic research to address unmet community needs and bridge divisions.[46] Church planting networks eventually began to recognize that whites living in the Midwest represented a declining percentage of the American population, while African American, Hispanic, and Asian populations were increasing. They also saw that younger people, even if conservative, were not staying in traditional churches. Church planting became a way to respond to those realities.[47]

The influence of "missional" and "emergent" church thinkers among Christian Churches/Churches of Christ further shaped and added strength to the church planting movement after 1995. Missional thinkers argued that the church, rather than attracting people to its programs, should go out into the community, meeting needs and bringing the presence of Christ into unfamiliar territory. Emergent church thinkers wrote about the need for new churches to experiment with post-modern worship styles to reach younger generations.[48]

While Christian Churches/Churches of Christ did not have a denominational office or assembly that issued social resolutions, many church plants were at the cutting-edge of the church's engagement with the wider culture. Leaders increasingly saw church planting as a way to attract young people disinterested in both traditional and mega-church styles of worship. While mega-church ministers often gathered similar people into a safe social space, a new generation of church planting ministers often assumed Christians should enter unfamiliar territory, take risks, and cross cultural boundaries. Many church planters sought to reach out to new populations—underrepresented ethnic communities, secularists, and the poor—people they had not targeted before.[49] Though the largest church planting groups focused their energies on growing white suburbs, others targeted African Americans and Hispanics in urban areas. In 1988, African American ministers formed the Fellowship of Christians in Urban Services (FOCUS) to rally Christian Churches/Churches of Christ to the cause of urban ministry, particularly among the African American population.[50]

However, building bridges to the African American community proved difficult for Christian Churches/Churches of Christ. Though many leaders looked for ways to eliminate barriers, they continued to reflect the group's dominant white makeup.[51] A number of African American leaders and supporters of racial reconciliation met in 1997 and petitioned the Executive Committee of the North American Christian Convention (NACC) for a meeting to address their concerns. As a result, the Executive Committee agreed that they would always have a person of color on their Committee, would always include at least one person of color on the platform, and pledged to address the history of discrimination against African Americans by NACC leaders at the 1998 Convention. When NACC leaders failed to issue a detailed apology at the 1998 Convention, some African American leaders resolved not to return. Others, however, saw the modest steps as the beginning of a more hopeful future. Articles on racial reconciliation followed in the *Christian Standard*, *Lookout*, and *Horizons* magazines.[52] At the beginning of the twenty-first century there were an estimated one hundred predominantly African American congregations in Christian Churches/Churches of Christ with a combined membership of 5,000.

The missional movement of the late 1990s saw church planters targeting areas outside the Midwest and experimenting with interracial congregations, innovative worship music, provocative sermons, and creating nonprofits to minister to physical needs. Church plants in Sterling, Virginia, and Gaithersburg, Maryland, reflected these impulses. In New Orleans, a number of church plants sought to address the physical, social, and spiritual needs of their communities. Responding to the devastation of Hurricane Katrina in 2005, each provided a place to serve the community's physical needs before launching public worship services. Members of both Christian Churches/Churches of Christ and Churches of Christ partnered to start the African American New Orleans East Church, another indication of the new ways of thinking for many in this stream of the Stone-Campbell Movement.[53]

The 2020 Vision of the Christian Church (Disciples of Christ)

Like other mainline Protestant denominations, Disciples membership dropped dramatically in the 1960s and following. From 1945 to 1965 Disciples established new congregations by a technique colloquially known as "swarming." A "swarm" would be composed of members willing to leave their previous congregation to form a new church. The swarm, like bees, would create a new "colony," usually located in the vicinity where the swarming members lived. Sometimes a city association or board coordinated the swarming, but often a single church, and sometimes two or three, also used this technique.[54]

However, by the mid-1960s the rate of new church starts using this practice slowed significantly. Regional organizations, which had helped to fund new church starts in the previous decade, were overextended. Offerings received by the regions often largely went to repay outstanding loans for existing church plants, leaving little money for new efforts. In addition, the Civil Rights Movement and the urban crisis commanded the attention of many congregations, directing financial resources and programs to the work of social reconciliation.[55]

Most significantly for the Disciples and churches such as the Methodists, Episcopalians, and Presbyterians, large numbers of America's most privileged college youth, disillusioned by the nation's participation in the Vietnam War, stopped going to church in the 1960s. Unlike earlier generations of youth who often stopped going to church during their college years, this group did not return.[56] The result was a significant loss in Disciples congregations of members from the Baby Boom generation—persons born between 1945 and 1965. Established congregations experiencing membership declines were not inclined to send remaining members to help establish a new congregation.

In 1971, the Louisville General Assembly passed Resolution 44, emphasizing development and renewal of existing congregations rather than starting new ones— effectively calling to a halt the planting of new churches. In response to this move, the National Convocation in 1973 issued a strong call for the establishment of new black congregations. This appeal was repeated and approved by the 1975 San Antonio General Assembly in Resolution 7569, which called Church Extension to begin a new program for planting churches. The driving factor that had prompted the National Convocation to make the proposal initially was their contention, stated in the resolution, that Disciples had "yet to mount an effective evangelistic thrust toward the masses of Blacks in urbanized areas."

The result of the San Antonio action was a consultation in spring 1979, which brought together seventy-five persons, including representatives from regional and general ministries and other selected individuals, both lay and ordained. The consultation determined that the new program would focus on reaching the unchurched in the United States and Canada. Guidelines for the new church plants stated that 15 percent of new congregations should be black, 10 percent Hispanic, 5 percent other ethnic groups, and 70 percent white. Church Extension and Homeland Ministries were to create a New Congregation Establishment Committee that would include representatives of regions, Disciples Hispanic and Asian-American organizations, the National Convocation, and the Church of Christ, Disciples of Christ.[57]

Soon known as Church Advance Now (CAN), this 1980s program employed pastor/developers (P/Ds), rather than the swarming technique of the post-World War II era. The initial goal was to have eight P/Ds trained and available by spring 1982. Raymond E. Brown, of the Church Extension staff, described the desired qualities of a P/D in the December 6, 1980, issue of *The Disciple* as "the ability to persevere, actively support the church beyond the congregation, be sensitive to the feelings of others, deal constructively with conflict, adapt well to new situations, have good administrative skills, be optimistic and a good organizer." He added that the program was seeking primarily experienced pastors who had served successful pastorates.[58] The committee set a goal of starting a minimum of one hundred new congregations during the 1980s. James L. Powell, who had been associate regional minister for the Christian Church (Disciples of Christ) in Indiana, became head of the program in February 1983.[59]

By the end of the decade, the number of new churches reached 128. However, the percentages for ethnic minorities had not been achieved: only thirty-six represented black, Hispanic, Korean, Filipino, and multi-cultural congregations. When Powell shifted to general administrative responsibilities with Church Extension in 1990, the board of the ministry selected Deborah Thompson to be director of new congregation establishment.

In the 1990s the program became CAN II, with a goal of two hundred new church starts. The New Congregation Establishment Team, with support from the National Convocation, called an African-American Summit in 1993 to identify issues related to starting African American congregations. The team also assessed the P/D model, concluding that while it was the preferred method, other techniques might work better in certain situations. With regions having fewer financial resources for supporting new congregations, Church Extension adopted a different approach during the last half of the 1990s: challenging established congregations to start new ones. This rebirth of a version of the swarming method, launched in 1996 in three regions with pilot studies of multi-site and parenting models, showed that "Congregations Starting Congregations" held promise for Disciples.[60]

The goal of two hundred new starts in the 1990s was not achieved, though one hundred eighty were attempted. At the end of the decade 148 were active: sixteen African American, twenty-four Asian-American, forty-eight Hispanic, two Haitian, two Native American, six multicultural, and fifty Caucasian.[61] Disciples were making progress on the call for new congregations among ethnic minorities. Nevertheless, between 1979 and 1999, while Disciples averaged twelve new church starts per year, they lost an average of forty-five congregations annually.[62]

In 2001, Richard L. Hamm, who had served since 1994 as General Minister and President, issued a challenge to the Christian Church (Disciples of Christ) to plant one thousand new congregations and transform one thousand existing congregations between 2000 and 2020. Hamm, who had been formulating his proposals since accepting the task of General Minister, published his ideas in a book titled *2020 Vision for the Christian Church (Disciples of Christ)*. Reaching back at least as far as the Disciples commitment to the Civil Rights Movement of the 1960s, the 2020 Vision also included the proposal that Disciples become a pro-reconciling/anti-racist church. In addition, it called for leadership development to ensure the success of the first three initiatives. All of these efforts were rooted in Hamm's vision for the Christian Church (Disciples of Christ): "To be a faithful, growing church that demonstrates true community, deep Christian spirituality, and a passion for justice."[63]

The 2001 General Assembly accepted Hamm's challenge and began to implement strategies to add an average of fifty new churches a year. CAN II became New Church Ministry, and Church Extension appointed Rick Morse, P/D and organizing minister of Lake Washington Christian Church, Kirkland, Washington, as director. In addition, the leadership team of New Church Ministry was expanded to include two assistant directors: Gilberto Collazo, minister of University Gardens Christian Church, Rio Piedras, Puerto Rico; and Judy Turner, a Homeland Ministries staff member assigned to Church Extension.[64]

Within two years 116 new churches had been added to Disciples rolls, and by 2007 the number had risen to 504. Roughly half were new church plants and the others were existing churches that decided to affiliate with

With funding from CAN, Rev. Cynthia L. Hale, who had previously served as a chaplain for correctional institutions in Colorado and North Carolina, was called by the Georgia Region in 1985 to establish a congregation in Dekalb County. Starting with a Bible study in her apartment in February 1986, membership of Ray of Hope Christian Church numbered almost 5000 by 2010, with an average worship attendance of 1100.

Disciples and were counted as new. As many as 80 percent of these new congregations were African American, Hispanic, Asian American, or Haitian.[65]

At a New Church Summit organized by Church Extension in November 2000, church consultant George Bullard asserted that the best method of planting churches is for churches to start churches.[66] One of the congregations that took this message to heart was the Mississippi Boulevard Christian Church in Memphis, Tennessee. In eight years, this African American congregation had launched four new congregations, one of which in 2010 had an average weekly attendance of over 6,000.[67]

The dramatic increase in the number of new Disciples congregations since 2001 slowed the numerical decline of the Disciples but did not reverse it. By 2009, total church membership had declined to slightly more than 680,000.[68] In addition, some Disciples wondered if the new churches that had been added to Disciples rolls were really Disciples churches. Reporting on her first meeting as a member of the Disciples General Board, Old Testament seminary professor Lisa Davison noted that many of the "new" congregations were not new at all, but existing congregations that had decided to become Disciples. "What no one mentioned," she remarked, "was that many of these congregations do not observe weekly communion, several have backward views about women, and some do not approach Scripture from a rational perspective." She concluded, "The prevailing attitude seems to be, if you are willing to put a red chalice [the Disciples' logo] on your sign and we can count you in our report to the Yearbook, we'll take you!"[69]

Responses to Davison in letters to the editor of *DisciplesWorld* ranged widely. One writer praised Davison's willingness "to speak up and reclaim our liberal Disciples heritage" and traditional practices such as weekly communion. Another offered the friendly suggestion, "In this time of intense partisanship both nationally and internationally, it is more constructive to include all who claim Christ as their lord in our communion and to learn to deal with the multitude of variation." Yet another respondent indignantly charged Davison with suggesting that Disciples refuse membership to Haitian, Hispanic, African American, and Asians simply because they do not meet her "theological expectations."[70] Clearly, Davison had raised significant issues. Disciples continued to wrestle with these issues while seeking to be "a faithful, growing church that demonstrates true community, deep Christian spirituality, and a passion for justice."

Starting a New Century

By the first decade of the twenty-first century the social change that had begun in the 1960s had deeply influenced each of the United States streams, as had each of their distinctive histories within the Stone-Campbell Movement. Churches of Christ, having gained increased access to graduate theological education, were divided over the emergence of a way of viewing Scripture that focused on Christ rather than positive law assumptions, and which supporters promised would help eliminate divisions over practices. It would also, they believed, help Christians relate more faithfully to contemporary social issues, deepen their relationship with God, and open the door to relationship with other Christians. In fact, this Christocentric approach to Scripture, while provoking the threat of separation by Churches of Christ that maintained the older hermeneutic, did build bridges between Churches of Christ and Christian Churches/Churches of Christ, the Christian Church (Disciples of Christ), and other Christians.

Christian Churches/Churches of Christ, working from the theories of Donald McGavran and subsequent church growth strategists, had grown significantly through the development of mega-churches and the planting of new churches through agencies such as Stadia. In the process, they had come to look and act quite differently from the Christian Churches/Churches of Christ that had emerged from the Disciples in 1971. Though much of their growth had been among conservative suburban whites, they were increasingly aware of the challenges of reaching beyond the culture of the majority of their current membership.

Disciples of Christ embodied a level of racial-ethnic and theological diversity never before witnessed in the U.S. Stone-Campbell Movement. Having decided in response to membership loses in the 1960s to focus on renewing existing churches rather than continuing to plant new congregations, they had been prodded by black members acting through the National Convocation to develop new strategies for church planting. Disciples had long championed unity in Christ that can bear real diversity. The challenge now was to see if in addition to adding new African American, Haitian, Hispanic, and Asian congregations, they could become a truly pro-reconciling/anti-racist church and develop the leadership to facilitate the growth of a faithful church that "demonstrates true community, deep Christian spirituality, and a passion for justice."

Continuing to live in an era of social change, Stone-Campbell Christians across the United States struggled with their identity in a pluralistic and polarized culture while pursing with new energy what they discerned to be God's calling in the twenty-first century.

13

Developments in the United Kingdom and British Commonwealth

As in the United States, the Stone-Campbell Movement in Britain, Canada, Australia, and New Zealand developed in multifaceted ways in the century following the centennial of Thomas Campbell's *Declaration and Address*. The Churches launched initiatives in ministerial education, experienced increased tension over issues of higher criticism and ecumenism, expanded their internal cooperative efforts, and pursued unions with other churches. The Statute of Westminster passed in 1931 by the Parliament of the United Kingdom granted the British dominions political independence, though they remained part of the empire through their continued allegiance to the monarchy. This shift, along with other social, economic, and political developments, affected the responses of the churches to the issues of war, gender, sexuality, and race, and influenced patterns of growth and decline.

Ministerial Education, Higher Criticism, Ecumenism, and Division

The Churches in Britain, Australia, and New Zealand developed ministerial education in remarkably similar ways. The call for more systematic training of ministers had been raised in the 1890s, and by the first decade of the twentieth century several British leaders were calling for the establishment of a Bible college. The Foreign Christian Missionary Society's warning to the Christian Association that it could no longer depend on American evangelists made the need even more urgent. Leaders urged the establishment of local schools to avoid losing candidates who traveled to the United States for ministerial education and stayed.

The first of the new schools began in 1907 when the Australian Churches founded the College of the Bible, with A. R. Main as principal from 1910 to 1938.

Churches in the U.K. began Overdale College in 1920, with William Robinson serving as principal until his retirement in 1949. In New Zealand the churches established a College at Glen Leith, Dunedin, in 1927, with Australian A.L. Haddon as principal until his sudden death in 1961. Despite the establishment of the new schools, the much larger U.S. movement continued to attract ministerial students. Even several teachers from the colleges moved to teach at American colleges or spent significant time in the United States, including William Robinson, J. G. Clague, and A. C. Watters.

The new colleges soon faced criticism from the Churches in regard to two issues that were also controversial in the United States: biblical higher criticism and ecumenism. Since each school was accountable to a committee of its national Conference rather than an independent board of trustees, the Churches themselves were directly involved in the debate over these matters. Though conservative members attacked Robinson and lecturer Joseph Smith in Britain, and Haddon in New Zealand for non-traditional views, the majority in the churches rallied to the colleges' support.

In Britain the first sign of controversy came in 1923 when two churches proposed that the training committee require Overdale College to withdraw from the Student Christian Movement (SCM) because of doctrinal views expressed in SCM Press books. Robinson strongly supported affiliation with the SCM to provide his students opportunities for contact with other churches and to make Churches of Christ more widely known. The Conference approved a resolution that took issue with some views expressed in SCM Press books, yet affirmed that the educational benefits of affiliation outweighed any disagreements. The following year, thirty-five churches again called on the school to separate from the SCM and expressed misgivings about Robinson's teaching. Nevertheless, the Conference reaffirmed its 1923 resolution. The controversy erupted again in 1925 when some churches threatened to withhold funds until the college discontinued its SCM affiliation. Chair of the training committee R.W. Black responded that no one had produced any evidence to substantiate charges of false teaching against the staff and accused those churches of trying to damage the college.

In 1926, teacher Joseph Smith came under attack for views of Scripture he had expressed in the *Christian Advocate* in 1925 and 1926. In August 1925 he interpreted Jeremiah 7:22 ("For in the day that I brought your ancestors out of the land of Egypt, I did not speak to them or command them concerning burnt offerings and sacrifices") to mean that the commands in Leviticus concerning animal sacrifices were an unauthorized addition to the original covenant with the patriarchs. In January and February 1926, he argued that the Christian sacraments did not come simply from Christ's commands but had more complex origins.

Though Smith had been writing in this vein for thirty years, Black resigned as chair of the training committee as a result of the controversy, labeling Smith's articles unnecessarily provocative. Robinson responded that if Black resigned, he would feel compelled to resign as principal, since the chair's resignation implied a loss of confidence in the college. As a compromise, Black agreed at a meeting of the training committee to withdraw his resignation if the college would dismiss Smith. When supporters of the college heard of the proposal, many condemned it, especially since Smith had not been given an opportunity to defend himself. The training committee met again and reversed its dismissal of Smith, leading Black and members of his family to resign from the committee and withdraw their financial backing. Overdale's supporters believed they had secured the school's academic freedom and that the Blacks had damaged their own credibility by their actions.[1]

Just as the Overdale controversy reached its climax, New Zealand Churches of Christ purchased property for their college and began looking for a principal. Among those considered was A. L. Haddon (1895-1961), Youth Director and Bible Schools Organizer for the New South Wales Churches in Australia. As Haddon became the selection committee's top candidate, the chair, John Inglis Wright, received a letter from "a prominent member" in New South Wales alleging that Haddon was "tainted with modernistic ideas." The accuser based the charge

on an editorial exchange in the *Australian Christian* about an article written by A.R. Main, principal of Glen Iris College of the Bible. Main had written negatively about higher critical methods of biblical study, and two former Glen Iris students wrote to defend the critical approach. Both of the students had been classmates of Haddon, and the writer suggested that Haddon shared the same views. Haddon responded that he rejected "the views of the German destructive critics" and was opposed to every theory of evolution that conflicted with the Word of God. With this assurance, the committee appointed him the school's first principal in 1927.

Four years after Glen Leith College opened, a letter signed simply "X" appeared in the *New Zealand Christian* asserting that Haddon's use of the term "Universal Father" for God showed he was a modernist. Haddon responded forcefully, labeling X's position both unscriptural and unacceptable. In his final sentence, Haddon asserted: "His chief complaint seems to be that the whole army is out of step but our John." Clearly Haddon was accusing Chairman of the College Board, John Inglis Wright, with being "X." From then on the two men were in open conflict. Wright resigned as chair and member of the College Board in 1932, but for the rest of his life continued to criticize "the canker of modernism" in the college.

Though delegates defeated a resolution attacking the college and its faculty at the 1934 Conference, the controversy polarized churches especially in the Dunedin area where the college was located. Opponents of the college began a new journal, *The Restorationist*, dedicated to criticizing the college and its principal. Supporters considered moving the college to Auckland, but the controversy began to subside when Haddon received an invitation to become principal of the New South Wales College in Sydney in 1943. His opponents again raised the accusations of modernism against Haddon, but when he made a strong statement to the Conference specifically denying them, his opponents backed down. Haddon stayed in New Zealand, and by 1950 the controversy had passed.[2]

In comparison to Robinson and Haddon, A. R. Main (1876-1945) in Australia faced little opposition. Like the other two, he served as editor of the chief journal for Churches of Christ, the *Australian Christian*, from 1914 to 1941, as well as principal of the College of the Bible at Glen Iris from 1910 to 1938. Earlier he had joined the Austral Publishing Company at the invitation of A.B. Maston and become evangelist of the

Ann Street congregation in Brisbane in 1900. Between 1903 and 1905 he served as evangelist at the Footscray church in Melbourne, began studies at the University of Melbourne, and lectured part-time at the Australian College of the Bible, then under the sponsorship of Swanston Street church. When the Victoria Conference formally established the College at Glen Iris in 1907, they appointed Main as a lecturer.

Main dominated the Federal Conference, not only because of his grasp of constitutional issues, but also because of the respect many in the churches had for his theological knowledge. A lack of contention characterized the *Australian Christian* during Main's editorship, partly because of his caution toward what he saw as liberal tendencies in the U.S. and his determination to keep them out of Australia. While the college did not escape criticism, it was never as intense as it was in Britain or New Zealand.[3]

A native of Scotland, Alexander Russell Main became one of the most influential leaders of the Australian Churches of Christ in the first half of the twentieth century.

The second issue the colleges faced was how to relate to the emerging ecumenical movement. Some insisted that ecumenical involvement would be an admission that Churches of Christ were merely "one of the sects."

Others argued that the participation of Churches of Christ would provide a broader platform to plead for the essentials of New Testament Christianity.

Churches of Christ participated in ecumenical activity primarily through the Faith and Order Movement. William Robinson, Reg Ennis, and David Moffatt Wilson represented British and Australian Churches of Christ at the first Faith and Order conference at Lausanne in 1927.[4] Robinson sent three articles from Lausanne for the *Christian Advocate*, revealing in one that Bishop Charles Gore of the Church of England had consulted attendees from Churches of Christ about the wording of a paragraph on creeds in the final conference report.[5]

The Union Committee of the Annual Conference wrote a response to the Lausanne Report, which the 1929 Conference discussed and approved. What proved to be more significant, however, was what happened before the body's formal approval of the response. In June, conservative minister R.K. Francis had published an article titled "That they may all be one," arguing that the only basis for legitimate unity was the restoration of New Testament Christianity as understood by Churches of Christ. Just before the Annual Conference began in August, six members of the committee that had written the Response to Lausanne published an article in the *Christian Advocate* urging Churches of Christ to accept persons not baptized by immersion as Christians. Yet the same issue contained a letter from Joseph Smith arguing for the traditional "closed communion" position.[6]

As discussion began at the 1929 Conference, someone read a letter from the Secretary of the Lausanne Committee of Reference, Canon H. N. Bate, in which he stated that the response from Churches of Christ was one of the best the committee had received. He commended its defense of believers' baptism coupled with the hope that the churches would find a way forward to mutual recognition. The Conference thanked William Robinson and Joseph Smith, who had been largely responsible for drafting the response.[7] But then a tense debate over communion broke out, fueled by the perception that former Christian Association churches had failed to abide by the terms of the 1917 agreement that required immersion for participation in the Lord's Supper.[8]

Among those most unhappy with the former Christian Association's alleged disregard of the 1917 agreement were the "Old Paths" churches, a term taken from Jeremiah 6:16: "ask for the old paths, where there is the good way, and walk therein" (KJV). This had been a favorite text of nineteenth-century leader David

King and was used frequently by Walter Crosthwaite, a twentieth-century leader among these conservative congregations. These Old Paths churches held a separate conference in 1924 and had been among the strongest critics of Overdale College for its affiliation with the Student Christian Movement.[9] By the time the second World Conference on Faith and Order met at Edinburgh in 1937, the Old Paths churches had virtually given up on the main body of British Churches of Christ, and four had formally withdrawn.[10]

Robinson, who served as President of the Annual Conference of the British Churches in 1935, was intimately involved in the Faith and Order discussions of the 1930s.[11] The *Christian Advocate*'s positive reports of the 1937 Faith and Order Conference provoked no negative comments. In 1938, the Union Committee of the Annual Conference also gave a positive report of the Edinburgh meeting, noting that the *British Weekly*, a widely read Free Church paper, had spoken favorably about the Churches of Christ. The conference agreed to prepare responses to Edinburgh jointly with the Disciples International Convention in the United States and Canada. William Robinson, James Gray, and W. J. Clague wrote the response, which was approved in 1940 by the International Convention, and by the British Conference the following year.

Despite majority approval of these moves, a minority opposed such ecumenism, which they believed was coming out of Overdale College. A letter from "Fairplay" in the September 23, 1938, *Christian Advocate* stated, "Our people want Christianity according to the Scriptures without the modernism, clericalism, and doubting of God's Word that is being taught at Overdale."[12] Beginning in 1943, Old Paths churches attempted to persuade other churches to withdraw from the Conference. The Argyle Street congregation at Hindley sent Robinson a list of fourteen questions, including, "Do you hold that every word in the Bible is true?" and, "Do you believe that members of the sects are Christians?" Though Robinson expressed surprise that those who professed to require no creed but Christ should demand answers to such a catechism, he responded with a confession of his own faith.[13]

In response to Robinson's answer, the Argyle Street church withdrew from the Annual Conference in 1945, though a minority of forty-six members began meeting in King Street and asked to be admitted at the same time.[14] The same year, Walter Crosthwaite condemned participation by Churches of Christ in the Free Church Federal Council.[15] A discussion between representatives

appointed by each side achieved little, and between 1943 and 1947 nineteen more churches withdrew from the Conference, and others followed.[16]

At Glen Leith, Haddon introduced in 1941 an eighty-lecture course on the origins, history, and ideals of the Stone-Campbell Movement that focused on Christian unity. He also became extremely active in the ecumenical movement, both in New Zealand and internationally.[17] He helped create the National Council of Churches in New Zealand, serving as chair in 1945-46. He also participated in the first New Zealand Life and Work Conference in Christchurch in 1945 and the first Faith and Order Conference in Wellington in 1947. The college granted Haddon leave to attend the third World Convention of Churches of Christ at Buffalo, New York, in 1947, and in 1952 he attended the fourth World Convention at Melbourne, which he served as First Vice-President. Then in 1954, he made a lecture tour to the U.S. that culminated in his participation in the Evanston Assembly of the World Council of Churches.[18]

In Australia, Main welcomed the 1927 Lausanne Conference's call to unity and publicized the prospectus of the World Council of Churches in 1937. He argued that Churches of Christ needed to be represented to present their New Testament plea for unity. He also argued that Churches of Christ shared much with other Protestants and warned against using "a New Testament name in a sectarian sense."[19]

In the late 1930s and 1940s the ecumenical initiative in Australia passed to T. H. Scambler (1879-1944), who succeeded Main as principal of Glen Iris in 1938. Born in Newstead, Victoria, Scambler had served as a preacher in the Melbourne area before moving to Perth. Recognizing his need for further education, he studied at Drake University in Iowa, then returned to Western Australia. After a ministry in Hawthorn, Victoria, he began to lecture at Glen Iris while continuing part-time pastorates. As early as 1916 Scambler had written in the *Australian Christian* that the Disciples' "plea for Christian Union is a recognition as Christian of all who sincerely love and serve the Lord Jesus, whether they coincide with us in doctrine and ordinance or not." By 1937 the Victorian Conference had established a Committee for the Promotion of Christian Union with Scambler as chair, and in 1946 the Federal Conference decided to affiliate with the newly formed Australian Committee for the World Council of Churches.[20]

In the minds of the critics, these ecumenical developments had arisen from modernistic views of Scripture that weakened faithfulness to traditional teachings.

At the Australian Federal Conference of 1938, R. O. Sutton accused Glen Iris College of producing students with "decidedly modernistic conceptions of Biblical interpretation" and urged the College Board to insure that all lecturers in biblical and doctrinal subjects were "fundamentalist rather than modernistic in their view of Biblical interpretation." In 1941, members of the New South Wales Conference, some of whom had misgivings about Glen Iris, established their own college. Evangelist E. C. Hinrichsen spoke for a number of dissidents when he asserted, "Some of us still believe that the Bible alone contains the religion of Protestants." Though the New South Wales Conference was careful to consult Glen Iris in its planning, B. G. Corlett, secretary of the new College Committee, said that the school would aim at "study of the Bible as the sole revelation of God's will" in "complete allegiance with the tenets of the Restoration Movement." Conference leaders persuaded Main to come out of retirement to serve as principal, which he did, hoping to avoid a complete break with Glen Iris.[21]

It was Arthur Stephenson (1900-1988), however, who brought reconciliation between the two schools. Born in Western Australia, he studied at Glen Iris and served two ministries before becoming a full-time student at the University of Melbourne from 1928 to 1933. He lectured part-time in church history at Glen Iris while Main was out of the country, and in 1941 became editor of the *Australian Christian*. When Scambler died, Stephenson lectured in Apologetics at Glen Iris and in 1951 became principal of the Bible College in New South Wales until his retirement in 1969. Like Scambler, he believed that Churches of Christ should involve themselves in union discussions, yet he was sensitive to the concerns of those who opposed such action. He tried to persuade them that such ecumenical concerns had been inherent to the Stone-Campbell Movement from its beginnings, highlighting the *Declaration and Address* as its foundational document.[22]

Within a year after Scambler's successor, E. Lyall Williams (1906-1994), had become principal of Glen Iris in 1945, critics began accusing the faculty of abandoning doctrinal beliefs that were the basis of the New Testament church. Williams encouraged student inquiry in his teaching by presenting arguments for and against accepted doctrinal positions, a practice that clearly disturbed many. Williams explained his theological stance in an article titled "The Witness of Churches of Christ," published in the seventieth anniversary booklet of the Kaniva District Churches of Christ. The truths for which Churches of Christ stand, he argued, began

with the conviction that the Church's primary task is to win others to a personal commitment to Christ as Savior and Lord. The second conviction was that the Church is essentially one and that its visible unity is the will of God.[23]

Williams wrote the article at the end of the 1950s when critics had once again targeted ecumenical involvement. Several churches in Victoria, led by Keith Macnaughtan, minister of Swanston Street church, criticized the World Council of Churches (WCC) for its support of Orthodox priests in Eastern Europe, its modernist leadership, and its alleged soft line on Roman Catholics. Nevertheless, the Victoria-Tasmanian Conference affiliated at the state level with the WCC in 1953. Some who opposed that move formed the Evangelical Fellowship to promote their understanding of restorationism and combat modernism, broadcasting a weekly radio program and supporting the International Council of Christian Churches headed by the American anti-communist fundamentalist Carl McIntire. The New South Wales Conference had withdrawn state support for the WCC in 1950, and despite re-establishing a state Committee for the Promotion of Christian Union in 1958, did not reaffiliate. New South Wales also decided against using Christian education material prepared by the Joint Board of Christian Education of the Presbyterian, Methodist, and Congregational Churches, reprinting instead material prepared by the emerging Christian Churches/Churches of Christ in the United States.[24]

New Bible colleges were established in Woolwich, New South Wales, in 1942; in Perth, Western Australia, in 1945; and in Kenmore, Queensland, in 1965. At first these schools maintained close cooperation with the college at Glen Iris, but gradually began to reflect the more conservative views of the states in which they were located. Provocative remarks about "brotherhood decay" by Kenmore Principal James Jauncey kept the issues alive. Though he later admitted that the majority in Australian Churches of Christ were theologically conservative, perceptions of a move away from traditional positions persisted and were sufficient to prevent the establishment of a Federal Consultative Board of Theological Studies among the colleges for fear that the "liberalism" of Glen Iris would stop the expression of conservative theology in New South Wales and Queensland.[25]

The connection between higher criticism of the Bible and modern ecumenism noted by conservatives in British Churches of Christ could not be denied. The young progressives in the British "Forward Movement" in the 1880s and early 1890s had insisted that Churches of Christ must confront the theological issues of the day, including higher biblical criticism. While Alexander Campbell's primitivism had struck a responsive chord with the British nonconformists who initially formed British Churches of Christ, it was this aspect of Campbell's thought that higher criticism most sharply challenged. As the British Churches were preparing in 1917 to establish a college, they sent future Principal William Robinson, who had a degree in chemistry, to Mansfield College, Oxford, to study theology. There he was trained in biblical criticism and the theology of P.T. Forsyth, whose critique of nineteenth-century Protestant liberalism prefigured later Neo-Orthodoxy.

Robinson's first book, *Essays on Christian Unity* (1922), began by declaring that although Christians had once regarded the New Testament as "a law-book, written to provide details of worship, belief and conduct," it was now a new and more valuable book because artificial theories about its origin had been abandoned. "The days of textual theology are gone. The historic method of interpretation has come to stay." The Bible, however, had not lost its position as "the norm by which to test all future Christianity." The New Testament, he concluded, must be seen in its proper historical relationship to the Church. Christian unity would come only through an appeal to Scripture, history, and reason.[26]

Following his career in Great Britain, William Robinson (second from left) taught Christian theology and doctrine at the Butler School of Religion from 1952 to 1956. Pictured here receiving a distinguished service citation from the Disciples of Christ Historical Society (DCHS) with Butler professor of missions A. C. Watters, DCHS trustee Eva Jean Wrather, and Butler School of Religion dean O. L. Shelton. *(Courtesy Christian Theological Seminary, Indianapolis)*

Robinson's *Religion and Life* (1925) engaged the biblical scholarship of the previous thirty years with no reference to the Campbells.[27] The same is true of his Louisa Curtis Lectures at Spurgeon's College, London, published as *Whither Theology? Some Essential Biblical Patterns* (1945). Even his U.S. lectures given at Butler University in September 1947, later published as *The Biblical Doctrine of the Church* (1948, revised 1960), though referencing Thomas Campbell's *Declaration and Address*, drew primarily from his 1937 Edinburgh Faith and Order paper "The Church and the Word of God." For Robinson, it was in the pursuit of Christian unity rather than restoration that the thought of Stone and the Campbells still had something to say.

In Australia, Arthur Stephenson did the same kind of work that Robinson had done in Britain by offering a critical appraisal of restoration principles in the light of contemporary circumstances. The New Testament contained principles, he insisted, not a blueprint for church government. Like Robinson, Stephenson argued for an interpretation of Scripture informed by "considered, qualified, catholic scholarship."[28]

Alexander Campbell had argued that the ancient faith was not the metaphysical dogmas of the creeds, but the gospel of what God had done through Jesus Christ. Robinson's statement that "The Word of God is as much an *acted* word as a *spoken* word" stood in that tradition. He went on to insist, however, that because God's speech and action are delivered "*in history*, the relativity of history is round about them," an assertion that mystified and troubled some of his critics.[29] Though viewed by conservatives as undermining the Stone-Campbell Movement, Robinson, Main, Stephenson, Williams, and Haddon—who dominated the Churches in Britain, Australia, and New Zealand from roughly 1920 to 1970—saw their task as offering to a new generation a vision of something worth advancing in the "position and plea" of Churches of Christ.

Developing a Cooperative Order

The Churches of Christ in Britain, Australia, and New Zealand established a conference system much earlier than the American Churches and did not hesitate to delegate responsibilities to committees appointed by those conferences. Among the reasons were the small scale of the organizations and the scarcity of resources. In Britain the Conference of Churches remained unincorporated during its entire existence, under the official umbrella of "excepted charity," though it did create legal structures to hold overseas missions property and to receive and distribute funds for the Chapel Building Committee. In Australia state conferences handled most of these responsibilities rather than the national organization.

Initially cooperative work in Britain, Australia, and New Zealand was for evangelization. After the churches had overcome early objections to settled preachers, cooperation became a way of helping congregations afford their own preacher. Cooperation in this quickly led to cooperation in Sunday school and youth work. The churches began channeling their support for foreign missions through the Conferences beginning in the 1880s. The churches hesitated, however, when it came to cooperative support of temperance and other social issues, even though most members were in sympathy with the causes. In Britain, the Annual Conference finally accepted the Temperance Committee formed in 1880 as a formal part of its work in 1919, but only after seventy-two churches had expressed their support.[30]

An even more troubling issue was cooperative support for constructing church buildings—called chapels in Britain. Two matters were at stake. One was the problem of a congregation being in debt to the Conference for the ownership of its building, including the possibility that the Conference might involve itself in internal church disputes. More serious, however, was the fact that English law required churches to state in a trust deed the beliefs of the congregation for which the building was held. This involved drawing up what amounted to a creed. Congregations did not feel uncomfortable about stating their beliefs, but the idea that the Annual Conference might state the beliefs of the churches collectively raised fears that such a statement could be imposed as a test of fellowship. The British Annual Meeting, having rejected in 1908 any responsibility for funding church buildings, did not absorb the privately run Chapel Building Fund until 1923.[31] In Australia and New Zealand the timing was different, but the issues were similar. An act of the New Zealand Parliament in 1929 authorized the Conference's Church Extension and Property Trust Board to act as trustee for local church properties.[32]

The British Sisters' Conference established in the late nineteenth century became part of the Annual Conference in 1939, with a Sisters' Committee reporting to the Conference. New Zealand women's work became a Conference responsibility in the same period. In Australia the first Women's Federal Conference met in Sydney in August 1938.[33] With the formation of the World Christian Women's Fellowship in 1955, national committees

changed their names to reflect that terminology.

The 1920s had been a time of considerable competition for funding among the committees of the British Conference. Though cooperative organizations existed, there was still wide leeway for local congregations, particularly wealthy ones, to act on their own. In 1930, the churches set up a Central Council with representatives from all standing committees to coordinate work and approve major expenditures. Due partly to the Depression, all the major committees incurred significant debt between the wars. In November of his 1935 term as conference president, William Robinson launched a campaign to eliminate just over £5,000 of debt within two years, a goal achieved by July 1937. Not until after World War II did the British churches consider unified fund-raising like that of American Disciples, establishing the national Finance Committee in 1956.[34]

Churches in the U.K. created the position of General Secretary in 1948. Leslie Colver, former Sunday school organizer, became the first General Secretary and proved an effective link between the churches and committees. Walter Hendry followed in 1962, and in 1967 Philip Morgan took the office. All had been full-time ministers, a shift from the earlier dominance of wealthy businessmen.[35] State Conferences, which had always taken priority over the office of Federal Secretary in Australia, appointed full-time organizers in the 1960s.[36] There was no comparable position in New Zealand.

The more official nature of Conferences in the British dominions led to the development of official magazines. In Britain the *Ecclesiastical Observer* and the *Christian Advocate* had been combined to form the *Bible Advocate* in 1890, run by the Publishing Committee of the Annual Conference. This represented a significant shift away from the previous pattern of individually owned and distributed magazines. A.B. Maston established the *Australian Christian* in 1898, and the New Zealand churches began the *New Zealand Christian* between the world wars.[37]

The Conferences also made attempts at producing official hymnbooks. The British Churches published *Hymns for Churches of Christ* in 1908 that replaced several earlier collections, succeeded in 1938 by *The Christian Hymnary*. Old Paths Churches began efforts to publish a hymnbook in 1948, but finances delayed it until 1957 when *Hymns for Churches of Christ* appeared.[38] Australian Churches published the *Churches of Christ Hymn Book* in 1931.[39]

The churches in Britain and its territories had almost no controversy over structure. When the majority of Old Paths Churches of Christ withdrew from the British Conference in 1947, they immediately established a Conference of their own.[40] However, when U.S. evangelist John Allen Hudson in his 1948 history of British Churches criticized David King's acceptance of the Conference and Committee system, it raised the issue among those churches.[41] By 1956 the Cleveleys Church proposed that the Evangelistic Committee be disbanded and its assets transferred to a trust fund. At the Spring Conference, A. E. Winstanley moved to disband the committee on the grounds that it was unscriptural and sectarian. The debate continued at the Autumn Conference with a motion to disband the committee and an amendment to retain it. Though the Spring Conference in 1957 retained it, the debate continued.[42] Gradually the organizational features of the British Old Paths churches disappeared in favor of the more local congregational emphasis of the U.S. Churches of Christ.

The Churches in both New Zealand and Australia significantly reduced their structures in the late twentieth and early twenty-first centuries. Though primarily responses to the realities of size and financial resources, these shifts also represented a sense among the churches that such moves could free them for new kinds of mission.[43]

Developments in Canada

The Canadian churches experienced a pattern of organizational development different from that of Britain, Australia, and New Zealand. As in Australia, the provincial cooperations were the driving force up to World War I. After the war, many in the scattered churches and organizations felt a strong need for some kind of national structure. The result was the formation of the All-Canada Committee in 1922, headquartered in Toronto. Fifty churches from British Columbia to the Maritimes had expressed support for the idea when it was formed; but, a team appointed later to gauge the churches' attitude toward the organization discovered a significant lack of trust in the committee's commitment to the churches in all parts of the country.[44]

The All-Canada Committee moved quickly to appoint a Continuation Committee that, working with the provincial boards, selected an All-Canada Secretary (H.B. Kilgour), began a merger of the Ontario *Christian Messenger* and the Maritime *Christian* into a single paper (the *Canadian Christian*), created an extension fund, and began consideration of either a Bible chair or an all-Canada college. By 1927 the committee had added national children's work and women's work and appointed organizers.[45]

Despite all the activity, the All-Canada Committee never became an effective organization. Though the vast size of the country has sometimes been given as the reason, the heartland for Canadian Churches of Christ was only about 600 miles across and centered in the east. A more likely explanation is that the closeness of all major Canadian cities to the United States made the American conventions a better option for feeling part of a larger fellowship. In 1948, dissatisfaction with the leadership of the All-Canada Committee, which many perceived to be theologically liberal because of its sympathy to open membership, led to the withdrawal of the majority of the churches in the Maritimes. After the restructure of North American Disciples in 1968, the Canadian churches chose not to have each province affiliate with the nearest U.S. region. Instead, they chose to become a separate region of the Christian Church (Disciples of Christ).[46]

As in Britain, the Canadian churches moved from reliance on successful businessmen to full-time ministers as conference executives. In the early period, the leading figure of the All-Canada Committee had been Winnipeg business leader George Stewart. But after his retirement, Oliver McCully, formerly a minister in churches in Manitoba and Ontario, became the All-Canada Secretary and served from 1941 to 1965. His plan was to visit every church at least once a year, as well as all Canadian students studying in seminary.[47]

Canadian churches gave no issue greater attention than ministerial education. As in Australia and New Zealand, the churches had experienced the loss of ministerial students who never returned after studying in the United States. The All-Canada Conferences in Poplar Hill, Ontario, in June 1922, and at Winnipeg in June 1923, agreed to consider establishing a Bible chair or an all-Canada Bible college and to appoint a committee of ten to work out a plan for it. The 1924 Toronto Convention appointed a provisional body of trustees, which reported to the next year's convention.

One idea had been to affiliate their new institution with the University of Toronto. But when the trustees discovered the school was not financially able to accept an affiliated college, they devised a new proposal. They would send students to another university for their general education, then to an approved theological college for ministerial education, adding a course of lectures in Disciples principles by someone appointed by the trustees. They named McMaster University, then in Toronto, as the appropriate school and appointed R. George Quiggin of Hillcrest Church, Toronto, dean of the lectureship beginning in September 1925. In 1927 the trustees purchased property and incorporated the All-Canada College in October. Quiggin retired in February 1928, and W. C. MacDougall assumed the role of principal. The school soon developed extension courses in places as far apart as Winnipeg and Halifax.

When McMaster University moved to Hamilton in 1930, the churches began using the University of Toronto and Victoria University. Toronto businessman Charles L. Burton chaired the Board of Trustees of the All-Canada College and raised financial support from members across the country. Nevertheless, by 1932 some were questioning MacDougall's doctrinal positions, and in view of the financial depression and a reduction of students, the Board closed the college temporarily. When it reopened in 1939 under Dean and Lecturer C. A. Lawson, students studied liberal arts at Victoria College, Toronto (the undergraduate college of Victoria University), followed by an additional two years at Emmanuel College, an accredited theological seminary also part of Victoria University.[48]

Beginning in 1958, the college began providing funds for ministerial candidates to study at any accredited university and seminary. Raymond Cuthbert described how "the College without Walls" operated in 1988, providing half the tuition fees at a university of the student's choice and full tuition at an accredited seminary, for which the student pledged to spend at least five years serving a church in Canada or mission overseas. The school also provided support for professional enrichment, and the College Institute of Religious Studies, directed by Melvin L. Breakenridge, provided introductory courses in Christian theology, history, doctrine, and practice for lay members.[49]

In 1932, the year of the All-Canada College's suspension, Charles H. Phillips, minister at First Christian Church in Lethbridge, founded Alberta Bible College to train preachers for the west. In 1936, the college had a student body of thirty-nine and began the process of incorporation. It also hired an assistant principal, J. M. Hill, who was a graduate of Northwest Christian College

in Eugene, Oregon. Within a year the number of students had increased to one hundred four. In 1937 the college moved to Calgary and Hill became principal, followed by Melvin Breakenridge in 1941.[50] The college drew students from all over Canada and continued to grow.

The faculty and student body of Alberta Bible College in 1936-37. Principal J. M. Hill is on the front row, fourth from left. ("ABC 1930's," from website of *Alberta Bible College*)

Alberta Bible College's original doctrinal statement defined the Bible as "a full, final and infallible revelation of the Divine will," asserted that "the New Testament is the divine constitution for the worship, discipline and government of the churches of Christ," and that "the actual unity of all believers in Christ on the basis set forth in the New Testament is an obligation laid on all Christians and its realization essential to the evangelization of the world."[51] Despite its conservative foundation, which reflected the theology of the emerging U.S. Christian Churches/Churches of Christ, the college provided ministers for all streams of the Stone-Campbell Movement in Canada. In the early twenty-first century, two-thirds of the leadership of the Christian Churches/Churches of Christ and the Christian Church (Disciples of Christ) in Canada had studied at Alberta Bible College.[52]

Canadian a cappella Churches of Christ also began educational institutions: Western Christian College in 1945 at Radville, Saskatchewan (which operated in Regina from 2001 until its closing in 2012), and Great Lakes Christian College (High School) at Beamsville, Ontario, in 1952. Both served students from all religious traditions.[53] Leaders chartered Great Lakes Bible College in 1987 and operated it out of the Waterloo Church of Christ.[54] In addition, Christian Churches/Churches of Christ operated Ontario Bible College (1939-1943), Toronto Christian Seminary (1958-64), and Ontario Christian Seminary (1972-98), using an arrangement similar to that between McMaster University and the earlier Canadian college.[55]

Instrumental Music

Instrumental music in worship was slow to emerge as an issue in the churches of the British Commonwealth. Initially most did not use instrumental music, reflecting the theological tradition of pioneer leaders, the general practice in British nonconformity, and the small number of wealthy church members. When differences did begin to emerge in the second quarter of the nineteenth century, they were essentially social, between upwardly mobile members who wanted worship to be more impressive, and the working classes who saw no reason to change the traditions.[56]

The churches in Australia and New Zealand generally regarded the matter as a question for local determination. Not until 1950 did local leaders in Australia, dissatisfied with the Associated churches, begin a specifically non-instrumental fellowship assisted by U.S. Churches of Christ.[57] In New Zealand, Paul Mathews from California led the formation of an a cappella fellowship in the 1950s.[58] In 1982 these churches, with help from the U.S., established South Pacific Bible College in Tauranga on the North Island. The school attracted students from New Zealand, Australia, Southeast Asia, and the Pacific islands who came to train to be ministers in existing Churches of Christ in their home countries or to plant new congregations.[59]

In Canada, links with nearby U.S. churches tended to be a stronger factor in determining worship practices than cross-Canadian connections. The churches in southwestern Ontario, for example, were mostly non-instrumental, reflecting their close contacts with Churches of Christ in Michigan. This identification with U.S. Churches of Christ could also be seen in the increasing unwillingness of these Ontario congregations to take part in All-Canada activities after 1922.

Efforts to Achieve Church Union

Though not without controversy, Churches of Christ in the British Commonwealth were active participants in union discussions with other church bodies during the twentieth century. Before 1960 such discussions were primarily with Baptists, but decreasing interest

in ecumenism by many Baptist churches in the late twentieth century increasingly redirected the union efforts of Churches of Christ toward other groups.

In Britain, R.W. Black had begun working in the 1910s toward a merger of Churches of Christ with the Baptist Union. Several ministers of the Christian Association had come from Baptist churches and supported Black's efforts. In 1917, however, several returned to the Baptist Union in protest to the Christian Association's union with the more conservative Co-operation. Black himself became increasingly frustrated by both the conservatism of many British Churches of Christ and the modernistic views on biblical criticism of William Robinson at Overdale College. In 1931 he took his church at Fulham Cross—the largest in the Conference—into the Baptist Union. [60] Black's two brothers, J. W. Black and H. Milner Black, however, remained important leaders in Churches of Christ.

In 1941, R.W. Black, then serving as president of the Baptist Union, suggested that union efforts between the two bodies be resumed. Each group appointed five members to a joint committee and talks began. Both bodies began encouraging interaction between local congregations, and in 1948 they jointly published *Infant Baptism Today*. The major challenge, however, in the words of the committee, was that "the practice of open membership in some Baptist Churches was a real barrier to any progress to organic union of the two bodies." Not only did British Churches of Christ practice closed membership, most strongly opposed admitting unimmersed persons to communion. The Baptists had neither the desire nor the constitutional ability to restrict the freedom of local churches to adopt their own policy on this matter and would have been happy for Churches of Christ to join the Baptist Union as individual congregations. The British Churches of Christ, on the other hand, had no desire to reopen a controversy that had seethed in the 1920s between the more open churches of the former Christian Association and the older British Churches of Christ. Though in 1951 the joint committee approved a proposal for an association that would preserve the identity of Churches of Christ, it was never enacted, and in 1957 the Baptist Union Council ended the project.[61]

Between 1940 and 1943, the New Zealand Churches also held union conversations with Baptists, but the talks ended when the groups were unable to come to an agreement on the relationship of baptism and salvation. In the previous decade they had held unsuccessful conversations with another group called Churches of

Christ who practiced weekly communion, but also believed in conditional immortality and the pre-millennial second coming of Christ.[62]

In 1954, the New Zealand Joint Standing Committee on Union of Methodists, Presbyterians, and Congregationalists prepared a Basis of Union and invited all churches that were members of the National Council to join them. Arthur Haddon persuaded the Dominion Conference of the New Zealand Churches of Christ at Palmerston North in 1955 to participate, then took a prominent role in the difficult process of preparing a set of principles acceptable to Churches of Christ. When the proposed union was presented to the churches in 1957, 75 percent of the membership of Churches of Christ voted in favor. Complications arose, however, when the Anglican Church joined the talks in 1959, necessitating a redrafting of the Basis of Union. Haddon, who died in 1961, did not live to see the new document. When the Churches of Christ voted on the revised Plan of Union in 1972, only 55 percent were in favor.[63] The eventual rejection of the Plan by the Anglicans meant that the union did not materialize. Yet at the end of the twentieth century, eleven out of the thirty-three churches in the New Zealand Association were in cooperating parishes with other partners in a union process.[64]

Efforts toward union with the Presbyterians and Congregationalists in the U.K. were facilitated by several earlier developments. The Faith and Order Movement had significantly influenced the British Churches of Christ, particularly in their understanding of ministry and ordination. During World War II, the churches had approved an important Report on Ordination, resulting in the formal ordination of all evangelists, increasingly called ministers, at a special session of the Annual Conference in 1943. A later Report on the Ministry, approved in 1953, discussed the relationship between ministers and elders and raised the question of women's ministry for the first time.[65]

In 1954, the Conference Paper at the meeting of the Association of Churches of Christ was on "Intercommunion."[66] Norman Walters, Secretary of the Union Committee, suggested that the time had come for an "adventure in faith" on the question of admission to communion and offered a proposal he called "Guest Communion." Two years later the Association adopted a recommendation from the Union Committee to approve Walters's proposal. Congregations could offer communion to occasional visitors from other churches that did not practice believers' baptism, with the condition that they would receive a tactful and charitable

explanation of the understanding of communion held by Churches of Christ after the service. This was the first officially approved departure from the closed communion position by British Churches of Christ.[67]

In 1963, at the suggestion of the Burnage church in Manchester, the Association asked the Union Committee to consider what was called "guest membership" or "ecumenical membership." This was not merely a theoretical question. It had been prompted by the matter of whether members of churches that practiced infant baptism could be admitted as members of Churches of Christ planted in new housing areas. The proposal attempted to retain the long-held opposition of the British churches to open membership by emphasizing that such "members" would be "guests" from another part of the "ecumenical" church. Church leaders held a weekend consultation in January 1964, which led to Conference Papers on the topic that year by James Gray and John Francis. Though no formal resolutions concerning "ecumenical membership" were presented to the Association at the time, by 1972 twenty percent of the churches had adopted the practice and eighty percent were practicing "guest communion." At that point the Union Committee prepared a formal statement endorsing ecumenical membership, which was adopted by the Annual Conference with only three dissenting votes.[68]

Meanwhile, new ecumenical initiatives had emerged in the U.K. in the mid-1960s. In Wales, a process called "Covenanting for Union" brought together Methodists, Anglicans, Presbyterians, and Independents in serious union conversations. Even more significant for Churches of Christ was an effort to unite British Presbyterians and Congregationalists. In 1966, the Congregational-Presbyterian Joint Committee sent an invitation to other churches to send observers to their meetings. The three observers from British Churches of Christ quickly discovered that the Joint Committee took their views on baptism very seriously, amending a clause in the Plan of Union in light of their comments.

In 1968 the Annual Conference approved a four-stage plan of "Steps towards Christian Unity." The first step was to seek the support of every congregation for a covenant to work and pray for Christian union. The second was to seek similar support for the opening of formal conversations with a particular church or churches. The third and fourth steps would consist of negotiations resulting in union proposals, followed by the decision of the Churches of Christ on those proposals.

Within a year, seventy-one churches out of one

hundred three had approved the covenant, and the 1971 Conference invited the churches to support conversations with the United Reformed Church (as the new Congregational-Presbyterian Church was to be known) when it was formed the following year.[69] Negotiations took place between 1972 and 1976. Although the General Assembly of the United Reformed Church (URC) supported the proposals for Churches of Christ to become part of the body by an overwhelming majority in 1977, by January 1978 it was clear that Churches of Christ had not achieved approval by the legally required two-thirds of the churches representing three-quarters of the membership. The Annual Conference of 1978 invited the churches that had not supported the proposals to reconsider their position in light of the majority view. If the numbers required for approval were still insufficient, it authorized the Central Council to arrange for a vote in the churches on the dissolution of the Association. This would allow each local church to make its own decision about the union.

When the votes needed to continue pursuit of union with the URC did not materialize, the Conference set in motion the procedure for dissolution. The churches voted fifty-four to twenty with one abstention to dissolve the Association, and the Annual Conference of 1979 took the necessary steps to implement the decision in March 1980.[70] The churches of the Glasgow District immediately invited all congregations who wished to join them in a reformed Association to seek union with the URC. In 1981 the new Association became part of the United Reformed Church at a Unifying Assembly in Birmingham.

The educational work of the British Churches of Christ had become part of the URC even before the Unifying Assembly. The Selly Oak Colleges of which Overdale was part had shifted their emphasis in the 1970s from training ministers for the U.K. to preparing overseas students for work in their own countries. The Training Committee considered the possibility of affiliating with the new Anglican-Methodist Queen's College, but decided in light of negotiations with the United Reformed Church that it made more sense to close Overdale College and merge its work with the United Reformed College in Manchester. Overdale's principal, J. E. Francis, joined the Manchester staff in 1977.[71]

The churches that did not become part of the United Reformed Church came together to form the Fellowship of Churches of Christ, with a conference structure modeled on that of the old Association. This structure surprised members of Christian Churches/Churches

of Christ from the U.S. who came to serve in Fellowship congregations. In 2001 the churches wrote a new constitution that replaced the old system of committees reporting to an annual conference with a National Leadership Team with Task Groups, an Annual Delegate Conference, and an Annual Celebration.[72] In 1980, the Fellowship of Churches of Christ had established Springdale College in Birmingham with assistance from the British-American Fellowship Committee headed by C. Robert Wetzel and supported by Christian Churches/ Churches of Christ in the United States. As had been the case with Overdale College, Springdale was affiliated with the Selly Oak Colleges. In 2000 Springdale merged with the Birmingham Bible Institute to form Birmingham Christian College, but later changed its focus to become an inter-denominational center for training church leaders for mission and evangelism.[73]

A. L. Haddon (center), founding principal of Glen Leith College in New Zealand, became a leader in the ecumenical movement. He is pictured here at the University of Chicago Disciples Divinity House Hoover Lectures on Christian Unity in 1961 with former student and fellow New Zealander Garfield Todd (right) and Divinity House dean W. Barnett Blakemore.

In Australia, the Victoria Committee for the Promotion of Christian Union applied for observer status in 1964 to the Australian Presbyterian-Methodist-Congregational conversations, and submitted observations on the proposed Basis of Union. Participants in these talks did not receive Churches of Christ with the same generosity as in Britain, nor was the commitment to union by Churches of Christ as great. The original participants in the conversations formed the Uniting Church of Australia in 1977 without the participation of Churches of Christ, though occasional informal conversations continued.[74] Beginning in 1964 some Australian churches, starting with a new congregation in the eastern suburbs of Melbourne now known as Knoxfield Church of Christ, adopted principles set out in a document titled "Christians in Fellowship." The document outlined a way of welcoming into local congregations those who had been baptized as infants, while retaining the right for them to be baptized by immersion if they wished.

From 1976 to 1986 Canadian Disciples participated in union conversations with the Anglicans and the United Church of Canada—formed in 1925 from Congregationalists, Presbyterians, and Methodists. Though the conversation produced a study document on Principles for Union, only four Disciples congregations indicated support for the effort, and the conversations were ended by mutual consent. During the union talks, a joint committee of Disciples and United Church members had formed three united congregations.[75] After the talks ended, the United Church closed two, leaving only the Campbell-Stone United Church in Calgary, Alberta. Despite the discouraging trend, in 1997 Ray Cuthbert formed the Broadway United Church in Winnipeg from two Disciples churches and one United Church congregation.[76]

Cuthbert, editor of the *Canadian Disciple*, was frustrated by what he saw as a void in the Canadian Disciples' sense of purpose after 1986, especially pointing to their failure to follow through on union with the United Church. Nova Scotia church planter Neil Bergman disagreed, suggesting that like the Presbyterians and Lutherans, Disciples should concentrate on unity within the Stone-Campbell Movement itself.[77] Executive Minister Robert Steffer focused his efforts on developing pastoral relationships with all the Canadian congregations to recreate a sense of purpose. He raised funds, streamlined committee work, and helped establish four new congregations, including a Haitian church in Montreal as well as Latino churches in Montreal and Toronto.[78]

Union talks and agreements reached by Churches of Christ throughout the British Commonwealth in the twentieth century usually created a dissenting minority. Those who worked for wider union did so because they believed they were being faithful to the call for unity issued by the earliest leaders of the Stone-Campbell Movement. Those who opposed it almost always did so on the ground that they were being faithful to the ideal of a restored New Testament church. By the end of the century, however, the personal antagonism that initially resulted from these clashes had often been replaced by more irenic attitudes.

Social Issues

In the midst of developing schools and organizational structures, grappling with higher criticism and ecumenism, and pursuing church union, the Churches of Christ of the British Commonwealth also found themselves confronted by issues of war, gender, sexuality, and race.

During World War II the British Churches included and ministered to both those who served in the armed forces and those who were conscientious objectors. Most of the Old Paths churches that eventually withdrew from the Conference were pacifist; yet some that remained also held pacifist sentiments. William Robinson, for example, who had served in the First World War, became a prominent pacifist in the inter-war years and wrote a book titled *Christianity Is Pacifism*, though not using traditional biblicist arguments.[79] A 1943 survey of the Conference Churches suggested that members serving in the military outnumbered pacifists by about two to one. The tribunal system provided more opportunities for alternative service than it had in World War I, which satisfied all but the most extreme pacifists.[80]

The introduction of compulsory military service in Australia did not occur until 1943, limiting the time the churches were forced to deal with the issue. In New Zealand, like in Britain, a much improved tribunal process was able to deal more humanely with conscientious objectors, alleviating the anxieties of most.[81] Canadian churches reflected the same spectrum of attitudes on the issue of Christians and warfare as the other Commonwealth countries, yet in none of these nations did positions on war become a central issue for Churches of Christ.

The development and use of atomic weapons at the end of World War II, however, introduced a new dimension to the pacifist argument. The massive destructive potential of these weapons raised the question of whether there could be any justifiable cause for using them. The development of the hydrogen bomb in the 1950s heightened the urgency of the matter.[82] The outbreak of the Korean War prompted the Old Paths Churches to advocate pacifism in a public meeting in Manchester in September 1951. At the meeting, several members who had not declared conscientious objector status and had served in the armed forces stated that they would never serve again.[83]

The war in Vietnam provoked even more controversy

than the use of atomic weapons. Britain, Canada, and New Zealand did not commit forces to fight with the United States in Vietnam, but Australia did, and even reintroduced compulsory service.[84] This provoked strong criticism from Australian churches generally. Churches of Christ in Victoria were members of the Inter-Church Committee on Peace, which offered advice to conscientious objectors. In 1967, members of the Melbourne vice squad stopped a group of young ministers from distributing pamphlets about American atrocities in Vietnam.[85] Arguments against the Vietnam War were not exclusively pacifist, based more often on political disagreements over strategy than the morality of war. Though the controversy became heated, it did not become a church-dividing issue.

The British churches also had a long history of discussion of women's ministries. As early as 1919, Albert Brown's Conference Paper on "The Place of Women in the Ministry of the Church" concluded that there was no decisive objection to an extension of all aspects of Christian ministry to women. He urged the churches to train every woman and man who was willing to work.[86] Partly due to the well-established women's organizations and the leadership exercised by women serving as overseas missionaries, the role of women did not become a pressing issue in the British Churches until after 1950.

Nevertheless, a younger generation of women protested what they saw as significant limitations on opportunities for service. Not until 1973 was a woman—Winnie Clark—selected president of the Annual Conference. The first women ordained to the ministry were Daphne Jones and Nellie Smith (a former missionary) at the Conference of the Reformed Association in 1980. More significant was the admission of women to the eldership, which was always a matter of local decision rather than national policy. A significant number of women elders in the British Churches became Auxiliary Ministers as a result of union with the United Reformed Church in 1981. Neither the Fellowship of Churches of Christ nor the Old Paths Churches had provisions for women ministers.

The churches in Australia and New Zealand, with the exception of a cappella churches, accepted both women elders and women ministers, though it was rare for women ministers to be called to the largest churches in Australia.[87] One indicator of the continued male-dominated attitudes was the unquestioned use of "brethren" and "brotherhood" in the Churches in Britain, Australia, and New Zealand until well into the 1990s. Though the churches of the Canada region of the

Christian Church (Disciples of Christ) operated under the gender-inclusive guidelines of that body, by the early twenty-first century scarcely any women ministers had served local congregations in the Disciples or any other Stone-Campbell stream in Canada. Probably the best-known woman from the Canadian Disciples was Jessie M. Trout (1895-1990) who served first as a missionary and then as an executive of the United Christian Missionary Society.

Issues related to human sexuality, artificial birth control, and abortion did not significantly affect the life of the British Churches of Christ. In Australia, Churches of Christ vigorously debated issues such as homosexuality, abortion, and feminism in the *Australian Christian* beginning in the 1960s. The attitude toward homosexuals in the Churches was moderately tolerant in comparison with national attitudes. In all these matters there were significant differences between the states, with Victoria generally being the most liberal.

Because of Britain's early abolition of slavery, the nations of the British Commonwealth had tended to assume a superior attitude toward the U.S. on the issue of race. Race relations in many British territories, however, reflected the same attitudes of white privilege seen in American society. In Australia, the Dawson Street church in Ballarat raised questions about the legal mistreatment of aborigines and their neglect by health services.[88] The Churches established a Federal Aborigines Mission Board in 1938 with stations primarily in Western Australia. In the 1960s they extended work among children and adults to Victoria, New South Wales, and Queensland. The best-known aboriginal member of Churches of Christ was Pastor Doug Nicholls, who in 1957 was awarded the rank of MBE (Member of the Order of the British Empire) and a knighthood in 1972 for his work for his people.

In 1976 the British government appointed Nicholls Governor of South Australia, though he was forced to retire early for health reasons.[89] Still, indigenous inhabitants were not allowed to vote in federal elections until 1962, and not in Queensland until 1965. Aboriginal land rights became a major issue in the late 1960s, and in 1976 the government passed the Aboriginal Land Rights (Northern Territory) Act. Attempts to restrict native land rights provoked a bitter political fight in the 1990s. The policy of separating aboriginal children from their parents also became a hotly debated issue that went to the heart of Australian national consciousness. Against this backdrop, the efforts of all the nation's churches, including Churches of Christ, appeared largely paternalistic.[90]

Following a career as a professional Australian football player, Doug Nicholls became a social worker in 1942 and eventually organized the first Aboriginal Church of Christ in Australia. As editor of the Aboriginal Advancement League's journal *Smoke Signals*, he helped draw Aboriginal issues to the attention of government officials and the general public. *(Photo of Douglas Nicholls and his wife, Gladys, courtesy of Disciples Historical Society.)*

In New Zealand, consciousness of the way white settlers had used the Treaty of Waitangi of 1840 to exploit the Maori population emerged in the 1970s. The New Zealand Churches had begun Maori Missions in the 1930s in the Pukekohe district and near the city of Tauranga, both south of Auckland on the north island.[91] Though many Maoris had sold their land by the 1970s, efforts to recover earlier loss of land to unscrupulous white settlers continued. New Zealand politicians were generally more open to admitting and correcting matters of racial discrimination than their Australian counterparts and made an attempt at a new beginning after the 150th anniversary of the Treaty of Waitangi in 1991.[92] The New Zealand Churches, however, gave little attention to the issue.

Increased immigration into the U.K. from the Caribbean, India, Pakistan, and African colonies beginning in the late 1940s transformed British society, exposing racial attitudes largely ignored since Britain's abolition of slavery in the nineteenth century. This transformation challenged the churches to decide whether or not they truly believed that in Christ all humanity is one. In cities like Birmingham, Leicester, Manchester, and London, congregations struggled with whether or not to stay in neighborhoods from which upwardly mobile white members were moving and where new immigrants were finding homes.

In the 1950s Australia confronted the implications of its "white Australia" policy as both Australia and New Zealand faced a significant increase in immigration from southeast Asia. The 1949 Communist revolution in China, the anti-colonial insurgency in Indo-China in the 1950s, and the Vietnam War that followed led to even more immigration. Both Australian and New Zealand Churches of Christ were slow to face the issue of white attitudes toward both indigenous inhabitants and non-white immigrants, partly because of the location of their congregations, but primarily because they did not see it as a significant issue.

The same was true of the Canadian Churches in relation to "First Nation" peoples. Since few surviving First Nation inhabitants lived in the areas of their numerical strength, the churches seldom thought about the matter. Still, race relations were often better in Canada than in the United States, reflected in the response of the churches to significant immigration from non-traditional sources in the late twentieth century. One example was the Home Street Church in Winnipeg. In 1968, the pastor Norma Hall welcomed a few Filipina women into the congregation, who had been members of the United Church of Christ in Manila. Increased immigration of Filipinos to that area of Canada led to an influx of others to the church, with several becoming church officers. Another example was the Hillcrest Christian Church in Toronto; by 1990, half the congregation's members were non-white.[93]

Numerical Growth and Decline

British Churches of Christ continued to grow in the 1920s, reaching a peak membership of 16,596 in 1930—an increase of nearly 50 percent since 1900. A decrease in emigration after World War I likely contributed to this growth, but it also reflected evangelistic efforts to start new churches in developing areas. Of the eleven new congregations begun after 1920, most were south of the Lancashire-Yorkshire/Cheshire-Nottinghamshire border, places not previously known as areas of strength for Churches of Christ.

The Great Depression slowed growth, and the World War II bombing damage to church buildings followed by inadequate damage compensation after 1945 hindered expansion even further. Nevertheless, attitudes about the future remained optimistic well into the 1950s. A few older congregations built new buildings and some moved to the suburbs. The number of ministers and missionaries grew between the wars, and arguments against the policy of short pastorates changed attitudes and allowed for longer ministries. A. C. Watters reported in 1936 that in 1914 none of the eighteen full-time ministers had spent the whole year with one church. By 1936, two-thirds of the then thirty-one ministers had been with one church for a year or more. He argued that this pattern of longer ministries was compatible with the practice of mutual ministry.[94] Still, it was unusual for a minister to stay in one church for more than five years.

In addition, a new emphasis on "special missions" grew, especially through the efforts of J.W. Black, Chair of the General Evangelist Committee (GEC). Beginning in 1928, Black began conducting evangelistic campaigns around the country. Two years later the GEC proposed a "Forward Movement" in evangelism, and, in October 1933, Black persuaded E. C. Hinrichsen of Australia to spearhead this effort. Hinrichsen and song leader V. B. Morris arrived in February 1935 and conducted evangelistic campaigns in Leicester, Chester, and Manchester, resulting in two hundred eighty-eight additions. Though Hinrichsen returned to Australia in October 1936, over one thousand were added to the churches during his campaigns.[95]

Other expansion of the work of the British Conference included the 1920 appointment of former missionary R. H. Parker as full-time Organizing Secretary of the Temperance and Social Questions Committee, the successor of the Temperance Committee. The churches also appointed Leslie Colver as full-time Sunday school organizer in 1933.[96] In many ways the inter-war period was a golden age of confidence for British Churches of Christ.

The second half of the twentieth century was largely shaped by the British government's desperate attempts to deal with the consequences of the two world wars. Much of the country's infrastructure had been destroyed and, because the national deficit had reduced public investment, Britain's staple industries of coal mining, iron and steel manufacture, shipbuilding, and textile manufacture had essentially collapsed. Even the new motor manufacturing and electronics industries of the 1930s struggled to compete after 1960, and were often acquired by multi-national firms based in other countries.

Under Margaret Thatcher's government in the 1980s, the country's traditional industries suffered even more as a result of the focus on development of international finance and information technology. These shifts had a dramatic effect on the distribution of population. The southeast experienced significant growth, while Scotland, Wales, the north of England, and to a lesser extent the Midlands became areas of long-term unemployment. These depressed areas were where Churches of Christ had been strongest, and as a result the churches suffered significant decline.

With expectations for full-time evangelists increasing among the congregations, the old tradition of establishing a congregation with half a dozen people virtually disappeared. In the second half of the twentieth century, British Churches of Christ founded only two new churches, one in the new town of East Kilbride in 1954, the other in the developing Leicester suburb of Oadby in 1965. In both cases, costs forced the congregations to build much smaller buildings than planned, showing at the congregational level the country's lack of economic development.

In contrast, members of Old Paths congregations established several new churches in the late twentieth century. One was at Corby in Northamptonshire when steelworks were established with Scottish labor from closed plants further north. Also, the presence of American military chaplains from Churches of Christ on U.S. Army and Air Force bases, the largest of which were in the south of England, helped spark the formation of such congregations. With increasing help from the United States, the number of Old Paths congregations rose to around sixty by the end of the twentieth century, with about two thousand members.[97]

The Fellowship of Churches of Christ, which separated from the larger body in 1980 rather than become part of the United Reformed Church, also established new congregations, often based on the Community Church model. Fellowship churches often used contemporary charismatic worship practices like praise songs and electric instruments. For a while the Fellowship cooperated closely with the churches in New Zealand and Australia. In the early twenty-first century, nationwide membership of the Fellowship numbered around one thousand.[98]

Membership in New Zealand peaked at 4,972 in 1938, a few years later than in Great Britain. This number was nearly double that of 1905. New Zealand's economy, however, suffered greatly in the inter-war depression, and beginning in the 1960s the development of new textiles and EU tariffs hurt traditional wool and lamb exports. Located primarily on the South Island where traditional industries suffered most, Churches of Christ experienced declines. By 2000, numbers in the Associated Churches had dropped to around 1,800, although a new congregation was established in Auckland in 2002. A cappella Churches of Christ in New Zealand numbered approximately one thousand members in twenty-five congregations.[99]

In Canada the development of the western states in the early twentieth century changed the economic balance of the country, particularly as a result of westward migration from the Maritimes and Ontario. Churches of Christ benefited from this shift, though they never developed the numbers that existed further east. Though never as complete as in the United States, the division of the North American Stone-Campbell Movement into three major streams was seen among the Canadian churches much more than in other parts of the Commonwealth. A cappella congregations were in the majority and those related to the Christian Church (Disciples of Christ) the smallest. Establishing new congregations that would become self-supporting, as the Disciples Board of Church Extension expected, proved difficult often because of a lack of consistent ministerial leadership. And despite the underwriting of church buildings by the Church of Christ Development Company, most new Disciples congregations did not survive.[100]

At the beginning of the twenty-first century, all Canadian Stone-Campbell streams combined numbered around 15,300 members in two hundred twenty-two congregations. More significantly, the balance of the streams had shifted. In 1938 Disciples had numbered 9,785 in eighty congregations. At the beginning of the twenty-first century, the total number of Disciples in Canada was less than 1,800.

The Australian pattern of growth and decline was similar to that of New Zealand, with membership doubling between 1900 and 1930. Nevertheless, in the 1930s when unemployment reached over 30 percent of the male population, membership declined as it had in Britain. Since World War II, the pattern of the Australian Churches of Christ, which had always been concentrated in the larger towns, was for larger churches to grow larger, while smaller ones declined. By the end of the twentieth century the membership of the Associated churches was 36,500 in four hundred forty-three congregations, representing a considerable increase over the pre-war period. In addition, there were around three thousand members in eighty-one a cappella congregations with ties to U.S. Churches of Christ.[101]

The post-World War II growth of the Australian Churches was a result of several factors. Australian Churches of Christ had long believed in the importance of regular evangelistic campaigns. Several of the Australian state conferences employed evangelists like G. T. Fitzgerald in South Australia beginning in 1946. E. C. Hinrichsen established himself as an evangelist between the wars, making evangelistic tours in Britain and New Zealand, as well as his native Australia.[102] The Billy Graham evangelistic crusades starting in the 1950s were also a factor. The Australian Churches of Christ cooperated closely with the Graham organization, engaging in systematic follow-up to make sure those converted were linked to local churches. The climax of post-war growth in the Australian churches in 1960 coincided with the Graham mission.[103]

"Visitation evangelism," originally borrowed from the United States, continued the impetus begun by the Graham Crusades. Members of congregations visited house-to-house, inviting neighbors to attend special church gatherings. Even more significant was the adaptation of Donald McGavran's church growth techniques to the Australian situation. Gordon Moyes had been converted during an evangelistic campaign following the Melbourne World Convention in 1952. While minister at the Cheltenham Church in Melbourne in 1975, he wrote the influential book *How to Grow an Australian Church*. As a result of the churches' use of these methods, several mega-churches developed in the 1980s and 1990s, including the Careforce Church in Melbourne, and the Kardinia Christian Church in Geelong, Victoria.

Looking to the Future

As the Stone-Campbell Movement in the British Commonwealth moved into the twenty-first century, it faced questions that were sharper than at any point in its history, involving in some cases its very survival. Throughout its history, the Movement had most often attracted Christians seeking a better understanding of the Christian faith. With the massive decline of Christianity in the West, including Britain and its former colonies, the Churches often found themselves ill-equipped to respond to non-Christians wondering what Christian faith had to offer. Since most Churches of Christ in U.K. and Commonwealth countries had come to reject the proselytizing of other Christians, the question before leaders was whether there were distinctive Stone-Campbell gifts they could use to faithfully witness to the gospel in a hurting world.

14

The Stone-Campbell Movement in Asia
Since the 1920s

By the 1920s, U. S., British, and Australian missionary societies of the Stone-Campbell Movement supported evangelism throughout Asia, especially in India, China, Japan, and the Philippines. North American Churches of Christ had begun direct support missions in Asia before the turn of the twentieth century, and by the 1920s, nascent Christian Churches/Churches of Christ were doing the same. Yet the quest for freedom from imperialism after World War I led many in Asia to view Western missionaries with suspicion. This fact, coupled with a growing conviction among key missionary leaders that the churches should reflect the culture in which they existed and ultimately be led by local Christians, accelerated the process of indigenization of Stone-Campbell missions.

Another major impulse in the twentieth century was the creation of national union Protestant churches—particularly in Japan, the Philippines, and India—into which many mission congregations entered. In the late twentieth century, the Christian Church (Disciples of Christ), the Churches of Christ in the UK, and the Churches of Christ in Australia and New Zealand maintained ecumenical partnerships with these national churches. North American Churches of Christ and Christian Churches/Churches of Christ did not join the national union churches. Yet these streams began important educational and medical missions in addition to evangelistic work and developed stronger partnerships between missionaries and national leadership.

India

By the 1920s, Stone-Campbell missions were spread throughout the Central Provinces and the United Provinces (British names from the period used throughout this chapter) in the northwest, with a small mission in

the Bombay Presidency on the western coast, making India one of the Movement's largest and most successful mission initiatives.

The work supported by the United Christian Missionary Society (UCMS) consisted of thirteen stations, each with an organized church. Although the congregations at Damoh and Mungeli had called Indian pastors in 1919, missionaries remained pastors of the other eleven. The mission operated primary and secondary schools, a Bible college at Jabalpur, dispensaries at all thirteen stations, several hospitals as well as a leper asylum and a tuberculosis sanatorium. Veteran missionaries Mary Kingsbury, John and Helen McGavran, Dr. Mary McGavran, and C. G. and Edith Elsam led a team of seventy-seven missionaries and more than three hundred Indian workers.[1]

The Foreign Missions Committee (FMC) of the British Churches of Christ supported three stations in the United Provinces by the 1920s. Each station had a small congregation under missionary leadership, and one had an orphanage. A. C. Watters (1887-1970) directed the work in all three stations, which also employed several Indian workers. Because of their relatively close proximity, the UCMS and FMC missions developed a close working relationship.[2]

Nearly a thousand miles to the southwest, the Australian Churches of Christ operated two mission stations by 1920. With some support from the FMC, five Australian missionaries served at Baramati and Shrigonda in the Bombay Presidency. Like the others, both stations had small, missionary-led congregations and numerous Indian workers. This Australian mission was especially known for its work among the Bhampta, a caste of thieves who survived by picking pockets in Indian railway towns.[3]

In 1925, UCMS leaders made the controversial decision to concentrate efforts in what they called the "preferred areas" of the mission. A shortage of missionary personnel and contributions, rising costs, and the distance between stations made managing the mission increasingly difficult. The UCMS closed the Maudha station, made one hospital into a dispensary, and discontinued their primary schools at Harda. The UCMS annual report stated unequivocally, "No church was abandoned… But some funds invested in educational and medical work were diverted to other places where our work will be more coordinated and less scattered."[4] Nonetheless, the decision angered some in the United States, especially those who already had doubts about the UCMS's mission policies.

In response, two couples separated from the UCMS and continued as direct-support missionaries. Sterling (1886-1928) and Dr. Zoena (1882-1979) Rothermel, who had served at the Maudha station between 1915 and 1922 as missionaries for the CWBM and the UCMS, vigorously opposed the station's closing. While on furlough in the United States they began raising support, and in 1927 negotiated the purchase of the Maudha station from the UCMS, returning to India as direct-support missionaries. Although Sterling died in 1928, Dr. Rothermel continued medical missions in Maudha and the surrounding villages until her retirement in 1965. Their daughter Jean (Rothermel) Roland (1920-2002), and her husband, William Roland, continued the work in Maudha until 1997.[5]

The other couple was Harry (d. 1946) and Emma Schaefer. Like the Rothermels, the Schaefers had served as CWBM and UCMS missionaries between 1913 and 1927. During their terms of service in Bilaspur, Harry had done evangelistic work and supervised the construction of several mission buildings, including the Jackman Memorial Hospital. Emma had taught in the schools and worked with Bible women. The Schaefers believed that the UCMS mission placed too much emphasis on medical and educational work and opposed its developing cooperation with other denominations. When they returned to Bilaspur as direct-support missionaries in 1928, they founded Central Provinces India Mission. With their son, Harry Schaefer, Jr., they focused on evangelism and church building into the 1960s in an area where UCMS missionaries also continued to work.[6]

Missionaries from the United States were not the only ones dissatisfied with the UCMS's decision to close some operations. Australian G. Percy Pittman, supported by the British FMC, openly charged that Harda had been "abandoned." The Australian churches assumed support of one UCMS missionary, Mary Thompson, an Australian woman who had served in Harda since 1891. Pittman eventually broke with the FMC, became a direct-support missionary, and in 1928 established a new station for the Australian Churches of Christ at Simla, in the northern Punjab Province.[7]

Even as the UCMS consolidated its mission work in India, British and Australian Churches of Christ were expanding theirs in the 1920s and early 1930s. In 1925, Australian Churches of Christ opened a new station in Dhond, including a hospital under the direction of Dr. G. H. Oldfield and two Indian physicians. A young Indian named Dr. Ratnaker Parkhe took over the administration of the hospital upon Oldfield's retirement in 1948. British Churches of Christ sent three additional workers to help at their stations in the 1920s: Elsie Francis to Dudhi, Bessie Melville to the orphanage at Daltonganj, and Anne Piggott who itinerated between all of the mission stations, working primarily with Bible women.[8]

When the practice of medicine by women in Europe and the United States was severely restricted, many women doctors served faithfully in missions across the globe. For more than five decades, Dr. Zoena Rothermel provided medical care to the people of Maudha, India.

The Great Depression greatly accelerated the indigenization of Stone-Campbell missions in India. As contributions from Western churches plummeted and the number of missionaries working in India decreased, Indian Christians assumed more leadership. The examples of UCMS workers Alfred Aleppa and George Harrison Singh are illustrative.

Mary Graybiel had brought Aleppa to Damoh around 1895 as a young boy orphaned during the famine. After graduating from the mission high school in Harda, he returned to serve as a native evangelist at several outstations around Damoh. Later Aleppa completed studies at the Bible college at Jabalpur and in 1921 became the first native pastor of the Damoh church and padre sahib (house father) of the orphanage. Ordained in 1924, his responsibilities expanded to include supervising all district evangelistic work where almost five hundred Christians lived. Known throughout the region as Bhayaji (big brother), Aleppa also served in a variety of civil service positions with the British. He worked faithfully with the India mission until his death in 1947.[9]

Singh received his early education in Indian mission schools and by 1920 had graduated from Hiram College and the College of Missions in the United States. He returned to India to serve as pastor of the mission's church at Barela, near Jabalpur. While there he and four other Indian "teacher-preachers" developed a program of evangelism in which they spent half the day teaching in village schools and the other half in house-to-house evangelism. Along with Methodist Episcopal Bishop J. Waskom Pickett and UCMS missionary Donald McGavran, Singh undertook important sociological studies of the mass movements in central India that were leading to significant growth in some churches. In 1938, he served as a delegate from India to the ecumenical mission conference in Tambaram, and was among the voices of the "younger churches" that stressed the importance of inter-religious dialogue for the future of Christian missions. He continued serving churches in the mission until his death, but also gained wide respect from Protestant missionaries of many denominations and his Indian contemporaries for his inter-denominational work.[10]

The growing popularity of the Indian Independence Movement in the 1920s and 1930s also accelerated the indigenization of the UCMS mission in India. Mohandas Ghandi's message of anti-colonialism and self-sufficiency emboldened Indian leaders to claim a greater role in leading the work of the missions and motivated mission leaders to create the space for them to do so. At the golden Jubilee convention at Jabalpur in 1932, UCMS leaders made a firm commitment to speed up the process of moving the church "toward self-support, toward self-government, and toward self-propagation." This process of indigenization continued for several decades, as leaders like Luther Shah, Samuel Massih, and Peter Solomon rose to assume leadership in the mission's churches, hospitals, and schools. By 1965, the churches and other institutions of the mission were almost entirely self-governing and self-supporting, and the way was prepared for them to enter the developing United Church of North India.[11]

George Hamilton Singh completed a sociological study of the caste system in India for his master's degree at Butler University in 1927. He is pictured here, shortly after his return to India, caring for a village child. (*World Call*, July-August 1934)

The work of British Churches of Christ in the Palamau District of the United Provinces remained remarkably stable, partly because of a committed group of missionaries that included J. C. and Dorothy Christie, Penry and Elsie Price, and Bessie Melville. In 1933, Percy and Naomi Pittman, who had served as part of the FMC work from 1909 to 1920, returned to the FMC mission after having worked for more than a decade as independent missionaries. Their return was welcomed, and they served six more years at no expense to the FMC until their retirement in 1939. Among the Indian leaders who worked faithfully alongside these missionaries was a "Bible woman" named Susanna Sahay, the wife of Indian evangelist Prabhu Sahay.[12]

Despite the financial challenges of the Great Depression, by the late 1930s the mission of the British Churches of Christ had expanded into several villages southwest of Daltonganj in the Bhandaria District. In each village, missionaries formed a small church that provided a base for evangelistic, educational, temperance, and medical work throughout the district.[13] In 1942 missionaries reorganized the Churches Representative Committee—which directed all the mission's activities—to include a two-thirds majority of Indian leaders. A new generation of Indians who supported Indian independence—especially Tapsi Lal, pastor of the Daltonganj church, and Babu Minz, superintendent of the Bhandaria schools—pushed aggressively for greater control of the churches, schools, and medical facilities. On the eve of Indian independence, the British Churches of Christ mission included eight churches, employed eight missionaries and almost thirty Indian workers, administered seven schools, and ministered to a Christian community of nearly 1,000 people. In 1956, the FMC relinquished the station in Daltonganj to the Swedish Independent Baptist Missionary Society, so that the remaining missionaries could concentrate their efforts in Bhandaria and Surguja. A year later, the Indian and British leadership of the mission agreed on a Five Year Plan by which the churches would become financially self-sufficient. During the 1960s, Indian leaders gradually assumed full responsibility for virtually every phase of the mission's work.[14]

In 1905, the Australian Churches of Christ had begun work in Baramati, 130 miles southeast of Bombay (present-day Mumbai), with the arrival of Henry Strutton and his wife. Within a year, the Struttons had established a church whose membership was drawn mainly from the Dalits, the lowest caste of Indian society. By the early 1920s, fifteen missionaries were working in Baramati, Shrigonda, and at least ten neighboring villages. Several served for decades, including Florence Cameron from 1915 to 1954, Elsie Caldicott from 1916 to 1949, and H. R. Coventry from 1916 to 1947. Organized as the Conference of Churches of Christ in West India (CCCWI) in 1927, the mission also employed twenty-six Indian evangelists and Bible women. The mission included an educational program for the Bhampta caste, orphanages for boys and girls, a hospital and dispensary, and schools at all levels of instruction.[15]

Two Australian women emerged as the primary leaders of the CCCWI for more than sixty years. Edna Vawser (1902-1994) arrived in India in 1926, with support from her parents, the Hindmarsh Place Christian Church, and her own work. Not until 1939 did she become a missionary of the Overseas Mission Board. For thirty years Vawser served in the orphanages at Baramati

and Shrigonda, joined by her colleague Hazel Skuce in 1949. In 1967, the two became founding members of the Baramati Agricultural Development Trust, an organization to sponsor water conservation projects and provide agricultural education.[16]

Australian Churches of Christ continued to provide support to this work in the early twenty-first century through their Global Mission Partners.[17] The Baramati and Shrigonda Children's Homes continued to provide care to children left orphaned by India's ongoing public health crises, especially HIV/AIDS. Ashwood Memorial Hospital continued operation in Dhond under Indian leadership, with help from occasional medical personnel from abroad. In 1985, Kiron Gaikwad began Hosanna Ministries and the Ankoor Home with some support from Australian Churches of Christ. She and her staff worked among the Yavatmai people of central India, providing medical care, an orphanage, and Bible training.[18]

Many Stone-Campbell mission leaders in India had long shared with other groups a desire for church union in India. As early as 1939, Samuel Maqbul Masih insisted that unity was the Indian church's greatest need. Division hindered evangelism, especially among the lower castes, who were already victims of a divided society. Overlapping work wasted personnel and money. Furthermore, the "new conditions in India arising out of her political and social awakening…make it imperative for the church in India to be united."[19] Obstacles to the proposed union for the churches of the Stone-Campbell Movement included the fact that most of the negotiating churches practiced infant as well as believer's baptism, the likelihood that the united church would adopt an episcopal rather than congregational polity, and would commit to a formal confession of faith.

The only real question for UCMS missionary Tom Hill was, what do the Indian church leaders want? "Will our American brethren allow them the same liberty we prize ourselves, or shall we insist upon dictation across the seas?"[20] According to Hill, the Indian context was key. Maintaining distinctive denominational doctrines was far less important than developing effective evangelism in the particular circumstances. "Faced by a world in crisis, by the large Indian majorities of Hindus and Mohammedans, [Indian church leaders] may count union of more moment than some of the items we have held dear," he explained. In addition, he insisted that the emphasis the U. S. and British churches placed on congregational polity was a byproduct of modern democracy and could not be "translated" to the Indian context. "India is definitely not democratic and will tend more and more to adopt episcopal-like systems of church government." Most important for Hill, however, was the mounting nationalism in India. Western Christians would have to face the fact that Indian churches were becoming more resistant to domination and were eager to align themselves with other Indian groups as the best way to free themselves from colonialism.[21]

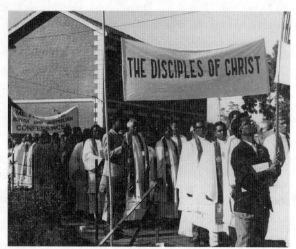

Representatives of the Disciples of Christ participate in the inaugural ceremony for the United Church of North India in 1970. The new united church included six denominations and claimed a total membership of more than a million.

In the two decades following Indian independence, this commitment to church union began to take institutional shape. Many formerly denominational schools, medical facilities, and presses became "union" institutions. Between 1947 and 1953, UCMS-supported missionaries joined the work at several of these institutions, including Allahabad Agricultural Institute (Presbyterian), Leonard Theological College (Methodist Episcopal), Vellore Christian Medical College (Reformed Church of America), and Ludhiana Christian Medical College and Hospital (Baptist).[22]

In the 1950s and 1960s, the UCMS also cooperated with the societies of other denominations to expand the work in India and elsewhere. As early as 1951, Methodist, Presbyterian, and Church of Scotland missionaries formed the Union Mission to Nepal. Five years later Elizabeth Hill, a registered nurse and North American Disciple, joined them and helped establish a cholera hospital in Katmandu. In the late 1950s and 1960s, the mission expanded to include education and social services in at least three additional locations as

other Protestant missionaries joined the effort. Though the Nepalese government prohibited direct evangelism and constructing church buildings, this cooperative work made significant inroads in planting Christianity in that nation.[23]

Another example of ecumenical cooperation began in 1952, when the UCMS joined the work of the London-based Baptist Missionary Society in Orissa, a region southeast of the Indian Central Provinces. By combining forces, the two societies were able to open a new station in Diptipur. UCMS missionaries L. Franklin and Ada White were the first to join the Baptist work, which expanded to include middle and secondary schools, and in 1957 a two-year Bible school at Balangir to train Indian pastors. By 1960, the UCMS was supporting three additional missionary couples, including Dr. Paul Detweiler, who opened the Diptipur Christian Hospital. When the Orissa congregations joined the United Church of North India in 1970, the mission claimed more than six thousand members.[24]

The formation of the United Church of North India was the most significant ecumenical development of the era. As early as 1929, leaders of the UCMS and Australian Churches of Christ missions participated in discussions about forming such a union church.[25] Anglicans, Congregationalists, Presbyterians, Methodists, and Baptists engaged in "roundtable conversations" throughout the 1930s, 1940s, and 1950s, forming in 1951 a negotiation committee to forge an actual union. Though the Australian Churches of Christ Mission had been one of the earliest conversation participants, many Stone-Campbell mission churches were reluctant to merge for the reasons noted above—the union church's acceptance of infant baptism, plus its plan to adopt an episcopal polity and produce a creed-like statement of belief.

In 1957, however, the UCMS-supported churches joined the conversations and eventually were convinced to become part of the emerging union church. The United Church of North India was formed in November 1970, with the participation of most UCMS, British, and Australian Stone-Campbell mission churches.[26] North American Disciples and British Churches of Christ continued to partner with the United Church by providing "fraternal workers" whenever requested.

The UCMS and FMC involvement in the church union discussions further alienated non-participating Stone-Campbell churches. By the early 1950s, direct-support missions were flourishing in strategic centers of the Central and United Provinces. The Schaefers continued their work through their Central Provinces Indian Mission in Bilaspur and the Rothermels through their Christian Mission to India in Ragaul. At least three new direct-support missions also had been established: the Church of Christ Mission at Kulpahar, the Assam Christian Mission, and the South India Church of Christ Mission in Travencore. Each of these followed the pattern of the Schaefers and Rothermels. Evangelism and church planting were the primary objectives, though these missions also provided medical care, education, and social services.[27]

After the formation of the United Church of North India, direct-support missions continued to grow through works like Benevolent Social Services of India, Inc., started in 1970 by David (1910-1976) and Lois (1916-2006) Rees. Natives of Alberta, Canada, they began mission work in 1946 among the Lisu people of southwestern China. When the Chinese Revolution brought communists into power in 1949 they fled to Burma, but moved to India in 1953 when Burmese communists rose to power after independence from Britain.[28]

Through the 1950s and 1960s the Reeses did "village evangelism" among the poor of the Shillong region of northeast India. In 1968, the local government imposed restrictions on Christian mission work that forced them to relocate to South India. There it was clear that the region's greatest need was medical care, especially for those suffering from leprosy. In 1970 the missionary couple established a thirty-bed Leprosy Hospital in Adhra Pradesh and outdoor clinics in surrounding villages. As their medical care and evangelistic efforts expanded, their mission became known as Benevolent Social Services of India, Inc. (BSSI). Though David was killed in an automobile accident in 1976, Lois continued leading BSSI for another sixteen years, retiring in 1992. Emrys and Usha Rees, the son and daughter-in-law of the founders, assumed leadership of the mission. In the last decades of the twentieth century BSSI expanded to help address HIV/AIDS and tuberculosis epidemics in India.[29]

Another example of direct-support work was the Central India Christian Mission (CICM). Vijai Lall (1933-1993) and his wife, Pushpa, served in the UCMS-supported mission for more than forty years, Vijai as Director of Christian Education for the Disciples of Christ India Mission (DCIM), and Pushpa as principal of the Christian high school in Damoh. As DCIM leaders became more enthusiastic about joining the union church, Vijai and Pushpa led several churches to become independent Christian congregations. Their

son, Ajai Lall, and his wife, Indu, established CICM with significant assistance from his parents. Under the direction of a board composed of Christian Churches/Churches of Christ leaders in the United States, CICM focused mainly on evangelism and church planting.[30]

The work of North American Churches of Christ in India, begun by E. S. Jelley and his missionary colleagues in Ahmednagar in the Bombay Presidency, had ended by the late 1920s. Several of the churches had followed their missionaries and Indian leaders into the Seventh-Day Adventists.[31] However, just when many Stone-Campbell missions were becoming part of the United Church of North India, North American Churches of Christ resumed mission efforts.

Already a successful evangelist in Canada, John Carlos Bailey was almost sixty years old when he first arrived in India in 1963. He is shown here at an evangelistic meeting wearing a pancha, the traditional dress of Tugulu men. (John Carlos Bailey, *My Appointment with Destiny*, 1975)

In 1963, Canadians John Carlos Bailey (1903-2001) and his wife Myrtle entered Shillong, the capital of Assam, a small state in the northeast. There they began work with three small congregations among the Khasi tribe that had broken with the Presbyterians in the 1930s.[32] The Baileys soon received a call to begin new work in Madras (now Chennai) more than a thousand miles to the southwest. They turned over the work in Assam to other Canadian missionaries, notably David Hallett, who led the mission work there for thirty years until his retirement in 1993.[33] In Madras the Baileys began evangelistic and church-planting work throughout the Tamil Nadu and Andrha Pradesh states of southeastern India. After only two years, the Baileys reported that more than 1,500 people had been baptized and at least seventy-five churches had been established. Encouraged by their initial successes, at least a dozen other Canadian missionaries joined the Baileys in the 1960s.[34] Also led by Indian evangelists, these Churches of Christ in India experienced explosive numerical growth. By the time the Baileys retired to Saskatchewan in 1972, the missionaries and Indian evangelists had helped establish more than seven hundred congregations in India.[35] So amazing was the growth that missionaries sometimes had to defend themselves against charges of exaggerated reports.[36]

Nehemiah Gootam and his brother Joshua emerged as two of the most important leaders of Churches of Christ in India. Baptized by J. C. Bailey in 1963, the brothers quickly became talented evangelists, educators, and church planters. Upon Bailey's retirement in 1972, Nehemiah assumed responsibility for leading several preacher training schools, especially Kakinada School of Preaching. Joshua began a daily Telegu-language radio broadcast that reached more than 100 million listeners. He already had been instrumental in helping North American missionaries establish Churches of Christ in Bombay. The Gootams published *Seatya Wahku* (*The Word of Truth*), a newspaper containing doctrinal teaching, devotional material, and news of the churches. At the beginning of the twenty-first century, both Nehemiah and Joshua Gootam continued to serve as significant leaders of Churches of Christ in India and effective spokespeople for India among North American Churches of Christ.[37]

Despite visa restrictions, hundreds of missionaries from U.S. Churches of Christ made one-to-three-month mission trips to India to conduct radio programs, distribute Bibles and devotional literature, assist with evangelism, and provide medical care. Participants in one such trip began evangelistic and church-planting work in New Delhi, which they turned over immediately to Indian evangelists.[38] Leadership training was a principal focus of most of these short-term missions.[39] In 1969, North American missionaries established the Madras School of Preaching, supported by the Sunset Church of Christ in Lubbock, Texas. Within two years, the school was meeting in its own facility and had received government recognition, permitting instructors from other nations, including the United States, to teach there.[40] In the 1990s, the school's curriculum expanded to include a full program of liberal arts and graduate theological studies. At the beginning of the twenty-first century, the school was known as The National Bible College.[41] From this teaching center, Bible correspondence courses have been offered to hundreds of thousands of people across

Beginning in 1972, Nehemiah Gootam directed the Kakinada School of Preaching, a two-year program emphasizing Bible study and memorization to equip Indian evangelists. He is pictured here with his wife Nalini. (John Carlos Bailey, *My Appointment with Destiny*, 1975)

India, greatly aiding the growth of Churches of Christ.

By the mid-1970s, missionaries from North American Churches of Christ generally agreed with J. C. Choate when he said of the work in New Delhi that they had "worked themselves out of a job."[42] Indian leaders, they believed, were sufficiently prepared to carry on the work without significant assistance from North American missionaries. Though missionaries have continued to assist with short-term mission trips, Indian leaders have been primarily responsible for establishing many of the 48,000 congregations in almost every state in India. At the beginning of the twenty-first century, the membership of Churches of Christ in India may have been as high as 1.14 million people.[43]

Prior to independence in 1947, Pakistan, then made up of eastern and western sections, had been part of British India. Predominantly Muslim, the nation adopted a constitution as an Islamic republic in 1956, though military leaders who seized the government in a coup two years later strengthened relations with the United States and other Western countries. In February 1961, Gordon and Jane Hogan and their family became the first missionaries to Pakistan from North American Churches of Christ when they moved to Lahore. They found the Lee Turner family, missionaries from North American Christian Churches/Churches of Christ, already working in the city. Others who moved to Pakistan included J. C. and Betty Choate in 1962, followed by Jim and Laura Waldron and Wayne and Deane Newcomb in 1967, all to Karachi. The missionaries soon established Bible training schools in Lahore and Karachi. By the late 1960s, however, the country's internal instability and wars with India, along with the difficulty of working in a Muslim land, led most of the missionaries to move to other fields, including the Hogans to Singapore and the Choates to Sri Lanka and later India.

The work of Churches of Christ continued under the leadership of Pakistani Christians, including Anwar Masih, who had studied at the Bible training school in Karachi and later directed the school at Lahore; Hadayat H. Din, who began preaching in his home town of Sialkot and later also began a preacher's training program; and Asghar Ali, baptized at Lahore in February 1962, who, after studying at Four Seas College from 1967-1968, returned to lead the church in Lahore. While missionaries from the United States were able to secure short-term visas to help with the work, and several native ministers received financial support from American Churches of Christ, Churches of Christ in Pakistan have been led primarily by native evangelists since the early 1970s. By 1993 around 500 persons had been baptized, though anti-Christian pressure led many to return to Islam. In 2004 there were an estimated twenty-five Churches of Christ congregations with approximately 250 members.[44]

Despite difficult conditions, in 1989 Pakistani Christian Saleem Massey returned to his country after graduation from Cincinnati Bible Seminary and founded Pakistan Christian Evangelical Services with the goal of planting churches throughout the country. With support from individuals and congregations of both the Christian Church (Disciples of Christ) and Christian Churches/Churches of Christ in North America, plus Australian and Scottish Churches of Christ, Massey had established eight churches with a total of more than 3,000 members by 2011. Many of the congregations provided schools for poor children and sponsored medical camps where visiting medical teams from the U.S. provided free care to Christians and Muslims.

China

By the end of the 1920s, Stone-Campbell missions in China had developed into one of the Movement's most significant efforts. The UCMS-supported China Mission was headquartered in Nanking, but operated stations in four other major cities in the Yangtse River Valley: Chuchow, Wuhu, Luchowfu, and Nantungchow. Scattered between these stations were fourteen congregations with a combined membership of 1,400. In Nanking the mission operated six day schools for girls and boys, and the UCMS participated in interdenominational educational work at the University of Nanking, Ginling College for Women, Nanking Theological Seminary, and the Bible Teachers' Training School. All of the stations except Wuhu also provided medical care through Christian hospitals and dispensaries. At its height in 1926, the UCMS supported sixty-four missionaries in China, assisted by hundreds of Chinese workers.[45]

At the annual convention of the UCMS-supported China Mission in 1921, leaders adopted a plan to begin transferring responsibility from the missionaries to Chinese Christian leaders. The goal was to create a true partnership in which both would work together "in the bond of a common fellowship and allegiance to a common Master." The reorganization created two administrative bodies, each with equal Chinese and missionary representation, that functioned for twenty-five years. The first was a fourteen-person council that served as a "board of managers" for the China Mission, reviewing the mission's work, making major decisions, and creating policy. The second was a six-person administrative committee that carried out the council's decisions.[46]

In this new structure, Li Hou-fu (d. 1939) distinguished himself as one of the most capable leaders of the China Mission. Son of an important government official, Li graduated from the mission school in Nanking in 1900. For many years he held a lucrative position as a translator for several railroad companies, though always involved with the Mission. He later served as pastor of the Chinese church at Hisakwan, taught at Nanking Theological Seminary, and served as an evangelist in many of the mission's outstations. In 1921 leaders elected him co-secretary of the mission along with missionary Edwin Marx (1885-1955), a position he held for nearly two decades. He suffered persecution by the Chinese government and in 1937 was forced to flee Nanking after the Japanese invasion, dying two years later as a refugee.[47]

Besides the UCMS-supported work in the north, North American Churches of Christ sent several missionaries to southern China in the 1920s. George (1898-1991) and Sallie (1896-1981) Benson were the first to arrive in 1925, establishing a base in Hong Kong. After learning Cantonese, the Bensons received permission from Chinese authorities to move inland, where they preached in the streets of the rural villages along the Xun River. Less than a year later, however, political turmoil in the region forced the Bensons to return to Hong Kong. In 1927, five other missionaries joined them there: Emmett (1896-1942) and Margaret (b. 1904) Broaddus; Lewis (1903-1985) and Grace Oldham; and Ethel Mattley (1887-1970).[48]

In Hong Kong, these missionaries soon found a small congregation of independent Chinese Christians under the leadership of Au Kwong-hon, who apparently had been converted by a Baptist missionary and lived for a time in Australia. The group readily welcomed the missionaries, and Benson convinced the church to abandon its use of instrumental music out of a commitment to restoring New Testament Christianity. The Shum Shui Po Church of Christ became the base of mission work, and soon the missionaries had established several other congregations in the suburbs of the city. As a British protectorate, the island offered some measure of safety from the Chinese civil war. Emmett Broaddus taught Bible and English at Munsang College, and several young men from his classes became leaders of the growing Hong Kong mission. Still, the missionaries—especially Mattley—never abandoned hopes of establishing an inland mission in southern China.[49]

Chinese political conditions in the late 1920s, however, were extremely unsettled. The revolutions of 1911 and 1919 failed to establish a stable national government, and warlords and their armies ruled most of China. Beginning in 1926, under the leadership of general Chiang Kai-shek, the Kuomintang, the Nationalist People's Party, attempted to overthrow these warlords and unite the nation under its political leadership. The civil war intensified, especially in the Yangtse River Valley cities of Luchowfu, Chuchow, and Nanking. Anti-foreign sentiment was strong among Nationalist leaders, and foreign institutions—including churches—came under attack. Most foreigners fled China. By 1928, the Kuomintang had succeeded and restored relative peace, but the relationship between foreign institutions and the new Nationalist government was extremely fragile.

The 1921 restructuring of the UCMS-supported China Mission proved advantageous. By the time Nationalist forces overtook the Yangtse River Valley five years later, much of the work had been transferred to Chinese leaders. Chinese leaders protected mission property and defended Christians after the missionaries left. Almost single-handedly, Min Chen His-ren preserved the Drum Tower Girls' School from destruction in Nanking, and Dr. Chen Dao Sen saved the mission's hospital and dispensary in Luchowfu.[50] In Chuchow, Ho Li-min petitioned and received orders from military officers to restrain occupying troops, personally posting the orders throughout the city.[51]

Though the global economic depression presented significant challenges, Stone-Campbell mission work in China continued to expand and thrive. In the early 1930s, the missionaries from North American Churches of Christ resumed work inland in south China, leaving the three Hong Kong congregations under the primary leadership of Chinese ministers. At Canton (now Guangzhou) the Bensons and Oldhams established two congregations and began the Canton Bible School and Canton English Finishing School for the training of Chinese Christian leaders. They also began publishing two journals: *The Canton Christian* (later renamed *The Oriental Christian*), an English-language periodical to solicit financial support for their work; and *The Defender*, a Chinese-language periodical for circulation in China, Australia, and the United States. Benson also translated several crucial works into Chinese, including J. W. McGarvey's *Commentary on Acts* and T. W. Philips's *The Church of Christ*. Some graduates of Harding College whom Benson had encouraged to become missionaries joined the work in Canton by the mid-1930s: Lowell (1910-2007) and Odessa (1911-2010) Davis; Roy and Ruth Whitfield; and Elizabeth (1890-1971) and Estella Bernard.[52] The Broaduses, Mattley, and several Chinese leaders from Hong Kong engaged in itinerant evangelistic work in villages around Canton, establishing several churches.

In the Yangtse River Valley, some UCMS-supported Chinese pastors began advocating Christianity as a "civil religion," insisting that the Christian faith supported the emerging Nationalist social and political order. Though the government occasionally confiscated church property, "the church people accepted the losses patiently and courteously...striving always to maintain and cultivate the utmost degree of amicable relations." When the Nationalist government ruled that to receive government approval the principal and a majority of directors of all educational institutions must be Chinese and that teaching of religion must stop, the leaders of the China Mission quickly conformed rather than risk closure. In addition, the China Mission began cooperating in interdenominational union efforts, especially the China

Christian Educational Association and the National Christian Council, often supplying leadership for these organizations.[53]

Beginning in 1937, the Imperial Japanese Army launched a full-scale invasion of China provoking the Second Sino-Japanese War. Although the Kuomintang army offered fierce resistance, the Japanese quickly overtook most of the northern coastline and the entire Yangtse River Valley. By 1939, the Japanese also had captured several important coastal cities in south China, including Canton (Guangzhou), which they would continue to occupy until the end of World War II. Most Stone-Campbell missionaries chose to leave China in the early years of Japanese occupation, though a handful remained until the United States entered World War II in December 1941.

Violence throughout China reached a peak with the occupation of Nanking in December 1937. For six weeks, Japanese soldiers massacred approximately 200,000 unarmed Chinese soldiers and civilians, and raped an estimated 50,000 Chinese women and young girls. Among Stone-Campbell missionaries who had remained was Miner Searle Bates (1897-1978), longtime faculty member at the University of Nanking. As a member of the International Committee for the Nanking Safety Zones, he worked to ensure the safety of more than 250,000 people living in the city during the Japanese occupation. Another was Minnie Vautrin (1886-1941), dean of the department of education at Ginling College. Nearly 10,000 people sought refuge on the Ginling campus, and for six months she coordinated efforts to meet their needs, negotiated their safety, and protected college resources from the Japanese. The emotional strain was too great for her to bear, and in 1941 she committed suicide while on furlough in Indianapolis.[54]

Shao Ching-San—better known as Luther Shao (d. 1958)—emerged as the most significant leader of the China Mission during the Japanese occupation. Having grown up in the Mission, he graduated from Nanking Theological Seminary in 1926 and became one of the pastors at Drum Tower Church. In 1930, he entered Yale Divinity School and was a frequent teacher and lecturer among Disciples in the United States. He received a Ph.D. from Yale in 1934 and returned to China and to the pastorate of the Drum Tower Church. During the Japanese occupation (1937-1945), he served refugees in the western province of Szechwan. Upon the death of Li Hou-fu in 1939, Shao also assumed the position of Chinese secretary of the mission, a position he held until the China Mission dissolved during the communist

takeover. Despite persecution, he continued to lead Chinese Christians until his death in 1958.[55]

Like their UCMS counterparts, missionaries from North American Churches of Christ remained in their stations in south China until the last possible moment. The Bensons already had left in 1937 so that George could become president of Harding College. But after the Imperial Japanese Army overtook Canton (Guangzhou) in 1939, all of the missionaries evacuated to Hong Kong, and many later joined the mission work of Churches of Christ in the Philippines. Emmett Broaddus remained in Hong Kong, however, where he died amid war conditions in 1942. Missionaries from Churches of Christ attempted to revive the work in Guangzhou after the war, but concentrated their efforts in Hong Kong beginning in the late 1950s.[56]

Even before the end of World War II, the UCMS began making plans to resume the China Mission. After a two-day meeting in spring 1944, China missionaries and UCMS executives decided to re-enter China as soon as possible.[57] The stream of missionaries who returned to China beginning in late 1945 found most of the mission property destroyed or badly damaged, and many of the churches in disarray. The UCMS launched an aggressive campaign to raise over $400,000 for the "reconstruction and rehabilitation" of the China Mission. Before significant work could resume, however, political conditions in China again deteriorated.[58]

Between 1946 and 1949, the communist People's Liberation Army under the leadership of Mao Zedong began its effort to control the nation. Beginning in Manchuria, the communists marched southward, gaining the sympathies of rural people and overtaking city after city. Badly weakened by its resistance to Japanese occupation, the armies of the Kuomintang offered little resistance. On October 1, 1949, Mao proclaimed victory and formed the People's Republic of China, forcing the remnant of the Kuomintang to seek refuge in Taiwan. Sweeping economic and social reforms followed, including the expulsion of all foreigners from China. An "iron curtain" had fallen, and for more than forty years China would be largely cut off from outside influence.

Amid these changes, the UCMS radically altered its involvement with the churches of the China Mission. Realizing that sending personnel to China would be impossible for the foreseeable future, the society committed itself to caring for missionaries who had served and preparing new ones for the future. The society also continued financial support of the Chinese churches as possible, but transferred ownership and full responsibility for the mission to the Chinese. By the middle of 1951, the last of the UCMS missionaries had left mainland China.[59]

As early as 1947, Lowell and Odessa Davis from North American Churches of Christ had returned to Guangzhou, primarily to provide humanitarian assistance. They were pleased to find that a small Church of Christ continued to meet there and that the Canton Bible School had resumed operation, both under Chinese leadership. For almost two years, they distributed clothing and food, established an orphanage, and assisted Chinese leaders in evangelistic work, especially among college students in the region. Hopes for an ongoing partnership between the Chinese and North American Churches of Christ in Guangzhou were cut short in 1949 when the communist revolution forced the Davises and their co-workers from mainland China.[60]

After the Communist Revolution, Chinese church leaders heroically continued the pastoral, educational, and medical work of the China Mission. At the 1951 ordination of Pan Chuin Chang (front row, center), Luther Shao (front row, left) and Disciples missionary James McCallum (back row, center) participated.

North American Churches of Christ had some success in reviving their mission work in Hong Kong after World War II, mainly because the island remained a British protectorate beyond the reach of communist control until 1999. The first missionary to arrive in 1949 was Elizabeth Bernard, who had come to China first in 1933. Though completely blind, she ran an orphanage in her home, distributed food and clothing to the poor, and helped lead two small congregations: Shum Shui Po and Hunghorn.[61] She labored alone until 1959, when additional missionaries began arriving for short-term assignments.[62]

Progress was slow; over the next twenty-five years, only five additional congregations were established: Wanchai (1967), Wa Fu Estate (1968), Kowloon (1971), Argyle Street (1973), and Yuen Long (1982). Beyond these church-planting efforts, missionaries from North American Churches of Christ fulfilled a dream of establishing preaching schools to train Chinese evangelists: China-Asia Preaching School and the Hong Kong Bible Institute.[63] Many of the students at these schools were refugee Christians fleeing from communist persecution in mainland China, including leaders like Tong Hin Chee and C. H. Kuan. These refuges sometime returned to mainland China and worked with churches despite government opposition.[64] At the beginning of the twenty-first century, membership in the Churches of Christ in Hong Kong was approximately four hundred.

During the 1980s and 1990s, the People's Republic of China emerged from its political and economic isolation under the leadership of third-generation Chinese communists like Jiang Zemin. China and the United States re-established amicable foreign relations, and rapid economic growth propelled China to a position of leadership in the world economy. Amid these developments, the Christian Church (Disciples of Christ) resumed mission work in the People's Republic of China on a limited scale. As early as 1979, a group of Christian leaders from China visited the Disciples general offices, and two years later four leaders of the Division of Overseas Ministries (DOM), successor to the Overseas Division of the UCMS, made a reciprocal visit to China, the first such contact in more than thirty years.[65] Many other similar visits were made through the 1980s and 1990s, primarily "to re-establish non-official but fervent ties with our Chinese Christian sisters and brothers, to give encouragement to them in a period of fast growth and unprecedented opportunity, and to stand in solidarity with them, as they experience more restrictions from their government."[66] To Disciples leaders, it was clear that partnership was developing between the Christian Church (Disciples of Christ) and the Chinese church.[67]

Beyond these visits, since the late 1970s, Disciples have worked in China through ecumenical bodies like the China Program of the National Council of Churches, the United Board for Christian Higher Education in Asia, and the Amity Foundation. Disciples workers have provided disaster relief, participated in community development projects, and taught in many educational institutions, including Nanjing Jingling Union Theological Seminary.[68] Additionally, in the 1980s and 1990s, Week of Compassion funds provided several scholarships for Chinese students to study at theological schools in the United States. Among those students were Xiao-ling Zhu, who graduated from Bethany College in 1988 and Candler School of Theology at Emory University in 1994. After serving Disciples churches of Chinese Americans, Xiao-ling was appointed in 2000 as executive secretary for East Asia and the Pacific of the Common Global Ministries Board.[69] This new board, modeled on relationships that had developed in Latin America and the Caribbean, was established in 1996 to unite all overseas ministries of the Christian Church (Disciples of Christ) and the United Church of Christ.

At the beginning of the twenty-first century, some congregations tracing their heritage to early Stone-Campbell missions survived on mainland China. One example is the congregation in Huili, a village in the Sichuan Province. Established in the 1920s by missionaries from the Australian Churches of Christ, by the 1950s it was operating under the Three-Self Patriotic Movement as the only authorized Protestant Church in the region. Surviving the Chinese civil war, communist suppression of the churches, and the Cultural Revolution of the 1960s and 1970s, the Christian community at Huili numbered more than 400 persons, and at the end of the twentieth century continued to meet in a building constructed in the 1940s with funds from the Australian Churches of Christ.[70]

Members of North American Churches of Christ and Christian Churches/Churches of Christ also continued to serve in the People's Republic of China in the early twenty-first century. Many went to China as teachers of English with the secondary purpose of strengthening churches and evangelization. Members of Churches of Christ began China Mission, with a focus on providing care for orphans and the elderly in a number of care centers. Likely because of the goodwill created by China Mission, the Chinese Director of Religious Affairs gave approval for establishment of a government-sanctioned Church of Christ in Beijing in connection with the 2008 Olympics.[71]

Tibet

In 1920, five missionary couples under the leadership of Dr. Albert Shelton served in the Tibetan Christian Mission in Batang. The mission consisted of a congregation, a day school, a hospital, and an orphanage, supported chiefly by the UCMS. After the fall of the Qing Dynasty in 1912, Tibet became a de facto independent nation under the leadership of the Dalai Lama, though his rule was unstable. In 1918 the Dalai Lama had invited

Shelton to expand the mission's work in Chamdo, near the capital city. Though civil unrest was common and the people were often hostile to foreign influence, it appeared the work in Tibet would continue to expand.

In 1922, however, while traveling between Batang and the Tibetan capital of Lhasa, armed robbers attacked Dr. Shelton and his Tibetan escorts. Though taken quickly to Batang for medical treatment, he died a few days later.[72] Shelton immediately became a "martyr for Tibet," and support for the mission increased dramatically. Friends established the Shelton Memorial Fund and by 1923 supporters had contributed enough funds to send seven additional missionaries to Tibet. Civil war continued along the Tibetan border, however, and both the U.S. and Chinese governments refused permission for additional stations, prompting several of the missionaries to return home out of frustration and disappointment. Nevertheless, the Shelton Memorial Fund financed a new building for the orphanage in Batang, permitted the mission to expand its agricultural education programs, and underwrote a faculty position at the College of Missions in Indianapolis.[73]

The Tibetan Christian Mission continued Shelton's focus on establishing an indigenous church. In 1930 the UCMS reported that the church in Batang had a native pastor, Li Gwei Gwang, and had in the previous year ordained native elders and deacons. Attendance at the Bible schools was 203, and two outstations had frequent preaching. The orphanage cared for fifty-seven boys, a girls orphanage had been opened in January, and the day school had an enrollment of ninety-three. Over the previous four years, the medical work had more than doubled to 23,115 annual treatments.[74]

However, there was also controversy within the mission. J. Russell (1898-1991) and Gertrude (1896-1977) Morse resigned from the UCMS in 1926 in opposition to "open membership," returning to Tibet as direct-support missionaries four years later. They opened a new work in the cities of the Yunnan Province, south of Batang. For the next twenty years, the Morses— including their sons Eugene, Robert, and Russell LaVergne—established churches among the Lisu people of the Mekong and Salween Valleys. Isabel Maxey and Dorothy Sterling assisted the Morses for most of those years. By the time World War II again destabilized western China, their Tibetan-Lisuland Christian Mission had established more than thirty churches with more than six thousand members. As the Communist Revolution spread to the Yunnan Province in 1949, most of the missionaries fled to northern Burma, though J. Russell Morse was arrested and imprisoned as a "foreign spy." These direct-support missionaries were the last from the Stone-Campbell Movement to evacuate China.[75]

Meanwhile, at the suggestion of the UCMS, the 1932 International Convention voted to close its Tibetan Christian Mission. Contributions to missions were declining because of the Great Depression, and the UCMS leadership believed that the dwindling resources were better spent in India, the Belgian Congo, China, and Japan. One report acknowledged frankly that the UCMS "cannot meet the present and added expenses necessary to carry on in Batang without drawing on the brotherhood for larger contributions than can now be made, or taking support from other equally important, less expensive, and far more stable fields." Furthermore, civil unrest and military clashes between Tibetan and Chinese soldiers and extremely slow communication and travel discouraged most potential missionaries from going.[76]

In the United States, opposition to the UCMS's decision was swift and strong. Some raised questions about the mission's property and the money remaining in the Shelton Memorial Fund. To them it seemed the UCMS was shirking its fiduciary responsibility, even though ownership of the property had been transferred to a committee of Tibetan Christians led by Lee Gway Gwang. Others appealed to the great sacrifices of former missionaries. Still others saw the decision as an indictment of missionary societies, where a "board of managers" could make such a capricious decision without regard for the missionaries or the people they served. Despite the protests, by 1935 the work of the UCMS Tibetan Christian Mission had ended.

In 1937, Dr. Norton Bare and his wife, Lois, attempted to revive the mission in Batang, believing that "it would be nothing short of tragic to lose gains already made" there.[77] Though unable to persuade the UCMS to release the remaining monies of the Shelton Memorial Fund for the revived mission, the Bares worked in Batang for several years. In early 1938, experienced missionaries Vernon and Mona Newland visited Batang and concluded that missionaries there should prioritize evangelism and church planting above medical work and other social services following the model of the Morses a decade earlier. Later that year a group of direct-support missionaries arrived in Batang, including Edgar Nichols, his wife and four children, Melba Palmer, and Gladys Schwake. For the next ten years this group was the only consistent missionary presence of any church in Batang.[78]

Though the work was interrupted by outbreaks of persecution, civil unrest, and World War II, the missionaries took these difficulties in stride. When the local lamas secured a government order to expel the missionaries in 1939, Vernon Newland wrote: "This move of the lamas at Yen Chin is but a passing incident. The lamas…are like a wall before us, but we are determined not to be discouraged or frightened away, but to preach on, teach on, and pray on until that wall is broken."[79]

In 1945, it seemed the wall had come down. Sixteen government leaders of the Sikang Province wrote an open letter to Christian Churches in the United States in which they pledged support of the Batang mission if the churches would expand the work. The leaders were especially interested in seeing the orphanage, medical care, and agricultural education programs re-established.[80] As a result, following World War II, at least seven additional missionaries began preparing for work along the Tibetan border. By 1947-1948, some of those missionaries were at work in Batang itself, while others labored in other parts of the borderland. Eventually some of these efforts developed into separate initiatives. Charles W. and Lois (1921-1996) Callaway led the Northern Burma Christian Mission, while Harold and Ada Taylor led the Yunnan-Chinese Christian Mission.

When the Communist Party under Chinese general Mao Zedong came to power in Beijing in late 1949, China began asserting control over Tibet. Guerilla warfare broke out, and eventually diplomatic negotiations between the governments broke down altogether. By late 1950, the People's Liberation Army (PLA) invaded Tibet, quickly overpowering the national army, imprisoning key Tibetan leaders, and confiscating property. The Dalai Lama was forced into an agreement that granted control to Mao's government and permitted the PLA to occupy Tibet. By 1959, he had repudiated the agreement and was forced into exile. Guerilla warfare continued into the twenty-first century, as Tibetan nationalists resisted continued occupation of the nation by the Chinese.

Leading up to the Chinese annexation of Tibet, the fighting throughout the Yunnan and Sikang Provinces became so intense that Stone-Campbell missionaries were forced to flee. Most made their way on foot over the Himalayas into northern Burma, where they planned to wait until the fighting subsided. Conditions in Tibet never improved enough to permit them to return, however, and most turned their missionary attention to Japan, Thailand, Korea, and the Philippines.

Japan

In the 1920s, it appeared that Japanese leaders had curbed the nation's imperialistic ambitions and had begun building a stable democratic empire. Because of the nation's limited role in World War I, Japan experienced economic growth, and a liberal-minded government implemented social reforms that expanded voting rights, encouraged the development of labor unions, and provided social welfare.[81]

In this context, Stone-Campbell mission work in Japan flourished. The UCMS-supported work was concentrated in three areas. First, in the Tōhoku region in the northeast of the mainland, the cities of Akita and Fukushima had thriving congregations, and other congregations were developing in Sendai, Haranomachi, and Yonezawa. Second, in Tokyo, the mission administered several schools, including the Seigakuin Bible Seminary (called Drake Bible College in English), Seigakuin boys' high school, and Joshi Seigakuin, the highly regarded school for girls.[82] The mission also operated the Asakusa (East Tokyo) Institute, a social welfare center that included a twenty-five-bed hospital, an outpatient clinic, a day nursery, and a small orphanage. Greater Tokyo had six congregations with Japanese pastors and a combined membership of around a thousand. Finally, in Osaka the mission supported three congregations and the Christy Institute, a night school where boys could learn clerical skills useful in the developing industrial city.[83] After visiting the mission in Japan in 1927-1928, Stephen Corey concluded that those in Tokyo and Osaka were within five years of being self-supporting ministries and recommended that missionaries be phased out of this work so they could concentrate on the Tōhoku region.[84]

Direct-support mission work in Japan also flourished through the 1920s. The Yotsuya Mission had six churches and eight outstations, conducting ministerial training classes in two outstations. William Cunningham was understandably proud of the progress of the mission: "the Yotsuya Mission has grown from nothing except a vision in the hearts and minds of two people, to its present size…the converts are numbered in thousands and the Bible Schools outnumber those of any other mission in Japan." In 1923, the Mission began working among Korean immigrants in Tokyo, and a year later expanded into Korea itself.[85]

Additionally, North American Churches of Christ supported a dozen missionaries to Japan in the early 1920s, mostly serving in the Ibaraki and Shizuoka prefectures.

The mission consisted of eleven congregations and five schools. J. M. McCaleb remained the leader of the work while others labored alongside him throughout the 1920s. Sarah Andrews (1892-1961) evangelized and worked with Lillie Cypert (1890-1954) in the schools, while O. D. Bixler (1896-1968), Herman J. Fox (1896-1960), his twin brother Harry Robert, Sr. (1896-1974), and E. A. Rhodes (1887-1981) focused on evangelism and church planting.[86]

With the collapse of the world economy in 1929, however, Stone-Campbell missions in Japan suffered greatly. Due to lack of funds, the UCMS withdrew missionaries until only two couples remained: Rollin (1878-1959) and Marie (1883-1949) McCoy, and Thomas (1881-1949) and Stella (1881-1969) Young. Whatever could not be sustained or turned over to Japanese leaders was simply abandoned. The four main stations at Akita, Tokyo, Fukushima, and Osaka remained open, but the UCMS abandoned the outstations and suspended itinerant evangelism. The missionaries and their Japanese colleagues focused on leading the existing churches and educational institutions.[87]

Direct-support missionary work also suffered during the Great Depression. By 1934, contributions to the Yotsuya Mission fell to a third of what they had been five years before, forcing the closure of some of the Mission's work. Amidst these financial pressures, a division developed in the Mission, primarily between W. D. Cunningham and John Chase (1905-1987), the Mission's main evangelist in Korea. Cunningham finally dismissed Chase and his wife Wahneta (1901-2002) "for opposing the policies of the Yotsuya Mission." Soon thereafter, three other Yotsuya missionaries—all women—resigned in protest. These developments touched off a storm of controversy in the United States, and led two Japanese congregations to withdraw from the Mission.[88]

Despite the reduction in personnel, several important developments occurred in direct-support missions in Japan during the Depression years. In 1934, the three women formerly associated with the Yotsuya Mission established Mabashi Christian Mission. Grace Farnham, Ruth Schoonover, and Vivian Lemmon began a church, a kindergarten, three Bible schools, a girls club, and several Bible classes for youth and adults in Matsudo, a fast-growing suburb of Tokyo. By 1939, the church had a Japanese pastor, Samuel Kawamura, who also accepted responsibility for much of the other work. The missionaries were preparing to expand the work of Mabashi Christian Mission into Tanabe, a coastal city in the Wakayama prefecture, when their work was cut short by Schoonover's death and Lemmon's return to the United States to care for her father. Farnham was forced out of Japan by the beginning of World War II. However, in 1947 she resumed her work with the Mabashi Mission and remained there until her retirement in 1960.[89]

Another important direct support work was the Osaka Christian Mission, formed in 1919 by Milton and Grace Madden who had just resigned from the FCMS. They had located the mission in Kita Ku, the North Ward of the city, which was virtually destroyed in 1934 by Typhoon Muroto. After raising money for recovery efforts, the Maddens reorganized in the Asahi Ku (Rising Sun Ward). By 1939, the mission included a church, a school for children, and the Osaka Bible Seminary.[90]

Both the Osaka and Mabashi Christian Missions included "women's work." In groups composed mainly of the mothers of children in the missions' schools—called fujinkai—female missionaries taught Christianity to, and fellowshipped, cooked, and sewed with Japanese women. "The value of this means of reaching our Japanese women cannot be put into words," one missionary claimed. The patriarchal structures of the Japanese family almost always prohibited the women of the household from attending church services, unless accompanied by their husbands or fathers.[91]

In the 1930s, however, military leaders took control of Japan and began building a militaristic empire. A strong belief in Japanese racial superiority gave these ultra-nationalists justification to dominate Southeast Asia. The Japanese occupation of Manchuria in 1931 and its full scale invasion of China in 1937 touched off the Second Sino-Japanese War, and by the early 1940s growing fear of Japanese imperialism escalated this regional conflict into the Pacific theater of World War II.[92]

These developments affected the Stone-Campbell Movement in Japan in a number of ways. First, the government sought greater control over Japan's religious organizations as it attempted to establish Shinto as the official state religion. In 1939, it enacted the Religious Organizations Law that stipulated a religious body must have at least fifty congregations and five thousand members to be authorized by the government. The Japanese Council of Churches had twenty-three member denominations, only seven of which met the qualifications. Many smaller missions not part of the Council also did not qualify. The Religious Organizations Law was a significant step toward expelling foreign influence from Japan, especially Christian missionaries.[93]

In 1940, the UCMS-supported work claimed only nineteen organized churches and 2,660 members.[94]

The direct support Yotsuya Mission claimed twenty-six congregations and around six thousand members. The work of North American Churches of Christ was considerably smaller. None of the Stone-Campbell missions in Japan, therefore, qualified for government authorization under the new law. Without it these groups would be categorized as "religious associations" and would risk persecution, closure of churches, confiscation of property, and possibly the execution or exile of their leaders. Stone-Campbell leaders in Japan chose different ways of adjusting to the developing political situation.

In 1936 Emily Cunningham formed two holding companies to protect assets of the Yotsuya Mission. The Church of Christ Yotsuya Mission Holding Corporation, known in Japanese as the Zaidan, served as trustee of property owned by the mission's churches, and was administered entirely by Japanese leaders. The Churches of Christ Cunningham Mission, Inc., served as trustee of funds raised in support of the mission. When the Japanese government began confiscating property of foreign nationals in the late 1930s, the assets of the Yotsuya Mission were safeguarded since the church property belonged to Japanese leaders, and banks in the United States held and distributed all of the mission's funds.[95]

UCMS leaders in Japan chose another alternative. In 1940, under considerable pressure from the Japanese government, thirty-five Protestant denominations, with a combined membership of about 240,000, united to become the *Nihon Kirisuto Kyōdan*, the United Church of Christ in Japan (or simply Kyōdan). Despite its coercive origins, most of the UCMS-supported churches in Japan joined the Kyōdan because of their commitment to Christian unity and the emerging ecumenical movement.

The churches of the Yotsuya Mission refused to enter the Kyōdan at first. Many leaders of the mission—including Japanese and Korean pastors—believed that entering the union church would force them to compromise essential matters of belief and practice. "This act of union makes things more difficult than ever for Yotsuya Mission," missionary Shirley Still observed in 1940, just after the Kyōdan came into being. "But we must continue as long as it is possible to work for God without any compromise of the faith."[96] Increasing pressure on Japanese ministers in the Yotsuya Mission led several to join the Kyōdan, and after the outbreak of the War, all but one entered the union.[97] Some Churches of Christ also joined the Kyōdan, and those that refused suffered persecution. Some had their buildings confiscated and were forced to continue meeting secretly in members' homes.[98]

At the outbreak of World War II, virtually all of the Stone-Campbell missionaries in Japan evacuated upon the advice of the U. S. government. At the Yotsuya Mission, Emily Cunningham and Owen Still remained, and both quietly continued teaching English and Bible classes. But by 1942, the situation in Japan had become so intense that even these two missionaries fled. Among missionaries from North American Churches of Christ, Sarah Andrews, who had worked in Japan since 1916, was forced by illness to remain in Japan during the entire war. Under house arrest for much of the time, Japanese Christians and her Japanese neighbors cared for Andrews though they were themselves suffering from the deprivations of war. A co-worker, Lillie Cypert, also remained interned by the Japanese government in Tokyo until evacuated in an exchange in 1943.[99]

During the war, many of the churches, schools, and other institutions of the Stone-Campbell Movement were destroyed. Those that remained continued under Japanese leadership as they were able. At Osaka, all of the direct-support mission's buildings were destroyed by Allied fire-bombing. A retired army captain and personal friend of the Maddens, Hiromu Sugnao, erected and lived in a shack on the mission property to prevent it from being confiscated by the Japanese government.[100] In Churches of Christ, Yunosuke Hiratsuka, then minister of the Kamitomizaka Church of Christ, continued as an important leader. In 1944, his congregation merged with Zoshigaya Church of Christ (established by J. M. McCaleb) to become part of the Kyōdan.[101]

Between 1945 and 1951 the Allied Powers under General Douglas MacArthur occupied Japan. During this time, at least fifteen missionaries from North American Churches of Christ returned to Japan with the encouragement of E. W. McMillan (1889-1991). Several were graduates of Pepperdine University, including Harry Robert Fox, Jr., Logan Fox, and R. C. Cannon. Others were recent graduates of Harding College, among them several with medical training, who were influenced for missions by the school's president, former missionary to China George Benson. These missionaries believed their efforts would be successful because the war had "chastened" the Japanese people and made them more receptive to the gospel.[102]

Within five years of re-entering Japan, missionaries from North American Churches of Christ had re-established more than two dozen congregations located mainly in the Tokyo, Ibaraki, and Shizuoka Prefectures. The missionaries focused on evangelism and training Japanese preachers, leaving much of the congregational leadership to Japanese Christians. About half of these churches were self-supporting, while the other half continued to receive financial support from North American congregations. These congregations served as bases for aggressive evangelism including radio and marketplace preaching, revival meetings, Bible correspondence courses, religious tracts and newspapers, and summer Bible camps. They also operated the Nazare-en Home for the Aged, Hosana-en Service Center for the Blind, and Nakuda Children's home.[103]

Perhaps the most significant development among Churches of Christ during the years of the Allied occupation was the formation of a school system that would become Ibaraki Christian University. In 1948, O. D. Bixler purchased for Japanese Churches of Christ thirty-five acres south of Hitachi, an important industrial city eighty-five miles northeast of Tokyo. There they established a high school known as Shion Gakuen, beginning with sixty students. By the early 1950s, the school had grown in popularity and expanded to include a Junior College. In 1967, Ibaraki Christian College was established with a liberal arts curriculum. The Omika Church of Christ met on campus. North American Churches of Christ, along with the Ibaraki Helper's Association—a group of wealthy and influential Japanese businessmen—administered the school in its earliest years. Although many faculty and staff of the school were at least nominally members of Churches of Christ, the majority of students were not.[104]

For more than thirty years, Ibaraki Christian College provided much-needed education in post-war Japan and served as an evangelistic mission of the Japanese Churches of Christ. By the 1970s, however, Churches of Christ in both North America and Japan found it increasingly difficult to sustain the growing school. Though eventually funding from Churches of Christ in the United States decreased significantly, the school maintained its historic ties to the churches through a number of teachers and administrators.[105]

The number of missionaries in Japan from North American Churches of Christ had dropped from thirty-eight in the late 1950s to thirteen in 1967. Though some missionaries resisted the shift, a well-trained and committed Japanese leadership was taking on greater responsibilities in the churches and other institutions. By 1970, Shunzo Asano, a Hitachi businessman who had been among the original founders of the school, was Ibaraki Christian College's president.[106] In 1989, the Japan School of Evangelism began operation in the building of the Tachikawa Church of Christ under a

Japanese administration, though funded significantly by contributions from North American Churches of Christ. At the beginning of the twenty-first century, about sixty *Kirisuto no Kyokai* (Churches of Christ) existed in Japan, located mainly in the Ibakari and Shizuoka Prefectures, with an estimated membership of one thousand.[107]

Leaders of the Churches of Christ Cunningham Mission (led by members of North American Christian Churches/Churches of Christ) also returned during the Allied occupation. At least a dozen missionaries arrived between 1947 and 1950, many recent graduates of Atlanta Christian College. With the help of Japanese leaders, they began rebuilding churches, reopening schools, and distributing food, clothing, and medical supplies. In 1948, the Yotsuya Mission opened Tokyo Bible Seminary with missionaries and Japanese church leaders serving as faculty. The seminary prepared approximately a hundred ministers and lay leaders before closing in 1958.[108]

In 1953, the Board of the Churches of Christ Cunningham Mission, Inc., instituted three major changes to hasten the independence and self-support of the Japanese churches. First, missionaries became responsible for maintaining their own living link support. The Mission's Funds would help churches maintain property and carry out their mission, but when the funds were depleted, the mission would offer no further financial support. Second, ownership of church property would be transferred from the Zaidan (Yotsuya Mission Holding Corporation) to the churches themselves, once they had "qualified elders and financial independence." Once the transfer of property was complete, the Zaidan would cease to exist. Finally, the Tokyo Bible Seminary was reincorporated as an institution independent of the mission, with its own board of trustees.[109]

At the beginning of the twenty-first century, there were approximately sixty churches that traced their heritage to the Churches of Christ Cunningham Mission. Even after the mission dissolved, North American Christian Churches/Churches of Christ continued to support a steady stream of evangelists, teachers, and other workers to assist these Japanese churches. Likewise Osaka Bible Seminary continued to train leaders for the churches with a faculty composed of both missionaries and Japanese pastors. Although the churches supported no benevolent institutions, they operated three Christian service camps: Karuizawa Christian Camp, Shinshu Bible Camp, and the Christian Shuyokai.[110]

During the Allied occupation of Japan, the UCMS supported ten missionaries to assist Japanese leaders in reconstructing churches and schools, and providing humanitarian aid, medical care, and social services.[111] But the precise relationship between these UCMS missionaries and the Japanese churches remained in question. In 1954, the UCMS sent a Commission of Friendly Inquiry to Japan to consult with the fourteen congregations historically related to the society's mission work, but now a part of the Kyōdan. Its purpose was to define the relationship between these congregations, Disciples missionaries, and the UCMS itself.[112]

Following this visit, in 1955 the Christian Churches (Disciples of Christ) entered into a new relationship with the Kyōdan. Rather than supporting only the work of the churches related historically to its mission, the UCMS would coordinate its support for the whole church through the Kyōdan's Interboard Committee for Christian Work. As in other contexts, UCMS personnel would no longer be called "missionaries," but "fraternal workers" to signal the new partnership.[113] Led by veteran workers Kenneth (1895-1993) and Grace (1892-1981) Hendricks, between ten and twenty such fraternal workers assisted the Kyōdan in programs of evangelism, education, and social service throughout the 1950s, 1960s, and 1970s.

At the beginning of the twenty-first century, the Christian Church (Disciples of Christ) maintained a partnership with the Kyōdan through its Common Global Ministries Board.[114]

Korea

After defeating both China and Russia in a series of wars between 1894 and 1905, Japan annexed Korea in 1910 and took control of the nation's political and economic life. Especially after World War I, the Korean people made periodic attempts to throw off Japanese colonialism, but the small, poorly equipped revolutionaries were no match for imperial forces. Japan suppressed Korean dissent with increasing brutality in the 1930s and 1940s, including use of labor camps, sexual slavery, and forced sterilization. Only after the defeat of Japan in 1945 did more than thirty-five years of Japanese colonialism end.[115]

Despite the hardships accompanying Japanese occupation, the Stone-Campbell Movement was established in Korea through the cooperative work of both North American missionaries and Korean evangelists. William Cunningham, the leader of Japan's Yotsuya Christian Mission, first visited Korea en route to Shanghai. There he witnessed the Great P'yŏngyang Revival, then underway among Korean Protestants, and first considered planting "undenominational" churches in Korea. In 1909 or 1910, the Yotsuya Mission had sent its first missionary to Korea—most likely a native Korean then living in Japan—and he baptized a few people. But a shortage of funds prevented the Mission from sustaining the work.[116]

Following World War I, the Yotsuya Mission began work among the increasing number of Korean immigrants to Tokyo, and by 1923 had organized its first Korean congregation. This initial success and the improving financial situation of the Mission inspired Cunningham to send a full-time missionary to Korea. Lee Wan Kyun began evangelistic work in 1924 and soon established four preaching points. His converts organized the Stone-Campbell Movement's first congregation in Korea in 1931.[117]

About the same time, a Korean evangelist for the Salvation Army named Sung Nak So (1890-1964) became disillusioned with his denomination because of preferential treatment of white cadets over their Korean counterparts. In 1927 he struck out on his own and founded a small congregation in Puyŏ, in the southern Ch'ungchŏ'ng Province, that he simply called a Christian Church (*kidok chi kyohoe*). When Sung learned of Cunningham and the Yotsuya Mission, he went to Japan in early 1930 and decided to join the Stone-Campbell Movement. The Mission appointed him pastor of its Korean immigrant congregation in Yokohama. A year later, he returned to Korea to establish the Mission's second congregation in Korea. After serving that church for less than three years, however, Sung became alienated from the Yotsuya Mission as well and returned to his work as an independent evangelist.[118]

In 1933, Cunningham sent another Korean evangelist, Lee In Pom, to conduct a survey of the religious situation in Korea to assess the future of the work there. A young man "full of fiery zeal for unity," Lee observed strong competition between denominational mission agencies, particularly the Methodists and Presbyterians. Korean Protestant Christians themselves, on the other hand, generally resisted this competition, leading him to conclude that the people of Korea were predisposed to the message of the Stone-Campbell Movement.[119] Lee In Pom soon joined Lee Wan Kyun in evangelism and church planting. Largely because of their work, by the end of the 1930s there were around 5,000 members, nearly twice the number in Japan, with a dozen congregations and eighteen evangelistic outstations.[120]

Dong Suk Kee (1881-1971), was another leader in the early Stone-Campbell Movement in Korea. As early as 1904, while working on sugar plantations in Hawaii, he was converted and baptized by a Methodist minister. He later studied at Garrett School of Divinity at Northwestern University, and after graduating in 1913 returned to Korea and served for fourteen years as a missionary for the Methodist Episcopal Church. In 1919 Dong participated in the anti-Japanese March First Movement and spent seven months in jail. While in prison he determined to return to the United States to further his education.[121]

In 1928, Dong enrolled in the newly founded Cincinnati Bible College. Under the influence of the faculty he was immersed and resigned his position in the Methodist Episcopal Church. He spent much of 1929 raising financial support to return to Korea as a missionary. Key leaders and their churches supported him, including Ralph L. Records (1883-1965), dean of the college; Edwin R. Errett (1891-1944), editor of the *Christian Standard*; and James Deforest Murch, founder and president of the Christian Restoration Association.

While in Birmingham, Alabama, he met T. B. Thompson and F. A. Decker who persuaded him to further his study of the Movement at Central Church of Christ in Nashville, Tennessee. There he studied with Charles R. Brewer (1890-1971), Hall L. Calhoun (1863-1935), and Sam Pittman (1876-1965)—all leaders in the Churches of Christ. They convinced Dong that using musical instruments in worship was unscriptural. With the support of several Nashville congregations, Dong then returned to Korea as an evangelist for the Churches of Christ, arriving in 1930.[122] Despite his doctrinal commitments, he continued to enjoy the support of his mentors at Cincinnati Bible College and their churches throughout his career.

Before the end of 1930, Dong had won over his family members and close friends in his hometown, Pukchŏng, in northern Korea and formed the Hamjŏn Church of Christ, the nation's first. In 1931, a missionary from Churches of Christ working in Japan—most likely J. M. McCaleb—came to Korea to help him baptize thirty new converts.[123] By 1940 Dong had founded seven Churches of Christ, all in what is now North Korea.

Dong was not the only evangelist working for the Churches of Christ in Korea in the late 1930s. Kang Myung (Moon) Suck also had been a promising young leader of the Methodist Episcopal Church.[124] After graduating from Vanderbilt University in 1935, and before returning to Korea, he visited several churches in Nashville, one of them a Church of Christ. There he was introduced to the Stone-Campbell Movement.

This experience led Kang to spend another year in the United States, studying at Freed-Hardeman College in Henderson, Tennessee. When he returned home to southeastern Korea in late 1936, he did so as an evangelist of the Churches of Christ.

Kang immediately established a church in Ulsan and eventually founded three more in the region before moving north to plant three churches in Seoul and another in Inch'ŏn.[125] Kang's zeal for the restoration ideals he had learned from North American Churches of Christ angered other Korean Christians, and several became critics of his work. In addition, some of his acquaintances sought to take advantage of him because of the financial support he received from North American churches. In 1944, Kang became embroiled in an intense conflict with a detractor. The stress of the clash put him into a state of severe exhaustion, which led to a fatal illness within the year. Of the congregations Kang established, only Ulsan continued as a viable body after his death.[126]

Before World War II, a small number of North American missionaries came to Korea to assist the developing Stone-Campbell Movement there. John and Wahneta Chase were among the first. Between 1927 and 1934, they had served with the Yotsuya Mission among Korean immigrants in Japan. After Cunningham dismissed them amid a quarrel over their salaries, the Chases returned to the United States and raised their own support. In 1936 they moved to Korea and founded the independent Korean Christian Mission with the purpose of training Korean evangelists.[127] In Seoul the Chases purchased a four-story building from the British and Foreign Bible Society, established a headquarters for the mission, and began a Bible Institute. Among those who studied at Chase's institute before the war were some of the most influential Korean leaders of the Stone-Campbell Movement: Sung Nak So, Kim Yo Han, and Ch'oe Sang Hyon. By the time World War II forced the Chase family out of Korea in 1940, there were six congregations affiliated with the Korean Christian Mission, all under the leadership of Korean pastors.[128]

The Japanese government tightened colonial control over Korea during the war, including an attempt to force State Shinto on the people. By 1940, Japanese leaders required Koreans to perform Shinto rituals before all school, church, or other public gatherings. Among Christians in Korea, whether or not to acquiesce became a matter of intense controversy. Some groups complied, including the Catholic Church and the Methodist Episcopal Church. Others, especially the Presbyterian Church, refused to submit, risking censure, imprisonment, and even execution.[129]

Many in the Stone-Campbell Movement also refused to comply, including leaders and churches associated with John Chase's Korean Christian Mission. In a 1941 report Chase wrote, "I am of the conviction that the churches…ARE NOT BOWING TO THE EAST. But they are bowing the knee, confessing that Jesus Christ is Lord…"[130] The government put Sung Nak So, Kim Munhwa, and Ch'oe Sang Hyon under surveillance for refusing to participate in Shinto rituals. Twice they were taken to a police station where officials interrogated and beat them.[131] Ch'oe Sang Hyon's son Chae Yoon Kwon told the story of his father's faithful service in a 1997 biography.[132] Undoubtedly the churches associated with the Yotsuya Mission and the work of Dong Suk Kee also resisted the imposition of State Shinto, but there is no specific evidence of it.

After being identified with different streams of the Stone-Campbell Movement, Dong Suk Kee became passionate about Christian unity, especially after World War II and the rise of communism in northern Korea. His efforts encouraged cooperation among members of different streams. (*Gospel Advocate*, September 3, 1931)

Stone-Campbell Movement churches in Korea suffered other hardships during the war. The colonial government strictly regulated all contact between Koreans and foreigners, and the presence of missionaries meant constant scrutiny for the churches, interrogations for their leaders, and censorship of their correspondence, making evacuation of the missionaries essential.[133]

Because Japanese law strictly forbade Koreans from accepting financial support from foreigners, after 1941 the Yotsuya Mission had to withdraw all financial support from its Korean evangelists. Devastated by these developments, Lee In Pom wrote the leaders of Yotsuya: "We thank you for your help for a long time to preach the Word of God and to establish the Church of Christ in Korea...I resolve to be faithful to the Lord till death and to be more enthusiastic in preaching the gospel."[134] The circumstances of the war years decimated the Korean churches associated with the Yotsuya Mission. By 1945 all of them had closed.

Though the Allied victory in World War II ended more than three decades of Japanese colonial rule in Korea in 1945, the Allies were unwilling to grant full independence to the nation. Against the vigorous protest of nearly all Koreans, they partitioned the nation along the 38th Parallel; the Soviet Union occupied the region to the north while the United States occupied the region to the south. The goal of the occupation was to stabilize the nation and prepare it for self-rule. Over the next five years, however, relations between the two superpowers deteriorated, and two nations developed. North Korea established a communist government with strong Soviet sympathies, while South Korea struggled to establish liberal democracy, develop a capitalist economy, and maintain diplomatic relations with Western Europe and the United States. Both nations claimed sovereignty over the whole Korean Peninsula, and between 1950 and 1953 a bloody civil war raged, fueled partly by the developing Cold War antagonism between the superpowers.[135]

Between the end of World War II and the Korean civil war, North American missionaries and Korean leaders worked to re-establish the Stone-Campbell Movement in the country. The rise of communism in the north forced members to abandon their churches and flee to the south. Among them were leaders like Dong Suk Kee, Koo Kwang So (d. 1994), Kang Byung Chun (d. 1993), and Lee Chong Man.[136] While Dong continued evangelistic and church-planting work in Seoul and the surrounding area, the other three took leadership positions in South Korean Christian educational institutions and social service agencies,. During the Korean War, Dong went to the United States to raise support and served as an army chaplain to Korean soldiers who came to Ft. Benning, Georgia, for training. While there, he influenced a number of people—most notably Dale Richeson and his family—who served as missionaries for Churches of Christ following the Korean War.[137] Nothing is known about the fate of the seven

congregations Dong established in the north.

These leaders from North Korea were particularly concerned about Christian unity. During the Japanese occupation, they had witnessed conflicts and rivalries between denominational missions. Moreover, Korean Christians themselves were sharply divided between those who submitted to State Shinto during World War II and those who did not. The North Korean leaders believed that the message of the Stone-Campbell Movement had particular relevance in this context. In 1946 they issued "The Declaration of Unity of all Churches of Christ," calling all churches to be united "under one name, one Bible, and the Biblical plan of salvation."[138] To their disappointment, few churches responded to their call.

North American missionaries also returned to Korea, beginning with John T. Chase in 1946. He resumed leadership of the Korean Christian Mission and laid definite plans for its future.[139] He soon discovered that only two of the churches associated with the mission before the war continued to meet: the Tonamdong Church and the Naesudong (or Pilundong) Church.[140] Nevertheless, he and fellow missionary John J. Hill (1913-2009) reopened the Mission's Bible Institute, which in 1949 was renamed the Korean Christian Bible Seminary.[141] With the help of Burris Butler, editor of the *Christian Standard*, Chase led a fund-raising campaign in 1949-1950 called "Chapels for Korea." In just over a year and a half, the campaign raised more than $50,000.00 to help rebuild the churches of Korea destroyed or damaged during World War II.[142] The efforts of these North American missionaries and dozens of Korean leaders revitalized the Korean Christian Mission. By the time the Korean War began, the number of churches associated with the mission had grown to forty-two.[143]

Once again between 1950 and 1953, wartime conditions presented significant challenges for the churches of the Stone-Campbell Movement. In the first month of the Korean War, communist forces overtook almost the entire peninsula. Missionaries evacuated as they watched the North Korean army burn church buildings—including the Korean Christian Mission's headquarters in Seoul—imprison church leaders, and confiscate church property. At least one leader of the Mission, Ch'oe Sang Hyon, was executed for his opposition to the communist takeover.[144] The only place where North Korean armies were not in control was the region around Pusan and the Jeju Island.[145]

With the entry of United Nations troops, North Korean forces were pushed back, and by the summer of 1951, the war reached a stalemate roughly around the 38th Parallel, the original line of partition. The Hills returned to re-establish the Mission's educational institutions, while Korean evangelists worked among the refugees in the south, evangelizing and re-establishing churches. To meet the pressing need created by the war, the Korean Christian Mission established a number of orphanages, the most significant of which were the Christian Mission Orphanage and the Taejon Orphanage at Pan Am Dong.[146] By the time the Korean War ended in 1953, 51 churches, 38 ministers, and 1,905 members were associated with the Korean Christian Mission.[147]

Aside from supporting Dong Suk Kee and Kang Myung (Moon) Suck, North American Churches of Christ did not send missionaries to Korea until after the war. One of the first issues they had to face was that of cooperation with the established missions. Largely because of the influence of Dong Suk Kee, the distinction between the instrumental and non-instrumental Stone-Campbell missions in Korea was not sharp. But this soon changed. When Dale Richeson came to Korea in 1954 as the first North American missionary from the Churches of Christ, he sought cooperation with existing missions. After two years of sharp criticism from his sponsoring congregations, Richeson simply left Korea.[148] It was clear that North American Churches of Christ wanted a mission distinct from those already established.

By 1960, seven full-time missionaries from North American Churches of Christ were working in Korea, several of whom had served in the U.S. military and had been stationed in Korea during the war: A. R. Holton (1891-1964); Haskell (1916-2003) and Enid (1923-1988) Chessir; Bill and Peggy Richardson; and Dan (1933-2006) and Joyce Hardin. The group established at least seventeen congregations in Seoul and surrounding cities, established Korea Christian Institute in 1958 near the Kimpo Air Force Base to train Korean evangelists and school teachers, and cared for hundreds of children orphaned by the war. These missionaries had particular success in evangelistic work among young people attending the colleges and universities in and around Seoul.[149] As in other global contexts, they also worked with U. S. military personnel stationed in Korea.

In the 1960s and 1970s, South Korea struggled to establish a stable democracy and a sense of national identity. Under President Park Chung Hee, elected in 1961, Korea industrialized, normalized relations with Japan, and developed strong diplomatic ties to the United States. When student groups and labor unions demanded an expansion of civil rights, the government restricted political freedoms, sometimes suppressing dissent through violence. Following Park's assassination in 1979, South Korea again entered a period of authoritarian rule and social instability. Beginning in the mid-1980s, however, South Korea elected a series of liberal civilian governments that led to greater social stability, economic growth, and cultural development. At the beginning of the twenty-first century, South Korea was one of the most significant diplomatic and economic powers in Asia.[150]

Inspired by such national trends, Stone-Campbell leaders in Korea in the 1960s moved away from dependence on missionary support toward a self-sustaining, autonomous movement. Chase retired from his leadership role in the Korean Christian Mission in 1955 as the Korean churches were organizing themselves into a cooperative structure that eventually became the Conference of Christian Churches and Churches of Christ. The Mission's new superintendent, Harold Taylor, sometimes found himself at odds with the Korean leadership in the 1960s and 1970s, particularly over the relocation of the headquarters and the administration of Seoul Bible Seminary. Missionaries from North American Churches of Christ experienced similar tensions during this period, partly because of their continued reluctance to cooperate with the established missions with whom they differed on matters of doctrine.[151]

Probably the most influential Korean leader during this period was Chae Yoon Kwon. Born to one of the Stone-Campbell Movement's first Korean evangelists, he grew up during the Japanese occupation, World War II, and the Korean War. After studying at San Jose Bible College and Lincoln Christian Seminary, he returned to Korea in 1961 to work with the Korean Christian Mission. In the early 1960s, he established thriving congregations in the Town-dong and To-dong areas of Seoul, the Hwanwon Christian Publishing Company, and the Geon Christian Children's Home.[152]

Differences between Chae and the missionaries led him to establish the Korean Christian Gospel Mission. In 1965 the new Mission established its own school— Korea Christian Seminary—led entirely by Koreans. Through a series of mergers with other institutions, by 1997 the seminary had become Seoul Christian University. In the early 1970s, the Mission began sending Korean evangelists throughout Asia, by the 1980s to parts of Africa and Latin America, and more recently into the former Soviet Union and China. Eventually Chae completed his doctorate through the Korean extension of Immanuel Baptist Theological Seminary.[153] Beginning in the late 1960s, the Overseas Mission Board of the Australian Churches of

Christ (now, Global Mission Partners) provided support to ministries under Chae's leadership.[154]

The role of the Korean Christian Mission at the beginning of the twenty-first century was minimal because Korean leadership had assumed responsibility for the evangelistic, church-planting, educational, and social services work begun by the Mission. The Conference of Christian Churches and Churches of Christ in Korea was a fully self-supporting organization, in 2003 claiming two hundred seventy-one churches.[155]

Throughout the 1960s and 1970s, North American missionaries from Churches of Christ continued to play a very significant role in the growth and development of that body in Korea. In Seoul they operated a middle school enrolling up to 150 students, a medical clinic, and a center for distributing free clothing and meals to the poor. The self-supporting Hyo Chang Dong Church of Christ under the leadership of Park Kyu Hyum was at the center of the work.[156] Churches of Christ continued to focus on training evangelists at their Korean Christian Institute, which by 1998 had expanded to include programs for public school teachers, social workers, information technology, music, and the liberal arts, and was renamed Korea Christian University.[157] In 1964, they established the Bible Correspondence Center that within ten years of operation was enrolling more than 20,000 people annually. By 2007, it had grown to be the largest ministry of its kind in Korea, with 160,000 students and extensive online offerings. And in 1977, they began a Korean-language radio broadcast, partly to support the ongoing work of the Bible Correspondence Center.[158]

Outside of Seoul, North American missionaries and Korean leaders in Churches of Christ continued evangelistic and church planting work. In the late 1960s and early 1970s, they conducted successful evangelistic campaigns, often assisted by college and seminary students from the United States.[159] They undertook significant church-planting work on Jeju Island off the southern tip of the Korean peninsula, where at least eight Churches of Christ had been established by the mid-1970s. In Busan, Churches of Christ also operated a home for widows and children that provided housing, food, instruction in English, and job placement services.[160] The numerical growth of the churches had not been spectacular, but it had been steady. In 1956, there were seven Korean Churches of Christ. In 1966 the number had increased to forty-three. A decade later the number had risen to seventy-nine, and by 1986, to eighty-six. In 2003, there were one hundred four Churches of Christ in Korea.[161] Though North American missionaries

found it difficult to cooperate across the streams of the Movement because of differences in doctrine and practice, the relationship among Korean members of the Stone-Campbell Movement was always strong. Partly because the Korean government was calling for increased cooperation between the nation's churches, in 1983 leaders of the instrumental and non-instrumental churches issued a joint proclamation declaring that the two groups had coalesced into a united Churches of Christ in Korea. Shortly thereafter, about half of the congregations of Korean Churches of Christ issued a statement nullifying the proclamation, stating that they had never been consulted about a union and that such an act would be unscriptural. Nevertheless, efforts at cooperation continued, and in November 2007 leaders of the two communities issued a statement that they would collaborate in the creation of educational materials and training events. Prospects for the growth and unity of the Stone-Campbell Movement in Korea continued to be hopeful.

Philippines

By the early 1920s, the Stone-Campbell Movement in the Philippines was concentrated in two areas of Luzon, the northernmost and largest of the nation's seven thousand islands. In the lowlands around Manila among the Tagalogs, the UCMS supported extensive medical work, evangelism and church-planting, and educational institutions, primarily to train Filipino church leaders. In Northern Luzon among the Ilocanos, the UCMS supported medical work, evangelism and church planting, schools for children, and a Christian service camp.[162] Following the rupture in the Philippine Mission over comity agreements and open membership, Leslie and Carrie Wolfe returned to the Philippines in late 1926 and reorganized most of the churches in Manila and the Tagalog-speaking provinces into the Christian Convention, whose congregations adopted the name "Churches of Christ." The Wolfes led the direct-support mission until Leslie's death in 1945. Carrie then continued work with the mission until her retirement in 1958. Leslie Wolfe trained a sizeable group of Filipino church leaders in the Manila Bible Institute to be fierce defenders of baptism by immersion and opponents of denominationalism, ecumenism, and theological liberalism.[163]

Wolfe also trained Filipino converts in attacking the Catholic Church, comparing what he viewed as its "superstitions" to the rational, biblical pattern of faith and practice of the Stone-Campbell Movement.[164] He believed the mission was saving Filipinos as much from Roman Catholicism as from unbelief and believed that the growth of "New Testament Christianity" in the predominantly Catholic Philippines would encourage religious and political democracy. In a 1927 report, Wolfe told of Catholic protesters burning Bibles and stoning an assembly of Stone-Campbell Christians in central Manila. The article appeared with the subtitle "[Rome] Offers Violent Interference to Preaching of Gospel in Philippines, Defying Stars and Stripes."[165] "Who can doubt," wrote Wolfe in 1938, "that if this people can have the stabilizing power of a higher faith their political and social future will be excellent?"[166] Supporters in the United States saw the Wolfe mission as contributing to an emerging American-style democracy.[167]

In the 1930s the churches associated with Wolfe's Christian Convention expanded, holding regional conventions, conducting Bible institutes, and constructing church buildings (usually bamboo "chapels"). Most growth occurred outside urban centers, where the Roman Catholic Church was less dominant. By 1941 there were eighty-eight congregations of the "undenominational" Churches of Christ spread across the Philippines, including most of the ten congregations in the Cagayan province that had been "abandoned" to the Methodist Episcopal Church in the comity agreement that had triggered the rupture in the Philippine Mission. On the eve of World War II, the Christian Convention led by the Wolfes was larger than the UCMS-supported mission.[168] The Wolfes were eager to share leadership of the mission with Filipinos. Among the earliest Filipino leaders were Ligoria Carmona, a longtime Bible woman, who "converted more souls than any other worker [the Wolfes] had known;" H. M. Mayor, a Filipino dentist, who served for many years as the president of the Christian Convention; and Faustino Peneyra, who had been instrumental in founding several schools and medical clinics. Filipino church leaders also had primary responsibility for publishing the Convention's monthly newspaper, *Ang Sulo ng Kristiano* (*The Torch of the Christian*).[169]

About the same time the Wolfes returned to the Philippines as direct-support missionaries, auto industry pioneer and philanthropist George Pepperdine (1886-1962) visited the islands and committed himself to the idea of beginning a mission of North American Churches of Christ. With Pepperdine's financial support, George Benson left China briefly to evangelize on the island of Mindoro, 86 miles southwest of Manila. Through an interpreter named José Cordova, Benson preached a nine-week revival in 1928, resulting in over 200 baptisms.[170]

Benson, however, believed he had been called to China, not the Philippines. So, Pepperdine convinced H. G. (b. 1889) and Marie (b. 1896) Cassell—members of the Los Angeles congregation where Pepperdine was an elder—to assume responsibility for the work Benson had begun. Between 1928 and 1945 the Cassells engaged in evangelism and church planting, first on Mindoro and later in Manila. Education, however, was particularly important to the Cassells. In one of their first reports, they observed that "we can baptize hundreds and hundreds of [Filipinos] as soon as we have men who are able to teach this nation and make disciples of them."[171] In addition to educational work, organizing a dozen churches, and conducting regular tent-meeting revivals, they taught in the Manila Bible Seminary administered by the Wolfe mission. For five years between 1933 and 1938, Orville Rodman (1881-1944) also worked with the Cassells in the mission. After being interned in a Japanese prison camp during World War II, the Cassells returned to the United States, but carried on regular correspondence with leaders of the churches.[172]

Believing that the Philippines was "better able than most fields to carry on without missionary leadership and with less financial support," by 1932 the UCMS, responding to the collapse of the global economy in 1929, had withdrawn all but two missionaries.[173] Harry (b. 1891) and Leith (1896-1969) Fonger remained for two years to assist Filipino leaders with evangelism and church planting among the mountain people. E. K. and Idella Higdon also remained in the Philippines, but as employees of Union Theological Seminary in Manila, not the UCMS.[174] At the time of the withdrawal of the UCMS missionaries, the Philippine Mission consisted of eighty-seven churches, located primarily in Northern Luzon, with a combined membership of 6,771.[175]

Without the support of resident missionaries, Filipino leaders including Simeon Rivera, Ruperto Innis, and Leon Bana took charge of evangelistic work, while Bible women including Mercedes Manglallan and Santiago Gaces taught Sunday schools, vacation Bible schools, and engaged in personal evangelism.[176] More than forty Filipino pastors led their congregations through very difficult times. In 1933 the churches launched Northern Luzon Christian College in Laoag to train leaders specifically for the Philippine Mission. The school was so popular that, by 1938, there were more than a hundred studying in Laoag and at least two extension sites in Northern Luzon.[177]

The Imperial Japanese Army invaded the Philippines in late1941. Over three-and-a-half years, the Japanese invasion, anti-occupation guerilla warfare, and the Allied liberation of the Philippines claimed the lives of nearly a million Filipinos, and destroyed every major city, including Manila. Most of the Stone-Campbell Movement's missionaries who remained in the Philippines were interned in prisoner-of-war camps for the duration of the war, including H. G. Cassell, Vernon and Mona Newland, Leslie and Carrie Wolfe, J. Willis and Velma Hale, Edith Shimmel, and Ethel Jones. Filipino Christians risked their lives by smuggling food, supplies, and money to sustain these missionaries during their imprisonment.[178]

In 1943, the Japanese government forced all Protestant denominations into a union church known as the Evangelical Church of the Philippines. Despite its coercive origins, some Filipino leaders saw the formation of this union church as a significant step toward greater Christian unity. Others saw the formation of the union church as "collaboration" with the Japanese, and resisted it as much as they resisted the occupation itself. The legacy of this conflict continued to hamper Stone-Campbell Movement churches in their pursuit of unity for several decades.[179]

After the war, at the request of some of the churches in northern Luzon, the UCMS sent a dozen missionaries to the Philippines between 1946 and 1950 to assist with recovery efforts. While some of the missionaries helped in schools, others worked with Filipino leaders to resume evangelism and church-planting in the mountains. Additionally, funds from a post-War Disciples capital campaign, the Crusade for a Christian World, bought supplies to rebuild more than twenty church buildings and five schools by 1950. Missionary John Chatfield coordinated these efforts in partnership with Filipino church leaders.[180] Beyond recovery and rebuilding, however, UCMS missionaries worked with Philippine leaders in 1946 to develop an aggressive five- and later ten-year plan that focused on training additional Philippine leaders, providing "old-age security" for church workers, and expanding evangelistic work among the "non-Christian tribes" of the rural lowlands.[181]

In 1948, the mission boards and Filipino churches of the Presbyterians, Congregational Christians, Evangelical United Brethren, Methodists, and the Christian Churches (Disciples of Christ) united to form the United Church of Christ in the Philippines (UCCP). These groups had been part of comity agreements from the beginning, and some had united in 1929 to form the United Evangelical Church.[182] Enrique Sobrepeña, long-time Filipino leader in the UCMS mission and well-respected theological educator, was elected the first presiding bishop of the UCCP.

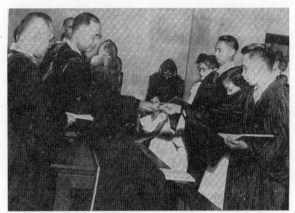

Presiding Bishop of the UCCP, Enrique Sobrepeña, commissions José Estoye to be the church's first missionary to Thailand in 1954. Sobrepeña emerged as a key Philippine leader and advocate of Christian unity after the UCMS withdrew most of its missionaries from the Philippines in 1932. (*World Call*, July 28, 1954)

In 1954, Sobrepeña published an article in the *Christian-Evangelist* to explain the church's polity and commitment to unity. Pointing to John 17:21-23 as a scriptural basis for unity, he also celebrated the comity agreements reached by the earliest Protestant missionaries as having "laid the foundation for unity and cooperation." Although preserving the heritages of their denominational missions, he asserted that the union church proclaimed its common faith and message as "Jesus Christ, the Son of the Living God, our Lord and Savior." In terms of polity, the United Church of the Philippines combined a "satisfactory measure" of local congregational autonomy, presbyterial representative democracy, and episcopal oversight and accountability.[183] The UCCP included about nine hundred congregations and more than fifty schools offering various levels of instruction. The church supported its own foreign missionary societies and sent Filipino evangelists to Korea, Thailand, Indonesia, Iran, and even the United States.[184] By the mid-1970s, the UCCP was entirely self-supporting, and the foreign missionary boards—including the UCMS—had transferred ownership of all church property. As the UCCP stabilized, the UCMS supported as many as sixteen workers in the Philippines to assist in a variety of administrative, evangelistic, social service, and educational ministries. [185]

This situation changed dramatically between 1972 and 1981, when President Ferdinand Marcos ruled the Philippines by martial law. Initially, the UCCP generally supported Marcos and spoke out only against his most egregious abuses, but more aggressive opposition developed among other Protestant groups and the Roman Catholic Church. Arrest and imprisonment of church leaders critical of the regime became common, and in the interests of their safety the Division of Overseas Ministries recalled all but a handful of its workers by the middle of the 1970s. Those who remained taught at church-related schools like Silliman University, Ellinwood College, and Union Theological Seminary. By the early 1980s, even the UCCP and the Christian Church (Disciples of Christ) became vocal critics of the Marcos regime, which came to an end in 1986. [186] Since that time, the DOM and the Common Global Ministries Board has continued its relationship with the UCCP primarily through ecumenical channels.

Throughout the 1940s and 1950s, Carrie Wolfe, along with her daughter Edith and son-in-law Benjamin Allison, continued to lead the Christian Convention. By 1948, the mission had expanded its work into Cotabato on the island of Mindanao, far to the south. There they assumed the work that missionaries from Churches of Christ H. G. and Marie Cassell had left in the hands of Pedro Azada when they left the Philippines three years before. They convinced these congregations that the Cassells had taught them "false doctrine" when they claimed "that the Bible condemns the use of musical instruments in worship."[187] By the mid-1950s, the direct support Christian Convention included ninety congregations.[188]

When failing health forced Carrie Wolfe to return to the United States in 1958, Diego Romulo and other Filipino leaders assumed responsibility for the Christian Convention.[189] Influenced by Holiness and Pentecostal revivalism, this movement experienced phenomenal growth over the next fifty years. In 2001, the Churches of Christ in the Philippines claimed more than 1,200 congregations with a combined membership of around 150,000.[190]

Beginning in the 1960s, North American Christian Churches/Churches of Christ established dozens of direct-support missions in the Philippines to support the growing Churches of Christ in the Philippines. These missions focused on leadership training, medical care, and social services. One of the earliest was Ambassadors for Christ Philippine Evangelism, founded in 1970 by Charles and Florence Littel. Located primarily on the island of Mindanao, they focused on evangelism among the island's growing Muslim population, began a training program for church leaders, and founded the Palm Haven Christian Children's Home.[191]

The establishment of Bible colleges and seminaries was one of the most significant parts of direct-support mission work. Three seminaries established during the Wolfe's tenure continued into the twenty-first century: Manila Bible Seminary (1926), Cebu Bible Seminary (1947), and Aparri Bible Seminary (1952). North American Christian Churches/ Churches of Christ also established and supported Philippine Bible Seminary (1971), Mindanao Christian Foundation College and Seminary (1979), Negros College of Evangelism (1985), Philippine College of Ministry (1992), and Central Philippines Bible College (2000).[192] In each case, missionaries cooperated with Filipino leaders to provide theological education.

After World War II, North American Churches of Christ resumed work in the Philippines when several former military personnel returned to the island as missionaries. Ralph (1908-1996) and Eunice (1912-1996) Brashears moved in 1948 to Baguio City in Northern Luzon. Further south, Victor and Mae Broaddus worked in Manila beginning in 1951. By the end of the 1950s, a dozen missionaries from North American Churches of Christ were working throughout the Philippines, doing evangelistic work and organizing churches. As in most other post-war mission contexts, many of these Churches of Christ consisted of U. S. military personnel.

In 1948, missionaries from North American Churches of Christ established the Philippine Bible College in Baguio City. For more than a decade, the college met in inadequate rented buildings while missionaries attempted to raise additional funding. By the late 1950s, the college operated out of additional locations in Manila and Quezon City. Finally in 1960, sufficient funds had been raised to build the college's first "all-purpose" building in Baguio City, including classrooms, offices, and dormitory space. Almost immediately, the new facility was "crowded to capacity," with dorms and classrooms overflowing with students.[193] Especially in the 1960s, North American Churches of Christ in the Philippines did extensive evangelistic, medical, social service, and educational work.[194] Small groups of missionaries descended on the islands to conduct short-term "campaigns" similar to ones used in other mission fields. Several students who participated in these campaigns returned later as long-term missionaries, including Jeff Shelton who founded Cebu Bible College in 1988, and Barry and Shari Murrell who worked in Cebu for three decades. In 1963 Charlie Garner, who had been working in the Philippines since 1958, raised a team of fifteen adult missionaries and their families with the goal of evangelizing "the entire population of Manila and Baguio City," in order to "wrest them from Catholic and Moslem hands."[195] Though only two of the families were able to go the next year—Bob and Barbara Buchanan and the Ray Bryans—these families provided long-term service, the Bryans spending twenty-eight years. Churches of Christ formed at least seven schools to train church leaders, including Philippine and Cebu Bible Colleges.[196]

In 1964 Filipino Churches of Christ began gathering annually for a Fil-American Lectureship, which brought together missionaries and Filipino leaders for worship, fellowship, and educational workshops.[197] Vigorous missionary work continued through the 1960s and 1970s, resulting in the planting of more than a hundred Churches of Christ. By 1994 there were over 10,000 members of Churches of Christ in the country, and by 2011 the numbers had reached nearly 40,000 members and seven hundred congregations. In addition, Filipino Churches of Christ operated fourteen Bible colleges and preacher training schools throughout Luzon, Mindanao, and Visayas.[198]

Southeast Asia

By the 1920s, the Stone-Campbell Movement maintained a small but stable presence in Southeast Asia through the mission of the British Churches of Christ in the Nakhon Pathom province in Thailand. Two experienced missionary couples led the work: Percy and Mark Clark, and Robert and Elizabeth Halliday (1869-1961). Along with numerous Thai evangelists and teachers, these missionaries led three congregations with a total membership of nearly 400, conducted several boarding schools for children, and administered thousands of medical treatments each year.

The reduction in contributions to the Foreign Mission Committee during the Great Depression was compounded in Thailand by poor exchange rates. As a result the mission closed some of its schools and focused on evangelistic and medical work. A small "Gospel Team" composed of Siamese and Chinese Christians did much of the evangelism, often spending days "tramping through the country singing and preaching."[199] In 1930, the mission completed the Hays Cottage Hospital in Nakhon Choom. Percy Clark continued to direct the

medical work, but a young Thai physician, Dr. H. T. Chen, gradually assumed responsibility.[200]

In 1934, after years of discussion, the churches of the Baptist, Congregationalist, and Presbyterian mission societies formed the Church of Christ in Siam. The British Churches of Christ did not join the union church because of its acceptance of infant baptism. Nevertheless, the British Churches of Christ passed a resolution that same year instructing churches and missionaries to cooperate with the union church through the National Christian Council.[201]

The Japanese Imperial Army invaded Thailand in 1941 with the full knowledge and cooperation of the Thai government. Thai nationalism, on the rise since the early 1930s, included a firm insistence that "none can be a true patriot who is not Buddhist." As a result of both Japanese occupation and rising Buddhist nationalism in Thailand, the government confiscated the mission's churches, schools, and hospital. Against the advice of the British Foreign Missions Committee, the Clarks and Esther Halliday (daughter of Robert and his first wife Agnes) chose to remain in Thailand. Shortly after the invasion they were interned in prisoner-of-war camps in Bangkok, where they remained until the end of World War II.

Leaders of the work in Nakhon Pathom included five nationalities in the early 1950s: Chinese, US, Filipino, English, and Thai. Veteran missionary Mary Clark is in the front row, second from the right.

In 1951, British Churches of Christ began the process of handing over responsibility for the mission in Thailand to the UCMS. The Clarks and Hallidays had announced their retirements. In 1952 the UCMS transferred Edna Gish (1894-1995), who had been driven out of China by the communist revolution, to serve the Chinese Christians in Nakhon Pathom. A year later, new recruits George (1914-2008) and Margaret (1921-2006) Cherryhomes also arrived from China. In addition, the UCMS took responsibility for paying the Thai evangelists, teachers, and doctors who worked for the mission. Throughout the 1950s, UCMS missionary staff in Thailand continued to grow, eventually including twelve workers from the United States, Great Britain, China, and the Philippines.

Almost immediately after taking over the work in Thailand, the UCMS began encouraging its congregations to join the union church. By 1962, ownership of the mission's property was transferred to the Church of Christ in Thailand, and the mission ceased to exist as a separate entity. However, the UCMS continued for many years to support fraternal workers to serve with the Church of Christ in Thailand. A Chinese pastor originally associated with the Disciples of Christ China Mission, David Luo (1915-2011), served between 1955 and 1981 as a rural pastor, church administrator, and professor at both Chiang Mai Theological Seminary and Bangkok Institute of Theology. Richard and Estelle (1925-1991) Carlson served from 1956 to 1974 as medical workers in a variety of hospitals and clinics sponsored by the church. From 1957 to 1992, Dr. Victor and Marian McAnallen—both ordained ministers—served a number of Thai congregations around Nakhon Pathom, taught in schools, and led the Office of Education Ministry of the Church of Christ in Thailand.[202] Allan and Joan Eubank also served as missionaries for the Christian Church (Disciples of Christ) from 1961 to 2000, planting churches among the Thai and Lao Song people in Nakorn Pathaom province and teaching at what is now Payap University. In 1981 Allan founded Christian Communications Institute to develop non-traditional ways to communicate the gospel to the Thai people, including folk drama and dance.[203]

Just as the Thailand mission of the British Churches of Christ and the UCMS was uniting with the union church, missionaries supported by Christian Churches/ Churches of Christ in North America were beginning their work in Thailand. As early as 1949, C. W. and Lois (1921-1996) Callaway relocated from China to begin work among the Mien people of northern Thailand. They remained until 1985, when they returned to the United States to assist Mien immigrants from Laos.[204] Other direct support missionaries in the late twentieth century included Jerry and Pam Headen who served with a team in the Sansai district of Chiang Mai. After

returning from furlough in 1995, they became convinced that they could best serve by ministering to people with HIV/AIDS and other disadvantaged people in Thai society. The Headens began Philokalia Ministries, which provided transportation, employment training, and support at funerals, in cooperation with other Christian AIDS ministries.[205]

The Morse family and their missionary colleagues who had left China during the Communist Revolution also served in Thailand. However, they first had served a group of Lisu and Rawang refugees from China living in northern Burma from 1950 to 1965. Because government restrictions had been minimal, the North Burma Christian Mission (NBCM) had conducted a preacher training school, produced Bibles and Christian literature in Lisu and Rawang, and provided limited medical care. They also had helped the refugees build homes, organize village life, and learn more effective agricultural techniques. When the government ordered the missionaries to leave Burma in 1965, the NBCM claimed a membership of around 30,000 scattered in more than 350 congregations.[206]

After serving the Lisu people in China, direct-support missionary Gertrude Morse and her family continued their work with the Lisu and Rawang people of northern Burma, eventually serving the same people groups in Thailand. *(Courtesy of Cincinnati Christian University)*

By 1973, Eugene and Robert Morse had relocated NBCM to northern Thailand to work among the Lisu and Rawang refugees living in the Chiang Mai, Mae Hong Sorn, and Chiang Rai provinces. By the early 1990s, they had established seventy congregations and Lisu and Rawang leadership was emerging for both the church and the schools.[207] Partly because of doctrinal differences with his brothers, Russell LaVerne Morse established the separate Southeast Asia Evangelizing

Mission (SEAM), later known as Asia Christian Services (ACS), in the early 1970s. This mission focused on radio broadcasting, literature translation and publication, village medical services, and leadership training.[208]

The first missionaries to begin work in Thailand from North American Churches of Christ were Parker and Donna Henderson, who arrived in Bangkok in 1958. By the early 1960s, these missionaries and Thai converts Chua and Nara Pramungwong had established a thriving congregation, and by 1969 the church had begun a school of preaching.[209] Additional missionaries arrived throughout the 1960s, including Dorsey and Ola Mai Traw, who arrived in December 1961 and became leaders in the work at Chiang Mai. By 1965, the work of North American Churches of Christ in Thailand claimed twelve congregations with a combined membership of 900 people. From the beginning, the Thai churches were almost entirely self-sufficient financially.[210]

In 1971, the work of North American Churches of Christ was greatly strengthened by the addition of Chai Voraritskul. Born into a prominent Chinese family in Bangkok, Voraritskul had been converted by the preaching of Parker Henderson. After graduating from Howard University in Washington, D.C., and beginning a career as a research chemist, he decided in 1968 to become a missionary to Thailand. Graduating from the Sunset School of Preaching in 1971, he returned with his wife, Sue, to Thailand to begin missionary work.[211] Many of his family also became leaders in Thai Churches of Christ, including his mother, his brother, and his sisters. Children and grandchildren of the family continued as leaders into the twenty-first century.

An intern program begun by Chiang Mai missionary David Allen and shared with fellow missionary Robert Reagan influenced a number of young Christians both from the United States and Asia to do mission internships in Thailand. One team, made up of three couples and one single woman, formed and moved to the northern city of Phayao in 2009. In the early twenty-first century there were over one hundred Churches of Christ congregations in Thailand scattered over the country.

Following World War II, missionaries from North American Churches of Christ established work in other parts of Southeast Asia. Ira Y. Rice, Jr. (1917-2001), began evangelistic work in Singapore in 1955. Almost immediately, he organized the Moulmein Road Church of Christ from among the earliest Malayan and Singaporean converts.[212] Before 1960, the Moulmein congregation held three separate services: one each in English, Teochew-Cantonese, and Mandarin. Rice and

former Methodist evangelist Lye Hong Meng led the growing congregation.[213]

By the early 1960s, Rice and several other missionaries from North American Churches of Christ—including A. L. Harbin and Pence Dacus—began focusing on educating evangelists. In 1964 Dacus established Malaysian Bible College as a preacher training school that two years later became Four Seas College of the Bible and Missions.[214] Though North American missionary Gordon Hogan served as the school's president from 1968 to 1985, Malaysian church leaders took on important responsibilities at the school, especially Tan Keng Koon (1924-1979). A former Buddhist and heir of a family fortune made in the rubber industry, Tan had been baptized by Ira Rice in 1955 and studied at Freed-Hardman College in the late 1950s. He returned to Singapore in 1961 to work as an evangelist with Churches of Christ. After four years he was appointed dean of Four Seas College, where he taught for almost fifteen years until his death in 1979.[215] Chinese, Indonesian, Vietnamese, and Indian graduates of Four Seas College were instrumental in establishing Churches of Christ in other parts of southeast Asia, especially Malaysia and Indonesia in the 1970s and 1980s. However, political turmoil and the dominance of Islam—the religion of the majority Malay population—hindered growth in these areas. In Singapore, however, which separated from Malaysia in 1965, Churches of Christ continued to grow through the 1980s, in many ways mirroring the social, economic, and cultural growth of the nation as a whole. At least sixteen additional congregations were established, most of which were self-supporting from the beginning.[216]

In 1964, North American Churches of Christ launched "Operation Saigon" just as the U.S. government was sending growing numbers of military personnel to South Vietnam to intervene in a bloody civil war. Maurice and Marie Hall, former missionaries in France, and Phil Carpenter began the work. The potential of Vietnam as a mission field seemed great, and by 1966 thirteen additional missionary personnel arrived.[217] In two years, these missionaries established seventeen churches in Saigon, Danang, and many of the surrounding villages, most military congregations. They also established the American-Vietnamese International School, especially for children of U.S. military personnel.[218] Eventually, however, Operation Saigon began efforts among the South Vietnamese.

Perhaps the most important project to reach the Vietnamese people was broadcasting weekly, 30-minute programs sponsored by World Radio with Vietnamese evangelist Phil Nhon. Nhon had a master's degree in English from the University of Saigon, and after serving as a translator for the U.S. military, he worked for the American Bible Society and helped produce a translation of the New Testament in modern Vietnamese. His radio Bible studies and preaching led directly to the organization of three Vietnamese congregations by 1966. Nohn also was instrumental in establishing the mission's first preacher training program for Vietnamese church leaders.[219]

From the beginning, Operation Saigon also included significant humanitarian relief. Several military congregations—especially Hong-Thap Tu Church of Christ—coordinated the distribution of food, clothing, and medical supplies regardless of religious belief.[220] With the help of the Village Church of Christ in Oklahoma City, Operation Saigon opened three homes for orphaned Vietnamese children. The homes, in Saigon, Trung My Tay, and Danang, eventually were recognized and approved by the South Vietnamese government.[221]

The U.S. Churches of Christ that supported the work in Vietnam recognized that it was a very dangerous place. In 1965, Viet Cong detonated a bomb near the U.S. Embassy in Saigon, injuring more than 200 people. All of the missionaries were evacuated briefly, but most returned with a heightened sense of urgency, especially for the training of Vietnamese evangelists.[222] By 1968, however, the war had escalated to the point that remaining in Vietnam was impossible for most of the missionaries. Some relocated to other Asian fields, including Singapore and Hong Kong, while others returned home.[223]

When U.S. troops began withdrawing after 1972, it was clear that the few remaining missionaries would have to leave. They stepped up efforts to distribute food, clothing, and medical supplies, virtually abandoning evangelistic and church-planting work. In 1973, they began a chaplaincy program at Noa Military Hospital in Saigon. Ralph Burcham and Vietnamese evangelists Vu Vinh Thung and Tran Van Can ministered to the "sea of suffering humanity," including both Vietnamese and U.S. soldiers injured in the war. The last of the missionaries from Churches of Christ evacuated Vietnam on April 25, 1975, just five days before the fall of Saigon. Even after the evacuation, missionaries remained optimistic about the future of Churches of Christ in Vietnam.[224]

Their optimism was not entirely misplaced. By the mid-1990s, reports began to surface that some Churches of Christ continued to meet in Saigon under the leadership of Ta Ngoc Quy with support from Tran Van Can, who was then a radio evangelist in the United States. In 1996, a new congregation was founded in Hanoi, the capital. Leaders hoped that through its ministries the church eventually would gain legal recognition and thus begin meeting openly.[225] While limited, members of Churches of Christ also began work in Laos and Cambodia by the late 1990s, sometimes aided by short-term visits by groups from other Asian countries.[226]

Pacific Islands

The growth of the Stone-Campbell Movement in the New Hebrides had slowed following the death in 1918 of the indigenous leader Willie Tabimancon. During the Great Depression, the Overseas Mission Board of the Australian Churches of Christ sent only a handful of missionaries to the islands, and a lack of funds and recurrent disease often cut their work short. David (1914-1984) and Doris Hammer, who served from 1930 to 1943, were the only consistent Stone-Campbell missionary presence on the Pacific Islands during these difficult years.[227]

Indigenous elders, commonly called "teachers" on the islands, carried on the work of the churches as best they could with meager resources. Because they received no salary from the churches, these elder-teachers provided their own livelihood. They taught in the churches and village schools, mediated disputes in the churches, and combated "witchcraft and superstition." Perhaps the most important elder-teacher of the period was Abel Barni, described as "a splendid preacher of the gospel backed by his deeply spiritual life of devotion and piety."[228]

For many years, missionaries of the Australian Churches of Christ had hoped to begin medical work in the New Hebrides. Treatable diseases such as malaria and tuberculosis had claimed the lives of several missionaries and many more of the indigenous population. In addition, because of unsanitary conditions during birth, the infant mortality rate was 20 percent. Yaws, a bacterial infection of the skin common in tropical climates, especially affected children and the elderly. Some feared that these conditions would lead to the extinction of the indigenous people of the New Hebrides.[229]

In 1942, the Overseas Mission Board of the Australian Churches of Christ sent two women nurses, Mary Clipstone and Violet Wakely, who itinerated throughout the islands of Pentecost, Aoba, and Maewo treating infections, providing education, and training indigenous women to be midwives. Their work became central to the churches and sparked a steady stream of medical missionaries through the 1970s. Because much of the medical work was done by women and for women, it opened opportunities for island women to exercise leadership in the church and community.[230] Missionaries established at least three hospitals—one each on Pentecost, Aoba, and Maewo—that treated patients and trained island medical personnel.[231] Though the churches transferred these hospitals to the government in 1982, medical personnel from Australian and U. S. Stone-Campbell churches continued to come as missionaries, serving especially in rural areas.

Missionaries from Australian Churches of Christ also revitalized the educational program of the mission in the years following World War II. In 1946, Jack and Dorothy Smith established a small primary school at Ranmawot on Pentecost Island. It soon added secondary grades, which in 1955 were relocated to a new building built on the site of Tabimancon's school. Australian missionaries administered the schools until 1986, when Silas Buli became the first indigenous principal, serving until 2009. In 2003, the secondary school was renamed Ranwadi Churches of Christ College and continued to receive partial support from Global Mission Partners of the Australian Churches of Christ.[232] Similar schools developed on Aoba and Maewo.

Missionaries also began two schools to prepare indigenous leaders. In 1949, Ron and Phyllis McLean established the Londua Training School on Ambae Island. Under pressure from the British government, the school expanded its curriculum and became the co-educational Londua Technical College in 1960, offering an academic course through grade ten, and two years of additional technical training in areas like mechanics, carpentry, and business.[233] More important for training church leaders was Banmatmat Bible College, founded by missionary David Eagling in 1964. The college offered a four-year program that included extensive evangelistic experience. Beginning in the early 1980s, indigenous leaders—including many women—did most of the teaching. In the early twenty-first century, charismatic leanings at the school concerned some church leaders and led to consideration of closing the Bible college.[234]

In the 1970s, a strong nationalist movement known as Nagriamel developed on New Hebrides, and its leaders sought independence from the joint British and French colonial government. When the nation received independence in 1980, it renamed itself Vanuatu. Partly because of nationalist pressure, in 1973 the churches had organized the Conference of Churches of Christ in the New Hebrides. The Overseas Mission Board of the Australian Churches of Christ transferred ownership of the churches, schools, and medical facilities to the new convention, and indigenous leaders assumed full leadership. In 1980, the Stone-Campbell Movement in Vanuatu was named the Vanuatu Conference of Churches of Christ.

After independence, indigenization of the churches in Vanuatu accelerated. The Conference published a Bislama-langauge New Testament and hymnal. Charismatic revivals centered at the Banmatmat Bible College transformed the character of some churches. The conference sent missionaries to Papua New Guinea, the Solomon Islands, New Caledonia, Fiji, and other nations of the Pacific Islands, and many members of Churches of Christ held important government positions. At the beginning of the twenty-first century, the Vanuatu Conference of Churches of Christ claimed ninety-two congregations with a combined membership of 8,047. It maintained a close relationship with the Australian Churches of Christ through the latter's Global Mission Partners.[235]

Since 1949, Papua New Guinea had been supervised by the United Nations under the provisions of the International Trusteeship System, administered by Australia. The goal was to promote political, economic, and social development to prepare the territory for self-government and independence. Motivated partly by this responsibility, in 1958 the Overseas Mission Board of the Australian Churches of Christ dispatched Frank Beale and Harold Finger to begin a mission. These veteran missionaries established a station in the village of Tung, in the East Sepik Province, where no major Protestant missions, schools, or medical facilities existed.[236]

The Australian churches were strongly committed to the new mission in Papua New Guinea. By the mid-1960s, the Board was supporting more than twenty missionaries working in six villages in the Ramu River basin, where they organized churches, established primary and secondary schools, and provided medical care, both at the Paternoster Memorial Hospital and in countless village clinics. By 1970, the mission consisted of a dozen congregations with a combined membership of at least five hundred, although many more people regularly attended worship services.[237]

After Papua New Guinea held its first democratic elections in 1972, and achieved full political independence three years later, Australian Churches of Christ began turning the work over to indigenous leaders. In 1972, primary leadership passed to a Mission Council, including both missionaries and indigenous leaders. Over the next decade the Council evolved into a conference of churches, adopted the name Melanesian Evangelical Churches of Christ (MECC), and began holding annual conventions in 1981 fully independent of the overseas Mission Board. Trained at the interdenominational Christian Leaders Training College near Banz, a talented group of indigenous leaders emerged to lead the MECC into an era of rapid growth. The MECC began Gandep Bible College, offering a three-year ministerial training program; translated and published a Rao-language New Testament; and developed literacy programs for rural areas. In 2011 the MECC claimed a membership of approximately 6,000 in 112 congregations, and continued a close relationship with the Australian Churches of Christ.[238]

Since the early 1970s, North American Churches of Christ also have engaged in evangelistic and church-planting work in Papua New Guinea. Supported by the Highland Street Church of Christ in Memphis, Tennessee, Joe and Rosabelle Cannon established a station in Lae in the Morobe Province, one of the largest cities in the nation. Over the next thirteen years, they established churches and trained indigenous leaders at their Melanesian Bible College. Dozens of other workers from North American, Australian, and Japanese Churches of Christ joined the growing mission; by the beginning of the twenty-first century, churches had been planted in about half of Papua New Guinea's twenty provinces. North American Churches of Christ continued to provide primary support for these congregations and trained indigenous leaders through several small Bible colleges, Bible correspondence courses, and preacher training programs. At the beginning of the twenty-first century, there were over one hundred Churches of Christ with a total of approximately five thousand members in the nation.[239]

In 1977 Papua New Guinea became the first mission focus of a new ministry established by members of Christian Churches/Churches of Christ the previous year. Originally led by Al Hamilton, Pioneer Bible Translators (PBT) was formed with the idea of using Bible translation and literacy training as strategies for church planting and church growth. The first missionary translators to arrive were David and Sharran Pryor, John and Bonita Pryor, and Ron and Lisa Augsburger, followed by over seventy-five others by 2011. These missionaries completed the translation of the entire Bible into Pidgin in 1990, and the New Testament into Kire in 2000. While PBT sent translators and support staff to scores of locations, especially in Africa, Asia, and the South Pacific, Papua New Guinea remained one of its strongest works.[240]

Conclusion

Amid the social upheaval and change of twentieth-century Asia, the Stone-Campbell Movement began thousands of independent congregations and contributed to the formation of union churches. Stone-Campbell Christians also led in the development of educational and medical institutions and in the delivery of social services. Indigenization occurred by intention and in response to the Great Depression, war, and social and political movements. At the beginning of the twenty-first century Stone-Campbell churches and union churches of Stone-Campbell lineage, having come through remarkable struggles, continued to make the Christian witness in cultures in which they almost always represented a distinct minority of the population.

15

The Stone-Campbell Movement in Latin America and the Caribbean Since the 1920s

By the 1920s, the Stone-Campbell Movement was well-established in several areas of Latin America and the Caribbean, mainly through the work of the United Christian Missionary Society (UCMS). In Jamaica, the society maintained the oldest continuous foreign mission of the North American Stone-Campbell Movement, characterized by growing ecumenical cooperation. In Mexico, the UCMS had relocated to the central part of the country after comity agreements reached at the 1916 Panama Conference, while direct-support missionaries had continued the original mission in the north. In Puerto Rico, the society focused on evangelism and church planting. Missions in South America—especially UCMS efforts in Argentina and Paraguay, and work by North American Churches of Christ in Brazil—had only begun.

Between the world wars, the nations of Latin America and the Caribbean struggled to achieve political and economic stability. Though most were technically independent, U. S. foreign policy—sometimes called "dollar diplomacy"—developed a new kind of colonialism by encouraging U.S. banks and businesses to invest heavily in regional markets, resulting in financial dependence on the United States. Especially after World War II, strong anti-imperialist movements emerged, often fueled by Marxist and other anti-capitalist ideologies. As national leaders struggled to gain greater control of their political and economic lives, religious leaders also began to assume greater responsibility for the churches.

Following World War II, North American Disciples slowly turned over responsibility for UCMS churches, schools, and other ministries to Latin American and Caribbean leaders. Beginning about 1960, Disciples developed partnerships with Pentecostal churches throughout the region, and with these and other ecumenical partners provided significant humanitarian assistance

to combat poverty, violence, civil war, and human rights violations.

At the same time, North American Churches of Christ greatly accelerated their evangelistic and church-planting work throughout Latin America and the Caribbean. Missionary families supported by individual congregations began work in South America in the 1950s, inspiring more organized and extensive efforts in the 1960s and 1970s. Beginning in 1963, the annual Pan American Lectureship brought together missionaries from all over Latin America and the Caribbean for education, mutual support, and strategic planning. In 1971, Ken Dye, then a missionary in Kingston, Jamaica, began the Caribbean Lectureship, which in 2010 attracted 2000 members of Churches of Christ from across the region, including Cuba—which hosted the Lectureship in 2005.[1] In 1976 the Continent of Great Cities ministry began equipping and sending mission teams to establish congregations in the largest cities of Latin America and the Caribbean. Especially since the 1980s, North American Churches of Christ also contributed significant humanitarian assistance to the region.

North American Christian Churches/Churches of Christ pursued similar evangelistic, church-planting, educational, and humanitarian objectives, especially in Mexico and Brazil. Though most of the work was through the direct support method, Christian Missionary Fellowship (CMF), an agency begun in 1949 as an alternative to the UCMS, also planted congregations in these and other countries. CMF efforts to indigenize its church plants in Brazil in the 1980s helped nurture a vibrant Brazilian network of churches that served as host to the 2012 World Convention.

In the 1990s the Church of Christ, Disciples of Christ began work in Jamaica and Panama. By the first decade of the twenty-first century the Christian Worship Center in Kingston, Jamaica, had become a certified church in that body, and a second congregation had been planted in St. Catherine parish. In Panama, seven churches had been planted in and around Panama City.

Though Disciples worked ecumenically around the globe, their efforts in Latin America and the Caribbean led to a special relationship with the United Church of Christ (UCC) that would influence the ministry of these churches worldwide. In the 1980s mission personnel from the Disciples and the UCC began a partnership that became the Common Ministry in Latin America and the Caribbean. This ministry was the model for the uniting in 1996 of all Disciples and UCC overseas ministries through the Common Global Ministries Board (CGMB).

Jamaica

In 1926, the Jamaica Mission had eight UCMS missionaries and twenty-three Jamaican pastors and teachers leading twenty-five churches with a combined membership of 3,606. The mission also administered nine elementary schools with a total enrollment of eight hundred eighty.[2] Though Jamaican leaders pushed for greater autonomy, the churches' dependency on financial support and personnel from the United States hindered such moves.[3]

The first major step toward the indigenization of the Jamaica Mission was the formation in 1929 of a delegate convention named the Jamaica Association of Christian Churches. A Central Committee of six Jamaican leaders and two missionaries oversaw the work of the churches between Association meetings. George Penso, an elder at the Duke Street Church in Kingston, served as the committee's first chair. The UCMS continued support with the understanding that Jamaican leaders would focus on growing through evangelism and stewardship. With the endorsement of the UCMS, the missionaries, and the Central Committee, the Association adopted an ambitious plan for the churches to be self-sufficient by 1935. No one foresaw the coming of the Great Depression.[4]

Because the island's economy was so closely tied to that of the United States, Jamaica felt the impact of the Great Depression almost immediately. Though the leaders of the Central Committee and many Jamaican pastors remained committed to the six-year plan, it was impossible to implement. Jamaican pastors made great sacrifices, sometimes taking boarders into their homes to supplement decreasing salaries. In 1932, the UCMS withdrew its last missionaries from Jamaica, leaving the

Association and its leaders to carry on the work.[5]

Friction soon developed among leaders of the Association, primarily between members of the Central Committee and some of the pastors. The stronger churches—especially the Duke Street and Torrington congregations—believed they should have greater autonomy because they were more financially self-sufficient. They resented the Association spending their apportionments to support poorer congregations. In response, the Central Committee began an attempt to exercise more authority over the churches by functioning more like a presbytery.[6]

The internal friction continued, and in 1938, the Association of Christian Churches in Jamaica asked the UCMS to mediate a conflict between it and the Duke Street Church in Kingston. The Central Committee had called for the resignation of George Penso, then serving as Duke Street's pastor, and the congregation had refused to comply. Despite UCMS doubts about the Central Committee's growing authority, it sent a veteran of the Disciples of Christ Congo Mission, Everard Moon (1879-1962), to assume the pastorate of the congregation. The struggle intensified after Moon's arrival, portrayed in local Kingston newspapers as a "fight between a Jamaican pastor and a foreign missionary."[7] The result of the incident, however, was to strengthen the Central Committee's authority over the Association's churches.

Another step in the process of indigenization was the formation of the Jamaican Christian Council in 1941, an ecumenical body composed of leaders from ten denominations, including Disciples.[8] Among the Council's objectives were: "To provide a means whereby Christian bodies in Jamaica may act together (a) to study problems and opportunities which challenge the Christian way of life; (b) to promote wherever possible cooperative action; (c) to make clear by public statement the spiritual issues involved in island problems."[9] In many ways, the formation of the Jamaican Christian Council was the first step in a fifty-year process that would result in a Protestant union church.

Education had been an important part of the Jamaica Mission's program from the beginning. Though local congregations had provided Bible schools and other opportunities for instruction, the desire for more led the Mission in 1895 to begin sending a steady stream of church leaders to Southern Christian Institute in Edwards, Mississippi, for general education.[10] Those who wanted to become ministers often continued their studies at other Disciples colleges, especially Drake, Hiram, and Eureka. By 1930, Disciples schools in the United States had educated twenty-five Jamaican leaders, including Louis Thomas Shirley and his sons, Charles and Herbert; Eric Walworth Hunt; and Edwin James Robertson.[11] This basic pattern for training Jamaican leaders continued into the 1960s. In 1962, Richmond Nelson completed his Bachelor of Divinity at Union Theological Seminary in New York, making him the first Jamaican Disciples leader to complete a graduate theological degree.[12]

Cyril Robertson served as the first Jamaican principal of Oberlin High School between 1948 and 1962. During these years Oberlin transitioned from being a missionary-controlled "industrial school" to a Jamaican administered academic high school.

As important as the connection with the U.S. schools was, by the early 1940s leaders believed it was time for similar schools in Jamaica. In 1943, the Central Committee applied to the UCMS to begin a high school in Kingston. The UCMS had considered similar plans since the mission's beginning, but none had ever materialized. Jamaican leaders proposed an academic high school, but UCMS executive E. K. Higdon (1887-1961) urged the agency and the Association to follow the "industrial education" model (eighth grade academic skills with a focus on manual labor) used for blacks in the American South. Though the UCMS recommendation clearly reflected racist assumptions, Jamaican leaders reluctantly agreed, and the Christian College opened in 1946. After two years of missionary leadership, Cyril Robertson, pastor of Duke Street Christian Church, became principal of the college. Under his leadership, the school pursued an uneasy middle course between the industrial school UCMS leaders wanted and the academic program Jamaican leaders wanted.[13]

Within a decade, however, the school had developed into a well-respected academic high school. From five

students in the first class, enrollment grew to more than 150. With its new emphasis on academics, leaders changed the school's name in 1955 to Oberlin High School. By 1957, Oberlin met the Department of Education's accreditation requirements, offering a curriculum that prepared students to pass the standard junior and senior level Cambridge examinations. Under the leadership of Canadian missionary Archie Allan, summer work crews from the United States cooperated with Jamaican leaders to build new facilities for the school, many of which continued in use at the beginning of the twenty-first century.[14]

The Association of Christian Churches in Jamaica participated in the ecumenical developments in the nation and region, though at first unofficially. In 1952, Jamaican Presbyterians, Methodists, Congregationalists, and Moravians formed the Church Union Commission to pursue cooperation and eventual organic union.[15] The Commission's first significant venture was founding Union Theological Seminary in 1955. The Association of Christian Churches was only an observer to the Commission's work, yet it contributed, along with the UCMS, $10,000 toward the founding of the school on the condition that Disciples students would be eligible to enroll.[16] Later the Association became a full member of the Commission, and by 1965 several other denominations—including the Anglican Church—had joined in supporting the seminary. Because a relationship had developed with the University of the West Indies in Mona, the school's administration changed its name to the United Theological College of the West Indies, and by the early 1970s had relocated to a campus adjacent to the university.[17]

In addition, the Association of Christian Churches in Jamaica was one of the first members of the World Council of Churches and a founding member of the Caribbean Conference of Churches (CCC).[18] The CCC emerged from an International Missionary Council meeting in Puerto Rico in 1957 that had helped create Christian Action for Development (CADEC), an organization of Caribbean churches to improve their nations' economies and record of justice. In 1973 CADEC leaders founded the Caribbean Conference of Churches in Kingston with eighteen member denominations, making human dignity, liberation, and social justice its priorities.[19]

Direct support missions began shortly after the UCMS withdrew its missionaries from Jamaica in 1932. About that time, a Congregationalist minister on the island named C. V. Hall had become aware of the Stone-Campbell Movement and was convinced of its restorationist principles. In 1935 he left the Congregationalist Church and began planting churches throughout Clarendon Parish, especially in the Mocho Mountains, making appeals to the *Christian Standard* for help in recruiting additional missionaries.[20] By 1938, Luke Elliott and his wife joined Hall in what they called the Jamaica Christian Mission. In the early years, whole congregations—usually Baptists and Pentecostals—affiliated with the Jamaica Christian Mission.[21]

After eighteen months, illness forced the Elliots to return to the United States, leaving Hall to continue the work alone.[22] They returned, however, in 1944, and together with Hall focused on "winning" denominational churches to "New Testament Christianity," establishing new churches according to their restoration vision, and providing theological education for Jamaican pastors and lay leaders. After five years, the Jamaica Christian Mission reported 6,210 baptisms and eighteen additional congregations in Clarendon Parish. They also had founded Jamaica Bible Seminary in Mocho and trained a dozen evangelists.[23]

For reasons not readily apparent, the *Christian Standard* distanced itself from the Jamaica Christian Mission in 1950 when the Elliotts resigned and returned to the United States. The new superintendents, Donald and Maxine Fream, had stipulated that they would assume all responsibility for supporting the work financially.[24] The *Standard* published regular reports about the mission's work but no appeals for support. In 1951, the mission relocated to Stony Hill, north of Kingston, after Hurricane Charlie destroyed many of the churches and the building that housed the seminary. The Freams and at least three other missionary couples worked in Jamaica through the 1950s, rebuilding churches, establishing a Christian preparatory school, teaching in Jamaica Bible Seminary, and broadcasting an evangelistic radio program. They also continued church planting, assisted by a number of Jamaican evangelists.[25]

Unable to raise sufficient support, the Jamaica Christian Mission closed Jamaica Bible Seminary in 1959. The Freams continued work with Jamaican evangelists, while Harold and Adele Hill administered the Christian preparatory school until it closed in 1997.[26] By the middle 1960s, the Jamaica Christian Mission also supported Harvey and Nancy Bacus who focused their work on Jamaican youth. They established a six-acre service camp near Kingston known as the Nine Palms Christian Camp, organized annual Youth Jamborees, and established the Jamaica Christian Boys Home.

In addition, they began an evangelistic outreach to Rastafarians, though with limited success.[27]

The Mission appointed Jamaican pastor Winston Scott administrator in 1990.[28] Under the leadership of an American Advisory Board established in 1988 and with financial support from Discovery Christian Church in Cocoa, Florida, the mission opened Jamaica Christian College in 1995. The administration and most of the faculty were leaders in North American Christian Churches/Churches of Christ. By the beginning of the twenty-first century, the school had trained pastors who served in more than a hundred congregations across the island.

North American Churches of Christ also worked in Jamaica, especially after Jamaican pastor Clifford Edwards broke with the Association in 1958, and invited missionaries from Churches of Christ to visit the island. Through the influence of these missionaries, ten ministers and their churches left the Association to form a Jamaican movement of Churches of Christ.[29] These churches grew with the support of dozens of missionaries from North America. The first new congregation was established in Mona in 1967, on property adjacent to the university. Three years later, Churches of Christ established the Jamaica School of Preaching in Kingston.[30] In the 1990s, there were at least forty-eight Churches of Christ in Jamaica with a combined membership of approximately 2,300.[31] In 2007 almost sixty congregations existed, most served by ministers trained at the Jamaica School of Preaching.[32]

Though it had participated in ecumenical activities since the early 1950s, the Association of Christian Churches did not join the United Church of Jamaica and the Grand Cayman when it was formed in 1965. This was due in part to the fact that the UCMS had not yet transferred ownership of church property to the Association.[33] When Jamaican Disciples became a legal corporation in 1974 and the UCMS completed the transfer of all properties in 1976, it paved the way for the Association to join the Presbyterian and Congregationalist Churches in the union if it chose to do so. The Association, then known as the Synod of Disciples of Christ in Jamaica, had become an autonomous, self-supporting church, though the successor to UCMS—the Disciples Division of Overseas Ministry (DOM)—continued to support fraternal workers in Jamaica when requested. In late 1992—after almost twenty years of discussion and debate—the Synod of Disciples of Christ entered the union church. Now called the United Church of Jamaica and the Cayman Islands, the national church claimed more than two hundred congregations and twenty thousand members. At the time of the merger, forty were historically Disciples congregations with approximately six thousand members.[34]

The Church of Christ, Disciples of Christ began work in Jamaica in the 1990s through the efforts of Elder Tony Smith, an associate minister of the New Covenant Church in Brooklyn, New York. Betty Cousins, producer of Smith's "Here's Life" program on WMCA radio, introduced him to her husband, Bishop Tony Cousins, who had a ministry in Jamaica—the couple's home country.[35] Through this contact, Smith and five others from the Northeastern District Assembly made a weeklong visit to Jamaica in 1994, conducting nightly "deliverance" services in impoverished areas of Kingston. Though Jamaica had a strong Christian presence, practitioners of Obeah (Jamaican voodoo) and the Spiritual Baptist Church (a fusion of Christianity and traditional African religion) strongly challenged the team. Despite attacks by seemingly demon-possessed people, swarms of stinging flies, and distractions by practitioners of Obeah, the team ministered to hundreds of people.

The 1994 visit resulted in the establishment of the Christian Worship Center in Kingston led by Cousins. Continued contact between Cousins and Smith led to the certification and induction of the Worship Center into the Church of Christ, Disciples of Christ in 2009. Smith, then General Evangelist for the General Assembly, returned to Jamaica in 2010 to strengthen the new connection and expand the deliverance services begun sixteen years earlier. Later that year, Cousins planted a second church in St. Catherine parish, named Mt. Carmel Christian Worship Center. As a mission of the Northeastern District Assembly, the Jamaican churches received aid and training through the Foreign Missions Ministry, directed by Smith. Cousins served both the Kingston and St. Catherine Worship Centers with a combined membership of two hundred, aired a weekly radio program called "Speaking from the Heart," and established a lunch program for impoverished children in Kingston.[36]

Mexico

Between 1914 and 1919, the Christian Woman's Board of Missions relocated its work from northern to central Mexico as part of a comity agreement finalized at the 1916 Panama Conference. To some leaders both in Mexico and the United States it appeared that the CWBM had abandoned its seven churches and their Mexican pastors. In response, several missionaries,

most notably Enrique Westrup (1880-1967), founded the Mexican Society for Christian Missions in 1917. The purpose of the organization was "to perpetuate and enlarge, as far as possible, the work formerly done in Mexico by the Christian Woman's Board of Missions for the restoration of primitive Christianity among the Mexican people."[37]

The *Christian Standard* took up Westrup's cause as part of the attack on "organized" mission work. At the first Restoration Congress that met just before the 1919 St. Louis Convention to oppose creation of the UCMS, Westrup received a standing ovation when introduced as a featured speaker. The *Standard* editorialized that this applause "revealed clearly the growing conviction…that an injustice has been done our Mexican brethren and the Restoration cause" and called for "loyal brethren" to support the abandoned mission. Less than a month after the Congress, Westrup returned to Mexico with almost $1,700 in support.[38] The *Christian Standard* and regional Restoration Congresses promoted the Mexican Society vigorously throughout the 1920s, collecting and distributing contributions through the magazine's Cincinnati offices.[39]

A 1920 report contrasted the missionaries of the Mexican Society with those of the UCMS. Unlike UCMS personnel, they were not spending money taking trips in comfortable Pullman train cars and staying in expensive hotels to attend denominational conferences or represent the "Disciples denomination" at interchurch and federation meetings. Instead, they were enthusiastically preaching the gospel. They were on fire, the report declared, with the plea "for the restoration of New Testament Christianity" in northern Mexico. Not surprisingly, the Mexican Society turned down an offer from the Methodist Episcopal Church to unite with its mission.[40]

The UCMS had relocated its missionary personnel and several Mexican workers into the central provinces of San Luis Potosí and Aguascalientes by 1920. Schools established by Presbyterian and Methodist missionaries—Colegio Morelos in Aguascalientes and Colegio Inglés in San Luis Potosí—became part of the UCMS's Mexico Christian Mission.[41] The churches, however, were a different matter. The Presbyterian congregation in Aguascalientes "was not disposed to cooperate" with the UCMS, so a small Stone-Campbell group under the leadership of Pilar Silva began meeting in the auditorium of Colegio Morelos. By early 1921, this congregation became an established church with a modest building. The UCMS mission also established a new congregation

Mexico

in San Luis Potosí in 1922. Leaders counted those who had been immersed as members, but included as affiliate members unimmersed Methodists who attended the mission church.[42]

The changing political situation following the Mexican Revolution dramatically affected the work of all missions in Mexico. The Mexican government had approved a new constitution in 1917, though its provisions were not fully implemented until the mid-1920s. Article 3 mandated, in part, that "educational services shall be secular and, therefore, free of any religious orientation," making it impossible for the UCMS to maintain its schools in Aguascalientes and San Luis Potosí. Both schools suspended religious instruction in 1926 and came under close government scrutiny. Colegio Inglés remained open, but was absorbed into the state education system in 1932. Under the direction of Mexican educators, especially Maria de J. Valero (d. 1961), the school continued until 1967. Colegio Morelos, however, closed in 1934. From the mid-1930s forward, the UCMS was unable to offer primary and secondary education in Mexico.[43]

Additionally, Article 130 of the Mexican Constitution required that ministers of all churches in the country be Mexican by birth. While intended to exclude Spanish and French Catholic clergy, it also barred all other non-Mexican missionaries.[44] The article further stipulated that ownership of all church property be transferred to the state. Again, while aimed at taking away the Catholic Church's vast colonial-era landholdings, it also affected the property of all other churches. In addition, the article required all churches to register and be approved by the Mexican government.[45]

These constitutional requirements accelerated the indigenization of Stone-Campbell mission work in Mexico. In the UCMS-supported work, for example, leadership was vested in El Consejo Central de Evangelismo (The Central Council on Evangelism) beginning in 1927. This seven-member council included only one missionary; the remaining members were Mexican pastors and laypeople. The council held responsibility for planning and directing all evangelistic and church-planting work in Aguascalientes and San Luis Potosí, including selecting, employing, paying, and disciplining

Mexican evangelists and their assistants.[46]

Because the UCMS Mexico Christian Mission could no longer operate religious schools, it shifted its focus to social services and medical care in the 1930s and 1940s. In Aguascalientes, missionaries opened the Morelos Social Center in the Colegio Morelos building in 1934, offering basketball leagues, night schools taught by Mexican teachers, English language classes, a library, and Boy Scouts. Mission leaders opened a similar facility, the Juarez Social Center, in San Luis Potosí in 1937.[47] In the 1940s, UCMS missionaries like Florine Cantrell (1899-1994) in Zacatecas helped establish, in addition to a small church and elementary school under Mexican leadership, a cooperative for farmers, a clinic for mothers and babies, and a community center.[48] In Aguascalientes missionaries established *Sanatorio Esperanza* (Hope Sanatorium), which evolved into Hope Hospital, as well as a home for girls and an agricultural education program for boys.[49]

At their annual convention in 1935, the churches of Aguascalientes and San Luis Potosí organized a missionary society under the leadership of Mexican evangelists and supported by the Mexican churches. The society's goal was "to train workers, both lay and ministerial, and to send them out to help evangelize the people of Mexico."[50] More significant was the participation of these churches in the National Evangelistic Crusade in 1941. Disciples, Methodists, Presbyterians, Baptists, and Nazarenes cooperated in visiting existing churches and challenging them to begin house-to-house evangelism. Participants targeted most major Mexican cities, and Disciples in Aguascalientes and San Luis Potosí were especially zealous workers.[51]

Though not part of the UCMS's comity area, missionaries maintained a presence in Mexico City as faculty of Union Evangelical Seminary. The seminary appointed Frederick J. Huegel (1889-1971) to its faculty in 1929 after he and his wife Alleen (1888-1980) had served as missionaries in both Aguascalientes and San Luis Potosí for almost a decade. Until his retirement in 1956, Huegel taught theology, preached, and engaged in prison evangelism. Among Mexican Disciples, he was the primary promoter of ecumenical cooperation in education, publishing, evangelism, and social services.

By the middle of the 1950s, the churches of the UCMS Mexico Christian Mission had made significant progress toward indigenization and self-support. All pastors were Mexican as required by law, but even the governing council—known then as the Union of Christian Workers—was comprised only of Mexican leaders. The pastor of Central Church in San Luis Potosí, Daniel Lopez de Lars, served for many years as the president of the union. In 1960 leaders committed to a three-year "Revolutionary Plan for Evangelism," which relied on a group of almost five hundred specially trained laypersons to organize monthly evangelistic meetings, conduct direct-mail appeals, and distribute devotional literature. At the end of the three-year period, the work had reached more than twelve thousand people, resulting in two hundred ninety baptisms and a new Disciples congregation in Mexico City.[52]

In 1963, the twenty churches of the UCMS Mexico Christian Mission organized themselves into *La Asociación de Iglesias Cristianas Evangélicas (Discíplos de Cristo)* [the Association of Evangelical Christian Churches (Disciples of Christ)]. The AICE held annual delegate conventions for worship, fellowship, and education, with a small executive committee composed of pastors and laypersons directing the work between conventions. UCMS personnel who remained in Mexico became "fraternal workers." Because the churches of the Association remained heavily dependent on financial support from the UCMS, it committed itself to a Six Year Plan of Advance in 1964. Among other things, the churches aimed at adding two thousand members, establishing twenty new churches, and collecting at least half of their annual expenditures from the churches themselves.[53] Though the churches made significant progress toward these goals before 1970, it would be another decade before they became self-sufficient.

In 1968, Union Evangelical Seminary helped create a consortium known as *La Comunidad Teológica de México* (the Theological Community of Mexico). All of Union's resources were relocated to San Angel, a suburb of Mexico City, and combined with those of the other participating seminaries. Like the other schools, Union retained a distinct identity and enjoyed considerable freedom to develop its programming. After the sale of its old property, the churches of the AICE placed the money in a scholarship fund to support ministerial students in the consortium.[54]

Almost a century of governmental hostility toward religious groups ended in 1992 when the Mexican legislature approved the "Law on Religious Associations and Public Worship." Reversing many of the restrictions of the 1917 Constitution, the law declared all religious associations to be equal and banned religious discrimination. More importantly, the law recognized the churches' right to hold property, as long as it was registered with the state and used for religious purposes. This provision, however, led to conflict within the AICE.

In addition to church buildings, the AICE had structures and land used for social, educational, recreational, medical, and other community programs and services. Though always understood as belonging to the church, legally these properties were owned by two non-profit associations formed by the AICE General Assembly. This arrangement had raised concerns among some Mexican Disciples, particularly when the associations made decisions contrary to the desires of other church leaders.

In 1993 differences over property ownership turned into a serious conflict. Nearly half of the AICE congregations registered under the new Mexican law as the *Confraternidad de Iglesias Cristianas (Discípulos de Cristo)* [Fellowship of Christian Churches (Disciples of Christ)], also known as the CICE, based in San Luis Potosí. The remaining congregations also registered under a new name, the *Alianza de Iglesias Cristianas Evangélicas (Discípulos de Cristo) en México* [Alliance of Evangelical Christian Churches (Disciples of Christ) in Mexico], based in Aguascalientes, but still known as AICE. The Division of Overseas Ministries/Global Ministries of the Christian Church (Disciples of Christ) in the United States and Canada helped facilitate dialogues and encourage reconciliation between the two groups, though at the beginning of the twenty-first century full reunification had not been achieved.[55]

In addition to the work of Enrique Westrup, the Mexican work of North American Christian Churches/Churches of Christ had roots in one of the converts of the UCMS mission in San Luis Potosí. Antonio Medina had studied for the priesthood before the Mexican government closed Catholic seminaries in 1916. From a wealthy and influential family, he served in the Mexican delegation to the League of Nations and studied at the University of Paris. Upon his return to Mexico, he was attracted to one of the UCMS-supported churches in San Luis Potosí where he was baptized in 1927.

Initially, Medina began evangelistic and church planting work for the UCMS, but persuaded by arguments against the society, soon became a direct-support missionary. After marrying Victoria Infante in 1932, the couple planted churches in the towns of Loreto, Salinas, Las Colonias, Ojocaliente, and Estancia. By the time they retired in 1957, Antonio Medina estimated that he had baptized more than 4,500 people and that he and his wife had established more than a dozen congregations.[56] Their daughter, Martha, settled in Salinas with her American husband Wayne Hayes in 1954, and organized her father's work into the direct-support Central Mexico Christian Mission, which continued at the beginning of the twenty-first century.

After hearing in 1944 that Westrup's Mexican Society for Christian Missions then had only eight Mexican evangelists with an average age of fifty-nine, Harlan and Frances Cary opened Colegio Biblico in Eagle Pass, Texas, in 1945.[57] The school trained dozens of Mexican evangelists using a curriculum like that of Cary's alma mater, Cincinnati Bible Seminary. By the early 1960s, more than forty churches with approximately two thousand members were active in the region, a remarkable number considering Mexican legal restrictions then in force that forbad public evangelism, distribution of literature, or advertising of services.[58]

In 1950, direct-support missionaries Gerald and Geneva Bowlin established a similar school in Nogales, Arizona. Their Mexican Bible Seminary affiliated briefly with Cary's Colegio Biblico, but by 1955 had relocated to Hermosillo in northwest Mexico and was incorporated as the Western Mexico Christian Mission. Though the Bowlins served as liaisons between the school and North American churches, Mexican evangelist Alejandro Julián served as president of the school. Extension campuses soon opened in Chihuahua, Baja, Salinas, and Estancia, all administered by Mexican leaders. Students began aggressive evangelistic efforts, and by the early 1960s had organized more than one hundred twenty house churches with as many as ten thousand members.[59]

When Harlan Cary retired from the presidency of Colegio Biblico in 1976, the school was the principal training center for Spanish-speaking leaders for Christian Churches/Churches of Christ in northern Mexico. Under the leadership of Cary's son John, Colegio Biblico opened an extension campus in Piedras Negras in 1996 for students unable to secure visas to study in Eagle Pass. In 1999, Jorge Mercado, a graduate of Colegio Biblico and long-time pastor, became the first Mexican president of the school. At the beginning of the twenty-first century, the school continued on both campuses, and offered four- and five-year degree programs in theology, ministerial science, sacred literature, and Christian education.[60]

In the 1950s Enrique Westrup continued as principal leader of the Mexican Mission of the Churches of Christ, formerly the Mexican Society for Christian Missions, centered in Monterrey. He served as pastor of Central Christian Church and provided oversight to other evangelists and lay leaders associated with the mission. Perhaps the most important of Westrup's colleagues in

Monterrey were Pablo Pacheco and his son, Lonnie, who assumed responsibility for the Mexican Mission in 1962.[61] Westrup continued to edit *La Vía de Paz* (*The Way of Peace*), a journal with devotional material and Bible lessons.[62] Missionaries from North American Christian Churches/Churches of Christ who wanted to work in Mexico often began by affiliating with Westrup's mission in Monterrey.

One such couple was Rodney and Masel Northrup, who first came to Mexico in 1949. Settling in Saltillo, fifty miles southwest of Monterrey, the Northrups began a publishing ministry producing Spanish-language tracts, educational materials, and other works to support the Mexican Mission of the Churches of Christ and other Latin American direct-support missions.[63] Though prohibited by Mexican law from serving as pastors, in 1952 they helped organize a church that sent Mexican evangelists to preach in the surrounding area. In the 1960s and 1970s, dozens of additional direct-support missionaries worked with the Northrups, who later established missions throughout northern Mexico.

Significant mission work by North American Churches of Christ did not begin until the 1930s. At the beginning of the twentieth century, there were a few scattered Churches of Christ in Mexico, composed mainly of U.S. citizens who had moved there for economic advancement. During the Mexican Revolution from 1910 to 1920, evangelists like W. A. Schultz had left the country, though they continued work among Mexicans living in the southwestern United States.[64]

In the 1920s, Churches of Christ expanded their presence among the Mexican population of southern Texas and northern Mexico, especially through the work of Abilene Christian College (ACC) professors Howard Schug (1881-1969) and J. W. Treat (1907-1998). Schug began work among Hispanic families in Abilene, Texas, in 1921, starting a Bible class for children and eventually forming the first *Iglesia de Cristo* (Church of Christ) in the city. Schug influenced a number of ACC students to train to preach in Spanish in both Texas and Mexico, among them Jesse B. and Mary Gill, and Hilario Zamorano.[65] Treat was known for translating hundreds of hymns into Spanish that were used in Spanish-speaking Churches of Christ worldwide throughout the twentieth century.[66]

One of the most important leaders of *Iglesias de Cristo* in Mexico in the early twentieth century was Pedro Rivas. He had fled to Los Fresnos, Texas, to escape the Mexican Revolution and came in contact with members of Churches of Christ who supported him financially and spiritually. Assisted to attend Freed-Hardeman College

in Henderson, Tennessee, for theological training, he graduated in May 1932 and returned to Mexico where he preached in the Rio Grande valley as a vocational missionary. He finally settled in Torreón, Coahuila, which became a center for Rivas's evangelistic work. In 1941, John F. Wolfe, minister in El Paso, Texas, conducted an evangelistic meeting in Rivas's home that brought in several converts and energized the small group already there. The next year the congregation constructed the first permanent church building of an Iglesia de Cristo in Mexico with the help of the Church of Christ in Midland, Texas.[67]

Among the early leaders of Churches of Christ work on the Texas-Mexico border was Mexican-born Hilario Zamorano. He had been a student at Abilene Christian College, where he studied with Howard Schug and J. W. Treat. (*World Vision*, November 1936)

With financial support from the Church of Christ in Brownsville, Texas, Rivas was able to devote full time to evangelism, preaching in Torreón and surrounding towns and villages. In addition, in the mid-1940s Rivas travelled among Churches of Christ in the United States soliciting funds for a school to train Mexican and other Spanish-speaking evangelists. With support from a U.S. Board of Trustees, Rivas established the Torreón School of Preaching in 1946. By the end of that year, Rivas had become editor of *La Vía de Vida* (*The Way of Life*), begun as an English language paper in 1945 by a young graduate of David Lipscomb College, Harris Goodwin, to inform U.S. churches of the Mexican work. L. Haven Miller of Abilene and John F. Wolfe of El Paso were major advocates for the work in Mexico, making frequent teaching trips to the new congregations, preaching in new places, and raising support for the salaries of local preachers. By 1959, forty *Iglesias de Cristo* existed in Mexico.[68]

Besides the School of Preaching in Torreón, church leaders established another in Monterrey. In addition, the Latin American Bible School established in 1962 in Lubbock, Texas (renamed Sunset School of Preaching in 1964, and Sunset International Bible Institute in 1995), provided Spanish language classes for U.S. missionaries and trained Mexican evangelists. Reflecting the growing model in Churches of Christ of forming and sending trained mission teams, the Sunset Church of Christ in Lubbock sent a seven-family church planting team to Mexico City in 1987. Other teams went to Toluca, Cuernavaca, Guadalajara, León, and Morelia. The Toluca congregation ordained elders in November 2001 and cast a vision for evangelizing the region by sending teams from the local congregation. By 2000 there were four hundred *Iglesias de Cristo* in Mexico with over twenty-five thousand members.[69]

As with all mission work in Churches of Christ, the group's strongly congregational nature made comprehensive surveys of the work in Mexico difficult. Brief reports in the *Christian Chronicle* in the late twentieth and early twenty-first centuries indicated a vigorous connection between churches in Mexico and the United States, with frequent short-term mission trips to assist local congregations, church-sponsored orphan homes, and other evangelistic and service activities. The rise of drug-related violence, however, greatly hindered such efforts in the twenty-first century. [70]

Puerto Rico

By the end of the 1920s, the UCMS-supported mission in Puerto Rico consisted of twenty-three congregations with a combined membership of 1,331. Although strong Puerto Rican leaders had begun to emerge—especially Augusto Cotto Reyes and Juan B. Ortiz—responsibility for the mission still rested with the missionaries. Since the United States government administered public education and healthcare in Puerto Rico, the church confined its work almost entirely to evangelism. Since 1919, the UCMS mission had participated with other denominations in the *Seminario Evangélico de Puerto Rico* (Evangelical Seminary of Puerto Rico), a union press and bookstore, and a union periodical entitled *Puerto Rico Evangélico*. Veteran missionaries Vere C. (1878-1966) and Mayme (1882-1956) Carpenter led a team of six missionaries and twenty-five Puerto Rican

ministers working on the island.[71]

Within a four-year period two devastating hurricanes struck Puerto Rico, dramatically affecting life on the island, including the UCMS mission. In 1928, Hurricane San Filipe killed more than three hundred people, left forty thousand homeless, and did nearly fifty million dollars in property damage (including the complete destruction of nearly half of the mission's church buildings). Recovery had barely begun when Hurricane San Ciprian struck the island in 1932. This storm killed another two hundred fifty-seven people, left fifty thousand homeless, and did another thirty million dollars in property damage. Together these storms devastated the island's economy, destroying its sugar, citrus, tobacco, and coffee plantations.[72]

The Great Depression further devastated Puerto Rico, forcing the UCMS to reduce its financial support by two-thirds, dramatically reducing the salaries of the four remaining missionaries and the fourteen Puerto Rican pastors.[73] Although members were able to rebuild some church buildings destroyed by the hurricanes before the Depression, many congregations continued without a meeting place until after World War II.

In the midst of this suffering and uncertainty, a small prayer group began meeting on Sunday evenings at the Calle Comerío Christian Church to confess sins and seek reconciliation with God. By early 1933, the prayer group had grown and included several leading pastors. At one of these prayer meetings, several people experienced glossolalia and dancing in the Spirit. Over the next eighteen months participants also fasted and prayed, engaged in aggressive evangelism, and spread their enthusiasm to other denominations. This development—known as *El Avivamiento del 33* (the Revival of '33)—completely redefined the spiritual identity of Puerto Rican Disciples. They moved away from the orderly worship of the missionaries and embraced a spontaneous style that included what they saw as physical manifestations of the Spirit's work.[74]

The revival scandalized the missionaries and UCMS leaders, who attempted to suppress it as inconsistent with Disciples teaching and practice. In 1934, missionaries organized a series of retreats for Puerto Rican pastors and lay leaders designed to "extinguish the fires of the revival" through re-education. They also attempted to force Puerto Rican pastors to sign a "Declaration of Purpose," pledging cooperation with the UCMS and its missionaries and re-establishing worship patterns consistent with what they had been taught. Disagreements between UCMS representatives and Puerto Rican church leaders led to sharp confrontations, culminating in January 1935, when missionaries with the help of local police tried to stop the services at Comerío Street and install another minister. The conflict became so intense that the annual convention of the churches, scheduled for February, had to be cancelled. Only the intervention of well-respected missionary Samuel Guy Inman succeeded in resolving the conflict. [75]

Rev. Carmelo Álvarez (1899-1979) was the pastor of the Calle Comerio church when *El Avivamiento del 33* began in his congregation. He is pictured here two years before with church member Amparo Torres (left) and UCMS missionary Hallie Lemmon. (*World Call*, May 1931)

Years later, in 1972, missionary C. Manly Morton (1884-1976) lamented his role in trying to suppress the revival, and admitted it had taken him more than thirty years to understand and appreciate it. To "old line Disciples" missionaries, the Pentecostal spirituality of the revival caused deep frustration. Mutual understanding became virtually impossible. Morton admitted that the missionaries had made mistakes in dealing with the revival, especially permitting a "holier than thou barrier"

to develop between the missionaries and the Puerto Rican leaders of the revival. He had wanted to crush it, he said, but "I now thank God that I was not capable of doing it." While he maintained that some leaders exploited the revival for their own advantage, "for the great mass of our people this was a real spiritual experience and out of it came a blessing greater than any other we have ever known."[76]

Membership in the churches grew dramatically following the revival. In 1932, the combined membership of the Puerto Rican congregations was 1,780. By 1947, membership had grown to more than five thousand, representing a 280 percent increase in fifteen years.[77] Beyond numerical growth, however, the revival and the resulting conflict galvanized the resolve of Puerto Rican leaders to develop self-sufficient churches independent of missionary control and UCMS financial assistance.

The institutional groundwork for indigenization had been laid as early as 1930. Against the advice of some UCMS executives and missionaries, the twenty-second Annual Convention established an eleven-member *Junta Administrativa* (Administrative Council) that included both missionaries and Puerto Rican pastors to oversee the work of the churches between conventions. By 1948, the Council expanded to include all ordained pastors, two seminarians, and one representative each from the men's, women's, and young people's groups.[78] This represented a shift from a majority of missionaries in 1930 to a majority of Puerto Rican leaders in 1948. With the Carpenters having retired in 1944, and the Mortons serving their last year in 1948, a new relationship was developing between the UCMS and the Puerto Rican churches.

In the early 1950s, the Administrative Council developed a constitution, and in 1955 legally incorporated as the "Administrative Board of the Churches of the Disciples of Christ in Puerto Rico." The first constitution called for greater cooperation between church leaders and the UCMS, and stipulated that the Administrative Council be composed of Puerto Rican leaders, the Executive Secretary for Latin America of the UCMS, one at-large member chosen by the UCMS, and UCMS missionaries called by the Board. Though the UCMS continued substantial financial support, the Administrative Board assumed full responsibility for the Puerto Rican work and determined the use of the funds.[79]

Disciples of Christ in Puerto Rico achieved full autonomy from the UCMS in the late 1960s as North American Disciples were undergoing restructure. The UCMS had withdrawn the last of its missionaries in 1965, and two years later Puerto Rican Disciples adopted a new constitution. Renamed the *Convención de las Iglesias Cristianas (Discíplos de Cristo)* [the Convention of Christian Churches (Disciples of Christ)], the new corporation was a convention of churches, not an Administrative Council functioning on behalf of those churches. The new constitution also stipulated that delegates to the annual conventions include equal numbers of ordained clergy and laypersons, and that all church members contribute to a Fondo Común (Common Fund) that supported the convention's work. Although the UCMS continued to provide some financial help, by 1967 Puerto Rican Disciples constituted a fully autonomous and largely self-supporting church.[80]

Between 1970 and 1975, a generational conflict arose over Christian involvement in political matters. Though older Puerto Rican Disciples generally adopted a "hands-off" policy, younger generations did not. They vigorously opposed the Vietnam War that had claimed the lives of more than a thousand Puerto Ricans serving in the U.S. military. They also protested the buildup of U.S. naval forces in Vieques and Culebra, strategic locations from which the navy frequently intervened in Latin American affairs. Many supported the Civil Rights Movement in the United States, embraced Latin American Liberation Theology, and endorsed ecumenical dialogue with the Roman Catholic Church. Some older leaders denounced this activism as disidencia juvenil (juvenile dissent), and the Administrative Council expelled fourteen young leaders—many pastors of churches—from the Convention.[81]

The generational conflict strained relationships between Puerto Rican Disciples and the Division of Overseas Ministry of the Christian Church (Disciples of Christ) in the United States and Canada (DOM). In 1975, the Administrative Council broke formal relations with the DOM and requested the removal of its Executive Secretary for Latin America and the Caribbean, William Nottingham, who expressed sympathies for the younger leaders. The group demanded a liaison who better represented the theological and political views of the majority. In 1976, DOM leadership reassigned Nottingham at his request to the position of Executive Secretary for East Asia and the Pacific. By 1985, the generational conflict had died down and, in a gesture of reconciliation, the Convention passed a resolution expressing its appreciation for Nottingham's contribution to the mission work of the Christian Church (Disciples of Christ), especially in Puerto Rico.[82]

Even in the midst of this generational conflict, Puerto Rican Disciples recognized their own missionary responsibility both in Latin America and among Spanish-speaking Disciples in the United States. A 1974 revision to the Convention's constitution called on the churches to "promote, protect, and sustain their own missionary work." A handful of Puerto Rican missionary leaders emerged in the late 1970s and 1980s, notably Juan Marcos and Flor Rivera; Felix and Maria Ortiz; Carmelo Álvarez and Raquel Rodriguez; Luis and Genoveva del Pilar; and Jorge Bardéguez. These leaders were instrumental in developing ecumenical partnerships between U.S. and Puerto Rican Disciples and Pentecostal churches throughout Latin America. In 1980, the Convention formally partnered with the DOM to work together in Latin America for economic and social justice.[83] At the beginning of the twenty-first century, that partnership remained strong, coordinated through the Common Global Ministries Board in cooperation with the Central Pastoral Office for Hispanic Ministries.

In 1919, Puerto Rican Disciples had joined five other denominations in establishing the *Seminario Evangélico de Puerto Rico*. The school provided theological education for most pastors, though beginning in the 1960s many Puerto Rican Disciples continued their education at U.S. seminaries and graduate schools affiliated with the Christian Church (Disciples of Christ). In addition, since 1948, the Convention employed a General Director of Christian Education to oversee congregation-based lay education, who also published *El Educador Cristiano* (*The Christian Educator*) and contributed to ecumenical initiatives in Christian education.

Lay education opened the door for greater participation of women in leadership roles. Puerto Rican Disciples ordained Juana Santana, their first woman pastor, in 1977. After having served in a Spanish-speaking congregation in Bridgeport, Connecticut, she returned to Puerto Rico to establish a congregation in Río Nuevo. Other women followed, many of whom had prepared for ministry first in these lay education programs.[84]

In 1984, the Convention restructured itself into the *Iglesia Cristiana (Discíplos de Cristo) en Puerto Rico* [Christian Church (Disciples of Christ) in Puerto Rico]. While the move did not significantly alter the denomination's administrative structure, it did create the office of Pastor General. This shift defined the church's primary leader as a pastor, not a denominational executive. In addition, the new constitution replaced the voluntary Common Fund with a mandatory *Fondo de la Hermandad* (Brotherhood Fund), which required every congregation to contribute at least 10 percent of its income to the work of the whole church. While this new constitution affirmed the autonomy of the local congregation, it also emphasized the essential unity of the global Church. In 2011, the Christian Church (Disciples of Christ) in Puerto Rico claimed one hundred four congregations with a combined membership of 22,059.[85] It maintained strong connections with Spanish-speaking congregations in the United States, especially in South Florida, New York City, and Chicago.

North American Churches of Christ *(Iglesias de Cristo)* began in Puerto Rico in the early 1950s when Burl Buckman, a U.S. soldier stationed on the island, began distributing evangelistic tracts in Spanish and eventually assembled a small congregation. At the same time, Clark Hannah, a commercial pilot who regularly flew between New York City and San Juan, began placing ads in local newspapers for free Bible correspondence courses. The number of responses led Hannah to contact ministers John Young and Joe McKissick from Texas, who visited in April 1953. McKissick taught and baptized a previous contact named Gregorio Rodriguez and secured support from the Dalhart, Texas, Church of Christ to support Winston Atkinson to work in San Juan. Other missionaries who served in the 1950s included Dwayne Davenport, Harlan Overton, and Jose Cuellar. Jack Fogarty led numerous short evangelistic campaigns to San Juan.[86] Figures for 2008 showed that the oldest existing *Iglesia de Cristo* congregation in Puerto Rico was established in 1954 in Vega Alta. The largest congregation was established in 1968 in Bayamon, with a weekly attendance of one hundred eighteen. The island had thirty-two congregations with 1166 adherents.[87]

North American Christian Churches/Churches of Christ began in Puerto Rico with the arrival of Gordon and Vivian Thompson in 1954, who quickly established a congregation and an elementary school. In the mid-1960s other missionaries began arriving who, along with Puerto Rican leaders, established ten new congregations in the 1970s and 1980s and two elementary schools. The four San Juan congregations began conducting weekly college-level leadership training sessions in the early twenty-first century. The 2007 Directory of the Ministry listed five American missionary families living and working in Puerto Rico.[88]

Cuba

The earliest Stone-Campbell Movement efforts in Cuba had ended in 1916 when the FCMS withdrew and transferred its property to the Presbyterian Church. Beginning in the late 1930s, however, work began again, this time through the efforts of two Cuban American members of U.S. Churches of Christ. José Ricardo Jímenez (1900-1974) and Ernesto Estévez returned to Cuba from Florida in 1937 and 1939, respectively, and worked as evangelists for nearly two decades with little assistance from North American Churches of Christ. Nevertheless they established one hundred sixty-one congregations—most meeting in homes—with a combined membership of around five thousand. One of their most effective evangelistic tools was a weekly, thirty-minute, Spanish-language radio program broadcast from Havana.[89] In 1958, two evangelists from North America—C. W. Scott and C. E. McCamie—came to Cuba to assist this indigenous movement.[90] However, a year later the Cuban Revolution brought Fidel Castro and eventually the communist party to power in Cuba, cutting short the prospect of cooperative work between Cuban and North American Churches of Christ.

Initially Cuban church leaders were optimistic about the revolutionary government's separation of church and state, proclamation of complete religious freedom, and promise to respect human rights.[91] Castro's government, however, viewed the churches with suspicion because of their failure to challenge the abuses of the dictator Fulgencio Batista. For more than thirty years Churches of Christ and other Christian groups in Cuba faced persecution and suppression. North American missionaries were prohibited entry, and partnerships with the churches in Cuba were impossible. Many members either left Churches of Christ or fled to other parts of Latin America as refugees. Those who remained in Cuba avoided government suspicion by refusing to comment on political issues. By the late 1980s, the number of churches had dwindled to fifteen, with a combined membership of no more than four hundred.[92]

One sign of hope for Cuban Churches of Christ was the March 1987 visit of Spanish church leader and evangelist Juan Monroy who had met with Fidel Castro in Nicaragua two years earlier to advocate religious freedom and discuss the future of Churches of Christ. As a result, the government allowed Monroy to make numerous short-term trips to Cuba throughout the late 1980s and early 1990s. He was able to support and encourage the struggling churches, and to help lay groundwork for developments that followed.[93]

During the same period, North American Disciples developed a cautious relationship with the *Iglesia Cristiana Pentecostal de Cuba* (ICPC), the Christian Pentecostal Church of Cuba. Venezuelan Juan Marcos Rivera, a DOM fraternal worker and ecumenical leader, made initial contact in 1971. In the early 1970s, the DOM began modest financial support for the ICPC, the *Seminario Evangélico de Matanzas* (Evangelical Seminary of Matanzas), and the *Concilio de Iglesias de Cuba* (Cuban Council of Churches). Fraternal visits in the late 1970s and early 1980s strengthened the relationship between the Christian Church (Disciples of Christ) and these Cuban ministries.[94] At the beginning of the twenty-first century, the Christian Church (Disciples of Christ) continued these partnerships through the Common Global Ministries Board.[95]

Following the collapse of the Soviet Union and the Eastern European bloc between 1989 and 1992, Cuba's economy and Castro's government weakened considerably. In response, Cuba loosened restrictions on trade with other nations and opened itself to tourism. Despite the impact on the Cuban poor, the U.S. government tightened economic sanctions against Cuba in hopes of toppling Castro's government. In 1973 the Christian Church (Disciples of Christ) had called for an end to such economic sanctions, and in the 1990s many Disciples joined the Cuban Council of Churches in denouncing them as a manifestation of racism.[96]

Following several devastating hurricanes—especially Lili (1996) and Irene (1999)—the Cuban government also began accepting foreign humanitarian aid, especially from the United States. While continuing to support its historic ministry partners in Cuba, the Christian Church (Disciples of Christ) also provided material aid through Church World Service, and additional financial assistance through the Week of Compassion offering. Between 1993 and 1999, the Global Ministries Board collected and shipped more than ten million dollars in food, medicine, medical equipment, school supplies, and other materials to the island to aid the recovery efforts under the direction of Cuban churches.[97]

These developments also provided an opportunity for Churches of Christ in Cuba, North America, and Jamaica to develop partnerships in evangelism, church planting, and leadership training. Though Juan Monroy had been involved in evangelistic efforts in the country since the late 1980s, North American Churches of Christ returned in early 1993 to help lead the first evangelistic campaign in Cuba since the work of Scott and McCamie over thirty years before. Due to ongoing government restrictions, however, no North American missionary could remain in Cuba for more than three months at a time.[98] The "Herald of Truth" began a radio ministry in Cuba, broadcasting from Miami, Florida, and Grand Cayman in 1995.[99] In 2001 Sunset International School of Preaching began a variety of educational ministries

aimed at developing church leaders. In cooperation with Cuban workers, these efforts resulted in one hundred twenty congregations with a membership of almost five thousand by 2009. The Cuban Churches of Christ hosted the 35th Caribbean Lectureship in 2005.[100] North American Churches of Christ were among the largest contributors of humanitarian relief to Cuba in the early twenty-first century, both by individual congregations and by ministries like Healing Hands International and the Christian Relief Fund.[101]

Argentina

In the late 1920s, the UCMS work in Argentina remained small, with only two organized churches, preaching points in four outstations, and one hundred thirty-nine members. Some argued that financial resources and personnel would be better invested in other areas, including neighboring Paraguay. Though the UCMS decided to continue support in 1931, by 1933 the Great Depression forced reduction of the missionary staff to two couples: John D. (1891-1978) and Anna (1893-1957) Montgomery; and Normal (1900-1964) and Mae Yoho (1900-1983) Ward. The UCMS also discontinued support of the ecumenical Instituto Modelo de Obreras Christianas, and reduced pastors' salaries.[102]

Between 1930 and 1943, four dictators rose to power through intimidation and electoral fraud. During this "Infamous Decade," the government suppressed political opposition and established economically disastrous relationships with foreign nations. In the midst of this extreme political instability, indigenization of the Argentine Mission accelerated. The Consejo Central de las Iglesias de los Discípulos (Central Council of Disciples Churches) formed in 1929 to guide the work of the churches and represent the mission in ecumenical endeavors, marked the first formal inclusion of Argentine Christians as national leaders. Membership included missionaries, Argentine pastors, and two elected laypersons from the churches. The Council in turn organized a delegate convention that first met occasionally, then annually after the Great Depression. Similar to the Disciples International Convention in the United States, the Argentine convention included worship, education, fellowship, and sessions for determining mission policy.[103]

By the early 1940s, the Argentine Mission had recovered from the Great Depression and began laying plans for expanding its work, despite the nation's ongoing political instability. Over the next decade and a half, the UCMS sent a dozen additional missionaries to Argentina, supported both by living link relationships with specific churches and by funds from the Crusade for a Christian World (1947-1950).[104] In 1943, the mission began publishing *River Plate Reflections*, an English-language quarterly for distribution in North America with news about the missions in Argentina and Paraguay. Leaders opened a station in Resistencia in 1944—a strategic location as the capital and largest city of the district, situated mid-way between Buenos Aires and Asuncíon, Paraguay, where the UCMS maintained a thriving mission. In 1946, the UCMS appointed T. J. (1919-2012) and Virginia (1918-2002) Liggett to serve in Resistencia, where they remained until 1957.[105]

Argentine pastor Feliciano Sarli led the work at Resistencia. He and the Liggetts established a small congregation and school and cooperated with the Methodist and Waldensian missions to begin work among the Toba people. Since the 1880s, the Argentine government had claimed ownership of Toba land, developing it for agricultural purposes and exploiting the Toba people as a cheap source of labor. Most of the station's work centered on legal assistance related to land claims, medical care, and drilling for water. Evangelism was minimal, mainly because most Tobas were already Pentecostal Christians.[106]

Disciples pastor, ecumenist, and educator Jorgelina Lozada teaching a course on the history of Argentina to a group of missionaries at Colegio Ward in the early 1950s. On the board she has highlighted the general election of 1951, the first one in which Argentine women were permitted to vote. (*World Call*, October 1952)

Another influential leader was Jorgelina Lozada (1906-1995). Baptized in the Belgrano Christian Church in 1921, she was one of the first women to graduate from the Instituto Modelo de Obreras Christianas four years

later. In 1930, the Argentine Mission ordained her as one of the first women pastors in the Rio de la Plata region. Initially serving as an evangelist and "home missionary," she became pastor of the Villa Mitre Christian Church in the La Paternal neighborhood. Under her leadership, the church developed a kindergarten and free health clinic for the poor. She was a delegate to the 1938 World Missionary Conference in Madras, India, and two years later published a book based on her observations of evangelical missions there, *La India Tradicionalista y el Servicio Social (Traditional India and Social Service)*. Serving for many years as executive secretary of the Confederation of Evangelical Churches in the River Plate region, she was the primary organizer of the first Latin American Evangelical Conference (CELA 1) in Buenos Aires in 1949. Her ecumenical involvement widened even further in the 1950s as she attended the World Sunday School Convention in 1950, the International Missionary Council in 1952, and the World Council of Churches in 1954. Her declining health kept her in Argentina beginning in the 1960s, but until her death in 1995 she continued her ministry with Argentine Disciples and several private social service organizations.[107]

By 1959 the Central Council of Disciples Churches had been reorganized into an autonomous, self-supporting convention of churches named *La Iglesia Evangélica de los Discípulos de Cristo en Argentina* (The Evangelical Church of the Disciples of Christ in Argentina). The church consisted of eight congregations with a combined membership of six hundred forty-six. Argentine Disciples continued to cooperate in the Colegio Ward and the Union Theological Seminary in Buenos Aires. Despite government opposition, they also continued to support interdenominational work among the Toba people in the Chacos region. UCMS personnel served as "fraternal workers" instead of missionaries after 1959.

Two years after its formation, the Evangelical Church of the Disciples of Christ in Argentina adopted a "Ten-Year Plan of Advance" to achieve self-support for existing churches and establish five new congregations.[108] Evangelism was especially successful in the Chacos region, where Argentine Disciples established three new congregations in the 1960s. In 1962 they established an agricultural school in Vilasoro in northeastern Argentina, for which the UCMS and Argentine churches purchased more than 300,000 acres. Pablo Navajas Artaza, one of Argentina's wealthiest agriculturalists, donated land and yerba crops to help finance the school's operation in its early years. Outside the small town of Vedia, two hundred miles west of Buenos Aires, Argentine Disciples also established a Christian service camp in 1963.[109]

Between 1976 and 1983, the political situation in Argentina reached its lowest point as three military dictators ruled the nation and instituted the National Reorganization Process, which opponents called *La Guerra Sucia* (the Dirty War). Though claiming to restore political and social order to the badly divided nation, the process degenerated into one of the most repressive regimes in Latin American history. The junta gave the military virtually unbridled authority over perceived political opponents. As many as thirty thousand people were imprisoned, tortured, exiled, or simply disappeared in a seven-year period. Most were social reformers, religious leaders, and human rights advocates. The continuing weakness of the Argentine economy coupled with the disastrous Falklands War with Great Britain in 1982 led to the rise of a moderate civilian government that began to restore genuine order.

Like many Protestant churches, Disciples in Argentina suffered considerably during National Reorganization. In 1976, military police arrested and imprisoned Claudia Peiró, the teenage daughter of pastor Angel Peiró, whose boyfriend had been accused of belonging to a student group suspected of subversive activities. At one time or another, all Argentine Disciples pastors appeared on the "death lists," forcing many into exile for a time. As late as 1986, a bomb exploded in the Colegiales Church, one of a long history of attacks on religious organizations intended to intimidate those advocating human rights.[110]

Yet many Protestants were actively involved in resisting the dictators and assisting their victims. In 1977, Argentine Disciples women participated in forming the Abuelas de Plaza de Mayo (Grandmothers of the Plaza de Mayo), an interdenominational organization to locate children who disappeared during National Reorganization. In its first years, the organization located more than three hundred children kidnapped by the military for illegal adoption or sale. In 1998, evidence the Abuelas had gathered over more than twenty years helped lead to the arrest of Jorge Videla, one of the three military dictators. In addition, Argentine Disciples helped organize the *Movimiento Ecuménico por los Derechos Humanos* (Ecumenical Movement for Human Rights), founded in 1976, to defend and promote human rights, mobilize churches, promote training and education, and provide social services for victims of human rights violations.[111]

Although Argentine Disciples had been involved in dialogues with Methodists concerning formation of a union church since the late 1960s, they began concrete actions in 1987. After three years of bi-lateral dialogue and experimental union worship services, the Villa Devoto Methodist and Villa Mitre Disciples congregations merged to form Iglesia Emmanuel, and the Colegiales Disciples and Belgrano Methodist congregations in Buenos Aires merged to form *Iglesia El Buen Pastor* (Good Shepherd Church). In the late 1980s, Argentine Disciples entered other union dialogues with the Church of God (Anderson, Indiana), the Reformed Church, and the Rio de la Plata Evangelical Church.[112] Though full organic union had not been achieved at the beginning of the twenty-first century, a number of union experiments at the congregational level had been successful.

The work of both Churches of Christ and Christian Churches/Churches of Christ in Argentina was small. Churches of Christ began in Argentina in 1957 with the baptism of a former Catholic priest, Silverio Ojeda, in Buenos Aires by H. L. Perry, a New York businessman. Later that year Harlan Overton visited Ojeda and arranged support for him to work as a full time evangelist. In 1958 Ronald Davis and Lionel Cortez from Abilene Christian University arrived to work with Ojeda. In the decades since these beginnings at least twenty-eight missionary families worked in the country. At the beginning of the twenty-first century, many of the fifteen congregations were under Argentine leadership. Reflecting the widespread pattern of Stone-Campbell missions, the Caballito Church of Christ in Buenos Aires began a ministry training school in 2011.[113]

Paraguay

Stone-Campbell work in Paraguay had begun in 1918 with CWBM missionaries holding English-language worship services and Bible studies in their homes. The next year they began a co-educational boarding school they named Colegio Internacional. In 1928 the mission began English and Spanish worship services in the four-hundred-seat auditorium in the school's recently constructed Mary Lyons Hall. Gradually, a church began to develop among students and their families. In 1939, the mission purchased land adjacent to the school, and the next year built the Peru Street Christian Church. While attitudes toward the school were generally positive, the church faced significant opposition, often inspired by local Catholic leaders. When the children of a prominent Paraguayan military officer who were studying at the school became interested in attending church and being baptized, local priests insisted that he withdraw them immediately. Prior to the dedication of the new building, local opponents vandalized the wall around the property with mud and ink.[114]

Both Paraguay and neighboring Bolivia claimed a large, sparsely populated lowland area between the two nations known as the Gran Chaco. When oil was discovered in the region in the late 1920s, conflict over its control led to the Chaco War between 1932 and 1935. The cost of the war, combined with the economic strains of the Great Depression brought both nations to the verge of total economic collapse. Shortly after the war, a disgruntled military forced Paraguayan President Eusebio Ayala to resign in the so-called February Revolution. For the next eighteen years, military dictators ruled Paraguay in ways inspired by European fascism.

During the Chaco War, Paraguayan nationalists seized the Colegio Internacional, using some of the buildings as hospitals. Several of the school's older students joined the army and were killed in the fighting. During the February Revolution, fighting in Asunción led church leaders to sequester the students, faculty, and administration on campus.[115] The experience of the war and political chaos strengthened the commitment of the school's leaders to its mission of producing "honest businessmen, self-sacrificing politicians, and peaceful citizens by teaching the tenets of evangelical Christianity."[116]

Hansen's disease—commonly known as leprosy—was common in Paraguay when the Disciples of Christ Mission began. Discrimination against its victims included denial of employment, housing, and medical care. For many, the only option was begging on the streets of the major cities. In 1934, Scottish missionary physician Dr. John Hay (1863-1943) and UCMS missionary Malcolm Norment (1890-1969) convinced the Paraguayan government to donate 2,500 acres to the Paraguay Mission to begin a leper colony. Located eight miles outside of Sapucay, Colonia Santa Isabel began in a boxcar that Hay and Norment converted into a residence for their first patients.[117]

Supported by donations from the Peru Street Christian Church, students at the Colegio Internacional, leading businessmen, and a growing medical community, the colony developed a reputation for compassionate treatment of leprosy patients. In 1941, an interdenominational council of Protestant ministers formed the *Patronato de Leprosos del Paraguay* (Board for Paraguayan Lepers), to oversee the colony's work under the leadership of UCMS missionary Robert Lemmon and the partnership of a women's group known as the *Comisión de Damas*. With the support of public health organizations in the United States, the Disciples of Christ Paraguay Mission built a leprosy hospital on the colony's grounds in 1948. By the early 1950s the growing number of patients forced the mission to turn the work over to the Paraguayan Ministry of Public Health and the Roman Catholic Church, though the UCMS continued to provide workers through the 1960s.[118]

Three UCMS missionary couples established a second station at Coronel Oviedo in 1946, which opened *Casa de Amistad* (Friendship House), a social center that held worship services, conducted a Sunday school for children, maintained a library, and provided social activities for the people of this rural area. They organized the Coronel Oveido Church in 1957, which began evangelistic work among the Guaraní people. Small Christian communities were established in Nuevo Londres, Tacuacorá, and Tuyu Pucú.[119] After progress on the Pan-American Highway in the mid-1950s made travel between Asunción and São Paulo, Brazil, much easier, new communities along the east-west route of the highway provided an opportunity to extend the Paraguay Mission. Missionaries and Paraguayan leaders evangelized and planted churches along this highway, reaching into the Paraná state of Brazil by the early 1960s.[120]

As the reputation of the Disciples of Christ Paraguay Mission grew in the 1950s and 1960s, evangelism and church planting became more effective in and around Asunción. As early as 1950, Agnes Fishbach (1900-1984) and a young Paraguayan woman named Ermelinda Rodríguez began Bible studies in their home in Colón, a suburb of Asunción. Within a year, they had established the Second Christian Church, better known as the Barrio Colón Church. Similar efforts in Arroyos y Esteros resulted in an agricultural ministry and church by 1960, and a year later a primary school and church in Villa Aurelia.[121] By 1970, the Disciples of Christ Paraguay Mission consisted of nine churches with a combined membership of four hundred fifty-eight.[122]

As early as 1956, the Mission had resolved that "Paraguayans should be more deeply involved in planning and implementing the work of the church."[123] Soon the churches were organized into the *Iglesia Cristiana Discípulos de Cristo en Paraguay* (Christian Church, Disciples of Christ in Paraguay), led entirely by Paraguayan pastors and laypersons. Former UCMS missionaries became "fraternal workers," concentrating their efforts in the Colegio Internacional and ecumenical work.

In 1953, J. Raymond (1905-1996) and Elizabeth (1900-1985) Mills established *Misión de Amistad* (Friendship Mission) in Asunción with the financial help of *Colegio Internacional* alumni. Similar to Friendship House in

Coronel Oviedo, this social service center developed a comprehensive program including worship, vacation Bible schools, medical and dental care, classes teaching domestic skills, and a variety of recreational activities. The mission drew international attention almost immediately because of its progressive integration of evangelistic and social services ministry.[124]

During the dictatorship of Alfredo Stroessner, human rights violations reached their worst. Between 1954 and 1989, he and his Colorado Party were responsible for the murder of at least fifty thousand people, the unexplained disappearance of thirty thousand others, and the imprisonment of more than four hundred thousand, mostly political opponents. They also enslaved whole tribes of indigenous people, notably the Aché of eastern Paraguay, to exploit natural resources for personal gain. Those who called attention to such human rights violations or provided assistance to victims risked government censure, exile, persecution, or even execution.

Because *Misión de Amistad* advocated the rights of indigenous people and peasant farmers, it became the target of government suspicion and harassment in the 1970s. In 1976, the Stroessner government arrested and imprisoned ten Disciples leaders—including mission director Victor Vaca and UCMS fraternal workers Frisco and Bertha Gilchrist—falsely charging them with supplying funds to purchase arms, teaching Marxist doctrine, and fomenting rebellion against the government.[125]

Though international pressure forced authorities to release the detainees after six months, the episode called attention to much greater human rights violations perpetrated by the Stroessner regime. Evangelical Christians, including Paraguayan Disciples, formed the *Comité de las Iglesias* in 1976. With the political support of the administration of U.S. President Jimmy Carter, the committee pressed for the release of all political prisoners and coordinated medical and psychological care for them. In its first three years, the committee secured the release of almost 1,500 persons held without cause.[126] Likely because of their involvement with the committee, Paraguayan Disciples and North American fraternal workers suffered persecution well into the 1980s, including the 1987 exile of *Misión de Amistad* Board member Armin Ihle, and the arrest of sixty persons associated with the *Comité* and *Misión de Amistad* on false accusations of subversive activities after an international delegation of church leaders visited Paraguay in 1988 to express support for their work.[127]

Misión de Amistad continued to receive financial support from the Division of Overseas Ministries of the Christian Church (Disciples of Christ) in the United States and Canada until 1992, when it became a self-supporting institution with its own constitution and board of directors.[128] Colegio Internacional continued to grow in both enrollment and reputation with an enrollment of almost 1,500 students. Leaders wrote a new school constitution in 1972 stipulating that the entire board of trustees be Paraguayan and Argentine, signaling its full independence of the DOM. At the beginning of the twenty-first century, Colegio Internacional had an enrollment of more than two thousand students.

The work of North American Churches of Christ in Paraguay was limited. Though some work began as early as 1965 by evangelists from Brazil and Uruguay, only two missionaries gave concentrated effort to the country— Luís Ramirez, who moved to Asunción from Montevideo in 1976 with the help of the Northside Church of Christ in Austin, Texas, and the Forrest McDonald family who worked in the country during 1981-1984. Not until 2003 when a team sent by the Continent of Great Cities ministry arrived did work by Churches of Christ in Paraguay receive a significant boost.[129]

Brazil

The Stone-Campbell Movement first arrived in Brazil in 1927, when three couples of the North American Churches of Christ began missionary work in the northeastern states. Orla S. (1893-1978) and Ethel (1892-1967) Boyer and Virgil (1902-2000) and Ramona Smith were the first to arrive, followed by George and Dallas Johnson two years later. Immediately they established headquarters in Mata Grande in the state of Alagoas, and soon had a growing congregation and printing press.[130] By 1931, the group had planted at least four other churches in the neighboring state of Pernambuco. "The gospel has been introduced in every village and town within a hundred miles of this station," they reported.[131] By the mid-1930s, the missionaries and at least four Brazilian evangelists also had preached in the neighboring states of Ceará, Rio Grande do Norte, and Paraíba.

Opposition from Catholic leaders was strong, labeling the church the "nova seita" (new sect). On one preaching tour in Jarsin, Ceará, a group under the leadership of the local priest threw stones at the missionaries and forcibly confined them to the house where they were staying. A few months later, in the nearby city of Juazeiro, a local military officer had to protect the missionaries so

Brazil

they could exercise their constitutional right to preach in public.[132] Some Brazilians affiliated with the mission also suffered persecution, including a Catholic woman who did washing for the missionaries who reported that when she went to confession, the priest refused to hear her unless she stopped working for them.[133]

As the missionaries expanded their work, Pentecostalism was also spreading throughout Brazil.[134] A 1932 report by Boyer to *Word and Work* raised suspicions in some readers' minds that Pentecostal doctrine and practice had influenced the Brazilian Churches of Christ. Supporters questioned Virgil Smith about this during his 1934 furlough to the United States. He reported that some Brazilian leaders had, in fact, experienced "baptism of the Spirit," including evangelists João Nunes and Manoel Pinheiro. More specifically, these leaders and some in their churches had spoken in tongues. Though the missionaries acknowledged these experiences as authentic, they denied teaching them as doctrines of Christian faith. The missionaries did not question the Brazilian leaders' commitment to restoring New

Testament Christianity, and advised their supporters to tolerate these differences.[135]

The antagonism with which U.S. church leaders confronted Smith about these experiences led him to visit the headquarters of the Assemblies of God in Springfield, Missouri. In conversations with officials there, he found their views more in line with his developing understandings of the Holy Spirit and was apparently ordained. By 1935 the Boyers and Smiths, along with many of the Brazilian leaders and their churches, had affiliated with the newly autonomous Brazilian Assembléia de Deus (Assembly of God), formerly a mission of Swedish Pentecostals.[136] When the missionaries later moved to southeastern Brazil, some of the congregations separated from the Assembléia de Deus and participated in the formation of the Igreja de Cristo Pentecostal do Brasil (the Pentecostal Church of Christ of Brazil).[137] Another twenty years would pass before North American Churches of Christ would begin new mission work in Brazil.

North American Christian Churches/Churches of

Christ entered Brazil when the fiftieth graduating class of Johnson Bible College (now Johnson University) established a fund to send classmates Lloyd David and Ruth Sanders as direct-support missionaries. The effort, named the Brazil Christian Mission, raised enough money to send the Sanderses to Rio de Janeiro in early 1948. Nine additional missionaries joined them over the next ten years.[138] From the beginning, the Brazil Christian Mission focused on training Brazilian evangelists and leaders to preach and establish churches.[139]

Antonio Santos Medeiros, president of the conference of the Church of Our Lord Jesus Christ, shakes hands with Christian Churches/Churches of Christ missionary Lloyd David Sanders in 1954. Mederios and Sanders negotiated the union between the congregations of the conference and the Brazil Christian Mission. (*Brazil Christian Mission*, February 1954)

Upon their arrival, the Sanderses spent several months in Rio de Janeiro studying Portuguese, then moved to the small city of Goiânia, one hundred twenty miles southwest of Brasília. With the assistance of a teacher in the local Catholic high school, Decio Jaime, the Sanderses rented a small home and began the Escola Biblica (Bible School) in the neighboring village of Vila Nova. Jaime would later be baptized and attend Lincoln Bible Institute (now Lincoln Christian University).[140] Enrollment in the Escola Biblica grew rapidly, but had to be capped at one hundred students due to limited funds and personnel. Meanwhile the Sanderses adopted Amancio Coqueiro, the youngest son of a destitute woman of Vila Nova, who became the first "convert" of the Brazil Christian Mission.

The Brazil Christian Mission began a weekly radio program known as Hora Cristã (the Christian Hour) in 1953. The Sanderses also opened a government-licensed Bible bookstore that distributed hundreds of Portuguese Bibles annually. To build support for the mission, the couple began the monthly *Brazil Christian Mission* for North American supporters. In 1955 the Sanderses built four permanent buildings to serve as mission headquarters on two acres donated by former Goias governor and senator Jeronimo Coimbro Bueno. One of the buildings included dormitory space, offices, and classrooms for the Instituto Cristão de Goiânia (Goiânia Christian Institute), a school to train Brazilian evangelists. By 1960, graduates had begun new work in surrounding villages, including Silvania, Botafogo, and Vila Operaria.[141]

In 1954, Abrahão Curry, leader of a São Paulo congregation affiliated with an indigenous restoration movement known as the "Church of Our Lord Jesus Christ," contacted the Brazil Christian Mission. Conversations with Curry and other leaders convinced Mission personnel that these thirteen congregations had arrived at the same basic doctrinal stances as Christian Churches "entirely ignorant of the Restoration Movement in the United States," and they immediately began cooperative work with them. These congregations traced their roots to a movement begun by Brazilian Christians in 1928, and had organized their first church in 1936. Whether these churches had a connection with the earlier mission of North American Churches of Christ is not certain. By the time the Sanderses encountered them, the Church of Our Lord Jesus Christ claimed around one thousand members, with ten ministers and forty-five workers preaching in thirty-four outstations.[142]

Though the Brazil Christian Mission was a direct-support mission governed by its own board, it made annual reports to the International Convention of the Christian Churches (Disciples of Christ) beginning in 1949. In 1961, the board of directors of the International Convention urged leaders of the Brazil Christian Mission to become fully integrated into the cooperative structures of the Disciples of Christ. "[The Brazil Christian Mission] cannot be involved in direct support and at the same time commit itself to the disciplines of unified methods of raising funds," they insisted. "It cannot be cooperative in its sympathies and independent in its procedures. It cannot accept all of the privileges of being identified with other agencies in a cooperative fellowship and not accept its share of the responsibility for the common cause."[143]

In response, the board of the Brazil Christian Mission voted in 1961 to terminate its relationship with the International Convention. The question of open membership and UCMS commitment to the ecumenical movement particularly troubled the Mission's leaders. They believed that leaders of the International Convention were trying to force them "to endorse…agencies which we cannot conscientiously and wholeheartedly support" and explained that their decision was "purely an action of doctrinal conviction."[144] Other supporters of the Brazil Christian Mission labeled the International Convention's appeal a "line-up-or-get-out ultimatum" that represented the kind of ecclesiastical domination to be expected from Disciples liberals.[145] At the time of its break with the International Convention, the Brazil Christian Mission included eleven congregations and preaching points, an average attendance of three hundred forty in a dozen Sunday schools, and five primary schools with an enrollment of one hundred seventy eight. Nine missionaries and six Brazilian evangelists led the work.[146]

The early successes of the Brazil Christian Mission inspired other direct-support missionaries to begin work there in the 1950s. William and Virginia Loft arrived in 1952 and established the Amazon Valley Christian Mission in Belém. They preached among the Amerindians of the region, planted churches, and established the Amazon Valley Christian Home for Children.[147] When the Lofts relocated to Brasilia, which became the federal capital in 1957, David and Beverly Bayless assumed responsibility for the mission and renamed it "Christ for the Amazon Valley." In addition to continuing the Lofts' work, in 1958 they also began training native evangelists at their Belém Bible Seminary (later named Pará Christian Institute).[148] The Christian Missionary Fellowship began sending workers to Brazil in 1957, beginning with John Nichols, son of veteran missionary Edgar Nichols of India and Tibet.[149] By 1960, North American Christian Churches/Churches of Christ supported no fewer than thirty missionaries in Brazil.

Eventually the Sanderses relocated to Brasilia, while other missionaries, especially Thomas and Elizabeth Fife, assumed responsibility for the work in Goiânia. In these two locations, the Brazil Christian Mission continued to thrive throughout the 1960s and 1970s, especially as Brazilian evangelists began to assume greater leadership roles. New mission initiatives began in Brasilia in particular. In 1980, the Brazil Christian Mission established the *Faculdad Teológica Cristã do Brasil* (Christian Theological Faculty of Brazil) at the Plano Piloto Christian Church in suburban Brasilia. Similar to Bible colleges in North America, the school trained Brazilian evangelists and other church leaders. In cooperation with the Brazilian government, the mission inaugurated the Integrated Life Project in 1986, which built dozens of homes for the underprivileged, especially the elderly.[150]

In 1961, missionaries from Christian Churches/Churches of Christ began yearly conferences that focused on worship, fellowship, and education, much like the North American Christian Convention with which they were familiar. At the first gathering, leaders also agreed to cooperate in the development of audio-visual educational materials and to form the Association of Christian Literature.[151] Between 1968 and 1980, missionaries from U.S. Churches of Christ began participating in the conferences. Often main speakers were chosen from the two groups, as in the 1972 gathering in Goiânia that featured Reuel Lemmons from Churches of Christ and Robert O. Fife from Christian Churches. To facilitate participation by Churches of Christ, conference worship was conducted without instrumental music. The conferences ended in the 1980s, however, when some missionaries and Brazilian leaders in Christian Churches/Churches of Christ began to embrace Pentecostal theology and practices, and a number of the missionaries returned to the United States.[152]

At length, a significant number of members and leaders in the Brazilian Christian Churches experienced the neo-Pentecostal or Charismatic renewal that swept through Christian bodies around the world in the 1970s and 1980s. Some fully embraced Pentecostal theology and practices, including speaking in tongues and miraculous gifts. Others continued to maintain that the Holy Spirit was received through baptism, but expanded their view of spiritual gifts, with some believing in a separate baptism of the Holy Spirit. All these groups adopted an exuberant charismatic style of worship. Those who rejected these developments felt themselves increasingly drawn toward fellowship with Churches of Christ. Some began attending an annual Missionary Conference sponsored by Churches of Christ, a biannual spiritual retreat for English-speaking leaders organized by the Continent of Great Cities ministry, and training schools operated by Churches of Christ.

As the earlier conferences held by Christian Churches were ending, Brazilian leaders and missionaries organized the *Concilio Ministerial das Igrejas de Cristo no Brasil* (Ministerial Council of the Churches of Christ in Brazil) in the late 1970s. Open to any minister, elder, or missionary who chose to participate, the council functioned as a fellowship of leaders that organized gatherings for men, women, youth, and missionaries in the Brazilian

Christian Churches, and conducted an annual June leadership retreat. Ministers and leaders from all parts of the Brazilian Christian Churches were members of the Ministerial Council, including both charismatics and non-charismatics. The Council provided primary leadership for the 2012 global gathering of the World Convention of Churches of Christ in Gioânia.[153] At the beginning of the twenty-first century, Brazilian Christian Churches consisted of four hundred forty congregations—including several mega-churches—with a combined membership of ninety thousand.

North American Churches of Christ returned to Brazil when Arlie and Alma Smith settled in São Paulo in 1956. They began holding a Bible study in their home and, with the help of Brazilian converts Marcelino dos Santos and Roberto Blanco, established a small congregation and began a weekly newspaper titled *Volta a Biblia* (*Return to the Bible*). By 1959, Ivan and Kitty Rude had joined the Smiths and the handful of Brazilian evangelists working with them in São Paulo.[154]

The Brazil work received a major boost when a group of Abilene Christian College (now University) students read reports about missionary opportunities in Brazil in 1957 and committed to becoming full-time missionaries upon graduation.[155] In 1961, these fourteen families—thirty-one adults and seventeen children— arrived in São Paulo.[156] Less than a year after their arrival, they established the *Escola da Biblia* (School of the Bible) to train Brazilian evangelists. Meeting in a rented building in the suburb of San Amaro, the school enrolled fifty-four students in its first year.[157] Almost immediately, Brazilian graduates of the school began assisting the missionaries in evangelism, resulting in thousands of baptisms and at least a dozen organized congregations by the mid 1960s.[158]

The missionaries began an aggressive building campaign in 1964, with the goal of raising $250,000 to build churches and establish a permanent base of operations in São Paulo. Coordinated through the Central Church of Christ in Amarillo, Texas, the leaders contacted more than three thousand North American congregations and urged each member to contribute one dollar toward the campaign.[159] In 1966, North American Churches of Christ purchased a network of twenty-eight radio stations broadcasting from São Paulo. The radio stations carried evangelistic preaching programs twice daily, daily Bible readings, children's programs, and offered free Bible correspondence courses. The programs could be heard throughout Latin America and the Caribbean, and the missionaries broadcast in both Portuguese and Spanish.[160]

Meanwhile, a second group of over one hundred was preparing to enter Belo Horizonte as a "missionary colony" to begin evangelism, educational services, and medical care in what they called "Operation/68 Brazil."[161] In the 1960s Belo Horizonte, the capital and largest city of the Minas Gerais state of southwestern Brazil, was developing quickly into a center of commerce, education, and culture. Seven missionary families arrived in 1967 as an advance guard, purchasing property, establishing relationships with local community leaders, and beginning evangelistic work in rural areas around the city.[162] A year later, the rest of the group arrived, and by 1970, evangelism and church planting had spread from Belo Horizonte to Curitiba, Porto Alegre, and Rio de Janeiro. Mission leaders established congregations, trained Brazilian leaders, and conducted correspondence courses with an enrollment of more than three thousand.

Encouraged by their early success, the missionaries and their Brazilian co-laborers committed themselves in 1969 to an aggressive program of missionary expansion they called "Breakthrough Brazil." Before 1980, they planned to expand missionary efforts into the capital cities of seven Brazilian states—especially Recife, Brasilia, and Salvador—and the federal capitals of three neighboring South American nations: Buenos Aires, Argentina; Montevideo, Uruguay; and Asunción, Paraguay.[163] In 1976, Ellis and Doris Long began leading the effort with significant support from the Central Church of Christ in Amarillo, Texas, and the Golf Course Road Church of Christ in Midland, Texas. Renamed the Continent of Great Cities ministry in 1979, it began sending missionary teams into key cities of Brazil in the 1980s, of Argentina in the 1990s, and of Paraguay, Mexico, and Central America in the 2000s.[164] As a result, at the beginning of the twenty-first century virtually every nation of South America had resident missionaries supported by North American Churches of Christ who helped lead congregations in cooperation with local evangelists.

Once established, Churches of Christ in Brazil developed important social service ministries to meet the needs of their communities. A representative example is *Lar Cristão de Assistência a Menores* (The Christian Children's Home). In 1971 a Brazilian woman named Maria Farias began taking needy and orphaned children into her home. Upon her death ten years later, the Comendador Soares Church of Christ in Rio de Janeiro—then led by Arlie and Alma Smith—purchased her home and opened the orphanage. For most of the 1980s and 1990s, the home provided care for a dozen or more children and teenagers. In 1997, responsibility for the Christian Children's Home was transferred from the congregation to Southern Christian Homes, a benevolent organization affiliated with Churches of Christ based in Morrillton, Arkansas. In 2000, Southern Christian Homes moved the orphanage to Cabreúva, in São Paulo state, on farmland donated by long-time missionaries in Brazil, Allan and Maria Dutton.[165]

Beginning in the 1960s, the Christian Church (Disciples of Christ) also supported social service ministries, along with community development and pastoral ministries, through fraternal workers. One of the most significant was Itoko Maeda (1918-2008). Born in Tokyo, she graduated from Joshi Sei Gakuin, Aoyama Gakuin University, and Japanese Women's Theological Seminary before coming to the United States in 1953, where she received degrees from Eastern Mennonite College and Lexington Theological Seminary. In 1956, she was ordained at Downey Avenue Christian Church in Indianapolis. Employed by the UCMS and the DOM, she served first in Okinawa, then in the 1960s and 1970s among Japanese communities in South America.[166] Between 1968 and 1978, Maeda served as the executive for women's ministries with the Federacão Evangelica Igrejas Japanesas do Brazil (Japanese Federation of Evangelical Churches of Brazil) in Sao Paulo, an interdenominational association composed mainly of Japanese expatriates living in Brazil.[167]

Building on Maeda's decade of service in Brazil, in the 1980s the Christian Church (Disciples of Christ) developed ecumenical partnerships with three autonomous Brazilian churches: the *Igreja Presbiteriana Unida do Brasil* (United Presbyterian Church of Brazil), the *Asociação da Igreja Metodista do Brasil* (Association of the Methodist Church of Brazil), and the *Igreja Evangélica Congregacional do Brasil* (Evangelical Congregational Church of Brazil). Since then, dozens of fraternal workers have served three- and four-year assignments in ministries with these churches. One example was David Blackburn (1943-1992), who served as pastor of a Methodist church in the slum of Alto da Bondade, near Recife, from 1971 until his death in 1992. He also taught in the local university and secondary schools, and organized a cooperative of local merchants.[168] Another example was Rev. Barbara de Souza, who in 1996 began the *Associação das Agentes Educadoras Comunitárias de Saúde* (Association of Community Health Educators). This ministry, fully staffed by Brazilian leaders after 1999, provided health education and medical services in shantytowns around Rio de Janeiro.[169]

After more than sixty years of work, almost six hundred churches of the Stone-Campbell Movement existed in Brazil at the beginning of the twenty-first century. Approximately one hundred twenty were largely the result of missions by North American Churches of Christ and four hundred forty from the foundational work of North American Christian Churches/Churches of Christ. Disciples worked with existing churches to provide educational, medical, and social services. Though missionaries continued to serve in Brazil, the vast majority of church leaders were Brazilians.

Venezuela

In the late 1940s, a Pentecostal preacher named Edmundo Jordán left Venezuela to serve several Hispanic churches in New York City, including the Macedonia Pentecostal Church in Harlem. There he met and established a friendship with Domingo Rodríguez, the Puerto Rican pastor of La Hermosa Christian Church (Disciples of Christ). Through Rodriguez's influence, in 1955 Jordán became a member of the Disciples of Christ in Puerto Rico.[170]

Jordán's church, the *Unión Evangélica Pentecostal Venezolana* (Evangelical Pentecostal Union of Venezuela), commonly called the UEPV, was founded in 1914 as an independent Pentecostal body, but had affiliated with the Assemblies of God in 1940. Under the leadership of Exeario Sosa and Frederico Bender, many UEPV pastors resisted attempts by Assemblies of God missionaries from the U.S. to control the church, resulting in the dissolving of its relationship with the Assemblies of God in 1957.[171] By 1959, discussions between Jordán, Rodriguez, Sosa, and Bender suggested that a partnership between the UEPV and Disciples could be possible. Meanwhile, UCMS president Dale Fiers made a survey trip to several Latin American nations—including Venezuela—and recommended that North American Disciples consider developing ecumenical partnerships with the growing Pentecostal churches throughout the region.[172]

For the next five years, leaders of the UEPV, the Christian Churches (Disciples of Christ), and Disciples of Christ in Puerto Rico explored ways in which the churches might enter into partnership. In 1960, a seven-member delegation of Disciples including UCMS executive Mae Yoho Ward, Evangelical Seminary of Puerto Rico president T. J. Liggett, four pastors of the Pentecostal Church in Cuba, and Jordán attended the UEPV convention to open official discussions.[173] Three years later when Liggett made another visit to Venezuela, the proposed partnership took more concrete form. Liggett noted that the UEPV lacked theologically trained pastors, and proposed that the partnership focus specifically on this issue. "This church is reaching outward and upward," he noted, "but yearns for fellowship, and support, and guidance."[174]

Recalling their earlier difficulties with the Assemblies of God, UEPV leaders were cautious about the developing partnership. Sosa, who in 1963 was president of the UEPV, recommended that the relationship remain "very informal…without any expectation that the Pentecostal Union would become a 'Disciples church.'"[175] As early as 1963, UEPV leader Freddie Briceño produced a statement to help the Disciples better understand the identity and mission of the UEPV, especially its commitments to ecumenism and social justice. Similarly, Liggett published articles in Disciples periodicals describing the emerging partnership and stressing the right of the UEPV to self-determination.[176]

Along with U. S. Disciples Vernon Baker (left) and Francis Lindell (center), Juan Marcos Rivera surveys the construction site for the Bender School outside Barquisimeto, Venezuela, in 1972. The Division of Overseas Ministries sponsored a two-month lay mission project to help in construction projects and strengthen the emerging partnership between U. S. Disciples and Venezuelan Pentecostals. (*World Call*, July-August 1972)

In 1963, UEPV leaders warmly welcomed Juan Marcos and Flor Rivera as the first fraternal workers from the Christian Churches (Disciples of Christ). For the next eleven years, this experienced missionary couple helped train church leaders, produced Christian education materials, and organized fraternal visits by delegations of North American and Puerto Rican Disciples to further develop the partnership.[177] Their work resulted in a

"well-established cooperation and mutual fellowship, while maintaining the integrity and identity of each denomination."[178]

Juan Marcos Rivera's service with the UEPV led to greater responsibilities in the developing ecumenical movement in Latin America. Beginning in 1972, he served on the *Comisión Evangélica Latinoamericana de Educación Cristiana* (Latin American Commission for Christian Education) and was instrumental in the 1978 formation of the Latin American Council of Churches.[179] As the Riveras' responsibilities increased, the DOM appointed other fraternal workers to the UEPV, including Dean E. and Grace Rogers who worked among indigenous congregations in the Guajiro region between Colombia and Venezuela from 1969-1972, and Puerto Rican pastor José Erazo who served from 1977-1981 as an advisor in administration and preaching.[180]

One of the most important dimensions of the partnership was providing theological education for UEPV pastors. In 1968, Emisael Álvarez became the first UEPV pastor to complete advanced theological education when he graduated from the Evangelical Seminary in Puerto Rico.[181] Beginning in the 1970s, many other UEPV pastors enrolled at the seminary. By the early 1980s, UEPV pastors also were studying at the *Seminario Bíblico Latinoamericano* (Latin America Biblical Seminary) in San Jose, Costa Rica, where Puerto Rican Disciples Carmelo Álvarez and Raquel Rodriguez served on the faculty. At both institutions UEPV students found that Disciples both valued and affirmed their Pentecostal faith and practice. Álvarez served as theological advisor to the UEPV for three decades, and became missionary-consultant for theological education in 2002.

Beginning in the 1980s, the DOM and later the Common Global Ministries Board and the Disciples of Christ in Puerto Rico maintained a close partnership with the UEPV, providing financial assistance, supporting lay and pastoral educational programs, and coordinating visits by church leaders. This partnership provided a model for similar relationships between Disciples and other Pentecostal denominations, especially in Cuba, Chile, and Nicaragua. The partnership also helped North American Disciples develop a theology of mission that integrated Pentecostal faith and practice with historic Disciples commitments to ecumenism and social justice.[182]

Central America

The Stone-Campbell Movement entered Central America when the Jerry Hill, Carl James, Floyd Hill, and Hignacio Huerta families from North American

Churches of Christ moved to Guatemala in 1959. In the first two years, they established five congregations, broadcast a daily radio program, published a newspaper called *Semanario de Restauración* (*The Restoration Weekly*), and conducted Bible correspondence courses.[183] Among the earliest Guatemalan leaders were Jose Francisco Hernandez Vasquez, Rosalio Dardon Morales, and Pedro Soto, all baptized by the missionaries in 1960. Vasquez had been expelled from a Roman Catholic seminary and disowned by his family for attending a Protestant worship service. Morales proved to be a capable preacher and helped plant a number of churches in Zaragosa, Nahualate, and Monte Cristo. Soto was president of a youth association for an English-speaking interdenominational church in the capital, but began coordinating the youth work for the new mission.[184] By the mid-1960s, these Guatemalan leaders together with the North American missionaries established a thriving mission including two dozen congregations located mainly in urban areas.[185]

In 1963, the first Pan American Lectureship was held in Guatemala City, the nation's capital. Coordinated by Reuel Lemmons (1912-1989) and modeled after lectureships held in Europe since the early 1950s, this gathering brought together missionaries from North American Churches of Christ and leaders from Latin America and the Caribbean for education, mutual support, and strategic planning. As in Europe, this lectureship emerged as an annual event and rotated between major cities in the region. At the beginning of the twenty-first century, Pan American Lectureships were still held as an important expression of the partnership between Churches of Christ in North America, Latin America, and the Caribbean.[186]

Missionaries made at least two important commitments at the 1963 Pan American Lectureship. First, they pledged to expand evangelism and church planting in Central America. Before the end of the decade, North American Churches of Christ were supporting missionary families in neighboring El Salvador (1965), Costa Rica (1967), and Honduras (1969). In 1970, four additional missionary families arrived to begin work among the Quiché people in the highlands of Guatemala. Second, the missionaries committed themselves to planting autonomous and self-supporting churches from the beginning. As a result, few appeals for financial support were made to North American Churches of Christ, and missionaries functioned as "roving teachers" among churches that were otherwise led by native leaders. Missionaries also partnered with local leaders in

producing radio broadcasts, newspapers, and educational opportunities to support the work of the churches.[187] These commitments continued to define the mission work of North American Churches of Christ in Central America at the beginning of the twenty-first century.

The Christian Church (Disciples of Christ) began cooperating in ecumenical work in Central America in 1975, when the DOM began funding two faculty positions at the *Seminario Bíblico Latinoamericano* (Latin America Biblical Seminary) in San Jose, Costa Rica. Carmelo Álvarez and Raquel Rodriguez were appointed—he teaching church history and later serving as president, she teaching pastoral counseling. Supported by the DOM, Álvarez also served on the Latin American Council of Churches, directed the *Departamiento Ecuménico de Investigaciones* (Ecumenical Research Department), and represented Disciples at Latin American ecumenical gatherings.[188]

For much of the time Stone-Campbell personnel worked in Central America, the region suffered significant social and political upheaval, including civil wars in Guatemala (1960-1996) and El Salvador (1980-1992), and Sandinista dominance in Nicaragua (1979-1990). In addition, natural disasters like the Guatemala earthquake of 1976 and Hurricane Mitch in 1998 created a long-term humanitarian and medical crises in the region. Stone-Campbell Movement churches responded to these developments in a variety of ways.

North American Churches of Christ offered substantial aid and medical care to the people of Central America through such initiatives as the Predisan Project, begun in 1986 by Dr. Robert and Doris Clark. Located in the town of Catacamas, Honduras, Predisan provided medical care through its Good Samaritan medical clinic and several "wilderness clinics" in remote areas, provided adult literacy classes, trained Honduran church leaders in basic medical care and midwifery, and offered a Christian-based model of recovery for drug and alcohol addictions.[189] Dozens of similar medical missions by North American Churches of Christ—both short- and long-term—served the people of Central America.[190]

Beginning in the 1980s, the Christian Church (Disciples of Christ) developed ecumenical partnerships to address the humanitarian crises resulting from war and natural disasters and joined other denominations in denouncing U.S. involvement in the militarization of the region. As early as 1981, the General Assembly adopted resolutions committing Disciples to work for peace in El Salvador. In response, the DOM supported an amicus brief drafted by the National Council of Churches in

Crockett v. Reagan (1983), a case that challenged U.S. military intervention in the nation. It also began supporting the Inter-religious Task Force on El Salvador and Central America, a New York City-based ministry to assist U.S. congregations "to interpret the situation in El Salvador and Central America from a Christian perspective."[191] Between 1984 and 1990, DOM-supported workers assisted Bishop Medaro Gómez of the Lutheran Church in El Salvador in providing refugee services, medical care, and other ministries to the war-torn nation.[192] Later, similar partnerships developed between DOM and the Baptist Church of El Salvador and the Roman Catholic Archdiocese of San Salvador.[193] Even after the civil war ended in 1990, Disciples supported recovery efforts in El Salvador, especially rebuilding of housing through Habitat for Humanity and the Week of Compassion offering. The Christian Church (Disciples of Christ) made similar efforts in other nations of Central America through the 1980s, and by 1990 the DOM supported seventeen workers in the region.[194]

The Church of Christ, Disciples of Christ entered Central America through the efforts of Timothy Peppers, a deacon in the Goldsboro-Raleigh District Assembly, who had served at a U.S. military base in Panama. After retiring from military service in the 1990s, Peppers returned annually from his home in North Carolina to help establish a church. Eventually, several members of the Goldsboro-Raleigh District moved to Panama and began holding monthly services. Panamanian Javier Waterfall, while on a visit to North Carolina, had been ordained by Bishop Chester L. Aycock, and with Peppers helped establish seven churches in and around Panama City, some of which met in open-air brush arbors.

In 2004, Bishop Aycock brought the seven congregations, then totaling eight hundred members, into the Church of Christ, Disciples of Christ, International. The anchor church, Bernabé Discípulo de Cristo in Panama City, had grown to support a multiple-ministry staff and developed a lunch program that fed one hundred twenty children daily. Church leaders from the United States conducted frequent teaching ministries with the congregations using interpreters, and the revised edition of the *General Assembly Church of Christ, Disciples of Christ International Ministry Manual* was translated into Spanish to serve these missions.[195]

Conclusion

All North American streams contributed to the twentieth-century growth and indigenization of the Stone-Campbell Movement in Latin America and the Caribbean. Disciples planted churches in Argentina and Paraguay. While continuing to offer various kinds of assistance, they transferred properties held by the United Christian Missionary Society to self-governing Disciples churches throughout the region. Christian Churches/Churches of Christ also planted churches in the region. In Brazil, they led in the union of Christian Churches/Churches of Christ with indigenous churches that had independently embraced beliefs and practices identified with the Stone-Campbell Movement. After World War II, North American Churches of Christ sent increasing numbers of missionaries to this part of the world. Through efforts such as the Pan American and Caribbean Lectureships and the Continent of Great Cities ministry, Churches of Christ in Latin America and the Caribbean grew significantly in the late twentieth and early twenty-first centuries. Many of these new Churches of Christ were autonomous and self-supporting from the start. The Church of Christ, Disciples of Christ certified an existing congregation in Jamaica and recognized congregations that had been planted in Panama by a member of the church.

Throughout the region, Stone-Campbell Christians developed and supported institutions to educate indigenous leaders and engaged in various forms of humanitarian relief and social service. Disciples supported and helped to form ecumenical organizations to defend human rights and to advance human dignity, liberation, and economic and social justice. In Puerto Rico, Disciples, and in Brazil, Christian Churches/Churches of Christ, integrated Pentecostal faith and practice with traditional Stone-Campbell commitments. Puerto Rican Disciples also helped to develop ecumenical partnerships between U.S. and Puerto Rican Disciples and Pentecostal churches throughout Latin America. At the beginning of the twenty-first century, there were Stone-Campbell churches and union churches of Stone-Campbell lineage witnessing to Jesus Christ across the region.

16

The Stone-Campbell Movement in Africa
Since the 1920s

By the 1920s, the Stone-Campbell Movement had established a solid presence in central and southern Africa aided partly by European colonialism. In the Belgian Congo, the United Christian Missionary Society (UCMS) maintained one of the Movement's largest and fastest growing missions, which included evangelistic, educational, and medical work. Further south, expressions of the Movement from the United States, Great Britain, Australia, and New Zealand participated in similar missions in the British colonies of Northern and Southern Rhodesia, Nyasaland, and the Union of South Africa.

As elsewhere, Stone-Campbell missions in Africa had only begun to indigenize by the 1920s, and the rise of both Pentecostalism and African Initiated Churches (AICs) was in its earliest stages. Stone-Campbell churches resisted partnership with AICs and Pentecostal churches for both political and theological reasons. Often AICs were associated with radical anti-colonial movements, and African Pentecostalism sometimes tolerated indigenous practices such as polygamy that churches associated with foreign missions long had rejected.[1]

Between the world wars, African leaders mobilized to resist European colonialism, and by the 1950s, independent nations had begun to emerge throughout the continent, at times by peaceful negotiation, but more often by revolution. In the midst of these profound political and social changes, responsibility for the churches, schools, and medical facilities of the Stone-Campbell missions quickly passed to African leaders. In some cases, new national public education and healthcare systems absorbed the mission schools and medical clinics.

In several countries, existing church bodies merged to form national union churches. The Christian Church (Disciples of Christ) in the United States and Canada, the Churches of Christ in Great Britain and Ireland (part of the United Reformed Church after 1981), and the Churches of Christ in Australia and New Zealand established ecumenical partnerships with these new churches, doing most of their work in Africa through these bodies. Meanwhile, North American Churches of Christ accelerated their African evangelistic and church planting efforts beginning in the 1950s, especially in Nigeria, Ghana, Tanzania, and Malawi. Those efforts produced sizeable Christian communities with African leaders, though churches in North America often continued significant financial support and control. Christian Churches/Churches of Christ also increased missions to Africa beginning in the 1950s. In addition, Stone-Campbell churches in Europe and the United States provided support and personnel in response to social, educational, and medical challenges such as the HIV/AIDS pandemic through both ecumenical partnerships and direct-support missions.

South Africa

By 1929, the Stone-Campbell Movement in South Africa had nine white congregations with a total membership of nearly eight hundred, and many black and colored churches scattered among the mining towns with a combined membership that may have reached five thousand.[2] Optimism about the future of the Stone-Campbell Movement ran high. "We come to South Africa," exclaimed UCMS executive Charles Richards,"with a plea not for a Dutch church, or for an English church, or for an American church, but for a Church of Christ in which all people can worship together in harmony." Based partly on underlying racist assumptions, Richards believed a strong presence of the Stone-Campbell Movement among white colonists was a prerequisite for the evangelization of black and colored South Africans.[3]

The Great Depression, however, exacted a heavy toll on Stone-Campbell missions in South Africa. Most of the missionaries active in the 1920s returned to the United States because of lack of funds. Leadership in the white churches fell primarily to lay leaders like Phil Van Niekerk in Boksburg and Jacob Duvenage in Benoni, both later ordained. In addition to preaching at their own churches, they itinerated between six other congregations during the 1930s. Though occasionally missionaries or preachers from the United States, Britain, or Australia visited, the churches "maintain[ed] themselves very creditably without any overseas help for a number of years."[4] Among black and colored congregations, Simon Sibenya (d. 1941), minister in the mining town of Kimberley, became one of the chief leaders. Along with

evangelists T. D. Mathibe and George Khosa, Sibenya continued preaching despite opposition from colonial authorities who feared potential anti-colonial violence from large gatherings of black South Africans.[5] These conditions continued through the end of World War II.

In 1945, the white South African Churches approached the UCMS for assistance, and in March the following year the Society sent Basil F. Holt (1902-1979) to provide leadership to the churches and evangelistic mission. Holt had joined the Thomas Mission in 1927, eventually serving as minister of the Linden Christian Church in Johannesburg. In 1930, he had gone to the United States in an unsuccessful attempt to raise support for the mission during the Great Depression. Remaining in the United States, he had served as minister of two large churches in the Midwest, and lectured for a time at Johnson Bible College (now Johnson University) near Knoxville, Tennessee. He had also completed three degrees at theological schools in Chicago.

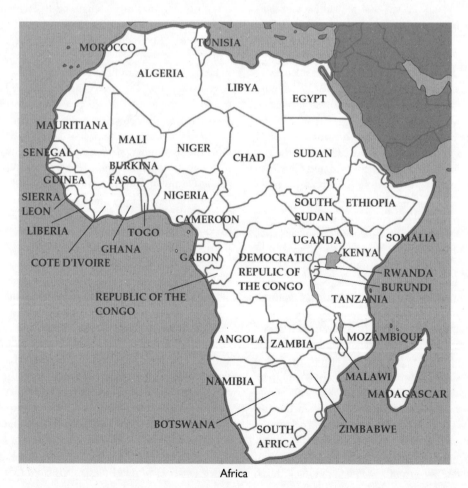

Africa

When he and his wife Margaret (1897-1961) returned to South Africa, he again became minister at the Linden Christian Church. Until his retirement in 1969, he worked as a congregational minister and Field Secretary for the UCMS, promoting Christian unity and working for improved race relations throughout South Africa.[6]

When the Holts arrived, the number of white congregations had declined from nine to eight, with a total of around three hundred members. He quickly organized the churches into the South African Association of Disciples of Christ (Churches of Christ), which then transferred ownership of all church property to the UCMS. From its beginning the association was ecumenical, cooperating in interdenominational organizations like the Christian Council of South Africa and, in 1952, sent a Fraternal Visitor to the World Conference on Faith and Order in Lund, Sweden. In 1954, these white churches began a mission to black and colored South Africans, and by the end of the 1960s, at least seven congregations had been established. Each church employed a black or colored minister, supported partly by the white churches. Though the churches remained racially segregated, the ministers regularly exchanged pulpits.[7] During the 1950s and 1960s, the South African churches took advantage of access to low-interest loans from the Board of Church Extension and received funds from the Capital for Kingdom Building Campaign to construct church buildings for both white and black churches, including one for Holt's own congregation.[8]

Holt also began publishing a newspaper for the Association titled *The South African Sentinel*.[9] Between 1946 and 1969, the paper was distributed widely not only in South Africa, but also in the United States, Great Britain, Australia, and New Zealand. Additionally, the Association began preparing a new generation of leaders in 1948 when it sent Percy Webber (1922-1972) and Bernard Barron to Rhodes University at Grahamstown in the Cape Province to complete their theological studies.[10] Both were ordained in 1951 and served many years as ministers. Upon Holt's retirement in 1969, Webber assumed the role of UCMS Field Secretary in South Africa. Webber was leading the process of integrating the Association's churches—white, black, and colored—into the United Congregational Church of Southern Africa when he died of a heart attack in 1972.

Holt was also a leading voice on the South African Institute of Race Relations, located at Witwatersrand University in Johannesburg. The Institute attempted to influence Parliament on issues of race relations, worked for better education for black and colored people, and advocated racial justice in the court system. He was also instrumental in beginning the annual Peter Ainslie Lecture on Christian Unity at the university, which often challenged the church to lead in opposing apartheid and working for racial justice in South Africa.[11]

About the time of the formation of the South African Association of the Disciples of Christ (Churches of Christ), two direct-support missionaries from Canada arrived to take responsibility for the work among black and colored workers in the mining district. William (1914-1970) and Melba (1913-2002) Rees had been direct-support missionaries in China when they were advised to leave in 1949 because of the communist revolution. By late 1950, they and another couple from the United States, Max Ward (1917-2000) and Gladys (1918-2002) Randall, had settled in Kimberley and begun their work. Upon their arrival, they found one hundred fifty black and colored congregations scattered throughout Pondoland, Natal, and the Transvaal, served by thirty evangelists. The leaders of these churches had been given little opportunity for ministerial training, and the missionaries reported "immorality, dishonesty, superstition, and polygamy" were commonplace. Evangelist George Khosa—at work in the region around Johannesburg since 1915—served as the superintendent of the mission, though the missionaries reported that many Africans resented his authoritarian style of leadership.[12]

The churches' annual conference in December 1950 elected Randall to replace Khosa as superintendent of the mission, a post he held for the next six years. As superintendent, he organized the work into the direct-support South African Christian Mission, began publishing the *South African Torch*, and successfully raised money to underwrite its operations. From the beginning, Randall emphasized the need for the South African churches to be self-governing and self-supporting. At its first annual conference at Idutywa in 1953, the South African Christian Mission adopted a constitution and chose a leadership committee of Africans. The constitution specifically stated that missionaries served only in an advisory capacity to the churches.[13]

Randall was convinced that the mission's greatest need was a school to train black and colored evangelists. He recruited Lynn (1918-2001) and Lucille Stanley, who in 1954 opened a Bible training school in the church at Kimberley. Five years later, the school was relocated and renamed the Umzumbe Bible Institute. Together with Patu Nicholas Qwemesha (d. 1994), their son, Michael, and other South African pastors, the Stanleys trained hundreds of evangelists until the school closed in 1994 amidst racial tensions related to the anti-apartheid movement. Three years later, the school was reopened in Kimberley as the South African Bible Institute, entirely under the leadership of Africans.[14]

The relationship between Holt's UCMS-supported work and Randall's direct-support mission was usually cordial. In 1951 Randall met with Holt at the Linden Christian Church, and the two men presented their theological positions—especially concerning baptism—in a private debate attended by key leaders. Though they reached no conclusion, each staked out the position followed in their respective missions. A less congenial encounter between Stone-Campbell missionaries occurred in 1953 when two evangelists from North American Churches of Christ arrived. In January Randall received an urgent telegram from Sydney Roji, minister of the East London church in Idutywa, claiming that the two missionaries were trying to convince his congregation

During long periods of missionary absence in the 1930s and 1940s, Sabina "Grandma" Sibenya often helped her husband, Simon, lead the black and colored churches around Kimberley, South Africa. She is pictured here outside her home with Maggie Watters, missionary from the British Churches of Christ, and Max Ward Randall around 1955. (*South African Torch*, January-February 1955, courtesy Cincinnati Christian University)

to leave and become part of their Church of Christ.[15] Tensions such as this were rare, however, and by the 1980s relations between the missionaries were generally friendly.

The churches of the Stone-Campbell Movement in South Africa had been shaped by the pervasive racism that sustained apartheid. As early as the 1954 meeting of

the South African Association of the Disciples of Christ (Churches of Christ), Dr. A. B. Xuma, a well-known African medical doctor, delivered an address entitled "What the African Expects of the Church Today." In the address, he condemned the segregated churches of South Africa for their part in implicitly sanctioning apartheid, demanding that the churches lead the way in a resistance movement.[16] Most white leaders in the Association did not receive his message well. In the 1960s when apartheid policies began requiring "sects" of African Christians to affiliate with European Protestant missions, a number of such groups applied to the Association for membership. Such groups were placed on "probation," and white churches and leaders viewed them with great suspicion, requiring them to "produce satisfactory evidence of their good character and acceptability." Often that meant toning down their African nationalism and abandoning their "extremes of Holy Spirit and healing influences."[17]

As early as 1962, leaders of the South African Association of the Disciples of Christ (Churches of Christ) considered joining the Congregational Union of Southern Africa, then being formed by most congregationalist denominations, not only in South Africa, but also in Botswana, Mozambique, Namibia, and Zimbabwe. Holt and his Linden Avenue church were immediately admitted to the Union as "associate" members, but discussions among the other Association churches continued until 1967 when the union church formally came into existence.[18] In 1972, when given the opportunity to become part of the fully integrated union church, most of the fifty black and colored congregations in the Association did so. Of the three white congregations then in existence, one chose to remain independent and closed shortly thereafter, one took three years to decide but finally joined, and the third joined the all-white Presbyterian Church of Southern Africa. The major problem for these churches, a disappointed Basil Holt explained, was that in the united church non-whites dominated numerically.[19] At the beginning of the twenty-first century, the Christian Church (Disciples of Christ) in the United States and Canada maintained a partnership with the United Congregational Church of Southern Africa through its Common Global Ministries Board.

Beginning in the late 1950s, dozens of direct-support missionaries from North American Christian Churches/ Churches of Christ served in South Africa. Among the first were Al and Jean Zimmerman, who began primary schools among black and colored children within a three-hundred-mile radius of Cape Town. By 1962, they also had established the Cape Bible Seminary to train South African evangelists and church planters. Among the early graduates of the seminary were David Matutu, B. J. Mguzulwa, and Stanley Thena, all of whom also studied at Bible colleges in the United States.[20]

Another example of such direct-support mission work was that of Dr. Stuart (d. 2010) and Marilyn Cook. In 1966, they began an inner-city mission in Johannesburg, later relocating to the Limpopo Province to begin evangelistic and church-planting work. In 1975, they began Aletheia International Ministries, through which they provided food, clothing, and spiritual counseling to thousands of South Africans. Still later, the ministry conducted weeklong Insight Seminars, designed to develop church leaders.[21] Others served in missions similar to the Cooks, though most worked in educational and social service ministries, responding especially to the HIV/AIDS pandemic.

With the help of South African Nic Qwemesha (seated left) and fellow missionaries like Robert Mills (seated center) Lynn Stanley (seated right) began a preacher training school in Kimberley. Later named Umzumbe Bible Institute, the school trained hundreds of black and colored evangelists for the direct-support mission in South Africa. (*South African Torch*, September-October 1957, courtesy Cincinnati Christian University)

North American Churches of Christ had established a presence in South Africa in 1943, when George and Ottis Scott moved from the mission in Northern Rhodesia to Cape Town and began work among the black and colored communities.[22] In the early 1950s, other missionaries arrived who fanned out from Johannesburg to preach and plant churches among white, colored, and black communities in Gauteng, Limpopo, Mpumalanga,

and Northwest Provinces. Among the early arrivals were John and Bessie Hardin, Guy and Jessie Caskey, Foy Short, and Eldred Echols. By the end of the 1950s, the missionaries had established a dozen white, fifteen colored, and fifty black congregations with a combined membership of as high as 2,600. One of the strongest was the white church in Port Elizabeth, which had a building and was nearly self-supporting.[23] Among later missionaries were Robert "Tex" (b. 1928) and Mary Jane (b. 1937) Williams who worked in Pietermaritzburg for fifteen years beginning in 1958. Tex served as minister of the Edendale Church of Christ and later directed the Natal School of Preaching that trained evangelists to work among the Zulu people.

Between 1946 and 1951, North American Churches of Christ broadcast a weekly radio program from Lourenço Marques in neighboring Mozambique, which could be heard throughout southern Africa. Many attribute the success of the Johannesburg missionaries partly to the influence of this program, in which Reuel Lemmons (1912-1989), editor of the *Firm Foundation*, was the featured speaker. Follow-up to responses to the radio program often resulted in opportunities for further evangelism. When the missionaries resumed the radio program in 1960, improved technology allowed the program to be heard for more than a thousand mile radius. By 1962, the Bible correspondence course offered through the program had four hundred students.[24]

Churches of Christ missionary Robert "Tex" Williams (back row, left) conducted the Natal School of Preaching in Pietermaritzburg. Graduates did evangelistic work among black, colored, Indian, and southeast Asian populations living in South Africa. He is pictured here with the faculty and students of the school in 1970. (*Firm Foundation*, September 1970)

By the mid-1970s, North American Churches of Christ had suspended most of their evangelistic and church-planting work in South Africa. They had already established seventy-five black, colored, and Indian congregations, and another twenty-five white ones. The missionaries began focusing instead on training evangelists and lay leaders for these churches. Leaders had established four "schools of preaching" for black and colored leaders in southern Africa: Umtali, in Southern Rhodesia; Manzini, in Swaziland; and Vendaland and Natal, both in the Union of South Africa. A fifth school was Southern Africa Bible School (now College) in Benoni, then exclusively for training white preachers. Beyond teaching in these schools, missionaries also conducted two annual Lectureships in South Africa, and maintained two Christian service camps. Like the schools of preaching, these institutions were then racially segregated.[25] The missionaries also directed evangelism and church planting toward the developing nations to the north, especially Botswana and Namibia.

At the beginning of the twenty-first century, there were an estimated five hundred congregations with a combined membership of thirty-three thousand that traced their beginnings to the mission work of North American Churches of Christ in South Africa.

Southern Rhodesia (Zimbabwe)

By the 1920s, the Foreign Mission Union of the New Zealand Churches of Christ was supporting a thriving mission in Southern Rhodesia under the leadership of F. L. Hadfield. John and Emma Sherriff had been working independently (though in co-operation with the New Zealand Mission) since the purchase of the Forrest Vale estate in 1906. The original work in Bulawayo had become entirely self-supporting before World War I, and John Tokwe served as minister of the growing congregation.[26] In 1919, the missionaries had relocated the headquarters of the Mission to Dadaya, ninety miles east of Bulawayo. This proved to be a strategic point from which to expand, and they had soon increased the number of native evangelists and outstations. Two new couples, Mr. and Mrs. C. A. Bowen and Mr. and Mrs. S. E. Riches, arrived in 1925 and 1926 respectively.[27] In 1928, Bowen began work in the Mashoko Reserve, a relatively undeveloped area in the malaria belt, two thousand feet lower than Dadaya.

On the eve of the Great Depression, the mission's twenty-two churches had a combined membership of around 1,200. In addition to fifteen schools and the Native Evangelist Teacher Training College, mission personnel had also begun work in Shabani, just outside the Reserve, where twenty thousand workers were employed in local asbestos mines. Because of language differences, mission leaders secured two evangelists from Nyasaland with the help of Mary Bannister of the Nyasaland British Mission.[28]

Plans for expanding the Dadaya Mission, however, were put on hold during the Great Depression. Although 1932 had been a record year for the Mission, with 1,343 decisions and 568 baptisms, declining contributions from the churches and poor rates of monetary exchange had created a financial crisis from which the mission did not recover until the early 1940s. In addition, John Sherriff died in 1935 after almost forty years of missionary work in Southern Rhodesia. Though Emma Sherriff remained, Sherriff's death took its toll on morale. Finally, the colonial government increased standards for both white and African teachers, which disqualified many who were serving. The government withdrew approval of Bowen as superintendent of the Mashoko mission, and the New Zealand Churches' financial inability to support other missionaries created a personnel crisis. The Mashoko Mission was closed between 1934 and 1940, but tribal leaders on the Reserve refused to permit other churches to establish missions in the area, saying "they had been married to the Church of Christ, and wanted no other husband."[29]

In 1934, R. S. Garfield (1908-2002) and Grace (1911-2001) Todd volunteered for missionary service with the New Zealand Foreign Mission Union, which sent them to Africa in June. Though originally slated to be superintendent only of the Dadaya Mission, the shortage of missionaries led to his appointment over the Mashoko Mission as well. Under the Todds' leadership, Dadaya grew significantly, especially its educational work. Grace Todd, a credentialed teacher, became Headmistress of the Dadaya School, and with government assistance began recruiting African teachers. Eventually the standards she set for teaching and curriculum at Dadaya were adopted as the standard for the entire country.

Under Todd's leadership, the Dadaya Mission focused on its schools. Beginning in the 1930s—largely because of Todd's influence in government circles—the mission began receiving annual government grants to pay teachers, purchase books and other supplies, and build better school facilities. The mission also received regular grants from the private Beit Trust for the same

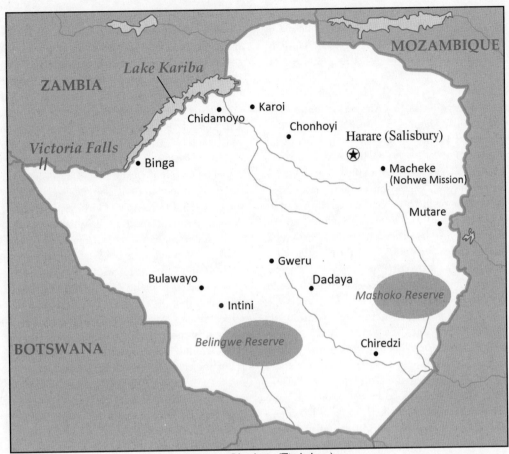

Southern Rhodesia (Zimbabwe)

purposes. As a result, the number of schools and their total enrollment doubled between 1934 and 1946, with the central boarding school at Dadaya alone reaching an enrollment of five hundred sixty.

The number of churches grew during the same period to thirty-three with a combined membership of more than three thousand. The Todds encouraged the development of African leaders, and, by 1946, the approximately one hundred fifty evangelists, Bible school teachers, and other African church workers carried the bulk of the responsibility for the mission's churches. Among the leaders who emerged at Dadaya during this time were David Mkwanazi, J. N. Hlambelo, and J. M. Sibanda.[30]

In 1946, Garfield Todd was elected to represent the Shabani District in the Southern Rhodesian Parliament, though he remained superintendent of Dadaya Mission.[31] Todd's record of leadership in education and politics resulted in his election as Prime Minister of Southern

Rhodesia in 1953. In that office, he continued to work to improve education for Africans, offering government grants to missions—including the Dadaya Mission—to expand schools, hire more and better trained teachers, and provide teacher training to Africans. Many whites, however, viewed him as a dangerous liberal, and he was ousted from power in 1958.[32]

Mr. and Mrs. Ray Knapp, and Mr. A.W. (Laddie) and Mrs. C.M. (Queenie) Ladbrook, became the main New Zealand missionaries in Southern Rhodesia after World War II, gradually assuming responsibility for the Mission after Todd became prime minister. Disagreements among the missionaries caused a crisis in 1953. Chair of the Missionary Council, D.N. Strawbridge, made a month-long visit to the Mission and recommended that all the missionaries be withdrawn. Though the Council did not accept the proposal, several missionaries resigned, reducing the number at Dadaya from fifteen to eight. This decrease made staffing of the Mashoko Mission very difficult. In 1956, the Mission celebrated its Golden Jubilee with Garfield Todd and F. L. Hadfield laying the foundation stone of the Jubilee Memorial Church, followed in August 1958 by the All Africa Convention of Churches of Christ in Bulawayo.[33]

In 1960 the Mission sent M. M. Nyoni to study in the U.S. before becoming the first African Headmaster of Secondary Schools at Dadaya. The same year Ladbrook wrote to New Zealand urging more training and official recognition for the native evangelists, as well as an increase in their salaries. Nyoni eventually completed a master's degree in New Zealand and became principal of all the Dadaya Schools in 1964, marking a major step in transfer of leadership to Africans. Ray Knapp's sudden death in the same year, however, raised the question of who would become Superintendent of the Mission. The Dadaya board was already composed of both Africans and missionaries, and it made the decision to discontinue the office of Superintendent.

The following year, 1965, the government of Ian Smith unilaterally declared Southern Rhodesia's independence. This immediately exposed differences of opinion among the white members of the churches. Though everyone expected that Africans would eventually assume responsibility for government, they differed significantly about the speed at which this should happen. The imposition of sanctions on Smith's government by Commonwealth countries restricted the amount of money the New Zealand mission board could send to Rhodesia. Increasing division between whites and blacks also raised serious questions about the Mission's prospects. In October 1967, the mission board held a two-day meeting with Garfield Todd about the future. Then, at the Dominion Conference later in the month the board committed itself to the Africanization of the work in Rhodesia, though only when they judged that the indigenous church was capable of taking over.[34]

In the decades leading up to the international community's recognition in 1980 of Zimbabwe's independence, issues of race, justice, and majority rule dominated the concerns of the missions supported by the Foreign Mission Board of the New Zealand Churches of Christ. As early as 1950, mission leaders held a conference in Rosetenville focusing on "Christian Citizenship in a Multi-Racial Society." For three days, representatives of many races and ethnicities in the country considered how they might work for a more just society. Reflecting, no doubt, the sentiments of the Universal Declaration of Human Rights issued by the United Nations in 1948, the leaders of the mission expressed their commitment to the principles that all people are created in God's image and therefore there existed an essential unity among all humanity, that persons belonging to a more "advanced social order" have a responsibility to assist those who belong to more "primitive" ones, that the franchise should be extended to "all capable of exercising it," that every child should have access to the best education possible, and that all people have the right to work in the sphere in which they can make the best use of their abilities for the common good.[35]

The growing violence associated with African independence movements throughout southern Africa in the early 1960s prompted Garfield Todd to ask whether African nationalism and Christianity were compatible. African nationalists were not rejecting Christianity per se, but disagreed with how the institutional church in Africa had aligned itself with colonial power, especially in its racial segregation. What was often missed, he said, is the fact that the church was instrumental in providing education for Africans, and education had fueled the nationalist movements. The time had come, he insisted, that the church side with the nationalist movements. "It is not persecution which saps the strength of the Church but the tolerance of evil and the withholding of religious action. The Church's strength may be based upon prayer and worship, but her vindication is seen in her practical, outgoing concern for the people of the land."[36]

Some of the students educated in the Dadaya Mission's schools went on to become important leaders in Zimbabwean education and politics. One such leader was Nadabaningi Sithole (1920-2000), who enrolled in the boys' boarding school in Dadaya in 1935 and returned to the school as a teacher after receiving his National Junior Certificate. In 1947, Garfield Todd fired him from the Dadaya Mission for leading a teacher's strike, though the two later reconciled and became political allies. When he returned to Southern Rhodesia in 1953 after three years of study in the United States, Sithole had been ordained in the Methodist Episcopal Church and completed his Doctor of Divinity degree. In 1960, he joined the African nationalist movement in Southern Rhodesia and served several terms in Parliament. He was a leading voice in the negotiations to transfer power to the black majority between 1978 and 1980. Falling out of favor with the Mugabe regime, he was exiled to the United States in 1987, where he continued to be an outspoken African nationalist.[37]

In the late 1960s and early 1970s, Ian Smith's Southern Rhodesian government became suspicious of several Protestant missions, including those of the Stone-Campbell Movement, suspecting them of fomenting black nationalism. Parliament enacted laws that directly threatened the existence of the Dadaya Mission, including drastic reduction of government subsidies to mission schools. Legislation also required parcels of land to be classified according to the race of their owners, effectively drawing firm boundaries around strictly segregated communities. Because they refused to identify with one race, missions like Dadaya were classified as "white" by the government, and non-whites were restricted from occupying those lands. Repeated attempts to challenge the laws through the court system proved unsuccessful. In 1972 the government, which had earlier placed Garfield Todd under house arrest, imprisoned Todd and his daughter Judith for thirty-six days for speaking out against the restrictive laws and white minority rule.[38]

In 1970 the government took over all schools, including those at Dadaya. This forced a change in mission policy and resolved a long-running tension among missionaries concerning whether education or evangelism should be the chief focus. It led to the mission board's "Partners with Africa in Christian Evangelism" program (PACE), approved by the Dominion Conference the following year. The New Zealand Churches of Christ missionaries in Southern Rhodesia, along with African church leaders, oversaw a two-year process by which the mission's work was completely transferred from the missionaries to the Africans. Though some missionaries remained as partners, by 1973 the churches had formed the fully self-supporting and independent Associated Churches of Christ in Zimbabwe—Zimbabwe being the name used by African nationalists beginning in the 1960s.[39]

For more than twenty years after his ouster as Prime Minister, Garfield Todd had continued his crusade against apartheid without an official position in government. Between 1980 and 1985, he served as a senator under Robert Mugabe, independent Zimbabwe's first Prime Minister. Decorated numerous times for his extraordinary civil service, he was knighted in 1989. After his 1985 retirement, Todd became increasingly critical of the Mugabe regime's repressive policies, leading to his being placed under house arrest and in February 2002 stripped of his Zimbabwean citizenship. He died the following October at a hospital in Bulawayo.

North American Churches of Christ also were working in two missions in Southern Rhodesia before World War II. Dewitt (1901-1972) and Dollie (1903-2003) Garrett settled in Salisbury, the colonial capital, in 1931,

assuming leadership of the work begun by New Zealand Churches of Christ some years before.[40] The Garretts worked among the local African people, and within ten years the mission consisted of four churches, a boarding school, and a hospital. Significantly, many of the people living in Salisbury at the time were Nyasalanders who came to work for a while, then return home.[41] From the beginning, then, the mission also had an impact on the spread of the Stone-Campbell Movement in Nyasaland (now Malawi).

In 1940, W. L. and Addie Brown established a second mission in Southern Rhodesia for the North American Churches of Christ. The Nhowe Mission included a medical clinic, a boarding school, and evangelistic work in surrounding villages. But by the mid-1950s, the mission was facing the possibility of closure due to a shortage of personnel and funding. Under the terms of the government lease, the mission had to be maintained to specific standards, and Nhowe no longer met them. At the time the mission maintained a half dozen schools with an enrollment of more than a thousand, Dr. Marjorie Sewell (b. 1923) served the clinic as physician, and several churches had been established in surrounding villages. By 1957, the University Avenue Church of Christ in Austin, Texas, had assumed responsibility for the Nhowe Mission, and a new group of missionaries arrived to revitalize the work, including the Nhowe Bible School.[42] Among the new missionaries was Dr. Anne Stricklin (1925-2008). After graduating from Abilene Christian College, she worked as a nurse at the Nhowe Mission between 1950 and 1957. She later worked for eight years for the colonial government in Northern Rhodesia until she returned to the United States in 1965 to complete a Master's degree in social work, and in 1970 a doctorate in clinical psychology. Through the 1980s and 1990s, she taught in several South African universities and offered psychological, social, and remedial teaching services for children, individuals, and families through a private practice. At her death in 2008, she left a large bequest to the Nhowe Mission that was used to establish a school of nursing.

One indigenous church-planting effort began in 1964 when Campion Mugweni, Saul Chaire, and Jonathan Chitendini—all of whom prepared at the Nhowe preacher training school—planted a church in Umtali (now Mutare). Their work was so successful that, in 1971, the preacher training school was moved from Nhowe to Umtali, where the three evangelists trained dozens of others to be church-planters.

At the beginning of the twenty-first century, the

Nhowe Mission included schools offering instruction at all levels to over 1,500 students, with the nursing school graduating nearly twenty nurses each year.[43] In addition, the Brian Lemons Memorial Hospital provided both inpatient and outpatient care to five thousand people each month, and an orphanage served the needs of children who had lost their parents to HIV/AIDS. The East Point Church of Christ in Wichita, Kansas, provided primary financial support for the mission.

First arriving in 1906, New Zealand missionary F. L. Hadfield continued to offer leadership to Stone-Campbell missions in southern Africa until his death in 1966. Hadfield was a tireless advocate of Christian unity and the full participation of Africans in leading the work of the churches. (*Central African Story*, February 1965)

At times, doctrinal differences strained relationships between the Stone-Campbell missions in Southern Rhodesia. A. C. Watters, a missionary for the British Churches of Christ, recalled one conflict in the early 1950s. Missionaries from North American Churches of Christ had been in Northern and Southern Rhodesia for over three decades and had cooperated in many ways with the missions of the other Stone-Campbell streams. After World War II, however, a new generation entered the field without appreciating that history. One missionary to Bulawayo "took more than half of the European congregation to form an anti-organ church a mile away," and "gained control of all the outlying mission schools." F. L. Hadfield convinced the three black congregations and the colored congregation to remain with the mission. Following this controversy, in 1957 the British Churches of Christ transferred responsibility for the European congregation to the UCMS, which sent Watters to help revitalize it.[44]

That same year the Foreign Mission Union of the New Zealand Churches of Christ transferred responsibility for the Mashoko Mission to direct-support missionaries from the United States. John and Marjorie Pemberton—both graduates of Kentucky Christian College—arrived in 1956 to work with the Ladbrooks who had served there for several years.[45] A year later, the Pembertons assumed full responsibility for the work in Mashoko, organizing it as the Southern Rhodesia Churches of Christ Mission and publishing a newsletter called the *Southern Rhodesia Story* (later renamed the *Central African Story*). In 1959 the Mission welcomed three more missionaries: Rod and Beverly Cameron and Dr. Dennis Pruett. With significant government grants, they established the Mashoko Christian Hospital, a one-hundred-thirty-bed facility that also included an outpatient clinic and a training school for African medical personnel.[46] In 1959, the white congregation at Bulawayo severed its relationship with the UCMS and aligned itself with the new Mission.[47]

The Southern Rhodesia Churches of Christ Mission grew steadily in the thirty years before independence, and by 1960 had incorporated the original Bulawayo mission and had been renamed Central African Mission. Eventually missions were established in ten additional locations. Typical of these missions was the one established on the Hippo Valley Estate near Chiredzi in 1964. Proprietors of the estate invited mission personnel to establish schools and a medical clinic to serve the Zulu and Ndebele workers on its vast sugar plantation. By 1980, the Mission consisted of one white and eleven black congregations with a total membership of around 1,200, seven elementary schools that served about five hundred students, and the Mashoko hospital and associated clinics in the region.[48] More than one hundred fifty missionaries had served in these stations before independence in a variety of evangelistic, educational, and medical roles.[49]

At the beginning of the twenty-first century, the work was known as the Mashoko/Hippo Valley Christian Mission. Bob Pemberton and Zebedee Togarepi served as leaders of the mission, including its thirty churches, twenty-five schools, and the hospital. The mission constructed two facilities to care for children orphaned by the HIV/AIDS pandemic: the Christian Children's Home and Chiredzi Christian Children's Village. Mission personnel also began evangelistic work among refugees from neighboring Mozambique.[50] In addition, North American Christian Churches/Churches of Christ participated in mission work in Zimbabwe through the Christian Missionary Fellowship, White Fields

Evangelism, Inc., and Fellowship of Associates of Medical Evangelism (FAME).[51]

Important partnerships developed between the Associated Churches of Christ in Zimbabwe and the Churches of Christ in Australia and New Zealand. In one such partnership begun in 1989, Australian and New Zealand churches provided tuition assistance for church leaders to receive training at theological colleges in Zimbabwe. In the 1990s, when Zimbabwe suffered severe drought that caused significant shortages of food, the Associated Churches of Christ in Zimbabwe partnered with churches in Australia, New Zealand, and Great Britain to provide relief.[52]

Northern Rhodesia (Zambia)

The Stone-Campbell Movement first arrived in Northern Rhodesia in the early 1910s. Peter Masiya and Jack Mzilwa, two of John Sherriff's converts, had begun evangelizing in villages around Livingstone, two hundred eighty miles northwest of Bulawayo. In the 1920s they moved to the area around Sinde, where Masiya led a church of two hundred African members and Mzilwa's preaching resulted in several hundred baptisms. After working for two years in Bulawayo with the Sherriffs, missionaries W. N. Short (1894-1980) and his wife, A'Delia (1896-1982), from North American Churches of Christ, relocated to Sinde in 1923 to build on the work begun by Masiya and Mzilwa.[53] Encouraged by reports of success at Sinde, the Sherriffs spent most of 1924 in Canada and the United States raising funds and recruiting personnel for the growing work in Northern and Southern Rhodesia. By the end of the decade, missionaries recruited by the Sherriffs had established a strong presence in Northern Rhodesia.

Among the first to arrive at Sinde were Ray (1887-1927) and Zelma (1894-1964) Lawyer. Shortly after their arrival they suffered a number of disasters, including the death of a son, the burning of their home, and serious illness. In 1927 tragedy struck again when Ray Lawyer was killed in a hunting accident, resulting in Zelma's

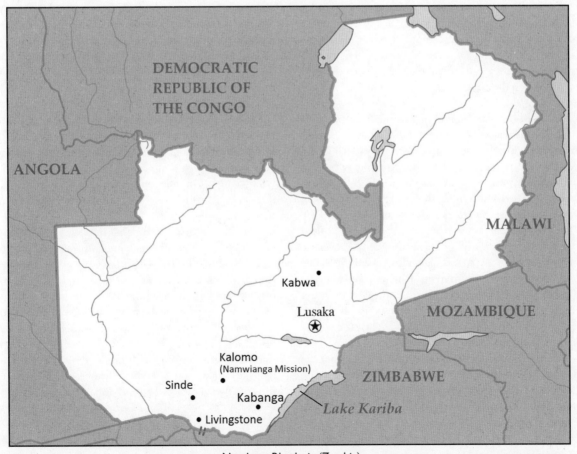

Northern Rhodesia (Zambia)

return to the United States. Before the mid-1930s, four additional missionary couples had arrived and begun work in three new stations: Dow (1894-1990) and Alice (1894-1941) Merritt opened the station at Kabanga; George M. (1874-1955) and Ottis (1882-1955) Scott opened the station at Livingstone in 1927; and Alva (1888-1976) and Margaret (1892-1972) Rees opened the station at Namwianga in 1932. Despite doctrinal differences between leaders, Stone-Campbell missions in Southern and Northern Rhodesia cooperated in virtually every aspect of their work.[54]

In addition to these pioneer African preachers and missionaries, two other African leaders were instrumental in developing Churches of Christ missions in Northern Rhodesia in the early years. Throughout the 1920s, Peter Masiya was the Shorts' co-worker at Sinde. Before he died unexpectedly, Masiya had converted Kambole Mpatamatenga, cook for Northern Rhodesia's Chief Medical Officer, during an evangelistic meeting at Mujala village. Not only did Mpatamatenga help build Sinde Mission, he also helped build Kabanga Mission, and worked with most of the missionaries who came in the 1930s and 1940s. He taught school at the Siamundele outstation and after his retirement he established a mission school at his home in Mutwanjili. His fluency in English and several African dialects equipped him to help translate the New Testament into Chitonga (1949) and Lozi (1951).[55]

As with other mission efforts worldwide, the Great Depression seriously hindered the work of North American Churches of Christ in Northern Rhodesia. By 1934, all the stations were operating at significant deficits, and merchants were beginning to refuse them credit. Food was in extremely short supply, partly because swarms of locusts had destroyed crops for several years. The government required missions to maintain their property at a high level or ownership would revert to the government. A "Missionary Distress Fund" raised by North American Churches of Christ helped alleviate immediate needs, but the work continued to suffer through the 1930s. Leaders finally closed the Kabanga Mission, leaving only the Sinde, Livingstone, and Namwianga stations.[56]

As the Depression years ended, other missionaries arrived in Northern Rhodesia and the work again stabilized. James Alvin (1909-1997) and Georgia Hobby immediately assumed leadership roles, developing a comprehensive school system out of the three mission schools at Namwianga, Kabanga, and Sinde; two town schools in Kalomo and Livingstone; and fourteen village

schools. Together these schools maintained an enrollment of about 2,500 throughout the 1940s and 1950s. These schools offered instruction in Chitonga and developed curriculum for children through sixth-grade equivalency. By the early 1940s, the school system also included a two-year teacher-training program, a school to train African preachers, and the Eureka School for the children of missionaries. In 1962, at the age many would begin considering retirement, the Hobbys completed nurses' training in the United States and returned to Namwianga to establish the mission's first clinic.[57] By the late 1960s, every station provided medical services, often supported by significant government grants.

Other missionaries who arrived to help in the work included James and Joyce Shewmaker in 1939, Jesse and Augusta Brittell in 1946, and Henry and Florence Pierce in 1950. When they arrived in 1949, Kenneth and Iris Elder assumed responsibility for the Kabanga mission. He was an engineer and carpenter, and set out immediately to build adequate facilities for the school and church. She was a teacher who had grown up in Northern Rhodesia as the daughter of Dow and Alice Merritt. Together with African leader Jim Mzumara, the Elders revitalized the Kabanga station that had been closed for more than a decade. In 1948, the mission work by North American Churches of Christ in Northern Rhodesia included twenty-five schools, served by forty-two native teachers, with a total enrollment of 2,133.[58]

After declaring independence from Great Britain in 1964, the colony of Northern Rhodesia became the Republic of Zambia. By then, the work begun by North American Churches of Christ had been consolidated at Namwianga. The mission operated twenty-six primary schools, all of which were immediately absorbed into the new government's public school system. At the request of the Zambian government, however, the mission established the Namwianga Christian Secondary School and the George Benson Christian College. Beginning in the early 1980s, the mission slowly increased the number of Zambians on the teaching staff of these schools, and by the early twenty-first century, the vast majority were Zambian. Also during the 1980s, the Namwianga mission began offering limited medical services with the help of significant grants from the Zambian government. Eventually the mission offered more advanced medical services through two clinics and a small inpatient hospital.[59]

Though most of the work of U.S. Churches of Christ centered in southern Zambia, new mission teams and personnel from the Namwianga mission began work in the northern part of the country in the twenty-first century. This included the establishment of Zambia Christian College in Kabwe, and reviving Mapepe Bible College in Lusaka, closed since 1964, both in 2005.[60] In 1980, there were two hundred eleven Churches of Christ in Zambia. By the beginning of the twenty-first century, there were as many as 1,300, with a combined membership of thirty thousand. A Ten Year Plan projected 2,500 congregations, with at least one Church of Christ in every city or town in the country. In addition, Zambian evangelists began working among Angolan refugees and targeting the countries surrounding them for church planting.[61]

Nyasaland (Malawi)

Because of its alleged connection with the 1915 Chilembwe uprising, the colonial government banned the mission of the British Churches of Christ in Nyasaland. Officials confiscated the mission's property, deported George Hollis, interned Mary Bannister and the Philpotts, and imprisoned several African leaders, including Ronald Kaunda, George Masangano (d. 1964), and Frederick Nkhonde (d. 1935). Despite efforts

by leaders of the British Foreign Missions Committee (FMC) to persuade the House of Commons to lift the ban in 1920, Parliament left the decision with the colonial administration. Influenced by members of the Church of Scotland mission who had always opposed the work of the Churches of Christ, the colonial government refused.

Nevertheless, several churches continued to meet in secret, baptizing converts under cover of night. The colonial government released Kaunda, Masangano, and Nkhonde in 1918, 1919, and 1920 respectively on the condition that they sign a pledge to submit to it. While officials permitted them to resume work, they were required to file quarterly reports and consult with the government before opening new village churches. The three leaders appealed to the British Churches of Christ to send missionaries, and when the ban was finally lifted in 1927, Mary Bannister returned to Nyasaland the following year. Upon her arrival, she learned that the native leaders had expanded the mission into the cities of Mlanje, Palombe, Ntondwe, and Dowa in southern Nyasaland, establishing congregations and schools, and moving the center of their work to the southern city of Namiwawa.[62]

The FMC had begun discussions with the Baptist Industrial Mission at Gowa in 1920 to purchase their station, but the government's expulsion of the British Mission stopped the talks until 1927. In 1929, the groups completed negotiations, and the British Churches of Christ acquired the Gowa Mission, including its forty-two village schools. The mission property included residences for missionaries and a chapel that would seat almost seven hundred people. Additional missionary staff began arriving in 1930, with Ernest and Louie Gray who served until 1956, followed by Wilfred and Elsie Georgeson, who served until 1947. Wilfred directed the school at Gowa, and because he was classified as a teacher rather than a missionary was eligible for a government grant for his work. Together the missionaries established a training school for evangelists and teachers. While the Georgesons worked with Mary Bannister at Gowa, the Grays assumed leadership of the work in Namiwawa. Soon, however, tensions arose between the new missionaries and the three principal African leaders who had sustained the work by themselves for more than a decade.[63]

The main problem stemmed from the

Nyasaland (Malawi)

colonial government's requirement that the missionaries had to become part of the Federated Missions for Nyasaland in order to return. Being part of that organization, however, included mutual acceptance of members—open membership. Almost as soon as Gray arrived, Frederick Nkhonde asked him if membership in the Federated Missions meant they would accept those baptized as infants. Gray, perhaps influenced by the fact that open communion had always been the practice at Gowa, said "Yes." The Namiwawa elders were dismayed, and Nkhonde immediately sent a letter to W. M. Kempster, editor of the *Bible Advocate*, via Hollis in Cape Town, informing him of Gray's "open membership" position.

In reality, Gray had quickly realized the problem and petitioned the Chief Commissioner in Zomba that the mission not be forced to join the Federation. The petition was granted, and the Churches of Christ did not join. The Gowa Mission also changed its open communion policy. Nevertheless, the Old Paths churches in Britain used the report that Gray supported open membership as part of their campaign against continued participation in the British Conference. Mary Bannister was furious with Nkhonde, and wrote that she felt betrayed "by one of my best friends." [64]

Though Nkhonde and Gray reconciled on this matter in December 1930, a second disagreement arose that was not resolved. Another condition of the Federated Missions was that they would not recruit from one another, and in particular should not accept anyone under discipline in another church. Gray had no problem with this, but Nkhonde was deeply offended. He also objected to the process of pre-baptism catechesis introduced by Gray that sometimes lasted a year or more. Nkhonde baptized two men under discipline from the Church of Scotland mission and was rebuked by Gray.

In December 1931, the three African leaders led several churches out of the mission and formed the African Church of Christ. Despite a letter from John Sherriff in Bulawayo trying to persuade Nkhonde that he had acted wrongly, he was unable to effect reconciliation. In Britain Kempster used the *Bible Advocate* to repeat allegations concerning open communion, and the FMC considered closing Namiwawa rather than continue with a divided mission. The Committee received a letter from Hollis and two other elders at the Loop Street Church of Christ in Cape Town charging the FMC with approving the allegedly "modernist" teachings of William Robinson at Overdale College. The FMC sent one if its members,

Harry Langton, who investigated the situation carefully, and as a result of his report formally excommunicated in 1933 the African Church of Christ. After Nkhonde's death in 1935, George Masangano seceded from the African Church of Christ to form the Church of God. [65]

The African leaders, supported by Hollis, insisted that their separation was in response to the Grays' theological liberalism. The missionaries, however, were convinced that the real agenda was a "determination to be free at all costs from anything in the nature of European control." [66] Undoubtedly Nkhonde did lose power as a result of the missionaries' return, particularly over the distribution of money for salaries. But the idea of "Africa for the Africans," which had moved Joseph Booth and convinced George Hollis, had certainly influenced Nkhonde as well. Kempster and the Old Paths group associated with the *Bible Advocate* used the controversy to attack not only the Nyasaland mission, but also Overdale College. Sherriff feared that Nkhonde's actions would lead to a repetition of the Chilembwe uprising of 1915. The episode reflected impulses that would lead to the formation of bodies known as African Instituted Churches. [67]

On March 17, 1937, the Gowa Mission opened the John Crook Memorial Hospital in a ceremony at which the Government District Commissioner officiated in the presence of the Paramount Chief. This marked a positive change in the relationship between Mission and Government. [68] Though always under-funded and understaffed, the hospital provided valuable medical care which otherwise was very limited in central Nyasaland. The mission of the British Churches of Christ became a charter member of the Christian Council of Nyasaland, founded in 1942 to facilitate ecumenical cooperation between its twenty-one members.

The short-lived Central Africa Federation that attempted to unite Nyasaland with Northern and Southern Rhodesia filled the late 1950s with political unrest. Still, the process of developing a self-governing Church in Nyasaland that began with the establishment of local Finance Committees in 1956 continued. By 1960, some of the Finance Committees were already self-supporting. Annual Conferences in the two Districts of Namiwawa and Gowa had been meeting for some time. At the Annual Conference of the Namiwawa District in August 1959, Wilfred Georgeson, then chair of the FMC, visited Nyasaland to mark the jubilee of the establishment of the Namiwawa Mission. All twenty-two congregations sent representatives, as did several neighboring missions. [69]

For thirty years the mission of the British Churches of Christ in Gowa and Namiwawa had grown steadily. Though the number of schools dropped from forty-four to thirty-three between 1934 and 1960, enrollment grew from 2,100 to over 3,800. Church membership grew from two thousand five hundred to four thousand, with thirty-four churches and fourteen African ministers in 1960. Though there were fewer African evangelists and teachers than the eighty there had been in 1934, the ministers in 1960 were better trained as a result of Ernest Gray's work. In addition to the Grays and the Georgesons, nine other missionaries served in this period along with the African evangelists. Foremost among African leaders were Moses Chinganga, Samuel Magowero, and Henry Masozo.[70]

Henry Masozo, pictured here with his wife, was elected the first African president of the Churches of Christ in Namiwawa in 1962. He is wearing the ornate collar of embroidered silk brocade that became symbolic of the office. (*Christian Advocate*, February 9, 1962)

The Nyasaland independence movement became a major preoccupation for leaders of the British Churches of Christ in the early 1960s. Though many local leaders seemed uncertain about whether or not voting was "worldly," some younger members became strongly involved in politics. In 1962 the first popular elections brought the Malawi Congress Party to power, and the new African Minister of Education set up local education committees to control the schools. The inevitable trend toward Africanization coupled with financial difficulties led the missionaries in 1966 to recommend to the FMC that the schools be handed over to the government, and

by 1968 only the Gowa School remained under mission control.[71]

After full independence in 1964, the new African government renamed the country Malawi. Henry Masozo had become the first African President of the Namiwawa Churches of Christ in 1962. To coincide with independence, Gowa and Namiwawa formally united into the Churches of Christ in Malawi. The first African to be ordained to the ministry had been Alfred Moffatt Phangaphanga by Ernest Gray before his departure in 1956. By 1965 there were ten ordained African ministers in the new nation.

The FMC sent five other missionaries after 1960, yet in 1976, all mission properties were formally transferred to the ownership of the Malawian Churches. After a visit to Malawi by Victor and Nellie Smith in 1980, the Churches of Christ in Malawi became a member of the Council for World Mission. In 2000, the Churches of Christ in Malawi relocated headquarters from Gowa to the capital Lilongwe to better facilitate the churches' ecumenical work, including union conversations with the Anglican and Presbyterian churches. In 2011, the Churches of Christ in Malawi reported forty-six congregations with a combined membership of forty thousand.[72]

In addition to the work of the British Churches of Christ, after World War II North American Churches of Christ also began work in Nyasaland. As mentioned, between 1946 and 1951 North American Churches of Christ broadcast a weekly radio program from Lourenço Marques, Mozambique, which could be heard throughout southern Africa. Two young men from Nyasaland—Ahaziah Apollo Ngwira and Timothy Zimba—were students in the medical school at Rhodes University in Grahamstown, South Africa, when they heard the broadcast. Determined to become evangelists for the Churches of Christ, both left their medical studies, returned to Nyasaland, and by 1950 had established several congregations in the northern districts of Mzimba, Nkhata Bay, and Rumphi.

One of Ngwira's converts was Godwin Mukwakwa who, although blind, became one of the most effective evangelists in the country.[73] At the request of Ngwira and Zimba, missionaries from North American Churches of Christ Eldred Echols and Guy Caskey visited Nyasaland in 1951. The Americans met Mukwakwa in Mzimba, then drove seventy miles north on a bush track, camping near a village beside a small lake. When they preached to the villagers that evening, they assumed it would be the first Christian message the people had ever heard. They were surprised to learn, however, that Mukwakwa had preceded them, having made the trip on foot.[74]

Ngwira and Zimba continued their work in northern Malawi without further support from North American Churches of Christ. In 1957, however, Andrew (1931-1992) and Claudene Connally, James (1926-2011) and Clydene Judd, and Doyle and Louise Gilliam arrived to help the African evangelists organize the churches into the Lubagha Mission. After its founding, dozens of missionaries and African leaders served in this mission. In 1992, the Mission began publishing tracts in the Chichewa and Chitumbuka languages, issuing and distributing nearly half a million annually. In addition, in 1994 the Mission established the Church of Christ Bible College at Mzuzu to train Malawian evangelists and church leaders, many of whom later accompanied North American missionaries into neighboring Tanzania.[75]

In southern Nyasaland, a number of congregations separated from Masangano's Church of God in the early 1950s and by 1955 were appealing to North American Churches of Christ to supply missionaries. Though then serving in Salisbury, Southern Rhodesia, C. B. Head of the non-Bible class Churches of Christ periodically made the three-hundred-fifty-mile trip to southern Nyasaland to work among these congregations during the late 1950s. In 1961, missionaries Roland and Wada Hayes and G. B. and Ruth Shelburne organized these congregations into the Namikango Mission at Thondwe. They immediately began a four-year Bible training program, opened a primary school, and established a maternity hospital. Later the Mission began a program of education and medical care for those suffering from HIV/AIDS.[76]

The African Church of Christ—founded by Kaunda and Nkhonde and "excommunicated" by the British Churches of Christ mission—consisted of a handful of struggling congregations in central Nyasaland in the late 1950s. Missionaries from North American Churches of Christ began working with them at the request of some of their Malawian leaders in 1958. Doyle and Louise Gilliam and F. P. and Marianne Higginbotham trained evangelists for the Lilongwe, Dowa, Dedza, and Mchinji districts of central Malawi in the 1960s. By 1967, this mission had organized a school to train Malawian evangelists at Mponela, which was under the control of African leaders from the beginning.[77] Efforts by Malawian evangelists resulted in tremendous growth, and by the beginning of the twenty-first century there were almost 4100 of these Churches of Christ in Malawi with a combined membership of nearly 205,000.[78]

As early as 1952, missionaries from North American congregations that would become non-institutional Churches of Christ also were working in Nyasaland. Paul and Wilma Nichols initially planned to work with congregations in the central districts, but because of disagreements—particularly over the use of multiple cups during the Lord's Supper—they began working in the southern districts instead. One African evangelist, E. C. Severe, joined the Nicholses in establishing the Wendewende Mission in the Mulanje District in 1953. When the Nicholses left Nyasaland in 1959, Severe accepted responsibility for the mission, though he continued to receive financial assistance from North American churches. Beginning in the mid-1960s, a number of other missionaries from non-institutional Churches of Christ also worked in southern Malawi headquartered in Blantyre. At the beginning of the twenty-first century, there were approximately nine hundred non-institutional Churches of Christ, most in the southern districts, with a combined membership of seventy-five thousand. Initially, congregations of institutional and non-institutional Churches of Christ maintained a sharp distinction, though since the 1980s the groups showed signs of lessening antagonism.

Belgian Congo (Democratic Republic of the Congo)

By the 1920s, the Disciples of Christ Congo Mission (DCCM) was the largest and fastest growing mission of any in the Stone-Campbell Movement. In less than twenty-five years, the mission had grown to include six stations scattered throughout the Congo River Basin, and the steamship *Oregon* facilitated travel between them. Forty-five missionaries and almost seven hundred native workers led the evangelistic, educational, and medical work for a Christian community that numbered almost ten thousand people. The mission press at Bolenge churned out thousands of pages of printed material annually, including two quarterly papers: the interdenominational *Congo Mission News*, and the Lonkundo-language *Ekim'ea Nsango*, for which both missionaries and Congolese leaders wrote. In cooperation with the neighboring Balolo Christian Mission, DCCM published a revised edition of the Lomongo-Lonkundo New Testament. Furthermore, in 1921 the Phelps-Stokes Commission, formed to promote the educational models used for blacks in the U.S., had praised the mission's educational program. North American Disciples were understandably proud of their work in the Belgian Congo.

One of the DCCM's greatest needs was an advanced program to train Congolese leaders. In the early 1920s, leaders made several attempts to launch a cooperative school with neighboring missions, but a shortage of funds and personnel hampered those efforts. After UCMS executive Cyrus Yocum (1883-1958) visited the DCCM in 1924, however, North American Disciples raised funds to help establish the *Institut Chrétien Congolais* (Congolese Christian Institute) in 1928.[79] The school offered a three-year course that included mathematics, science, Bible, church history, French, geography, and agriculture. The goal was not simply to train ministers, but to prepare teachers, doctors, nurses, agriculturalists, and business people.[80] Students paid by raising cash crops to sell in local markets. The first class included eighteen men and sixteen women. Wives and children participated in a course of study that emphasized domestic arts.[81]

Some of the earliest Congolese leaders were graduates of the Congo Christian Institute, including Iso Timothy, Pierre Bokomboji, Natanaele Bongelemba, and Sarah Bombongo Bofale, the daughter of Mark Njoji.[82]

By the late 1920s, leaders of the DCCM were becoming increasingly concerned about the expansion of Islam in the areas around their stations, especially Mondombe. Most Muslims in the region had come for purposes of trading, but the missionaries feared Islam would attract their Congolese converts because it, like African traditional religions, permitted polygamy. In 1926, Royal Dye warned Christians in North America about the threat he believed Islam posed to Christianity in equatorial Africa. He compared the "idle, contentious church" in North Africa in the fourth and fifth centuries to the "poorly equipped" Protestant missions of his day. Islam overran the former, and, unless more was invested in the latter, he warned, Islam would triumph over it too.[83] Similarly, Everard Moon urged North American

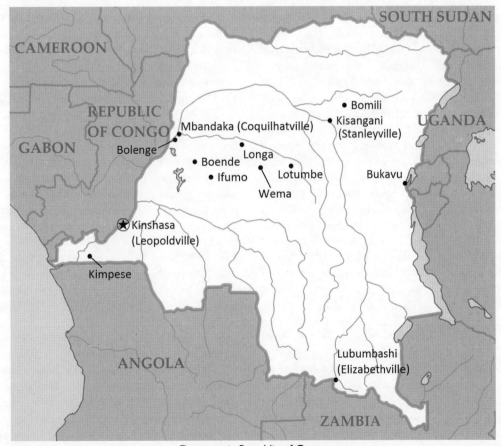

Democratic Republic of Congo

Disciples to increase their commitment to the DCCM, "so that Mohammed shall find on his arrival a well established church of Christ."[84]

By 1934, however, the effects of the Great Depression had reduced the mission's overall budget to half of what it had been four years before, resulting in drastic reductions in missionary salaries, cancelled furloughs, and a scarcity of supplies for hospitals and schools. The missionaries and Congolese leaders kept all the stations open at great personal sacrifice. In fact, the Depression years saw tremendous growth for the DCCM. Between 1929 and 1939, total Congolese membership of DCCM congregations rose to over forty-eight thousand.[85] The mission also increased cooperation with neighboring missions. In 1933, DCCM missionary Emory Ross (1887-1973) began editing *L'Évangile en Afrique*, the first inter-denominational paper for Congolese Christians. Two years later DCCM cooperated in opening a union bookstore in Leopoldville called *La Librairie Évangélique au Congo*.[86] The Depression years clearly increased the ecumenical commitment of the missionaries and Congolese leaders.

Perhaps the most significant development of the Depression years—for the DCCM and for Protestantism in the Belgian Congo generally—was the formation of the Église du Christ au Congo (Church of Christ in Congo). Since 1902, a council of missionaries had coordinated the work of all the denominational missionary societies, which in 1924 adopted the name Congo Protestant Council. With the growing number of experienced Congolese leaders, the missionaries reorganized the council in 1934 and changed its name to the Église du Christ au Congo. This move signaled the transitioning of Protestantism in the Belgian Congo from a missionary movement to an indigenous one.[87]

Changes in the Congo Christian Institute illustrate the process of indigenization begun in the 1930s. When the school opened in 1928, only missionaries served as trustees and faculty. By 1940, the faculty included six missionaries and four Congolese leaders, and the board of trustees was nearly balanced in representation. Reflecting commitments that the missionaries had made years before, H. Gray Russell (1890-1978) explained in 1941, "we feel that the control of all policies should pass gradually into the hand of those most affected."[88]

By the early 1940s, a custom had developed in the churches of the DCCM to take up monthly a collection called mpoji e'isei, or "gifts of mercy." First begun at the Bolenge church, this special offering helped meet the financial needs of the mission during the Great Depression, but later expanded to include nearby missions whose support had been reduced or cut off altogether by World War II. DCCM missionary Herbert Smith reported:

> The *mpoji e'isei* helped the "orphaned" missions of the Congo; they provided milk through the Red Cross to the babies of Belgium and the Greek towns mentioned in the New Testament; they helped evangelize the Congo; they built a substantial church at Wedji; they aided the great Bible societies in the publication and distribution of the Scriptures; they cheered soldiers in their camps and in prisons; they bought presents for one of our own missionaries who was a prisoner of war.[89]

Healthy stewardship always had been a hallmark of the Congolese Christians. The Depression and war years strengthened the Congolese Christians' commitment to stewardship and enlarged their vision of the church's mission.

Immediately after World War II, UCMS executive Virgil Sly (1901-1978) made a three-and-a-half month tour of the DCCM. After visiting the mission's union work in Leopoldville, he toured most of the stations, observing their evangelistic, educational, and medical work. Impressed, he called on the UCMS to commit over $190,000 from the Crusade for a Christian World to finance several building projects for the mission. He also called on the UCMS to recruit more and better equipped missionaries to expand the work of DCCM, which at the time had only twenty-eight missionaries for a Christian community of almost sixty thousand.[90] As a result, eighteen additional missionaries arrived by 1950, and two additional stations opened: Bosobele (1945) and Ifumo (1947). The DCCM caught the attention of *Life* magazine in 1947, and the June 2 issue featured a nine-page photographic essay on the work at Moneika.[91]

In 1949, the DCCM celebrated its Golden Jubilee at Bolenge. Planned by missionary H. C. Hobgood (1886-1979) and Congolese pastor Mbowina Mattieu, the festivities featured an address by the first DCCM missionary, Ellsworth Faris (1874-1953), the Congo Christian Institute's graduation exercises, and a range of social activities. The Jubilee had deep symbolic significance. Virgil Sly described it as "not a conference of missionaries, but of churches, which were represented by Congolese from each of the nine stations and from many of the back country areas. It marked the beginning of the adult life of these churches."[92]

In the 1950s, DCCM began participating in two new cooperative ventures. For many years Baptist missionary societies in Congo had considered establishing a cooperative medical training school, but the Great Depression and World War II had prevented them from doing so. In 1946, five societies, including the UCMS, each contributed $20,000 toward the building of the *Institut Médical Évangélique* (Evangelical Medical Institute) in Kimpese, and a sizeable grant from the Belgian government made up the difference. Opening in 1953, the Institute's main building included classrooms and a clinic, with other buildings providing housing for students and medical instructors. At the beginning of the twenty-first century, the Christian Church (Disciples of Christ) in the United States and Canada continued to support the Institute by sponsoring doctors and teachers, and by providing financial support through the Common Global Ministries Board.[93]

A second cooperative endeavor was the Protestant Theological Faculty at Elizabethville founded in 1959. Political turmoil during the 1960s forced the Faculty to move several times and delayed development of its education program. The secularization of education in 1974 under President Joseph Mobutu nearly forced the school to cease operations, but the *Église du Christ au Congo* assumed full responsibility for its operation as a private enterprise. Settling finally in Kinshasa in 1979, the Faculty helped build a comprehensive undergraduate humanities program, and in 1994 reorganized itself into the *L'université Protestante au Congo* (the Protestant University of Congo, or UPC). At the beginning of the twenty-first century, UPC included faculties in theology, business and economics, law, and medicine.[94]

The DCCM also expanded its own work in the 1950s. With $2.8 million raised through the Disciples' "Capital for Kingdom Building" program, DCCM was able to undertake almost four hundred individual projects. It added missionaries, bringing the total to eighty-eight at its height in 1957-1959. It opened a new station at Boende in 1957 and opened schools to train pastors at three other stations. All mission stations received radios, and the mission began scores of building projects resulting in new churches, schools, and medical facilities, including the Dye Memorial Church in Bolenge.[95] By 1959, DCCM reported impressive statistics, with over nine hundred places of worship accommodating more than 107,000 members, three hundred eight schools serving 14,400 students, and medical facilities providing more than 530,000 treatments annually.[96]

DCCM leaders took decisive steps in the late 1950s to transfer responsibility for the mission to Congolese Christians, partly in response to rising nationalism. In 1957, DCCM implemented a plan first suggested by the leaders of the Moneika station in which groups containing both missionaries and Congolese leaders made all decisions. In 1958, the mission held the first Congress of the Disciples of Christ Congo Mission in Bolenge. This legislative body consisted of all missionaries and three Congolese delegates from each of the mission's ten stations. Between biennial meetings of the Congress, a Central Committee consisting of one missionary and one Congolese leader from each station made decisions on issues affecting the mission.[97] Although representation on the Central Committee was equally divided, in the Congress missionaries still outnumbered Congolese nearly three-to-one. In 1959, the DCCM established a Central Fund administered by Congolese leaders to collect and distribute money from the mission's churches for salaries, travel costs, missions outside the Congo, and other church expenses.[98] The UCMS no longer controlled all funds supporting the DCCM.

Meanwhile, the political situation in the Belgian Congo became increasingly volatile. A strong desire for independence from colonial rule had been developing since the 1930s, especially among the évolués, the educated middle class. In response, the Belgian government adopted in 1955 a thirty-year plan that would result in independence. Nationalist leaders unilaterally rejected the plan, and by 1959 resistance to colonial rule turned violent as riots broke out in most major cities, especially Leopoldville. After a series of "roundtable discussions" between the Belgian government and nationalist leaders, Belgium granted independence on June 20, 1960. Almost immediately, Congo plunged into six years of civil war as various military factions vied for control of the new nation.[99]

Within a month of independence, unrest had become so severe that the UCMS recalled all but seven of its missionaries from Congo, leaving the mission's schools, medical facilities, and other institutions to Congolese leaders.[100] When missionaries returned in late 1960, their first task was to cooperate with these Congolese leaders in writing a new constitution for the DCCM. Leaders began forming a completely autonomous church organization under Congolese leadership and transferring ownership of all mission property to that church.[101] Missionaries soon learned to their surprise just how much Congolese church leaders wanted independence.[102] "We are children no longer, and we do not want to be treated as children," they exclaimed. "We need you, as our older brothers in the faith, and we welcome you; but many of you will have to change your attitude toward us if you want us to work with you."[103] The lessons learned in Congo contributed significantly to the UCMS's adoption in 1961 of *The Strategy of World Mission* with its theological foundation that the mission belongs to God, not the missionaries.

The most important Congolese leader in the era of independence was Itofo Jean Bokeleale (1919-1997). Born and raised near Lotumbe, he entered the mission school there in 1937. After completing the curriculum in just two years, he began studies at Institut Chrétien Congolais (Congolese Christian Institute or ICC), graduating in 1942. For almost fifteen years he taught at ICC, but in 1956 the DCCM's largest church at the time at Coquilhatville called him to be an assistant pastor. In the early 1960s, he studied at the Free University of Brussels, completing his doctorate in 1964. When he returned to the Congo, he assumed leadership of the 200,000-member community of Disciples. Under Bokeleale the church developed a strong infrastructure administered by Congolese leaders, expanded its educational work—especially for women—and laid the groundwork for Disciples to enter the union church then developing in the nation.[104]

As political and social unrest continued following independence, UCMS leaders sent a five-member commission to the Congo in 1963 to evaluate the situation. The commission recommended that the UCMS accelerate efforts to help Congolese Disciples become a self-supporting and self-governing church with a "missionary witness" of its own. They advised the UCMS to prioritize sending personnel to assist with educational programs, especially the training of church leaders. Because of ongoing political strife, however, they also advised the UCMS to continue sending medical personnel and supporting the hospitals and clinics.[105]

Meanwhile, in a series of meetings beginning in 1964 known as the "Consultation for Church Union," missionary and Congolese representatives from the largest denominational missions, most of whom had related to each other through the Congo Protestant Council, known as the *Église du Christ au Congo* since 1934, met to discuss the possibility of forming a union Protestant Church. Led by Bokeleale, the group had drafted a constitution for the new church by early 1965. Evangelical and fundamentalist groups strongly opposed the union efforts, but in the end sixty-two different bodies united to form the *Église du Christ au Congo* in 1970. Because he was "without doubt, the chief player in the formation of the ECC," the body elected Bokeleale its

first president.[106] The various parts of the union church continued to reflect the origins, theologies, and worship practices of their respective historic missions. At the beginning of the twenty-first century, the churches that traced their origins to the DCCM were known as the *Communaute des Disciples du Christ* (the Community of Disciples of Christ) within the Église du Christ au Congo and reported a membership of 650,000.[107]

A 1965 Congo Consultation in Indianapolis addressed the relationship between the UCMS, the community of Disciples of Christ in Congo, the *Église du Christ au Congo*, and larger ecumenical church bodies. Congolese and U.S. Disciples leaders determined that the UCMS would continue to provide financial support and personnel according to Congolese desires, that the Community of Disciples of Christ in Congo would continue to participate in the Disciples International Convention and the World Convention of Churches of Christ, and that the Community of Disciples of Christ in Congo should build relationships with ecumenical bodies such as the All-Africa Council of Churches and the World Council of Churches. Though the Consultation did not settle every issue, it did result in the transfer of ownership of all DCCM property to the Congolese church.[108]

The political situation in the Democratic Republic of the Congo continued unstable. Riots, internal military strife, and assassinations were common, despite United Nations intervention. Sometimes the unrest directly affected the DCCM, as in the Simba Rebellion of 1964. Backed by Chinese communists, a political faction in the northeast mounted a rebellion against the Congolese central government that forced missionaries to evacuate the stations in Moembe, Moende, and Coquilhatville. U.S. and Belgian military personnel eventually ended the rebellion, but the incident demonstrated the instability of the central government and the dangers of working in the Congo.[109]

In 1965, Joseph-Désiré Mobutu gained control of the country and quickly established an authoritarian regime that lasted for more than thirty-five years. Pursuing an ideology known as Authenticité, his regime attempted to purge the nation of all vestiges of European colonialism and create a unified national identity, renaming the nation the Republic of Zaire in 1971. Mobutu secularized the nation's education and healthcare, required all religious bodies to join one of four "umbrella" organizations of which *Église du Christ au Zaire* was one, and built a strong military that was extremely loyal to him. Most churches—especially the Roman Catholic Church—interpreted Authenticité as an attack on Christianity, and therefore opposed Mobutu. The regime proved disastrous for Zaire as Mobutu amassed a personal fortune at the expense of the nation's economy.

At the request of the Community of Disciples of Christ in Zaire, the Division of Overseas Ministries (DOM) of the Christian Church (Disciples of Christ) supported dozens of "fraternal workers" in Zaire during the 1970s and 1980s. Most came on short-term

Former Disciples fraternal worker Millard Fuller addresses a crowd in Ntondo, Zaire in 1979, with Mompongo Mo Imana serving as translator. Based on his pioneering work in Zaire, Fuller developed Habitat for Humanity when he returned to the United States. *(From website of the Fuller Center for Housing)*

assignments to assist with educational, medical, and evangelistic work. One example is the Bokotola Housing Project begun in the Mbanddaka district in 1973. DOM workers Millard and Linda Fuller forged a coalition of charitable organizations—including Koinonia Partners, the Lilly Endowment, *Guidepost* magazine, and the Mennonite Central Committee—to raise money for over a hundred houses for impoverished people in the district. The Fund for Humanity, administered through the Community of Disciples of Christ in Zaire, managed all donations.[110] Upon their return to the United States in 1976, the Fullers established Habitat for Humanity, based on the operational model that they developed as Disciples fraternal workers in the Congo.[111]

Tensions remained between the Community of Disciples of Christ in Zaire and the Christian Church (Disciples of Christ) in the United States and Canada, however. In the 1970s a number of official delegations met—sometimes in Zaire and other times in the United

States—so that the two groups could come to a better understanding of one another. A continuing concern for U.S. Disciples was the episcopal polity of the *Église du Christ au Zaire.* The Community of Disciples in Zaire, on the other hand, was troubled over the failure of some U.S. Disciples to work with them as full partners, especially in handling of funds. By 1981, the two churches had adopted a "covenant of agreement" to clarify the terms of the ongoing relationship between them.[112] Particularly important in this covenant were DOM support for fraternal workers, scholarship assistance to Congolese leaders pursuing higher education in Europe and the United States, and regular participation of Zairian delegates in the General Assemblies of the Christian Church (Disciples of Christ). In 1989, the Community of Disciples of Christ in Zaire began its first "foreign mission" by sending a missionary to the People's Republic of the Congo, a communist nation across the river.[113]

The political situation in Zaire again became extremely unstable in the 1990s and early 2000s. In 1991, economic collapse drove food prices so high that violent demonstrations broke out in most major cities, and army troops stationed in Kinshasa mutinied when the government was unable to pay their salaries. Three years later, one and a half million refugees settled in eastern Zaire as they fled the genocide in neighboring Rwanda. Mobutu died in exile in 1997 during the First Congo War (1996-1997), and various political and military factions vied for control of the nation. Leaders changed the name of the nation back to the Democratic Republic of the Congo, and a Second Congo War (1998-2003) involving most of the nations of central Africa resulted in a fragile transitional government.

By late 1992, the Division of Overseas Ministries had evacuated the last of its fraternal workers from Zaire. For most of the following decade, responsibility for leading the churches and related institutions fell entirely to Zairian leaders. Reflecting the unsettled situation in Zaire generally, the Community of Disciples of Christ also suffered as various factions vied to control the church and to dictate the terms of its relationship with the Christian Church (Disciples of Christ).[114] In 2000, the DOM reported that these leaders nevertheless had "done a remarkable job continuing medical, church, and educational ministries without mission personnel assistance." For this reason, DOM leaders were "convinced that not sending mission staff back to the Congo was a wise and prudent decision."[115] Nevertheless, at the beginning of the twenty-first century, the Christian Church (Disciples of Christ) in the United States and

Canada continued in partnership with the *Église du Christ au Congo,* especially with the Community of Disciples of Christ. The Common Global Ministries Board supported projects like the Bolenge Evangelical Hospital, educational institutions for women, and programs addressing violence against women and girls in Congo.

Furthermore, new models for partnership between Disciples in North America and the Congo emerged in the early twenty-first century. For example, in 2008, the Christian Church (Disciples of Christ) in Indiana entered into a partnership agreement with the Mbandaka District of the *Communité des Disciples du Christ.* Often referred to as a "jumelange"—literally, a "twinning"—of the churches, this partnership included periodic reciprocal visits, sharing of resources and personnel, and cooperation in a variety of ministries.[116]

North American Christian Churches/Churches of Christ began a small direct-support mission in the Belgian Congo in 1948. Because the government would not admit missionaries not supported by a legally recognized missionary society, they formed the African Christian Mission to coordinate the work. Guy and Eula Humphreys settled in Bomili, a village in northeastern Congo, and by 1950 had organized eight churches with a combined membership of six hundred under the leadership of native evangelists. The mission was located on a one hundred sixty-eight-acre plot with a church building, a missionary residence, a school, and a clinic to treat lepers. In 1951, the Belgian government granted official recognition to the mission.[117]

As the Africa Christian Mission expanded, a dozen additional missionaries served with the Humphreys before 1964. By the end of the first decade more than thirty churches had been established among the Babali tribe in Bomili and the surrounding villages, with a membership of five thousand.[118]

Like DCCM, the direct-support Africa Christian Mission suffered during the political upheavals following independence. After two years of teaching in the mission's school, Phyllis Rine (1939-1964) was shot to death in Stanleyville during the Simba Rebellion, and several missionary couples taken hostage. Most of the others were evacuated to safety, and Congolese Christians protected the mission property from being destroyed.[119] For almost three years, the work in the region around Bomili continued under Congolese leadership.

When Africa Christian Mission personnel returned to the Democratic Republic of the Congo in 1967, they relocated to Bukavu, the capital of the South Kivu Province, three hundred miles southeast of Bomili. From here they provided support to the Congolese leadership in Bomili, preached and planted churches, taught at schools, and provided medical services for more than thirty years. Missionaries were evacuated permanently in 1995 after tensions related to the Rwandan Genocide sparked renewed civil war in the eastern Congo. At the beginning of the twenty-first century, the Alliance of Christian Missions International—the new name for the African Christian Mission—supported two missionary couples in Bomili.[120]

Probably as a result of contacts with direct-support missionaries in the Democratic Republic of the Congo, the Stone-Campbell Movement spread south into neighboring Angola in the late 1970s. During the Angolan War of Independence (1961-1975), thousands of Angolan refugees settled in the Democratic Republic of the Congo. A small group from the Bakongo tribe came to view themselves as "Christians only" and formed an association eventually known as Igreja de Cristo em Angola (the Church of Christ in Angola—ICA). By the 1980s, significant partnerships were developing between the ICA and Christian Churches in both Brazil and North America. At the beginning of the twenty-first century, the ICA numbered about thirty congregations, mostly in Uige and Luanda provinces in northwestern Angola.[121]

West Africa

In the years following World War II, North American Churches of Christ began aggressive mission work throughout West Africa with significant cooperation from African leaders. Beginning in Nigeria among an indigenous Christian movement, this mission spread quickly into Ghana, and later into several other nations of West Africa. In addition, African Americans from the Church of Christ, Disciples of Christ entered Liberia in the 1930s, and Ghana and Togo in the 1980s, establishing significant evangelistic and social service ministries in these West African nations. At the beginning of the twenty-first century, both groups continued strong missions in the region despite its ongoing political upheaval, ethnic conflict, and inter-religious tension.

In 1948, a Nigerian named Coolidge Akpan Okon Essien (1915-1960) enrolled in a Bible correspondence course offered by the Lawrence Avenue Church of Christ in Nashville, Tennessee. Born in the Efik tribe of eastern Nigeria, he attended schools administered by the Scottish Presbyterian mission working near his village and eventually became an evangelist for the mission. When he enrolled in the correspondence course, he was leading a sizeable evangelistic work without support from European or North American missionaries. In his correspondence with the Nashville congregation, Essien insisted that the work he had started needed the assistance of experienced missionaries if it were to continue and expand. "We can teach our people but we need teaching ourselves. Send men to teach us and we shall take Nigeria for the truth."[122]

At the request of the Lawrence Avenue church, missionaries Boyd Reese (1888-1974) from Southern Rhodesia and Eldred Echols (1920-2003) from South Africa visited Essien in 1950. They learned that he and five other Nigerian evangelists had baptized more than ten thousand people, established at least forty-nine churches, and begun a preacher training school. Reese and Echols reported, "In Nigeria a remarkable chain of events has, without the conscious direction of any human agency, produced an opportunity for the spread of New Testament Christianity which has no parallel in the history of Africa. In three and a half short years they have established more congregations than we have in the whole of southern Africa after thirty years of labor by white missionaries."[123] This realization led North American Churches of Christ to develop an exceptionally strong commitment to educating and supporting African evangelists.

In 1952-1953, the first four missionary families from North American Churches of Christ arrived in Nigeria: Howard and Mildred Horton, Jimmy and Rosa Lee Johnson, Eugene and Glenna Paden, and Elvis and Emily Huffard.[124] Soon they established Ukpom Bible College and the Bible Training College at Onicha Ngwa, which offered two-year preacher training programs. In addition they began numerous three-month Bible studies in the churches that served as "feeder" programs to the schools. The missionaries also established a system of village schools that enrolled thousands of children. Before the end of the decade, two additional missionary families arrived to assist with the church's educational programs. Though government grants and contributions from North American Churches of Christ provided most of the funds to establish these schools, eventually they were sustained by student tuition. The teachers were most often graduates of the Bible college and leaders in Churches of Christ.[125] In 1959, the missionaries organized the Nigerian Christian Schools Foundation, Inc., to "further the work of the village Christian schools that already exist in Nigeria." When the foundation began, the mission schools had a combined enrollment of 2,500 students.[126]

In 1960 the British government granted full independence to the Federation of Nigeria. Though the new Republic of Nigeria was a unified nation, its three major regions retained a substantial measure of self-government and remained divided ethnically and religiously. The result was an unstable political and social order, plagued by frequent unrest and government corruption. After the discovery of vast oil reserves in the Niger River Delta, various factions vied for control of the government and the nation's oil, leading to civil war from 1967 to 1970.

Despite the deteriorating political situation, mission work by Churches of Christ thrived in Nigeria. Before the Nigerian Civil War, nearly thirty missionary families worked in cooperation with the movement begun by Essien and his colleagues.[127] Nigerian leaders did most of the evangelism and church planting, while missionaries taught in the Bible colleges and administered a growing education system that by 1964 included ten elementary schools, thirty-nine Bible chairs in government schools, two Bible colleges, and a Bible correspondence school with a combined enrollment of nearly ten thousand students. These programs had a reputation for being of the highest quality. When missionaries launched Nigerian Christian Secondary School in 1964, it received four hundred applications for the seventy available openings.[128] The same year, Dr. Henry and Grace Farrar arrived in Nigeria with support to build a hospital. The next year two nurses, Iris Hayes and Nancy Petty, joined the Farrars and they launched Nigerian Christian Hospital at Onicha Ngwa, treating thousands of patients annually.[129] Churches of Christ in the United States and Great Britain provided significant support for the hospital at the end of the twentieth century.[130] In addition, by 1965, small groups of students from colleges affiliated with U.S. Churches of Christ had begun arriving in Nigeria—sometimes for months—to conduct aggressive evangelistic campaigns known as "Conquest for Christ" in cooperation with Nigerian church leaders.[131]

Most missionaries from North American Churches of Christ evacuated Nigeria during the civil war.[132] Some, along with a group of Nigerian leaders, settled in neighboring Cameroon where they continued evangelism, planted churches, and provided aid to refugees.[133] In Nigeria, the fighting destroyed one hundred thirty churches and killed approximately four thousand members, including twelve preachers.[134] One Nigerian evangelist lost twenty-six relatives, while another witnessed his five-year-old child bayoneted to death. Fighters badly damaged the buildings of Upkom Bible College, looting furnishings and supplies.[135] Still, in light of the fact that the Nigerian civil war and its aftermath are considered one of the worst humanitarian disasters of the twentieth century, losses to the mission were relatively small.

Though they had difficulty obtaining visas to re-enter the nation after the war, missionaries from North American Churches of Christ resumed work in Nigeria in 1971. During the war financial support for Nigerian evangelists had plummeted and needed to be re-established. Dr. Farrar reopened the Nigerian Christian Hospital, but needed additional help to meet the growing demand for services. Nigerian evangelist Stephen Okoronkwo was prepared to reopen the Bible college in Onicha Ngwa, but lacked funds to support the thirty students. Nigerian Christian Secondary School had no principal, and dozens of children of church families were orphaned and needed care.[136] By early 1974, much of the work of rebuilding had been completed, largely because of the financial support provided by North American congregations, and administered by Nigerian church leader Moses Oparah.[137] Despite the aftermath of the war, North American Churches of Christ resumed active cooperation with Nigerian leaders, considering Nigeria to be one of the most promising mission fields.[138]

Soon after the civil war, however, the Nigerian government confiscated the elementary and secondary schools of all missions throughout the nation, incorporating them into the state system. Although this was a blow, the missionaries then established the Christian Trade Technical School in Oyubia in 1972. When the government took it too in 1975, only Upkom Bible College remained. By the late 1970s, under the leadership of Nigerian evangelist Andrew Isliip, the school expanded its curriculum to include "secular" subjects, especially math and the sciences. All of the teachers, however, were still either North American missionaries or Nigerian leaders of Churches of Christ.

The standards of the preacher-training program at Ukpom Bible College were raised significantly in the early 1980s, and in 1988 administrators renamed it Nigerian Christian Bible College (NCBC), which became a constituent school of the University of Calabar.[139] By the mid-1990s, NCBC had graduated its first students in a fully accredited bachelor's degree program and opened a second campus in Abeokuta.[140] Despite the fact that NCBC grew to include programs only indirectly related to the mission, African Christian Schools Foundation, Inc., retained a significant interest in the school at the beginning of the twenty-first century, and many former

missionaries to Nigeria served on its board of directors.[141]

Missionary to Nigeria and professor of missions at Abilene Christian University, Wendell Broom explained what he believed were advantages Churches of Christ had in their evangelism and church planting in the country. First, proclaiming a simple, evangelical message that appealed to the New Testament alone as its foundation was unique among Protestant missions in Nigeria. Second, Churches of Christ emphasized congregational autonomy, not only permitting, but encouraging laypersons to take active roles in leading the church, even in administering the sacraments. In these ways Churches of Christ distinguished themselves from other Protestant missions in Nigeria, especially those of the dominant Anglican Church. [142]

Broom also claimed that as a result of their experience in Nigeria, North American Churches of Christ developed a new mission strategy that directly impacted their work across Africa. The missionaries came to make the top priority of their extensive school system the preparing of a large body of Nigerian evangelists to preach the gospel and establish churches. Once trained, North American Churches of Christ supported these leaders financially, a policy that caused considerable controversy both in North America and Africa. Nonetheless, the mission strategy that Essien had recommended as early as 1948 seemed to be working: North American missionaries trained and supported African evangelists, who in turn "[took] Nigeria for the truth." By the year 2000, Churches of Christ in Nigeria claimed over three thousand congregations with a combined membership of nearly 265,000—nearly a third of all Protestants in the nation.[143]

In June 1958, Broom and Sewell Hall, both then serving as missionaries in Nigeria, traveled to Nkum in the Central Region of Ghana to visit a man named John Gaidoo (d. 1961), then a major in the Salvation Army. Gaidoo's initial contact with Churches of Christ had been through a Bible correspondence course he had studied with Alabama minister Bennie Lee Fudge. After subsequent missionary visits, Gaidoo was baptized, then traveled to Nigeria to study with American missionaries before returning to Ghana to preach.[144] Gaidoo baptized fifty-five people and established at least three congregations traveling and preaching at his own expense.[145] By the time missionaries Jerry Reynolds and Dewayne Davenport arrived in Accra in 1961 to work with him, Gaidoo had died.

Reynolds and Davenport eventually settled in Kumasi, not far from the Kwame Nkrumah University of Science and Technology. Working closely with Samuel Buahin Obeng who had been introduced to Churches of Christ by Gaidoo and Hall in 1961 and had also studied in Nigeria, they began "open-air preaching" that sometimes drew audiences as large as six hundred people, distributed literature, began a Bible correspondence course, and in 1962 established Ghana Bible College. By the end of their first year of work, they had established twelve congregations and preached to an estimated seventy thousand people.[146]

The missionaries' stay in Ghana was short-lived, however. By May 1965, none of the missionaries remained, and most who followed came on short-term trips and worked with the few trained Ghanaian evangelists. Nevertheless, between 1966 and 1986, the number of Ghanaian Churches of Christ grew rapidly as a result of the work of indigenous evangelists with American support and encouragement. The fastest growth was in the 1980s, spurred by World Bible School correspondence courses and follow-up campaigns as well as food and medical aid by American Churches of Christ during the drought and famine of that period.

At the beginning of the twenty-first century, the Churches of Christ in Ghana consisted of one thousand fifty congregations with a combined membership of seventy-two thousand.[147] The largest of these congregations was the Nsawam Road Church of Christ in Accra with over 1,200 members. The congregation operated Heritage Christian College (formerly National Bible Institute), a school that had trained hundreds of Ghanaian evangelists since it opened in 1982. Graduates of Ghana Bible College and Heritage Christian College planted scores of congregations throughout Ghana and West Africa. Ghanaian Christians established schools, coordinated medical clinics, drilled thousands of wells for deprived communities in northern Ghana, planted more than forty congregations composed of former Muslims, and operated Village of Hope orphanage to care for orphaned and destitute children, including street children from Accra.

In addition, Ghanaian evangelists from Churches of Christ planted churches in countries such as Togo, Cote d'Ivoire, Burkina Faso, Benin, The Gambia, Senegal, Mali, Gabon, Central African Republic, Mauritania, and Equatorial Guinea. Outside the African continent, members of Ghanaian Churches of Christ planted churches and served as missionaries in the United Kingdom, Italy, Germany, the Netherlands, Belgium, Canada, and the United States. In 2011 there were congregations of Churches of Christ made up entirely of Ghanaians and worshipping in local Ghanaian dialects in the Bronx, New York; Hyattsville, Maryland; Columbus, Ohio; and Atlanta, Georgia. Ghanaian Christians who migrated to Europe and North America also served as elders, deacons, and ministers in predominantly European or American congregations.

The twentieth-century rise of Pentecostalism in Africa affected all churches, including those of the Stone-Campbell Movment. In Ghana, some in Churches of Christ were especially drawn to Pentecostal style prayer groups and prayer camps for healing and financial prosperity. Beginning in 1993, members of several congregations formed prayer groups that challenged traditional understandings in Churches of Christ of the cessation of miracles and the work of the Holy Spirit in the lives of Christians. Ecstatic experiences, speaking in tongues, spirit possession, and divination became part of some of the groups. These developments caused the formation of pro-Pentecostal and anti-Pentecostal factions in many congregations. Though their congregational structure made it difficult for Churches of Christ to respond as a whole, a Ministers' Association of national leaders appointed a committee to resolve conflicts. In 2010, an uneasy peace existed between the groups.[148]

The first contact between Ghanaians and North American Christian Churches/Churches of Christ was a letter requesting a Bible from a young man from Shama in the Western Region of Ghana in December 1961 to National Bible College, a correspondence school in Wichita, Kansas. When others made similar requests, the Ark Valley Christian Church in Wichita began sending Bibles and large quantities of Christian literature. The first missionaries from Christian Churches/Churches of Christ came in August 1963. Their goal was to foment a Ghanaian Restoration Movement, establishing "a positive and productive association with the churches in Ghana" without controlling them. To a great extent, this challenge was met through the establishment of Ghana Christian College in 1966. The college's stated purpose was to "assist a variety of indigenous churches through training their leaders, hoping to influence these churches toward New Testament Christianity."[149] Christian Churches in Ghana also operated the Christian Leadership Training Institute, offering seminars for church leaders and resources for evangelism and discipleship.

Christian Churches in Ghana formed themselves into a "Fellowship of Christian Churches" with a national secretariat in Accra to coordinate their affairs run by an executive committee and assisted by committees on finance and business, missions/evangelism, Christian education, convention planning, and public relations. The body zoned the country into "Areas" from which representatives of the churches formed a "National Council." In 2011, the Fellowship of Christian Churches in Ghana had two hundred congregations in twenty-two Areas.

A mission of the Church of Christ, Disciples of Christ in Ghana began through the efforts of Ebenezer Sefah of Sekondi-Takoradi, Ghana, and Bishop Chester Aycock of the Goldsboro-Raleigh District Assembly of North Carolina. In the mid-1980s, Sefah established the Refreshing Times Christian Centre to reach rural and remote areas in the Takoradi region. Sefah was ecumenically minded, seeking to create a consortium of parachurch groups and evangelists.

In March 1988, Sefah reported receiving a vision to establish a ministry to "bring times of refreshing to our generation and beyond." Despite limited support and encouragement, he went on a three-day fast to confirm his vision, and after additional weeks of prayer, organized the Refreshing Hour International Church on May 1, 1988, with an initial membership of five people. Within a year, Sefah and others had established three additional churches and increased membership dramatically. In less than a decade, other churches were begun and the headquarters in Baka-Ekyir constructed a new building named the Cathedral of Dreams in 2005.[150]

Bishop Aycock was introduced to Bishop Sefah by Rev. J. Do-Right Dudley at a Gospel Crusade in Florida in 1998. Aycock, determined to expand his district's international outreach, visited the Refreshing Hour churches in Ghana in 1998 along with a team of volunteers. Two years later, Sefah received ministerial certification from the Church of Christ, Disciples of Christ at the Goldsboro-Raleigh District Assembly, and brought all of the Refreshing Hour Churches under the jurisdiction of the Goldsboro-Raleigh Assembly.

Estimates varied on the number of Ghanaian members. The Cathedral of Dreams had five hundred members in 2010, and according to Bishop Aycock, there were one hundred fifty churches affiliated with Refreshing Hour, with a total of ten thousand members. Many of the churches and pastors had been affiliated with other denominational groups before aligning themselves with the Refreshing Hour Churches. Refreshing Hour Social Foundation (RESOF) actively partnered with the government to alleviate social and economic problems,

including matters of health, aging, and community development. Sefah became bishop in 2009, and in 2011 opened churches in South Africa, Belize, and England.[151]

Church of Christ, Disciples of Christ congregations and prayer centers in Togo developed with the support of the Northeastern District Assembly through the efforts of one man and his family. In the 1970s Atsu Mawussi Awadzie worked as a secondary school English teacher and as a choirmaster in the Catholic Church in Kpalimé, Togo. In the 1980s Mawussi was appointed youth and project coordinator of a voluntary work camp organization named the Association Togolaise des Volontaires Chretiens au Travail (Association of Christian Volunteers at Work) in Kpalimé. This position enabled him to travel all over the world to represent the association and encouraged him to begin his own not-for-profit organization in Togo called the Union of Young Christians in 1989.[152]

During his travels, he met Tiombe Tallie, a member of the Northeastern District Assembly of the Church of Christ, Disciples of Christ, at a World Council of Churches Committee meeting in 1991. Three years later, in August 1994, Mawussi received an invitation from Tiombe Tallie to participate in the Church of Christ, Disciples of Christ Youth Fellowship's World Ecumenical Youth Summit, held in Newburgh, New York. Mawussi attended Sunday services at Mt. Carmel Church of Christ, Disciples of Christ, where the preaching of the pastor, Elder Thermond Herring, touched him. Mawussi concluded that despite all his spiritual projects he had never had a direct encounter with Christ nor accepted Jesus as his Savior and Lord. He gave his life to Christ and returned to Togo to begin a church. Discouraged by the challenges of church planting, he began a school in Gape later that year.

In March 2002, Mawussi returned to Mt. Carmel Church of Christ, Disciples of Christ in Newburgh at the invitation of Pastor Thermond Herring. Mawussi engaged in intensive training in administration, Bible, and doctrine from Herring and the Disciples of Christ Learning Center of the Northeastern District Assembly and was ordained by Bishop Marvin Creech in September 2002. Elder Mawussi returned to Togo in November 2002, and within three months began an intensive church-planting program. By 2004 Mawussi had trained and ordained seven elders, and by 2011 had organized seven churches and missions.[153]

Between political and social instability resulting from a military coup in 2005, devastating floods in 2009, and rigid restrictions on churches and evangelism by the government, the Togolese churches and prayer centers found themselves in difficult circumstances. By 2010, the ministerial staff had dwindled to two people—Elder Mawussi and his brother-in-law, Evangelist Victor Koffi Kugblenu. Despite these difficulties, by October 2011 the ministry had grown to two thousand members.[154]

While Elder Mawussi struggled to minister to the churches, the Northeastern District reassessed their commitment to international evangelism. General Evangelist Sheila H. Gillams visited Togo in 2004, and in 2010, presiding district bishop Leonard E. Brown and four other church officials, known as the Togo Now Team (TNT), made an official visit from the Northeastern District Assembly. Bishop Brown presided over the ordination of Elder Mawussi's wife, Elder Pauline Adzovi Kugblenu, and the Team met with professors from the University of Lomé, the Minister of the Interior, and several tribal chiefs. The TNT's report commended Elder Mawussi's accomplishments and led to a more centralized approach to international evangelism by the newly elected presiding bishop of the Northeastern District Assembly, Bishop Andrew J. Boomer, Jr. In November 2010, Bishop Boomer instituted a separate subsidiary for foreign missions in his district to support the Togo mission.

As in Ghana, Togolese ministers had a keen sense of the importance of serving the needs of people in the broadest sense. They frequently raised funds for medical aid, secondary schools, clean drinking water, and women's education and employment. Elder Mawussi and General Evangelist Gillams also set up a series of ecumenical conferences for the churches in Togo in January 2012.[155]

The Church of Christ, Disciples of Christ was also active in Liberia. In 1986, Elder Johnny Jbehmie of Liberia approached General Bishop of the Assembly Churches in the United States, MacDonald Moses, with a request to bring twenty-one churches into the General Assembly. The churches could not be accepted, however, without an official visit. Though Moses was not reelected General Bishop in 1989, he led a delegation of ten church officials to Liberia to receive the churches into the General Assembly, to create the "African Soul Winning District Assembly" headquartered in Monrovia, and to consecrate Elder Johnny Jbehmie as Bishop of the new District.[156]

East Africa

In much the same way as in West Africa, missionaries from North American Churches of Christ began

evangelism and church planting in East Africa in the years following World War II. Missionaries working in the Union of South Africa established a foothold in Tanzania in the early 1950s, and from there spread throughout East Africa by the middle of the 1960s.

In 1948, missionaries to South Africa Eldred Echols and Guy Caskey attempted to establish a mission in Dar-es-Salaam, the capital city of what was then known as Tanganyika. Though the government initially denied them permission to stay, they discovered that because the nation was a United Nations trust territory, foreigners who purchased property belonging to Germans (former colonizers of the area) could stay. Though unsuccessful in their appeal for funds from North American Churches of Christ, Echols and Caskey returned in 1952 and purchased two farms near the town of Chimala with their own money. They farmed the five-hundred-acre Chosi property to produce income to support their mission. The second property was the three-hundred-acre Ailsa farm atop the Rift Valley Escarpment, on which they built the Tanganyika Bible School (TBS) in 1956. Instead of focusing on building Christian communities by establishing primary and secondary schools, they gave primary attention to training Africans committed to evangelizing Africa as the most successful way of spreading Christianity.[157]

Tanganyika Bible School (TBS) offered a two-year program to train African men to preach and offered classes for their wives to serve in supportive roles. Initially only missionaries composed the faculty at TBS, but by the early 1960s Nyasaland evangelist Ahaziah Apollo Ngwira and South African evangelist Al Horne had joined them. By 1964 forty-four students from Tanganyika, Nyasaland, and Northern Rhodesia were training at TBS, along with their wives and families.

As at the Nhowe Mission, TBS organized student evangelistic campaigns during breaks between semesters. One Nyasaland student, Grandwell Ngulube, preached in Mbeya town during one break and was arrested for preaching without a license. When the District Commissioner threatened to put Ngulube in jail, he replied, "even if you do, I will still preach in prison." The Commissioner released Ngulube with orders to leave him to his preaching in peace. Another student, Efron Mtonga, chose to preach among the warrior Wasangu people of the plains area. The Wasangu listened politely to Mtonga's sermons, but refused to share their meager food supplies with him. After three days of preaching he headed back to Ailsa but collapsed from hunger halfway up the trail. Other returning students found him and carried him to the school where he reported that many Wasangu were ready to consider the gospel. Later, when he received an offer for American support, Mtonga stated, "Like Paul, I have no choice of whether to preach or not. I do have a choice of whether I accept support or not. My gift to the Lord will be giving the word to people free of charge."[158]

In 1971, TBS closed due to lack of financial support and opposition from the socialist government. As Churches of Christ continued to spread into the southwest region in the early 1980s, the need for a school to train preachers became critical, leading to the opening of the Chimala School of Preaching in 1987. During the first year, fifteen enrolled in the Swahili-language program. By the beginning of the twenty-first century, the school had graduated more than two hundred fifty evangelists who served in churches throughout the country. The success of this school led the mission to establish a partnership with Bear Valley Bible Institute in Denver, Colorado, in 2004 to begin Chimala Bible College. This school offered a four-year undergraduate curriculum taught mainly by educators from U.S. Churches of Christ. Missionaries in the country later expanded their work to include elementary and secondary schools as well.[159]

Tanganyika acquired its independence from Great Britain in 1961, and the name of the nation changed to Tanzania in 1964. The new government stipulated that churches must conduct benevolent work or missionaries would be required to leave the country. Because the Chimala mission was four hundred fifty miles away from the nearest hospital, leaders decided to open a medical facility. Nyasaland missionaries Andrew and Claudene Connally began raising funds to build and staff a hospital. In 1962, they negotiated the purchase of a hotel with four hundred ninety acres of land, and, less than a year later, Drs. Jerry Mays and Ronald Huddleston arrived to begin the medical work. In 1964 the two doctors opened an outpatient clinic on the newly purchased property and a year later began operating the sixty-bed Chimala Hospital.[160] At the beginning of the twenty-first century, the hospital had expanded to a one-hundred-twenty-bed facility that served more than twenty thousand patients annually. The hospital also offered special educational and treatment programs for patients with tuberculosis and HIV/AIDS.[161]

In 1963, Echols and Caskey developed a mission strategy known as the "Safari for Souls" campaign. For five months, a group of twelve college students from Fort Worth Christian College and Abilene Christian College went to Tanzania to assist missionaries in evangelism. With a rudimentary knowledge of Swahili, the group made three trips of twenty or more days each, preaching from village to village accompanied by experienced missionaries and African evangelists. They took with them a slide projector and generator with which they showed biblical filmstrips. The safari's goal was one thousand conversions before the end of the year, which they apparently met.[162] Through such campaigns and individual efforts, TBS students and teachers established churches in villages around Chimala in southern Tanzania, Northern Rhodesia, and Nyasaland.

When Eldred Echols and his family moved to Benoni, South Africa, in 1964, the Connallys assumed responsibility for the Chimala work, leading it through difficult times in the 1970s and 1980s. Tanzania's socialist prime minister, Julius Kambarage Nyerere (1922-1999) initiated social reforms collectively known in Swahili as Ujamaa ("familyhood"). The most radical of these measures forced Tanzanians between 1973 and 1976 to move from private property onto collective farms, seriously disrupting village life throughout the nation. A brief war between Tanzania and Uganda in 1978-1979 and political corruption in Nyerere's government left Tanzania one of the poorest nations in the world by the time Nyerere retired in 1985.

Though the two decades of social and political turmoil greatly impeded the work of Churches of Christ in Tanzania, after the return of political and economic stability many churches were re-established, due mainly to the efforts of evangelists trained at the Chimala School of Preaching. Also, in the 1990s, a mission team began work in the Mwanza Region of northern Tanzania focusing on creating a truly indigenous church. Within twenty years that movement grew to over six thousand members in more than one hundred twenty village congregations among the Sukuma Tribe, with local leaders making decisions concerning everything from worship styles to church organization.[163] This focus on rapid indigenization reflected a growing trend among mission teams from U.S. Churches of Christ in Africa.[164]

Missionaries to Ethiopia from North American Churches of Christ focused their work in two major areas: training African leaders to evangelize and plant churches, and development of educational programs for the deaf. Carl Thompson and Bob Gowen and their families arrived in 1960, settling in the capital, Addis Ababa, and purchasing church property in the Makanisa neighborhood. By 1962, Ethiopian Princess

Tenanya Worq Haile Selassie had leased property to the missionaries and they had opened Amha Desta School for the Deaf, named after the eldest son of the princess. From the beginning, Ethiopian Christian Demere Chernet administered the school in cooperation with the missionaries. Their goal was to provide education for the estimated thirty-five thousand deaf people in Ethiopia. Students from the school of social work in the University of Addis Ababa often did internships at the school. By 1969, the demand was so great that the missionaries opened a second school for the deaf at Mazoria.[165]

Ato Shongeh Sadaybo had converted to Christianity and begun evangelistic work in the Sidamo Province of southern Ethiopia shortly after the Italian occupation of Ethiopia in 1937. Some reports claim that he may have had as many as twenty thousand followers by the end of World War II. Already familiar with the work of Churches of Christ in southern Africa, Sadaybo travelled to the United States to seek help in leading the movement he had begun. He reported that churches that had left their former denominational missions to accept his restorationist message were suffering persecution, that schools run by other Christian groups refused to admit their children, and that mission hospitals would not treat them. Sadaybo's appeal to Emperor Haile Selassie prevented many of his followers from being imprisoned and executed, but hostilities toward them continued.[166]

In response, North American Churches of Christ—primarily in and around Los Angeles, California—sent a number of missionaries in the 1960s to help Sadaybo and other workers already there to continue their evangelistic work. Consistent with the mission strategy of Churches of Christ, the new arrivals placed emphasis on training Ethiopian evangelists.In 1968, John Young, minister of the Central Church of Christ in Stockton, California, led a one-hundred-day intensive preacher-training program. Congregations in North America sponsored twenty Ethiopian church leaders, allowing them to leave secular employment, attend the program, and become full-time evangelists. Following the training program, Young led the group into the villages of the Kambaata Province, where their evangelistic efforts met with considerable success.[167]

Besides Sadaybo, perhaps the most important Ethiopian leader was Behailu Abebe. Born the son of a state governor, he became alienated from his aristocratic family when he affiliated with Churches of Christ, first as a translator and later as one of its most successful evangelists and administrator of its deaf schools. During the Ethiopian famine of 1984-1985, Abebe coordinated extensive humanitarian assistance by Churches of Christ worldwide. Suffering through the hardships of communist rule—including exile to Kenya for a time—he remained an outspoken church leader. Later, two schools affiliated with Churches of Christ in the United States awarded him honorary doctorates, and he served as dean of the Ethiopian branch of Sunset International Bible Institute in Addis Ababa.[168]

Between 1974 and 1991, Mengistu Haile Mariam ruled Ethiopia as a communist military dictator. He expelled all Christian missionaries from Ethiopia, closed down churches, and imprisoned Ethiopian religious leaders who spoke against him. Government restrictions on travel within Ethiopia virtually cut off Churches of Christ from one another. However, Abebe, Chernet, and other Ethiopian leaders were generally able to secure permission to travel to administer the two schools for the deaf. Often, small groups of rural church leaders from the Sidamo and Kambata Provinces would slip into the mission compound at Mazoria under cover of night for encouragement, planning, and instruction.

Between 1984 and 1987, a lack of rainfall and socialist farming practices combined to produce one of the worst famines in modern history. Some of the most affected areas were the Sidamo and Kambata districts. Members of the Makanisa church in Addis Ababa literally saw many of their fellow Christians starving to death on government television. With much prayer and fasting the church sent Abebe to the United States with a goal to raise $100,000 in relief funds from the churches. The Central Church of Christ in Stockton, California, and the White's Ferry Road Church of Christ in Monroe, Louisiana, partnered with Abebe in a nationwide effort that eventually raised over $8 million for Ethiopian famine relief. The Ethiopian Church of Christ, under Abebe's direction, administered this and other aid totaling over $15 million. Their relief program fed over 130,000 Ethiopians in distribution points in Kambata, Jido, and Fursi Provinces.[169]

Abebe was also instrumental in developing inter-religious dialogue and cooperation between Christians and Muslims and administering support for Ethiopian refugees in Britain, the Netherlands, Uganda, Kenya, and the United States.[170] Due to the continued work of Abebe and other Ethiopian leaders, at the beginning of the twenty-first century Churches of Christ in Ethiopia had six hundred seventy congregations and as many as fifty thousand members.[171]

North American Christian Churches/Churches of Christ also worked in Ethiopia beginning in 1963, when Mont and Elaine Smith entered Ethiopia with the Christian Missionary Fellowship (CMF).[172] The Smiths, the first of almost two dozen missionary families to serve in the country, began their ministry in the Wollega Province among the Oromo and Kazza (Gumuz) people. Another early CMF family was Eddie and Donna Elliston who served in Ethiopia from 1969 to 1977, then moved to Kenya. Elliston described the work as including first evangelism, then social services and "culture lift," together with education and medicine.[173] Doug Priest, Jr., another Ethiopian missionary, later became executive director for CMF. When CMF missionaries left Ethiopia in 1977 due to the Marxist takeover, four thousand Ethiopians were members of Christian Churches.

In 1992, a new CMF team entered Ethiopia to expand the work among unreached people of the Gumuz tribe and to begin planting churches and ministering to the urban poor of Addis Ababa. Steve and Doretha Limiero oversaw a combination Bible college/conference center in Kiramu that provided intensive training and fellowship for Oromo Christians. Shelly Hilvety worked with the church's Community Health Evangelism program, a ministry that cared for both physical and spiritual needs of those living in the slums of the capital. Also in Addis Ababa, David and Marsha Van Wagenen taught cell church principles and trained leaders for launching a movement of rapidly multiplying cell-church groups, which was facilitated through the Kristos Andinet congregation.[174]

The Stone-Campbell Movement arrived in Kenya at a time of significant transition for the new nation. After Kenya gained independence from Great Britain in 1963, most white and Indian colonists left, and the new government redistributed their landholdings to native farmers. President Jomo Kenyatta led the nation as it developed into a representative democracy, often fighting against political rivals who advocated African socialism. Economically, Kenya prospered in the years following independence, mainly because the government was able to attract significant foreign investment. By the time Kenyatta died in office in 1978, Kenya had developed into one of the most politically and economically stable nations on the continent.

North American Churches of Christ sent Van and Jean Tate and Ted and Martha Ogle to Kenya in 1965, shortly after independence. The couples arrived in the capital Nairobi in 1965 and began evangelistic work that quickly led to the formation of three congregations. The government granted legal recognition to Churches of Christ the following year. The territory the missionaries sought to cover was vast. The nearest missionaries from Churches of Christ were eight hundred miles to the north in Addis Ababa and eight hundred miles to the south in Tanzania. To the west lay Uganda, Rwanda, and Burundi, where no missionaries from Churches of Christ were then working.[175]

By the early 1970s, six additional missionary couples were working in western Kenya, three in Kakamega and Kisumu, and three in Sotik. In all cases, the missionaries worked with the people of the region in their own languages, including Kiswahili and Kalinjin. Their evangelistic program was village-based and focused on church planting and training indigenous leaders. This team also employed church growth strategies propagated by Donald McGavran's Fuller School of World Mission.[176] The Sotik team set the tone for subsequent Kenyan mission teams working in Kisii, Kitale, Eldoret, Meru, Malindi, Kalifi, and Mombasa.[177] Gailyn Van Rheenen, after serving fourteen years in Sotik, returned to Abilene Christian University as a professor of missions. Through his teaching and writing, Van Rheenen influenced another generation of contextualizing mission teams, both in Churches of Christ and the broader evangelical world.[178]

At the request of missionaries, in 1983 the government of Kenya donated five acres of land in the heart of Nairobi for the development of a church, school, and social service program. North American Churches of Christ began an aggressive campaign called "Target Nairobi" to raise $1 million for the cost of building the needed facilities. Coordinated by the Eastwood Church of Christ in Hutchinson, Kansas, the campaign took three years, with construction sometimes delayed or stopped altogether because of rising costs. By the late 1980s, however, construction had been completed.[179] Partly because of the delay in completing the projects promised in "Target Nairobi," Churches of Christ lost government recognition in 1988 after more than twenty years. Negotiations to reregister the church were successful, and government recognition was again granted in 1994.[180]

North American Churches of Christ began two significant schools in Kenya in cooperation with local church leaders. Berkley Hackett (1941-2012) established the Kenya Christian Industrial Training Institute in 1991.[181] The main campus was located on five acres in the Eastleigh area of Nairobi. Students took certificate courses in automotive repair, applied electrical engineering, electronics, and computing systems. All were required to take Bible courses as well as participate in sports and cultural programs. At the beginning of the twenty-first century, the Kenya Christian Industrial Institute enrolled over 2,400 students and had plans to expand its programming to accommodate four thousand.

A second school, the Nairobi Great Commission School (NGCS), began in 1990 when national leaders saw the need for more extensive training for church leaders. The vision of NGCS was to provide an accredited program of education in Bible, missions, and congregational ministry that balanced quality academics with practical, experiential training. The school offered a baccalaureate degree in cooperation with Daystar University in Nairobi, an advanced two-year diploma, and a certificate program through a series of rural extension campuses in Kenya, Uganda, and Tanzania. Its students came from Kenya, Uganda, Rwanda, Zambia, Sudan, South Africa, Botswana, Ghana, and Tanzania. At the end of the first decade of the twenty-first century, there were almost fifteen hundred congregations of Churches of Christ in Kenya with a combined membership of nearly forty thousand.

North American Christian Churches/Churches of Christ also began mission work in Kenya in the years following independence. Supported through Africa Christian Mission, Howard and June Crowl arrived in Nairobi in 1965 and remained there at the beginning of the twenty-first century. Their work focused first on developing African leaders in evangelism and church planting, but later expanded to include a number of other ministries. One, operated by their daughter Christine, was Kris's Kids Kare, caring for children left orphaned by the HIV/AIDS pandemic. Howard Crowl also taught theology at Kenya Christian Industrial Training Institute and served as pastor of the French-speaking church of Congolese refugees in Nairobi. In addition, the Crowls ran a program for ex-street boys, called Ahadi Boys (formerly Rainbow Children of Promise), which provided education until the boys were ready for formal schooling. After high school, the ministry helped them go to university or special trade schools.

In addition to the work of the Crowls, North American Christian Churches/Churches of Christ supported a number of missionaries in Kenya through the Christian Missionary Fellowship (CMF). In the late 1970s, CMF began sending missionaries to work among the pastoral Masai and Turkana tribes of western Kenya. CMF worked under the registration of the African Christian Churches of Kenya until the Kenya government abruptly deregistered that association in 1987. At that time, CMF began work under the umbrella of the Kenya Church of Christ.[182] The CMF churches received their own registration with the Kenya government in 2006. Called Community Christian Church, this fellowship consists of eighty Maasai churches and forty-three Turkana churches with about 9,500 members, all under Kenyan leadership.

Some of the nearly five hundred church leaders and members from Churches of Christ from thirteen African countries who attended the 2008 Africans Claiming Africa Conference in Badagry, Nigeria. *(Courtesy Sam Shewmaker, Missions Resource Network)*

Perhaps one of the most important outgrowths of the Stone-Campbell Movement in Kenya was a regular ten-day conference of African evangelists and missionaries. Africans Claiming Africa (ACA) conferences met every four years to mobilize Stone-Campbell Movement churches in Africa for more effective evangelism. Kenyan missionaries spearheaded the first conference in 1992, held at Thuci River Lodge near Meru, Kenya.[183] Subsequent conferences were held in Zimbabwe in 1997, South Africa in 2000, Ghana in 2004, Nigeria in 2008, and Zambia in 2012.[184]

In the 1990s, the Stone-Campbell Movement spread to other nations of East Africa, mainly because of the work of African evangelists associated with the work in Tanzania, Kenya, Ethiopia, and Malawi. Efforts included humanitarian relief amid the ongoing warfare in the region, especially in Uganda and Sudan. At the beginning of the twenty-first century, small congregations of Churches of Christ were developing across the region.

Mozambique

In 1959, a Mozambican named Dias Bento Feliciano moved to neighboring Nyasaland, where he became a member of a Church of Christ and probably attended one of the mission's preacher training schools. In 1968, he returned to the village of Mihawa in the Zambezia Province of Mozambique, where he attempted to work with the Baptist mission of which his father was a leader. Doctrinal differences soon became apparent, and Feliciano and his father led several of their congregations out of the mission. For this Feliciano was taken to court and imprisoned by Portuguese colonial authorities. Nevertheless, these congregations had begun worshipping together as Churches of Christ by the mid-1960s. [185]

At the time Feliciano was developing this indigenous movement, guerilla forces in Mozambique were fighting a protracted war of independence against Portugal, who had colonized the region since the late fifteenth century. During the Mozambican War of Independence (1962-1975) the nation was virtually cut off from contact with Western nations, including the United States. After gaining independence in 1975, Mozambique descended into a seventeen-year civil war until 1992. During this conflict as well, the communist government prohibited Westerners from entering the nation. U.S. Stone-Campbell missionaries never directly impacted Feliciano's movement.

Working closely with Feliciano in the late 1960s and early 1970s, however, was a young Portuguese missionary named Carlos Esteves. The two spent time together in prison because their evangelistic work was perceived to be a threat to the fragile communist government. Other missionaries from Churches of Christ in Portugal and Brazil also helped Feliciano in the early years of the mission. By 1969, the Evangelical Swiss Mission of Christ had withdrawn from Mozambique because of the war of independence, leaving their churches without missionary support. Feliciano convinced many of these congregations to join the Churches of Christ. Throughout the early 1970s, leaders of this new mission planted churches throughout the Zambezia and Tete Provinces of central Mozambique. Leading evangelists of the mission at this time included Faria Raul, Cruz Nicola, and Anducaue Vasco. As many as thirty evangelists from Churches of Christ in Mozambique and Malawi

participated. In the early 1980s, Feliciano conducted a preacher training school at Nauela. [186]

During the Mozambican civil war, Feliciano fled to Malawi. During his absence Sozinho Macuaria conducted the preacher training school and prepared a new generation of Mozambican evangelists to serve the growing Churches of Christ. By the time Feliciano returned to Mozambique, he had adopted a theology likely influenced by Oneness Pentecostals whose missions were flourishing in southern Malawi by the 1970s. He began teaching that converts should be baptized only in the name of Jesus the Son, not in the name of the "Father, Son, and Holy Spirit." So insistent was he on this point that he attempted to require the other leaders of the Churches of Christ in Mozambique to be rebaptized. In addition, influenced by one-cup Churches of Christ also flourishing in southern Malawi, he insisted on using only one cup in the celebration of the Lord's Supper. At the beginning of the twenty-first century, at least four different groups of Churches of Christ were registered with the government of Mozambique. Although there were five hundred congregations with a combined membership of around twenty thousand in Mozambique, there was little cooperation among them. [187]

At the end of the Mozambican civil war, missionaries from North American Christian Churches/Churches of Christ began working in the country through Good News for Africa (*Boa Nova Para África*). Among the missionaries who arrived in 1992 were Jacob and Jaynie Michael, Cecil and Betty Byrd, and Jon and Bonna Ray. Their primary work was administering the Maputo Biblical and Theological Seminary to help train Mozambican evangelists. [188] This partnership continued at the beginning of the twenty-first century between North American Christian Churches/Churches of Christ and an indigenous movement in Mozambique that had approximately three hundred congregations with a combined membership of around ten thousand people. [189]

Conclusion

All parts of the Stone-Campbell Movement participated in the twentieth-century shift of the numerical center of Christianity to the global south, especially to Africa. Churches of Christ in Africa outnumbered those in the United States by the early twenty-first century. The Community of Disciples of Christ in Congo alone was nearly equal to the membership of the Christian Church (Disciples of Christ) in the United States and Canada. The Church of Christ, Disciples of Christ welcomed into fellowship indigenious churches and their leaders. Stone-Campbell Christians had led in the establishing of educational institutions and the provision of medical and health services. In Southern Rhodesia, Nyasaland, and South Africa, missionaries supported by the Foreign Mission Union of the New Zealand Churches of Christ, the Foreign Missionary Committee of the British Churches of Christ, and the UCMS had supported the human rights of the black majorities. These missionaries, along with missionaries from North American Churches of Christ and Christian Churches/Churches of Christ had embraced the difficult work of evangelization in cultures and languages immensely different from their own. In every case, missionaries had traveled to distant places, learned languages, taught the people, and often risked danger and death to witness to the gospel of Jesus Christ. Though substantial funding continued to come from overseas, by the beginning of the twenty-first century indigenous churches of the Stone-Campbell lineage were flourishing across Africa.

17

The Stone-Campbell Movement in Europe
Since the 1920s

By the 1880s Stone-Campbell mission societies largely had withdrawn from work begun in Europe, believing efforts in "non-Christian lands" to be more urgent. In France, the struggling mission closed amid the turmoil of World War I, and in Scandinavia most of the churches were absorbed into larger denominational bodies.

However, a religious movement in the Russian Empire and Eastern Europe formed a significant body of churches that would eventually identify itself with the Stone-Campbell Movement. Surviving the political, social, and economic uncertainties of World War II, the rise and fall of communism, and the ongoing inter-religious conflicts of the region, these expressions of the Stone-Campbell Movement continued in Russia, Belarus, Ukraine, Poland, and other nations of Eastern Europe in the twenty-first century.

As with other parts of the world, leaders in North American Churches of Christ had begun planning new mission work in Germany and Italy before the end of World War II. Having a foothold in the region because of U. S. military personnel stationed there, these churches sent hundreds of missionaries to evangelize, establish churches and schools, and provide social services to people devastated by the war. Between 1948 and 1978, the number of missionaries from Churches of Christ grew in Europe from twelve to more than two hundred. North American Christian Churches/Churches of Christ also engaged in European missions, though on a smaller scale.

Beginning in the late 1970s, however, missionary zeal for Europe by both North American Churches of Christ and Christian Churches/Churches of Christ began to wane. Many congregations withdrew financial support because of rising costs, increasing conviction that more

results could be obtained in "non-Christian lands," and the belief that the European churches ought to sustain themselves. Nevertheless, even in the first decade of the twenty-first century both streams continued to support a wide variety of mission work throughout Europe.

Because of growing commitment to the ecumenical movement, Disciples did not engage in church planting in Europe after the 1920s. Instead, they worked alongside existing denominations through the World Council of Churches and the Division of Overseas Ministries, later part of the Common Global Ministries Board. In the years immediately following World War II, this work focused on relief of the massive humanitarian crisis resulting from the destruction of Europe's industrial infrastructure and the collapse of its economy. Eventually fraternal workers served with European churches in a variety of roles.

Russia and Ukraine

In the mid-1870s, British missionary Granville Waldegrave (1833-1913) held evangelistic meetings in the homes of the nobility around St. Petersburg at the invitation of Elizaveta Chertkova, a member of the Russian nobility. Waldegrave—also known as Lord Radstock—was a member of the Plymouth Brethren, a conservative evangelical group emphasizing religious freedom, lay leadership in the church, weekly observance of the Lord's Supper, and opposition to creeds. A significant number accepted his preaching, resulting in the emergence of an evangelical revival.[1]

Among those converted was a high-ranking member of the Russian military, Vasili Alexandrovich Pashkov (1830-1902). Under Pashkov's leadership the revival continued, even after Lord Radstock fled Russia during revolutionary unrest in 1878. To avoid government suspicion and opposition from Orthodox leaders, Pashkov named the developing movement the "Society for the Encouragement of Spiritual Reading," though the popular label for his followers was "Gospel Christians." The group's principal aim was to provide Russian Bibles and instruction in how to read them to all who were interested. In addition to preaching evangelical Protestantism, these Gospel Christians began social services for the poor, including shelters, orphanages, and schools. Despite these services, Russian officials forced Pashkov to renounce his military position and persecuted him and his followers.[2]

Informal connections soon developed between the Gospel Christians around St. Petersburg and other evangelical Protestant groups in Russia, especially in the Caucasus. In Odessa (present-day Ukraine), for example, a movement among German Baptists called Stundism had been teaching baptism by immersion and local church autonomy since the late 1860s. At Tiflis (now Tbilisi, capital of Georgia), a convert named Mikitia Veronin had been organizing congregations since the early 1870s. In 1884, Pashkov called the leaders of these

evangelical Protestants together for a congress in St. Petersburg, hoping to form a united movement. The Russian police, with the approval of the Orthodox Church, broke up the meeting and exiled Pashkov.[3]

Although outlawed, the Gospel Christian movement continued. Sometime before 1890, Ivan Stepanovich Prokhanov (1869-1935), a mechanical engineer who had studied theology in Bristol and London, England, and in Berlin, Germany, assumed leadership of the movement. Because the Gospel Christians were unable to meet publicly, Prokhanov began publishing an underground newspaper in 1901 named *The Conversation*, mailing it to scattered disciples in registered letters. The next year, while visiting the United States as an employee of the Westinghouse Electric Company, he came in contact with members of the Stone-Campbell Movement in Pittsburgh and Chicago. He returned to Russia convinced he could develop a partnership between the Gospel Christians and the Disciples in the United States.[4]

During the turmoil of the Russo-Japanese War (1904-1905), Russian revolutionaries issued the October Manifesto, demanding basic human rights for all,

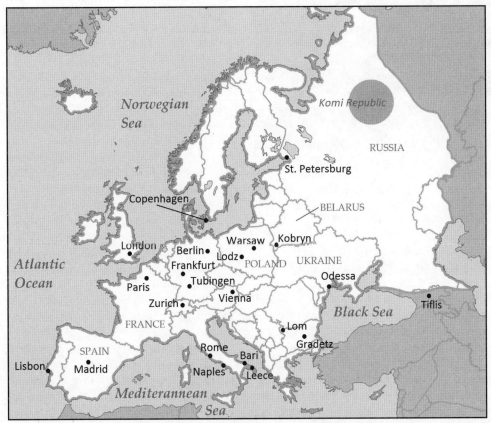

Europe

including religious freedom. When the first Russian constitution was ratified in 1906, it included a guarantee of complete religious freedom. Almost immediately, the Gospel Christian movement emerged from hiding, with Prokhanov taking a very public role as leader and spokesperson. In 1906 he began publishing a monthly periodical called *The Christian* and in 1910 added a weekly Bible study called *The Morning Star*. In addition he organized the Christian Evangelical Publishing Association to print and distribute Russian-language Bibles, hymnbooks, and educational materials and opened the first Protestant bookstore and Bible school in Russia in 1913. In 1909, Pashkov also led in organizing the evangelicals he had called together in 1884 into the All-Russian Evangelical Christian Union headquartered in St. Petersburg. Despite constitutional guarantees of religious freedom, however, Prokhanov and the Gospel Christians experienced severe persecution, both by the Russian government and the leadership of the Orthodox Church.

Ivan Stepanovich Prokhanov (center, in white) and many others suffered persecution because of their involvement with the Gospel Christians. Imprisoned at Tver around 1910, two of these leaders proudly hold their Bibles. (From *The Gospel in Russia*, 1936)

Meanwhile, members of the Gospel Christian Movement who had immigrated to the United States began teaching other Russian immigrants in New York City and Chicago. As early as 1906, John Johnson had established a small congregation in New York City that was committed to restoring New Testament Christianity. Two years later, this congregation merged with the West Fifty-Sixth Street Church of Christ and formed the City Mission Society, dedicated specifically to evangelistic work among the city's Russian immigrants. In 1911, the American Christian Missionary Society began supporting

the congregation's efforts and employed Johnson as a full-time missionary. By 1916, the mission was publishing a monthly magazine, *The Russian Christian Herald*.[5] In Chicago, missionary Basil Keusseff began work among Russian immigrants in 1909. With support from the American Christian Missionary Society, he helped organize what would become the Crystal Street Church of Christ, and in 1920 founded the Brotherhood House, a center for immigrant social services.

The Chicago and New York communities served as points of contact for a developing relationship between the Gospel Christians in Russia and the Stone-Campbell Movement in the United States. In 1912, Alexander Persianov and Martin Schmidt appealed to the Disciples International Convention meeting in Louisville, Kentucky, for help in sustaining the Gospel Christian Movement in Russia. In response, the Convention appointed a Russian Emergency Committee, led by Z. T. Sweeney (1849-1926), to visit Russia and determine the best course of action. Sweeney reported that the Gospel Christians in Russia were as dedicated to restoring New Testament Christianity as any of the Movement's leaders in the United States. Many influential people in the Russian government were sympathetic to the Gospel Christians, he asserted, and the Gospel Christians had an efficient and effective organization. "One hundred thousand dollars put into Russia in the next ten years," he reported, "would develop a half million Gospel Christians in less than a quarter of a century."[6] Others spoke in similarly glowing terms about the potential of such a partnership.[7] In rapid succession the outbreak of World War I, the Russian Revolution (1917), and severe famine in Russia in the early 1920s blocked the proposed partnership from developing beyond helping meet some of the Gospel Christians' most basic needs.

Despite the extreme difficulties, Prokhanov remained optimistic about the future of the All-Russian Evangelical Christian Union. In 1922, he led the Union in issuing "The Gospel Call," a statement written to the Supreme Council of the Russian Orthodox Church. In this conciliatory letter, he called on the leaders of the state church to acknowledge that they had "forgotten Christ" during the recent years of persecution and made unhelpful compromises with the Russian government. Accordingly the Gospel Christians "stretch[ed] their brotherly hand" to the state church and invited its leaders to join the national reformation movement. They held prayer meetings in major cities throughout Russia, in which leaders of both the All-Russian Evangelical

Christian Union and the Russian Orthodox Church participated. "For the first time in Russian history," Prokhanov wrote, "the representatives of the persecuted church prayed together with the leaders of the state church, which had been guilty of terrible persecutions of the past."[8] In 1926, Prokhanov began publishing *The Gospel in Russia* to share news of the Gospel Christian Movement both in Russia and the United States.

At this point the Gospel Christians claimed six hundred missionaries and a membership of two million people scattered throughout the empire. Prokhanov was particularly proud of the movement's successful mission work among Russian Jews and the non-Christian tribes of Scandinavia and Eastern Europe.[9] Such developments, however, were soon overshadowed by other social and political forces.

By the mid-1920s, a powerful atheistic movement known as the League of the Militant Godless was growing in the Russian Empire. Inspired by Bolshevik ideology, the league recruited disillusioned members of the working class, peasants, and students to oppose religious institutions of all kinds, especially those of the Russian Orthodox Church. Claiming that the "struggle against religion is a struggle for socialism," the league sought to neutralize the influence of religious faith in the emerging social order of post-revolutionary Russia. Beginning in 1932, the league vigorously pursued a Five-Year Plan that sought to close all churches in Russia, imprison church leaders, and re-educate the Russian populace. By the beginning of World War II, the league boasted a membership of over three million and staffed ninety-six thousand offices scattered throughout the empire.[10]

Prokhanov's Gospel Christians were not spared during this period of intense persecution. In Leningrad, for example, the government closed all but one of the Gospel Christians' seventeen places of worship under pressure from the League of the Militant Godless. Many of the movement's leaders were exiled or sent to Siberian labor camps. Russian officials exiled Prokhanov himself to the United States in 1928, and he never returned to Russia. The government often refused to issue food cards during the Great Depression to those who remained—both lay leaders and clergy. Effectively, this meant starvation because others were afraid to help them. Prokhanov compared the persecution of early Christians to that of modern Russia. "In the hearts of the Evangelical Christians in Russia now the same faith is to be found which was in the hearts of the Apostles, the faith which overcomes the world and gains victory

through Jesus Christ."[11] When Prokhanov died in 1935, no one of his stature emerged to lead the All-Russian Evangelical Christian Union.

In 1944, the Stalinist government began forcing all Protestants into a government-approved umbrella organization known as the All-Union Council of Evangelical Christians and Baptists, a development that met with mixed reactions from the Gospel Christians. Many simply chose to go underground again, much as they had done before. Throughout the Cold War (1947-1991), the so-called "iron curtain" effectively cut off all communication between the descendants of the Gospel Christians and the Stone-Campbell Movement in the United States, a relationship that had been extremely important in the life of the Russian churches. Apparently many of the congregations of the Gospel Christian Movement simply disbanded. At the beginning of the twenty-first century, however, there appeared to be about one hundred fifty congregations in western Russia that traced their heritage to Prokhanov's movement. The combined membership of these churches was around three thousand.[12]

As early as 1953, North American Churches of Christ learned that some five thousand Christians, primarily in Ukraine, were meeting together as "churches of Christ" separately from the government approved All-Union Council. In summer 1958, a group under the leadership of Otis Gatewood (1911-1999) met with leaders of these churches and discovered that "their work and worship was remarkably like ours here in the United States."[13] Despite government opposition, North American Churches of Christ tried to maintain contact with and support these churches. One of the most effective ways was through radio broadcasts, featuring leaders like Henry Ciszek and Jozef Naumiuk in Poland, and later Ukrainian Stephan Bilak (1926-2004).[14]

Between 1988 and 1991, the Soviet Union underwent significant political and economic restructuring under the leadership of Mikhail Gorbachev, ushering in an era of more openness in government dealings. Amid these developments, North American Churches of Christ began distributing Bibles through Texas-based European Mission and Bible Foundation, increased their Russian-language radio and television broadcasts, and expanded Bible correspondence courses.[15] Following the dissolution of the Soviet Union in late 1991, these and similar efforts accelerated quickly with the full cooperation and participation of Russian Christians. The "Let's Start Talking" ministry and "Herald of Truth" undertook several evangelistic campaigns in Ukraine, as well as in Kiev, Moscow, and St. Petersburg, Russia, baptizing and organizing churches.[16] By the mid-1990s, more than twenty experienced missionaries and ministry organizations were working in the former Soviet Union on behalf of North American Churches of Christ. Evangelistic work continued throughout western Russia and Lithuania, but also reached as far as south central Siberia, especially in the Komi Republic.[17]

At the beginning of the twenty-first century, North American Churches of Christ continued to support significant evangelistic, church-planting, and humanitarian missions throughout the former Soviet Union and Ukraine. In 2005, leaders from U.S. and Russian Churches of Christ began the Institute of Theology and Christian Mission (ITCM) in St. Petersburg to provide training for Russian Christians. Affiliated for three years with St. Petersburg State University, the University's 2008 restructuring led ITCM to shift its programs to on-line delivery. ITCM served churches in Belarus, Ukraine, and Estonia with conferences and training workshops. In 2011, ITCM President Igor Egirev reported fifty-three Churches of Christ in Russia.[18] About fifty congregations affiliated with the U.S. Churches of Christ were also meeting in Ukraine.[19]

Poland and Belarus

In the opening years of the twentieth century, thousands of Poles left the Roman Catholic Church to form the Mariavite Church of Poland. Among the reforms they sought were greater freedom of conscience, higher moral standards, the right of the clergy to marry, and celebration of the liturgy in Polish. In 1910, one of the leaders of that church, Waclaw Zebrowski, became convinced that even the Mariavite Church was not fully reformed. On a visit to St. Petersburg, Russia, in 1911-1912, he came in contact with Ivan Prokhanov, whose ideas of religious reform influenced him greatly. Upon his return to Poland, Zebrowski developed a small community of followers dedicated to the restoration of apostolic Christianity, much like Prokhanov's Gospel Christians.[20]

In spring 1913, a delegation of Disciples from the United States visited Zebrowski and his followers in Warsaw. They discussed with the group the principles of the Stone-Campbell Movement in the United States, persuading Zebrowski and a number of his followers to accept immersion and establishing the first church related to the Stone-Campbell movement in Poland. Z. T. Sweeney presided over Zebrowski's ordination

that same year. Within a year, the group had formed a second congregation and developed significant ministries among the poorest people of Warsaw. In addition, the Church of Christ in Poland and the Disciples in the United States began to form a lasting partnership. The turmoil of World War I delayed the growth of Zebrowski's movement, and after the war some of his followers joined other Protestant groups. Nevertheless, by 1930, Zebrowski's movement had grown to include seventy congregations in central and western Poland, with a combined membership of around six thousand.[21]

Waclaw Zebrowski (left) served as a Roman Catholic priest for more than ten years before he was excommunicated for criticizing the clergy for its immorality. Louis Patmont (right), European correspondent for the *Christian Standard*, helped the churches in the United States become aware of Zebrowski's movement in Poland. (*Christian Standard*, June 21, 1913)

About the time Zebrowski's movement began taking shape, a young Polish immigrant to the United States named Konstantin Jaroszewicz (1891-1984) began attending the Second Church of Christ in Brooklyn, New York, where Joseph Keevil (1872-1931) was minister. Keevil baptized Jaroszewicz in 1912, and soon afterward sent the young man to Johnson Bible College near Knoxville, Tennessee. After his graduation in 1916, Jaroszewicz returned to New York City to join Keevil in evangelistic work among the city's growing number of eastern European immigrants. In 1921, he returned to his native village of Starowieś in northeastern Poland to begin a "vigorous program of evangelism, church planting, and humanitarian relief."[22] Despite persecution, slander, and eviction from their home because of his preaching, Jaroszewicz and his wife, Ksenia, eventually succeeded in establishing a small congregation in the village.[23]

In 1923, Jaroszewicz and his wife relocated the center of their work to Kobryń to join forces with two other evangelists, Jerzy Sacewicz (1903-1986) and Jan Bukowicz (1890-1950). Educated in an Orthodox seminary and baptized by Baptist missionaries, Sacewicz and his wife Lidia were leading a small congregation in their home by 1921. Bukowicz had returned to Kobryń after being converted at an evangelistic meeting in Chicago in 1911 and completing theological studies at Moody Bible Institute in Chicago and the International Bible College in Minneapolis (renamed Crossroads College in 2002). Finding they shared similar theological views, the three evangelists and their wives established the Home Mission Office at Kobryń, and undertook well-organized, aggressive evangelistic work during the 1920s and 1930s. Between 1926 and 1939 they published *Christianskiĭ Soyuz* (*The Christian Union*), a monthly Russian-language periodical dedicated to the restoration of the New Testament church as the basis of Christian unity.[24]

At the Home Mission Office at Kobryń, the publishing staff turned out at least 5,000 copies each month of the Russian-language *Christianskiĭ Soyuz*. (Paul Baiko, *History of the Churches of Christ in Poland*, 2001)

The establishment and early growth of this movement coincided with a period of relative political stability and growth in Poland. The nation had come into being as a democratic republic in 1918, and adopted its first constitution three years later. Among other guarantees, the constitution promised religious freedom, even for the nation's significant Jewish minority. During the 1920s, Poland's economy grew stronger, its system of public education improved, and a sense of national identity developed. Despite frequent regional conflicts over the precise borders of the nation, Poland was emerging from the devastation of World War I as one of the strongest nations of Europe.[25]

By 1929, the mission had established more than thirty Churches of Christ throughout eastern Poland and Western Belarus. That year, representatives of these churches met for their first annual convention and established the Union of Churches of Christ of Evangelical Confession. They appointed a board to promote evangelism, produce and distribute Christian literature, educate pastors, organize congregations, and provide social services, especially to orphans and homeless persons. Later, this board also maintained contact with other churches of the Stone-Campbell Movement globally through the World Convention of Churches of Christ. The board was particularly vigorous in its educational and publishing work. In the 1930s, the union offered annual Bible training classes for pastors and lay leaders using a curriculum similar to that taught in Stone-Campbell Bible colleges in the United States. In 1938, the Union replaced its Russian-language paper with one published in Polish. The new paper, *Słowo Pojednania* (*The Word of Reconciliation*) had a circulation of more than five thousand when it began. One of the unique features of the Union's evangelistic work was its music ministry. Brass bands and choral groups of all sizes toured the region leading public song services that sometimes turned into evangelical revivals.[26]

Despite the rise of the Great Depression, in the 1930s Stone-Campbell Movement churches in North America began making significant financial contributions to the Churches of Christ in Poland, without which much of their work would have been impossible. Appeals for financial assistance appeared regularly in the journals, often claiming that Churches of Christ in Poland were the nation's chief "bulwark" against the spread of atheism and secularism.[27]

The political situation in Poland began to deteriorate in the 1930s as the economic depression put pressure on the government to abandon its commitments to democracy and become increasingly authoritarian. Though Poland never embraced totalitarianism as fully as Germany and Italy, the nation's 1935 constitution greatly increased the powers of the Polish president, while diminishing those of the legislature. Suppression of opposition became increasingly common, anti-semitism was on the rise, and communism became an attractive option for some influential Polish leaders of the era. Generally speaking, however, the government continued to tolerate evangelical Protestant groups, even exempting their leaders from compulsory military service.[28]

Churches of Christ in Poland continued to thrive. Its leaders focused on evangelism, requiring every member to give full time to the task for a certain period. In addition to annual conventions, the churches also held regional conventions. The highlight of these regional gatherings was the baptismal service. Thousands paraded through the town—always following one of the brass bands—to the banks of the nearest river. Candidates were immersed, followed by an "agape feast" in which the whole church gathered to celebrate. As a result of their enthusiasm and dedication, the Churches of Christ in Poland grew significantly. By the eve of World War II, the movement claimed seventy-eight established congregations, more than four hundred mission stations, and an estimated membership of forty thousand.[29]

During World War II, both Germany and the Soviet Union occupied parts of Poland. Between 1939 and 1941, the eastern provinces—where most Churches of Christ were located—fell under Soviet control. Although the occupying armies sometimes attempted to confiscate church property and prohibit worship services, church leaders were usually successful in negotiating peace. As the war intensified, however, Soviet officials sent many leaders to labor camps in Siberia, Kazakhstan, or the Ural Mountains, and most never returned. The churches continued to meet, though always under fear of persecution by the communist Red Army.

In the Nazi-dominated western provinces, the government outlawed services of Churches of Christ. Many congregations continued to meet in secret, however, and a few church leaders were able to secure permission to continue their work under close government scrutiny. Between 1941 and 1945, German occupation of Poland expanded into the eastern regions as well, where the army pursued similar policies. Like all Polish churches during the occupation, Churches of Christ survived by remaining detached from politics, to the point of raising no protest to the Holocaust.[30]

Poland again underwent significant transformation in the aftermath of World War II. The Soviet Union annexed most of the territory in the eastern provinces in 1945. The western provinces, including territory formerly a part of Germany, were reconstituted as an independent nation. By 1948, the communist party had gained control and established the People's Republic of Poland as a dependent satellite state of the Soviet Union. In 1955, Poland joined the Warsaw Pact, a treaty in which the eight communist nations of Eastern Europe agreed to mutual defense against Western military domination. An overhaul of the Polish economy brought the rapid expansion of industry, the collectivization of agriculture, and the redistribution of the nation's vast land resources. A Soviet-controlled secret police supervised virtually

every aspect of Polish society, and a communist-controlled system of public education taught Stalinist propaganda. The government made regular attempts to consolidate both Roman Catholic and evangelical Protestants into one single state-controlled church.[31]

The Union of Churches of Christ of Evangelical Confession also underwent significant transformation because of these developments. Seventy of its churches remained in the eastern provinces, and the Soviet government simply forced these churches to join the Russian All-Union Council of Evangelical Christians and Baptists. The handful of Churches of Christ in the western provinces by 1948 had reconstituted the Union of Churches of Christ of Evangelical Confession, received reluctant authorization from the government to resume their activities, and relocated their administrative offices from Kobryń to Warsaw. Congregations that had been meeting underground resurfaced and joined the Union. By 1948, the Union included forty congregations scattered throughout the republic, with a combined membership of approximately twenty thousand.[32]

In the immediate post-war years, the Churches of Christ in Poland continued their focus on evangelism and church building, but also rallied to meet the social needs of the Polish people, providing food, clothing, housing, and medical care for those orphaned by the fighting. Churches of Christ began a new journal, *Jedność* (*Unity*), and established a theological seminary in Warsaw. In the late 1940s, the group began new forms of youth work, establishing camp programs, holding rallies and conventions, and engaging in other activities designed to attract young people to the movement.[33]

The communist government of Poland, however, consistently suspected the Churches of Christ of subversive activities. In 1950 the Ministry of Public Security arrested key leaders on charges of espionage and treason, closing their churches and confiscating their property. Warsaw pastor and president of the Union Jerzy Sacewicz, leading missionary Mikolaj Korniluk (1903-1971), and prominent youth worker Boleslaw Winnik were imprisoned in Rakowiecka for more than three years without trial. Only the death of Josef Stalin in 1953 secured their release.[34]

To meet the opposition of the communist government in Poland, some evangelical Protestant leaders concluded that the best strategy would be to form one United Evangelical Church (UEC). After two years of deliberation, Polish Churches of Christ voted to enter the umbrella organization in 1953. Leaders were uneasy about being part of the organization because of doctrinal convictions regarding baptism and church structure. Nevertheless, practical considerations motivated them to remain part of the UEC until the fall of communism forty-five years later. The UEC succeeded in creating opportunities for greater cooperation between evangelical churches, especially in publication, training pastors, youth work, and the building of Home Betania, a retirement home in Ostróda.[35]

A strong working relationship between the Churches of Christ in Poland and the Christian Churches/Churches of Christ in the United States developed beginning in the 1950s, largely because of the work of Paul and Adela Bajko. Bajko was raised in Polish Churches of Christ, the son of a preacher in Targoszyce. As a student at the Slavic Evangelical-Baptist Seminary in Lüdenscheid, Germany, in the late 1940s, he came into contact with Earl Stuckenbruck (1916-2008), missionary to Germany who maintained ties with both the Disciples and the emerging Christian Churches/Churches of Christ. As a result of this connection, Bajko immigrated to the United States and continued his studies at Eastern Christian Institute (then in East Orange, New Jersey) and Milligan College, from which he graduated in 1953. A year later, he and Adela returned to New Jersey, where he began teaching in Eastern's Department of Missions and serving as pastor of the Czech Church of Christ.[36]

The Bajkos moved again in 1960 when Eastern Christian Institute relocated to Bel-Air, Maryland, to become Eastern Christian College. They toured Poland that year to learn about the needs of the Polish Churches of Christ. Returning to the United States, Paul raised funds to support a steady stream of young people from Poland who were coming to attend Bible colleges in the United States. and to prepare programs to be broadcast over short-wave radio. Adela edited *Guidepost*, a monthly English-language periodical to support their work, translated hymns from English into Polish, and published devotional works. Their efforts evolved into Polish Christian Ministries (PCM), with the goal of establishing and supporting churches in Poland "according to the model found in the New Testament." The Bajkos led PCM for almost forty years, until their retirement in 1992.[37] Beginning in 1994, Wayne Murphy began serving as executive director of PCM under a board of directors made up primarily of pastors and lay leaders in Christian Churches/Churches of Christ. The work of PCM was chronicled in a quarterly magazine, *The Polska Herald*.[38]

North American Churches of Christ entered Poland when four preachers from the U.S. conducted an evangelistic tour of the nation in the summer of 1957.

Two leaders in the Polish Methodist Church, Henry Ciszek and Jozef Naumiuk (d. 1965), served as translators for the Americans, and as a result left their positions to become evangelists for the new effort by U.S. Churches of Christ. Supported by the Urbandale Church of Christ in Dallas, Texas, the two experienced initial success in their evangelism and church planting. However, laws enacted by Poland's communist government in the late 1950s, including the strict prohibition of evangelism and religious conversion, limited the growth and influence of the church. By 1959, Ciszek and Naumiuk were under suspicion for "heading an illegal organization." For six years a legal battle dragged on, both evangelists serving periodic prison sentences and church leaders in North America attempting to intervene on their behalf. In 1964, the communist government ordered Ciszek to leave Poland, and a year later Naumiuk died of pneumonia. The few Churches of Christ that resulted from their evangelistic work continued to meet underground because the government considered them an illegal organization.[39]

The government of the People's Republic of Poland became increasingly unstable in the 1970s and 1980s because of internal corruption, a stagnant economy, and pressure from popular resistance movements. A loose federation of trade unions slowly developed into a political party known as *Solidarność* (Solidarity), whose power grew to rival that of the communist government. This movement of reform received significant support from the Roman Catholic Church, especially from the Archbishop of Krakow, Cardinal Karol Józef Wojtyła (1920-2005), who became Pope John Paul II in 1978. Initially, government leaders tried to suppress the resistance by declaring martial law. By the late 1980s, however, resistance was so strong that the communist government was forced to negotiate with the leaders of Solidarity. As a result of Roundtable Discussions, in 1989 Poland held its first free elections in more than half a century and communist control of the nation came to an end.[40]

The Polish Churches of Christ associated with North American Christian Churches/Churches of Christ generally refused to become involved in the social and political upheaval, sparing them from significant government scrutiny. With the assistance of Polish Christian Ministries, the churches began a number of new initiatives. In 1971, Churches of Christ purchased property outside of Ostróda and developed a Christian service camp. By the early twenty-first century, more than fifteen thousand young people had participated in its programs. In 1982, the churches launched Child's World Mission, which served an interdenominational constituency by developing lesson plans, training teachers, and establishing vacation Bible schools throughout Eastern Europe and Russia. Child's World Mission also established and supported emergency care facilities for abandoned and neglected children. Because of the increasing difficulty and expense of sending students to the United States for theological education, Polish Churches of Christ established the Christian Bible Institute in Warsaw. The Institute's faculty included both Polish and foreign church leaders and academics, some of whom were from Christian Churches/Churches of Christ in the United States. The Institute's programs eventually expanded to include cooperative work with the International Institute of Biblical Studies in Vienna, Austria, and Cincinnati Christian University in the United States.[41]

During the political and social upheavals of the early 1980s, food was in extremely short supply throughout Poland. Churches of the Christ in the United States, Canada, and Europe made direct appeals to their congregations beginning in the fall of 1981 to assist the Churches of Christ begun by Ciszek's and Naumiuk's work. Coordinated by Hans Nowak of the Mannheim, Germany, congregation, the "Food for Poland" program raised more than $1.7 million in less than six weeks. After purchasing more than one hundred forty tons of food in West Germany, volunteers illegally drove fifty semi-trailers into Poland with the help of a Czech military escort. Once across the border, they assisted church leaders in distributing the food where it was most needed among their own people, and then to others, especially to orphanages and hospitals.[42] Similar efforts on a smaller scale continued throughout the early 1980s. In all, the churches distributed more than four hundred sixty tons of food in twenty-six Polish cities. The humanitarian concern shown by the global network of Churches of Christ impressed the Polish government so much that, in early 1982, it recognized these Churches of Christ as a legal religious body.[43] At the beginning of the twenty-first century, six Polish Churches of Christ traced their beginnings to the evangelistic work of Ciszek and Naumiuk.[44]

In 1987, the United Evangelical Church dissolved, and Churches of Christ in Poland renamed themselves the Church of the Congregation of Christ. Now fully independent and also recognized legally, the church immediately accelerated evangelistic efforts and established five new congregations in places formerly closed off to such efforts, including Łódź, an important industrial city. Additionally, the Church began a new periodical, *Słowo i Życie* (*Word and Life*). The quarterly publication carried devotional materials, articles of historical interest, and news of the churches. By 1995 this renewed evangelistic zeal led the Church to establish the Foreign Mission and Charity Ministry under the leadership of Sławomir Rynkowski. This ministry established churches among and provided assistance to Polish expatriates living throughout eastern Europe, especially in Lithuania, Belarus, Ukraine, and Russia. The Church considered the Foreign Mission and Charity Ministry an extension of the work begun by Jerzy Sacewicz in the 1930s that was interrupted by World War II and the communist domination of Poland for more than forty years.[45]

Created in 1989, the Republic of Poland approved a new constitution in 1997 that explicitly protected religious freedom while acknowledging the importance that Christianity—particularly Roman Catholicism—has played in the development of Polish national identity. Part of the European Union since 2004, Poland's economy strengthened in the early twenty-first century, though there was a growing gap between the wealthy and the poor.[46]

In the 1990s, the Church of the Congregation of Christ in Poland experimented with a number of organizational structures, partly in response to the shifting political situation in the nation. By the beginning of the twenty-first century, the church had settled on a quasi-presbyterian polity: a national Synod that included representatives from each congregation met every four years. Between meetings of the Synod, a biennial Collegium of Pastors with an elected Secretariat that included a Head Presbyter, a Secretary, and a Treasurer, governed the church. The body held annual non-legislative church conferences, providing opportunities for members to worship, fellowship, and participate in educational workshops. As the churches adapted this new structure, the leadership again changed the name of the church in 2004 to Wspólnoty Kościołów Chrystusowych, usually translated as the Fellowship of Christian Churches. In 2010 the Fellowship was under the leadership of Head Presbyter Andrzej Bajenski, and included thirty-two churches and mission stations with an estimated membership of five thousand.[47]

Germany

Beginning in the late nineteenth century, some members of U. S. Churches of Christ began calling for a mission to Germany. Joseph Baumann (ca. 1850-1912), a

German immigrant who had been baptized and become a member of Churches of Christ in Texas, returned to his homeland for a short period in the 1890s to preach to his family and the people with whom he had grown up. Disappointed at his lack of success, he returned to his Texas farm and evangelized in Texas, Colorado, and Mississippi. In 1910 R. H. Boll published a call from Baumann for two volunteers to do mission work in Germany with a pledge to provide part of their support, but no one responded.[48]

World War II, however, provided the catalyst needed for U.S. Churches of Christ to begin preparing for mission work in Germany. U. S. military personnel stationed in Europe had begun organizing churches and calling for support from home. In early 1943, G. C. Brewer (1884-1956) announced that his congregation, the Broadway Church of Christ in Lubbock, Texas, would sponsor a plan for the post-war evangelization of Europe. According to the plan, Broadway would receive and distribute funds collected from any congregation that wanted to support the effort. Some criticized the "sponsoring church" plan as an unauthorized concentration of power in one congregation, but Brewer replied, "We are only agreeing to help increase the vision, strengthen the faith and enlarge the hearts of the Lord's people for an opportunity that we hope will come to the churches."[49]

The Lubbock congregation sent Otis Gatewood (1911-1999) and his wife Alma (1908-1963) to Germany in 1947 as missionaries of the Churches of Christ. With the permission of the commanders of the U. S. armed forces in the "American Zone" of occupied Germany, they evangelized in tent meetings and established congregations in Frankfurt and the surrounding area. These congregations included both British and American military personnel and German citizens. The Gatewoods also developed a personal style of evangelism that included befriending individuals and teaching one-on-one or in small groups, which they found effective with the war-ravaged people.[50] In the first ten years, the Gatewoods' work in Germany attracted more than forty additional missionaries, resulting in the establishment of twenty congregations. By 1956, *Gemeinden Christi* had been established in Frankfurt, Berlin, Münich, Heidelberg, Mannheim, Weisbaden, Stuttgart, and other important cities.[51]

Beyond evangelism and church planting, the missionaries provided social services and educational ministries. They coordinated efforts by North American Churches of Christ to provide food and clothing to an estimated six hundred thousand people in the years immediately following the war.[52] Their work also included a boys' home, a summer camp at Gemünden, vacation Bible schools, and a newspaper titled *Der Christ im Zwanzigsten Jahrhundert* (*The Twentieth Century Christian*). Finally, missionaries and German co-workers organized a Bible training school to prepare leaders for the developing churches. For their efforts, Otis Gatewood received the *Bundesverdienstkreuz* (the Order of Merit of the Federal Republic of Germany) in 1952, the highest honor bestowed by the West German government on a non-citizen.[53]

Thirty-eight German evangelists also helped lead the mission and its churches in the first decade. One of the most important was Hans Godwin Grimm, who came from a family of persecuted dissenters. Educated in comparative religion at some of Germany's best theological schools, Grimm was the author of books, articles, and inspirational devotional works. In 1933 the Gestapo imprisoned him for preaching against Hitler and the Nazi Party. After World War II, the government of East Germany arrested him in Leipzig for preaching against communism, and he spent four years in jail and concentration camps. Upon his release in 1952, he fled to West Germany and associated with Churches of Christ in Frankfurt. Throughout the 1950s, he served as an evangelist for the congregations at Kaiserslauten and Mannheim, and in the 1960s led the expansion of the mission into Biel, Switzerland, from which he retired in 1970. Due largely to his evangelistic efforts, Churches of Christ established at least six congregations in the former East Germany.[54]

During the 1960s and 1970s, U.S. Churches of Christ in Germany developed a highly successful program of evangelism. City-wide "campaigns" brought together missionaries, German Christians, and volunteers from the United States (mainly college students from Lubbock Christian, Abilene Christian, and Harding Universities) for month-long periods of intense evangelistic work. Campaigns began with the mass mailing of tracts and German-language copies of the *Firm Foundation* (*Das Feste Fundament*) and the distribution of handbills in the streets. Two-week revivals then followed, often attracting thousands of spectators. After the revival, leaders of the campaign made house-to-house calls, using Gatewood's methods of "personal evangelism." Often these campaigns resulted in dozens of baptisms and significant increases in church membership.

Beyond the evangelistic campaigns, Churches of Christ began a radio ministry in 1965 that was directed by Gottfried Reichel), one of Otis Gatewood's earliest contacts in Frankfurt. A 1953 graduate of Harding University, Reichel developed and broadcast a program titled *Es grüßen euch die Gemeinden Christi* (The Churches of Christ Greet You) for thirty-five years. Transmitted over the powerful Radio Luxembourg, his program reached an estimated seventy million people each week, and mail responses came from Europe, Asia, Africa, and North America. Upon his retirement in 2000, Reichel received numerous awards and recognitions for his pioneering work in radio ministry among Churches of Christ.[55]

During this same period, Churches of Christ in Germany developed institutions to train leaders for their growing congregations. As early as 1951, annual "lectureships" met in Frankfurt, bringing together missionaries, German Christians, and educators from North America for two-week periods of training, worship, and fellowship. Beginning in the mid-1960s, these lectureships assembled hundreds of leaders from Churches of Christ all over Europe. In 1970, the churches launched the Heidelberg Preacher Training School, housed until its close in 1982 in Pepperdine University's Moore Haus, a learning center for Pepperdine students. Most German leaders, however, preferred to study at institutions operated by Churches of Christ in the United States.[56]

Beginning in the 1980s, missionary zeal for Europe among Churches of Christ began to lag. Gradually, increasing responsibility for the churches passed to German leaders, although significant partnerships with Churches of Christ in North America and other parts of Europe remained. In the second decade of the twenty-first century German Churches of Christ continued ministries in twenty-five German cities, though many of the congregations were small and continued to rely on financial assistance and limited missionary leadership from North American congregations. Nevertheless, Churches of Christ in Germany cooperated to begin their own evangelistic work in Thailand, Poland, Ghana, Pakistan, and India, and to offer humanitarian relief to the nations of Eastern Europe after the collapse of communism.[57]

In addition to efforts of U.S. Churches of Christ, Disciples also began evangelistic work in Germany in the years following World War II, inspired by Prussian nobleman Ludwig von Gerdtell (1872-1954). During doctoral studies in New Testament at the University of Erlangen, von Gerdtell began embracing some of the commitments of the Stone-Campbell Movement. In the 1910s and 1920s, he published works criticizing

the idea of a state church and advocating freedom of conscience, repudiating creeds and confessions of faith, and calling for the restoration of New Testament Christianity. Highly critical of Nazism, he fled to the United States in 1934, where he met Dean Walker and Frederick D. Kershner at the Butler School of Religion in Indianapolis. So convinced were they that von Gerdtell would develop his small group of German followers into a significant movement, they formed the German Evangelical Association (GEA), intending to "form an alliance between Disciples in America and the new groups of Christians brought together by von Gerdtell." The continued rise of Nazism and the outbreak of World War II prevented von Gerdtell from returning to Germany, however. Between 1935 and 1944, he served as lecturer in church history and doctrine at Butler. During those nine years of teaching, a number of significant theological differences with U. S. Disciples surfaced which led to Gerdtell's loss of Disciples support.[58]

Commitment to a German mission continued to be a priority among some Disciples, however. After World War II, Walker and Kershner convinced two students at the Butler School of Religion—Earl Stuckenbruck (1916-2008) and his wife, Ottie Mearl (b. 1922)—to go to Germany as missionaries of the GEA, renamed the European Evangelistic Society (EES) in 1946. Their aim was to establish an institute through which the plea of the Stone-Campbell Movement could be presented in the context of a major European research university. Beyond the institute, however, the mission would include traditional evangelistic efforts in central Europe. After several years of preparation, the Stuckenbrucks began work in 1950 not far from the historic University of Tübingen.

The Stuckenbrucks pursued their objectives with vigor. They bought a plot of ground and made plans for a building, gathered a small church named *Christliche Gemeinde* (the "Christian congregation"), and began publishing a monthly English-language newsletter titled the *European Evangelist*. They also developed a relationship with Adolf Köberle (1898-1990), a leading theologian among Lutheran Pietists and a member of the Tübingen faculty. Disciples in the United States, however, did not support the EES as its leaders had hoped, and the sixty thousand dollars needed to carry out the building project never materialized.[59]

One of the most important early developments in the EES was the addition of evangelist Theodore Mosalkow (1892-1984) to the staff in 1955. Born in Russia to an evangelical family and trained in medicine,

Mosalkow came to Germany just before World War I to continue his education at the University of Hamburg. After his parents perished during the Russian Revolution in 1917, he decided to remain in Germany. He taught briefly at the Slavic Bible College (an institution affiliated with Prokanov's Gospel Christian Movement), then went into private medical practice. From 1935 to 1955 he served as a full-time missionary for the German Tent Mission.[60] Between 1955 and his retirement from the EES in 1979, Mosalkow engaged in aggressive evangelism among Slavic-speaking people of Germany and eastern Europe, serving also as a link between the EES, its supporting churches in North America, and the Churches of Christ in Poland.[61]

By the 1970s, the Institute for the Study of Christian Origins brought many Stone-Campbell scholars into contact with the world-renowned theological faculty at the University of Tübingen. Former director S. Scott Bartchy teaches a course in New Testament at the university in 1980. (*European Evangelist,* January-March 1982)

By 1962, the Stuckenbrucks had developed sufficient resources to launch what would eventually be called the *Institut zür Erforschung des Urchristentums* (the Institute for the Study of Christian Origins). The Institute functioned like a German Stift, a residential center supported by church funds for theological students, but connected to a major research university. Unlike the other institutes at Tübingen, this one provided resources for the study of Christian origins, encouraging the critical study of rabbinic Judaism, the New Testament, and patristics. Although ecumenical in outlook, the institute focused specifically on providing these resources for members of the Stone-Campbell Movement, and support came

entirely from the United States. The Institute related formally to the University of Tübingen through the Department of Missiology and Ecumenical Theology, where Gerhard Rosenkranz (1896-1983) was the leading scholar.[62]

The Institute was located in the EES's newly purchased building adjacent to the university on Wilhelmstrasse, the main thoroughfare in Tübingen. Through the mid-1960s, the Stuckenbrucks assembled an impressive library and toured the United States to raise money. They entrusted the care of the *Christliche Gemeinde* to a doctoral student named James Crouch, who served the church for five years. A growing number of university students and their families began attending the church, attracted mainly by Crouch's preaching. The EES began sponsoring study tours so that members of the Stone-Campbell Movement could visit historical sites throughout Germany and experience the work in Tübingen firsthand. By the late 1960s, the *Christliche Gemeinde* was thriving, and the Institute was poised to become a flourishing center of academic and church life.[63]

After the Stuckenbrucks relocated to the United States in 1968 for Earl to assume a teaching position at Milligan College, S. Scott Bartchy (b. 1936) and Fredrick Norris (b. 1941) served as directors of the Institute for over a decade and brought its programming to maturity. Under their leadership, the Institute began offering fellowships that brought Stone-Campbell Movement scholars to Tübingen to attend classes at the university, research and write, and engage in other scholarly activities. The Institute began hosting regular colloquia, bringing leading scholars from Europe and the United States—including Hans Küng, Heiko Oberman, Helmut Koester, Otto Betz, Langdon Gilkey, and David Aune—to lead discussions of their current research.

Yet the scholarly work of the Institute was never separated from the life of the church. Both Bartchy and Norris had significant pastoral experience in addition to academic credentials, and the *Christliche Gemeinde,* under the leadership of Bruce Shields from 1970 to 1975 and Werner Hausen from 1975 to 1987, provided a constant reminder that scholarship must always be in service of the church.[64] This scholarly activity, the ministry of the congregation, and Mosalkow's evangelistic work brought together all parts of the Stuckenbrucks' vision for the work in Tübingen.[65]

Beginning in 1981, the European Evangelistic Society began sponsoring a lectureship that rotated between the North American Christian Convention, the General Assembly of the Christian Church (Disciples of Christ), and the World Convention of Churches of Christ. The aim of this lecture series was similar to the goal of the Institute: to encourage scholarly research into Christian origins, especially as it informed the identity and mission of the Stone-Campbell Movement. This lectureship also created a forum in which scholars from the three major North America streams could engage in dialogue and promote mutual understanding. In 1988, the lectureship was named to honor the work of Dean E. Walker, who served as the president of EES from 1947 to 1974. Between 1989 and 2000, patristics scholar Ronald Heine served as director of the Institute.[66]

After the fall of communism in Eastern Europe, the EES entrusted the work of the *Christliche Gemeinde* to a Russian-born evangelist, Gennadij Dück, and his wife Lilia because the two were well-suited to resume the evangelistic work that ended with Mosalkow's retirement in 1979. For more than a decade beginning in 1992, the Dücks not only served as effective ministers of the Tübingen congregation, but led a half dozen evangelistic, church-planting, and social service missions throughout eastern Europe, especially in the Czech Republic, Poland, Belarus, and their native Lithuania. In 2010, EES merged with TCM International Institute (described below).[67]

Austria and Switzerland

By the mid-1950s, the work of North American Churches of Christ in Germany began to expand into Austria. After working for five years in Münich, Bob (1920-1995) and Ruth (b. 1921) Hare relocated to Vienna in 1956, where several other missionary families soon joined them. One hundred fifty miles to the west, a young German evangelist Rudolph Rischer (b. 1937) and his wife Cristel (1938-2000) established the work in Salzburg in 1958. A native of Czechoslovakia, Rischer and his family fled to Münich shortly after World War II. In 1950, Bob Hare baptized him and he joined the *Gemeinde Christi* there. After studying briefly at David Lipscomb College, he returned to Germany as an evangelist, and by the mid-1960s he and Cristel were serving the congregations in Salzburg and Branau. Within a decade, both of Rischer's congregations were self-supporting and were sponsoring a Christian service camp. Additionally, Rischer's preaching could be heard on radio broadcasts from Luxembourg during the 1960s and 1970s. In 1983 the Rischers moved to Augsburg where they served one of the congregations there.[68] As a result of these efforts, six congregations had been established in Austria by 1970, including in Vienna and Graz.

In addition to the Eastern European Mission sponsored by U.S. Churches of Christ, Gene Dulin (1925-2007) and his wife Lenora established TCM International in Vienna as a mission of North American Christian Churches/Churches of Christ. Founded in 1957, initially TCM (Toronto Christian Mission) was an evangelistic and church planting mission in Toronto, Canada, where the Dulins had gone as missionaries. In 1963, they met John Huk, a Russian who ministered in an independent evangelical church made up of eastern European immigrants in Toronto. Together they made a tour of Russia and Eastern Europe, and developed a new mission for TCM. Changing the organization's name to Taking Christ to Millions, the Dulins relocated the mission to Vienna in 1971. From Vienna, missionaries crossed into Eastern Europe to distribute Bibles, conduct evangelistic campaigns, and provide food and clothing to impoverished Christian communities.[69]

After the fall of communism and the retirement of the Dulins in 1991, TCM again revised its mission and changed its name. Training Christians for Ministry focused primarily on educating pastors who served in congregations throughout Eastern Europe. Beginning in the early 1980s, TCM conducted "summer seminaries": two-week programs that by the 1990s had matured into a comprehensive theological curriculum through TCM International Institute, affiliated with the University of Vancouver. Under the leadership of Tony Twist, at the beginning of the twenty-first century the Institute educated almost eight hundred students annually, and leading academics and pastors of the North American Christian Churches/ Churches of Christ regularly taught in the Institute. In 2008 TCM International Institute was accredited and operated a dozen satellite campuses in eleven nations in Central and Eastern Europe.[70]

U.S. Churches of Christ also launched a Vienna-based educational institution called European Christian College that offered a traditional liberal arts curriculum with a special emphasis on global awareness. Otis Gatewood was the school's founder and served as its first president from 1980-1988. Under the leadership of Wil Godheer, satellite campuses were established across the globe and the name of the school was changed to International University. At the beginning of the twenty-first century, the school's curriculum focused on programs in business administration and international diplomacy, both of which enrolled students from around the world. Though the school had not lost the distinctly Christian focus of its curriculum, its mission statement suggested a broader focus of "Preparing students from around the world to serve in the world."[71]

A handful of congregations of *Gemeinde Christi* scattered throughout Switzerland trace their history to the collaborative work of both U.S. and German missionaries from Churches of Christ. In the early 1950s, Heinrich Blum relocated to Zürich from Germany, where he had been a leader in Churches of Christ for several years. In 1955, John and Joanne McKinney joined Blum, who was hosting Bible studies in his home. In 1960, the Swiss churches opened a Christian camp outside of Thun, and for more than three decades young people from Churches of Christ in Germany, Switzerland, Italy, and the United States gathered in two-week sessions of worship, learning, fellowship, and service. With the assistance of missionaries from both Germany and the United States, by the late 1960s, the work had expanded into six other Swiss cities, including Basel, Bern, and Schaffhausen.[72]

Southeastern Europe and the Balkans

Throughout the late nineteenth and early twentieth centuries, southeastern Europe was in a continuous state of political and social upheaval. Fierce nationalisms along ethnic and linguistic lines inspired regular revolts against the two major powers in the region: the Ottoman Empire and the Austro-Hungarian Empire. Additionally, these ethnic groups often clashed with one another. Religion also played a major role in this upheaval because for centuries the people of the region had been more or less evenly divided between Orthodoxy, Roman Catholicism, and Islam, with small communities of Jews also struggling to maintain existence. In this context, faith traditions had become an important element of national identities. Before World War I, the nations of Serbia and Monetenegro (1878), Romania (1881), Bulgaria (1908), and Albania (1912) had come into being.

Out of this political and social upheaval, a flood of immigrants from southeastern Europe entered the United States between the 1880s and 1910s. Among those immigrants was John Kovacs, a Presbyterian minister. He was serving a small Hungarian community outside of Baton Rouge, Louisiana, when he came across a copy of the *Christian Standard* sometime around 1905. Convinced by its call to restore New Testament Christianity, Kovacs left his congregation in 1909, presumably to begin work as an itinerant evangelist among Eastern European immigrants in the Baton Rouge area. He published a small tract in Hungarian titled *Herald of the True Gospel*

in order to acquaint his "fellow-countrymen with the basal principles of the Restoration."[73] Apparently, this tract circulated not only among Hungarian immigrant communities in the United States, but also found its way back to southeastern Europe.

Another Hungarian immigrant to the United States was Basil Keusseff. Born in the village of Gradetz, Bulgaria, he received an education in England before going back to his homeland to begin mission work for the American Baptist Missionary Union. In the early 1890s, he served as pastor of the Baptist churches at Lom and Sofia, though opposition from local Orthodox priests was strong. He immigrated to the United States around the turn of the century, settling in Pittsburgh. Shortly thereafter, he met Robert Bamber, then pastor of the Turtle Creek Christian Church, and soon began missionary work for the Stone-Campbell Movement among the city's immigrant communities. In 1909, the City Missionary Society in Chicago called Keusseff to lead the Bulgarian Christian Society they had established two years before. Along with other Bulgarian immigrants—most notably Paul Mishkoff and Zaprian Vidoloff—Keusseff administered a shelter for immigrants that provided food and clothing, regular preaching, and help in finding jobs.

This work among immigrant communities in the United States was a critical factor in establishing the Stone-Campbell Movement in southeastern Europe. In 1909, Peter Poppoff, then pastor of a church at Lom, Bulgaria, initiated correspondence with Basil Keusseff. Poppoff described a growing "restoration" movement in and around Lom and called for help from U. S. churches: "We beg most earnestly the American brethren to make some sacrifices, take up this work and organize it thoroughly."[74] The progress of the movement in Bulgaria was reported on the pages of the *Christian Standard* up to the time of World War I. In 1910, Poppoff began publishing a Bulgarian-language newspaper titled in English *The Christian Banner.* Further, he reported that many Orthodox priests were secretly working for the restoration of apostolic Christianity.[75] Following the First Balkan War (1912-1913), leaders in Bulgaria and the United States proposed building an orphanage and a school where children could "receive a true Christian education."[76]

In 1914, however, government officials imprisoned Poppoff on the charge of having "designated himself as a priest of the Evangelical Christian Church" and issuing illegal certificates of marriage. Prior to approval of the first Bulgarian constitution in 1879, issuing certificates of marriage was the sole responsibility of the Bulgarian Orthodox Church, though the issue was hotly contested. In the end, Poppoff proved that he had the right to do so under Articles 40 and 42 of the nation's constitution.[77] The outbreak of World War I and the Great Depression, however, hindered further expansion of the Stone-Campbell Movement in southeastern Europe at the time.

Stone-Campbell mission work in southeastern Europe resumed in the late 1930s with the work of direct-support missionary Frank Vass (1880-1957). Vass immigrated from Hungary to the United States in 1910, and in 1919 affiliated with Stone-Campbell Movement churches in Los Angeles. After serving as a lay leader for fifteen years, he was ordained by the Figueroa Boulevard Christian Church in 1934.[78] Efforts to support Vass soon were organized into the Central Europe Christian Mission. About the same time, Paul Mishkoff began the Bulgarian Gospel Mission with some support from Stone-Campbell congregations in both the United States and Australia. He claimed to have approximately three hundred followers in Sofia, though they were under severe persecution.[79]

The work in Bulgaria begun by Peter Poppoff and his family was disrupted by persecution by Orthodox church leaders, World War I, and the Great Depression. (*Christian Standard,* June 25, 1910)

With the support of several Los Angeles congregations, Vass returned to central and southeastern Europe in 1938 to do evangelistic and church-planting work in Romania, Czechoslovakia, Yugoslavia, and Austria. Formerly a Baptist, he typically worked with existing congregations; the entire Baptist congregation in Irsa

City, Hungary, became a part of the Stone-Campbell Movement as a result of Vass's preaching in 1939.[80] Nevertheless, like his predecessors in southeastern Europe, Vass experienced significant opposition from government officials and the clergy of the Orthodox and Roman Catholic churches. While working in the Balkan states in 1938, he was imprisoned four times because of his preaching against the state churches. After two years Vass had influenced eighty-five congregations in central Europe to become part of the Stone-Campbell Movement.[81] The *Christian Standard* credited him with winning "over a thousand converts in the Balkan states and…developing an unknown number of churches of the New Testament order."[82]

The outbreak of World War II forced Vass to return to the United States, where he worked with immigrants from southeastern Europe living in Cleveland and Pittsburgh. He wrote a steady stream of sermons, tracts, Bible study lessons, and other Christian literature in Slavic languages for the native leadership he had left behind.[83] After the war, Vass and other direct-support missionaries were eager to re-enter southeastern Europe, though the spread of communism throughout the region largely prevented them from doing so.[84]

By the early 1960s, North American Churches of Christ were attempting limited mission work in southeastern Europe and the Balkans, using their mission in Vienna, Austria, as a base of operation. Bob Hare made periodic trips behind the "iron curtain" and wrote of the great possibilities for mission work in the region.[85] Radio stations in Western Europe broadcasted Slavic-language religious programs that offered listeners free Bible correspondence courses, and European Christian College in Vienna provided leadership training beginning in 1978. Perhaps the most significant initiative was the Eastern European Mission and Bible Foundation (EEM). Established in 1961 by John Sudbury (1925-2010) and supported by North American Churches of Christ, EEM printed and distributed Bibles, devotional works, and other Christian literature to people living in the nations of Eastern Europe, then under Soviet control. Initially operating out of Dallas, Texas, EEM relocated to Vienna in 1974. After the fall of communism in Eastern Europe in the early 1990s, EEM began conducting evangelistic trips, supporting congregations, conducting Christian service camps, and doing other more direct forms of mission work. EEM relied on a very large network of Churches of Christ across the globe, translators and agents in Eastern Europe, and its Vienna staff to support and carry on the work. It its first fifty years of work,

EEM was credited with translating the Bible into twenty dialects and distributing approximately eight million copies throughout Eastern Europe.[86]

In 1969, David Gatewood (1942-2000) and Bud Pickle—both members of U.S. Churches of Christ—enrolled as exchange students at the University of Zagreb in Croatia. In 1971, they influenced one of their professors, Mladen Jovanovic, and his wife Dragica to be baptized. With this couple, Gatewood and Pickle began subtle evangelistic work in Zagreb and the surrounding region. Slowly an underground church meeting in homes began to develop, and experienced missionaries like Otis Gatewood (David's father) and Bob Hare visited regularly from Germany and Austria to support their work. As communist control in Croatia weakened, the government granted legal recognition to the Church of Christ in Croatia in 1985, and the congregation began meeting openly in a three-bedroom apartment in Zagreb.

A total of fourteen Churches of Christ were established in Croatia after legalization. One of the strongest was the Kuslanova congregation in Zagreb. In addition to hosting an evangelistic radio broadcast, the church housed the *Biblijski Institut* (Biblical Institute) accredited by the Ministry of Education of Croatia. In 2007 the Institute partnered with the Evangelical Theological Seminary in Osijek and began publishing *Kairos: Evangelical Journal of Theology* in both English and Croatian.[87]

Many in North American Churches of Christ interpreted the collapse of communism, symbolized by the tearing down of the Berlin Wall in December 1989, as a providential opportunity. Leaders announced that April 29, 1990, would be the first "World Day of Prayer and Giving for Eastern Europe," and they set a goal of raising fifteen million dollars to support at least forty-eight existing missionaries and other ministries in the region. Congregations held World Days of Prayer and Giving regularly for the next several years. Because of funds raised in this effort, Eastern European Mission, for example, was able to expand its work to include church planting, conversational English courses, Slavic-language material for the World Bible School, and Bible distribution. This fund-raising momentum continued into the twenty-first century, as EEM held periodic "Million Dollar Sundays," challenging North American Churches of Christ to raise one million dollars in a single special offering.[88]

Similarly, the Yugoslav War, which raged in the Balkans from 1991 to 1995, inspired North American Churches of Christ to begin a wide variety of humanitarian relief efforts in the war-torn region. For example, in Albania, a missionary team led by Dick Ady entered the capital Tirana in 1992, offering food, medical services, and supplies.[89] "Operation Albania" sent several long-term missionary families who began educational work and established small congregations in Tirana, Vlore, Berati, Korce, Reps, and Elbasan.[90] North American Churches of Christ began similar efforts in Slovenia, Croatia, Bosnia and Herzegovina, Yugoslavia, Macedonia, and Bulgaria.

Italy

While stationed in Italy between 1943 and 1945, Guy Mayfield (1909-1984), a member of North American Christian Churches/Churches of Christ then serving as a U.S. air force chaplain, was permitted to preach in Baptist and Waldensian congregations in Manduria, Latiano, and Oria. He and Giuseppe Settembrini (1896-1977), a representative of the British Bible Society, also began evangelistic work in the province of Brindisi. Mayfield became convinced that the majority of Italians were Roman Catholic in name only and had been taught a bias against Protestants by their priests. He also believed that the few Protestants he encountered could easily be led out of what he viewed as their denominationalism. In 1945, he urged Christian Churches in the United States to begin a direct-support mission to Italy.[91]

Two years later, Mayfield returned to Italy with his wife, Thelma (1911-2008), as leaders of the newly formed Mediterranean Christian Mission. Four other missionaries joined them: Betheen Grubaugh, Evelyn Jones, and Charles and Mary Frances Phipps. Establishing a headquarters in Bari, a port city on the Adriatic Sea, the missionaries returned to the congregations in which Guy Mayfield had preached several years before, and by 1948 had convinced them to unite with the mission as Christian Churches. That same year the mission ordained Settembrini.[92]

Believing that Rome would be a better site for the mission headquarters, the Mayfields relocated there in 1950, just as the Phipps were returning to the United States because of Mary's health. Once settled in Rome, the Mayfields began a Bible study in their home and, with the help of Italian evangelist Luigi Lisi, also began a preaching ministry. Evelyn Jones and Betheen Grubaugh established a school in which Italian young people could learn English.[93]

After Mayfield was transferred to Sheppard Air Force Base in Wichita Falls, Texas, in 1952, two new missionary couples arrived in 1953 to assume leadership of the Mediterranean Christian Mission. Malcolm (1923-1985) and Wilma Coffey settled in Bari, and Charles (1923-1988) and Jessie Lee (1924-2010) Troyer settled in Lecce, another coastal city on the Adriatic Sea, eighty-five miles to the south. Eventually the Troyers' organized their work separately as the Lecce Christian Mission, though the couples continued to cooperate closely with one another. Laboring for more than forty years as direct-support missionaries, these couples established and helped support at least twelve congregations throughout Brindisi and the surrounding provinces. [94]

At the beginning of the twenty-first century, North American Christian Churches/Churches of Christ supported two missionary couples whose work grew out of the Mediterranean and Lecce Christian Missions: Harold and Enid Fowler, who had been in Matelica since 1964, and James and Karen Wolsieffer, who had been in Oria since 1971. They continued evangelistic work and church planting, and supported the ministries of the Italian pastors. Additionally, they supported Pino and Evelina Neglia of the congregation at Lecce. Working with the Fowlers, Pino Neglia translated numerous Bible commentaries into Italian and published religious journals. By the beginning of the twenty-first century, twenty congregations existed with an estimated total membership of around five hundred. [95]

North American Christian Churches/Churches of Christ also supported missionaries through Team Expansion. Centered primarily in Ancona and Verona, these younger missionaries employed the "cell church model" of evangelism. They gathered small groups of inquirers in their homes for worship, prayer, and Bible study; worked on developing intimate personal relationships; and began immediately to reach out in service and evangelism. At the beginning of the twenty-first century, no church had yet been organized as a result of their pioneering work. [96]

Italy had been a focus of extensive planning for evangelism by North American Churches of Christ during World War II. In 1947, former army chaplain Cline Paden (1919-2007) led a team to Italy to determine strategies for beginning work there. A number of Texas congregations sponsored the trip, but the Crescent Hill Church of Christ in Brownfield, Texas, quickly became the primary promoter of post-war missions in Italy. Despite strong support, the work began slowly because of difficulties securing permission from the Italian government, which opposed the work. [97]

Two years later, Paden and eleven other missionaries from U.S. Churches of Christ arrived in Naples. They soon acquired property in the town of Frascati near Rome as a base of operations and established an orphanage for boys that they named Villa Speranza (House of Hope). They also began distributing relief supplies received from U.S. Churches of Christ to local Italians still suffering the aftermath of World War II. By the end of 1949, they had accepted twenty-two boys into the orphanage, baptized two hundred sixty former Roman Catholics, and distributed over one hundred thousand dollars worth of food and clothing. [98]

Authorities in the Italian government and leaders of the Roman Catholic Church—especially members of the arch-conservative group *Azione Cattolica* (Catholic Action)—viewed the success of these missionaries with alarm. They targeted the missionaries for harassment, forced the closure of their churches and other institutions, and prohibited their educational activities during the 1950s. Sometimes the opposition turned violent. Local priests stirred parishioners to attack the evangelists' vehicles as they rode through Castelgandolfo, cut the brake line on Paden's brother's car, and even plant a bomb under Paden's jeep. [99] When the Italian government shut down the orphanage and tried to deport the evangelists, a group of ministers from U.S. Churches of Christ flew to Washington to pressure the federal government to intervene. Liberal political leaders and other Protestant leaders in Italy rallied around the missionaries, as did anti-Catholic Protestant leaders in the United States. With pressure from the U.S. State Department, the Italian government allowed the orphanage to reopen with the provision that it accept no other children, and reluctantly extended Paden's visa. [100]

At least one conflict between the missionaries from Churches of Christ and the Italian government received international attention. In 1954, the police in Rome removed a sign that simply read *Chiesa di Cristo* (Church of Christ) from the church building. As often as Paden replaced the sign, the police returned to remove it. The conflict eventually reached the Italian Supreme Court. At issue was the interpretation and application of Articles 3 and 20 of the Italian Constitution of 1948, which allegedly guaranteed a level of religious freedom in Italy similar to that in the United States. [101] After three years of legal battles, the Court finally ruled in favor of the Churches of Christ. *Time* magazine, however, accused Paden of failing to comply with Italian law, and support for him began to falter. [102] The Italian government forced Paden to leave Italy in October 1957 and he never returned, though his brothers Harold and Gerald continued work in Italy for many years.

Despite this opposition, missionaries continued to arrive, an Italian leadership developed, and the churches grew. During the 1960s, there were between twenty-five and thirty missionaries from North American Churches of Christ working in Italy. They led evangelistic meetings, published literature, helped plant churches, and provided social services and medical care. Of particular importance were the mission's educational institutions. First opened in 1959, *La Scuola Biblica di Firenze* (Florence Bible School) educated Italian evangelists for leadership in the churches. Churches of Christ opened a similar school in Milan two years later in cooperation with the *Facoltà Teologica di Milano* (Theological Faculty of Milan). The graduates of these Bible schools eventually became the most prominent leaders of the Churches of Christ in Italy, including Salvatore Puliga (1914-1986), Otello Pandolfini (1923-1999), Luca Bonanno Leo (1924-1991), and Giulio Pistolesi (1919-1991). Together the missionaries and Italian evangelists served in more than fifty churches that had a combined membership of about 1,500 people.[103]

As Italian leaders began to emerge, they also became the targets of government persecution and censure. In 1962, Pandolfini was accused of offending the state church by distributing a polemical, anti-Catholic tract entitled "Priestism." The tract referred to the Roman Catholic priesthood as an "insatiable polyp" that daily "plunges its tentacles into the live flesh of the country."[104] Though Pandolfini was acquitted, he accumulated significant legal costs for his defense. In the mid-1960s, another evangelist from Civitavecchia, Gian Luigi Giudici, had been instrumental in convincing a number of Roman Catholics to become members of Churches of Christ, including a young, well-educated priest. Government authorities indicted Giudici on charges of publicly criticizing the Roman Catholic Church. By 1967, he had exhausted his appeals, and the Supreme Court found him guilty. U. S. Churches of Christ rallied to pay the fifteen thousand dollar fine and all of his legal costs so that he could avoid the six-year prison sentence.[105]

By the early 1970s, most of the missionaries from North American Churches of Christ had left Italy, largely because of rising costs, ongoing opposition from the Italian government and the Roman Catholic Church, and a shortage of personnel. Leadership of the churches fell mainly to a handful of Italian ministers, with occasional support of missionaries sponsored by short-term mission programs like Project Italy and Avanti Italia. Leaders of the Italian Churches of Christ assembled annually in national and regional "lectureships" for worship, study, and fellowship; maintained the Bible Schools in Florence and Milan in partnership with Harding University in the United States; published the monthly magazines *La Buona Notizia* (*The Good News*) and *Le Chiese Informa* (*The Churches Speak*); conducted radio ministries in Ferarra and Forlí; and engaged in medical and humanitarian mission work in Africa and Eastern Europe, especially in the Ivory Coast, Romania, and Albania. Because of increasing immigration from Africa—mainly Christians from Nigeria and Ghana—Churches of Christ in Italy experienced significant growth.[106] At the beginning of the twenty-first century the Churches of Christ in Italy had a combined membership of approximately two thousand, with sixty-four congregations concentrated in Sicily, Lazio, Puglia, Tuscany, and Emilia Romagna.

The Netherlands and Belgium

The presence of the Stone-Campbell Movement in the Low Countries was almost exclusively the result of work by missionaries from U.S. Churches of Christ that began in the late 1940s. In 1942, a Dutch immigrant to the United States named Jacob Vandervis attended a debate between evangelist Otis Gatewood and Mormon elder Kenneth Farnsworth in Salt Lake City. Vandervis was so convinced by Gatewood's argument that he left the Church of Jesus Christ of Latter-day Saints and joined the Churches of Christ. In 1946 he returned to the Netherlands and began evangelistic work, establishing congregations in both Haarlem and Amsterdam. More than sixty missionaries from U.S. Churches of Christ worked in the Netherlands during the last decades of the twentieth century, establishing congregations in Eindhoven, Maastricht, Utrecht, The Hague, and Groningen.[107]

Similarly, U.S. Churches of Christ began work in the French-speaking regions of Belgium in 1948, when Samuel F. Timmerman (1918-2009) and his wife Maxine (1918-2012) settled in Pepinster in the Province of Liège.[108] In the first decade, their evangelistic work led to the formation of three congregations: Pepinster, Liège, and Verviers. Two other missionary couples came to Belgium in the early 1950s and inaugurated the work in Brussels. Hilton (1925-2003) and Wanda (b. 1927) Terry and Donald Earwood and his wife established two congregations in the capital city. The Timmermans worked in Liege until 1970, when leadership of the congregation passed to Jean-Marie Frerot.[109] The short-lived School of the Bible in Verviers closed in 1970, but Bible correspondence courses, which had played a significant role in the mission's work from the beginning, continued as an evangelistic tool.

In the Flemish-speaking regions of Belgium in the north, Roy and Rita Davison began work in Oostende and Roeselare in 1961 with the cooperation of their colleagues in the Netherlands. Later, congregations were established in Brugge, Turnhout, Merksem, and Leuven.[110] At the beginning of the twenty-first century there were twenty small congregations in cities including Brussels, Amsterdam, Rotterdam, and Utrecht with a combined membership of about three hundred.

France

While studying at Abilene Christian University in 1949, Maurice Hall and Melvin Anderson committed themselves to becoming the first missionaries from North American Churches of Christ to France. By the end of that year, both of the young missionaries and their families had arrived in Paris with enough funds to sustain their work for three years. Because they had only a basic working knowledge of French and virtually no acquaintance with the culture, they initially evangelized among English-speaking military personnel who remained on occupation duty. "Pockets of military servicemen," Hall recalled many years later, "were a daily encouragement to the newly-arrived missionaries."[111]

A steady stream of missionaries from North American Churches of Christ followed, and by 1960 there were twenty-one workers and their families scattered in cities throughout the nation, including Orleans, Lyon, Nice, and Marseille.[112] One of these families was that of Don Daugherty (1929-1986), who first came to Orleans in 1953. He quickly mastered the French language and eventually married a French woman, Collette le Cardinal. His thirty years of service in France included editing and publishing *Vie et Verite* (*Life and Truth*) from 1955 to 1969, a magazine that served French-speaking Churches of Christ across the globe. Additionally he translated and wrote hundreds of hymns, eventually assembling them into a hymnal. Though Daugherty died in 1986, Collette remained active in the work.

Because the membership in several of the French congregations was composed mainly of U.S. military personnel who moved frequently, they often closed shortly after opening. Moreover, a French leadership for these churches was very slow in developing. Throughout the 1960s and 1970s, several city-wide "campaigns" resulted in the addition of more French citizens to the congregations. The churches launched a French-language radio program in 1963, broadcast throughout northern Africa, France, and Belgium on Transworld

Radio in Monte Carlo, but it ceased after only a few years because of insufficient financial support.

Critics accused the French mission of a lack of productivity, despite protests from its leaders.[113] One significant outcome of the French mission, however, was the awareness that it raised among North American Churches of Christ of the importance of the French language for mission. Leaders began to speak of *le monde francophone* (the French-speaking world) to highlight the fact that the French language was crucial for work in parts of Canada, the Caribbean, Polynesia, and Africa.[114] At the beginning of the twenty-first century there were nine Èglise du Christ congregations in France with a combined membership of around four hundred.

Spain and Portugal

After overthrowing the democratic government in Spain and abolishing its parliament, Francisco Franco ruled the nation as a military dictator between 1936 and 1975. Seeking to foster a nationalist spirit in a country torn apart by civil war, he intentionally isolated Spain from the international community, violently suppressed political opposition, and attempted to purge foreign influence from Spanish culture. In 1953, Franco struck a concordat with the Vatican that greatly strengthened the relationship between the Catholic Church and the Spanish state. Roman Catholicism became the only legal religion in Spain; other religious bodies were not permitted to own property, publish written materials, or meet openly. The government was granted almost complete authority in the appointment of personnel in the Spanish church. Civil laws were rewritten to conform to Roman Catholic social teachings, most notably making divorce and the sale of contraceptives illegal. Perceived to be a pernicious influence, Spain's small Protestant minority experienced severe persecution under Franco's regime.[115]

Even under these adverse circumstances, the Stone-Campbell Movement established a modest but lasting presence in Spain. In 1951, Juan Antonio Monroy (b. 1929), an atheist and journalist, was converted to evangelical Christianity in Tangier, Morocco, and quickly became a zealous preacher. Initially working primarily among Plymouth Brethren churches in both Morocco and Spain, he gained a reputation as a defender of religious liberty with his 1958 book *Defensa de los Protestantes Espanoles* (*A Defense of the Spanish Protestants*), which detailed the oppressive treatment of non-Catholics by the Spanish government. Against much opposition from the Spanish government, he published and distributed a religious magazine, *Luz y Verdad* (*Light and Truth*) and conducted a weekly radio show, *La Estrella Matutina* (*The Morning Star*).[116]

In 1964, Monroy came to the United States on a speaking tour. While he was in New York City, the Spanish Consulate asked him to come to the Spanish pavilion at the New York World's Fair to sign copies of one of his popular books, *La Biblia en El Quijote* (*The Bible in Don Quixote*). There he met representatives from Highland Church of Christ in Abilene, Texas. For more than a decade, that congregation had sponsored the "Herald of Truth" radio and television ministry, then broadcast across more than two hundred radio and fifty television stations in the English-speaking world. Hoping to expand the outreach of this ministry, the congregation began supporting Monroy in 1965, and he quickly began Spanish-language radio broadcasts and established a Church of Christ in Madrid. Monroy soon discovered at least seven congregations in Spain and northern Morocco "worshipping very close to the New Testament pattern." Along with the Highland church, other Texas congregations began supporting the evangelists serving these churches and vested Monroy and the *Iglesia de Cristo* in Madrid with significant responsibility for training them and overseeing their work.[117] By 1974, the Churches of Christ in North America were supporting evangelists in eleven cities in Spain, distributing thousands of Bibles annually, and conducting Bible correspondence courses throughout the Spanish-speaking world.[118]

In Portugal, the political situation was nearly identical to that of Spain during the mid-twentieth century. António de Oliveira Salazar established an authoritarian, right-wing government that ruled the nation from 1933 to 1974. The Salazar regime struck a concordat with the Vatican in 1940 similar to the one with Spain thirteen years later.

In 1969, Arlie and Alma Smith left more than a decade of work sponsored by U.S. Churches of Christ in Brazil to relocate to Lisbon. There they established a small *Igreja de Cristo* and began a program to train preachers.[119] The Smiths returned to Brazil after two years, and for the next eight years, several missionaries attempted to carry on the work. Several groups of students from the United States also came to help with aggressive city-wide evangelistic campaigns.[120] Nevertheless, in 1977, the Lisbon church disbanded. In Porto, a coastal city one hundred seventy miles north of Lisbon, a Church of Christ developed as a direct result of Monroy's "Herald of Truth" radio program in 1973. Two years later the Highland Church of Christ in Abilene, Texas, sent Lou Seckler, a Brazilian who was among the

earliest converts of the Churches of Christ in São Paulo, Brazil, to assume leadership of the work in Porto. Just over a year later, Seckler left Portugal to begin mission work in Central America through his own organization, Harvest Ministries.[121] Despite lack of missionary support, the small congregation in Porto continued under the leadership of Adelino L. Da Silva.[122]

Juan Antonio Monroy (left) was a leader in the effort to secure religious liberty for Evangelicals in Spain. He influenced Spanish-speaking Churches of Christ worldwide through his extensive evangelism and publications. Shown here with leaders of Churches of Christ in Cuba. (Courtesy Center for Restoration Studies, Abilene Christian University)

After the fall of the Franco regime in 1975, Spain began making the transition to a modern democracy. Spain's 1978 constitution provided for free elections, protected fundamental human rights, disestablished the Roman Catholic Church, and guaranteed religious liberty. Spanish Protestants enjoyed unprecedented freedoms and the Stone-Campbell Movement flourished. In the 1980s and 1990s, Juan Monroy greatly expanded his publication efforts, and began three additional religious magazines. The most important of these was *Restauración*, a publication designed to advance the cause of restoring New Testament Christianity. He also continued his *"Heraldo de la Verdad"* ("Herald of Truth") broadcast on a weekly basis across nearly a hundred Spanish-speaking radio stations around the world, some available on the Internet. Largely as a result of his evangelistic work, the number of Churches of Christ in Spain had grown by the beginning of the twenty-first century to almost thirty with a combined membership of approximately two thousand five hundred. This made the Stone-Campbell Movement one of the fastest growing religious bodies in the nation. Monroy and other leaders of the Spanish congregations were also instrumental in establishing mission work in other Spanish-speaking nations, especially in Cuba, Mexico, and Colombia.[123]

In 1986, the year Spain joined the European Union, a group of Protestants formed the Federación de Entidades Religiosas Evangélicas de España (the Federation of Evangelical Religious Entities of Spain) as an umbrella organization to represent the interests of its member churches with the Spanish government. In the 1990s, Monroy served as the president of the Federación. At least one of the congregations in Madrid opposed his serving because of perceived latitudinarianism in doctrine that such a position required, causing a controversy to erupt among Churches of Christ. Yet, Monroy's leadership among Spanish Protestants was widely recognized. In 1997, he was granted an audience before the Spanish King Juan Carlos I, where he advocated increased religious freedom and human rights.[124]

In 1980, experienced missionaries William and Virginia Loft began work in Murcia on behalf of the North American Christian Churches/Churches of Christ. A handful of missionaries joined them in the 1980s, helping the Lofts establish a congregation and begin evangelistic work in nearby Alcantarilla. Bill Loft died of yellow fever in 1989, and his wife subsequently returned to the United States. At the beginning of the twenty-first century, Erick and Sira Gutierrez led the small congregation in Murcia, with significant, ongoing support from Bill Loft Mission, Inc.[125]

Ecumenical Ministries

In September 1945—just four months after the end of World War II in Europe—the UCMS sent leading Disciples ecumenist George W. Buckner (1893-1981) on a survey tour to determine what might be done to foster "the rehabilitation and strengthening of the continental churches." Buckner was the director of the Association for the Promotion of Christian Unity (later renamed the Council on Christian Unity) and the editor of *World Call.* He also served on the Provisional Committee of the World Council of Churches (WCC) while it was in the process of forming (1944-1948). For more than three months, he witnessed firsthand the destruction and human misery caused by the war, and called for U.S. Disciples to provide food, clothing, medical supplies, and other goods.[126] Beginning immediately upon his return,

Buckner published a number of articles in *World Call* written by Robert Root, then a correspondent of the WCC working in Geneva, to dramatize the dire needs of war-weary Europeans.[127]

Disciples rallied to this cause. The International Convention's Committee on Relief Appeals coordinated aggressive efforts to raise money through the Week of Compassion offering and through the Crusade for a Christian World. Beyond raising money, Disciples also collected "material aid"—mostly food, clothing, and medical supplies—coordinated through the Department of Social Welfare of the UCMS. By mid-1948, Disciples had raised $500,000 and shipped five tons of material aid.[128] While the majority of funds raised went to Western Europe, some funds and most of the material aid went to China, Japan, and Eastern Europe. Along with most other Protestant denominations in the United States, Disciples worked through Church World Service, an interdenominational agency formed in 1946 to be the ecumenical "relief and service arm" of U. S. churches.[129] Disciples also participated in the interdenominational relief efforts of the Christian Rural Overseas Program (C.R.O.P.), Cooperative for American Remittances to Europe (C.A.R.E.), and "Heifers for Relief."[130] At the beginning of the twenty-first century, these agencies continued to be important partners with the Christian Church (Disciples of Christ) in its ministries of humanitarian relief.

In 1948, the U.S. government committed itself to the four-year European Recovery Program—popularly known as the Marshall Plan—and provided thirteen billion dollars in aid, mostly to Great Britain, France, Germany, Italy, and the Netherlands. This figure roughly matched the amount of aid already provided to European nations by U.S. churches, humanitarian organizations, and other agencies of the private sector.[131] Because of their government's enormous commitment to rebuilding Western Europe, many U.S. churches—including the Disciples—focused their relief assistance in other areas, including Eastern Europe.

One example was Greece. Between 1941 and 1944, three of the Axis Powers—Germany, Italy, and Bulgaria—occupied almost the whole nation. Especially in the northern provinces, the occupiers had retaliated against all resistance with brutal severity: destroying crops, burning down whole villages, and executing resistance leaders (including hundreds of clergy). After liberation, Greece plunged into civil war from 1946 to 1949, further escalating the humanitarian crisis.[132] Even before the end of the Greek Civil War, the Department of Reconstruction and Inter-church Aid of the WCC began providing assistance in cooperation with the Greek Orthodox Church, one of its member churches.[133]

As early as 1949, U.S. Disciples participated in sending aid to Greece through the Week of Compassion offering. Two years later the UCMS cooperated with the WCC to begin a pilot program in Ioannina, the largest city of Epirus in northwestern Greece. A team of a dozen young men and women with various skills volunteered for work in agricultural and community development programs. Working in cooperation with the bishop of the Greek Orthodox Church in Ioannina, the "Greek Team" focused on service, stating that they had "not come to preach but to help their fellow men develop a better life in the spirit of partnership." One of their first tasks was to unclog an "ancient Turkish drainage tunnel" to improve the irrigation of more than two hundred acres of prime farmland outside the city. Later team members developed the land into an "experimental farm" that taught local people improved agricultural skills. For more than a decade the Disciples, the WCC, and the Greek Orthodox Church cooperated in this innovative program, modeled after similar programs of the Mennonite Central Committee, the American Friends Service Committee, and Brethren Disaster Services.[134]

One of the most significant ways in which Disciples maintained a presence in Europe following World War II was their involvement in the WCC itself. George W. Buckner served on its Central Committee (1948-1961), represented the Disciples at two WCC assemblies, and served on the board of directors of the Ecumenical Institute in Bossey, Switzerland. This commitment to conciliar ecumenism through the WCC continued through Buckner's successors in the Council on Christian Unity—George Beazley, Paul Crow, and Robert Welsh—and through many other Disciples who were associated with the WCC and its work.[135]

By the early 1950s, the UCMS no longer supported "missionaries" to Europe. Instead, working with the Commission on Inter-Church Aid of the WCC, the UCMS committed to a program of sending "fraternal workers" to Europe for the purpose of "sharing the churches' spiritual and material resources, of deepening understanding and fellowship, and of witnessing and renewing our common faith."[136] Supported by funds from the annual Week of Compassion offering, these fraternal workers served on two- and three-year assignments on special projects overseas under the auspices of the WCC

and partner churches, especially in Europe. One of the earliest special projects of the fraternal worker program was the Paris-based *Comité Inter-Mouvements Auprès Des Évacués* (Interdenominational Committee for Assistance to Evacuees), commonly known as CIMADE. Begun in 1939 as a ministry of the French Reformed Church, this committee initially assisted refugees from Alsace-Lorraine during the German occupation and provided relief to those interned in Nazi concentration camps in France, including Jews. In 1945, Robert Tobias (1919-2010), who later became a leading Disciples ecumenist and theological educator, began working with CIMADE, and provided a model for the emerging fraternal worker program. Between 1951 and 1970, the UCMS continued to send a steady stream of fraternal workers to CIMADE, including William Nottingham (b. 1927) who served a four-year term as associate director. These workers assisted with the resettlement of refugees fleeing the former French colonies in Africa amidst revolutions and ongoing post-revolutionary civil wars. The Christian Church (Disciples of Christ) continued to send fraternal workers to CIMADE through the early 1990s.[137]

An ecumenical ministry, CIMADE included young people from all over Europe and the United States. Disciple Bill Nottingham (wearing glasses), confers with fellow CIMADE workers from France, Spain, and Switzerland in 1959. (*World Call*, May 1959)

The UCMS began sending fraternal workers to West Germany in 1951 through an ecumenical partnership with the *Evangelische Kirche der altpreußischen Union* (Evangelical Church of the Old-Prussian Union, or EKU). Before 1970, a dozen such workers were assigned to major urban centers—especially West Berlin—to a variety of church-related programs: schools, orphanages, homes for the elderly, and especially the *Sozialpfarramt*, a ministry that advocated the rights of industrial workers and the unemployed. Occasionally, these fraternal workers assumed responsibilities of leading parish-based youth ministries as well.[138]

Throughout the 1970s and into the 1980s, the Division of Overseas Ministries (DOM) supported fraternal workers on two- and three-year appointments at *Aktion Sühnezeichen Friedensdienste* (Action Reconciliation Service for Peace) in West Berlin. Founded in 1958, this organization worked in cooperation with the Evangelical Church of Germany to mobilize students internationally to pursue reconciliation and peace, and to fight against racism and discrimination. Disciples fraternal workers typically helped prepare students for work in English-speaking countries, facilitated inter-religious dialogue between Christian and Jewish young people, and helped coordinate relief efforts for Christians behind the "iron curtain."[139] After the Berlin Wall fell in 1989, DOM began supporting fraternal workers serving in parish churches in the former East Berlin. There the work focused primarily on alleviating German hostility to foreigners and resolving tensions between the German people of the formerly communist East and the capitalist West. This work continued at the beginning of the twenty-first century, led by Steven and Lisa Smith, twenty-year veterans of the German work and partners with the Common Global Ministries Board.[140]

From 1972 to 1976 Fred (1934-2005) and Marguerite Bronkema directed a documentation and study project called "The Future of the Missionary Enterprise," an initiative of the International Documentation of the Contemporary Church. Based in Rome and financed by the missionary boards of several Protestant denominations and the Roman Catholic Church, the project convened conferences all over the globe, bringing together church leaders from Asia, Africa, and Latin America to help shape the future of Christian missions. The Bronkemas also supervised the translation and publication of the proceedings from these conferences. This work resulted in a nineteen-volume publication that helped give voice to global leaders and shape the mission theology and strategies of Western churches in the late twentieth century.[141]

Looking to the Future

In the post-World War II era, much of Europe—both Eastern and Western—became a post-Christian society, most citizens having no active connection to any Christian tradition. Yet in the early years of the twenty-first century, Christian immigrants to Europe from Africa and Asia brought their experience of faith into the European churches, including the churches of the Stone-Campbell Movement.[142] Christians from several streams of this heritage continued to respond to needs and opportunities presented them in a complex and changing landscape.

18

The Quest for Unity

The early leaders of the Stone-Campbell Movement viewed division among Christians as sin. They believed that the issues dividing them were illegitimate and ungodly obstacles to evangelism. The wish "to die, be dissolved, and sink into union with the Body of Christ at large" of *The Last Will and Testament of the Springfield Presbytery* (1804) and the affirmation that "the Church of Christ upon earth is essentially, intentionally, and constitutionally one" of Thomas Campbell's *Declaration and Address* (1809) were central to the Stone-Campbell Movement's identity from its beginning.

Yet precisely how to end Christian division and embrace visible Christian unity became the issue. For Barton Stone the answer was to remove the creeds and structures that prevented Christian unity. Alexander Campbell agreed, but insisted that "the restoration of the ancient order of things" was also necessary. Because of this, he often found himself more at home contending with other Christians about the right ordering of the Church than taking the gospel to those who had not heard it. Nevertheless, it was the Stone-Campbell Movement's persistent concern for evangelism that often drove leaders back to its early emphasis on Christian unity. As the Movement itself suffered division, each of its developing streams appropriated and adapted in different ways their shared commitment to the unity of Christ's church.[1]

The Stone-Campbell Movement's founders addressed their appeals for unity to the whole church. Both *The Last Will and Testament* and the *Declaration and Address* were published as pamphlets intended to be distributed widely among all believers. When given the opportunity, Stone addressed his call to unity to Baptist associations, many of which gave up the name Baptist and united with Stone's Christians. The Campbells united with the Baptists in 1813 and would have continued to pursue reform and visible unity as Baptists if escalating tensions had not led to their exclusion from many Baptist associations.

The union of the Stone and Campbell churches in the 1830s was itself an example of the unity they sought. It was not a merger of denominational structures, but a coming together of Christians based on each group's recognition of the Christian faith and practice of the other and a shared commitment to visible unity based on the apostolic witness alone. Initiated by meetings of Christians and Reformers in Georgetown and Lexington, Kentucky, in December 1831, the union became a reality when hundreds of local congregations from the two groups united, urged on by the energetic work of "Reformer" John Smith and "Christian" John Rogers.

In 1835, Stone endorsed Congregationalist Lyman Beecher's call for a meeting of delegations from all Christian denominations to bring an end to sectarian strife.[2] Though nothing came of this initiative, Stone took up the call for a meeting of delegates from all denominations to discuss terms of Christian union. In 1841 he announced that the Christians in Kentucky had called "a convention of all denominations of Christians" for April 2, 1841. Alexander Campbell addressed the convention, but participation was disappointing.[3] Undeterred, Stone again called for a meeting of delegates of the churches in 1843, advising, "Let the churches select their wisest and best men" and let them "come together in the Spirit, and in the spirit of meekness confer on this all important subject."[4] To Stone's great disappointment such a convention of the churches did not materialize.

Shortly before his death in 1866, Alexander Campbell learned of a meeting in Richmond, Virginia, between church leaders of the Stone-Campbell Movement and Baptists to discuss union. "There was never any sufficient reason for a separation between us and the Baptists," he responded. "We ought to have remained one people, and to have labored together to restore the primitive faith and practice."[5] Despite Campbell's view that the separation of Reformers and the Baptists should never have happened, this reunion effort also failed to achieve visible unity.

The chief difficulty with the Stone-Campbell call to unity was that the churches of the Movement themselves inevitably came to function as a denomination—an identifiable body with unique historical and doctrinal characteristics. Their call to unity often appeared to other Christians as nothing more than a call to join their denomination. Meanwhile, issues of self-understanding among the Stone-Campbell churches became volatile and divisive in the late nineteenth century and again in the twentieth. Both the first North American division that took shape after the American Civil War, and the second, which became visible in the first half of the twentieth century, involved conflict over concepts of the nature of the church and legitimate ways of carrying out the church's mission.

Informal structures, such as journals and schools, and influential leaders had widespread influence in creating a shared identity among Stone-Campbell churches from the very beginning. Annual conventions, missionary societies, and other agencies eventually began to provide a basis for a more formal institutional identity as well. Though the group's radical congregational polity meant that both division and unity occurred fundamentally at the local congregational level, many Stone-Campbell churches around the world would eventually create structures through which to participate in cooperative ministry and in twentieth-century ecumenical efforts.

Internal Unity Efforts: Christian Churches (Disciples) and Churches of Christ

The bitter irony of division in a movement committed to visible Christian unity was not lost on members of the Stone-Campbell Movement. Unity overtures began even as the first North American division reached its final stages. In Tennessee, a state in which the division had been especially acute, the Tennessee State Missionary Convention created a Commission on Unity in 1914 under the leadership of state evangelist E. H. Koch. John B. Cowden, while editor of the *Tennessee Christian*, wrote tracts urging unity and issued a call for a conference for fraternal discussion.[6] Most leaders in Churches of Christ, however, insisted that the Christian Churches had left them by adding unauthorized practices like instrumental music in worship. They insisted that only if the Christian Churches returned to the positions they all had once occupied could they be one again.[7]

The efforts of the Commission on Unity in Tennessee ended with two debates in 1923 and 1926. The first took place in Nashville between N. B. Hardeman from Churches of Christ and Ira M. Boswell from Christian Churches, and was published by the Gospel Advocate Company the following year. The second was a written debate between H. Leo Boles representing Churches of Christ and Merrell D. Clubb representing Christian Churches, published in serial form in the *Gospel Advocate* and *Christian-Evangelist* in 1926. Both debates focused on instrumental music in worship, and both reflected hardening exclusive attitudes that prevented significant moves toward unity, though, at a personal level, fraternal relations often continued.

The next major unity effort began in 1933, when Ernest Beam, a judge in Long Beach, California, and minister of the Central Church of Christ, and William Jessup, then President of San Jose Bible College affiliated with Christian Churches, organized a three-day "Unity Rally" in Visalia, California, that brought one thousand members of the two groups together. The two also jointly wrote and published a booklet titled *We Are One in Christ: The Task Before Us*, in which they explained their view of how visible unity could be achieved.

The meetings continued in California for two decades despite attacks on Beam and Jessup by some in both groups.[8] Beam's congregation alternated between instrumental and a cappella services, and in 1950 he began publishing *The Christian Forum* to fight sectarian division. Beam's death in 1957, likely hastened by strong condemnation of his unity efforts by leaders in Churches of Christ, ended the meetings.[9]

In 1933, the same year the Jessup-Beam meetings began and the year before the creation of the Disciples Commission on Restudy, James DeForest Murch of the Christian Churches, then editor of the *Christian Standard*, launched what he called the "Christian Action Crusade." Motivated by the admonition of Romans 12:2 to "be transformed by the renewing of your mind," Murch saw the Crusade as an effort to promote Christian unity through spiritual renewal. Through Bible study materials, articles in the *Christian Standard*, and other venues, Murch reached out to Disciples, Churches of Christ, and Baptists, hoping that leaders of all these groups would see the importance of focusing on spiritual commonalities.[10] By 1936, however, the efforts of Christian Action had become focused on what historians would label the Murch-Witty meetings.

In 1936 Murch and Claude F. Witty, minister of the West Side Central Church of Christ in Detroit, began personal conversations that led to a series of five regional unity meetings beginning in February 1937, in Cincinnati, Ohio. From these meetings grew a five-point "Approach to Unity" (prayer, survey, friendliness, cooperation, study and discussion) and the idea for a national meeting. Witty hosted the first national meeting on May 3-4, 1938, in his Detroit church, with more than one thousand in attendance, and leaders hosted another national meeting the next year in Indianapolis.[11] Other gatherings followed in Lexington, Kentucky, and Columbus, Ohio, in 1940 and 1941.[12]

John B. Cowden (1876-1965, left) worked for reconciliation between Churches of Christ and Christian Churches after the initial division. He wrote six books between 1920 and 1939, including examinations of the concept of Christian unity in the writings of Paul and John, and through worship. Pictured here with Don Carlos Janes, mission leader in Churches of Christ.

Wartime gasoline and travel restrictions brought the first round of these national meetings to a halt. Participants continued the work, however, though "neighborhood conferences" in such places as Detroit, Toledo, Lansing, and Ontario. In 1943 Murch and Witty began a journal they titled *Christian Unity Quarterly* that continued until 1947. They also published a widely distributed tract titled *Christian Unity: Churches of Christ and Christian Churches*. After the end of World War II, supporters held three more national Conferences on Christian Unity in 1946 and 1947 in Cincinnati and Los Angeles.

The *Christian Standard* strongly endorsed the Murch-Witty efforts. The *Christian-Evangelist*, as well as two papers published by members of Churches of Christ—the *Christian Leader* and *Word and Work*—were also supportive. But the *Gospel Advocate* and *Firm Foundation*, the most widely read papers among Churches of Christ, first

opposed and then ignored the meetings. In addition, the second major North American division that would separate Christian Churches/Churches of Christ from Disciples was already well underway. These factors contributed to the struggle of the Murch-Witty meetings to gain wide support, and by the end of the 1940s the meetings had ended.

While the Beam-Jessup and Murch-Witty unity meetings produced few visible institutional results, they reflected a deep longing on the part of many across the North American streams to be one. That longing would lead some in each group to continue to seek ways of connecting with their estranged sisters and brothers and of manifesting the unity they so desired.

Internal Unity Efforts: Churches of Christ and Christian Churches/Churches of Christ

The second North American division was virtually complete with the 1968 restructure of the Christian Church (Disciples of Christ). The efforts to maintain internal unity within Disciples had largely ended. Yet cordial relationships between leaders nurtured by those efforts continued in many places. In Hartford, Illinois, "rank and file" members of all three streams held a local forum annually from 1957 to 1972. Another Annual Unity Forum, usually held on campuses of colleges of the three major North American streams, met from 1966 to 1975, beginning and ending at Bethany College. These meetings in some ways set the stage for the longest running effort at internal unity—the Restoration Forums.

In 1983, Allen Cloyd, director of the Restoration Leadership Ministry sponsored by the Vultee Church of Christ in Nashville, Tennessee, contacted Don DeWelt, president of College Press in Joplin, Missouri, and teacher at Ozark Bible College. Cloyd proposed organizing a meeting between one hundred leaders—fifty each from Churches of Christ and Christian Churches/Churches of Christ—"to establish dialogue for mutual understanding and appreciation."[13] Dennis Randall from Churches of Christ along with Chris DeWelt and Ken Idleman from Christian Churches/Churches of Christ joined Cloyd and DeWelt to plan what they called the Restoration Summit. The invitation-only meeting took place on the campus of Ozark Bible College in Joplin, August 7-9, 1984.

Though participants were frank about differences, attendees conducted the meeting in a thoroughly irenic spirit. The fact that the two bodies shared many conservative stances provided a basis for exploring possibilities for future cooperation. Leaders from

Christian Churches/Churches of Christ carefully explained to those from Churches of Christ their perception of the differences between them and the Christian Church (Disciples of Christ), something most from Churches of Christ knew little about. The generally enthusiastic response of those who participated in the Restoration Summit led organizers to plan other meetings, but with two major changes. Critics had been suspicious of the Summit's invitation-only nature and the name's implication of a high-level decision making body. In response, planners changed the gathering's name to the "Restoration Forum" and opened all meetings to anyone who wanted to attend.

Between 1984 and 2007, the Restoration Forum met twenty-five times in cities across North America. Eventually the meetings included Disciples and members of smaller divisions within Churches of Christ. One of the largest Forum gatherings took place in Lubbock, Texas, in October 2002. During the meeting, several hundred people signed a "Covenant of Unity" pledging "to share our Lord's passion and urgency for unity" and "to turn away from any kind of divisive or factious spirit which is not characteristic of the Spirit of Christ (Galatians 5:20)."[14]

By 2005, many had come to believe that the Forums had achieved the goals leaders had envisioned at the beginning. They had helped facilitate benevolent and evangelistic cooperation between Stone-Campbell churches in several parts of the United States. Mission teams in a number of locations outside North America included members of both Churches of Christ and Christian Churches/Churches of Christ, and the groups cooperated in evangelism in places like east Africa. Several congregations in Mississippi, Texas, and Washington had united. The Stone-Campbell Dialogue, begun in 1999, included many leaders from the Restoration Forums and included all three of the North American streams. In light of these successes, supporters held the final Restoration Forum at Ozark Christian College, the site of its beginning, in September 2007.

The previous year, Forum leaders had held the meeting as part of the Abilene Christian University Lectureship, focusing on the 1906 Census of Religious Bodies that had recorded the first division. Leaders addressed the historical and theological circumstances of that important event, and spoke of the hope of continuing reconciliation in the twenty-first century. In June, the North American Christian Convention meeting in Louisville, Kentucky, also marked the centennial of the 1906 Census with a push to invite members of Churches of Christ and to declare that for many in the two bodies, the division was no longer in force.

Unity Efforts Within Churches of Christ

Beginning in 1955, Leroy Garrett initiated a series of unity meetings at the Wynnewood Chapel in Dallas, Texas. Though Garrett and others had begun the congregation in 1951 as a protest to the "pastor system" they saw in mainstream Churches of Christ, the group had become increasingly concerned over divisions in the Stone-Campbell Movement. The gatherings consisted of members of most of the sub-groups within Churches of Christ. Though limited in scope, the meetings proved to be transformative to many, moving leaders like J. Ervin Waters, a hard-hitting debater for the one-cup churches, to stop denouncing those who differed from their beliefs and to become advocates for unity in diversity.[15]

Meanwhile, the non-institutional schism in Churches of Christ, which took shape in the same era, resulted in the separation of about 10 percent of the congregations from the mainstream. The issues reflected the same fears about missionary societies and other para-church agencies that had arisen a century before. Churches of Christ had "crossed the tracks" in the post-World War II economic and educational boom, leading many members to dream of more effective ways of doing evangelism, missions, and benevolence. Institutions like orphans' homes and cooperative evangelistic efforts like the national radio program "Herald of Truth" proliferated, prompting attacks on what some saw as a move away from a simple and scriptural congregational structure. The "sponsoring church" plan of pooling the resources of many congregations through the oversight of the eldership of one also drew fire. Rancorous articles and debates pushed the sides apart, producing a clear division by the 1960s.

In January 1968 leaders of the antagonistic parties organized a small dialogue meeting in Arlington, Texas, in which two teams of thirteen men presented papers focusing on their differences. The following year the Guardian of Truth Foundation published the essays as "The Arlington Meeting."[16] Little resulted from that gathering, however, and no others occurred for two more decades. In 1988 and 1990 leaders from the two groups organized open meetings in Nashville, Tennessee, and Dallas, Texas, respectively, to discuss the issues and attempt to build bridges. Each of the meetings drew around 800 attendees and resulted in increased contact between mainstream and non-institutional leaders. Still, they produced only limited rapprochement.

Another effort at internal unity in Churches of Christ took place at the 2004 and 2005 Abilene Christian University Lectureship. The school sponsored a series of "Faithful Conversations" between leaders of the International Churches of Christ (ICOC) and of mainstream congregations. The ICOC, with roots in the 1960s Crossroads Church of Christ in Gainesville, Florida, had experienced considerable growth under the leadership of Kip McKean starting in the late 1970s in the Boston Church of Christ. Internal ICOC leadership crises in the 1990s culminated with the forced departure of Kip McKean as the group's autocratic leader in 2002. The crisis led to a decentralization of the body and more openness to other churches. The ACU Lectureship conversations were one of a series of events taking place around the globe that brought the two groups together. Many students from the ICOC attended mainstream schools, and speakers from each body appeared on one another's lectureship programs.[17]

The Stone-Campbell Dialogue

One internal unity effort focused from its beginning on developing closer relationships and greater trust between all the major streams of the Stone-Campbell Movement in North America. The idea for the Stone-Campbell Dialogue grew initially out of a comment made by the General Minister and President of the Christian Church (Disciples of Christ), Richard Hamm, at the 1998 Board meeting of the World Convention of Churches of Christ. Hamm raised the question of how Disciples could legitimately claim to be ecumenical if they consistently avoided relations with those with whom they shared the same history. The comment elicited a favorable response from several others on the World Convention Board.

Hamm and the President of the Disciples Council on Christian Unity, Robert Welsh, working with Henry Webb and John Mills from Christian Churches/Churches of Christ, made initial inquiries and pulled together a group of three leaders from each of the three major North American streams to meet in Cincinnati, Ohio, on June 25, 1999. As the conversation progressed, each participant committed to pursuing the unity of the fractured Movement. Those present composed a purpose statement that explained the Dialogue's goal as developing "relationships and trust within the three streams of the Stone-Campbell Movement through worship and through charitable and frank dialogue." The statement explicitly denied that the Dialogue was seeking any kind of organizational or structural merger.

The initial group agreed to expand the number to include twenty people, six from each of the streams, and two observers who transcended the divisions because of their work or nationality. To the surprise of participants, who had stated in their first meeting that they would not seek to produce written agreements or common statements, at their June 2000 meeting at the Madison Church of Christ in Nashville, Tennessee, Dialogue members were able to write a "Confession of Sin and Affirmation of Faith" acknowledging the "special trust" to promote unity among Christians that had been given to the Stone-Campbell Movement, with the confession that each of the streams had betrayed that trust.[18]

The Dialogue met twice a year from December 1999 to June 2002, then began yearly meetings that took the conversation into local churches wherever the group was meeting. The group produced materials for congregations to use in creating dialogues in their own locations, and originated the idea for the October 2009 "Great Communion" to celebrate the bicentennial of Thomas Campbell's call for unity in the *Declaration and Address* and mark the 1909 communion service at the Pittsburgh Centennial Convention.[19] In 2009, after ten years of dialogue and initiatives to expand the conversation, the Dialogue recommitted to continuing its work and refocused its energies toward promoting joint service and worship among congregations of the Stone-Campbell Movement and beyond.

North American Disciples of Christ

Meanwhile, leaders of specific streams of the global Stone-Campbell Movement had sought to advance the visible unity of the whole church in ways that reflected different concepts of the church and ways of promoting its mission.

Disciples leaders influenced by the higher criticism of the Bible and the ecumenical movement accepted the idea that the gospel message would inevitably and legitimately look different in different times and circumstances. They confessed that Disciples too participated in the "sin of denominationalism," and were therefore more humble about their own understandings and more tolerant than some of their forebears of the religious expressions of others. They declared themselves to be ready to work with other denominations toward the goal of visible unity.

As a result of this emphasis, Disciples were charter members of the Federal Council of Churches of Christ in America (FCC), founded in 1908. They were also founding members of the National Council of Churches of Christ in the USA (NCC) when it succeeded the Federal Council in 1950. Disciples were part of United Church Women, later known as Church Women United, from its founding in 1941. Disciples also filled key leadership roles in each of these organizations. Edgar DeWitt Jones served as President of the FCC, and Roy G. Ross, Joan Brown Campbell, and Michael Kinnamon each served as General Secretary of the National Council of Churches. J. Irwin Miller served as president. Mossie Wyker, Mary Louise Rowand, and Susan Mix each served as President of United Church Women.

Though Disciples were not officially represented at the 1910 Edinburgh Missionary Conference, often identified as the beginning of the modern ecumenical movement, a number of Disciples were present as visitors, including Archibald McLean, Herbert L. Willett, James H. Garrison, C.C. Morrison, and Leslie W. Morgan, the latter a minister serving the Christian Association in England.[20] Disciples promoted an Anglo-American Conference on Christian Union in London on July 4-5, 1910, which included major leaders in the British churches like Hanmer William Webb-Peploe, leader of the Evangelical party in Anglicanism, and C. Silvester Horne, Congregational minister and Member of Parliament.[21]

Through the Disciples Council on Christian Union, Peter Ainslie, along with Bishop Charles Henry Brent of the Episcopal Church, took the lead in calling for a World Conference to discuss matters of Faith and Order to be organized along the lines of the Edinburgh Missionary Conference. Between December 1913 and February 1914, Ainslie met with leaders of British Churches of Christ in London, Leicester, and Edinburgh to secure their support for the Faith and Order initiative.[22] As a result, British Churches of Christ sent representatives to the 1920 Preparatory Conference, including William Robinson who would later play an important role in international ecumenism.

When the First World Conference on Faith and Order met at Lausanne, Switzerland, in 1927, Stone-Campbell churches in the United States, Great Britain, and Australia sent representatives. Among the ten American Disciples present were B. A. Abbott, Peter Ainslie, and John B. Cowden. George A. Klingman, a member of U.S. Churches of Christ, also attended.[23] William Robinson represented British Churches of Christ, and Reg Ennis and David Moffatt Wilson the Australian Churches of Christ.[24] American Disciples also sent delegates to the first Life and Work Conference at Stockholm in 1925, by which time Ainslie's role as a

world ecumenical leader had been clearly established. In 1937 members of the Oxford Conference on Church, Community and State and the Edinburgh Faith and Order Conference proposed that the Faith and Order movement join with the Life and Work movement to form a World Council of Churches. William Robinson made the motion at Edinburgh to vote on the Report approving the establishment of the WCC.[25]

North American Disciples took their work in the World Council of Churches very seriously, sending full delegations to every meeting and responding in writing to its published statements. Representatives to the WCC Central Committee included Council on Christian Unity presidents George Walker Buckner, George G. Beazley, Jr., and Paul A. Crow, Jr.; as well as J. Irwin Miller, Raymond Cuthbert, Jean Woolfolk; and Disciples general ministers and presidents Richard L. Hamm and Sharon E. Watkins. The Council on Christian Unity frequently provided staff to the World Council offices in Geneva, including Robert Tobias in Interchurch Aid, Lucy Griffith in World Youth Projects, Rosemary Roberts in Scholarships, Donald Newby and William J. Nottingham in the Youth Department, John Fulton in Communication, and Robert Welsh, Stephen V. Cranford, Michael Kinnamon, and Thomas F. Best in the Faith and Order Commission.

Peter Ainslie (center) with Disciples F. W. Burnham, R. H. Miller, Finis S. Idleman, and H. C. Armstrong on their way to the preliminary meeting for the World Conference on Faith and Order in Geneva, Switzerland, in August 1920.

The Council on Christian Unity was also significantly involved in the WCC's Ecumenical Institute at Bossey, Switzerland, especially in offering scholarships and sending Disciples to its Graduate School for Ecumenical

Studies and seminars. Four presidents of the Council—Buckner, Beasley, Crow, and Welsh—served on Bossey's board, the latter two each serving as moderator. Howard E. Short and Clark Williamson were sent as tutors to the Graduate School.

A new development in the ecumenical movement in the early twenty-first century was the inclusion of Christian communities not previously present at the table, including Evangelical and Pentecostal bodies. Two initiatives were prominent. Internationally, the Global Christian Forum (GCF) brought together Roman Catholic, Reformed, Orthodox (Eastern and Oriental), Anglican, Evangelical, and Pentecostal churches to begin the process of getting acquainted and witnessing to their common faith in Jesus Christ. Robert Welsh, as President of the Disciples Council on Christian Unity, and B.J. Mpofu, President of the World Convention of Churches of Christ from 2008 to 2012, served as official representatives of the Disciples Ecumenical Consultative Council (DECC) to the first meeting of the GCF in Limuru, Kenya, in 2007.[26]

In the United States, a similar initiative begun in 2001 called Christian Churches Together in the USA (CCT), included historic Protestant, Roman Catholic, Pentecostal, Evangelical, and Orthodox churches for the first time as full members in one ecumenical organization. This effort focused on how the churches could respond to issues of domestic poverty as a common witness across the traditions. The CCT Board chose Richard Hamm, General Minister and President of the Christian Church (Disciples of Christ) in the U.S. and Canada from 1993 to 2003, to serve as its first Executive Director.[27]

In 1911 Peter Ainslie began publication of *The Christian Union Quarterly.* An independent journal, Ainslie remained editor until his death in 1934, when Charles Clayton Morrison took over and renamed it *Christendom*. It later became *The Ecumenical Review* of the World Council of Churches.[28] In 1961 George Beazley renewed the lineage of Ainslie's quarterly with a publication named *Mid-stream: An Ecumenical Journal*. Across its history *Mid-Stream* had three editors: Beazley (1961-73), Paul Crow (1974-98), and Robert Welsh (1999-2002). In 2003 the CCU ended *Mid-Stream* and launched a new publication titled *Call to Unity: Resourcing the Church For Ecumenical Ministry*. This journal ceased print publication in 2011 with a move to develop an e-journal to provide online resources for ecumenism.

Disciples have a long history of relationships and unity efforts with Baptists. Twentieth-century efforts began with a meeting between Disciples and Freewill

Baptists in 1904 that seemed to have great promise. However, Freewill Baptist efforts to reunite with the American Baptists, completed in 1909, diverted that group's focus away from efforts with the Disciples. Extremely promising efforts begun in 1928 with the American (formerly Northern) Baptist Convention ended when the Baptist Convention of 1930 declined to recommend unity as long as Disciples held to baptism for the remission of sins.[29]

Further serious discussions between American Baptists and Disciples in the 1940s led to several joint ministry efforts, including publication of a hymnal, cooperative ministry on several college campuses, and congregations cooperating in local ministries. The two groups even held conventions in the same city in 1952, but, shortly afterward, the discussions dissolved. Though the two churches continued to have theological differences related to baptism, and practical differences related to the Lord's Supper and creeds, conversations seem to have ended primarily over anxieties about the continued existence of each group's denominational institutions.[30]

Between 1918 and 1920, Disciples in the United States participated in conversations with Presbyterians and seventeen other churches concerning a plan to unite under the name "The United Churches of Christ in America," also known as the "Philadelphia Plan." Though providing initially only for a federation much like that of the Federal Council of Churches, the plan stated the ultimate goal as organic union. To accomplish that goal, leaders from the participating groups proposed a set of progressive steps whereby denominations could begin to submit to the oversight of a central body. None of the churches involved, however, was able to secure approval from their governing bodies and constituencies, and the plan died for lack of support.[31]

Yet interest in such efforts was not dead. The Association for the Promotion of Christian Unity (the name adopted by the Council on Christian Union in 1916 and used until 1954) secured the adoption by the International Convention at Columbus, Ohio, in 1946 of a resolution accepting the invitation of the Congregational Christian Churches to a conference on organic union of Churches that recognized one another's ministries and sacraments. Then, in 1949 Disciples were part of a historic meeting at Greenwich, Connecticut, that began work on another plan of union. Since the FCC declined to host the meetings, the interested churches formed a separate conference to pursue conversations. Disciples leader C.C. Morrison, editor of *The Christian*

Century, presented the initial form of a plan in which each denomination would retain its own identity at first, but would be expected to find a way to merge quickly into a united church. The groups pursued the Greenwich Plan for over a decade, but representatives of the participating church bodies were never able to develop a plan they felt was ready for presentation to their respective groups.[32]

Disciples efforts next focused on a Consultation on Church Union (COCU) formed in response to a sermon by Presbyterian Eugene Carson Blake in December 1960 titled "A Proposal Toward the Reunion of Christ's Church." In 1970, COCU sent to its nine member churches *A Plan of Union for the Church of Christ Uniting*, but the bodies resisted the document's proposal to cluster parishes from different traditions under local parish councils. In the 1980s the body produced a theological statement, *The COCU Consensus: In Quest of a Church of Christ Uniting*. It proposed a new form of church union called "covenant communion," which would be organic and visible, but not organizational. In 2002 the participating bodies formally ended COCU and created a new structure named Churches Uniting in Christ (CUIC) that focused on mutual recognition and the eradication of racism. At every point in the life of COCU/CUIC Disciples provided key leadership, including George Beazley who served as President from 1970-1973, Paul Crow who served as General Secretary from 1968-1974, and Michael Kinnamon who served as General Secretary from 2000-2002.

In 1962, the Christian Church (Disciples of Christ) and the United Church of Christ (UCC) initiated church union conversations. These talks were a continuation of discussions and close relationships with the Congregational Christian Church begun in 1946 before the creation of the UCC in 1957. The groups temporarily suspended talks in 1966 to give full attention to the COCU process in which both were involved, but resumed in earnest in 1977. This bilateral process resulted in a "Declaration of Ecumenical Partnership" in 1985 and the decision in 1989 to declare themselves to be in "full communion." Since the 1960s the Division of World Mission of the UCMS, which later became the Division of Overseas Ministries of the Christian Church (Disciples of Christ), shared joint executive offices for geographical regions with the United Church Board of World Ministries, later named Wider Church Ministries of the United Church of Christ. In April 1996, these ministries entered into full cooperation, with the chief executive officer of each serving as co-executive of the Common Global Ministries Board of the Christian Church (Disciples of Christ) and the United Church of Christ.

Between 1967 and 1973 the Christian Church (Disciples of Christ) and the U.S. Catholic Bishops' Commission for Ecumenical Dialogue conducted a bilateral dialogue in the U.S inspired by George G. Beazley, Jr., and Archbishop (later Cardinal) William Baum of Washington. The two bodies published a joint report of the dialogue titled *An Adventure in Understanding*. This national dialogue provided the foundation for the establishment of an international Disciples-Catholic dialogue, which began in 1977.

In 1987 representatives from Disciples of Christ and the Russian Orthodox Church began a conversation under the sponsorship of the Council on Christian Unity. A delegation of ten Disciples, including General Minister and President John O. Humbert, traveled to the USSR for the first session at the Department of External Relations at the St. Danilov Monastery in Moscow and with the theological faculties at Zagorsk, Leningrad, and Odessa. Participants addressed the themes of "Baptism, Eucharist and Ministry" and "Peacemaking in a Nuclear Age." The second session in 1990 took place at Orthodox theological communities in St. Petersburg and Moscow just as the transition from rigid Marxism to *perestroika* was happening in the Russian Communist party. The themes that year were "The Renewal of Parish Life" and "The Church's Diaconal Ministry in Society."

Churches in the United Kingdom and British Commonwealth

Churches of the Stone-Campbell tradition in other parts of the world did not embrace ecumenical activity as quickly as U.S. Disciples. Nevertheless, many became participants in ecumenical conversations at both the national and international levels, and several eventually became part of union churches. In Britain the union of the Conference Churches with the Christian Association in 1917 led the latter to withdraw from active participation in activities with the British Free Churches. Yet the newly united Conference appointed delegates to the Faith and Order Preparatory Conference in Geneva in 1918, and did the same for the 1927 World Conference on Faith and Order in Lausanne. By the 1930s William Robinson had become an established figure on the British ecumenical scene, and the British Churches joined the Free Church Federal Council when it was formed in 1940, and the British Council of Churches in 1942. After unsuccessful discussions with the Baptist Union in the 1940s, British Churches of Christ began a process in the 1960s that eventually led in 1981 to the majority of congregations becoming part of the United Reformed Church.

The British Churches were also actively involved in the discussions begun in response to the call to the churches issued by the Nottingham Faith and Order Conference of 1964 to covenant for unity. Churches of Christ were also represented in the Churches Unity Commission, created by the newly formed United Reformed Church in 1974 to work for the unity of all British churches. When the Unity Commission formed the Churches Council for Covenanting that worked from 1978 to 1982 to produce a document for moving forward, Churches of Christ were members. Though these efforts were unable to secure the support needed for full implementation, they reflected the commitment of the British Churches of Christ to the pursuit of visible unity.[33] In 1980 Philip Morgan became General Secretary of the British Council of Churches and initiated the process that led to the reconstruction of the ecumenical councils in Britain and the inclusion of the Roman Catholic Church.

Church union leaders in Jamaica who helped create the United Church in Jamaica and the Cayman Islands. Left to right: S. A. Webley, Secretary of the Jamaica Council of Churches; Richmond I. Nelson, pastor of Duke Street Christian Church and secretary of the Church Union Commission; Paul A. Crow, Jr., general secretary of the Disciples Council on Christian Unity; Herbert S. Shirley, Disciples pastor serving a union congregation; and Ashley A. Smith, pastor of the United Church of Jamaica and chair of the Church Union Commission.

In New Zealand, Churches of Christ associated with the Annual Conference were involved in multilateral discussions on church union in the 1960s, though these eventually ended when the Anglicans withdrew in the 1980s. Though Churches of Christ in Australia did not join the Uniting Church in Australia, they sent

observers to the discussions that led to its formation in 1977. The small number of Churches of Christ with British roots in South Africa became part of the United Congregational Church of Southern Africa in the 1970s. British-sponsored missions in India became part of the Church of North India in 1970. Disciples in Jamaica joined with a union of Congregationalists and Presbyterians to form the United Church in Jamaica and the Cayman Islands in 1992.

In 1922, Canadian Disciples had formed the All-Canada Committee of the Christian Church. The Committee allowed for more extensive cooperation among congregations and organizations that had been largely unconnected. In 1925, Canadian Congregationalists, Methodists, and Presbyterians came together to create the United Church of Canada. Though Canadian Disciples were not directly involved in that effort,[34] the All-Canada Committee became the vehicle for Disciples to participate in the official union talks that began between the Anglican Church and United Church of Canada in 1943. Disciples joined the process first as Observers in 1949, and in 1959 became a full party to the talks, with the Disciples Council on Christian Unity providing staff leadership. Representatives of the three churches published a Plan of Union in 1973, but three years later the Anglican Church withdrew from negotiations. The United Church and Disciples continued, however, establishing three joint congregations, one in each of the three Areas of the Christian Church (Disciples of Christ) in Canada. Nevertheless, when the union committee polled the constituencies of the two bodies, they found little support for the union. Upon recommendation by the committee, both national bodies approved ending the negotiations in 1985.[35]

Canadian Disciples were active participants in local ecumenism during much of the twentieth century, and were founding members of the World and Canadian Councils of Churches as well as the Women's Inter-Church Council. For their size, Canadian Disciples provided a disproportionately high number of leaders to the ecumenical movement in that country. This included presidents and executive staff of the Canadian Council of Churches, presidents of the Women's Inter-Church Council of Canada, chairs of ecumenical commissions, and representatives and member delegates to the assemblies of the World Council of Churches.

Worldwide Stone-Campbell Organizations

Besides the many inter-denominational efforts, some leaders showed an increasing concern for connections between the worldwide Stone-Campbell family of churches. By the early twentieth century, internal tensions strained relations in a number of places, including between the North American Foreign Christian Missionary Society (FCMS)-related Christian Association and the older Conference of Churches of Christ in Britain, and between Disciples and Churches of Christ in the United States. The union of the FCMS-related Christian Association churches with the Conference Churches in 1917 strengthened trans-Atlantic links with North American Disciples that were reflected in the many visits by American evangelists. One of those evangelists was Jesse Bader, an enthusiastic young Disciple who would become Director of Evangelism for the Federal Council of Churches in the U.S.A. in 1932.

In 1924, Bader conceived the idea of a World Convention of Churches of Christ and persuaded the British Annual Conference of 1926 to support the idea. J.W. Black, chair of the General Evangelist Committee in the U.K., visited the Disciples Convention in Memphis, Tennessee, in November 1926 as a fraternal delegate, beginning a tradition that would last until most British churches became part of the United Reformed Church in 1981. The Memphis Convention appointed a Pentecost Committee of Fifteen to direct the 1900th Anniversary Observance of Pentecost, and the group decided to make that commemoration part of the proposed World Convention. Bader visited Australian and New Zealand Churches of Christ in 1927 and secured their support. As a result, Bader and others began making plans for the first World Convention to meet in Washington, D.C., in October 1930, following the Disciples International Convention. Eight thousand delegates from thirty-five countries attended, and planners agreed to hold a second Convention in Leicester, England, in 1935, with J.W. Black as President.[36]

World War II prevented the meeting planned for Toronto in 1940, so the next World Convention was at Buffalo in 1947, followed by Melbourne in 1952 and Toronto in 1955. Edinburgh hosted the 1960 Convention, and Puerto Rico followed in 1965.[37] Bader became full-time General Secretary in 1954, followed by Larry Kirkpatrick in 1963, and Alan Lee in 1971. The World Convention Board appointed Lyndsay and Lorraine Jacobs from New Zealand as General Secretary and Associate General Secretary in 1992, the first non-Americans to serve in that position. Australian Jeff Weston followed them in 2005, and in 2010, Gary Holloway became the first person from U.S. Churches of Christ to lead the body in the renamed office of Executive Director.

The World Convention was primarily a gathering for fellowship, welcoming members of all Stone-Campbell traditions and possessing no binding authority. Nevertheless, in the early 1960s the Second Vatican Council invited the World Convention to send representatives to its sessions. As General Secretary, Bader attended the first session in 1962. William G. Baker, of Edinburgh, Scotland, along with W. Barnett Blakemore and Howard E. Short from the United States attended the second and third sessions in 1963 and 1964, with Blakemore and Basil Holt of Johannesburg present for the final gathering in 1965.

By the 1970s, Stone-Campbell Churches active in the global ecumenical movement felt the need for a body that could act in a more formally representative way. This led to the formation of the Disciples Ecumenical Consultative Council (DECC) in 1975. This body was responsible for, among other things, international theological dialogues with the Roman Catholic Church. In 1977, at the initiative of Paul Crow of the DECC and Cardinal Johannes Willebrands of the Vatican's Pontifical Council for Promoting Christian Unity, representatives of the two bodies began the International Disciples of Christ–Roman Catholic Dialogue, which by 2008 had completed four multi-year rounds of talks and produced "agreed accounts" of the proceedings. The documents reflected the focus of each round and were titled: *Apostolicity and Catholicity* (1977-82), *The Church as Communion in Christ* (1983-1992), *Receiving and Handing on the Faith: The Mission and Responsibility of the Church* (1993-2002), and *The Presence of Christ in the Church, with Special Reference to the Eucharist* (2003 -2008). The group scheduled a fifth round for 2013.

In March 1987 the DECC and the World Alliance of Reformed Churches convened an international dialogue in Birmingham, England. Some United Churches were already members of both bodies. The Dialogue explored common doctrinal roots, the sacraments of baptism and the Lord's Supper, the ministry, and models of Christian unity, concluding that there were "no theological obstacles" between these two traditions. The dialogue's report declared, "The Disciples of Christ and the Reformed Churches recognize and accept each other as visible expressions of the one Church of Christ."

In 2010 the World Alliance of Reformed Churches united with the Reformed Ecumenical Council to form the World Communion of Reformed Churches. Disciples from the United States and Britain were present at the Uniting General Council as the DECC became the first associate member of the new Reformed body. This membership category was designed specifically to recognize the relationship of the DECC to the Reformed Churches and was described as including "Fellowships of churches that affirm a Reformed identity" and include in their membership churches that are members of the World Communion of Reformed Churches.[38]

U.S. Churches of Christ and Christian Churches/Churches of Christ

In the streams of the Stone-Campbell Movement that rejected the kinds of institutions necessary for participation in formal ecumenical efforts, individuals, congregations, or informal groups could and often did initiate unity efforts without securing authorization from any larger authoritative body. Leaders from those streams generally were not able to take part in formal bodies like National Councils of Churches or the World Council of Churches because of the lack of a recognized appointing body. One notable exception, however, was the involvement of a small number of scholars from Churches of Christ and Christian Churches/Churches of Christ in the Faith and Order Commission of the National Council of Churches in the United States. In most cases the participants' academic institutions supported their work, and each acted in one sense as an individual. Still, though they had no delegated authority such as that possessed by representatives of most churches active in the ecumenical movement, they did represent their streams as knowledgeable and committed members.[39] Such representation was possible because the Faith and Order movement had always included people from church bodies that could not or chose not to become members of the Federal Council and later National Council of Churches. Those from Churches of Christ who served on the NCC Faith and Order Commission included Lynn Mitchell of the University of Houston, Douglas Foster from Abilene Christian University, and Ron Highfield from Pepperdine University. From Christian Churches/ Churches of Christ, Frederick Norris and Paul Blowers from Emmanuel Christian Seminary participated.[40]

As the participation of members of Churches of Christ and Christian Churches/Churches of Christ in the NCC Faith and Order Commission illustrated, Stone-Campbell streams that lacked the expected structures through which to do ecumenical work often provided ecumenists in the form of their scholars. Engaging leaders from other Christian bodies in the context of scholarly discourse seemed less threatening to both participants and their schools, even when taking place in formal ecumenical settings. These contacts resulted in fruitful participation by those who would otherwise have been excluded from ecumenical dialogue, bringing the voices of "non-conciliar" Christian traditions into the ecumenical conversation.

The lack of formal representative structures made it difficult for Churches of Christ and Christian Churches/ Churches of Christ to initiate anything other than local relationships with other groups of Christians. In the second half of the twentieth century a few leaders in Churches of Christ began to take steps to initiate conversation with Baptist leaders, mostly in the Southern Baptist Convention, since many areas of numerical strength for the two bodies overlapped. As early as the 1960s some ministers in Churches of Christ began informal breakfast meetings with Baptist counterparts, sometimes growing out of acquaintances made through local ministerial associations. On March 20-21, 1975, Leroy Garrett, editor of the monthly *Restoration Review* that circulated widely in all parts of the Stone-Campbell Movement, participated with two Baptist professors at Baylor University, C. W. Christian and James Leo Garrett, in what was advertised as a "Church of Christ/ Baptist Dialogue."[41] The same year a small group of leaders of the two groups in Houston held a "Day of Study" that included Baptist theologian G. R. Beasley-Murray.[42] In the 1980s, J. Harold Thomas, then minister of the College Church of Christ in Conway, Arkansas, held a series of unity meetings that involved Baptist speakers as well as others from various church bodies.[43] All of these events were occasional and essentially local in nature.

By the end of the 1980s, however, leaders from each of the two groups had begun a national dialogue. In the late 1980s, Gary Leazer, then Director of the Inter-faith Witness Department of the SBC Home Mission Board, and Douglas Foster, then teaching at Lipscomb University in Nashville, met at meetings of the Faith and Order Commission of the National Council of Churches and began pursuing the possibility of a formal Southern Baptist–Churches of Christ Conversation. The proposed Conversation would be structured like one Southern Baptists had conducted with Roman Catholics since 1971. Each team would consist of seven members, drawn from academics and ministers, with the group meeting once a year for serious consideration of a mutually agreed upon theological topic. Though Southern Baptist participants were funded by the SBC Interfaith Witness Department, members from Churches of Christ secured their own funding through the churches or schools where they worked, and sometimes paid expenses out of their own pockets.

Team members gathered for their first meeting in January 1992 in Nashville, Tennessee, on the campus of Lipscomb University. Planners had set up the initial session as a get-acquainted meeting in which each member of the Conversation would tell personal stories of relations with people and churches of the other group. The planned one-hour session soon stretched to three and paved the way for substantive and frank discussions based on the mutual trust and respect that had been created. The next day formal papers detailed ways in which each group perceived the other, followed by descriptions of the current status of each body. The group planned to continue meeting yearly on the last weekend of January, but to keep meetings low-key and unpublicized because of potential opposition. The yearly Conversation meetings focused on topics such as hermeneutics, baptism, and the Holy Spirit from 1993-1996.

The Southern Baptist Convention, however, was experiencing serious internal struggles during this time, which resulted in a restructure of the denomination and the end of the Conversation. Paul Gritz, church historian at Southwestern Baptist Theological Seminary (SWBTS) in Fort Worth, Texas, and Douglas Foster began discussing possibilities for continued meetings sponsored by Southwestern and Abilene Christian University. A small planning committee organized two meetings, billed as the "Interlaced Histories Project," that convened February 7-8, 1997, on the campus of SWBTS, and January 30-31, 1998, on the campus of Abilene Christian University. At the end of the 1998 meeting, Baptist leaders announced the possibility of a resumption of the Conversation since restructuring of the SBC had been completed. The Home Mission Board, which had sponsored Baptist participation in the Conversation, was now named the North American Mission Board, and its parent organization Interfaith Witness was now Interfaith Evangelism.

Though leaders from both groups met the following year to map out a four-year agenda, the Conversation met only one more time. Scheduled for the traditional last weekend in January, the group gathered at the North American Mission Board offices in suburban Atlanta and engaged papers focused on "The Eternal Security of the Believer." Plans to meet the following year were dropped, however, when Director of the Southern Baptist Interfaith Evangelism Department Rudy Gonzalez informed the teams that in his judgment the meetings did not "fit within our clear objectives," ending the ten-year effort.[44]

This action led to a new effort begun by the Graduate School of Theology of Abilene Christian University and Logsdon School of Theology at Hardin-Simmons University, also in Abilene. Ronnie Prevost of the Logsdon faculty and Douglas Foster of ACU, along with seminary deans Vernon Davis and Jack Reese, formed a committee to plan a new "dialogue" that would include faculty, students, and ministers from the two church bodies in Texas. The Baptist–Churches of Christ Dialogue in Texas began in November 2002 as an annual meeting to discuss important issues of theology and polity. A major difference, however, between the Dialogue and the earlier Conversation was the focus on exploring ways the two groups had worked together and could expand their cooperation in ministry.[45]

In 1983 a group of ten leaders in North American Christian Churches/Churches of Christ met to discuss the future of the Stone-Campbell Movement. After extensive discussion the group planned an Open Forum of fifty representative leaders for the following April in St. Louis, Missouri. The enthusiastic response to that meeting led to a series of annual gatherings for frank discussion about the status of Christian Churches/Churches of Christ. Significant doctrinal and attitudinal differences began to surface in the conversations, leading planners to focus the 1988 session on the concept of Christian unity and to invite Disciples ecumenist Michael Kinnamon to address the issue. Kinnamon issued a sharp challenge to Forum participants, charging that Christian Churches/Churches of Christ had remained on the sidelines of worldwide unity efforts despite their professed passion for unity and urging them to enter the ecumenical process.

Spurred by Kinnamon's challenge, the Open Forum's Convening Committee suggested inviting representatives from the Church of God (Anderson, Indiana) to engage in dialogue at the 1989 meeting. A shared conservative theology as well as the personal friendship of Leonard Wymore, former North American Christian Convention Director, and David Lawson, Associate General Secretary of the Church of God, made this a logical choice.[46] Open Forum meetings between the two churches took place in 1989, 1990, 1991, and 1993.

While the groups discovered that they held much in common, serious differences also surfaced, including understandings of the purpose of baptism, ordination of women in ministry (a practice affirmed by the Church of God), and church polity. From 1992 to 1996 a smaller

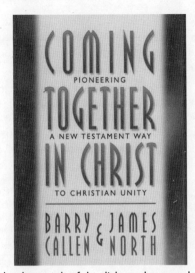

This book, a result of the dialogue between leaders from Christian Churches/Churches of Christ and the Church of God (Anderson, Indiana), was a strong call for conservative Christians to participate seriously in ecumenical efforts.

group of twelve, named the "Task Force on Doctrinal Dialogue," met twice yearly to discuss these differences and seek ways of pursuing unity. In 1996 the Task Force wrote a "Consensus Statement of Faith" specifying the areas of agreement, and urging continued dialogue on matters of difference. The following year College Press published a book of essays and documents detailing the progress of the Forum titled *Coming Together in Christ*.[47] Though a restructuring of the Church of God in 1997 ended this round of Open Forums, when the formation of a North American Stone-Campbell Dialogue began in 1998, the members from Christian Churches/Churches of Christ had all been participants in the Open Forums.[48]

Into the Twenty-First Century

At its beginning the Stone-Campbell Movement made the visible unity of all followers of Christ a priority. In the midst of striving for unity, circumstances and experiences inevitably shaped Christians in significantly different ways. Though the development of different ecclesiologies and the distinctive twentieth century experiences of different streams of the worldwide Stone-Campbell Movement led to a variety of approaches, members of Stone-Campbell churches around the globe continued to pursue the vision and calling of Christian unity. The quest for unity continued.

Toward a Stone-Campbell Identity

The Stone-Campbell Movement became remarkably diverse during the nineteenth and twentieth centuries. Emerging in the early years of the American Republic, it quickly connected with similar movements in Britain and spread to Canada, Australia, and New Zealand. By the early twentieth century the Movement had established missions in Europe, Asia, Africa, Latin America, and the Caribbean, and had suffered divisions in Britain and North America. Differences in doctrine, practice, and understandings of the relation of church and culture evident by the 1909 Centennial of Thomas Campbell's *Declaration and Address* continued to develop over the next century.

In light of this complex global history, is it possible to speak of a common Stone-Campbell identity that transcends the differences regarding doctrine, practice, race, ethnicity, gender, and sexuality that have divided this movement? At first glance, the answer may seem to be no. Yet, over the course of this study, four values have remained more or less prominent in the Stone-Campbell Movement and can be seen as transcending marks of the Movement's identity: unity, evangelism, restoration, and peace and justice.

In 1804, Barton Stone's Springfield Presbytery expressed its desire "to die, be dissolved, and sink into union with the Body of Christ at large." Five years later Thomas Campbell declared that "the Church of Christ upon earth is essentially, intentionally, and constitutionally one." And in 1832, when some in the Christian movement opposed union with the Reformers because of differences over the purpose of baptism, Barton Stone exhorted: "Let the Unity of christians be our polar star. To this let our eyes be continually turned, and to this let our united efforts be directed—that the world may believe, and be saved." As the Movement in North America divided into two streams in the late nineteenth and early twentieth centuries, each stream continued to claim the goal of unity. Later, as the Commission on Restudy of the Disciples of Christ sought to head off a second major division of the Movement in North America, Dean E. Walker urged Disciples to see themselves as a manifestation of the unity Christ willed for the entire church. Echoing Stone, Walker exhorted

Disciples to remember that their plea for unity on the simple confession of faith in Christ was not merely for unity's sake or to put an end to human creeds, but so that the world could see Christ, believe in him, and be saved.

Not stopping with exhortations, Stone-Campbell churches across the globe have been in the forefront of efforts to unite Christians in national and world councils of churches and through unions and cooperative efforts with churches of other Christian traditions. Even members of Stone-Campbell churches that opposed those forms of union have participated in dialogues with Christians from other traditions in local, regional, and national contexts. At the heart of the Stone-Campbell commitment to unity has been the conviction that unity is both the gift and will of God, and the inescapable calling of all Christians.

As seen in the statements of Stone and Walker above, the value of unity in the Stone-Campbell Movement has been inseparable from a commitment to evangelism. Jesus' prayer in John 17:20-21, that those who believe in him may be one, that the world may believe, has often been quoted by leaders of the Stone-Campbell Movement. For Stone, the Great Revival in the West demonstrated the relationship between unity and evangelism. The revival, born out of union sacramental meetings led by Presbyterians and Methodists, had been God's answer to prayers for revival at the beginning of the nineteenth century. The Campbells shared Stone's view of the connection between unity and evangelism. Thomas Campbell's *Declaration and Address* was a call for Christians of all denominations to come together to "promote simple evangelical Christianity." Though methods have differed, Stone-Campbell Christians across the globe commissioned evangelists and church planters from the earliest days of the Movement. Among the most influential missiologists of the last century was former Disciples missionary to India, Donald McGavran. Though taking diverse forms, evangelism, like unity, has been an enduring mark of the Stone-Campbell Movement.

Closely related to the Stone-Campbell commitments to unity and evangelism has been a commitment to the restoration of apostolic Christianity—a third value or mark of the Movement. For Barton Stone the heart of this commitment was the replacement of human confessions with what he perceived to be the New Testament confession of faith: that Jesus is the Christ. Stone believed that submission to that simple confession was critical to the transformation needed for both the unity and evangelism of the church. The Campbells also insisted on this simple confession, as did Walter Scott, who became the best-known early evangelist of the Campbell movement.

Alexander Campbell took the restoration of apostolic Christianity a step further. For him, the restoration of apostolic Christianity also included the restoration of ancient practices of the Church, such as weekly observance of the Lord's Supper and a New Testament order of ministry. Campbell believed that the restoration of these practices was key to the spread of the gospel by which God had willed to reconcile sinners and transform the world.

Authority for these practices was rooted in the notion of positive law, an approach that could, and sometimes did, result in a legalism that worked against unity. In response, some Disciples came to reject the whole idea of restoration. By the 1960s, however, Disciples scholar Ronald Osborn had recast the goal of restoration as that of seeking apostolicity. Apostolic faith and order, Osborn argued, points to what is essential to the life of the church as opposed to those things that are peripheral or transitory. This idea drew from Thomas Campbell's assertion that "nothing ought to be inculcated upon Christians as articles of faith; nor required of them as terms of communion; but what is expressly taught and enjoined upon them, in the word of God." Osborn counseled that contemporary Christians must avoid both insisting on beliefs and practices that the apostolic church did not require and overlooking concerns to which it gave attention. Instead, they were to distinguish what was historically conditioned and therefore transitory from what bore witness to the gospel. Many scholars and leaders in North American Churches of Christ came to share similar views.

Both Stone and the Campbells saw unity, evangelism, and restoration as essential to God's coming reign of peace and justice. Thus, a fourth mark of the Stone-Campbell movement has been a commitment to peace and justice, though often clearly a faltering one. As is the case with unity, evangelism, and restoration, peace and justice has been understood and pursued by Stone-Campbell Christians in often vastly different ways. In the 1820s and 1830s both Alexander Campbell and

Barton Stone identified slavery as an injustice that any government embodying Christian principles would set right. In the 1840s, growing sectional strife led Campbell to moderate his position in an effort to maintain the unity of church and nation that he believed were essential to the ultimate establishment of justice. Stone, on the other hand, adopted the antigovernment stance advocated in the early 1840s by the most radical of Northern abolitionists. In the 1850s, differences over obedience to the Fugitive Slave Law and opposition to slavery led to the formation of the abolitionist Christian Missionary Society as an alternative to the moderate American Christian Missionary Society. Barton Stone, Alexander Campbell, and David Lipscomb ultimately advocated pacifism as the most effective means of achieving both peace and justice. Different responses to participation in the Civil War would contribute to the first division of the Movement in North America. In the twentieth century, Stone-Campbell Christians in North America and in the U.K. and British Commonwealth continued to address the issue of war, while also engaging concerns of race, ethnicity, religious pluralism, gender, and sexuality. In Africa, Stone-Campbell missionaries increasingly came to support the human rights of black majorities.

At the beginning of the twenty-first century the Stone-Campbell Movement remained significantly divided. Multiple North American streams existed, each related to different parts of the global church. Theological, social, and cultural differences within streams also divided the churches. Yet, as this study demonstrates, in many places around the world Stone-Campbell Christians were coming together with each other and with Christians from other heritages to demonstrate the unity that God gives through Jesus Christ and in response to contemporary challenges of evangelism, the pursuit of apostolic Christianity, and issues of peace and justice. As Stone-Campbell Christians find this common ground, this Movement will continue to move, witnessing to the gospel of reconciliation and the reign of Jesus Christ in and for the world.

Notes

Introduction

[1]William Thomas Moore, *A Comprehensive History of the Disciples of Christ, Being an Account of a Century's Effort to Restore Primitive Christianity in Its Faith, Doctrine, and Life* (London and Edinburgh: Fleming H. Revell, 1909), 19.

[2]Alexander Campbell, "A Restoration of the Ancient Order of Things, no. I," *Christian Baptist* (February, 1825): 128.

[3]Moore, *Comprehensive History,* 31-32.

[4]Moore, *Comprehensive History,* 31-32.

[5]For a review of some of these early histories, see Paul M. Blowers, Douglas A. Foster, and D. Newell Williams, "Stone-Campbell History over Three Centuries: A Survey and Analysis," in *The Encyclopedia of the Stone-Campbell Movement* (Grand Rapids: Eerdmans, 2004), xxi-xxiii.

[6]John Rowe, *History of Reformatory Movements Resulting in a Restoration of the Apostolic Church with a History of the Nineteen General Church Councils* (Cincinnati: G. W. Rice, 1884); also the 9th ed., which added to the title *...also A History of All Innovations, from the Third Century Down* (Cincinnati: F. L. Rowe, 1913), 160-161.

[7]*A Debate on the Roman Catholic Religion: Between Alexander Campbell, and the Rt. Rev. John B. Purcell* (Cincinnati: J.A. and U.P. James, 1837; reprinted 1851), 65-69.

[8]James DeForest Murch, *Christians Only: A History of the Restoration Movement* (Cincinnati: Standard Publishing, 1962), 9-18.

[9]Moore, *Comprehensive History,* 35.

[10]James H. Garrison, *The Story of a Century* (St. Louis: Christian Publishing, 1909), 246-249 and 263-269.

[11]James H. Garrison, *Christian Union: A Historical Study* (St. Louis: Christian Publishing, 1906), 127-207.

[12]Garrison, *Christian Union,* 164-186.

[13]David Lipscomb, *Christian Unity: How Promoted, How Destroyed* (Nashville: McQuiddy Printing, 1916), 19-29 and 58-64.

[14]On the maturation of historicism in the nineteenth and early twentieth centuries, see Michael Bentley, *Modern Historiography* (London and New York: Routledge, 1999), 1-102; Ernst Breisach, *Historiography: Ancient, Medieval, and Modern,* 2nd ed. (Chicago: University of Chicago Press, 1994), 199-322; and Georg G. Iggers, *Historiography in the Twentieth Century: From Scientific Objectivity to the Postmodern Challenge* (Hanover and London: Wesleyan University Press, 1997), 23-35. Iggers's description of historicism is particularly instructive: "Historicism was more than a theory of history. It involved a total philosophy of life, a unique combination of a conception of science, specifically of the human or cultural sciences, and a conception of the political and social order" (p. 29).

[15]Iggers, *Historiography,* 30.

[16]Winfred Garrison, *Heritage and Destiny: An American Religious Movement Looks Ahead* (St. Louis: Bethany Press, 1961), 35.

[17]See the analysis of the different "vectors" of the early Movement in Anthony Dunnavant, "Continuities, Changes, and Conflicts: The Founders' Understanding of the Disciples Movement," in Anthony Dunnavant, Richard Hughes, and Paul Blowers, *Founding Vocation and Future Vision: The Self-Understanding of the Disciples of Christ and Churches of Christ* (St. Louis: Chalice Press, 1999), 1-19; and Mark G. Toulouse, *Joined in Discipleship: The Shaping of Contemporary Disciples Identity,* revised ed. (St. Louis: Chalice Press, 1997), 37-135.

[18]Breisach, *Historiography,* 363-369.

[19]On Turner's contribution to the "New History" of America, see Breisach, *Historiography,* 313-315 and 369-370.

[20]Frederick Jackson Turner, "The Significance of the Frontier in American History" (1893), reprinted in his *The Frontier in American History* (New York: Henry Holt, 1920), 2.

[21]Winfred E. Garrison, *Religion Follows the Frontier: A History of the Disciples of Christ* (New York: Harper & Brothers, 1931), 49-58, 59-86, and 199-200.

[22]Winfred Garrison and Alfred T. DeGroot, *The Disciples of Christ: A History* (St. Louis: Christian Board of Publication, 1948), 59-78; Murch, *Christians Only,* 19-34; Lester G. McAllister and William E. Tucker, *Journey in Faith: A History of the Christian Church (Disciples of Christ)* (St. Louis: Bethany Press, 1975), 38-60; Henry E. Webb, *In Search of Christian Unity: A History of the Restoration Movement,* revised ed. (Abilene: Abilene University Press, 2003), 35-59; James B. North, *Union in Truth: An Interpretive History of the Restoration Movement* (Cincinnati: Standard Publishing, 1994), 3-6; Toulouse, *Joined in Discipleship,* 17-36; Leroy Garrett, *The Stone-Campbell Movement,* revised ed. (Joplin: College Press, 1994), 47-95. More recently see Douglas Foster and Michael Casey, "The Renaissance of Stone-Campbell Studies: An Assessment and New Directions," in Michael Casey and Douglas Foster, *The Stone-Campbell Movement: An International Religious Tradition* (Knoxville: University of Tennessee Press, 2002), 35-39; and D. Duane Cummins, *The Disciples: A Struggle for Reformation* (St. Louis: Chalice Press, 2009), 14-22.

[23]Blowers, Foster, and Williams, "Stone-Campbell History over Three Centuries," xxx-xxxi.

[24]Nathan Hatch, *The Democratization of American Christianity* (New Haven: Yale University Press, 1989), 68-81, 163, 167-70.

[25]Casey and Foster, "The Renaissance of Stone-Campbell Studies," 1-65.

[26]Moore, *Comprehensive History,* 25, 27.

[27]Thomas Bender, "Introduction," in Thomas Bender, ed., *Rethinking American History in a Global Age* (Berkeley and Los Angeles: University of California Press, 2002), 5-6.

[28]Iggers, *Historiography,* 97-117; Dorothy Ross, "The New and Newer Histories: Social Theory and Historiography in an American Key," in Anthony Mulho and Gordon S. Wood, ed., *Imagined Histories: American Historians Interpret the Past* (Princeton: Princeton University Press, 1998), 85-106; Thomas C. Holt, "Explaining Racism in American History," in Mulho and Wood, *Imagined Histories,* 117-119; Philip Gleason, "Crèvacoeur's Question: Historical Writing on Immigration, Ethnicity, and National Identity," in Mulho and Wood, *Imagined Histories,* 120-43; Robin D. G. Kelly, "How the West Was Won: The African Diaspora and the Re-Mapping of U.S. History," in Bender, ed., *Rethinking American History in a Global Age,* 123-147.

[29]Robert G. Nelson, *Disciples of Christ in Jamaica, 1858-1958* (St. Louis: Bethany Press, 1958).

[30]Daisy L. Machado, *Of Borders and Margins: Hispanic Disciples in Texas, 1888-1945* (New York: Oxford University Press, 2003), viii.

[31]Machado, *Of Borders and Margins,* xiii, 3-87.

[32]Debra Hull, *Christian Church Women: Shapers of a Movement* (St. Louis, Missouri: Chalice Press, 1994); Loretta Long, *The Life of Selina Campbell: A Fellow Soldier in the Cause of Restoration* (Tuscaloosa: University of Alabama Press, 2001).

[33]Mary Ellen Lantzer Pereira, *Women Preaching in the Christian Church: An Examination of the 1892-93* Christian Standard *Controversy* (Edmonds: Candlelight Publishing, 2000). See also C. Leonard Allen, "Silena Moore Holman (1850-1915), Voice of the 'New Woman'

among Churches of Christ," *Discipliana* 56 (1996): 3-11; and Fran Craddock, Martha Faw, and Nancy Heimer, *In the Fullness of Time: A History of Women in the Christian Church (Disciples of Christ)* (St. Louis: Chalice Press, 1999).

[34]Edward J. Robinson, *To Save My Race from Abuse: The Life of Samuel Robert Cassius* (Tuscaloosa: University of Alabama Press, 2007); Edward J. Robinson, *To Lift Up My Race: The Essential Writings of Samuel Robert Cassius* (Knoxville: University of Tennessee Press, 2008).

[35]D. Duane Cummins, *Dale Fiers: Twentieth Century Disciple* (Fort Worth: TCU Press, 2003); and Duane Cummins, *Kenneth L. Teegarden: The Man, the Church, the Times* (Fort Worth: TCU Press, 2007).

[36]Richard Hughes, *Reviving the Ancient Faith: The Story of Churches of Christ in America* (Grand Rapids: Eerdmans, 1996).

[37]See most notably the essays in William R. Baker, ed., *Evangelicalism and the Stone-Campbell Movement* (Downers Grove: InterVarsity Press, 2002); see also Richard Hughes, "Are Restorationists Evangelicals?" in Donald Dayton and Robert Johnston, ed., *The Variety of American Evangelicalism* (Downers Grove: InterVarsity Press, 1991), 109-134.

[38]For a promotion of the utility of the "Evangelical" identity, see Stanley Grenz, *Renewing the Center: Evangelical Theology in a Post-Theological Era* (Grand Rapids: Baker Academic, 2000); for a substantial criticism of its utility, see D.G. Hart, *Deconstructing Evangelicalism: Conservative Protestantism in the Age of Billy Graham* (Grand Rapids: Baker Academic, 2004). See also Donald Dayton, "Some Doubts about the Usefulness of the Category 'Evangelical,'" in Dayton and Johnston, *The Variety of American Evangelicalism*, 245-251.

[39]"National Profiles," World Convention of the Churches of Christ, accessed August 3, 2011, http://www.worldconvention.org/nationalprofiles.php.

1: Emergence of Stone-Campbell Movement

[1]Leonard J. Trinterud, *The Forming of an American Tradition: A Re-Examination of Colonial Presbyterianism* (Philadelphia: Westminster Press, 1948); Randall Balmer and John R. Fitzmier, *The Presbyterians* (Westport: Greenwood Press, 1993), 25-30.

[2]D. Newell Williams, *Barton Stone: A Spiritual Biography* (St. Louis: Chalice Press, 2000), 9-24.

[3]Barton W. Stone, *The Biography of Eld. Barton Warren Stone, Written by Himself, with additions and Reflections by Eld. John Rogers* (Cincinnati: Published for the author by J.S. and U.P. James, 1847); reprinted in Hoke S. Dickinson, ed., *The Cane Ridge Reader,* (n.p., 1972), 8-11. For information on Hodge, see Williams, *Barton Stone,* 27.

[4]Stone, *Biography,* 12. Stone and Holmes appear to have been assigned a treatise in a Latin work by Witsius, later translated as *Sacred Dissertations on What is Commonly Called the Apostle's Creed,* 2 vols., trans. from the Latin and followed with notes, critical and explanatory, by Donald Fraser (Edinburgh: A. Fullarton and Co., 1823), 1:121-143.

[5]Stone, *Biography,* 13.

[6]Stone, *Biography,* 13.

[7]Isaac Watts, "The Christian Doctrine of the Trinity; or, Father, Son, and Spirit, Three Persons and One God, Asserted and Proved, with Their Divine Rights and Honours Vindicated, by Plain Evidence of Scripture, Without the Aid or Encumbrance of Human Schemes," in *The Works of the Late Reverend and Learned Isaac Watts,* 6 vols. (London: J. and T. Longman, 1757), 4:417, 426, 461-465, 491.

[8]Watts, "The Christian Doctrine of the Trinity," 417, 461-465, 472-484.

[9]Williams, *Barton Stone,* 30.

[10]Stone, *Biography,* 14.

[11]Stone, *Biography,* 14-16, 29.

[12]Richard Beard, *Brief Biographical Sketches of Some of the Early Ministers of the Cumberland Presbyterian Church,* second series (Nashville: Cumberland Presbyterian Board of Publication, 1874), 13-15.

[13]Williams, *Barton Stone,* 44.

[14]Stone, *Biography,* 29-31. See also Williams, *Barton Stone,* 40-44.

[15]Williams, *Barton Stone,* 44-45.

[16]Paul Conkin, *Cane Ridge: America's Pentecost* (Madison: University of Wisconsin Press, 1990), 56-63. For an account of the Scottish lineage of the American Presbyterian Sacramental meeting see Leigh Eric Schmidt, *Holy Fairs: Scottish Communions and American Revivals in the Early Modern Period* (Princeton: Princeton University Press, 1989).

[17]Stone, *Biography,* 34-35.

[18]Williams, *Barton Stone,* 23-27.

[19]Barton W. Stone, *A Reply to John P. Campbell's Strictures on Atonement* (Lexington: Joseph Charles, 1805), 6; Williams, *Barton Stone,* 53-55.

[20]Stone, *A Reply,* 6.

[21]Stone, *Biography,* 36; Williams, *Barton Stone,* 55-57.

[22]Conkin, *Cane Ridge,* 88-92; Ellen T. Eslinger, "The Great Revival in Bourbon County, Kentucky" (Chicago: University of Chicago, 1988), 345-346, 350.

[23]Williams, *Barton Stone,* 61-63.

[24]James R. Rogers, *The Cane Ridge Meeting-house* (Cincinnati: Standard Publishing Company, 1910), 33.

[25]Stone, *Biography,* 45-46; see also Barton W. Stone, *History of the Christian Church in the West,* reprint ed. (Lexington: College of the Bible, 1956), 4-5.

[26]Williams, *Barton Stone,* 71-72.

[27]Williams, *Barton Stone,* 72-76.

[28]"Minutes of the Synod of Kentucky, 1802-1811," in William Warren Sweet, *Religion on the American Frontier, 1783-1840,* vol. 2, *The Presbyterians* (Chicago: University of Chicago Press, 1936), 318-319. See also "An Apology for Renouncing the Jurisdiction of the Synod of Kentucky. To which is added a Compendious View of the Gospel, and a few remarks on the Confession of Faith," in Stone, *Biography,* 169-171.

[29]Williams, *Barton Stone,* 84-87.

[30]Stone, *History,* 26.

[31]"Last Will and Testament of Springfield Presbytery," in Stone, *Biography,* 53.

[32]Williams, *Barton Stone,* 99-101.

[33]Joseph Thomas, *The Travels and Gospel Labors of Joseph Thomas* (Winchester: J. Foster, 1812), 80-81.

[34]Robert Marshall and John Thompson, *A Brief Historical Account of Sundry Things in the Doctrines and State of the Christian, or as it is Commonly Called, the Newlight Church, Containing their Testimony Against Several Doctrines Held in that Church, and its Disorganized State; Together with Some Reasons Why those Two Brethren Purpose to Seek for a More Pure and Orderly Connection* (Cincinnati: J. Carpenter, 1811), 255-256.

[35]Williams, *Barton Stone,* 77, 98-99.

[36]B.W. Stone to Samuel Rennels, Cane Ridge Preservation Project Museum, Cane Ridge, Bourbon County, Kentucky.

[37]David C. Roos, "The Social Thought of Barton Warren Stone and Its Significance Today for the Disciples of Christ in Western Kentucky" (DMin thesis, Vanderbilt University, 1973), 83.

[38]Stone, *Biography,* 59; Williams, *Barton Stone,* 107-109, 118-119.

[39]Stone, *History,* 45; Stone, *Biography,* 64.

[40]Stone, *Biography,* 63; Williams, *Barton Stone,* 121-128.

[41]Letter from William Lamphier to the *Herald of Gospel Liberty,* May 12, 1809, ed. Elias Smith, Portsmouth, N.H., quoted in Roos, "Social Thought of Barton Stone," 88.

[42]Stone, *Biography,* 60; Williams, *Barton Stone,* 130. Believers' immersion, in which the candidate is fully immersed in water, was the form of baptism practiced by Baptists, who argued that it was the only form of baptism described in the Bible.

[43]Stone, *History,* 47.

[44]Marshall and Thompson, *Brief Historical Account,* 11-12.

[45]Marshall and Thompson, *Brief Historical Account,* 13-14. See also Stone, *History,* 48.

[46]Williams, *Barton Stone,* 134-135.

[47]Marshall and Thompson, *Brief Historical Account,* 15.

[48]Stone, *Biography*, 65-66.

[49]Stone, *Biography*, 67-68, 72-75; Williams, *Barton Stone*, 139-140.

[50]Williams, *Barton Stone*, 149-150.

[51]*National Intelligencer*, January 4, 1817, quoted in Roos, "Social Thought of Barton Stone," 96; See also George M. Frederickson, *The Black Image in the White Mind* (New York: Harper & Row, 1971), 11.

[52]J. W. Roberts and R. L. Roberts, Jr., "Like Fire in Dry Stubble—The Stone Movement 1804-1832," *Restoration Quarterly* (1963): 148-154; and *Restoration Quarterly* (1965): 32-35.

[53]Frank M. Masters, *A History of the Baptists in Kentucky* (Louisville: Kentucky Baptist Historical Society, 1953), 171-172.

[54]Michael G. Kenney, *The Perfect Law of Liberty: Elias Smith and the Providential History of America* (Washington: Smithsonian Institution Press, 1994). For a discussion of the Christians in New England and the Christians in Virginia and North Carolina see Nathan O. Hatch, *The Democratization of American Christianity* (New Haven: Yale University Press, 1989). Older works include Milo True Morrill, *A History of the Christian Denomination in America* (Dayton: The Christian Publishing Association, 1912) and W.E. MacClenny, *The Life of Rev. James O'Kelly and the Early History of the Christian Church in the South* (Raleigh: Edwards and Broughton, 1910).

[55]Stone, *History*, 49.

[56]George Miller, *The Campbell Genealogy*, Campbell Mansion, Bethany, West Virginia. cites 1710 as the date of Thomas Campbell's immigration to northern Ireland. Eva Jean Wrather, *Alexander Campbell: Adventurer in Freedom* (Ft. Worth: Disciples of Christ Historical Society and TCU Press, 2005) quotes from unnamed records that say this Thomas was born in County Down, indicating the family already was in Ireland.

[57]Alexander Campbell, *Memoirs of Elder Thomas Campbell* (Cincinnati: H.S. Bosworth, 1861), 8; and Robert Richardson, *Memoirs of Alexander Campbell*, 2 vols. (Philadelphia, J. B. Lippincott & Co., 1868-70), 1:21.

[58]Alexander Campbell, *Memoirs of Elder Thomas Campbell*, 8.

[59]Callum G. Brown, *Religion and Society in Scotland Since 1707* (Edinburgh: Edinburgh University Press, 1997), 23.

[60]Thomas Sommers, *Observations on the Meaning and Extent of the Oath Taken at the Admission of Every Burgess in the City of Edinburgh* (Edinburgh: William Turnbull, 1794), 7-8.

[61]Sommers, *Observations on the Meaning and Extent*, 24.

[62]John D. Brewer and Gareth I. Higgins, *Anti-Catholicism in Northern Ireland, 1600-1998: The Moat and the Beam* (New York: St. Martin's Press, Inc., 1998), 45.

[63]Brewer and Higgins, *Anti-Catholicism*, 41, 47-48, 57.

[64]Richardson, *Memoirs of Alexander Campbell*, 1:24.

[65]Campbell, *Memoirs of Elder Thomas Campbell*, 22; Richardson, *Memoirs of Alexander Campbell*, 1:41-45.

[66]David Hempton and Myrtle Hill, *Evangelical Protestantism in Ulster Society 1740-1890* (London: Routledge, 1992), 15-16.

[67]Hempton and Hill, *Evangelical Protestantism*, 15-16.

[68]Hiram J. Lester, "The Form and Function of the *Declaration and Address*," in Thomas Olbricht and Hans Rollman, ed., *The Quest for Christian Unity, Peace and Purity in Thomas Campbell's "Declaration and Address"* (Lanham: The Scarecrow Press, 2000), 184-185. See also "The Irish Background to Thomas Campbell's *Declaration and Address*," *Journal of the United Reformed Church History Society*, 3:6 (May, 1985), 215-225.

[69]Peter Brooke, *Controversies in Ulster Presbyterianism, 1790-1836* (PhD diss., University of Cambridge, 1980), available at www.peterbrooke.org.uk/p%26t/Northern%20Ireland/controversies/content, accessed December 16, 2011.

[70]Richardson, *Memoirs of Alexander Campbell*, 1:57; Lester, "The Form and Function of the *Declaration and Address*," 186.

[71]Richardson, *Memoirs*, 78-80.

[72]Kerby A. Miller, et al., *Irish Immigrants in the Land of Canaan: Letters and Memoirs from Colonial and Revolutionary America, 1675-1815*

(New York: Oxford University Press, 2003), 7.

[73]Miller, et al., *Irish Immigrants*, xxii.

[74]Marianne Wokeck, *Trade in Strangers: The Beginnings of Mass Migration to North America* (University Park: Penn State University Press, 1999), 194.

[75]The General Associate Synod had revised its *Narrative and Testimony* in 1804, noting, "That, as no human composure, however excellent and well expressed, can be supposed to contain a full and comprehensive view of divine truth; so, by this adherence, we are not precluded from embracing, upon due deliberation, any further light which may afterward arise from the word of God, about any article of divine truth." *Narrative and Testimony, Enacted by the General Associate Synod*, 1804, 12-13, quoted in John M'Kerrow, *History of the Secession Church* (Glasgow: A. Fullerton, 1841), 443.

[76]"Minutes of the Chartiers Presbytery," 124, quoted in William Herbert Hanna, *Thomas Campbell: Seceder and Christian Union Advocate* (Cincinnati: Standard Publishing Company, 1935), 33ff.

[77]"Minutes of the Chartiers Presbytery," 132-137, quoted in Hanna, *Thomas Campbell*, 39-43.

[78]Hanna, *Thomas Campbell*, 91-93.

[79]Thomas Campbell, *Declaration and Address* (St. Louis: Mission Messenger, 1975), 25-27.

[80]Campbell, *Declaration and Address*, 34-35.

[81]The Synod also cited their disapproval of sentiments in the *Declaration and Address*, Thomas's objections to sections of the Westminster Confession and to infant baptism, and the fact that Synods were not authorized to form connections with ministers, churches, or associations. Minutes of the Synod of Pittsburgh, October 4-5, 1810. Cited in Richardson, *Memoirs of Alexander Campbell*, 1:327-328.

[82]Wrather, *Alexander Campbell: Adventurer in Freedom*, 1:165.

[83]Alexander Haldane, *Memoirs of the Lives of Robert Haldane of Airthrey, and of his Brother, James Alexander Haldane* (New York: R. Carter and Brothers, 1853), 357-358; Richardson, *Memoirs of Alexander Campbell*, 1:392.

[84]Richardson, *Memoirs of Alexander Campbell*, 1:371-373.

[85]Richardson, *Memoirs of Alexander Campbell*, 1:250.

[86]Richardson, *Memoirs of Alexander Campbell*, 1:395-398, 403-404.

[87]Alexander Campbell, "Anecdotes, Incidents and Facts," *Millennial Harbinger* (June, 1848): 345-346.

[88]Richardson, *Memoirs of Alexander Campbell*, 2:90.

[89]Alexander Campbell, *The Sacred Writings of the Apostles and Evangelists of Jesus Christ, Commonly Styled the New Testament. Translated From the Original Greek, by George Campbell, James Macknight, and Philip Doddridge, Doctors of the Church of Scotland. With Prefaces to the Historical and Epistolary Books; and an Appendix, Containing Critical Notes and Various Translations of Difficult Passages* (Buffaloe, Brooke County, Virginia, Printed and Published by Alexr. Campbell, 1826); Alexander Campbell, *Psalms, Hymns and Spiritual Songs* (Bethany, Va., A. Campbell, 1828). For an analysis of Campbell's early publishing efforts, see Gary Holloway, "Alexander Campbell as a Publisher," *Restoration Quarterly* (January,1995): 28-35 and Scott Seay, "Breaking Up Fallow Ground or Sowing the Seeds of Discord," *Discipliana* (Winter, 2001), 113-127.

[90]See Alexander Campbell's thirty-two part series entitled "A Restoration of the Ancient Order of Things" in the *Christian Baptist*, especially No. VI (August, 1825): 3:193-195; No. VII (September, 1825): 3:208-213; No. VIII (October, 1825): 3:231-238; No. IX (November, 1825): 3:254-256; No. X (January, 1826): 3:299-302; No. XII (April, 1826): 3:358-362; No. XIII (June, 1826): 3:383-386; No. XIV (August, 1826): 4:5-8; and No. XIX (May, 1827): 4:234-236. All notes citing the *Christian Baptist* refer to the original, 7-volume series, paginated serially in each volume.

[91]Alexander Campbell, "The Foundation of Hope and Christian Union," *Christian Baptist* (April, 1824): 1:220-223.

[92]Alexander Campbell, "A Restoration of the Ancient Order of Things—II," *Christian Baptist* (March, 1825): 3:69.

[93]Campbell, "A Restoration—II,"134-135.

[94]Between October 1823 and February 1824, Campbell wrote a five-part critique entitled "The Clergy." See *Christian Baptist* (October, 1823): 1:61-71; (November, 1823): 1:91-96; (December, 1823): 1:109-112; (January, 1824): 1:133-139; and (February, 1824): 1:157-1613. See also Alexander Campbell, "The Third Epistle of Peter, to the Preachers and Rulers of Congregations" *Christian Baptist* (July, 1825): 2:280-285.

[95]Alexander Campbell, "The Origin of the 'Christian Clergy," Splendid Meeting Houses, and Fixed Salaries, Exhibited from Ecclesiastical History" *Christian Baptist* (August, 1823): 1:28-31.

[96]Alexander Campbell, *Order*, Millennial Harbinger Extra, No. 8, (Bethany, Va., 1835): 504-506.

[97]Alexander Campbell, *Christian Baptist* (June, 1824): 1:271.

[98]Alexander Campbell, *The Christian System*, 5th ed. (Cincinnati: Standard Publishing Company, 1901), 291.

[99]Alexander Campbell, "A Reply to R[obert] B S[emple]," *Christian Baptist* (April, 1826), 3:356-357; "A Restoration of the Ancient Order of Things—XXXII," *Christian Baptist* (September, 1829): 7:43-46.

[100]Alexander Campbell, "The Clergy—I," *Christian Baptist* (October, 1823): 1:61-71; "A Restoration—XII," *Christian Baptist* (April, 1826): 3:358-362; Alexander Campbell, "A Restoration of the Ancient Order of Things—XIII," *Christian Baptist* (June, 1826): 3:383-386. See also Weldon Bailey Bennett, "The Concept of Ministry in the Thought of Representative Men of the Disciples of Christ" (PhD diss., University of Southern California, 1971), 115-116; Campbell, *Order*, 503-504.

[101]Campbell, *Order*, 507.

[102]Campbell, *Christian System*, 61-63; Campbell, *Order*, 522-524, 526-527; Bennett, "The Concept of Ministry," 256-257.

[103]Alexander Campbell, "Prospectus," *Millennial Harbinger* (January, 1830): 1.

[104]William K. Fox, Sr. "African Americans in the Movement," in Douglas Foster, et al., ed., *The Encyclopedia of the Stone-Campbell Movement* (Grand Rapids: Eerdmans, 2004), 10-11.

[105]Alexander Campbell, *Christian Baptist* (August, 1823): 1:25.

[106]Campbell, "Prospectus," 1.

[107]Alexander Campbell, "The Crisis," *Millennial Harbinger* (February, 1832): 86-88.

[108]Selina H. Campbell, *Home Life and Reminiscenes of Alexander Campbell* (St. Louis: John Burns, Publisher, 1882), 454-455; Alexander Campbell, "Our Position to American Slavery," *Millennial Harbinger* (June, 1845): 259.

[109]See Rick Cherok, *Debating for God: Alexander Campbell's Challenge to Skepticism in Antebellum America* (Abilene: Abilene Christian University Press, 2008).

[110]For a thorough analysis of the development of Alexander Campbell's baptismal theology as developed in the Walker and Maccalla debates, see David W. Fletcher, ed., *Baptism and the Remission of Sins* (Joplin: College Press, 1990).

[111]Alexander Campbell, "Miscellaneous Letters—No. 1," *Christian Baptist* (October, 1827): 5:70.

[112]William Baxter, *Life of Elder Walter Scott* (Cincinnati: Bosworth, Chase, and Hall Publishers, 1874), 79-80; and Dwight E. Stevenson, *The Voice of the Golden Oracle* (St. Louis: Christian Board of Publication, 1946), 103.

[113]Richard L. Harrison, Jr., *From Camp Meeting to Church: A History of the Christian Church (Disciples of Christ) in Kentucky* (St. Louis: Published for the Christian Church (Disciples of Christ) in Kentucky by the Christian Board of Publication, 1992), 45-47.

[114]Williams, *Barton Stone*, 167-161.

[115]Barton Stone, *Christian Messenger* (September, 1829): 261-262.

[116]Williams, *Barton Stone*, 171-173; Barton Stone to Prochorus [pseud.], *Christian Messenger* (June, 1827): 186; Barton Stone to Philip [Walter Scott], *Christian Messenger* (January 1827): 49-52.

[117]W. T., "Extract of a Letter to the Editor," *Christian Baptist* (January, 1830): 7:139.

[118]F [pseud.] to Alexander Campbell, *Millennial Harbinger* (May, 1830): 199-200.

[119]Barton Stone, *Christian Messenger* (August, 1830): 201.

[120]Alexander Campbell to B [Barton Stone], *Millennial Harbinger* (August, 1830): 372-373.

[121]Alexander Campbell to B [Barton Stone], *Millennial Harbinger* (August, 1830): 372.

[122]Alexander Campbell, "Opinion," *Millennial Harbinger* (February, 1831): 102-103.

[123]Barton Stone, "Answer to Elder John Scott," *Christian Messenger* (September, 1830): 228-229.

[124]Barton Stone, "Union," *Christian Messenger* (August, 1831):181-185.

[125]Stone, "Union," 180.

[126]Alexander Campbell, "Reply on Union, Communion, and the Name Christian," *Millennial Harbinger* (August, 1831): 389-390.

[127]Campbell, "Reply," 390.

[128]Barton Stone, "Union of Christians," *Christian Messenger* (January, 1831): 6. For an account of the life of John T. Johnson, see John Rogers, *The Biography of Elder J. T. Johnson* (Cincinnati: Privately printed, 1861).

[129]Williams, *Barton Stone*, 190-191.

[130]John Augustus Williams, *Life of Elder John Smith* (St. Louis: Christian Publishing Company, 1870), 449-454.

[131]Williams, *Life of Elder John Smith*, 454-455.

[132]Williams, *Life of Elder John Smith*, 455.

[133]Barton Stone, "Union of Christians," *Christian Messenger* (January, 1832): 6-7; and Barton Stone, "Remarks on the Above Communication," *Christian Messenger* (January, 1830): 30.

[134]Barton Stone, "Advice," *Christian Messenger* (April, 1832): 110.

[135]Alexander Campbell, "Letters to Dr. James Otey, Bishop of Tennessee, Letter III," *Millennial Harbinger* (July, 1835): 289-295; and Alexander Campbell, "Letters to Dr. James Otey, Bishop of Tennessee, Letter VII," *Millennial Harbinger* (December, 1835): 590-594. See also George R. Phillips, "Differences in the Theological and Philosophical Backgrounds of Alexander Campbell and Barton W. Stone and Resulting Differences of Thought in Their Theological Formulations" (PhD diss., Vanderbilt University, 1968), 167-168.

[136]Barton Stone, "Reply to Broth J— M—," *Christian Messenger* (January, 1833): 4-6.

[137]Benjamin Franklin Hall, *The Autobiography of B.F. Hall* (unpublished manuscript held in the archives of Christian Theological Seminary, Indianapolis, Indiana), 50-51.

[138]Alexander Campbell, "The Spirit of God," *The Christian System* (1866; reprint, Salem: Ayer Company Publishers, 1988), 23-25, 63-67, 266-267; Alexander Campbell, *A Connected View of the Principles and Rules by which the Living Oracles May Be Intelligibly and Certainly Interpreted* (Bethany: M'Vay and Ewing, 1835), 346-351. See also D. Newell Williams, "The Gospel as the Power of God to Salvation: Alexander Campbell and Experimental Religion," in James M. Seale, ed., *Lectures in Honor of the Alexander Campbell Bicentennial, 1788-1988* (Nashville: Disciples of Christ Historical Society, 1988), 127-148.

[139]Barton Stone, "Reply to Dr. S. Roach's Letter," *Christian Messenger* (February, 1832): 61-63; Barton Stone, "An Address to the Churches of Christ," *Christian Messenger* (September, 1832): 263-266; Barton Stone, "Reply," *Christian Messenger* (May, 1834): 135-146. See also Alexander Campbell, "Union," *Millennial Harbinger* (September, 1831): 385-389; Alexander Campbell, "Reply on Union, Communion, and the Name Christian," *Millennial Harbinger* (September, 1831): 389-396; Alexander Campbell, "The Christian Messenger," *Millennial Harbinger* (December, 1831): 557-558.

[140]Barton Stone, "Remarks on Elder David Purviance's Communication," *Christian Messenger* (January, 1833): 18-19; Williams, *Barton Stone*, 197-200.

[141]Barton Stone, "An Address to the Churches of Christ," *Christian Messenger* (September, 1832): 265-266.

[142]Mathew Gardner, *The Autobiography of Elder Matthew Gardner: A Minister in the Christian Church* (Dayton, Ohio: Christian Publishing Association, 1874), 74.

[143]Vincent L. Miller, *Religious Denominations of the World* (Philadelphia: J.W. Bradley, 1860), 142.

2: Developments in U.S. to 1866

[1]Alexander Campbell, "Any Christians among the Protestant Parties," *Millennial Harbinger* (September, 1837): 412.

[2]Alexander Campbell, "Christians among the Sects," *Millennial Harbinger* (December, 1837): 565.

[3]Campbell, "Any Christians among the Protestant Parties," 412, 414.

[4]Campbell, "Christians Among the Sects," 507-508.

[5]Perry Epler Gresham, *Campbell and the Colleges* (Nashville: Disciples of Christ Historical Society, 1973), 19-38.

[6]For more information on the authority of Baptist associations in the early United States, see the Philadelphia Confession of Faith (1743), Article 27, "Of the Church," Sections 14 and 15; and Benjamin Griffith, *A Short Treatise Concerning a True and Orderly Gospel Church* (1743), available at http://www.founders.org/library/polity/griffith.htm, accessed August 4, 2011.

[7]Robert Richardson, *Memoirs of Alexander Campbell*, 2 vols. (Philadelphia: J. B. Lippincott, 1868-1870), 1:329; Alexander Campbell, "Mahoning Association," *Millennial Harbinger* (September 6, 1830): 411-416.

[8]Alexander Campbell, "The Co-Operation of Churches—No. 1," *Millennial Harbinger* (May, 1831): 237-238.

[9]Alexander Campbell, "General Meeting in New Lisbon," *Millennial Harbinger* (October, 1831): 445-446.

[10]A. B. G. and F. W. E., "Cooperation of Churches—No. V," *Millennial Harbinger* (May, 1832): 201.

[11]See, for example, Aylett Raines and William Hayden, "Progress of Reform," *Millennial Harbinger* (October,1832): 512-515.

[12]Alexander Campbell, "The Nature of the Christian Organization, No. I," *Millennial Harbinger* (November, 1841): 533-534.

[13]Alexander Campbell, "Five Arguments for Church Organization," *Millennial Harbinger* (November, 1842): 523.

[14]Alexander Campbell, "Church Organization—No. I," *Millennial Harbinger* (February, 1849): 93; "Church Organization—No. II," *Millennial Harbinger* (April, 1849): 222-223.

[15]Alexander Campbell, "Church Organization—No. III," *Millennial Harbinger* (May, 1849): 272-273.

[16]Alexander Campbell, "Convention," *Millennial Harbinger* (August, 1849): 475-476.

[17]W. K. P[endleton] and Alexander Campbell, "The Convention of Christian Churches," *Millennial Harbinger* (December, 1849): 689-695.

[18]Alexander Campbell, "The Christian Missionary Society," *Millennial Harbinger* (May, 1850): 282-284.

[19]Herman Norton, *Tennessee Christians* (Nashville: Reed and Company, 1971), 47-59.

[20]Alexander Campbell, "The Christian Religion," *Christian Baptist* (August 3, 1823): 15

[21]Alexander Campbell, "Conventions—No. V," *Millennial Harbinger* (November 1850): 638.

[22]David E. Harrell, Jr., *Quest for a Christian America, 1800–1865: A Social History of the Disciples of Christ*, 2 vols. (Tuscaloosa: University of Alabama Press, 2003 [1966]), 1:116.

[23]Paul M. Blowers, "'Living in a Land of Prophets': James T. Barclay and an Early Disciples of Christ Mission to Jews in the Holy Land," *Church History* 62 (1993): 494-513.

[24]James Barclay, "Letter to Alexander Campbell," *Millennial Harbinger* (January, 1854): 6; James Barclay, *The City of the Great King, or Jerusalem as it Was, as it Is, and as it Is to Be* (James Challen and Sons, 1858).

[25]James Barclay, "The Welfare of the World Bound Up in the Destiny of Israel," 7 parts, *Millennial Harbinger* (December, 1860): 661-669; (January, 1861): 6-14; (February, 1861): 61-69; (March, 1861): 121-128; (May, 1861): 241-246; (June, 1861): 301-307; and (July, 1861): 361-365.

[26]"A Mission Station in Jerusalem," *Christian-Evangelist* (April 12, 1928): 463.

[27]Alexander Campbell, "An Address Delivered to the Christian Missionary Society," *Millennial Harbinger* (November, 1857): 601-615, quoted at 613-614.

[28]*They Went to Africa: Biographies of Missionaries of the Disciples of Christ* (United Christian Missionary Society, 1952), 5; Alonzo Fortune, *Disciples in Kentucky* (The Christian Churches in Kentucky, 1932), 349-350.

[29]Robert Nelson, *Disciples of Christ in Jamaica, 1858-1958* (St. Louis: Bethany Press, 1958), 29-32.

[30]J. O. Beardslee, "Infant Sprinkling," *Millennial Harbinger* (January, 1857): 32-37.

[31]Nelson, *Disciples of Christ in Jamaica*, 32-36. Alexander Campbell, "A Missionary for Jamaica," *Millennial Harbinger* (April, 1857): 231-233.

[32]Nelson, *Disciples of Christ in Jamaica*, 40-42.

[33]Nelson, *Disciples of Christ in Jamaica*, 42.

[34]Barton Stone, "Address to the People of the United States on Slavery," *Christian Messenger* (April, 1835): 82.

[35]Barton Stone, "Emancipation of Slaves," *Christian Messenger* (July 1835): 160-161. See Patrick Richardson, *Empire and Slavery* (London: Longmans, Green, and Co., Ltd., 1968), 94-95.

[36]Barton Stone, "Emancipation of Slaves in the French Colonies," *Christian Messenger* (July, 1835): 161-163.

[37]Barton Stone, "An Explanation," *Christian Messenger* (November, 1835): 263.

[38]Raymond James Krohn, "Nonresistance," in Paul Finkleman, *Encyclopedia of African American History, 1619-1895: From the Colonial Period to the Age of Frederick Douglass*, 2 vols. (New York: Oxford University Press, 2006), 2:462-463.

[39]Barton Stone, "Reply to T. P. Ware," *Christian Messenger* (October, 1844): 169-171; Barton Stone, "An Interview Between and Old and Young Preacher," *Christian Messenger* (December, 1844): 227-228.

[40]James Gifford, "Emily Tubman and the African Colonization Movement in Georgia," *Georgia Historical Quarterly* (1975): 10-24; Joseph Richard Bennett, "A Study of the Life and Contributions of Emily H. Tubman" (BD thesis, Butler School of Religion, 1958), 41-47.

[41]Alexander Campbell, "Millennium—No. I," *Millennial Harbinger* (February, 1830): 58.

[42]Thomas Campbell, "Elder Thomas Campbell's Views of Slavery," *Millennial Harbinger* (January, 1845): 3-8.

[43]Alexander Campbell, "Our Position to American Slavery, No. VIII," *Millennial Harbinger* (June, 1845): 263.

[44]Alexander Campbell, "Our Position to American Slavery, No. V;" *Millennial Harbinger* (May, 1845): 234.

[45]Frederick Douglass, "The Free Church of Scotland and American Slavery: An Address Delivered in Dundee, Scotland, on January 30, 1846," published in the *Dundee Courier*, February 3, 1846, available at http://www.yale.edu/glc/archive/1066.htm, accessed August 3, 2011.

[46]Richardson, *Memoirs of Alexander Campbell*, 2:552-566. Thomas Chalmers, *Alexander Campbell's Tour in Scotland* (Louisville: Guide Printing and Publishing Company, 1892).

[47]Alexander Campbell, "Our Position on American Slavery," *Millennial Harbinger* (January, 1851): 49-50.

[48]Alexander Campbell, "Disturbance in Bethany College,"

Millennial Harbinger (January, 1856): 51, 56-57, 59.

[49]Rosetta B. Hastings, ed. *Personal Recollections of Pardee Butler* (Cincinnati: Standard Publishing Co., 1889), 321.

[50]Lester McAllister and William Tucker, *Journey in Faith: A History of the Christian Church (Disciples of Christ)* (St. Louis: Bethany Press, 1975), 199-200.

[51]John G. Fee, *An Anti-Slavery Manual, or, The Wrongs of American Slavery Exposed By the Light of the Bible and of Facts, with A Remedy for the Evil*, 2d ed. (New York: William Harned, 1851), available at http://medicolegal.tripod.com/feeasm1851.htm, accessed January 11, 2012.

[52]Jane Campbell McKeever to John Boggs, *North-Western Christian Magazine* (November, 1854): 153-154. For more on McKeever's abolitionist activities, see John H. Hull, "Jane Campbell McKeever," *Discipliana* (Spring, 1992): 7-12.

[53]John H. Hull, "Underground Railroad Activity Among Western Pennsylvania Disciples," *Discipliana* (Spring, 1997): 7-8.

[54]McAllister and Tucker, *Journey in Faith*, 196.

[55]*Annual Report of the American and Foreign Anti-Slavery Society* (New York: William Harned, Office Agent, 1851), 56. See also Harrell, *Quest for a Christian America*, 1:93ff.

[56]B. F. Manire, "Mississippi State Meeting," *Millennial Harbinger* (October, 1868): 583.

[57]Edward E. Gacey to Alexander Campbell, September 12, 1861, Campbell Collection, Bethany College.

[58]Harrell, *Quest for a Christian America*, 1:4.

[59]Lawrence A. Q. Burnley, *Cost of Unity: African American Agency and Education in the Christian Church, 1865-1914* (Macon: Mercer University Press, 2008), 111. See also Robert Jordan, *Two Races in One Fellowship* (Detroit: United Christian Church, 1944), 23.

[60]Burnley, *Cost of Unity*, 111-113. See also Hap Lyda, "A History of Black Christian Churches (Disciples of Christ) in the United States Through 1899," (PhD diss., Vanderbilt University, 1972), 8-9.

[61]See Richard L. Harrison, Jr., *From Camp Meeting to Church: A History of the Christian Church (Disciples of Christ) in Kentucky* (St. Louis: published for the Christian Church [Disciples of Christ] in Kentucky by the Christian Board of Publication, 1992), 128-129; McAllister and Tucker, *Journey in Faith*, 186.

[62]Lyda, "A History of Black Christian Churches," 23-35, 37, 173.

[63]Alexander Campbell, "The Cherokee Indians," *Millennial Harbinger* (January, 1830): 44-46.

[64]James J. Trott, "To the Editor of the Millennial Harbinger," *Millennial Harbinger* (February, 1832): 85.

[65]Tolbert Fanning, "James J. Trott: Messenger of the Church of Christ at Franklin College, Tennessee, to the Cherokee Nation," *Gospel Advocate* (March 25, 1869): 271-274.

[66]J. J. Trott, "The Indian Mission," *Christian Record* (August, 1856): 244.

[67]J. J. Trott, "The Indian Mission," *Millennial Harbinger* (September, 1860): 505-507.

[68]Stephen Thurston, "Letter to Colonel Joseph Ames, September 27, 1834," *Christian Messenger* (July, 1835): 157-159.

[69]J. McFarland, "Congress of Nations," *Christian Messenger* (September, 1835): 201-203; "Congress of Nations," *Christian Messenger* (June, 1841): 358.

[70]"Queries Proposed for Investigation by a Worthy Brother," *Christian Messenger* (December, 1827): 36; Peter Brock, *Pacifism in the United States: From the Colonial Era to the First World War* (Princeton: Princeton University Press, 1968).

[71]Barton Stone, "Civil and Military Offices Sought and Held by Christians," *Christian Messenger* (May, 1842): 204-205.

[72]"Lectures on Matt[hew] VI, VI, and VII Chapters," *Christian Messenger* (July, 1844): 65-66.

[73]Stone, "Civil and Military Offices," 202.

[74]Barton Stone, "Kingdom of Heaven or Church of God," *Christian Messenger* (September, 1840): 30; Barton Stone, "Reflections on Old Age," *Christian Messenger* (August, 1843): 123; Stone, "Interview," 225-226.

[75]Stone, "Civil and Military Offices," 203.

[76]Stone, "Reflections on Old Age," 124-125.

[77]Stone, "Reply to T. P. Ware," 168. Stone's view of the contrast between the limited power of earthly governments and the rule of Christ may have been influenced by an article by Missouri preacher Jacob Creath, Jr. See Jacob Creath, "Essay No. III," *Christian Messenger* (February, 1841): 189-191.

[78]Stone, "Civil and Military Offices," 202-204.

[79]Stone, "Civil and Military Offices," 202; Stone, "Reply to T. P. Ware," 167-170.

[80]Alexander Campbell, "The Christian Religion," *Christian Baptist* (August, 1823): 1:24.

[81]Alexander Campbell, "Address on War," in *Popular Lectures and Addresses by Alexander Campbell* (Philadelphia: James Challen and Son, 1863), 357.

[82]Campbell, "Address on War," 362-363.

[83]Alexander Campbell, "An Address on War," *Millennial Harbinger* (July, 1848): 361-386; Campbell, *Popular Lectures and Addresses*, 357.

[84]Campbell, *Popular Lectures and Addresses*, 365

[85]Alexander Campbell, "The Fugitive Slave Law," *Millennial Harbinger* (January, 1851): 27; and Alexander Campbell, "Slavery and the Fugitive Slave Law," *Millennial Harbinger* (April, 1851): 202.

[86]Alexander Campbell, "The Spirit of War," *Millennial Harbinger* (June, 1861): 339.

[87]Alexander Campbell, "Wars and Rumors of Wars," *Millennial Harbinger* (June, 1861): 348.

[88]McAllister and Tucker, *Journey in Faith*, 200-207.

[89]Tolbert Fanning, "Churches of Christ and World Powers," *Gospel Advocate* (July 3, 1866): 417ff. See also Norton, *Tennessee Christians*, 103-104; Harrell, *The Quest for Christian America*, 151.

[90]Joan Jenkins Perez, "Stone, Barton Warren, Jr.," *Handbook of Texas Online*, http://www.tshaonline.org/handbook/online/articles/SS/fst63.html, accessed August 3, 2011; R. Edwin Groover, *The Well-Ordered Home: Alexander Campbell and the Family* (Joplin: College Press Publishing Company, 1988), 143-144.

[91]Moses E. Lard, "Can We Divide?" *Lard's Quarterly* (April, 1866): 331.

[92]Lard, "Can We Divide?" 335-336.

[93]Tolbert Fanning, "Cooperation," *Gospel Advocate* (October, 1855): 110.

[94]Norton, *Tennessee Christians*, 55-61.

[95]Tolbert Fanning, "Annual Meeting of the American Christian Missionary Society," *Gospel Advocate* (November, 1859): 333.

[96]Tolbert Fanning, "Ministers of Peace in the World's Conflicts," *Gospel Advocate* (November, 1861): 347-348; David Lipscomb, "I Did Wrong," *Gospel Advocate* (March 13, 1866): 170-171.

3: African American Institutions to 1920

[1]For biographical sketches of Preston Taylor's life, see Clement Richardson, *The National Cyclopedia of the Colored Race* (Montgomery: National Publishing Company, 1919), 334-335; and Todd W. Simmons, "Preston Taylor: Seeker of Dignity for Black Disciples," *Discipliana* (Winter, 2000): 99-109.

[2]Robert E. Hooper, *A Distinct People: A History of the Churches of Christ in the 20th Century* (West Monroe: Howard Publishing, 1993), 258-259.

[3]Lester C. Lamon, *Black Tennesseans, 1900-1930* (Knoxville: University of Tennessee Press, 1977); Howard N. Rabinowitz, *Race Relations in the Urban South, 1865-1890* (New York: Oxford University Press, 1978), 218.

[4]Edward J. Robinson, *To Save My Race from Abuse: The Life of Samuel Robert Cassius* (Tuscaloosa: University of Alabama Press, 2007), 11-16.

[5]Robinson, *To Save My Race*, 20-21.

[6]Robinson, *To Save My Race*, 81-131.

[7]Hap C. S. Lyda, "African Americans in the Movement," in Douglas Foster, et al., ed., *The Encyclopedia of the Stone-Campbell Movement* (Grand Rapids: Eerdmans, 2004), 11-13; Annie C. Tuggle, *Our Ministers and Song Leaders of the Church of Christ* (Detroit: n.p., 1945), 71.

[8]Jeanne Scott Duke, "Journey of Faith: The Freedmen Congregations of Davis Bend," *Discipliana* (Summer, 2006): 49.

[9]Duke, "Journey of Faith," 39-43, 44-47.

[10]Hap C. S. Lyda, "A History of Black Christian Churches (Disciples of Christ) in the United States Through 1899" (PhD dissertation, Vanderbilt University, 1972), 63.

[11]William T. Withers, "A Great Work Among the Freedmen," *The Ecclesiastical Observer* XXVI, Sixth Series (September 1, 1873): 294-295.

[12]Duke, "Journey of Faith," 47-49.

[13]Duke, "Journey of Faith," 49.

[14]Richard L. Harrison, Jr., *From Camp Meeting to Church: A History of the Christian Church (Disciples of Christ) in Kentucky* (St. Louis: Christian Board of Publication, 1992), 131, 138.

[15]Harrison, *From Camp Meeting to Church*, 138-139.

[16]Harrison, *From Camp Meeting to Church*, 140.

[17]Harrison, *From Camp Meeting to Church*, 138-139.

[18]Harrison, *From Camp Meeting to Church*, 140-142.

[19]Harrison, *From Camp Meeting to Church*, 139.

[20]Samuel Robert Cassius, *The Letter and Spirit of Giving and the Race Problem* (1898), in Edward Robinson, ed., *To Lift Up My Race: The Essential Writings of Samuel Robert Cassius* (Knoxville: University of Tennessee Press, 2008), 74.

[21]Samuel Robert Cassius, "A Colored Brother's Protest," *The Christian-Evangelist* (November 14, 1889): 726.

[22]Robinson, *To Save My Race from Abuse*, 61-64, 75-76.

[23]Sheila Hope Gillams, "Principle and Practice: The Quandary of African American Restorationists in the History and Theology of the Church of Christ, Disciples of Christ, 1850-1950" (PhD diss., Union Theological Seminary, 2002), 69-72.

[24]Gillams, "Principle and Practice," 49-50.

[25]Gillams, "Principle and Practice," 49, 60-63.

[26]Gillams, "Principle and Practice," 49-51.

[27]Gillams, "Principle and Practice," 118.

[28]Gillams, "Principle and Practice," 121-122; General Assembly, *Proceedings of the Twenty-Seventh General Assembly of the Disciples of Christ, 1897*, 16.

[29]Gillams, "Principle and Practice," 115-116, 118-122.

[30]Gillams, "Principle and Practice," 117-118.

[31]Gillams, "Principle and Practice," 94, 111-112.

[32]Gillams, "Principle and Practice," 134, 154-155.

[33]Gillams, "Principle and Practice," 135-136.

[34]David Edwin Harrell, *The Social Sources of Division in the Disciples of Christ, 1865-1900* (Atlanta: Publishing Systems, Inc., 1973), 170, 184.

[35]Lewis Pinkerton, "Kentucky," *Christian Standard* (May 19, 1866): 53.

[36]Harrell, *Social Sources of Division*, 165-166.

[37]David Lipscomb, "The Freedmen—Their Condition," *Gospel Advocate* (February 13, 1868): 147-148; Harrell, *Social Sources of Division*, 172.

[38]In cooperation with the city's school board, Second's Sunday school was transformed into "Public School #23." Lyda, "African Americans," 12.

[39]Lyda, "A History," 65 and 99.

[40]Lawrence A. Q. Burnley, *Cost of Unity: African-American Agency and Education in the Christian Church, 1865-1914* (Macon: Mercer University Press, 2008), 211-212.

[41]Burnley, *Cost of Unity*, 212. See also J. C. Power, "A Warning," *Christian Standard* (December 4, 1869): 389; "Tennessee Manual Labor University," *Christian Standard* (December 18, 1869): 404; "The Murfreesboro School," *Christian Standard* (January 29, 1870): 36; and Samuel Lowery, "A Calumniating Slanderer," *Christian Standard* (January 29, 1870): 34-35.

[42]*Report of Proceedings of the Twenty-fourth Anniversary Meeting of the General Christian Missionary Convention, 1872,* (Cincinnati: Bosworth, Chase and Hall, 1872), 17-18, quoted in Harrell, *Social Sources of Division*, 182.

[43]Burnley, *Cost of Unity*, 192.

[44]*Proceedings of the General Missionary Convention* (Cincinnati: Chase and Hall, 1877), 25, quoted in Harrell, *Sources of Division*, 180.

[45]Duke, "Journey of Faith," 49, 51.

[46]John Long, "Disciples and Negro Education," *World Call* (April, 1943): 13-14.

[47]Arlene Goodwin, "Biography of Randal Faurot, A.M.," in *History of De Kalb County, Indiana* (Chicago: Inter-State Publishing Company, 1885), 707-709; Elmer C. Lewis, "A History of Secondary and Higher Education in Negro Schools Related to the Disciples of Christ" (PhD dissertation, University of Pittsburgh, 1957), 44.

[48]Joel B. Lehman, "The Work of the CWBM among the Negroes," *Missionary Tidings* (November, 1910): 232.

[49]Andrew R. Wood, "Southern Christian Institute (1875-1954)," in Douglas Foster, et al., ed., *The Encyclopedia of the Stone-Campbell Movement* (Grand Rapids: Eerdmans, 2004), 694-695. By 1932 SCI had developed its curriculum sufficiently to be classed as a junior college with an enrollment of 19 college students. In 1954 SCI merged with Tougaloo College in Jackson, Mississippi, a black liberal arts college founded by the Congregationalist-supported American Missionary Society.

[50]C. C. Smith, "History of Our Mission Work among the Negroes," *American Home Missionary* (March, 1900): 17.

[51]R. B. Neal, "The Colored Bible School," *Gospel Advocate* (October 10, 1888): 1, quoted in Burnley, *Cost of Unity*, 217

[52]John W. Jenkins, "Colored Schools and Missions," (report presented to the Board of the General Christian Missionary Convention, 1889), quoted in Burnley, *Cost of Unity*, 217.

[53]Lyda, "A History," 124-125. Also see Harrell, *The Social Sources of Division*, 193-194; Elmer Lewis, "A History of Secondary and Higher Education," 49; John C. Long, "The Disciples of Christ and Negro Education" (PhD diss., University of Southern California, 1960), 145-147.

[54]Burnley, *Cost of Unity*, 220; Effie Cunningham, "Work of Disciples of Christ with Negro Americans," (St. Louis: United Christian Missionary Society, ca. 1922), 10-11; Robert G. Sherer, *Black Education in Alabama, 1865-1901* (Tuscaloosa: University of Alabama Press, 1997), 90. See also Harrell, *Social Sources of Division*, 195; Lewis, "Disciples of Christ and Negro Education," 67; and Lyda, "A History," 134.

[55]Burnley, *Cost of Unity*, 219.

[56]Burnley, *Cost of Unity*, 216-217.

[57]Burnley, *Cost of Unity*, 224. The dating here is based on James H. Thomas' report "The Piedmont School of Industry," *Gospel Plea* (October 30, 1901): 7. Lewis dates the opening on October 1, 1900, (p. 69); and Long cites a published a report by W. A. Cole in which he stated "we made preliminary arrangements for the final opening of the Piedmont School of Industry on Friday, October 4, 1900." W. A. Cole, *American Home Missionary*, VI (November, 1900): 79, quoted in Long, "Disciples of Christ and Negro Education," 180.

[58]Burnley, *Cost of Unity*, 224.

[59]Burnley, *Cost of Unity*, 228.

[60]"National Colored Christian College," *Christian Standard* (January 14, 1888): 29. Also see Burnley, *Cost of Unity*, 218; Harrell, *Social Sources of Division*, 193; Lyda, "A History," 166; D. Duane Cummins, *The Disciples: A Struggle for Reformation* (St. Louis: Chalice Press, 2009), 90.

[61]Burnley, *Cost of Unity*, 234; and Mary Alphin, "The Opening of Jarvis Christian Institute," *Missionary Tidings* (May, 1913): 13.

[62]Bertha M. Fuller, *Sarah Lue Bostick: Minister and Missionary*, (Private Printing, 1949), 8, on file at the Disciples of Christ Historical Society, Nashville, Tennessee, quoted in Burnley, *Cost of Unity*, 236.

[63]Fran Craddock, Martha Few, and Nancy Heimer, *In the Fullness of Time: A History of Women in the Christian Church (Disciples of Christ)* (St. Louis: Chalice Press, 1999), 50. See also Burnley, *Cost of Unity*, 237.

[64]Mary Alphin, "Report to the Board," *Gospel Plea* (June, 1910): 35, quoted in Burnley, *Cost of Unity*, 237.

[65]Burnley, *Cost of Unity*, 241. Jarvis became an accredited four-year college in 1938.

[66]Samuel Robert Cassius, *Negro Evangelization and the Tohee Industrial School* (Cincinnati: Christian Leader, 1898).

[67]Robinson, *To Save My Race from Abuse*, 100-110.

[68]G. P. Bowser, "Putnam County Normal, Industrial, and Orphan School, Silver Point, Tenn.," *Gospel Advocate* (July 29, 1915): 745; G. P. Bowser, "Work among the Colored People," *Gospel Advocate* (February 20, 1908): 125; G. P. Bowser, "Work among the Colored Disciples," *Gospel Advocate* (April 30, 1908): 285. For a thorough study of African Americans' quest for education in the post-Civil War South, see James D. Anderson, *The Education of Blacks in the South, 1860-1935* (Chapel Hill: University of North Carolina Press, 1988).

[69]G. P. Bowser, "The Colored Bible School," *Gospel Advocate* (May 7, 1914): 508.

[70]A. M. Burton, "The Prospects and Needs of the Putnam County Industrial School for Negroes," *Gospel Advocate* (February 10, 1916): 132. Regarding Burton's business acumen, see Don H. Doyle, *Nashville in the New South, 1880-1930* (Knoxville: University of Tennessee Press, 1985), 57-58.

[71]"Report of Silver Point Bible School for Negroes," *Gospel Advocate* (July 27, 1916): 748-749.

[72]G. P. Bowser, "Among the Colored People," *Gospel Advocate* (May 4, 1916): 458.

[73]Wood, "Southern Christian Institute," 695. This last effort led to the establishment of Southwestern Christian College in Terrell, Texas, in 1950. The school achieved accreditation as a junior college in 1977 and senior college status for Bible and religious education in 1980. At the beginning of the twenty-first century, Southwestern had an enrollment of approximately 200 students.

[74]"Goldsboro Christian Institute," *The North Carolina Christian* (December, 1956): 11; Gillams, "Principle and Practice," 158.

[75]Burnley, *Cost of Unity*, 214.

[76]Burnley, *Cost of Unity*, 215-216.

[77]Burnley, *Cost of Unity*, 198-199; General Christian Missionary Convention, "Work among Negroes in the United States, 1864-1892" (unpublished manuscript), 33-38, quoted in Lyda, "A History," 117.

[78]Joel B. Lehman, "The Work among Negroes," *Missionary Tidings* (December, 1909): 365; Lehman, "The Work of the CWBM," 232.

[79]Preston Taylor, "The Status and Outlook of the Colored Brotherhood," in *Report of the First General Convention of Christian (Colored) Churches in the U.S.A., held at Nashville, Tennessee August [sic] 5th to 9th, 1917* (Nashville: n. p., 1917), 24. See Burnley, *Cost of Unity*, 246-249 for an extended quotation and analysis of Taylor's address.

[80]Taylor, "Status and Outlook," 21-22.

[81]Taylor, "Status and Outlook," 23.

[82]Taylor, "Status and Outlook," 24.

[83]Brenda Cardwell and William Fox, Sr., *Journey Toward Wholeness: A History of Black Disciples of Christ in the Mission of the Christian Church* (Nashville: National Convocation, 1990), 20.

[84]Rayford W. Logan, *The Betrayal of the Negro, from Rutherford B. Hayes to Woodrow Wilson* (New York: Collier Books, 1965).

[85]See Neil R. McMillen, *Dark Journey: Black Mississippians in the Age of Jim Crow* (Urbana: University of Illinois Press, 1990) and Leon F. Litwack, *Trouble in Mind: Black Southerners in the Age of Jim Crow* (New York: Knopf, 1998).

[86]Quoted in Harold Bradley, *The United States From 1865* (New York: Charles Scribner's Sons, 1973), 146.

[87]See Benjamin E. Mays, *Born to Rebel: An Autobiography* (New York: Charles Scribner's Sons, 1971), 83-88, 149, and 251; and C. Vann Woodward, *The Strange Career of Jim Crow* (New York: Oxford University Press, 1966), 170-171.

[88]See Philip Dray, *At the Hands of Persons Unknown: The Lynching of Black America* (New York: Random House, 2002) and Charles Chesnutt, "Lynching Statistics," http://faculty.berea.edu/browners/chesnutt/classroom/lynchingstat.html, accessed August 8, 2011.

[89]John Hope Franklin and Alfred A. Moss, Jr., *From Slavery to Freedom: A History of African Americans* (1947; reprint, Boston: McGraw-Hill, 2000), 323. In the first fourteen years of the twentieth century, only 315 victims of lynching were accused of rape or attempted rape. More than 500 were accused of robbery, insulting white persons, and numerous other offenses.

[90]Franklin and Moss, *From Slavery to Freedom*, 352-355.

[91]Harrell, *Social Sources of Division*, 205.

[92]"The Problem of the Negro," *The Christian-Evangelist* (June 1, 1899): 677.

[93]Washington included Preston Taylor "among the members of the Negro race that may serve to encourage other men and women of the race to go forward and win success in business directions." See Booker T. Washington, *The Negro in Business* (New York: AMS Press, 1907), 3.

[94]Quoted in Louis Harlan, *Booker T. Washington: The Making of a Black Leader, 1865-1901* (New York: Oxford University Press, 1972), 218. See Burnley, *Cost of Unity*, 171-172.

[95]"Indianapolis Convention," *The Christian-Evangelist* (October 28, 1897): 674, in Harrell, *Social Sources of Division*, 179.

[96]E. S. L. Whitfield, *A Message to the Negro Disciples of Christ of Eastern North Carolina* (Charlotte: privately published, 1906), 10-11.

[97]Annie C. Tuggle, "Another Appreciation of Booker T. Washington," *Gospel Advocate* (March 30, 1916): 225. Here Tuggle is in part responding to Cassius's eulogy of Booker T. Washington's death. See Samuel Robert Cassius, "An Appreciation of Booker T. Washington," *Gospel Advocate* (December 23, 1915): 1302.

[98]Lamon, *Black Tennesseans*; and Rabinowitz, *Race Relations in the Urban South*, 218. See also Edward L. Wheeler, *Uplifting the Race: The Black Minister in the New South, 1865-1902* (Lanham: University Press of America, 1986).

[99]Annie C. Tuggle, "Review," *Gospel Advocate* (January 18, 1923): 65; Annie C. Tuggle, *Another World Wonder* (n.p., 1973), 78 and 91.

4: Role of Women in U.S., 1874–1920

[1]Susan Hill Lindley, *You Have Stept Out of Your Place: A History of Women and Religion in America* (Louisville: Westminster John Knox Press, 1996), 48-116.

[2]Debra B. Hull, *Christian Church Women: Shapers of a Movement* (St. Louis: Chalice Press, 1994), 117-142; and Fran Craddock, Martha Faw, and Nancy Heimer, *In the Fullness of Time: A History of Women in the Christian Church (Disciples of Christ)* (St. Louis: Chalice Press, 1999), 8-9.

[3]Mother [Eliza Daniel] Stewart, *Memories of the Crusade, A Thrilling Account of the Great Uprising of the Women of Ohio in 1873, Against the Liquor Crime* (Columbus: Wm. G. Hubbard & Co., 1873).

[4]"Woman's Christian Temperance Union: Early History," available at http://www.wctu.org/earlyhistory.html, accessed August 20, 2010.

[5]Barbara Welter, "The Cult of True Womanhood: 1820-1860," *American Quarterly* (Summer, 1966): 151-174.

[6]See for example, Alexander Campbell, "Women's Rights," *Millennial Harbinger* (April, 1854): 203-206; Selina Campbell, "Women Preachers," *Christian Standard* (December 18, 1880): 402.

[7]Isaac Errett, "How Shall Women Labor in the Gospel," *Christian Standard* (April 6, 1872): 108.

[8]Elijah Goodwin, "Woman Preaching," *The Christian* (July 8, 1875): 2-3.

[9]Caroline Neville Pearre, "Our Beginning," *Missionary Tidings* (August, 1899): 102-103; Ida Withers Harrison, *Forty Years of Service: A History of the Christian Woman's Board of Missions* (Indianapolis: United Christian Missionary Society, 1920), 5-41.

[10]Isaac Errett, "Help These Women," *Christian Standard* (July 11, 1874): 220.

[11]David Lipscomb, "Card of Invitation," *Gospel Advocate* (October 6, 1892): 628.

[12]David Lipscomb, "Home Life, Home Duties, Home Religion," *Gospel Advocate* (May 27, 1897): 325.

[13]J. W. Sewell, "Infidelity in Young Men," *Gospel Advocate* (February 18, 1892): 103.

[14]David Lipscomb, "Woman's Work in the Church," *Gospel Advocate* (March 14, 1888): 7.

[15]David Lipscomb, "Woman's Work," *Gospel Advocate* (December 1, 1892): 756.

[16]Selina Campbell, "Women Preachers," *Christian Standard* (December 18, 1880): 402.

[17]Annie C. Tuggle, *Another World Wonder* (n.p., 1973), 14-16.

[18]Candace Lhamon Smith, "Whom We Serve," *Missionary Tidings* (December, 1896): 219; Ella Huffman, "The Higher Conquest," *Christian Oracle* (November 9, 1893): 708-709.

[19]Emma Campbell, "Our Work—Past and Future, *The Christian* (October 3, 1878): 1.

[20]Marcia Melissa Bassett Goodwin, "From My Standpoint," *Christian Standard* (June 11, 1881): 186.

[21]Smith, "Whom We Serve," 217.

[22]Louise Kelley, "The Growth and Present Status of the C.W.B.M.," *Missionary Tidings* (December, 1896): 202.

[23]Goodwin, "From My Standpoint," 186.

[24]Cindy Dougherty, "National Benevolent Association of the Christian Church (Disciples of Christ)," in Doug Foster, et al., ed., *The Encyclopedia of the Stone-Campbell Movement* (Grand Rapids: Eerdmans, 2004), 553-554.

[25]Mrs. J. A. C. Merriman, "Washington," *Missionary Tidings* (Christmas, 1894): 10.

[26]Lura V. Thompson, "Illinois," *Missionary Tidings* (December, 1896): 163.

[27]Mrs. E. S. Lattimore, "Maryland," *Missionary Tidings* (November, 1902): 251.

[28]Rachel Crouch, "How to Present the Work," *Missionary Tidings* (December, 1897): 184.

[29]Anna M. Hale, "The Field Worker, Her Qualifications," and Mary Lyons, "The Fieldworker, Her Preparation," *Missionary Tidings* (December, 1897): 183.

[30]Millie Vercoe, "South Dakota," *Missionary Tidings* (November, 1902): 252.

[31]Susie Sublette, "Kentucky," *Missionary Tidings* (Christmas, 1893): 17.

[32]T. D. Butler, "The Choice of Officers," *Missionary Tidings* (November, 1903): 283.

[33]Anna M. Hale, "Illinois," *Missionary Tidings* (November, 1902): 250.

[34]Cora Brunson, "South Carolina," *Missionary Tidings* (November, 1904): 269.

[35]Maria Jameson, *Missionary Tidings* (December, 1896): 200.

[36]Louise Kelly, "The Vital Significance of Our Woman's Work," *Missionary Tidings* (November, 1903): 280.

[37]Clara H. Hazelrigg, "Kansas," *Missionary Tidings* (December, 1897): 152.

[38]Bertha Mason, "Texas," *Missionary Tidings* (November, 1904): 267.

[39]"Miss Lura V. Thompson's Report," *Missionary Tidings* (November, 1902): 249.

[40]Sudie E. Flint, "Colorado," *Missionary Tidings* (November, 1912): 252.

[41]Crouch, "How to Present the Work," 184.

[42]"Sunday Service," *Missionary Tidings* (December, 1892): 37. See also Mrs. S. B. Baxter, "2nd District Convention," *Missionary Tidings* (Christmas, 1893): 38.

[43]Rachel Crouch, "Conditions of Membership," *Missionary Tidings* (November, 1903): 282.

[44]Millie Vercoe, "South Dakota," *Missionary Tidings* (November, 1902): 253; and Lydia A. Hopkins, "Washington," *Missionary Tidings* (November, 1899): 211.

[45]Olivia A. Baldwin, "Texas," *Missionary Tidings* (December, 1897): 153.

[46]Mrs. T. I. Stockman, "Indiana," *Missionary Tidings* (Christmas, 1893): 16.

[47]Cordie B. Knowles, "How May We Best Develop the Missionary Spirit in Our Children," *Missionary Tidings* (Christmas, 1894): 33.

[48]Annie Paul Carson and Affra B. Anderson, "California South-Arizona," *Missionary Tidings* (November, 1914): 323.

[49]Stockman, "Indiana," 16.

[50]Knowles, "How May We Best Develop," 33.

[51]Mrs. I. A. Conkin, "California," *Missionary Tidings* (December, 1889): 7.

[52]Baldwin, "Texas," 153.

[53]Alice A. Peak, "Iowa," *Missionary Tidings* (Christmas, 1895): 193.

[54]Affra B. Anderson, "California South," *Missionary Tidings* (November, 1916): 305.

[55]Mrs. R. F. Hill and Etta Nunn, "North Carolina," *Missionary Tidings* (November, 1913): 281.

[56]Richard Harrison, *From Camp Meeting to Church: A History of the Christian Church (Disciples of Christ) in Kentucky* (St. Louis: Christian Board of Publication, 1992), 138-139; Hull, *Christian Church Women*, 128-129.

[57]Sarah L. Bostick, "Beginning of the Missionary Work and Plans in Arkansas, 1896, Historical Sketch up to 1918," (n.p., n.d.), 1; Hap Lyda, "A History of Black Christian Churches (Disciples of Christ) in the United States Through 1899" (PhD diss., Vanderbilt University, 1972), 105-111, 154, and 165.

[58]Bertha Mason Fuller, *The Life Story of Sarah Lue Bostick* (Little Rock: n.p., 1949), 31, 33-34.

[59]Harrison, *From Camp Meeting to Church*, 138, 142.

[60]Brenda M. Cardwell and William K. Fox, Sr., *Journey Toward Wholeness: A History of Black Disciples of Christ in the Mission of the Christian Church* (Nashville: National Convocation of the Christian Church [Disciples of Christ], 1990), 14-22.

[61]Laura Gerould Craig, "New York and New Jersey," *Missionary Tidings* (November, 1906): 287.

[62]Mrs. R. F. Hill and Etta Nunn, "North Carolina," *Missionary Tidings* (November, 1915): 313.

[63]Mary Lyons, "Ohio," *Missionary Tidings* (November, 1913): 281; Elsie L. Taylor, "Pennsylvania," *Missionary Tidings* (November, 1914): 325; Hill and Nunn, "North Carolina," 313.

[64]Craig, "New York and New Jersey," 287.

[65]Louise Kelly, "Mrs. Kelly's Report," *Missionary Tidings* (November, 1903): 250.

[66]Francis "Birdie" Farrar Omer, *Mother or the Aloe Plant* (Louisville: Standard Publishing Company, 1925), 70.

[67]Omer, *Mother*, 69-70.

[68]Omer, *Mother*, 69-70.

[69]Clara H. Hazelrigg, "Kansas Letter," *Christian-Evangelist* (June 7, 1900): 725.

[70]Isabelle Goodacre, handwritten answers on Board of Pensions questionnaire, Biography File for Isabelle Goodacre, held at Disciples of Christ Historical Society, Nashville, Tennessee.

[71]Mattie Pounds, "The Children, News and Notes from the Young People's Department," *Missionary Tidings* (September, 1912): 149.

[72]Nathan S. Haynes, *History of the Disciples in Illinois 1819-1914* (Cincinnati: Standard Publishing, 1915), 464-466. Records actually show that she was not ordained until August 1889. See Glenn Zuber, "The Gospel of Temperance: Early Disciple Women Preachers and the WCTU 1887-1912," *Discipliana* 53 (Summer, 1993): 50-52.

[73]Zuber, "The Gospel of Temperance," 55-60.

[74]Hull, *Christian Church Women*, 34.

[75]Colby D. Hall, *Texas Disciples* (Fort Worth: Texas Christian University Press, 1953), 213, 217, 320.

[76]Cardwell and Fox, *Journey Toward Wholeness*, 24.

[77]Hull, *Christian Church Women*, 107-110.

[78]J. Cy Rowell and Jack L. Seymour, "Identity and Unity: Disciples Church Education," in D. Newell Williams, ed., *A Case Study of Mainstream Protestantism: The Disciples' Relation to American Culture, 1880-1989* (Grand Rapids: Eerdmans, 1991), 319-321.

[79]Tuggle, *Another World Wonder*, 45.

[80]Gillams, "Principle and Practice: The Quandary of African American Restorationists in the History of the Church of Christ, Disciples of Christ" (PhD diss., Union Theological Seminary, 2002), 109-110, 173-174.

[81]Gillams, "Principle and Practice," 109-110, 180-181.

[82]Good examples are R. C. Bell, "Woman's Work," *The Way* (August 6, 1903): 775-777; and Henry Hawley, "Woman and Her Work," *The Way* (August 20, 1903): 810.

[83]James A. Harding, "Woman's Work in the Church," *Christian Leader & the Way* (March 8, 1904): 8.

[84]Daniel Sommer, "Woman's Religious Duties and Privileges in Public," *Octographic Review* (August 20, 1901): 1.

[85]Silena M. Holman, "Wanted—Mothers," *Gospel Advocate* (April 1, 1897): 198.

[86]David Lipscomb, "Woman's Work in the Church," *Gospel Advocate* (March 14, 1888): 6-7.

[87]Silena M. Holman, "A Peculiar People," *Gospel Advocate* (May 2, 1888): 12.

[88]Holman, "A Peculiar People," 12.

[89]A. A. Bunner, "Woman's Work in the Church," *Gospel Advocate* (June 20, 1888): 5.

[90]David Lipscomb, "Woman's Station and Work," *Gospel Advocate* (October 10, 1888): 6-7.

[91]A collection of some of her writings and some of Lipscomb's responses are available at http://www.mun.ca/rels/restmov/people/sholman.html, accessed August 13, 2011.

[92]"Brother Larimore's Tribute to Mrs. Silena Moore Holman," *Gospel Advocate* (October 14, 1915): 1027.

[93]"Women and Preaching: The Caskey-Briney Discussion," *Christian Evangelist* (October, 1892): 646.

[94]"Women and Preaching: The Caskey-Briney Discussion," *Christian Evangelist* (December, 1892): 758.

[95]Clara Babcock, "Women in the Pulpit," *Christian Standard* (June 4, 1892): 483.

[96]Morgan Hayden, "Women Pastors and Evangelists," *Christian Standard* (June, 1893): 470.

[97]N. S. Haynes, "The Privilege of Women to Preach: Or Her Duty to Keep Silent—Which?" *Christian Standard* (September 16, 1893): 730.

[98]Thinking Cap, "A Protest," *Christian Standard* (July 1, 1893): 518.

[99]"List of Women Preachers," *The American Home Missionary* (December, 1906): 602 and *The American Home Missionary* 13 (December, 1907): 627. Beginning the next year, the publication became known as the *Yearbook*, and publication of the list continued. See *The Yearbook of the Disciples of Christ* (Cincinnati: American Christian Missionary Society, 1909), 149-150; *Yearbook* (1910), 145-146; *Yearbook* (1911), 128-

129; and *Yearbook* (1912), 254.

5: Divisions in North America

[1]Lester McAllister and William Tucker, *Journey in Faith: A History of the Christian Church (Disciples of Christ)* (St. Louis: Chalice Press, 1975), 217-219.

[2]Alexander Campbell, "Sketch of a Tour of 75 Days," *Millennial Harbinger* (July, 1835): 331-333; Alexander Campbell, "Notes on a Tour to the North-East—No. 1," *Millennial Harbinger* (July, 1836): 330-333.

[3]Richard T. Hughes, *Reviving the Ancient Faith: The Story of Churches of Christ in America* (Grand Rapids: Eerdmans, 1996), xii and 117-119.

[4]David Lipscomb, *Civil Government: Its Origin, Mission, and Destiny and the Christian's Relation to It* (Nashville: McQuiddy Printing Company, 1913), 27.

[5]James A. Harding, "The Kingdom of Christ vs. The Kingdoms of Satan," *The Way* (October 15, 1903): 930.

[6]David Lipscomb, *Queries and Answers*, ed. J. W. Shepherd, 5th ed. (Nashville: Gospel Advocate Co., 1963), 247.

[7]David Lipscomb, "The Kingdom of God," *Gospel Advocate* (May 21, 1903): 328.

[8]Lipscomb, *Civil Government*, 133-135; John Mark Hicks and Bobby Valentine, *Kingdom Come: Embracing the Spiritual Legacy of David Lipscomb and James Harding* (Abilene: Leafwood Publishers, 2006).

[9]Tolbert Fanning, "Reply to G. W. Elly's Protest," *Gospel Advocate* (February 20, 1866): 122.

[10]Hughes, *Reviving the Ancient Faith*, 134.

[11]Tolbert Fanning, "Ministers of Peace in the World's Conflicts," *Gospel Advocate* (November, 1861): 348.

[12]Lipscomb, "The Advocate and Sectionalism," *Gospel Advocate* (May 1, 1866): 273.

[13]"The Consultation Meeting in Murfreesboro," *Gospel Advocate* (June 26, 1866): 401-403.

[14]Robert E. Hooper, *Crying in the Wilderness: A Biography of David Lipscomb* (Nashville: David Lipscomb College, 1979), 91.

[15]Gilbert Randolph, "The Gospel Advocate," *Gospel Advocate* (January 9, 1866): 25.

[16]David Lipscomb, "Nathan W. Smith," *Gospel Advocate* (August 24, 1899): 537.

[17]David Lipscomb, "The New Hymn Book," *Gospel Advocate* (February 27, 1866): 133 and 135.

[18]David Lipscomb, "The Advocate," *Gospel Advocate* (January 1, 1866): 2.

[19]The material in this section is drawn from John Mark Hicks, Johnny Melton, and Bobby Valentine, *A Gathered People: Revisioning the Assembly as Transforming Encounter* (Abilene: Leafwood Publishers, 2007), 118-122.

[20]H. Turner, "Does the New Testament Determine the Elements of the Public Worship?" *Christian Quarterly* (January, 1870): 250-258.

[21]Benjamin Franklin, "Positive Divine Law," in *Gospel Preacher: A Book of Twenty-One Sermons*, vol. 2 (Cincinnati: G. W. Rice, Publisher, 1877), 195-217, quoted at 215.

[22]David Lipscomb, "The Organ in Worship," *Gospel Advocate* (September 11, 1873): 855.

[23]D. Newell Williams, *Ministry Among Disciples; Past, Present, and Future* (Indianapolis: Council on Christian Unity, 1985), 17-18.

[24]Weldon Bailey Bennett, "The Concept of Ministry in the Thought of Representative Men of the Disciples of Christ" (PhD diss., University of Southern California, 1971), 258, 264-265, and 292.

[25]David Lipscomb, *Gospel Advocate* (April, 1891): 261

[26]Robert Richardson, "Nature of Christian Faith," *Millennial Harbinger* (March, 1856): 154.

[27]Terry Miethe, "Slogans," in Douglas Foster, et al., ed., *The Encyclopedia of the Stone-Campbell Movement* (Grand Rapids: Eerdmans, 2004), 688.

[28]McAllister and Tucker, *Journey in Faith*, 263-276.

[29]See David Edwin Harrell, Jr., *The Social Sources of Division in the Disciples of Christ 1865-1900* (Atlanta: Publishing Systems, Inc., 1973).

[30] James H. Garrison, "Prerogatives of Mission Boards," *Christian-Evangelist* (May 24, 1894): 322.

[31]"Is there a Missing Link?" *Christian-Evangelist* (December 6, 1906): 1569; "A Study of our Present-Day Problems," *Christian-Evangelist* (January 6, 1908): 36.

[32]Two versions of the "Address and Declaration" were published shortly after the meeting at the Sand Creek Church. The versions contain minor differences in wording, but one very significant difference. The first version *does not* include "the use of instrumental music" among the innovations against which the signers are protesting. See "Address and Declaration," *Octographic Review* (September 5, 1889): 8. The second version *does*. See "Address and Declaration," *The Christian Leader* (September 10, 1889): 2. The reason for the difference between the versions is not clear. For a line-by-line comparison of the two versions, see http://stone-campbell.org/address/Address%20and%20Declaration.htm, accessed August 16, 2011.

[33]This paragraph comes from the *Octographic Review* version referenced above. It does not differ substantively from the same paragraph in the *Christian Leader* version.

[34]"The Seceders—Who Are They?" *Christian-Evangelist* (October 10, 1889): 648. An anonymous author similarly ridiculed the signers of the "Address and Declaration." See "The Sand Creek Chronicles," *Christian Standard* (September 28, 1889): 646.

[35]David Lipscomb, *Christian Unity: How Promoted, How Destroyed. Faith and Opinion* (Nashville: Gospel Advocate Printing Co., 1890), 28-29. See also David Lipscomb, "Sand Creek Address and Declaration," *Gospel Advocate* (November 17, 1892): 725.

[36]David Lipscomb, "Convention Thoughts," *Gospel Advocate* (November 10, 1892): 709.

[37]Kevin J. Christiano, "Numbering Israel: The U.S. Census and Religious Organizations," *Social Science History* (Autumn, 1984): 342-343.

[38]David Lipscomb, "The 'Church of Christ' and the 'Disciples of Christ,'" *Gospel Advocate* (July 18, 1907): 450. North probably consulted Benjamin Lyon Smith, George B. Ranshaw, and William Wright, eds., "Yearbook, 1906," *American Home Missionary* (December, 1906). Lipscomb's and Elam's names appear in the list of Tennessee preachers on p. 537.

[39]Lipscomb, "The Church of Christ," 450.

[40]James H. Garrison, "Things Which Make for Division," *The Christian-Evangelist* (December, 1907): 1645.

[41]David Lipscomb, "The *Christian-Evangelist* and Christian Unity," *Gospel Advocate* (January 23, 1908): 57.

[42]Garrison, "Things Which Make for Division," 1645.

[43]Lipscomb, "The *Christian-Evangelist* and Christian Unity," 58.

[44]"Death Calls G. A. Hoffmann," *Christian Standard* (January 1, 1938): 15.

[45]David Lipscomb, "United States Church Statistics," *Gospel Advocate* (November 7, 1907): 713.

[46]See for example J. W. Shepherd, "Editorial," *Gospel Advocate* (February 20, 1908): 117; and G. A. Hoffmann, "Statistics of the Churches of Christ," *Christian Standard* (March 28, 1908): 565.

[47]*Religious Bodies* (Washington: Government Printing Office, 1906), 15, 30.

[48]*Religious Bodies*, 46.

[49]Alexander Campbell, "Work among the Colored People," *Gospel Advocate* (December 2, 1909): 1523; Marshall Keeble, "Keeble to be Here," *Gospel Advocate* (December 25, 1941): 1242.

[50]T. G. M'Lean, "Among the Colored Folks," *Gospel Advocate* (April 15, 1920): 389, quoted in Edward Robinson, "'The Two Old Heroes' Samuel W. Womack, Alexander Campbell and the Origins of Black Churches of Christ in the United States," *Discipliana* (Spring, 2005): 13.

[51]Robinson, "'The Two Old Heroes,'" 4.

[52]S. W. Womack, "Church News" *Gospel Advocate* (July 10, 1902): 445.

[53]S. W. Womack, "Work among the Colored People" *Gospel Advocate* (January 3, 1918): 18.

[54]R. Vernon Boyd, *Undying Dedication: The Story of G. P. Bowser* (Nashville: Gospel Advocate Co., 1985), 22-24.

[55]"A Paper for the Colored Brethren," *Gospel Advocate* (February 6, 1902): 92.

[56]In a ministry spanning nearly seventy years, Keeble is estimated to have baptized as many as 30,000. See Don Haymes, "Marshall Keeble," in Douglas Foster, et al., ed., *The Encyclopedia of the Stone Campbell Movement* (Grand Rapids: Eerdmans, 2004), 441.

[57]Douglas A. Foster, "The 1906 Census of Religious Bodies and Division in the Stone-Campbell Movement: A Closer Look," *Discipliana* (Fall, 2006): 83-93.

[58]On this point, see Clark M. Williamson and Charles R. Blaisdell, "Disciples Contributions and Responses to Mainstream Protestant Theology, 1880-1953," in D. Newell Williams, ed., *A Case Study of Mainstream Protestantism: The Disciples Relation to American Culture, 1880-1989* (Grand Rapids: Eerdmans, 1991), esp. 109-114. See also Eugene Boring, *Disciples and the Bible: A History of Disciples Biblical Interpretation in North America* (St. Louis: Chalice Press, 1997), 221-253.

[59]Henry E. Webb, *In Search of Christian Unity: A History of the Restoration Movement* (Cincinnati: Standard Publishing, 1990), 251. For a collection of McGarvey's essays against the critics, see McGarvey, *Short Essays in Biblical Criticism, Reprinted from the Christian Standard, 1893-1904* (Cincinnati: The Standard Publishing Co., 1910).

[60]J. W. McGarvey, "Biblical Criticism," *Christian Standard* (February 8, 1902): 14.

[61]J.W. McGarvey, "Biblical Criticism," *Christian Standard* (April 20, 1895): 11.

[62]James B. North, *Union in Truth: An Interpretive History of the Restoration Movement* (Cincinnati: Standard Publishing Company, 1994), 264-266.

[63]Joseph R. Jeter, *Alexander Procter: The Sage of Independence* (Claremont: Disciples Seminary Foundation, 1983), quoted at 124.

[64]Samuel C. Pearson, "The Cave Affair: Protestant Thought in the Gilded Age," *Encounter* (Spring, 1980): 180.

[65]James H. Garrison, "The Difficulty in the Central Church," *Christian-Evangelist* (December 26, 1889): 820.

[66]J. W. McGarvey, "Grounds on Which We Receive the Bible as the Word of God, and the Only Rule of Faith and Practice," in James H. Garrison, *The Old Faith Restated* (St. Louis: Christian Publishing Company, 1891), 11-48.

[67]G. W. Longan, "Grounds on Which We Accept Jesus as the Messiah, the Son of God and Savior of the World," *The Old Faith Restated*, 49-97, esp. 57-58, 69-82.

[68]Garrison, "Lessons From Our Past Experience; or, Helps and Hindrances," in *The Old Faith Restated*, 421-456; the indented quote is on 455.

[69]Isaac Errett, *Our Position: A Brief Statement of the Distinctive Features of the Plea for Reformation Urged by the People Known as Disciples of Christ* (Cincinnati: Standard Publishing Company, 1873), 290.

[70]Isaac Errett, "Inspiration," in *Missouri Christian Lectures*, 5 vols. (St. Louis: Christian Publication Company, 1882-1891), 2:167, 183.

[71]B. B. Tyler, "The Promise of Christian Union in the Signs of the Times," in *Addresses Delivered at the World's Congress and General Missionary Conventions of the Church of Christ Held at Chicago, in September, 1893* (Chicago: S. J. Clarke, 1893), 157-176, quoted at 174.

[72]W. T. Moore, "The Church of the Future," in *Addresses*, 53 and 77.

[73]Errett Gates, "The Philosophy of our History—III," *Christian Century* (October 23, 1902): 1271-1272. Among such efforts were the Episcopal Church's 1887 Chicago-Lambeth Quadrilateral and the newly formed National Federation of Churches and Christian

Workers.

[74]"Mr. Sheldon on Christian Unity," *Christian-Evangelist* (March 23, 1900): 356.

[75]"The Biggest Idea of the Convention: Disciples Renewing their Study of the Basis of Union," *Christian Century* (November 4, 1909): 5.

[76]F. M. Rains, "Forward!" *Christian-Evangelist* (February 11, 1915): 169.

[77]"Christ's World Purpose," *Christian-Evangelist* (February 18, 1915): 207.

[78]Samuel H. Church, "Progress and Achievements of a Century," *Christian Century* (November 18, 1909): 1143-1147.

[79]Addison Clark, "Letter to the Editor," *Christian Century* (December 2, 1909): 1195.

[80]In 2010, the Council, having changed its name in 1916 to the Association for the Promotion of Christian Unity, and in 1954 to the Council on Christian Unity, celebrated one hundred years of promoting a Disciples witness to Christian unity.

[81]Peter Ainslie, "Our Fellowship and The Task," *Christian Standard* (November 3, 1910): 325-326, 336; continued in "Our Fellowship and The Task," *Christian Century* (November 10, 1910): 349-350.

[82]"The Approach to Christendom," *Christian Century* (September 15, 1910): 153.

[83]Quoted in McAllister and Tucker, *Journey in Faith*, 280.

[84]J. H. Hughes, "Our Plea," *Christian Standard* (May 24, 1902): 745.

[85]Mark G. Toulouse, "Open Membership," in Douglas Foster, et al., ed., *The Encyclopedia of the Stone-Campbell Movement* (Grand Rapids: Eerdmans, 2004), 576-577.

[86]"Unifying the Progressive Forces," *Christian Century* (March 7, 1918): 3-6.

[87]David Lipscomb, "Bible School," *Gospel Advocate* (June 17, 1891): 377.

[88]Don Carlos Janes, "J. A. Harding," *Gospel Herald* (May 14, 1914): 1.

[89]This material is dependent upon John Mark Hicks, "The Gracious Separatist: Moral and Positive Law in the Theology of James A. Harding," *Restoration Quarterly* (Summer, 2000): 129-147.

[90]Daniel Sommer, "The Signs of the Times," *Octographic Review* (October 5, 1897): 1; and David Lipscomb, "The Churches Across the Mountains," *Gospel Advocate* (January 7, 1897): 4.

[91]Daniel Sommer, "A Record of My Life—(No. 44)," *American Christian Review* (July 15, 1941): 9-10.

[92]Daniel Sommer, "College, What Is It?" *Octographic Review* (March 1, 1910): 3.

[93]Austin McGary, "Five Years Work," *Firm Foundation* (September 3, 1889): 4.

[94]Sommer, "A Letter with Comments," *Octograhic Review* (February 2, 1904): 3.

[95]Daniel Sommer, "Let Patience Have Her Perfect Work," *Octographic Review* (June 29, 1897): 1, 8.

[96]J. D. Tant, "Too Many Papers," *Firm Foundation* (January 10, 1899): 23.

[97]Austin McGary, "Editorial," *Firm Foundation* (September 13, 1898): 284.

[98]Austin McGary, "The Firm Foundation—Its Aims and Principles," *Firm Foundation* (January 8, 1901): 8.

[99]George Savage, "Brother Burnett's Charges," *Firm Foundation* (November 28, 1905): 4.

[100]David Lipscomb, "Bible Schools," *Gospel Advocate* (June 16, 1910): 712-713.

[101]James A. Harding, "What a Brother Editor Thinks, With Some Comments Thereon," *The Way* (July, 1900): 98.

[102]James A. Harding, "Questions and Answers," *The Way* (July 17, 1902): 122.

[103]John W. Durst and J. C. McQuiddy, *The Faith that Qualifies for*

Valid Baptism: A Discussion (Nashville: McQuiddy Printing Company, 1914).

[104]L. F. Bittle, "The Gift of the Holy Ghost," *Octographic Review* (November 26, 1901): 4; Daniel Sommer, "Concerning What the Holy Spirit Says to Sinner and Saints," *Octographic Review* (July 14, 1903): 1.

[105]G. T. Walker, "The Indwelling of the Spirit," *Firm Foundation* (June 20, 1899): 385.

[106]L. C. Chisholm, "Spiritual Influence," *Firm Foundation* (November 14, 1905): 2.

[107]J. W. Denton, "Bro. Burnett's Muddle Again," *Firm Foundation* (September 6, 1898): 282.

[108]J. W. Denton, "The Spirit and the Word," *Firm Foundation* (July 4, 1905): 1.

[109]T. R. Burnett, "Owen to the Rescue," *Gospel Advocate* (April 21, 1898): 251.

[110]James A. Harding, "Another Effort to Get Dr. Holloway Out of the Fog," *Christian Leader & the Way* (October 24, 1905): 8; and James A. Harding, "Saving Souls, Special Providence, Dr. Holloway," *Christian Leader & the Way* (January 29, 1904): 8.

[111]R. H. Boll, "The Spirit's Indwelling," *Christian Leader and the Way* (May 16, 1905): 1.

[112]L. C. Chisholm, "Spiritual Influence," *Firm Foundation* (November 14, 1905): 2.

[113]Daniel Sommer, "Signs of the Times. Eleventh Article," *Octographic Review* (August 26, 1902): 1, 8; and Daniel Sommer, "Signs of the Times. Tenth Article," *Octographic Review* (August 19, 1902): 1.

[114]Daniel Sommer, "Sunday-Schools and Sunday-School Literature," *Octographic Review* (February 26, 1901): 1.

[115]Daniel Sommer, "Signs of the Times. Ninth Article," *Octographic Review* (August 12, 1902): 1.

[116]Daniel Sommer, "A Serious Letter," *Octographic Review* (July 18, 1905): 3.

[117]Sommer, "Signs of the Times. Ninth Article," 1.

[118]J. D. Tant, "Information Wanted," *Firm Foundation* (March 21, 1911): 6.

[119]Glenna Matthews, *"Just a Housewife": The Rise and Fall of Domesticity in America* (Oxford: University Press, 1987). See Kathy J. Pully, "Gender Roles and Conservative Churches: 1870-1930," 443-483; and Fred A. Bailey, "The Cult of True Womanhood and the Disciple Path to Female Preaching," 485-517, in *Essays on Women in Earliest Christianity*, vol. 2 (Joplin: College Press, 1995).

[120]Good examples are R. C. Bell, "Woman's Work," *The Way* (August 6, 1903): 775-777; and Henry Hawley, "Woman and Her Work," *The Way* (August 20, 1903): 810; James A. Harding, "Woman's Work in the Church," *Christian Leader & the Way* (March 8, 1904): 8.

[121]James A. Harding, "Woman's Work in the Church," *Christian Leader & the Way* (March 8, 1904): 8.

[122]Daniel Sommer, "Woman's Religious Duties and Privileges in Public," *Octographic Review* (August 20, 1901): 1.

[123]See, for example, J. C. Frazee, "Your Women," *Octographic Review* (July 5, 1904): 2.

[124]T. B. Larimore, "Reply to O. P. Spiegel's Open Letter," *Christian Standard* (July 24, 1897): 965-967.

[125]Byron Lambert, "Frederick D. Kershner," in Douglas Foster, et al., ed., *The Encyclopedia of the Stone-Campbell Movement* (Grand Rapids: Eerdmans, 2004), 444-446.

6: U.K./British Dominions to the 1920s

[1]Andrew Reed and James Matheson, *A Narrative of the Visit to the American Churches*, 2 vols. (New York: Harper and Brothers, 1835); and Francis Augustus Cox and James Hoby, *The Baptists in America* (London: T. Ward and Company, 1836).

[2]British Churches of Christ published the Maccalla Debate in 1842, the year of the first Cooperation Meeting. "Notice of the Debate on Baptism," *Christian Messenger and Reformer* (October, 1842):

268-273. Campbell's version of the New Testament had been published in London in March 1838 through the efforts of a Baptist minister. *The Sacred Writings of the Apostles and Evangelists…with Prefaces and an Appendix by A. Campbell* (London, 1838); "Version of the New Testament," *Christian Messenger and Reformer* (March, 1838): 35-36.

[3]The phrase comes from William Chillingworth, *The Religion of Protestants a Safe Way to Salvation* (London, 1637), a defense of the Church of England.

[4]"News from Reforming Brethren," *Christian Messenger and Reformer* (April, 1838): 72; and "News from Reforming Brethren and Churches," *Christian Messenger and Reformer* (December, 1837): 357-360.

[5]Almost all Stone-Campbell groups outside of the United States labeled themselves "Churches of Christ" and should not be equated with North American Churches of Christ after the division with Disciples.

[6]Alexander Campbell, "Attempt at the Restoration of the Ancient Order," *Christian Baptist* (November, 1827), 5:87-88; (December, 1827), 5:107-109; (January, 1828), 5:133-135; (February, 1828), 5:155-157; and (March, 1828), 5:190-192.

[7]The Scotch Baptists followed the teachings of Archibald McLean and Robert Carmichael, who withdrew from the Glasite congregation in Glasgow in 1763 and by 1765 had concluded that only believer's baptism could be justified from the New Testament. They founded the first Baptist congregation in Edinburgh, hence the label "Scotch." They spread to England and North Wales in the next half-century, so were not confined to Scotland. They were highly Calvinistic.

[8]William Jones, ed., *The Millennial Harbinger and Voluntary Church Advocate*, 2 vols. (London: G. Wightman, 1835), 1:1, 1:10-14; see also D. W. Bebbington, ed., *The Baptists in Scotland: A History* (Glasgow: Baptist Union of Scotland, 1988), 97, 163-164.

[9]Alexander Campbell, "A Restoration of the Ancient Order of Things," *Christian Baptist* (June, 1825), 2:254-259. Later, James Wallis would reprint the article in his *Christian Messenger and Reformer* (March, 1837): 14-19.

[10]"Letters from England—No. V," *Christian Messenger and Reformer* (July, 1838): 164-171; see also William Jones, *Primitive Christianity Illustrated in Thirty Sermons* (London: G. Wightman, 1837), 487-490.

[11]Andrew Fuller (1754-1815) was the first Secretary of the Baptist Missionary Society (1792), and was responsible for the moderate Calvinism that justified preaching the gospel to the heathen in his *The Gospel Worthy of all Acceptation* (1785).

[12]"Extract of a Letter to J. Wallis," *Christian Messenger and Reformer* (September, 1837): 247-249; and Jones, *Sermons on Primitive Christianity*, 502-503. Campbell commends Grew's work in "A Tribute to the Memory of the Apostles," *Millennial Harbinger* (May 1832): 239.

[13]The name was changed to the *British Millennial Harbinger and Family Magazine* in 1848.

[14]In English and Welsh nonconformity the name "Church of Christ" was not distinctive, particularly among Scotch Baptists. Many early nonconformist congregations used this description beginning in the late seventeenth century, though it was sometimes modified by words such as "of the Baptist (or Independent) denomination." But see A. C. Watters, *History of the British Churches of Christ* (Birmingham: Berean Press, 1948), 17. See also William Robinson, "A Short History of the Churches of Christ in the Furness District," *Christian Monthly* (January, 1920): 3-4.

[15]*George C. Reid, Our First Evangelist* (Southport: Powell and Green, 1885), 3-13.

[16]The total was probably nearer 1,600 if numbers from the non-reporting churches are included: David M. Thompson, *Let Sects and Parties Fall: A Short History of the Association of Churches of Christ in Great Britain and Ireland* (Birmingham: Berean Press, 1980), 31.

[17]"Co-operative Meeting at Edinburgh," *Christian Messenger and Reformer* (September, 1842): 247-249; and "Meeting of Messengers," *Christian Messenger and Reformer* (October, 1842): 279-284.

[18]"Report of General Meeting," *British Millennial Harbinger* (September 2, 1861): 463-464. The term "Co-operation," reflecting Alexander Campbell's use, simply described the gathering of the churches to coordinate evangelism and other activities. Later in the nineteenth century, "Annual Meeting" and "Annual Conference" became the common designations.

[19]John Aitken, "Memoir of Thomas Hughes," *British Millennial Harbinger* (August 1, 1866): 274-279.

[20]David King, "On the Life and Death of James Wallis," *British Millennial Harbinger* (July 1, 1867): 221 and 226.

[21]"Report of the General Meeting," *British Millennial Harbinger* (September 2, 1861): 464; Henry S. Earl, "Camden Town, London," *British Millennial Harbinger* (June 1, 1864): 218-219; "Earl on King," *British Millennial Harbinger* (September 1, 1869): 317-320; David King, "The Editor of the British Harbinger to the Disciples of Christ in America," *British Millennial Harbinger* (October 1, 1869): 347-352; and "H. S. Earl and the Editor," *British Millennial Harbinger* (May 1, 1870): 163-166.

[22]"Reviews, Notes on Passing Events, and Correspondence," *British Millennial Harbinger* (September 1, 1865): 314.

[23]"Annual General Meeting," *British Millennial Harbinger* (September 1, 1866): 320. The *Christian Advocate* was not published in 1866, so there is no alternative report available.

[24]Reports of the meeting became part of the controversy. W. T. Moore, *Life of Timothy Coop* (London: Christian Commonwealth Publishing, 1889), 247 and 266; reviewed by Lancelot Oliver, "The Life of Timothy Coop," *Christian Advocate* (1889): 244-247 and 278-288.

[25]"Intelligence of the Churches, Etc.," *Ecclesiastical Observer* (1876): 13, 77, and 265; "Letter from H. S. Earl to W. T. Moore," *Christian Advocate* (1876): 394; "The General Annual Meeting," (resolution 17), *Christian Advocate* (September 1883): 366.

[26]Bartley Ellis, "The Eastern Pilgrims," *Christian Advocate* (1877): 142-143 and 249-250; "Annual Meeting," *Ecclesiastical Observer* (August 15, 1877): 220; and William Linn, Gilbert Tickles, and David King, "Letters to Churches of Christ in America" in 3 parts, *Ecclesiastical Observer* (1878): 5-6, 16-19, 33-35, and 47-49.

[27]"Intelligence of the Churches, Etc.," *Ecclesiastical Observer* (1878): 82, and 209-210; Moore, *Life of Timothy Coop*, 325; and "The General Annual Meeting," *Christian Advocate* (September, 1883): 366.

[28]Moore, *Life of Timothy Coop*, 326-328; Archibald McLean, *The History of the Foreign Christian Missionary Society* (New York: Fleming Revell, 1919), 53-54.

[29]McLean, *History*, 54; Henry Varley, *Henry Varley's Life Story* (London: Pickering and Inglis, 1913), 65-87, 128-129.

[30]Moore, *Life of Timothy Coop*, 396-397.

[31]McLean, *History*, 125-126.

[32]McLean, *History*, 129; "Missionary Experiences," *Christian Monthly* (November, 1920): 176.

[33]Varley, *Life Story*, 129-130.

[34]T.S. Buckingham, "The Coming Union," *Christian Monthly* (July, 1917): 108.

[35]Leslie W. Morgan, "The Late William Durban," *Christian Monthly* (January, 1913): 3-7.

[36]L.W.M., "The Barnabas of our Churches," *Christian Monthly* (June, 1917): 90-91; *Centennial Convention Report: One Hundredth Anniversary of the Disciples of Christ* (Cincinnati: Standard Publishing, 1909), 168.

[37]None of the Forms of Service suggested for Sunday morning worship in 1916 included communion (although it is possible that it was normally done as an "after-service," as in many Baptist and Congregational churches at that time). See "The Editor's Page," *Christian Monthly* (September, 1916): 128 and insert.

[38]T.S. Buckingham, "The Crying Need of the British Churches," *Christian Monthly* (September, 1912): 137-138.

[39]*Churches of Christ Year Book and Annual Report* (Birmingham:

40"Resolution 21," *Churches of Christ Year Book and Annual Report* (Birmingham: Churches of Christ, 1890), 61; and "General Annual Meeting," *Bible Advocate* (September 1, 1890): 233-234 and 236.

41"What Does it Mean?" *Bible Advocate* (October 1, 1890): 254-255 and 305-307. When King died in June 1894, however, this new journal, then titled *The Christian at Work*, ceased publication.

42Positive appraisals were made by George Collin and T. K. Thompson; the more critical one comes from John Crockatt. "In Memoriam of David King," *Bible Advocate* (July 24, 1894): 261-275; and "Editorial Notes," *The Christian at Work* (August, 1894): 171; "David King," *The Christian at Work* (August, 1894): 178-181.

43"Sister's Conference," *Christian Advocate* (1881): 394-397.

44*Churches of Christ Year Book and Annual Report* (Birmingham: Churches of Christ, 1889), 33; "The General Annual Meeting," *Christian Advocate* (1889): 372-374; and "The Recent Annual Meeting," *Ecclesiastical Observer* (October 1, 1889): 140.

45Thompson, *Let Sects and Parties Fall*, 94-97.

46A Son of the Forge [pseud.], "Socialism and Christianity," 6 parts, *Bible Advocate* (1908): 5, 51-52, 113-115, 161-163, 210-213, 241-244. There is little evidence before World War I of many politically Conservative members of Churches of Christ. The increasing diversity within British Churches of Christ reflected the fracturing of Liberal politics. The evidence seems to challenge the argument that Churches of Christ were a "Labour Sect" before World War I. See Ackers, "The Churches of Christ as a Labour Sect," 199-206.

47See Tickle's articles in the "News and Views" section of the *Bible Advocate* (1899): 796, 814, 835, 855, 896; *Bible Advocate* (1900): 40, 55, 74, 93; See also *Churches of Christ Year Book* (1900), 79-80.

48*Churches of Christ Year Book* (1901), 46-47.

49T. E. Entwistle, "Report of the Annual Meeting," *Bible Advocate* (September 14, 1914): 513.

50"Do the Circumstances Justify Christians in Engaging as Soldiers in the Present War?" *Bible Advocate* (September 11, 1914): 577.

51William Mottlershaw, "Brethren in Camp," *Bible Advocate* (1914): 645, 665, 669, 681.

52John Rae, *Conscience and Politics: The British Government and the Conscientious Objector to Military Service, 1916-1919* (London: Oxford University Press, 1970), 1-4, 13-32, 61-63.

53Robert Price, "Brethren and an Anti-War Attitude," *Bible Advocate* (March 16, 1916): 157; Robert Price, "The Tribunals," *Bible Advocate* (1916): 204-205, 221.

54J. B. Kendrick, "Platt Bridge," *Bible Advocate* (April 28, 1916): 270; "A Conference of Brethren Opposed to Rendering Military Service," *Bible Advocate* (June 2, 1916): 349; "Conscientious Objectors," *Bible Advocate* (June 16, 1916): 381; "Brethren in Need of Help," *Bible Advocate* (July 14, 1916): 445.

55Julian Elwes, "Fellowship in Sympathy," *Bible Advocate* (July 28, 1916): 476.

56"In Sympathetic Remembrance," *Bible Advocate* (August 25, 1916): 532.

57*Churches of Christ Year Book* (1916), 148-149; "The Annual Meeting of 1916," *Bible Advocate* (1916): 519, 557-558.

58Robert Price, "Rough Treatment of Conscientious Objectors," *Bible Advocate* (1916): 413-414, 467, 493, 589; *For His Name's Sake: Being a Record of the Witness Given by Members of Churches of Christ in Great Britain Against Militarism During the European War, 1914-1918* (Heanor: W. Barker, 1921), 65-69. This resource is also available at www.netcomuk.co.uk/~pdover/fhnsidx.htm, accessed August 19, 2011.

59William Robinson, "In Memoriam: William Wilson," *Bible Advocate* (November 10, 1916): 685-686; T. E. Entwistle, "False Sentiment," *Bible Advocate* (November 17, 1916): 705. The editors issued an apology for their part in promoting the controversy. See "Letters to the Editor," *Bible Advocate* (November 17, 1916): 717.

60T. E. Entwistle, "The Case of the Absolutist," *Bible Advocate* (November 2, 1917): 523.

61"Obituary," *Bible Advocate* (January 10, 1919): 15; *For His Name's Sake*, 71-76.

62Ackers, "Who Speaks for the Christians?" 488; see also the account by Michael Casey in Joe Nisbet, *Historical Survey of Churches of Christ in the British Isles* (Aberdeen: privately printed, 2000), 191-210; "The Overlooked Pacifist Tradition of the Old Paths Churches of Christ," Part I, *Journal of the United Reformed Church History Society* (May, 2000): 446-460.

63"Remarks on Recent Events," *Young Christian* (April, 1891): 64; "Editorial Notes," *Young Christian* (July, 1891): 117; Bartley Ellis, "Drafting," *Bible Advocate* (July 1, 1891): 173.

64Joseph Smith, "The Higher Criticism, VII The New Testament Evidence," *Young Christian* (December, 1892): 271.

65L. Oliver, "Biblical Criticism," *The Old Paths* (October, 1892): 129-141.

66"Bro. Oliver's Address," *Young Christian* (September, 1892): 194.

67Oliver, "Biblical Criticism," 131; R. P. Anderson, "The Other Side," *Young Christian* (May, 1892): 61-63. Eight other articles followed.

68Joseph Smith, "In What Form and Emphasis on What Aspects Ought the Gospel to be Preached Today so as to Stay the Alienation of the Masses from the Church and to Win them for Jesus Christ?" *Churches of Christ Year Book* (1910), 36.

69Charles Greig, "A Review of the Work of the Higher Criticism and its Bearing on New Testament Christianity," *Churches of Christ Year Book* (1911), 28-46, quoted at 40 and 45.

70"The Conference Paper," *Bible Advocate* (August 18, 1911): 518.

71T. E. Entwistle, "The Verity and Value of Miracles," *Bible Advocate* (September 1, 1911): 546-547; Walter Crosworth, "The Chairman's Address and Conference Paper," *Bible Advocate* (September 15, 1911): 589; R. Lucas Swaby, "Brother Batten's Annual Meeting Paper," *Bible Advocate* (November 10, 1911): 715-716; C. W. Batten, "Brother Batten's Annual Meeting Paper," *Bible Advocate* (November 24, 1911): 749.

72"Resolution of the Christian Association," *Bible Advocate* (October 25, 1901): 855.

73*Churches of Christ Year Book* (1902), 97.

74*Churches of Christ Year Book* (1905), 144-166; "Letter from Philadelphia, U.S.A.," *Bible Advocate* (August 18, 1905): 535-536, and 644. There is no reference to this in accounts of the C.A. Cheltenham Conference in *Christian Quarterly* (October, 1905), and only a notice of the report without indication of its content in *Christian Quarterly* (July, 1905): 171.

75*Churches of Christ Year Book* (1910), 165; *Churches of Christ Year Book* (1911), 169; *Churches of Christ Year Book* (1912), 176-177; *Churches of Christ Year Book* (1913), 178; See also "Training Committee Report," *Bible Advocate* (August 15, 1913): 517-518.

76*Churches of Christ Year Book* (1914), 164-165; George W. Buckner, "Watchman, What of the Night?" *Christian Monthly* (October, 1916): Insert 5. For the Faith and Order conversation see "Dr Ainslie and the C.A. Executive," *Christian Monthly* (March 1914): 42-43.

77"Conference of Representatives at Leicester," *Bible Advocate* (May 4, 1917): 206-207; *Churches of Christ Year Book* (1917), 62-63.

78"The Conference: Special Features," *Christian Monthly* (August, 1917): 122; *Churches of Christ Year Book* (1917), 152; and "72nd Annual Meeting of the Churches of Christ," *Bible Advocate* (August 15, 1917): 387-388.

79"Editorial Notes," *Christian Monthly* (November, 1914): 164.

80"Reviews, Notes on Passing Events, Correspondence, Etc., Annual General Meeting," *British Millennial Harbinger* (September 1, 1865): 315-317.

81See Grant Foreman, "Settlement of English Potters in Wisconsin," *The Wisconsin Magazine of History* (June, 1938): 375-396.

82James Wallis, "Emigration and Christianity," *British Millennial Harbinger* (1849): 285-286, 329-331, 423-425, 476.

83"Reviews, Notes on Passing Events, Correspondence," 317.

84There were also some from "English Baptist" congregations

in Scotland that had developed after 1800. These groups were small or non-existent in the U.S. since most Scottish emigrants went to Canada between 1800-1830 instead of the United States.

[85]Ash's *Reminiscences* originally appeared as a series of 21 articles in the *Christian Worker* between 1882 and 1884 and were reprinted as Joseph Ash, *Reminiscences: History of Our Rise and Progress of Our Cause in Canada* (Beamsville: Gospel Herald Foundation, 1998), 74. See also Samuel D. Clark, *Church and Sect in Canada* (Toronto: University of Toronto Press, 1948), 278.

[86]Reuben Butchart, *The Disciples of Christ in Canada since 1830* (Toronto: Canadian Headquarters' Publication, Churches of Christ [Disciples], 1949), 96. See also G. H. Ellis, "A Note on the Distinction between 'Scotch Baptist' and 'Scottish Baptist,'" in Claude Cox, ed., *The Campbell-Stone Movement in Ontario* (Lewiston: Edwin Mellen, 1995), 413-419.

[87]Phillip Griffin-Allwood, "To Hear a Free Gospel," in Michael W. Casey and Douglas A. Foster, eds., *The Stone-Campbell Movement: An International Religious Tradition* (Knoxville: University of Tennessee Press, 2002), 549-553.

[88]Regular Baptists were Calvinist or "Particular" Baptists from England that organized in the U.S. and Canada and became the largest Baptist group in North America. They generally practiced closed communion.

[89]Phillip Griffin-Allwood, "Canadian Disciple Roots Among Maritime Regular Baptists" (2003), 1-5, available at www.glinx.com/~grifwood/CDNROOTS.PDF, accessed August 15, 2010; Butchart, *Disciples of Christ in Canada*, 122-123, 284-286; Ronald Fraser, Stewart Lewis, and Claude Cox, "The Movement in Canada," in Douglas Foster, et al., ed., *The Encyclopedia of the Stone-Campbell Movement* (Grand Rapids: Eerdmans, 2004), 151-163.

[90]Butchart, *Disciples of Christ in Canada*, 286-288. See also *The American Home Missionary 1916 Containing The Year Book of Churches of Christ (Disciples)* (Cincinnati: The American Christian Missionary Society, 1916), 709.

[91]Eugene C. Perry, *A History of Religious Periodicals in the Restoration Movement in Canada* (Beamsville: Gospel Herald Publications, 2003), 14-16.

[92]See "Granville Street Baptist Church Record Book 1827-1842," 1-10, cited in Griffin-Allwood, "Canadian Disciples Roots," 9 at www.glinx.com/~grifwood/CDNROOTS.PDF, accessed August 18, 2011.

[93]Griffin-Allwood, "Canadian Disciples Roots," 5-9; R. E. Shaw, "History of the Disciples of Christ in Halifax, Nova Scotia," *Collections of the Nova Scotia Historical Society* (1963): 121-139.

[94]Butchart, *History of Disciples of Christ in Canada*, 309-311, 318-319.

[95]Butchart, *History of Disciples of Christ in Canada*, 314-317.

[96]George Yuille, *History of the Baptists in Scotland from Pre-Reformation Times* (Glasgow: Baptist Union of Scotland, 1926), 70; and Bebbington, *The Baptists in Scotland*, 283-284. See also Dugald Sinclair, *Journal of Itinerating Exertions in Some of the More Destitute Parts of Scotland*, 6 vols. (Edinburgh, 1814-1817); Butchart, *Disciples of Christ in Canada*, 404; Donald E. Meek, "Dugald Sinclair: The Life and Work of a Highland Itinerant Missionary," *Scottish Studies* (1991): 59-91.

[97]Bebbington, *Baptists in Scotland*, 283-284 and 292. Meek emphasizes the importance of the distinction between "Scotch Baptists" and "Scottish Baptists" in his "Dugald Sinclair," 87-88. It is unlikely that the church in Aldborough was Scotch Baptist, as Butchart implies (p. 385). McVicar was not a Scotch Baptist in Scotland. Butchart wrongly identifies the Lochgilphead church as Scotch Baptist (p. 139). For Black's moves, see G. H. Ellis, "James Black's Life and Times," in Claude E. Cox, ed., *The Campbell-Stone Movement in Ontario*, 101-142.

[98]Edwin Broadus, *How the Disciples Came Together in Early Ontario* (Beamsville: Gospel Herald, 2009), 92; Butchart, *Disciples in Canada*, 476-477.

[99]Butchart, *Disciples of Christ in Canada*, 393-395; Broadus, *How the Disciples Came Together*, 95.

[100]Broadus, *How the Disciples Came Together*, 43-61; Butchart, *Disciples of Christ in Canada*, 389-392.

[101]Broadus, *How the Disciples Came Together*, 78-79. For the secession at Shuter Street, see Geoffrey H. Ellis, "The Restoration Churches in Toronto," paper presented at the 2004 annual meeting of the Canadian Churches of Christ Historical Society, available at www.ccchs.ca/papers/TORONTORestorationFullDocument.pdf, accessed January 6, 2012.

[102]Broadus, *How the Disciples Came Together*, 117-129.

[103]Ash, *Reminiscences*, 7-11; Broadus, *How the Disciples Came Together*, 144-151.

[104]Broadus, *How the Disciples Came Together*, 3-7, 177-180.

[105]Butchart, *Disciples of Christ in Canada*, 79-80, 97-99, 104; Claude Cox, "The Movement in Canada," in Douglas Foster, et al., ed., *The Encyclopedia of the Stone-Campbell Movement* (Grand Rapids: Eerdmans, 2004), 153.

[106]Butchart, *Disciples of Christ in Canada*, 606-607, 611-614, 630-632, 636-637, 644-660, 668-669.

[107]Butchart, *Disciples of Christ in Canada*, 543.

[108]Butchart, *Disciples of Christ in Canada*, 86-91.

[109]Lane Scruggs, "Trouble in Canada: The Higher Criticism Dispute at the Disciples College in St. Thomas," (unpublished essay, University of Toronto, 2011).

[110]Butchart, *Disciples of Christ in Canada*, 148-154.

[111]Butchart, *Disciples of Christ in Canada*, 234; Eugene C. Perry, *A History of Religious Periodicals in the Restoration Movement in Canada* (Beamsville: Gospel Herald Foundation, 2003), 82-84, 87, 95-96, 98-100.

[112]Perry, *Religious Periodicals*, 139-160.

[113]Perry, *Religious Periodicals*, 135.

[114]Butchart, *Disciples of Christ in Canada*, 105.

[115]E. L. Broadus, "The Beamsville Church at the Beginning of the 20th Century: A Study of One Congregation's Response to Division," in *Campbell-Stone Movement in Ontario*, 278-285; Shelley L. Jacobs, "Pacifism in Churches of Christ in Western Canada During World War II and the Influence of Nashville Bible School," *Restoration Quarterly* (2006): 215-219; Claude Cox, "The Division between Disciples and Churches of Christ in the Disciples Church at Meaford, Ontario," *Restoration Quarterly* (1984): 29-36.

[116]Lane Scruggs, "Understanding the Division of the Stone-Campbell Movement in Ontario," (MTS thesis, University of Toronto, 1911), 72-73.

[117]Lyndsay Jacobs, "The Movement in New Zealand," in Douglas Foster, et al, ed., *The Encyclopedia of the Stone-Campbell Movement* (Grand Rapids: Eerdmans, 2004), 563-566.

[118]T. Jackson, "Letter to the Editor," *Christian Messenger and Family Magazine* (June, 1845): 93-94; "Items of News: Letter from Congregation at Nelson, New Zealand," *Christian Messenger and Family Magazine* (November, 1846): 528; "Home News: Letter from Auckland, New Zealand," *Christian Messenger and Family Magazine* (June, 1847): 287; and Godfrey Fretwell, ed., *Centenary Historical Souvenir: Associated Churches of Christ in New Zealand, 1844-1944* (Wellington: G. Deslandes, 1944), 16.

[119]Fretwell, *Centenary Historical Souvenir*, 16-17; A.B. Maston, ed., *Jubilee Pictorial History of Churches of Christ in Australasia* (Melbourne: Austral Publishing Company, 1903), 375-376.

[120]Fretwell, *Centenary Historical Souvenir*, 19; Maston, *Jubilee History*, 393-396.

[121]Fretwell, *Centenary Historical Souvenir*, 20; Maston, *Jubilee History*, 353, 358-360.

[122]A. L. Haddon, *Centenary Historical Souvenir: Associated Churches of Christ in New Zealand, 1844-1944* (Wellington: Churches of Christ, 1944), 26-33.

[123]Haddon, *Centenary Historical Souvenir*, 38-39.

[124]Haddon, *Centenary Historical Souvenir*, 34-37.

[125]Geoffrey W. Rice, ed., *The Oxford History of New Zealand* (Melbourne: Oxford University Press, 1992), 255-259.

[126]Haddon, *Centenary Historical Souvenir*, 37-38.

[127]Graeme Chapman, "The Movement in Australia," in Doug Foster, et al., *The Encyclopedia of the Stone-Campbell Movement* (Grand Rapids: Eerdmans, 2004), 47-53.

[128]Jackson's letter was dated April 4, 1849, and refers back to July-August the previous year. See "Extracts of a Letter from South Australia," *The British Millennial Harbinger* (1849): 525; H. R. Taylor, *The History of Churches of Christ in South Australia, 1846-1959* (Adelaide: Churches of Christ Evangelistic Union, 1959), 1-7; and Trevor Lawrie, *From Soil and Seed* (Adelaide: privately published, 1983), 40.

[129]Lawrie, *From Soil and Seed*, 32-33; Maston, *Jubilee History*, 19-20, 37-39.

[130]"Extract of a Letter from South Australia," *The British Millennial Harbinger* (October, 1853): 477.

[131]Taylor, *Churches of Christ in South Australia*, 9-13.

[132]Maston, *Jubilee History*, 305 and 338; and Harold Hayward, "Whatever happened to Albert: The Life and Legacy of Albert Griffin," *Australian Churches of Christ Historical Society's Historical Digest* (2001), unpaginated, available at http://www.cctc.edu.au/Historical/Digest%202011%20Monograph%20on%20NSW%20founders.pdf, accessed August 18, 2011.

[133]Maston, *Jubilee History*, 311, 341; A.W. Stephenson, ed., *One Hundred Years: A Statement of the Development and Accomplishments of the Churches of Christ in Australia* (Melbourne: Austral Publishing Company, 1946), 21-22; Hayward, "Whatever Happened to Albert?"

[134]Maston, *Jubilee History*, 311, 317-319; Stephenson, *One Hundred Years*, 22; Hayward, "Whatever Happened to Albert?"

[135]H. G. Picton, "Letter from Australia," *British Millennial Harbinger* (March, 1853): 142.

[136]Maston, *Jubilee History*, 246-248, 260-262.

[137]Grame Chapman, *One Lord, One Faith, One Baptism: History of the Churches of Christ in Australia* (Melbourne: Vital Publications, 1979), 87.

[138]H. R. Taylor, *The History of Churches of Christ in South Australia, 1846-1959* (Adelaide: Sharples Printers, 1959), 15-16.

[139]Maston, *Jubilee History*, 405; "News,"*Australian Christian Pioneer* (December, 1870): 119-120; "Letter from W. Hindle," *Australian Christian Pioneer* (June, 1871): 259; "Letter from W. Hindle," *Australian Christian Pioneer* (October, 1872): 85-86.

[140]Thomas Bates, "Letter from T. H. Bates," *Australian Christian Pioneer* (December, 1870): 116; "News," *Australian Christian Pioneer* (January, 1873): 157; "News," *Australian Christian Pioneer* (June, 1873): 277-278; and Maston, *Jubilee History*, 85, 360.

[141]Graeme Chapman, *Ballarat Churches of Christ, 1859-1993: A History* (Mulgrave North: Churches of Christ Theological College, 1994), 18-22.

[142]"News," *Australian Christian Pioneer* (May, 1873): 252-255.

[143]Taylor, *Churches of Christ in South Australia*, 20-22.

[144]Taylor, *Churches of Christ in South Australia*, 39-42.

[145]Chapman, *One Lord, One Faith, One Baptism*, 80-83; Maston, *Jubilee History*, 81-83, 103-105, 133-134.

[146]"News," *Australian Christian Pioneer* (December, 1870): 116; "The Co-Editor's Resignation," *Australian Christian Pioneer* (August, 1872): 7-8; Taylor, *Churches of Christ in South Australia*, 34.

[147]Chapman, *One Lord, One Faith, One Baptism*, 85-86; Taylor, *Churches of Christ in South Australia*, 33-36.

[148]Maston, *Jubilee History*, 182-185, 308.

[149]Taylor, *Churches of Christ in South Australia*, 79-80.

[150]Maston, *Jubilee History*, 157, 182-183, 408-411; Chapman, *One Lord, One Faith, One Baptism*, 83-84; Taylor, *Churches of Christ in South Australia*, 58-60.

[151]A.M. Ludbrook, "Australian Echoes," *The Young Christian* (November. 1892): 260-261; "Mission Work among the Kanakas,"

The Young Christian (December, 1892): 266-268; "Mission Work among the Kanakas," *The Young Christian* (January 1893): 5-7.

[152]Maston, *Jubilee History*, 411-423; Chapman, *One Lord, One Faith, One Baptism*, 84-85; Taylor, *Churches of Christ in South Australia*, 59-61.

[153]Chapman, *One Lord, One Faith, One Baptism*, 94-99.

[154]Butchart, *Disciples of Christ in Canada*, 62-63; Chapman, *One Lord, One Faith, One Baptism*, 42-45, 51-53, 61-64, 97-99.

[155]Thompson, *Let Sects and Parties Fall*, 70.

[156]Graeme Chapman, *One Lord, One Faith, One Baptism*, 15, 51. Australia and New Zealand suffered from a lack of such persons. The church in Auckland, New Zealand, wrote James Wallis in 1856 complaining, "We have no one who is qualified to proclaim the gospel out of doors," and a few months later, "We have no one of much gift of speech among us." One consequence of this lack of speakers in the early years in Australia was a greater emphasis on the Lord's Supper than on preaching.

[157]Brian Talbot, *Search for a Common Identity: The Origins of the Baptist Union of Scotland, 1800-1870* (Eugene: Wipf and Stock, 2007), 259-265.

7: World Missions, 1874 to 1929

[1]David Filbeck, "Direct Support Missions," in Douglas Foster, et al., *The Encyclopedia of the Stone-Campbell Movement* (Grand Rapids: Eerdmans, 2004); David Filbeck, *The First Fifty Years: A Brief History of the Direct-Support Missionary Movement* (Joplin: College Press Publishing Co., 1980).

[2]Don Haymes, "Janes, Don Carlos," in Douglas Foster, et al., *The Encyclopedia of the Stone-Campbell Movement* (Grand Rapids: Eerdmans, 2004), 423-424; Jeremy Hegi, "Don Carlos Janes: One Man Missionary Society" (MA thesis, Abilene Christian University, 2011). A deep commitment to dispensational premillennialism fueled Janes's urgency for taking the gospel to the world, but also provoked strong opposition to his efforts when most Churches of Christ rejected premillennial theology between the1920s and the 1940s.

[3]Paul Allen Williams, "College of Missions," in Douglas Foster, et al., *The Encyclopedia of the Stone-Campbell Movement* (Grand Rapids: Eerdmans, 2004), 226-227; Henry Shaw, *Hoosier Disciples: A Comprehensive History of the Christian Churches (Disciples of Christ) in Indiana* (St. Louis: Bethany Press, 1966), 343-345.

[4]"Our Missionary to Denmark," *Christian Standard* (May 6, 1876): 148-149.

[5]O. C. Mikkelsen, "Religious Prospect in Denmark," *Christian Standard* (November 1, 1884): 346.

[6]A.C. Watters, *History of British Churches of Christ* (Indianapolis: School of Religion, Butler University, 1948), 88-89; Archibald McLean, *History of the Foreign Christian Missionary Society* (New York: Fleming Revel, 1919), 132.

[7]"Dr. Holck, First Missionary to Scandinavia," *Christian Standard* (August 12, 1944): 500-501; Watters, *History of British Churches of Christ*, 88-89; A. Holck, "Denmark," *Missionary Intelligencer* (November, 1904): 426.

[8]R.P. Anderson, "Christiania," *Missionary Tidings* (November, 1905): 405; "Norway," *Missionary Intelligencer* (November, 1909): 544. For more on the spread of Pentecostalism in Scandinavia, see Allan Anderson, *An Introduction to Pentecostalism* (Cambridge: Cambridge University Press, 2004), 84-90.

[9]Stephen Corey, "Disciples in the Land of the Midnight Sun," *Christian-Evangelist* (September 6, 1923): 1139; Robert Hopkins, "Robert Hopkins in Copenhagen," *Christian-Evangelist* (December 25, 1946): 1274-1275; "Disciples Unite with Baptists in Denmark," *Christian-Evangelist* (August 18, 1948): 835.

[10]McLean, *History*, 57-58; Jules DeLaunay, "Our French Mission," *Christian Standard* (January 25, 1879): 26; J. A. Myers, "The Paris Mission," *Christian Standard* (September 20, 1879): 298.

[11]McLean, *History*, 136-138; Isaac Errett, "Foreign Christian

Missionary Society," *Christian Standard* (October 22, 1886): 337; David Thompson, *Let Sects and Parties Fall: A Short History of the Association of Churches of Christ in Great Britain and Ireland* (Birmingham: Berean Press, 1980), 85.

[12]Alfred Seddon,"The Hors-de-Rome Movement in France," *Christian Standard* (May 15, 1909): 859-861. Before Seddon's arrival in Paris in 1909, Hautefeuille was the editor of a monthly religious magazine entitled *L'Exode: Restauration du Christianisme Primitif, sa Doctrine, ses Ordinances, ses Fruits.*

[13]"G. N. Shishmanian," *History of Fresno, California,* 2 vols. (Los Angeles: Historic Records Company, 1919), 2:1185-1186; J. W. McGarvey, *Lands of the Bible* (Philadelphia: J. B. Lippincott, 1881), 501; McLean, *History,* 59.

[14]McLean, *History*, 139, 141.

[15]McLean, *History*, 139; M. Baghdasarian, "Persian Letter," *The Christian-Evangelist* (January 5, 1899): 16; M. Baghdasarian, "Persian Letter," *Christian-Evangelist* (September 7, 1899): 1138; "Educator Dies," *World Call* (May, 1937): 33.

[16]Charles Louis Loos, "Some Facts about American Missions in Armenia," *Christian Standard* (June 19, 1886): 196; Charles Louis Loos, "The Charge Against Our Armenian Missionaries," *Christian Standard* (November 12, 1887): 364. This conflict with the Congregationalists was complicated by the fact that Shishmanian, at least, had been educated at Babeck Seminary, administered by the Congregationalist ABCFM. Before his affiliation with the Stone-Campbell Movement, he probably was expected to serve as a Congregationalist missionary. See "Shishmanian," *History of Fresno,* 2:1185-1186.

[17]G. N. Shishmanian, "Hinderances in Mission Fields," *The Christian-Evangelist* (July 11, 1901): 873; McLean, *History,* 140-141. Shishmanian retired to Fresno, California, in 1907, where he cultivated a small vineyard and orange grove. "Shishmanian," *History of Fresno,* 2:1185-1186.

[18]"Bleeding Armenia," *Christian Standard* (January 29, 1916): 594-595; Alva W. Taylor, "The Armenian Massacre," *Christian-Evangelist* (November 25, 1915): 1499; and "Armenian Horror Grows," *Christian-Evangelist* (December 2, 1915): 1532.

[19]"Armenian and Syrian Relief," *Christian Standard* (January 24, 1920): 426; "Armenian Children Saved—Orphans through the Cruelty of the Turk—by Christian America," *Christian Standard* (February 23, 1918): 674; "Armenian Christians Fleeing from Turkey," *Christian Standard* (March 23, 1918): 806; "An Armenian Family that Escaped the Turks," *Christian Standard* (April 6, 1918): 870; "Tragedy in Armenia and Syria," *Christian Standard* (April 12, 1919): 683.

[20]Donald West, "India Portfolio: Disciples of Christ India Mission," (Indianapolis: United Christian Missionary Society, 1954), n.p.; Lela Taylor, *Disciples of Christ in India: A Brief Resume of Missionary Work with a List of Missionaries* (Indianapolis: United Christian Missionary Society, 1922), 3-10; Elmira Dickinson, *Historical Sketch of the Christian Woman's Board of Missions* (Indianapolis: Christian Woman's Board of Missions, 1911), 17-18.

[21]Emma Wharton, "Home Life in India," *Missionary Tidings,* (August, 1883): 1; Ada Boyd, "Letter from India," *Missionary Tidings,* (July, 1885): 1, 3; "India," *Missionary Tidings* (December, 1887): 4; "India," *Missionary Tidings* (August, 1889): 8; "India Items," *Missionary Tidings* (January, 1891): 7-8; West, *India Portfolio,* n.p.; Archibald McLean, "Official Statement Concerning the India Mission," *Christian-Evangelist* (June 28, 1883): 9; Edith Yocum, *They Went to India: Biographies of Missionaries of the Disciples of Christ* (Indianapolis: United Christian Missionary Society, 1947), 7-21.

[22]Emma Wharton, *Life of G. L. Wharton* (New York: Fleming Revell, 1913), 75-76.

[23]"Letter from Miss Graybiel," *Missionary Tidings* (February, 1888): 2.

[24]McLean, *History,* 89, 142; "India," *Missionary Tidings* (July, 1892): 7; "India," *Missionary Tidings* (December, 1892):12; "India," *Missionary Tidings* (December, 1893): 21. "Bai" is a suffix of respect,

sometimes connoting "teacher."

[25]"India," *Missionary Tidings* (December, 1893): 21; "India," *Missionary Tidings* (April, 1890): 7.

[26]"India," *Missionary Tidings* (September, 1888): 6-7; "India," *Missionary Tidings* (September, 1889): 8-9; "India," *Missionary Tidings* (May, 1890): 14; "Notes from India," *Missionary Tidings* (September, 1893): 10-11; "Report of the Superintendent of the Young People's Department of the CWBM," *Missionary Tidings* (December, 1894): 32; "Auxiliary Program for August," *Missionary Tidings* (July, 1895): 56. An account of the origin of the orphanage can be found in Mary Kingsbury, "Our Orphan Work in India," *Missionary Tidings* (January, 1897): 247-248.

[27]"Letters from India," *Missionary Tidings* (March, 1884): 3; "Letter from India," *Missionary Tidings* (June, 1885): 3; "Letter from Miss Graybiel," *Missionary Tidings* (February, 1888): 2; "India," *Missionary Tidings* (December, 1892): 11-12; McLean, *History,* 146.

[28]West, *India Portfolio,* n.p.; Yocum, *They Went to India,* 26-60; "Report of the Annual Meeting of the National Executive Committee," *Missionary Tidings* (December, 1896): 190-191.

[29]West, *India Portfolio,* n. p.; W. M. Forrest, "Some Contributions to Christian Unity from Mission Fields," *Christian Standard* (November 25, 1899): 1500; W. M. Forrest, "Does India Need Christian Union?" *Christian Standard* (June 22, 1901): 780. For a description of the typical work in these orphanages at the turn of the twentieth century, see *Damoh Doings: Sketches of Orphan Life* (Cincinnati: Foreign Christian Missionary Society, 1900).

[30]McLean, *History,* 164; West, *India Portfolio,* n.p.

[31]Donald McGavran, *The Bridges of God: A Study in the Strategy of Missions* (New York: Friendship Press, 1955), 45-67.

[32]G. L. Wharton, "Our Bible College in India," *Christian-Evangelist* (November 26, 1903): 702; Yocum, *They Went to India,* 44-45.

[33]Morton D. Adams, "Bilaspur Convention Notes," *Christian-Evangelist* (May 23, 1907): 668; West, *India Portfolio,* n.p.

[34]For a full biography, see Leta May Brown, *Hira Lal of India: Diamond Precious* (St. Louis: Bethany Press, 1954).

[35]A. B. Maston, *Jubilee Pictorial History of Churches of Christ in Australasia* (Melbourne: Austral Publishing Company, 1903), 408-415; H. R. Taylor, *The History of the Churches of Christ in South Australia, 1846-1959* (Adelaide: Churches of Christ Evangelistic Union, 1959), 61; K. Bowes, ed., *Partners, One Hundred Years of Mission Overseas by Churches of Christ in Australia, 1891-1991* (Melbourne: Overseas Mission Board, 1990), 16.

[36]"Report of the Foreign Missions Committee," *Churches of Christ Year Book and Annual Report* (Birmingham: Churches of Christ, 1909), 89-90; *Churches of Christ Year Book* (1911), 88-99; Thompson, *Let Sects and Parties Fall,* 99; Watters, *History,* 98.

[37]*Churches of Christ Year Book* (1913), 85, 95, 96.

[38]*Churches of Christ Year Book* (1914), 77, 91; Margaret Watters, *Winged Feet* (privately published, 1981), 13, 15-16, 22-23; *Churches of Christ Year Book* (1915), 102-104.

[39]E. S Jelley, "Bitter-Sweet," *Gospel Advocate* (February 20, 1913): 188-189; "Biographical Sketch of E. S. Jelley's Work," *Firm Foundation* (August 21, 1917): 3; and Earl West, *The Search for the Ancient Order: A History of the Restoration Movement,* 4 vols. (Indianapolis: Religious Book Service, 1949), 3:348.

[40]J. C. McQuiddy, "An Open Door," *Gospel Advocate* (December 8, 1910): 1362; E. S. Jelley, "The Work in India," *Gospel Advocate* (May 23, 1912): 551; E. S. Jelley, "Report from India," *Gospel Advocate* (February 27, 1913): 207.

[41]W. Hume McHenry, "A Visit to Brother Armstrong-Hopkins," *Gospel Advocate* (January 11, 1917): 30; W. Hume McHenry, "Concerning Brother and Sister Armstrong-Hopkins," *Christian Leader* (January 16, 1917): 12-13; West, *Search for the Ancient Order,* 3:350-353.

[42]E.S. Jelley, "Concerning the Work in India," *Gospel Advocate* (November 30, 1913): 1130; E. S. Jelley and W. H. McHenry, "Report of Jelley and McHenry from 1915," *Gospel Advocate* (May

18, 1916): 495; W. H. McHenry, "Work in the Nizam Dominions," *Gospel Advocate* (April 26, 1917): 418-419; J.C. McQuiddy, "The Janes-McHenry-Martin-Jorgenson Combination," *Gospel Advocate* (March 6, 1919): 224-226.

[43]J. C. McQuiddy, "Exonerating Brother Jelley," *Gospel Advocate* (February 7, 1918): 878; West, *Search for the Ancient Order*, 3:354-357; E. S. Jelley, "Wanted: Advice from Fathers and Mothers in Israel," *Christian Standard* (May 2, 1925): 751.

[44]A 1930 list of Churches of Christ missionaries probably refers to Jelley when it says that "a brother whom we are not prepared to commend" was working in India. *Missionary Messenger* (December, 1930): 323. Three years later, a similar list includes Jelley among "retired" missionaries of the Churches of Christ. *Missionary Messenger* (November, 1933): 512. Jelley died in India in 1962.

[45]John Wolfe, "Our Work in India," *Gospel Advocate* (December 27, 1928): 1227-1229; *Booster's Bulletin* (June, 1927): 22.

[46]McLean, *History*, 93-95; "San" is added to names in Japanese as a title of respect, most closely corresponding to "Mr.," "Mrs." etc., in English.

[47]"Japan Portfolio" (Indianapolis: United Christian Missionary Society, 1957), a pamphlet held in the archives of Christian Theological Seminary, Indianapolis, Indiana, 126:2. See also McLean, *History*, 199.

[48]McLean, *History*, 199-200.

[49]"Japan Portfolio," n. p.

[50]McLean, *History*, 200. See also Charles Robinson, *Forty Years of Missionary Work* (Japan: n.p., 1923), 4; Maston, *Jubilee History*, 414.

[51]W. K. Azbill, "Work of a Japanese Preacher," *Gospel Advocate* (September 6, 1894): 557; David Filbeck and Robert S. Bates, "Asia, Missions in," in Douglas Foster, et al., ed., *The Encyclopedia of the Stone-Campbell Movement* (Grand Rapids: Eerdmans, 2004), 34.

[52]John M. McCaleb, "Notes from Japan," *Gospel Advocate* (February 23, 1893): 126; Ed Matthews, "John Moody McCaleb," in Douglas Foster, et al., ed., *The Encyclopedia of the Stone-Campbell Movement* (Eerdmans, 2004), 505-506; Gary Turner, "Pioneer to Japan: A Biography of J. M. McCaleb" (MA thesis, Abilene Christian University, 1972). See also McCaleb's account of his missionary work in *Once Traveled Roads* (Nashville: Gospel Advocate, 1934).

[53]Genevieve Brown, ed. *They Went to Japan: Biographies of Missionaries of the Disciples of Christ* (Indianapolis: United Christian Missionary Society, 1949), 12-14; Mrs. F. E. Hagan, "Lavenia Oldham," *World Call* (August, 1927): 1.

[54]McLean, *History of the Foreign Christian Missionary Society*, 215; Brown, *They Went to Japan*, 25; Harvey Hugo Guy, "Mr. Kakujiro Ishikawa," *Japan Harbinger* (July, 1906): 3; Fred Eugene Hagin, *The Cross in Japan: A Study of Achievement and Opportunity* (New York: Fleming Revel, 1914), 258.

[55]McLean, *History*, 216-218.

[56]At the beginning of the twenty-first century both schools had been incorporated into the Christian-oriented Seigakuin University and Schools. See the English-language website: www.seig.ac.jp/english/, accessed November 29, 2007.

[57]W. R. Warren, ed., *Survey of Service: Organizations Represented in International Convention of Disciples of Christ* (St. Louis: Christian Board of Publication, 1928), 346; Brown, *They Went to Japan*, 16-17.

[58]Rose T. Armbruster, "Editorial," *Japan Harbinger* (January, 1906): 2.

[59]This *Missionary Messenger* is not to be confused with the paper of the same name published by Don Carlos Janes in Louisville, Kentucky, beginning in 1929.

[60]J. M. McCaleb, "Our Work in Japan," *Gospel Advocate* (November 24, 1910): 1306; J. M. McCaleb, "Zoshigaya Gakuin," *Christian Standard* (July 29, 1911): 1254-1255; Mac Lynn, *Churches of Christ around the World: Exclusive of the United States and Her Territories* (Nashville: 21st Century Christian Publication, 2003), 116.

[61]John McCaleb, "Seven Years' Experience—Native Evangelists," *Gospel Advocate* (December 1, 1898): 771; "Seven Years' Experience—Facing the Problem," *Gospel Advocate* (December 22, 1898): 807. See also George Pepperdine, "Mission Work in Japan—No. 3," *Gospel Advocate* (August 30, 1928): 818. McCaleb also resisted the attempt by Clara Bishop to continue leading the Kamitonizaka Church of Christ mission after William died unexpectedly in 1913. See J. M. McCaleb, "The Future of Our Work in Japan," *Gospel Advocate* (August 7, 1913): 751.

[62]W. J. Bishop, "Bishop Hiratsuka Japan Mission, Tokyo, No. 2," *Gospel Advocate* (May 19, 1910): 614. In 1910 Bishop, McCaleb, and Hiratsuka collaborated to translate J. W. McGarvey's commentary on Acts into Japanese. W. J. Bishop, "My Publication Work in Japan, Past and Prospective," *Gospel Advocate* (November 17, 1910): 1275; W. J. Bishop, "Commentary on Acts Issued in Japanese," *Gospel Advocate* (April 28, 1910): 531; "That Commentary in Japanese," *Gospel Advocate* (July 14, 1910): 819; Yonnosuke [sic] Hiratsuka, "A Personal History of Hiratsuka," *Gospel Advocate* (January 30, 1947): 82-83. A brief autobiography in English is Yunosuke Hiratsuka, "History of the Church in Japan, 1952 ('The History of Kamitomizaka Church of Christ in Tokyo, Japan' and 'The Autobiography of Yunosuke Hiratsuka')." Unpublished manuscript. Center for Restoration Studies, Brown Library, Abilene Christian University.

[63]Emily Cunningham and Florence Still, *Flaming Torch: The Life Story of W. D. Cunningham* (Yotsuya Mission, 1939), 28; Mattie Pounds, "Minutes of the Executive Committee from July 17, 1901," *Missionary Tidings* (September, 1901):138.

[64]Cunningham and Still, *Flaming Torch*, 33.

[65]W. D. Cunninghamn, "Declaration of Independence," *Tokyo Christian* (November, 1903): 2; "Our New Missionaries," *Tokyo Christian* (June, 1915): 1; Henry Webb, *In Search of Christian Unity: A History of the Restoration Movement* (Cincinnati: Standard Publishing Company, 1990), 322.

[66]McLean, *History*, 97-99.

[67]By 1896, E. T. Williams had resigned from the China Mission to pursue a career of scholarship and U.S.-China diplomacy. See Dimitri Lazo, "An Enduring Encounter: E. T. Williams, China, and the United States," (PhD diss., University of Illinois, 1977).

[68]McLean, *History*, 100; Maston, *Jubilee History*, 414; Taylor, *Churches of Christ in South Australia*, 60-62.

[69]Immanuel Hsü, *The Rise of Modern China* (New York: Oxford, 1999), esp. chs. 11-14.

[70]McLean, *History*, 100-101, 223-234; "Shi Kwei-piao," *Biography Set Series Seven: Our Workers in China* (United Christian Missionary Society, 1940), n.p.; Elliott Osgood, *Shi, the Storyteller: The Life and Work of Shi Kwei-piao, Chinese Storyteller and Pastor* (New York: Powell and White, 1926).

[71]McLean, *History*, 223-224.

[72]McLean, *History*, 226.

[73]The uprising was finally put down on August 14, 1900, by a coalition force of 19,000 sent by European and Japanese powers. See Samuel Hugh Moffett, *A History of Christianity in China: Vol. II, 1500-1900* (New York: Orbis, 2005), 484-488.

[74]*Disciples on the Rim of Asia* (Indianapolis: United Christian Missionary Society, 1962), 62.

[75]W.R. Hunt, "How Our Missionaries Helped Save Nanking," *The Christian-Evangelist* (January 18, 1912): 80-81; E.I. Osgood and Edwin Marx, *The China Christian Mission: Completing Fifty Years of Service* (Indianapolis: United Christian Missionary Society), 16-17.

[76]Osgood and Marx, *China Christian Mission*, 9, 13-14, 23; McLean, *History*, 231; Warren, *Survey of Service*, 368-369; Lois Ely, *Disciples of Christ in China* (Indianapolis: United Christian Missionary Society, 1948), 61.

[77]Warren, *Survey of Service*, 370-371, 374, 376, 379; Osgood and Marx, *China Christian Mission*, 11.

[78]Warren, *Survey of Service*, 370; McLean, *History*, 244-245; Osgood and Marx, *China Christian Mission*, 12; Elliott Osgood, "Results

of the Chuchow Revival," *Christian-Evangelist* (August 5, 1909): 992; William Renfrey Hunt, "Revival in China," *Christian-Evangelist* (June 23, 1910): 909.

79Osgood and Marx, *China Christian Mission*, 25; *Disciples on the Rim of Asia*, 63-64.

80Osgood and Marx, *China Christian Mission*, 25; *Disciples on the Rim of Asia*, 65.

81"Dr. Susie Rijnhart Moyes," in Geniveve Brown, ed., *Biography Set Series Five: Our Workers in Jamaica, Tibet, and the Philippine Islands* (Indianapolis: United Christian Missionary Society, 1937), n.p.; Susie Rijnhart, *With the Tibetans in Tent and Temple* (New York: Fleming Revell, 1901); Isabel Stuart Robson, *Two Lady Missionaries in Tibet* (London: S. W. Partridge and Company, 1909).

82Warren, *Survey of Service*, 396. See also from the annual reports of the Foreign Christian Missionary Society, published in the *Missionary Intelligencer* between 1904 and 1909.

83"Tibet," *The Missionary Intelligencer* (November, 1908): 498; Albert Shelton, *Pioneering in Tibet: A Personal Record of Life and Experience in Mission Fields* (New York: Fleming Revel, 1921), 39-40; Warren, *Survey of Service*, 395; "Tibet," *The Missionary Intelligencer* (November, 1914): 446.

84"The Department of Foreign Missions," *Yearbook and Annual Reports* (St. Louis: United Christian Missionary Society, 1921), 39-40; Bert Wilson, "Shelton of Batang," *World Call* (June, 1919): 10-15.

85"The Way Open to Lhasa!" *World Call* (February, 1919): 18.

86Albert Shelton, "From the Roof of the World," *World Call* (February, 1919): 19. For more on Albert Shelton and the early years of the Tibetan Christian Mission, see Douglas Wissing, *Pioneer in Tibet: The Life and Perils of Dr. Albert Shelton* (New York: Palgrave, 2004).

87Michael Charney, *A History of Modern Burma* (New York: Cambridge University Press, 2009), 5-45.

88"Report of the Foreign Missionary Committee," *Churches of Christ Year Book and Annual Report* (Birmingham: Churches of Christ, 1895), 30. Hereafter cited as *Churches of Christ Year Book*.

89Watters, *History of the British Churches of Christ*, 96-97; David Thompson, *Let Sects and Parties Fall*, 96-97; *Churches of Christ Year Book* (1897), 56-64; "Robert Halliday," in John Taylor and Clyde Binfield, eds., *Who They Were: In the Reformed Churches of England and Wales, 1901-2000* (Donington: United Reformed Church History Society, 2007), 94.

90*Churches of Christ Year Book* (1901), 69-70; *Churches of Christ Year Book* (1904), 56-64; "Industrial Mission at Ye, Lower Burma," *The Bible Advocate* (February 12, 1904): 103-104.

91"The General Annual Meeting," *Bible Advocate* (1906): 522-525, 668-669, 749; *Churches of Christ Year Book* (1907), 50-54; Thompson, *Let Sects and Parties Fall*, 98.

92*Churches of Christ Year Book* (1910), 74-75; *Churches of Christ Year Book* (1911), 78-79; *Churches of Christ Year Book* (1915), 89-90; "Burma," *Bible Advocate* (May 10, 1912): 300.

93*Churches of Christ Year Book* (1903), 63-65; *Churches of Christ Year Book* (1904), 64-68; *Churches of Christ Year Book* (1905), 73-78; Thompson, *Let Sects and Parties Fall*, 98.

94"Percy Clark," *Christian Advocate* (October 18, 1957): 493-494; "Fifty-Five Years in Thailand," *Christian Advocate* (October 25, 1957): 508; W. Crockatt, "Siam as a Mission Field," *The Bible Advocate* (August 4, 1905): 488-490; "Percy and Mary Clark," in Taylor and Binfield, eds., *Who They Were*, 34-35. Mary Clark published a collection of reminiscences about her experiences as a missionary in Thailand: *Stories from Pagoda Land* (Leed: Churches of Christ Foreign Missions Committee, 1920).

95*Churches of Christ Year Book* (1906), 52-53; *Churches of Christ Year Book* (1907), 50-58; *Churches of Christ Year Book* (1910), 79.

96*Churches of Christ Year Book* (1914), 81-88; *Churches of Christ Year Book* (1915), 91-101; *Churches of Christ Year Book* (1918), 66-71.

97Chris Baker and Pasuk Phongpaichit, *A History of Thailand* (New York: Cambridge University Press, 2009), 105-139.

98*Churches of Christ Year Book* (1918), 66-71.

99*Churches of Christ Year Book* (1918), 70. Robert Halliday is generally recognized as the "father of Mon studies" because of his mastery of the language and his intimate knowledge of the Mon communities of Burma and Thailand. He was the author of numerous books, including *The Talaings* (Rangoon: Government Printing, 1917) and *A Mon-English Dictionary* (Bangkok: The Siam Society, 1922). Because most of his works were published by American Baptist publishing companies, he is often incorrectly identified as an American Baptist missionary.

100Kathleen Nadeau, *The History of the Philippines* (Westport: Greenwood Press, 2008), 33-66.

101McLean, *History*, 112; Hermon Williams, "Beginnings in the Philippines," *Christian Standard* (September 26, 1931): 940.

102Mark Maxey, "History of the Christian Mission in the Philippine Islands" (BD thesis, Cincinnati Bible Seminary, 1943), 12-15.

103Ely, *They Went to the Philippines*, 13-14, 16-17; McLean, *History*, 336-339, 343-346; "History of Nursing in the Philippines," Nursing Portal Philippines, available at www.nursing.ph/history-of-nursing-in-the-philippines.html, accessed September 5, 2011.

104Lois Ely, *They Went to the Philippines* (Indianapolis: United Christian Missionary Society, 1950), 8-13; Maxey, "History of the Christian Mission," 15-19; See also *The Philippine Mission* (Cincinnati: Foreign Christian Missionary Society, 1908), a tract held in the archives of Christian Theological Seminary, 102:4.

105McLean, *History*, 351.

106Stephen Corey, *Among Asia's Needy Millions* (Cincinnati: Foreign Christian Missionary Society, 1915), 31.

107Maxey, "The Christian Mission," 19-22, 31.

108Virgil A. Sly, "The Philippines—A Christian Opportunity," (Indianapolis: The United Christian Missionary Society, 1950), 11; Warren, *Survey of Service*, 438.

109*Disciples Year Book* (1925), 71-74.

110Maxey, "The Philippine Mission," 78.

111Maxey, "The Philippine Mission," 83-84.

112Webb, *In Search of Christian Unity*, 307. Among Filipino Christians especially, the Wolfes have been celebrated for their resistance to theological liberalism. See Abraham Ventura, "Church of Christ in the Philippines: A History," *The Golden Book: Church of Christ, 1901, Philippines* (Cruzada: Cruzada Church of Christ, 1958); Diego Romulo, "Churches of Christ in the Philippines," *The Centennial Book of the Churches of Christ in the Philippines, 1901-2001* (Manila: Churches of Christ, 2002), 66-72; Charlie Ayuno, "History of the Churches of Christ in the Philippines," *Centennial Book*, 105-120.

113Sly, "The Philippines," 11; Dwight E. Stevenson, *Christianity in the Philippines: A Report on the Only Christian Nation in the Orient* (Lexington: The College of the Bible, 1956), 38.

114"Suggested Kanaka Mission," *Christian Pioneer* (1891): 347; "Our Kanaka Missionary and His Work," *Christian Pioneer* (1896): 100. These articles have been reprinted in Graeme Chapman, *No Other Foundation: A Documentary History of Churches of Christ in Australia, 1846-1990* (Mulgrave, Victoria: Privately published, 1993), 399-401. See also C. R. Burdeu, "Missionary John Thompson," in Wilkie Thompson, ed., *The Digest of the Australian Churches of Christ Historical Society* (February, 1967): 3-4.

115Graham Warne, "Pentecost Kanakas," *Australian Christian* (July, 2003): 16. See also John Thompson, "My Tour through the New Hebrides," *Australian Christian* (1904): 275, 300, 310, 357, 385, 423, 440.

116Ronald Saunders, "How the Gospel Came from Australia to the New Hebrides," *Christian Standard* (May 19, 1945): 1, 13; John Garrett, *Footsteps in the Sea: Christianity in Oceania to World War II* (Geneva: WCC Publications, 1992), 104-106.

117Saunders, "How the Gospel Came from Australia," 1; R. S. A. McLean, *Preaching Christ in the New Hebrides*, Provocative Pamphlets

No. 26 (Melbourne: Federal Literature Committee of the Churches of Christ in Australia, 1957), 2. This pamphlet is held in the archives of Christian Theological Seminary, Indianapolis, Indiana.

[118]Garrett, *Footsteps in the Sea*, 105.

[119]Saunders, "How the Gospel Came from Australia," 1; McLean, *Preaching Christ*, 2; A. W. Stephenson, ed. *One Hundred Years: A Statement of the Development and Accomplishments of Churches of Christ in Australia* (Melbourne: The Austral Printing and Publishing Company, 1946), 75-84.

[120]C. C. Smith, *The Life and Work of Jacob Kenoly* (Cincinnati: The Methodist Book Concern, 1912), 1-60; *They Went to Africa: Biographies of Missionaries of Disciples of Christ* (Indianapolis, United Christian Missionary Society, 1952), 6-8.

[121]Smith, *Life and Work*, 61-113.

[122]Smith, *Life and Work*, 114-124.

[123]Smith, *Life and Work*, 114-124; C. C. Smith, "Jacob Kenoly and His Work in Liberia, Africa," *Christian Standard* (February 26, 1910): 366-367; C. C. Smith, "Building Blocks," *Christian Standard* (January 1, 1910): 23; C. C. Smith, "Life and Work of Jacob Kenoly in Africa," *Christian Standard* (June 10, 1911): 958-959.

[124]*They Went to Africa*, 12-13.

[125]"Liberia, Africa," *Missionary Tidings* (August, 1911): 134-135; "Liberia Africa," *Missionary Tidings* (October, 1911): 197-199.

[126]Smith, *Jacob Kenoly*, 60-144; "Liberia, Africa," *Missionary Tidings*, (July, 1912): 92; C. C. Smith, "Jacob Kenoly Memorial," *Christian Standard* (January 6, 1912): 20-21.

[127]*They Went to Africa*, 8-12; "Africa," *Missionary Tidings* (April, 1917): 476.

[128]"Can this be True?" *Christian Standard* (January 3, 1920): 352-353; "Ruth Kenoly Chapter," *Christian Standard* (June 19, 1920): 940-941; Joel Lehman, "Open Letter Concerning the Kenoly Case," *Christian Standard* (August 14, 1920): 1134.

[129]Leonard Thompson, *A History of South Africa* (New Haven: Yale University Press, 2001), 70-109.

[130]Thompson, *History of South Africa*, 110-153.

[131]Most recent histories of the Stone-Campbell Movement in South Africa mistakenly attribute the founding of Cape Town Church of Christ to New Zealander John Sherriff, who arrived in 1896, four years after Tickle. These histories appear to follow Murray Savage, *Achievement: Fifty Years of Missionary Witness in Southern Rhodesia* (Wellington: A. H. and A. W. Reed, 1949), 21-22. Even Fred Cowin, one of the Movement's earliest missionaries in the colony, seems to have been unaware of Tickle's early efforts. See Fred Cowin, "Concerning the Church of Jesus Christ in Cape Town," *Bible Advocate* (June 15, 1906): 374.

[132]"Church Intelligence," *Bible Advocate* (May 1, 1893): 178; "Report of the Annual Meeting," *Bible Advocate* (August 15, 1893): 311-312; Edgar Horwood, "South Africa," *Bible Advocate* (May 15, 1894): 196; "General Annual Meeting," *Bible Advocate* (August 21, 1896): 397; "Church Intelligence," *Bible Advocate* (November 13, 1896): 549-550; Charles Allen, "Cape Town," *Bible Advocate* (November 19, 1897): 752; H. Elliott Tickle, "Church Intelligence," *Bible Advocate* (May 6, 1898): 286.

[133]H. Elliott Tickle, "Evangelization in South Africa," *Bible Advocate* (March 13, 1903):173; H. Elliott Tickle, "Evangelization in South Africa," *Bible Advocate* (May 8, 1903): 300; "Johannesburg," *Bible Advocate* (August 28, 1903): 576.

[134]*Churches of Christ Year Book* (1904), 68-74; *Churches of Christ Year Book* (1905), 78-80; R.K. Francis, "From Cape Town to Johannesburg," *Bible Advocate* (February 26, 1904):136-137; "Church Intelligence," *Bible Advocate* (March 11, 1904): 175; R.K. Francis, "From Johannesburg to Durbin and Back," *Bible Advocate* (April 29, 1904): 276-278; R.K. Francis, "Bulawayo, Cape Town, and Home," *Bible Advocate* (July 15, 1904): 459; "The General Annual Meeting," *Bible Advocate* (August 18, 1905): 527-529.

[135]"Church Intelligence," *Bible Advocate* (May 10, 1907): 302-303; "Native Mission, Roodepoort, Transvaal," *Bible Advocate* (January 24, 1908): 57-58; "Church Intelligence," *Bible Advocate* (July 10, 1908): 448.

[136]Barron, "History of Disciples," 235-236. *The Disciples of Christ in South Africa* (Indianapolis: United Christian Missionary Society, 1954), a pamphlet held in the archives of Christian Theological Seminary, 84:19.

[137]W. H. Book, "A Man Sees the Light," *Christian Standard* (September 20, 1913): 1546; W. H. Book, "The True Story of Thomas Kalane," *Christian Standard* (February 26, 1922): 3267; W. H. Book, "The Acts of a Black Apostle," *Christian Standard* (May 6, 1922): 3501; and "Thomas Kalane Vindicated," *Christian Standard* (July 29, 1922): 3789-3790.

[138]O. E. Payne, "Tidings from the Other USA: Thomas Kalane Deported," *Christian Standard* (April 26, 1924): 747; "His Zeal Shamed Us," *Christian Standard* (September 20, 1924): 1279; "An Ambassador of Christ in Africa," *Christian Standard* (September 10, 1921): 2637, 2651.

[139]M. P. Hayden, "The Facts of the Case," *Christian Standard* (December 30, 1911): 2172; Carl Lewis, Clara Lewis, and C. B. Titus, "African Christian Missionary Society," *Christian Standard* (March 24, 1928): 280; C. B. Titus, "Native Work in South Africa," *Christian Standard* (December 31, 1927): 1074. Titus recounts some of his experiences as a missionary in his *Christ's One Church Forever: A China-Africa Mission Story* (Cherokee: Titus, 1934).

[140]J. R. Kellems, "The Thomas Mission's Plans for Africa," *South African Christian* (January, 1928): 44, 49; Jesse Kellems, "South African Christian Convention," and G. Erikkson, "A Program for Native Work," *Christian Standard* (October 1, 1927): 739-740; and Carroll C. Roberts, "Retrospect and Prospect for the Cause in South Africa," *Christian Standard* (January 5, 1929): 1-4, 6.

[141]Chengetai Zvobgo, *A History of Zimbabwe, 1890-2008* (New York: Cambridge, 2009), 11-53.

[142]Savage, *Achievement*, 21-27; Earl West, *The Search for the Ancient Order: A History of the Restoration Movement*, 4 vols. (Indianapolis: Religious Book Service, 1949), 3:340-344.

[143]John Sherriff, "A Letter from South Africa," *Christian Leader and the Way* (November 21, 1905): 9; Savage, *Achievement*, 28-34; Thompson, *Let Sects and Parties Fall*, 98; West, *Search for the Ancient Order*, 3:344.

[144]H. Elliot Tickle, "Mission Enterprise at Bulawayo," *Bible Advocate* (January 15, 1904): 39-40; R. K. Francis, "South Africa for Christ and His Church," *Bible Advocate* (March 17, 1905): 167-168. Reports of the work in Bulawayo often were included alongside of those in South Africa. See, e.g., "Church Intelligence," *Bible Advocate* (March 18, 1904):190-191; "Church Intelligence," *Bible Advocate* (May 26, 1905): 335; "Church Intelligence," *Bible Advocate* (February 9, 1906): 92-93.

[145]John Sherriff, "The New Work in South Africa," *Christian Leader and the Way* (July 23, 1907): 2; Savage, *Achievement*, 39-40, 42.

[146]Savage, *Achievement*, 53-54, 61-62.

[147]Savage, *Achievement*, 35-41, 58, 63-64.

[148]Savage, *Achievement*, 46-54, 60-74; A. C. Watters, "Disciples Missionary Becomes Prime Minister," *World Call* (December, 1953): 26.

[149]F. L. Hadfield, "John Sheriff—Christian Pioneer," *The South African Sentinel* (July, 1950): 5.

[150]Savage, *Achievement*, 76.

[151]J. McCracken, *Politics and Christianity in Malawi, 1875-1940* (New York: Cambridge University Press, 1977); Andrew C. Ross, *Blantyre Mission and the Making of Modern Malawi* (Blantyre: Christian Literature Association in Malawi, 1996); Bengt Sundkler and Christopher Steed, *A History of the Church in Africa* (New York: Cambridge University Press, 2000), 467-482.

[152]McCracken, *Politics and Christianity*, 187-188; Ernest Gray, "The Early History of the Churches of Christ Missionary Work

in Nyasaland, Central Africa, 1907-1930," Churches of Christ Historical Society, Occasional Paper No. 1 (Cambridge: Churches of Christ Historical Society, 1981), n.p.

[153]Gray, "Early History," n.p.

[154]"The Appeal from Brother Joseph Booth," *Bible Advocate* (March 30, 1906): 203; H. Langworthy, *Africa for the African: The Life of Joseph Booth* (Blantyre: Christian Literature Association in Malawi, 1996), 189-193; Gray, "Early History," n. p.

[155]Andrew Young, "Church of Christ Central Africa Mission," *Bible Advocate* (September 20, 1907): 620.

[156]J. Potts, "Appeal on Behalf of Native Mission Work," *Bible Advocate* (June 12, 1908): 382; "Interesting News from Central Africa," *Bible Advocate* (October 9, 1908): 667-668; *Churches of Christ Year Book* (1908), 87-88; Gray, "Early History," n. p.

[157]*Churches of Christ Year Book* (1908), 87.

[158]*Churches of Christ Year Book* (1908), 87, 160; *Churches of Christ Year Book* (1909), 90-91, 166; Thompson, *Let Sects and Parties Fall*, 98-99.

[159]*Churches of Christ Year Book* (1910), 85.

[160]*Churches of Christ Year Book* (1910), 83-86; *Churches of Christ Year Book* (1911), 90-93; *Churches of Christ Year Book* (1912), 80-82, 95-97; *Churches of Christ Year Book* (1913), 100-103; *Churches of Christ Year Book* (1914), 92-94.

[161]G. A. Shepperson and T. Price, *Independent African: John Chilembwe and the Origin, Setting, and Significance of the Nyasaland Native Uprising of 1915* (Edinburgh: University Press, 1958).

[162]*Churches of Christ Year Book* (1915), 90-91, 109-114; *Churches of Christ Year Book* (1916), 58-61, 75-77; *Churches of Christ Year Book* (1917), 71-72; Shepperson and Price, *Independent African*, 341-355, Gray, "Early History," n.p.; G.B. Shelburne, "History of the Church in Malawi, Africa," http://www.bible.acu.edu/ministry/centers_institutes/missions/page.asp?ID=412, accessed June 29, 2010.

[163]*Churches of Christ Year Book* (1927), 81, 191.

[164]Warren, ed., *Survey of Service*, 494-495; Herbert Smith, *Fifty Years in Congo: Disciples of Christ at the Equator* (Indianapolis: United Christian Missionary Society, 1949), 3; *They Went to Africa*, 14; Paul Williams, "Disciples and Red Rubber: The Disciples of Christ Congo Mission, the Congo Free State, and the Congo Reform Campaign of 1987-1908," *Discipliana* (Spring, 2006): 3-18.

[165]"Report of the Committee on Africa," *The Missionary Intelligencer* (November, 1899): 302; Smith, *Fifty Years in Congo*, 16.

[166]Polly Dye, *In His Glad Service: The Story of Royal J. and Eva N. Dye* (Eugene: Northwest Christian College, 1975), 13-71.

[167]For a detailed analysis of polygamy in the early DCCM, see Elonda Efefe, "La doctrine Biblique du mariage et le problème de la polygamie au Zaire" [The Biblical doctrine of marriage and the issue of polygamy in Zaire] (PhD diss., University of Strasbourg, 1976).

[168]Smith, *Fifty Years in Congo*, 22-24.

[169]Eva Dye, *Bolenge: A Story of Gospel Triumphs in the Congo* (Indianapolis: Foreign Christian Missionary Society, 1909), 133-139; Myrta Pearson Ross, "The Ordination of Mark Njoji," *World Call* (January, 1921): 30; "Mark Njoji," *Biography Set*, Series One, Leaflet Eleven (Indianapolis: United Christian Missionary Society, 1933); James Merrill, "Bolenge—The Little Church that Wouldn't Stop Growing," *World Call* (November, 1955): 22-23.

[170]Adam Hochschild, *King Leopold's Ghost* (New York: Houghton Mifflin, 1998); Georges Nzongola-Ntalaja, *The Congo from Leopold to Kabila: A People's History* (New York: Zed Books, 2002), 13-60.

[171]Williams, "Disciples and Red Rubber," 8; Nzongola-Ntalaja, *Congo*, 23-26.

[172]Williams, "Disciples and Red Rubber," 15.

[173]Eva Dye, "Bonkanda wa Nzakomba Book of God," *World Call* (February, 1921): 34-35; Tobitha Hobgood, "The Lomongo-Lonkundo New Testament," *World Call* (July, 1921): 36-37.

[174]Virgil Sly, "Farewell to the Oregon," *World Call* (January 1950): 22-23. The growing cost of maintaining the *S. S. Oregon*, along with improving systems of transportation throughout the Congo,

forced DCCM leaders in 1949 to retire the steamship from service.

[175]William Holder, "The Church in Congo," *World Call* (October, 1926): 15-17.

[176]He records some of his early experiences in Andrew Hensey, *Opals from Africa* (Cincinnati: Foreign Christian Missionary Society, 1910).

[177]After leaving the Congo in 1931, Andrew Hensey taught at the College of Missions in Indianapolis, Indiana, and the Kennedy School of Missions in Hartford, Connecticut. *They Went to Africa*, 24-25.

[178]*They Went to Africa*, 34-36.

[179]*They Went to Africa*, pp. 30-32; 45-46; 48-51; Ernest B. Pearson, "The Healing of Africa," *World Call* (May, 1920): 22-24; G. J. P. Barger, "Fighting Yaws, A Mission Service," *World Call* (December, 1925): 31-34.

[180]Smith, *Fifty Years in Congo*, 43-44; Myrta Pearson Ross, "The Union Mission House," *World Call* (June, 1924): 29.

[181]Mark Toulouse, "Stephen Corey," in Douglas Foster, et al., ed., *The Encyclopedia of the Stone-Campbell Movement* (Grand Rapids: Eerdmans, 2004), 242-243; Smith, *Fifty Years in Congo*, 44-45; Emory Ross, "Phelps-Stokes Educational Commission in Congo," *World Call* (January, 1922): 21-23. See especially Edward H. Berman, "American Influence on African Education: The Role of the Phelps-Stokes Fund's Education Commissions," *Comparative Education Review* 15 (June 1971): 132-145.

[182]"Through the Years," *World Call* (January, 1934): 38-39.

[183]"Jamaica Mission," *British Millennial Harbinger* (June 1, 1864): 215-218; "Annual Meeting in Jamaica," *British Millennial Harbinger* (September 1, 1865): 322-326; "Letter from Jamaica," *British Millennial Harbinger* (July 1, 1866): 252-253; "Letter from Jamaica," *British Millennial Harbinger* (June 1, 1867): 212-214; "Jamaica," *British Millennial Harbinger* (September 1, 1869): 335; "The Jamaica Mission," *British Millennial Harbinger* (November 1, 1869): 390-392; Brian Stanley, *History of the Baptist Missionary Society* (Edinburgh: T and T Clark, 1992), 96-99; Robert Nelson, *Disciples in Jamaica, 1858-1958: A Centennial of Missions in the Gem of the Caribbean* (St. Louis: Bethany Press, 1958), 43-46.

[184]Ida Harrison, *Forty Years of Service: A History of the Christian Woman's Board of Missions* (n.p., n.d.), 31-32; Nelson, *Disciples in Jamaica*, 53; 71-75.

[185]Nelson, *Disciples in Jamaica*, 64-66.

[186]Nelson, *Disciples in Jamaica*, 58-59. The original constitution of the JCMA, adopted on May 16, 1865, was printed in "Annual Meeting," *British Millennial Harbinger* (1865): 323.

[187]Nelson, *Disciples in Jamaica*, 60, 62-66.

[188]Harrison, *Forty Years of Service*, 35-37; Nelson, *Disciples in Jamaica*, 75-77.

[189]Nelson, *Disciples in Jamaica*, 80.

[190]*Disciples Year Book* (1927), 37; Warren, *Survey of Service*, 480-482.

[191]Nelson, *Disciples in Jamaica*, 86.

[192]M. L. Hoblit, "Mexico as a Mission Field," an address given at the Texas Christian Convention, June 17, 1895, and published in *Missionary Tidings* (February, 1896): 249-250.

[193]"Our Mexican Mission," *Missionary Tidings* (February, 1896): 234-235; M. L. Hoblit, "Mexico for Christ," *The Christian-Evangelist* (April 30, 1896): 285; "Mexico," *Missionary Tidings* (March, 1896): 267-268; and M. L. Hoblit, "Our Work in Mexico," *Missionary Tidings* (September, 1899): 132.

[194]M. L. Hoblit, "Mexico," *Missionary Tidings* (December, 1897): 162-163; M. L. Hoblit, "Mexico," *Missionary Tidings* (December, 1898): 183; "M. L. Hoblit," *They Went to Latin America* (Indianapolis: United Christian Missionary Society, 1947), 9.

[195]M. L. Hoblit, "Our Work in Mexico," *Missionary Tidings* (September, 1899): 132-133; A. G. Alderman, "General Report of the Monterey Mission," *Missionary Tidings* (November, 1901): 227-228.

[196]Elma Irelan, *Fifty Years with our Mexican Neighbors* (Indianapolis:

United Christian Missionary Society, 1944), 23-24.

[197]"Mr. Thomas M. Westrup and Family," *They Went to Latin America*, 13-14; Irelan, *Fifty Years*, 29-30.

[198]Irelan, *Fifty Years*, 26.

[199]The mission typically paid the Mexican teachers half the rate of their missionary colleagues. A. G. Alderman, "Mexico," *Missionary Tidings* (November, 1903): 228-229.

[200]"Mr. and Mrs. Samuel Guy Inman," *They Went to Latin America*, 16-17. The best account of the partnership between Inman and Jimenez can be found in S. G. Inman, "The Passing of Felipe Jimenez," *Missionary Tidings* (December, 1916): 317.

[201]J. C. Mason, "Annual Address of the Corresponding Secretary of the Texas Christian Missionary Society Board," *Texas Missions* (June, 1906): 12; Warren, *Survey of Service*, 121; Daisy Macahdo, *Of Borders and Margins: Hispanic Disciples in Texas, 1888-1945* (New York: Oxford, 2003), 88-101.

[202]Irelan, *Fifty Years*, 58-62; W. I. Mellinger, "The Situation in Mexico," *Christian Standard* (October 14, 1911): 1694; E. T. Westrup, "Affairs in Mexico," *Christian Standard* (April 6, 1912): 577.

[203]"Mexico," *Missionary Tidings* (March, 1907): 430.

[204]S. G. Inman, "The Passing of Felipe Jimenez," *Missionary Tidings* (December, 1916): 317.

[205]Irelan, *Fifty Years*, 63-64.

[206]Samuel Guy Inman, "The Panama Conference and the Disciples of Christ," *Missionary Tidings* (November, 1916): 260-263; Stephen J. Corey, *Fifty Years of Attack and Controversy: The Consequences among Disciples of Christ* (Committee on Publication of the Corey Manuscript, 1953), 56-57; Warren, *Survey of Service*, 456.

[207]Warren, *Survey of Service*, 450; Archibald McLean, "A Visit to Mexico," *The Christian-Evangelist* (April 27, 1919): 401.

[208]E. T. Westrup, "Facts About the Mexico Mission," *Christian Standard* (September 6, 1919): 1201; E. T. Westrup, "Wreck of the Christian Institute, Monterrey, Mexico," *Christian Standard* (September 20, 1919): 1253; Irelan, *Fifty Years*, 31.

[209]Warren, *Survey of Service*, 452-454.

[210]West, *Search for the Ancient Order*, 2:362-370.

[211]McLean, *History*, 108-109.

[212]Lowell C. McPherson, "Letter from Cuba," *Christian-Evangelist* (February 22, 1900): 242; "Cuba," *Missionary Intelligencer* (November, 1918): 209-212.

[213]McLean, *History*, 319-324.

[214]McLean, *History*, 324; "Cuba," *The Missionary Intelligencer* (November, 1918): 515.

[215]J. A. Erwin, "A New Star—Puerto Rico for Christ," *Christian Standard* (October 29, 1898): 1409-1410.

[216]Joaquin Vargas, *Los Discipulos de Cristo en Puerto Rico* [Disciples of Christ in Puerto Rico] (San Jose, Costa Rica: Iglesia Cristiana [Discipulos de Cristo] en Puerto Rico, 1988), 32.

[217]C. Manly Morton, *Kingdom Building in Puerto Rico* (Indianapolis: United Christian Missionary Society, 1949), 98; Vargas, *Los Discipulos*, 63.

[218]For example, medical missionary Dr. W. A. Alton complained of violations of the comity agreement, accusing Lutherans, Presbyterians, and Episcopalians of encroaching into Disciples areas. W. A. Alton, "Comity in Porto [sic] Rico," *Christian Standard* (May 25, 1907): 890.

[219]Vargas, *Los Discipulos*, 33.

[220]Morton, *Kingdom Building*, 21-22.

[221]Vargas, *Los Discipulos*, 37.

[222]Morton, *Kingdom Building*, 27-30.

[223]Morton, *Kingdom Building*, 29; Vargas, *Los Discipulos*, 45.

[224]Morton, *Kingdom Building*, 42-45; Vere C. Carpenter, *Puerto Rican Disciples* (Tampa: The Christian Press, 1960); *They Went to Latin America*, 48-50.

[225]Mae Yoho Ward, *Puerto Rico Looks Up* (Indianapolis: United Christian Missionary Society, 1947), 7; Morton, *Kingdom Building*, 31.

[226]Morton, *Kingdom Building*, 89, 102.

[227]Vargas, *Disciplulos*, 63-65, 179-191.

[228]Vargas, *Disciplulos*, 65.

[229]Morton, *Kingdom Building*, 57.

[230]Morton, *Kingdom Building*, 55-56.

[231]J. Dexter Montgomery, *Disciples of Christ in Argentina, 1906-1956* (St. Louis: Bethany Press, 1956), 48-57.

[232]Montgomery, *Disciples of Christ in Argentina*, 75-76. After several decades of development and increasing ecumenical cooperation, in 1969, the union seminary was reorganized as *Instituto Superior Evangelico de Estudios Teologicos* (Evangelical Institute of Theological Studies).

[233]Montgomery, *Disciples of Christ in Argentina*, 77; Warren, *Survey of Service*, 461.

[234]Montgomery, *Disciples of Christ in Argentina*, 78-81; Hugh McWilliams, "The Result of Vision and Labor," *World Call* (March, 1926): 44.

[235]C. Manly Morton, "Don Jose," *World Call* (1921): 41; Montgomery, *Disciples of Christ in Argentina*, 83.

[236]Montgomery, *Disciples of Christ in Argentina*, 84.

[237]Inman borrowed the title of his address from Rafael Barrett (1876-1910), a Spanish journalist, who published a work by the same title in 1910, exposing the social and economic injustice in Paraguay at the time.

[238]C. Manly Morton, *Paraguay: The Inland Republic* (Cincinnati: Powell and White), 143-153.

[239]Elizabeth Eastman Mills, *Adventuring with Christ in Paraguay: Fifty Years of Service, 1920-1970* (privately published, 1973), 8-9.

[240]"New Buildings at Asunción, Paraguay," *Christian-Evangelist* (June 7, 1928): 740; "New University Building Completed," *Christian-Evangelist* (November 22, 1928): 1508.

[241]Warren, *Survey of Service*, 464.

8: Churches of Christ

[1]Thomas Olbricht, "Churches of Christ," in Douglas Foster, et al., ed., *The Encyclopedia of the Stone-Campbell Movement* (Grand Rapids: Eerdmans, 2004), 215.

[2]Olbricht, "Churches of Christ," 215-216.

[3]J. D. Tant, "Too Many Papers," *Firm Foundation* (January 10, 1899): 23.

[4]J. D. Tant, "What We Teach and Why We Teach It," *Firm Foundation* (June 1 1899): 350.

[5]T. B. Larimore, "My Latest Trip to Texas," *Gospel Advocate* (July 26, 1917): 719-720.

[6]Foy E. Wallace, "Disposed to Boycott Tennessee Preachers and Papers," *Gospel Advocate* (August 9, 1917): 764-765.

[7]William T. Owen, "Brevities," *Firm Foundation* (August 29, 1933): 4.

[8]J. N. Armstrong, "Who and What We Are," *Gospel Herald* (October 31, 1912): 4.

[9]R. L. Whiteside and C. R. Nichol, *Christ and His Kingdom* (Clifton: Mrs. C. R. Nichol Publisher, 1925).

[10]Robertson L. Whiteside, *A New Commentary on Paul's Letter to the Saints at Rome* (Clifton: Published by Mrs. C. R. Nichol, 1945), originally appearing in the 1930s as a series in the *Gospel Advocate*; and with C. R. Nichol, *Sound Doctrine: A Series of Bible Studies for Sunday School Classes, Prayer Meetings, Private Studies, College Classes, etc.*, 5 volumes, 6th edition (Abilene: Abilene Christian University Bookstore, 1980-1987; originally published 1920-1952).

[11]Foy E. Wallace Jr., *The Christian and the Government* (Nashville: Foy E. Wallace, Jr., Publications, 1968), 46.

[12]J. D. Tant, "In the Lower Rio Grande Valley," *Firm Foundation* (March 21, 1933): 2.

[13]Foy E. Wallace, Jr., *God's Prophetic Word: A Series of Sermons Delivered in the Music Hall in Houston, Texas, January 21-28, 1945, Exposing Modern Millennial Theories* (Houston: Roy E. Cogdill, 1946).

[14]Richard Hughes, *Reviving the Ancient Faith: The Story of Churches*

of Christ in America (Grand Rapids: Eerdmans, 1996), 3.

[15]R. L. Whiteside, "Indwelling of the Holy Spirit," *Gospel Herald* (August 28, 1913): 2.

[16]James A. Harding, "What I Would Not, I Do," *Gospel Advocate* (July 11, 1883): 442.

[17]James A. Harding, "Notes on the Holy Spirit's Work, with a Remarkable Illustration," *Christian Leader & The Way* (August 1, 1905): 8.

[18]K. C. Moser, "Brother Colley Seeks Information," *Firm Foundation* (March 11, 1930): 3.

[19]K. C. Moser, "Reply to Brother Colley," *Firm Foundation* (May 6, 1930): 3.

[20]H. Leo Boles, *The Holy Spirit, His Personality, Nature, Works* (Nashville: Gospel Advocate, 1942).

[21]Robert H. Boll, *The Kingdom of God: A Survey-Study of the Bible's Principal Themes* (Louisville: Word and Work, 1924).

[22]R. L. Whiteside and C. R. Nichol, *Christ and His Kingdom: A Review of R.H. Boll* (Clifton: Mrs. C.R. Nichol, c. 1924). Shreveport: Lambert Book House, 1984 reprint.

[23]H. Leo Boles and R. H. Boll, *Unfulfilled Prophecy: A Discussion on Prophetic Themes* (Nashville: Gospel Advocate, 1928), 5-6.

[24]H. Leo Boles, "The Issue Now—And Then," *Gospel Guardian* (October 1, 1935): 5.

[25]G. C. Brewer, "A Plea for Unity," *Abilene Christian College Bible Lectures 1934* (Austin: Firm Foundation Publishing House, 1934), 182-184; Charles M. Neal and Foy E. Wallace, Jr., *Neal-Wallace Discussion on the Thousand Years Reign of Christ* (Nashville: Gospel Advocate Company, 1933), 346-349.

[26]W. W. Otey, "Meaning of 'Mark' and 'Turn Away From'," *Firm Foundation* (December 10, 1935): 3.

[27]L. L. Briggance, "The Boll Evil," *Gospel Advocate* (August 23, 1934): 814.

[28]Lipscomb, *Civil Government*, 131.

[29]Michael W. Casey, "From Religious Outsiders to Insiders: The Rise and Fall of Pacifism in Churches of Christ," *Journal of Church and State* (Summer, 2002): 455-475.

[30]G. H. P. Showalter, "So-Called Conscientious Objectors," *Firm Foundation* (June 18, 1918): 3.

[31]Whiteside as quoted in Foy E. Wallace Jr., *The Christian and the Government* (Nashville: Foy E. Wallace, Jr., Publications, 1968), 67.

[32]R. H. Boll, "War, Pacifism, and Christianity," *Word and Work* (March, 1923): 71-76.

[33]G. C. Brewer, "Christians and War," *Gospel Advocate* (July 4, 1940): 626.

[34]C. Leonard Allen, *Distant Voices: Discovering a Forgotten Past for a Changing Church* (Abilene: Abilene Christian University Press, 1993), 163.

[35]K. C. Moser, *The Way of Salvation: Being an Exposition of God's Method of Justification Through Christ* (Nashville: Gospel Advocate, 1932), 115.

[36]R. L. Whiteside, "Lessons on the Roman Letter," *Gospel Advocate* (July 6, 1933): 630.

[37]R. L. Whiteside, *A New Commentary on Paul's Letter to the Saints at Rome* (Denton: Miss Inys Whiteside, 1945), 92.

[38]Foy E. Wallace, Jr., "'The Way of Salvation'," *Gospel Advocate* (April 24, 1932): 494.

[39]Foy E. Wallace, Jr., *The Present Truth* (Fort Worth: Foy E. Wallace, Jr., Publications, 1977), 1036.

[40]G. C. Brewer, "Read this Book," *Gospel Advocate* (May 11, 1933): 434.

[41]G. C. Brewer, "Grace and Salvation," in *Abilene Christian College Bible Lectureship* (Austin: Firm Foundation Publishing Co., 1952), 102-103.

[42]G. C. Brewer, "The Righteousness of God," *Gospel Advocate* (March 7, 1946): 224.

[43]Brewer, "Righteousness of God," 224.

[44]R. C. Bell, "Honor to Whom Honor is Due," *Firm Foundation* (November 6, 1951): 6.

[45]Daniel Sommer, "Address," *Octographic Review* (September 5, 1889): 1, 5, 8.

[46]Foy E. Wallace, Jr., "Broken Cisterns," *Firm Foundation* (September 1, 1936): 1.

[47]James A. Harding, "Scraps about Important Matters," *Christian Leader & The Way* (August 23, 1904): 9; James A. Harding, "Concerning Six Bible Schools," *The Way* (November 26, 1903): 1025-1027.

[48]J. N. Armstrong, "A New Bible School—Change of Location," *Gospel Advocate* (October 27, 1904): 681.

[49]Stockholders opened Southwestern Christian College in October 1904. Though financial difficulties led trustees to reorganize and rename the school Southland University in 1908, they were forced to close it the following year. Stephen D. Eckstein, Jr., *History of the Churches of Christ in Texas 1824-1950* (Austin: Firm Foundation Publishing House, 1963), 219.

[50]J. B. Inman, "West Tennessee Christian College," *Gospel Advocate* (September 16, 1885): 588.

[51]James Marvin Powell and Mary Nelle Hardeman Powell, *N.B.H.—A Biography of Nicholas Brodie Hardeman* (Nashville: Gospel Advocate, 1964).

[52]N. B. Hardeman, *Hardeman's Tabernacle Sermons*, 5 vols. (Nashville: Gospel Advocate, 1922-1943).

[53]William Woodson, *Standing for Their Faith: A History of Churches of Christ in Tennessee, 1900-1950* (Henderson: J and W Publications, 1979), 74-75.

[54]Hardeman, *Tabernacle Sermons*, 4:9.

[55]Ira Boswell and N. B. Hardeman, *Boswell-Hardeman Discussion on Instrumental Music in the Worship* (Nashville: Gospel Advocate Company, 1924).

[56]William Banowsky, *The Mirror of a Movement: Churches of Christ as Seen Through the Abilene Christian College Lectureship* (Dallas: Christian Publishing Co., 1965), 257.

[57]Guy N. Woods, *Questions and Answers: Open Forum* (Henderson: Freed-Hardeman College, 1976) and Guy N. Woods, *Questions and Answers: Volume 2* (Nashville: Gospel Advocate, 1986).

[58]Leroy Brownlow, *Why I Am a Member of the Church of Christ* (Fort Worth: Brownlow Publishing Co., 1945).

[59]James A. Harding, "The Right Hands of Fellowship," *Gospel Advocate* (February 22, 1883): 118.

[60]James A. Harding, "Laying on of Hands—The Grounds of Unity," *The Way* (September 26, 1901): 203.

[61]Lee P. Mansfield, "Then and Now," *Firm Foundation* (March 14, 1916): 3.

[62]*Census of Religious Bodies*, 1926 (Washington: U.S. Government Printing Office, 1928), 1:125.

[63]Daniel Sommer, "The Sunday School Question Considered" (in three chapters), *Octographic Review* (November 3, 1903): 8; (November 10, 1903): 8; and (November 17, 1903): 8.

[64]N. L. Clark, "Editorial Notes," *Firm Foundation* (January 29, 1907): 4.

[65]N. L. Clark, "What Shall We Do About It?" *Firm Foundation* (March 12, 1907): 4.

[66]Larry Hart, "A Brief History of a Minor Restorationist Group: The Non-Sunday School Churches of Christ," *Restoration Quarterly* (Winter, 1979): 222; Ronny F. Wade, *The Sun Will Shine Again Someday* (Springfield: Yesterday's Treasures, 1986), 44.

[67]Carl H. Royster, *Churches of Christ in the United States, 2009* (Nashville: 21st Century Christian, 2009), 23.

[68]J. Curtis Pope, "Evangelism, Evangelists," in Douglas Foster, et al., ed., *The Encyclopedia of the Stone-Campbell Movement* (Grand Rapids: Eerdmans, 2004), 319-320; Lipscomb, "Preachers and Their Work," *Gospel Advocate* (April 11, 1911): 232.

[69]M. C. Kurfees, "What Does It Mean?" *Gospel Advocate* (July 5,

1900): 418-419.

[70]G. K. Wallace and W. Carl Ketcherside, *Wallace-Ketcherside Debate* (Longview: Telegram Book Co., 1953); G. K. Wallace and W. Carl Ketcherside, *Wallace-Ketcherside—St. Louis Debate* (Longview: Telegram Book Co., 1954).

[71]Royster, *Churches of Christ, 2009*, 23.

[72]David Lipscomb, "Individual Communion Services," *Gospel Advocate* (July 27, 1911): 812-813.

[73]H. C. Harper, "Individual Communion," *Firm Foundation* (March 5, 1912): 6.

[74]G. C. Brewer, "Did G. C. Brewer Introduce the Individual Communion Cup Among the Churches?" *Gospel Advocate* (February 3, 1955): 85-87.

[75]Royster, *Churches of Christ, 2009*, 23.

[76]M. Norvel Young, "The 1946 Religious Census," *Gospel Advocate* (November 21, 1946): 1109; M. Norvel Young, "A Report on the Census and Appeal," *Gospel Advocate* (October 9, 1947): 813.

[77]M. Norvel Young, "Encyclopedia Britannica Carries Story on Churches of Christ," *Firm Foundation* (April 23, 1957): 264.

[78]B. C. Goodpasture, "Our Rapid Growth," *Gospel Advocate* (January 15, 1959): 34.

[79]Bernard Quinn, et al., ed., *Churches and Church Membership: 1980* (Atlanta: Glenmary Research Center, 1980), 2; Carl H. Royster, *Churches of Christ in the United States, 2006* (Nashville: 21ˢᵗ Century Christian, 2006), 19.

[80]David Edwin Harrell, *Churches of Christ in the Twentieth Century: Homer Hailey's Personal Journey of Faith* (Tuscaloosa: University of Alabama Press, 2000), 73.

[81]David Edwin Harrell, Jr., *The Emergence of the 'Church of Christ' Denomination* (Athens: C.E.I. Publishing Company, 1972).

[82]Foy E. Wallace, Jr., "Broken Cisterns," *Firm Foundation* (September 1, 1936): 1.

[83]Athens Clay Pullias, *Information Concerning Financial Gifts to David Lipscomb College by Congregations of the Church of Christ, 1891-1968* (Nashville: David Lipscomb College, 1969).

[84]Harrell, *Churches of Christ*, 76.

[85]Foy E. Wallace, Jr., "Man and Education," *Gospel Advocate* (June 4, 1931): 676-677.

[86]G. C. Brewer, "Evangelizing the World in the Post War Period," *Firm Foundation* (February 16, 1943): 1-2.

[87]N. B. Hardeman, "Position of Freed-Hardeman College Regarding 'Bible Schools'," *Gospel Advocate* (February 13, 1947): 132, 144; Cled E. Wallace, "Putting the Schools Where They Belong," *Bible Banner* (March, 1947): 2; Robert L. Whiteside, "Churches and Colleges," *Bible Banner* (June, 1947): 1.

[88]J. D. Tant, "Who Are the Cowards," *Firm Foundation* (October 14, 1947): 8-9.

[89]Foy E. Wallace, Jr., *A Review of the New Versions, Consisting of an Exposure of the Multiple New Translations* (Fort Worth: Foy E. Wallace, Jr., Publications, 1973).

[90]Harrell, *Churches of Christ*, 89.

[91]Brewer, "Evangelizing," 1.

[92]J. E. Choate and Lewis S. Maiden, *The Anchor that Holds: A Biography of Benton Cordell Goodpasture* (Nashville: Gospel Advocate, 1971).

[93]John C. Hardin, "Common Cause: B. C. Goodpasture, the *Gospel Advocate*, and Churches of Christ in the Twentieth Century" (PhD diss., Auburn University, 2009).

[94]Roy E. Cogdill and Guy N. Woods, *Woods-Cogdill Debate* (Nashville: Gospel Advocate Company, 1958).

[95]James W. Adams and Reuel Lemmons, *The Arlington Meeting* (Marion: Cogdill Foundation Publications, 1976).

[96]Harrell, *Churches of Christ*, 145.

[97]Royster, *Churches of Christ, 2009*, 23.

[98]W. Carl Ketcherside, *Pilgrimage of Joy: An Autobiography of Carl Ketcherside* (Joplin: College Press, 1991).

[99]Leroy Garrett, *A Lovers Quarrel, An Autobiography: My Pilgrimage of Freedom in Churches of Christ* (Abilene: Abilene Christian University Press, 2003).

[100]Robert Meyers, ed., *Voices of Concern: Critical Studies in Church of Christism* (St. Louis: Mission Messenger, 1966).

[101]Kenney Carl Moser, *Christ Versus a "Plan"* (Searcy: Harding College Bookstore, 1952).

[102]Kenney Carl Moser, *The Gist of Romans* (Delight: Gospel Light Publishing, 1958).

[103]G. P. Bowser, "Better Outlook for the Colored People" *Gospel Advocate* (August 30, 1928): 836.

[104]Edward J. Robinson, *Show Us How You Do It: Marshall Keeble and the Rise of Black Churches of Christ in the United States, 1914-1968* (Tuscaloosa: University of Alabama Press, 2008), 11-21.

[105]R. Vernon Boyd, "Interview with R. N. Hogan" (1968 or 1969) in Boyd Collection at the Center for Restoration Studies at Abilene Christian University, Abilene, Texas.

[106]R. Vernon Boyd, *Undying Dedication: The Story of G. P. Bowser* (Nashville: Gospel Advocate Company, 1985), 66-67; Annie C. Tuggle, *Another World Wonder* (n.p., n.d.), 66.

[107]R. Vernon Boyd, "Interview with Thelma M. Holt" (April 10, 1972) in the Boyd Collection in the Center for Restoration Studies at Abilene Christian University in Abilene, Texas.

[108]F. B. Shepherd, "Work among the Negroes" *Gospel Advocate* (December 18, 1930): 1226.

[109]Marshall Keeble, "Among the Colored Brethren" *Gospel Advocate* (July 26, 1951): 638-639. See also Marshall Keeble, *From Mule Back to Super Jet with the Gospel* (Nashville: Gospel Advocate, 1962); Edward J. Robinson, ed., *A Godsend to His People: The Essential Writings and Speeches of Marshall Keeble* (Knoxville: University of Tennessee Press, 2008), 87-101.

[110]Robinson, *Godsend*, 87-101.

[111]Marshall Keeble, "From the Brethren," *Gospel Advocate* (April 9, 1925): 354. See also Robinson, *A Godsend to His People*, 21; and Robinson, *Show Us How You Do It*, 22-30.

[112]Edward Robinson, *The Fight Is on in Texas: A History of African American Churches of Christ in the Lone Star State* (Abilene: Abilene Christian University Press, 2008), 134.

[113]Quoted in Robinson, *Show Us How You Do It*, 132.

[114]Robinson, *Fight Is on in Texas*, 105-106, 113.

[115]Robinson, *Show Us How You Do It*, 132-133.

[116]Robinson, *Fight Is on in Texas*, 67-77.

[117]Robinson, *Show Us How You Do It*, 142-145, 171.

[118]Royster, *Churches of Christ, 2009*, 16.

9: Disciples of Christ

[1]James H. Garrison, *The Story of a Century* (St. Louis: Christian Publishing Company, 1909), 256-258.

[2]W. T. Moore, *A Comprehensive History of the Disciples of Christ* (New York: Fleming H. Revell Company, 1909), 767.

[3]Henry E. Webb, *In Search of Christian Unity: A History of the Restoration Movement* (Cincinnati: Standard Publishing, 1990), 289.

[4]Lester McAllister and William Tucker, *Journey in Faith: A History of the Christian Church (Disciples of Christ)* (St. Louis: Bethany Press, 1975), 398-399.

[5]"Resolutions Passed by the Convention," *The Christian-Evangelist* (November 9, 1939): 1218-1219.

[6]*License and Ordination of the Christian Ministry: Suggested Standards, Procedures and Preparatory Reading Course* (Indianapolis: The United Christian Missionary Society, 1948), 18.

[7]*Disciples Year Book* (1964), 60.

[8]David Chidester, *Salvation and Suicide: Jim Jones, the People's Temple, and Jonestown* (Bloomington: Indiana University Press, 2003), 3-5; "Service of Ordination," and "Ordination Certificate," held in the James W. Jones biography file in the archives of Christian Theological Seminary, Indianapolis, Indiana. An eyewitness description of Jones's

Indianapolis ministry can be found in Catherine Hyacinth Thrash, *The Onliest One Alive: Surviving Jonestown, Guyana* (Indianapolis: Marian Towne, 1995), 47-60. See also Scott Seay, "Jim Jones and the Disciples of Christ in Indianapolis," unpublished paper presented at Christian Theological Seminary, January 19, 2012.

[9]Chidester, *Salvation and Suicide*, 6-8; Katherine Willis Pershey, "Jim Jones and the Disciples: Could It Happen Again?" *DisciplesWorld* (November, 2008): 9.

[10]Chidester, *Salvation and Suicide*, 6-8; Thrash, *Onliest One Alive*, 61-79.

[11]Chidester, *Salvation and Suicide*, 6-7; Pershey, "Jim Jones and the Disciples," 9.

[12]Chidester, *Salvation and Suicide*, 9-11; Thrash, *Onliest One Alive*, 83-124.

[13]Pershey, "Jim Jones and the Disciples," 10-11.

[14]Lillian Moir, "The Guyana Mass Murder-Suicide Tragedy," (Indianapolis: November 22, 1978), a press release held in the James W. Jones biography file in the archives of Christian Theological Seminary, Indianapolis, Indiana; "Disciples Shamed by Jones Tie; To Ask Policy Review," *Indianapolis Star* (November 28, 1978); Gordon Witkin, "Disciples of Christ Church Face Problems in Cutting Ties with 'Straying' Congregations," *Indianapolis Star* (December 3, 1978); Kenneth Teegarden, "To Look Back at Jonestown," *The Disciple* (February 4, 1979): 15.

[15]D. Duane Cummins, *The Disciples: A Struggle for Reformation* (St. Louis: Chalice Press, 2009), 241-242; Pershey, "Jim Jones and the Disciples," 11-12; "Statement of the General Minister and President to the Administrative Committee of the General Board, March 12, 1979," held in the James W. Jones biography file in the archives of Christian Theological Seminary, Indianapolis, Indiana.

[16]Brenda M. Cardwell and William K. Fox, Sr., *Journey Toward Wholeness; A History of Black Disciples of Christ in the Mission of the Christian Church* (Nashville: National Convocation of the Christian Church [Disciples of Christ], 1990), 25-29, 39.

[17]Cardwell and Fox, *Journey Toward Wholeness*, 21, 33, 38, 53-55.

[18]Cardwell and Fox, *Journey Toward Wholeness*, 61-64.

[19]Cardwell and Fox, *Journey Toward Wholeness*, 64-67.

[20]Cardwell and Fox, *Journey Toward Wholeness*, 66, 69-72.

[21]Cardwell and Fox, *Journey Toward Wholeness*, 91-92.

[22]Cardwell and Fox, *Journey Toward Wholeness*, 81, 83-85.

[23]Cardwell and Fox, *Journey Toward Wholeness*, 92-94.

[24]Cardwell and Fox, *Journey Toward Wholeness*, 94, 97-98.

[25]Cardwell and Fox, *Journey Toward Wholeness*, 118, 122-123.

[26]Cardwell and Fox, *Journey Toward Wholeness*, 123-125.

[27]Quoted in Cardwell and Fox, *Journey Toward Wholeness*, 98.

[28]See, for example, *The American Home Missionary* (January, 1910): 140-142.

[29]Washington-Norfolk District, *Minutes of the Forty-Third Annual Assembly of the Washington and Norfolk District of the Colored Disciples of Christ, 1913*, 8.

[30]For a discussion of Campbell's efforts to unite the Church of Christ, Disciples of Christ and the Disciples, see Sheila Gillams, *Principle and Practice: The Quandary of African American Restorationists in the History and Theology of the Church of Christ, Disciples of Christ, 1850-1950* (PhD diss., Union Theological Seminary, 2002), 187-202.

[31]National Christian Missionary Convention, *Minutes of the Eleventh Annual Christian Missionary Convention of the Churches of Christ of the United States, 1927*, 12-13. For Whitefield's efforts to unite the two fellowships, see Gillams, *Principle and Practice*, 203-208.

[32]Goldsboro-Raleigh District, *Minutes of the Fifty-Sixth Annual Assembly of the Goldsboro-Raleigh District, 1927*, 4, 6, quoted in Gillams, *Principle and Practice*, 204.

[33]Gillams, *Principle and Practice*, 204.

[34]Gillams, *Principle and Practice*, 201, 204-206.

[35]Gillams, *Principle and Practice*, 207.

[36]Gillams, *Principle and Practice*, 239-240, 280-282.

[37]Gillams, *Principle and Practice*, 286-287. Davis was the first chief elder to be addressed as "bishop" after the assemblies changed the designation of the office in 1946.

[38]Cardwell and Fox, *Journey Toward Wholeness*, 130-131, 144, 153-155.

[39]Oscar Lucas, *The Disciple's Voice* (East Orange: privately published, 1950), 39.

[40]"District Assemblies," available at www.cocdocintl.org, accessed October 13, 2011; "Church History: History and Tradition," available at http://disciplesintl.org/ChurchHistory.html, accessed October 13, 2011.

[41]Gillams, *Principle and Practice*, 1, 22-24, 34-37, 40-42.

[42]Sheila H. Gillams, ed., *General Assembly Church of Christ, Disciples of Christ International Ministry Manual* (White Plains: General Assembly of the Church of Christ, Disciples of Christ, International, 2003), 19.

[43]Hazel Lewis and Cynthia Maus, "For Those Whom It Concerns," a letter dated January 7, 1927, UCMS Collection, Box 60, held at Disciples of Christ Historical Society in Nashville, Tennessee.

[44]"A Statement of Factors to be Considered in a Study of the Relationship of the Christian Woman's Board of Missions to the United Christian Missionary Society," UCMS Collection, Box 60, held at Disciples of Christ Historical Society, Nashville, Tennessee.

[45]"Dear Friend," a letter of the Christian Woman's Board of Missions, March 2, 1933, UCMS Collection, Box 60, held at Disciples of Christ Historical Society, Nashville, Tennessee.

[46]Effie L. Cunningham, letter to Lela Taylor, October 27, 1931, UCMS Collection, Box 60, held at Disciples of Christ Historical Society, Nashville, Tennessee.

[47]"Service and Status of Women in Disciples of Christ," a report dated June 1, 1953, UCMS Collection, Box 62, held at Disciples of Christ Historical Society, Nashville, Tennessee.

[48]"The Proportion of Men and Women in the Administration and Staff of the United Christian Missionary Society," a report dated 1956, UCMS Collection, Box 29, held at Disciples of Christ Historical Society, Nashville, Tennessee.

[49]*Disciples Year Book* (2007), 705.

[50]Mossie A. Wyker, *Church Women in the Scheme of Things* (St. Louis: Bethany Press, 1953), 5. See also Debra B. Hull, *Christian Church Women: Shapers of a Movement* (St. Louis: Chalice Press, 1994).

[51]Fran Craddock, Martha Faw, and Nancy Heimer, *In the Fullness of Time: A History of Women in the Christian Church (Disciples of Christ)* (St. Louis: Chalice Press, 1999), 81ff.

[52]Oma Lou Myers, *Rosa's Song: The Life and Ministry of Rosa Page Welch* (St. Louis: CBP Press, 1984).

[53]Margaret Cherryhomes, "Application for Missionary Service," dated June 17, 1946, UCMS Collection, Disciples of Christ Historical Society, Nashville, Tennessee.

[54]James A. Crain, *The Development of Social Ideas Among the Disciples of Christ* (St. Louis: The Bethany Press, 1969).

[55]W. Clark Gilpin, "Issues Relevant to Union in the History of the Christian Church (Disciples of Christ)," *Encounter* (Winter, 1980): 15-23.

[56]Dwight E. Stevenson, *Lexington Theological Seminary, 1865-1965: The College of the Bible Century* (St. Louis: Bethany Press, 1964). Calhoun eventually became part of Churches of Christ. See Adron Doran and Julian Ernest Choate, *The Christian Scholar: A Biography of Hall Laurie Calhoun* (Nashville: Gospel Advocate Company, 1985).

[57]*Disciples Year Book* (1945), 42-46.

[58]Charles Berry, Jr., and E. W. Rand, "An Abstract of Negro Education in the Disciple Brotherhood, a Comparative Study," (Bloomington: Bureau of Educational Research, Indiana University, 1949), 29, quoted in Cardwell and Fox, *Journey Toward Wholeness*, 46.

[59]"Resolutions Adopted by the Restoration Congress," *Christian Standard* (October 25, 1919): 1, 6; J. Michael Utzinger, *Yet Saints Their Watch Are Keeping: Fundamentalists, Modernists, and the Development of Evangelical Ecclesiology, 1887-1937* (Macon: Mercer University Press,

2006), 220-221.

[60]Frederick D. Kershner, "The North American Christian Convention Is Not Schismatic," *Christian Standard* (June 8, 1940): 545; Dean E. Walker, "The North American Christian Convention," *Shane Quarterly* (January, 1942): 65-72.

[61]A. D. Harman, "A Century of Conscious Entity," *The Christian-Evangelist* (November 18, 1926): 1449-1451, 1463-1464.

[62]Stephen Corey's Travel Diary for 1928, UCMS Collection, Disciples of Christ Historical Society, Nashville, Tennessee.

[63]Daisy L. Machado, *Of Borders and Margins: Hispanic Disciples in Texas, 1888-1945* (New York: Oxford University Press, 2003), xiii, 92-99.

[64]Pablo A. Jiménez, "Hispanics in the Movement," in Douglas Foster, et al., ed., *The Encyclopedia of the Stone-Campbell Movement* (Grand Rapids: Eerdmans, 2004), 395-399.

[65]"Where East and West Meet," (Indianapolis, Christian Woman's Board of Missions n.d.), 4.

[66]Ben E. Watson, *A Story of the Japanese Christian Churches in the United States as Adventures, Discoveries, Achievements, Aspirations* (Indianapolis: United Christian Missionary Society, n.d.).

[67]"Filipino Christian Church: 65th Anniversary, 1933–1998," a booklet produced by Filipino Christian Church in 1998; "History: The Filipino (Disciples) Christian Church" available at www.fdccla.org, accessed July 6, 2010.

[68]In 1948 the disbanded Japanese Christian Church was reconstituted as West Adams Christian Church (Disciples of Christ). "And only after considerable pleading was our church allowed to begin as the West Adams Christian church," Joe Nagano to Dr. Geunhee Yu (n.d., North American Pacific Asian Disciples Ministries, Division of Homeland Ministries, Christian Church [Disciples of Christ]).

[69]"Where We Have Shared," March 26, 1953. Responding to the fears of white Americans that Chinese immigrants were stealing "American" jobs, Congress passed the Chinese Exclusion Act in 1882 which limited Chinese immigrants to one hundred five per year for ten years. This legislation was strengthened in 1884 with additional provisions that limited the ability of any person of Chinese descent to freely leave and enter the United States. Other restrictive acts would follow.

[70]For informative anecdotes on All Peoples Church—what became of Japanese Christian Church after 1942—see Dan B. Geunung, *A Street Called Love: The Story of All Peoples Christian Church and Center, Los Angeles, California* (Pasadena: Hope Publishing House, 2000).

[71]"Justice," in Kagiwada memorial Sunday and NAPAD Ministry Week Materials for September 12-18, 1999; Homeland Ministries, Christian Church (Disciples of Christ), 5.

[72]Quoted in Sandhya Jha, *Room at the Table: Struggle for Unity and Equality in Disciples History* (St. Louis: Chalice Press, 2009), 84.

[73]Sydney E. Ahlstrom, *A Religious History of the American People* (New Haven: Yale University Press, 1972), 782.

[74]Edward Scribner Ames, *The New Orthodoxy* (Chicago: The University of Chicago Press, 1917), 11, 27, 50-51.

[75]Clark Williamson and Charles Blaisdell, "Disciples and Mainstream Protestant Theology," in D. Newell Williams, ed., *A Case Study in Mainstream Protestantism: The Disciples' Relation to American Culture, 1880-1989* (Grand Rapids: Eerdmans, 1991), 120-123. See also Edward Scribner Ames, *The Divinity of Christ* (Chicago: Bethany Press, 1911).

[76]Edward Scribner Ames, *Beyond Theology: The Autobiography of Edward Scribner Ames*, Van Meter Ames, ed. (Chicago: The University of Chicago Press, 1959).

[77]See the lengthy discussion of Willett compared to J. W. McGarvey in Eugene Boring, *Disciples and the Bible: A History of Disciples Biblical Interpretation in North America* (St. Louis: Chalice Press, 1997), 221-253.

[78]Herbert Lockwood Willett, *Basic Truths of the Christian Faith* (Chicago: Christian Century Co., 1903), 122.

[79]Herbert Lockwood Willett, "Introduction," in Herbert L. Willett, Orvis F. Jordan, and Charles M. Sharpe, eds., *Progress: Anniversary Volume of the Campbell Institute on the Completion of Twenty Years of History* (Chicago: Christian Century Press, 1917), 14.

[80]This expression is found in Willett's autobiography, *The Corridor of Years* (unpublished manuscript, 1967), 160. See also Leo Perdue, "The Disciples and Higher Criticism: The Formation of an Intellectual Tradition," in Williams, ed., *Case Study*, 77.

[81]Willett, *Basic Truths*, 78, 116, 124.

[82]Charles Clayton Morrison, *What Is Christianity?* (Chicago: Willett, Clark, and Company, 1940), 21, 58.

[83]Charles Clayton Morrison, *Can Protestantism Win America?* (New York: Harper & Brothers Publishers, 1948); Charles Clayton Morrison, *Unfinished Reformation* (New York: Harper and Brothers, 1953). See also Williamson and Blaisdell, "Disciples and Mainstream Protestant Theology," esp. 129-137.

[84]Samuel C. Pearson, Jr., "The Campbell Institute: Herald of the Transformation of an American Religious Tradition," *The Scroll* (Spring, 1978): 1-63.

[85]Forrest also served as the executive secretary of the Board of Education founded by the Convention in 1894 (now Higher Education Leadership Ministries). She and her husband, J. D. Forrest, were associated with the Chicago School of Philosophy, and were active members of the Chicago Philosophy Club.

[86]Pearson, "The Campbell Institute," 26.

[87]For a detailed account of the work of the Commission, see D. Newell Williams, "Overcoming a Liberal-Conservative Divide: The Commission on Restudy of the Disciples of Christ," in James O. Duke and Anthony L. Dunnavant, ed., *Christian Faith Seeking Historical Understanding: Essays in Honor of H. Jack Forstman* (Macon: Mercer University Press, 1997), 247-276.

[88]"Minutes of July 13, 14, 1939," Frederick Doyle Kersner Collection, Box 16, Folder 3, held in the archives of Christian Theological Seminary, Indianapolis, Indiana.

[89]"Commission on Restudy of the Disciples of Christ," *Disciples Year Book* (1946), 119.

[90]"Commission on Restudy," *Disciples Year Book* (1946), 119.

[91]"Commission on Restudy," *Disciples Year Book* (1946), 118.

[92]"Commission on Restudy," *Disciples Year Book* (1946), 120.

[93]"Commission on Restudy's Report Assumes Brotherhood To Be a Denomination," Frederick Doyle Kershner Collection, Box 16, Folder 4, held at Christian Theological Seminary, Indianapolis, Indiana.

[94]"Commission on Restudy of the Disciples of Christ," *Disciples Year Book* (1947), 117.

[95]"Commission on Restudy of the Disciples of Christ," *Disciples Year Book* (1948), 121-122.

[96]"Minutes of Study Meeting, July 5th and 6th, 1949," Frederick Doyle Kershner Collection, Box 16, Folder 4, held in the archives of Christian Theological Seminary, Indianapolis, Indiana.

[97]"The Report of the Commission on Restudy of the Disciples of Christ Authorized by the International Convention of the Disciples of Christ, San Francisco, 1948," Orman L. Shelton Collection, Box 1, Folder 3, held in the archives of Christian Theological Seminary, Indianapolis, Indiana.

[98]"Minutes of the Business Session, Y.M.C.A., Cincinnati, Ohio, Centennial Convention October 26, 1949," Orman L. Shelton Collection, Box 1, Folder 3, held in the archives of Christian Theological Seminary, Indianapolis, Indiana.

[99]Pearson, "The Campbell Institute," 35-36.

[100]James Duke and Joseph Driskill, "Disciples Theologizing amid Currents of Mainstream Protestant Thought, 1840-1980," in Williams, ed., *Case Study*, 146.

[101]Duke and Driskill, "Disciples Theologizing," 146-149.

[102]Ronald E. Osborn, "One Holy Catholic and Apostolic Church," in William Barnett Blakemore, ed., *The Renewal of the*

Church: The Panel of Scholars Reports, 3 vols. (St. Louis: Bethany Press, 1963), 1:315-316.

[103]Osborn, "One Holy Catholic and Apostolic Church," 1:316-318.

[104]Osborn, "One Holy Catholic and Apostolic Church," 1:318-319.

[105]Osborn, "One Holy Catholic and Apostolic Church," 1:319.

[106]Osborn, "One Holy Catholic and Apostolic Church," 1:318-320.

[107]Osborn, "One Holy Catholic and Apostolic Church," 1:321-322.

[108]A fuller consideration of this shift in the Disciples theology of mission is found in Mark Toulouse, *Joined in Discipleship: The Shaping of Contemporary Disciples Identity* (St. Louis: Chalice Press, 1997), 189-217, esp. 205-213.

[109]W. B. Blakemore, "The Issue of Polity for Disciples Today," in William Barnett Blakemore, ed., *The Renewal of the Church: The Panel of Scholars Reports,* 3 vols. (St. Louis: Bethany Press, 1963), 3:75-76.

[110]Toulouse, *Joined in Discipleship,* 219-243.

[111]D. Duane Cummins, *The Disciples: A Struggle for Reformation* (St. Louis: Chalice Press, 2009), 204-223. See also Webb, *In Search of Christian Unity,* 365-373; Anthony Dunnavant, *Restructure: Four Historical Ideals in the Campbell-Stone Movement and the Development of the Polity of the Christian Church (Disciples of Christ)* (New York: Peter Lang, 1993), 220-236.

[112]Roger W. Stump, "Spatial Patterns of Growth and Decline among the Disciples of Christ, 1890-1980," in Williams, ed., *Case Study,* 451-453.

[113]Stump, "Spatial Patterns of Growth," 449, 453-456.

[114]Stump, "Spatial Patterns of Growth," 457-458

[115]Stump, "Spatial Patterns of Growth," 462-466.

[116]Lorraine and Lyndsay Jacobs, "The World Convention of Churches of Christ" in Foster, et al., ed., *The Encyclopedia of the Stone-Campbell Movement,* 785-786.

[117]James M. Seale, "Disciples of Christ Historical Society," in Foster, et al., ed., *The Encyclopedia of the Stone-Campbell Movement,* 275-276.

10: Christian Churches/Churches of Christ

[1]Robert Sutton and Mark Chaves, "Explaining Schism in American Protestant Denominations, 1890-1990," *Journal for the Scientific Study of Religion* (June, 2004): 172.

[2]Eugene Boring, *Disciples and the Bible: A History of Disciples Biblical Interpretation in North America* (St. Louis: Chalice Press, 1997), 221-253.

[3]Conrad Wright, "The Growth of Denominational Bureaucracies: A Neglected Aspect of American Church History," *Harvard Theological Review* (April, 1984): 177-194.

[4]Robert K. Murray, *Red Scare: A Study in National Hysteria, 1919-1920* (Minneapolis: University of Minnesota Press, 1955); Allan J. Lichtman, *White Protestant Nation: The Rise of the American Conservative Movement* (New York: Grove Press, 2008), 26-30.

[5]David Siebenaler, "Indiana Disciples of Christ and the Modernist-Fundamentalist Controversy, 1919-1930," *Discipliana* (December, 2004): 99.

[6]Joel Carpenter, "Propagating the Faith Once Delivered: The Fundamentalist Missionary Enterprise, 1920-1945," in Joel Carpenter and Wilbert Shenk, eds., *Earthen Vessels: American Evangelicals and Foreign Missions, 1880-1980* (Grand Rapids: Eerdmans, 1990), 92-132.

[7]Max Ward Randall, *Light for a Dark Country: A Story of Evangelism and Mission Survey and Expansion in Southern Africa* (Joliet: Mission Services Press, 1960), 103-106.

[8]David Filbeck, *The First Fifty Years: A Brief History of the Direct-Support Missionary Movement* (Joplin: College Press, 1980), 194-210.

[9]"Articles of Incorporation of the Christian Missionary Fellowship" (dated February 28, 1949), held in the Emmanuel Christian Seminary Archives, Johnson City, Tennessee.

[10]"Christian Missionary Fellowship," *Christian Standard* (May 5, 1951): 282.

[11]O. D. Johnson, "Concerning an Organized Missionary Fellowship" (unpublished paper), 2, held in the Emmanuel Christian Seminary Archives, Johnson City, Tennessee.

[12]O. D. Johnson, "CMF Attitudes, Basis, Structures, Policies" (Kansas City: Christian Missionary Fellowship, 1951), 3-6, held in the Emmanuel Christian Seminary Archives, Johnson City, Tennessee. This essay is a revised reprint from Johnson's editorial series appearing in *Missionary Fellowship* from 1950 to 1955.

[13]Mark Maxey, *The Christian Missionary Fellowship: Its First Fifteen Years* (San Clemente: Go Ye Books, 1965), 16.

[14]O. D. Johnson, "To Think About: How Should a Mission Function," Pt. V: "In Promoting Christian Unity," *Missionary Fellowship* (March, 1954), 2, 4.

[15]Johnson, "To Think About," 4.

[16]On the ethos of biblical study in the Bible colleges, see Boring, *Disciples and the Bible,* 372-375.

[17]James B. North, "Cincinnati Bible College and Seminary," in Douglas Foster, et al., ed., *The Encyclopedia of the Stone-Campbell Movement* (Grand Rapids: Eerdmans, 2004), 220-221.

[18]Reuben G. Bullard, "Camps: Christian Churches/Churches of Christ," in Foster, et al., ed., *Encyclopedia,* 148.

[19]W. Ray Kelley, "African Americans in the Movement: Christian Churches/Churches of Christ," in Foster, et al., ed., *Encyclopedia,* 18-19; Lisa W. Davidson, "College of the Scriptures," in Foster, et al., ed., *Encyclopedia,* 227.

[20]On the Bible colleges' own understanding of their functions, see Gerald Tiffin, "The Interaction of the Bible College Movement and the Independent Disciples of Christ Denomination" (PhD diss., Stanford University, 1968), 106-112. Tiffin notes eight identifiable functions: (1) reopening closed congregations; (2) reclaiming congregations from the Disciples denomination; (3) beginning new congregations; (4) strengthening existing congregations; (5) providing regional organizational centers for "independent" Disciples congregations; (6) supplemental religious training for students eventually attending university; (7) ministerial training; and (8) anti-communism.

[21]In some instances they cultivated relationships with state universities to create joint degree programs. Examples include Pacific Christian College [now Hope International University] and California State University–Fullerton; Manhattan Christian College and Kansas State University; Northwest Christian College [now University] and the University of Oregon; Alberta Bible College and the University of Alberta; and Lincoln Christian University with Illinois State University. Several opted to drop "Bible College" for "Christian University." Examples include Roanoke Bible College (est. 1948), now Mid-Atlantic Christian University. Minnesota Bible College (est. 1913) renamed itself Crossroads College.

[22]James Deforest Murch, *Christians Only: A History of the Restoration Movement* (Cincinnati: Standard Publishing), 263-277.

[23]The official title was *Directory of the Ministry of the Undenominational Fellowship of Christian Churches and Churches of Christ* (Pattonville: privately published, 1955). The internal title page included two important clarifications: "The question of some, concerning this new publication, will be answered by the statement that the listing in this volume pertains, in large part, to the group or fellowship known to the U.S. Census as the 'Disciples of Christ.' The use of the name, 'Churches of Christ' does not here refer to the congregations of those various groups, of the same name, who make the use of musical instruments in worship a test of fellowship." The Directory became an annual publication in 1963. On the importance of this development, see A. T. DeGroot, *Church of Christ Number Two* (Birmingham: Birmingham Printers, 1956), 1-2; and A. T. DeGroot, *New Possibilities for Disciples and Independents* (St. Louis: Bethany Press, 1963), 24-28.

[24]Because of the informal status of these meetings, the participants themselves arranged for publication of the papers from at least the first five Consultations. Charles Gresham of Christian Churches/Churches of Christ took the lead in editing the volumes.

[25]"What Brotherhood Cooperation Means," (St. Louis: International Convention of the Christian Churches [Disciples of Christ], n.d.), 1, a pamphlet held in the archives of Emmanuel Christian Seminary, Johnson City, Tennessee.

[26]"What Brotherhood Cooperation Means," 5, 8-9.

[27]"What Brotherhood Cooperation Means," 13.

[28]"What Brotherhood Cooperation Means," 15-16.

[29]William Tucker and Lester McAllister, *Journey in Faith: A History of the Christian Church (Disciples of Christ)* (St. Louis: Bethany Press, 1975), 443-447; Henry Webb, *In Search of Christian Unity: A History of the Restoration Movement* (Cincinnati: Standard Publishing, 1990), 355-371; Leroy Garrett, *The Stone-Campbell Movement: The Story of the American Restoration Movement* (Joplin: College Press, 2002), 495-524; Mark Toulouse, *Joined in Discipleship: The Shaping of Contemporary Disciples Identity*, 2nd ed. (St. Louis: Chalice Press, 1997), 235-240.

[30]William Lown, "Biblical Authority and Restructure" (Manhattan: privately published, 1964), 4-10, a pamphlet held in the archives of Emmanuel Christian Seminary, Johnson City, Tennessee; James Strauss, "The Restoration Principle in the Light of Theology of Restructure: The Restoration of Biblical Christianity. Possible?? Necessary??" (Lincoln: privately published, 1965), a pamphlet held in the archives of Emmanuel Christian Seminary, Johnson City, Tennessee.

[31]Dean E. Walker, "The Tradition of Christ," in William Richardson, ed., *Adventuring for Christian Unity and Other Essays* (Johnson City: Emmanuel School of Religion, 1992), 542-545; William Lown, *The Restoration Movement and Its Meaning for Today* (B. D. Phillips Memorial Lectures, 1970; Kimberlin Heights: Johnson Bible College, 1971), 31-36 and 43-45.

[32]Walker, "The Tradition of Christ," 545-546.

[33]Walker, "The Tradition of Christ," 546.

[34]"Restructuring the Brotherhood," *The Seminary Review* (Fall, 1965): 8-18.

[35]Garrison first used the analogy in an address before the International Convention in 1964, then in 1967 indicated his suspicion that the Provisional Design of the Restructure was a "wrong fork." Winfred E. Garrison, *A Fork in the Road* (Indianapolis: Pension Fund of the Christian Churches, 1964); Robert O. Fife. *Ecclesiastical Issues in the Restructure of the Christian Church (Disciples of Christ)* (Los Angeles: Westwood Christian Foundation, 1981), 1-10. See also Edwin Hayden, "Overdriving," *Christian Standard* (May 18, 1968): 306.

[36]Dean E. Walker, "The Nature of the Church and Restructure" (paper delivered at the North American Christian Convention, Louisville, June 1966), held in the Emmanuel Christian Seminary Archives; Robert O. Fife, "Restoration and Restructure" (informal address delivered at the Ministers' Breakfast, T.H. Johnson Memorial Lectures), appended to *Christ Our Hope* (T.H. Johnson Memorial Lectures, Manhattan Bible College, 1964; Manhattan: Manhattan Bible College, 1964).

[37]Webb, *In Search of Christian Unity*, 370.

[38]See the editorials of Edwin Hayden, *Christian Standard* (1968): 242, 306, 402, 498, 658, 674, 706, 770; and *Christian Standard* (1969): 130, 146, 178, 290, 594, 818. See also Karl Lutz, "Restructure Will Destroy the Brotherhood," *Christian Standard* (1968): 483-484, 505-506, 553-554.

[39]"One Church's Resolution," *Christian Standard* (June 1, 1968): 342.

[40]Robert Friedly and Duane Cummins, *The Search for Identity: Disciples of Christ—The Restructure Years* (St. Louis: CBP Press, 1987), 63-64; Toulouse, *Joined in Discipleship*, 239; Roger W. Stump, "Spatial Patterns of Growth and Decline among the Disciples of Christ, 1890-1980," in D. Newell Williams, ed., *A Case Study of Mainstream*

Protestantism (Grand Rapids: Eerdmans, 1991), 461.

[41]David Edwin Harrell, Jr., "Restorationism and the Stone-Campbell Tradition," in Charles H. Lippy and Peter W. Williams, ed., *The Encyclopedia of the American Religious Experience*, 2 vols. (New York: Charles Scribner's Sons, 1988), 2:857.

[42]Stump, "Spatial Patterns," 459-461.

[43]B. D. Phillips, "An Open Letter to the Board of Trustees of the Disciples of Christ Historical Society," *Christian Standard* (May 18, 1968): 311.

[44]Edwin Hayden, "Giving Up What?" *Christian Standard* (August 10, 1968): 498.

[45]James DeForest Murch, correspondence with Charles Gresham, 1968; "Minutes of the Chaplaincy Endorsement Commission, 1973"; and *Chaplaincy Endorsement Commission of the Christian Churches and Churches of Christ* (n.p, n.d.), each held in the archives of Emmanuel Christian Seminary, Johnson City, Tennessee.

[46]Charles Gresham, "What Do Independents Have in Common? or The Unity of the Independent Movement," in Charles Gresham, ed., *The Second Consultation on Internal Unity* (Oklahoma City: privately published, 1960), 34-37.

[47]A. T. DeGroot critically analyzed these divergences among "independents," deemed "Church of Christ Number Two," in his *New Possibilities for Disciples and Independents*, 45-67, 92-97. Later, three studies attempted to define ideological groupings in the Christian Churches/Churches of Christ: C. J. Dull, "Intellectual Factions and Groupings in the Independent Christian Churches," *The [Cincinnati Bible] Seminary Review* (1985): 91-118; G. Richard Phillips, "From Modern Theology to a Post-Modern World: Christian Churches and Churches of Christ," *Discipliana* (Fall, 1994): 83-95; Paul Blowers, "Christian Churches, Churches of Christ," in Hans Hillerbrand, ed., *The Encyclopedia of Protestantism*, 2 vols. (New York: Routledge, 2004), 1:398-402.

[48]Dull labels them "Independent Fundamentalists," whereas for Phillips they would be a strident subset of "classic Restorationism." Here they are being termed "foundationalist" restorationists to avoid the label "fundamentalist," which could create confusion with other Fundamentalists with whom they had some significant theological differences. They were foundationalists in the sense of a fervent commitment to a purely objective, original, and comprehensive New Testament platform of faith and practice.

[49]E. C. Cameron, "Fundamentalism and the Disciples of Christ," *Christian Standard* (June 8, 1929): 532-533.

[50]For a good profile of Foster in relation to Fundamentalism of the time, see Kevin Kragenbrink, "Dividing the Disciples: Social, Cultural, and Intellectual Sources of Division in Disciples of Christ, 1919-1945" (PhD diss., Auburn University, 1996), 176-180.

[51]R. C. Foster, *The Revised Standard Version of the New Testament: An Appraisal* (Pittsburgh: The Evangelical Fellowship, 1946); R. C. Foster, *The Battle of the Versions* (Cincinnati: Cincinnati Bible Seminary, 1953; reprinted from *Christian Standard*, January–March 1953).

[52]Foster, *The Battle of the Versions*, 4, 9.

[53]R. C. Foster, *Controversy versus Pacifism* (Cincinnati: Cincinnati Bible Seminary, 1958); R. C. Foster, *The Everlasting Gospel* (Cincinnati: Standard Publishing, 1929), 139.

[54]Foster, *Everlasting Gospel*, 214-260.

[55]Kragenbrink, "Dividing the Disciples," 174.

[56]Quoted in Webb, *In Search of Christian Unity*, 298.

[57]Robert Elmore, "Christianity Versus Rationalism," in *The Watchword of the Restoration Vindicated: Five Masterly Arguments* (Cincinnati: Standard Publishing, 1939), 73-91.

[58]Elmore, "Christianity Versus Rationalism," 76.

[59]Filbeck, *The First Fifty Years*, 175-210.

[60]Elmore, "Christianity Versus Rationalism," 79.

[61]Foster, *Christianity Versus Pacifism*, 16. On restorationist infighting, see also DeGroot, *New Possibilities*, 46-67.

[62]See the *1971 Sessions of the Kiamichi Clinic* (Dallas: Bible Book

Store, 1971).

[63]"Our Philosophy," and "Our Position," 2011-2012 Florida Christian College online catalogue, 11, available at www.fcc.edu/academics/documents/College_Catalog_2011_2012.pdf, accessed January 10, 2012.

[64]"Statement of Faith for Selected CCU Faculty and Staff," Cincinnati Christian University, available at www.ccuniversity.edu/about/statement-of-faith, accessed January 10, 2012.

[65]"Heritage of CCU," Cincinnati Christian University, available at www.ccuniversity.edu/about/heritage-of-ccu, accessed January 10, 2012.

[66]Victor Knowles and William Paul, *Taking a Stand: The Story of the Ottumwa Brethren* (Joplin: College Press, 1996); also Victor Knowles, *Archie Word: Voice of Thunder, Heart of Tears* (Joplin: College Press, 1992).

[67]Knowles and Paul, *Taking a Stand*, 301-331.

[68]This would subsume the group that Dull calls the "Midwestern Pragmatics" and the two groups that Phillips identifies respectively as "Evangelicals" and "Church Growth Pragmatists."

[69]James DeForest Murch, *Adventuring for Christ in Changing Times: An Autobiography of James DeForest Murch* (Louisville: Restoration Press, 1973), 65, 84-58.

[70]Kragenbrink, "Dividing the Disciples," 193-206.

[71]James DeForest Murch, *The Protestant Revolt: Road to Freedom for American Churches* (Arlington: Crestwood Books, 1967); James DeForest Murch, *The Free Church* (Louisville: Restoration Press, 1966); and Murch, *Christians Only*, 9-18.

[72]Murch, *Protestant Revolt*, 178-211.

[73]James DeForest Murch, "Progress toward Brotherhood Unity," *Christian Standard* (January 8, 1938): 29.

[74]Murch, *Adventuring for Christ*, 148-152.

[75]On the coalition of "Neo-Evangelicals" taking over the mantle from earlier Fundamentalists in American Protestantism at mid-century, see George Marsden, *Understanding Fundamentalism and Evangelicalism* (Grand Rapids: Eerdmans, 1991), 62-64, 73-77, and 100-109.

[76]James DeForest Murch, *The World Council of Churches: An Analysis and Evaluation* (Wheaton: National Association of Evangelicals, 1961),10.

[77]D. G. Hart, *Deconstructing Evangelicalism: Conservative Protestantism in the Age of Billy Graham* (Grand Rapids: Baker Academic, 2004).

[78]Donald W. Dayton and Robert K. Johnson, *The Variety of American Evangelicalism* (Knoxville: University of Tennessee Press, 1991); and William Baker, "Christian Churches (Independent): Are We Evangelical?" in William Baker, ed., *Evangelicalism and the Stone-Campbell Movement* (Downers Grove: InterVarsity Press, 2002), 36-43.

[79]An example is the failure of *Christianity Today*, a key journalistic voice of American Evangelicalism, to publish a feature story on Alexander Campbell during the Campbell bicentennial in 1988.

[80]James DeForest Murch, "The Restoration Plea in an Ecumenical Era," in Charles Gresham, ed., *Second Consultation on Internal Unity*, 128-141, where he argues that the restoration plea was *the* answer to the churches' ecumenical urge.

[81]Jack Cottrell and Myron Taylor, "Inerrancy as a Restoration Principle" (debate manuscript), North American Christian Convention, Indianapolis, July 8-9, 1985. Cottrell clarified, however, that inerrancy should be a restoration principle but not a "term of salvation." Cf. also Jack Cottrell, *The Authority of the Bible* (Grand Rapids: Baker, 1978).

[82]Dull, "Intellectual Factions and Groupings," 95-98; C.J. Dull, "The *Declaration and Address* among Independents," in Thomas Olbricht and Hans Rollmann, eds., *The Quest for Christian Unity, Peace, and Purity: Thomas Campbell's* Declaration and Address (Lanham: Scarecrow Press, 2000), 417-423.

[83]Phillips, "From Modern Church to Post-Modern World," 88.

[84]Byron Lambert, "The 'Middle Way' of Frederick D. Kershner," in Dan Lawson, ed., *Emmanuel at 40: Heritage and Promise*

(Johnson City: Emmanuel School of Religion Press, 2005).

[85]Paul Blowers, "Restoring the One, Holy, Catholic and Apostolic Church: The *Declaration and Address* as Interpreted by William Robinson and Frederick Doyle Kershner," in Olbricht and Rollman, *Quest for Christian Unity*, 365-388.

[86]Walker, *Adventuring for Christian Unity*, 147-150 and 525-550.

[87]James Van Buren, "Restorationism," *Christian Standard* (May 28, 1949): 349-350.

[88]"Views and Reviews: The National Association of Evangelicals," *Christian Standard* (October 6, 1951): 638-639.

[89]Taylor and Cottrell, "Inerrancy as a Restoration Principle," n.p.

[90]Robert Fife, *Celebration of Heritage* (Los Angeles: Westwood Christian Foundation, 1992).

[91]Robert Fife, "The Inclusiveness of Church Membership," in Charles Gresham, ed., *Consultation on Internal Unity of the Christian Churches* (Manhattan: n.p., 1963), 11-24.

[92]C. Robert Wetzel, "Christian Churches/Churches of Christ at 2001: In Search of a Theological Center," *Stone-Campbell Journal* (Winter, 2001): 3-12. See also the *Christian Standard* (July 13, 2008), a special issue entitled "Does the Restoration Movement Matter?"

11: Responses to U.S. Social Change

[1]Alejandro Portes and Rubén G. Rumbaut, *Immigrant America: A Portrait*, 2d ed. (Berkeley: University of California Press, 1997); Diana Eck, *A New Religious America: How a 'Christian Country' Has Become the World's Most Religiously Diverse Nation* (San Francisco: Harper San Francisco, 2001), 2-3.

[2]Quoted in D. Duane Cummins, *Dale Fiers: Twentieth Century Disciple* (Fort Worth: TCU Press, 2003), 117.

[3]Cummins, *Fiers*, 117.

[4]Cummins, *Fiers*, 119, 121-122, 124.

[5]Clarice Campbell and Oscar Rogers, *Mississippi: The View From Tougaloo* (University of Mississippi Press, 1979), 198-217.

[6]Keith Watkins, *Christian Theological Seminary, Indianapolis: A History of Education for Ministry* (Zionsville: Guild Press of Indiana, 2001), 151-152.

[7]Richard L. Harrison, Jr., *From Camp Meeting to Church: A History of the Christian Church (Disciples of Christ) in Kentucky* (St. Louis: Christian Board of Publication, 1992), 284-285.

[8]Cummins, *Fiers*, 121-122.

[9]Cummins, *Fiers*, 119.

[10]Minutes of the Business Session National Board of the 50th Annual Assembly National Christian Missionary Convention, Chicago, Illinois, August 1966, 12-13.

[11]Lester McAllister and William Tucker, *Journey in Faith: A History of the Christian Church (Disciples of Christ)* (St. Louis: Christian Board of Publication, 1975), 453. In the early 2000s Reconciliation evolved into Reconciliation Ministry, charged with advancing the Pro-Reconciliation/Anti-Racism initiative adopted by the Disciples General Board.

[12]This attitude reflected the position of the Presbyterian Church in the United States (the Southern Presbyterians). See the Confession of Faith of the Presbyterian Church in the United States, chapter 33, paragraph 4. Ernest Trice Thompson, *The Spirituality of the Church: A Distinctive Doctrine of the Presbyterian Church in the United States* (Richmond: John Knox Press, 1961).

[13]Reuel Lemmons, "The Church and Integration," *Firm Foundation* (March 31, 1964): 194; James F. Fowler, "From the Midst of the Crises," *Firm Foundation* (March 31, 1964): 199.

[14]R. N. Hogan, "The Sin of Being a Respecter of Persons" *Christian Echo* (June, 1959): 2, 5.

[15]Fred Gray, *Bus Ride to Justice: Changing the System by the System, the Life and Works of Fred Gray* (Montgomery: Black Belt Press, 1995).

[16]Richard T. Hughes, *Reviving the Ancient Faith: The Story of Churches of Christ* (Grand Rapids: Eerdmans, 1996), 293-294; Theodore Wesley

Crawford, "From Segregation to Independence: African Americans in Churches of Christ" (PhD diss., Vanderbilt University, 2008).

[17]"Dr. Molefe Kete Asante," available at http://www.asante.net, accessed January 6, 2012.

[18]Edward Robinson, *The Fight Is on in Texas: A History of African American Churches of Christ in the Lone Star State* (Abilene: Abilene Christian University Press, 2008), 162-165; Edward Robinson, *Show Us How You Do It: Marshall Keeble and the Rise of Black Churches of Christ in the United States, 1914-1968* (Birmingham: University of Alabama Press, 2008), 165-170.

[19]David Jones, Jr., "Report on Race Relations Workshop" *Supplement to Christian Chronicle* (May 10, 1968): 2-4.

[20]Lawrence L. (Bud) Stumbaugh, "Report on Race Relations Workshop" *Supplement to Christian Chronicle* (May 10, 1968): 5.

[21]Douglas A. Foster, "Justice, Racism & Churches of Christ," in Gary Holloway and John York, eds., *Unfinished Reconciliation: Justice, Racism and Churches of Christ* (Abilene: Abilene Christian University Press, 2006), 117-135.

[22]Douglas A. Foster, "An Angry Peace: Race and Religion," *ACU Today* (Spring 2000): 8-20, 39.

[23]See, for example, John McRay, "Race or Grace," *Mission* (July, 1968): 5.

[24]"The Right Thing to Do: A Special Report," *ACU Today* (Spring, 2000): 2-5.

[25]Steve Carr, "An Urban Conversation for the Restoration Movement," *Christian Standard* (August 10, 2008): 606-608.

[26]James DeForest Murch, "Today in Christendom: Fruits of the Social Gospel," *Christian Standard* (April 19, 1969): 247.

[27]"A Racist Pronouncement," *Christian Standard* (March 7, 1970): 227; James DeForest Murch, "Today in Christendom: Handwriting on the Wall," *Christian Standard* (January 24, 1970): 97.

[28]"One More Time," *Christian Standard* (July 19, 1969): 450.

[29]"What System?" *Christian Standard* (May 3, 1969): 274.

[30]"Call to Action," *Christian Standard* (May 4, 1968): 274.

[31]Robert Fife, *Teeth on Edge* (Grand Rapids: Baker Book House, 1971), 133; Robert Fife, "Racism: A Continuing Challenge to the Lordship of Jesus Christ," *Conveying the Incarnation* (Joplin: College Press, 1993), 181-187.

[32]James Van Buren, "The Church and Culture," *Christian Standard* (August 16, 1970): 743.

[33]Leland Tyrrell, "Who Will Work This Field?" *Christian Standard* (November 29, 1969): 758; W. Ray Kelley, "Racism Is a Sin!" *Christian Standard* (July 31, 1994): 657-658; W. Ray Kelley, "African American Evangelism: Where Are We and Where Are We Going?" *Christian Standard* (February 12, 2006): 102-103.

[34]See, for example, Paul Williams, "The Time Has Come. The Time is Now!" *Christian Standard* (September 10, 1989): 831-832.

[35]Denzil D. Holness, *The Jonah Syndrome: White Churches Running from the Inner City* (Joplin: College Press, 1998). In 2003, Holness began publication of a quarterly newsletter, *Voice in the Wilderness*, examining a variety of issues of race in the Christian Churches/Churches of Christ.

[36]Debbie Brunsman, "Building Bridges to a Different World," *Christian Standard* (July 31, 1994): 659-661.

[37]Robert Hull, "The Hidden Wound and the Healing Table," *Christian Standard* (February 12, 2006): 100-101.

[38]Darrell Rowland, "White as Snow? Guilty as Sin?" *Christian Standard* (October 3, 2010): 721-723. This special issue bears the title "All White Is Not All Right."

[39]Mark Moore, "Half-Pure Religion and the Unpopularity of the Poor," *Christian Standard* (April 5, 2009): 246-248.

[40]Doug Priest, "Care for the Earth Is Bringing Good News to the Poor," *Christian Standard* (September 20, 2009): 662; Doug Priest, "Balancing Word and Deed," *Christian Standard* (April 5, 2009): 244-245, 248; Carr, "An Urban Conversation for the Restoration Movement," 607-608.

[41]For examples, see Philip Kenneson, "Cultivating a Generous Heart," *Christian Standard* (April 24, 2005): 260-263; Mike Faust, "Will Work for Food," *Christian Standard* (May 20, 2007): 308-309, 314; John Sloper, "Three Sides of Community Ministry," *Christian Standard* (November 18, 2009): 782-783, 787; Jennifer Taylor, "City Centered: Making a Difference One Relationship at a Time," *Christian Standard* (November 18, 2009): 784-786; Ash Barker, "Will We Make Poverty Personal?" *Christian Standard* (December 13, 2009): 878-881.

[42]"Center for Urban and Global Outreach," http://www.ccuniversity.edu/cugo/, accessed January 14, 2012.

[43]For example, see, B. C. Goodpasture, "It Happened Here," *Gospel Advocate* (August 14, 1969): 518, 527.

[44]Hughes, *Reviving the Ancient Faith*, 261-263.

[45]Ronnie F. Wade, *The Sun Will Shine Again Someday: A History of the Non-Class, One-Cup Churches of Christ* (Springfield: Yesterday's Treasures, 1986), 153-157.

[46]Alexander Campbell, "Address on War" (Washington: Government Printing Office, 1937); Bennie Lee Fudge, "Can a Christian Kill for His Government?" (Athens, privately published, 1943).

[47]Batsell Barrett Baxter, "When War Comes," *20th Century Christian* (November, 1938): 1-3.

[48]Batsell Barrett Baxter, "The Christian and Warfare," a message delivered in chapel at David Lipscomb College, Nashville, Tennessee, March 8, 1968, held in the Center for Restoration Studies, Leaders Files, Baxter, Batsell Barrett.

[49]Lee M. Rogers, *God and Government* (Tuscumbia: Lee M. Rogers, 1971), 1-6.

[50]Rogers, *God and Government*, 106-109.

[51]C. G. Ross, *War: A Trilogy: Three Perspectives, One Biblical Position* (Ft. Worth: Star Bible Publications, 1994); Lee C. Camp, "Pacifism: The Case for Christian Non-Violence," *New Wineskins* (January/February, 2002), available at www.wineskins.org/filter.asp?SID=2&fi_key=36&co_key=277; and *Mere Discipleship: Radical Christianity in a Rebellious World* (Grand Rapids: Brazos Press, 2003).

[52]The display of the U. S. flag in worship spaces has been a source of controversy for both mainline and evangelical churches. See "Rally Round the Flag," *Christianity Today* (November 12, 2001): 36.

[53]David Allen, pulpit minister for Northside Church of Christ, San Antonio, e-mail conversation with Douglas Foster, August 2010.

[54]Lee Camp, professor at Lipscomb University College of the Bible and Ministry, e-mail to Douglas Foster, August 3, 2010.

[55]This informal survey was conducted by Douglas A. Foster, Associate Professor of Church History in the Graduate School of Theology at Abilene Christian University, Abilene, Texas.

[56]Jack Cottrell, "The Errors of Pacifism," 2 parts, *Christian Standard* (1982): 716, 742.

[57]Laurence Keene, *Heirs of Stone and Campbell on the Pacific Slope* (Claremont: Disciple Seminary Foundation in Association with the School of Theology at Claremont, 1984), 67.

[58]Paul Butler, *What the Bible Says About Civil Government* (Joplin: College Press, 1990), 236. Aaron S. Chambers, "The Path of Pacifism: A Synoptic Study of the Fate of the Tradition of Pacifism in the Churches of Christ and Christian Churches/Churches of Christ in the Stone-Campbell Movement (MA thesis, Abilene Christian University, 2000).

[59]Robert Wuthnow, *The Struggle for America's Soul: Evangelicals, Liberals, & Secularism* (Grand Rapids: Eerdmans, 1989), 33-34.

[60]D. Duane Cummins, *The Disciples Colleges: A History* (St. Louis: Christian Board of Publication, 1987), 123; Lester G. McAllister, *Bethany: the First 150 Years* (Bethany: Bethany College Press, 1991), 360; William Jerry MacLean, *Barton College: Our Century* (Wilson: Barton College, 2002), 251-254.

[61]Mark G. Toulouse, Jeffrey Williams, and Dyan Dietz, eds., *Institutional Change in Theological Education: A History of Brite Divinity School* (Fort Worth: Texas Christian University Press, 2011), 122-125.

[62]Robert L. Friedly and D. Duane Cummins, *The Search for Identity: Disciples of Christ—The Restructure Years* (St. Louis: Christian Board of Publication, 1987), 133-134.

[63]See Charles Cochran, "Assembly Approves Anti-War Resolution, available at www.disciplesworldmagazine.com/node/8745, accessed January 9, 2012. The full text of Resolution 0728 can be found in "The Church's Response to the War in Iraq, Revised," *Disciples Year Book*, 248-249.

[64]Daisy L. Machado, "From Anglo-American Traditions to a Multicultural World," *Discipliana* (March, 1997): 47-48, 55-57.

[65]Howard Bowers, editor of the *Disciples Year Book and Directory*, e-mail to Newell Williams, January 4, 2012.

[66]Howard Bowers, editor of the *Disciples Year Book and Directory*, e-mail to Newell Williams, January 3, 2012.

[67]Mark S. Massa, "Disciples in a Mission Land: The Christian Church in New York City," in *A Case Study of Mainstream Protestantism*, 486-487.

[68]Massa, "Disciples in a Mission Land," 488.

[69]Participants included General Minister and President Sharon Watkins, Executive Secretary of the National Convocation Timothy James, representatives from Home Missions and the New Church Ministry program of Church Extension, regional ministers from the Northeastern and Florida regions, and ten Haitian pastors. Roster attached to e-mail from Charlie Wallace to Newell Williams, August 5, 2010.

[70]Wallace, e-mail to Williams, August 4, 2010.

[71]Howard Bowers, e-mail to Newell Williams, January 5, 2012.

[72]Paul M. Blowers, "Hispanics in the Movement," in Douglas Foster, et al., ed., *The Encyclopedia of the Stone-Campbell Movement* (Grand Rapids: Eerdmans, 2004), 400.

[73]See, for example, Jim Tune, "Intentionally International," *Christian Standard* (October 3, 2010): 730-731.

[74]Brad Dupray, "Interview with Byron Davis," *Christian Standard* (October 3, 2010): 730-731.

[75]"FriendSpeak: Creating Life, Changing Conversations," available at http://www.friendspeak.org, accessed November 16, 2011.

[76]See for example, Lindy Adams, "Asian Congregations Increasing in United States," *Christian Chronicle* (June, 2004): 8.

[77]Robert Wilonsky, "Bilingual in the Branch? Say It Ain't So," *Dallas Observer* blog, November 20, 2006, available online at http://blogs.dallasobserver.com/unfairpark/2006/11/bilingual_in_the_branch_say_it.php?print=true, accessed November 16, 2011.

[78]Chris Siedman, minister at Farmer's Branch Church of Christ, e-mail to Douglas A. Foster, August 20, 2010.

[79]*Churches of Christ in the United States, 2009 Edition* (Nashville: 21st Century Christian, 2009), 16; Adams, "Asian Congregations," 8.

[80]See, for example, Eric Tryggestad, "Breaking the Language Barrier, and the Trend," *Christian Chronicle* (May, 2007): 1, 6; "Laotians Find Faith, Challenges in United States," *Christian Chronicle* (January, 2006): 1, 29.

[81]Massa, "Disciples in a Mission Land," 487.

[82]Sharon Watkins, "Women and Leadership in the Christian Church (Disciples of Christ)," paper presented at the Stone-Campbell Dialogue, Cincinnati Bible College, November 27-28, 2000. Available at http://www.disciples.org/ccu/programs/documents/2000Watkins.html, accessed January 14, 2012.

[83]"15 Greatest Black Women Preachers: Experts and Leading Blacks Name Select Group of Ministers," *Ebony* (November, 1997): 102-114.

[84]"Issues Identified by Black Clergywomen for Discussion at the Convocation," *Selah* (August, 1988): 9.

[85]Sheila Hope Gillams, "Principle and Practice: The Quandary of African American Restorationists in the History and Theology of the Church of Christ, Disciples of Christ, 1850-1950" (PhD diss., Union Theological Seminary, 2002), 315.

[86]Jha published *Room at the Table: Struggle for Unity and Equality in Disciples History* (St. Louis: Chalice Press, 2009).

[87]Nohemí Colón-Pagán, ed., *Tú Sobrepasas de Todas: Contribución de Las Mujeres a la Iglesia Cristiana (Discípulo de Cristo) (1989-1998)* [You are the best of all: contributions of women to the Christian Church (Disciples of Christ), 1989-1998] (Iglesia Cristiana Discípulo de Cristo in Puerto Rico: 1999), 116.

[88]Rita Nakashima Brock, Claudia Camp, and Serene Jones, eds., *Setting the Table: Women in Theological Conversation* (St. Louis: Chalice Press, 1995),

[89]Stephen V. Sprinkle, *Disciples and Theology: Understanding the Faith of a People in Covenant* (St. Louis: Chalice Press, 1999), 123.

[90]"10 Inspiring Women Religious Leaders," Huffington Post, available at www.huffingtonpost.com/2011/08/15/women-religious-leaders_n_924807.html?#s327348&title=Dr_Ingrid_Mattson, accessed October 25, 2011.

[91]Robert R. Taylor, "ERA, Churches, Christian Education, and the Home," *Gospel Advocate* (February 27, 1975): 134-136.

[92]Betty Burton Choate, "Women's Rights," *Gospel Herald* (June, 1998): 10, 13.

[93]LeVan Shoptaw, "ERA and the Military Draft," *Gospel Light* (February ,1977): 26-27.

[94]Wallace Alexander, "That Houson Conference—And the Radical 'Feminists'," *Gospel Light* (December, 1977): 179; B. LaVerne Wade, "Christian Women Confront a Contemporary Crisis," *Firm Foundation* (January 17, 1978): 8.

[95]Irene C. Taylor, "Thoughts from Christian Women: The Women's Movement—Then and Now," *Firm Foundation* (October, 1992): 22-23; "Thoughts from Christian Women: The Equal Rights Philosophy—Door to Confusion," *Firm Foundation* (November, 1992): 22-23; "Thoughts from Christian Women: The Women's Movement: Current Status," *Firm Foundation* (December, 1992): 20-21.

[96]Lindy Adams, "Churches' Study of Women's Issue Evokes Varying Conclusions, Practice," *Christian Chronicle* (October, 2004): 1, 29.

[97]Ronnie Wiggins, "The Role of Women," *Christian Chronicle* (June, 1998): 18-19.

[98]"Gender Justice and Churches of Christ," available at http://gal328.org/index.html, accessed November 16, 2011; and "The Women in Ministry Network" available at http://womeninministrycc.com/contact, accessed November 16, 2011.

[99]Melanie W. Wright "Voices of Canadian Concern: What Has Happened to the Churches of Christ in Ontario?" in Warren Lewis and Hans Rollmann, eds., *Restoring the First-century Church in the Twenty-first Century: Essays on the Stone-Campbell Restoration Movement, in Honor of Don Haymes* (Eugene: Wipf & Stock, 2005), 539-542.

[100]Lindy Adams, "A Conversation with Jeanene Reese," *Christian Chronicle* (January, 2002): 20.

[101]Katie Hays, "Opening Doors: The Journal of a Minister," in Billie Silvey, ed., *Trusting Women: The Way of Women in the Churches of Christ* (Orange: New Leaf Books, 2002), 39-42. Hayes was later ordained in the Christian Church (Disciples of Christ).

[102]Izetta Sams, "Christian Woman in the Home and in the Church," *Christian Echo* (November/December 1990): 7.

[103]Josephine Decierdo-Mock, "The Abundant Life," in Billie Silvey, *Trusting Women*, 73-84.

[104]This data was compiled by Douglas A. Foster, Associate Professor of Church History, Abilene Christian University, Abilene, Texas, in fall 2010.

[105]D'Esta Love, Chaplain at Pepperdine University, e-mail conversation with Douglas A. Foster, August 2010.

[106]Stephen Johnson and Lynette Sharp Penya, "Gender Inclusivity in Church of Christ Congregations," An Executive Summary of the Research Project, October 2010, 6.

[107]Love to Foster, August, 2010.

[108]Grayson Ensign, "Of Feminine Leadership," *Christian Standard*

(April 13, 1975): 319.

[109]Brad Dupray, "Interview with Eleanor Daniel," *Christian Standard* (June 24, 2007): 396-397.

[110]For examples of how Christian Church leaders have debated the role of women leaders, see Peter J. Isenberg, "From Ephesus to America," *Christian Standard* (October 8, 1989): 917; Lewis Foster, "Woman—Where's She Going Today?" *Christian Standard* (December 11, 1988): 1144-1147; Jack Cottrell, "Male and Female Roles" *Christian Standard* (January 19, 1986): 52-54; Joseph M. Webb, "Where Is the Command to Silence?" Part I *Christian Standard* (May 21, 1989): 5; and his "Where Is the Command to Silence?," Part II *Christian Standard* (May 28, 1989): 7.

[111]James B. North, "The Anderson Open Forum," *Christian Standard* (June 24, 1990): 557.

[112]In John T. Brown, *Who's Who in Churches of Christ: Biographical Sketches and Portraits of Ministers and Other Leaders* (Cincinnati: Standard Publishing, 1929), see the following biographical sketches: "Riggs, Helen Robbins," 229, "Etta, Mrs. William D. (Angie)," 200, "Raum, Carrabelle O'Neal," 221, Mrs. Edward Clutter, 57. Elizabeth Johnson served as President of Johnson Bible College. See Robert E. Black, *The Story of Johnson Bible College* (Kimberlin Heights: Tennessee Valley Printing Co., 1951); Alva Ross Brown, *Standing on the Promises* (privately published, 1928).

[113]Eleanor A. Daniel, "Women in Ministry: Christian Churches/Churches of Christ," in Douglas Foster, et al., ed., *The Encyclopedia of the Stone-Campbell Movement* (Grand Rapids: Eerdmans, 2004), 780.

[114]Brad Dupray, "Interview with Marsha Relyea Miles," *Christian Standard* (February 10, 2008): 115-116.

[115]See "Louisville Gospel," available at http://louisvillegospel.com/profiles/blogs/annual-christian-womens, accessed October 26, 2011.

[116]*Our Bodies, Ourselves: A Book by and for Women* (New York: Simon and Schuster, 1976), 216.

[117]This discussion follows Cummins, *The Disciples: A Struggle for Reformation*, 239-241, 261.

[118]James Guth and Helen Lee Turner, "Pastoral Politics in the 1988 Election: Disciples as Compared to Presbyterians and Southern Baptists," in D. Newell Williams, ed., *A Case Study of Mainstream Protestantism* (St. Louis: Chalice Press, 1991), 378, 404.

[119]Craig Churchill, "Churches of Christ and Abortion: A Survey of Selected Periodicals," *Restoration Quarterly* (July, 1996): 129.

[120]Silbano Garcia, "What Does the Word of God Say About Homosexuality?" Churches of Christ Internet Ministries, available at http://church-of-christ.org/homosexuality.htm, accessed January 9, 2012.

[121]Charles A. Holt, "Gay and Lesbian Members of the Church of Christ," *The Examiner* (September, 1987): 23-25.

[122]Lynn Mitchell, "Coming Out in Houston: The A Cappella Chorus," *Mission* (October, 1979): 59-64.

[123]Leroy Garrett, "Our Changing World," *Restoration Review* (December, 1985): 198; Leroy Garrett, "Our Changing World," *Restoration Review* (April, 1986): 279.

[124]Abilene's student handbook, for example, listed "sexual immorality, including pre-martial sex (heterosexual and homosexual activity)" as a Category Three offense subject to suspension or dismissal from the University. See "ACU Student Handbook" available at www.acu.edu/campusoffices/studentlife/studenthandbook/index.html#Student%20Conduct, accessed November 16, 2011.

[125]Caitlin MacIntyre, "Three Equality Riders Arrested at Heritage Christian University," available at www.soulforce.org/article/1449, accessed November 16, 2011.

[126]Richard Lindsay, "Dialog Begins on Ending Abilene Christian's Discriminatory Policy," available at http://www.soulforce.org/article/776, accessed November 16, 2011.

[127]Center Peace "Welcome" available at www.centerpeace.net/welcome, accessed January 8, 2012.

[128]David Kirkpatrick, "The Evangelical Crackup," *The New York Times Magazine* (October 28, 2007): 10, available at www.nytimes.com/2007/10/28/magazine/28Evangelicals, accessed on December 15, 2007.

[129]Robert Rea, Professor of Church History and Historical Theology, Lincoln Christian University, e-mail to D. Newell Williams, June 20, 2011.

[130]Frederick Norris, "Abortion, No—But Then What?" *Christian Standard* (June 7, 1990): 8-9; David Grubbs, "Legal, Safe, and Rare," *Christian Standard* (May 9, 1993): 399-400.

[131]See, for example, Howard Casteel, "Abortion, an Affront to God," *Christian Standard* (July 21, 1991): 612-613; Ed Charlton, "Abortion: An Appeal to the Practical Conscience of America," *Christian Standard* (July 4, 1993): 570-571; Don Kimbro, "The *Imago Dei*," *Christian Standard* (April 14, 2002): 310-311.

[132]See, for example, Henry Hill, "Pro Choice," *Christian Standard* (October 27, 1991): 912-913; Carlie Butler, "Choice," *Christian Standard* (July 3, 1994): 570-571.

[133]Susan Page, "Shaping Politics from the Pulpits," *USA Today*, available at www.usatoday.com/news/washington/2005-08-02-christian-cover_x.htm, accessed December 15, 2007.

[134]Darinka Aleksic, "The Megachurch as a Social Space: A Case Study of Exurban Enclave Development," a paper presented at First International Conference of Young Urban Researchers, June 5, 2007, available at http://conferencias.iscte.pt/viewabstract.php, accessed December 1, 2009.

[135]The organizers of Disciple Renewal were concerned by what they believed to be a liberalizing trend among Disciples on such issues as the lordship of Jesus Christ, the authority of the Bible, and homosexuality. In 1995 they established the Disciples Heritage Fellowship as an organization of autonomous churches. In 2002 the DHF officially included sixty member congregations and one hundred supporting churches. See Kevin D. Ray, "Disciple Renewal: The First Decade 1985-1995," (MA thesis, Lincoln Christian Seminary, 2001); "Disciples Heritage Fellowship," available at www.dhfchurches.org/index.htm, accessed November 16, 2011.

[136]Clark M. Williamson, *A Guest in the House of Israel* (Louisville: Westminster John Knox, 1993), 250.

[137]"A Sacred Obligation: Rethinking Christian Faith in Relation to Judaism and the Jewish People," in John Merkle, ed., *Faith Transformed: Christian Encounters with Jews and Judaism* (Collegeville: Liturgical Press, 2003).

[138]*A Study Guide to Accompany the Report "Disciples of Christ and Interreligious Engagement"* (Indianapolis: Council on Christian Unity, 2006), 2.

[139]"Islam Revealed," available at www.islamunveiled.info, accessed November 16, 2011.

[140]Evertt L. Huffard, *Christ or the Qur'an?* (Jackson: Evertt L. Huffard, 2001), v-vi, 104.

[141]Gover Shipp, *Christianity and Islam Bridging Two Worlds* (Webb City: Covenant Publishing, 2002), 118.

[142]Lee Camp, *Who Is My Enemy? Questions American Christians Must Face About Islam—and Themselves* (Grand Rapids: Brazos Press, 2011).

[143]"History and Mission," Gülen Institute, available at www.guleninstitute.org/index.php/About-Us.html, accessed November 16, 2011.

[144]*Aliens and Light*, 104th Annual Summit, Abilene Christian University (September 19-22, 2010), 9, 19, 22, 28.

[145]J. D. Long, "Fethullah Gülen and Interfaith/cultural Dialog: The Lubbock Christian University Experience," Third Annual Conference on Islam in the Contemporary World, University of Texas at San Antonio, November 3, 2007.

[146]Robert Rae, Professor of Church History and Historical Theology, Lincoln Christian University, e-mail to D. Newell Williams, October 17, 2011.

12: Theological and Institutional Shifts

[1]Roy Bowen Ward, "'The Restoration Principle': A Critical Analysis," *Restoration Quarterly* (Winter, 1965): 210.

[2]Batsell Barrett Baxter, "The Training of Preachers," *Firm Foundation* (June 23, 1970): 387.

[3]William Woodson, Alan E. Highers, Monroe Hawley, and Rubel Shelly, *The Restoration Movement and Unity* (Henderson: Freed-Hardeman College, 1986), 140.

[4]J. D. Thomas, *Harmonizing Hermeneutics* (Nashville: Gospel Advocate, 1991).

[5]J. D. Thomas, *We Be Brethren: A Study in Biblical Interpretation* (Abilene: Biblical Research Press, 1958); J. D. Thomas, *Heaven's Window: Sequel to We Be Brethren* (Abilene: Biblical Research Press, 1974).

[6]F. LaGard Smith, *The Cultural Church* (Nashville: 20th Century Christian, 1992).

[7]*Papers Presented to the Christian Scholars Conference Hosted by Pepperdine University, July 19-21, 1989* (Malibu: Christian Scholars Conference, 1989); *Papers Presented to the Christian Scholars Conference Hosted by Abilene Christian University, July 19-21, 1990* (Abilene: Christian Scholars Conference, 1990).

[8]Thomas H. Olbricht, *Hearing God's Voice: My Life with Scripture in the Churches of Christ* (Abilene: Abilene Christian University Press, 1996).

[9]Lindy Adams, "Instrumental Worship: Isolated or Key Trend?" *Christian Chronicle* (September 2003): 1, 29. In October and November 2010 the online journal *New Wineskins* carried articles examining the issue and interviewing ministers at churches that had added instrumental services. See "Accompanied or *A Capella*?" available at www.wineskins.org/page.asp?SID=2&Page=375, accessed January 10, 2012.

[10]Tim Woodruff, *The Church That Flies* (Orange: New Leaf Books, 2000), 17-18.

[11]Bill Love, *The Core Gospel: On Restoring the Crux of the Matter* (Abilene: Abilene Christian University Press, 1992); Jeff Childers, Douglas A. Foster, and Jack R. Reese, *The Crux of the Matter: Crisis, Tradition and the Future of Churches of Christ* (Abilene: Abilene Christian University Press, 2001).

[12]Rubel Shelly, *I Just Want to Be a Christian* (Nashville: 20th Century Christian, 1984).

[13]Leonard Allen and Lynn Anderson, eds., *The Transforming of a Tradition: Churches of Christ in the New Millennium* (Orange: New Leaf Books, 2001).

[14]Kenneth L. Cukrowski, Mark W. Hamilton, and James Thompson, *God's Holy Fire: The Nature and Function of Scripture* (Abilene: Abilene Christian University Press, 2002); Jeff Childers and Frederick Aquino, *Unveiling Glory: Visions of Christ's Transforming Presence* (Abilene: Abilene Christian University Press, 2003); Mark Love, Douglas A. Foster, and Randall J. Harris, *Seeking a Lasting City: The Church's Journey in the Story of God* (Abilene: Abilene Christian University Press, 2005).

[15]John Mark Hicks, *Come to the Table: Revisioning the Lord's Supper* (Orange: New Leaf Books, 2001); John Mark Hicks and Greg Taylor, *Down in the River to Pray: Revisioning Baptism as God's Transforming Work* (Siloam Springs: Leafwood Press, 2004); and John Mark Hicks, Johnny Melton, and Bobby Valentine, *A Gathered People: Revisioning the Assembly as Transforming Encounter* (Abilene: Leafwood Press, 2007), 9-16.

[16]*Memphis Meeting with the Representatives of the Herald of Truth: September 10, 1973* (Memphis: Getwell Church of Christ, 1973).

[17]Reuel Lemmons, "Finis," *Firm Foundation* (August 23, 1983): 2.

[18]*Wineskins* would later become an online journal and be renamed *New Wineskins* in 2001, available at www.wineskins.org, accessed January 10, 2012.

[19]See, for example, "Life Aboard the Fellow-Ship," *Upwords: The Teaching Ministry of Max Lucado*, available at www.maxlucado.com/articles/topical/life_aboard_the_fellow-ship, accessed December 14, 2011.

[20]Rick Atchley and Bob Russell, *Together Again: Restoring Unity in Christ After a Century of Separation* (Leafwood Publishers and Standard Publishing, 2006). Reflecting the conservative Evangelical leanings of both of these megachurch pastors, suspicion toward the Christian Church (Disciples of Christ) led them to keep that group at arms length even while calling for a "reunion" within the Stone-Campbell Movement.

[21]"The Bible Today," *Abilene Christian College Annual Bible Lectures* (Abilene: Students Exchange, 1966).

[22]Douglas A. Foster, "Waves of the Spirit Against a Rational Rock: The Impact of the Pentecostal, Charismatic and Third Wave Movements on Churches of Christ," *Restoration Quarterly* (January, 2003): 99-110.

[23]See accounts in *The Acts of the Holy Spirit in the Church of Christ Today* (Los Angeles: Full Gospel Business Men's Fellowship International, 1971).

[24]Rick Rowland, "The History of Campus Ministry in Churches of Christ," in Tim Curtis and Mike Matheny, eds., *Ministering on the College Campus* (Nashville: 20th Century Christian, 1991), 13-20.

[25]Rowland, "History of Campus Ministry," 22-23; Lawrence "Bud" Stumbaugh, "Cost of Discipleship," sermon at Dallas Campus Evangelism Seminar, December 1966, quoted in Michael W. Casey, "Solution…Revolution: Campus Evangelism and the Rise of Evangelicalism in Churches of Christ," presented at the Churches of Christ in the Post-Modern Age Seminar, Nashville, Tennessee, July 1991, 3-4.

[26]Jim Bevis, Charles Shelton, Dudley Lynch, "A Statement to the Supporters of Campus Evangelism from the CE Staff," *Go* (April, 1970): 1, 3. Leaders continued to seek support for the ministry, renamed Campus Advance, a name also used by the Crossroads campus ministry starting in 1967.

[27]S. David Moore, *The Shepherding Movement: Controversy and Charismatic Ecclesiology* (New York: Continuum, 2004); and S. D. Moore, "Shepherding Movement," in *The New International Dictionary of Pentecostal and Charismatic Movements*, revised edition (Zondervan, 2003).

[28]For a description and critical analysis, see Flavil R. Yeakley, Jr., *The Discipling Dilemma: A Study of the Discipling Movement Among Churches of Christ* (Nashville: Gospel Advocate Company, 1988).

[29]Richard N. Ostling and Sophronia Scott Gregory, "Keepers of the Flock," *Time* (May 18, 1992); Michael Paulson, "Campuses Ban Alleged Church Cult," *Boston Globe*, February 23, 2001.

[30]Kevin S. Wells, "International Churches of Christ," in Douglas Foster, et al., ed., *The Encyclopedia of the Stone-Campbell Movement* (Grand Rapids: Eerdmans, 2004), 418-419. A leadership crisis led to a decentralization of the body and a move to reconcile with mainstream Churches of Christ in 2002. See "ICOC Cooperation Churches" available at www.icocco-op.org, accessed on December 4, 2011. A number of websites operated by former members of the ICOC are also available. See, for example, "Reveal: A Not-for-Profit Organization," available at www.reveal.org, accessed February 12, 2012.

[31]Douglas A. Foster, Mel E. Hailey, and Thomas L. Winter, *Ministers at the Millennium: A Survey of Preachers in Churches of Christ* (Abilene: Abilene Christian University Press, 2000), 70, 165-166.

[32]John Mark Hicks, "1900-2000: Change and Growing Diversity," in Lindy Adams and Scott LaMascus, eds., *Decades of Destiny: A History of Churches of Christ from 1900-2000* (Abilene: Abilene Christian University Press, 2004), 124-125.

[33]Henry Webb, "Christian Churches/Churches of Christ," in Foster, et al., ed., *Encyclopedia*, 185.

[34]John E. Wasem, "NNCC: A 37-Year Journey of Passion and Vision," *Christian Standard* (August 6, 2006): 8-9.

[35]Donald A. McGavran, *Understanding Church Growth: Third Edition*, revised and edited by C. Peter Wagner (Grand Rapids: Eerdmans, 1970), vii-xi.

[36]"History," Southeast Christian Church, available at www.southeastchristian.org/?page=3442, accessed January 10, 2012.

[37]C. Peter Wagner, "Preface to the Third (1990) Edition," in *Understanding Church Growth*, ix.

[38]Elmer Towns, "Effective Evangelism View: Church Growth Effectively Confronts and Penetrates the Culture," in Gary McIntosh and Paul Engle, eds., *Evaluating the Church Growth Movement: Five Views* (Grand Rapids: Zondervan, 2004), 43.

[39]Gary I. McIntosh, "Introduction: Why Church Growth Can't Be Ignored," in McIntosh and Engle, *Evaluating the Church Growth Movement*, 21.

[40]Wasem, "NNCC: A 37-year Journey," 8-9.

[41]Jennifer Taylor, "Getting Strong: The National New Church Conference's 'Exponential' Development," *Christian Standard* (October 12, 2008): 764-765, 768.

[42]Greg Marksberry, "Stadia: New Church Strategies: A Time for Cooperation," *Christian Standard* (November 2, 2003): 726-727.

[43]Patricia Leigh Brown, "Megachurches as Minitowns," *The New York Times*, May 9, 2002, available at www.nytimes.com/2002/05/09/garden/megachurches-as-minitowns.html, accessed December 20, 2011.

[44]"10Q with Bob Russell of Southeast Christian Church," available at http://churchrelevance.com/10q-with-bob-russell-of-southeast-christian-church, accessed December 14, 2011.

[45]Clifford Grammich, "Many Faiths of Many Regions: Continuities and Changes Among Religious Adherents Across U.S. Counties" available at www.rand.org/pubs/working_papers/2005/RAND_WR211.pdf, accessed December 14, 2011.

[46]Susan Page, "Shaping Politics from the Pulpits," available at www.usatoday.com/news/washington/2005-08-02-christian-cover_x.htm, accessed on December 14, 2011; David Kirkpatrick, "The Evangelical Crackup," available at http://query.nytimes.com/gst/fullpage.html?res=9C04EEDE1738F93BA15753C1A9619C8B63-&scp=2&sq=Evangelical+Crackup&st=nyt, accessed on December 14, 2011. See also Scott Thuma and Dave Travis, *Beyond Megachurch Myths: What We Can Learn from America's Largest Churches* (San Francisco: John Wiley & Sons, 2007), 143.

[47]Promoters of church planting see it addressing a number of short-comings in the Christian Churches. For examples, see Alan Ahlgrim, "It's Time," *Christian Standard* (February 18, 2007): 100-101, 109; Bob Russell, "Let's Celebrate," *Christian Standard* (October 28, 2007): 676-678, 687.

[48]On emerging generations and worship, see Dan Kimball, *Emerging Worship: Creating Worship Gatherings for New Generations* (Grand Rapids: Zondervan, 2004), 1-11. On the history and principles of the missional movement, see Craig Van Gelder, "Gospel and Our Culture View," 75-102, in McIntosh and Engle, *Evaluating The Church Growth Movement*.

[49]Ahlgrim, "It's Time," 101.

[50]W. Ray Kelley, "African-Americans in the Movement," in Foster, et al., ed., *Encyclopedia*, 20.

[51]W. Ray Kelley, "African-American Evangelism: Where Are We and Where Are We Going?" *Christian Standard* (February 12, 2006): 102-103, 108.

[52]Kelley, "African-Americans in the Movement," in Foster, et al., ed., *Encyclopedia*, 20.

[53]"About," EnrichNova, available at http://enrichnova.wordpress.com/about, accessed December 14, 2011; Mark Wilkinson, "Where Did We Come From?" *Starting Point* (n.p.: Journey's Crossing, 2008), 2; Rick Grover, "Double-Espresso Church Planting in New Orleans," *Christian Standard* (October 12, 2008): 758-760.

[54]Harold R. Watkins, *Continuity, Conservation, Cutting Edge: A Research Book Surveying the History of the Board of Church Extension (aka Church Extension) of the Christian Church (Disciples of Christ)* (Indianapolis: Church Extension, 2005), 94, 109.

[55]Watkins, *Continuity*, 99.

[56]D. Newell Williams, "Christianity in Twentieth Century America: Implications for the Twenty First Century," *Encounter* (Summer 2002): 247-261.

[57]Watkins, *Continuity*, 101-102.

[58]Watkins, *Continuity*, 103-104.

[59]Watkins, *Continuity*, 103.

[60]Watkins, *Continuity*, 107-109.

[61]Watkins, *Continuity*, 110.

[62]Duane Cummins, *The Disciples: A Struggle for Reformation* (St. Louis: Chalice Press, 2009), 248-249, 264.

[63]Richard L. Hamm, *2020 Vision for the Christian Church (Disciples of Christ)* (St. Louis: Chalice Press, 2001), 25-86.

[64]Watkins, *Continuity*, 111.

[65]Cummins, *Disciples*, 264; Ayanna Johnson, "New Churches Inspire, Challenge Disciples," *Disciples World* (July-August 2006): 8-10.

[66]Watkins, *Continuity*, 111.

[67]Rick Morse, "Ever Thought of Giving Birth?" *The Journey: A Publication of Church Extension and New Church Ministry* (Fall, 2010): 4.

[68]*Year Book and Directory of the Christian Church (Disciples of Christ)* (Indianapolis: Office of the General Minister and President, 2009), 550.

[69]Lisa Davison, "General Board...or Walking the Plank?" *Disciplesworld* (October, 2004): 21.

[70]"Response to Davison's Speak Out," *Disciplesworld* (December, 2004): 5, 42; "What Makes Us Disciples?" *Disciplesworld* (January/February 2005): 5.

13: Developments in U.K. and Brit. Commonwealth

[1]David Thompson, *Let Sects and Parties Fall: A Short History of the Association of Churches of Christ in Great Britain and Ireland* (Birmingham: Berean Press, 1980), 131-134.

[2]Murray J. Savage, *Haddon of Glen Leith: An Ecumenical Pilgrimage* (Dunedin: Associated Churches of Christ of New Zealand, 1970), 32-35, 44-45, 60-62.

[3]Graeme Chapman, *One Lord, One Faith, One Baptism: A History of the Churches of Christ in Australia* (Keysborough: Vital Publications, 1979), 121-129.

[4]Chapman, *One Lord, One Faith, One Baptism*, 111, 167; Graeme Chapman, *No Other Foundation: A Documentary History of the Churches of Christ in Australia, 1846-1990*, 3 vols. (Mulgrave, Victoria: privately published, 1990), 2:506; "Churches of Christ Fourth World Convention," *Christian Advocate* (September 5, 1952): 281.

[5]William Robinson, "Conference on Faith and Order," *Christian Advocate* (August 19, 1927): 527.

[6]R. K. Francis, "That they may all be one," with subsequent letters from W. J. Cullen, R. K. Francis, and Dudley A. Elwes, *Christian Advocate* (1929): 356, 372, 405, 437, 459, 469, 484-485.

[7]The response is found in "Churches of Christ in Great Britain and Ireland," in Leonard Hodgson, ed., *Convictions: A Selection from the Responses of the Churches to the Report of the World Conference on Faith and Order Held at Lausanne, 1927* (New York: Macmillan, 1934), 66-78.

[8]Thompson, *Let Sects and Parties Fall*, 137-141.

[9]David Thompson, "Churches of Christ in Great Britain and Ireland," in Douglas Foster, et al., ed., *The Encyclopedia of the Stone Campbell Movement* (Grand Rapids: Eerdmans, 2004), 371.

[10]Thompson, "Churches of Christ," 371.

[11]William Robinson, "The View of Disciples or Churches of Christ," in Roderic Dunkerley, ed., *The Ministry and the Sacraments* (London: SCM Press, 1937), 253-268.

[12]Fairplay [pseud.], "Letter to the Editor," *Christian Advocate* (September 23, 1938): 599.

[13]Argyle Street Church of Christ, letter to William Robinson, dated February 18, 1945. A copy of this letter is held in the private files of David Thompson, Cambridge, England.

[14]"Minutes of the 99th Conference," *Churches of Christ Year Book and Annual Report* (Birmingham: Churches of Christ, 1945), 93-94

(resolutions 4 and 10). The Argyle Street church (having reported a membership of 129 in 1944) reported an average attendance of 40 at the Lord's Supper in "Faith that Removes Mountains," Insert in *Scripture Standard* (August, 1946).

[15]Walter Crosthwaite, "Free Church Federal Council," *Scripture Standard* (1945): 73.

[16]Thompson, "Churches of Christ in Great Britain and Ireland," 371.

[17]This was partly reflected in his pamphlet, A. L. Haddon, *The Coming of the World Church: A Brief Introduction to the Ecumenical Movement* (Dunedin, N.Z.: Youth Committee of the New Zealand Council of Religious Education, 1942).

[18]Savage, *Haddon of Glen Leith*, 65-88.

[19]Chapman, *One Lord, One Faith, One Baptism*, 136-137. After 1913, Main was not personally involved in unity initiatives other than discussions with Baptists.

[20]Chapman, *One Lord, One Faith, One Baptism*, 153-155.

[21]Chapman, *One Lord, One Faith, One Baptism*, 155-157.

[22]Graeme Chapman, "A. W. Stephenson," *Digest of the Australian Churches of Christ Historical Society*, nos. 98-99 (July, 1988).

[23]*Kaniva District Churches of Christ Seventieth Anniversary: Historical Reflections* (Kaniva: 1959), inside cover.

[24]Chapman, *One Lord, One Faith, One Baptism*, 174-175.

[25]Chapman, *One Lord, One Faith, One Baptism*, 176-177. In 1989, the school at Glen Iris, later known as the Churches of Christ Theological College, relocated to Mulgrave, Victoria.

[26]William Robinson, *Essays on Christian Unity* (London: James Clarke, 1924), 10-11 (italics original).

[27]William Robinson, *Religion and Life: A Study of Christian Conduct in Relation to Belief* (London: Elliott Stock, 1925), 20-27, 36, 54-73. He did refer to one of Rotherham's translations in *The Emphasized Bible*.

[28]William Robinson, *Religion and Life*, 157-158. See also William Robinson, *Biblical Doctrine of the Church*, 2nd edition (St Louis: Bethany Press, 1960), 231; A. W. Stephenson, "Truth in Love," in A. W. Stephenson, ed., *One Hundred Years: A Statement of the Development and Accomplishments of the Churches of Christ in Australia* (Melbourne: Austral Publishing, 1946), 7-18.

[29]William Robinson, *Whither Theology? Some Essential Biblical Patterns* (London: Lutterworth Press, 1945), 44-45. See also Frederick W. Norris, "Work and Influence in the United States," in J. Gray, ed., *W. R.: The Man and His Work* (Birmingham: Berean Press, 1978), 66-74.

[30]Thompson, *Let Sects and Parties Fall*, 119.

[31]Thompson, *Let Sects and Parties Fall*, 119-120, 149. A revised Model Trust Deed was approved by Conference in 1952, which removed the list of beliefs in the 1923 Deed, referring simply to the beliefs and practices "commonly held by the Churches associating under the name Churches of Christ." *Churches of Christ Year Book* (1952), 112-14, 138 (resolution 8). See also *Churches of Christ Year Book* (1923), 141-148; *Churches of Christ Year Book* (1951), 121.

[32]Lyndsay Jacobs, *Understanding the Associated Churches of Christ/Christian Churches in New Zealand* (Melbourne: Joint Board of Christian Education, 1969), 12-13.

[33]Stephenson, *One Hundred Years*, 172-173.

[34]*Churches of Christ Year Book* (1956), 167 (resolution 25), 181-183; *Churches of Christ Year Book* (1957), 55-58, 161 (resolution 29); *Churches of Christ Year Book* (1958), 48-58, 159 (resolution 38); *Churches of Christ Year Book* (1959), 54-57, 158-159 (resolution 32).

[35]P. A. W. Smith, "President's Overdraft Redemption Fund," *Churches of Christ Year Book* (1961), 133-135, 158 (resolution 6). On the origins of the Fraternal Aid plan, see *Churches of Christ Year Book* (1955), 59.

[36]Chapman, *One Lord, One Faith, One Baptism*, 163.

[37]At the beginning of the twenty-first century financial realities forced both the *New Zealand Christian* and the *Australian Christian* to become fully on-line publications.

[38]"The New Hymn Book," *Scripture Standard* (November,1948): 168; "The New Hymn Book," *Scripture Standard* (August, 1957): 125.

[39]Stephenson, *One Hundred Years*, 162-163.

[40]See, for example, "The Wigan Conference," *Scripture Standard* (November, 1948): 162-169; "The Blackburn Conference" (June, 1949): 81-88.

[41]J. A. Hudson, *The Church in Great Britain* (Old Paths Book Club, 1948), 69; book review by C. Melling, *Scripture Standard* (August, 1948): 118-119.

[42]"The Wigan Conference," *Scripture Standard* (May, 1956): 65-67; "Conference and Rally," *Scripture Standard* (September, 1956): 133; "The Spring Conference 1957," *Scripture Standard* (June, 1957): 83-84; W. Brown, "The Organisation and Government of the Church of Christ," *Scripture Standard* (October 1957): 150-152.

[43]These moves reflected the reduction in central organization in the 1990s of the Fellowship of Churches of Christ in Britain that would be formed from churches that did not enter the United Reformed Church in 1981, described below.

[44]"75 Years of Service," *Canadian Disciple* (Spring, 1997): 2.

[45]Reuben Butchart, *Disciples of Christ in Canada* (Toronto: Churches of Christ [Disciples], 1949), 175-185.

[46]"Ken Wills Remembers," *Canadian Disciple* (Summer, 1997): 9.

[47]"1941-1965, The McCully Years," *Canadian Disciple* (Spring, 1997): 4-6.

[48]Butchart, *Disciples in Canada*, 155-165. In the first decade of the twenty-first century Disciples were still, on occasion, educated at Emmanuel, and in 2009 Disciples historian and theologian Mark Toulouse was named Emmanuel's principal.

[49]R. A. Cuthbert, "The College without Walls," *Canadian Disciple* (Fall, 1988): 9-11.

[50]Butchart, *Disciples in Canada*, 169-171; D. A. Barrie, "A History of the Christian Church and Christian Church (Disciples of Christ) in Alberta, Canada" (MA thesis, Lincoln Christian Seminary, 1975), 147-153.

[51]Butchart, *Disciples in Canada*, 171.

[52]Ronald Fraser, "Alberta Bible College," in Douglas Foster, et al., ed., *Encyclopedia of the Stone-Campbell Movement* (Grand Rapids: Eerdmans, 2004), 23-24.

[53]See Lillian M. Torkelson and Roger W. Peterson, "Western Christian College: Background and Historical Perspective 1931 to 1995," available at www.oldpaths.com/Archive/WCC, accessed December 21, 2011; and "Great Lakes Christian High School: Our History," available at www.glchs.on.ca/index.php/aboutus/history, accessed December 21, 2011.

[54]A Christian Churches/Churches of Christ school with the same name was started in Michigan in 1949. In 1992 the Michigan school changed its name to Great Lakes Christian College.

[55]Ronald Fraser, Stewart Lewis, and Claude Cox, "The Movement in Canada," in Douglas Foster, et al., ed., *Encyclopedia of the Stone-Campbell Movement* (Grand Rapids: Eerdmans, 2004), 156.

[56]James Marsden, "Conference Paper," *Churches of Christ Year Book and Annual Report* (Birmingham: Churches of Christ, 1909), 25-52, 169-170 (resolutions 36, 43).

[57]Chapman, *One Lord, One Faith, One Baptism*, 177-178; Jacobs, *Understanding*, 15.

[58]For a full discussion of the post-World War II beginning and growth of a cappella Churches of Christ in New Zealand, see Mark Willis, *From Cottages to Congregations: A History of Churches of Christ in New Zealand from 1844 to 2004* (n.p., c. 2004), 107-245.

[59]"About SPBC" available at www.spbc.org.nz/AboutSPBC.htm, accessed December 21, 2011.

[60]*Churches of Christ Year Book* (1931), 181 (resolution 3); Thompson, *Let Sects and Parties Fall*, 140-141; Henry Townsend, *Robert Wilson Black* (London: Carey Kingsgate Press, 1954), 71.

[61]"Baptists and the Churches of Christ," *Christian Advocate* (January 28, 1942): 46; "The Week in Review," *Christian Advocate*

(February 4, 1942): 52; "Free Church Union," *Christian Advocate* (March 18, 1942): 97-98; "Baptists and Churches of Christ Confer," *Christian Advocate* (April 8, 1942): 128; "Resolution Recommending Closer Association with Baptist Churches," *Christian Advocate* (August 18, 1950), 274; "Baptists and Churches of Christ," *Christian Advocate* (May 18, 1951), 169-170; *Churches of Christ Year Book* (1942), 113 (resolution 16); *Churches of Christ Year Book* (1948), 87-88; *Churches of Christ Year Book* (1950), 38-39, 127-128 (resolution 23); *Churches of Christ Year Book* (1952), 43; *Churches of Christ Year Book* (1957), 113; Thompson, *Let Sects and Parties Fall*, 184-186; Townsend, *R. W. Black*, 103-114, 136-43; E.A. Payne, *The Baptist Union: A Short History* (London: Carey Kingsgate Press, 1959), 221.

[62]*Centenary Historical Souvenir*, 48; Thomas Hagger, "Primitive Christianity in New Zealand," *Christian Advocate* (October 9, 1936): 646.

[63]Savage, *Haddon of Glen Leith*, 65-88.

[64]Jacobs, *Understanding*, 13-14. See "Christian Churches New Zealand: Our History," available at http://www.ccnz.org/index.php?option=com_content&task=view&id=12&Itemid=28, accessed December 21, 2011.

[65]Thompson, *Let Sects and Parties Fall*, 177-180.

[66]"Association" became the official term used for the British Churches of Christ in the Revised Rules and Regulations adopted in 1948.

[67]Norman Walters, "Conference Paper," *Churches of Christ Year Book* (1954), 39-50; *Churches of Christ Year Book* (1956), 119-121, 166 (resolution 8); P. Morgan, "Union Committee Report," *Christian Advocate* (August 17, 1956): 455-456; Thompson, *Let Sects and Parties Fall*, 186-187.

[68]*Churches of Christ Year Book* (1963), 172 (resolution 44); James Gray, "What Is God Requiring of Us Now?" *Churches of Christ Year Book* (1964), 55-67; *Churches of Christ Year Book* (1972), xviii (resolution 14); D. M. Thompson, "Churches of Christ in the British Isles, 1842-1972," *Journal of the United Reformed Church History Society* (1972-1973): 33; Thompson, *Let Sects and Parties Fall*, 188-189.

[69]*Churches of Christ Year Book* (1967), 168, 195 (resolution 19), 199 (resolutions 55-55); *Churches of Christ Year Book* (1968), 66-68; *Churches of Christ Year Book* (1969), 59-60, 65-70, 81-82; *Churches of Christ Year Book* (1970), 57-58, 73; *Churches of Christ Year Book* (1971), 69, 132 (resolution 8); *Churches of Christ Year Book* (1972), 7-8, xviii (resolution 21); *Churches of Christ Year Book* (1973), xv-xvi (resolution 41–which wrongly states that 74 churches rather than 72 voted in favor of opening negotiations); Thompson, *Let Sects and Parties Fall*, 190-91.

[70]Thompson, *Let Sects and Parties Fall*, 195-197.

[71]Thompson, *Let Sects and Parties Fall*, 173; *Churches of Christ Year Book* (1975), 28-30.

[72]"Fellowship of Churches of Christ Constitution," *Fellowship of Churches of Christ in Great Britain and Ireland Year Book* (2001-2002), 12-18.

[73]C. Robert Wetzel, "Springdale College," in Douglas Foster, et al., ed., *The Encyclopedia of the Stone-Campbell Movement* (Grand Rapid: Eerdmans, 2004), 695-696. Martin Robinson became principal in 2002. See also the current Springdale College website, available at http://springdalecollege.org.uk/about/, accessed December 10, 2010, which makes no mention of Churches of Christ in explaining its origins. See "A Brief History of BCC," at http://www.bhxc.org.uk/about/a-brief-history-of-bcc.html, accessed December 22, 2011.

[74]Chapman, *One Lord, One Faith, One Baptism*, 173-174.

[75]Gordon Murray, "St. Timothy Lower Sackville," *Canadian Disciple* (Summer, 1987): 4-6. The Union Church at St Timothy, Lower Sackville, Nova Scotia, was a joint Disciples–United Church congregation that met in the same building as St. Elizabeth Seton Catholic Church.

[76]Ronald A. Fraser, Stewart J. Lewis, and Claude Cox, "The Movement in Canada," in Douglas Foster, et al., ed., *The Encyclopedia of the Stone-Campbell Movement* (Grand Rapid: Eerdmans, 2004), 156;

Neil Bergman, "Letter to the Editor," *Canadian Disciple* (Fall, 1990): 8-9; Ray Cuthbert, "A New Disciple-United Witness in Winnipeg," *Canadian Disciple* (Summer, 1997): 10-12; "The Elmer Stainton Years," *Canadian Disciple* (Fall, 1997): 4.

[77]"Churches and People," *Canadian Disciple* (Winter, 1990): 7; Raymond Cuthbert, "Editorial," *Canadian Disciple* (Summer, 1990): 4-5; Neil Bergman, "Letters," *Canadian Disciple* (Fall, 1990): 9.

[78]Robert Steffer, "Dear Canadian Disciples," *Canadian Disciple* (Winter, 1996): 4-8.

[79]William Robinson, *Christianity in Pacifism* (London: Allen and Unwin, 1933), 66, 92; William Robinson, *Pacifism in the Old Testament and Afterwards* (London: Fellowship of Reconciliation, 1933), 26.

[80]Thompson, *Let Sects and Parties Fall*, 154-156.

[81]Keith Sinclair, *A History of New Zealand* (London: Oxford University Press, 1961), 284.

[82]Regarding discussions of atomic weapons, see *Churches of Christ Year Book* (1945), 99 (resolution 54, passed on 8 August 1945); for the hydrogen bomb, see *Churches of Christ Year Book* (1957), 163-164 (resolutions 48-49); for the Partial Nuclear Test Ban Treaty, see *Churches of Christ Year Book* (1963), 172 (resolution 45).

[83]A. L. Frith, "The Drift towards War," *Scripture Standard* (September, 1950): 131-132; A. L. Frith, "These Forty Years," *Scripture Standard* (October, 1951): 149; (December, 1951): 184-185; (February, 1952): 21-23; Editor, "Churches of Christ and War," A. L. Frith, "The War Bug," A. H. Odd, "War," *Scripture Standard* (November 1951): 161-167; M. W. Casey, "The Overlooked Pacifist Tradition of the Old Paths Churches of Christ, Part II," *Journal of the United Reformed Church History Society* (December, 2000): 523-528.

[84]Stuart Macintyre, *A Concise History of Australia* (Cambridge: Cambridge University Press, 1999), 214-215.

[85]Chapman, *One Lord, One Faith, One Baptism*, 167.

[86]Albert Brown, "Conference Paper," *Churches of Christ Year Book and Annual Report* (Birmingham: Churches of Christ, 1919), 26-43.

[87]Congregations that viewed instrumental music in worship to be a violation of scriptural norms often associated with U.S. Churches of Christ.

[88]Graeme Chapman, *Ballarat Churches of Christ, 1959-1993* (Mulgrave, Victoria: Churches of Christ Theological College, 1994), 268.

[89]Chapman, *One Lord, One Faith, One Baptism*, 148-149.

[90]Macintyre, *Concise History*, 231, 236, 267-268, 287-290. Not surprisingly this is one of the most contested areas of recent Australian historical writing.

[91]Godfrey Fretwell, A. L. Haddon, and Milton Vickery, *Centennial Historical Souvenir: Being a Brief History of the Associated Churches of Christ in New Zealand, 1844-1944* (Wellington: G. Deslandes, 1944), 44; Stephenson, *One Hundred Years*, 151-152.

[92]Sinclair, *New Zealand*, 318-321.

[93]"Churches and People," *Canadian Disciple* (Spring, 1990): 10; "The Disciples in Winnipeg," *Canadian Disciple* (Fall, 1993): 8.

[94]A. C. Watters, "The Need for More Evangelists," *Christian Advocate* (August 28, 1931): 545-546; A. C. Watters, "How We May Increase Whole-Time Ministry and at the Same Time Preserve Mutual Ministry in Our Churches," *Churches of Christ Year Book* (1936), 37.

[95]Thompson, *Let Sects and Parties Fall*, 145-146.

[96]*Churches of Christ Year Book* (1920), 133; *Churches of Christ Year Book* (1933), 154.

[97]David M. Thompson, "Churches of Christ in Great Britain and Ireland," in Douglas Foster, et al., ed., *The Encyclopedia of the Stone-Campbell Movement* (Grand Rapids: Eerdmans, 2004), 372.

[98]Denis R. Lindsay, "Missions in Europe," in Douglas Foster, et al., ed., *The Encyclopedia of the Stone-Campbell Movement* (Grand Rapids: Eerdmans, 2004), 312.

[99]Lyndsay Jacobs, "The Movement in New Zealand," in Douglas Foster, et al., ed., *The Encyclopedia of the Stone-Campbell Movement* (Grand

Rapids: Eerdmans, 2004), 566.

[100]*Helping Build Churches in Canada: A Report of the First Thirty Years, 1957-1987* (London: Church of Christ Development Co. Ltd., n.d), 2-4; "Ken Wills Remembers," *Canadian Disciple* (Summer, 1997): 6; Melvin Breakenridge, "Thirty Years Later: The Churches of Christ Development Company," *Canadian Disciple* (Summer, 1987): 11-12.

[101]Graeme Chapman, "The Movement in Australia," in Douglas Foster, et al., ed., *Encyclopedia of the Stone-Campbell Movement* (Grand Rapids: Eerdmans, 2004), 53.

[102]Herbert R. Taylor, *Churches of Christ in South Australia, 1846-1959* (Adelaide: Churches of Christ Evangelistic Union, 1959), 30-31.

[103]Graeme Chapman, *One Lord, One Faith, One Baptism*, 167.

14: Movement in Asia Since 1920s

[1]"First Annual Report of the United Christian Missionary Society," *Disciples Year Book* (1921), 29-34.

[2]A.C. Watters, *History of the British Churches of Christ* (Indianapolis: Butler University School of Religion, 1948), 118-119; David Thompson, *Let Sects and Parties Fall: A Short History of the Association of Churches of Christ in Great Britain and Ireland* (Birmingham: Berean Press, 1980), 99, 144.

[3]"Foreign Mission Enterprises of Australian Churches," *Christian Standard* (July 21, 1928): 718; H.R. Taylor, *The History of the Churches of Christ in South Australia, 1846-1959* (Adelaide: Churches of Christ Evangelistic Union, 1959), 61.

[4]*Disciples Year Book* (1929), 29-30.

[5]*Medical Missionaries in India: Dr. Zoena May Rothermel* (Christian Woman's Board of Missions, n.d.), a pamphlet held in the archives of Christian Theological Seminary, Indianapolis, Indiana; *They Went to India: Biographies of Missionaries of the Disciples of Christ* (Indianapolis: United Christian Missionary Society, n.d.), 74; Sterling Rothermel, "Rothermels Purchase Maudha Station from UCMS," *Christian Standard* (May 26, 1928): 514; Zoena Rothermel, "Maudaha Mission Faces Eviction after Thirteen Years of Service," *Christian Standard* (February 18, 1928): 147. See also Henry Webb, *In Search of Christian Unity: A History of the Restoration Movement* (Cincinnati: Standard Publishing, 1990), 325.

[6]*They Went to India*, 69; Webb, *In Search of Christian Unity*, 324-325; Harry Schaeffer, "Our Ideals for Missionary Work in Central Provinces, India," *Christian Standard* (June 11, 1927): 558; "Schaefers to Use the Apostolic Method," *Christian Standard* (February 25, 1928): 169; "Third Annual Report of the Central Provinces Mission of the Churches of Christ," *Christian Standard* (March 7, 1931): 242.

[7]G. Percy Pittman, "Let There Be No More Hardas!" *World Call* (March, 1932): 19-20; Fred Saunders, "Australian Mission Stations in China and India Report Progress," *Christian Standard* (December 6, 1930): 1182.

[8]"Dr. Oldfield Resigns," *Australian Christian* (June, 1948): 257; "Dhond Work Increases," *Australian Christian* (June, 1948): 281; Thompson, *Let Sects and Parties Fall*, 144.

[9]Mary McGavran, "The Second Generation," *World Call* (January, 1923): 47; Ray Rice, "Work and Worship in Damoh," *World Call* (June, 1925): 35-36; "A Modern Timothy Speaks," *World Call* (August, 1925): 37; "Newsroom," *World Call* (April, 1947): 40.

[10]J.W. Pickett, D.A. McGavran, and G.H. Singh, *Christian Missions in Mid-India: A Study of Nine Areas with Special Reference to Mass Movements* (Jubbulpore: The Mission Press, 1938).

[11]*Disciples Year Book* (1965), 215.

[12]Maggie Watters, *Winged Feet: Archie and Maggie Watters Story of Adventures Following in the Service of the Cross* (privately published, 1981), 111-113.

[13]*Churches of Christ Year Book*, (1939), 59.

[14]*Churches of Christ Year Book* (1942), 60; *Churches of Christ Year Book* (1946), 57; *Churches of Christ Year Book* (1956), 73-74; *Churches of Christ Year Book* (1957), 72.

[15]Bruce Coventry, *A Commentary on Churches of Christ in Western India* (Melbourne: Federal Literature Committee of Churches of Christ in Australia, 1962), a pamphlet held in the archives of Christian Theological Seminary, Indianapolis, Indiana.

[16]Jeff May, "Edna Vawser, 1902-1994," *Australian Christian* (April 23, 1994): 141.

[17]Australian Churches of Christ Global Mission Partners, Inc., formerly known as the Australian Churches of Christ Overseas Mission Board, Inc., began in 1891 as the Churches of Christ Foreign Mission Committee. See "About Us," Global Mission Partners Churches of Christ in Australia, available at www.inpartnership.org.au/about-us, accessed February 12, 2012.

[18]"India," Global Mission Partners, Churches of Christ in Australia, available at www.inpartnership.org.au/countries/india, accessed July 31, 2011.

[19]Samuel Maqbul Masih, "A Task for the Church in India," *World Call* (February, 1939): 13-14.

[20]Tom Hill, "Church Union in North India," *World Call* (September, 1941): 21-22.

[21]Tom Hill, "Unity in India: Whither?" *World Call* (October, 1941): 19-20, 22.

[22]Telfer Mook, "A Proud People in Search of Friends," *The Disciple* (February, 1983): 13; *India Portfolio: Cooperative Work* (Indianapolis: United Christian Missionary Society, 1954), a pamphlet held in the archives of Christian Theological Seminary, Indianapolis, Indiana, 126:13.

[23]*India Portfolio: Nepal* (Indianapolis: United Christian Missionary Society, 1954), a pamphlet held in the archives of Christian Theological Seminary, Indianapolis, Indiana, 126:13.

[24]*India Portfolio: Orissa* (Indianapolis: United Christian Missionary Society, 1954), a pamphlet held in the archives of Christian Theological Seminary, Indianapolis, Indiana, 126:13.

[25]*Plan of Church Union in North India and Pakistan* (Madras: The Christian Literature Society, 1965), iii.

[26]T. J. Liggett, "Enlarging the Partnership in India," *World Call* (July-August, 1970): 6-7.

[27]"Preaching the Word in India," *Christian Standard* (August 16, 1952): 518-522.

[28]"A Brief History of the Rees Family," 2-3, unpublished paper provided by Jim and Carol Young, Forwarding Agents for Benevolent Social Services of India, Inc., P.O. Box 475, Lapel, Indiana 46051.

[29]"A Brief History of the Rees Family," 3, 5-6.

[30]William A Griffin, "How CCIM Came to Be: Family Backgrounds on Ajai and Indu Lall with the Beginning of the Mission," unpublished paper dated September 17, 2001, provided by L.V. Spencer, Administrator of the Central India Christian Mission, 9911 Emnora Lane, Houston, Texas 77080.

[31]Charles F. Scott, "Christ and India—First and Twentieth Centuries," *Gospel Advocate* (January, 1993): 15.

[32]J.C. Bailey, "India: The Closed Door Is Being Opened," *Christian Chronicle* (January 18, 1963): 1, 3.

[33]David Hallett, *The Serpentine Road* (Crossville: Crossville Church of Christ, n.d.), a tract held in the archives of Christian Theological Seminary, Indianapolis, Indiana.

[34]Unlike U.S. citizens, Canadians were able to secure long-term visas for India throughout the Cold War period (1947-1991) because of the historic relationship of India to the British Commonwealth.

[35]J.C. Choate, "India Growth Is Amazing," *Christian Chronicle* (April 9, 1965): 1; "Sensational News of the Church in India," *Firm Foundation* (October 6, 1964): 644; Charles Scott, "J.C. Bailey and C.F. Scott in Joint India Labors," *Christian Chronicle* (November 18, 1975): 1, 10; Charles Scott, "Christ and India—First and Twentieth Centuries," *Gospel Advocate* (January, 1993): 15; Lloyd Smith, "Indian Work Exploding," *Firm Foundation* (February 20, 1968): 126; J.C. Bailey, "Forty Years a Canadian Preacher," available at www.oldpaths.com/Archive/Bailey/John/Carlos/1903/40years, accessed January 27, 2011.

[36]James Johnson, "A Comprehensive View of the Work in South India," *Firm Foundation* (June 18, 1968): 390-391.

[37]"Church in Bombay, India, Receives Legal Recognition," *Firm Foundation* (October 5, 1965): 638; "The Communists Were Defeated?" *Firm Foundation* (July 18, 1967): 462; "India Broadcast Announced," *Firm Foundation* (1967): 127; "How to Start an Independent Church in India," *Firm Foundation* (March 26, 1968): 202; Gootam's Telegu Broadcast in India Generates High Response," *Christian Chronicle* (July, 1992): 19.

[38]"Six Months in New Delhi," *Firm Foundation* (June 3, 1969): 348-349.

[39]J.C. Choate, "Bible Schools in India," *Firm Foundation* (February 27, 1968): 138; Truitt Adair, "Let God Involve You in India," *Firm Foundation* (November 4, 1969): 693; J.C. Choate, "We Can Now Preach to All India Through Radio," *Christian Chronicle* (May 31, 1977): 3-4; Charles F. Scott, "Group Teaching in India Report Progress," *Christian Chronicle* (April 5, 1977): 1, 5;

[40]"Sunset Church in Lubbock Assumes Responsibility for Preacher Training Program in Madras, India," *Firm Foundation* (1969): 203; "Memorial Building Dedicated at Madras, India," *Firm Foundation* (August 18, 1970): 523; Truitt Adair, "Successful Trip to India," *Firm Foundation* (September 7, 1971): 572

[41]"Brief History," National Bible College, available at www.thenationalbiblecollege.in/index.html, accessed February 4, 2011.

[42]"J.C. Choate," "We Have Worked Ourselves Out of a Job," *Firm Foundation* (August 6, 1974): 509.

[43]Erik Tryggestad, "In Global Terms, the Church Is Booming," *Christian Chronicle* (January, 2008): 22.

[44]"Islamic Republic of Pakistan," World Convention Country Profiles, at www.worldconvention.org/newsite/resources/profiles/pakistan/, accessed October 9, 2011; Jim Waldron, "Pakistan Newsletter," at www.waldronmissions.org/NL_pdf_files/1996newsletters/nl1996_04.pdf accessed October 9, 2011.

[45]William Warren, ed., *Survey of Service* (St. Louis: Christian Board of Publication, 1928), 355-385; *Disciples Year Book* (1930), 37.

[46]E.I. Osgood and Edwin Marx, *The China Christian Mission: Completing Fifty Years of Service* (Indianapolis: United Christian Missionary Society, 1935), 25-26.

[47]"Li-Hou-fu," *Biography Set, Series Seven, Leaflet Eighteen,* (Indianapolis: United Christian Missionary Society, 1940).

[48]"From the Brethren," *Gospel Advocate* (September 24, 1925): 936; "Brief Word from Missionaries," *Firm Foundation* (April 27, 1926): 4; George Benson, "Word from China," *Firm Foundation* (April 10, 1928): 11.

[49]Emmett Broaddus, "Hong Kong Mission," *Word and Work* (March, 1928): 90; and Emmett Broaddus, "Conditions in China," *Gospel Advocate* (September 16, 1928): 854; Earl West, *The Search for the Ancient Order: A History of the Restoration Movement,* 4 vols. (Germantown: Religious Book Service, 1949-1987), 4:307-308.

[50]Searle Bates, "The Ordeal of Nanking," *The Christian-Evangelist* (April 28, 1927): 583, 615; Stephen Corey, "Our Chinese Brothers Carry On," *The Christian-Evangelist* (February 2, 1928): 143-144, 158.

[51]Osgood and Marx, "The China Christian Mission," 27.

[52]West, *Search for the Ancient Order,* 4:316-317; L. Edward Hicks, *Sometimes Wrong, But Never in Doubt: George S. Benson and the Education of the New Religious Right* (Knoxville: University of Tennessee Press, 1994), ch. 1.

[53]Osgood and Marx, "China Christian Mission," 29-33; quoted at 29.

[54]Iris Chang, *The Rape of Nanking* (New York: Putnam, 1998); "Uncensored Reports too Grim Story of Nanking," *Christian Evangelist* (January 3, 1938): 91-92; *They Went to China: Biographies of Missionaries of the Disciples of Christ* (Indianapolis: United Christian Missionary Society. 1948), 41-42, 62-63.

[55]Jospeh Boone Hunter, "A Man for the Job," *World Call* (December, 1934): 27; "Introducing Luther Shao," *World Call* (October, 1947): 27; "Witness in Red China," *World Call* (June, 1959): 16.

[56]West, *Search for the Ancient Order,* 4:322-325.

[57]"China Missionaries Meet in Indianapolis," *Christian-Evangelist* (May 17, 1944): 484-485.

[58]*Reconstruction and Rehabilitation of the China Mission* (Indianapolis: United Christian Missionary Society, 1946), a pamphlet held in the archives of Christian Theological Seminary, Indianapolis, Indiana, 84:25.

[59]"Our Missionary Task in China," *Christian-Evangelist* (December 6, 1950): 1201-1202; *Disciples on the Rim of Asia* (St. Louis: Christian Board of Publication, 1962), 73.

[60]West, *Search for the Ancient Order,* 4:364-365. See also Odessa Davis, *To China and Beyond: A Spiritual Journey* (Austin: Nortex Press, 2000).

[61]Tom Tune, *Elizabeth Bernard: Forty Years Among the Chinese* (privately published, 1975) available at www.oldpaths.com/Archive/Tune/Myles/Thomas/1929/bernard.html, accessed July 15, 2011; "Sister Bernard Practices Christianity," *Firm Foundation* (May 28, 1963): 350.

[62]"Plans for Hong Kong at Last," *Firm Foundation* (August 12, 1958): 508; "Mission Work in China," *Firm Foundation* (October 14, 1958): 654; George Benson, "Hong Kong Today," *Firm Foundation* (February 7, 1961): 87, 91.

[63]George Benson, "Hong Kong Christian College Plans Laid," *Firm Foundation* (March 7, 1961): 157.

[64]Gus Eoff, "Thirtieth Baptism," *Firm Foundation* (September 13, 1960): 588; Paul H. F. Hui, "A Story of the Struggle for Freedom," *Firm Foundation* (November 8, 1966): 714.

[65]William Nottingham, "Changing China: Disciples Visitors Find a Lively, Faithful Church," *The Disciple* (January 17, 1982): 10-11, 17.

[66]C. William Nichols, "The General Minister Visits China: They Remember Us Well!" *The Disciple* (May, 1992): 24-26, quoted at 24.

[67]"One Fifth of the World's People: When Will Missions Return to China?" *The Disciple* (February, 1993): 4-9.

[68]*Disciples Year Book* (1987), 200; *Disciples Year Book* (1992), 207; *Disciples Year Book* (1994), 248; *Disciples Year Book* (2003), 202.

[69]William Nottingham, "Entering the 'China Century': Disciples Mission Work Survives Repression to Begin a New Day," *The Disciple* (January/February, 2001): 30-31.

[70]Jeff Weston, "A Lasting Investment," *Australian Christian* (July, 1997): 235.

[71]"China Update: Beijing Church of Christ," *Gospel Advocate* (October 2008): 37-38; "Beijing Church of Christ," available at http://beijingchurchofchrist.com/gpage.html, accessed November 2, 2011; "China Mission" available at http://china-mission.com/home.aspx, accessed November 2, 2011.

[72]"Dr. A. L. Shelton, Martyr for Tibet," *World Call* (May, 1922): 7-13. See also Douglas Wissing, *Pioneer in Tibet: The Life and Perils of Dr. Albert Shelton* (New York: Palgrave Macmillan, 2004), 225-238.

[73]Stephen Corey, "Recent Developments in the Tibetan Mission," *World Call* (December, 1926): 36; Marion Duncan, "A Quarter Century in Tibet," *World Call* (June, 1930): 18-19; Marion Duncan, "The New Orphanage at Batang," *World Call* (July, 1931): 23.

[74]Warren, *Survey of Service,* 395; *Disciples Year Book* (1931), 29-30.

[75]J. Russell Morse, "Why Are We Going Back to Tibet?" *Christian Standard* (January 12, 1929): 25; J. Russell Morse, "New Converts and New Workers in Tibetan Mission," *Christian Standard* (September 5, 1931): 869-871; J. Russell Morse, "Evangelistic Fervor Joined with Emphasis on Christian Living," *Christian Standard* (January 11, 1941): 42-43; Eugene Morse, *Exodus to a Hidden Valley* (New York: E.P. Dutton, 1974); "1921-1991: Seventy Years of Missionary Service," *North Burma Christian Mission Newsletter* (July, 1991), 1-2.

[76]"A Statement Concerning the Tibetan Situation," *World Call*

(May, 1932): 23-24.

⁷⁷Vernon Newland, "I Visit Batang," *Christian Standard* (November 5, 1938): 1074.

⁷⁸Vernon Newland, "Batang Again Occupied as Brotherhood Mission Post," *Christian Standard* (September 30, 1939): 933-934; Edgar Nichols, "Witnessing on the Tibetan Border," *Christian Standard* (April 19, 1947): 285-286.

⁷⁹Newland, "Batang Again Occupied as Brotherhood Mission Post," 933-934.

⁸⁰"Batang's Leading Citizens Ask Help," *Christian Standard* (July 7, 1945): 417-419.

⁸¹Andrew Gordon, *A Modern History of Japan: From Tokugawa Times to the Present* (New York: Oxford, 2008), 139-181.

⁸²"History," Seigakuin University, available at www.seigakuin. jp/english/ab_his.html, accessed November 29, 2011.

⁸³Warren, *Survey of Service*, 334-354.

⁸⁴Stephen Corey, *Report of a Visit to Japan, China, Philippines, and India* (unpublished manuscript, 1928) held in the archives of Christian Theological Seminary, Indianapolis, Indiana.

⁸⁵Mark Maxey, "Christians in Japan: 100 Years," available at www.bible101.org/japanmissions/index.html, accessed February 4, 2011.

⁸⁶West, *Search for the Ancient Order*, 4:283-303.

⁸⁷*Japan Portfolio: The United Church of Christ in Japan* (Indianapolis: United Christian Missionary Society, 1957), a pamphlet held in the archives of Christian Theological Seminary, Indianapolis, Indiana, 126:2; Genevieve Brown, *They Went to Japan: Biographies of Missionaries of the Disciples of Christ* (Indianapolis: United Christian Missionary Society, 1949).

⁸⁸Maxey, "Christians in Japan"; Emily Cunningham and Florence Still, *The Flaming Torch: The Life Story of W. D. Cunningham* (Tokyo: Yotsuya Mission, 1939), 102; "Division in the Yotsuya Mission," *Christian Standard* (November 10, 1934): 816; "Miscellaneous," *Tokyo Christian* (November, 1934): 2.

⁸⁹Grace Madden, "Mabashi Church of Christ," *Christian Standard* (August 26, 1939): 821.

⁹⁰Grace Madden, "Osaka Christian Mission," *Christian Standard* (August 26, 1939): 821. Osaka Bible Seminary's first Japanese President, Akinori Nakano, served from 2001 to 2010, followed by Daiki Kishimoto. See "Osaka Bible Seminary," available at www. jesus4greaterasia.com/OsakaBibleSeminary.htm, accessed February 12, 2012.

⁹¹Harold Cole, "Forty-four Years in Japan," *Christian Standard* (January 13, 1940): 46-47.

⁹²Gordon, *Modern History of Japan*, 182-203. Japanese historiography uses the label "Greater East Asia War."

⁹³Richard Drummond, *A History of Christianity in Japan* (Grand Rapids: Eerdmans, 1971), 257.

⁹⁴Jessie M. Trout, *Forward in Missions and Education* (Indianapolis: United Christian Missionary Society, 1942), 106.

⁹⁵"Changes in Policy and Methods to Take Place in Cunningham Mission," *Tokyo Christian* (March, 1953): 1.

⁹⁶Shirley Still, "Japanese Union Church," *Tokyo Christian* (December, 1940): 4.

⁹⁷Emily Cunningham, "Church Union in Japan," *Tokyo Christian* (April—June 1943): 1.

⁹⁸Maxey, "Christians in Japan."

⁹⁹Don Carlos Janes, "On Foreign Fields," *Word and Work* (January, 1944): 24. A photo of Andrews with Japanese Christians in 1944 appears in Shizuko Ide, ed. *Misu Sera Andoryusu no Senkyo no Shogai wo Shinobu* [In memory of Miss Sarah Andrews' Missionary Life] (Shimizu, Shizuoka: Okitsu Kirisutonokyokai, 1999), 15.

¹⁰⁰Maxey, "Christians in Japan."

¹⁰¹West, *Search for the Ancient Order*, 4:356. Yunosuke Hiratsuka was one of the most important leaders in Stone-Campbell churches in Japan. See *Kamini Yorite Yasushi: Hiratsuka Yunosuke Jiden* [Peace

through God: An Autobiography of Yunosuke Hiratsuka] (Tokyo: Yorudansha, 1989).

¹⁰²E.W. McMillan, "Status of the Work in Japan," *Firm Foundation* (June 1, 1948): 4; E.W. McMillan, "Present Conditions, Future Plans for Japan," *Firm Foundation* (August 24, 1948): 3-4; E.W. McMillan, "The Voice of Opportunity: China and Japan," *Firm Foundation* (July 19, 1949): 1-2.

¹⁰³Charles Doyle, "Preacher Training in Japan," *Firm Foundation* (December 24, 1957): 823; Charles Doyle, "Mission Methods in Japan—A Review," *Firm Foundation* (October 17, 1961): 664; "School for the Blind Started in Japan," *Firm Foundation* (July 24, 1967): 475; "The Completion of Hosana-En Service Center for the Blind," *Firm Foundation* (January 13, 1970): 1.

¹⁰⁴"The Ibaraki Story," *Firm Foundation* (May 20, 1958): 310-311, 315.

¹⁰⁵"Brief History of Ibaraki Christian Education Community," Ibaraki Christian College, available at www.icc.ac.jp/english/history. html, accessed January 27, 2011; two Japanese histories of the schools are *Shion no Oka Gojunen: Ibaraki Kirisutokyogakuen Kotogakko Gojunen, Chugakko Sanjugonenshi* [The hill of Shion, 50 years: a history of the first 50 years of Ibaraki Christian High School and the first 35 years of Ibaraki Christian Junior High School] (Hitachi, Ibaraki: Ibaraki Kirisutokyogakuen Kotogakko, 1997); and *Ibaraki Kirisutokyo Gakuen 60 Nenshi Hensaniinkai*, ed. Ibaraki Kirisutokyo Gakuen 60 Nenshi Zuroku: *A Pictorial History of Ibaraki Christian Community: Celebrating Our 60th Anniversary* (Hitachi, Ibaraki: Ibaraki Kirisutokyo Gakuen, 2010).

¹⁰⁶"Ibaraki Christian College Names Japanese President," *Firm Foundation* (December 1, 1970): 763. See also "Ibaraki Accredited Four-Year System," *Christian Chronicle* (March 24, 1967): 1.

¹⁰⁷Erik Tryggestad, "Taking Root in a Land of Thorns: Japan by the Numbers," *Christian Chronicle* (March, 2004): 18. An important history of Churches of Christ in Japan told by Japanese leaders is *Kirisutonokyokaishi (Ibarakiihokuban) Hensaniinkai*, ed. *Kirisutonokyokaishi (Ibaraki Ihoku Ban)* [A History of Churches of Christ in Ibaraki and Further North Regions in Japan] (Hitachinaka, Ibaraki: Kirisutonokyokaishi (Ibarakiihokuban) Hensaniinkai, 1997).

¹⁰⁸"Tokyo Mission Bible College Launched," *Tokyo Christian* (May-June, 1948): 1; "Interesting Autobiographies," *Tokyo Christian* (November-December, 1948): 1.

¹⁰⁹"Changes in Policy and Methods to Take Place in Cunningham Mission," *Tokyo Christian* (March-April, 1953): 1, 3.

¹¹⁰Maxey, "Christians in Japan."

¹¹¹*Disciples Year Book* (1950), 56.

¹¹²*Japan Portfolio: The United Church of Christ in Japan* (Indianapolis: United Christian Missionary Society, 1957), a pamphlet held in the archives of Christian Theological Seminary, Indianapolis, Indiana, 126:2.

¹¹³*Disciples Year Book* (1955), 196.

¹¹⁴The most comprehensive Japanese account of the Stone-Campbell Movement in Japan, particularly Disciples, is Misao Akiyama, ed., *Kirisutokyokai (Disaipurusu) Shi* [A history of Kirisutokyokai (Disciples of Christ in Japan)] (Tokyo: Kirisutokyokaishi Kankoiinkai, 1973).

¹¹⁵Carter J. Eckert, et. al., *Korea Old and New: A History* (Seoul: Ilchokak, 1990; distributed by Harvard University Press), 327.

¹¹⁶W.D. Cunningham, "Visit to Korea," *Christian Standard* (May 24, 1924): 863; "About People," *Tokyo Christian* (October, 1929): 1; "Korean Notes," *Tokyo Christian* (July, 1935): 3; Cunningham and Still, *The Flaming Torch*, 45; Timothy S. Lee, "The Great Revival of 1907 in Korea: Its Evangelical and Political Background," *Criterion: A Publication of the University of Chicago Divinity School*, 40:2 (Spring, 2001): 10-17.

¹¹⁷Cunningham and Still, *The Flaming Torch*, 84, 87; "Korean Work," *Tokyo Christian* (February, 1932): 2.

¹¹⁸Roh Bong Ook, ed., *Mission to Korea: John J. Hill* (Seoul: Han'guk kŭrisdo kyohoe ŭi yuji chaedan, 2006), 42; "Korean Work,"

Tokyo Christian (December, 1931): 2.

[119]W.D. Cunningham, "Awakening Korea," *Christian Standard* (October 28, 1933): 866.

[120]*Tokyo Christian* (November, 1933): 2-3; *Tokyo Christian* (May, 1935): 1; *Tokyo Christian* (November 1937): 4; Emily Cunningham, "A Year in World Missions: Yotsuya Mission, Japan," *Christian Standard* (March 19, 1938): 1.

[121]Kim Sebok, *Han'guk kŭrisdo ŭi kyonoe kyohoesa* [A History of Korean Churches of Christ], (Seoul: Ch'ambitsa, 1966), 47; and Kim Ikchin, "Dong Suk Kee wa han'guk 'kŭrisdoŭi kyohoe'" [Dong Suk Kee and the Korean "Churches of Christ"], in *Han'guk kidokkyowa yŏksa* [Korean Christianity and History], Vol. 8 (1998), 220. On his involvement in the 1919 uprising, see Timothy S. Lee, "A Political Factor in the Rise of Protestantism in Korea: Protestantism and the 1919 March First Movement," *Church History* (March, 2000): 116-142.

[122]Kim Ikchin, "Dong Suk Kee," 223-227; S. K. Dong, "The New Work in Korea," *Gospel Advocate* (September 3, 1931): 1106-1107.

[123]Kim Ikchin, "Dong Suk Kee," 228. Kim only mentions the last name of this Japan missionary, which is transliterated into Korean as "maekallaem."

[124]His Korean first name was "Myung" (or "Myŏng" in McCune-Reischauer transliteration), but the word was difficult for his American acquaintances to pronounce, so they called him "Moon" and Kang was resigned to it, writing his name as "Kang Moonsuck" when corresponding with the Americans. Kim Sebok, *Han'guk kŭrisdo ŭi kyonoe kyohoesa* [A History of Korean Churches of Christ], 50, 54.

[125]Bak Dae Soon, *Kan'ch'urin han'guk kŭristo ŭi kyohoesa* [An Abridged History of the Churches of Christ in Korea] (Seoul: onŭl ŭi munhwasa, 1998), 35.

[126]Kim Sebok, *Han'guk kŭrisdo ŭi kyonoe kyohoesa* [A History of Korean Churches of Christ], 51.

[127]J.T. Chase, "Korea for Christ," *Christian Standard* (May 9, 1936): 452.

[128]John J. Hill, "A Short History of the Churches of Christ in Korea," available at www.kccs.pe.kr/rmes002.htm, accessed on December 13, 2007.

[129]Lee Kun Sam, *The Christian Confrontation with Shinto Nationalism* (Philadelphia: Presbyterian and Reformed Publishing Co., 1966).

[130]John T. Chase, "The Situation in Korea," *Christian Standard* (May 31, 1941): 573 (emphasis original).

[131]Roh, *Mission to Korea*, 44.

[132]Yoon Kwon Chae, *A Short History of Korean Christian Churches and Churches of Christ (My Witness)* (Seoul: Hwanwŏn chulpansa, 1997), 113-114. Also see, Lee Eun Dae, *Ilche sidae minjok honŭl ilkkaeun chidoja: Ch'oe Sanghyŏn moksa ŭi Sasang kwa sinhak* [A Leader Who Has Awakened the Nation's Soul during the Japanese Colonial Period: Reverend Choi Sang Hyun's Thought and Theology] (Seoul: Kumnan, 2007).

[133]John T. Chase, "Why the Missionary Exodus?" *Christian Standard* (June 14, 1941): 621.

[134]Emily Cunningham, et al., "Our Work in Korea," *Tokyo Christian* (February, 1941): 2-4.

[135]Kim, *A History of Korean Churches*, 141-180.

[136]Yoon Kwon Chae, "Short History of the Korean Christian Churches and Churches of Christ," available at www.kccs.info/rmes004.htm, accessed July 20, 2011; Ch'oe Chaeun, *Han'guk kŭrisdo ŭi Kyohoesa: yuakki kurisdo ŭi kyohoerul chungsim ŭro* [A History of the Churches of Christ in Korea: Centering on the Instrumentalist Churches of Christ], 72.

[137]Kim Ikchin, "Dong Suk Kee," 229-230; Roh, *Mission to Korea*, 44.

[138]Chae, "Short History."

[139]John T. Chase, "Post-War Plans Outlined for Evangelism in Korea," *Christian Standard* (March 17, 1945): 166.

[140]Hill, "A Short History."

[141]John T. Chase, "John Chase Reports Bright Prospects for Return of Mission Property," *Christian Standard* (November 20, 1948): 1; John J. Hill, "Korean Missionary Begins Repairs on Damaged Mission Property," *Christian Standard* (December 9, 1950): 771.

[142]John T. Chase, "Proposed Goal Reached in Chapels for Korea Campaign," *Christian Standard* (July 8, 1950): 420.

[143]Kim Ch'anyong, *Han'guk Kŭrisdo ŭi kyohoe ch'ogi yŏksa: William D. Cunningham ŭi saengaerŭl chungsim ŭro, 1864-1936* [The Early History of Korean Christian Church: Centering on the Life of William D. Cunningham, 1865-1936] (Seoul: T'aekwang, 1991), 132; Ch'oe Chaeun, *Han'guk kŭrisdo ŭi Kyohoesa: yuakki kurisdo ŭi kyohoerul chungsim ŭro* [A History of the Churches of Christ in Korea: Centering on the Instrumentalist Churches of Christ], 91-93.

[144]Lee Eun Dae, *Ilche sidae minjok honŭl ilkkaeun chidoja: Ch'oe Sanghyŏn moksa ŭi Sasang kwa sinhak* [A Leader Who Has Awakened the Nation's Soul during the Japanese Colonial Period: Reverend Choi Sang Hyun's Thought and Theology] (Seoul: Kumnan, 2007), 59; Yoon, *Short History*, 115-116.

[145]Chae, "Short History," available at http://kccs.info/rmes004.htm, accessed July 20, 2011.

[146]Ch'oe Chaeun, *A History of the Churches of Christ in Korea*, 83; John J. Hill, "Korean Christian Mission," *Christian Standard* (May 19, 1951): 309-310; John J. Hill, "A Short History."

[147]Roh Bong Ook, ed., *Mission to Korea: John J. Hill* (Seoul: Han'guk kŭrisdo kyohoe ŭi yuji chaedan, 2006), 46.

[148]Kim Sebok, *Han'guk kŭrisdo ŭi kyonoe kyohoesa* [A History of Korean Churches of Christ], (Seoul: Ch'ambitsa, 1966), 56-57.

[149]Chae Yoon Kwon, *A Short History of Korean Christian Churches and Churches of Christ (My Witness)*, 37; A.R. Holton and Haskell Chessir, "Korea: Its Significance for the Gospel of Jesus Christ," *Firm Foundation* (November 12, 1957): 726-727, 731; Haskell Chessir, "They Said It Couldn't Be Done," *Gospel Advocate* (December 22, 1960): 808-810; Houston Ezell, "Let Us Tell You What's Missing in Korea," *Gospel Advocate* (November 30, 1961): 760-761.

[150]Don Oberdorfer, *The Two Koreas: A Contemporary History* (Basic Books, 2002), 47-138.

[151]Chae, "Short History."

[152]"Biography of Yoon Kwon Chae," available at www.kcgm.org/dr_chae.html, accessed July 21, 2011. Chae describes his early experiences as a Christian in Korea in "What the Cross Meant to Me Under Communist Rule," *Christian Standard* (February 18, 1961): 99-100.

[153]"Biography of Yoon Kwon Chae."

[154]"South Korea," Global Mission Partners Churches of Christ in Australia, available at www.inpartnership.org.au/countries/south-korea, accessed July 30, 2011.

[155]Ch'oe Chaeun, *A History of the Churches of Christ in Korea*, 170.

[156]A.R. Holton, "Korean Mission Work Evidences Church Growth in the Far East," *Christian Chronicle* (February 1, 1963): 11; "Self-Supporting Church in Seoul, Korea," *Firm Foundation* (February 25, 1964): 122.

[157]"History," Korea Christian University, available at http://eng.kcu.ac.kr/eng/aboutkcu/02_2history.php, accessed October 8, 2011.

[158]O.P. Baird, "Open Doors in Korea," *Gospel Advocate* (August 8, 1974): 505.

[159]"Korea Receives Christ," *Firm Foundation* (November 25, 1969): 750; "160 Baptized in Two Korean Campaigns," *Firm Foundation* (October 13, 1970): 652; "50-Day Campaign Sees Four New Congregations Established," *Firm Foundation* (November 20, 1973): 748.

[160]Baird, "Open Doors in Korea," 504-505.

[161]Ch'oe Chaeun, *A History of the Churches of Christ in Korea*, 78, 168.

[162]*Disciples Year Book* (1923), 70; *Diamond Jubilee: Church of Christ in the Philippines, Southeast Luzon Conference, United Church of Christ in the Philippines* (n.p., 1984), n.p., a convention program held in the archives

of Christian Theological Seminary, Indianapolis, Indiana.

[163]"Manila Bible Institute Opens," *Christian Standard* (May 15, 1926): 461.

[164]Leslie Wolfe, "The Fellowship of His Suffering: Perversions of Christianity Rampant in the Philippines," *Christian Standard* (June 11, 1927): 559.

[165]Leslie Wolfe, "Rome Never Changes—Just Dissembles," *Christian Standard* (April 9, 1927): 337.

[166]Leslie Wolfe, "The Philippines on the March," *Christian Standard* (March 19, 1938): 266.

[167]Henrietta Heron, "A 'Trip Around the World'—'The Pearl of the Antilles': September Missionary Program," *Christian Standard* (August 29, 1931): 846-848.

[168]Leslie Wolfe, "Philippine Churches Disfellowshiped by Comity Agreement Hold Their First Convention" (including formal written protest of the churches to the UCMS, April 1941), *Christian Standard* (June 7, 1941): 598, 604; Stevenson, *Christianity in the Philippines,* 38; Mariano Apilado, *Revolution, Colonialism and Mission: A Study of the Role of Protestant Churches Role in the Philippines* (PhD diss., Vanderbilt University, 1976), 379-386.

[169]Leslie Wolfe, "Pearl of the Orient" (Cincinnati: Standard Publishing Company, 1935), a pamphlet held in the archives of Christian Theological Seminary, Indianapolis, Indiana, 77:32.

[170]George Benson, "From the Philippines," *Gospel Advocate* (December 6, 1928): 1159. On Benson's nine-week revival on Mindoro, see also George Benson, "Word from the Philippines," *Gospel Advocate* (September 27, 1928): 927; George Benson, "Word from the Philippines," *Gospel Advocate* (November 15, 1928): 1094.

[171]H.G. Cassell, "Philippine Missions," *Gospel Advocate* (February 26, 1931): 244

[172]H.G. Cassell, "The Men of the Philippines for the Man of Galilee," *Gospel Advocate* (April 16, 1931): 466-467; H.G. Cassell, "A Great Light in the Philippines," *Gospel Advocate* (November 15, 1931): 1298-1299; West, *Search for the Ancient Order,* 4:322-325.

[173]"Disciples of Christ in the Philippine Islands," (Indianapolis: United Christian Missionary Society, 1948), a pamphlet held in the archives at Christian Theological Seminary, Indianapolis, Indiana, 118:19. The quote comes from p. 24.

[174]Lois Ann Ely, *They Went to the Philippines: Biographies of Missionaries of the Disciples of Christ* (Indianapolis: United Christian Missionary Society, 1950), 21-22, 30-31.

[175]*Disciples Year Book* (1933), 18.

[176]Daisy and Allen Huber, "Forty Years in the Philippines," *World Call* (June, 1941): 28-29.

[177]Juan Santos, "College Established in Laoag," *World Call* (January, 1947): 26.

[178]John Cuttrell, "Letter from Service Man Tells of Wolfes' Prison Camp Experience," *Christian Standard* (July 7, 1945): 9, 16; Carrie Wolfe, "The Results of Persecution," *Christian Standard* (March 16, 1946): 166-167.

[179]Norwood Tye, *Journeying with the United Church of Christ in the Philippines: A History* (Quezon City: United Church of Christ in the Philippines, 1994), 12-16.

[180]*Disciples Year Book* (1946), 40; "UCMS Missionaries Aid Philippine Rebuilding," *The Christian-Evangelist* (May 17, 1950): 493.

[181]*Disciples Year Book* (1947), 37; *Disciples Year Book* (1949), 58.

[182]Virgil Sly, *The Philippines—A Christian Opportunity* (Indianapolis: United Christian Missionary Society, c. 1950), 17, a pamphlet held in the archives of Christian Theological Seminary Indianapolis, Indiana, 84:26; Tye, *Journeying with the United Church of Christ in the Philippines,* 30-34; Donald West, "New Unity in the Philippines: Historic Action Brings Tagalog Disciples into United Church of Christ," *World Call* (May, 1962): 28; Wayne Moss, "New Chapter in the Philippines," *World Call* (March, 1963): 31. For a treatment of Disciples missions in the Philippines with documents and extensive photos, see Samuel G. Catli, *Silent Heroes, Remote Places, Disciples* (Laoag City, Philippines:

Crown Printers, 2004).

[183]Enrique Sobrepeña, "Unity in Diversity—Church Solution in the Philippines," *Christian-Evangelist* (July 28, 1954): 708-710, 724; *The Growing World Mission of Disciples of Christ* (Indianapolis: United Christian Missionary Society, 1958), 60.

[184]Juan Santos, "Filipino Christians Want Church Union," *World Call* (March, 1957): 13-14; Sobrepeña published a fuller explanation of the United Church's commitment to unity in *That They May Be One: A Brief Account of the United Church Movement in the Philippines* (Manila: United Church of Christ in the Philippines, 1955).

[185]*Disciples Year Book* (1973), 169.

[186]Victor Aguilan, "The Church Under the Gun: A Critical Historical Analysis of the Relationship Between the United Church of Christ in the Philippines and the Marcos Regime," (unpublished paper, 2002); *Disciples Year Book* (1976), 156; *Disciples Year Book* (1978), 162; *Disciples Year Book* (1987), 200.

[187]H.G. Cassell, "Why Were We Here?" *Gospel Advocate* (February 12, 1948): 155; Benjamin Allison, "The Isles Shall Wait for His Law," *Christian Standard* (January 17, 1948): 42.

[188]"Missionaries Report Progress in Philippine Islands," *Christian Standard* (April 23, 1949): 262; Carrie Wolfe, "Builders in God's Work," *Christian Standard* (February 6, 1954): 89-90; Diego Romulo, "Bringer of Good Tidings," *Christian Standard* (June 18, 1966): 3-4.

[189]"Carrie Wolfe Retires," *Christian Standard* (September 20, 1958): 544; Tye, *Journeying with the United Church of Christ,* 210-212.

[190]Charles Ayuno and Larry Arienzano, *History of the Churches of Christ in the Philippines* (n.p., 2001), 105-120; and David Filbeck and Robert Bates, "Missions in Asia," in Douglas Foster, et al, ed., *The Encyclopedia of the Stone-Campbell Movement* (Grand Rapids: Eerdmans, 2004), 38.

[191]"History," Ambassadors for Christ Philippine Mission, Inc., available at www.ambassadorsforchristphilippines.org/home.aspx?igid=4021, accessed July 25, 2011.

[192]Diego Romulo, "Churches of Christ in the Philippines," in *A Centennial Book of the Churches of Christ in the Philippines, 1901-2001* (Manila, Philippines: Centennial Book of the Churches of Christ in the Philippines, 2002), 68. A number of theses and dissertations have been completed on the importance of these colleges and seminaries to the growth of the Churches of Christ in the Philippines. See, for example, Samson Bernabe Lubag, "The Role of the Philippine Bible Seminary in the Churches of Christ in Ilocos Region," (MDiv thesis, Emmanuel School of Religion, 1991); Elpidio Batalla, "A History of Davao Bible Seminary: Its Role in the Growth of the Churches of Christ in Mindanao, Philippines," (MAR thesis, Emmanuel School of Religion, 1981).

[193]Ralph Brashears, "Baguio Situation Precarious," *Firm Foundation* (March 8, 1960): 155; "Southwest Church Outlines Goals in the Philippines," *Firm Foundation* (April 4, 1961): 20; Ralph Brashears, "Philippine Situation Described," *Firm Foundation* (August 1, 1961): 493.

[194]Don Gardner, "Help Distribute Bibles," *Gospel Advocate* (July 2, 1959): 425; Olaf Wick, "The Famine in the Philippines," *Gospel Advocate* (August 6, 1959): 499-500; "Philippine Famine Is Grave," *Firm Foundation* (July 28, 1959): 478.

[195]"Plans Ready for Philippine Islands," *Firm Foundation* (January 28, 1964): 61.

[196]Mac Lynn, *Churches of Christ Around the World* (Nashville: Gospel Advocate, 1990), 172.

[197]"Philippine Preachers Meet at Clark A.F.B.," *Firm Foundation* (April 17, 1966): 236.

[198]Mac Lynn, *Churches of Christ,* 18; Eusebio Tanicala, *Directory Churches of Christ Philippines 1999*; Eusebio Tanicala, e-mail to Doug Foster, October 14, 2011. For an overview of Stone-Campbell church history in the Philippines, see "A Preacher's Blog" available at http://mountainviewcoc.wordpress.com/church-history, accessed November 2, 2011.

[199]*Churches of Christ Year Book* (1933), 64.

[200]*Churches of Christ Year Book* (1931), 66.

[201]*Churches of Christ Year Book* (1935), 66.

[202]"Death of Rev. David Luo, Former Missionary to Thailand," Global Ministries, available at http://globalministries.org/news/losses/death-of-reverend-david-luo.html, accessed January 7, 2012; "Estelle Carlson, Former Nurse, Worked at Clinic in Thailand," *The Daily Gazette* (Schenectady, New York), May 13, 1991.

"The History of Our Congregation," Oak Hills Christian Church (Disciples of Christ), available at www.butlerdisciples.org/about.htm, accessed January 7, 2012. See also the annual reports of the UCMS and DOM in the *Disciples Year Book*.

[203]L. Allan Eubank, *God! If You Are Really God, Ask and Receive* (Chiang Mai, Thailand: TCF Press, 2003); L. Allan Eubank, *Dance-Drama Before the Throne: A Thai Experience* (Chiang Mai, Thailand: TCF Press, 2004).

[204]Harvey Hoekstra, "The Mien Bible to be Recorded in Audio," available at http://www.assistnews.net/Stories/2010/s10110088.htm, accessed November 9, 2011. See also, Joyce Bhang, *Mother Teacher: From the Memoirs of Lois Callaway, Missionary to the Mien People of Southeast Asia* (Maitland: Xulon Press, 2004).

[205]"Jerry and Pam Headen: Missionaries to Thailand," Salem Church of Christ, available at www.churchofchristsalem.org/missions/jerry_headen.html, accessed February 4, 2011.

[206]"1921-1991: Seventy Years of Missionary Service," *North Burma Christian Mission Newsletter* (October, 1991): 1-2; Eugene Morse, *Exodus to a Hidden Valley* (New York: E. P. Dutton, 1974).

[207]"1921-1991: Seventy Years," 2.

[208]See "Asia Christian Services," available at www.asiachristianservices.org/whoarewe.html, accessed March 10, 2012. In the late 1960s and early 1970s, the Morse brothers differed in their evaluation of the Pentecostal spirituality common among Christians in southeast Asia. By the late 1970s, reconciliation had been achieved and their respective missions fully cooperated. See the mission file on "North Burma Christian Mission," held in the archives of Cincinnati Christian University.

[209]Kenneth Rideout, "An Open Door: Thailand," *Gospel Advocate* (May 17, 1962): 312-313.

[210]Clyde Jones, "McClungs Depart for Thailand," *Firm Foundation* (June 22, 1965): 396.

[211]"Thailand Native Plans to Return," *Firm Foundation* (April 20, 1971): 254.

[212]The British granted Singapore partial self-government in 1955, but in 1963 it merged with Malaya, Sabah, and Sarawak to form Malaysia. Racial tensions led the Malaysian Parliament to expel Singapore in 1965. The island has existed as an independent nation since.

[213]"Opportunity in Singapore," *Firm Foundation* (April 28, 1959): 267; "Brother Lye Hong Meng," *Firm Foundation* (September 2, 1958): 555.

[214]"Pence Dacus and the Singapore School," *Firm Foundation* (February 21, 1967): 114.

[215]"In Memory of Brother Tan Keng Koon (1924-1979)," Four Seas College of the Bible and Missions, available at www.fourseas.edu.sg/FourSeas/index.php?option=com_content&view=article&id=11%3Amemory-tankk&Itemid=5, accessed July 25, 2011.

[216]"Singapore: Church Growing," *Christian Chronicle* (August, 1982): 10; Joy McMillon, "Singapore: Church Celebrates 20th Year," *Christian Chronicle* (October, 1984): 9; Glover Shipp, "Singapore Church Has High Goals for Evangelism in Decade of the 90s," *Christian Chronicle* (April, 1992): 15.

[217]"Thirteen Proves Luck for Vietnam's Missionaries," *Firm Foundation* 83 (October 4, 1966): 639.

[218]"Viet Nam Potentially 'Greatest Work of Decade,'" *Christian Chronicle* (April 17, 1964): 5; "Missionaries to Start American School in Saigon in September," *Firm Foundation* (September 28, 1965): 622;

"AVIS Re-Opened," *Firm Foundation* (January 3, 1967): 11.

[219]"Broadcast in Vietnam," *Firm Foundation* (September 21, 1965): 605; "Radio Vietnam Offers Church Free Time," *Firm Foundation* (August 17, 1965): 524; Gene Conner, "Three New Military Congregations Now Meeting in South Vietnam," *Firm Foundation* (April 26, 1966): 267; Ralph Burcham, "Two Wars Being Staged in Vietnam," *Christian Chronicle* (January 6, 1967): 2; "Vietnam's First Preacher Training Program a Success," *Firm Foundation* (November 7, 1967): 724.

[220]Maurice Hall, "Churches Aid Hungry Vietnamese Children," *Firm Foundation* (June 15, 1965): 380; Maurice Hall, "Vietnam Mission Took Huge Steps During First Year," *Christian Chronicle* (January 29, 1965): 2.

[221]"Vietnam Government Approved Orphans' Program," *Firm Foundation* (July 18, 1967): 459; "Child Care in Vietnam Unified," *Firm Foundation* (July 11, 1967): 446; Ralph Burcham, "Vietnam Missionaries Care for War Orphans," *Christian Chronicle* (October 7, 1966): 4.

[222]Maurice Hall, "While U. S. Embassy Burns, Wealthy Buddhist Is Baptized," *Firm Foundation* (April 13, 1965): 237; "Missionaries Return to Saigon," *Firm Foundation* (March 30, 1965): 204.

[223]Wayne Briggs, "Vietnam Mission Picture: Safety, Disorganization," *Christian Chronicle* (March 1, 1968): 1, 8.

[224]Ralph Burcham, "A Sea of Suffering Humanity," *Firm Foundation* (September 4, 1973): 570; "Escape from Saigon," *Firm Foundation* (August 5, 1975): 490-491.

[225]Glover Shipp, "Vietnam Church Worships in Spite of Persecution," *Christian Chronicle* (May, 1992): 19; Glover Shipp, "New Church Begins in Viet Capital," *Christian Chronicle* (January, 1996): 26; Glover Shipp, "Vietnam," *Christian Chronicle* (December, 1997): 1, 14.

[226]Megan Canfield, "Imprisoned in Laos," West Ark Church of Christ, available at www.westarkchurchofchrist.org/library/persecution.htm, accessed November 2, 2011; Erik Tryggestad, "Camp Cambodia: Teens in Asia Serve," *Christian Chronicle* (May, 2010): 17.

[227]Saunders, "How the Gospel Came from Australia," 13. The Hammers later returned to Australia to serve as missionaries to the aborigines and vocal advocates of their civil rights.

[228]Saunders, "How the Gospel Came from Australia," 13.

[229]Saunders, "How the Gospel Came from Australia," 13.

[230]Dorothy Smith, "Changed Womanhood," *The Australian Christian* (June 12, 1951): 269; Loreen Stanhope, "Our Responsibility," *The Australian Christian* (June 13, 1961): 360; Helen Maiden, "Heal the Sick," *The Australian Christian* (June 18, 1963): 374.

[231]McLean, *Preaching Christ*, 4.

[232]"Vanuatu," Global Mission Partners, Churches of Christ in Australia, available at www.inpartnership.org.au/countries/vanuatu, accessed July 30, 2011.

[233]Ron McLean, "The White Man's Legacy," *The Australian Christian* (June 10, 1952): 268; "This Is Big Business," *The Australian Christian* (June 13, 1961): 353.

[234]David Eagling, "Wanted: Men of Action," *The Australian Christian* (June 15, 1968): 304; John Liu, "Progress at Banmatmat," *The Australian Christian* (June 16, 1973): 240; "Revival in the South Pacific," *Renewal Journal* (2002), available at http://www.pastornet.net.au/renewal/journal20/20f.htm, accessed August 1, 2011.

[235]Graham Warne, "Pentecost Kanakas," *The Australian Christian* (July, 2003): 216.

[236]Frank Beale and Harold Finger, "Vision and Venture in New Guinea," *The Australian Christian* (June 10, 1958): 336.

[237]R.S.A. McLean, "Then and Now," *The Australian Christian* (June 19, 1965): 5; "Missionaries Required: New Guinea and New Hebrides," *The Australian Christian* (June 10, 1972): 220.

[238]"New Guinea," Global Mission Partners, Churches of Christ in Australia, available at www.inpartnership.org.au/countries/papua-new-guniea, accessed August 1, 2011; "Then and Now," *Conference*

News of the Churches of Christ in Victoria and Tasmania (October, 2008): 6 available at http://cofcaustralia.org/cofc-cms/images/stories/CofCVicTas/oct%202008%20conference%20newsletter.pdf, accessed August 1, 2011.

[239]Lynn, *Churches of Christ*, 18, 168-169.

[240]"Papua New Guinea," World Convention of Churches of Christ Resources, available at www.worldconvention.org/newsite/resources/profiles/papua-new-guinea; "Heritage," Pioneer Bible Translators, available at www.pioneerbible.org/cms/tiki-index.php?page=PBT+History, accessed February 12, 2012.

15: Latin Am./Caribbean Since 1920s

[1]Erik Tryggestad, "Around the World, October 2010," *Christian Chronicle* (October, 2010): 9; "After 35 Years and One Hurricane, Lectureship Reaches Cuba," *Christian Chronicle* (August, 2005): 1, 29.

[2]"Tabular View of Foreign Missions," *Year Book of the International Convention of Disciples of Christ* (St. Louis: United Christian Missionary Society, 1927), 37; William Warren, *Survey of Service: Organizations Represented in International Convention of Disciples of Christ* (St. Louis: Christian Board of Publication, 1928), 480-482.

[3]Robert Nelson, *Disciples of Christ in Jamaica, 1858-1958* (St. Louis: Bethany Press, 1958), 86.

[4]Nelson, *Disciples of Christ in Jamaica*, 108-111; Stephen Corey, "Our First Foreign Field Plans for Self-Support," *World Call* (August, 1929): 12, 23.

[5]Nelson, *Disciples of Christ in Jamaica*, 116.

[6]Nelson, *Disciples of Christ in Jamaica*, 117-118.

[7]Nelson, *Disciples of Christ in Jamaica*, 119.

[8]Nelson, *Disciples of Christ in Jamaica*, 166.

[9]Quoted in Nelson, *Disciples of Christ in Jamaica*, 167.

[10]P. H. Moss, "The Island of Springs," *World Call* (January, 1928): 35; Oswald Penso, "Lights and Shadows in Jamaica," *World Call* (May, 1930): 9.

[11]"Another Hand Across the Sea," *World Call* (May, 1930): 20.

[12]"United Christian Missionary Society Annual Report," *Year Book of the Christian Churches (Disciples of Christ)* (St. Louis: Christian Board of Publication, 1962), 276. (Hereafter *Disciples Year Book*).

[13]Nelson, *Disciples of Christ in Jamaica*, 128-142; E. K. Higdon, "Jamaicans on the March," (Indianapolis: United Christian Missionary Society, 1947), 20-22.

[14]J. Edward Moseley, "A Mission School Is Built," *World Call* (March, 1951): 19-21; J. Edward Moseley, "A New School Begins to Make Its Mark," *World Call* (May, 1952): 12; Archie Allan, "Seven Years Have Changed Jamaica," *World Call* (November, 1958): 29-30.

[15]Nelson, *Disciples of Christ in Jamaica*, 170.

[16]Nelson, *Disciples of Christ in Jamaica*, 170-176; James Lollis, "Jamaicans Have a Mind to Cooperate," *World Call* (March, 1955): 14-15.

[17]Arthur Charles Dayfoot, *The Shaping of the West Indian Church 1492-1962* (Gainesville: University Press of Florida, 1999), 215-218.

[18]"About CCC—Introduction," available at www.ccc-caribe.org/eng/intro.htm, accessed February 15, 2011.

[19]Carmelo Álvarez, "Theology from the Margins: A Caribbean Response, A People of God in the Caribbean," in María Pilar Aquino and Roberto S. Goizueta, eds., *Theology: Expanding the Borders* (Mystic: Twenty-Third Publications, 1998), 272-274.

[20]L. L. Myers, "Remarkable Movement to the New Testament Church in Jamaica," *Christian Standard* (September 7, 1935): 853; C. V. Hall, "Open Door in Jamaica," *Christian Standard* (June 26, 1936): 616; E. A. Watts, "Story of the Church in Jamaica," *Christian Standard* (May 8, 1937): 389.

[21]"Eight Denominational Churches Have Stepped Out," *Christian Standard* (October 10, 1938): 956; "Two More Churches Step Out into the Restoration Movement," *Christian Standard* (August 23, 1941): 876.

[22]Luke Elliott, "Jamaica and the Restoration Movement," *Christian Standard* (July 1, 1945): 451, 464.

[23]"Jamaica Christian Mission Celebrates Tenth Anniversary," *Christian Standard* (January 1, 1949): 4.

[24]"Notice Regarding Funds for Jamaica Christian Mission," *Christian Standard* (August 26, 1950): 531.

[25]Donald Fream, "132 Lives Lost and Buildings Damaged in Hurricane in Jamaica," *Christian Standard* (December 8, 1951): 565; "Jamaica Christian Mission Moves to New Location Near Kingston," *Christian Standard* (November 24, 1951): 741.

[26]"Jamaica Christian Mission, Then and Now," Jamaica Christian Mission, available at www.jamaicachristianmissionltd.com/history.html, accessed December 15, 2011.

[27]"From the Field," *Christian Standard* (May 28, 1966): 378; Harvey Bacus and Harold Hill, "Christ Died for Them, Too," *Christian Standard* (June 2, 1962): 345-346.

[28]"Jamaica Christian Mission, Then and Now."

[29]C. D. Davis, "Restoration Has Come to Jamaica," *Firm Foundation* (November 11, 1958): 709.

[30]"Jamaica School of Preaching Opens," *Firm Foundation* (June 2, 1970): 348.

[31]Mac Lynn, *Churches of Christ Around the World* (Nashville: Gospel Advocate, 1990), 132.

[32]Erik Tryggestad, "Preachers of the Caribbean," *Christian Chronicle* (August, 2007): 21.

[33]*Disciples Year Book* (1974), 152.

[34]"Jamaica Disciples Part of New Union," *The Disciple* (February, 1993): 43; *Disciples Year Book* (1994), 261-262.

[35]Deliverance Ministries focus on casting out demons or evil spirits believed to be responsible for physical, mental, and financial affliction.

[36]Telephone interview with Elder Tony Smith, General Evangelist of the Church of Christ, Disciples of Christ, and pastor of Faithful Church of Christ, Disciples of Christ, by Sheila H. Gillams, September 29, 2011.

[37]"The Mexican Society for Christian Missions: Its Origin and the Nature of Its Work," (n.p., 1926), a tract held in the archives of Christian Theological Seminary, Indianapolis, Indiana.

[38]"To the Rescue of the Mexican Mission." *Christian Standard* (November 1, 1919): 119.

[39]Enrique Westrup, "Northern Mexico," *Christian Standard* (August 14, 1920): 1152.

[40]"Evangelism in Mexico," *Christian Standard* (April 24, 1920): 760; Enrique Westrup, "Shall We Join Others?" *Christian Standard* (May 8, 1920): 804.

[41]Etta Nunn, "A Chronicle of Colegio Ingles," *World Call* (August, 1931): 26.

[42]Elma Irelan, *Fifty Years with Our Mexican Neighbors* (St. Louis: Bethany Press, 1944), 83-84, 92-94.

[43]"Closing of School Challenges Disciples of Christ in Mexico," *World Call* (May, 1968): 48; Irelan, *Fity Years*, 84-88.

[44]"Status of Missionaries in Mexico Explained," *World Call* (April, 1926): 51.

[45]Mae Yoho Ward, *Mexico Looks Forward* (Indianapolis: United Christian Missionary Society, 1945), 3-5.

[46]Irelan, *Fifty Years*, 108-109.

[47]Irelan, *Fity Years*, 113-116; Howard Holroyd, "Centro Social Juarez," *World Call* (December, 1938): 46.

[48]Ward, *Mexico Looks Forward*, 13-16; "Miss Florine Cantrell," *They Went to Latin America* (Indianapolis: United Christian Missionary Society, 1947), 37-38.

[49]Irelan, *Fifty Years*,117-118.

[50]"Mexican Churches Form Missionary Society," *Christian-Evangelist* (November 14, 1935): 1501.

[51]F. J. Huegel, "Mexico's Evangelistic Crusade," *World Call* (November, 1942): 21; Frederick J. Huegel, "Evangelism in Mexico," *Christian-Evangelist* (January 9, 1941): 50-51.

[52]*Disciples Year Book* (1961), 276; *Disciples Year Book* (1963), 258.

[53]*Disciples Year Book* (1965), 218.

[54]*Disciples Year Book* (1982), 218.

[55]David Vargas, retired president of Common Global Ministries Board, e-mail to Douglas A. Foster, December 6, 2011.

[56]William Nottingham and William Morgan, "Missions in Latin America and the Caribbean," in Douglas Foster, et al., ed., *The Encyclopedia of the Stone-Campbell Movement* (Grand Rapids: Eerdmans, 2004), 456.

[57]Harlan Cary, "Our Mexican Neighbors," *Christian Standard* (March 20, 1948): 189.

[58]James DeForest Much, *Christians Only: A History of the Restoration Movement* (Cincinnati: Standard Publishing, 1962), 327; Harlan Cary, "Mexican Evangelism," *Christian Standard* (March 15, 1952): 170-171.

[59]"Bowlin Applies for Passport," *Christian Standard* (June 25, 1955): 411; "Boal and Bowlin Meet," *Christian Standard* (September 8, 1962): 572-573; Much, *Christians Only*, 327.

[60]Cary, "Mexican Neighbors," 189; Harland Cary, "Witnessing in the United States," *Christian Standard* (January 7, 1950): 15; Harland Cary, "Preaching the Word in Latin America and the Caribbean," *Christian Standard* (March 15, 1952): 170. See also "About Us," Colegio Biblico, available at www.colegiobiblico.net/history.html, accessed December 15, 2011.

[61]Cary, "Mexican Neighbors," 189.

[62]E. T. Westrup, "Monterrey, Mexico," *Christian Standard* (March 15, 1952): 171.

[63]Rodney Northrup, "Missionary Makes Preparation for Spanish Publishing House," *Christian Standard* (December 10, 1949): 789; Rodney Northrup, "Witnessing in Saltillo," *Christian Standard* (March 25, 1950): 191.

[64]Earl Irvin West, *The Search for the Ancient Order*, 4 vols. (Indianapolis: Religious Book Service, 1949-1987), 3:362-370.

[65]West, *The Search for the Ancient Order*, 4:392-393.

[66]The hymnal, *Cantos Espirituales* was expanded and remained in print in the early twenty-first century. See "Cantos Espirituales" available at www.cantosespirituales.com/default.aspx, accessed February 5, 2011.

[67]West, *Search for the Ancient Order*, 4:392; Gary L. Green, "Missions in Latin America and Caribbean: Churches of Christ," in Douglas Foster, et al., ed., *The Encyclopedia of the Stone-Campbell Movement* (Grand Rapids: Eerdmans, 2004), 465.

[68]Green, "Missions," 465.

[69]Mac Lynn, *Churches of Christ Around the World: Quick Reference* (Nashville: 21st Century Christian, 2003) 17, 146-148.

[70]Erik Tryggestad, "Drug-Related Violence in Mexico Fails to Deter the Peace of Jesus," *Christian Chronicle* (May, 2009): 14.

[71]On his work in Puerto Rico, see Vere Carpenter, *Puerto Rican Disciples: A Personal Narrative of Fifty Years with Christ in the Island of Enchantment* (Tampa: The Christian Press, 1960).

[72]For the perspective of Stone-Campbell missionaries on these hurricanes, see "40,000 Homeless in Puerto Rico," *World Call* (November, 1928): 27; "A Personal Account of the Disaster," *World Call* (November, 1928): 28.

[73]Joaquín Vargas, *Los Discipulos de Crista en Puerto Rico* [The Disciples of Christ in Puerto Rico] (San Jose, Costa Rica: DEI, 1988), 88-89; C. Manly Morton, *Kingdom Building in Puerto Rico* (Indianapolis: United Christian Missionary Society, 1949), 64-65.

[74]Daisy Machado, "El gran avivamiento del '33: The Protestant Missionary Enterprise, Revival, Identity, and Tradition," in Orlando O. Espín and Gary Macy, eds., *Futuring Our Past: Exploration in the Theology of Tradition* (Maryknoll: Orbis Books, 2006), 249-275.

[75]Vargas, *Los Discipulos*, 95.

[76]C. Manly Morton, *Somewhere a Voice Is Calling: The Story of the Life of One Who Listened* (Fort Lauderdale: The Hamilton M. and Blanche C. Forman Christian Foundation, 1972), 103-104; Vargas, *Los Discipulos*, 100.

[77]Vargas, *Los Discipulos*, 82.

[78]Vargas, *Los Discipulos*, 106.

[79]Vargas, *Los Discipulos*, 107-111; *Disciples Year Book* (1955), 197-198.

[80]Vargas, *Los Discipulos*, 112-115.

[81]Vargas, *Los Discipulos*, 144-150.

[82]Vargas, *Los Discipulos*, 151-154, 159-160.

[83]Vargas, *Los Discipulos*, 115-116.

[84]Vargas, *Los Discipulos*, 129-135; Samuel Silva Gotay, *Protestantismo y Política en Puerto Rico, 1898-1930* [Protestantism and politics in Puerto Rico, 1898-1930] (San Juan: Editorial Universidad de Puerto Rico, 1997), 179-182, 215-223.

[85]Esteban González Doble, Pastor General, Iglesia Cristiana (Discípulos de Cristo) en Puerto Rico, e-mail message to Scott Seay, March 3, 2011.

[86]Green, "Missions Latin America and Caribbean," 465.

[87]Carl H. Royster, *Churches of Christ in the United States, Inclusive of Her Commonwealth and Territories* (Nashville: 21st Century Christian, 2009), 495-497.

[88]Clinton J. Holloway, "Commonwealth of Puerto Rico," World Convention Country Profiles, available at www.worldconvention.org/newsite/resources/profiles/puerto-rico/, accessed August 19, 2011.

[89]"Radio Opportunity in Cuba," *Firm Foundation* (July 7, 1959): 428.

[90]"Floridians Preach in Cuba," *Christian Chronicle* (April 15, 1958): 1; Erik Tryggestad, "Seeing the Light in Cuba," *Christian Chronicle* (January, 2006): 17-19.

[91]J. R. Jimenez and Ernest Estevez, "A Brief Report on the Cuban Situation," *Firm Foundation* (June 2, 1959): 341.

[92]Glover Shipp, "Historic Cuba Campaign Results in 94 Baptisms," *Christian Chronicle* (August, 1993): 1; Lynn, *Churches of Christ Around the World*, 54.

[93]Monroy was known throughout Latin America for his Spanish language radio broadcasts sponsored by the Herald of Truth ministries based in Abilene, Texas. He also traveled extensively throughout the region preaching. Juan Antonio Monroy, *Juan Antonio Monroy: An Autobiography* (Abilene: Abilene Christian University Press, 2011), 169-173.

[94]*Disciples Year Book* (1976), 162; *Disciples Year Book* (1977), 177; *Disciples Year Book* (1981), 195.

[95]Carmelo Álvarez, "Cuba: A Celebration of Hope," *The Disciple* (October, 1998): 42-44. See also "Cuba," Global Ministries, available at http://globalministries.org/lac/countries/cuba, accessed December 23, 2011.

[96]*Disciples Year Book* (1994), 260.

[97]*Disciples Year Book* (2000), 225.

[98]Glover Shipp, "Historic Cuba Campaign," *Christian Chronicle* (August, 1993): 1.

[99]*Christian Chronicle* (September, 1995): 24.

[100]"Cuban Church Growth Passes Old Mark," *Christian Chronicle* (May, 1999): 30; Jonathan Cannon, "Ministries Discuss Future of Cuba Work," *Christian Chronicle* (December, 2007): 3; Erik Tryggestad, "As Restrictions Ease, Churches Consider Future in Cuba," *Christian Chronicle* (May, 2009): 3, 15.

[101]Erik Tryggestad, "Cuban Officials Recognize Work of U. S. Churches," *Christian Chronicle* (July, 2002): 1, 29.

[102]Montgomery, *Disciples of Christ in Argentina*, 89-90; 95-96.

[103]Montgomery, *Disciples of Christ in Argentina*, 92-93.

[104]W. K. Azbill used "living link" as early as 1890 to refer to congregations that provided funds earmarked for specific missionaries or indigenous workers. The FCMS and CWBM used "living link" programs to encourage support for missions, and the program continued under the UCMS. The method became a major strategy for direct support missions as opposition to UCMS policies increased, using a "forwarding agent" instead of the society to transfer funds. David Filbeck, *The First Fifty Years: A Brief History of the Direct Support*

Missionary Movement (Joplin: College Press Publishing Company, 1980), 196-210. The Crusade for a Christian World was initiated at the International Convention at Columbus, Ohio, August 6-11, 1946. Objectives included raising fourteen million dollars, much of it designated to recruit and train 3,000 new ministers and missionaries. Charles Crossfield Ware, *A History of Atlantic Christian College: Culture in Coastal Carolina* (Wilson: Atlantic Christian College, 1956): 181.

[105]Montgomery, *Disciples of Christ in Argentina*, 135-136; *They Went to Latin America*, 76-77.

[106]S. S. McWilliams, "Opportunity in Argentina," *World Call* (July, 1944): 23; Margaret Owen, "Gateway to the Chaco," *World Call* (November, 1944): 22; "New Work in the Chaco," *World Call* (December, 1946): 29.

[107]Margaret Richards Owen, *The Reverend Jorgelina Lozada: Ecumenical Witness* (privately published, 1991), a pamphlet held at Disciples of Christ Historical Society, Nashville, Tennessee.

[108]*Disciples Year Book* (1962), 275-276.

[109]Allin Sharp, "Argentine Disciples Opening New Work," *World Call* (June, 1961): 32-33.

[110]"Courage in Argentina," *The Disciple* (February 20, 1977): 11-12; *Disciples Year Book* (1989), 207.

[111]*Movimento Ecumenico por los Derechos Humanos*, available at www.derechos.net/medh, accessed February 22, 2011.

[112]*Disciples Year Book* (1989), 207.

[113]Erik Tryggestad, "Latin America: From Dirt Roads to Urban Pavement, Churches of Christ Take Root," *Christian Chronicle* (July, 2011): 21.

[114]Mills, *Adventuring with Christ*, 39-45.

[115]Mills, *Adventuring with Christ*, 14-15.

[116]Malcolm Norment, "*Colegio Internacional* in the Future of Paraguay," *World Call* (October, 1933): 12.

[117]Mills, *Adventuring with Christ*, 114-116; Agnes Henderson, "The Leper Work in Paraguay," *World Call* (July, 1938): 27.

[118]Mills, *Adventuring with Christ*, 118-120; "Provisions for Leper Colony," *World Call* (January, 1942): 37; Malcolm Norment, "Improvements at the Leper Colony," *World Call* (July, 1943): 22; "Lepers Receive Loving Care at Sapucay," *World Call* (September, 1951): 46.

[119]Mills, *Adventuring with Christ*, 75-82; Allin Sharp, "House of Friendship," *World Call* (March, 1955): 43; Grace Rogers, "Friendship House," *World Call* (June, 1957): 46.

[120]Mills, *Adventuring with Christ*, 82-83.

[121]Mills, *Adventuring with Christ*, 66-73.

[122]*Disciples Year Book* (1970-71), 185.

[123]Mills, *Adventuring with Christ*, 57.

[124]Mills, *Adventuring with Christ*, 88-113.

[125]"Disciples Workers Charged in Paraguay," *The Disciple* (July 4, 1976): 16; Frisco Gilchrist, "Guilty—But Not as Charged," *The Disciple* (October 17, 1976): 6; "Nine of Ten Prisoners Released," *The Disciple* (December 19, 1976): 22.

[126]"Paraguay: A Conversation with Ann Douglas about the Crisis and Its Meaning," *The Disciple* (February 6, 1977): 11-12; *Disciples Year Book* (1980), 210.

[127]*Disciples Year Book* (1990), 212.

[128]*Disciples Year Book* (1989), 221.

[129]Green, "Missions in Latin America and Caribbean," 461; Erik Tryggestad, "Latin America: From Dirt Roads," 21.

[130]Virgil Smith, "Words from Brazil," *Gospel Advocate* (January 5, 1928): 7, 14; O. S. Boyer, "A Long Time Coming," *Gospel Advocate* (July 26, 1928): 710-711.

[131]Virgil Smith, "Flashes from a Neglected Continent," *Gospel Advocate* (June 4, 1931): 690.

[132]Ramona Smith, "Adventures in Ceara," *Gospel Advocate* (March 5, 1931): 277.

[133]Virgil Smith, "Interior Mission of Northern Brazil," *Word and Work* (June, 1931): 170.

[134]Paul Freston, "Pentecostalism in Brazil: A Brief History," *Religion* (April, 1995): 119-133.

[135]O.S. Boyer, "Interior Brazil Mission," *Word and Work* (February, 1932): 52; "O. S. Boyer Letter," *Word and Work* (August, 1932): 206-207; R. H. Boll, "Virgil Smith of Brazil—His Work and Experiences," *Word and Work* (July, 1934): 142-144.

[136]Virgil F. Smith, letter to Bro. Frodsham, Lewisville, Ky., July 11, 1935, Correspondence, Assemblies of God World Missions Archives, Springfield, Missouri; "A Contrast in Missions," *The Pentecostal Evangel* (April 15, 1950): 8; "Short-term Bible School in Lavras, Brazil," *The Pentecostal Evangel* (September 23, 1950): 10.

[137]"Nossa História" [Our History], Igreja de Cristo Pentecostal no Brasil [Pentecostal Church of Christ in Brazil], available at at http://icpb.com.br/index.php/nossa-historia, accessed January 10, 2012.

[138]"JBC Class Backs Member for South America Mission Field," *Christian Standard* (August 14, 1943): 1; "Tenth Anniversary Sees Brazil Christian Mission Opening Work in New Capital of Brazil," *Brazil Christian Mission* (January, 1958): 1, 3.

[139]Lloyd D. Sanders, "Brazil—Colossus of the South," *Christian Standard* (October 18, 1947): 722.

[140]L. David Sanders, Missionary, Commends Former Catholic Professor," *Christian Standard* (December 3, 1949): 771.

[141]"What Is the Brazil Christian Mission?" *Brazil Christian Mission Study Booklet* (January, 1957): 2-3.

[142]"New Testament Churches Discovered in Brazil," *Christian Standard* (January 9, 1954): 24; Carolee Ewing, "Thirteen Congregations Now 'Christians Only'," *Christian Standard* (June 19, 1954): 390; "Thirteen Congregations Join the Restoration Movement," *Brazil Christian Mission* (February, 1954): 1, 3.

[143]A. Dale Fiers, "What Price Cooperation?" *World Call* (July-August, 1961): 11, 48.

[144]"BCM Withdraws from Convention," *Christian Standard* (June 24, 1961): 404; "Important Notice," *Brazil Christian Mission* (July-August, 1961): 2.

[145]"Instructive Document," *Christian Standard* (August 19, 1961): 522-523.

[146]"Study Booklet," *Brazil Christian Mission* (May-June, 1959): 1, 3.

[147]"William Loft to Establish Mission Among Indians in Amazon Valley," *Christian Standard* (August 12, 1950): 501.

[148]"Belem Bible Seminary Organized," *Christian Standard* (January 11, 1958): 24.

[149]"Missionary Recruits to Brazil," *Christian Standard* (March 3, 1957): 201.

[150]"History," Brazil Christian Mission, available at www.bcmission.org/history2.htm, accessed August 27, 2008.

[151]"Brazil Missionaries Meet," *Christian Standard* (April 22, 1961): 252.

[152]Leon Tester, "Missionaries of the Churches of Christ and Christian Churches Hold Joint Meeting in Brazil," *Firm Foundation* (March 15, 1968): 154; Jeff Fife, e-mail to Douglas A. Foster, December 7, 2011.

[153]Jeff Fife, e-mail to Douglas A. Foster, December 7, 2011; Bryan Gibbs, e-mail to Douglas A. Foster, December 7, 2011.

[154]Orlan Miller, "Ivan Rude to Brazil," *Firm Foundation* (June 9, 1959): 364.

[155]"Second Annual Fort Worth Missionary Lectureship," *Firm Foundation* (August 9, 1960): 507.

[156]"They Go with the Gospel to Brazil in June," *Firm Foundation* (April 25, 1961): 264-265; "Thirteen Families to Sail to Brazil," *Christian Chronicle* (May 19, 1961): 1, 6.

[157]"Escola da Biblia," *Firm Foundation* (July 28, 1964): 484; Ted Stewart, "Bible Course Effective in Brazil Work," *Christian Chronicle* (April 3, 1964): 7.

[158]Leon Tester, "Group-Evangelism Proven in Brazil," *Christian*

Chronicle (June 5, 1964): 23.

159"Building Plans Spark Interest in Brazil Work," *Christian Chronicle* (October 23, 1964): 1, 3; "Brazil Mission Group Announces Sizeable Building Program," *Firm Foundation* (November 17, 1964): 741; "All-Church Fund Raising," *Firm Foundation* (February 16, 1965): 107; Ellis Long, "Brazil Group Purchases Top Sao Paulo Property," *Christian Chronicle* (February 19, 1965): 14.

160"Brazilian Radio Network Purchased," *Firm Foundation* (June 7, 1966): 364; Alton Howard, "Brazilian Christians Buy Network," *Christian Chronicle* (June 10, 1966): 12.

161"104 in New Mission Group Select Brazil," *Firm Foundation* (May 7, 1963): 299; "Operation 68 to Work among Brazilians," *Christian Chronicle* (May 10, 1963): 1, 4.

162Bill Youngs, "Advance Group Sails on Liner," *Firm Foundation* (August 1, 1967): 490; "New Brazil Group Settles In," *Firm Foundation* (October 17, 1967): 667; "A Restoration Movement Is Born," *Firm Foundation* (November 28, 1967): 782; Leon Tester, "New Building Opened in Sao Paulo," *Christian Chronicle* (March 3, 1967): 1; Leon Tester, "Land Bought in Brazil to Further Youth Work," (March 10, 1967): 1, 11; "Operation '68 Vanguard Sails," *Christian Chronicle* (August 4, 1967): 1.

163"Breakthrough Brazil Announced," *Firm Foundation* (January 14, 1969): 29; "Mega-Cities Provide Target for Project," *Christian Chronicle* (January 6, 1969): 6.

164Glover Shipp, "Belo Horizonte Mission Team Celebrates Tenth Anniversary," *Christian Chronicle* (April 4, 1978): 6; Joy McMillon, "Belo Horizonte Mission Team Celebrates Twentieth Anniversary," *Christian Chronicle* (October, 1987): 10; See also "Timeline," Continent of Great Cities, available at www.greatcities.org/template.php?filename=history.html, accessed February 27, 2011.

165R. Scott LaMascus, "Smiths Serve Orphanage, Alabama Christians Help," *Christian Chronicle* (September, 1998): 13; Glover Shipp, "Brazil Children's Home Will Migrate," *Christian Chronicle* (November, 1999): 28. See also "Christian Children's Home," available at http://childrenshome.randal.fastmail.fm/, accessed February 11, 2011.

166"Death of Otoko Maeda," Global Ministries, available at http://www.globalministries.org/news/losses/death-of-itoko-maeda.html, accessed December 15, 2011.

167*Disciples Year Book* (1970-1971), 181; *Disciples Year Book* (1979), 167; Marilynne Hill, *Itoko Maeda: Woman of Mission* (St. Louis: Chalice Press, 1997), esp. ch. 5.

168*Disciples Year Book* (1994), 258.

169"History," AECS, available at http://www.aecsprojetobrasil.com.br/pag%20history.htm, accessed December 15, 2011.

170Carmelo Álvarez, "Ecumenism of the Spirit and Mission: Disciples of Christ and Pentecostals in Venezuela," in Peter Heltzel, ed., *Chalice Introduction to Disciples Theology* (St. Louis: Chalice Press, 2008), 289. For more on Jordán, see Juan L. Lugo, *Pentecostés en Puerto Rico o la vida de un misionero* [Pentecost in Puerto Rico or the life of a missionary] (San Juan, Puerto Rico, 1951), 99.

171Carmelo Álvarez, "Sharing in God's Mission: The Evangelical Pentecostal Union of Venezuela and the Christian Church (Disciples of Christ) in the United States, 1960-1980" (PhD diss., University of Amsterdam, 2006), 90-108.

172Dale Fiers, "Report of Latin American Trip" (Indianapolis: Minutes of the Board of the UCMS, 1959), Item 10, 4, held in the archives of Christian Theological Seminary, Indianapolis, Indiana.

173Gregario Uzcátegui, "Hitos para la historia," [Milestone in history], (unpublished manuscript, 1999), 1; Thomas J. Liggett, telephone interview with Carmelo Álvarez, June 11, 1997.

174Thomas J. Liggett, "Report of the Visit to Churches and Leaders of the Pentecostal Union of Venezuela, July 12-14, 1963," 5, held in the archives of Christian Theological Seminary, Indianapolis, Indiana.

175Liggett, "Report," 5.

176Freddie Briceño, "Mi visión de la UEPV a los primeros siete años de fundada," [UEPV: My visión of its first seven years of existence] in Gamaliel Lugo, ed., *Presencia Pentecostal en Venezuela* [Pentecostal presence in Venezuela] (Maracaibo, Venezuela: Ediciones UEPV, 1997), 15; T. J. Liggett, "New Era Dawns in Latin America," *World Call* (January, 1962): 19-20; T. J. Liggett, "Protestant Dilemmas in Latin America," *World Call* (January, 1964): 19-20. See also Luis F. del Pila, *Lo hizo El: Testimonios I* [It did him: testimonials 1] (Bayamon, Puerto Rico: Impresas Quintana, 1999), 149-153.

177Carmelo E. Álvarez and Carlos Cardoza, *Llamados a construir el reino de Dios* [Called to build the Kingdom of God] (Bayamon, Puerto Rico: Convention of the Christian Church, 2000). 101-133; "New Partners in Venezuela," *World Call* (September 1963): 26.

178Álvarez, "Ecumenism of the Spirit," 291.

179Juan Marcos Rivera, telephone interview with Carmelo Álvarez, June 11, 1997.

180Biographical information: Dean Earl Rogers, UCMS Archives, 1980; Grace and Dean Rogers, "Missionary Notes," *World Call* (January, 1970): 33-34; *Disciples Year Book* (1979), 168.

181*Disciples Year Book* (1968), 288.

182Álvarez, "Ecumenism of the Spirit," 292; David Vargas, "¿Por qué una consulta?" a paper presented at a Disciples/UCC Consultation with Pentecostal Partners in Latin America and the Caribbean, "Sharing of Hope: An Ecumenism of the Spirit," Indianapolis, October 3-November 1, 1997), 1-2.

183"Report on Survey Trip to Guatemala, Central America," *Firm Foundation* (March 29, 1960): 206; "Missionary Tells of the Guatemala Situation," *Firm Foundation* (January 17, 1961): 45.

184"Guatemalan Ex-Priest to Enter ACC," *Firm Foundation* (February 7, 1961): 92; "Denominational Preacher Converted in Guatemala City," *Firm Foundation* (July 11, 1961): 444; "Growth Snowballing in Guatemala," *Firm Foundation* (August 8, 1961): 507.

185Lane Cubstead, "Guatemala: A Sturdy Foothold Secured," *Christian Chronicle* (November 19, 1965): 1-2.

186Thomas Olbricht, "Pan American Lectures," in Douglas Foster, et al., ed., *The Encyclopedia of the Stone-Campbell Movement* (Grand Rapids: Eerdmans, 2004), 588.

187Glover Shipp, "Groundwork for Mission Is Laid in El Salvador," *Christian Chronicle* (February 14, 1964): n.p.; Jerry Hill, "Guatemalan Church Does Without U. S. Aid," *Christian Chronicle* (November 10, 1967): 1; David Stewart, "Guatemala: The Indigenous Approach," *Christian Chronicle* (May 12, 1969): 1-3; "Unchurched Indians Target for Missionaries," *Christian Chronicle* (February 16, 1970): 8; "Spanish Language Training Center Established in Honduras," *Christian Chronicle* (May 3, 1977): 1, 4; "Nicaragua: Indigenous Chruch Flourishes," *Christian Chronicle* (December, 1987): 12.

188*Disciples Year Book* (1979), 166.

189"The Predisan Project," *Christian Chronicle* (September, 1995): 16-17; "Predisan's Mission and Vision," available at www.predisan.org, accessed July 14, 2011.

190"Guatemala Quake Relief," *Christian Chronicle* (March 9, 1976): 1, 4; "Guatemala Quake," *Christian Chronicle* (March 23, 1976): 9; "Salvadoran Christians Displaced," *Christian Chronicle* (September, 1983): 1, 4; "Churches, Members Aid Central America," *Christian Chronicle* (January, 1999): 1, 14.

191*Disciples Year Book* (1984), 184.

192*Disciples Year Book* (1985), 190.

193*Disciples Year Book* (1991), 194-195; Kenneth Kennon, "Salvadorans Return to Make Peace," *The Disciple* (December, 1990): 10-11; Daniel Dale and Nancy Jones, "El Salvador: Hope Beyond Pain," *The Disciple* (March, 1991): 26-27.

194Lillian Moir, "Poverty and Violence: Central American Legacy," *The Disciple* (November, 1990): 24-25.

195Telephone interview with Bishop Chester Aycock, presiding bishop of the Goldsboro-Raleigh District Assembly, by Sheila H. Gillams, September 28, 2011; and Goldsboro-Raleigh Church

Directory (circa 2005), from Goldsboro-Raleigh file binder 2, General Assembly Church of Christ, Disciples of Christ Archives, Brooklyn, New York.

16: Movement in Africa Since 1920s

[1]Bosela Eale, "Mission in Africa: An African Disciples Perspective," in Peter Heltzell, ed., *Chalice Introduction to Disciples Theology* (St. Louis: Chalice Press, 2008), 266-267; Eliki Bonanga, President of the Community of Disciples of Christ in the Congo, personal interview with Scott Seay, Mbandaka, Democratic Republic of Congo, May 30, 2011; Sandra Gourdet, Africa Executive for the Common Global Ministries Board, e-mail correspondence with Scott Seay, October, 2011.

[2]Hugh McCallum, "Those South African Churches Heroically Carry On," *Christian Standard* (January 16, 1932): 59.

[3]Charles Richards, "The South African Mission," *Christian-Evangelist* (January 15, 1931): 105.

[4]"United Society Seconds Basil Holt to Race Relations," *The South African Sentinel* (April, 1948): 4-5.

[5]McCallum, "Those South African Churches," 59.

[6]"UCMS Plans New Service to South Africa," *Christian-Evangelist* (December 5, 1945): 1181; "Our Minister: Basil Holt, M.A., B.D.," *The South African Sentinel* (November, 1950): 4-5.

[7]"Annual Report of the United Christian Missionary Society," *Year Book of the International Convention of Christian Churches (Disciples of Christ)* (St. Louis: Bethany Press, 1957), 239. (Hereafter *Disciples Year Book*).

[8]Robert Hopkins, "Basil Holt Going to South Africa," *World Call* (January, 1946): 19; "The South Africa Churches of Chirst (Disciples)," *South African Sentinel* (October, 1946): 12; "The South Africa Churches of Christ (Disciples)," 11; "Basil Holt, 'Disciples in South Africa,'" *Christian Advocate* (April 22, 1960): 198-199; "South African Association of Disciples of Christ," *South African Sentinel* (May, 1956): 274-275; Basil Holt, "Our First Six Years in South Africa," *South African Sentinel* (January, 1953): 112; E. Jones, "Dedication and Opening of Orlando Christian Church," *South African Sentinel* (May, 1956): 270-272; "New Church Buildings in the Republic of South Africa," *World Call* (July-August, 1970): 40-41.

[9]"Introducing Ourselves," *South African Sentinel* (January, 1946): 2.

[10]"First Ministerial Students Leave for Rhodes University," *South African Sentinel* (April, 1948): 1-3, 5.

[11]Basil Holt, "Race Relations in South Africa," *World Call* (March, 1948): 11; Basil Holt and Horton Davies, "Racial Division and Christian Unity," *World Call* (December, 1951): 18-19.

[12]Max Ward Randall, *We Would Do It Again* (Joliet: Mission Services, 1965), 86, 89, 94-95.

[13]Randall, *We Would Do it Again,* 140-141; William Rees, "Missionaries Stress Need for Workers in Africa," *Christian Standard* (July 1, 1950): 405; Max Ward Randall, "Evangelism Is the Only Answer for Africa," *Christian Standard* (December 2, 1950): 757; Max Ward Randall, "Church of Christ Mission, South Africa," *Christian Standard* (September 20, 1952): 599.

[14]This story is told in the mission's newsletter *South African Torch.* See especially Lynn Stanley, "Background of Umzumbe Bible Institute," (Second Quarter, 1979): 1; Michael Stanley, "Winds of Change Reach Gale Force," (Second Quarter, 1993): 1-2; and Duane Stanley, "Celebrating Thirty-Five Years on the Field," (Fourth Quarter, 2006): 1-3. Mission leaders decided to close Umzumbe Bible Institute following a 1993 incident in which a student assaulted Principal Michael Stanley.

[15]Randall, *We Would Do it Again,* 140-141.

[16]Robert Webber, "The All-Southern Convention of Disciples of Christ," *South African Sentinel* (November, 1954): 204.

[17]*Disciples Year Book* (1961), 271; *Disciples Year Book* (1964), 268; *Disciples Year Book* (1965), 211.

[18]*Disciples Year Book* (1963), 252.

[19]Bernard Spong, *Sticking Around: An Autobiography* (Pietermaritzburg: Cluster Publications, 2006), 83-84.

[20]Al and Jean Zimmerman, "South African Christian Mission," (privately published, 1986), a pamphlet held in the archives of Emmanuel Christian Seminary, Johnson City, Tennessee; "About Us," South African Christian Mission, available at http://sacmonline. org/index.php/sacm-history, accessed November 11, 2011. Steve Zimmerman, Director of South African Christian Mission, e-mail correspondence with Scott Seay, September, 2011.

[21]Stuart and Marilyn Cook, "Mission to South Africa History," available at www.mission2sa.org, accessed September 4, 2010.

[22]Glover Shipp, "Some Eighty Churches Working in South Africa," *Christian Chronicle* (September 2, 1960): 5-6.

[23]Glover Shipp, "80 Churches, 2,600 Members Count in Union of South Africa," *Christian Chronicle* (October 5, 1962): 5; Vance Fox, "Austin Church Sends Its Preacher to Africa," *Firm Foundation* (June 4, 1957): 359.

[24]L. C. Burns, "Great African Radio Program Revived," *Firm Foundation* (June 14, 1960): 375; and "Radio Work in Africa Produced Results," *Firm Foundation* (May 8, 1962): 302.

[25]Joe Watson, "The Church in South Africa," *Gospel Advocate* (March 3, 1976): 154; Joe Watson, "Bible School Has Great Impact in South Africa," *Christian Chronicle* (November 16, 1976): 1, 6.

[26]In 1937 the Mission Board handed over the Bulawayo property to the Associated Churches of Christ of Southern Rhodesia.

[27]Murray J. Savage, *Achievement: 50 Years of Missionary Witness in Southern Rhodesia* (Wellington: Associated Churches of Christ of New Zealand, 1949), 60-71.

[28]Savage, *Achievement,* 72-76; J. M. McCaleb, *On the Trail of the Missionaries* (Nashville: Gospel Advocate, 1930), 137.

[29]Savage, *Achievement,* 78-81; "Forty Years of Progress," *New Zealand Christian* (September 11, 1946), n.p.

[30]"Missionary Achievement," 4-5; "Dadaya Needs Your Help," *New Zealand Christian* (September 11, 1945): n.p. The Beit Trust was established in 1906 after the death of Albert Biet, a British philanthropist. At first, the trust financed railways, bridges, and roads in the British colonies in southern Africa, later funding education and other charitable initiatives. In 1949, for example, the Dadaya mission received a £10,000 grant from the Beit Trust. See "Crusading in Rhodesia," *New Zealand Christian* (September, 1949): n.p.; and "The Biet Trust," available at www.beittrust.org.uk, accessed January 21, 2011.

[31]A. C. Watters, "Disciples Missionary Becomes Prime Minister," *World Call* (December, 1953): 26; "Missionary Achievement," *New Zealand Christian* (January 20, 1954): 4-6. Frank Hadfield had also been a member of the Legislative Council between 1920 and 1928.

[32]Patrick Keatley and Andrew Meldrum, "Sir Garfield Todd: Liberal Rhodesian Premier Brought Down Over Black Reforms," available at www.guardian.co.uk/news/2002/oct/14/guardianobituaries.obituaries1, accessed November 2, 2010; On Todd's political vision for Zimbabwe, see Michael Casey, *The Rhetoric of Sir Garfield Todd: Christian Imagination and the Dream of an African Democracy* (Waco, Baylor University Press, 2007).

[33]Murray Savage, *Forward into Freedom* (Nelson: Associated Churches of Christ in New Zealand, 1979), 13-46.

[34]Savage, *Forward into Freedom,* 47-100.

[35]"Race Relations in South Africa," *New Zealand Christian* (January 20, 1950): 12.

[36]Garfield Todd, "Can Christianity Survive in Africa?" *New Zealand Christian* (February 20, 1963): 1-2.

[37]Michael West, "Nbadaningi Sithole, Garfield Todd and the Dadaya School Strike of 1947," *Journal of Southern African Studies* (June, 1992): 297-316.

[38]"Overseas Mission News," *New Zealand Christian* (February, 1970): 8-9; "The Struggle for Justice in Rhodesia," *New Zealand*

Christian (August, 1970): 3-4; W. S. Lowe, "Why the Todds Went to Prison," *New Zealand Christian* (April, 1972): 9.

[39]Savage, *Forward into Freedom*, 120-130; Casey, *Rhetoric of Sir Garfield Todd*, 4-5, 117-123.

[40]Savage, *Achievement*, 73; "The Missionaries," *World Vision* (February, 1937): 9.

[41]"Report of the African Work: Salisbury," *World Vision* (October-December, 1942): 27-28.

[42]Ray Tenpenny, "Nhowe Mission Faces Official Intervention," *Gospel Advocate* (December 10, 1954): 990-991; J. Douglas Williams, "A Statement Concerning Nhowe," *Gospel Advocate* (November 15, 1956): 915; and "Nhowe Mission to Continue," *Firm Foundation* (July 2, 1957): 422.

[43]"School of Nursing," Nohwe Mission, Zimbabwe, available at·www.nhowemission.org/school_of_nursing, accessed February 2, 2011.

[44]A. C. Watters, "Our Mission in Southern Rhodesia," *Christian Advocate* (September 16, 1960): 447-448; Robert McNeill, "Retirement in Southern Rhodesia," *Christian-Evangelist* (June 24, 1957): 822-823.

[45]C. M. (Queenie) Ladbrook, *Tools in the Hands of God* (Glen Iris, Vic.: Vital Publications, 1983).

[46]Max Ward Randall, "Progress on the Zambezi," *Christian Standard* (October 31, 1959): 608; "A Hospital for $100,000," *Christian Standard* (October 31, 1959): 605-606; and A. C. Watters, "Our Mission in Southern Rhodesia," *Christian Standard* (November 19, 1960): 755.

[47]A. C. Watters, "Unity Preserved in Southern Rhodesia," *Christian Standard* (October 31, 1959): 607.

[48]"Update—Zimbabwe, Rhodesia," *Christian Standard* (February 3, 1980): 98.

[49]John Pemberton, "A Decade: 1956-1966," *Central African Story* Special Issue (August, 1966): 1-12; John Pemberton, "Destroyed for Lack of Knowledge," *Christian Standard* (September 8, 1974): 807; Jack Pennington, "The Dream Goes On," *Central African Story* (March, 1980): 1-3; "History," *Central African Christian* (June, 1980): 10-11.

[50]"Hippo Valley Christian Mission," available at www.hippovalley.com, accessed February 4, 2011.

[51]See "FAME: Our History," at www.fameworld.org/who-we-are/our-history, accessed January 1, 2012.

[52]"Overseas Mission Heads to Visit Zimbabwe," *New Zealand Christian* (September, 1989): 10; "Training Ministers in Zimbabwe," *New Zealand Christian* (November, 1989): 10; "Two New in Zimbabwe," *New Zealand Christian* (February, 1990): 11.

[53]"The Prospector Who Became a Preacher," *World Vision* (February, 1937): 6-7; "Peter Masiya—Zambia," in Sam Shewmaker, ed., *A Great Light Dawning* (Searcy: Drumbeat Publications, 2002), 12; Ellen Baize, "Will and Delia Short—Pioneers," in Shewmaker, *Great Light*, 24-25.

[54]"Ray and Zelma Lawyer," *Booster's Bulletin* (October, 1927): 1; "The Death of Ray Lawyer," *Booster's Bulletin* (November, 1927): 47; Zelma Lawyer, *I Married a Missionary* (Abilene: Abilene Christian College Press, 1943); "The Missionaries," *World Vision* (February, 1937): 9; On the earliest Churches of Christ work in Northern Rhodesia, see also Earl West, *The Search for the Ancient Order*, 4 vols., (Germantown: Religious Book Service, 1946-1987), 4:257-282.

[55]Allen Avery, "Kambole: Apostle to the Tonga," Shewmaker, *Great Light*, 17-23.

[56]"Missionary Distress Fund," *Missionary Messenger* (February, 1934): 1-2.

[57]"Report of the African Work," *World Vision* (October-December, 1942): 20-29; Georgia Hobby, *They Called Him Muluti: The Life and Times of Alvin Hobby, A Teacher in Africa* (Winona: J.C. Choate, 2000); George S. Benson, *Missionary Experiences* (Delight: Gospel Light, 1987); and Georgia Hobby, *Give Us This Bread* (Winona: J. C. Choate Publications, 1988).

[58]"Directory of American Missionaries in Africa," *World Vision* (September, 1952): 4-6; "Report of the African Work: Kabanga Mission," *World Vision* (October-December, 1942): 26; "Church of Christ Missions of Northern Rhodesia," *World Vision* (March, 1948): 12.

[59]"A Short History of Namwianga Mission," Zambia Mission, available at www.zambiamission.org/history.html, accessed February 1, 2011.

[60]"Zambia Missions," at http://www.zambiamissions.org/, accessed January 2, 2012.

[61]"Umtali Being Unshackeled," *Firm Foundation* (March 8, 1966): 157; Ira North, "Umtali School of Preaching," *Gospel Advocate* (October 20, 1970): 661; "Nearly Completed Rhodesian Mission to Be Focus of Preacher Training," *Christian Chronicle* (August 31, 1970): 1, 6; Loy Mitchell, "Umtali School of Preaching Commiting the Word to Faithful Men," *Christian Chronicle* (March 23, 1976): 8; "Ten Year Plan," at http://www.zambiamission.org/10year.html, accessed January 2, 2012.

[62]"Report of the Foreign Missions Committee," *Churches of Christ Year Book and Annual Report* (Birmingham: Churches of Christ, 1926), 100-101. (Hereafter *Churches of Christ Year Book*).

[63]*Churches of Christ Year Book* (1930), 65, 82-83.

[64]"The Nyasaland Mission: A Plain Statement," *Our Missions Overseas*, 16 (1946: 8. This was published in response to the *Scripture Standard Supplement* (November 1945), containing a copy of the letter written by Frederick Nkhonde to Kempster, published in the *Bible Advocate* for January 1931, along with a letter from Ronald Kaunda describing the incident below concerning baptism of those under discipline later in 1931, but omitting any reference to the agreement between Gray and Frederick in December 1930.

[65]*Churches of Christ Year Book* (1933), 67; G. B. Shelburne, III, "History of the Church in Malawi Africa," at http://www.bible.acu.edu/ministry/centers_institutes/missions/page.asp?ID=412. Mary Bannister resigned in 1934 because of declining health likely exacerbated by the strain of the previous years during which even she had been attacked by the *Bible Advocate*. She died in 1940. Laurie Grinstead, "Resignation of Miss Bannister," *Christian Advocate* (June 15, 1934): 375.

[66]*Churches of Christ Year Book* (1933), 67.

[67]Also known as African Independent Churches, African Indigenous Churches, and African Instituted Churches. Most often, simply the acronym AIC is used. Victor E W Hayward, *African Independent Church Movements* (London: World Council of Churches, 1963).

[68]*Churches of Christ Year Book* (1937), 92.

[69]*Churches of Christ Year Book* (1956), 81; *Churches of Christ Year Book* (1958), 71-73; *Churches of Christ Year Book* (1960), 71.

[70]These generalizations are based on statistics from the *Churches of Christ Year Book* (1934), 85; *Churches of Christ Year Book* (1948), 60; *Churches of Christ Year Book* (1960), 75.

[71]*Churches of Christ Year Book* (1966), 895; *Churches of Christ Year Book* (1968), 86-87; *Churches of Christ Year Book* (1966), 895.

[72]"Churches of Christ in Malawi," CWM: A Partnership of Churches in Mission, available at www.cwmission.org/africa-region/churches-of-christ-in-malawi, accessed November 2, 2011.

[73]"Blind African Preacher Baptizes Fifty-Three People in a Series of Meetings," *Firm Foundation* (May 15, 1956): 327.

[74]Eldred Echols, *Wings of the Morning* (Fort Worth: Wings Press, 1989), 105-106.

[75]Doyle Gilliam, "The Church Grows in Malawi," *Firm Foundation* (May 3, 1966): 283; Erik Tryggestad, "President of Malawi Helps Churches Celebrate 100 Years of Evangelism," *Christian Chronicle* (February, 2007): 12; Erik Tryggestad, "The Face of Malawi," *Christian Chronicle* (January, 2011): 1, 16.

[76]Shelburne, "History."

[77]Shelburne, "History."

[78]Mac Lynn, *Churches of Christ Around the World: Quick Reference*

(Nashville: 21st Century Christian Publications, 2003), 17, 137-139.

[79]Herbert Smith, "Training Leaders for Tomorrow's Africa," *World Call* (March, 1936): 14.

[80]Herbert Smith, "How Shall the Congo Christian Institute Develop?" *World Call* (October, 1929): 19-20.

[81]Herbert Smith, *Fifty Years in Congo: Disciples of Christ at the Equator* (Indianapolis: United Christian Missionary Society, 1949), 72-74, and 83-84.

[82]*Biography Set Series Four: Our Workers in Africa,* Leaflet Fifteen (Indianapolis: United Christian Missionary Society, 1936), held in the archives of Christian Theological Seminary, Indianapolis, Indiana.

[83]Royal Dye, "The Crescent Conquest or the Cross Triumphant?" *World Call* (October, 1926): 8-10.

[84]E. R. Moon, "Breaking the Wilderness for Christ," *World Call* (October, 1926): 11-14.

[85]*Disciples Year Book* (1930), 56; *Disciples Year Book* (1940), 22.

[86]Smith, *Fifty Years in Congo,* 76, 110.

[87]Smith, *Fifty Years in Congo,* 90.

[88]H. Gray Russell, "A Christian School in the Belgian Congo," *World Call* (January, 1941): 12-13, 16.

[89]Smith, *Fifty Years in Congo,* 104, 106.

[90]Virgil Sly, "Report on the Congo Mission," (Indianapolis: United Christian Missionary Society, 1946); Donald Baker, "Personnel Needs in Congo," *World Call* (June, 1946): 26-27; *Disciples Year Book* (1948), 52.

[91]Donald Burke and N. R. Farbman, "Photographic Essay: Congo Mission," *Life* (June 2, 1947): 105ff.

[92]Virgil Sly, "Congo Golden Jubilee," *World Call* (September, 1949):12-13.

[93]Gene Johnson, *Congo Centennial: The Second Fifty Years* (privately published, 1999): 37.

[94]"Historique de l'UPC," Université Protestante au Congo, available at www.upc-rdc.cd/historique.php, accessed February 3, 2011.

[95]Johnson, *Congo Centennial,* 52-54; "Barbara Bates Dade, "Capital for the Congo," *World Call* (March, 1960): 19-20.

[96]"To a Changing Continent," *World Call* (September, 1959): 9.

[97]Johnson, *Congo Centennial,* 47; *Disciples Year Book* (1958), 239; *Disciples Year Book* (1960), 272.

[98]"Congolese Churches Set Up Central Fund," *World Call* (January, 1959), 5.

[99]Johnson, *Congo Centennial,* 70.

[100]*Disciples Year Book* (1961), 269-271.

[101]*Disciples Year Book* (1962), 268-269.

[102]Betsy Hobgood, "Returning Missionaries See Changes in Congo," *World Call* (December, 1959): 36.

[103]Kabeye Noé, "Congolese Leader Agrees that Partnership Is Needed," *World Call* (February, 1960), 38.

[104]Johnson, *Congo Centennial,* 138; "Bokeleale—African Christian," *World Call* (July, 1967): 11.

[105]Johnson, *Congo Centennial,* 90-91; W. A Welsh, "Words to Remember," *World Call* (September, 1963): 20; "Congo's Doors are Wide Open: A Letter from Jean B. Bokeleale," *World Call* (September, 1963): 21.

[106]Johnson, *Congo Centennial,* 102; Philip Kabongo-Mbaya, *L' Église du Christ au Zaire* (Paris: Éditions Karthala, 1992), 197.

[107]"Church of Christ in Congo—Community of Disciples of Christ," World Council of Churches, available at www.oikoumene. org/gr/memberchurches/regions/africa/democratic-republic-of-congo/church-of-christ-in-congo-community-of-disciples-of-christ-in-congo.html, accessed February 12, 2011.

[108]Johnson, *Congo Centennial,* 104-105; "Congo Disciples Look to the Future," *World Call* (May, 1965): 31.

[109]Johnson, *Congo Centennial,* 99-101.

[110]Johnson, *Congo Centennial,* 134-137; *Disciples Year Book* (1975), 145.

[111]"The History of Habitat," Habitat for Humanity, available at www.habitat.org/how/historytext.aspx, accessed January 3, 2012.

[112]Johnson, *Congo Centennial,* 154-156; *Disciples Year Book* (1973), 168; *Disciples Year Book* (1978), 160; and especially *Disciples Year Book* (1982), 210.

[113]Dan Hoffman, "Zairians Open Own 'Foreign Mission,'" *The Disciple* (September, 1990): 17-19.

[114]Robert Friedly, "Crisis in Zaire: Are We and Our Money Part of the Problem?" *The Disciple* (September, 1991): 24-26.

[115]*Disciples Year Book* (1993), 206; *Disciples Year Book* (2000), 220.

[116]"Congo Partnership," Christian Church (Disciples of Christ) in Indiana, available at http://indianadisciples.org/about/congo-partnership, accessed January 3, 2012.

[117]Guy Humphreys, "Progress of African Mission Reported," *Christian Standard* (January 21, 1950): 37; "A Brief History of African Christian Mission: The Formatiave Years," *The African* (Winter, 1990): 4-6.

[118]"The Progressive Fifties: Continuation of a Brief History of African Christian Mission," *The African* (Summer, 1992), 6, 12; June Crowl, "History of African Christian Mission," *The African* (Winter, 1992): 3, 6.

[119]"Missionaries Evacuated," *Christian Standard* (August 29, 1964): 557; "Some Workers Return to Congo," *Christian Standard* (October 10, 1964): 653; "Doors and Adversaries," *Christian Standard* (December 19, 1964): 806; and "Miss Rine Killed in Congo, Schaubs are Safe," *Christian Standard* (December 19, 1964): 816.

[120]"A Brief History," Alliance of Christian Missions, available at www.acmint.com/history.html, accessed February 3, 2011.

[121]"Angolan Mission Team, Angola Partnerss," at http://www. angolateam.org/the-workers/angolan-partners/, accessed January 27, 2012.

[122]On the Scottish Presbyterian mission in eastern Nigeria, see William Taylor, *Mission to Educate: A History of the Scottish Presbyterian Mission in East Nigeria, 1846-1960* (Leiden: Brill, 1996); Reda Goff, *The Great Nigerian Mission* (Nashville: Lawrence Avenue Church of Christ, 1964), 8.

[123]Goff, *Great Nigerian Mission,* 8, 15

[124]Reda C. Goff, *The Great Nigerian Mission* (Nashville: Lawrence Avenue Church of Christ, 1964), 16-17.

[125]"Our Story," Africa Christian Schools, available at http:// africanchristianschools.org/about-us/our-story, accessed November 11, 2011; Roy Drennett, "Forty Natives Enrolled in Iboland Bible College," *Christian Chronicle* (April 9, 1957): 1, 6; "Rees Bryant Family Arrives in Nigeria," *Firm Foundation* (April 29, 1958): 264; and "Six Missionary Families Now in Nigeria," *Christian Chronicle* (December 1, 1959): 4-5.

[126]"Nigerian Christian Schools Foundation, Inc.," *Firm Foundation* (November 3, 1959): 696; Bill Curry, "December Marks 10th Year for Nigerian Work," *Christian Chronicle* (December 21, 1962): 3.

[127]J. W. Nicks, "Post-War Nigeria," *Gospel Advocate* (October 15, 1970): 660-661.

[128]"Drive Launched for Nigerian School," *Firm Foundation* (December 8, 1964): 787; Glenn Martin, "Huffard Opens Nigerian Christian School," *Christian Chronicle* (April 24, 1964): 1.

[129]Bill Curry, "Mission Force in Nigeria Is Expanding," *Christian Chronicle* (August 14, 1964): 4; "Dr. Farrar to Receive Help for Hospital in Nigeria," *Firm Foundation* (November 30, 1965): 766; "Three Facets Highlight Nigeria Break-Through," *Christian Chronicle* (November 19, 1965): 4.

[130]Stafford North and Russell Fountain, "The Church in Nigeria: A Long and Inspiring Story of Dedication and Progress," *Christian Chronicle* (October, 1995): 28; "Nigerian Christian Hospital," at http://www.ihcf.net/nigerian-hospital.html, accessed January 27, 2012.

[131]William Youngs, "Conquest for Christ to Begin in August," *Firm Foundation* (May 26, 1964): 342.

[132]Rees Bryant and Howard Horton, "Work in Nigeria not Uprooted," *Firm Foundation* (October 8, 1968): 650; Rees Bryant, "Nigeria 1968: War and Faith," *Firm Foundation* (October 22, 1968): 682; and "Christians Die in the Land of Horrors," *Christan Chronicle* (September 9, 1968): 4-5.

[133]"Nigerian Missions' Pullout Benefits Cameroon Church," *Christian Chronicle* (January 5, 1968): 1; "Cameroon Program Boosted by Campaign," *Christian Chronicle* (May 17, 1968): 1.

[134]Nicks, "Post-War Nigeria," 660-661.

[135]Jim Massey, "The Demanding Challenge in Biafra," *Christian Chronicle* (January 26, 1970): 1, 4; "Nigerian School of Preaching Re-Opens," *Firm Foundation* (February 16, 1971): 110.

[136]"A Few Dollars will Supply a Great Need in War-Torn Nigeria," *Firm Foundation* (January 15, 1971): 10; "Immigration Thaw in Nigeria," *Firm Foundation* (Seprtember 7, 1971): 570; "Okoronkwo Named Head of Nigerian Bible School," *Christian Chronicle* (February 8, 1971): 1.

[137]"Capsule Portrait of Unconquered Nation: Ibo Churches Flourish in Ravaged Nigeria," *Christian Chronicle* (August 3, 1970): 1, 4, 7; J. W. Nicks, "Among Ibos in Nigeria, West Africa," *Firm Foundation* (June 18, 1974): 394.

[138]John Beckloff, "Nigerian Churches: Incredible Growth and Opportunities," *Christian Chronicle* (January 15, 1973): 1, 3; Bill Hicks, "Nigeria 1978: Churches Growing," *Christian Chronicle* (May 2, 1978): 8.

[139]"Our Story," African Christian Schools.

[140]Glover Shipp, "First Nigerian Students Take BA Course," *Christian Chronicle* (July, 1995): 24; "Nigerian College Graduates 57 Students," *Christian Chronicle* (July, 1996): 24; "Nigeria College to Open New Branch," *Christian Chronicle* (July, 1998): 28; "Nigerian College Builds Second Campus," *Christian Chronicle* (December, 1999): 32.

[141]"Our Story," African Christian Schools.

[142]Wendell Broom, "Growth of Churches of Christ among Ibibios of Nigeria," (MS thesis, Fuller Theological Seminary, 1970).

[143]Mark Berryman, "Status of Churches of Christ in Sub-Saharan Africa" (a report compiled for the Africans Claiming Africa for Christ conference in Johannesburg, May, 2000). The statistical table in Berryman's report is available at www.harding.edu/cwm/archives/resources/articles/AFRICA2000STATISTICSPDF.PDF, accessed February 7, 2011.

[144]Augustine Tawiah, Samuel Twumasi-Ankrah, and Dan McVey, *The Churches of Christ in Ghana: Where Did We Come From and Where Are We Going?* (Accra: World Literature Publications, 1992), 19-20.

[145]Sewell Hall, *Christianity Magazine* (1984), 287.

[146]Jane Ann Derr, *Trailblazing with God: Learning to Walk on the Water* (Maitland: Xulon Press, 2008), 210; "Going to Ghana with the Gospel," *Firm Foundation* (May 2, 1961): 276; Dewayne Davenport, "Ghana Pioneer Preacher Passes Before First Workers Arrive," *Christian Chronicle* (September 8, 1961): 1, 4; "The Gospel in Ghana—The First Year in Review," *Firm Foundation* (November 13, 1962): 732.

[147]Berryman, "Status of Churches of Christ."

[148]Albert Douglas Ofori, "The Development of Pentecostalism in Ghana and Its Effect on Churches of Christ" (MA thesis, Abilene Christian University, 2009), 94-128; see also Ogbu Kalu, *African Pentecostalism: An Introduction* (New York: Oxford University Press, 2008).

[149]David Clarence Couch, "Something Is Better than Nothing: The History of Ghana Christian College and Seminary" (MA thesis, Cincinnati Christian Seminary, 1985), iii, 18-23, 42.

[150]"Refreshing Hour International Church, Ghana, West Africa," available at http://www.rehic.com, accessed September 30, 2011; Refreshing Hour Life Bible College Fifth Graduation Ceremony Program, Refreshing Hour Church, Cathedral of Dreams, Baka-Ekyir, Sekondi, September 13, 2008, held in the private collection of Dr. Sheila Gillams, Assistant Professor of Religious Studies, Medgar Evers College, City University of New York.

[151]Bishop Chester Aycock, Pastor of St. Paul Church of Christ, Disciples of Christ and General Vice Bishop Malcolm Johnson of the Church of Christ, Disciples of Christ, telephone interview with Dr. Sheila H. Gillams September 28, 2011; "Refreshing Hour."

[152]Elder Atsu Mawussi Awadzie, Togolese leader of the Church of Christ, Disciples of Christ, e-mail communication with Dr. Sheila H. Gillams, April 23, 2007.

[153]Elder Atsu Mawussi Awadzie, Togolese leader of the Church of Christ, Disciples of Christ, e-mail communication with Sheila H. Gillams, December 13, 2004.

[154]Elder Atsu Mawussi Awadzie, Togolese leader of the Church of Christ, Disciples of Christ, telephone interview with Sheila H. Gillams, September 29, 2011.

[155]"Refreshing Hour." General Vice Bishop Malcolm Johnson, Church of Christ, Disciples of Christ, telephone interview with Dr. Sheila Gillams, September 28, 2011.

[156]Telephone interview with General Bishop MacDonald Moses by Sheila H. Gillams, October 3, 2011.

[157]"Historical Sketch of Mission Efforts in Tanzania," *Christian Chronicle* (June 17, 1975): 9-10; Guy V. Caskey, *Along Tanganyika Trails* (Pampa: n.d.), 3; Donna Horne, *Meanwhile Back in the Jungle: Tanganyika Tales* (Winona: J.C. Choate, 1986).

[158]Eldred Echols, *Wings of the Morning* (Fort Worth: Wings Press, 1989), 180-182.

[159]"Chimala School of Preaching," Chimala Mission Hospitals and Schools, available at www.chimalamission.com/schoolofpreaching.html, accessed November 11, 2011; and "Chimala Bible College," Chimala Mission Hospitals and Schools, available at www.chimalamission.com/biblecollege.html, accessed November 11, 2011.

[160]Charles Hill, "Medical Doctor Ready to Go to Chimala, Tanganyika," *Firm Foundation* (January 15, 1963): 42.; "Another Physician Plans Mission Work in Africa," *Firm Foundation* (February 12, 1963): 109; R. Scott Lamascus, "Chimala Hospital Celebrates 25 Years in Tanzanian Work," *Christian Chronicle* (September, 1987): 15; "History of Chimala Mission," www.nyachurchofchrist.com, accessed July 15, 2008.

[161]"Chimala Hospital," Chimala Mission Hospitals and Schools, available at www.chimalamission.com/hospital.html, accessed July 8, 2011.

[162]Claude Gild, "The Timothys Are Coming," *Firm Foundation* (July 9, 1963): 443; Claude Gild, "Welcome Planned for African Missionaries," *Firm Foundation* (November 26, 1963): 763.

[163]Stanley Granberg, "A Survey of Work in East Africa," in Wendell Broom and Stanley Granberg, eds., *100 Years of African Missions* (Abilene: Abilene Christian University Press, 2001), 124; "Ministry," Mission Mwanza, available at http://missionmwanza.org, accessed January 3, 2012.

[164]Erik Tryggestad, "Burkina Faso: New Life in a Land of Wooden Crosses," *Christian Chronicle* (September 2009): 20-21.

[165]J. C. Moore, "Emphasis on Education in Ethiopia," *Firm Foundation* (October 29, 1963): 701; "Mission Terminated," *Firm Foundation* (November 26, 1963): 764; and Stanley Granberg, "A Survey of Work in East Africa," in Wendell Broom and Stanley Granberg, eds., *100 Years of African Missions* (Abilene: Abilene Christian University Press, 2001).

[166]"Congregations in Ethiopia," *Firm Foundation* (May 7, 1963): 300; Carl Thompson, "'We Have Found the True Church!' Report on Ethiopia Group Says," *Christian Chronicle* (April 26, 1963): 1, 7.

[167]John Young, "64 Ethiopians Baptized in 5 Days," *Firm Foundation* (November 29, 1966): 766; John Young, "The Eunuch's Land Opens Its Doors," *Firm Foundation* (May 23, 1967): 334; "Ethiopian Preaching School," *Firm Foundation* (November 14, 1967): 747; "Crash Preacher Training Program Successful," *Firm Foundation* (May 7, 1968): 298.

[168]Stanley E. Granberg, "Behailu Abebe: Called to Serve, Leadership Emergence in Ethiopia, 1943-1993," (unpublished manuscript, Fuller Theological Seminary, 1993).

[169]"Ethiopia: Famine Programs Organize," *Christian Chronicle* (November, 1984): 1, 12; R. Scott Lamascus, "Ethiopia Recieves $2.4 Million," *Christian Chronicle* (December, 1984): 1.

[170]Roy Jones, "Ethiopian Church Leader Recognized as Humanitarian," *Christian Chronicle* (September, 1996): 19; Glover Shipp, "Ethiopian Work Takes New Dimension," *Christian Chronicle* (January, 1998): 28; Glover Shipp, "Ethiopian Work Shows Maturity," *Christian Chronicle* (August, 1999): 28; and Erik Tryggestad, "A Conversation with Behailu Abebe," *Christian Chronicle* (September, 2002), 20.

[171]Berryman, "Status of Churches of Christ."

[172]"Make Disciples of All the Nations" pamphlet, n.d. CMF was organized in 1949 as an agency of what would become Christian Churches/Churches of Christ to fund missionaries.

[173]Edgar J. Elliston, "An Ethnohistory of Ethiopia: A Study of the Factors Which Affect the Planting and Growth of the Church," (MA thesis, Fuller Theological Seminary, 1968).

[174]"A Short History of Christian Missionary Fellowship," www.cmfi.org, accessed July 15, 2008.

[175]"A Missionary Story Repeated," *Firm Foundation* (January 18, 1966): 43.

[176]"Church Growth among the Kipsigis," unpublished manuscript.

[177]Kenya Mission Team, *Church Planting, Watering, and Increasing in Kenya* (Firm Foundation, 1980).

[178]Gailyn Van Rheenen, *Missions: Biblical Foundations and Contemporary Strategies* (Grand Rapids: Zondervan, 1996).

[179]"Nairobi, Kenya," a special advertising insert to the *Christian Chronicle* (1983). Periodic reports on "Target Nairobi" appeared in the *Christian Chronicle* throughout the 1980s.

[180]R. Scott Lamascus, "Kenya: Leaders Scramble to Save Church Status," *Christian Chronicle* (July, 1988): 1; "Kenya Churches Regain Government Recognition," *Christian Chronicle* (January, 1995): 22.

[181]"Kenya Christian Industrial Training Institute," available at www.kciti.edu, accessed July 15, 2008.

[182]Larry L. Niemeyer, ed., "The Status of the American Mission Activity of Christian Churches/Churches of Christ in Africa" (1989), Ozark Christian College Library.

[183]William Searcy, "The Nairobi Great Commission School," in 100 Years of African Missions.

[184]Sam Shewmaker, ed., *Africans Claiming Africa: Claiming the Vision* (Queensland: Drumbeat Publications, 1999); "Africans Claiming Africa for Christ," available at http://aca-zambia.org/ accessed January 27, 2012.

[185]Chad Westerholm, "A Brief History of the Churches of Christ in Mozambique," available at http://www.makuateam.org/MT/News/CofC%20History%20in%20Mozambique.pdf, accessed February 8, 2011.

[186]Westerholm, "A Brief History of the Churches of Christ in Mozambique."

[187]Westerholm, "A Brief History of the Churches of Christ in Mozambique."

[188]Glover Shipp, "Mozambique Church Survey Reveals Restoration Effort," *Christian Chronicle* (November-December, 1991): 17; Donna Mitchell, *Among the People of the Sun: Our Years in Africa* (Winona: Choate Publications, 1995); and Glover Shipp, "Mozambican Church Leaders Trained," *Christian Chronicle* (February, 1997): 26.

[189]Glover Shipp, "Mozambican Churches Survive War," *Christian Chronicle* (November, 1994): 22.

17: Movement in Europe Since 1920s

[1]David Fountain, *Lord Radstock and the Russian Awakening* (Southampton: Mayflower Christian Books, 1988), 35-46.

[2]Fountain, *Lord Radstock*, 57-68.

[3]Geoff Ellis and Wesley Jones, *The Other Revolution: Russian Evangelical Awakenings* (Abilene: Abilene Christian University Press, 1996); Robert Reeves, "The Restoration Movement in Russia," *Christian Standard* (May, 1959): 297.

[4]I. S. Prokhanov, *In the Cauldron of Russia, 1869-1933* (New York: All-Russian Evangelical Christian Union, 1933), 119-128.

[5]Reeves, "Restoration Movement in Russia," 298; Joseph Keevil, "The Story of Our Russian Mission," *Christian Standard* (January 4, 1913): 4; "A New Russian Paper," *Christian Standard* (July 15, 1916): 1432.

[6]Reeves, "Restoration Movement in Russia," 298.

[7]Louis Patmont, "Christian Only Movement in Russia," *Christian Standard* (January 4, 1913): 5; Grant Lewis, "The American Christian Missionary Society and the Russians in New York City," *Christian Standard* (March 9, 1912): 422.

[8]I. S. Prokhanov, "The Movement to Restore Pure Christianity in Russia," *Christian Standard* (April 21, 1923): 1.

[9]Prokhanov, *Cauldron of Russia*, 140-177; "Forward with the Restoration Forces," *Christian Standard* (January 2, 1926): 1.

[10]Daniel Peris, *Storming the Heavens: The Soviet League of the Militant Godless* (Ithaca: Cornell University Press, 1998).

[11]Prokhanov, *Cauldron of Russia*, 253-255.

[12]Reeves, "The Restoration Movement in Russia," 297-299; L. Wesley Jones, "Gospel Christians in Russia," in Douglas Foster, et al., ed., *The Encyclopedia of the Stone-Campbell Movement* (Grand Rapids: Eerdmans, 2004), 661-662.

[13]"Iron Curtain Trip Charted," *Christian Chronicle* (April 29, 1958): 1-2; Otis Gatewood, "5,000 Members of Church Found in Russia by Group," *Christian Chronicle* (September 23, 1958): 1, 5; Glover Shipp, "Iron Curtain Countries Are Frontier of Huge Magnitude for the Church," *Christian Chronicle* (May 10, 1960): 3.

[14]Philip Patterson, "Iron Curtain: Church Continues to Grow in Russia," *Christian Chronicle* (November, 1982): 15.

[15]Candy Holcombe, "USSR: *Glasnost* Widens Doors for Evangelism," *Christian Chronicle* (June, 1988): 1, 7; "Russian Radio Grants Christians Free Air Time," *Christian Chronicle* (September, 1990): 16; "Russian Mission Efforts Gain Momentum," *Christian Chronicle* (November-December, 1991): 1, 4.

[16]"Herald of Truth Workers Campaign in the Ukraine," *Christian Chronicle* (June, 1991): 17; Jennifer Wolford and Glover Shipp, "Campaigns Augment Soviet Churches," *Christian Chronicle* (August, 1991): 1, 4; "Church in Former Soviet Union Continues to Expand," *Christian Chronicle* (August, 1992): 18.

[17]"Russian Center Established," *Christian Chronicle* (April, 1992): 1, 4; Jim Mettinbrink, "Churches Meet in Komi Republic," *Christian Chronicle* (December, 1996): 24; "Testing the Winds of Change: How Russia's Demise Opened the Door to Christianity," *Christian Chronicle* (November, 1996): 16-17.

[18]"Institute of Theology and Christian Mission," available at www.itcm.ru/english/seminar.html, accessed September 20, 2011.

[19]See "Ukraine Directory of the Churches of Christ" available at http://church-of-christ.org/churches/Ukraine/Ukraine_S.htm, accessed January 11, 2012; "Kyiv Church of Christ," available at http://www.ueckyiv.org/church-of-christ, accessed January 11, 2012; "Obolon Church of Christ," available at http://www.obolon-church.kiev.ua/?q=en, accessed January 11, 2012.

[20]John Stratton, "On Foreign Fields," *Word and Work* (August, 1914): 15-16; Louis Patmont, "The Restoration Movement in Poland," *Christian Standard* (June 21, 1913): 995-996.

[21]Waclaw Zebrowski, "The Work in Poland," *Christian Standard* (March 14, 1914): 478; "The Churches of Christ in Poland," *Christian Standard* (February 15, 1930): 153.

[22]Dennis Lindsay, "Missions in Europe," in Foster, et al., ed., *Encyclopedia*, 310.

[23]Paul Bajko, *A History of the Churches of Christ in Poland* (Bel Air: Polish Christian Ministries, 2001), 18-20.

[24]Bajko, *History*, 21-23. See also "The Churches of Christ in Poland," *Christian Standard* (February 15, 1930): 153.

[25]Jerzy Lukowski and Hubert Zawadski, *A Concise History of Poland* (New York: Cambridge University Press, 2001), ch. 6.

[26]Bajko, *History*, 27-31.

[27]R. Graham Keevil, "Our Brethren in Poland," *Christian Standard* (May 7, 1932): 445-446; Konstantin Jaroszewicz, "The Union Churches of Christ a Bulwark Against the Spread of Anarchy," *Christian Standard* (June 19, 1937): 553; Konstantin Jaroszewicz, "Europe Is a Fugitive from Justice," *Christian Standard* (April 27, 1940): 402, and (May 4, 1940): 429.

[28]Lukowski and Zawadski, *Concise History*, ch. 6.

[29]Bajko, *History*, 37-41.

[30]Bajko, *History*, 47-51; quoted at p. 50.

[31]Lukowski and Zawadski, *Concise History*, ch. 7.

[32]Bajko, *History*, 52-54.

[33]Bajko, *History*, 57-59; Jerzy Sacewicz, *The Churches of Christ in Poland* (Warsaw, 1981), 90-95.

[34]Jerzy Sacewicz, "Prison Notes," *Word and Life* (1992). *Word and Life* is a Polish-language quarterly publication of the Community of Christ Churches. Rough English translations of some issues are available online at www.slowoizycie.pl, accessed January 11, 2012.

[35]Bajko, *History*, 61-66, 96-97.

[36]Bajko, *History*, 73-75; Paul Bajko, "Report from Poland," *Christian Standard* (February 19, 1955): 123.

[37]Bajko, *History*, 73-78; Paul Bajko, "Following Fellowship in Poland: Personal Visit Adds to Contacts Already Established," *Christian Standard* (December 21, 1963): 809-810.

[38]"Polish Christian Ministries," available at www.pcmusa.org, accessed November 1, 2010.

[39]R. J. Smith, "Two Influential Poles Converted," *Christian Chronicle* (May 20, 1958): 1; "Naumiuk, Ciszek Face Trial in Warsaw October 9," *Christian Chronicle* (September 22, 1961): 1; R. J. Smith, "Ciszek Acquitted; Naumiuk Gets Suspended Sentence," *Christian Chronicle* (October 27, 1961): 1; "Naumiuk Arrested Again; Sentence Review in May," *Christian Chronicle* (May 11, 1962): 1; "Polish Court Confirms Naumiuk's Prior Convictions," *Christian Chronicle* (August 10, 1962): 1; R. J. Smith, "The Church in Poland—1962 Brought Harder Times," *Christian Chronicle* (February 1, 1962): 8; James Betts, "Henryk Ciszek Forced to Leave Poland," *Christian Chronicle* (March 6, 1964): 1-2; Henryk Ciszek, "A Leader Falls in Poland," *Christian Chronicle* (June 11, 1965): 1-2.

[40]Lukowski and Zawadski, *Concise History*, ch. 7.

[41]Bajko, *History*, 96-110.

[42]"Poland: 140 Tons of Food Delivered and Church Legalized," *Firm Foundation* (November 10, 1981): 714; "Poland: Food Program Continues," *Christian Chronicle* (January, 1982): 1-2.

[43]"Church Legally Recognized in Poland," *Firm Foundation* (July 20, 1982): 458; "Poland: Church Recognized by Government," *Christian Chronicle* (May, 1982): 11. On the ambiguities of this "legal recognition," see Don Haymes, "Caesar and Christ," *Integrity* (December, 1983): 95-96.

[44]George Bajenski, e-mail to Victor Knowles, February 28, 2011. This e-mail was forwarded to Scott Seay with the permission of the original author and the recipient.

[45]Bajko, *History*, 109-110.

[46]Lukowski and Zawadski, *Concise History*, ch. 7.

[47]Bajko, *History*, 87-95; George Bajenski, e-mail to Victor Knowles, February 28, 2011. This e-mail was forwarded to Scott Seay with the permission of the original author and the recipient.

[48]R. H. Boll, "Brother Baumann's work in Germany," *Gospel Advocate* (June 28, 1900): 415; R. H. Boll, "A Call to Germany," *Gospel Advocate* (April 21, 1900): 481; E. H. Rogers, "A Great and Good Man Gone," *Gospel Advocate* (December 5, 1912): 1320-1321.

[49]Earl Irvin West, *The Search for the Ancient Order: A History of the Restoration Movement*, 4 vols. (Religious Book Service, 1949-1987), 3:376-377; Richard Hughes, *Reviving the Ancient Faith: The Story of Churches of Christ in America* (Grand Rapids: Eerdmans, 1996), 234-235. The quote comes from G. C. Brewer, "Evangelizing the World in the Post-War Period," *Firm Foundation* (February 16, 1943): 1-2.

[50]See Otis Gatewood, *You Can Do Personal Work* (n.p., 1956).

[51]Otis Gatewood, "First Tent Meeting in Germany This Summer a Success," *Gospel Advocate* (July 20, 1950): 470; Harvie Pruitt, "Germany: The First Years," *Gospel Advocate* (October, 1997): 22-26.

[52]"Report from Europe," *Gospel Advocate* (June 7, 1956): 523-533; Pruitt, "Germany," 23.

[53]Richard Hughes and R. L. Roberts, "Otis Gatewood," *The Churches of Christ* (Westport: Greenwood Press, 2001), 220-221.

[54]Hans Nowak, "A Noble Preacher in Germany," *Gospel Advocate* (March 29, 1956): 310.

[55]"Gottfried Reichel," *Firm Foundation* (August 31, 1965): 558; "Biographical Information: Gottfried Reichel," available at www. oldpathsmedia.org, accessed December 2, 2010.

[56]Howard White, "Preacher Training Program in Germany," *Firm Foundation* (June 9, 1970): 362; "Training German Preachers," *Firm Foundation* (October 27, 1970): 684; Howard White, "Heidelberg Preacher Training School," *Firm Foundation* (December 26, 1971): 59.

[57]Jack Fogarty, "Germany," *Christian Chronicle* (June, 1985): 10-11; Harvie Pruitt, "Germany: Current Work," *Gospel Advocate* (October, 1997): 24.

[58]Keith Watkins, *Christian Theological Seminary, Indianapolis, Indiana: A History of Education for Ministry* (Zionsville: Guild Press of Indiana, 2001), 102.

[59]"College of the Church in Tübingen," *European Evangelist* (August, 1950): 1; "Society Secures Significant Building," *European Evangelist* (April, 1962): 1-2.

[60]"Theodore Mosalkow," *European Evangelist* (December, 1961): 4.

[61]Earl Stuckenbruck, "A Faithful Co-Worker," *European Evangelist* (October, 1958): 1; "Dr. Theodore Mosalkow," *European Evangelist* (August, 1962): 2-4.

[62]Robert Shaw, "Thus It Began," in David Fiensy and William Howden, eds., *Faith in Practice: Studies in the Book of Acts, a Festschrift in Honor of Earl and Ottie Mearl Stuckenbruck* (Atlanta: European Evangelistic Society, 1995), 21-22.

[63]"James E. Crouch to Join Earl Stuckenbruck," *European Evangelist* (July, 1961): 1; "Society Secures Significant Building," *European Evangelist* (April, 1962): 1-2.

[64]Shaw, "Thus It Began," 34-38.

[65]Since its beginning, the EES has received support from all three of the North American streams of the Stone-Campbell Movement.

[66]Beth Langstaff, "Farewell to Dr. Ronald E. Heine," *European Evangelist* (Fall, 2000): 2, 4.

[67]"New Missionary Family," *European Evangelist* (Summer, 1992): 1-2.

[68]Bob Hare, "Veteran Missionary Needs Your Help," *Firm Foundation* (October 17, 1972): 666.

[69]"History," Training Christians for Ministry, available at http://www.tcmi.org/history, accessed July 6, 2011.

[70]"History," Training Christians for Ministry.

[71]"About MIUV," Megatrend University, available at http://www.megatrendvienna.at/401_EN-Megatrend-University-About-MIUV.61A206049815cef6f90597e54d06c38abdae3f20, accessed January 11, 2012.

[72]Jack McKinney, "Prospect of the Work in Switzerland," *Gospel Advocate* (June 7, 1956): 539; Jerry Earnhart, "Swiss Mission Materialized Right After World War II," *Christian Chronicle* (March 27, 1964): 3.

[73]"An Opening Among the Hungarians," *Christian Standard* (August 14, 1909): 1427-1428.

[74]"The Ancient Gospel in Bulgaria," *Christian Standard* (October 9, 1909): 1772-1773.

[75]"Home Missions Abroad," *Christian Standard* (April 23, 1910): 705-706.

[76]Peter Poppoff, "Appeal from Bulgarian Christians," *Christian Standard* (November 8, 1913): 1862-1863; Peter Poppoff, "Providential Opening for Christian Work in Bulgaria," *Christian Standard* (January 10, 1914): 44.

[77]"The Restoration Movement in Bulgaria," *Christian Standard* (January 10, 1914): 43-44.

[78]"New Missionary Work in Central Europe," *Christian Standard* (November 14, 1936): 1113.

[79]Thomas Hagger, "The Movement in Bulgaria," *Christian Standard* (July 3, 1937): 585.

[80]"Entire Congregation Becomes New Testament Church," *Christian Standard* (August 5, 1939): 762.

[81]"Delegation Greets Brother Vass as He Enters Hungary," *Christian Standard* (October 15, 1938): 1021.

[82]"Frank Vass Is Returning," *Christian Standard* (March 30, 1940): 296.

[83]Morris Book, "Morris Book Urges Support for Vass, Hungarian Missionary," *Christian Standard* (February 28, 1948): 132.

[84]Ben Schiller, "Central Europe Calls," *Christian Standard* (September 20, 1947): 653.

[85]See, for example, Bob Hare, "Missionary Sees Possibility of Work in Czechoslovakia," *Christian Chronicle* (January 15, 1965): 5.

[86]"Holding Up the Hands of Our Persecuted Brethren," *Christian Chronicle* (June 29, 1976): 1, 5; Ben Jones, "Printing Mission for Eastern Europe," *Christian Chronicle* (November 30, 1976): 1, 4; and Otis Gatewood, "European Christian College To Begin in Vienna, Austria," *Christian Chronicle* (April 18, 1978): 1.

[87]Lindy Adams, "A Conversation with Mladen Jovanovic," *Christian Chronicle* (April, 2003): 20; "Biblijski Institute," at http://bizg.hr/, accessed February 2, 2012.

[88]"Churches Plan Global Effort," *Christian Chronicle* (March, 1990): 1. Much of this issue is dedicated to interpreting how the collapse of communism required Churches of Christ to rethink their mission work in southeastern Europe and the Balkans. See also, "Eastern European Mission Expands Outreach Program," *Christian Chronicle* (July, 1991): 15; and *Eastern European Mission News* (Spring, 2011), available at http://www.eem.org/newsletters/EEM_Newsletter_Vol_50_No_2.pdf, accessed July 6, 2011.

[89]Russ Burcham, "Opportunity in Albania," *Gospel Advocate* (February, 1993): 51.

[90]"Albanian Evangelism Enters New Church-Planting Phase," *Christian Chronicle* (June, 1992): 21; Bob Hare, "Churches Thrive in Eastern Europe," *Gospel Advocate* (March, 1994): 60.

[91]Guy Mayfield, "Chaplain Mayfield Writes of Opportunity in Italy," *Christian Standard* (March 28, 1945): 205.

[92]"New Testament Church Is Planted at Latiano, Italy," *Christian Standard* (February 28, 1948): 131; "Second Church Planted by Workers in Italy," *Christian Standard* (February 28, 1948): 143; "Italian Evangelist Ordained by Mediterranean Missionaries," *Christian Standard* (April 24, 1948): 267.

[93]Guy Mayfield, "Mayfields to Continue Teaching in Rome, Italy," *Christian Standard* (April 15, 1950): 230.

[94]Guy Mayfield, "New Mission Station," *Christian Standard* (October 18, 1952): 664; Cheryl Trueblood Barboza, *A Glimpse of His Story: The History of Cross-Cultural Missions at Roanoke Bible College* (Maitland: Xulon Press, 2010), 92-96.

[95]"Fowlers in Italy," available at www.hefowler.com/who.html, accessed January 28, 2012; Julie Fowler, Forwarding Agent for Italy for Christ Mission, e-mail correspondence with Scott Seay, November, 2010; Pino Neglia, Director of Leece Christian Mission,

e-mail correspondence with Scott Seay, November, 2010."

[96]"Missionary Websites," TEAM Expansion, available at http://web.teamexpansion.org/#/about-us/missionary-websites, accessed October 5, 2012.

[97]Cline Paden, "Rome: The Beginning," *Gospel Advocate* (October, 1997): 13.

[98]"Italians Harass U.S. Evangelists," *Life* (February 20, 1950): 95-99.

[99]"Beachhead," *Time* (January 23, 1950): 53.

[100]"Italy Fifty Years in Retrospect," *Christian Chronicle* (February, 1999): 18-19; Roy Palmer Domenico, "'For The Cause of Christ Here in Italy': America's Protestant Challenge in Italy and the Cultural Ambiguity of the Cold War," *Diplomatic History* (September, 2005): 638-639, 343-346.

[101]"Religious Freedom in Italy," *Gospel Advocate* (February 25, 1954): 146; M. Norvel Young, "An Italian Lawyer Speaks," *Gospel Advocate* (March 4, 1954): 169-170.

[102]"Religion: The Sign," *Time* (March 14, 1955); Letter, Cline R. Paden to Editor of *Time*, March 14, 1955, in Personal Papers of Reuel Lemmons, Box 1, Center for Restoration Studies, Abilene Christian University; Orville McDonald, *Report of Trip to Rome*, booklet in Personal Papers of Reuel Lemmons, Box 1, Center for Restoration Studies, Abilene Christian University, Abilene, Texas.

[103]"1960 Alphabetical Directory of American Missionaries Abroad," *World Vision* (November, 1960): 17-28; "Introduzione al Movimento di Restaurazione," [Introduction to the Restoration Movement], available at http://www.cesnur.org/religioni_italia/r/restaurazione_01.htm, accessed January 11, 2012.

[104]"Italian Preacher Faces Court," *Firm Foundation* (October 2, 1962): 632; "Pandolfini Convicted in Rome Tribunal," *Christian Chronicle* (December 21, 1962): 1, 4.

[105]"Ex-Priest Baptized in Civitavecchia," *Firm Foundation* (November 12, 1963): 732; "Giudici Threatened with Imprisonment in Italy," *Firm Foundation* (March 21, 1967): 190; "Italian Evangelist on Trial," *Firm Foundation* (January 7, 1967): 750; Gerald Paden, "Conviction of Giudici Is Confirmed," *Christian Chronicle* (November 20, 1967): 1, 3; "Gian Giudici Still Under Indictment," *Firm Foundation* (January 7, 1968): 14; "Gian Giudici on Trial for the Gospel's Sake," *Firm Foundation* (January 28, 1968): 62.

[106]"Italian Efforts," *Gospel Advocate* (October, 1997): 15.

[107]Jacob C. Vandervis, *Why I Left the Mormon Church* (World Vision Publishing, 1944); "Report from Europe," *Gospel Advocate* (June 7, 1956): 536-537; Jim Krumrel, "Belgium and Holland," *Gospel Advocate* (October, 1997): 20-21.

[108]"Report from Europe," *Gospel Advocate* (June 7, 1956): 533-534; S. F. Timmerman, "Belgium Work Ten Years Old," *Christian Chronicle* (February 25, 1958): 3.

[109]Clyde Redmon, "Ye Ministered to My Needs," *Gospel Advocate* (November 30, 1978): 757.

[110]S. F. Timmerman, "Belgium: Yesterday and Today," *Gospel Advocate* (March 7, 1968): 155.

[111]Maurice Hall, "The Challenge of Paris and France," *Gospel Advocate* (June 7, 1956): 534-535; Maurice Hall, "France Shows Friendship; Still Working with America," *Christian Chronicle* (March 4, 1958): 1, 3; Maurice Hall and Doyle Kee, "France" *Gospel Advocate* (October, 1997): 18.

[112]"1960 Alphabetical Directory of Missionaries Abroad," *World Vision* (November, 1960): 17-28.

[113]"Campaign in France Planned," *Firm Foundation* (June 19, 1962): 397; L. D. Lawrence, "French Language Gospel Radio Program Launched," *Firm Foundation* (March 26, 1963): 205; "Campaign Plans Developing for French World," *Firm Foundation* (March 12, 1968): 173; Doyle Kee, "European French Work Coming of Age," *Firm Foundation* (July 3, 1979): 424, 427.

[114]*Le Monde Francais:* The French World Awaits Us," *Christian Chronicle* (July, 1999): 18-19.

[115]Stanley Payne, *The Franco Regime, 1936-1975* (Madison: University of Wisconsin Press, 1987), 421-422.

[116]Juan Antonio Monroy, *Juan Antonio Monroy: An Autobiography* (Abilene: Abilene Christian University Press, 2011), 32, 66.

[117]Lane Cubstead, "New Work in Spain Uncovered," *Christian Chronicle* (February 19, 1965): 1, 15.

[118]Monroy, *Autobiography*, 121-31; Juan Monroy, "Preaching the Gospel in Spain," *Gospel Advocate* (1974): 174.

[119]Arlie Smith, "The Church in Lisbon, Portugal," *Gospel Advocate* (September 10, 1970): 580. The cover of the November 3, 1970, edition of *Firm Foundation* includes a photo of the Lisbon congregation on its first anniversary. It appears that about 50 people are present at the service.

[120]Arlie Smith, "Lisbon Campaign," *Firm Foundation* (August 3, 1971): 490.

[121]"On the Job in Portugal," *Firm Foundation* (March 4, 1975): 140.

[122]Staff Reports, "Portugal," *Christian Chronicle* (September, 2008): 10.

[123]Julian Garcia Hernando, *Pluralismo Religioso en Espa*ña, vol. 1 (Madrid: Sociedad de Educación Atenas, 1981).

[124]Monroy received by the King of Spain," *Christian Chronicle* (June, 1998): 28.

[125]"Latin American Mission," available at www.lamtoday.org/index.html, accessed September 30, 2010. This website gives information about the continuing work of Bill Loft Mission, Inc., in Spain.

[126]"Editor in Europe," *World Call* (September, 1945): 2; "George Walker Buckner, Jr.," *World Call* (December, 1945): 2; Paul A. Crow, "George Walker Buckner," in Douglas Foster, et al., ed., *The Encyclopedia of the Stone-Campbell Movement* (Grand Rapids: Eerdmans, 2004), 101-102.

[127]See, for example, Robert Root, "Czechoslovakia—Seven Years After Munich," *World Call* (April, 1946): 21-22; "Symbols of Central Europe," *World Call* (May, 1946): 28; "German Church vs. Goliath," (September, 1946): 12; "Thanks, America," *World Call* (February, 1947): 29.

[128]*Disciples Year Book* (1948), 118-119.

[129]Ronald Stenning, *Church World Service: Fifty Years of Help and Hope* (New York: Friendship Press, 1996), 3.

[130]*Disciples Year Book* (1948), 119.

[131]Alan Milward, *The Reconstruction of Western Europe, 1945-1951* (New York: Routledge, 2006), 46.

[132]Mark Mazower, *Inside Hitler's Greece: The Experience of Occupation* (New Haven: Yale University Press, 2001); David Close, *The Greek Civil War, 1943-1950: Studies in Polarization* (New York: Routledge, 1989); Mark Mazower, ed., *After the War Was Over: Reconstructing the Family, Nation, and State in Greece, 1943-1960* (Princeton: Princeton University Press, 2000).

[133]J. B. Gaselee, "Toward Reconstruction in Greece," *World Call* (July-August, 1949): 20-21.

[134]Robert Tobias, "Disciples Help Greeks Rebuild a Torn Nation," *World Call* (November, 1953): 26-27; John Taylor, "Greek Team Serves Ten Years," *World Call* (July-August, 1961): quoted at 28.

[135]Paul Crow, "George Beazley," in Foster, et al., ed., *Encyclopedia*, 71-72.

[136]Christian Berg and Franz von Hammerstein, *Leibhaftige Ökumene: Berichte ausländischer Mitarbeiter und Studenten in unserer Kirche* [Embodied ecumenism: reports of foreign staff and students in our church] (Berlin: Lettner-Verlag, 1963), quoted in *The History of Fraternal Workers, Christian Church (Disciples of Christ)* (unpublished manuscript prepared by the Division of Overseas Ministries, 1988), 2.

[137]Lester McAllister, "The Story of CIMADE," *World Call* (November, 1945): 8-9; William Nottingham, "CIMADE—Christian Trouble Shooter," *World Call* (May, 1959): 29-30. Generalizations about the Disciples' ongoing work with CIMADE have been made from the annual reports of the DOM included in the *Year Book and Directory of the Christian Church (Disciples of Christ)*.

[138]*History of Fraternal Workers*, 3.

[139]Robert Friedly, "German Youth—They Don't Want a Second Holocaust," *The Disciple* (January 15, 1978): 4-6. These generalizations are based mainly on the annual reports of the Division of Overseas Ministries included in the annual *Year Book and Directory of the Christian Church (Disciples of Christ)* from 1974 to 1991. See also, "History of ASRP in Germany," Action Reconciliation Service for Peace, available at www.asf-ev.de/en/about-us/history.html, accessed November 22, 2011.

[140]These generalizations are based on the annual reports of the Division of Overseas Ministries and the Common Board of Global Ministries included in the annual *Year Book and Directory of the Christian Church (Disciples of Christ)* from 1992 to 2005.

[141]*Disciples Year Book* (1974), 138.

[142]For an analysis of the demise of Christendom in Europe, see Phillip Jenkins, *God's Continent: Christianity, Islam and Europe's Religious Crisis* (Oxford: University Press, 2005). For example, the Church of Christ in Graz, Austria, doubled its membership between 2004 and 2008 with the arrival of a group of Nigerian refugees, resulting in changes in both the worship and governance styles of the congregation.

18: Quest for Unity

[1]Douglas A. Foster, "The Struggle for Unity During the Period of Division of the Restoration Movement: 1875-1900" (PhD dissertation, Vanderbilt University, 1987).

[2]Lyman Beecher, "A Proselyting Spirit Dangerous to the Prosperity of the Church," *Christian Messenger* (December, 1835): 281-283.

[3]Barton Stone, "The Disunion of Christians," *Christian Messenger* (March, 1841): 246-247; John Gano, letter to Barton Stone dated March 18, 1841, *Christian Messenger* (April, 1841): 281; John T. Johnson, letter to Barton Stone, dated May 14, 2841, *Christian Messenger* (June, 1841): 355.

[4]Barton Stone, "Unity," *Christian Messenger* (May, 1843): 8-9.

[5]Robert Richardson, *Memoirs of Alexander Campbell*, 2 vols. (Philadelphia: J. B. Lippincott & Co., 1870), 2:675.

[6]Herman Norton, *Tennessee Christians* (Nashville: Reed and Company, 1971), 234-235, 250-251.

[7]See, for example, the speech that H. Leo Boles made at the Murch-Witty unity meeting in May 1939, later published as "The Way of Unity Between 'Christian Church' and Churches of Christ," *Christian Standard* (1939): 529-530, 555-556, 571, 580-581, 586; and "The Way of Unity," *Gospel Advocate* (1939): 508-509, 516, 532-533, 554-555. Later the Gospel Advocate Publishing Company issued the speech as a tract by the same name.

[8]Victor Knowles, "A Look Back at the Beam-Jessup Unity Meetings," *One Body* (Spring, 1991).

[9]Letter from Bill Jessup to Galen Farnsworth, January 5, 1990, cited in Victor Knowles, *A Biography: Archie Word, Voice of Thunder, Heart of Tears* (Joplin: College Press, 1992), 445; Jessup, "A Look Back at the Beam-Jessup Unity Meetings," 9.

[10]James DeForest Murch, *Adventuring for Christ in Changing Times* (Louisville: Restoration Press, 1972).

[11]James DeForest Murch, *Christians Only: A History of the Restoration Movement* (Cincinnati: Standard Publishing, 1962), 274-247.

[12]Richard Cobb, "The Failure of the Murch-Witty Unity Movement in the Stone-Campbell Tradition, 1937-1947: Was the Church in the Way?" (MA thesis, Abilene Christian University, 1996).

[13]Victor Knowles, "Don't Know Much About History: Reviewing 70 Years of Rapprochement Between A Cappella Churches of Christ and Conservative Christian Churches 1933-2004," Pepperdine University Bible Lectures, May 6-7, 2004, available at http://www.poeministries.org/pages/Lectures/

Don%27tKnowMuchAboutHisto.htm, accessed December 21, 2011.

[14]For a list of the dates, locations of all the Restoration Forums, as well as the text of the Covenant of Unity, see "Peace on Earth Ministries," available at http://www.poeministries.org/Restoration-Archives.html, accessed December 21, 2011.

[15]Leroy Garrett, *A Lover's Quarrel: An Autobiography* (Abilene: Abilene Christian University Press, 2003), 132-133.

[16]*The Arlington Meeting* (Orlando: Cogdill Foundation, 1970).

[17]"A Meeting of the Minds," *Christian Chronicle* (March, 2004): 17-19; see also the "International Churches of Christ" issue of *Leaven: A Journal of Christian Ministry* (Second Quarter, 2010): 70-113.

[18]"Confession of Sin and Affirmation of Faith: An Invitation from the Stone-Campbell Dialogue," Council on Christian Unity, available at www.disciples.org/ccu/programs/documents/2000Con fessionStatement.html, accessed December 21, 2011.

[19]"Stone-Campbell Dialogue," Council on Christian Unity, available at www.disciples.org/ccu/programs/stonecampbell, accessed December 21, 2011

[20]Richardson, *Memoirs*, 2:178.

[21]Richardson, *Memoirs*, 2:179-80; Archibald McLean, *History of the Foreign Christian Missionary Society* (New York: Fleming Revell, 1919), 127-128; Winfred Garrison and Alfred DeGroot, *Disciples of Christ: A History* (St. Louis: Christian Board of Publication, 1948), 565.

[22]W. Mander, "The Larger Religious World," *Christian Monthly* (August, 1920): 123.

[23]Jimmie Moore Mankin, "Little Man with a Great Brain," *Discipliana* (January, 1995): 25ff.

[24]H. N. Bate, ed., *Faith and Order: Proceedings of the World Conference, Lausanne, August 3-21, 1927* (New York: G. H. Doran Co., 1927), 508-526.

[25]Leonard Hodgson, *The Second World Conference on Faith and Order, Held at Edinburgh, August 3-18, 1937* (London : Student Christian Movement Press, 1938), 204.

[26]"The Global Christian Forum," available at www.globalchristianforum.org, accessed December 21, 2011; Huibert van Beek, ed., *Revisioning Christian Unity—The Global Christian Forum* (Eugene: Wipf & Stock, 2009).

[27]"Christian Churches Together in the USA," available at www.christianchurchestogether.org, accessed December 21, 2011.

[28]Winfred Garrison, *Christian Unity and the Disciples of Christ* (St. Louis: Bethany Press, 1955), 160-163.

[29]Franklin M. Rector, "Baptist-Disciple Conversations Toward Unity," in Nils Ehrenstrom and Walter G. Muelder, eds., *Institutionalism and Church Unity* (New York: Association Press, 1963), 255-256.

[30]Rector, "Baptist-Disciple Conversations," 257-273.

[31]Garrison, *Christian Unity*, 57-58.

[32]Garrison, *Christian Unity*, 168-169.

[33]Kenneth Hylson-Smith, *Evangelicals in the Church of England, 1734-1984* (Continuum International Publishing Group, 1989), 341.

[34]Albert E. Smith, "Why Are the Disciples of Christ Out of the United Church of Canada?" *World Call* (May, 1926): 7.

[35]Files of Canada Region of the Christian Church (Disciples of Christ), held at Disciples of Christ Historical Society, Nashville, Tennessee.

[36]H. B. Holloway, "An Adventure in World Fellowship," *Program of the Second World Convention of Churches of Christ, August 7-12, 1935, Leicester, England.*

[37]For information on all World Conventions from 1930 to 2008, see Clinton J. Holloway, *Together in Christ: A History of the World Convention of Churches of Christ 1930-2008* (Nashville: privately published, 2008).

[38]"Constitution, Article VI. D.," World Communion of Reformed Churches, available at www.reformedchurches.org/docs/WCRC-Constitution0709.pdf, accessed December 21, 2011.

[39]Gilbert W. Stafford, "The Faith and Order Movement," Appendix H in Barry Callen and James North, eds., *Coming Together in Christ* (Joplin: College Press Publishing Company, 1997), 203.

[40]Douglas A. Foster, "Ecumenical Leadership in a Postmodern and Post –Christian Age: The Potential for the Churches of the Stone-Campbell Movement," Dean E. Walker Lecture, North American Christian Convention, July 5, 2007, Kansas City, Missouri.

[41]Leroy Garrett, "Drama on Both Sides of the Border," *Restoration Quarterly* (May, 1975): 96-97.

[42]Lynn Mitchell, Jr., "Beasley-Murray, Baptism, and the Baptists," *Mission* (August, 1975): 36-39.

[43]Leroy Garrett, Denton, Texas, letter to Douglas Foster, Abilene, Texas, April 9, 2003, personal files of Douglas A. Foster, Abilene Christian University, Abilene, Texas; Leroy Garrett, "Back to Back Conferences on Freedom," *Restoration Review* (February, 1985): 28-29.

[44]Rudy Gonzalez, Alpharetta, Georgia, letter to Douglas Foster, Abilene, Texas, September 11, 2000, personal files of Douglas A. Foster, Abilene Christian University, Abilene, Texas.

[45]Douglas A. Foster, "Efforts at Repairing the Breach: Twentieth-Century Dialogues of the Churches of the Stone-Campbell Movement with Baptists and Presbyterians," *Discipliana* (Winter, 2003): 103-107.

[46]Leonard Wymore, e-mail to Douglas Foster, November 26, 2010.

[47]Barry Callen and James North, *Coming Together in Christ: Pioneering a New Testament Way to Christian Unity* (Joplin: College Press Publishing Company, 1997).

[48]See also John Mills, *The History of the Open Forum on the Mission of the Church: Christian Churches/Churches of Christ 1983-2009* (Middleburg Heights: Open Forum/Southwest Christian Church, 2011).

Index

Page numbers in **bold** indicate a photograph. Page numbers in *italics* indicate a map.

N